W9-ANB-749

2nd edition

ENCYCLOPEDIA OF
PHILOSOPHY

7

volume

2nd edition

ENCYCLOPEDIA OF
PHILOSOPHY

DONALD M. BORCHERT

Editor in Chief

MACMILLAN REFERENCE USA
An imprint of Thomson Gale, a part of The Thomson Corporation

THOMSON

GALE

Detroit • New York • San Francisco • San Diego • New Haven, Conn. • Waterville, Maine • London • Munich

Encyclopedia of Philosophy, Second Edition

Donald M. Borchert, Editor in Chief

For permission to use material from this product, submit your request via Web at http://www.gale-edit.com/permissions, or you may download our Permissions Request form and submit your request by fax or mail to:

Permissions
Thomson Gale
27500 Drake Rd.
Farmington Hills, MI 48331-3535
Permissions Hotline:
248-699-8006 or 800-877-4253 ext. 8006
Fax: 248-699-8074 or 800-762-4058

Since this page cannot legibly accommodate all copyright notices, the acknowledgments constitute an extension of the copyright notice.

While every effort has been made to ensure the reliability of the information presented in this publication, Thomson Gale does not guarantee the accuracy of the data contained herein. Thomson Gale accepts no payment for listing; and inclusion in the publication of any organization, agency, institution, publication, service, or individual does not imply endorsement of the editors or publisher. Errors brought to the attention of the publisher and verified to the satisfaction of the publisher will be corrected in future editions.

LIBRARY OF CONGRESS CATALOGING-IN-PUBLICATION DATA

Encyclopedia of philosophy / Donald M. Borchert, editor in chief.—2nd ed.
 p. cm.
  Includes bibliographical references and index.
  ISBN 0-02-865780-2 (set hardcover : alk. paper)—
  ISBN 0-02-865781-0 (vol 1)—ISBN 0-02-865782-9 (vol 2)—
  ISBN 0-02-865783-7 (vol 3)—ISBN 0-02-865784-5 (vol 4)—
  ISBN 0-02-865785-3 (vol 5)—ISBN 0-02-865786-1 (vol 6)—
  ISBN 0-02-865787-X (vol 7)—ISBN 0-02-865788-8 (vol 8)—
  ISBN 0-02-865789-6 (vol 9)—ISBN 0-02-865790-X (vol 10)
  1. Philosophy–Encyclopedias. I. Borchert, Donald M., 1934-

B51.E53 2005
103–dc22

                                                2005018573

This title is also available as an e-book.
ISBN 0-02-866072-2
Contact your Thomson Gale representative for ordering information.

Printed in the United States of America
10 9 8 7 6 5 4 3 2 1

contents

OAKESHOTT, MICHAEL
(1901–1990)

Michael Oakeshott, a wide-ranging thinker mostly known for his work in social and political philosophy, was born in Chelsfield, Kent, on December 11, 1901. Oakeshott read history at Gonville and Caius College, Cambridge, and graduated in 1923. He returned as a fellow in 1925. In 1940 he enlisted in the British Army and served with "Phantom," an intelligence unit that worked on artillery spotting. In 1949 he went to Oxford as a fellow of Nuffield College and in 1951 he was appointed to the chair of political science at the London School of Economics. He retired in 1969, but continued to be active from his retirement home in Acton, Dorset, where he died on December 18, 1990.

EXPERIENCE AND ITS MODES

Experience and Its Modes (1933) was Oakeshott's first major work. In the book Oakeshott creates some of the major distinctions that mark his social/political philosophy. The most important concerns experience itself. Influenced by the holism of Plato and Hegel (especially the *Phenomenology of Spirit*) and the idealism of Francis Bradley (*Appearance and Reality*), Oakeshott posits that "experience is a single whole, within which modifications may be distinguished, but which admits of no final or absolute division; and that experience everywhere, not merely is inseparable from thought, but is itself a form of thought" (1933, p. 10). Within the unity of experience people attempt to make sense of it via interpretative devices such as "history research," "scientific experimentation," and "practical reasoning." But all of these paths will ultimately fail. This is demonstrated by a relentless skepticism. The futile interpretative modes rely upon a false understanding of the primacy of Enlightenment-style rationalism. Instead, the agent finds herself in the midst of her own reflections and poetic imaginings. This agent-centered construction creates a tension in a world of other minds. The result is a necessary travail to reconcile one's own experience with that of others. This process is necessary to make social existence coherent.

Along with this amalgam of skeptical idealism Oakeshott posits freedom:

> The starting place of doing is a state of reflective consciousness, namely, the agent's own understanding of his situation, what it means to him. And, of course, it is no less *his* situation even though it may be a concern with what he understands to be the situation of another or of oth-

ers. ... And it is in this respect of this starting-place in an understood contingent situation that the agent in conduct may be said to be "free." (1975, p. 37)

Freedom is thus one of the properties of consciousness that allows the interpretative awareness of consciousness to develop.

Because freedom is a precondition of people's experience of the world, it is vain for totalitarian dictators to endeavor to suppress it. To do so would mean that the dictator tries to suppress an aspect of human nature that underlies the possibility of human experience. It just can't happen. Freedom will exhibit itself in one form or another. This is not a teleological expression of human nature but rather an indication that people will interpret and respond to what life presents them. This is a concrete and practical vision. Though some may be drawn to the modes to make sense of it all (a vain endeavor), the primary imperative (á la Berkeley) is first to accommodate the primary data of experience as it presents itself: "And no matter how far we go with it, we shall not easily forget the sweet delight which lies in the empty kisses of abstraction" (1933, p. 356).

RATIONALISM IN POLITICS

The essays in *Rationalism in Politics* (1991) form the core of Oakeshott's social/political thought. In the title essay Oakeshott extends some of the concepts of his earlier work to critique Enlightenment rationalism as a device that is serviceable for guiding social and political thinking. He proclaims this Hobbesian skepticism of rationalism as a useful tool for politics in language that is reminiscent of Aristotle (*EN* I.1).

> Every science, every art, every practical activity requiring skill of any sort, indeed every human activity whatsoever, involves knowledge. And universally, this knowledge is of two sorts. ... The first sort of knowledge I will call technical knowledge or knowledge of technique. ... The second sort of knowledge I will call practical, because it exists only in use, is not reflective and (unlike technique) cannot be formulated into rules. (1991, p. 12)

This essay then goes on to evaluate these two aspects of reason with a critique of traditional accounts that aspire to make rationalism a transcendent tool. Instead, Oakeshott insists, reason is merely the handmaiden of free holistic experience.

In "The Tower of Babel" Oakeshott sets out a Hegelian understanding of the existing community and its proper influence on the individual. Two sorts of morality are posited: The first represents the existing moral community (akin to the German *Sittlichkeit*). The second is a philosophical critique that may alter the first. Alan Donagan contends that Oakeshott (like Hegel) misses the force of deontological commands by favoring the *Sittlichkeit* over *Moralität*. By being biased toward experience, as such, Donagan believes that fundamental principles that supercede morality are not given their due. The mere existence of the second (philosophical) form of morality is not adequate. This much resembles the Kant-Hegel debate on the proper place of experience in evaluating the moral community. Oakeshott's position of affirming the existing moral community puts him into the camp of political conservatism. How much one is to make of this is still a subject of critical debate.

"The Voice of Poetry in the Conversation of Mankind" is another key essay in the collection that proclaims an aesthetics that is disinterested. It is not for the sake of instruction nor is it a conscious imitation of nature. "The poet does not recognize and record natural or conventional correspondencies or use them to 'explore reality'; he does not invoke equivalencies, he makes images" (1991, p. 528). In this way, the work of art is for the sake of the pleasurable contemplation of images. In some ways Oakeshott's aesthetic stance is reminiscent of Schiller and some readings of Kant. It is consistent with the holism standpoint that was established in *Experience and its Modes*.

CONCLUSION

Michael Oakeshott may be best known as a conservative political writer in the tradition of Hobbes. However, as the comments above suggest, he is more than that. He grounds his thinking in a comprehensive epistemological theory that also supports other explorations (such as aesthetics, history, and education). To evaluate his work, it is important to view Oakeshott within this larger context.

See also Aristotle; Berkeley, George; Bradley, Francis Herbert; Enlightenment; Epistemology, History of; Hegel, Georg Wilhelm Friedrich; Hobbes, Thomas; Idealism; Kant, Immanuel; Plato; Rationalism; Social and Political Philosophy.

Bibliography

MAJOR WORKS BY OAKESHOTT

Experience and Its Modes. Cambridge, U.K.: Cambridge University Press, 1933. Reprinted in 1966; paperback edition 1986.

The Social and Political Doctrines of Contemporary Europe. Cambridge, U.K.: Cambridge University Press, 1939.

Rationalism in Politics and Other Essays. London: Methuen, 1962. Revised by Timothy Fuller. Indianapolis: Liberty Press, 1991.

On Human Conduct. Oxford: Clarendon Press, 1975. Paper ed., Oxford: Clarendon Press, 1990.

On History and Other Essays. Oxford: Basil Blackwell, 1983.

The Voice of Liberal Learning: Michael Oakeshott on Education, edited by Timothy Fuller. New Haven, CT: Yale University Press, 1989.

"Introduction" to Thomas Hobbes, *Leviathan.* Oxford: Basil Blackwell, 1946. Included in *Rationalism in Politics,* 1991.

A complete bibliography to 1968 is available in *Politics and Experience: Essays Presented to Professor Michael Oakeshott on the Occasion of his Retirement,* edited by Preston King and B. C. Parekh. (Cambridge, U.K.: Cambridge University Press, 1968). An online bibliography is available from the Michael Oakeshott Association (available from www.michael-oakeshott-association.org).

WORKS ABOUT OAKESHOTT

Auspitz, Josiah Lee. "Individuality, Civility, and Theory: The Philosophical Imagination of Michael Oakeshott." *Political Theory* 4 (3) (1976): 261–294.

Donagan, Alan. *The Theory of Morality.* Chicago: University of Chicago Press, 1977.

Flathman, Richard E. *The Practice of Political Authority.* Chicago: University of Chicago Press, 1980.

Franco, Paul. *The Political Philosophy of Michael Oakeshott.* New Haven, CT: Yale University Press, 1990.

Fuller, Timothy. "Authority and the Individual in Civil Association: Oakeshott, Flathman and Yves Simon." In *NOMOS 29: Authority Revisited,* edited by Roland Pennock and John Chapman, 131–151. New York: New York University Press, 1987.

Grant, Robert. *Oakeshott.* London: Claridge Press, 1990.

King, Preston, and B. C. Parekh, eds. *Politics and Experience: Essays Presented to Professor Michael Oakeshott on the Occasion of His Retirement.* Cambridge, U.K.: Cambridge University Press, 1968.

Letwin, Shirley Robin. "Morality and the Law." *Ratio Juris* 2 (1) (March 1989): 55–65.

Minogue, Kenneth Minogue. "Michael Oakeshott." In *Contemporary Political Philosophers,* edited by Zbigniew Pelczynski and John Gray, 120–146. New York: St. Martin's Press, 1984.

Nardin, Terry. *The Philosophy of Michael Oakeshott.* University Park, PA: Penn State University Press, 2001.

Podoksik, Efriam. "The Voice of Poetry in the Thought of Michael Oakeshott." *Journal of the History of Ideas* 63 (4) (2002): 717–733.

Wells, Harwell. "The Philosophical Michael Oakeshott." *Journal of the History of Ideas* 55 (1) (1994): 129–145.

Worthington, Glen. "Michael Oakeshott and the City of God." *Political Theory* 28 (3) (2000): 377–398.

Michael Boylan (2005)

OBJECTIVISM

See *Objectivity in Ethics*

OBJECTIVITY IN ETHICS

What objectivity in ethics is depends, in part, on what ethics is. On the narrowest understanding, ethics consists in judgments about moral constraints, which govern a person's treatment of other people, as such. On the broadest understanding, ethics includes all normative judgments, which say which responses one ought to have, and all evaluative judgments, which assess people and things against standards, as good or bad, beautiful or ugly, and so on. While it may seem strained to interpret "ethics" so broadly, many of the questions about the objectivity of ethics in the narrow sense apply to normative and evaluative judgments in general.

In one sense, what is objective is what is so independently of one's particular attitudes or position. But this idea can be specified in different ways. In one sense, a particular ethical judgment is objective if and only if it is correct, where this is an evaluation of the judgment itself, not of how it is formed or sustained. If ethical judgments are beliefs, then it is natural to think that they are correct if and only if they are true. Scholars might call this *objectivity as truth.* But ethical judgments might be correct in some way other than being true. Immanuel Kant held that some ethical judgments are correct, even though ethical judgments are commands, which cannot be true or false. Scholars might call this more inclusive conception *objectivity as correctness.*

In another sense, a particular ethical judgment is objective if and only if it is formed and sustained in response to factors that tend to make such judgments correct. An ethical judgment is objective in this sense if it results from the judger's responsible assessment of the relevant ethical considerations, not unduly influenced by his or her desires, emotions, or affiliations. Scholars might call this *objectivity as justification.*

A different kind of objectivity, described by Thomas Nagel (1979), is possessed, in the first instance, not by particular judgments themselves, but instead by what those judgments are about. Something has objective value, in this sense, if it gives everyone reason to respond to it in the same way, regardless of his or her relation to it. For example, human suffering gives everyone reason to do what he or she can to alleviate it. Scholars might call this *objectivity as impersonality* and the associated values "impersonal" or "neutral" values. They contrast with things of "personal" or "relative" value, which give persons who stand in special relations to them reason to respond to them in special ways. For example, a child's suffering gives that child's parent more pressing reason to alleviate it than it gives others. There is a tendency, Nagel (1986) observed, to assimilate impersonality with justification and correctness, which misleadingly suggests that judgments of personal value, such as that a parent has reason to care specially for his or her child, are necessarily biased or false.

So far this entry has been considering the objectivity of particular ethical judgments and their contents. But some ask whether ethics as a whole, the sum of humankind's actual or possible ethical judgments taken together, is objective. Vaguely put, the question is whether ethical judgments are answerable to anything independent of them.

One might interpret this question as asking, "Is there an ethical reality?" where this "reality" is what ethical judgments would be answerable to. This question can be construed, in turn, as asking, "Are there ethical entities existing out there, in the world?" But this may be a tendentious formulation. What makes judgments distinctively ethical is not that they are about entities of a distinctive kind, which might exist somewhere, but instead that they predicate properties of a distinctive kind. What the question "Is there an ethical reality?" more plausibly asks is, "Do things actually have ethical properties?" And this seems to boil down to the questions "Are some actual or possible ethical beliefs, which predicate ethical properties of things, true? Can it be so that something is good or bad, right or wrong?" This is objectivity as truth, generalized to the domain as a whole. Note that in order for ethics to be objective in this sense, it is not enough that ethical judgments be either true or false. The "error theory" that J. L. Mackie (1977) proposed, which denies this kind of objectivity to ethics, asserts that all ethical judgments are false because they all contain a mistaken presupposition that something's having an ethical property is something that can be so.

Those who deny that ethical judgments are beliefs may still affirm that they can be correct, in some way other than being true. There are right and wrong answers to ethical questions, they may say, even if there is no eth-

ical reality that makes them right or wrong. They affirm objectivity as correctness generalized to the domain as a whole.

In another sense, ethics is objective if some actual or possible ethical judgments are or could be justified. This is objectivity as justification generalized. If ethics lacks justification, it does not follow that it lacks correctness. The fact that no ethical beliefs are justified, for example, does not mean that no ethical beliefs are true. But it may seem to have similar practical implications. Even if one's ethical beliefs might be true, one has no reason to treat them as true.

In still another sense, ethics is objective if it does not "depend on" one's psychology. Scholars might call this *objectivity as mind independence*. Since the claim that ethics is mind independent is just the denial of the claim that ethics is mind dependent, the way to come to terms with the former is to come to terms with the latter. To understand what it might mean to deny that ethics "depends on" one's psychology, in other words, one needs first to understand what it might mean to assert it. It cannot be to assert that ethical judgments depend on one's psychology. This is a truism; all judgments are psychological phenomena. Nor can it be to assert that the things about which one makes ethical judgments depend on one's psychology. No one denies that some ethical judgments can be about psychological states, such as intentions to harm others.

A more promising interpretation of the idea that ethics "depends on" one's psychology—of what is denied by the claim that ethics is objective in the present sense—is that ethical judgments predicate some property involving human psychology. An extension of this idea, which scholars might call *mind dependence of properties*, might capture the sense in which noncognitivism represents ethics as mind dependent. According to noncognitivism, ethical judgments only appear to predicate properties of things, while they in fact only express the judger's decisions or feelings regarding those things. Noncognitivists, therefore, will not agree that ethical judgments predicate psychological properties. But they may say something that approximates this: that in place of predicating properties, ethical judgments express judgers' psychological states.

Another possible interpretation of the idea that ethics "depends on" one's psychology, which scholars might call *mind dependence of correctness*, is that what makes ethical judgments correct, when they are, is something about one's psychology. The mind dependence of ethical properties entails the mind dependence of ethical correctness. If ethical judgments predicate psychological properties, then what makes those judgments true or false are psychological facts. But one might deny that ethical judgments predicate properties, while still holding, first, that they can be correct and, second, that their correctness is mind dependent. A Kantian theory might claim that ethical judgments do not predicate special ethical properties of actions, but instead command that they be done. But it might hold first that these commands can be correct and, second, that what makes them correct is something about the human will.

A natural way of spelling out the thought that ethical properties are mind dependent, which David Lewis (1989) explored in his work, is dispositionalism. Dispositionalism holds that what it is for something to have an ethical property (to be good, say) just is for it to be the case that subjects in certain conditions would respond to it in a certain way (such as by approving of or desiring it). One reservation about dispositionalism is whether the relevant response can be specified without appealing to the ethical property at issue. If approving of or desiring something consists in believing it to be good, for example, then dispositionalism appears to be circular.

Another reservation is that dispositionalism seems to imply, implausibly, that the extension of ethical properties varies with dispositions to respond, so that if the relevant subjects in the relevant conditions were not to approve of, say, kindness, it would no longer be good. One proposal to overcome this reservation, considered by David Wiggins (1998), is to identify actual dispositions as the relevant dispositions. If dispositions in the actual world are held fixed, then the extension of goodness does not vary across possible worlds, even ones in which dispositions vary. Does this mean, however, that as the identity of the actual world varies, the extension of goodness also varies? If so, then, as Lewis (1989) and Christopher Peacocke (2004) observed, the source of the original reservation seems only to have been relocated. If not, then, as Barry Stroud (2000) argued, it is unclear in what sense goodness is still being said to "depend" on dispositions. The dispositions that are held fixed are held fixed, it seems, simply because they are responsive to goodness.

Dispositionalism, it is sometimes said, is compatible with the correctness—indeed the truth—of ethical judgments. According to dispositionalism, the judgment that something is good is true if and only if subjects in the relevant conditions would approve of it. It might be said, however, that dispositionalism does not allow ethics to be correct in a more thoroughgoing sense. Although dispositionalism holds that judgments about the relevant responses can be correct, it also holds that there is no sense in which the responses themselves can be correct.

Some theories attempt to make mind dependence hospitable to a more thoroughgoing kind of correctness. John McDowell (1985) and Wiggins (1998) suggested that the relevant responses can be "merited" by their objects, and they proposed that what it is for something to be have an ethical property is, in part, for it to "merit" a certain response. In what way, then, are ethical properties still mind dependent? It is a necessary truth about any property that something has that property only if it "merits" a certain response: at very least, the judgment that it has that property. Perhaps the claim is that while this may be a necessary truth about every property, it is not an essential truth about every property. It is not part of "what it is" for something to have a shape property, for example, that it merits a response, whereas it is part of "what it is" for something to have an ethical property.

Kantians also argue for a mind dependence that is hospitable to a more thoroughgoing kind of correctness than dispositionalism allows. What makes an ethical judgment correct, according to Christine Korsgaard (1996), is that endorsing that judgment is constitutive of rational, reflective agency. Thus, the correctness of ethical judgments depends not on contingent tendencies of particular minds, as dispositionalism supposes, but instead on the necessary structure of a mind that is capable of asking ethical questions at all.

So much for what it might mean to assert or deny that ethics, as a whole, is objective. Why might one assert or deny it? Some have thought that ethics could be correct if and only if God laid down ethical laws. There are laws only where there is a lawgiver, the reasoning may go, and mortal lawgivers can establish only conventional laws. Therefore, God alone can establish ethical laws. Do all laws, however, require a lawgiver? Perhaps ethical laws, like logical laws, are not chosen by anyone. Moreover, it is unclear whether God could choose all ethical laws, for reasons given in the *Euthyphro* of Plato. If God chose certain ethical laws without regard for their goodness, then those laws would appear to be arbitrary, which it seems ethical laws cannot be. If instead God chose certain ethical laws because they were good, then God would appear to have been responding to prior and independent ethical laws, which he did not choose.

Others are anxious to deny that ethical judgments can be correct because they wish to justify tolerance of different ethical judgments. It is true that if no ethical judgment is correct, then one cannot ground one's intolerance of differing judgments on the claim that one's own judgments are correct. However, this shows only that there is a false premise in one argument for intolerance. It does not provide any positive justification for an ethical principle of tolerance. Moreover, to justify such an ethical requirement would seem to amount to establishing the correctness of at least one ethical judgment. So it is not clear whether the denial that ethical judgments can be correct is even compatible with the attempt to justify an ethical principle of tolerance.

A more prevalent concern among contemporary academic philosophers is that the objectivity of ethical judgments is incompatible with the apparent link between making an ethical judgment and being motivated to act accordingly. For example, Mackie (1977) denied that ethical judgments can be true, on the grounds that they presuppose "queer" properties: properties such that when someone believes that an object possesses one, he or she necessarily is moved in a particular way. Perhaps what is "queer" here, however, is the unqualified claim that making an ethical judgment entails being motivated to act accordingly. More plausible, as Michael Smith (1994) and Korsgaard (1986) argued in their works, is the thesis that making an ethical judgment entails being motivated, insofar as one is not irrational, to act accordingly. Smith and Korsgaard appeared to believe, however, that this revised thesis can be explained only if the content or correctness of ethical judgments is in a way mind dependent: dependent not on the tendencies of particular contingent minds, but instead on the structure or content of ideally rational psychology.

Other philosophers are impressed by disagreement in ethics. Ethical disagreement alone, however, does not entail that ethical judgments cannot be correct, any more than scientific disagreement entails that scientific judgments cannot be correct. The thought may be—as Mackie (1977), for example, seemed to pursue it—that ethical disagreement is in some way different from other kinds of disagreement, and that this difference is evidence that ethical judgments are explained by something other than their subject matter, or that ethics cannot settle the questions that it asks. As this entry will discuss, however, these claims—that ethics can be given an "unmasking explanation" and that it cannot resolve its own questions—may seem plausible even in the absence of actual disagreement.

Still other philosophers, such as Gilbert Harman (1977), Bernard Williams (1985), and Crispin Wright (1992), doubted that ethics can be objective, on the grounds that its subject matter does not provide causal explanations. That an action was wrong, for example, does not seem to explain why anything that followed took place.

While causal powers might be required by a stipulated sense of "objectivity," it is not immediately obvious how they are relevant to objectivity intuitively understood as answerability to something independent of judgment. To be sure, some judgments are about causal powers, and so the possession of such powers is straightforwardly relevant to the correctness of such judgments. If celestial events have no influence on the fates of men, for example, then astrological beliefs are false. But as Ronald Dworkin (1996) and T.M. Scanlon (2003) noted, ethics does not purport to make judgments about causal powers. So whether ethical properties possess such powers does not seem to be similarly relevant to the correctness of ethical judgments.

What seems more plausibly relevant to objectivity is the power of the subject matter of ethics to explain, specifically, ethical judgments. If ethical beliefs, for example, are explained by something other than their putative subject matter—if, as Stroud (2000) put it, an "unmasking explanation" can be given of ethics—then it may seem that ethical beliefs are not suitably responsive to their subject matter. And if ethical beliefs are not suitably responsive to their subject matter, then they are not justified. Moreover, an unmasking explanation may be reason to doubt that ethical beliefs are true: to conclude that ethics, as a whole, is a kind of illusion. Such is the upshot of more familiar unmasking explanations of beliefs about, for example, ghosts and desert oases.

Dworkin (1996) and Scanlon (2003) questioned the assumption that beliefs can be suitably responsive to a subject matter, and hence justified, only if they are causally explained by it. Mathematical beliefs, by analogy, seem to be justified without being caused by their subject matter. Stroud (2000) doubted that an unmasking explanation of ethics can even be given. He argued that one cannot recognize ethical beliefs—the *explanandum*—without accepting some ethical claims, which the "unmasking" *explanans* was supposed to avoid.

A final concern, as Wiggins (1995) and Scanlon (2003) have suggested, is simply that ethics may seem unable to settle any, or enough, of the questions it asks. It may seem, for example, that no argument could settle whether lying to one's friend to spare her feelings in a certain kind of situation is the right thing to do. Here there seems to be a sharp contrast with mathematics, which is able to settle many of the questions it asks. The failure of ethical argument might suggest that ethical judgments cannot be justified: that we lack sufficient reason to hold them. Or it might suggest that ethical judgments cannot be correct: that the subject matter of ethics does not con-strain unique answers to the questions that can be asked about it.

This is a "first-order" or "substantive" doubt, which arises within ethical thought itself, about the prospects of its success. It is often distinguished from "second-order" or "metaethical" doubts, such as those raised by Mackie (1977) and Harman (1977), which are supposed neither to be based on, nor to imply anything, about the prospects of "internal" ethical argument. Dworkin (1996) doubted that this distinction can be sustained, concluding that purportedly "second-order" positions about the objectivity of ethics are, if they are intelligible at all, simply substantive positions within ethics.

See also Error Theory of Ethics; Ethical Naturalism; Ethical Relativism; Ethical Subjectivism; Metaethics; Moral Principles: Their Justification; Moral Realism; Noncognitivism; Rationalism in Ethics (Practical Reason Approaches); Response-Dependence Theories.

Bibliography

Darwall, Stephen, Allan Gibbard, and Peter Railton. "Toward *Fin de Siècle* Ethics: Some Trends." In *Moral Discourse and Practice*. Oxford: Oxford University Press, 1997.

Dworkin, Ronald. "Objectivity and Truth: You'd Better Believe It." *Philosophy and Public Affairs* 25 (2) (1996): 87–139.

Harman, Gilbert. *The Nature of Morality: An Introduction to Ethics*. Oxford: Oxford University Press, 1977.

Korsgaard, Christine. "Skepticism about Practical Reason." *Journal of Philosophy* 83 (1) (1986): 5–25.

Korsgaard, Christine. *The Sources of Normativity*. Cambridge, U.K.: Cambridge University Press, 1996.

Lewis, David. "Dispositional Theories of Value." *Proceedings of the Aristotelian Society* Supp. Vol. 63 (1989): 113–137.

Mackie, J. L. *Ethics: Inventing Right and Wrong*. Harmondsworth, Middlesex: Penguin, 1977.

McDowell, John. "Values and Secondary Qualities." In *Morality and Objectivity*, edited by Ted Honderich. London: Routledge & Kegan Paul, 1985.

Nagel, Thomas. *The Possibility of Altruism*. Princeton, NJ: Princeton University Press, 1979.

Nagel, Thomas. *The View from Nowhere*. New York: Oxford University Press, 1986.

Peacocke, Christopher. "Moral Rationalism." *Journal of Philosophy* 101 (10) (2004): 499–526.

Scanlon, T. M. "Metaphysics and Morals." *Proceedings and Addresses of the American Philosophical Association* 77 (2) (2003): 7–22.

Shafer-Landau, Russ. *Whatever Happened to Good and Evil?* Oxford: Oxford University Press, 2004.

Smith, Michael. *The Moral Problem*. Oxford: Blackwell, 1994.

Stroud, Barry. *The Quest for Reality: Subjectivism and the Metaphysics of Color*. New York: Oxford University Press, 2000.

Wiggins, David. "Objective and Subjective in Ethics, with Two Postscripts about Truth." *Ratio* 8 (3) (1995): 243–258.

Wiggins, David. "A Sensible Subjectivism?" In *Needs, Values, Truth*. 3rd ed. Oxford: Oxford University Press, 1998.

Williams, Bernard. *Ethics and the Limits of Philosophy*. Cambridge, MA: Harvard University Press, 1985.

Wright, Crispin. *Truth and Objectivity*. Cambridge, MA: Harvard University Press, 1992.

Niko Kolodny (2005)

OCCASIONALISM

See *Cartesianism*; *Geulincx, Arnold*; *Malebranche, Nicolas*

OCKHAM, WILLIAM OF

See *William of Ockham*

OCKHAMISM

"Ockhamism" is a term used by some historians of medieval philosophy to characterize the critical and skeptical attitude toward natural theology and traditional metaphysics that became prevalent in the fourteenth century and is ascribed to the influence of William of Ockham (c. 1285–1349). There is little historical basis for speaking of an Ockhamist school, since Ockham had scarcely any avowed disciples; nor was the critical attitude toward natural theology initiated by him, although his logical criteria of demonstration and evidence undoubtedly gave it a powerful implementation. With these reservations one may, in a general sense, attach Ockham's name to the movement of thought that, in the fourteenth century, closed out the medieval enterprise of synthesizing Aristotelian philosophy with Christian theology and initiated new lines of development that led toward the scientific empiricism of the seventeenth century. The Ockhamist or nominalist movement was known in the fourteenth and fifteenth centuries as the "modern way" (*via moderna*), and was contrasted with the "old way" (*via antiqua*) associated with thirteenth-century Scholasticism.

One may distinguish two main phases of this movement of fourteenth-century thought. The first phase, occurring between 1330 and 1350, was marked by the rapid spread of Ockham's doctrines and method among the theologians and philosophers teaching at the universities of Oxford and Paris, where Ockham's logical techniques were used in criticism of the older scholastic tradition. The second phase, less directly associated with Ockham's own teachings, commenced around 1350 and involved what may be described as a reconstruction of philosophy, and of theology as well, on foundations compatible with Ockham's empiricism and nominalism.

CRITIQUE OF SCHOLASTICISM

The influence of Ockham's logic and of his nominalistic critique of the thirteenth-century metaphysical syntheses of philosophy and theology was exhibited at Oxford in the work of Adam Wodeham (d. 1349), a Franciscan who had studied with Ockham, and of Robert Holkot (d. 1349), a Dominican theologian who lectured at Oxford around 1330 and later taught at Cambridge. Holkot was an outspoken nominalist who minced no words in stating that theology is not a science and that its doctrines can in no way be demonstrated or even comprehended by human reason. Christian dogma, for Holkot, was accepted by an act of will, on the authority of the church.

Thomas Bradwardine (c. 1290–1349) reacted against what he regarded as a new Pelagianism embodied in the Ockhamist interpretation of revealed theology, but he used Ockham's logical techniques to draw deterministic consequences from the doctrine of divine omnipotence, invoking the authority of Augustine for his views. Other Oxford teachers influenced by Ockham, and particularly by his logical methods, included Richard Swineshead ("the Calculator"), John Dumbleton, William Heytesbury, and Richard Billingham.

THE "MODERN WAY"

It was at Paris, more than at Oxford, that Ockham's influence led, after an initial resistance, to establishment of a relatively stable, and in some respects scientifically fruitful, philosophical school that endured and spread through central Europe in the late fourteenth and early fifteenth centuries.

One of the first Parisian theologians to embrace Ockham's doctrines was John of Mirecourt, a Cistercian monk who lectured on Peter Lombard's *Sentences* in 1344–1345. His skeptical treatment of the arguments of traditional theology led to a condemnation by the theological faculty at Paris of articles taken from his lectures. In many respects Mirecourt's positions resembled those of Holkot, by whom he may have been influenced.

Another victim of disciplinary action by the authorities of the University of Paris was Nicolas of Autrecourt, who was condemned to burn publicly, in November 1347, his letters to Bernard of Arezzo and his treatise

Exigit ordo executionis. Nicolas, reacting to the Ockhamist thesis that God, by his absolute power, could cause an intuitive cognition of a nonexistent object, or could cause sensible qualities to exist without any substance being qualified by them, held that the only things of which man can have certain knowledge are the qualities perceived by his five senses, the acts or affections of his own mind, and those propositions logically evident by the principle of contradiction. From this he argued that we have no ground for belief in substances or for making inferences on the basis of causal relations, and he asserted that the whole philosophy of Aristotle is a fictitious construction devoid of any evidence or even of probability, since it rests on the assumption of substances and of causal necessities that are neither logically nor empirically evident. Preferring certainty to the Ockhamist "hypothesis of nature," Nicolas turned Ockham's critique of metaphysical necessity against Ockham's own empiricism and was rebuked by John Buridan for demanding absolute evidence, or logical necessity, in a domain of inquiry in which only conditional evidence based on the assumption of a common course of nature is appropriate.

In the hands of Buridan, a teacher on the faculty of arts at Paris, Ockham's logic, theory of knowledge, and nominalistic ontology were made the basis of a natural philosophy or physics of empirical type, within which Buridan developed the impetus theory of projectile motion and gravitational acceleration and subjected the assumptions of Aristotelian physics and cosmology to critical analysis in terms of empirical criteria of evidence. Buridan's reconstruction of natural philosophy as a positive and empirically based science of observable phenomena undermined the Aristotelian tradition and provided some of the main starting points for the development of modern mechanics in the seventeenth century.

At the same time a theologian of Paris, Gregory of Rimini (d. 1358), who became general of the order of Augustinian Hermits, made a constructive use of Ockhamist methods and doctrines in a theological synthesis of nominalism and Augustinianism; although he took issue with both Ockham and Buridan on some issues of metaphysics, the later Scholastics regarded him as a modern theologian of the nominalist group.

Natural philosophy, as distinguished from theology, was dominated by the moderately Ockhamist tradition established at Paris by Buridan, developed by Albert of Saxony and Nicholas of Oresme, and carried to the new universities of central Europe by Albert, Marsilius of Inghen, Henry of Hainbuch, and Henry of Oyta. A document drawn up by the faculty of the University of

Cologne in 1425 speaks of the period of preeminence of the *via moderna* as the century of Buridan (*saeculum Buridani*), indicating that the Ockhamism of the later fourteenth century had become associated with Buridan and his followers more than with Ockham.

RELIGIOUS INFLUENCE

The Ockhamist divorce of Christian theology from Aristotelian metaphysics, with the corresponding emphasis on religious faith and the tradition of the Church Fathers as foundation of Christian doctrine, was reflected in the popular religious movement associated with the school of Deventer and the *devotio moderna* and in the criticisms of the scholastic methods of theological disputation and argument made by Jean de Gerson at the end of the fourteenth century. Gabriel Biel (c. 1410–1495) was the last influential theologian of the Ockhamist school, and in his work the influence of Gerson, Gregory of Rimini, Holkot, and of Ockham himself brought together the diverse strands of this nominalist tradition in a doctrine with strong religious emphasis.

Ockhamism, as a well-developed philosophical and religious tradition, was submerged by the Reformation and the Counter-Reformation, as well as by the humanist revolt against the medieval cultural tradition. However, its leading ideas, in the liberation of both the Christian faith and the scientific investigation of nature from dogmatic Aristotelianism, remained operative outside the schools and bore fruit in the seventeenth and eighteenth centuries.

See also Buridan, John; Gregory of Rimini; John of Mirecourt; Nicolas of Autrecourt; William of Ockham.

Bibliography

HISTORICAL SURVEYS

Ashworth, E. J. *Language and Logic in the Post-Medieval Period.* Dordrecht: Reidel, 1974.

Courtenay, W. J. "The Reception of Ockham's Thought at the University of Paris." In *Preuve et raisons à l'Université de Paris,* edited by Z. Kaluza and P. Vignaux, Paris: Vrin, 1984, pp. 43–64.

Courtenay, W. J. "Was There an Ockhamist School?" In *Philosophy and Learning: Universities in the Middle Ages,* edited by M. J. F. M. Hoenen, J. H. J. Schneider, and G. Wieland, Leiden: Brill, 1995, pp. 263–92.

Courtenay, W. J., and K. Tachau. "Ockham, Ockhamists and the English-German Nation at Paris, 1339–1341." *History of Universities* 2 (1982): 53–96.

Klima, G. "The Medieval Problem of Universals." *The Stanford Encyclopedia of Philosophy (Winter 2004 Edition),* edited by Edward N. Zalta. <http://plato.stanford.edu/archives/win2004/entries/universals-medieval/>.

Nuchelmans, G. *Late-Scholastic and Humanist Theories of the Proposition.* Amsterdam: North Holland, 1980.

Scott, T. K. "Nicholas of Autrecourt, Buridan and Ockhamism." In *Journal of the History of Philosophy* 9 (1971): 15–41.

Thijssen, J. M. M. H. *Censure and Heresy at the University of Paris, 1200–1400.* Philadelphia: University of Pennsylvania Press, 1998.

Zimmermann, A., ed. *Antiqui und Moderni: Traditionsbewusstsein und Fortschrittsbewusstsein im späten Mittelalter.* Berlin: de Gruyter, 1974.

OCKHAM

Adams, M. M. *William Ockham.* 2 vols. Notre Dame, IN: University of Notre Dame Press, 1987; 2nd ed., 1989.

Panaccio, C., ed. *The Cambridge Companion to Ockham.* New York: Cambridge University Press, 1999.

Panaccio, C. *Le discours intérieur: De platon à Guillaume d'Ockham.* Paris: Éditions de Seuil, 1999.

Panaccio, C. *Les mots, les concepts et les choses. Le sémantique de Guillaume d'Occam et le nominalisme d'aujourd'hui.* Montréal-Paris: Bellarmin-Vrin, 1991.

Panaccio, C. *Ockham on Concepts.* Hampshire/Burlington: Ashgate, 2004.

Panaccio, C. "Some Epistemological Implications of the Burley-Ockham Dispute." *Franciscan Studies* 35 (1975): 212–22.

Panaccio, C. "Synonymy and Equivocation in Ockham's Mental Language." *Journal of the History of Philosophy* 18 (1980): 9–22.

Panaccio, C. "Three Versions of Ockham's Reductionist Program." *Franciscan Studies* 56 (1998): 335–46.

Spade, P. V. "Ockham's Distinctions between Absolute and Connotative Terms." *Vivarium* 13 (1975): 55–76.

BURIDAN

Friedmann, R. L., and S. Ebbesen, eds. *John Buridan and Beyond: Topics in the Language Sciences 1300–1700.* Copenhagen: The Royal Danish Academy of Sciences and Letters, 2004.

Klima, G. "Buridan's Logic and the Ontology of Modes." In *Medieval Analyses in Language and Cognition,* edited by R. L. Friedmann and S. Ebbesen, Copenhagen: The Royal Danish Academy of Sciences and Letters, 1999, pp. 473–495.

Klima, G. "The Essentialist Nominalism of John Buridan." *The Review of Metaphysics,* 58 (2005): 301–315.

Klima, G. "Latin as a Formal Language: Outlines of a Buridanian Semantics." *Cahiers de l'Institut du Moyen-Age Grec et Latin.* Copenhagen, 61 (1991): 78–106.

Normore, C. "Buridan's Ontology." In *How Things Are: Studies in Predication and the History and Philosophy of Science,* edited by J. Bogen and J. E. McGuire, Dordrecht: Reidel, 1985, pp. 189–203.

Pinborg, J., ed. *The Logic of John Buridan.* Copenhagen: Museum Tusculanum, 1976.

Thijssen, J. M. M. H., and Jack Zupko, eds. *The Metaphysics and Natural Philosophy of John Buridan.* Leiden: E. J. Brill, 2001.

Zupko, J. "Buridan and Skepticism." *Journal of the History of Philosophy* 31 (1993): 191–221.

Zupko, J. *John Buridan: Portrait of a 14th-Century Arts Master.* Notre Dame, IN: University of Notre Dame Press, 2003.

NICHOLAS OF AUTRECOURT

Grellard, C. *Croire et savior: Les principes de la connaissance selon Nicolas d'Autrecourt.* Paris: Vrin, 2005.

Kaluza, Z. "Nicolas d'Autrecourt. Ami de la vérité." In *Histoire littéraire de la France*, vol. 42, fasc. 1. Paris, 1995.

Scott, T. K. "Nicholas of Autrecourt, Buridan, and Ockhamism." *Journal of the History of Philosophy* 9 (1971): 15–41.

Tachau, K. H. *Vision and Certitude in the Age of Ockham. Optics, Epistemology and the Foundations of Semantics, 1250–1345.* Leiden: Brill, 1988.

Thijssen, J. M. M. H. "John Buridan and Nicholas of Autrecourt on Causality and Induction." *Traditio* 43 (1987): 237–255.

Thijssen, J. M. M. H. "The Quest for Certain Knowledge in the Fourteenth Century: Nicholas of Autrecourt against the Academics." In *Ancient Scepticism and the Sceptical Tradition*, edited by J. Sihvola, Helsinki: Societas Philosophica Fennica, 2000, pp. 199–223 (*Acta Philosophica Fennica*, 66).

Thijssen, J. M. M. H. "The 'Semantic Articles' of Autrecourt's Condemnation." *Archives d'histoire doctrinale et littéraire du moyen âge*, 65 (1990): 155–175.

Zupko, J. "How It Played in the rue de Fouarre: The Reception of Adam Wodeham's Theory of the *Complexe Significabile* in the Arts Faculty at Paris in the Mid-Fourteenth Century." *Franciscan Studies* 54 (1994–97): 211–225.

Ernest A. Moody (1967)
Bibliography updated by Gyula Klima (2005)

OGYŪ SORAI
(1666–1728)

Ogyū Sorai, or Butsu, was a Japanese Confucianist of the *kogakuha* ("school of ancient learning"), and famous as a political thinker. Ogyū was born in Edo (Tokyo). He was a gifted pupil and soon mastered classical Chinese; the classical style is characteristic of his writings. Proud by nature, Ogyū distinguished himself in the defense of official Zhu Xi Neo-Confucianism in polemics against Itō Jinsai. In 1716, however, his views changed, and in *Bendō* (Defining the way) and *Bemmei* (Definitions of terms) he supports most of Itō's ideas. All of Ogyū's other works were inspired by the ancient sages in accord with the maxim "back to antiquity," a maxim applicable to many of his innovations. These innovations were expressed in *Taiheisaku* (A policy for great peace) and *Seidan* (Discourses on government). Ogyū's cosmological views differ little from Itō's; Ogyū, too, rejects the dichotomy of *ri*, the principle, and *ki*, the material energy.

Ogyū holds a positivist and historicist conception of the Way (*dō*); it became for him the factual order of society, with its positive laws and institutions. He rightly points out how Confucius stressed the societal implications of the Way. Ogyū goes much further, excluding personal ethics until only "rites," that is, propriety and social behavior, combined with obedience to the government, remain. In this sense he comes very close to the Chinese Legalists in utilitarian ethics. Although he was apparently inspired by Xunzi c. 295–c. 238 BCE), he does not mention the name. For Ogyū, human nature cannot be much corrected; in this only social institutions are of any use. The sole meaning of "humaneness" is the giving of peace and prosperity to the people, and "virtue" is the virtue of the ruler in discerning able men. His political and economic ideas have little in common with Confucian moralizing. Government is a practical technique (*jutsu*), and the economy is not based on thrift but on sound social policies. He was against the idea of fanatic loyalty to the lord and advocated some social mobility, believing that the lower samurai but not the common people should be allowed to improve their status.

Ogyū's views of history are distinguished by the same practical approach. The founder of a dynasty plays a great role because of the public institutions he has to establish, yet rulers often fall because of the difficulty of preventing economic decline. Living under the Tokugawa shogunate, Ogyū rejected even the nominal sovereignty of the emperor (an opinion his best pupil, Dazai Shundai [1680–1747], concurred in). Shintoism for Ogyū was an invention of Yoshida Kanetomo (1435–1511). Ogyū's stand in favor of the Tokugawa government and his rejection of Shintoism explain why he was not repressed for his daring ideas and anti-Zhu Xi doctrine.

See also Chinese Philosophy; Itō Jinsai; Japanese Philosophy; Xunzi; Zhu Xi (Chu Hsi).

Bibliography

The principal works of Ogyū Sorai can be found in several collections. See *Nihon rinri ihen* (Library on Japanese ethics), edited by Inoue Tetsujirō (Tokyo: Ikuseikai, 1902), Vol. VI, pp. 11–203; *Nihon keizai taiten* (Classics on Japanese economics), edited by Takimoto Seiichi (Tokyo: Shishi Shuppansha, 1928), Vol. IX, pp. 3–375; *Ogyū Soraishū* (Collected works of Ogyū Sorai; Tokyo, 1937).

Two secondary sources in English are J. R. McEvan, *The Political Writings of Ogyū Sorai* (Cambridge, U.K.: Cambridge University Press, 1962) and W. T. de Bary, Ryusaku Tsunoda, and Donald Keene, eds., *Sources of*

Japanese Tradition (New York: Columbia University Press, 1958), pp. 342–343, 422–433.

Gino K. Piovesana, S.J. (1967)

OKEN, LORENZ
(1779–1855)

Lorenz Oken, a German biologist and philosopher, was born at Bohlsbach, Baden. He was graduated from the faculty of medicine at Freiburg in 1804 and obtained his first professorship in medicine at Jena in 1807. Oken left Jena in 1819 because as editor of the liberal periodical *Isis* he had incurred the disfavor of the authorities. He traveled in Germany and France, lectured at the University of Basel in 1821 and 1822, and after a brief appointment at the University of Munich he became professor of physiology in Zürich, where he remained until his death.

After a few years in Jena, Oken was asked to transfer from medicine to philosophy. Yet ten years later, in his second term at Basel, he was listed as professor of medicine only, with no reference to philosophy. These changes reflect Oken's development and the superseding of romantic nature philosophy by a more objective study of natural phenomena. Under the influence of Friedrich von Schelling and the thinkers of the romantic school, Oken's imagination—rather than a genuine philosophical bent—swept him on to his own version of philosophy of identity. If in his time Oken was thought to be a greater philosopher than even Schelling, it was because he had a much wider knowledge of the natural sciences to illustrate and support his metaphysics. His most significant book in this connection is the *Lehrbuch der Naturphilosophie* (*Elements of Physiophilosophy*). This work aroused great interest, especially among the New England transcendentalists. Oken tried to establish a correspondence between mathematical structures and nature, and between metaphysical essences and nature. Fond of Pythagorean mysticism, he argued that all life is cast in the mold of mathematical symbols. Zero is nothingness and the infinite at the same time. The evolution of positive and negative numbers out of zero is the counterpart of a descending and ascending order of things—the descent being from matter (heavenly bodies, rocks, minerals, etc.) to some primeval mucus, while the ascent is from this mucus, seminated by infusoria and helped along by galvanism, through the whole scale of plant and animal life to man.

Metaphysically, zero is God. The disintegration of matter to mucus and the evolution of living beings illustrate God's desire to manifest himself in nature—when he comes to man, he meets himself; man is a god created by God. Theogony turns into hylogeny, the creation of matter. By the same token, all that exists is embedded in and permeated by an everlasting stream of vitality—pantheism and vitalism combine in Oken's view of the universe and its parts.

A poet in science, Ralph Waldo Emerson called Oken admiringly. The appropriateness of this remark is underlined by Oken the physiologist, who regarded man as an assembly of all the sense organs and other bodily parts developed along the ascending path; and by Oken the psychologist, who saw all animals as contributing to the psychology of the crowning organism, man. Mollusks gave man prudence and caution; from the snails man received seriousness and dignity; courage and nobility came from the insects; and the fish brought him the dowry of memory. Oken as a scientist with imagination may have had his merits, but as a philosopher he was unable to raise thought from the level of matter, chemistry, physiology, and cosmogony to a level of creative independence. Mind for Oken was merely a mirror in which God and nature could behold themselves.

In his less poetic moods, Oken came close to being a modern scientist. He held, with Johann Wolfgang von Goethe but independently of him, that the cephalic bones are a repetition of the vertebrae, and he was not far from establishing the cellular structure of living organisms. His publications after *Physiophilosophy-Lehrbuch der Naturgeschichte* and *Allgemeine Naturgeschichte für alle Stände*—reverted to the method of his earlier works: close observation and faithful description. If in Oken's days the natural sciences had to extricate themselves from preconceived mystical notions wrongly called philosophy, they beg today to be understood again in some wider context. The wheel has come full circle, as it must according to Oken's belief in the alternating processes of dynamic expansion and nostalgic reduction to a state of absolute quietness, a belief reminiscent of Friedrich Nietzsche's eternal recurrence of the same. The difference is that for Oken the fascination of this unending spectacle ended where Nietzsche's interest in it began, with the arrival of man and the search for values.

See also Emerson, Ralph Waldo; Goethe, Johann Wolfgang von; New England Transcendentalism; Nietzsche, Friedrich; Realism and Naturalism, Mathematical; Schelling, Friedrich Wilhelm Joseph von; Structuralism, Mathematical; Value and Valuation.

Bibliography

PRINCIPAL WORKS BY OKEN

Lehrbuch der Naturphilosophie, 3 vols. Jena: F. Frommann, 1809–1811; improved and final ed., 1843. Translated by Alfred Tulk as *Elements of Physiophilosophy.* London: Ray Society, 1847.

Lehrbuch der Naturgeschichte, 5 vols. Leipzig and Jena, 1813–1826.

Allgemeine Naturgeschichte für alle Stände, 13 vols. Stuttgart: Hoffman, 1833–1841.

WORKS ON OKEN

Ecker, Alexander. *Lorenz Oken. Eine biographische Skizze.* Stuttgart, 1880.

Hübner, Georg Wilhelm. *Okens Naturphilosophie prinzipiell und kritisch bearbeitet.* Borna-Leipzig, 1909.

Schuster, Julius. *Oken. Der Mann und sein Werk.* Berlin, 1922.

Hermann Boeschenstein (1967)

OLIVI, PETER JOHN
(1248–1298)

Peter John Olivi was one of the most original philosophers of the late thirteenth century. Despite the influence his ideas had in the Middle Ages and in the formation of the early modern thought, his own writings have been studied little. The Council of Vienne (1311–1312) and Pope John XXII (in 1326) condemned some of his views, and after this his works (most of which have survived in the Vatican library) remained mostly in obscurity. His innovative ideas on the philosophy of history, on Aristotelian metaphysics, and especially on human freedom were developed by other philosophers whose texts had a more constant and wider circulation (e.g., John Duns Scotus, William Ockham, and Peter Aureol).

As a twelve-year-old youth in 1261, Olivi entered the Franciscan order and thereby also one of the best educational systems of the time. From 1267 to 1272 he studied in Paris with St. Bonaventure and other famous thinkers. Possibly because of arrogant opinions, he did not receive a doctorate. Nevertheless, he moved on to teach at different Franciscan schools in southern France. After some of his views were condemned in 1283, he withdrew from such duties. He was rehabilitated in 1288 with the help of his former teacher, Cardinal Matthew of Aquasparta, and taught in Florence for two years before returning to Montpellier and later Narbonne, where he stayed until his death on March 14, 1298.

Readers of Olivi's works have often noted that Olivi had a very distinctive writing style. Though his works clearly belong to the genres of medieval academic writing, they contain a very personal tone that seems to spring from Olivi's intimate experiential touch to philosophical thinking. Olivi clearly had a liking for arguments, and often he refrained from making a determinate solution, although he did not hesitate to take strong stances on some very controversial issues. In general, his habits of thought have a surprisingly modern feel.

SOCIAL PHILOSOPHY

Olivi's most important innovations in social philosophy are related to the Franciscan ideal of poverty. In his commentary on the Apocalypse and already in the early *Questions on Evangelical Perfection* he formulated a theory of how the Franciscans used the necessities of life without having property in them (*usus pauper*). The theory differs in its detail to what John Duns Scotus and William Ockham presented later, but the crucial philosophical innovations can be found already in Olivi's works.

The idea of subjective right is often connected to early modern political philosophy, but it was developed already in the discussions concerning Franciscan poverty. Olivi's view concerning rights differed from the Aristotelian orthodoxy of the time, for according to him the natural order does not imply rights. Rather, they must be constituted by an act of a free will. This view becomes clear in his theory of property acquisition and of political power. Though Olivi taught for the Franciscans absolute obedience to the superiors, he qualified that the power of the superiors must accord with the purpose of the power. This makes obedience in fact an issue that each person must weigh in his or her own conscience.

Olivi was a theologian, and he wrote many biblical commentaries, often with an apocalyptic message. He also had a historical view of the Church as a changing institution. He has often been understood as claiming that the Antichrist will be a pope.

HUMAN FREEDOM

The human free will is a topic that receives a large share of what can be called Olivi's main philosophical work, the commentary on Peter of Lombards *Sentences*. Some of Olivi's strongest anti-Aristotelian formulations come form this context. Like apparently all the texts where he explicitly opposes Aristotelian thought, it was written soon after the bishop Etienne Tempier's condemnation of 1277 against 219 more or less Aristotelian theses. Olivi showed no knowledge of the documents of the condemnation themselves, but attacked the Aristotelian positions and apparently also Thomas Aquinas's views quite openly.

According to Olivi's main argument for the freedom the human will, the ground for human social practices like friendship and gratitude, and even personhood, would collapse if human beings denied the freedom of the will. In Olivi's view, free choice is a real possibility open for all mentally healthy adult humans in their normal condition. Unlike the animals, humans can make choices self-reflexively as their own choices. Olivi discussed the Aristotelian practical syllogism and accepted that humans consider rationally what would be the best course of action given a certain end. But even after this consideration, humans remain free to follow the best course of action or to do something else. Also, the human will is always free to posit a new ultimate end. In Olivi's example, if one hates one's enemy and reasons the best way to harm the person, one remains free not to inflict harm, or even to begin loving the person for his or her own sake. Every human has an almost infinite moral worth based on such freedom, and as a free agent can be treated as a person.

METAPHYSICS

Olivi's ontological view of the human soul was rejected by the fourteenth-century Church as too dualist. He was understood to have claimed that the soul is not the form of the body, though his point was subtler. According to his metaphysics, all individuals consist of matter and form. However, he distinguished two kinds of matter: corporeal and spiritual. The human soul informs matter of both kinds, but the intellectual soul does not inform any corporeal matter. The human soul is thus a form of the corporeal body only in respect to its sensitive part. Thus, Olivi accepted the Aristotelian metaphysics of form and matter, but thought that the human intellectual soul is a full individual capable of existence and activity even without the body. This tradition of thought was continued by later Franciscans like Scotus and Ockham, although they gave up the idea of spiritual matter and with it also the universality of the form-matter metaphysics, making the intellectual soul an immaterial substance. In this way, Olivi's theory can be seen as direct predecessor of René Descartes's seventeenth-century dualist view.

In the philosophy of mind, Olivi's most important starting point was that the mind is active and the corporeal bodies are passive. He described sensory perception in terms of an intentional relation where the mind comports to the world, thus rejecting the standard Aristotelian model that the corporeal things act upon the cognitive systems. Olivi also developed a relatively elaborated theory of the self and human self-understanding.

Olivi was a well-educated intellectual working in a way similar to his contemporaries. In most of the topics he treated he refrained from putting forward a full theory. Rather, he aimed at deeper, though incomplete, understanding on the complexity of the problems, and called for recognition of the imperfections of the human reasoning capacities. Olivi did not oppose rational thought, but he saw its limits. Much of his philosophical originality lies in the way he strove for a rationally un-Aristotelian way of thinking at a time in which basic university education was based on Aristotle's texts.

See also Aristotelianism; Bonaventure, St.; Descartes, René; Determinism and Freedom; Duns Scotus, John; Matthew of Acquasparta; Medieval Philosophy; Peter Aureol; Peter Lombard; Philosophy of History; Philosophy of Mind; Thomas Aquinas, St.; William of Ockham.

Bibliography

WORKS BY PETER JOHN OLIVI

For a listing of Olivi's writings, see *Archivum Franciscanum historicum* 91 (3–4) (1998).

Quaestiones in secundum librum Sententiarum. Bibliotheca Franciscana Scholastica 4–6. Edited by B. Jansen. Quaracchi: Collegium S. Bonaventurae, 1922–1926.

Quodlibeta quinque. Edited by S. Defraia. Grottaferrata: Editiones Collegii S. Bonaventurae ad Claras Aquas, 2002.

WORKS ABOUT PETER JOHN OLIVI

Boureau, A., and S. Piron, eds. *Pierre de Jean Olivi (1248–1298).* Paris: Vrin, 1999.

Burr, David. *Olivi and Franciscan Poverty: The Origins of the Usus Pauper Controversy.* Philadelphia: University of Pennsylvania Press, 1989.

Lagerlund, H., and M. Yrjönsuuri, eds. *Emotions and Choice from Boethius to Descartes.* Kluwer: Dordrecht, 2002.

Pasnau, Robert. *Theories of Cognition in the Later Middle Ages.* Cambridge, U.K.: Cambridge University Press, 1997.

Putallaz, François-Xavier. *Insolente liberté. Controverses et condamnations au XIIIe siècle.* Paris: Cerf, 1995.

Yrjönsuuri, Mikko (2005)

OMAN, JOHN WOOD
(1860–1939)

John Wood Oman, the philosopher of religion and theologian, was a Scotsman from the Orkney Islands. After being educated at Edinburgh and Heidelberg universities and serving for seventeen years in a rural pastorate in

Northumberland, he taught for twenty-eight years at Westminster College, Cambridge, the seminary of the English Presbyterian Church. The chief influence on his developing thought was that of Friedrich Schleiermacher, whose *Reden* Oman translated into English.

In the massive *The Natural and the Supernatural* (1931) Oman portrays the root of religion as man's immediate sense of the Supernatural. The primary religious awareness is not inferential but is, in words that Oman used to describe the similar conception of Schleiermacher, "intuition of reality, an intercourse between a universe, present always in all its meaning, and a spirit, responding with all its understanding" (p. 36). By the Supernatural, Oman does not mean the mysterious, the uncanny, or the miraculous but a larger environment than physical nature, "a special kind of environment, which has its own particular sanctions" (p. 23), through commerce with which man receives his characteristically human degree of independence within his natural environment.

The Supernatural is variously conceived in different types of religion, as is the character of the redemption that the supernatural makes possible. In primitive religion redemption is found by seeking the Supernatural in nature as an animistic force indefinitely many and yet vaguely one. In polytheism the Supernatural consists of individual spirits that rule different parts of nature, and redemption means the managing of nature through its many divine masters. Cosmic pantheism accepts nature in its wholeness as the Supernatural, while the acosmic mysticism of India wholly excludes nature from the Supernatural, as illusion. Religions of the ceremonial-legal type, such as priestly Judaism and Islam, divide the Natural into a sacred realm and a secular realm, cultivating the sacred or religious while leaving the secular outside the sphere of redemption. Finally, for the prophetic monotheism of the Hebrew prophets and of Christianity redemption is reconciliation to the Natural by finding within it the purpose of the one personal Supernatural. To be reconciled to God is to accept all the experiences of one's life as of God's appointing, and one's duties as divine commands. Thus, prophetic religion is intensely practical and this-worldly. Speaking of its Old Testament representatives, Oman says, "What determines their faith is not a theory of the Supernatural, but an attitude towards the Natural, as a sphere in which a victory of deeper meaning than the visible and of more abiding purpose than the fleeting can be won" (p. 448).

Oman emphasizes that knowledge of our environment, whether the natural or the Supernatural, does not consist in the mere registering of "impacts" but always consists in a perception of "meaning." In order to become aware of our environment, we must rightly interpret its impingements upon us. "Thus knowledge is not knowledge as an effect of an unknown external cause, but is knowledge as we so interpret that our meaning is the actual meaning of our environment" (p. 175). In this interpretative process, the mind exercises a degree of freedom. That degree is established by the individual frontiers of each mind, which are largely controlled from within and across which the meaning of the environment can pass only as a meaning recognized by the individual.

The Supernatural presents itself to the human mind with the quality of the sacred or of absolute worth. To be aware of the Supernatural is to recognize some sacred value that lays an absolute claim upon us, even if in the early stages of man's dealings with the Supernatural this is only an irrational taboo. Religion is "essentially a dealing with an unseen environment of absolute worth, which demands worship" (p. 23). This recognition of and allegiance to the sacred frees man from the dominance of his physical surroundings: "He obtained firm footing to deal with his environment the moment he regarded anything as sacred, because he could say 'No' and was no longer its mere creature" (p. 85).

While man's sense of the Supernatural gives him a fixed point amid the evanescent and a degree of freedom in relation to the natural, he can gain this only by exercise of his own freedom. For "The peculiarity of the supernatural environment is that we cannot enter it except as we see and choose it as our own" (p. 309).

Oman makes no use of the attempted logical coercion of the traditional theistic proofs. He does not try to establish the truth of religion independently of religious experience. Rather he starts from the fact of the religious man's awareness of a larger supernatural environment, in terms of which he lives, and argues that this awareness has no greater need or possibility of philosophical justification than has our awareness of the natural environment. "Among Western thinkers from [René] Descartes onwards, attempts have been made to prove the existence of a material world by other evidence than the way it environs us, but the result was no more reassuring for the reality of the natural world than for the reality of the supernatural" (p. 51).

The same basic standpoint is evident in Oman's contributions to doctrinal theology, especially his *Grace and Personality* (1919). Oman was the first of a series of twentieth-century Christian thinkers—such as Karl Heim, Emil Brunner, H. H. Farmer, and John Macmurray—to treat as a normative principle of his theology the insight that God is the supremely personal reality, that his dealings with men take place in the personal realm, and that the great central Christian terms—revelation, faith, grace, sin, reconciliation—are to be understood as part of the language of personal relationship and are perverted when construed in nonpersonal ways. Oman taught that religious truths are not infallibilities declared authoritatively from heaven but claim acceptance only because they irresistibly impress our minds as true, and that God seeks our trust only by showing himself to be trustworthy.

There are in Oman's works the elements of a religious philosophy that might well appeal to many today because it is consistently empiricist, being based upon what is given in human experience. However, it is often expressed in Oman's pages on a higher level of generality, and with less detailed precision, than has become customary since he wrote, and there is therefore scope for the development of these same themes in more contemporary terms.

See also Brunner, Emil; Descartes, René; Heim, Karl; Religion, Naturalistic Reconstructions of; Schleiermacher, Friedrich Daniel Ernst.

Bibliography

WORKS BY OMAN

Vision and Authority. London: Hodder and Stoughton, 1902; 2nd ed., 1928.

The Problem of Faith and Freedom in the Last Two Centuries. London: Hodder and Stoughton, 1906.

The Church and the Divine Order. London: Hodder and Stoughton, 1911.

The War and Its Issues. Cambridge, U.K.: Cambridge University Press, 1916.

Grace and Personality. Cambridge, U.K.: Cambridge University Press, 1919; 4th ed., 1931.

The Paradox of the World: Sermons. Cambridge, U.K.: Cambridge University Press, 1921.

The Book of Revelation. Cambridge, U.K.: Cambridge University Press, 1923.

The Office of the Ministry. London: Student Christian Movement Press, 1928.

The Text of Revelation. Cambridge, U.K.: Cambridge University Press, 1928.

The Natural and the Supernatural. Cambridge, U.K.: Cambridge University Press, 1931.

Concerning the Ministry. London: Student Christian Movement Press, 1936.

Honest Religion. Cambridge, U.K.: Cambridge University Press, 1941.

A Dialogue with God. London: James Clarke, 1951. Sermons.

WORKS ON OMAN

Bevons, Stephen. *John Oman and His Doctrine of God.* Cambridge, U.K.: Cambridge University Press, 1992.

Healey, F. G. *Religion and Reality: The Theology of John Oman.* Edinburgh: Oliver and Boyd, 1965.

Hood, Adam. *Baillie, Oman, and Macmurray: Experience and Religious Belief.* Burlington: Ashgate, 2003.

Langford, Thomas. *In Search of Foundations: English Theology 1900–1920.* Nashville: Abington Press, 1969.

Langford, Thomas. "The Theological Methodology of John Oman and H. H. Farmer." *Religious Studies* 1 (1965): 229–240.

Tennant, F. R. "John Wood Oman, 1860–1939." *Proceedings of the British Academy* 25 (1939): 333–338.

John Hick (1967)
Bibliography updated by Christian B. Miller (2005)

ONTOLOGICAL ARGUMENT FOR THE EXISTENCE OF GOD

The Ontological Argument for the existence of God was first propounded by Anselm (c. 1033–1109), abbot of Bee and later archbishop of Canterbury, in his *Proslogion* (Chs. 2–4) and in his *Reply* to a contemporary critic.

He begins (*Proslogion* 2) with the concept of God as "something than which nothing greater can be conceived" (*aliquid quo nihil maius cogitari possit*, and other equivalent formulations). It is clear that by "greater" Anselm means "more perfect." (Sometimes he uses *melius*, "better," instead of *maius*, "greater": for instance, *Proslogion* 14 and 18.) Since we have this idea, it follows that "Something than which nothing greater can be conceived" at least exists in our minds (*in intellectu*) as an object of thought. The question is whether it also exists in extramental reality (*in re*). Anselm argues that it must so exist, since otherwise we should be able to conceive of something greater than that than which nothing greater can be conceived—which is absurd. Therefore "Something than which nothing greater can be conceived" must exist in reality.

In *Proslogion* 3 Anselm adds that "Something than which nothing greater can be conceived" exists in the truest and greatest way (*verissime et maxime esse*); for whereas anything else can be conceived not to exist (and thus exists only contingently), "Something than which nothing greater can be conceived" cannot be conceived not to exist (and thus exists necessarily). For that which cannot be conceived not to exist is greater than that which *can* be conceived not to exist, and therefore only that which cannot be conceived not to exist is adequate to the notion of "Something a greater than which cannot be conceived."

Anselm explains (in his *Responsio*) that by a being which cannot be conceived not to exist he means one that is eternal in the sense of having no beginning or end and always existing as a whole, that is, not in successive phases. He argues that if such a being can be conceived, it must also exist. For the idea of an eternal being that has either ceased to exist or has not yet come into existence is self-contradictory; the notion of eternal existence excludes both of these possibilities. This latter argument has been revived and developed in our own day (see below).

Many of the earliest manuscripts of the *Proslogion* contain a contemporary criticism (attributed in two of the manuscripts to one Gaunilo of Marmoutier) together with Anselm's reply. The criticism, summed up in the analogy of the island, is directed against Anselm's argument as presented in *Proslogion* 2. Gaunilo sets up what he supposes to be a parallel ontological argument for the existence of an island more perfect than any known island: such an island must exist, since otherwise it would be less perfect than any known island, and this would be a contradiction. In reply Anselm develops the reasoning of *Proslogion* 3. His argument cannot be applied to islands or to anything else whose nonexistence is conceivable, for whatever can be conceived not to exist is *eo ipso* less than "Something than which nothing greater can be conceived." Only from this latter notion can we (according to Anselm) deduce that there must be something corresponding to it in reality.

Perhaps the most valuable feature of Anselm's argument is its formulation of the Christian concept of God. Augustine (*De Libero Arbitrio* II, 6, 14) had used the definition of God as one "than whom there is nothing superior." The Ontological Argument could not be based upon this notion, for although it is true by definition that the most perfect being that there is, exists, there is no guarantee that this being is God, in the sense of the proper object of man's worship. Anselm, however, does not define God as the most perfect being that there is but as a being than whom no more perfect is even conceivable. This represents the final development of the monotheistic conception. God is the most adequate conceivable object of worship; there is no possibility of another reality beyond him to which he is inferior or subordinate and which would thus be an even more worthy recipient of man's devotion. Thus metaphysical ultimacy and moral ultimacy coincide; one cannot ask of the most

perfect conceivable being, as one can of a first cause, necessary being, unmoved mover, or designer of the world (supposing such to exist) whether men ought to worship him. Here the religious exigencies that move from polytheism through henotheism to ethical monotheism reach their logical terminus. And the credit belongs to Anselm for having first formulated this central core of the ultimate concept of deity.

DESCARTES'S ARGUMENT

Anselm's argument was rejected by Thomas Aquinas in favor of the Cosmological Argument and as a consequence was largely neglected during the remainder of the medieval period. It was, however, again brought into prominence by René Descartes in the seventeenth century, and most subsequent discussions have been based upon Descartes's formulation. Descartes made explicit the presupposition of the argument that existence is an attribute or predicate which, like other predicates, a given *x* can meaningfully be said to have or to lack. He claims that just as the idea of a triangle necessarily includes among the defining attributes of a triangle that of having its three internal angles equal to two right angles, so the idea of a supremely perfect being (a different formula from Anselm's) necessarily includes the attribute of existence. Consequently we can no more think, without contradiction, of a supremely perfect being which lacks existence than of a triangle which lacks three sides.

Descartes considers the following objection: From the fact that in order to be a triangle a figure must have three sides it does not follow that there actually are any triangles; and likewise in the case of the concept of a supremely perfect being. His reply is that whereas the notion, or essence, of a triangle does not include the attribute of existence that of a supremely perfect being does, and that therefore in this special case we are entitled to infer existence from a concept.

KANT'S CRITICISM

Descartes's version of the Ontological Argument had some important contemporary critics—for example, Pierre Gassendi and Johannes Caterus (Johan de Kater)—but the classic criticism is that of Immanuel Kant. This moves on two levels. First, leaving the argument's presuppositions for the moment unchallenged, he grants the analytic connection that Descartes had affirmed between the concept of God and that of existence. In the proposition "A perfect being exists" we cannot without contradiction affirm the subject and reject the predicate. But, he points out, we can without contradiction elect not to affirm the subject together with its predicate. We can reject as a whole the complex concept of an existing all-perfect being.

Second, however, Kant rejects the assumption that existence is a real predicate. If it were a real, and not merely a grammatical, predicate, it would be able to form part of the definition of God, and it could then be an analytic truth that God exists. But existential propositions (propositions asserting existence) are always synthetic, always true or false as a matter of fact rather than as a matter of definition. Whether any specified kind of thing exists can be determined only by the tests of experience. The function of "is" or "exists" is not to add to the content of a concept but to posit an object answering to a concept. Thus, the real contains no more than the possible (a hundred real dollars are the same in number as a hundred imagined ones); the difference is that in the one case the concept does and in the other case it does not correspond to something in reality.

RUSSELL'S ANALYSIS. Essentially the same point—so far as it affects the Ontological Argument—was made in the twentieth century by Bertrand Russell in his theory of descriptions. This involves an analysis of positive and negative existential propositions, according to which to affirm that x's exist is to affirm that there are objects answering to the description "x," and to deny that x's exist is to deny that there are any such objects. The function of "exists" is thus to assert the instantiation of a given concept. "Cows exist" is not a statement about cows, to the effect that they have the attribute of existing, but about the concept or description "cow," to the effect that it has instances. If this is so, then the proper theological question is not whether a perfect being, in order to be perfect, must together with its other attributes have the attribute of existence but whether the concept of an (existing) perfect being has an instance. This question cannot be determined a priori, as the Ontological Argument professes to do, by inspection of the concept of God. The nature of thought on the one hand and of the extramental world on the other, and of the difference between them, is such that there can be no valid inference from the thought of a given kind of being to the conclusion that there is in fact a being of that kind. This is the fundamental logical objection to the Ontological Argument.

HEGELIAN USE OF THE ARGUMENT

Prior to Kant, the Ontological Argument had been used by Benedict de Spinoza and Gottfried Wilhelm Leibniz. Since Kant, the form of it that he discussed has remained under the heavy cloud of his criticism. However, G. W. F. Hegel and his school put the argument to a somewhat different use. As Hegel himself expressed it, "In the case of the finite, existence does not correspond to the Notion (*Begriffe*). On the other hand, in the case of the Infinite, which is determined within itself, the reality must correspond to the Notion (*Begriffe*); this is the Idea (*Idee*), the unity of subject and object" (*Vorlesungen über die Philosophie der Religion*, Vol. II, p. 479). Otherwise stated, Being itself, or the Absolute, is the presupposition of all existence and all thought. If finite beings exist, Being exists; when beings think, Being comes to self-consciousness; and in the reasoning of the Ontological Argument, finite thinking is conscious of its own ultimate ground, the reality of which it cannot rationally deny.

The defect of this argument is that its conclusion is either trivial or excessively unclear. It is trivial if the reality of Being is synonymous with the existence of the sum of finite beings; but on the other hand, it is so unclear as to be scarcely interesting if Being is regarded as a metaphysical quantity whose distinction from the sum of finite beings cannot be explicated.

The use of the argument in early twentieth-century French "reflexive" philosophy (see bibliography) has affinities with the Hegelian use.

CONTEMPORARY DISCUSSIONS

Discussion of the Ontological Argument has continued throughout the modern period and is perhaps as active today as at any time in the past. For there is perennial fascination in a piece of reasoning that employs such fundamental concepts, operates so subtly with them, and professes to demonstrate so momentous a conclusion.

Among theologians, attempts have been made to maintain the value of the argument, not as a proof of God's existence but as an exploration of the Christian understanding of God. Thus, Karl Barth regards the proof as an unfolding of the significance of God's revelation of himself as One whom the believer is prohibited from thinking as less than the highest conceivable reality. On this view Anselm's argument does not seek to convert the atheist but rather to lead an already formed Christian faith into a deeper understanding of its object. Again, Paul Tillich treated the theistic proofs as expressions of the question of God that is implied in our human finitude. They analyze different aspects of the human situation, showing how it points to God. Thus, the Ontological Argument "shows that an awareness of the infinite is included in man's awareness of finitude." This is in effect a Hegelian use of the argument.

HARTSHORNE AND MALCOLM. At the same time, some contemporary philosophers—especially Charles Hartshorne and Norman Malcolm—revived the second argument, or second form of the argument, found in Anselm's *Proslogion* (3) and in his *Responsio* to Gaunilo. As they have reconstructed it, this argument starts from the premise that the concept of God as eternal, self-existent being is such that the question whether God exists cannot be a contingent question but must be one of logical necessity or impossibility. A being who exists, but of whom it is conceivable that he might not have existed, would be less than God; for only a being whose existence is necessary rather than contingent can be that than which nothing greater is conceivable. But if such a necessary being does not exist, it must be a necessary rather than a contingent fact that he does not exist. Thus God's existence is either logically necessary or logically impossible. However, it has not been shown to be impossible—that is, the concept of such a being has not been shown to be self-contradictory—and therefore we must conclude that God necessarily exists.

Hartshorne formalizes the argument as follows:

(1) $q \rightarrow Nq$	"Anslem's principle": perfection could not exist contingently
(2) $Nq \vee \sim Nq$	Excluded middle
(3) $\sim Nq \rightarrow N \sim Nq$	Form of Becker's postulate: modal status is always necessary.
(4) $Nq \vee N \sim Nq$	Inference from (2, 3)
(5) $N \sim Nq \rightarrow N \sim q$	Inference from (1): the necessary falsity of the consequent implies that of the antecedent (modal form of *modus tollens*)
(6) $Nq \vee N \sim q$	Inference from (4, 5)
(7) $\sim N \sim q$	Intuitive postulate (of conclusion from other theistic arguments): perfection is not impossible
(8) Nq	Inference from (6, 7)
(9) $Nq \rightarrow q$	Modal axiom
(10) q	Inference from (8, 9)

In this formalization q stands for $(\exists x)Px$ ("There is a perfect being" or "Perfection exists"); N means "analytic or L-true, true by necessity of the meanings of the terms employed"; and $\rightarrow$ signifies strict implication.

CRITICISM. The above argument seems to depend upon a confusion of two different concepts of necessary being. The distinction involved is important for the elucidation of the idea of God and represents one of the points at which study of the Ontological Argument can be fruitful even though the argument itself fails. The two concepts are those of logical necessity and ontological or factual necessity. In modern philosophy, logical necessity is a concept that applies only to propositions; a proposition is logically necessary if it is true in virtue of the meanings of the terms composing it. And it is a basic empiricist principle that existential propositions cannot be logically necessary. In other words, whether or not a given kind of entity exists is a question of experiential fact and not of the rules of language. On this view, the notion of a logically necessary being is inadmissible, for it would mean that the existential proposition "God exists" is logically true or true by definition. Anselm's principle, however, which is used as the first premise of Hartshorne's argument, was not that God is a logically necessary being (in this modern sense) but that God is an ontologically or factually necessary being, For, as noted above, Anselm was explicit that by a being whose nonexistence is inconceivable he meant a being who exists without beginning or end and always as a whole. (This is virtually the scholastic notion of *aseity*, from *a se esse*, "self-existence," that is, eternal and independent existence.) Interpreting "For God to exist is for him to exist necessarily" (prop. 1) in this way, we can validly infer from it that God's existence is ontologically either necessary or impossible (prop. 6). For if an eternal being exists, he cannot, compatibly with the concept of him as eternal, cease to exist: thus his existence is necessary. And if such a being does not exist, he cannot, compatibly with the concept of him as eternal, come to exist: thus his existence is impossible.

However, it does not follow from this that an eternal being in fact exists but only that if such a being exists, his existence is ontologically necessary, and that if no such being exists, it is impossible for one to exist. Hartshorne's argument can advance from proposition 6 to its conclusion only by assuming at this point that it has been established that the existence of God is (not, or not only, ontologically but) *logically* necessary or impossible. He can then rule out the latter alternative (prop. 7), and conclude that God necessarily exists (prop. 8) and hence that he exists (prop. 10). Thus, in propositions 1–6 "necessary" means "ontologically necessary"; in propositions 6–10 it means "logically necessary"; and proposition 6 itself is the point at which the confusion occurs. (The same illicit shift between the notions of ontological and logical necessity can be observed in Malcolm's version of the argument.)

The conclusion to be drawn is that the Ontological Argument, considered as an attempted logical demonstration of the existence of God, fails. In both of the forms that are found in Anselm, and which are still matters of discussion today, the flaw in the argument is that while it establishes that the concept of God involves the idea of God's existence, and indeed of God's necessary (in the sense of eternal) existence, it cannot take the further step of establishing that this concept of an eternally existent being is exemplified in reality.

See also Anselm, St.

Bibliography

For the general history of the Ontological Argument, see M. Esser, *Der ontologische Gottesbeweis und seine Geschichte* (Bonn, 1905); J. Kopper, *Reflexion und Raisonnement im ontologischen Gottesbeweis* (Cologne, 1962); and C. C. J. Webb, "Anselm's Ontological Argument for the Existence of God," in *PAS* 3 (2) (1896): 25–43. On its alleged origin in Plato, see J. Moreau, "L'argument ontologique" dans le *Phédon*," in *Revue philosophique de la France et de l'étranger* 137 (1947): 320–343, and J. Prescott Johnson, "The Ontological Argument in Plato," in *Personalist* (1963): 24–34. The main passage in Augustine which may have influenced Anselm (in relation to the Ontological Argument) is *De Libero Arbitrio*, Book II, translated by J. H. S. Burleigh as "On Free Will," in *Augustine: Earlier Writings*, edited by J. H. S. Burleigh (London and Philadelphia, 1953).

Anselm's version of the argument occurs in *Proslogion*, Chs. 2–4, and in his exchange with Gaunilo. The Latin text is in Dom F. S. Schmitt's critical edition of the *Opera Omnia*, Vol. I (Edinburgh, 1945), pp. 101–104 and 125–139. The best English translations of the *Proslogion* as a whole are those of Eugene R. Fairweather in *A Scholastic Miscellany: Anselm to Ockham* (Philadelphia: Westminster Press, 1956); A. C. Pegis in *The Wisdom of Catholicism* (New York: Random House, 1949); M. J. Charlesworth, *St. Anselm's "Proslogion" with "A Reply on Behalf of the Fool" by Gaunilo and "The Author's Reply to Gaunilo,"* with an introduction and philosophical commentary by Charlesworth (Oxford: Clarendon Press, 1965); and A. C. McGill in *The Many Faced Argument*, edited by John Hick and A. C. McGill (New York: Macmillan, 1967), where McGill, as well as translating *Proslogion* 2–4, has translated Anselm's exchange with Gaunilo, arranging the texts so as to present Anselm's replies in relation to the specific criticisms to which they refer. The translations by S. N. Deane in *St. Anselm: Basic Writings*, 2nd ed. (La Salle, IL, 1962) include, in addition to the *Proslogion*, Gaunilo's *On Behalf of the Fool* and Anselm's *Reply*. Anselm's dialogue *De Veritate* is also relevant; there is an excellent English translation by Richard McKeon in *Selections from Medieval Philosophers*, Vol. I (New York: Scribners, 1929).

On the interpretation of Anselm, the most important older writings are Charles Filliatre, *La philosophie de saint Anselme* (Paris, 1920); Alexandre Koyré, *L'idée de Dieu dans la philosophie de S. Anselme* (Paris, 1923); Karl Barth, *Fides Quaerens Intellectum: Anselms Beweis der Existenz Gottes in Zusammenhang seines theologischen Programms* (Zürich, 1930; 2nd ed., 1958), translated by Ian Robertson as *Anselm:*

Fides Quaerens Intellectum (Richmond, VA: John Knox Press, 1960); A. Stolz, "Zur Theologie Anselms im Proslogion," in *Catholica* (1933): 1–21, translated by A. C. McGill in *The Many Faced Argument* (see above); Étienne Gilson, "Sens et nature de l'argument de saint Anselme," in *Archives d'histoire doctrinale et littéraire du moyen âge* 9 (1934): 5–51; and Adolf Kolping, *Anselms Proslogion— Beweis der Existenz Gottes im Zusammenhang seines Spekulativen Programms: Fides Quaerens Intellectum* (Bonn, 1939).

For more recent historical studies, see *Spicilegium Beccense*, Proceedings of the Congrès International du IXe Centenaire de l'arrivée d'Anselme au Bec (Paris: J. Vrin, 1959).

For the view that there are two different arguments in *Proslogion*, see Charles Hartshorne, introduction to *St. Anselm: Basic Writings* (see above); "What Did Anselm Discover?," in *Union Theological Seminary Quarterly Review* (1962): 213–222; and *The Logic of Perfection* (La Salle, IL: Open Court, 1962), Ch. 2. See also Norman Malcolm, "Anselm's Ontological Arguments," in *Philosophical Review* 69 (1 (1960): 41–62, reprinted in Malcolm's *Knowledge and Certainty* (Englewood Cliffs, NJ: Prentice Hall, 1963). St. Thomas's criticism of the argument occurs in his *Summa Contra Gentiles* I, 10 and 11, and *Summa Theologiae* I, 2, 1.

For the argument after Anselm, see O. Paschen, *Der ontologische Gottesbeweis in der Scholastik* (Aachen, 1903); John Duns Scotus, *De Primo Principio*, translated by E. Roche (St. Bonaventure, NY: Franciscan Institute, 1949); I. Hislop, "St. Thomas and the Ontological Argument," in *Contemplations Presented to the Dominican Tertiaries of Glasgow* (London, 1949), pp. 32–38; P. L. M. Puech, "Duns Scotus et l'argument de saint Anselme," in *Nos Cahiers* (1937): 183–199; A. Runze, *Der ontologische Gottesbeweis, kritische Darstellung seiner Geschichte seit Anselm bis auf die Gegenwart* (Halle, 1882); O. Herrlin, *The Ontological Proof in Thomistic and Kantian Interpretation* (Uppsala: Lundquistska bokhandeln, 1950); Robert Miller, "The Ontological Argument in St. Anselm and Descartes," in *Modern Schoolman* (1954–1955): 341–349, and (1955–1956): 31–38; and Alexandre Koyré, *Essai sur l'idée de Dieu et les preuves de son existence chez Descartes* (Paris: E. Leroux, 1922).

Descartes's own version of the argument occurs in his *Meditations* (V, but see also III). Spinoza uses the argument in his *Ethics*, Part I, Props. 7–11. Leibniz's version is found in his *New Essays concerning Human Understanding*, Book IV, Ch. 10 and Appendix X, and in his *Monadology*, Secs. 44–45. Kant's criticism of the argument (in its Cartesian form) occurs in his *Critique of Pure Reason*, Transcendental Dialectic, Book II, Ch. iii, Sec. 4.

The Hegelian use of the argument is to be found in Hegel's *Vorlesungen über die Philosophie der Religion*, edited by P. Marheineke (Berlin, 1832), Appendix: "Beweise für das Dasein Gottes," Vol. II, pp. 466–483, translated by E. B. Speirs and J. B. Sanderson as *Lectures on the Philosophy of Religion* (London: K. Paul, Trench, Trubner, 1895), Vol. III. pp. 347–367; and in *Vorlesungen über die Geschichte der Philosophie*, edited by K. L. Michelet (Berlin, 1836), Vol. III, pp. 164–169, translated by E. S. Haldane and F. H. Simson as *Lectures on the History of Philosophy* (London, 1896), Vol. III, pp. 62–67; Edward Caird, "Anselm's Argument for the Being of God," in *Journal of Theological Studies* 1 (1899):

23–39; E. E. Harris, *Revelation through Reason* (New Haven, CT: Yale University Press, 1958); Paul Tillich, "The Two Types of Philosophy of Religion," in his *Theology of Culture* (New York: Oxford University Press, 1959); and R. G. Collingwood, *An Essay on Philosophical Method* (Oxford: Clarendon Press, 1933). Collingwood's use of the argument was criticized by Gilbert Ryle in "Mr. Collingwood and the Ontological Argument," in *Mind*, n.s., 44 (174) (1935): 137–151. There is a reply to Ryle by E. E: Harris in *Mind*, n.s., 45 (180) (1936): 474–481, and a rejoinder by Ryle in *Mind*, n.s., 46 (181) (1937): 53–57. This discussion is reprinted in *The Many Faced Argument* (see above).

For the argument in recent French "reflexive" philosophy, see M. Blondel, *L'action* (Paris, 1893 and 1950), *L'être et les êtres* (Paris, 1935), and *La pensée* (Paris, 1934 and 1948); J. Paliard, *Intuition et réflexion* (Paris, 1925); and A. Forest, "L'argument de saint Anselme dans la philosophie réflexive," in *Spicilegium Beccense*, pp. 273–294, translated by A. C. McGill in *The Many Faced Argument* (see above).

Some important contemporary philosophical discussions are C. D. Broad, "Arguments for the Existence of God," in *Journal of Theological Studies* 40 (157) (January 1939); J. N. Findlay, "Can God's Existence Be Disproved?," in *Mind*, n.s., 57 (226) (1948): 176–183, reprinted in *New Essays in Philosophical Theology* edited by A. G. N. Flew and Alasdair MacIntyre (London, 1958); Nicholas Rescher, "The Ontological Proof Revisited," in *Australasian Journal of Philosophy* 37 (2) (1959): 138–148; William P. Alston, "The Ontological Argument Revisited," in *Philosophical Review* 69 (4) (1960): 452–474; Norman Malcolm, "Anselm's Ontological Argument" (see above); Charles Hartshorne, *The Logic of Perfection* (see above); Jerome Shaffer, "Existence, Predication and the Ontological Argument," in *Mind*, n.s., 71 (283) (1962): 307–325, reprinted in *The Many Faced Argument* (see above); and a discussion by R. E. Allen, Raziel Abelson, Terence Penelhum, Alvin Plantinga, and Paul Henle in *Philosophical Review* 70 (1) (1961): 56–109.

On the notions of "existence" and "necessary existence," see Bertrand Russell, "The Philosophy of Logical Atomism" (1918), in his *Logic and Knowledge*, edited by R. C. Marsh (London: Allen and Unwin, 1956); G. E. Moore, "Is Existence a Predicate?," in *PAS*, Supp., 15 (1936), reprinted in *Logic and Language*, 2d series, edited by A. G. N. Flew (Oxford, 1959); William Kneale, "Is Existence a Predicate?," in *PAS*, Supp., 15 (1936), reprinted in *Readings in Philosophical Analysis*, edited by Herbert Feigl and Wilfrid Sellars (New York: Appleton-Century-Crofts, 1949); George Nakhnikian and W. C. Salmon, "'Exists' as a Predicate," in *Philosophical Review* 66 (4) (1957): 535–542; John Hick, "God as Necessary Being," in *Journal of Philosophy* 57 (22–23) (1960): 725–734; and Terence Penelhum, "Divine Necessity," in *Mind*, n.s., 69 (274) (1960): 175–186.

John Hick (1967)

ONTOLOGICAL ARGUMENT FOR THE EXISTENCE OF GOD [ADDENDUM]

Work on the ontological argument since 1970 has been mainly concerned with the so-called modal ontological argument for the existence of a perfect being.

THE CONCEPT OF A PERFECT BEING

Descartes defined a (supremely) perfect being as a being that possesses all perfections. But if a property F is a perfection, it would seem that a being that is F but might not have been F falls short of perfection. Hence a better definition of a perfect being would be as follows: a being that has all perfections and could not have lacked any perfection—a perfect being is a being that has all perfections *essentially* (has all perfections in every possible world in which it exists).

THE LOGICAL VALIDITY OF THE MODAL ONTOLOGICAL ARGUMENT

The argument has two premises: (1) A perfect being is possible (exists in some possible world); (2) Necessary existence (existence in every possible world) is a perfection.

Plantinga (1974) has shown that the existence of a perfect being is logically deducible from these two premises. (The proof presupposes the strongest system of modal reasoning, S5. [For more discussion on S5, see the entry "Modal Logic."] Here we assume without argument that a modal argument that is valid in no weaker system than S5 is not objectionable on that ground. For a contrary view, see Salmon [1989].) Suppose a perfect being exists in some possible world w [premise (1)]. This being is necessarily existent in w [premise (2)], and must therefore exist in every possible world, for if there were some world in which it did not exist, it would not be *necessarily* existent in w. This being has in w all perfections [premise (1)]. It must therefore have all perfections in every possible world in which it exists (that is, in every possible world), for if there were some world in which it existed but failed to have all perfections, it would not have all perfections *essentially* in w. This being therefore exists in the actual world and in every other possible world, and has all perfections in the actual world and in every other possible world. It is therefore necessarily existent in the actual world (if it were not necessarily existent in the actual world, there would be some world in which it did not exist) and has all perfections essentially in the actual world (if it did not have all perfections essentially in the actual world, there would be some world in which it did not have all perfections). That is to say— there exists a perfect being.

THE PREMISES OF THE ARGUMENT

The conclusion of the argument follows (in S5) from its two premises. But are the two premises true? Critics of the argument are typically willing to grant premise (2) but see no reason to accept premise (1).

Plantinga has conceded that there seems to be no way to demonstrate the possibility of a perfect being. (And he recognizes that one may not simply presume that a concept is possible in the absence of a demonstration of its impossibility. So to presume can in fact lead one into contradiction, because there are pairs of concepts, neither of which can be *shown* to be impossible and at least one of which must *be* impossible. If it cannot be shown that a perfect being is impossible, the concept of a perfect being and the concept of a being who knows that there is no perfect being are such a pair.) Plantinga contends, however, that it is not irrational to believe that a perfect being is possible (just as it is not irrational to believe that a private language is possible or that free will is possible: a philosopher who believes in the possibility of these things is not *ipso facto* irrational). He further contends that it is not irrational to believe the demonstrated logical consequences of things that are not rational to believe, and that it is therefore not irrational to believe that there is a perfect being. He concludes that although the modal ontological argument is not a proof that a perfect being exists, its logical validity in effect constitutes a proof that it is not irrational to believe that a perfect being exists. This conclusion has been disputed by van Inwagen (1977).

GÖDEL'S POSSIBILITY PROOF

The most important recent attempt to prove that a perfect being is possible occurs in a brief note (unpublished in his lifetime) by Kurt Gödel ("Ontological Proof" in Fefferman, ed. [1995]). The argument (slightly modified) is this: Necessary existence and the "essentialization" of every other perfection (having that perfection essentially) are all positive properties, and any set of positive properties is consistent or possible because the set of all positive properties is possible. This last statement is a consequence of two "axioms": (1) The set of all positive properties is closed under entailment; and (2) If a property is positive, its negation is not positive. (A set of properties entails the property F if it is impossible for something to

have all the properties in that set and to lack F. A set of properties is closed under entailment if it contains every property entailed by any of its subsets.)

PROOF. Suppose that the set of all positive properties is impossible or inconsistent. We show that this entails a contradiction. Since an impossible set of properties entails any property, the only set of properties that is both impossible and closed under entailment is the set of all properties: the set of all positive properties is the set of all properties. But the negation of a positive property is not a positive property: the set of all positive properties is not the set of all properties.

Unfortunately, Gödel's attempts to explain the idea of a positive property are compressed and cryptic. They leave the reader with no reason to suppose that there is a set of properties such that (1) necessary existence and the essentialization of every other perfection are members of that set, (2) that set is closed under entailment, and (3) if a property is member of that set, its negation is not. The modal ontological argument therefore remains inconclusive.

See also Degrees of Perfection, Argument for the Existence of God; Descartes, René; Gödel, Kurt; Gödel's Theorem; Modal Logic; Plantinga, Alvin.

Bibliography

Feferman, Solomon; John W. Dawson Jr., Warren Goldfarb, Charles Parsons, Robert N. Solovay, eds. *Kurt Gödel: Unpublished Essays and Lectures Collected Work.* Vol. 2 of *Collected Works.* Oxford: Oxford University Press, 1995.

Gödel, Kurt. "Ontological Proof." In Feferman *et al.*, 303–304.

Plantinga, Alvin. *God, Freedom, and Evil.* New York: Harper & Row, 1974.

Plantinga, Alvin. *The Nature of Necessity.* Oxford: Clarendon Press, 1974.

Salmon, Nathan. "The Logic of What Might Have Been." *The Philosophical Review* 97 (1989): 3–34.

van Inwagen, Peter. *Metaphysics.* 2nd ed. Boulder, CO: Westview, 2002.

van Inwagen, Peter. "Ontological Arguments." *Noûs* 11 (1977): 375–395.

Peter van Inwagen (2005)

ONTOLOGY

Ontology is the most general science or study of Being, Existence, or Reality. An informal use of the term signifies what, in general terms, a philosopher considers the world to contain. Thus it is said that Descartes proposed a dualist ontology, or that there were no gods in d'Holbach's ontology. But in its more formal meaning, ontology is the aspect of metaphysics aiming to characterize Reality by identifying all its essential categories and setting forth the relations among them.

BEING QUA BEING

Existence, as the most comprehensive category of all, should embrace members with the least in common. Nevertheless, Western philosophy long sought some substantive common content present in anything just in virtue of its existence. The history of these attempts to identify the common character of being qua being is not encouraging.

In *The Sophist*, Plato's Eleatic Stranger proposes that a role in the world's causal network is the necessary and sufficient condition for existence, that "Power is the mark of Being." This idea has had some currency in the twentieth century, particularly in the work of David Lewis (1986) and D. M. Armstrong (1978, 1989, 1997). This *Eleatic principle* is an attractive test for reality in the natural world, for whatever is real in nature should be able to make a difference. It might be necessary to weaken the requirement and admit a passive space-time that provides the arena within which the active beings exert themselves. Even so, the Eleatic principle seems to be at best a contingent aspect of the world because there seems to be no impossibility involved in the idea of a completely inert being. It also begs the question against abstract entities such as numbers, or geometric points, or sets, which, if they exist, lie outside the causal nexus.

For Samuel Alexander (1920), to be is to be the exclusive occupant of a volume of space-time. This rules out not only abstract entities, but even a field theory of the natural world, for force fields occupy regions of space-time, yet do not exclude one another.

J. M. E. McTaggart (1921–1927) argued that the mark of being is to stand in a determining correspondence with all of one's infinite parts. A determining correspondence ensures that from a sufficient description of anything, a sufficient description of any of its parts can be derived. This requirement implies that space, the natural world, and most of the contents of minds are unreal. From this consequence the conclusion to be drawn is that McTaggart's proposed mark of being is excessively demanding.

The problem of a substantive content for being qua being is reflected in the idiosyncratic behavior of the verb "to exist." Consider singular negatives: "Aristotle does not

speak Spanish" is true because the predicate "does not speak Spanish" applies to the item referred to by the subject term. But "Pegasus does not exist" cannot be true because its predicate applies to the item referred to by the subject term. If the subject term refers to anything, that item exists, which would make the whole statement false.

Kant famously declared that existence is not a property, and this view has become widely accepted. The modern logic that descends from Gottlob Frege and the *Principia Mathematica* (1910–1913) of Alfred North Whitehead and Bertrand Russell replaces all expressions using "exists" with others using "There are." Thus, "Lions exist" becomes "There are lions," while "Dragons do not exist" becomes "There are no dragons."

In technical terms, this process replaces any existence claim with one using a quantifier ranging over a domain (the world), so that to exist becomes a matter not of possessing the special property *existence*, but of possessing some other, ordinary, properties. The determination to restate all claims to existence or nonexistence with "There are …" and "There are no …" is expressed in W. V. Quine's dictum: "To be is to be the value of a variable."

If existence is not a property, it cannot be a perfection. This undercuts those versions of the ontological argument for the existence of God that rely on existence being among the perfections. A recent response has been to argue that, even if existence is not a property, necessary existence is (Plantinga 1974, 1975; van Inwagen 1993).

REALITY AND ACTUALITY

Is existence all there is, or should we recognize categories even broader that that of Being? In Plato, and even earlier, is to be found the distinction between Reality (What is) and Appearance (What is not nothing, yet only seems to Be). Aristotle distinguishes the fully existent (Being), from that which is still in formation (Becoming). These distinctions are perhaps best seen as advocating different grades of reality within the one category of Being.

Aristotle also distinguishes the fully Real (Act) from that which may be (Potency). This distinction is the forerunner of a strong strand in ontology that recognizes possible worlds in addition to the actual world, the one we inhabit. In the Neoplatonists, and again in Alexius Meinong, the realm of the existent is augmented by that of the subsistent, which encompasses what does not exist although it might have done so, such as golden mountains.

A full-scale ontology of this kind, in which the realm of Essence is wider than that of Existence, was presented by James K. Feibleman in 1951. In the work of Richard Sylvan (1980), this is extended even further. In Sylvan's system, the individual variables range over not only the actual and the possible, but the impossible as well.

POSSIBLE WORLDS. Gottfried Wilhelm Leibniz was the first to make systematic use of the idea that all the possibilities can be regarded as forming worlds—each a complete internally consistent realm that may combine some elements matching the actual world with others in which it differs. The actual world is one of the possible worlds, distinguished from all others by the fact that none of its elements is merely possible. If one is able to refer to possible worlds, it is easy to define *necessary beings*, otherwise so difficult to characterize, as those present in all possible worlds (see below).

MODAL REALISM. Possible worlds make available explanations of causal powers, of counterfactual conditionals, of unexercised dispositions, and of real uninstantiated properties. Such advantages led David Lewis (1986) to embrace modal realism, which affirms the literal reality of all possible worlds.

Other philosophers, while appreciating these advantages, have balked at the apparently infinite expansion of the ontology that this requires. This has led to accounts of ersatz possible worlds: Rudolf Carnap and others have proposed that a possible world is a maximally consistent set of sentences. Armstrong and others have developed Wittgenstein's idea that a possible world is a nonactual recombination of the elements of this world. Peter Lopston (2001) advances a reductive realism, which expands the kind of property assigned in the actual world to include might-have-had features. The success of these approaches is subject to continuing controversy.

MANY WORLDS IN QUANTUM THEORY. The notion that the world we live in is not the only one has also been canvassed recently in the interpretation of some otherwise baffling paradoxes in quantum physics. On these accounts the world is not a single unified entity, but one subject to continual bifurcation, a process that generates an ever-increasing number of worlds. Many-world views of this kind are in an important way different from modal realism: all these quantum worlds are supposed to be actual but mutually inaccessible.

THE CATEGORIES OF BEING

The principal task of ontology is to furnish an inventory of the categories, the most general divisions of Reality. The most important of these are:

SUBSTANCES. An individual or particular substance is an object, a thing in its own right. Common everyday things, such as bricks and bedsteads, provide a model for the category of substance. Substances are required to have several basic features, although it is not clear that these features are compatible with one another.

Particularity and individuality. A substance is both a particular and an individual; not just some duck or other, but this very duck. An object is of the *kind* it is (a duck) on account of its properties. But if these properties are universals, shared by many particulars, they cannot themselves confer particularity. Some philosophers, most notoriously Locke, proposed a constituent of substances that would perform this role, a *substratum* that would confer both particularity and individuality. A substratum would be a bare particular, an item inherently particular and individual, yet without any other feature. It is difficult to see how such bare particulars could be distinguished from one another, but if bare particulars are all exactly alike, how could any one of them individualize its own substance? More generally, bare particulars conflict with Aristotle's dictum that the minimum of being, the least thing there can be, is a "this-such," a particular having a property.

Another proposal is that substances are individuated by their location. Locations—space-time points and regions—are themselves unique particulars; if they can have primitive particularity, that raises the question why other particulars require a substratum or other particularizer. There are other difficulties with location also: Location will not individuate force fields or other physical entities that do not monopolize their space. It fails also for any items of an immaterial kind.

Either individuality—and hence particularity—are primitive, or there are bare particulars, or each substance has a special property, known as *haecceity* or *thisness*, which can bestow particularity and individuality on its bearer. For a discussion see chapter fifteen of John Heil's *From an Ontological Point of View* (2003).

Indivisibility. Individual substances must be distinguished from compounds, so a single substance must be indivisible, in the sense that it has no parts that are themselves substances. This disqualifies ordinary things as individual substances. This simplicity requirement is much emphasized in Aquinas's doctrine of God. It leads in Leibniz to the monadology, and in Roger Joseph Boscovich to the doctrine of material points.

Persistence. Substances are distinguished from their properties by a capacity to persist, that is, to retain their identity through at least some changes. A fire truck can change in color, yet remain the fire truck it always has been. The ordinary compound substances of everyday life have some persistence, but cannot survive all changes. A fire truck dismantled and scrapped is no longer a fire truck. Complete persistence belongs only to the fundamental substances.

Independence. Any substance could be the only thing in existence. If this independence is interpreted causally, no ordinary object is a substance, for they are all brought into being, and hence depend for their existence on their causes. Space-time and its fields might qualify, yet even these depend, in theistic systems, on the creative activity of God. So in Thomism, God is the substance par excellence, but the natural world includes created substances, dependent on God, but otherwise existent in their own right. Spinoza, insisting on absolute independence, concluded that there can be only one substance, the all-embracing totality, God-or-Nature.

If one takes the independence of substances in a logical, rather than a causal sense, a substance is anything that, in principle, could stand alone. This was David Hume's requirement, and anything meeting it is a Humean substance. For compounds, the requirement is that the thing, including all its parts, could exist alone. This requirement is much less rigorous than causal independence and requires no persistence.

No-substance theories. There have been attempts to dispense with substances. Russell has proposed that an ordinary concrete object is no more than a bundle of all its properties. There is always an issue over what it is that binds the bundle. Moreover, as the properties are universals, this theory implies that no two things can be exactly alike.

In Donald Williams's version of the bundle theory (1966), the properties are particular instances or tropes (see below). This avoids any problem with the possibility of there being two exactly resembling objects, but it requires that all members of the bundle be "compresent"—all at the same place in space-time. There are difficulties in treating a space-time location as just one further trope in the bundle, but if it is given special treatment it becomes a substantializing substratum.

Russell also advocated an event ontology as a no-substance view. He used "event" for the occurrence of a property at a place and a time; such events are not happenings, but states of affairs (see below). He proposed that ordinary substances, and their more fundamental parts, are sequences of clusters of such events.

The basic elements in these ontologies may not be simple or indivisible, and they lack persistence. Nevertheless, these states of affairs or events are Humean substances. Indeed, unless there is nothing at all, something must be a Humean substance, and in that sense, any *no substance* theory must fail.

PROPERTIES AND RELATIONS. Properties are the intrinsic features or characteristics of things, which belong to them considered singly. Relations, involving two or more terms, are the ways in which things stand to one another. In many respects, properties and relations can be treated together.

Properties as universals. Properties are usually thought of as universals that can characterize indefinitely many instances. There is but one Eiffel Tower, but the tower's height, weight, and iron constitution are features it has in common with many other things. The Problem of Universals is the problem of explaining how any one real entity could possibly exist, fully and completely, in many different instances. This problem has attracted three different proposed solutions: nominalism, conceptualism, and realism. Nominalism and conceptualism both deny that properties are genuinely universal. According to nominalism, the only element common to all iron things is that they can all be described using the predicate "iron," or all are members of the class *iron things*, or all resemble some typical iron objects. According to conceptualism, the universal element consists in an impulse of our minds to group several things together. These reductive theories have had adherents since the time of Plato and were particularly prevalent among the British Empiricists and their descendents. Nominalism and conceptualism were explicitly challenged by Russell in *Problems of Philosophy* (1912). The most thorough case against such views is presented in D. M. Armstrong, *Universals and Scientific Realism* (1978).

Realism regarding universals is at least as old as Plato. His theory of Forms presents a thoroughgoing realism that accords to genuine properties both a real existence, in a realm of their own, and a status superior to any this-worldly instantiations of them there may be. The Forms exist *ante rem*—that is, whether or not they are instantiated. The traditional account of Aristotle ascribes to him a modified realism, according to which properties are real, and universal, but can exist only *in rebus*, as the properties of concrete instances. Here one encounters again his view that the least that is "apt for being" is a this-such, a union of particular with universal.

Realism has always faced two principal objections. First, that it is uneconomical, especially in its Platonist form. The question of economy is a current issue in the philosophy of science, as it at least appears that our best physical and chemical theories involve uninstantiated properties. The second objection is that it can provide no coherent account of the link between a property and the substance that bears it, the *inherence* relation. Inherence cannot be a normal relation, for then it is just one further universal standing in need of an inherence link to its terms, the substance and the original property. But if it is not a relation in the ordinary sense, what is it? The problem with inherence lends support to versions of realism in which properties are particulars.

Properties as particulars. Even if the property *iron* is universal, the particular case of *being iron* that occurs in the Eiffel Tower belongs to the tower alone and is as particular as the tower itself. Trope theory, as developed first by Donald Williams, treats the instance not as a dependent entity arising from the instantiation of a universal, but as a Humean substance in its own right.

When this approach is coupled with a bundle or compresence account of ordinary many-featured substances, the problem of any inherence relation disappears. There is a further significant economy, for there is no need for a separate category of substance. These possibilities are explored further in Keith Campbell's book *Abstract Particulars* (1990).

Relations. When Russell reanimated the realism debate he accorded to relations a status fully equal to that of inherent properties. Indeed, it was his reflections on the role of relations in the foundations of mathematics and of logic that led him to his realism. Armstrong's realism takes the same form.

There is, nevertheless, a long tradition that accords primacy to the intrinsic properties. Aristotle held that relations are "the least of the things that are"; Hobbes and others held that the existence of relations depends on a mental act of comparison; and Leibniz's view was that every relation has its foundation in an intrinsic feature of one or both of its terms. This reductive program is expounded in Campbell (1990).

Relations do seem to be dependent in the sense that they must have substances as their terms, and these substances must have intrinsic properties. So unless there are intrinsic properties there can be no relations, but not vice

versa. Bundle theories of ordinary things concern only the intrinsic properties. To include relations in the bundles leads to problems over where to assign the relations, and this in turn induces a tendency towards a monism such as Francis Herbert Bradley's, in which ordinary substances are absorbed into a single all-embracing totality.

Powers. Some properties, such as *square*, seem to belong to how an object is. Others, such as *being a solvent*, seem to refer to what an object can do. This is the distinction between categorical and dispositional properties. One line of thought takes up the Eleatic principle, and identifies real properties as those that confer on their bearer a disposition to act or to be acted upon. Such dispositions are *powers*; a metaphysic of powers is set forth in George Molnar's *Powers* (2003) and in Brian Ellis's *Scientific Essentialism* (2001).

COMPLEXES. *Substance* and *property* are basic categories. In combination, they can provide a richer ontology.

States of affairs. A basic state of affairs consists in a particular having a property, or in two (or more) particulars standing in a relation. A single property inhering in a single particular is a minimal "this-such." Wittgenstein's *Tractatus Logico-Philosophicus* (1921) presented an ontology in which the world is composed of minimal relational states of affairs: those that actually obtain being facts, those merely possible being the remaining states of affairs. These themes—that the basic categories only ever occur in combination, and that these combinations constitute reality—are taken up in D. M. Armstrong's *A World of States of Affairs* (1997).

Events and processes. A state of affairs is static. To account for the dynamic aspects of the world requires an account of change. This can be done by using sequences of states of affairs: stability consists in successive states of affairs closely resembling one another, whereas change consists in the states of affairs at one time being replaced by others systematically different. An event is a single change, involving a pair of states of affairs; a process is a more complex series of events.

Whitehead, in *Process and Reality* (1929) accorded priority to the dynamic; all apparently persisting substances are actually slowly evolving processes. The status of space-time is still controversial. It may be a Humean substance; however, some accounts of matter assign it a place as a process, a sequence of complex, changing relations between particulars.

ABSTRACT OBJECTS

Human thought, particularly in mathematics and logic, seems to involve entities that have no apparent place in the natural spatiotemporal world, and no causal role. To admit such items challenges the principle of economy, yet successful reductions are difficult to accomplish.

NUMBERS AND SETS. Because all numbers can be represented in set theory, there is no need to admit both sets and numbers. Russell had proposed to eliminate sets in favor of propositional functions, but this proved impossible for more than a fragment of mathematics (Goodman and Quine 1947, Quine 1969). Because the variables of set theory have sets as their values, and to be is to be the value of a variable, we are committed to their reality—this is Platonism about sets and numbers. The most important work in attempting to avoid Platonism is Hartry Field's (1980, 1989).

GEOMETRICAL OBJECTS. Unlike anything in the natural world, the objects of geometry—Euclidian cubes, for example—are thought of as perfect, changeless, timeless, and without any physical causal powers. Moreover, there are geometries, and corresponding geometrical objects, with many more dimensions than this world has. A geometrical space can be divided and subdivided into an infinity of different shapes of different sizes. Platonism in geometry thus involves an infinite expansion in ontology.

One approach to this issue is to consider geometrical objects as abstracted objects, that is, objects taken from a context. On this view, every cube is just a particular spatial fragment of space-time and every triangle a fragment of one of space-time's spatial surfaces. One problem with this is that not all shapes will be available. If our space-time is nowhere perfectly Euclidean, there will be no real Euclidean cubes. We can treat these nonexistent objects as imaginary variations on the actually existing ones, and geometries that quantify over such things, as not literally true.

LOGIC. The philosophy of logic makes reference to propositions, operators, functions, and inferences. These are abstract entities, related to reasoning in much the same way as numbers are related to counting and measuring. The problems and prospects of a reductive treatment of them are also parallel.

NECESSARY BEINGS

Ordinary things are usually held to exist contingently; that is, they do exist, but might not have. Had our world's initial conditions or laws of nature been different, there would have been a different group of contingent beings. But some things seem to be immune from the vagaries of cause and chance; being outside the causal net, they cannot be brought into being and cannot be destroyed. These are "necessary beings." If Platonism is correct regarding any of the abstract objects, these will be necessary beings, even, paradoxically, the null class.

For Aristotle, anything that exists through an infinite time is necessary because he held that over infinite time every possibility would at some point be actualized. For Plotinus, any divine being would be outside time, and as such could not change, could not cease to exist, and thus would be A necessary being. For Aquinas, God's necessity derives from his simplicity: God's essence and his existence are identical; in this way he is a kind of being that must exist. For Spinoza, every genuine substance is *causa sui*, containing within itself the sufficient explanation for its own being, and thus it can guarantee its own existence under all possible conditions.

Duns Scotus, then Descartes, linked necessary being with logic: A necessary being is one, the denial of whose existence would be self-contradictory. "Real"—i.e., existing—"beans do not exist" is a self-contradiction, but only trivially because existence has been inserted into the definition of the subject. This does not make beans necessary beings. If existence is not inserted into the subject term's definition, it is doubtful whether any denial of existence would be a self-contradiction. The best discussion of necessary being is in Alvin Plantinga (1974, 1975).

See also Metaphysics.

Bibliography

Adams, R. M. "Primitive Thisness and Primitive Identity." *The Journal of Philosophy* 76 (1979): 5–26.

Alexander, Samuel. *Space, Time, and Deity: The Gifford Lectures at Glasgow.* 2 vols. London: Macmillan, 1920.

Armstrong, D. M. *A Combinatorial Theory of Possibility.* Cambridge, U.K.: Cambridge University Press, 1989.

Armstrong, D. M. *Universals and Scientific Realism.* 2 vols. Cambridge, U.K.: Cambridge University Press, 1978.

Armstrong, D. M. *A World of States of Affairs.* Cambridge, U.K.: Cambridge University Press, 1997.

Campbell, Keith. *Abstract Particulars.* Oxford: Blackwell, 1990.

Ellis, Brian. *Scientific Essentialism.* Cambridge, U.K.: Cambridge University Press, 2001.

Feibleman, James K. *Ontology.* Baltimore: Johns Hopkins Press, 1951.

Field, Hartry. *Realism, Mathematics and Modality.* Oxford: Blackwell, 1989.

Field, Hartry. *Science without Numbers: A Defence of Nominalism.* Oxford: Blackwell, 1980.

Forbes, Graeme. *The Metaphysics of Modality*. Oxford: Clarendon Press, 1985.

Goodman, N., and W. V. Quine. "Steps Towards a Constructive Nominalism." *Journal of Symbolic Logic* 12 (1947): 105–122.

Heil, John. *From an Ontological Point of View*. Oxford: Clarendon Press, 2003.

Lewis, David K. *On the Plurality of Worlds*. Oxford: Blackwell, 1986.

Loptson, Peter. *Reality: Fundamental Topics in Metaphysics*. Toronto: University of Toronto Press, 2001.

McTaggart, J. M. E. *The Nature of Existence*. 2 vols. Cambridge, U.K.: Cambridge University Press, 1921–1927.

Molnar, George. *Powers: A Study in Metaphysics*. New York: Oxford University Press, 2003.

Plantinga, Alvin. *God, Freedom, and Evil*. London: Allen and Unwin, 1975.

Plantinga, Alvin. *The Nature of Necessity*. Oxford: Clarendon Press, 1974.

Quine, W. V. *From a Logical Point of View: 9 Logico-Philosophical Essays*. 2nd ed. Cambridge, MA: Harvard University Press, 1961.

Quine, W. V. *Set Theory and Its Logic*. Cambridge, MA: Belknap Press of Harvard University, 1969.

Russell, Bertrand. *The Analysis of Matter*. London: Kegan Paul, Trench and Trubner, 1927. Event ontology.

Russell, Bertrand. *An Inquiry into Meaning and Truth*. London: Allen and Unwin, 1940. Substances as bundles of universals.

Russell, Bertrand. *The Problems of Philosophy*. London: Oxford University Press, 1912. Realism about universals

Sylvan, Richard. *Exploring Meinong's Jungle and Beyond*. Canberra: Australian National University, 1980.

Van Inwagen, Peter. *Metaphysics*. Boulder, CO: Westview Press, 1993.

Whitehead, A. N. *Process and Reality: An Essay in Cosmology*. Cambridge, U.K.: Cambridge University Press, 1929.

Williams, Donald C. *Principles of Empirical Realism: Philosophical Essays*. Springfield, IL: Thomas, 1966.

Wittgenstein, Ludwig. *Tractatus Logico-Philosophicus*. London: Routledge and Kegan Paul, 1921.

Keith Campbell (2005)

ONTOLOGY, HISTORY OF

The term *ontologia* was coined by scholastic writers in the seventeenth century. Rudolf Goclenius, who mentioned the word in 1636, may have been the first user, but the term was such a natural Latin coinage and began to appear so regularly that disputes about priority are pointless. Some writers, such as Abraham Calovius, used it interchangeably with *metaphysica*; others used it as the name of a subdivision of metaphysics. Johannes Clauberg (1622–1665), a Cartesian, coined instead the term *ontosophia*. By the time of Jean-Baptiste Duhamel (1624–1706), ontology was clearly distinguished from natural theology. The other subdivisions of metaphysics are cosmology and psychology, from which ontology is also distinguished. Thus, *ontologia* as a philosophical term of art was already in existence when it was finally canonized by Christian Wolff (1679–1754) and Alexander Gottlieb Baumgarten (1714–1762).

WOLFF

For the authors mentioned above, the subject matter of ontology was being as such. "Being" was understood univocally, as having one single sense. Ontology can therefore claim as ancestors John Duns Scotus and William of Ockham, rather than Thomas Aquinas. In the case of Wolff himself, Gottfried Wilhelm Leibniz was a stronger influence than scholasticism, but in his *Philosophia Prima Sive Ontologia*, Wolff refers explicitly to Francisco Suárez. According to Wolff, the method of ontology is deductive. The fundamental principle applying to all that is, is the principle of noncontradiction, which holds that it is a property of being itself that no being can both have and not have a given characteristic at one and the same time. From this, Wolff believed, follows the principle of sufficient reason, namely, that in all cases there must be some sufficient reason to explain why any being exists rather than does not exist. The universe is a collection of beings each of which has an essence that the intellect is capable of grasping as a clear and distinct idea. The principle of sufficient reason is invoked to explain why some essences have had existence conferred on them and others have not. The truths about beings that are deduced from indubitable first principles are all necessary truths. Thus, ontology has nothing to do with the contingent order of the world.

The influence of late scholasticism (or of what Étienne Gilson calls "essentialism") on rationalist metaphysics was repaid in kind, for the division of metaphysics into ontology, cosmology, and psychology found its way back into scholastic manuals, where it has persisted until very recently. Along with this division, there persisted the view that being constitutes an independent subject matter over and above the subject matter of the special sciences. The persistence of this view is perhaps to be explained by cultural rather than by intellectual factors. In the eighteenth and nineteenth centuries scholasticism was isolated in seminaries until Pope Leo XIII guided Thomism back into intellectual debate. Only in this way was scholasticism able to avoid the nemesis (in the form of Immanuel Kant) that awaited rationalist metaphysics.

KANT

In the written announcement of lectures given from 1765 to 1766, Kant treated ontology as a subdivision of metaphysics that included rational psychology but was distinguished, in his case, from empirical psychology, cosmology, and what he called the "science of God and the world": "Then in *ontology* I discuss the more general properties of things, the difference between spiritual and material beings." But when Kant came to write the *Critique of Pure Reason,* he settled matters with ontology once and for all. The two key passages are the discussion of the second antinomy of pure reason and the refutation of the ontological argument. Wolff had argued a priori that the world is composed of simple substances, themselves neither perceived nor possessing extension or shape, and each of them different, and that physical objects are composite, collections of such substances. In the second antinomy the thesis is that "every composite substance in the world consists of simple parts, and nothing exists anywhere that is not either simple or composed of simple parts"; and the proof that Kant presented is effectively Wolffian. But he presented an equally powerful proof for the antithesis, namely, that "no composite thing in the world consists of simple parts, and there exists nothing simple anywhere." In exposing the shared fallacy of both proofs, Kant made it impossible ever again to accept ontology as a deductive body of necessary truths that is akin to geometry in form but has being as its subject matter. His analysis of existence in his refutation of the Ontological Proof is a counterpart to this.

Since Kant, the most influential use of the term *ontology* outside scholastic manuals has been in the writings of Martin Heidegger and W. V. Quine. Both have been greeted by scholastic writers as engaged in essentially the same enterprise as they themselves, Father D. A. Drennen taking this view of Heidegger, and Father I. M. Bocheński of Quine.

HEIDEGGER

In regard to Heidegger's ontology, Father Drennen is perhaps partly correct. Heidegger wished to explain what character being must have if human consciousness is to be what it is. He began by quarreling with the principle of sufficient reason in its Leibniz-Wolff form. This, he said, is an inadequate starting point for ontology because the question "Why is there something rather than nothing?" presupposes that we already know what being and nothing are. Heidegger treated "Being" and "Nothing" as the names of contrasted and opposed powers whose existence is presupposed in all our judgments. In negative judgments, for example, to speak of what is not the case is implicitly to refer to Nothing. Heidegger's ontology, however, was not deductive or even systematic in form. It proceeds at times by the exegesis of poetry or of the more aphoristic fragments of the pre-Socratic philosophers and is thus very different from scholastic ontology.

QUINE

In the case of Quine, the name *ontology* has been in fact given to a quite different set of preoccupations. Quine has been concerned with two closely allied questions: To the existence of what kind of thing does belief in a given theory commit us? And what are the relations between intensional and extensional logic? His answer to the first question is that to be is to be the value of a variable: We have to admit the existence of that range of possible entities for which names could occur as values for those variables without which we could not state our beliefs. His answer to the second question is that intensional logics and extensional logics involve the admission not merely of different but of incompatible types of entity. "Both sorts of entity can be accommodated in the same logic only with the help of restrictions such as Church's, which serve to keep them from mixing, and this is very nearly a matter of two separate logics with a universe for each" (*From a Logical Point of View,* p. 157).

It is clear that Quine's logical preoccupations are in fact relevant to Wolff and the scholastics only in that an understanding of Quine's inquiries would preclude one from trying to construct a deductive ontology in the mode of Suárez or Wolff.

See also Baumgarten, Alexander Gottlieb; Church, Alonzo; Clauberg, Johannes; Cosmology; Gilson, Étienne Henry; Heidegger, Martin; Kant, Immanuel; Leibniz, Gottfried Wilhelm; Ontology; Psychology; Quine, Willard Van Orman; Suárez, Francisco; Thomas Aquinas, St.; Thomism; Wolff, Christian.

Bibliography

PRIMARY SOURCES

Baumgarten, Alexander Gottlieb. *Metaphysica.* Halle, 1740.

Clauberg, Johannes. *Opera Omnia,* edited by J. T. Schalbruch. 2 vols., 281. Amsterdam, 1691.

Duhamel, Jean-Baptiste. *De Consensu Veteris et Novae Philosophiae.* Paris, 1663.

Duns Scotus, John. *Opera Omnia.* 12 vols. Paris, 1891–1895. Vol. III, *Quaestiones Subtillissimae Super Libros Metaphysicorum Aristotelis.*

Heidegger, Martin. *Being and Time.* Translated by John Macquarrie and Edward Robinson. New York: Harper, 1962.

Heidegger, Martin. *Existence and Being.* Translated by D. Scott, R. Hall, and A. Crick. Chicago: Regnery, 1949.

Kant, Immanuel. *Critique of Pure Reason.* Translated by Norman Kemp Smith. London: Macmillan, 1929.

Quine, Willard Van Orman. *From a Logical Point of View.* Cambridge, MA: Harvard University Press, 1953.

Wolff, Christian. *Philosophia Prima Sive Ontologia.* Frankfurt and Leipzig, 1729.

Wolff, Christian. *Philosophia Rationalis, Sive Logica Methodo Scientifica Pertractata et ad Usum Scientiarum Atque Vitae Aptata.* Frankfurt and Leipzig, 1728.

SECONDARY SOURCES

Bocheński, I. M. *Philosophy—An Introduction.* Dordrecht, Netherlands, 1962.

Drennen, D. A., ed. *Modern Introduction to Metaphysics.* New York: Free Press of Glencoe, 1962.

Ferrater Mora, José. "On the Early History of Ontology." *Philosophy and Phenomenological Research* 24 (1963): 36–47.

Geach, P. T., A. J. Ayer, and W. V. Quine. "Symposium: On What There Is." *PAS,* Supp., 25 (1951): 125–160.

Gilson, Étienne. *Being and Some Philosophers.* Toronto: Pontifical Institute of Mediaeval Studies, 1949.

Martin, Gottfried. *Immanuel Kant: Ontologie und Wissenschaftstheorie.* Cologne: University of Cologne, 1951. Translated by P. G. Lucas as *Kant's Metaphysics and Theory of Science.* Manchester, U.K., 1955.

Marx, Werner. *Heidegger und die Tradition.* Stuttgart: W. Kohlhammer, 1961.

Owens, Joseph. *The Doctrine of Being in the Aristotelian Metaphysics.* Toronto: Pontifical Institute of Mediaeval Studies, 1951.

Alasdair MacIntyre (1967)

OPERATIONALISM

"Operationalism" is a program that aims at linking all scientific concepts to experimental procedures and at cleansing science of operationally undefinable terms, which it regards as being devoid of empirical meaning. Scientists adopted the operational approach to their subject before the principles of operationalism were made articulate. Operationalist theory was erected not on the basis of independent philosophical considerations but upon what was already implicit in the working practice of scientists. P. W. Bridgman, the Nobel Prize–winning physicist who is commonly regarded as the founder of operationalism, emphasized this point when he said, "it must be remembered that the operational point of view suggested itself from the observation of physicists in action" ("The Present State of Operationalism," in *The Validation of Scientific Theories,* edited by Philipp Frank, Boston, 1956, p. 79).

A fairly nontechnical illustration of the kinds of development in science in which one can discern an implicit operational point of view is the manner in which physicists treated the concept of physical length. In the nineteenth century it was discovered that Euclid's geometry was not logically unique and that other geometries based on different axioms were not necessarily internally inconsistent. The question was raised about the nature of physical space. Do lines and figures in physical space obey the theorems of Euclid?

At first sight this seems a perfectly sensible question to which there must be a definite answer. Even today some amount of sophistication is required to ask whether we have a clear notion of what could be done to find out whether space has a certain set of properties. Unless we can give an affirmative answer to this question, we should not take it for granted either that space has or that it lacks certain geometrical properties. By the end of the nineteenth century, however, scientists had accepted the view that if we cannot devise operations that would disclose whether or not space was Euclidean, then no definite geometrical properties can be assigned to space at all.

It is clear that in order to determine the geometrical properties of physical figures we must be able to compare distances. If we are unable to say whether distance *AB* is greater, smaller, or equal to distance *CD,* where *AB* and *CD* do not lie alongside one another, then we cannot even begin to investigate the geometrical nature of space. We take it for granted, however, that in order to compare distances we need a rigid measuring rod, that is, a rod which can be relied upon not to change in length while being transported from place to place. But the question whether the lengths of transported rods are preserved cannot be settled unless we presuppose the possession of some other standard of measurement to which these rods could be compared, but it is agreed that the sole standard of length is a rigid rod. Thus, there are no rigid rods except by fiat, and distances consequently cannot be spoken of as being objectively equal or unequal to one another, and the nature of space cannot uniquely be determined. From an operational point of view, therefore, space has no intrinsic metric, and it is a matter of convention whether we say space obeys this or that set of geometrical axioms.

THE OPERATIONALIST THESIS

Although the idea that physical entities, processes, and properties do not have an independent existence transcending the operations through which we may ascertain their presence or absence played an influential role in the thoughts of scientists before the 1920s, it was not until

1927 that Bridgman, in his celebrated *Logic of Modern Physics,* stated operationalism as an explicit program, made an articulate case for it, and undertook extensive operational analyses of the foundations of numerous physical concepts.

Bridgman soon had to retreat from his first extreme statement of operationalism. He had maintained that every scientifically meaningful concept must be capable of full definition in terms of performable physical operations and that a scientific concept is nothing more than the set of operations entering into its definition. The untenability of this view was quickly noticed—for example, by L. J. Russell, who in 1928 pointed out that in science one often speaks of certain operations as being better than others and that one cannot do so except in relation to something existing over and above them. Moreover, useful physical concepts do not as a rule lend themselves to an exhaustive definition. Any connection they have with instrumental operations may be loose and indirect: statements in which the concepts appear may, in the context of a set of other statements (but not on their own), entail statements describing physical operations. Consequently, in his later writings Bridgman freely permitted "paper and pencil operations," by which he meant mathematical and logical maneuverings with the aid of which no more is required of a concept than that it should be "indirectly making connection with instrumental operations."

It is not hard to see how by taking as one's model a physical concept like the length of a body one arrives at Bridgman's original position. But suppose someone objected that the stepping-off procedure carried out by measuring rods is not the only way to compute the length of a body. We may, for example, define it equally well in terms of the result obtained by timing the body's oscillation when it is allowed to swing as a pendulum and by using the well-known equation connecting the length with the period of oscillation. Length, after all, may enter into all sorts of relationships with other physical parameters, some of which we perhaps have not yet discovered.

To this objection it would have been replied that there is a fundamental difference between the ways in which the two sets of operations are related to the concept of length. The length of a body is "synonymous" with the number of times one can lay a rigid standard of length alongside it; when we speak of the length of a body we mean no more nor less than the number obtained through the stepping-off procedure performed by a measuring stick. When, however, we time a pendulum and then make the appropriate calculations, we merely measure length indirectly, via the relationship of length to other physical parameters. The second approach does not define length but rather inserts the already defined concept of length into an equation accepted as representing a genuine physical relationship.

It is much more difficult to maintain this distinction in the case of such concepts as temperature. One way to give an operational definition of temperature is in terms of measurements made by a mercury thermometer; another way is in terms of measurements made by a platinum-wire thermometer. The first way relies on the theory that the length of bodies varies with temperature; the second, on the theory that electrical resistance varies with temperature. It is easy to see that the concept of temperature is no more than partially interpreted through each of these, and doubtless other, sets of operations to which it is linked by relevant theories. This same position has become generally adopted toward all physical concepts.

We may thus distinguish three stages in scientific theorizing. In the first, preoperational stage, the universe was thought to contain many things and processes that transcend our theories about them and the operations and manipulations through which we may catch a glimpse of them in the mirror of experience. In the second, "naive" operational stage, the other extreme was taken, and all the terms of science were regarded as no more than abbreviations for our experimental results. In the third stage, scientific terms are still not regarded as standing for things and processes having an independent existence of their own, but the meaning of scientific terms is given by a more or less elaborate system of empirical theories in which the terms appear, together with the observations on which the theories embodying the terms are grounded. It is recognized that the concepts of science can never be fully grasped as long as the theories which contain them are open to further development.

The three stages in scientific theorizing are perhaps more dramatically accentuated in psychology than in the physical sciences. Until the early twentieth century the prevailing view was that psychology is a unique discipline dealing with a very special class of events, processes, and entities: the constituents of the realm of consciousness, to which no one but the experiencing individual has access. Although this realm is out of the reach of objective public operations and experimentations, many theorists regarded it as real—indeed, as more real than anything else—and believed that it should be studied by a unique method, introspection.

The radical behaviorism that replaced this mentalistic psychology is a form of naive operationalism and is based on the tenet that psychology is the study not of mental events, processes, or entities but of behavior. Psychologists were not to be concerned with publicly unobservable phenomena, and introspection—at best a private method of inquiry—was completely outlawed.

Today, in the third stage, sensations, images, and thought processes are no longer regarded as beyond the reach of scientists. They are studied through overt behavior, just as in physics nonobservables are studied indirectly through what is observed. The situation in psychology is very much like that in physics. That which is conceptualized need not be completely defined in terms of operations, although it must make contact with the world of public experience.

OPERATIONALISM AND VERIFICATIONISM

Operationalism is a movement within the philosophy of science. It is instructive to study its development in conjunction with a parallel movement in general philosophy: logical positivism, or logical empiricism. Central to logical positivism is the principle of verifiability, according to which any statement that is not a tautology must be verifiable or else is meaningless. It was thought that through the extensive employment of this principle it would be possible to show that many of the traditional unsolved problems of philosophy could be dealt with by demonstrating that they are simply meaningless. It was soon found, however, that the principle as originally conceived would get rid not only of troublesome problems but also of much useful discourse. The principle consequently underwent a number of revisions in rapid succession.

Rudolf Carnap's paper "The Methodological Character of Theoretical Concepts" embodies all the significant revisions. Carnap clearly exhibits a desire not to prescribe what should be regarded as meaningful from some metascientific or philosophical point of view but rather to describe what is commonly and usefully regarded as empirically meaningful. As mentioned earlier, operationalism from the beginning sought to explicate an approach already implied in the work of practicing scientists. Whereas verificationists previously tried to embrace all human discourse, they now, like the operationalists, confine their attempts to designing a criterion that will faithfully reflect what is meaningful discourse within empirical science. It has been realized that meanings are contextual and that one is therefore not to inquire whether a given sentence or word has or lacks meaning by itself but rather whether it has or lacks meaning relative to a specified system of theoretical, observational, and mixed statements.

A third important change, also clearly enunciated for the first time in Carnap's paper, is the departure from the original policy of inquiring directly into the meaningfulness of whole sentences. Instead, like the operationalists, Carnap deals with individual terms. He distinguishes between logical and empirical terms and also between observational-empirical and theoretical-empirical terms. Theoretical-empirical terms are not admitted into empirical discourse unless they can be shown to be anchored in observation. They need not be completely defined observationally, but a sentence must be constructible that, in conjunction with other sentences, logically implies that certain observations take place. A theoretical-empirical term is then regarded as having passed the test of empirical meaningfulness. The empirical significance of a sentence is now made dependent on the possession of significance by the terms it contains: Any syntactically well-formed sentence in which every term is significant (that is, is either a logical, an observational-empirical, or a theoretical-empirical term which has passed the test of empirical meaningfulness) is itself significant in the context of the group of sentences forming our system of science.

The only issue that divides operationalism from logical positivism is that operationalism seems to associate meaningfulness with linkability to experimental activities, whereas the principle of verifiability is satisfied if an expression is anchored to mere passive observation. However, this particular requirement of operationalism can safely be discarded, leading to a complete merger of these two contemporary offshoots of empiricism.

CRITICISM

Even in its present form, operationalism has not gone uncriticized. The chief complaint is that in the course of weakening its demands in order to accommodate highly theoretical but useful terms that would otherwise have been excluded from science, it has become so watered down as to lose all significance. Operationalism, according to its critics, says nothing we did not know all along. Even in a discipline less precise than physics—for example, in the social sciences—and in a period when standards of rigor had not reached their present stringency, if anyone had advanced a theory employing concepts which had no bearing whatsoever on observables, his theory would have been rejected. It is admitted that operationalism as originally conceived did have practical impact;

there are concrete results, especially in psychology, whose production was motivated by the naive operationalistic distrust of anything remote from experience—for example, results obtained in the investigation of subaudible speech. Psychologists came to this area of inquiry chiefly through their search for objective, nonmentalistic alternatives to thought processes. But now, with the liberalization of the criterion for empirical significance—so the complaint goes—when all that is stipulated is that no term qualifies for membership in the vocabulary of science unless it is in some way connected to the universe of operations, observables, and experience, the principle of operationalism is merely platitudinous.

In attempting to reply to this, we must not forget that the scope of operationalism is not confined to the weeding out from scientific vocabulary of terms devoid of empirical significance. Once we have adopted the operational point of view, we have formed in our own minds a particular image of the nature of scientific concepts, which colors our expectations and influences in all sorts of ways our practical approach and methodology.

The world of experience and observation was at one time looked upon as containing mere dim reflections of the world that is conceptualized in physics and whose real existence was on a transcendental plane ultimately beyond our reach. Admittedly, that which is without any observable manifestations whatsoever, which, so to speak, casts no shadow onto the plane of experience, would never have been considered as being of any use to science. Nevertheless, it is not unimportant whether we regard our operations as capturing at most the shadows of the furniture of the universe or as dealing with the furniture itself. Objects totally dissimilar in substance and even in size and shape may under particular circumstances cast identical shadows. Therefore, from the similarity of shadows one cannot infer a similarity in the corresponding objects or even that these objects always cast similar shadows. Similarly, so long as we regard as mere reflections the observations to which physical concepts are linked, the finding of resemblances between some of them will not give rise to the expectation that they resemble in all particulars. On adopting the operational point of view, on the other hand, we think we are looking not at reflected shadows but at the very entities and processes that are conceptualized in science, and our attitude changes accordingly.

To give an illustrative example, the properties of gravitational force and the laws governing it had been exhaustively investigated in the seventeenth and eighteenth centuries. Electromagnetic forces were comparative newcomers in science. Were they to be expected to behave like mechanical forces? There are excellent grounds for saying no: the sources from which electromagnetic forces arise, the systems with which they are associated, and the means by which they are generated are totally different from those involving mechanical forces. However, operationalists tend to see in the product of mass and acceleration (that is, in the measure of force) the very substance of force, although others might see in it no more than force's most immediately apparent reflection. Indeed, as soon as it was observed that electromagnetic phenomena are accompanied by the forcelike effect of accelerating masses, it was taken for granted that they are fully governed by all the laws of Newtonian mechanics, even though the latter was developed to deal with an effect of totally different origin.

An important aim of operationalism besides the practical one is philosophical. For philosophical purposes, it is far from sufficient to state generally that every empirically significant term must somehow be linked to observables—one must precisely articulate the nature of this link and construct in full detail a criterion of meaningfulness. Therefore, many concepts in the various sciences were analyzed in detail in order to clarify the exact role instrumental operations and observations play in the definition or explication of them. Believers in the ultimate formalizability of empirical significance hoped that the results would be generalized and expressible in a philosophically satisfactory way. It is, however, by no means clear that such work has been entirely successful. In fact, some philosophers are of the opinion that such efforts are altogether in vain and that although when faced with any individual term we are able quite easily to judge whether it is empirically significant, we shall never succeed in explicating the general criterion distinguishing meaningful from meaningless utterances.

There is thus unquestionably much scope for operationally clarifying basic concepts. The skeptic might try to show that just as there are no formal criteria by which to distinguish a fertile from a sterile theory, so there is no criterion by which to distinguish the empirically significant from the meaningless. One who believes that the contact empirical concepts must make with operations or experience in general can be precisely formalized might try to show that if our demands are modest enough and we do not expect the criterion of empirical significance to provide guidance for future scientific research, there are in principle no obstacles in the way of such formalization. Their next step would be to execute this formalization in a manner that would stand up to all criticism.

See also Bridgman, Percy William; Carnap, Rudolf; Logical Positivism; Scientific Theories; Verifiability Principle.

Bibliography

Bridgman, P. W. *The Logic of Modern Physics.* New York: Macmillan, 1927.

Bridgman, P. W. *The Nature of Physical Theory.* Princeton, NJ: Princeton University Press, 1936.

Bridgman, P. W. *The Nature of Some of Our Physical Concepts.* New York: Philosophical Library, 1952. Many individual concepts carefully analyzed.

Bridgman, P. W. *The Nature of Thermodynamics.* Cambridge, MA: Harvard University Press, 1941. Carefully analyzes many individual concepts.

Bridgman, P. W. *Reflections of a Physicist.* New York: Philosophical Library, 1950. A collection of papers.

Bures, C. E. "Operationism, Construction, and Inference." *Journal of Philosophy* 37 (1940): 393–401.

Carnap, Rudolf. "The Methodological Character of Theoretical Concepts." In *Minnesota Studies in the Philosophy of Science,* Vol. 1, edited by Herbert Feigl and Michael Scriven, 38–76. Minneapolis: University of Minnesota Press, 1956.

Carnap, Rudolf. "Testability and Meaning." *Philosophy of Science* 3 (1936): 419–471, and 4 (1937): 1–40.

Crissman, P. "The Operational Definition of Concepts." *Psychological Review* 46 (1939).

Dingle, Herbert. "A Theory of Measurement." *British Journal for the Philosophy of Science* 1 (1950). An extreme operationalist viewpoint.

Feigl, Herbert. "Operationism and Scientific Method." *Psychological Review* 52 (1945). A lucid and fair assessment of operationalism. Written as a contribution to "Symposium on Operationism," presented in the same issue.

Frank, Philipp. *Modern Science and Its Philosophy.* Cambridge, MA: Harvard University Press, 1949. On p. 44 the work of Bridgman is likened to that of Carnap.

Frank, Philipp, ed. *The Validation of Scientific Theories.* Boston: Beacon Press, 1956. Various writers assess the significance of operationalism in the 1950s.

Hearnshaw, L. J. "Psychology and Operationalism." *Australasian Journal of Psychology and Philosophy* 18 (1941).

Hempel, C. G. "A Logical Appraisal of Operationalism." *Scientific Monthly* 79 (1954): 215–220. Reprinted with modifications in his *Aspects of Scientific Explanation,* 123–133. New York, 1965.

Lindsay, L. B. "A Critique of Operationalism in Science." *Philosophy of Science* 4 (1937). Important and fair criticism of operationalism.

Margenau, Hans. *The Nature of Physical Theory.* New York, 1952. On p. 232, expresses impatience with operationalism.

Pap, Arthur. "Are Physical Magnitudes Operationally Definable?" In *Measurements, Definitions, and Theories,* edited by C. West Churchman. New York, 1959. Argues for the abolition of the demand for active operations.

Peters, Richard. "Observationalism in Psychology." *Mind* 68 (1959).

Reichenbach, Hans. *Experience and Prediction.* Chicago: University of Chicago Press, 1938.

Russell, L. J. Review of Bridgman's *The Logic of Modern Physics. Mind* 47 (1938).

Schlesinger, Georg. *Method in the Physical Sciences.* London: Routledge and Paul, 1963. Chapter 4 is devoted to a discussion of the practical scope of operationalism.

Skinner, B. F. "Behaviorism at Fifty." *Science* (1963).

Skinner, B. F. "The Operational Analysis of Psychological Terms." *Psychological Review* 52 (1945): 270–277.

Spence, K. W. "The Postulates and Methods of 'Behaviorism.'" *Psychological Review* 55 (1948): 67–78.

Stevens, S. S. "The Operational Basis of Psychology." *American Journal of Psychology* 46 (1935).

Stevens, S. S. "The Operational Definition of Psychological Concepts." *Psychological Review* 42 (1935). A major spokesman for operationalism in psychology.

G. Schlesinger (1967)

OPTIMISM AND PESSIMISM

See *Pessimism and Optimisim*

ORDER

See *Chaos Theory*; *Measurement and Measurement Theory*; *Teleological Argument for the Existence of God*

ORESME, NICOLE
(c. 1320–1382)

Nicole (Nicholas) Oresme was a Master of Arts and Theology at the University of Paris, royal counsellor, translator into French of Aristotle's works, and bishop of Lisieux. Of humble origin, he was admitted in the College of Navarre in 1348, where he became Grand Master in 1356, after having obtained the license of Master of Theology. He was born in Normandy probably no later than 1320, in a village near Caen (Allemagne, today Fleury-sur-Orne). His ecclesiastical career depended on his university teaching as well as on his connections with the royal court. The first benefice was granted by Pope Clement VI in 1342, in reply to a supplication list of the University of Paris in order to obtain support for master and students (Oresme is recorded as master); the election to the bishop's chair of Lisieux in 1377 was Charles V's (1364–1380) reward for Oresme's translations of Aristotle's works, made by royal request. His main ecclesiastical functions were in Normandy, a region with high strategic importance during the wars between France and England. He was appointed canon of Rouen Cathedral in 1362, and two years later he was chosen as dean. He reduced, but did not cut short, his connections with the university and with the royal court in Paris. In 1370 he disputed at the university a quodlibetal question; in 1375 he was charged, together with Simon Fréron and Richard Barbe, to find out if Marsilius of Padua's *Defensor Pacis* had been translated into French. Oresme translated and commented upon Aristotle's *Ethics* (*Le livre de ethiques d'Aristote*), *Politics* (*Les politiques*), *Economics* (*Le livre de yconomique d'Aristote*), and *De Caelo* (*Le livre du ciel et du monde*). He wrote also in French an elementary treatise on astronomy (*Livre de l'éspere*), and a treatise against the astrologers (*Livre de divinacions*). He died on July 11, 1382, in Lisieux.

His commentaries on Aristotle's physical writings (*Physics*, *On the heaven*, *On coming to be and passing away*, *On the soul*, and *Methereologics*), as well as his treatises (*Ad pauca respicientes*, *De proportionibus proportionum*, *De commensurabilitate motuum caeli*, *De configurationibus qualitatum*) bear witness to his prevailing scientific interests, and above all to his conviction of the importance of using mathematics in dealing with physical problems (qualitative changes, motion, duration). In his commentaries, Oresme discusses the main philosophical issues debated at the University of Paris after the dissemination of William of Ockham's works and the condemnations of John of Mirecourt (1347) and Nicolas of Autrécourt (1348).

THE SUBJECT OF HUMAN KNOWLEDGE AND THE CERTITUDE OF PHYSICAL SCIENCE

Oresme offered rather original solutions to two very important problems traditionally discussed in the opening questions of medieval commentaries on the physical writings of Aristotle: the subject of human knowledge, and the degree of certitude of physical science. Concerning the first, Oresme rejects the reductionist view, usually attributed to William Ockham, according to which human knowledge concerns exclusively the conclusion of a syllogism, as well as the claim that it deals with singular objects. He believes that human knowledge concerns properly what can be expressed through a proposition (*complexe significabile*) rather than through a single term.

On the certitude of physical science, Oresme shares the common position, strongly attacked by Nicolas d'Autrécourt, according to which it does not need the highest degree of certitude typical of mathematics and metaphysics.

The convenience of having recourse to mathematics in physical inquiries, however, permits one in some way to extend to physics this highest degree of certitude.

The possibility of applying mathematics to physics is warranted either by widening the field of physical inquiries to a hypothetical, non contradictory state of things, or by assuming the geometrical model of perspective in explaining physical actions like heating. The extension of imaginary cases to physical inquiries actually increases the potential of physics, whose limits coincide with the law of noncontradiction. In his *Quaestiones de spera* (q. 2), Oresme explicitly upholds the use of mathematical fictions (*imaginationes*), like points and lines, in physics, stating that in astronomy (and in the so called *scientiae mediae*) truth can not be reached without the aid of mathematics and geometry (he quotes for this solution the authority of Aristotle's *De coelo*).

The plurality of worlds and the daily rotation of the earth on its axis while the heavens remain stationary—two of the topics to which Oresme owes his celebrity among historians of science since Pierre Duhem—are such hypothetical cases. Oresme amply discussed the possibility of such hypotheses, concluding always in favor of the traditional view. The relativity of motion is a central issue in the astronomical hypothesis of the earth's daily rotation; Oresme's position concerning the nature of motion is an original attempt to maintain an absolute notion.

MATHEMATICS AND PHYSICS

One of Oresme's major contributions to natural philosophy is his solution concerning the "intension and remission of qualities"—that is the variation of intensity of qualities, motion, velocity, and every kind of successive thing. *De configurationibus qualitatum* opens by confirming the utility of making recourse to mathematics in physical inquiries: Intensities of qualities can be easily measured by representing them through geometrical figures, whose one line represents the subject where the quality is distributed (*extensio*), on which there are perpendicularly erected lines representing the intensities of the quality (*intensio*). The line connecting the higher points of the intensities (*linea summitatis*) can immediately inform us about the type of change (uniform, uniformly difform, difform).

Oresme avails himself of this method of graphing the varying of intensities of qualities and motions in order to explain the diversity of actions of physical agents, and also of human passions, occult virtues, aesthetic problems, and magical operations. In his effort to reduce uniformly difform types of variation to uniform ones, Oresme proposes a geometrical demonstration of the so called mean-speed theorem (the distances traversed by two moving objects, the former moving uniformly/difformly and the latter uniformly with the mean speed of the former, is the same). Galileo used an analogous geometric demonstration for freely falling bodies in his *Discorsi e dimostrazioni matematiche intorno a due nuove scienze.*

Oresme adhered to Thomas Bradwardine's solution, according to which velocity depends on a proportional change of the force as well as of the resistance. In order to double velocity, it is not enough to double force or to halve resistance, but the square of the proportion between force and resistance must also be obtained.

In *De proportionibus proportionum* III, prop.10, Oresme resorts to mathematics to argue for the high degree of probability of the incommensurability of any two unknown ratios: "because if many unknown ratios are proposed it is most probable that any one would be incommensurable to any other" (E. Grant's translation, p. 247). He proposes a similar argument in *De commensurabilitate* to support the incommensurability of heavenly circular motions in order to invalidate astrological predictions based on planetary conjunctions, which would be unpredictable.

MODI RERUM

Oresme's *Physics* commentary contains an original philosophical doctrine concerning the nature of motion, place, and time, and more generally the ontology of natural things. Evidently dissatisfied by the two opposing solutions—the reductionist, inspired by Ockham, according to which motion is nothing different than the moving object; and the realist, according to which motion is a quality inherent to the moving object—Oresme proposed to consider motion, as well as place, time, and other continuous natural things, as complex objects or events rather than as simple qualities and properties. To do that he availed himself also of semantical tools like the meaning of the proposition (*complexe significabile*). Oresme was convinced that his solution was able to avoid some ontological problems in natural philosophy: He explicitly quotes intension and remission of qualitative forms, with qualities considered as *modi* of the substance and not accidental properties inhering to the substance.

See also Aristotle; Bradwardine, Thomas; Duhem, Pierre Maurice Marie; Galileo Galilei; John of Mirecourt; Marsilius of Padua; Mathematics, Foundations of; Medieval Philosophy; Nicolas of Autrecourt; William of Ockham.

Bibliography

On Oresme's biography see: F. Neveux, "Nicole Oresme et le clergé normand du XIVe siècle." In *Autour de Nicole Oresme*, pp. 9–36, edited by J. Quillet. Paris: Vrin, 1990; W. J. Courtenay, "The Early Career of Nicole Oresme," *ISIS* 91 (2000), pp. 542–548.

French translations and commentaries: *Le livre de ethiques d'Aristote*, A. D. Menut, ed. (New York: G. E. Stechert, 1940); *Le livre de yconomique d'Aristote*, A. D. Menut ed. with English transl., in *Transactions of the American Philosophical Society*, N. S. Vol. 47, Part 2 (Philadelphia: American Philosophical Society, 1957); *Le livre de Politiques d'Aristote*, A. D. Menut, ed., in *Transactions of the American Philosophical Society*, N. S. Vol. 60, Part 6 (Philadelphia: American Philosophical Society, 1970); *Le livre du ciel et du monde*, A. D. Menut and A. J. Denomy, eds. with English transl. (Madison: Univ. of Wisconsin Press, 1968); *Le traité des monnaies* (French transl. of *De mutationibus monetarum*), ed. L. Wolowski, *Petit traité de la première invention des monnaies de Nicolas Oresme*, Paris, Guillaumin 1864 (Slatkine Reprints, 1976).

French treatises: *Traité de l'espere*, ed. J. V. Myers (Syracuse Univ., 1940), and L. M. McCarthy (Toronto Univ., 1943); *Le livre de divinacions*, G. W. Coopland ed. (Cambridge, MA: Harvard Univ. Press, 1952).

Latin commentaries and other writings in form of university questions: *Quaestiones super Geometriam Euclidis*, H. L. L. Busard, ed., (Leiden: Brill, 1961); *Quaestiones de sensu*, J. Agrimi, ed. (Firenze, 1983); *Expositio et Quaestiones in Aristotelis "De anima,"* B. Patar ed. (Louvain-Paris: Éditions de l'Institut Supérieur de Philosophie-Éditions Peeters, 1995); *Quaestiones super De generatione et corruptione*, S. Caroti ed. (München: Bayerische Akademie der Wissenschaften, 1996); *Quaestiones super Physicam*, S. Kirschner ed. (Stuttgart: Franz Steiner, 1997), the complete edition is in preparation; *Quaestio contra divinatores horoscopios*, S. Caroti, ed. in *Archives d'histoire doctrinale et littéraire du Moyen Âge*, 43, 1976, pp. 201–310; *Quodlibeta*, B. Hansen (Toronto: Pontifical Institute of Mediaeval Studies, 1985, partial ed.); *Quaestiones super de coelo*, C. Kren ed. (Univ. of Wisconsin, 1965); *Quaestiones super de spera*, G. Droppers ed. (Univ. of Wisconsin, 1966); *Quaestiones super quatuor libros Meteororum*, S. C. McCluskey ed. (Univ. of Wisconsin, 1974, partial ed.); *De visione stellarum*, D. E. Burton ed. (Indiana Univ., 2000); *Questio utrum aliqua res videatur*, J. B. Watson ed. (Harvard Univ., 1973).

Not yet identified is his commentary on the *Sentences*; the *De perfectione specierum* to which Oresme alludes in his *De configurationibus* (I, 20) is probably part of this commentary. Other theological writings: *Tractatus de communicatione idiomatum*, E. Borchert, ed. In *Beiträge zur Geschichte der Philosophie und Theologie des Mittelalters*, 35, München: Aschendorff, 1940, H. 4–5; *Determinatio facta in resumpta in domo Navarrae*, ms.

Latin treatises: *Algorismus proportionum*, M. Curtze ed. (Berlin: Calvary, 1868) and E. Grant ed. (Univ. of Wisconsin, 1957, partial ed.); *De proportionibus proportionum*, *Ad pauca respicientes*, E. Grant ed. with English transl. (Madison: Univ. of Wisconsin Press, 1966); *De configurationibus qualitatum et motuum*, M. Clagett ed. with English transl. (Madison: Univ.

of Wisconsin Press, 1968); *De commensurabilitate vel incommensurabilitate motuum celi*, E. Grant ed. with English transl. (Madison: Univ. of Wisconsin Press, 1971); *Tractatus contra iudiciarios astronomos*, H. Pruckner ed. (Leipzig-Berlin: Teubner, 1933) and G.W. Coopland ed. with English transl. (Cambridge, MA: Harvard Univ. Press, 1952); *Tractatus de mutationibus monetarum*, C. Johnson, ed. with English transl. (London: T. Nelson, 1956).

In addition to the pioneer studies of P. Duhem, *Le système du monde*, 10 vols. (Paris: Herman, 1913–1959, Vols. IV, VII, VIII, and IX) and A. Maier, *Studien zur Naturphilosophie der Spätscholastik*, 5 vols. (Rome: Edizioni di Storia e Letteraturea, 1949–1958), where Oresme's role in the history of science was highly appreciated, and to the volume of O. Pedersen's *Nicole Oresme og hans natufilosofiske System* (Copenhagen: Munksgaard, 1956, with a French summary), much new material can be found in the introductions to the editions of his works (above all in Clagett's introduction to *De configurationibus*). Two conferences have been dedicated to Oresme: *Nicolas Oresme. Tradition et innovation chez un intellectuel du XIVe siècle*, P. Souffrin, A. Ph. Segonds, eds. (Padova-Paris: Programma e Editori-Les Belles Lettres, 1988, with a very important contribution of H. Hugonnard-Roche, *Modalités et argumentation chez Nicole Oresme*) and *Autour de Nicole Oresme*, J. Quillet ed. (Paris: Vrin, 1990). The n. 3 (2000) of the review *Oriens-Occidens. Sciences, mathématiques et philosophie de l'Antiquité à l'Âge classique* is partly dedicated to Nicole Oresme's *Physics*. New material is also in the proceedings of the Parma conference: *Quia inter doctores est magna dissensio. Les débats de philosophie naturelle à Paris au XIVe siècle*, S. Caroti, J. Celeyrette eds. (Florence: Olschki, 2004).

Stefano Caroti (2005)

ORGANISMIC BIOLOGY

The term *organismalism* was coined by the zoologist W. E. Ritter in 1919 to describe the theory that, in his words, "the organism in its totality is as essential to an explanation of its elements as its elements are to an explanation of the organism." Subsequent writers have largely replaced *organismal* with the more euphonious *organismic* as a title for this theory, for the many variations on its main theme, and for some subordinate but supporting doctrines concerning the teleological and historical character of organisms.

Ritter regards Aristotle as the founder and most distinguished exponent of the organismic theory. But Aristotle is also claimed as the father of vitalism, a view that organismic biologists in general reject. In fact, there is considerable affinity between the two schools. They both agree that the methods of the physical sciences are applicable to the study of organisms but insist that these methods cannot tell the whole story; they agree that the "form" of the single whole organism is in some sense a factor in embryological development, animal behavior, reproduction, and physiology; and they both insist on the propriety of a teleological point of view. On all of these points, Aristotle not only agrees but presents, in his own terminology, careful and persuasive arguments in their favor. But organismic biology and vitalism differ in one fundamental respect: The latter holds (and the former denies) that the characteristic features of organic activity—all of which fall under the heading of "regulation"—are caused by the presence in the organism of a nonphysical but substantial entity. There are different interpretations of Aristotle (which we cannot examine here) on the question of whether he believes there are such vital entities. In this writer's view, Aristotle is clearly a vitalist.

The affinity between vitalism and organismic biology is more than an accident. In the history of biology it is difficult to disentangle vitalistic and organismic strands, since both schools are concerned with the same sorts of problems and speak the same sort of language. The distinction between them was drawn clearly only in the twentieth century. Organismic biology may be described as an attempt to achieve the aims of the murky organismic-vitalistic tradition, without appeal to vital entities.

The writings of contemporary organismic biologists present a number of difficulties for a philosophical commentator. The position of organismic biology is usually stated in a vocabulary that plays little or no theoretical role in the working language of biology. For example, "whole," "unity," "integrity," "part," "form," "principle," "understanding," and "significance" all occur frequently in their works. Now any biologist will use these terms occasionally in the course of his professional writing, just because they are perfectly good words in the English language. But they are not technical expressions; they are not, in ordinary usage, laden with biological theory; and they are trouble-free only when employed in contexts that make clear their function as items in the common language. The organismic biologist, however, makes them bear a heavy burden in the description of the nature of living organisms. And many, but by no means all, organismic biologists also assign a great deal of weight to some rather mysterious formulas. Here are a few: "The whole acts as a causal unit … on its own parts" (W. E. Agar); "The living body and its physiological environment form an organic whole, the parts of which cannot be understood in separation from one another" (J. S. Haldane); "No part of any organism can be rightly interpreted except as part of an individual organism" (W. E. Ritter). And here are a few more that are characteristic but not direct quotations: "The organic whole is greater than the sum of its parts"; "Knowledge of the goal of an animal's behavior is necessary for understanding its significance"; "Biological theory should be autonomous, with concepts and laws of its own." These formulas may be termed "mysterious" because, according to their most natural interpretations (as will be argued), they are all the barest of truisms.

Two additional points should be mentioned. Organismic biologists have employed some of the more obscure technical conceptions of speculative philosophy, such as "formal cause," "emergence," "hormic," "telic," and so on. And since their writings are a minority report on biological phenomena, organismic biologists are often polemical, engaging in denunciations of other biologists—"mechanists," "elementalists," and "reductionists"—whose positions they leave just as obscure as their own. For all of these reasons, an account of the organismic position that aims at answering the questions likely to be raised by philosophers of science involves elements of reconstruction and interpretation. Thus, a fuller description of the position and an interpretation designed to do justice both to the letter and spirit of the organismic tradition follows.

THE POSITION OF ORGANISMIC BIOLOGY

All organismic biologists hold that there is a gulf between organic and inorganic phenomena in one or more of the following respects.

ORGANIC UNITY. Organic systems are so organized that the activities of the whole cannot be understood as the sum of the activities of the parts. All members of the school agree on this point. As the term *organismic* implies, the most important example of such wholes is the single organism, but there are others, such as cells, organs, colonies, and some populations.

J. H. Woodger, whose *Biological Principles* is the most careful and extensive exposition of organismic biology, explains the conception of organic unity in the following way. Consider a system W that is *totally* composed of physicochemical parts—elementary particles, for example. The activities of these parts are described by the laws of physics. These particles may be the sole constituents of other systems (for example, molecules) which also totally compose W and which exhibit, in addition to activities described by the laws of physics, other activities described by the laws of chemistry. Molecules may similarly be the sole constituents of other systems, which are in turn the constituents …, up to the whole system W. In Woodger's terminology, W exhibits a series of "levels of organiza-

tion." The parts of W belong to a particular level, its physical parts to the physical level, its chemical parts to the chemical level, and so on. System W constitutes a perfect "hierarchy" of parts from levels 0 (zero) to n (a finite number), if 0-level parts are the sole constituents of all 1-level parts, and if every part at each level i (any given level) except the 0-level is totally composed of parts at level $i-1$.

Woodger points out that organisms are not perfect hierarchies, since some parts of the organism at an i-level may have parts at the $i-2$ level, while the $i-2$ parts are *not* organized into $i-1$ parts (for instance, blood has cellular *and* chemical but noncellular parts). Nevertheless, he contends, organisms approximate to a hierarchical organization. If we ignore deviations from the perfect hierarchy, we may let W represent a whole organism, and we may say that its 0-level parts are physical parts. Now this analysis permits us to say that the organism is composed totally of physical parts. Perhaps some philosophical materialists would be content with this thesis; at any rate, if it is true, it rules out vitalism. But it is false that the organism is composed *only* of physical parts, for there are parts at higher levels of organization. It is Woodger's contention, and a general thesis of organismic biology, that the laws which determine the behavior of the parts at a given level of organization are silent about some aspects of the behavior of the parts at the higher levels. To use an extreme example, the laws of quantum physics have nothing to say on the question of why honeybees kill their drones. According to Woodger, it is necessary to study the relations between the relata at *each* level of organization. In order to understand the behavior of cells during morphogenesis, for example, we must develop a theory of cell relations and not be content, for example, with only a theory of the relations between molecules.

DETERMINING FEATURES OF THE WHOLE. The parts of organic wholes not only exhibit patterns of behavior in virtue of their relations to other parts at the same level of organization, but in addition, *some* of the features of the parts at a given level are determined by the pattern of organization at *higher* (and, of course, at lower) levels of organization. This is the general form of the special thesis that the properties of the whole determine the properties of the part; and it seems to have the methodological consequence that a theory of the elements at a given level could not be complete without a theory of the elements at the higher levels. Woodger puts the point this way: the parts of organisms must be studied in situ, for we cannot learn how they would behave in situ by studying them in isolation.

TELEOLOGICAL BEHAVIOR OF ORGANISMS. One kind of activity, which is a consequence of organization at a level higher than that of the organism's physical parts, is directive or teleological behavior. Directiveness is an aspect of organisms that is shown in their physiology, in the behavior of individual animals, and in the social systems of some animals; and an account of directiveness is not only legitimate but necessary. E. S. Russell argues that since directiveness (processes aimed at the production and maintenance of organic unities) is a fact, then a physiological process, or piece of animal behavior, cannot be understood until we understand its function or its goal.

INTERPRETATION OF ORGANISMIC BIOLOGY

It was remarked above that if we give the slogans of organismic biology their most direct interpretations, they are nothing more than truisms. Consider, for example, the statement that the whole (if it is an organic unity) is more than the sum of its parts. This looks like a simple warning against the fallacy of composition: we are being warned, for example, that from the premise "No part of a bird can fly" we cannot infer "No whole bird can fly." No weighty volume is required to convince us that a whole may have numberless properties that its parts lack. Of course, there are other possible interpretations of the slogan. It might be taken to mean, especially in the form "The behavior of the whole is more than the sum of the behavior of its parts," that no description of the behavior of the parts could be a description of the behavior of the whole. So far from being a truism, this is obviously false. Finally, it might be taken to mean something like the following. Employing an analysis of Ernest Nagel, we might say that the behavior B of a system S is more than the sum of the behavior $b_1, b_2, \cdots, b_n$ of its parts $s_1, s_2, \cdots, s_n$, with respect to an antecedently specified theory T, if (1) B is an instance of a law L; (2) L is not part of T: (3) the laws in T describe $s_1, s_2, \cdots, s_n$ in such a way that they explain $b_1, b_2, \cdots, b_n$; and (4) L is not deducible from a description of $s_1, s_2, \cdots, s_n$ together with laws in T. An important point to notice here is that B can be identical with events $b_1, b_2, \cdots, b_n$, and yet the law of which B is an instance is not derivable from the laws of which $b_1, b_2, \cdots, b_n$ are instances.

This account makes the "more than" relation relative to a body of theory. Relative to existing physical and chemical theories, it is true (but perhaps not a truism) that much organic activity is more than the sum of the physical and chemical activities of its parts. The thesis that there are cases of higher-level behavior that will remain greater than the sum of the behavior of its physical parts, for all possible physical theories, is the doctrine of emergence, which many organismic biologists believe to be true. But it is essential to note two points—first, that the thesis is dubious and unproved, and second, that one can be an organismic biologist without believing it (L. von Bertalanffy is an example).

Let us now look at two more formulas of the organismic biologists. Woodger holds that an organic part, such as a cell, has properties in the organism that it does not have in isolation from the organism. This, too, is a truism: An excised eye lacks the property of contributing to the sight of its former owner. Now if we add, as Woodger does, that the properties of the part in the whole could not be uncovered by studying the part outside the whole, the thesis reduces to the thesis of emergence. And certainly, one of the commonest scientific procedures consists in predicting the behavior of a part in a system that has not yet been studied, although this prediction is assuredly made on the basis of knowledge gained by studying the part—not in "isolation," but as a part of other systems. For instance, the behavior of an electron in a cathode ray tube allows us to predict the electron's behavior in a cyclotron.

Finally, we may consider E. S. Russell's remark that understanding the significance of an animal's behavior requires understanding its goal. This, at least on Russell's interpretation, is a truism, for he connects the notion of a goal with the notion of adaptive value for the animal and identifies "significance" with adaptive value.

Omitting specific discussion of the other formulas cited, the general point is clear: Organismic biology seems to collapse either into doctrines that are not controversial or into unclarified, unproved, and dubious assertions about emergence, unpredictability, and irreducibility. Nevertheless, organismic biology is an important and valuable movement, for the following reasons.

First, organismic biology is perfectly correct in pointing out that there are levels of organization above the chemical level which exhibit laws of behavior that are not exhibited at lower levels (for example, molecules do not sting other molecules to death). Higher-level behavior can be treated without reference to behavior at lower levels, which means that the biologist can (and indeed does) construct concepts that are tailored to the description of higher-level behavior. The principles at the higher levels must be formulated before the question of their reducibility to lower level principles can even be considered. A biochemical geneticist is not only a biochemist; he is also a geneticist, because he is involved in elucidating the processes involved in the sort of gross biological phenomena studied by Gregor Mendel.

Second, the insistence of organismic biologists on the importance of functional analysis is well founded. Focusing on the biological ends of physiological and behavioral processes provides the only means for developing the conceptual schemes that are needed in morphology, ethology, evolution theory, and other branches of biology. This point is developed in detail in Morton Beckner's *Biological Way of Thought.*

Third, although organismic biology is a set of truisms, it is none the worse for being so. The trouble with truisms is their great number: there are so many that we easily overlook, sometimes systematically, some of the most important ones. Even though in fact many biologists agree with the organismic position, they will say that they disagree. This leads to the position (generally deleterious in the sciences) of the scientist's doing one thing and describing it as if he were doing something else.

To sum up, organismic biology is to be interpreted as a series of methodological proposals, based on certain very general features of the organism—namely, the existence in the organism of levels of organization with the biological ends of maintenance and reproduction. These features are sufficient to justify "a free, autonomous biology, with concepts and laws of its own," whether or not the higher levels are ultimately reducible to the lower ones.

See also Aristotle; Bertalanffy, Ludwig von; Philosophy of Biology; Teleology; Vitalism; Woodger, Joseph Henry.

Bibliography

Agar, W. E. *A Contribution to the Theory of Living Organisms.* 2nd ed. Melbourne, 1951.

Beckner, Morton. *The Biological Way of Thought.* New York: Columbia University Press, 1959.

Bertalanffy, Ludwig von. *Modern Theories of Development.* London: Oxford University Press, 1933.

Haldane, J. S. *Mechanism, Life, and Personality,* 2nd ed. New York: Dutton, 1923.

Lillie, R. S. *General Biology and Philosophy of Organism.* Chicago: University of Chicago Press, 1945.

Nagel, Ernest. "Mechanistic Explanation and Organismic Biology." In *Philosophy and Phenomenological Research* 2 (1951): 327–338.

Ritter, W. E. *The Unity of the Organism.* 2 vols. Boston: R.G. Badger, 1919.

Russell, E. S. *The Behaviour of Animals.* 2nd ed. London: E. Arnold, 1938.

Woodger, J. H. *Biological Principles.* London, 1948.

Morton O. Beckner (1967)

ORIGEN
(c. 185–253)

Origen, the Christian theologian and exegete of the Bible, was the foremost member of the catechetical school at Alexandria. Born of Christian parents in Alexandria, he was made head of a Christian school there in 204. He taught until 231, when conflict with the bishop forced him to leave for Caesarea in Palestine, where he taught until his death. He apparently heard lectures by Ammonius Saccas, founder of Neoplatonism, although he regarded philosophy as essentially preparatory to theology in the same way that other studies were prerequisite to philosophy itself. However, the influence of philosophy (primarily Platonic but also Stoic) on his thought was highly significant; it can be observed much more clearly in his presuppositions and arguments than in explicit quotations, which are relatively unusual except in the apologetic treatise *Contra Celsum*. The most important of his voluminous writings are *De Principiis*, a treatise on first principles and the earliest extant Christian systematic theology; the treatise *On Prayer*; and *Contra Celsum*.

DE PRINCIPIIS

A relatively early work, *De Principiis* begins with the statement that apostolic doctrine, as found in the New Testament, is incomplete because the apostles intentionally left some matters untouched for the sake of their spiritual successors. Origen devotes the first book to a consideration of the spiritual hierarchy consisting of the Father, who acts on all beings; the Logos (Word or Reason), who acts upon rational beings; the Spirit, who acts upon those rational beings who are sanctified, and the angels. The second book deals with the material world. Man, created because the angels fell, is a preexistent fallen spirit in a material body. After Adam's transgression came redemption by the incarnate Logos; later there will be resurrection, the last judgment, and the life of all men restored to spiritual bodies (a succession of other worlds may follow as it has gone before). The third book discusses freedom, characteristic of creatures but not of the Creator. When a soul is in a body, it can struggle for victory, helped by angels and hindered by demons. Since it possesses free will, it is capable of choosing the good. After a brief summary, Origen turns in the fourth book to an explanation of how the Scriptures can be shown to have various levels of meaning. Like man himself, they have flesh (literal meaning), soul (moral meaning), and spirit (allegorical-spiritual meaning). The exegetical difficulties in Scripture were placed there by their ultimate author, God, in the way that similar obstacles to faith were placed in the cosmos so that man could use his mind.

Origen's work, written in Greek, is extant only in fragments (Book IV is almost entire). The Latin version by Tyrannius Rufinus was severely criticized by St. Jerome on the ground that it lacks unorthodox passages that were in the original, but it has come to be regarded more favorably by modern scholars. The title *De Principiis* has parallels in second-century philosophy, as do many of the subjects Origen discusses; his approach, however, seems to be essentially Christian.

ON PRAYER

In *On Prayer*, written later in his life, Origen discusses prayer in general (Chs. 3–17) and the Lord's Prayer in particular (Chs. 18–30). The principal problem is that presented by prayer to an omniscient God who has foreordained everything. Once again, Origen insists upon God's gift of free will; the primary purpose of prayer is not petition as such but sharing in the life of God. Origen classifies prayer as petition, adoration (only of the Father), supplication, and thanksgiving. In each case he emphasizes—as do contemporary middle Platonists—the spiritual attitude of the one who prays.

CONTRA CELSUM

The late apologetic treatise against Celsus, written in 248, reveals the extent to which Origen was able to argue on grounds shared by his philosophical opponents; there is actually a wide measure of agreement between him and Celsus. Both are opposed to anthropomorphism, to idolatry, and to any crudely literal theology. Origen, however, consistently defends Christianity as he sees it and does not hesitate to attack philosophies and philosophers.

ORIGEN AND PHILOSOPHY

The precise extent of Origen's debt to philosophy was discussed in antiquity; the Neoplatonist Porphyry claimed (according to Eusebius, *Historia Ecclesiastica* VI, 19, 8) that Origen drew upon Plato, Numenius, Cronius, Apollophanes, Longinus, Moderatus, Nicomachus, Chaeremon the Stoic, and Cornutus. Since Origen does refer to many of these writers, whose names occur in Porphyry's description of the Neoplatonic curriculum, Porphyry may be attempting to demonstrate both the extent and the correctness of Origen's Neoplatonism. The systems and works of various philosophers—except for the "atheists"—were studied thoroughly in Origen's school. Origen himself often made use of philosophical dictionaries for the definitions of various terms, but he also studied the writings of the philosophers themselves, not only those of Plato and the Platonists but also those of the Stoics and, occasionally, the Peripatetics.

It is sometimes claimed that there were two Origens, one a pupil of Ammonius Saccas and the other the Christian theologian. It is more likely that both aspects were combined within one person, the first Christian to be a genuinely philosophical theologian.

See also Celsus; Eusebius; Neoplatonism; Numenius of Apamea; Patristic Philosophy; Peripatetics; Platonism and the Platonic Tradition; Porphyry; Stoicism.

Bibliography

TEXTS AND TRANSLATIONS

De la Rue, C. *Opera Omnia.* 4 vols. Paris, 1733–1759, reprinted in J. P. Migne, *Patrologia Graeca* XI–XVII. Paris, 1857–1866.

Critical editions of individual works in *Die griechischen christlichen Schriftsteller der ersten drei Jahrhunderte.* Leipzig: Hinrichs: Hinrichs, 1897–1941; Berlin and Leipzig, 1953; Berlin: Akademie-Verlag: Akademie-Verlag, 1954–.

English translations in *Ante-Nicene Christian Library.* Edinburgh: T. and T. Clark, 1864–.

STUDIES

Benjamins, Hendrik S. *Eingeordnete Freiheit: Freiheit und Vorsehung bei Origene.* Leiden: E.J. Brill, 1994.

Berner, Ulrich. *Origenes.* Darmstatt: Wissenschaftliche Buchgesellschaft, 1981.

Bienert, W. and U. Kühneweg, ed. *Origeniana septima: Origenes in den Auseinandersetzungen des 4. Jahrhunderts.* Leuven: Leuven University Press, 1999.

Brox, Norbert. "Spiritualität und Orthodoxie: Zum Konflikt des Origenes mit der Geschichte des Dogmas," in Ernst Dassmann and K. Suso Frank, eds, *Pietas: Festschrift für Bernhard Kötting = Jahrbuch für Antike und Christentum.* Ergänzungsband 8 (1980): 140–54.

Clark, Elizabeth A. *The Origenist Controversy: The Cultural Construction of an Early Christian Debate.* Princeton, NJ: Princeton University Press, 1992.

Crouzel, Henri. *Origène.* Paris: Lethielleux, 1985.

Crouzel, Henri. *Origène et la philosophie.* Paris, 1962.

Crouzel, Henri. *Origène et Plotin: Comparaisons doctrinales.* Paris: Aubier, 1991.

Dively, Elizabeth. *The Soul and Spirit of Scripture within Origen's Exegesis.* Leiden, 2005. Boston: Brill, 2005.

Edards, Mark. *Origen Against Plato.* Aldershot: Ashgate, 2002.

Hällström, Gunnar af. *Charismatic Succession: A Study on Origen's Concept of Prophecy.* Helsinki, 1985.

Hällström, Gunnar af. *Fides Simpliciorum according to Origen of Alexandria.* Helsinki: Societas Scientiarum Fennica, 1984.

Harl, Marguerite. *Origène et la fonction révélatrice du Verbe incarné.* Paris, 1958.

Jonas, Hans. *Gnosis und spätantiker Geist, vol. 2, Von der Mythologie zur mystischen Philosophie.* Edited by Kurt Rudolph, reprint, Göttingen: Vandenhoeck & Ruprecht, 1993.

Kannengiesser, Charles, ed. *Origen: His World and His Legacy.* Notre Dame, IN: University of Notre Dame Press, 1988.

Lange, Nicholas R. M. de. *Origen and the Jews: Studies in Jewish–Christian Relations in Third-Century Palestine.* Cambridge, 1976.

Lubac, Henri de. *Histoire et Esprit: L'intelligence d'Écriture d'après Origène.* Paris: Aubier, 1950.

Neuschäfer, Bernhardt. *Origenes als Philologe. Schweizerische Beiträge zur Altertumswissemchaft* 18. 2 vols. Basel, 1987.

Peri, Vittorio. *Omelie origeniane sui Salmi.* Vatican City: Biblioteca apostolica vaticana, 1980.

Stroumsa, Guy G. *Hidden Wisdom: Esoteric Traditions and the Roots of Christian Mysticism.* Leiden: E.J. Brill, 1996.

Strutwolf, Holger. *Gnosis als System: Zur Rezeption der valentinianischen Gnosis bei Origenes = Forschungen zur Kirchen- and Dogmengeschichte* 56. Göttingen: Vandenhoeck & Ruprecht, 1993.

Torjesen, Karen Jo. *Hermeneutical Procedure and Theological Method in Origen's Exegesis.* Berlin: De Gruyter, 1986.

Trigg, Joseph W. "The Angel of Great Counsel: Christ and the Angelic Hierarchy in Origen's Theology." *Journal of Theological Studies* n.s. 42 (1991): 35–51.

Trigg, Joseph W. *Origen: The Bible and Philosophy in the Third-Century Church.* Atlanta: J. Knox, 1983.

Robert M. Grant (1967)
Bibliography updated by Scott Carson (2005)

OROBIO DE CASTRO, ISAAC

(c. 1617–1687)

Isaac Orobio de Castro was born Baltazar Orobio de Castro in Braganza, Portugal. He grew up among crypto-Jews who were trying to preserve some of their heritage in the face of the Spanish Inquisition. He became an important Spanish doctor and a professor of metaphysics. He was arrested by the Inquisition for secretly practicing Judaism. After being tortured and tried, he was released. He then fled Spain for France, where he became professor of pharmacy at Toulouse (c. 1660). Finally, deciding to abandon living as a Christian, he moved to Holland, where in 1662 he changed his name from Baltazar to Isaac and became one of the leading intellectual figures and a medical practitioner in the Spanish-Portuguese Jewish community in Amsterdam. When he arrived in the Jewish community, he learned that there had been trouble about a former classmate of his from Spain, Juan de Prado. Prado was apparently involved with the young Spinoza and they were both charged with various heresies. Orobio wrote an answer, now lost, to one of Prado's works and against a work by Prado's son. Prado and his son held that the law of nature takes precedence over the law of Moses, and Orobio criticized their deism.

Orobio also wrote a metaphysical defense of his religion, based on mainly Spanish-Catholic Scholastic works and an answer to Alonso de Cepeda. His most famous works are an extremely rationalistic and Scholastic answer to Spinoza in geometrical form, *Certamen Philosophicum Propugnatum Veritatis Divinae ac Naturalis* (1684), which was published with Fénelon's *Demonstration de l'existence de Dieu*. The *Certamen* is the only critique of Spinoza by any member of the Jewish community that has survived and was considered one of the most important criticisms of Spinoza at the time.

Orbio engaged in a dialogue with one of the liberal Protestant leaders in the Netherlands, Philip van Limborch. They debated the truth of the Christian religion in 1687. This was a public debate where John Locke was present. The debate was published by Limborch under the title *Amica Collatio cum Erudito Judaeo* (1687) just after his opponent died, and Locke wrote a long review of it. Limborch met Orobio in Amsterdam in the 1680s and was much affected by his report of the Inquisition, which, through Limborch's *Historia Inquisitionis*, became for the next two centuries the best-known study of Inquisitorial investigation and torture methods. Orobio's most important anti-Christian work was *Prevenciones divinas contra la vana idolatria de las gentes.* He did not publish it because, as he explains in the note written in his own hand, he did not want to cause scandal, but he sent it to the Jesuits in Brussels, who liked it very much. It was published in French under the title *Israel vengé* (1770) by Baron d'Holbach. This work was used as important ammunition by French atheists against Christianity.

Through his works, Orobio de Castro showed an extremely acute understanding of metaphysics, using his knowledge of Spanish Scholasticism to buttress his religion against freethinkers and liberal and orthodox Christians. Some of his arguments against the doctrine of the Trinity are close to Spinoza's arguments against the plurality of substance.

See also Jewish Philosophy; Metaphysics.

Bibliography

WORKS BY OROBIO DE CASTRO
Additional works include *La observancia de la divina ley de Mosseh* (Coimbra, 1925), which has a preface by Moses

Bensabat Amzalak. There is also an English translation of the Limborch-Orobio debate (Farnborough, Gregg, 1969).

WORKS ABOUT OROBIO DE CASTRO

Angelis, Enrico de. "Crisi di conscienza fra I seicentisti per il metodo geometrico." *Annali della Scuola Normale Superiore di Pisa, lettere, storia e filosofia*, 2nd ser., 31 (1962): 253–271.

Carvalho, Joaquim de. *Orobio de Castro e o espinosismo.* In *Memorias da Academia das Ciências de Lisboa, Classe de letras.* Vol. 2. Lisbon: Academia das Ciências de Lisbon, 1937. A study on Orobio de Castro that includes the 1721 Spanish translation of Certamen Philosophicum.

Cohen, Monique-Lise, Ruth Attias, and Elie Szapiro. *Isaac Orobio de Castro et son temps: 1617–1687: juif portugais d'Espagne, de Toulouse et d'Europe.* Toulouse, France: Bibliotheque Municipale de Toulouse, 1992.

Kaplan, Yosef. *From Christianity to Judaism: The Story of Isaac Orobio de Castro.* Translated by Raphael Loewe. Oxford: Oxford University Press, 1989.

Révah, I. S. *Spinoza et Juan de Prado.* Paris: Mouton, 1959.

Richard Popkin (1967, 2005)

ORPHISM

"Orphism" is a modern term attached to two connected phenomena of Greek religion. The first is a body of traditional poetry, possibly from as early as the seventh century BCE, ascribed to a mythical singer called Orpheus and containing an account of the creation of the world and of the afterlife of the soul, its judgment and punishment for sins on Earth, and its final reincarnation in another living body. The second is the way of life adopted by those who accepted the truth of these writings, such truths being regarded with as much respect as the revelations in the traditional Greek "mysteries" at Eleusis and elsewhere.

CONTENTS OF ORPHIC WRITINGS

A number of fragments of the Orphic poems have survived, some of which belong to the poems as they were known in Athens in the fifth and fourth centuries BCE. However, these writings, in the manner of popular poetry, were constantly growing by accretion, and they seem to have become a general compendium of poetical accounts of theogony, cosmogony, and the soul's nature and fate. The contents of the poems as they existed in the fifth and fourth centuries BCE must be derived mainly from evidence in contemporary literature and, to a certain extent, in painting and sculpture.

ORPHEUS. It was in Greek art and literature of the sixth century BCE that Orpheus first appeared as a famous singer. The tradition that Orpheus sang while Musaeus wrote down his master's songs may reflect the moment of transition from oral to written literature—which probably occurred in the second half of the seventh century BCE—and this may be the time when these songs were composed.

To the poets of classical Greece, Orpheus was the singer possessed of supernatural powers. As such, he was enrolled among the Argonauts. According to an Alexandrian poet, Orpheus soothed his quarreling companions by singing to them of the creation of the world and of the dynasties of the gods. Euripides wrote of Orpheus's special connection with the underworld. A Naples bas-relief, executed at the end of the fifth century BCE, depicts his attempt to bring back his wife Eurydice from the dead. A little earlier in the same century, Polygnotus executed his famous picture of the underworld in which Orpheus was shown lyre in hand, amidst a group of legendary musicians.

It seems likely that this figure of Orpheus reflected the existing body of Orphic poetry, that his traits in fact represent its contents—a theogony which is an account of creation and a description of the underworld and of the soul's fate there.

THEOGONY. Plato's quotation of passages from an Orphic poem (in the *Cratylus* and *Philebus*) and Isocrates' description (in the *Busiris*) of what Orpheus wrote about suggest an Orphic theogony very like the one which is preserved as the work of Hesiod, the eighth-century BCE oral poet. From much later writers (Athenagoras, of the second century CE, and Damascius, of the fifth century CE) we learn of Orphic theogonies that contain non-Hesiodic elements—the cosmic egg and the creator Phanes. Since Phanes seems to be identifiable with the figure Eros that appears, together with the cosmic egg, in a cosmogony related in Aristophanes' fifth-century play *Birds*, both elements may accordingly be regarded as ancient. Three Orphic fragments joined by Otto Kern, which present a picture of the universe, may also be early since this picture of the universe, may also be early, since this picture bears a marked resemblance to Plato's image of the universe in the myth of Er at the end of the *Republic*. According to these fragments, the heaven, the earth, the sea, and the "signs with which the heaven is ringed" are abound round with a bond of Aether.

AFTERLIFE OF THE SOUL. Whereas Hesiod's *Theogony* contained a description of the underworld, inserted nominally in connection with the story of Zeus's overthrow of the Titans, this possibly traditional element was developed in the Orphic poems into a detailed account of the soul's fate after death, its judgment and its reincarnation. Plato, throughout his writings, plainly drew on an account of the soul's late which he had read about in Orphic literature. In the *Gorgias* (493B) he refers to "one of the wise, who holds that the body is a tomb" and he also reports the story that the soul of an uninitiated man is like a sieve: In Hades the uninitiated is most miserable, being doomed to an eternity of filling sieves with water, by means of other sieves. Quoting the same story in the *Republic* (363D), he speaks of Musaeus and Eumolpus enlarging on the rewards of the righteous in the other world, and he also speaks of other who "when they have sung the praises of justice in that strain … proceed to plunge the sinners and unrighteous men into a pool of mud in the world below, and set them to fetch water in a sieve." In the *Phaedo* (69E) he says that "the man who reaches Hades without experiencing initiation will lie in mud, whereas the initiated when he gets there will dwell with the gods." In the *Cratylus* (420B) Plato attributes specifically to the Orphic poets the theory that the body is the tomb of the soul. Two surviving Orphic fragments (Kern Fr. 222) speak of the differing fates of the just and the unjust in the afterlife, and several (Kern Fr. 223ff.) deal with the rebirth of the soul in various forms. Plato must certainly have been referring to Orphic poems when he said in the *Meno* (81A) that among others "Pindar and many another poet who is divinely inspired … say that the soul of man is immortal, and at one time comes to an end, which is called dying, and at another is reborn, but never perishes. Consequently a man ought to live his life in the utmost holiness."

THE ORPHIC LIFE

For those who believed the eschatological dogma contained in the Orphic poems, there followed certain consequences for the conduct of life.

PROHIBITIONS. *Adikia,* injustice against any living creature, had to be strictly avoided. In Euripides' *Hippolytus* the diet "of food without soul," which was required of followers of Orpheus, is mentioned. Herodotus referred to the Orphic practice, which was also Pythagorean, of avoiding the use of wool (robbed from sheep) in burial. Men who observed these scruples might be described as living as "Orphic life," in the words of Plato in the *Laws.*

INITIATIONS. Proclus spoke of those who were initiated under Orpheus's patronage with Dionysus or Kore (in the case of the latter, at Eleusis). In Euripides' play *Rhesus,* Orpheus's amanuensis Musaeus is an Athenian, and

Orpheus himself is closely connected with the Eleusinian initiations. It is certainly to these initiations that Aristophanes referred in the play *Frogs* when a character says, "Orpheus taught *teletai* [initiations] and abstinence from killing."

Evidently, the Orphic initiation had an essentially written character. Euripides referred to the person who observes Orphic scruples as "honoring the smoke of many writings." Plato mentioned "a mass of books" of Orpheus and Musaeus. Later writers contrasted this written initiation with the visual revelation at Eleusis, as when Pausanias wrote, "Whoever has seen an initiation at Eleusis or read the writings called Orphic knows what I mean." The Orphic literature seems to have borne the same relation to visual and oral instruction as a correspondence course bears to "live" teaching, and it appears to have been freely available.

Initiation into the mysteries was supposed to give a revelation of truth that would enable men to reach the next world in a state of guiltlessness. Plato reported that mendicant seers, who "frequented the doors of the rich," capitalized on this belief by offering cities and individuals the means of purification from sins committed. Among these are no doubt to be reckoned the *Orpheotelestai,* of whom Theophrastus spoke.

SIGNIFICANCE OF ORPHISM

Was Orphism, then, either a philosophy or a religion? It certainly was not a philosophical system, since in had no developed doctrine—merely a mythical account, derived from the popular oral poetry of the past, of the nature of the universe and of the afterlife of the soul. The philosophical importance of the Orphic literature lies in its influence, first of Pythagoras and Empedocles and then on Plato.

Pythagoras seems to have taken over the Orphic stories so completely that they could be referred to by Aristotle as Pythagorean stories, and earlier Ion of Chios could say that Pythagoras had fathered his writings on Orpheus. The immortality and transmigration of the soul is the one doctrine which can certainly be attributed to the earliest Pythagorean society; Plato spoke of a Pythagorean way of life, based, as we know from other sources, on ritual prescriptions designed to ensure the purity and blamelessness of the soul.

Empedocles, who lived in Sicily in the fifth century BCE, exhibited a similar belief in the soul's immortality and transmigration.

In the *Symposium* Plato does not appear to believe in the soul's immortality, but in the *Meno* he accepts the preexistence and survival of the soul on the authority of "divinely inspired poets," among whom Orpheus in certainly to be reckoned. This doctrine became a cornerstone of Plato's entire metaphysical system.

Orphism was not in itself a religion, although it was closely related to the initiations at Eleusis and elsewhere, which were perhaps the most striking religious manifestations of classical Greece. The Orphic element was, however, merely a traditional poetical account that provided the eschatological dogma that was the basis for certain observances to the described as a way of life. The religious depth of this way of should not be exaggerated. There were no organized rituals, religious communities, or priesthood. In the sense in which we ordinarily use the word *religion* in the study of the ancient world, Orphism was not a religion.

See also Aristotle; Empedocles; Plato; Proclus; Pythagoras and Pythagoreanism.

Bibliography

Guthrie, W. K. C. *Orpheus and Greek Religion.* London: Methuen, 1935.

Kern, Otto. *Orphicorum Fragmenta.* Berlin, 1922; reprinted 1963.

Linforth, Ivan M. *Arts of Orpheus.* Berkeley: University of California Press, 1941.

Nilsson, M. P. "Early Orphism and Kindred Religious Movements." *Harvard Theological Review* 28 (1935): 181–230.

John Morrison (1967)

ORPHISM [ADDENDUM]

A number of archaeological discoveries in the second half of the twentieth century have considerably supplemented our knowledge about Orphism.

OLBIA BONE PLATES

The bone plates, found in Olbia on the Black Sea and dated to the fifth century BCE, probably functioned as tokens for those who received initiation. The inscription on one of them suggests that initiates could identify themselves as Orphics, even if the initiation did not necessarily imply any radical reform in their lifestyles.

GOLD LEAVES

The gold leaves are tiny inscribed gold strips buried with the dead containing instructions on what to do and what to say in the underworld. Gold leaves were found in Southern Italy, in Thessaly, and on Crete. Though there was a period of skepticism, newly found specimens make it likely that gold leaves were used by Orphic initiates.

THE DERVENI PAPYRUS

The Derveni papyrus was found in 1962 in a small sepulchral site near Thessalonica. The text was probably composed in the first half of the fourth century BCE, and its author might have been one of the Orphic initiates (*orpheotelestai*) that Plato and Theophrastus talked about. The first part of the text develops a rationalizing explanation of ritual acts, and quotes Heraclitus' fragments B3 and B94 in such a way that suggests that these fragments originally formed one sentence. In the second part the author interprets verses from a poem he attributes to Orpheus, some of which we know from other Orphic theogonies. The poem focuses on an episode when Zeus swallows all existing beings, so that for a moment everything is contained in him. Zeus then brings them back to light, and the story continues with the birth of new gods. This allows the poet to say, "Zeus is the head, Zeus is middle, and from Zeus all things get their being" (frag. 14.2, Bernabé). This episode expresses in the language of myth some central concerns of the pre-Socratic philosophers, such as the one/many problem and the question of the ultimate source of everything. The commentator interprets the poem allegorically, claiming that it propounds a cosmological theory. He argues that the different divine names in the poem designate the different cosmic functions of a unique god who created the present world order from primordial chaos. This unique god is called Mind (Nous) and is identified with the element air. The commentator's interpretation is heavily influenced by Anaxagoras and, to a lesser extent, Archelaus and Diogenes of Apollonia.

See also Anaxagoras of Clazomenae; Diogenes of Apollonia.

Bibliography

Bernabé, Alberto. "Orphisme et présocratiques: Bilan et perspectives d'un dialogue complexe." In *Qu'est-ce que la philosophie présocratique*, edited by André Laks and Claire Louguet. Villeneuve-d'Ascq, France: Presses universitaires du Septentrion, 2002.

Betegh, Gábor. *The Derveni Papyrus: Cosmology, Theology, and Interpretation.* Cambridge, U.K.: Cambridge University Press, 2004.

Gábor Betegh (2005)

ORTEGA Y GASSET, JOSÉ
(1883–1955)

José Ortega y Gasset, the Spanish essayist and philosopher, was born in Madrid of a patrician family. He was educated at a Jesuit college near Málaga and at the University of Madrid, where he received a doctorate in philosophy in 1904. Ortega spent the next five years at German universities in Berlin and Leipzig and at the University of Marburg, where he became a disciple of the neo-Kantian philosopher Hermann Cohen. Appointed professor of metaphysics at the University of Madrid in 1910, he taught there until the outbreak of the Spanish Civil War in 1936. During those years he was also active as a journalist and as a politician. In 1923 he founded the *Revista de occidente,* a review and series of books that was instrumental in bringing Spain into touch with Western, and particularly German, thought. Ortega's work as editor and publisher, as a contribution toward "leveling the Pyrenees" that isolated Spain from contemporary culture, ranks high among his achievements.

Ortega led the republican intellectual opposition under the dictatorship of Primo de Rivera (1923–1930), and he played a part in the overthrow of King Alfonso XIII in 1931. Elected deputy for the province of León in the constituent assembly of the second Spanish republic, he was the leader of a parliamentary group of intellectuals known as *La agrupación al servicio de la república* (In the service of the republic) and was named civil governor of Madrid. This political commitment obliged him to leave Spain at the outbreak of the Civil War, and he spent years of exile in Argentina and western Europe. He settled in Portugal in 1945 and began to make visits to Spain. In 1948 he returned to Madrid, where, with Julián Marías, he founded the Institute of Humanities, at which he lectured. By the time of his death, Ortega was the acknowledged head of the most productive school of thinkers Spain had known for three centuries, and he had placed philosophy in Spain beyond the reach, not of opposition and criticism, but of the centuries-old reproach that it was un-Spanish or antinational and therefore either a foreign affectation or a subversive danger.

WRITINGS AND STYLE

Ortega was a prolific writer. His numerous volumes consist mostly of essays and newspaper or magazine articles of general cultural interest. He wrote fewer strictly philosophical works; his vast influence on Spanish philosophy was exercised chiefly through his teaching.

All of Ortega's works are written in magnificent prose. He wrote in a clear, masculine style, and his mastery of Castilian has seldom been surpassed. On the other hand, he had a tendency to be wordy and to be content with literary brilliance and striking metaphor when argument and explanation were crucial.

Ortega's literary gifts had other, more important consequences. He used them to create a philosophical style and technical vocabulary in a tongue that until then had lacked models for philosophical writing and words for many modern concepts. But his literary virtuosity disarmed criticism in much of the Spanish-speaking world, so that his followers have often confounded philosophy with fine writing and emotional declamation.

RATIO-VITALISM

Ortega called his philosophy the "metaphysics of vital reason," or "ratio-vitalism." By metaphysics he meant the quest for an ultimate or radical reality in which all else was rooted and from which every particular being derived its measure of reality. He found this ultimate reality in Life, a word that he first used in a biological sense, like the vitalists, but which soon came to mean "my life" and "your life"—the career and destiny of an individual in a given society and at a certain point in history. In his first philosophical book, *Meditaciones del Quijote* (1914), Ortega sought to go beyond the opposition of idealism (which, he claimed, asserted the ontological priority of the self) and realism (which asserted the priority of the things the self knows). He asserted that in truth self and things were constitutive of each other, each needing the other in order to exist. The sole reality was the self-with-things: *Yo soy yo y mi circunstancia* (I am I and my circumstances). The things around me, he said in the *Meditaciones,* "are the other half of my personality." The experience-matrix comprising self and things is not simply one of coexistence, because the self acts on things and realizes itself in so doing. This activity is life, the dynamic interaction of mutually dependent self and things in the course of which the self carries out a mission of self-fulfillment.

PERSPECTIVISM

Ortega called his theory of knowledge "perspectivism." The world can be known only from a specific point of view. There is no possibility of transcending one's relative perspectives through absolute or impartial knowledge. "The definitive being of the world is neither mind nor matter nor any determinate thing but a perspective." Each perspective is unique, irreplaceable, and necessary, and all are equally true: "The only false perspective is the one that claims to be the one and only perspective." Ortega joined perspectivism to his notion of life as comprising the matrix self-with-things in the declaration, "Each life is a point of view on to the universe."

REASON AND LIFE

Although the *Meditaciones* seemed to place Ortega in the vitalist tradition, he dissociated himself from its antirationalism. Rather, just as he reconciled idealism and realism, he proposed to reconcile rationalism and vitalism. He agreed with the vitalists to "dethrone Reason," to dismiss abstract reason and bring it back to its rightful role as "only a form and function of Life." Yet Ortega stressed so strongly the rationality of the élan vital at the human level and underscored so firmly man's dependence on reason as an instrument for coping with life that he appeared to enthrone reason again beneath a vitalist disguise. He used the terms "Life" and "Vitality" to describe man's restless search for knowledge, understanding, and spiritual satisfaction, which others would have called "intelligence" or "practical reason." In fact, Ortega seemed to identify vitality and reason: Thus, in *En torno a Galileo* (1933), he wrote, "Living means being forced to reason out our inexorable circumstances." Therefore, ratiovitalism was more rationalism than vitalism, and Ortega's thought was far removed from the irrationalist, romantic vitalism that flourished after World War I.

EXISTENTIALISM

Later, when Ortega appeared to have joined the existentialists (or, as he would have said, was joined by them), his insistence on the role of reason in the existential predicament gave his theories a distinctive color and allowed him to pour scorn on the sentimentalism of French existentialism. Ortega's dissociation from vitalism became complete when he took account of "the historical horizons of human life"—that is, of the social and cultural conditions of vitality in humankind. He gradually came to prefer the term "historical reason" to "vital reason." Life for Ortega now meant not biological vitality but "one man's life," and the vocation of the self was now conceived as what it must

do with things—a mission of self-realization. This is the language of existentialism, and Ortega spoke it with a rare eloquence.

> Man does not have a nature, but a history.... Man is no thing, but a drama.... His life is something that has to be chosen, made up as he goes along, and a man consists in that choice and invention. Each man is the novelist of himself, and though he may choose between being an original writer and a plagiarist, he cannot escape choosing.... He is condemned to be free.... Freedom is not an activity exercised by an entity that already possessed a fixed being before and apart from that activity. Being free means ... being able to be something else than what one is and not being able to settle down once and for all in any determined nature.... Unlike all the other things in the universe which have a pre-fixed being given to them, man is the only and almost inconceivable reality that exists without having an irrevocably pre-fixed being.... It is not only in economics but also in metaphysics that man must earn his living [*ganarse la vida*, win his life]. (*Historia como sistema*)

Each man has one best choice, and this is his imperative vocation or mission. "'Mission' means the awareness that each man has of his most authentic self which he is called upon to realize. The idea of mission is a constitutive ingredient of the human condition.... The being of man is at one and the same time natural and extranatural, a sort of ontological centaur" (*Obras completas*, Vol. V, pp. 209, 334). Ortega's moral theory thus derives directly from his anthropology; and indeed it is difficult, as with other existentialists, to separate his metaphysics from his anthropology and ethics. The moral life is the authentic one, the one that stays faithful to a life project or vocation; the immoral life is to abandon oneself to transient, outside influences, to drift instead of realizing a personal destiny. The choice of one personality out of the various possible personalities engages the whole of a man's reasoning powers and requires perpetual lucidity and concentration. This helps to explain Ortega's emphasis on the rationality of the élan vital at the human level. It is by intelligent reckoning with his circumstances that a man gains his being and becomes himself. Reasoned choice is constitutive of human personality.

SOCIAL THEORY

Life is always a problem, an insecurity, a "shipwreck," not only for the individual but for societies too. The desperate measures society takes to struggle against perpetual foundering constitute human culture. It was Ortega's social theory, set forth in *La rebelión de las masas* in 1930 (*The Revolt of the Masses,* New York, 1931), that first brought him international recognition. Ortega started from the belief that culture is radically insecure and that a constant effort is required to prevent it from lapsing into barbarism and torpor. That effort is beyond most men, who can merely contribute to it by accepting the leadership of a liberal aristocracy, which does most of humanity's works. The fact that men have no essence or fixed nature but each must choose himself implies their inequality. "Because the being of man is not given to him but is a pure imaginary possibility, the human species is of an instability and variability that make it incomparable with animal species. Men are enormously unequal, in spite of what the egalitarians of the last two centuries affirmed and of what old-fashioned folk of this century go on affirming" (*Meditación de la técnica,* p. 42).

Ortega distinguished interindividual from social relations. In the former, which include love and friendship, individuals behave as rational and responsible persons, whereas in social relationships, which include customs, laws, and the state, we encounter the irrational and impersonal, the imposed and anonymous. The resulting contrast of man and people (*El hombre y la gente*), of the individual and the collectivity, betrayed Ortega's aristocratic distrust of democracy and contemporary mass society. There is no collective soul, he said, because "society, the collectivity, is the great soulless one, because it is humanity naturalized, mechanized and as if mineralized." Everything that is social or collective is subhuman, intermediate between genuine humanity and nature; it is a "quasi-nature." Nevertheless, social relationships have their uses; they make other people's behavior predictable, they carry on inherited traditions, and by automatizing part of our lives, they set us free for creation in the important interindividual sphere. These gains of socialization need constant defense, for men's antisocial drives are never vanquished. Society is neither spontaneous nor self-perpetuating. It has to be invented and reinvented by a minority that, however, must be able to procure the cooperation of the masses. The elite is essential to any society; by proposing a project for collective living, it founds the community and then governs and directs it.

The masses are incapable of framing a project, for they live without plan or effort. When they revolt and claim to govern themselves, society is threatened with dissolution. Ortega thought this was happening in twentieth-century democracies, whether totalitarian, communist, or parliamentary. Nationalism was exhausted as a collective project, and the next plan had to be supranational. Ortega favored the "Europeanization of Spain" in a supranational entity governed by an irreligious intellectual elite. Catholicism was to be extirpated, but gradually and cautiously, with a first stage of "liberal religion" leading toward the secular state.

The sensitive intellectual would have as little as possible to do with governing, for it was inevitably degrading. "There is no political health when the government functions without the active cooperation of majorities. Perhaps this is why politics seems to me a second-class occupation" (*Invertebrate Spain,* p. 201).

ARISTOCRATIC LOGIC

The notion of an aristocracy of talents is the key to Ortega's logic. In *Ideas y creencias* ("Ideas and Beliefs," in *Obras completas,* Vol. V, pp. 377–489), he claimed that ideas are the personal creation of the thinking minority, while the mass lazily accepts plain commonsense beliefs that in reality are vulgar ruling opinions imposed by "a diffuse authoritarianism." The archetype of mob belief is empiricism, or as Ortega called it, "sensualism." Sensualism is a reliance on the evidence of the senses, on self-evident truisms, on experiments in science or on documents in history. Philosophy since Parmenides has been a reaction against the vulgar prejudice in favor of the senses. "Against the *doxa* of belief in the senses, philosophy is, constitutionally and not accidentally, *paradox*" (*La idea de principio,* p. 285).

These views were developed with remarkable vigor in his unfinished, posthumously published magnum opus, *La idea de principio en Leibniz y la evolución de la teoría deductiva* (Buenos Aires, 1958; *The Idea of Principle in Leibniz and the Evolution of Deductive Theory,* New York, 1971). He assailed every form of the belief that principles or axioms can be founded on sensible intuition, taking Aristotle as the first representative of this belief and following its transmission through the Stoics and Scholastics. Such a belief, Ortega declared, is "idiot," "plebeian"; it results from a mental derangement akin to catalepsy, in that it entails sitting bemused before brute reality instead of thinking creatively. The only principles available to us, he held, are posed arbitrarily by the mind. They are assumptions that cannot be proved to the satisfaction of the senses, but "prove themselves" by allowing the deduction of a coherent corpus of propositions. This is the advance of post-Cartesian thought over traditional realism. "Modern philosophy no longer begins with

Being but with Thought" (*La idea de principio*, p. 263). The only proof modern philosophy knows is theoretical use: If axioms or methods give good results, there is no more to be said.

> Principles can only come from the understanding itself as it is before and apart from any acquaintance with sensible things. From these purely intellectual principles may be deduced consequences that form a whole world of intellectual determinations, that is, of ideal objects. … The activity of knowing used to seem to consist in an effort to reflect, mirror, or copy in our mind the world of real things, but it turns out to be just the opposite, namely, the invention, construction, or fabrication of an unreal world. (*La idea de principio*, p. 394)

Since he considered this idealist logic a characteristically aristocratic attitude, Ortega thought it significant that Plato and René Descartes, the two men who did most to construct it, were of noble blood. In contrast, the empiricism of Aristotle was popular, vulgar, "demagogic." "It is the criteriology of Sancho Panza. Faith in the senses is a traditional dogma, a public institution established by the irresponsible and anonymous opinion of the People, the collectivity" (*La idea de principio*, p. 286). Even the principle of contradiction, "that dogma of ontological sensualism," was a mere commonplace of the collective mind, unsupported by reasons and anything but self-evident. Aristotle had failed to prove the principle of contradiction, that *A* could not both be and not be *X,* and Immanuel Kant's transcendental deduction of it had no force. Ortega was not seeking to dispense with that principle but to argue that it could not be proven. Logic is a calculus tested by coherence, not an abstraction from sensible experience. Principles are assumptions that are useful for particular purposes.

Philosophy, science, and mathematics are "pure exact fantasy" based on principles that are arbitrary conventions. They are phantasmagoria, not far removed from poetry. They are the creation of an aristocracy of intellect that reveals the characteristics of all aristocracies: playfulness, lack of seriousness, and love of sport and games. Ortega meant quite literally that logic and science were games played according to strict but perfectly gratuitous rules by a minority that seeks to escape the tedium, vulgarity, and deadly seriousness of the world of beliefs. We never really believe in science or philosophy; they remain "mere ideas" to play with, and they are always somewhat spectral and unserious compared with the visceral faith we put into beliefs. Theory, like any fantasy, is by definition always revocable. Therefore, we ought to play at philosophy, jovially and without pathos, with the mock seriousness required to "obey the rules of the game."

See also Aristotle; Descartes, René; Existentialism; Idealism; Kant, Immanuel; Marías, Julián; Parmenides of Elea; Plato; Rationalism; Realism; Vitalism.

Bibliography

WORKS BY ORTEGA

Meditaciones del Quijote. Madrid: Ediciones de la Residencia de Estudiantes, 1914. Translated by E. Rugg and D. Marin as *Meditations on Quixote.* New York: Norton, 1961.

España invertebrada. Madrid: Calpe, 1922. Translated by M. Adams as *Invertebrate Spain.* New York: Norton, 1937.

El tema de nuestro tiempo. Madrid: Calpe, 1923. Translated by James Cleugh as *The Modern Theme.* London: C.W. Daniel, 1931.

La deshumanización del arte. Madrid: Revista de Occidente, 1925. Translated by W. Trask as *The Dehumanizatian of Art.* New York, 1956.

En torno a Galileo. Madrid, 1933. Translated by M. Adams as *Man and Crisis.* New York: Norton, 1958.

Meditación de la técnica. Madrid, 1933.

Estudios sobre el amor. Madrid, 1939. Translated by T. Talbot as *On Love.* New York: Meridian, 1957.

Del imperio romano. Madrid, 1940–1941. Translated by H. Weyl as *Concord and Liberty.* New York: Norton, 1946.

Historia como sistema. Madrid: Revista de Occidente, 1941. Translated by H. Weyl, E. Clark, and W. Atkinson as *Toward a Philosophy of History.* New York: Norton, 1941. 2nd ed., *History as a System.* New York: Norton, 1961.

El hombre y la gente. Madrid: Revista de Occidente, 1957. Translated by W. Trask as *Man and People.* New York: Norton, 1959.

Que es filosofia? Madrid: Revista de Occidente, 1957. Translated by M. Adams as *What Is Philosophy?* New York; Norton, 1960.

Obras ineditas. 7 vols. Madrid and Buenos Aires, 1957–1961. Contains the later and posthumously published works.

The Idea of Principle in Leibniz and the Evolution of Deductive Theory. Translated by Mildred Adams. New York: Norton, 1971.

Obras completas. Vols. 1–12. Madrid: Alianza Editorial, 1983.

The Revolt of the Masses. Translated by Anthony Kerrigan; edited by Kenneth Moore. Notre Dame, IN: University of Notre Dame Press, 1985.

WORKS ON ORTEGA

Borel, J. *Ratson et vie chez Ortega y Casset.* Neuchâtel, 1959.

Cascalès, Charles. *L'humanisme d'Ortega y Gasset.* Paris, 1956.

Ceplecha, C. *The Historical Thought of José Ortega y Gasset.* New Haven, CT, 1957.

Dobson, Andrew. *An Introduction to the Politics and Philosophy of José Ortega y Gasset.* New York, 1989.

Donoso, A., and H. C. Raley. *José Ortega y Gasset: A Bibliography of Secondary Sources.* Bowling Green, OH: Philosophy Documentation Center, 1986.

Guy, Alain. *Ortega y Gasset, critique d'Aristote.* Paris, 1963.

Holmes, Oliver W. *Human Reality and the Social World: Ortega's Philosophy of History.* Amherst: University of Massachusetts Press, 1975.

Marías, Julián. *La escuela de Madrid.* Buenos Aires, 1959.

Marías, Julián. *Historia de la filosofía.* Madrid, 1941.

Marías, Julián. *Ortega, circunstancia y vocación.* Madrid, 1960.

Marías, Julián. *Ortega y tres antípodas.* Buenos Aires, 1950.

Ouimette, Victor. *José Ortega y Gasset.* Boston: Twayne, 1982.

Ramírez, Santiago. *La filosofía de Ortega y Gasset.* Barcelona, 1958.

Ramírez, Santiago. *Un orteguismo católico.* Salamanca, 1958.

Ramírez, Santiago. *La zona de seguridad.* Madrid, 1959.

Rodríguez Huéscar, Antonio. *José Ortega y Gasset's Metaphysical Innovation.* Trans. and ed. by Jorge García-Gómez. Albany: SUNY Press, 1995.

Silver, Philip W. *Ortega as Phenomenologist: The Genesis of "Mediations on Quixote."* New York: Columbia University Press, 1978.

Weintraub, Karl J. "Ortega y Gassét." In *Visions of Culture.* Chicago: Chicago University Press, 1966.

Neil McInnes (1967)
Bibliography updated by Philip Reed (2005)

OSTWALD, WILHELM

(1853–1932)

Wilhelm Ostwald was a German chemist, philosopher, and historian of science whose main scientific achievement was his pioneer work in physical chemistry, particularly in electrochemistry. With J. H. van't Hoff he founded the *Zeitschrift für physikalische Chemie* in 1887. He was awarded the Nobel Prize in chemistry in 1909.

ENERGETISM

Ostwald's philosophical outlook, known as energetism or energetic monism, was strongly influenced by his scientific background and by the state of physical science at the end of the nineteenth century. In particular, the first and second laws of thermodynamics—the law of conservation of energy and the law of entropy—decisively influenced his thought. Ostwald claimed that energy is the substrate of all phenomena and that all observable changes can be interpreted as transformations of one kind of energy into another. This claim was based on both epistemological and physical considerations. Ostwald pointed out that we never perceive anything but energy, or more accurately, differences in energy. One never perceives a material substance itself, but only its energetic interaction with his own organism.

In an argument similar to a classical argument of René Descartes's, Ostwald showed that even impenetrability, which, according to mechanists, is the constitutive feature of matter, is a mere sensory quality that is perceived only when there is a difference in kinetic energy between a piece of matter and one's own organism. No sensation of hardness would arise if a piece of matter which one tried to touch retreated at the same velocity with which his finger moved toward it. Ostwald interpreted all aspects of matter in terms of energy: Mass is the capacity of kinetic energy; occupancy of space is "volume-energy"; gravity is energy of distance. Thus, matter is nothing but a "spatially ordered group of various energies" which do not require any material substrate. Material substance belongs with caloric, phlogiston, and electric and magnetic fluids in the category of discarded and useless fictions. Ostwald prophesied that ether too would soon disappear from science, as the increasing difficulties in constructing a satisfactory model of it indicated.

This difficulty was for Ostwald only one symptom of mechanism's general failure to provide a satisfactory explanation of physical phenomena. He even doubted the usefulness of kinetic explanations of thermal phenomena, although the mechanical theory of heat had been extremely successful. The atom itself was for Ostwald only a convenient methodological fiction, which he refused to reify. (Only around 1908, under the growing pressure of new experimental confirmations of the discontinuous structure of matter, did he modify his view.)

The ubiquity and constancy of energy make it "the most general substance," and the conservation of energy underlies the validity of the law of causation. The succession of cause and effect is nothing but the transformation of one form of energy into another, the total amount of energy remaining constant. The law of conservation of energy guarantees the quantitative equality of cause and effect; and the direction of transformations is determined by the law of entropy, according to which all forms of energy are being gradually transformed into heat. Ostwald rejected all attempts to limit the application of the law of entropy; opposition to applying it to the whole of cosmic history was, in his view, nothing but emotional reluctance to accept the eventual death of civilization and even of humankind. The mechanistic view, which regards all processes as in principle reversible, fails to account for the irreversibility of time embodied in the law of entropy.

Ostwald belonged to a generation of philosophers of science that included Ernst Mach, Pierre Duhem, and J. B. Stallo, who were acutely aware of the limitations of mechanistic explanations. They overlooked the power and fruitfulness of mechanical and particularly of corpuscular models even on the molecular level, and atomic physics was not yet advanced enough to show the inadequacy of corpuscular models of subatomic phenomena. When this inadequacy became apparent, the crisis of the traditional scheme proved to be far more profound than Ostwald expected. While claiming to reduce all manifestations of matter to energy, he still retained mass, the basic concept of mechanism, under the disguised form of "capacity of energy." He anticipated the later relativistic fusion of mass and energy only in a hazy and qualitative way.

In this respect Ostwald can be compared with Herbert Spencer, with whom he shared other ideas: the substantialization of energy, the deduction of the causal law from the law of conservation of energy, an energetist approach to social science and ethics, and a determinist monistic metaphysics disguised by positivistic and agnostic formulas. Ostwald, however, lacked Spencer's philosophical sophistication; this is especially visible in his approach to the mind-body problem. Ostwald believed that he had refuted materialism by identifying consciousness with neural energy; he did not realize that his view was only a variant of physicalism. Like Ernst Haeckel, whom he greatly respected, Ostwald believed that his view was identical with Benedict de Spinoza's double-aspect theory, but this is not true. The haziness of Ostwald's monism invited criticism from antagonistic camps; Hans Driesch called it disguised materialism, and V. I. Lenin denounced it as "sheer idealism."

Ostwald devoted much time to propagating his views on monism. He founded the pantheistically oriented League of German Monists in 1906, and in 1911 he began to publish the series Monist Sunday Sermons (*Monistische Sonntagspredigten*).

ETHICS AND SOCIAL THOUGHT

Ostwald regarded the law of entropy as the basis for the theory of values. What we term *mind* or *consciousness* is nothing but a form of neural energy and is subject to the same laws as other forms of energy. In a temporally reversible world the concept of value would be meaningless, whereas it acquires a precise scientific meaning in the framework of energetism. Evolutionary advance consists in the fact that increased coordination between increasingly specialized organs results in increased efficiency of the organism and a minimum waste of energy. The same law—increased coordination resulting in maximum efficiency—determines the progress of civilization. Immanuel Kant's categorical imperative should be replaced by the "energetic imperative": "Do not waste your energy." Ostwald's applications of his energetic imperative to social thought were even more ambiguous than his views on the mind-body problem. Prior to 1914 Ostwald regarded war and conflict as a wasting of energy, and he favored internationalism and pacifism. But during World War I he justified his militant nationalism by claiming that the organization, efficiency, and minimum waste of energy of the German state represented the highest existing evolutionary form of human society.

HISTORY OF SCIENCE

In history of science Ostwald deserves credit for editing *Ostwalds Klassiker der exacten Wissenschaften*, a series of reprints of important scientific writings. His own classification of creative scientific minds into "classics" and "romantics," however, is probably oversimplified although interesting. Ostwald also founded and edited the journal *Annalen der Philosophie* (1901–1921).

See also Causation: Philosophy of Science; Chemistry, Philosophy of; Descartes, René; Duhem, Pierre Maurice Marie; Energy; Haeckel, Ernst Heinrich; Lenin, Vladimir Il'ich; Mach, Ernst; Materialism; Mind-Body Problem; Nationalism; Philosophy of Science, History of; Spinoza, Benedict (Baruch) de.

Bibliography

WORKS BY OSTWALD

Die Überwindung des wissenschaftlichen Materialismus. Leipzig: Veit, 1895.

Vorlesungen über die Naturphilosophie. Leipzig, 1895; 2nd ed., Leipzig, 1902.

Individuality and Immortality. Boston: Houghton Mifflin, 1906. The Ingersoll Lecture.

Grundrisse der Naturphilosophie. Leipzig, 1908.

Die energetische Grundlagen der Kulturwissenschaften. Leipzig, 1909.

Der energetische Imperativ. Leipzig: Akademische Verlagsgesellschaft, 1912.

Monism as the Goal of Civilization. Hamburg, 1913.

Die Philosophie der Werte. Leipzig: A. Kröner, 1913.

Lebenslinien. 3 vols. Leipzig, 1926–1927. Autobiography.

Wissenschaft und Gottesglaube. Edited by F. Herneck. Leipzig, 1960.

WORKS ON OSTWALD

Adler, F. W. *Die Metaphysik in der Ostwaldschen Energetik.* 1905.

Delbos, Victor. *Une théorie allemande de culture: W. Ostwald et sa philosophie.* Paris, 1916.

Driesch, Hans. *Naturbegriffe und Natururteile.* Leipzig: Wilhelm Engelmann, 1904.

Duhern, Pierre. *L'évolution de la mécanique.* Paris: A. Joanin, 1903. Esp. p. 179.

Lasswitz, K. "Die moderne Energetik in ihrer Bedeutung für die Erkenntniskritik." *Philosophische Monatshefte* 39: 1–30, 177–197.

Lenin, V. I. *Materialism i Empirio-krititsizm.* Moscow: Zveno, 1909. Translated by David Kirtko and Sidney Hook as *Materialism and Empirio-Criticism.* London: Lawrence, 1927. Esp. Ch. 5

Meyerson, Émile. *L'identité et réalité.* 5th ed. Paris, 1951. Esp. Ch. 10. Translated from the 1908 edition by Kate Loewenberg as *Identity and Reality.* London, 1930.

Rey, Abel. *La théorie de la physique chez les physiciens contemporains.* 2nd ed. Paris, 1923.

Rolla, A. *La filosofia energetica.* Turin, 1908.

Schnehen, Wilhelm von. *Energetische Weltanschauung.* Leipzig, 1908.

Milič Čapek (1967)

OTHER MINDS

The question of how all of us know that there are other beings besides themselves who have thoughts, feelings, and other mental attributes has been widely discussed, especially among analytic philosophers in the English-speaking world. At least three of the most influential German philosophers—namely, Edmund Husserl, Max Scheler, and Martin Heidegger—have also dealt with this problem. The problem of "other minds" becomes a serious and difficult one because the traditional and most obvious solution to it, the argument from analogy, is open to grave objections. At the present time it would seem that a majority of the philosophers who have concerned themselves with the question consider the traditional solution—that our belief in other minds can be adequately justified by an analogical argument—at least inadequate, if not radically and unremediably defective.

ARGUMENT FROM ANALOGY

In general terms to argue by analogy is to argue on the principle that if a given phenomenon *A* has been found to be associated with another phenomenon *B*, then any phenomenon similar to *A* is very likely to be associated with a phenomenon similar to *B*. In the particular case of other minds, it is said, I observe that there is an association between my mental states, on the one hand, and my behavior and the physical state of my body, on the other. I then notice that there are other bodies similar to mine and that they exhibit behavior similar to my own. I am justified, therefore, in concluding by analogy that mental states like the ones I experience are associated with those other bodies in the same way that my mental states are associated with my body. I notice, for example, that when I have a pain in my tooth, it is likely to be decayed and that I am likely to groan, complain, and hold my jaw. Observing another body like my own that has a decayed tooth and behaves as my body behaves when I have a toothache, I conclude that this body, like mine, is the body of a being that has a toothache.

OBJECTIONS TO THE ANALOGY ARGUMENT. The first and least radical objection to the argument from analogy is that it does not establish its conclusion with an adequate degree of certainty. The argument, it is said, would be relatively strong if the correlation of the mental and the physical was observed to hold in a large and varied collection of instances before it was concluded that it also held in other similar cases. But this is not so. If I use the argument from analogy, I have only one case, my own, as a basis for my inference. Moreover, the characteristics and behavior of the other bodies vary markedly from my own. How can I be sure that the differences between myself and others are not associated with the presence of mental attributes in my own case and with the absence of them in other cases?

The other difficulties in the argument from analogy concern two features of that argument—first, that it is logically impossible to check up on the correctness of the conclusion of the argument and, second, that the argument's validity implies that one must learn from one's own case alone what it is to have a mental attribute. Let us elaborate a little on each of these points.

In the case of a normal analogical argument, it makes good sense to suppose that one might check up directly on the conclusion of the argument; in principle one could always dispense with reasoning by analogy, even though this may not be practicable in some cases. Of course, one who says that we know of the existence of other minds by analogy must deny that we can check up on our conclusion in some more direct way, for if we could, the argument by analogy with ourselves could be dispensed with. It also seems that he cannot say that our inability to check up is merely a practical matter. Such checking up cannot consist in making further observations of a person's behavior and body; this we can often do sufficiently well in practice. It would have to consist in some other operation that we cannot in fact perform but which we can conceive of ourselves performing; perhaps it would be something like telepathy.

But aside from any difficulty in making clear sense of the notion of telepathy, why should telepathy be regarded as a more direct way of checking up than ordinary observation of behavior? Indeed, it seems that one's grounds for thinking that one has telepathic knowledge of another person's state of mind must include the knowledge that what one seemed to know telepathically generally correlates well with what one knows as a result of ordinary observation. The same would also seem to apply to any other extraordinary but conceivable way of knowing about another's mental state. Granted, then, that the supporter of the argument from analogy must hold that the impossibility of checking the conclusion more directly is not any variety of empirical impossibility, why is this held to destroy the argument? Perhaps there is a difference here between this argument and other valid analogical arguments, but why does this difference make this argument unacceptable? The answer given is that this difference renders the conclusion of the argument senseless. What can the phrase "He is in pain" mean to me if no conceivable observation I could make would show that it was true or false, if I have no criterion for its truth, and if I have no idea of what would count for or against it? It will not do to say that the sentence means that he has the same as I have when I am in pain, for, again, what counts as being the same here?

The other main difficulty in the analogical argument centers, as we have said, on the necessity, implied by that argument, for each of us to learn from his own case alone what it is to have a mental attribute. Two arguments have been advanced to show that this is impossible.

According to the first, which derives from Ludwig Wittgenstein, the analogical argument requires that one be able to pick out something (for example, a pain or a state of anger) and thereafter to identify it, when it recurs, as a pain or a state of anger. The trouble is, however, that this account leaves no room for a distinction between a correct and an incorrect identification. Behavioral and other checks are ruled out, leaving no conceivable means of deciding whether a mistake has been made. But a distinction between a correct and a mistaken identification is surely essential to the very notion of identification itself. In this way the analogical argument, which requires that we be able to make correct identifications of our inner states, also deprives the notion of identification of any meaning.

The second argument, which has been advanced by P. F. Strawson, is more complex. According to him, the idea of a predicate involves the idea of a range of individuals to which that predicate can be significantly applied. In the case of mental attributes, this range includes both oneself and others; one cannot have the notion of a mental attribute unless one has a notion of oneself and a notion of another. Since the notion of oneself is the notion of a subject of mental and other attributes, one cannot have the notion of oneself without the notion of some mental attributes. Therefore, one cannot have a notion of oneself without also having the notion of another subject of mental attributes. This notion, however, can be possessed only if one knows how to ascribe mental attributes to such subjects. Hence, until one knows how to do this, one has no notion either of oneself or of another. But the argument from analogy requires that one should first have a notion of oneself, of one's own case, and then discover how to ascribe mental attributes to others by arguing analogically from correlations that are found to hold in one's own case. A person without a notion of his own case could indeed argue analogically. He could find that pain was to be expected when a certain body (his own, as *we* say) was branded with a hot iron. He could infer that there would also be a pain when another similar body was similarly affected. But he would soon find out that he was mistaken in this conclusion, for he would detect no pain when the hot iron was applied to any body other than his own.

DEFENSES OF ANALOGY ARGUMENT. Some persistent attempts (especially by A. J. Ayer) have been made to defend the argument from analogy against the charges laid against it. To counter the charge of weakness, the following suggestions have been made. Emphasis has been laid upon the special feature of the argument from analogy—that people can speak and that their descriptions of their mental states are very like those I would give of some of my own. This, it is claimed, is something more telling than a mere similarity of behavior. Against this it is pointed out that speech can be regarded as something understood by the speaker only if it is accompanied by the appropriate nonverbal behavior.

Another defense is that conclusions drawn analogically from behavioristic similarities are powerfully reinforced by like conclusions drawn by arguments based on similarities in the state of the nervous system. This consideration hardly meets the main complaint—namely, that I base my inference on one case only, my own.

According to a rather more convincing attempt to meet this complaint, no more can be asked of any method of inference than that I be able to test its conclusion more directly in some cases and that when I do so, the conclusion usually turns out to be correct. The argument from analogy satisfies this test. I can suppose that there are, as there seem to be, other people besides myself and that these people argue analogically that I have certain thoughts and feelings. I can check on these imagined inferences and find that their conclusions are generally true. Whether these inferences are in fact made is neither here nor there; I can see that the method would work if it were used. Nor need I be worried because I can check only those cases in which the conclusion is about myself. In all or most inferences there will be a restricted class of cases that I can check up on. It is, for instance, logically impossible that I should make a direct check on a change of color that occurred where I could not observe it. But it would be a mistake to argue that any analogical argument that a color change had occurred was weak because it was based upon one sort of case only—the sort that I was able to observe. Why should it make a difference to the strength of the other minds argument that the relevant class of case is my own mental states as opposed to what I myself observe?

An argument similar to this one can also be used to rebut the charge that there is no conceivable means of checking up on the conclusion of the argument from analogy. There are in fact some cases in which I can make a check—namely, those cases that concern myself. Moreover, although it is logically impossible for me to be some other person and hence to make a direct check on that other person's mental states, this is unimportant, for it is never logically impossible that I should check on the truth of a psychological statement when the subject is referred to by a descriptive phrase, even though that description fits someone other than myself. It is logically impossible, perhaps, that I should be Robinson, but it is not logically impossible that I should now be the man flying a certain aircraft, even though Robinson is in fact that man. Moreover, it is claimed, when I make a statement about Robinson, what is stated is, in effect, that someone who answers to such and such a description has had such and such an experience. To this it has been objected that the only interpretation of this claim that yields the desired conclusion is untrue, namely, the interpretation that "Robinson has a pain" means the same thing as some sentence of the form "The so and so has a pain." However, this objection clearly fails to settle the matter, as can be seen by considering the following statements:

(1) The man sitting in this chair is angry.

(2) Robinson is the man sitting in this chair.

(3) Robinson is angry.

Statement (1) cannot be said to be unintelligible to me on the ground that I, not being the man in question, cannot check up directly, for it is conceivable that I might have been sitting in the chair; statement (2) can also be checked on by me; statement (3) follows from (1) and (2). It is surely quite implausible to hold that statement (3) is unintelligible to me, whereas statements (1) and (2) are not.

There is, however, another possible difficulty in the argument from analogy that is usually not at all clearly distinguished from the one just considered—namely, that it is in principle impossible for more than one person to check directly on the conclusion. It is often said that publicity is the essential requirement. But does this mean that it must be logically possible for each person to make the check, or is it the more stringent requirement that it be possible for everyone, or at least more than one, to do so? If the latter, then the difficulty has not been overcome. Equally it has not been shown clearly why publicity should be required in the more, rather than in the less, stringent form.

This brings us to the reasons given for holding that one cannot understand psychological predicates from one's own case alone, which is a requirement of the argument from analogy. One of these reasons, as we have seen, is that there is no sense in the idea of an identification that is subject to no check, where there is no criterion of correctness. This view has been questioned on two grounds. Strawson has argued that a criterion of correctness is not needed in all cases of identification, and according to Ayer, an identification of a sensation can be satisfactorily checked, without recourse to anything publicly observable, by means of other private sensations.

OTHER SOLUTIONS TO THE PROBLEM

BEHAVIORISM. Assuming that the argument from analogy is unacceptable, the most obvious alternative is to adopt some form of that variety of behaviorism according to which all psychological expressions can be fully understood in terms of behavior. If behaviorism is correct, there is clearly no room or need for the argument from analogy. In ascribing a pain to someone, for example, one is asserting something that is in principle subject to a public check—something about the way the individual is behaving, about how he would behave in certain circumstances, about what the circumstances in fact are, or the like. There is no need to make any inference from the publicly observable to something radically different.

This is not the place for a general discussion of behaviorism. Any objection to a given form of behaviorism will, of course, be an objection to that form of behaviorism as a solution to the problem of other minds. There is, however, one difficulty that has given rise to a number of closely related attempts to deal with the problem—namely, that it is implausible to give a behavioristic account of some first-person psychological statements. When, for example, I say that I have a terrible pain, I do not say this on the basis of observation of my own behavior and the circumstances in which I am placed. Nor am I speculating about how I would behave in other, hypothetical circumstances.

This difficulty has become of central importance for many philosophers who are impressed by some or all of the arguments that purport to refute the argument from analogy. They regard such arguments as showing, not only that this argument fails, but, more positively, that the connection between mental states, on the one hand, and behavior and circumstances, on the other, is logical or conceptual, not contingent. What is needed to remove the difficulty about our knowledge of other minds, it is thought, is to clear away the obstacles that prevent us from seeing clearly that this connection *is* a conceptual one. The primary obstacle in this instance is the peculiar nature of first-person psychological statements. It is this obstacle that prevents us from wholeheartedly accepting the true view and that makes us always hark back to the picture of mental states as objects to which the owner has privileged access.

There are at least two points involved here. First, if my own statements about my mental states are not about private happenings to which only I have access and if they are not about my behavior either, then what account *is* to be given of them? Second, the statement "I am in pain," made by me, contradicts the statement "He is not in pain," made about me by someone else. If one admits that the former is not about my behavior, how can one avoid the conclusion that the latter also is not about my behavior? But if the latter is not about my behavior, how can it be maintained that the connection between my pain and my behavior is a logical one?

WITTGENSTEIN. In dealing with the question "How do words refer to sensations?" Wittgenstein suggested, "Here is one possibility: words are connected with the primitive, the natural, expressions of sensation and used in their place" (*Philosophical Investigations*, Sec. 244). This sug-

gestion, which is not elaborated much by Wittgenstein, has sometimes been treated as an attempt to deal with the first point stated above and has had certain merits ascribed to it—for example, by Norman Malcolm. It explains how the utterance of a first-person psychological statement can have importance for us; such an utterance has the importance that natural expressions of sensation and emotion have. It is also said to explain certain features of the logic of psychological statements, the absurdity of someone's concluding that he has a pain from the observation of his own behavior, and the impossibility of someone's being mistaken about whether he has a pain or of wondering whether he has a pain. However, whatever its merits, this stress on the likeness of first-person sensation statements to natural expressions of emotion and sensation merely sharpens the second of the difficulties noted above—namely, that "I am in pain" can contradict "He is not in pain." It even makes it hard to see how the former can be a statement at all; a cry of pain is not a statement.

This difficulty is obviously insuperable for one who, unlike Wittgenstein, adopts the extreme position that apart from being verbal and learned responses, first-person sensation statements are exactly like natural expressions of sensation. Wittgenstein, however, appears to hold that a statement like "My leg hurts" is never in all respects like a cry of pain but is sometimes more like it and sometimes less, depending on the context of utterance. There seem to be three main likenesses that he wanted to stress in all first-person present-tense expressions of sensation and in many such expressions of emotion—namely, (1) the impossibility of these expressions being mistakenly uttered; (2) the possibility of their being insincere or pretended; and (3) the fact that such statements can justifiably be made without a basis of self-observation. The problem that arises in formulating a successful defense of his views is showing how a statement that bears the above likenesses to a cry of pain can yet be different enough to contradict another statement for which the criteria of truth lie in the realm of the publicly observable—that is, in the behavior of the speaker.

It cannot be said that Wittgenstein himself made a serious attempt to cope with this difficulty. Others have made the attempt, but no attempt has been very convincing. The second and third points of likeness present no great difficulty (see Douglas Gasking, "Avowals"). Any statement can be made insincerely, and there are many nonautobiographical statements that a person can justifiably make without observing that the criteria for their truth are satisfied. For example, some people can tell you that a certain note is middle C without first carrying out the tests that determine whether it has the appropriate frequency. For such statements to be justified, it is necessary only that those who make them are usually right in such cases.

Alleged incorrigibility. The first difficulty, which arises from the alleged incorrigibility (as it is termed) of first-person present-tense statements, is not so easily disposed of. The most hopeful approach—indeed, the only approach—is to exploit the fact that the natural expressions of sensation and emotion can be feigned. An insincere groan is akin to a lie, and a lie is a false statement. Perhaps a verbal expression can reasonably be called false if it is insincere and true if it is sincere, the distinction between sincerity and insincerity being a matter of the behavior of the speaker. In this way a plausible account could be given of how something very like a groan could also in some ways be like a statement and be regarded as such. The incorrigibility of such statements would then be accounted for.

But this is not enough; it does not explain how such a "statement" can be the contradictory of another statement that is logically connected with statements about the behavior of the maker of the "statement." For (1) "I have pain," said by me about myself, is the contradictory of (2) "I have not a pain," said by me about myself. Therefore, since (3) "He has a pain," said about me by someone else, is also the contradictory of (2), (1) and (3) must both be the same statement. Consequently, if (3) is logically connected with certain behavioral statements, (1) must also have these connections. This makes it difficult to see how (1) can be incorrigible. If I can be mistaken about my own behavior, as is the case, and if there is a logical connection between my pain and my behavior, then, it would seem, I can be mistaken about my pain. This difficulty is not overcome by assimilating the truth of a first-person pain statement to the sincerity of a groan. For (4) "I am sincere in saying I have a pain," said by me about myself, is the same statement as (5) "He is sincere in saying he has a pain," said about me by someone else. Therefore, if (5) is logically connected with statements about my behavior, so is (4), and, if (4) is so connected, it must, it seems, be corrigible. For to claim sincerely that p is to think that p when one makes the claim, and to claim insincerely that p is to think that not-p when one makes the claim. If (4) is corrigible, then someone might think he is sincere in claiming he has a pain when in fact he is insincere—that is to say, he might think that he thinks that he has a pain, although in fact he thinks that he has not a pain. If, however, one cannot be mistaken about one's own pain, then to think that one thinks one has a pain is to think one has a pain, and to think one has not a pain is not to have a pain. It follows that if (4) is corrigible, someone might think that he has a pain although, in fact, he has not a pain. In short, if (4) is corrigible and (1) is not, then (1) is corrigible.

There are apparently only two ways out of these difficulties that do not involve abandoning the thesis of the incorrigibility of first-person psychological statements and thus ceasing to attach much value to the assimilation of such statements to natural expressions of emotion and sensation. One might deny that (1) and (3) are the same statement, or one might maintain that although (1) is logically connected with behavioral statements about which I can be mistaken, yet I cannot be mistaken about (1). The first of these alternatives would involve finding a satisfactory explanation of why I cannot assert the same thing that someone else does when he asserts (3). The second would require an account of the notion of a logical connection that would allow for the existence of statements that, when made by myself, are incorrigible, but which are logically connected with other statements that, when made by myself, are not incorrigible.

In fact it has been argued by some that there are no psychological statements that are incorrigible and that the problem we have just been discussing is therefore an unnecessary one. It seems to be quite true that there are some ways in which one can be mistaken when one says one has, say, a pain. But the matter has not yet been clarified sufficiently for anyone to be justified in saying with confidence that this renders the problem unnecessary. Even if first-person present-tense pain statements are corrigible, this does not show that they are corrigible in all the ways that other statements are corrigible. Nor has it been shown convincingly that they are corrigible in such a way as to obviate any difficulty that may arise from the fact that "I have a pain," said by me, contradicts "He has a pain," said about me.

In addition to the above objections to Wittgenstein's views on the subject of psychological statements, there is another one that is of a less definite character and to which Wittgenstein himself alludes when he puts into the mouth of an imaginary objector such words as "and yet you again and again reach the conclusion that the sensation itself is a *nothing*" (*Philosophical Investigations*, Sec. 304). He protests, of course, that this is not the sort of impression he wishes to create and that it arises from his "setting his face against the picture of the inner process." Nevertheless, it cannot be said that he altogether succeeds in dispelling this impression. His problem might indeed be described in just these terms—to set his face against the inner process picture without creating the impression that he wishes to deny the existence of sensations. It does not seem that he succeeds in this.

P. F. STRAWSON. It is perhaps Wittgenstein's failure that in part gives rise to another attack on the problem—namely, that of P. F. Strawson. Strawson, like Wittgenstein, is convinced that the argument from analogy is mistaken and that skepticism about other minds is senseless or at least empty and pointless. Like Wittgenstein, he holds that the relation of the behavior of other people to their mental states is not contingent: "the behavior-criteria one goes on [in assigning P-predicates—that is, psychological predicates] are not just signs of the presence of what is meant by the P-predicate, but are criteria of a logically adequate kind for the ascription of the P-predicate" (*Individuals*, p. 106).

In spite of this he is out of sympathy with Wittgenstein in many ways. He considers that the assimilation of first-person present-tense psychological statements to the natural expressions of sensation and emotion "obscures the facts and is needless" (*Individuals*, p. 107). He is unconvinced by Wittgenstein's reasoning against the idea of a private language that might serve as a basis for the argument from analogy. He sees little difficulty in the notion of a person's inventing for himself a private language in which he has names for his sensations even when such sensations have no outward expressions: "He might simply be struck by the recurrence of a certain sensation and get into the habit of making a certain mark in a different place every time it occurred" (*Individuals*, p. 85). Nor does he consider the notion of a person's continuing to exist in a disembodied state as logically absurd (*Individuals*, pp. 115–116). He accuses Wittgenstein of hostility to the idea of what is not observed and of a "a prejudice against the inner" ("Critical Notice," p. 91).

All these criticisms of Wittgenstein suggest that Strawson holds the view that the connection between behavior and mental states is, after all, a contingent one. But this, as we have seen, is not so. How, then, does Strawson reconcile these apparently conflicting aspects of his thought? His line of thought appears to be approximately that general agreement in judgment is necessary before it is possible to have a common language. Such general agreement exists about, for example, "what it looks like here," and this agreement makes possible our common impersonal language of, for example, color. There is no such general agreement about "whether or not 'it's painful here,' " and there is thus no possibility of a com-

mon impersonal pain language. However, there is something available (namely, pain behavior) on which general agreement is possible, and if we are therefore to have a common pain language, we must each ascribe pain to others on the basis of their behavior. In this way a common personal language becomes possible.

In discussing Strawson's thought, it is crucial to emphasize that until a person decides to ascribe pains to others on the basis of their behavior, he has not got and cannot have our concept of pain, for part of that concept is that a pain is something that someone possesses. Nevertheless, he can have a concept (or perhaps something more rudimentary than a full-fledged concept) that is akin to our concept of pain but does not involve the idea of something that is had or possessed by either himself or others.

Perhaps this can be made more intelligible by considering a conceivable though unlikely case, that of a young child who has not yet got our concept of pain but is on the way to getting it. When he falls and knocks his head or scrapes his knee, he says, "It hurts." He has learned this sentence, perhaps as a replacement for natural cries of pain, and he uses it to get picked up and otherwise comforted. However, when his twin brother or a brick falls off the table, and the child is asked, "Does it hurt?" he replies, "No." Nevertheless, he cannot be said to mean by "It hurts" what is meant by "It hurts me," even though he says the former only when the latter is true, for he attaches no sense to "Does it hurt John?," as opposed to "Does it hurt me?" Nor, with regard to what he calls hurting, does he see any difference between John and a brick. If John says, "It hurts," when he himself is feeling all right, he regards what John says as simply untrue. In order for this child to make the transition to the concept of pain as something that either he or someone else has, he must learn to say, "It hurts John," when John bumps his head and cries and to say, "It hurts me," when formerly he said only, "It hurts." Until this linguistic convention is acquired, the child cannot be said to have the concept of pain as a property of persons at all, not even as a property of himself.

Thus, the argument from analogy breaks down because it assumes not only that a person can have a private language but that this language contains our concept of pain (ascribed pain). But such a language could contain at best only a concept of what we may call unascribed pain. The connection between unascribed pain and my behavior is a contingent one, but the connection between behavior and ascribed pain is not. We can see now why Strawson says, "I have argued that such a … 'justification' [of our beliefs about others] is impossible, that the demand for it cannot be coherently stated" (*Individuals*, p. 112). To talk about other people's pains at all is to accept and use the concept of ascribed pain, and it is an integral part of this concept that behavior shows any person whether that concept applies to other people.

Criticisms of Strawson. Strawson's views are open to some of the criticisms that have been directed against opinions that are the same as his own. In addition, Ayer has directed a number of criticisms specifically against Strawson's positions, asserting that his notion of logical adequacy is obscure and arguing that this obscurity is irremediable. It is certainly true that Strawson does not make the notion of logical adequacy as clear as he might, but Ayer's reasons for thinking that this obscurity could not be remedied are themselves inconclusive. Ayer's other main criticism is directed against Strawson's reason for holding that neither the argument from analogy nor the philosophical skepticism that arises from this argument can be stated coherently. This criticism is based on a failure properly to understand Strawson's position, which in turn leads to the mistaken idea that Strawson cannot allow for the existence of someone with the concept of a person "who was invariably mistaken in ascribing states of consciousness to others" (*The Concept of a Person and Other Essays*, p. 106).

There is nothing in Strawson's position to prevent him from holding that analogy is used in the ascription of states of consciousness to others; the only thing that he rules out is analogical *argument* of the traditional pattern. To understand this, let us use the words "upain" and "utickle" for the concepts of unascribed pains and tickles. According to Strawson, in order to pass from these concepts to those of (ascribed) pains and tickles, I must adopt verbal rules according to which I say "I have a pain" when there is a "upain" and "He has a pain" when another body exhibits certain behavior, and so on. But what sort of behavior, and so forth? There is no reason that Strawson's answer should not be along some such lines as "behavior, etc., that is like the behavior, etc., that this body (i.e., mine) exhibits when there is a upain." In accepting such a rule, I am not *arguing* by analogy. Now, I can adopt such a rule and thus have the concept of a person, but I can still fail to realize that all the objects I regard as persons are in fact unlike myself in ways that I have not noticed.

Ayer describes an imaginary child who is brought up and taught to speak by lifelike robots and who never meets real people. He argues, quite correctly, that this child would have the concept of a person and yet always

be mistaken when he ascribes mental attributes to anything. But no consequences fatal to Strawson's views follow from this. The child has adopted the verbal rule whose acceptance, according to Strawson, is necessary for the possession of the concept of a person. The child mistakenly thinks that the robots are persons because he believes that they are much more like himself than in fact they are. This gives no ground for the skeptical conclusion that I may here and now be mistaken in my belief that there are other people besides myself. If one accepts Strawson's position, such skepticism need be justified only if what I think to be other people are a great deal less like me in behavior, etc., than I take them to be. If there is a doubt left here, according to Strawson it can have nothing very specifically to do with other minds. The basis of Ayer's misunderstanding is his mistaken belief that Strawson "infers that any attempt to justify the belief that there are other persons by relying on the premiss that one knows oneself to be a person would be circular; the premiss would already assume what the argument is supposed to prove" (ibid., p. 104). But Strawson's objection to the argument from analogy is not that it is a circular argument. According to him, the trouble is that the argument both uses the concept of a person and rejects the verbal rule that is a necessary part of that concept, namely, the rule that mental attributes are to be ascribed to things on the basis of their behavior, and so on.

JOHN WISDOM'S VIEWS. Finally, something should be said of John Wisdom's very important work on this problem. It is quite impossible to summarize Wisdom's contribution as another solution to the problem of other minds. This impossibility is inherent in his views about philosophy and in the method he used in conformity with these views. All that can be done here is to give some idea of what is to be found in his writings on the problem of other minds by sketching his method of dealing with it.

Wisdom was much influenced by Wittgenstein, especially in regard to the idea that the treatment of a philosophical problem is in some ways like the treatment of an illness. Such a problem or puzzle is a symptom of deepseated intellectual disorder that consists in a persistent tendency to think about a certain area of thought and language in accordance with a misleading and partially inappropriate model. The puzzle is dissipated when one is "cured" of this tendency. Inattention, however, is not the only remedy, nor is the taking of drugs. The only "cure" available to a philosopher qua philosopher is a certain form of insight. The misleading model that distorts one's thinking is largely an unconscious one. Insight and freedom from its grip are obtained by bringing it into the open, by making quite clear in detail how our thought is governed by it, and by giving us a proper view of the nature of, for example, our knowledge of other minds.

Thus, Wisdom's first aim is to induce and sharpen philosophical perplexity by showing how it arises precisely out of the sort of position that is at first sight the most attractive to us. For example, the most natural answer to the question about other minds is the traditional one. But it is from this answer and the way of thinking that goes with it that philosophical skepticism most easily arises. Skepticism is satisfactorily removed only when we are brought to see that knowing about other minds is not altogether like other ways of knowing that are by analogy and that it need not be. It might be thought that the aim of a philosopher should be to find a correct model that does not mislead. But according to Wisdom, this is not so. Although every statement has its own logic, the logic of every statement is in some degree like that of every other. We cannot usefully create a limited set of pigeonholes into one of which goes our knowledge of other minds along with, say, our knowledge of the past, while our knowledge of any theoretical entity goes into another. The matter cannot come to this sort of a conclusion. There will be important differences that will make inappropriate any such pigeonhole, as well as the likenesses that make it possible. To get a true grasp of the nature of our knowledge of other minds, it is necessary to make a very large number of detailed comparisons between the various ways in which we know or might know things and between the logic of various types of statements. Only then will we see psychological statements and the ways in which we know of the existence of other people's thoughts and feelings in all their idiosyncrasies and in all their similarities to other statements and to other ways of knowing things. Until this is done, we cannot be entirely freed from our tendency to see things as they are not.

As may be deduced, Wisdom's writings about other minds are almost as much about induction, the past, perception, philosophy of science, and so on as they are about other minds. He used his method with subtlety, inventiveness, and imagination. Many points made by later writers on the problem of other minds are little more than elaborations or oversimplifications of points already made by Wisdom.

See also Private Language Problem.

Bibliography

ENGLISH-SPEAKING PHILOSOPHERS

Ayer, A. J. *The Concept of a Person and Other Essays*. London: Macmillan, 1963. Ch. 4. Criticizes Strawson's views.

Ayer, A. J. *The Problem of Knowledge*. London: Macmillan, 1956. Ch. 5. Defends the argument from analogy.

Bilgrami, Akeel. "Dummett, Realism, and Other Minds." In *The Philosophy of Michael Dummett*, edited by Brian McGuinness. Dordrecht: Kluwer, 1994.

Brewer, Bill. "Emotion and Other Minds." In *Understanding Emotions: Mind and Morals*, edited by Peter Goldie. Brookfield, U.K.: Ashgate, 2002.

Buford, T. O., ed. *Essays on Other Minds*. Chicago: University of Illinois Press, 1970.

Dennett, Daniel C. "Beliefs about Beliefs." *Behavioral and Brain Sciences* 1 (1978): 568–570.

Dretske, Fred. "Animal Minds." *Philosophic Exchange* 31 (2000–2001): 21–33.

Fodor, Jerry. "A Theory of the Child's Theory of Mind." *Cognition* 44 (1992): 283–296.

Foley, Richard. *Intellectual Trust in Oneself and Others*. New York: Cambridge University Press, 2001.

Gasking, Douglas. "Avowals." In *Analytical Philosophy*, edited by R. J. Butler, 154–169. Oxford, 1962.

Ginet, Carl. "Plantinga and the Philosophy of Mind." In *Alvin Plantinga*, edited by James E. Tomberlin. Dordrecht: Reidel, 1985.

Goldman, A. "In Defense of the Simulation Theory." *Mind and Language* 7 (1992): 104–119.

Heal, Jane. "Other Minds, Rationality, and Analogy." *Proceedings of the Aristotelian Society*, supplement 74 (2000): 1–19.

Heal, Jane. "Understanding Other Minds from the Inside." In *Current Issues in Philosophy of Mind*, edited by Anthony O'Hear. New York: Cambridge University Press, 1998.

Hill, Christopher. "On Getting to Know Others." *Philosophical Topics* 13 (1985): 257–266.

Leslie, A. M. "Pretense and Representation: The Origins of 'Theory of Mind.'" *Psychological Review* 94 (1987): 412–426.

Malcolm, Norman. "Knowledge of Other Minds." *Journal of Philosophy* 55 (1958): 969–978. A radical criticism of the argument from analogy and the traditional viewpoint.

Malcolm, Norman. "Wittgenstein's Philosophical Investigations." *Philosophical Review* 63 (4) (1954): 530–559. Defends Wittgenstein's views on private languages.

McDowell, John. "Criteria, Defeasibility, and Knowledge." *Proceedings of the British Academy* 68 (1982): 455–479.

McGinn, Colin. "What Is the Problem of Other Minds?" *Proceedings of the Aristotelian Society*, supplement 58 (1984): 119–137.

Mill, J. S. *An Examination of Sir William Hamilton's Philosophy*. London: Longmans Green, 1865. Ch. 12. Contains a straightforward version of the argument from analogy.

Nichols, Shaun. "Mindreading and the Cognitive Architecture underlying Altruistic Motivation." *Mind and Language* 16 (2001): 425–455.

Sober, Elliot. "Evolution and the Problem of Other Minds." *Journal of Philosophy* 97 (2000): 365–386.

Strawson, P. F. "Critical Notice of Wittgenstein's Philosophical Investigations." *Mind* 63 (249) (1954): 70–99. A criticism of Wittgenstein's views on private languages.

Strawson, P. F. *Individuals.* London: Methuen, 1959. Ch. 3.

Wisdom, John. "Other Minds." *Mind* 49 (196): 369–402; 50 (197): 1–22; 50 (198): 97–122; 50 (199): 209–242; 50 (200) 313–329; 51 (201): 1–18 (1940–1942).

Wisdom, John. "Other Minds." *Logic and Reality, PAS*, Supp. 20 (1946): 122–147.

Wisdom, John. *Other Minds.* Oxford: Blackwell, 1965. Reprints all the above.

Wittgenstein, Ludwig. *Philosophical Investigations.* Oxford: Blackwell, 1953.

GERMAN PHILOSOPHERS

Husserl, Edmund. *Cartesianische Meditationen. Husserliana*, Vol. I. The Hague, 1950. Meditation V. Translated by Dorion Cairns as *Cartesian Meditations; An Introduction to Phenomenology.* The Hague, 1960.

Scheler, Max Ferdinand. *Zur Phänomenologie und Theorie der Sympathiegefühle und von Liebe und Hass.* Halle, 1913. Appendix.

J. M. Shorter (1967)
Bibliography updated by Benjamin Fiedor (2005)

OTTO, RUDOLF

(1869–1937)

Rudolf Otto, the German theologian, was born at Peine in Hanover. He studied at Erlangen and Göttingen, where he became a *Privatdozent* in systematic theology in 1897. In 1904 Otto was appointed professor of systematic theology at Göttingen. He accepted similar posts at Breslau in 1914 and at Marburg in 1917, where he remained until his death. In addition to his philosophical work, Otto published works on Christ, on Indian religious thought and its relation to Christianity, and on various theological topics.

RELIGIOUS FEELING AND RELIGIOUS KNOWLEDGE

Otto's most significant philosophic contribution is to be found in his discussion of religious feeling and religious knowledge—a discussion that begins with his earliest work and culminates in *The Idea of the Holy*.

In *Naturalism and Religion* (1904) Otto discusses the relation of religion to a naturalism that demands that everything be explained on the basis of mathematical-mechanical laws, thus excluding the beyond, purpose, and mystery, which are essential to religion.

COGNITIVE CLAIMS OF RELIGION. Religion makes certain claims—that the world is conditioned and dependent, that there is a providence, that there is a side other than that which appears to us. These claims are not put forward as poetry but as truths. They cannot, however, be justified by, nor derived from, a consideration of nature in any straightforward sense. Reason may show that science does not conflict with these claims and even that science is unable to consider their truth-value. Reason may also point out hints in nature that suggest that these claims are true; reason cannot, however, justify them. These truths differ in kind from those of science and common sense and have their own grounds—the heart and conscience, feeling and intuition. Correlations can be made between various feelings, on the one hand, and religious claims, on the other. Corresponding to the claim that the world is conditioned and dependent is the feeling of the dependence and conditionally of all things. The claim that there is a providence, or teleological order, in things implies that certain value judgments are true and these value judgments rest on feeling and intuition. Corresponding to the claim that there is a beyond is piety—a feeling and intuition, which is bound up with our experience of the beautiful and the mysterious, that there is a reality behind appearances.

RELIGIOUS FEELINGS AND INTUITIONS

In *Naturalism and Religion* it is not entirely clear just what these feelings and intuitions are. Otto sometimes talks of them as if they were feelings in a straightforward sense. At other times he talks of them as if they were half-formulated judgments that carry with them an inescapable sense of conviction, and at still other times he talks of them as if they were cognitive experiences in somewhat the same way that visual experiences are cognitive.

CATEGORIES AND IDEAS. The notion of religious feelings and intuitions receives a more complete treatment in *The Philosophy of Religion Based on Kant and Fries* (1909), in which Otto follows the position of Jakob Friedrich Fries. We have an immediate knowledge of reality, the noumenal world, which shows itself in "feelings of truth." These feelings can be brought to full consciousness as ideas. An idea is a concept that can be applied to reality. When temporally schematized, the categories of theoretical reason can be applied to appearances and can also, when schematized by the principle of completeness (a principle based on reason's "perception and knowledge" that real existence is necessary, one, and complete), be applied to reality itself. A category thus schematized is an idea. These ideas are essentially negative. In effect, they exclude certain characteristics—temporality, contingency, and so on—from reality.

In the case of the practical reason the "feeling of truth" cannot be completely conceptualized. Practical reason does, however, derive the idea of reality as "the reign of purpose" from the principle of the dignity of the person that underlies the concept of duty. The idea is again presumably negative.

The negative judgments obtained through applying the ideas of theoretical and practical reason to reality must be supplemented by positive knowledge, which is gained through feelings or perceptions that cannot be adequately expressed although they can be communicated. These feelings, or perceptions, again seem to be, simultaneously, feelings in an ordinary sense, the ability to make judgments according to criteria that cannot themselves be formulated, and a direct perception of an objective existence—in this case, reality. Otto distinguishes between the feeling of beauty and of the sublime, on the one hand, and religious feelings, on the other. Although the discussion is somewhat obscure, it would seem that all three of these feelings either directly or indirectly disclose reality.

NUMINOUS FEELINGS

In *The Idea of the Holy* (1917), Otto attempts to make a clear distinction between numinous, or religious, feelings and feelings that might be confused with them, such as the feeling of the sublime. Numinous feelings have two primary aspects—a feeling of religious dread and a feeling of religious fascination. The closest analogue to religious dread, or awe, is the feeling of uncanniness—the feeling one has when the hair on the back of one's neck rises, the shudder or terror on hearing a ghost story, the dread of haunted places. The feeling of fascination by, attraction to, and prizing of the object that arouses the feeling in question creates both the desire to approach the object and the feeling that one possesses no value when considered in relation to the fascinating and prized object.

Otto's attempt to describe the various feelings must be distinguished from his theory about numinous feelings. Numinous feelings are unique; they cannot be analyzed as a complex of such nonnuminous feelings as love, fear, horror, a feeling of sublimity, and so on. Second, the capacity for numinous feelings is unexplainable; although the capacity may appear in the world only when certain conditions are fulfilled, the conditions do not constitute an adequate explanation of the capacity in question.

Numinous feelings are also cognitive. Two claims are made at this point. First, the feelings are the source of the concept of the numinous—the concept of something that is both a value and an objective reality. The numinous feelings are also cognitive in the sense that they are like visual experiences. They have "immediate and primary reference to an object outside the self"—the numinous quality or object, which is an object of numinous feelings in somewhat the same way that visible objects and qualities might be said to be the object of visual experiences.

INTERPRETATIONS. The relation between these two claims is not clear. At least two interpretations are possible. The first interpretation makes central the claim that numinous feelings disclose the numinous object. The encounter with the numinous object through numinous experiences gives rise to the concept of the numinous in much the same way that encounters with objects and qualities through visual experiences are thought to give rise to the concepts of those objects and qualities. The concept of the numinous is, then, a posteriori in the sense that it is derived from the experience of an object or quality. It is, however, a priori in the sense that it is not derived from any sense experience. In this interpretation the feeling is the source of the concept only in the sense that it discloses the object of the concept, the encounter with the object producing the concept of the object.

In the second interpretation the feeling gives rise to both the concept and the disclosure of the numinous object, yet it is not the encounter with the numinous that gives rise to the concept of the numinous. Rather, the feeling furnishes the concept in much the same way that Immanuel Kant's theoretical reason furnishes the various a priori categories. The concept of the numinous is, then, a priori in a standard sense. The feeling does more than this, however. The feeling that furnishes the concept also discloses the object to which the concept applies. How are these two functions of numinous feelings related? Neither the concept nor the object is, it would seem, given in isolation. Rather, the object is given through the concept or as structured by the concept. The two are given together although one is not derived from the other. In either interpretation Otto makes the claim that feeling puts us in contact with, discloses, is an awareness of, intuits something outside ourselves. In this respect feeling is like visual and auditory experiences. It has an objective referent whether this is structured by an a priori concept or whether it simply gives rise to a concept. Unfortunately, the difficulties involved in this claim are not discussed. Obvious disanalogies with ordinary perception (the absence of tests for "mis-seeing," the fact that no sense organ is tied to numinous experiences, the fact that nonpsychological predictions cannot be based on numinous experiences in the way in which they can be based on visual experiences, and so on) are ignored.

THE NUMEN

Otto calls the object of numinous feelings the numen, something that is both value and object but which can be only indirectly characterized by means of "ideograms"—that is, by designating properties which would appropriately call forth a feeling response analogous to that evoked in the encounter with the numen. For example, the encounter with the numen evokes religious dread. This is analogous to fear. Accordingly, we indicate the property of the numen that arouses religious dread by *wrath,* a term that refers to a property which often produces fear. In addition to this, however, we can and should "schematize" the numen by means of such rational concepts as goodness, completeness, necessity, and substantiality. That is, concepts of this sort may be predicated of the numen. The resulting judgment is synthetic a priori. It may be suggested that the cash value of the last claim is that we just "see" the connection to be appropriate if we possess numinous feelings.

THE HOLY

When the concept of the numinous and the schematizing concepts are brought together in this way, we have the "complex category of the 'holy' itself." The category is a priori in the sense that (1) the connection between the notion of the numinous and the schematizing concepts is a priori, (2) the concept of the numinous is a priori in that although it arises "amid the sensory data … of the natural world, … it does not arise out of them," and (3) the schematizing concepts are a priori.

The last claim is difficult to maintain, however, for Otto's examples of the schematizing concepts seem to make this impossible. It could perhaps be argued that schematizing concepts such as completeness, necessity, substantiality, and goodness are a priori. Otto also wishes to say, however, that the concepts of love, mercy, and moral will can function as concepts that schematize various aspects of the numinous. It is difficult to maintain that a concept such as love is a priori. What Otto maintains is that although "love" as applied to the numen and "love" as applied in ordinary situations have the same

content, their form differs. When referred to the numen, the term is taken absolutely; when it is applied in ordinary situations, it is not. Otto seems to mean that love in the ordinary sense admits of degrees that can be arranged on a scale. The love of the numen is the limit of this scale. Since the limit (whatever this might be) is not given to us in sense experience, we may call it a priori.

RELIGIOUS FEELINGS AND THE NUMEN

We can now explicate more fully the role that religious or numinous feelings play in religious knowledge. They disclose the numen to us. They are the source of the concept of the numinous. Finally, they appear to warrant the synthetic a priori judgments that link the schematizing concepts to the concept of the numinous.

The relation between the account presented in *The Philosophy of Religion* and *The Idea of the Holy* is, I think, clear. The ideas have become the "Idea of the Holy" (which breaks down into the concept of the numinous and the schematizing concepts), reality has become the numen, and feelings and intuitions have become numinous feelings.

AUTONOMY OF THE SPIRIT

Another theme, although less philosophically interesting, is of central concern to Otto himself—the autonomy of the spirit and of the spirit's religious capacities. In asserting that the spirit is autonomous, Otto is claiming that the laws of the spirit are fundamentally different from those of the natural world. In effect, they are the prescriptive laws of logic and ethics (and of religion?) rather than the descriptive laws of physics and psychology. Insofar as a spirit determines itself by prescriptive laws, it is free. Otto is further claiming that spirit is the source of concepts, principles, intuitions, and valuations that cannot be derived from sense experience. And, finally, he is claiming that although spirit develops under the influence of external stimuli, it is something unique in its own right. Spirit cannot be explained by, nor can its occurrence be predicted on, the basis of a consideration of sense experience alone. Spirit and its operations "emerge" under certain conditions but are not explained by these conditions.

See also A Priori and A Posteriori; Fries, Jakob Friedrich; Kant, Immanuel; Mysticism, Nature and Assessment of; Naturalism.

Bibliography

WORKS BY OTTO

Naturalistische und religiöse Weltansicht. Tübingen: Mohr, 1904. Translated by J. A. Thomson and M. R. Thomson as *Naturalism and Religion.* New York: Putnam, 1907.

Goethe und Darwin, Darwinismus und Religion. Göttingen: Vandenhoeck and Ruprecht, 1909. *Darwinismus und Religion* translated by S. G. Cole and E. M. Austin as "Darwinism and Religion" in *Crozer Quarterly* 8 (1931): 147–161.

Kantisch-Fries'sche Religionsphilosophie und ihre Anwendung auf die Theologie. Tübingen: Mohr, 1909. Translated by E. B. Dicker as *The Philosophy of Religion Based on Kant and Fries.* London: Williams and Norgate, 1931.

Das Heilige; über das Irrationale in der Idee des Gottlichen und sein Verhältnis zum Rationalen. Breslau: Trewendt and Granier, 1917; 25th ed. Munich, 1936. The later editions contain additional material. Translated by J. W. Harvey as *The Idea of the Holy: An Inquiry into the Nonrational Factor in the Idea of the Divine and Its Relation to the Rational.* New York, 1958.

Aufsätze das Numinose betreffend. Gotha: Klotz, 1923.

West-Östliche Mystik. Vergleich und Unterscheidung zur Wesensdeutung. Gotha: Klotz, 1926. Translated by B. L. Bracey and R. C. Payne as *Mysticism, East and West. A Comparative Analysis of the Nature of Mysticism.* New York: Macmillan, 1932.

Das Gefühl des Überweltlichen (Sensus Numinis). Munich, 1932. The first part of the fifth and sixth editions of the *Aufsätze* with some added material.

Sunde und Urshuld und andere Aufsätze zur Theologie. Munich, 1932. The second part of the fifth and sixth editions of the *Aufsätze* with some added material.

Religious Essays. A Supplement to the "Idea of the Holy," by Rudolf Otto. Translated by B. Lunn. London: Oxford University Press, 1931. This consists primarily of translations of essays found in the *Aufsätze* and the two preceding works.

Freiheit und Notwendigkeit, Ein Gespräch mit Nicolai Hartmann über Autonomie und Theonomie der Werte. Tübingen: Mohr, 1940.

WORKS ON OTTO

Almond, Philip. *Rudolf Otto: An Introduction to his Philosophical Theology.* Chapel Hill: University of North Carolina Press, 1984.

Ballard, Steven. *Rudolf Otto and the Synthesis of the Rational and the Non-Rational in the Idea of the Holy.* New York: Peter Lang, 2000.

Davison, R. F. *Rudolf Otto's Interpretation of Religion.* Princeton, NJ: Princeton University Press, 1947.

Feigel, F. C. *"Das Heilige." Eine kritische Abhandlung über Rudolf Otto's gleichnamiges Buch.* Haarlem, Netherlands, 1929.

Gooch, Todd. *The Numinous and Modernity: An Interpretation of Rudolf Otto's Philosophy of Religion.* New York: de Gruyter, 2000.

Haubold, W. *Die Bedeutung der Religionsgeschichte für die Theologie Rudolf Ottos.* Leipzig, 1940.

Moore, J. M. *Theories of Religious Experience with Special Reference to James, Otto and Bergson.* New York: Round Table Press, 1938.

Poland, Lynn. "The Idea of the Holy and the History of the Sublime." *Journal of Religion* 72 (1992): 175–197.

Proudfoot, Wayne. *Religious Experience.* Berkeley: University of California Press, 1985.

Raphael, Melissa. *Rudolf Otto and the Concept of Holiness.* Oxford: Clarendon Press, 1997.

Schlamm, Leon. "Numinous Experience and Religious Language." *Religious Studies* 28 (1992): 533–551.

Schlamm, Leon. "Rudolf Otto and Mystical Experience." *Religious Studies* 27 (1991): 389–398.

Siegfried, T. *Grundfragen der Theologie bei Rudolf Otto.* Gotha, 1931.

Sommer, J. W. E. *Der heilige Gott und der Gott der Gnade bei Rudolf Otto.* Frankfurt, 1950.

William J. Wainwright (1967)
Bibliography updated by Christian B. Miller (2005)

OUSIA

In classical Greek philosophy, *ousia* (a noun derived from the present participle of the Greek verb "to be") most often expresses one or another of four closely connected concepts: (1) what something is in itself, its being or essence; (2) an entity which is what it is, at least with respect to essential attributes, on its own and without dependence on any more fundamental entity of another type outside itself (in Plato's middle dialogues, the forms; for Aristotle, substance; for the Stoics, the material substrate); (3) for Plato, being as opposed to becoming; and (4) for the Stoics in some instances, existence as opposed to nonexistence. Depending on the context, *ousia* may be translated as "being," "essence," "reality," or "substance."

Employed in ordinary Greek to speak of a person's wealth and possessions, the word *ousia* was put to philosophical use by Plato in his early dialogue *Euthyphro* to state a requirement on definitions. Asked what piety is, Euthyphro answers that it is what is loved by all the gods. Socrates responds with a clear statement of concept (1), saying that Euthyphro has mentioned merely something that qualifies piety externally and has failed to give the *ousia* of piety (11a4–b1), what it is in itself that leads the gods to love it.

The transition from concept (1) to concept (2) occurs most clearly in the *Phaedo*, a dialogue of Plato's middle period. There the character Socrates introduces several forms, including the just itself and the beautiful itself (65d4–8), and speaks of them as the *ousia* of other things (65d13), in the sense that other things become just or beautiful, for example, only by participation in, or dependence on, the corresponding form (101c3–4). Each such form is an *ousia* according to concept (2) (76d9, cf. 77a2), a being or reality (78d1) that is always the same and unchanging (78d1–7), an object of thought rather than sensation.

In the *Republic* a similar picture obtains, but there the character Socrates speaks of the forms collectively as *ousia*, with the exception of the form of the good (VI, 509b8–9), and contrasts this invariant, unqualified, and cognitively reliable being first with the many sensible things, which can appear, for example, beautiful in one respect but ugly in another (V, 479c7, cf. 479b6–d1), and then with the collective becoming and decaying of these sensibles (VI, 485b21). This use of the word *ousia* to express concept (3), being as opposed to becoming, is frequent in book VII, where the study of the mathematical sciences serves to lead the prospective philosopher-rulers to turn away from becoming and toward being (VII, 525b5, cf. 525c6, 526e6, 534a3). This strong distinction in the *Republic* between being and becoming has been questioned by some scholars. In any case, it is considerably attenuated in some of Plato's later dialogues, including the *Philebus*, where the character Socrates asserts "Every process of generation … takes place for the sake of some particular being [*ousias tinas hekastēs*]" (54c2–3).

In the *Categories*, Aristotle uses the word *ousia* occasionally in the concept (1) sense of essence (e.g., at 1a1–2), but at the center of the discussion in the *Categories* is concept (2), and *ousia* in this sense becomes a technical term rendered by most translators as "substance." Moving even further from the view of the *Republic* than Plato does in his later dialogues, Aristotle argues that *ousia* in sense (2) belongs primarily and most of all to sensible entities like a particular human or a particular horse (2a11–14), since these "primary substances" (2a35) are substrates, or ontological subjects, not only of their own essential attributes but also, differently, of inherents from other categories, such as a certain quality or a certain quantity, that happen to be "in" them at one time or another (2a34–b5). He concludes that everything else under discussion in the *Categories*, including the species and genera of primary substances (called "secondary substances" at 2a14) as well as all the inherents in other categories, depend on primary substances for their being, in the sense that without primary substances, none of the others could be (2b5–6). (For an even stronger claim that all depends on substance, the focal or referential theory of the meaning of "being" [Gk. "to on," the participle], see *Metaphysics*, IV, 1003b5–10; cf. Devereux, pp. 220, 232.)

Aristotle's other extended discussion of *ousia* (*Metaphysics*, VII, VIII) accepts the view of the *Categories* that particular animals and plants fall under *ousiai* in sense (2) (VII, 1028b8–10). But book VII, having brought in the distinction between matter and form introduced in the *Physics* (190b1–191a22) to explain the coming-to-be and passing-away of particular sensible substances, subsequently regarded as composites of matter and form, says that such composite sensible substances are "posterior" to both matter and form (1029a30–32). It then argues at length for the thesis that form is primary substance (1037a5–7 and 1037a27–30, cf. 1032b1–2). This thesis raises two important questions. How does the thesis fit with Aristotle's position in the *Categories* that entities like particular horses and particular humans are primary substances? And is the primary substance the form of the species, which, though not a universal (1038b1–16), is nevertheless present in all the particular members of that species, or is it the particular form of a particular member of the species, unique to it and not present in any other member? These issues have been much debated since the 1950s, but in the 1980s and 1990s the weight of scholarly opinion shifted somewhat toward the particular-forms view, even as the widespread assumption that *Metaphysics* VII–VIII is a later work than the *Categories* came into question. (On these issues, see both Frede and Wedin; for a different view, see Loux.) The thesis that form is primary substance opens up the possibility of an inquiry, promised in book VII (1028b27–33), as to whether there can be any substance entirely separate from matter. This inquiry, carried out in book XII, leads Aristotle to conclude that there are not only eternal material substances (e.g., the planets, on his view) but also eternal immaterial substances (1071b4–5), including Aristotle's god, the first unmoved mover whose ceaseless thinking upon thinking (1072b1–30) inspires the movement of the outer sphere of fixed stars (1073a23–30).

Among the Stoics, by contrast, *ousia* in sense (2) is the single material substrate of all things, considered in abstraction from all qualities and relations depending on it (Calcidius, see Long and Hedley, Vol. 1, p. 269–270; for the Stoics' debt here to Plato, *Timaeus* 50a5–c6, see Menn, p. 216). Some Stoics also use the word *ousia* in sense (4), existence as opposed to nonexistence, to distinguish objects of thought that exist, objects that are peculiarly qualified portions of the material substrate *ousia*, for example, a particular horse, from objects of thought that are purely fictional and do not exist, for example, a centaur (Seneca, see Long and Hedley, Vol. 1, p.162).

See also Aristotle; Essence and Existence; Plato; Stoicism; Substance and Attribute.

Bibliography

Aristotle. *The Complete Works of Aristotle*, edited by Jonathan Barnes. Princeton, NJ: Princeton University Press, 1984.

Devereux, Daniel. "The Primacy of *Ousia*: Aristotle's Debt to Plato." In *Platonic Investigations*, edited by Dominic J. O'Meara. Washington, DC: Catholic University Press, 1984.

Frede, Michael. "Individuals in Aristotle." In his *Essays in Ancient Philosophy*. Minneapolis: University of Minnesota Press, 1987.

Long, Anthony A., and David N. Sedley. *The Hellenistic Philosophers*. 2 vols. Cambridge, U.K.: Cambridge University Press, 1987. This book includes both Calcidius's *Plato's Timaeus: Translation And Commentary*, sections 292–293, p. 269–270; and Seneca's *Letters*, 58.13–15.

Loux, Michael J. *Primary Ousia: An Essay on Aristotle's "Metaphysics" Z and H*. Ithaca, NY: Cornell University Press, 1991.

Menn, Stephen. "The Stoic Theory of Categories." In *Oxford Studies in Ancient Philosophy*. Vol. 17, edited by David Sedley. Oxford, U.K.: Oxford University Press, 1999

Plato *Plato: Complete Works*, edited by John Cooper. Indianapolis, IN: Hackett, 1997.

Wedin, Michael. *Aristotle's Theory of Substance: The "Categories" and "Metaphysics" Zeta*. Oxford, U.K.: Oxford University Press, 2000.

John Driscoll (2005)

OWEN, G. E. L

1922–1982

Gwilym Ellis Lane Owen was a major force in the post–World War II upsurge of analytically oriented philosophical work on ancient philosophy. The author of articles of enduring value, the subject of much discussion and controversy, many of them among the classics of the philosophical study of pre-Socratic philosophy, Plato, and Aristotle, he was concerned principally with the logic of argument, metaphysics, and philosophy of language; he had no substantive interests in ethics, political theory, or aesthetics. He understood the ancient philosophers as engaged in conceptual investigations of live philosophical interest. Raised in a Welsh family in Portsmouth, England, he matriculated at Corpus Christi College, Oxford, in 1940, completing his bachelor of arts degree in 1948, after war service in the Pacific arena. In 1950 he received a bachelor of philosophy degree under Gilbert Ryle's supervision, with an epoch-making thesis on logic, philosophy of language, and metaphysics in Plato's *Theaetetus, Parmenides, Sophist, Statesman*, and *Philebus*. Its main ideas formed the basis of his influential, though controversial, first publication, "The Place of the *Timaeus* in Plato's Dialogues."

After postdoctoral research at the University of Durham, Owen returned to Oxford in 1953 as university lecturer in ancient philosophy (from 1958, also nontutorial fellow of Corpus Christi), university reader (1957), and professor of ancient philosophy as first incumbent of that chair (1963). In 1966 he went to Harvard as professor of philosophy and the classics to direct a new PhD program in classical philosophy. In 1973 he returned to Great Britain as Laurence Professor of Ancient Philosophy in the Classics Faculty at Cambridge, and as fellow of King's College, where he remained until his early death in 1982.

Owen's year-long Oxford lectures on pre-Socratic philosophy, and his courses and seminars on Plato and Aristotle throughout his career, were famously exhilarating, challenging, and fast-paced explorations of central texts and topics in the study of ancient philosophy. A remarkably high percentage of the leading ancient philosophers of the next generation learned their craft and drew their initial inspiration from these classes. More than any of his contemporaries, Owen's example and personal influence shaped the growth and expansion in the philosophical study of ancient philosophy in the late twentieth century.

More than half of Owen's published work concerned Aristotle primarily, but his work on Plato and the pre-Socratic philosophers Parmenides and Zeno of Elea was equally ground breaking. He rejected the traditional idea that Plato's *Timaeus*—with its conception of the physical world as a "copy" drawn by a creator god from his intellectual vision of Forms existing in a separate nonphysical realm—was the culmination and permanent legacy of Plato's work in metaphysics. Rather, he read the dialectical and logical investigations of the *Parmenides* and *Sophist*, and others of what under his influence came to be referred to simply as the "late" dialogues, as containing deeper and more adequate reflections on issues of being and not-being, unity and multiplicity, becoming and change.

Confused ideas about these issues had motivated the "middle-period" theory of Forms, of *Symposium, Phaedo, Republic*, and *Timaeus*. Owen argued that *Timaeus* was in fact composed, not, as traditionally assumed, toward the end of Plato's life, but rather as a premature copestone to the middle-period theory, which was to be undermined and reconsidered in the "late" dialogues. His influential essays, "Notes on Ryle's Plato" and "Plato on Not-Being," dealing respectively with *Parmenides* and *Sophist*, cast new light on these intriguing but very obscure works, and spearheaded a generation of subsequent scholarly and philosophical work on them. His essays "Eleatic Questions," "Zeno and the Mathematicians," and "Plato and Parmenides on the Timeless Present" had a similar effect on studies of Parmenides and Zeno.

Owen's work on Aristotle concentrated on logic, methodology, physics, and metaphysics, but included one provocative paper on "Aristotelian Pleasures." This investigates Aristotle's idea that pleasure is to be conceived not as a passive experience but is itself an activity. Owen advanced the challenging thesis that Aristotle's two discussions of pleasure in *Nicomachean Ethics* VII and X have interestingly divergent conceptions of the relationship between the activity that pleasure itself is and whatever one takes pleasure in. In "Logic and Metaphysics in some Earlier Works of Aristotle" he paid careful attention to logical and philosophical details in some of Aristotle's earliest works and showed that the then popular picture of Aristotle's development (due to Werner Jaeger) was unacceptable. Far from only gradually freeing himself from a committed belief in a universal science of being, gained through the knowledge of middle-period Platonic Forms, Aristotle began by rejecting both the existence of such Forms and the possibility of any universal science of being.

It was only much later, with the employment of what Owen called a theory of "focal meaning" for *being*, that Aristotle could reconcile himself to any general science of being, or metaphysics. It was, however, the being of Aristotelian substances, not Platonic Forms, which provided the linchpin and focus of that science. In "The Platonism of Aristotle" and "Particular and General," he carried this analysis forward, finding in the middle books of Aristotle's *Metaphysics* an avowed sympathy with Plato's general metaphysical program—with Aristotelian forms, not Platonic Forms, at the center of the enterprise. Other well-known papers proposed an influential analysis of the "appearances" that Aristotle notoriously made the basis for the use of dialectical inquiry in physics, ethics, and other areas of philosophy ("*Tithenai ta phainomena*"), and argued that in his theory of categories Aristotle countenanced nonrepeatable individuals only in the category of substance. In other categories the "individuals" were such things as specific, narrowest *shades* of colors, not color-instances possessed uniquely by individual sub-

stances ("Inherence"). His paper "Aristotle on Time" also generated much discussion.

Owen was a moving force for the founding in 1957 of the Symposium Aristotelicum, a triennial select meeting of British, European, and North American scholars for concentrated joint study of a single Aristotelian text or topic. These meetings have done much to bring the diverse national traditions of Aristotelian scholarship into mutual communication. Several of Owen's articles originally appeared in the Symposium's triennial volumes. Many of his papers were reprinted in collections too numerous to list. After his death, they were all published together in 1986 (as *Collected Papers*); details of the original and other prior publications can be found there.

See also Aristotle; Parmenides of Elea; Philosophy of Language; Plato; Pre-Socratic Philosophy; Ryle, Gilbert; Zeno of Elea.

Bibliography

WORKS BY G. E. L. OWEN

"The Place of the *Timaeus* in Plato's Dialogues." *Classical Quarterly* NS 3 (1953): 79–95.

"Zeno and the Mathematicians." *Proceedings of the Aristotelian Society* 58 (1957–1958): 199–222.

"Eleatic Questions." *Classical Quarterly* NS 10 (1960): 84–102.

"Logic and Metaphysics in some Earlier Works of Aristotle." In *Aristotle and Plato in the Mid-Fourth Century*, edited by Ingemar Düring and G. E. L. Owen, 163–190. Göteborg, Sweden: Elanders Boktryckeri, 1960.

"Tithenai ta phainomena." In *Aristote et les problèmes de méthode*, edited by S. Mansion, 83–103. Louvain, Belgium: Publications Universitaires de Louvain, 1961.

"Inherence." *Phronesis* 10 (1965): 97–105.

"Plato and Parmenides on the Timeless Present." *The Monist* 50 (1966): 317–340.

"The Platonism of Aristotle." *Proceedings of the British Academy* 51 (1966): 125–150.

"Notes on Ryle's Plato." In *Ryle*, edited by O. P. Wood and George Pitcher, 341–372. Garden City, NY: Doubleday, 1970.

"Plato on Not-Being." In *Plato I*, edited by G. Vlastos, 223–267. Garden City, NY: Doubleday, 1970.

"Aristotelian Pleasures." *Proceedings of the Aristotelian Society* 72 (1971–1972): 135–152.

"Particular and General." *Proceedings of the Aristotelian Society* 79 (1978–1979): 1–21.

Logic, Science, and Dialectic: Collected Papers in Greek Philosophy. Edited by Martha C. Nussbaum. London: Duckworth, 1986.

John M. Cooper (2005)

PACIFISM

"Pacifism" is moral opposition to war. The concept embraces a wide range of positions from an absolute prohibition of all use of force against persons to a selective and pragmatic rejection of particular forms of such force under varying circumstances. Pacifists vary on their moral grounds for rejecting war and on their commitments to varieties of nonviolence.

Etymologically, pacifism comes from the Latin *pax, pacis,* "peace" (originally "compact") + *facere,* "to make," and literally means "peacemaking." Often, pacifism is incorrectly identified as passivism, which derives from the Latin *passivus,* "suffering," and means being inert or inactive, suffering acceptance. Pacifists may be passivists but often are activists, choosing nonviolent means to resolve conflict and achieve personal and social goals.

Pacifism consists of two parts: the moral opposition to war and the commitment to cooperative social and national conduct based on agreement. Beyond the mere absence of war, peace is a condition of group order arising from within by cooperation among participants rather than order imposed from outside by domination by others. Pacifism's opposition to war is much more frequently reflected in philosophic literature than is its active creation of peace.

Moral opposition to war is discussed across the history of Western philosophy. While early considerations of the morality of war can be found in ancient Greek texts (e.g., Plato, *Republic,* Book IV, 469c–471c), more thorough treatments are much later—notably from Desiderius Erasmus in the sixteenth century and Immanuel Kant in the late eighteenth. Adin Ballou articulated pragmatic pacifism in the mid-nineteenth century, and William James explored pacifist philosophy in the early twentieth. Arguments for pacifism tend to focus on the evils of war, including human suffering—especially of innocents—and moral degradation of participants as well as the uncontrollability of modern warfare.

The case for pacifism varies with the form of pacifism being put forth. Absolute pacifism, the view that it is wrong under all circumstances to use force against persons, may rest on one interpretation of Kant's categorical imperative, on Mohandas Gandhi's Satyagraha (truth force), on Martin Luther King Jr.'s notion of Christian love, or on other moral bases. Weaker forms of pacifism may rest on interpretations of these same principles or on other grounds. Epistemological pacifists stress the impossibility of knowing sufficiently to warrant taking lives, while pragmatic pacifists trace the empirical history of war to emphasize failures in achieving the ends that were to justify carnage. Nuclear pacifists focus on the projected effects of thermonuclear exchange, and ecological pacifists consider the effects of modern war on ecosystems.

See also Erasmus, Desiderius; James, William; Just War Theory; Kant, Immanuel; King, Martin Luther; Love; Peace, War, and Philosophy; Plato; Russell, Bertrand Arthur William; Social and Political Philosophy; Violence.

Bibliography

Ballou, A. "Christian Non-Resistance." In *Nonviolence in America: A Documentary History,* edited by S. Lynd. Indianapolis: Bobbs-Merrill, 1966.

Cady, D. L. *From Warism to Pacifism: A Moral Continuum.* Philadelphia: Temple University Press, 1989.

Cromartie, Michael, ed. *Peace Betrayed?: Essays on Pacifism and Politics.* Washington, DC: Ethics and Public Policy Center, 1990.

Erasmus, D. *Complaint of Peace.* 1517.

Erasmus, D. *Praise of Folly.* 1512.

Gandhi, M. K. *Non-violent Resistance.* Edited by B. Kumarappa. New York: Schocken, 1951.

Holmes, Robert L. *On War and Morality.* Princeton, NJ: Princeton University Press, 1989.

Holmes, Robert L. "Pacifism for Nonpacifists." In *Social and Political Philosophy,* edited by James P. Sterba. New York: Routledge, 2001.

James, W. "The Moral Equivalent of War" (1910). In *War and Morality,* edited by R. Wasserstrom. Belmont, CA: Wadsworth, 1970.

Kant, I. *Perpetual Peace* (1795). Edited and translated by L. W. Beck. New York: Liberal Arts Press, 1957.

King, M. L., Jr. *A Testament of Hope: The Essential Writings of Martin Luther King Jr.* Edited by J. M. Washington. San Francisco: Harper and Row, 1986.

Ruddick, S. *Maternal Thinking: Toward a Feminist Peace Politics.* Boston: Beacon Press, 1989.

Sharp, Gene. *Power and Struggle,* part 1 of *The Politics of Nonviolent Action.* Boston: P. Sargent, 1973.

Teichman, J. *Pacifism and the Just War.* Oxford: Blackwell, 1986.

Tolstoy, L. *The Kingdom of God and Peace Essays* (1909), 2nd ed. Oxford, 1951.

Duane L. Cady (1996)
Bibliography updated by Philip Reed (2005)

PAIN

There is no consistent philosophical view concerning the nature of pain, how to understand it, or what an understanding of pain might mean for philosophy of mind. Just about every conceivable position concerning the nature of pain is held by some leading thinker. Each of these positions has become grist for someone's mill in arguing either that pain is a paradigm instance of a conscious state or that pain is a special case and should not be included in any general theory of consciousness.

PHILOSOPHICAL VIEWS OF PAIN

Some philosophers and psychologists hold that pain is completely subjective: Either it is essentially private and completely mysterious, or it does not correlate with any biological markers but is completely nonmysterious. The International Association for the Study of Pain (IASP), the formal organization charged with defining pain, has articulated a paradigm subjective view. They write: "Pain is always subjective. . . . Many people report pain in the absence of tissue damage or any pathophysiological cause; usually this happens for psychological reasons. There is usually no way to distinguish their experience from that due to tissue damage if we take the subjective report. . . . [Pain] . . . is always a psychological state" (1986).

However, if one holds that pain does not correlate in some way with some sort of bodily state or event, one becomes a dualist. If pain just is a private experience, and that experience has no consistent underlying physical cause or correlate, then any interesting connection between the mind and the body over pain is lost.

Philosophers can eschew dualism by retreating to so-called token-token identity theory. Every experience in some creature is correlated with—identical to—some event or other in that creature's brain. And every experience in some other creature is correlated with—identical to—some event or other in that creature's brain. If the subjectivists are right, then there is no identifiable neural activity that is the same across all experiences of a type of pain. There is no brain correlate for the type "having a migraine headache," for example. Generic headache experiences occur only at a level of abstraction above brain activity—namely, in the mind and its cognitive states.

However, if philosophers deny type-type identity for larger brain structures across organisms, then they are also denying any hope of discovering mind-brain connections. For mental event-physical state correlations taken one at a time are all a robust token-token identity theory allows.

At the same time, scientists do believe that there are areas in the brain dedicated to pain processing, just as there are other areas dedicated to vision, audition, touch, and so forth. They believe that these areas are basically the same across humans, despite individual variation. Thus, even though a strict type-type identity might fail for particular sensory experiences, it still underlies views of our sensory systems taken as a whole. Types in science are allowed some play in them. They have to, or else there would be no mechanism by which to pick out any sort of cognitive processing in the brain at all.

All these lessons are missed by proponents of the subjective view, for they identify pain with the experience of pain and then explicitly deny that that experience has any correlation with any particular bodily reaction. But insofar as they want to be materialists interested in a scientific understanding of pain, they will have to permit generalizations connecting something in the body with the sensation of pain (see Hardcastle 1999).

Other philosophers and neurophysiologists argue that pain is completely objective; it is either intrinsic to the injured body part, a functional state, a set of behavioral reactions, or a type of perception. Pain is something that can be measured in bodies or behavior. As such, its connection to mentality, to sensations of pain, is secondary at best. Humans might recognize pain in terms of how it feels—the skin burns, for example. But, according to objective views that take pain as intrinsic to the injured body part, the pain itself is in the tissue. Hence, beliefs or judgments about the condition of the tissue are derivative—that is, pain is inferred from peripheral nociceptive or pain information (Annad and Craig 1996, Derbyshire 1996).

Similarly, if pain is understood as a type of perceptual process, then it works no differently than vision or olfaction. Animals receive some sort of perceptual input on their transducers, manipulate that information in their brains, and then use that manipulated information to alter motor reactions and other mental states. Part of the manipulated information might come into conscious awareness, but that sensation would constitute only a subset of what is meant by pain processing. According to this view, conscious experiences of pain, the damaged tissue itself, and the bodily and emotional reactions are all fundamental to pain processing. Each is one component in a larger process. Working together, these components take pressure, temperature, and chemical readings of tissues and use this information to track what is happening in bodies (Wall and Melzack 1989).

In these cases and most other instances of the objective view, pain is something entirely physical. Prima facie, it appears that the states or processes identified with pain could occur without any awareness of them at all. Most

objective views of pain have the unintuitive consequence of divorcing pain from sensations of pain or making the mental events associated with pain processing secondary to and dependent upon the pain processing itself.

There are a few objectivist philosophers who hold that pain is not a purely physical event. Instead, it is something like an attitudinal relation. Pain requires both a bodily state and then cognition over that state. Pain itself is the attitude, the belief, regarding one's bodily condition. This approach gets around the intuitive difficulties of the objective views by identifying pain with the consequent mental state. "Pain" then just refers to the mental event associated with pain processing. According to this view, there is pain processing and then pain proper.

CENTRAL PHILOSOPHICAL ISSUES

There are three large philosophical difficulties in defending any of the theories about pain processing outlined above: the problem of mental causation, the problem of naturalizing content, and the threat of eliminativism.

The difficulty with mental causation is roughly as follows. If one drops a hammer on one's foot and subsequently experiences pain, *that experience* is the proximal cause of one's writhing, cursing, and gnashing of teeth. Dropping a hammer on one's foot leads to pain behavior only if it causes in one the sensation of pain and the belief that one is in pain. If one were unconscious or otherwise oblivious to one's surroundings, then one could not sense any pain, nor could one believe that one were in pain. One could manifest no pain-related behavior either.

On the other hand, a neurophysiological view of the hammer-dropping incident seems be able to explain exactly the same events without appealing to mentality or any sort of psychological entities at all. Neurophysiologists might talk about how the intense pressure of the hammer head on a foot stimulates various nerve endings and thus causes action potentials to travel up a leg to a spinal column, where other nerves are then stimulated to fire. These nerves transmit the firing pattern to other nerves, and so it goes until nerves that cause muscles to contract are likewise stimulated and one gets the writhing, wincing, and teeth-gnashing behavior. Why doesn't the possibility of this sort of more precise, purely physical explanation rule out the higher-level, more general mental account? Or why doesn't it make the mental account nothing more than a placeholder until the details of our central nervous system get figured out? As long as one is persuaded by reductionism, then pain provides an exemplar case for why psychological explanations appear so tricky.

There is some evidence that depression is related to pain processing. One view is that untreatable chronic pain causes depression, which in turn increases the sensations of pain. This is a (grossly oversimplified) mentalistic explanation of how a mood causally interacts with other psychological states. At the same time, we know that depression is correlated with a decrease in the neurotransmitter serotonin. Persons suffering from just an imbalance of a neurotransmitter and sensations of pain are some neural state or other, then it seems that the relation between depression and pain should be explained in terms of neurotransmitters affecting neural activity. In this case, the mentalistic explanation is just a stand-in until all the more basic neurphysiological details are revealed.

Mental events causing other mental events seems to be a natural part of the explanatory world. At the same time, accounts of mental causation appear to be nothing over and above a sloppy characterization of more fine-grained and little understood physical details. The difficulty for those who would like to keep the mind intact as an explanatory unit is explicating how it is that mental causation has a legitimate place in an understanding of the universe above and beyond being a surrogate for the real causal story.

Though most philosophers of mind treat mental causation separately from issues concerning reference, explaining the causal powers of the mind really piggybacks on the problem of naturalizing content. What makes the question of mental causality peculiar is that the content of the mental states is relevant to their efficacy. One winces and nurses one's foot because one's corresponding mental states are about one's foot. If they were about something else, then one would most likely be doing something else. To explain exactly how it is that mental events cause other things, philosophers are first going to have to explain how it is they refer. That is, to justify privileging a mentalistic explanation of sensations and beliefs over a lower-level physicalistic one of neuronal firing patterns or ionic flow, first philosophers have to have a clear grasp on what it means to have mental events with content, since their content is what is causally relevant to subsequent behavior.

The question about the power of the content of beliefs and other mental states is quite important to understanding pain processing (Gamsa 1994). What one is thinking and believing about the world strongly influences how much pain one feels. Athletes intently focusing on their game can break large bones and not even notice it. But the same athletes, alone in their living rooms, will writhe on the floor if they stub their toes. Chronic pain patients can be trained to diminish their sensation of pain by changing their focus of attention and their beliefs about death and disease. Those suffering congenital indifference to pain often lead short and unpleasant lives both because they can't sense painful stimuli but also because they cannot form appropriate beliefs about the meaning of the vague tinglings they do feel. How pain feels depends to a large extent on the current doxastic milieu. Hence, understanding pain is going to require understanding what beliefs and desires (and other mental states) are and how they refer.

One implication of current scientific theories of pain is that folk ways of describing pains are inadequate and people would be better off eliminating the descriptors from everyday practices (Dennett 1978). The claim is that folkways of talking about pain comprise a rough and ready theory of pain. This theory assumes that pains are identical to the sensations of pain and that the word *pain* can capture the essence of that sensation. From the perspective of some objective views of pain, both assumptions are dubious. Pain processing is enormously complicated, and sensations of pain form only a tiny subset of what these processors do. But even if one focuses exclusively on sensations, the most important to folkways of being, the folk theory is still inadequate. Words to express all the dimensions of pain experiences simply do not exist. The descriptors used are either metaphorical or nonexistent. The folk theory of pain needs to be replaced by something commensurate with the phenomenology.

Consider that not only can the sensory, affective, and cognitive dimensions of pain be distinguished phenomenologically, but they can also be manipulated independently of one another. Mammals can feel a shooting pain in their legs but not suffer in the least from it; they can be in agony from pain without feeling any particular sensation localized to any part of their bodies. Philosophers could just decide by fiat that *pain* is going to refer to the localized sensations, or they could just decide that *pain* is going to refer to the suffering. But either way they do violence to folk notions of pain, which require that a single simple sense datum both seem to occur in some place and be unpleasant.

In response to these sorts of claims, some have argued that folk views of pain do not constitute a theory in any meaningful sense. Some believe that certain introspective facts are known indubitably. Pain is touted as one of those things. Perhaps there are some sensory states, like pain, about which people have special first-person apprehension; no inference of judgment is required.

However, it is quite easy to demonstrate that introspective knowledge of pain can be mistaken. If one burns one's hand by touching something hot, one jerks one's hand away from the heat source. This is a reflex action; the nociceptive information travels up the arm to the spinal column and then back down again. It takes about 20 to 40 msec from stimulus to behavior. The information also travels up the spinal column to the brain. One feels the burn as well. Unlike the reflex movement, this processing is more complicated and takes about 200 to 500 msec from stimulus to percept, a full order of magnitude longer.

Nevertheless, if one introspectively reports on what the incident feels like, one says that one moved one's hand away after one felt the pain; feeling pain initiated the motor sequence. For whatever reason, brains backdate pain sensations so that they seem causally relevant to reflex behavior. But clearly the effect is not caused after it occurs, so the introspective report has to be wrong. There is not any special, first-person knowledge of pains. Whatever knowledge is had is embedded and informed by a conceptual framework of the brains' devising. Despite protests to the contrary, pain experiences have all the earmarks of being at least prototheoretical in nature.

Other detractors point out that even if a completed science of pain does not use folk terms for pain, that would not imply that those sorts of mental states do not exist; they just would not be referred to in scientific discourse. The notion of pain would be analogous to ideas about tables and chairs, germs and gems, and birthday presents and birthday cake. These are perfectly legitimate terms. Science just does not use them. Being cultural artifacts of one stripe or another, they do not refer to things about which there are laws. There might not be a mental science or laws about pains, but folk psychology could still be used as it is now, in everyday explanations of behavior.

There is something undoubtedly right about this charge. In many ways, pain experiences are environmentally determined. Puppies raised without ever experiencing pain and without ever seeing any other dog in pain will exhibit no pain behavior. They will repeatedly sniff a lighted match without fear and then show no reaction when burned. Children learn both pain behaviors and the emotional concomitants to pain from the reactions of others around them. Expressions of pain and reports of sensation and experience are significantly different across cultures. Most of pain experiences and expressions are socially relative, a cultural artifact of sorts.

However, social relativity is not enough to show that folkways of understanding pain are adequate. Different cultures have different experiences; they also have different ways of understanding these experiences. Nevertheless, the burden falls on the folk psychologist to demonstrate how folk theories of pain are actually successful. This work has not just begun.

THE ETHICS OF PAIN TREATMENT

One of the most hotly debated subjects in pediatric care concerns whether infants are insensitive to pain (cf. Lawson 1988). The presumption historically has been that because young infants are not conscious, they cannot sense pain. As a result, analgesics and anesthesias are rarely used, even in the most invasive of procedures.

At first, this presumption of insensitivity is curious because infants' reactions to painful stimuli are well documented. Even premature neonates exhibit stress responses, hormonal fluctuations, and slowed recovery to painful interventions. In fact, the afferent nociceptive system is up and running by twenty-nine weeks of gestation, even though the pain inhibitory systems do not come on line until later. If anything, infants should be more sensitive to pain than adults. At least, by all indications, infants are sensitive to pain in some sense or other.

However, the question for many doctors is whether infants are aware of their pain. Some argue that unless neonates can consciously apprehend pain, then any sort of response they give to noxious stimuli are merely reflexes. Hence, there is no reason to treat infants' pain because the infants cannot feel anything.

Suppose they are right, even though there is much that goes on in brains that is neither conscious nor mere reflex. It is still the case that infants react to pain, both behaviorally and physiologically, that these reactions can be modified with relatively simple treatments, and that treating pain has an impact on recovery. Early exposure to pain, whether remembered or not, affects later experiences of and reactions to pain by altering the developmental course of the nervous system. Infants, like other newborn animals, learn to attach particular meanings or emotions or importance to particular experiences in virtue of what is associated with those experiences. This sort of behavioral malleability is very important if an organism is going to survive in a complex environment. Consequently, manipulating early experiences can have drastic effects later on, as animal studies show. Merely by changing the smells associated with suckling, scientists can alter adult sexual behavior in male rats, for example. Similar changes occur with pain processing in young infants. Nociceptive stimuli increase the size of the somatic receptive fields for neurons sensitive to pain and help maintain dendritic connections that would otherwise be eliminated over time. Perhaps, as some believe, chronic pain and hypersensitivity can result from early acute pain episodes, given how the neural receptors change. Early pain experiences have been shown to influence later personality and temperament. Something as common as circumcision can have lasting effects on pain sensitivity if done without anesthesia.

Given the impact early pain processing can have on later development, doctors have every reason to prevent infant pain, even if it feels dissimilar to an adult's, even if it feels like nothing at all to the infant. Whether infants consciously experience pain—and whether they are aware of some noxious stimulus or their own suffering—is a red herring. Available evidence converges around the idea that infants process pain, though perhaps not in the same way adults do. This processing has an impact on current behavior and later development. Because this influence is generally negative, insofar as we are able to prevent or alleviate some of their pain, we should.

See also Qualia.

Bibliography

Anand, K. J. S., and K. S. Craig. "New Perspectives on the Definition of Pain." *Pain* 67 (1996): 3–6.

Deberyshire, S. W. G. "Comment on Editorial by Anand and Craig." *Pain* 67 (1996): 210–211.

Dennett, D. C. "Why You Can't Make a Computer That Feels Pain." *Synthese* 38 (1978): 449.

Gamsa, A. "The Role of Psychological Factors in Chronic Pain, I and II." *Pain* 57 (1994): 5–29.

Hardcastle, V. G. *The Myth of Pain*. Cambridge, MA: The MIT Press, 1999.

International Association for the Study of Pain (IASP). Subcommittee on Classification. "Pain Terms: A Current List with Definitions and Notes on Usage." *Pain* (supplement) 3 (1986): 217.

Lawson, J. "Pain in the Neonate and Fetus." *New England Journal of Medicine* 318 (1988): 1, 398.

Wall, P. D., and R. Melzack, eds. *Textbook of Pain*. 2nd ed. New York: Churchill Livingstone, 1989.

Valerie Gray Hardcastle (2005)

PAIN, ETHICAL SIGNIFICANCE OF

Pain is a paradigm of an intrinsically bad mental state: It is an experience that is harmful to those who undergo it and makes their life go worse. Virtually all moral theories recognize norms to assist those who suffer from pain and to avoid inflicting unnecessary pain on others, though there is some disagreement about the source of these norms, their exact content, and their scope. The moral status of the pain of animals, for instance, remains a matter of controversy.

Pain has ethical significance when it is understood as an affective experience that is unpleasant or disliked in itself. Thus understood, pain belongs to a family of distinct but overlapping evaluative notions such as distress and suffering. The word "pain," however, is also used to refer to a type of bodily sensation typically associated with damage to body tissue. We normally find such sensations unpleasant, but when they are unaccompanied by an affective response (as reported by patients after frontal lobotomy) or when they are very mild, they are not experienced as unpleasant and no longer have this ethical significance. Furthermore, many hurtful experiences, both physical (nausea, electric shock) and mental (fear, regret) have a negative affective dimension without possessing the specific sensory quality common to cuts and burns. It is thus only pain in the broader, affective sense that is of direct interest to ethics.

The experience of pain is bad in itself but pain is also associated with other ills. Physical pain often accompanies bodily injury, and pain generally tends to incapacitate agents. It is important to distinguish the intrinsic badness of pain from these further harms. We also need to distinguish the badness of pain from a range of goods in which pain can play a part. Pain is instrumentally good insofar as it alerts us to bodily injury, for example. Many regard the painful aspect of just punishment as good, and some view pain as a necessary condition for the development of moral character and spiritual growth, for example. In all of these cases, however, pain can still be said to retain its badness for the agent. Thus pain justly inflicted on those who deserve it counts as punishment, and as good overall, only because it is also bad in itself for the offender. Other cases, such as masochism and the pain of grief, are harder to interpret.

Pain is often contrasted with hedonic states of positive value, such as pleasure and enjoyment. It should not be assumed, however, that pain and pleasure are simple contraries, since the occurrence or prospect of pain appears to have a different moral status, and to give reasons of greater force and urgency, than the occurrence or prospect of pleasure of equal intensity.

Pain also raises questions of ascription and measurement. It is often thought that subjects' sincere reports about their own pain are authoritative. There are also objective, largely behavioral criteria for ascribing pain. These used to be our exclusive means of detecting pain in animals and infants. These first- and third-person criteria seem ill-equipped, however, to deal with some of the cases reported by doctors and scientists, such as frontal lobotomy and hypnosis. The increased availability of devices that can directly detect the neural correlates of pain may present further challenges to our everyday practice of ascribing and assessing pain.

See also Happiness; Hedonism; Intrinsic Value; Pleasure.

Bibliography

Cassell, Eric J. *The Nature of Suffering and the Goals of Medicine.* New York: Oxford University Press, 1991.

Hare, Richard M. "Pain and Evil." In his *Essays on the Moral Concepts.* London: Macmillan, 1972.

Mayerfeld, Jamie. *Suffering and Moral Responsibility.* Oxford, U.K.: Oxford University Press, 1999.

Pitcher, George. "The Awfulness of Pain." *Journal of Philosophy* 68 (1970): 481–492.

Wall, Patrick. *Pain: The Science of Suffering.* London: Weidenfeld and Nicolson, 1999.

Guy Kahane (2005)

PAINE, THOMAS
(1737–1809)

Thomas Paine, the author, deist, and American revolutionary leader, was born at Thetford, Norfolk, in England. After an inconspicuous start in life as corset maker and customs officer, Paine emigrated at the age of thirty-seven from England to Philadelphia, carrying a letter of recommendation from Benjamin Franklin. Caught up almost immediately in the turmoil of the developing revolution, Paine published *Common Sense* (January 1776), the first public appeal for American independence as well as the pioneer enunciation of the diplomatic doctrine of avoiding European entanglements. In addition to attacking hereditary aristocracy, Paine expounded the theory that government and society are distinct entities and are not to be confounded, a theory also developed by Jean-Jacques Rousseau and later by William Godwin.

During subsequent stages of the American Revolution, Paine wrote a number of influential newspaper essays, including a famous series, the *Crisis,* concerned with particular political, economic, and military issues. In order to extend his reputation to Europe, Paine wrote the *Letter to the abbé Raynal, on the Affairs of North America*

(1783), refuting among other concepts of the French *philosophes,* the assertion that the Revolution concerned only economic issues and had no moral foundation. A confident affirmation of the idea of progress was incorporated in Paine's notions that the circle of civilization was soon to be completed and that commerce and science had already combined to improve the world to the point where there no longer existed a need to make war for profit.

After the American victory, Paine proceeded to France to seek financial support for an iron bridge of his own invention, once again carrying letters of recommendation from Franklin. In January 1790 he began a work defending Lafayette and the principles of the revolution that had broken out in France, a work that he later converted to an attack on Edmund Burke's highly critical *Reflections on the French Revolution.* The resulting treatise, *The Rights of Man* (Part I, 1791; Part II, 1792), gave a solid theoretical basis to the contingent appeals of Paine's American journalism. Affirming that government should be founded on reason rather than on tradition or precedent, Paine argued that democracy—a society in which all men have equal rights and in which leadership depends upon talent and wisdom—is superior to aristocracy. Although his political principles resemble those of John Locke, Paine later maintained that they were based entirely on his own reasoning and that he had never read the works of the English philosopher.

As a result of his republican writings, Paine was made an honorary citizen of France and in September 1792 he was elected to the French National Convention, taking his seat later that month.

Disturbed by the dogmatic atheism of the French revolutionary leaders, Paine began a treatise on religion, *The Age of Reason,* ostensibly a defense of deism but primarily an attack on Christianity. In Part I (1794), he rejected all forms of supernatural revelation in favor of the religion of nature, elevating, as he put it, reason and scientific observation over the three modes of superstition in Christianity: mystery, miracle, and prophecy. In Part II (1795), Paine continued to praise "the Perfection of the Deity," even though he exposed the abuses of Christianity with such vehemence that he brought upon himself the inaccurate accusation of opposing religion itself.

Although Paine dismissed the miracles of Christianity, he was later ready to believe that providence intervened in his own life. The story is incredible, but it reflects Paine's egoism. Because of his moderate policies in the Convention, particularly in an appeal to save Louis XVI from the guillotine, he was dismissed from the Convention and incarcerated in Luxembourg Prison. On his return to America, Paine explained that the cell doors of prisoners destined for execution were customarily marked with a number, and he argued that divine providence had protected him by causing his jailer to place the fatal number by mistake on the inside of his door so that it could not be seen the next morning.

One must turn to Paine's minor works to discover the positive side of his deism. His proof of the existence of God (in "A Discourse at the Society of Theophilanthropists") adopts essentially the same reasoning that Isaac Newton had used in a series of letters to an Anglican clergyman, Richard Bentley. Since the laws of mechanics, the argument runs, cannot explain the origin of motion, there must have been an external first cause to give the planets their original rotation. Paine stressed the concept of the plurality of worlds and assumed absolute moral laws. In "Private Thoughts on a Future State," he expressed a faith in an immortality strikingly different from that of most deists. The good people, he believed, would be happy in another world; the wicked would be punished; and those in between—the indifferent ones—would be "dropped entirely." Although contending that religion should be a private affair between each man and his creator, he insisted that no rational mind could logically reconcile new science and old Christianity.

Unable to adjust to French political life under Napoleon Bonaparte, Paine returned to America in 1802, where he was welcomed by liberal Jeffersonians but excoriated by most Federalists. Although he contributed extensively to newspapers under his revolutionary pseudonym of "Common Sense," he failed to regain his earlier influence and died in obscurity.

Paine, as much as any thinker of his age, was obsessed with the notion of the order and uniformity of nature, and he delighted in establishing parallels between one branch of learning and another. He believed that the fundamental laws of nature operative in religion, natural science, and politics were clear, simple, and within the reach of the average man. He developed no epistemology as such but combined a type of Quaker inner light with deistic reason. The fundamental weakness of his system—a weakness shared by most deists—is that he nowhere took up the problem of evil. Although he lavishly praised God for the regularity of the universe, the only suffering he noticed is that caused by social injustice.

Yet even though Paine was more influential as an agitator than as a theorist, he certainly understood and upheld the ideals of the Enlightenment and deserves to be ranked as one of America's outstanding *philosophes*.

See also Deism; Democracy; Egoism and Altruism; Enlightenment; Evil, The Problem of; Franklin, Benjamin; Godwin, William; Locke, John; Newton, Isaac; Political Philosophy, History of; Rousseau, Jean-Jacques.

Bibliography

WORKS BY PAINE

Writings of Thomas Paine. 4 vols, edited by Moncure D. Conway. New York. 1894–1896.
Complete Writings of Thomas Paine. 2 vols, edited by Philip S. Foner. New York: Citadel Press, 1945.

WORKS ON PAINE

Aldridge, Alfred Owen. *Man of Reason: The Life of Thomas Paine.* New York, 1959.
Ayer, A. J. *Thomas Paine.* Chicago: University of Chicago Press, 1988.
Claeys, Gregory. *Thomas Paine: Social and Political Thought.* London: Routledge, 1989.
Conway, Moncure D. *Life of Thomas Paine.* 2 vols. New York: Putnam, 1892.
Dyck, Ian, ed. *Citizen of the World: Essays on Thomas Paine.* New York: St. Martin's Press, 1988.
Foner, Eric. *Tom Paine and Revolutionary America.* Oxford: Oxford University Press, 1976.
Russell, Bertrand. "The Fate of Thomas Paine." In *Why I Am Not a Christian.* New York: Simon and Schuster, 1957.

Alfred Owen Aldridge (1967)
Bibliography updated by Christian B. Miller (2005)

PALÁGYI, MENYHERT
(1859–1924)

Menyhert (or Melchior) Palágyi, a scientist, literary critic, and philosopher, was born in Paks in west central Hungary. He studied science at Budapest, but his main activity there was as a literary critic. After 1900 he spent much time in Germany, studying informally with philosophers in many places. For a time he held a readership in physics and mathematics in Kolozsvár, Hungary (now Cluj-Napoca, Romania). He had little contact with Hungarian philosophers, however, and eventually returned to Germany, where he died in Darmstadt.

Throughout Palágyi's philosophical works, psychological doctrines and speculations on theoretical physics are mingled with his main interest in epistemology. He interpreted and criticized the then new theory of relativity from the point of view of epistemology, and epistemology from the point of view of his psychological theory. As he expressed his views in response to the new developments in these fields, he became somewhat lost in their transitional stages, and the fact that he criticized them from his own particular standpoint hindered his understanding of them. The central dominating idea throughout his works is a broadly Hegelian principle of polarity. It asserts an interdependence of opposites, a sort of cooperative unity, and it was applied by Palágyi with no apparent consistency and even more liberally than Hegelian dialectics would be. Palágyi was a monist who held a curious version of the denial of the distinction between the a priori and a posteriori.

His most purely philosophical work is *Der Streit der Psychologisten und Formalisten in der modernen Logik* (Leipzig, 1902). In it, among other things, he criticized Edmund Husserl for "tearing" logic away from psychology and "submerging" it in mathematics, and for his "ideal meaning" and his distinction between real and ideal laws. (Husserl himself reviewed this book in *Zeitschrift für Psychologie und Physik des Sinnesorgane* 31 [1903].) In the same year Palágyi wrote his *Die Logik auf dem Scheidewege* ("Logic at the Crossroads," Berlin and Leipzig, 1903). In these works Palágyi's main concern was not, despite his criticisms of Husserl, a return to psychologism but his principle of polarity. In his psychology, in fact, he tried to rescue from psychologism that which he termed "mental" (even though he only obscurely described the term). The source of all error is to mistake what is mental for what is merely vital (and, in the spirit of "polarity," what is vital for what is merely mental). He distinguished between mechanical and vital processes and consciousness. The mechanical is publicly observable, and the vital indirectly observable, but consciousness escapes observation by the methods applicable to the other processes: consciousness "punctuates" the vital process and is discontinuous. (He nevertheless explicitly affirmed the unity of the self, although it is doubtful how he could maintain this.) Our knowledge depends on the speed of these punctuations. God is the limiting case who grasps the whole time process instantaneously; for him all punctuations are one. This led Palágyi to such metaphysical claims as that our knowledge catches eternity in the fleeting moment, which is both temporal and eternal.

At the base of this theory of perception was his notion of imagined movement. Touch being the basic sense, all perception depends on our ability to trace the object in the imagination. He mistakenly supported this view by reference to the Kantian role of imagination in perception. His theoretical physics, in which his main interest was our perception of space-time (space-time being a unity in polarity), can best be understood if approached through this theory of perception.

See also A Priori and A Posteriori; Epistemology; Hegelianism; Husserl, Edmund; Imagination; Philosophy of Physics; Psychologism; Relativity Theory; Touch.

Bibliography

Ausgewahlte Werke, 3 vols. (Leipzig, 1924–1925), contains Palágyi's most important works.

Works on Palágyi are Werner Deubel, "Die Philosophie und Weltmechanik von Melchior Palágyi," in *Preussische Jahrbuch* 203 (1926): 329–356, with complete bibliography; W. R. Boyce Gibson, "The Philosophy of Melchior Palágyi," in *Journal of Philosophical Studies* 3 (1928): 15–28, 158–172; L. W. Schneider, *Der erste Periode in philosophischen Schaffen M. Palágyis* (Würzburg, 1942); and A. Wurmb, *Darstellung und Kritik der logische Grundbegriffe der Naturphilosophie Melchior Palágyis* (Leipzig, 1931).

Julius Kovesi (1967)

PALEY, WILLIAM
(1743–1805)

William Paley was an English theologian and moral philosopher. His father, William, was vicar of Helpston, Northamptonshire, and a minor canon of Peterborough; he later became headmaster of Giggleswick grammar school, where the younger Paley was educated. Paley entered Christ's College, Cambridge, in 1759, where he studied mathematics and became a senior wrangler. After an interlude of school teaching, he was elected a fellow of his college in 1766 and was ordained a priest in the established church in 1767. He taught at Cambridge for nine years, leaving the university only on his marriage. He held successively a number of different offices in the church, rising to be the archdeacon of Carlisle. Paley was the author of three books, one on morals and two defending Christian belief, all of which were widely read and accepted as textbooks. As late as 1831, Charles Darwin, studying for his BA examination at Cambridge, had to "get up" Paley's *A View of the Evidences of Christianity*, *The Principles of Moral and Political Philosophy*, and *Natural Theology*. The *Moral and Political Philosophy* contains Paley's famous satire on property, in which he describes the plight of a flock of pigeons in which private property is permitted. Although he immediately proceeds to list the advantages of a system of private property, his satire is savage ("the weakest perhaps, and worst pigeon of the flock" controls and wastes all the grain as he pleases), and Paley's friends are said to have assured him (correctly) that the publication of the passage would cost him a bishopric. It did earn him the nickname "Pigeon Paley."

Paley's *The Principles of Moral and Political Philosophy* (London, 1785) is a handbook on the duties and obligations of civil life rather than a philosophical treatise. The subtlety of the work may be gauged by its opening sentence: "Moral philosophy, Morality, Ethics, Casuistry, Natural Law, mean all the same thing; namely, that science which teaches men their duty and the reasons of it." Paley's definition of duty follows from his theological utilitarianism. The nature of the human frame implies that it is God's will for us to be happy in this life as well as in the next. Virtue is doing good to humankind, in obedience to the will of God and for the sake of everlasting happiness. Allegiance to God's will and a desire for everlasting happiness are sufficient grounds for moral obligation. Paley offers this account of moral obligation after finding that such obligation follows from the command of a superior, which is made persuasive by the prospect of a reward.

We may discover the will of God by consulting either Scripture or "the light of nature," both of which lead to the same conclusion. The will of God with regard to any action may be found by inquiring into its "tendency to promote or diminish the general happiness." We should carry out those actions that promote the general happiness and avoid those which diminish it. Promoting the general happiness requires paying attention to the general consequences of our actions. Paley offers a rule for assessing general consequences that resembles Immanuel Kant's categorical imperative: "The general consequence of any action may be estimated by asking what would be the consequence if the same sort of actions were generally permitted."

Paley believed that no special faculty is required to enable us to have moral knowledge. Thus he dismissed the views of those who have argued that morality requires either a moral sense, or an intuitive perception of right and wrong, or any other innate or instinctive capacity. All that is required for the foundation of morality is that each man has the wit to see that certain actions are beneficial to himself. Then the sentiment of approbation that naturally arises when these actions benefit him will continue to accompany his perception of these actions when they benefit someone else. Thus the custom of approving certain actions is begun, and children, who learn everything by imitating their elders, carry it on.

The bulk of the *Principles* is a detailed discussion of our duties to others, to ourselves, and to God. The final part is an outline of the elements of political knowledge. The wide acclaim accorded Paley's work is said to have stirred Jeremy Bentham to bring out his own version of the utilitarian doctrine in *Introduction to the Principles of Morals and Legislation* (1789).

Paley is the author of two theological works with the word *evidence* in their titles. The first, *A View of the Evidences of Christianity* (2 vols., London, 1794), is an essay in apologetics. The second, *Natural Theology; or, Evidences of the Existence and Attributes of the Deity, Collected from the Appearances of Nature* (London, 1802), is, as its title implies, an essay on natural theology. The books, which are similar in tone (they are both presented as judicious, lawyerlike statements of a case) doubtless owe much to Paley's lifelong interest in trials and the art of advocacy.

A View of the Evidences of Christianity demonstrates what can be said on behalf of Christian belief by an appeal to the behavior of the earliest Christians. Paley asks his readers to grant the possibility that God should have destined his human creation for a future state and that he should acquaint human beings with their destiny. If these possibilities are granted, then the need for miracles is clear, for they are the certification of revelation. The credibility of the Christian revelation hangs, therefore, on the issue of whether its miracles are genuine.

It is Paley's claim that the miracles on which Christianity is based (including those of the Old Testament) are genuine; and that indeed the only genuine miracles are those of Christianity (including its Jewish origins). Paley accepts David Hume's contention that the believability of Christianity rests ultimately on the reliability of the testimony of the earliest Christians, but he rejects Hume's thesis that no testimony for a miracle can ever be relied on because such testimony goes against universal experience. He argues that universal experience is too strong a test. By definition, miracles must be exceptions to universal experience or they would not be miracles. The real issue is whether there is a test for the reliability of witnesses who report an event that necessarily only they could have experienced. Paley finds such a test in our observation of whether the person who reports a miracle will cling to his report at the risk of his comfort, his happiness, and even his life. According to Paley, the original witnesses of the Christian miracles pass this test, since they labored and suffered "in attestation of the accounts which they delivered, and solely in consequence of their belief of these accounts."

Paley's hospitality for miracles is not quite so broad as we might at first think. The miraculous event must be in support of a revelation that is important to human happiness. Mere wonders are thus ruled out; and Paley also holds out against any event that may be resolved into a false perception and against any report that is guilty of exaggeration. But even after setting these limits, Paley maintains that a significant core of miracles stands as the guaranty of the Christian revelation. But the acceptance of these miracles must finally rest on the steadfastness of the original Christians; and the weakness of Paley's argument can be seen when we consider its close resemblance to a lawyer's defending his client by calling for the testimony of none but character witnesses. *A View of the Evidences of Christianity* had a huge success, and the bishops made Paley a prebendary of St. Pancras in the Cathedral of St. Paul's and the subdean of Lincoln.

In his *Natural Theology,* Paley appeals to a number of natural phenomena to establish the existence of a god. He states his argument at the very outset, and the remainder of the work is a train of examples illustrating that argument. The line of the argument runs as follows. If I found a stone while crossing a heath, and if I "were asked how the stone came to be there, I might possibly answer, that, for any thing I knew to the contrary, it had lain there forever; nor would it perhaps be very easy to show the absurdity of this answer. But suppose I had found a watch upon the ground, and it should be enquired how the watch happened to be in that place, I should hardly think of the answer which I had before given, that, for anything I knew, the watch might have always been there. Yet why should not this answer serve for the watch, as well as for the stone?" Paley answers, "For this reason, and for no other, viz. that when we come to inspect the watch, we perceive (what we could not discover in the stone) that its several parts are framed and put together for a purpose"—that is, to tell the time. The care with which the parts have been made and the fineness of their adjustment can have only one implication, namely, that the watch must have had a maker who understood its construction and who designed it for the use for which it is fitted. The conclusion would not be weakened if we had never seen a watch being made or could not conceive of how to make one. Nor would it be weakened if there were parts of the watch whose purpose we could not understand, or even if we could not ascertain whether these parts had some effect in the general purpose of the watch. Nor should we be satisfied if we were told either that the existence of the watch is to be explained by a principle of order which exists in things and disposes the parts of the watch into their present form and situation, or that the

watch is the result of the laws of "metallic nature." Finally, we should be surprised to hear that the mechanism of the watch is no proof of contrivance, but "only a motive to induce the mind to think so." In short, where there is mechanism, instrumentality, or contrivance, there must have been an intelligence who designed and made the machine, the instrument, the contrivance.

Paley then turns to nature with this argument in hand and, in his own words, applies it to adduce evidences of the existence of God. The bones and muscles of human beings, animals, and their insect equivalents, are of special interest to Paley, for the fitting together of joints and the adaptation of muscles are mechanisms that imply most forcefully a designing intelligence. The chemical side of physiology does not interest him much, for chemical action does not suggest the work of a divine mechanic. But Kiell's *Anatomy* is ransacked for appropriate examples, and the hare's backbone is picked apart at the end of the meat course to show the finesse of divine contrivance. The example that most interests Paley, and to which he often returns, is the eye, in its various parts and in the combination of these parts and their adaptation to function as an instrument of sight. As he remarks, he offers many examples of natural mechanism, but a single instance, the eye alone, should suffice to convince us of the existence of the divine intelligence that designed it.

The evidence drawn from nature, in addition to establishing the existence of God, permits us to infer certain of his characteristics. Because God has a mind, he must be a person. That there is a single intelligence at work is shown by the uniformity of the divine plan, as it is applied to all parts of the world. Finally, God's goodness is shown both by the fact that most contrivances are beneficial and by the fact that pleasure has been made an animal sensation.

At bottom, Paley's argument rests on his original decision to regard certain parts of nature as mechanisms or contrivances. If this decision is unquestioned, then his argument takes a long stride toward plausibility. Everything depends, however, on whether the human eye, for example, is analogous to a machine, and if so, how far this analogy takes us in the inference of other characteristics that the analogy might imply. These questions are raised and examined with devastating effect by Hume in the *Dialogues concerning Natural Religion,* a work published a quarter of a century before Paley's *Natural Theology.* It is to be regretted that Paley does not meet Hume's arguments head-on in the *Natural Theology,* in the same way that he meets Hume squarely on the issue of the believability of miracles in *A View of the Evidences of Christianity.*

See also Bentham, Jeremy; Darwin, Charles Robert; Hume, David; Kant, Immanuel; Miracles; Moral Sense; Revelation; Teleological Argument for the Existence of God; Utilitarianism.

Bibliography

WORKS BY PALEY

William Paley's collected writings are in *Works*, 8 vols. (London, 1805–1808). See also his *Natural Theology*, edited by Frederick Ferré (Indianapolis: Bobbs-Merrill, 1963).

WORKS ON PALEY

Barker, Ernest. "Paley and his Political Philosophy." In *Traditions of Civility.* Cambridge, U.K.: Cambridge University Press, 1948.

Clarke, Martin. *Paley: Evidences for the Man.* Toronto: University of Toronto Press, 1974.

LeMahieu, Dan. *The Mind of William Paley.* Lincoln: University of Nebraska Press, 1976.

Nuovo, Victor. "Rethinking Paley." *Synthese* 91 (1992): 29–51.

Oppy, Graham. "Paley's Argument for Design." *Philo* 5 (2002): 161–173.

Schneewind, Jerome. *Sidgwick's Ethics and Victorian Moral Philosophy.* Oxford: Clarendon Press, 1977.

Sweet, William. "Paley, Whately, and 'Enlightenment Evidentialism.'" *International Journal for Philosophy of Religion* 45 (1999): 143–166.

Elmer Sprague (1967)
Bibliography updated by Christian B. Miller (2005)

PALMER, ELIHU
(1764–1806)

Elihu Palmer was a radical spokesman for the Age of Reason and Revolution in America, who along with Thomas Paine and Ethan Allen gave expression to the ideals of deism and republicanism. Born in Canterbury, Connecticut, Palmer was graduated from Dartmouth in 1787. Originally a minister, he was persecuted for his extreme religious views and forced to flee the pulpit. In 1793 he was admitted to the bar. Blinded by disease, he spent the last years of his life defending deism. He edited the deistic weekly journal *Prospect, or View of the Moral World* and helped to organize the Deistical Society in New York.

Palmer's religious radicalism stemmed from his reaction to Calvinism. He rejected the doctrine of original sin as well as the idea of a punitive and arbitrary divine being. This reaction developed into a militant anti-Christianity and anticlericalism. Palmer rejected the claims of divine revelation, miracles, and prophesies, and he accused the Bible of inconsistency, contradiction, and vagueness. Not only did he deny the divinity of Christ, but he considered Jesus, Moses, and Muḥammad indecent and immoral and Christian salvation absurd and irrational. He attacked organized and institutionalized religion for its hypocrisy and self-interest.

Like other deists, Palmer defended a religion of nature, in which the order and harmony of the universe is believed to proclaim the existence of one supreme being, the divine creator. Palmer maintained that evil is not inherent in man or in nature but is due to corrupt social institutions and to defective human knowledge, which can both be corrected. He had boundless faith and optimism in reason, science, and education, believing that man possesses the capacities for intellectual and moral progress. In place of the traditional religious depreciation of human ability and dignity, he proposed a humanistic ethics. With others of this period, he held an empiricist epistemology, locating the source of all knowledge in sensation, and he was sympathetic to scientific and materialistic philosophy. Palmer was an ardent supporter of liberty and republicanism and saw in the American Revolution the inception of a new era for humanity.

See also Deism; Paine, Thomas; Progress, The Idea of; Republicanism.

Bibliography

Palmer's works include *Political Miscellany* (New York, 1793); *The Examiners Examined: Being a Defence of the Age of Reason* (New York: Printed for the author and sold by L. Wayland and J. Fellows, 1794); *An Enquiry Relative to the Moral and Political Improvement of the Human Species* (New York: John Crookes, 1797); *The Political Happiness of Nations: An Oration* (New York: n.p., 1800); *Principles of Nature: Or, a Development of the Moral Causes of Happiness and Misery among the Human Species* (New York, 1801); *Prospect, or View of the Moral World for the Year 1804* (New York: E. Palmer, 1803–1805), which he edited; and *Posthumous Pieces* (London, 1826).

For literature on Palmer, see G. Adolf Koch, *Republican Religion: The American Revolution and the Cult of Reason* (New York: Holt, 1933).

Paul Kurtz (1967)

PANAETIUS OF RHODES
(c. 185–110 BCE)

Panaetius of Rhodes was a pupil of Diogenes of Babylon and Antipater of Tarsus, both heads of the Stoic school in

Athens, and he succeeded Antipater as scholarch in 129. Little is known about his life though it is clear that he spent considerable time in Rome and in the circle of P. Cornelius Scipio Aemilianus. None of his writings survive, but traces of his importance do.

First, isolated testimony from antiquity reveals that Panaetius was especially willing to disagree with earlier Stoics about central matters of doctrine. He rejected the Stoic belief in divination, and against the earlier account that the cosmos would be consumed periodically in flames, he insisted that the world is everlasting. He maintained that virtue is not sufficient for happiness, since health, some resources, and strength are also necessary, and he divided virtues into the contemplative and practical, which sits uneasily with traditional Stoic intellectualism.

These examples suggest that Panaetius was keen to incorporate more Platonic and especially Aristotelian doctrines into his Stoicism, and many ancient sources directly attest to this desire. This feature of Panaetius's philosophy links him to his pupil Posidonius, the polymath who showed similar willingness to infuse pre-Stoic ideas into his Stoicism. Together, Panaetius and Posidonius have been taken to epitomize Middle Stoicism, which stands between early Greek Stoicism and later Roman Stoicism, but this periodization is of limited utility because there are more than three ancient Stoicisms. Nevertheless, the affinities between Panaetius and Posidonius distinguish them from most other Stoics. Their broadly shared approach is also linked to the syncretizing philosophy of the first century BCE that is typified by Antiochus of Ascalon. Such thought has been disparaged as *eclectic*, but there is nothing unworthy in the attempt to produce a well-grounded synthesis of a rich and varied philosophical tradition.

The second trace of Panaetius is due to Cicero, who has characters call Panaetius "a great and extremely learned man" (*Leg* III 14) and "chief among the Stoics" (*Acad* II 107). Cicero based the first two books of his *On Duties* (*De Officiis* on Panaetius's *On Duty or Appropriate Action* (*Peri tou kathêkontos*), and this makes Panaetius influential since, as Henry Sidgwick notes: "There is probably no ancient treatise which has done more than [Cicero's] *De Officiis* to communicate a knowledge of ancient morality to medieval and modern Europe" (Sidgwick 1902, p. 95).

Among the prominent features of *De Officiis* that are likely due to Panaetius, the following three are especially important. First, Cicero notes that anyone who is beneficent must choose his beneficiaries carefully, and he insists that one should help some people more just because one stands in a naturally closer relationship with them. He develops the point by suggesting a hierarchy of natural relationships, from the closest (marriage) to the most remote (the relationship one shares with all other human beings). The later Stoic Hierocles imagines the hierarchy as a series of concentric circles, but Cicero's version of the probably Panaetian idea that one's duties of beneficence are tied to certain relational facts independent of how one feels about those relationships has proven enormously influential.

Second, after identifying the traditional virtue of temperance or moderation with seemliness (*decorum*), Cicero insists that to display *decorum*, one must act in accordance with all of one's roles (*personae*). So, one must consider not only the role that all human beings share in common but also the particular role one has on account of one's peculiar natural talents. Additionally, one must consider the role that fortune assigns by giving one power, wealth, standing, and their opposites, and one must consider the demands of the role one chooses by taking up a particular career. With this schema, Cicero, no doubt inspired by Panaetius, takes the traditional Stoic concern to act appropriately in the particular circumstances, and he incorporates special attention to the ways in which social roles and individual talents matter to the circumstances.

Third, Cicero spends much of *De Officiis* II providing advice about how to pursue honor or glory. Earlier Stoics generally agreed that although honor might be useful, it has no intrinsic attraction. Cicero rejects that view in favor of a more Platonic line, according to which humans are naturally drawn to honor. Because the honorable is dependent upon what other people honor, this line generally ties one's pursuit of natural aims to the values of others in one's society. It also represents an especially concrete way in which the Panaetian approach of Cicero's *De Officiis* moves away from the paradoxical excellences of the early Stoics' sage and closer to the virtues of Roman politicians.

There is a final trace of Panaetius's importance, for he seems to be central to the eventual diffusion of Stoic thought. Most obviously, as a member of the Scipionic Circle, Panaetius helped to spread Stoicism in Rome. More speculatively, one might think that he contributed decisively to the decentralization of the Stoic school. There is no record that Panaetius had a successor as head of the Stoic school in Athens. His student Posidonius attracted pupils not to Athens but to Rhodes, which, curiously enough, was Panaetius's but not Posidonius's hometown. Did Panaetius arrange to have the school leave Athens? Did he otherwise let it die? Whatever his intentions, later Stoics studied and taught in a variety of places around the Mediterranean, and Stoicism continued to seep into a broad array of intellectual currents.

See also Antiochus of Ascalon; Aristotle; Cicero, Marcus Tullius; Diogenes Laertius; Plato; Posidonius; Sidgwick, Henry; Stoicism.

Bibliography

Cicero, Marcus Tullius. *Acadamica*. Hildesheim, Gg. Olma, 1966.

Cicero, Marcus Tullius. *On Duties* (*De Officiis*), edited by M. T. Griffin and E. M. Atkins. Cambridge, U.K.: Cambridge University Press, 1991.

Cicero, Marcus Tullius. *On the Commonwealth; and, On the Laws*, edited by James E.G. Zetzel. New York: Cambridge University Press, 1999.

Sidgwick, Henry. *Outlines of the History of Ethics for English Readers*. London: Macmillan, 1902.

TEXTS

Alesse, F. *Panezio di Rodi e la Tradizione Stoica*. Naples: Bibliopolis, 1994.

Straaten, M. van, ed. *Panaetii Rhodii Fragmenta*. Leiden: E. J. Brill, 1952.

Straaten, M. van. *Panétius*. Amsterdam: H. J. Paris, 1946.

STUDIES

Gill, Christopher. "Panaetius on the Virtue of Being Yourself." In *Images and Ideologies: Self-Definition in the Hellenistic World*, edited by A. Bulloch, et al. Berkeley: University of California Press, 1993, pp. 330–353.

Gill, Christopher. "Personhood and Personality: The Four-Personae Theory in Cicero, *De Officiis*." In *Oxford Studies in Ancient Philosophy*. Vol. VI. Oxford: Oxford University Press, 1988, pp. 169–199.

Eric Brown (2005)

PANENTHEISM

See *Emanationism; Krause, Karl Christian Friedrich*

PANNENBERG, WOLFHART
(1928–)

The thought of Wolfhart Pannenberg follows in the tradition of twentieth-century German systematic theology in replying to the secularizing nature of post-Enlightenment thought. Pannenberg's writings, however, unlike those of his near contemporaries, most notably Karl Barth and Rudolf Bultmann, do not reject the characteristic intel-lectual developments of Enlightenment thought. Rather, Pannenberg seeks to incorporate many of the key components of the Enlightenment into his comprehensive theological world view. Born in 1928, Pannenberg began his education as the University of Berlin. In 1950 he studied theology under Barth in Basle, and in 1951 he moved to Heidelberg where he completed his doctoral studies on the doctrine of predestination in Duns Scotus. Following this, he took up a teaching post at Heidelberg, later becoming Professor of Systematic Theology successively at Wuppertal, Mainz, and finally, in 1968, Munich.

Pannenberg's philosophical development was transformed by what he has described as an "intellectual conversion" to Christianity. This conversion, which was driven by his reading of philosophical as well as theological texts in his youth, has had two important influences on the development of his thought. First, Pannenberg's initial concerns are not with the Church and ecclesial theology. Instead, his thought centers on the role of religious experience on the individual within a created world defined by God. This *anthropological* aspect to Pannenberg's thought lies at the heart of his theological and philosophical system. Second, Pannenberg has been more receptive than many of his contemporaries in understanding and the developments in secular philosophical thought. Through all his writings, Pannenberg argues that many of the problems of modern secular thought can be resolved if God is reestablished as the defining principle of all creation. Pannenberg's most profound contribution to this debate has been through his dialogue with the secular aspects of critical history and latterly with the philosophy of science.

THE ANTHROPOLOGY OF RELIGIOUS EXPERIENCE

The starting point of Pannenberg's thought is his anthropological account of religious belief. Pannenberg's thought is based on the belief that God can be found naturally and freely within all aspects of human experience. This anthropological approach comes out most clearly in Pannenberg's 1983 work *Anthropology in Theological Perspective*. His main impetus in approaching theological questions in this manner is to address directly the implicit atheism of much post-Enlightenment thought. Pannenberg argues that the philosophical atheism of the Left-Hegelians, especially Ludwig Feuerbach, is in essence misguided anthropology. The philosophical atheism of Feuerbach defines God as merely the creation of the historically developing human mind. Pannenberg takes issue with this, arguing that it crucially misinterprets the place and role of God in human thought. By concentrating on the social and cultural uses of religious forms and structures, Pannenberg argues that the Left-Hegelians were able to dismiss these as constructs of the alienated human mind. Therefore Feuerbach, in particular, was able to collapse theology into anthropology, asserting the form of the divine as God simply a construct of the human mind (Pannenberg 1973, p. 87).

To counter this powerful philosophical criticism of theology and religion, Pannenberg argues that we must consider humans in the first instance without recourse to religious categories or structures. He argues that such an approach is a necessary part of thinking about religion in the post-Enlightenment world, because the Enlightenment moved humans away from the traditional structures and forms of religious belief. Consequently, Pannenberg argues, we must look for God in all parts of human experience, not simply those that are exclusively religious. This approach, which he characteristically describes as coming to God "from below," places Pannenberg in opposition to the theology of Barth. Barth's solution to the dilemma presented by philosophical atheism was to stress God as "Wholly Other," inaccessible to man accept through the initiative of Jesus Christ.

Pannenberg argues that it is self-contradictory to talk of God in a manner that makes him completely inaccessible to humans. If God is the creative force of all creation, he must be accessible to people in all parts of creation. In the first instance one is able to come to this realization, Pannenberg argues, through a process of self-examination. By carrying out this anthropological enquiry, Pannenberg believes that people are able to recognize in themselves transcendent categories such as imagination that draw the human mind above and beyond a simple, mundane corporeal existence. It is through grasping this natural sense of transcendence that the human mind first comes to comprehend the existence of God. In doing this, Pannenberg is not rejecting traditional theological forms; rather he argues that the natural human desire to comprehend the divine is driven by very real human characteristics that God places in the human mind. Pannenberg's anthropology of religious experience places him between the philosophical atheism of the Left-Hegelians and the Christian supremacy of Barth, stressing the real existence of the divine in all parts of the created world, a world in which humans are intimately and definitively involved.

HISTORY AS REVELATION

Pannenberg's primary contribution to the philosophy of religion has been in his attempts to build on this anthropological position to show the unity of human history with the experience God. Pannenberg's work on this subject is, in the first instance, a reaction to post-Enlightenment critical history. It is also defined in reaction to the rejection of historicism as a category within theology by Barth and, in particular, Bultmann. Pannenberg rejects the belief that historical research, even in areas such as the historical Jesus, do not provide any theological insight. Pannenberg argues that if God is the author of creation, he must be discernible in all parts of creation. Therefore to stress the eschatological and a historic nature of Christ as Bultmann does, is to remove God from the created world that is, by definition historical in form (Pannenberg 1970, p. 87).

The culmination of this work was the publication in 1961 of *Revelation as History*. In this collection of essays, which Pannenberg edited and contributed to, Pannenberg argues that theology, correctly understood, can reconcile the Hegelian understanding of history as the self-disclosure of the *Absolute* with twentieth-century developments in secular critical history. Pannenberg believes he is able to reconcile these two opposing understandings of history by stressing what he believes to be the defining principle of the human history: the desire to comprehend oneself within the created world in which we live. This essentially dialectical understanding of history, Pannenberg argues, underpins the subject areas, method, and approach of secular, critical history. At the most basic level, he argues, the modern secular historian makes judgments about the place and role of actions and events on history. Through this intellectual judgment the historian is implicitly assuming, Pannenberg's argues, that human history has a fundamental source and purpose. Consequently, the narrowly defined terms of critical history always assume, even at the most basic level, the existence of a suprahistorical intellectual structure. No historical person or event can define this structure; this can only be achieved by God who transcends and encompasses all history within himself. Pannenberg therefore believes one can reconcile theology with history if one accepts that they are different methods of understanding the self-disclosure of God within history. Therefore when we engage with the historical world in any way we are, by definition, understanding something of God's revelation to the world.

The Hegelian basis of this argument is clear; however, Pannenberg differs crucially from Hegel in two key components with his argument. First, looking back to his anthropology, Pannenberg asserts a narrower understanding of human reason than the version of reason we find in Hegel. This allows Pannenberg to retain a greater critical distance between the rational nature of God and ability of human reason to comprehend form and nature of God. Second, Pannenberg argues that although God reveals himself to humankind through the process of history this is, unlike in Hegel, not a necessary, but rather a contingent relationship. This more orthodox understanding of the human faculties and of God's relation to creation allows Pannenberg to reclaim something of the Hegelian understanding of universal history from the Left-Hegelian conflation of the God of universal history into anthropology.

This historicism has, inevitably, created new problems that Pannenberg's thought has not fully answered. Most importantly, Pannenberg's view of the contingent nature of God to human history opens up the problem of how to account for the existence of evil in a divinely ordained world. Pannenberg has countered, and to a limited extent answered this criticism by stressing that one has to understand the positive nature of human endeavor and action before one can understand the perversions. That is, we can only understand why humans turn from God if we first know how we are defined in relationship to God in the first instance (Tupper 1973).

CONCLUSION

The culmination of Pannenberg's intellectual output came with the publication of his three-volume *Systematic Theology* between 1988 and 1993. In this work, which completes the intellectual process begun in his earliest writings, Pannenberg argues that the pursuit of truth, the fundamental object of theology, can only come about within a rigorous and thoroughgoing philosophical framework. Through this framework Pannenberg has argued that it is possible to reconcile scientific research to theology in much the same way as he argues the critical history can be brought into the theological understanding of universal history. By stressing the systematically metaphysical form of theology, Pannenberg argues that theology can save science from intellectual narcissism by providing the overarching structure of truth within which the specific insights of scientific research can be comprehended. Although perhaps not as influential as his writings on theology and history, this engagement with modern science highlights the refreshing willingness, identifiable in all Pannenberg's work, to enter into dialogue with those intellectual disciplines of the post-Enlightenment world that sit outside the traditional corpus of religious and theological thought.

See also Barth, Karl; Bultmann, Rudolf; Duns Scotus, John; Enlightenment; Feuerbach, Ludwig Andreas; Hegel, Georg Wilhelm Friedrich; Hegelianism; Historicism; Philosophy of Religion; Philosophy of Science, History of; Philosophy of Science, Problems of.

Bibliography

WORKS BY PANNENBERG

Jesus—God and Man. Translated by Lewis L. Wilkins and Duane Priebe. London: SCM Press, 1968.

Revelation as History, edited by Wolfhart Pannenberg. Translated by David Granskou. New York: Macmillan, 1968.

What Is Man? Translated by Duane A. Priebe. Philadelphia: Fortress Press, 1970.

Basic Questions in Theology. 3 vols. Translated by George H. Kelm. London: SCM Press, 1970–1973.

Theology and the Philosophy of Science. Translated by Francis McDonagh. London: Darton, Longman and Todd, 1976.

Anthropology in Theological Perspective. Translated by Matthew J. O'Connell. Philadelphia: Westminster, 1985.

Christianity in a Secularized World. Translated by John Bowden. London: SCM, 1989.

Systematic Theology. 3 vols. Translated by Geoffrey W. Bromiley. Edinburgh, U.K.: T and T Clark, 1991–1998.

WORKS ABOUT PANNENBERG

Galloway, Allan D. *Wolfhart Pannenberg*. London: Allen and Unwin, 1973.

Tupper, Frank E. *The Theology of Wolfhart Pannenberg*. Philadelphia: Westminster Press, 1973. Contains a postscript by Wolfhart Pannenberg.

Benjamin Carter (2005)

PANPSYCHISM

"Panpsychism" is the theory according to which all objects in the universe, not only human beings and animals but also plants and even objects we usually classify as "inanimate," have an "inner" or "psychological" being. The German philosopher and psychologist G. T. Fechner wrote:

> I stood once on a hot summer's day beside a pool and contemplated a water-lily which had spread its leaves evenly over the water and with an open blossom was basking in the sunlight. How exceptionally fortunate, thought I, must this lily be which above basks in the sunlight and below is plunged in the water—if only it might be capable of feeling the sun and the bath. And

why not? I asked myself. It seemed to me that nature surely would not have built a creature so beautiful, and so carefully designed for such conditions, merely to be an object of idle observation. … I was inclined to think that nature had built it thus in order that all the pleasure which can be derived from bathing at once in sunlight and in water might be enjoyed by one creature in the fullest measure. (*Religion of a Scientist,* pp. 176–177)

To many readers this may seem to be merely charming poetry, but Fechner was writing in defense of a philosophical theory for which he argued with great passion and resourcefulness. "Where we see inorganic Nature seemingly dead," wrote the American panpsychist Josiah Royce, "there is, in fact, conscious life, just as surely as there is any Being present in Nature at all" (*The World and the Individual,* second series, p, 240). "All motion of matter in space," in the words of Hermann Lotze, "may be explained as a natural expression of the inner states of beings that seek or avoid one another with a feeling of their need.... The whole of the world of sense … is but the veil of an infinite realm of mental life" (*Microcosmus,* Vol. I, p. 363).

PANPSYCHISM AND RELATED DOCTRINES

Although panpsychism seems incredible to most people at the present time, it has been endorsed in one way or another by many eminent thinkers in antiquity as well as in recent times. Among those who were either outright panpsychists or who inclined to a position of this kind, in addition to Fechner, Royce, and Lotze one may count Thales, Anaximenes, Empedocles, several of the Stoics, Plotinus and Simplicius; numerous Italian and German Renaissance philosophers (including Paracelsus, Girolamo Cardano, Bernardino Telesio, Giordano Bruno, and Tommaso Campanella); G. W. Leibniz, F. W. J. von Schelling, Arthur Schopenhauer, Antonio Rosmini, W. K. Clifford, Harald Høffding, C. B. Renouvier, Eduard von Hartmann, and Wilhelm Wundt; the German freethinkers Ernst Haeckel, Wilhelm Bölsche, and Bruno Wille; C. A. Strong, Erich Adickes, Erich Becher, Alfred Fouillée, C. S. Peirce, and F. C. S. Schiller; and, in the twentieth century, A. N. Whitehead, Samuel Alexander, Bernardino Varisco, Paul Haeberlin, Aloys Wenzel, Charles Hartshorne, and the biologists Pierre Teilhard de Chardin, C. H. Waddington, Sewall Wright, and W. E. Agar.

Few panpsychists, writing in recent years, would make the claim that their position can be proven, but they do assert that the available evidence favors their theory or at the very least enables it to be a serious contender. According to Fechner, it is the best, clearest, most natural, and most beautiful account of the facts of the universe. According to Schiller, who was both a pragmatist and a panpsychist, the doctrine "renders the operation of things more comprehensible" and also enables us to "act upon them more successfully" (*Studies in Humanism,* p. 443). Similarly, Whitehead, after quoting a passage in which Francis Bacon declared his belief that "all bodies whatsoever, though they have no sense … yet have perception," claims that this line of thought "expresses a more fundamental truth than do the materialistic concepts which were then being shaped as adequate for physics" (*Science and the Modern World,* p. 56). Agar, who was a follower of Whitehead's, conceded that there can be "no coercive demonstration" of the truth or falsehood of panpsychism, but it "leads to a more consistent and satisfying world picture than any of the alternatives"; and, unlike these alternatives, panpsychism is not committed to the paradoxical view that "the mental factor … made its appearance out of the blue at some date in the world's history" (*The Theory of the Living Organism,* pp. 109–110).

Modern panpsychists have been quite aware that their theory ran counter to what Fechner's distinguished follower Friedrich Paulsen called "the obstinate dogmatism of popular opinion and of the physical conception of the universe" (*Introduction to Philosophy,* p. 93). This obstinacy they attributed to the prevalence of the "nightview" of the universe—an outlook natural in a mechanized civilization in which people are incapable of noticing and appreciating anything that cannot become the subject of measurement and calculation. In arguing for panpsychism, Fechner and Paulsen (among others) believed that they were counteracting a pernicious tendency in modern life, not merely defending a philosophical viewpoint. Fechner conceived of himself as "awakening a sleeping world" (*Religion of a Scientist,* p. 130) and frequently appealed to his readers to "meet nature with new eyes" (p. 211). Whether plants have souls is not, in the opinion of these writers, an idle or trivial question but on the contrary has a "broader bearing," and its answer decides many other questions and indeed determines one's "whole outlook upon nature" (Fechner, op. cit., p. 163). It is only by accepting panpsychism that a modern man (who finds it impossible to believe in the claims of traditional religion) can escape the distressing implications of materialism.

Unlike Fechner and Paulsen, Lotze supported the traditional religious doctrines of a personal, immaterial deity and a substantival, immortal soul; and hence he did not claim that we had to embrace panpsychism in order to avoid materialism. Lotze also repeatedly insisted, quite unlike Royce and Schiller, that we must not introduce panpsychism into science. Nevertheless he, too, greatly emphasized the emotional benefits accruing from the acceptance of panpsychism. Although science may and should set aside all reference to the "pervading animation of the universe," the "aesthetic view of Nature may lawfully fill out the sum of what exists." If we are panpsychists we no longer "look on one part of the cosmos as but a blind and lifeless instrument for the ends of another," but, on the contrary, find "beneath the unruffled surface of matter, behind the rigid and regular repetitions of its working, … the warmth of a hidden mental activity." Lotze was particularly concerned to vindicate "the fullness of animated life" in such lowly things as "the dust trodden by our feet [and] the prosaic texture of the cloth that forms our clothing." Dust, Lotze declares, is "dust only to him whom it inconveniences," and he asks us to remember that human beings who are "confined" in a low social position, in which the outflow of intellectual energy is greatly impeded, are not by any means deprived of their "high destiny." If in the case of such "oppressed fragments of humanity," of "this dust of the spiritual world," we may yet affirm a divine origin and a celestial goal, then we have far less reason to deny an inner life to physical dust particles; uncomely as these "may appear to us in their accumulations, they at least everywhere and without shortcoming perform the actions permitted to them by the universal order" (*Microcosmus,* Vol. I, pp. 361–363).

HYLOZOISM. Panpsychism is related to but not identical with hylozoism. "Hylozoism" is sometimes defined as the view that matter is "intrinsically" active and in this sense is primarily opposed to the view of philosophers, like Plato and George Berkeley, who asserted that matter is "essentially" inert or passive. More frequently, it refers to the theory that all objects in the universe are in some literal sense alive. Any panpsychist who endorses the usual view that mind implies life would automatically be a hylozoist in the latter sense, but the converse does not hold. In fact most panpsychists have been quite ready to have themselves labeled hylozoists, but there are some exceptions, of whom Schopenhauer is perhaps the most famous. According to Schopenhauer, all objects have an inner nature that he calls "will," but although this will may be described as psychic or mental, it is not necessar-

ily a form of life. "I am the first," Schopenhauer wrote, "who has asserted that a *will* must be attributed to all that is lifeless and inorganic. For, with me, the will is not, as has hitherto been assumed, an accident of cognition and therefore of life; but life itself is manifestation of will" (*On the Will in Nature,* p. 309).

William James is responsible for some terminological confusion that should be cleared up before we go any further. In several of his later writings James strongly supported a theory he stated in the following words: "there is a continuum of cosmic consciousness, against which our several minds plunge as into a mother-sea or reservoir. … we with our lives are like islands in the sea, or like trees in the forest" (*Memories and Studies,* p. 204). Not only psychical research, he held, but also metaphysical philosophy and speculative biology are led in their own ways to look with favor on some such "panpsychist view of the universe as this." Elsewhere he remarks that the evidence from normal and abnormal psychology, from religious experience and from psychical research combine to establish a "formidable probability in favor of a general view of the world almost identical with Fechner's" (*Varieties of Religious Experience,* p. 311). It is true that Fechner held to a theory of a cosmic reservoir of consciousness, regarding God as the universal consciousness in which all lesser souls are contained, but it was not the acceptance of this theory that made him a panpsychist, and James himself was *not* a panpsychist. He nowhere maintained that plants and inanimate objects have an inner psychic life, and it is not easy to see how the reservoir theory by itself logically implies panpsychism.

WORLD SOUL. It should also be pointed out that the theory of the "world soul" is not identical with and does not necessarily follow from panpsychism. A number of panpsychists have in fact maintained the existence of a world soul, and they regarded it as a natural extension of panpsychism. Thus, Fechner in his *Zend-Avesta* (Vol. I, p. 179) concluded that "the earth is a creature … , a unitary whole in form and substance, in purpose and effect … and self-sufficient in its individuality." It is related to our human body as "the whole tree is to a single twig, a permanent body to a perishable, small organ." "Nothing," in the words of Zeno the Stoic (as approvingly quoted by Cicero), that "is destitute itself of life and reason, can generate a being possessed of life and reason; but the world does generate beings possessed of life and reason; the world therefore is not itself destitute of life and reason" (*On the Nature of the Gods,* Bk. II, Sec. VIII). In a very similar vein Paulsen argues that Earth, since it "produces all living and animated beings and harbors them as parts of its life," may itself be plausibly regarded as "alive and animated." Only the person who is "not open to the inner life of things" will find it difficult to regard Earth as a unitary organism with an inner life as well as a body (*Introduction to Philosophy*, p. 108). To demand to be shown the eyes and ears, the mouth and digestive system, the skin and hair, the arms and legs, the nervous system and the brain of Earth is quite improper. Unlike an animal, Earth does not need a mouth and a stomach because it does not have to take in substances from outside. An animal pursues its prey and in turn attempts to escape its pursuers, and hence it needs eyes and ears, but Earth is not a pursuer and is also not pursued. An animal needs a brain and nerves in order to regulate its movements in response to its environment, but Earth moves around without any such aid. Much like Fechner, Paulsen concludes that "it has regulated its relations to the external world in the most beautiful and becoming manner." "Please do not," he adds, slightly hurt by the irreverent objections of some critics, "please do not ask it to do what is contrary to its nature and cosmical position" (ibid.). This elevated idea of Earth soul has not won general acceptance among panpsychists. Charles Hartshorne, a twentieth-century panpsychist who, like Fechner, is a friend of religion, pays tribute to the "eloquence" of Fechner's account but questions whether "the advances of science since his time have served to confirm" his view. While it may be plausible to regard an electron as "a rudimentary organism," the larger systems that Fechner and Paulsen dealt with so enthusiastically "seem to contemporary knowledge rather too loosely integrated to be accepted as sentient subjects." A tree, it seems plausible to argue, has less unity than one of its own cells, and, similarly, Earth has less unity than the animals which inhabit it ("Panpsychism," p. 447). Hartshorne, as just observed, is a religious thinker, but there have also been atheistic and agnostic panpsychists, and there is no doubt that they would dismiss the theory of the world soul as quite absurd and as an illegitimate extension of panpsychism.

DEGREES OF CONSCIOUSNESS. There is one other terminological confusion against which we should be on guard. Rudolf Eisler, in the article on panpsychism in his *Wörterbuch der Philosophischen Begriffe*, first supplies the definition that we have adopted here and that is the one generally accepted. Later, however, he remarks that many panpsychists merely assert that all matter has a "disposition towards the psychological"—that is, that they ascribe to inorganic things no more than a "hypothetical" or low-grade mentality. Now, panpsychists have indeed generally emphasized that there are degrees of "mentality" or "soul

life" and that the mentality or psychic nature of inanimate objects is of an exceedingly simple order, but a low degree or level of mentality must be distinguished from "hypothetical mentality" or the capacity to become the subject of mental activities. To qualify as a panpsychist a person must claim that all bodies actually have an inner or psychological nature or aspect. That all matter is potentially the subject of mental activities or characteristics is something that many other philosophers, including not a few materialists, would concede. To say that a stone is made of elements which, when suitably combined, form an entity that thinks and feels is not the same thing as to say that the stone itself has an inner, psychological being.

Royce is a notable exception to the statement that panpsychists regard the psychic character of inorganic bodies as much lower than that of human beings or animals. He thought that the difference was mainly one of speed and that the "fluent" nature of the inner life of inorganic systems tends to go unnoticed because of its "very vast slowness." To this he added, however, that slowness does not mean "a lower type of consciousness" (*The World and the Individual,* second series, pp. 226–227).

NAIVE AND CRITICAL PANPSYCHISM. Eisler distinguishes between "naive" and "critical" panpsychism—by the former he means the animism of primitive peoples and of children, by the latter he means panpsychist theories that are supported by arguments. In this article we are, of course, concerned exclusively with the "critical" or philosophical variety of panpsychism. Most critical panpsychists would probably endorse Agar's judgment that although primitive animism was "in its analogical way of thinking basically sound," it was also "full of errors" and "ludicrously mistaken in detail" (*The Theory of the Living Organism,* p. 109).

It should be observed that some philosophical panpsychists are not consistently "critical" in the sense just indicated. Thus, while offering elaborate arguments and conceding quite explicitly on numerous occasions that the inner psychic processes of plants and inanimate objects are not given to us in immediate experience but have to be inferred, both Schopenhauer and Fechner occasionally take the opposite position. In a remarkable passage, Schopenhauer tells us that if we consider various inanimate objects "attentively," we shall observe (among many other things) the "strong and unceasing impulse with which the waters hurry to the ocean, [the] persistency with which the magnet turns ever to the North Pole, [the] readiness with which iron flies to the magnet,

[the] eagerness with which the electric poles seek to be reunited, and which, just like human desire, is increased by obstacles [as well as] the choice with which bodies repel and attract each other, combine and separate, when they are set free in a fluid state, and emancipated from the bonds of rigidity." Furthermore, if we attend to the way in which a load "hampers our body by its gravitation towards the earth," we shall "feel directly [that it] unceasingly presses and strains [our body] in pursuit of its one tendency." This passage is taken from the early first volume of *Die Welt als Wille und Vorstellung* (Bk. II, Sec. 23). His later work *Über den Willen in der Natur* consists largely of lists of scientific facts "proving" Schopenhauer's assorted philosophical theories, including his panpsychism. Here we are told to "*look* attentively at a torrent dashing headlong over rocks," whose "boisterous vehemence" can arise only from an "exertion of strength" (p. 308). As for the celestial bodies, if we observe them carefully we shall see that they "play with each other, betray mutual inclination, exchange as it were amorous glances, yet never allow themselves to come into rude contact" (p. 305). Fechner, a milder man than Schopenhauer and more interested in plants than in boisterous torrents or burdensome loads, records experiences in which "the very soul of the plant stood visibly before me," in which he "saw" not only a special "outward clarity" of the flowers but also "the inward light" that in all likelihood caused the outer appearance (op. cit., pp. 211–212).

To see what is at issue between panpsychists and their opponents, it is important to point out that passages such as these are aberrations. It may indeed be held that in addition to the more familiar properties, to which philosophers refer as the primary and secondary qualities, physical objects possess a further set of qualities that are not noticed by observers who lack certain gifts or a suitable training. Such a view need not be mystical and has been plausibly defended in the case of the so-called tertiary qualities, especially those of artistic productions and performances. However, the initial definitions of "soul," "psychic," and "inner," or of any of the other terms used by panpsychists in statements of their position, preclude them from adopting a position of this kind. The "soul," the "inner" nature of an object, its "mental side" is by definition—a definition to which the panpsychists subscribe—something private that only the object itself can experience or observe. Hence, even if one grants that panpsychists possess gifts of which other mortals are deprived, these cannot possibly be the means of directly perceiving the inner qualities or states of any object external to the observer. Moreover, the great majority of panpsychists, including Schopenhauer and Fechner, do

not, in their more considered presentations, claim any special faculty for themselves that the opponents of panpsychism supposedly lack. On the contrary, it is implied that, starting from certain generally accessible facts, sound reasoning will lead a person to a panpsychist conclusion.

ARGUMENTS FOR PANPSYCHISM

The arguments for panpsychism may be conveniently grouped according to whether they presuppose the acceptance of a particular metaphysical system or some controversial epistemological theory or whether they are or purport to be of an empirical or inductive character. Some of the arguments of Leibniz and Royce are based on their respective versions of metaphysical idealism, and some of the arguments of Schopenhauer and Paulsen presuppose a Kantian theory of knowledge. It is impossible to evaluate any such arguments without getting involved in an appraisal of their particular metaphysical or epistemological framework, and we shall therefore confine our discussion to arguments of the other kind. It is perhaps worth noting in this connection that, especially since the mid-1800s, many panpsychists have regarded themselves as opponents of metaphysics, or, if they did not object to being labeled metaphysicians, they took care to add that theirs was an "inductive," not a speculative, variety of metaphysics. Fechner in particular prided himself on dispensing altogether with "a priori constructions," and he was a leading figure, along with von Hartmann and Wundt, in a movement to renounce any claim to a special philosophical method distinct from the method employed in the natural sciences. The only method that, on his view, could lead to a tenable theory about the universe as a whole was "generalization by induction and analogy, and the rational combination of the common elements gathered from different areas," as he observes in *Zend-Avesta*. Furthermore, even some of the panpsychists who were also speculative metaphysicians appealed to empirical considerations. They thought that panpsychism could be supported in different ways that were logically independent of one another. Royce was one of the philosophers who adopted this approach. Insisting that his "Idealistic Theory of Being … furnishes a deep warrant" for panpsychism, he nevertheless regarded panpsychism as also resting on "a merely empirical basis" (op. cit., p. 213). "Wholly apart from any more metaphysical consideration of the deeper nature of Reality," certain empirical facts suggest panpsychism as the conclusion of "a rough induction." In this connection, the theory should be treated as a "hypothesis for further testing" (ibid., pp. 223–224).

GENETIC ARGUMENTS. The arguments that have been most widely urged in defense of panpsychism, and which go back at least as far as Telesio and Campanella, rely, in one way or another, on the assumption that mental facts can be causally explained only in terms of other mental facts. Philosophers who have arrived at a parallelistic answer to the body-mind problem have been specially prone to endorse such arguments, but these can be stated independently of any commitment to parallelism. It is perhaps interesting to note in passing that many early champions of Darwinism (for example, Clifford in England and Haeckel and L. Büchner in Germany) were attracted by reasoning of this kind, although they were frequently repelled by the analogical arguments considered later in the present article. We shall here examine two such genetic arguments—one advanced by Paulsen, the other by a twentieth-century British scientist.

How, asks Paulsen, did soul life originate? Modern biology assumes, quite rightly in Paulsen's opinion, that organic life had a beginning on Earth and that the "first creations" arose from inorganic matter. The question then arises how "psychic life" came into being. "Is the first feeling in the first protoplasmic particle something absolutely new, something that did not exist before in any form, of which not the slightest trace was to be found previously?" (*Introduction to Philosophy*, pp. 99–100). To suppose that the first feeling in the first protoplasmic particle was something "absolutely new" would, however, imply a "creation out of nothing," which would be totally at variance with the basic (and well-founded) principles of science. You might as well, Paulsen remarks, ask the natural scientist "to believe that the protoplasmic particle itself was created out of nothing." The natural scientist rightly assumes that natural bodies arise from preexisting elements. These enter into new and more complicated combinations, and as a result the bodies are capable of performing "new and astonishing functions." Why does the natural scientist "not make the same natural assumption" in the case of the inner psychic processes as well? Why does he not say that "an inner life was already present in germ (*keimhaft*) in the elements, and that it developed into higher forms?"

It is not easy to appraise this line of reasoning because of the vagueness of the expression "absolutely new." As Ernest Nagel and others have pointed out, it is frequently not at all clear whether two processes or occurrences are to be counted as different instances of the same property or as different properties—whether they are or not usually depends on the purpose of the particular investigation. Furthermore, what may be "absolutely new," in the sense of not being predictable from certain initial conditions in conjunction with a certain set of laws, may at the same time not be absolutely new in the sense of being predictable from these initial conditions together with a different set of laws. However, let us assume that in a given case all parties agree that if at a moment T_1 the features of a system were of a certain kind and if at a subsequent moment T_2 they were of a certain different kind, something "absolutely new" came into being at T_2. More specifically, let us assume that the conditions at T_1 do not include any mental fact but that at T_2 they include "the first feeling" in the first protoplasmic particle. Now, according to Paulsen's argument, anybody who supposes that this is the kind of thing that actually happened—and a person who accepts certain scientific facts while rejecting panpsychism has to suppose that this is what happened—is committed to the view that something came from nothing. But to suppose that something came from nothing is unscientific and absurd.

There is a simple answer to this. By saying that something must always come from something and cannot come from nothing, we may mean either (1) that every phenomenon or event has a cause or (2) the scholastic principle that any property residing in an effect must also have been present in its cause. If we suppose that at time T_1 there was no mental fact in the universe while at a later time T_2 the first feeling occurred in a protoplasmic particle, we would indeed be violating proposition (2), but we would not at all be violating proposition (1). Yet if anything can here be regarded as "unscientific" or "absurd" it would be exceptions to (1). For reasons explained earlier, it is not easy to state (2) or its denial with any precision, but, in the most familiar sense of "new," experience seems to show that there are any number of effects possessing new properties—properties not present in the cause. The very course of evolution, to which Paulsen and other proponents of the genetic argument appeal, provides a multitude of illustrations of this. At any rate, an opponent of panpsychism would deny proposition (2) and would insist that such a denial is in no way unempirical or unscientific. To assume the opposite without further ado would surely be to beg one of the basic questions at issue.

Let us now consider a more recent version of a genetic argument: "Something must go on in the simplest inanimate things," writes the distinguished British geneticist C. H. Waddington, "which can be described in the same language as would be used to describe our self-awareness" (*The Nature of Life,* p. 121). It is true, he continues, that we know nothing of its nature, but the conclusion is forced on us by the "demands of logic and the application of evolutionary theory" (p. 122). Waddington's argument opens with the declaration that the phenomenon of self-awareness is a "basic mystery." This is so because awareness "can never be constructed theoretically out of our present fundamental scientific concepts, since these contain no element which has any similarity in kind with self-consciousness." But self-awareness undoubtedly exists, and hence we must infer that the mode we experience "evolved from simple forms which are experienced by non-human things." It is not difficult to accept this conclusion as far as animals like dogs and cats are concerned. But, Waddington proceeds, we cannot stop there if we take the theory of evolution seriously. According to the initial premise it is inconceivable that self-awareness "originated from anything which did not share something in common with it and possessed only those qualities which can be objectively observed from outside." Hence, we are forced to conclude that "even in the simplest inanimate things there is something which belongs to the same realm of being as self-awareness." Waddington's argument is not overtly based, as Paulsen's was, on the contention that somebody who accepts evolution but rejects panpsychism is committed to the absurd proposition that something comes from nothing. According to Waddington such a person would be committed to the view that self-awareness is not a mystery—that is, that it is explicable in physical terms—and this Waddington takes to be plainly false.

In reply it should be pointed out that Waddington appears to use the word *explanation* in two very different senses in the course of his argument. Sometimes when we ask for the explanation of a phenomenon we are looking for an account of its makeup, of how its parts are related and how they work. We use the word *explanation* in this sense when we want to have the nature of a car or a clock or perhaps a human eye explained to us. At other times, and more frequently, in asking for the explanation of a phenomenon we are looking for its cause. It is not easy to see why awareness should be said to be a "mystery" just because it cannot, in the first sense of "explanation," be explained in physical terms (this betrays a strange materialistic bias that regards a phenomenon as properly explicable, in the first sense, only if it is something material—one wonders why physical objects are not equally mysterious, since they cannot be explained in terms of predicates that are applicable only to mental states). But waiving this point—allowing, that is, that awareness cannot be adequately characterized by the kinds of predicates

usually applied to material objects and that this makes awareness incapable of explanation in the first of the two senses distinguished, none of this implies that awareness cannot be explained, in the second sense of the word, in terms of purely physical factors. Avoiding the word *explanation,* the point can be expressed very simply: Granting that awareness is not a physical phenomenon, it does not follow that it cannot be produced by conditions that are purely physical. When the matter is put in this way, it becomes clear that we are back to the difficulty besetting Paulsen's form of the argument. Waddington's argument does not, aside from the acceptance of the evolutionary theory, depend merely on the admission that awareness is not a physical phenomenon, that it "cannot be constructed" out of physical concepts: It also depends on the maxim that any property of the effect must also be present in the cause. We have already mentioned reasons for rejecting this principle, but perhaps it is worth adding that in the context of the body-mind relationship it seems particularly implausible. Brain tumors and other damage to the body, to give some very obvious examples, lead to all kinds of psychological states, but we do not for this reason refuse to regard them as explanations of the latter.

ANALOGICAL ARGUMENTS. The second set of arguments commonly employed by panpsychists, independently of any metaphysical system, purport to be of an analogical kind. Here the more systematic panpsychists usually proceed in two steps: The first consists in arguing that plants are in "essential" respects so much like animals that one cannot consistently attribute a psychic or soul life to animals but refuse it to plants; it is then maintained that the borderline between animate and inanimate objects is not sharp and that a careful examination of inanimate objects reveals them to have many impressive likenesses to animals and plants, indicating the existence of inner psychic being there also.

Plants manifest many of the same vital processes that are found in animals: nutrition, growth, reproduction, and many more. Like animals, plants are born and also die. Moreover, it is simply not true that plants lack the power of spontaneous movement that we observe in animals. "Does not the plant," asks Paulsen, "turn its buds and leaves to the light, does it not send its roots where it finds nourishment, and its tendrils where it finds support? Does it not close up its petals at night or when it rains, and does it not open them in sunshine?" If there is so great a "correspondence" between the visible processes, why should there not be a similar correspondence in "the invisible processes"? (op. cit., pp. 96–97). If it is argued that these analogies are too vague and trifling, because plants have neither a brain nor a nervous system, the answer is surely that there are animals that also lack brains and nervous systems. Fechner was particularly concerned to exhibit the weakness of this counterargument. He observes that if we remove the strings of a piano or a violin it becomes impossible to obtain any harmonic sounds from these instruments. If somebody concluded from this that the presence of strings is essential to the production of musical tones, he would be completely mistaken, because there are many instruments, like flutes and trombones, with which we can produce musical sounds although they have no strings; but this argument would be not one whit worse than that of the critic of panpsychism.

There are, to be sure, differences between plants and animals, and these a panpsychist has no wish to deny, but, according to Paulsen, they "may be conceived as indicating a difference in inner life also" rather than the absence of any inner processes. The differences indicate "that plants possess a peculiar inclination to receptivity and a decentralized extensity, whereas the psychical life of the animal shows more spontaneity and centralized intensity" (ibid., p. 98). Fechner is even more specific and compares the difference in psychical life between animals and plants to the difference in the psychology of men and women. Elsewhere he compares the former difference to that between the emotions of travelers and those who are "homebodies," between the pleasures associated with "running hither and thither" and those accompanying a "quiet and sedentary sphere of endeavor" (*Religion of a Scientist*, pp. 178–179). Paulsen adds, however, it does not really matter what we think about the details of the inner processes, since all such attempts at conceiving the nature of the psychic life of plants are "at best feeble." It should be remembered that we do not really fare any better if we try to "interpret" the psychical life of animals, especially that of the lower species. We know very little, Paulsen remarks, "about the inner experiences of a jelly-fish or the feelings of a caterpillar or a butterfly."

When we come to inanimate objects, Paulsen continues, the first thing to note is that organic and inorganic bodies must not be regarded as belonging to two separate worlds. There is constant interaction between them. They are composed of the same ingredients and acted on by the same forces. If this were all, however, the analogy would not be strong enough. It would be objected that unlike animals and plants, objects like stones are lifeless and rigid, that they lack all spontaneous activity. This opinion, Paulsen argues, is totally mistaken and is based on the Aristotelian-scholastic theory, taken over by material-

istic scientists of the eighteenth and nineteenth centuries, that matter is inherently and absolutely passive. This theory, whether in its original or in its modern atomistic form, is quite untenable. In fact a stone is not an "absolutely dead and rigid body" and devoid of "inner impulses." Modern physics has discarded such a view. Its molecules and atoms are "forms of the greatest inner complexity and mobility." Not only are the constituents of an apparently rigid object like a stone in continuous motion, but the entire system is "in constant interaction with its immediate surroundings as well as with the remotest system of fixed stars" (pp. 101–102). In the light of this it is not only not absurd but quite plausible to conclude that "corresponding to this wonderful play of physical forces and movements" there is a system of inner psychic processes "analogous to that which accompanies the working of the parts in an organic body." We thus arrive, on the basis of scientific evidence, at a view substantially like that of Empedocles that "love and hate form the motive forces in all things"—not, to be sure, quite as we know them in ourselves, but nevertheless in a form that is "at bottom similar" to these human emotions.

It is natural to object to such arguments that the analogies are altogether inconclusive. It is true that there are certain similarities between, say, a stone and a human body, but there are also all kinds of differences. Paulsen assures us that the similarities are "essential," but if "essential" here means that, as far as the inference to an inner psychic process is concerned, the similarities count and the differences do not, that they are relevant whereas the differences are irrelevant, one may well ask how Paulsen knows this. Surely no proposition has been or could have been established to the effect that inner physical movement is always and necessarily connected with psychic activity. Any such general proposition is precisely what the opponent of panpsychism would deny or question. Furthermore, leaving aside any discussion of whether those who regard matter as "active" and those who maintain it to be "passive" are engaging in a factual dispute (so that one party could be said to be right and the other wrong), it must be emphasized that in rejecting panpsychism one is in no way committed to the view that matter is devoid of "inner activity." The view that matter has no inner psychic aspect in no way precludes the admission of inner physical processes such as those postulated by modern physical theory.

These criticisms, however, do not go far enough. They assume, what seems very doubtful, that the arguments under discussion are of a genuinely empirical character. In this connection it is pertinent to raise the question what the universe would have to be like so that there would be no evidence for panpsychism, or, more strongly, so that the evidence would clearly favor the opposite position. We saw that Paulsen considered the fact that human bodies and inanimate objects are composed of the same elements to be evidence for his position. He also regarded the internal movements of the particles of apparently stationary objects as evidence of their inner life. But suppose that stones and human bodies were not composed of the same elements; would this constitute evidence against panpsychism or would it at least deprive panpsychism of evidence that is at present supporting it? Suppose that electrons were not buzzing inside the stone; would this show or would it be any kind of evidence for the view that the stone does not have a psychic life? From the writings of panpsychists it seems probable that the answer to these questions would be in the negative: If the elements of stones were quite different from those of human bodies, it might be an indication that the psychic processes in stones are even more different in detail from those of human beings, and if the internal constituents of the stones were not in constant motion it might indicate a more restful psychic life, but it would not indicate that no psychic life at all is going on. If this is an accurate presentation of the panpsychist position, it shows that the analogical arguments we have been considering are not genuinely empirical, that the facts pointed to are not, in any accepted sense, evidence for the conclusion. This is a far stronger criticism than the claim that the analogies are weak or the arguments inconclusive.

IS PANPSYCHISM AN INTELLIGIBLE DOCTRINE?

Some contemporary philosophers who have given more thought to the conditions of meaningful discourse than was customary in previous times are inclined to dismiss panpsychism not as false or unproven but as unintelligible. Thus, in his *Philosophical Investigations* Ludwig Wittgenstein raises the question "Could one imagine a stone's having consciousness?" and comments that if anyone can imagine this, it would merely amount to "image-mongery" (Sec. 390, p. 119 e). Such image-mongery, Wittgenstein seems to imply, would not show at all that in attributing consciousness to a stone one is making an intelligible statement. It would probably be pointless to try to "prove" that panpsychism is a meaningless doctrine. Any such attempt is liable to involve one in an elaborate and inconclusive defense of some controversial

meaning criterion. However, it may be of some interest to explain more fully, without intending to settle anything, why not a few contemporary philosophers would maintain that the panpsychists do not succeed in asserting any new facts and in the end merely urge certain pictures on us.

To this end let us first consider the following imaginary disputes about the "inner" nature of a tennis ball. *A* holds the common view that the ball is made of rubber and not of living tissue, while *B* holds the unusual opinion that if we were to examine the inside of the tennis ball under a powerful microscope we would find a brain, a nervous system, and other physiological structures usually associated with consciousness. Furthermore, *B* maintains that if we listened very attentively to what goes on while tennis balls are in their can we would hear one ball whispering to the other, "My brother, be careful—don't let them hit you too hard; if you roll into a bush on the other side of the fence you may spend the rest of your days in blissful peace." There is genuine empirical disagreement between *A* and *B* and, as far as we know, *A* would be right if the ball or balls in question are of the familiar kind. Let us next suppose that *C,* after reading Paulsen and Waddington, becomes converted to panpsychism and starts saying such things as "the tennis ball is not a mere body—it has an inner psychic life, it is moved by love and hate, although not love and hate quite as we know them in human beings." To an uncritical outsider it may at first appear, chiefly because of the images one associates with the word *inner,* that *C*, like *B*, is asserting the existence of strange goings on inside the ball, never suspected by the ordinary man or the physicist. In fact, however, if *C* is a philosophical panpsychist, he will not expect to find a brain or a nervous system or any kind of living tissue inside the ball, and he will disclaim any such assertion. Nor will he expect that tennis balls whisper gentle warnings to one another when they are alone. If he should start serving less forcefully in order to avoid hurting the ball, a professional panpsychist would undoubtedly advise him not to be silly, explaining that although their lives are governed by love and hate, balls do not get hurt in any sense that need concern a sympathetic human being. In other words, *C* does not disagree with *A* about what would be found inside the ball or about the ball's behavior while it is in the can, and he is also not treating the ball any differently from the way *A* does—or at any rate no different treatment is logically implied by his opinion that the ball has an inner psychic life. *B* really contradicts *A* and, at least in the case of the balls we all know, he is quite certainly mistaken. *C* is not mistaken, but one begins to wonder whether he is asserting any facts not allowed for in the ordinary, nonpanpsychist view of the ball. A semantically sensitive observer might comment that ordinary people (and uncritical philosophers) are apt to suppose that they understand well enough what panpsychism asserts and that they proceed to dismiss it as silly or incredible (that is, as plainly false) because they regard panpsychism as a theory like *B*'s unusual opinion about the tennis ball. In fact, panpsychism is not like *B*'s opinion but like *C*'s, and the appropriate criticism seems to be not that it is a false theory but that one does not really know what, if anything, has been asserted.

SCHILLER. Let us now turn to the procedure of an actual panpsychist to see the full relevance of the preceding reflections. F. C. S. Schiller argued that inanimate objects, contrary to the usual opinion, take notice of other inanimate objects, as well as of human beings. "Inanimate objects," he wrote, "are responsive to each other and modify their behavior accordingly. A stone is not indifferent to other stones" (*Logic for Use,* p. 447). Nor are stones indifferent to human beings: "In a very real sense," he wrote elsewhere, "a stone must be said to know us and to respond to our manipulation" (*Studies in Humanism,* p. 443). It is "as true of stones as of men" that if you treat them differently they behave differently (*Logic for Use,* p. 447). It must be emphasized, however, that the responsiveness, the nonindifference, of stones is not quite what we mean when we talk about the responsiveness and nonindifference of human beings. How does a stone exhibit its nonindifference to other stones? Very simply: in being gravitationally attracted to them (ibid.). Nor are we "recognized" by the stone "in our whole nature." It does not "apprehend us as spiritual beings," but this does not mean that the stone takes no note whatever of our existence. "It is aware of us and affected by us on the plane on which its own existence is passed." In the physical world we and stones share, "'awareness' can apparently be shown by being hard and heavy and colored and space-filling, and so forth. And all these things the stone is and recognizes in other bodies" (*Studies in Humanism,* p. 442). The stone "faithfully exercises" all its physical functions: "it gravitates and resists pressure, and obstructs ether vibrations, etc., and makes itself respected as such a body. And it treats us as if of a like nature with itself, on the level of its understanding, i.e., as bodies to which it is attracted inversely as the square of the distance, moderately hard and capable of being hit." The stone does not indeed "know or care" whether a human being gets hurt by it; but in those operations that are of "interest" to the stone, as, for example, in house building, "it plays its part and responds according to the measure of its capacity." What is true of stones, Schiller continues, is also true of atoms and electrons, if they really exist. Just as the stone responds only "after its fashion," so atoms and electrons also know us "after their fashion." They know us not as human beings but "as whirling mazes of atoms and electrons like themselves." We treat stones and atoms as "inanimate" because of "their immense spiritual remoteness from us" and "perhaps" also because of "our inability to understand them" (ibid., pp. 442, 444).

Some of his readers, Schiller realizes, will "cry" that the views just reported amount to "sheer hylozoism," but he does not regard this as any reason for concern. "What," he answers, "if it is hylozoism or, still better, panpsychism, so long as it really brings out a genuine analogy," and this, he is convinced, it does. "The analogy is helpful so long as it really renders the operations of things more comprehensible to us, and interprets facts which had seemed mysterious" (ibid., p. 443). Schiller illustrates his claim by considering the chemical phenomenon of catalytic action. It had "seemed mysterious" and "hard to understand" (presumably prior to the publication of Schiller's "humanistic" panpsychism), that two bodies *A* and *B* may have a strong affinity for each other and yet refuse to combine until the merest trace of a third substance *C* is introduced, which sets up an interaction between *A* and *B* without producing an alteration in *C* itself. But, asks Schiller, "is not this strangely suggestive of the idea that *A* and *B* did not know each other until they were introduced by *C,* and then liked each other so well that *C* was left out in the cold?" To this he adds—and here surely not even the most hostile critic would disagree—that "more such analogies and possibilities will probably be found if they are looked for." Nevertheless, panpsychism does not merely render the operation of things more comprehensible. It has a further virtue, to which Schiller alludes later in the same discussion: "The alien world which seemed so remote and so rigid to an inert contemplation, the reality which seemed so intractable to an aimless and fruitless speculation, grows plastic in this way to our intelligent manipulations" (ibid., p. 444).

Perhaps the most striking features of Schiller's presentation are the constant modifications or retractions of what at first appear truly remarkable assertions. Inanimate objects are "responsive to each other," but not the way in which human beings or animals are—they are responsive in being gravitationally attracted by other inanimate objects. The stone is "aware of us," but not, of course, in the sense in which human beings are aware—it is aware on "*its* plane"; the stone "recognizes" other bodies and is "interested" in operations such as house building, but "on the level of *its* understanding"; it "plays its part," but "according to the measure of *its* capacity"; atoms and electrons know us no less than we know them, but "after *their* fashion." It is not, perhaps, unfair to say that Schiller takes away with one hand what he gives with the other, and it may be questioned whether anything remains. When one is told that the stone is aware of us one reacts with astonishment and is apt to suppose that a statement has been made that contradicts what an ordinary nonpanpsychist believes; but this turns out to be more than doubtful since the stone's awareness, on its plane, seems to consist simply in being hard, heavy, space-filling, and colored. The stone makes itself respected and is interested in operations like house building, but in its own fashion, and this consists in gravitating, resisting pressure, and all the usual characteristics of stones, which are not questioned by those who do not subscribe to panpsychism. Schiller plainly believed that the panpsychist asserts (if he has not in fact discovered) facts about stones and atoms that are denied by, or whose existence is unknown to, the ordinary person and the materialist. He evidently did not believe that it was just a question of using words in different senses. But, if so, what are the facts he asserts and his opponents deny? Schiller's qualifications remind one of a song in the musical *Kiss Me, Kate* in which a lighthearted lady sings of her numerous and constantly changing amorous involvements, adding at the end of each verse, "But I'm always true to you, darling, in my fashion; yes, I'm always true to you, darling, in my way." How does the stone's awareness in its own way differ from what other people would refer to as absence of awareness?

EMPIRICAL PRETENSIONS OF PANPSYCHISTS. Even if one is disinclined to go so far as to dismiss panpsychism as meaningless, there is surely good reason to dispute the empirical and pragmatic pretensions of certain panpsychists. We saw that Royce regarded panpsychism (among other things) as a hypothesis "to be tested," but unfortunately he did not tell us anything about the way or ways in which this was to be done. Royce did indeed guard himself by maintaining that the mental processes in physical systems occur over "extremely august" temporal spans (*The World and the Individual,* second series, p. 226), so that a human being would be unable to detect a process of this kind. However, making the fullest allowance for this qualification and granting ourselves or some imaginary observer the "august" time span required by Royce's "hypothesis," this would still not do, since

Royce omitted to inform us what such an observer should look for.

Schiller, it will be remembered, assured us that as a result of accepting panpsychism the previously "remote" and "rigid" reality "grows plastic … to our manipulations." But he did not explain how and where these happy transformations would take place. Is a bricklayer who has been converted to panpsychism going to lay bricks more efficiently? Does a tennis player's game improve if he becomes a disciple of Schiller? No, but perhaps the chemist will find catalytic action more comprehensible, and "more such analogies and possibilities" will make other "intractable" processes less "mysterious." Regrettably, the opinion that panpsychism makes any of these phenomena easier to understand is the result of a confusion that hinges on an ambiguity in "comprehensible" and related expressions. Sometimes we attempt to make phenomena or correlations of events more comprehensible. In this sense, a phenomenon (for example, a certain disease or a plane crash) is comprehended or understood if its cause is discovered, and a correlation or a law becomes comprehensible if it is subsumed under a wider law (if, for example, the administration of a certain drug has in many cases been followed by the cure of a given condition, the correlation becomes comprehensible if we determine what it is about the drug that has this effect; and this is another way of saying that we subsume the correlation under a law). But at other times when we talk about making something comprehensible, we are concerned with explaining the meaning of theories or statements, not with the explanation of phenomena or of correlations. Unlike the first, this kind of problem may be regarded as pedagogical, and here all kinds of analogies may be helpful that do not or need not shed any light on the causes of the phenomena dealt with in the statements we are trying to make more comprehensible. It cannot, of course, be denied that an analogy such as the one Schiller offers may well make catalysts more comprehensible in this pedagogical sense—it may, for example, help schoolchildren to understand what a chemist is talking about. It is equally clear that such an analogy does absolutely nothing to make catalytic action more comprehensible in the earlier sense we mentioned, and it was surely in this sense that Schiller claimed panpsychism to make things less mysterious and easier to understand. It is difficult to believe that either Schiller or any other champion of panpsychism would be satisfied to have the theory regarded as no more than a pedagogical device in the teaching of natural science.

See also Alexander, Samuel; Anaximenes; Berkeley, George; Bruno, Giordano; Campanella, Tommaso; Cicero, Marcus Tullius; Clifford, William Kingdon; Empedocles; Fechner, Gustav Theodor; Fouillée, Alfred; Haeckel, Ernst Heinrich; Hartmann, Eduard von; Høffding, Harald; James, William; Leibniz, Gottfried Wilhelm; Lotze, Rudolf Hermann; Macrocosm and Microcosm; Materialism; Nagel, Ernest; Pantheism; Paracelsus; Paulsen, Friedrich; Peirce, Charles Sanders; Plato; Plotinus; Renouvier, Charles Bernard; Rosmini-Serbati, Antonio; Royce, Josiah; Schelling, Friedrich Wilhelm Joseph von; Schiller, Ferdinand Canning Scott; Schopenhauer, Arthur; Simplicius; Teilhard de Chardin, Pierre; Telesio, Bernardino; Thales of Miletus; Varisco, Bernardino; Whitehead, Alfred North; Wittgenstein, Ludwig Josef Johann; Wundt, Wilhelm.

Bibliography

The fullest systematic defenses of panpsychism since the mid-1800s are found in the writings of Paulsen, Fechner, Lotze, and Royce. Paulsen's arguments are presented in his very influential *Einleitung in die Philosophie* (21st ed., Stuttgart and Berlin, 1909), translated by F. Thilly as *Introduction to Philosophy* (2nd American ed., New York, 1906, with a preface by William James). Fechner's main writings on the subject are *Nanna: oder über das Seelenleben der Pflanzen* (3rd ed., Leipzig, 1903) and *Zend-Avesta: oder über die Dinge des Jenseits* (2nd ed., Hamburg: L. Voss, 1906). There is an English translation of selections from Fechner's works by W. Lowrie titled *Religion of a Scientist* (New York: Pantheon, 1946). Fechner's ideas are discussed in some detail in G. Stanley Hall, *Founders of Modern Psychology* (New York: Appleton, 1912); G. F. Stout, *God and Nature*, edited by A. K. Stout (Cambridge, U.K., 1952); Otto Külpe, *Die Philosophie der Gegenwart in Deutschland* (Leipzig: Teubner, 1902), translated by M. L. Patrick and G. T. W. Patrick as *Philosophy of the Present in Germany* (London: G. Allen, 1913); and G. Murphy, "A Brief Interpretation of Fechner," in *Psyche* 7 (1926): 75–80. Although Wilhelm Wundt condemned Fechner's speculations about the souls of the stars and Earth as "a fantastic dream," he himself concluded that mental life can arise only out of conditions that are themselves mental (*System der Philosophie*, Leipzig, 1889). Lotze's defense of panpsychism is contained in Vol. I of *Mikrokosmus* (Leipzig, 1856–1864), translated by E. Hamilton and E. E. C. Jones as *Microcosmus* (New York, 1890). Royce's panpsychism is presented in Lecture V of *The World and the Individual*, second series (New York: Macmillan, 1901). The American neorealist W. P. Montague, a student of Royce, relates how he "jumped with almost tearful gratitude" at Royce's "hypothesis about the varying time-spans in nature." He regarded this "hypothesis" as "a new and challenging contribution to the great panpsychist tradition," as "a clear and great thought" that "might even be true" (*The Ways of Things*, London, 1940, p. 669). Montague referred to his own position as "animistic materialism," and he is sometimes classified as a panpsychist, but in fact it is

very doubtful whether his animism implies panpsychism as we have here defined it.

Little was said in this article about A. N. Whitehead, probably the most distinguished champion of panpsychism in the twentieth century, chiefly because his views on the subject could not have been discussed without consideration of other features of his difficult system. Whitehead would have disagreed with many other panpsychists about the "units" that are to be regarded as the bearers of psychic life. These, he held, are not stars or stones but the events out of which stars and stones are constituted and that Whitehead calls "occasions." His views are presented in *Science and the Modern World* (New York: Macmillan, 1925), *Process and Reality* (New York: Macmillan, 1929), and, most fully, in "Nature Alive," Lecture 8 of *Modes of Thought* (New York: Macmillan, 1938). Panpsychistic views strongly influenced by Whitehead are put forward in Charles Hartshorne, *Beyond Humanism* (Chicago: Willett Clark, 1937) and *Man's Vision of God* (Chicago: L Willett Clark, 1941), and in W. E. Agar, *The Theory of the Living Organism* (Melbourne, 1943). Samuel Alexander, whose metaphysical position has many similarities to Whitehead's, also expresses views akin to panpsychism in his British Academy lecture "The Basis of Realism," reprinted in *Realism and the Background of Phenomenology* edited by R. M. Chisholm (Glencoe, IL: Free Press, 1960).

Of works by earlier panpsychists, special mention should be made of G. W. Leibniz, *Monadology* (various editions), and Arthur Schopenhauer, *Die Welt als Wille und Vorstellung*, 3 vols. (Leipzig, 1818), translated by R. B. Haldane and J. Kemp as *The World as Will and Idea* (London: Trubner, 1883), as well as his *Über den Willen in der Natur* (Frankfurt, 1836), translated by K. Hillebrand as *On the Will in Nature* (London, 1889).

Giordano Bruno's panpsychist views are presented in the second dialogue of *De la causa, Principio e uno*; for translations see Sidney Greenberg's *The Infinite in Giordano Bruno* (New York: King's Crown Press, 1950) and Jack Lindsay's version in *Cause, Principle and Unity* (New York: International, 1964). The works by Telesio and Campanella in which their panpsychism is expounded are not available in English. There is a very clear summary of their arguments in Harald Høffding, *A History of Modern Philosophy*, Vol. I (London, 1908). The texts of the pre-Socratics, some of whom were hylozoists rather than panpsychists, are available in English translation in G. S. Kirk and J. E. Raven, *The Presocratic Philosophers* (Cambridge, U.K.: Cambridge University Press, 1957). Because of his remarks about the "plastic nature in the universe" in *The True Intellectual System of the Universe*, Ralph Cudworth is described as a panpsychist in various reference works, but it is doubtful that this classification is accurate. Cudworth appears to have postulated the "plastic nature" for living things only and he should be labeled a "vitalist" in a sense in which this theory does not automatically imply panpsychism. C. B. Renouvier's panpsychism, which is in many ways similar to that of Leibniz, is expounded in several of his works, most fully in *La nouvelle monadologie* (Paris: A. Colin, 1899). Eduard von Hartmann advocates the view that even atoms possess an unconscious will in *Grundriss der Naturphilosophie*, Vol. II of *System der Philosophie im Grundriss* (Bad Sachsa im Harz, 1907). Benedict de Spinoza and Henri Bergson were not listed as panpsychists in the text because there is some doubt as to how some of their remarks are to be interpreted. In Spinoza's case there is at least one passage (*Ethics*, Pt. II, Note 2, Prop. XIII) supporting such a classification. Similarly, some of the remarks in "Summary and Conclusions," in Bergson's *Matter and Memory* (London: Allen and Unwin, 1910), may be construed as an endorsement of panpsychism.

C. H. Waddington's genetic argument is presented in *The Nature of Life* (London: Allen and Unwin, 1961). W. K. Clifford advocates very similar arguments in his essays "Body and Mind" and "On the Nature of Things-in-Themselves," in *Lectures and Essays,* Vol. II (London, 1903). The American critical realist C. A. Strong also employs genetic arguments in support of panpsychism in *The Origin of Consciousness* (London: Macmillan, 1918). Sewall Wright, a distinguished contemporary biologist, defends panpsychism on scientific grounds in "Gene and Organism," in the *American Naturalist* 87 (1953). Hackel's views are found in *Natürliche Schöpfungsgeschichte* (4th ed., Berlin, 1892), translated by E. Ray Lankester as *The History of Creation* (London, 1892), and in *Zellseelen und Seelenzellen* (Leipzig, 1909). Panpsychism is also defended on the basis of an appeal to continuity in nature in Harald Høffding, *Outlines of Psychology* (London, 1919). Høffding, however, is rather more diffident than the other writers mentioned in this paragraph. Schiller's defenses of panpsychism are contained in his *Studies in Humanism* (London: Macmillan, 1907) and *Logic for Use* (London: G. Bell, 1929). There is a full discussion of William James's views on panpsychism and various related theories in W. T. Bush, "William James and Panpsychism," in *Columbia University Studies in the History of Ideas,* Vol. II (New York, 1925).

A defense of the scholastic doctrine that an effect cannot possess any perfection which is not found in its cause is contained in G. H. Joyce, *Principles of Natural Theology* (London: Longmans, Green, 1923), Ch. 3. The question of what may be meant by the claim that an effect contains a "new" property is discussed in Arthur O. Lovejoy, "The Meanings of 'Emergence' and Its Modes," in *Proceedings of the Sixth International Congress of Philosophy* (New York, 1927); Ernest Nagel, *The Structure of Science* (New York: Harcourt Brace, 1961); and Arthur Pap, *An Introduction to the Philosophy of Science* (New York: Free Press of Glencoe, 1962). Certain contemporary arguments about the alleged causal inexplicability of human actions, similar to the genetic arguments by Paulsen and Waddington, are examined in Bernard Berofsky, "Determinism and the Concept of a Person," in *Journal of Philosophy* 61 (1964): 461–475.

General surveys of panpsychism are found in A. Rau, *Der moderne Panpsychismus* (Berlin, 1901), and Charles Hartshorne, "Panpsychism," in *A History of Philosophical Systems,* edited by V. T. A. Ferm (New York: Philosophical Library, 1950). Almost all extended discussions of panpsychism occur in the works of writers who accept the theory or who are at least sympathetic to it. One of the few highly critical discussions is contained in Alois Riehl, *Zur Einführung in die Philosophie der Gegenwart* (Leipzig: Teubner, 1903). Eisler's article on panpsychism in his *Wörterbuch der Philosophische Begriffe* (4th ed., Berlin: E. S.

Mittler, 1929) contains a very elaborate list of panpsychists and their writings.

Paul Edwards (1967)

PANTHEISM

"Pantheism" is a doctrine that usually occurs in a religious and philosophical context in which there are already tolerably clear conceptions of God and of the universe and the question has arisen how these two conceptions are related. It is, of course, easy to read pantheistic doctrines back into unsophisticated texts in which the concept of the divine remains unclarified, but it is wise to be skeptical about the value of such a reading. Some commentators have confidently ascribed pantheistic views to the Eleatics simply because they assert that what is, is one. But even if one considers Xenophanes, the most plausible candidate for such an ascription, it is clear that considerable care must be exercised. Thales and Anaximenes had some idea of objects in the world being infused with a divine power or substance that conferred life and movement. Xenophanes took over this idea and added to it a critique of Homeric and Hesiodic polytheism, attacking both their anthropomorphism and the immorality in which they involved the gods; his own consequent view of deity remains mysterious, however. Aristotle said that Xenophanes "with his eye on the whole world said that the One was god," but he also complained that Xenophanes "made nothing clear." It seems likely that Xenophanes, like other early Greek thinkers, did not distinguish clearly between asserting that an object was divine and asserting that a divine power informed the object's movement.

A failure by commentators themselves to observe this distinction makes it misleadingly easy to present both earlier pre-Socratic and later Stoic philosophers as recruits to the ranks of pantheism. But even Marcus Aurelius, the only notable thinker among them who can plausibly be represented as a pantheist, when he addressed the Universe itself as a deity did not clearly address it in the sense of all that is rather than in the sense of some principle of order that informs all that is.

VEDIC PANTHEISM

As in Greek thought, the approach to pantheism in Indian thought is a systematic critique of polytheism. Although there are also conceptions of a god who reigns as the highest deity—Indra at one time held this position—what emerged with the growth of theological reflection was the notion of Brahman. Brahman is the single, infinite reality, indefinable and unchanging, behind the illusory changing world of perceived material objects. The equation of plurality and change with imperfection is an assumption of the Vedanta teachings. From it there is drawn a proof of the illusory character of the material world, as well as of its imperfection. Were the material world real, it must, being neither self-existent nor eternal, have originated from Brahman. But if Brahman were such that from within it what is multifarious, changing, and therefore imperfect could arise, then Brahman would be imperfect. And what is imperfect cannot be Brahman.

We take the illusory for the real because our knowledge is itself tainted with imperfections. Our ordinary knowledge is such that knower and known, subject and object, are distinct. But to know Brahman would be for subject and object to become identical; it would be to attain a knowledge in which all distinctions were abolished and in which what is known would therefore be inexpressible. Two features of the pantheism of the Vedanta scholars deserve comment. The first is the affinity between their logical doctrines and those of F. H. Bradley, whose treatment of the realm of appearance is precisely parallel to the Vedanta treatment of the realm of illusion (*māyā*); Bradley's Absolute resembles Brahman chiefly in that both must be characterized negatively. As with Bradley's doctrine, the natural objection to Vedanta pantheism is to ask how, if Brahman is perfect and unchangeable, even the illusions of finitude, multiplicity, and change can have arisen. The Vedanta doctrine's answer is circular: Ignorance (lack of enlightenment) creates illusion. But it is, of course, illusion that fosters the many forms of ignorance.

Yet if the explanation of illusion is unsatisfactory, at least the cure for it is clear; the Vedanta doctrine is above all practical in its intentions. It will be noteworthy in the discussion of other and later pantheisms how often pantheism is linked to doctrines of mystical and contemplative practice. The separateness of the divine and the human, upon which monotheists insist, raises sharply the problem of how man can ever attain true unity with the divine. Those contemplative and mystical experiences, common to many religions, for whose description the language of a union between human and divine seems peculiarly appropriate—at least to those who have enjoyed these experiences—for that very reason create problems for a monotheistic theology, problems that have often been partly resolved by an approach to pantheistic formulations. It is at least plausible to argue that the essence of the Vedanta doctrine lies in its elucidation of mystical experience rather than in any use of metaphysical argument for purely intellectual ends.

WESTERN PANTHEISM TO SPINOZA

The pantheism of the Vedanta argues that because God is All and One, what is many is therefore illusory and unreal. The characteristic pantheism and near pantheism of the European Middle Ages proceeded, by contrast, from the view that because God alone truly is, all that is must in some sense be God, or at least a manifestation of God. Insofar as this view implies a notion of true being at the top of a scale of degrees of being, its ancestry is Platonic or Neoplatonic. It would be difficult to call Neoplatonism itself pantheistic because although it views the material world as an emanation from the divine, the fallen and radically imperfect and undivine character of that world is always emphasized.

ERIGENA AND AVERROES. However, the translation of Neoplatonic themes of emanation into Christian terms by John Scotus Erigena (c. 810–c. 877) resulted in *De Divisione Naturae,* which was condemned as heretical precisely because of its break with monotheism. It might be argued that Erigena does not seem to be wholly pantheistic in that he did not treat every aspect of nature as part of the divine in the same way and to the same degree. This would be misleading, however, for on this criterion no thinker could ever be judged a pantheist.

According to Erigena the whole, *natura,* is composed of four species of being: that which creates and is not created, that which is created and creates, that which is created and does not create, and that which is not created and does not create. The first is God as creator; the last, God as that into which all created beings have returned. The second and third are the created universe, which is in process of passing from God in his first form to God in his last form. Erigena wrote as if each class of beings belongs to a different period in a historical unfolding, but he also treated this as a misleading but necessary form of expression. *Natura* is eternal; the whole process is eternally present; and everything is a *theophania,* a manifestation of God.

Pope Honorius III condemned *De Divisione Naturae* in 1225 as "pullulating with worms of heretical perversity," and much earlier Erigena's other work had been described by the Council of Valence (855) as "Irish porridge" and "the devil's invention." Clearly, part of what perturbed them was Erigena's ability to interpret in a pantheistic sense both the biblical doctrine of creation and the biblical notion of a time when God shall be all in all.

A similar problem arose for the Islamic interpreter of Aristotle, Ibn Rushd (Averroes), whose discussions of the relation of human to divine intelligence aroused suspicion of pantheism and whose assertions of fidelity to the Qur'an did not save him from condemnation. A Christian Aristotelian such as Meister Eckhart, the Dominican mystic, was also condemned. Both Eckhart and Johannes Tauler spoke of God and man in terms of a mutual dependence that implies a fundamental unity including both. However, in every medieval case after Erigena the imputation of pantheism is at best inconclusive. Only since the sixteenth century has genuine pantheism become a recurrent European phenomenon.

BRUNO. Giordano Bruno (1548–1600) was an explicitly anti-Christian pantheist. He conceived of God as the immanent cause or goal of nature, distinct from each finite particular only because he includes them all within his own being. The divine life that informs everything also informs the human mind and soul, and the soul is immortal because it is part of the divine. Since God is not distinct from the world, he can have no particular providential intentions. Since all events are equally ruled by divine law, miracles cannot occur. Whatever happens, happens in accordance with law, and our freedom consists in identifying ourselves with the course of things. The Bible, according to Bruno, insofar as it errs on these points, is simply false.

BOEHME. Jakob Boehme (1575–1624) was a shoemaker, a mystic, and a Lutheran whose wish to remain within the church was shown by the fact that to the end he received the sacraments. The pantheism of Erigena or Bruno was founded upon a view that the universe must necessarily be a single all-inclusive system if it is to be intelligible. Their pantheism derived from their ideal of explanation. Boehme, by contrast, claimed that he was merely recording what he has learned from an inward mystical illumination. He saw the foundation of all things in the divine *Ungrund,* in which the triad of Everything, Nothing, and the Divine Agony that results from their encounter produces out of itself a procession of less ultimate triads which constitute the natural and human world. Boehme made no distinction between nature and spirit, for he saw nature as entirely the manifestation of spirit. It is not at all clear in what sense the propositions that Boehme advanced can have been the record of vision; it is clear that both in claiming authority for his vision and in the content of his doctrine he was bound to encounter, as he did, the condemnation of the Lutheran clergy.

SPINOZA. Benedict de Spinoza's pantheism had at least three sources: his ideal of human felicity, his concept of explanation, and his notion of the degrees of human knowledge. His explicit aim was to discover a good that would be independent of all the ordinary contingencies of chance and misfortune. Only that which is capable of completely filling and occupying the mind can be the supreme good in Spinoza's sense. The only knowledge that could satisfy these requirements would be the knowledge that the mind is part of the total system of nature and is at one with it when recognizing that everything is as it must be. Felicity is the knowledge of necessity, for if the mind can accept the necessity of its own place in the whole ordering of things, there will be room neither for rebellion nor for complaint. Thus, from the outset Spinoza's characterization of the supreme good required that his philosophy exhibit the whole universe as a single connected system.

So it is with his concept of explanation. To explain anything is to demonstrate that it cannot be other than it is. To demonstrate this entails laying bare the place of what is to be explained within a total system. Spinoza made no distinction between contingent causal connections and necessary logical connections. A deductive system in which every proposition follows from a set of initial axioms, postulates, and definitions mirrors the structure of the universe, in which every finite mode of existence exemplifies the pattern of order that derives from the single substance, *Deus, sive natura* (God, or nature). There can be only one substance, not a multiplicity of substances, for Spinoza so defined the notion of substance that the relation of a property to the substance of which it is a property is necessary, and therefore intelligible and explicable; however, the relation of one substance to another must be external and contingent, and therefore unintelligible and inexplicable. But for Spinoza it is unintelligible that what is unintelligible should be thought to exist. Hence, there can be only one substance; "God" and "Nature" could not be the names of two distinct and independent substances.

It follows that God cannot be said to be the creator of nature, except in a sense quite other than that of Christian or Jewish orthodoxy. Spinoza did distinguish between nature as active (*natura naturans*) and nature as passive product (*natura naturata*), and insofar as he identified God with nature as creative and self-sustaining rather than with nature as passive, he could speak of God as the immanent cause of the world. But this is quite different from the orthodox conception of divine efficient causality. Also, in Spinoza's view, there can be no divine providential intentions for particular agents and there can be no miracles. What, then, of the Bible?

Spinoza regarded the Bible as an expression of truth in the only mode in which the ordinary, unreflective, irrational man is able to believe it or be guided by it. Such men need images, for their knowledge is of the confused kind that does not rise to the rational and scientific explanation of phenomena, let alone to that *scientia intuitiva* (intuitive knowledge) by which the mind grasps the whole necessity of things and becomes identical with the *infinita idea Dei* (infinite idea of God). Freed from all those passions that dominated his actions so long as he did not grasp them intellectually, man is moved only by a fully conscious awareness of his place in the whole system. It is this awareness that Spinoza also identified as the intellectual love of God.

In using theological language to characterize both nature and the good of human life, Spinoza was not concealing an ultimately materialistic and atheistic standpoint. He believed that all the key predicates by which divinity is ascribed apply to the entire system of things, for it is infinite, at once the uncaused *causa sui* and *causa omnium* (cause of itself and cause of everything) and eternal. Even if Spinoza's attitude to the Bible was that it veils the truth, he believed that it *is* the truth that it veils. He considered his doctrine basically identical with both that of the ancient Hebrew writers and that of St. Paul. This did not save him from condemnation by the synagogue in his lifetime, let alone from condemnation by the church afterward.

GERMAN PANTHEISM

Erigena, Bruno, Boehme, Spinoza—each of these, no matter how much he may have made use of material drawn from earlier philosophical or religious writing, was a thinker who was independent of his specifically pantheist predecessors and who revived pantheism by his own critical reflections upon monotheism. It was only in the eighteenth century that something like a specifically pantheist tradition emerged. The word *pantheist* was first used in 1705 by John Toland in his *Socinianism truly stated*. Toland's hostile critic, J. Fay, used the word *pantheism* in 1709 and it speedily became common. With the increased questioning of Christianity, accompanied by an unwillingness to adopt atheistic positions, pantheism became an important doctrine, first for Johann Wolfgang von Goethe and Gotthold Ephraim Lessing, both of whom were influenced by Spinoza, then for Friedrich Schleiermacher, and finally for Johann Gottlieb Fichte, Friedrich von Schelling, and Georg Wilhelm Friedrich Hegel.

GOETHE AND LESSING. Goethe's aim was to discover a mode of theological thinking, rather than a theology, with which he could embrace both what he took to be the pagan attitude to nature and the redemptive values of Christianity. Suspicious as he was of Christian asceticism, he also recognized a distinctive Christian understanding of human possibility, and his various utterances about Christianity cannot be rendered consistent even by the greatest scholarly ingenuity. In the formulas of pantheism, which he was able to interpret in the sense that he wished precisely because he failed to understand Spinoza correctly, Goethe found a theology that enabled him both to identify the divine with the natural and to separate them. The infinite creativity Goethe ascribed to nature is what he took to be divine; but while the seeds of a consistent doctrine can be discerned in this aspect of Goethe's writings, it would be wrong to deny that part of pantheism's attraction for him was that it seemed to license his will to be inconsistent.

Lessing, by contrast, was consistent. He found the kernel of truth in all religions in a neutral version of Spinozism, which allowed him to see Judaism, Christianity, and Islam as distorted versions of the same truth, distorted because they confuse the historical trappings with the metaphysical essence.

SCHLEIERMACHER. Schleiermacher's quite different preoccupation was to make religion acceptable to the cultured unbelievers of his own time. The core of religion, on his view, is the sense of absolute dependence; to that on which we are absolutely dependent he gave a variety of names and titles, speaking of God in both monotheistic and pantheistic terms. However, he committed himself to pantheism by asserting that it is the Totality that is divine.

FICHTE. It is clear from Goethe, Lessing, and Schleiermacher that Spinoza's writing had become a major text for philosophical theology, but for these writers he was an inspiration rather than a precise source. With the advent of German idealism, the attempt to criticize the deductive form of Spinoza's reasoning while preserving the pantheistic content became a major theme of German philosophy. Nowhere is this more evident than in Fichte's writing, in which God and the universe are identified because the world is nothing but the material through which the Ego realizes its infinite moral vocation, and the divine is nothing but the moral order that includes both world and Ego. The divine cannot be personal and cannot have been the external creator of the world. Fichte poured scorn on the unintelligibility of the orthodox doctrine of creation ex nihilo (out of nothing). He distinguished sharply between the genuinely metaphysical and the merely historical elements in Christianity. It is the theology of the Johannine Gospel that he treated as the expression of the metaphysical, and to this he gave a pantheistic sense.

SCHELLING AND HEGEL. Schelling's pantheism was cruder than Fichte's—according to him, all distinctions disappear in the ultimate nature of things. The divine is identified with this ultimate distinctionless merging of nature and spirit, a unity more fundamental than any of the differences of the merely empirical world.

Hegel was subtler and more philosophically interesting than either Fichte or Schelling. Like Boehme and Schleiermacher, he remained within orthodox Protestant Christianity, claiming to be engaged in the interpretation rather than the revision of its dogmatic formulas. The Hegelian Absolute Idea preexists its finite manifestations logically but not temporally, and it receives its full embodiment only at the end of history, when it is incorporated in a social and moral order fully conscious of its own nature and of its place in history. This phase of self-consciousness is already reached at the level of thought in Hegel's *Logic*. But the Absolute Idea has no existence apart from or over and above its actual and possible manifestations in nature and history. Hence, the divine is the Totality.

After Hegel pantheism was less in vogue. The critique of Christianity became more radical, atheism became a more acceptable alternative, and Spinoza dominated the intellectual scene far less. In England a poetic pantheism appeared in Percy Bysshe Shelley and William Wordsworth, but in Shelley it coexisted with something much closer to atheism and in Wordsworth with a Christianity that displaced it. In any case, the intellectual resources of such a pantheism were so meager that it is not surprising that it did not survive in the nineteenth century.

CRITICISMS OF PANTHEISM

Pantheism essentially involves two assertions: that everything that exists constitutes a unity and that this all-inclusive unity is divine. What could be meant by the assertion that everything that exists constitutes a unity? It is first and most clearly not a unity derived from membership of the same class, the view that seems to have been taken by Boehme. "There is no class of all that is," wrote Aristotle. Why not? Because existence is not a genus. To say that something exists is not to classify it at all. When Boehme asserted that the universe includes both existence and nonexistence, he both anticipated a long tradition that culminated in Martin Heidegger and remained unintelligible. The notion of *a* unity that includes all that exists— or even all that exists and all that does not exist—is a notion devoid of content. What could be unitary in such an ostensible collection?

The unity might be of another kind, however. In Spinoza the unity of the universe is a logical unity, with every particular item deducible from the general nature of things. There is a single deductive web of explanation—there are not sciences; there is science. About such an alleged unity two points must be made. First, the contingent aspect of nature is entirely omitted. Even a total description of the universe in which every part of the description was logically related to some other part or parts (assuming for the moment such a description to be conceivable) would still leave us with the question whether the universe was as it was described; and if it was as it was described, this truth would be a contingent truth that could not be included in the description itself and that could stand in no internal conceptual relationship to the description. The fact of existence would remain irreducibly contingent. Second, the actual development of the sciences does not accord with Spinoza's ideal. The forms of explanation are not all the same; the logical structure of Darwinian evolutionary theory must be distinguished from the logical structure of quantum mechanics. Thus, the kind of unity ascribed by Spinoza to the universe seems to be lacking.

In Fichte and Hegel the unity ascribed to the universe is one of an overall purpose manifest in the pattern of events, as that pattern is discovered by the agent in his social and moral life. In order for this assertion to be meaningful it must be construed, at least in part, in empirical terms; in Fichte's case as a hypothesis about moral development, in Hegel's case as a hypothesis about historical development. Neither hypothesis appears to be vindicated by the facts.

Suppose, however, that a unity of some kind, inclusive of all that is, could be discovered. In virtue of what might the pantheist claim that it was divine? The infinity and the eternity of the universe have often been the predicates that seemed to entail its divinity, but the sense in which the universe is infinite and eternal is surely not that in which the traditional religions have ascribed these predicates to a god. What is clear is that pantheism as a theology has a source, independent of its metaphysics, in a widespread capacity for awe and wonder in the face both of natural phenomena and of the apparent totality of things. It is at least in part because pantheist metaphysics provides a vocabulary that appears more adequate than any other for the expression of these emotions that pantheism has shown such historical capacity for survival. But this does not, of course, give any warrant for believing pantheism to be true.

See also Aristotle; Averroes; Boehme, Jakob; Bradley, Francis Herbert; Brahman; Bruno, Giordano; Darwinism; Eckhart, Meister; Erigena, John Scotus; Eternity; Fichte, Johann Gottlieb; Goethe, Johann Wolfgang von; God, Concepts of; Hegel, Georg Wilhelm Friedrich; Heidegger, Martin; Indian Philosophy; Infinity in Theology and Metaphysics; Jacobi, Friedrich Heinrich; Lessing, Gotthold Ephraim; Marcus Aurelius Antoninus; Neoplatonism; Pantheismusstreit; Schelling, Friedrich Wilhelm Joseph von; Schleiermacher, Friedrich Daniel Ernst; Shelley, Percy Bysshe; Spinoza, Benedict (Baruch) de; Tauler, Johannes; Toland, John; Xenophanes of Colophon.

Bibliography

Boehme, Jakob. Works. Edited by C. J. Barber. London, 1909–.

Bruno, Giordano. "Concerning the Cause, Principle, and One." Translated by Sidney Greenberg in The Infinite in Giordano Bruno. New York: King's Crown Press, 1950.

Bruno, Giordano. "On the Infinite Universe and Worlds." Translated by Dorothea W. Singer in Giordano Bruno: His Life and Thought. New York: Schuman, 1950.

Eckhart. Meister Eckhart. Edited, with introduction, by O. Karrer. Munich, 1926.

Erigena, John Scotus. Opera. In Patrologia Latina, edited by J. P. Migne. Paris, 1844–1864. Vol. 122.

Fichte, J. G. Die Schrifte zu J. G. Fichte's Atheismusstreit. Edited by H. Lindau. Munich, 1912.

Fichte, J. G. The Science of Knowledge. Translated by A. E. Kroeger. Philadelphia, 1868.

Flint, Robert. Antitheistic Theories. London, 1878. Baird lectures.

Hegel, G. W. F. Lectures on the Philosophy of Religion. Translated by E. B. Speirs and J. B. Sanderson, 3 vols. London: K. Paul, Trench, Trubner, 1895.

Schelling, Friedrich. Werke. Edited by M. Schröter. 8 vols. Munich: Beck, 1927–1956.

Schleiermacher, Friedrich. On Religion: Speeches to Its Cultured Despisers. Translated by J. W. Oman. London: K. Paul, Trench, Trubner, 1893.

Spinoza, Benedict de. The Chief Works. Translated by R. H. M. Elwes, 2 vols. New York: Dover, 1951.

Alasdair MacIntyre (1967)

PANTHEISMUSSTREIT

Pantheismusstreit or the pantheism controversy, came to the attention of the public in 1785 when Friedrich Heinrich Jacobi published *Ueber die Lehre des Spinoza,* his correspondence with Moses Mendelssohn concerning Gotthold Ephraim Lessing's late Spinozist phase. Other prominent writers, including Immanuel Kant, Johann Gottfried Herder, Johann Wolfgang von Goethe, Johann Kaspar Lavater, and Johann Georg Hamann, became involved in this dispute, which led to an objective reappraisal of Spinozism. The first important reaction to Benedict de Spinoza's influence in Germany had been Gottfried Wilhelm Leibniz's *Theodicy* (1710). At the time of the pantheism controversy, the distorted image of Spinoza, the "satanic atheist," was definitely destroyed. This image had been created by Pierre Bayle and cultivated in Germany by Theophil Gottlieb Spitzel (1639–1691), Johann Christophorus Sturm (1635–1703), Johann Konrad Dippel (c. 1672–1734), and Christian K. Kortholt (1633–1694), whose *De Tribus Impostoribus Liber* (1680) had attacked Herbert of Cherbury, Thomas Hobbes, and Spinoza as "impostors."

INCEPTION OF THE CONTROVERSY

Jacobi's book constituted one stage in the struggle waged by the supporters of Hamann (whose sentimentalist faith Jacobi attempted to combine with Kant's critical philosophy) against the religious rationalism of the Berlin Enlightenment, whose proponents were grouped around Friedrich Christian Nicolai and the *Berlinische Monatsschrift.* In his *Golgotha und Scheblimini* (1784), Hamann had attacked the theistic rationalism of Mendelssohn's *Jerusalem* (1783). A work prized by Kant, Herder, Mirabeau, and Christian Garve, *Jerusalem* was directed against state-imposed creeds and religions of revelation.

Jacobi's hasty publication of his correspondence with Mendelssohn, too, was indirectly inspired by Hamann. The latter informed Jacobi on June 29, 1785, that the first part of Mendelssohn's *Morgenstunden* was already being printed. Wrongly suspecting that Mendelssohn had mentioned their controversy over Lessing in this work, Jacobi committed a dual breach of trust. To his *Ueber die Lehre des Spinoza* he appended anonymously a fragment from Goethe's unpublished "Prometheus" (1774) that Jacobi had shown Lessing during a conversation at Wolfenbüttel on July 7, 1780.

It was this conversation that served as the starting point and focus of the pantheism controversy. To the report of this conversation Jacobi added a digest of an argument with Mendelssohn that had ensued from a report by Elise Reimarus (February 1783) to the effect that Mendelssohn was busy with a work on Lessing. Through her, Jacobi led Mendelssohn to believe that "Lessing had been a Spinozist" but had never admitted it to his friend Mendelssohn because the latter had never taken seriously a relevant hint concerning the Spinozist purport of Paragraph 73 of Lessing's *Erziehung des Menschengeschlechts*. Mendelssohn, through Elise Reimarus, then addressed precise questions to Jacobi regarding the character of Lessing's alleged Spinozism. He considered it unlikely that, one, Lessing had been a Spinozist and that, two, he would have remained silent about it to a friend of many years' standing (Mendelssohn) while confiding it to the first stranger that had come along (Jacobi). Mendelssohn suggested courteously that perhaps Lessing, as was his nature, had made in jest certain paradoxical statements to Jacobi. However, if Jacobi could conclusively demonstrate Lessing's Spinozism, then, Mendelssohn allowed, he would have to give precedence to the truth in the work he planned to write about his friend.

In his reply of November 4, 1783, Jacobi again gave details of his conversations with Lessing. But in so doing, he misjudged his own situation. It was obvious that Lessing, tired of hearing Spinoza treated "like a dead dog," had been attempting to provoke Jacobi into a refutation of Spinozism. Jacobi, however, had declared himself helpless against the geometrical reasoning of Spinoza, which seemed unanswerable to him. Although he rejected Spinoza's "fatalism" and the concept of a God who created without insight and without will, he could find no counterarguments. To this Lessing had replied, "I note that you would like to have your will free; I do not crave free will." Lessing characterized the tendency to give thought the precedence over other life forces as a human prejudice. He asked Jacobi whether he thought he could derive the concept of an extramundane rationally creative deity from Leibniz. "I fear," Lessing added, "that Leibniz himself was fundamentally a Spinozist." He recalled "a passage in Leibniz where it is said of God that he himself is in a state of everlasting expansion and contraction, and that this constitutes the creation and existence of the world." Hard-pressed by the logic of Lessing as well as that of Spinoza, which "admits of no cause of things separate from the world," Jacobi saved himself by a leap into a sentimentalist faith in the God of Christianity who orders the world teleologically. With unconcealed irony, Lessing remarked that such a leap of faith ending up in a somersault was something he could no longer exact of his "old legs and heavy head." Derisively, he professed to find

agreements with his own system even in Charles Bonnet's *Palingénésie*, which Lavater—without the author's permission—had translated and had dedicated to Mendelssohn in an ill-fated attempt at proselytizing. Lessing also claimed to discern "obvious Spinozism" in Frans Hemsterhuis's *Aristée*. Jacobi himself believed he recognized in the disputed Paragraph 73 of Lessing's *Erziehung des Menschengeschlechts* his Spinozist interpretation of Christ as reality (*natura naturata*) and of God as the infinite substance (*natura naturans*).

Seven months after his reply to Mendelssohn (June 1784), Jacobi learned from Elise Reimarus that Mendelssohn had put aside his *Lessing* "in order first to venture a round with the Spinozists or 'all-in-one'rs.'" In August of that year, Mendelssohn wrote his *Erinnerungen* and sent them to Jacobi without, however, publishing them at that time. (They first appeared in 1786 in *Moses Mendelssohn an die Freunde Lessings,* pp. 36–56). In the *Erinnerungen* Mendelssohn marshaled rationalistic arguments against Spinoza and again expressed his disbelief in Lessing's Spinozism. He dealt sarcastically with Jacobi's "honorable retreat under the flag of faith" as a device necessary for Christian philosophers; Mendelssohn's own religion, on the other hand, allowed him to "raise doubts on grounds of reason" and did not dictate to him "any belief in eternal verities." Mendelssohn left unanswered Jacobi's *Lettre à M. Hemsterhuis,* a copy of which the author had sent him on September 5, 1784. But he notified his correspondent once again that pantheism would indeed come under discussion in the first part of the *Morgenstunden,* although their mutual correspondence would be disregarded. Mendelssohn requested that Jacobi delay publishing his "counterrecollections" until after the publication of the *Morgenstunden.*

Jacobi again sent Mendelssohn an exposition of Spinozism, in forty-four paragraphs, which ended in an enthusiastic identification of Christian faith, love, and—surprisingly—knowledge (in the sense of knowledge of nature). Mendelssohn, astonished at Jacobi's proselytizing zeal, called on Reimarus to act as arbiter in the matter of the controversy over Lessing. Reimarus counseled silence about the whole affair so as not to dishonor the memory of Lessing. Still another exegesis of Spinozism by Jacobi in six paragraphs began with the traditional thesis: "Spinozism is atheism."

Despite Mendelssohn's renewed assurances to Elise Reimarus on May 24, 1785, that he would not make use of his correspondence with Jacobi, the latter with an utter lack of consideration published the letters on August 28, 1785. Jacobi's account reads like an exorcism of the magnetic powers of Spinozism, whereas Mendelssohn's concern in the controversy was only to clear Lessing of the charge of Spinozism and to contrast his own religion of reason with Jacobi's visionary religion of sentiment, as well as to polemicize against Spinoza with Wolffian arguments. Mendelssohn's main proof for the existence of a rational God (in Part I of the *Morgenstunden*) was that all that is real must first be thought as real by some being, hence there exists an infinite intellect.

RESULTS OF THE CONTROVERSY

The pantheism controversy spread to wider circles of German intellectual life with the anonymous publication in 1786 of *Die Resultate der Jacobi'schen und Mendelssohn'schen Philosophie* by Thomas W. Wizenman, a young follower of Hamann and a Pietist, who had been induced by Jacobi to read Spinoza. Wizenman, under the guise of a disinterested spectator, openly took Jacobi's side. As Kant later revealed it, Wizenman launched into an *argumentum ad hominem* against Mendelssohn, attempting to destroy deism with atheism, and atheism with deism. For the fideist Wizenman, it was impossible to demonstrate the existence or the nonexistence of God and his relationships to the world. He tried to define the concept of reason in such a fashion that the rationality of a belief in revealed religion would proceed from this definition, once historical evidence of the revelation was at hand.

Compelled by Wizenman's publication to express an opinion, Kant in "Was heisst: sich im Denken orientieren?" (*Berlinische Monatsschrift,* October 1786) rejected both Jacobi's sentimentalist faith and Mendelssohn's rationalist faith as subjective views that conceal in themselves the danger of fanaticism. As in the later *Critique of Judgment* (Paragraph 80), Kant declared that pantheism did not provide a teleological explanation of things, so in the *Monatsschrift* article he defended himself against the reproach that his *Critique of Pure Reason* had promoted Spinozism: "Spinozism speaks of thoughts that themselves think and thus of an accidental thing that still at the same time exists for itself as subject—a concept that is not to be found at all in the human understanding and cannot be brought into it." Kant disapproved of Mendelssohn's attempt to reduce the quarrel of freedom of will versus determinism to a matter of pure logomachy (*Einige Bermerkungen zu Jakobis Prüfung der Mendelssohnschen Morgenstunden,* Leipzig, 1786).

More important than the polemics of the pantheism controversy were its effects on Herder and Goethe and later on Friedrich Schleiermacher, Friedrich von Schelling, and G. W. F. Hegel. Herder, in his five conversations titled *Gott* (1787), deplored Spinoza's terminological dependence on René Descartes, but he accepted Spinoza's concept of God, whom he regarded as the primal power from which all other powers derive. Thus in his own way he came close to the concept of the primal phenomenon that Goethe, as a metaphysical philosopher of nature, was seeking to investigate.

Goethe himself had reread Spinoza in January 1785 and had found in him the foundations for his own holistic or antimechanistic, anti-Newtonian concept of the universe. He had already, on June 4, 1785, objected to Jacobi: "You acknowledge the highest reality, which is the basis of Spinozism, on which all else rests, from which all else flows. He does not prove the Being of God, Being *is* God. And if for this reason others scold Spinoza for being an atheist, I should like to name him and praise him as *theissimum,* indeed, *christianissimum.*" On October 21 of the same year, Goethe sharply attacked Jacobi's play on the word *believe* as the behavior of a "faith-sophist," admonished him to apply himself to "clarity and distinctness of expression," and admitted "that while by nature I do not share Spinoza's mode of conception, if I had to cite a book that, more than any I know, agrees most fully with my own conception, I should have to name the *Ethics.*" On May 5, 1786, he expressed his disagreement with Jacobi:

> I cling more and more firmly to the reverence for God of the atheist [Spinoza] … and I cede to you [Christians] all that your religion enjoins and must enjoin … When you say that one can only *believe* in God … then I say to you that I lay great weight on *looking and seeing* and when Spinoza, speaking of *scientia intuitiva,* says *Hoc cognoscendi genus procedit ab adaequata idea essentiae formalis quorundam Dei attributorum ad adaequatam cognitionem essentiae rerum* [This manner of knowing moves from the adequate idea of the formal essence of some attributes of God to the adequate knowledge of the essence of things], these words give me courage to devote my entire life to the contemplation of the things that I can reach and of whose *essentia formali* I can hope to fashion an adequate idea

Just as Goethe, who, inspired by the pantheism controversy to make a study of Spinoza, became conscious of his own holism while reading the *Ethics,* so pantheism, thanks to its contact with Spinozism, progressed from its traditional manifestation as Neoplatonic emanation to a concept of evolution, which in Hegel's philosophy (and in the twentieth century, that of Henri Bergson) entails the development of the Absolute in and with the world.

See also Hamann, Johann Georg; Jacobi, Friedrich Heinrich; Mendelssohn, Moses; Spinoza, Benedict (Baruch) de.

Bibliography

Jacobi, Friedrich Heinrich. *Ueber die Lehre des Spinoza in Briefen an den Herrn Moses Mendelssohn.* Breslau, 1785. 2nd ed., revised and enlarged, Breslau: G. Löwe, 1789.

Mendelssohn, Moses. *An die Freunde Lessings.* Berlin: C. Voss, 1786.

Mendelssohn, Moses. *Morgenstunden, oder über das Daseyn Gottes.* Berlin: C. Voss, 1786.

Scholz, H. *Die Hauptschriften zum Pantheismusstreit zwischen Jacobi und Mendelssohn.* Berlin: Reuther and Reichard, 1916.

Kurt Weinberg (1967)
Translated by Albert E. Blumberg

PAPINI, GIOVANNI
(1881–1956)

Giovanni Papini, an Italian pragmatist philosopher and literary figure, was born in Florence into a family of modest means and had no formal education. Papini described himself in his *Un uomo finito* (Florence, 1913; translated by Virginia Page as *Failure; Un Uomo Finito*, New York, 1924), a book that was frankly and painfully biographical, as self-taught, urged on by an insatiable curiosity and a burning desire to investigate the various forms of knowledge. He quickly made a name for himself in Italian culture at the beginning of the twentieth century with his attack on the then prevailing positivist philosophy of Roberto Ardigò and his support of nationalistic tendencies and opposition to the ideals of democracy. He became a close friend of Giuseppe Prezzolini and other young writers who advocated doing away with the old oligarchies and giving a new impetus to the spiritual life of the country. The fruit of this collaboration was the birth in 1903 of *Leonardo,* a nonconformist review that published the most important contemporary thinkers. They chose Friedrich Nietzsche, Henri Bergson, William James, and F. C. S. Schiller as their exemplars and leaders, but the interests of the *Leonardo* group embraced the avant-garde currents in art and literature as well.

In his writings, later gathered together in a book titled *Pragmatismo* (Milan, 1913), Papini defined the essential aspects of his thought. His is a kind of magic pragmatism, markedly different from the logical and sci-entific pragmatism of C. S. Peirce. This pragmatism rejects the positivists' agnosticism concerning issues that go beyond experience; that metaphysical problems lack meaning does not indicate a lack in our intellectual capabilities but rather how very human the nature of knowing is. Instead of striving for definitive explanations in the manner of the traditional philosophies, the pragmatist is concerned with the methods and instruments that aid in defining the various forms of knowledge and activity. He does not believe in absolute principles or immutable truths; neither does he stop at mere description and generalization of the facts of experience. His aim is to develop laws and predictions, with the sole purpose of increasing the power of man over nature. No metaphysical hypothesis, observed Papini, is more valuable than another, and none can be recognized as true. On the contrary, the pragmatist viewpoint is one of maximum freedom and advocates a plurality of attitudes. Papini's celebrated definition of pragmatism was praised and quoted by William James:

> Pragmatism is a *corridor theory*, a corridor of a great hotel where there are 100 doors that open onto 100 rooms. In one there is a faldstool and a kneeling man who wants to regain his faith, in another a writing-desk and a man who wants to kill every metaphysic, in a third a laboratory and a man who wants to find new vantage points on the future. (*Pragmatismo*, p. 82)

Papini's *Leonardo* period, with neo-Hegelians such as Benedetto Croce and Giovanni Gentile aiding the attack on positivism, terminated in 1906. But this was only the beginning of a painful intellectual journey in which Papini sought, without success, to give form and coherence to his thought. He participated in the battle of ideas of *La voce,* directed by his friend Prezzolini; then he broke away and in 1911, in collaboration with Giovanni Amendola, directed a review with a strong moral bent, *L'anima;* and finally he founded *Lacerba,* an avant-garde journal violently opposed to the prevailing order of things. In the meantime, his literary output was enriched by numerous works, including *Il crepuscolo dei filosofi* (The twilight of the philosophers; Milan, 1906), *La cultura italiana* (Florence, 1906), written in collaboration with Prezzolini, and *L'altra metà* (The other half; Ancona, 1912). In addition to these books, a great number of articles testify to his zeal and his cultural interests. In this period Papini drew further away from the idealism gaining popularity in Italy, intensified his dissent with the school of Croce, and supported the futurist movement in accordance with his rebellion against traditional aesthetic rules.

Papini strongly favored Italian intervention in World War I because he saw the war as a decisive conflict between the old and the new. However, the war led him to a reassessment of Christian values and to embrace the works of the fathers of the church, and in particular those of St. Augustine. He regarded Augustine, to whom he devoted a book (*S. Agustino,* Florence, 1929), as a defender of the faith, an uncompromising polemicist, and an unsurpassable model of humanity reaching out toward the divine. Papini's activity did not diminish after his religious "conversion," but gradually became less and less concerned with philosophical matters, and concentrated instead on literary and scholarly subjects. Stricken by a disease that deprived him almost completely of the use of his senses but left his mind as active as ever, Papini bore up bravely until his death.

See also Ardigò, Roberto; Augustine, St.; Bergson, Henri; Croce, Benedetto; Gentile, Giovanni; James, William; Nietzsche, Friedrich; Peirce, Charles Sanders; Pragmatism; Schiller, Ferdinand Canning Scott.

Bibliography

See Michele Federico Sciacca, *Il secolo XX,* 2nd ed. (Milan, 1947), Vol. I, pp. 22–25; Eugenio Garin, *Cronache di filosofia* (Bari: G. Laterza, 1955); Antonio Santucci, *Il Pragmatismo in Italia* (Bologna: Mulino, 1963).

Antonio Santucci (1967)
Translated by Robert M. Connolly

PARACELSUS
(1493–1541)

Paracelsus was the pseudonym of Philippus Aureolus Theophrastus Bombastus (Baumastus) von Hohenheim, the reformer of medicine and pharmacology, chemist, philosopher, iconoclast, and writer. If he himself assumed this name, it could signify "higher than high," or "higher than Hohenheim," a jibe at his illegitimate paternal grandfather. Born in Einsiedeln, Switzerland, where his father practiced medicine, Paracelsus later lived at Villach in Carinthia (Austria), a center of mining, smelting, and alchemy—metal lores that were to occupy him for the rest of his life. From the age of fifteen his life was migratory. After medical studies at various German and Austrian universities, he seems to have completed his doctorate in 1515 at Ferrara under a faculty that was Scotist, Platonist, and humanist.

For the next eleven years, Paracelsus traveled throughout Europe, jeopardizing his authority as a physician by practicing surgery (then a craft, not a learned profession) in the army of Charles V and by experimental prescriptions. He visited spas, analyzed the waters, treated by hypnosis, and sometimes alleviated pain with laudanum. At Salzburg he narrowly escaped execution for participating in a peasants' revolt. When, in 1526, he settled at Strasbourg to establish himself in medical practice, he was famous as an object of superstitious distrust. But his spectacular cure of the printer Johann Froben quickly led to friendships with such men as Desiderius Erasmus and Oecolampadius and an appointment—against the will of the faculty—as medical lecturer at the University of Basel.

His eminence was short-lived. Lectures in German (rather than Latin), rejection of the canonical theory of Avicenna and Galen, denunciation of the apothecaries, and a public burning of the works of Avicenna were topped by the death of Froben. Those whose vested interests had been threatened tricked Paracelsus into behavior that could justify dismissal and arrest.

From 1528 until his death, his life was once again nomadic. Unkept promises and unstable patronage led him to Colmar, Nuremberg, Saint Gall, Villach, Vienna, and finally to Salzburg, where he died, probably of cancer, perhaps of metal poisoning.

Among his medical innovations were chemical urinalysis; a biochemical theory of digestion; chemical therapy; antisepsis of wounds; the use of laudanum, ether (without awareness of its anesthetic properties), and mercury for syphilis; and the combining of the apothecary's and surgeon's arts in the profession of medicine.

Paracelsus's numerous books are mostly variants on the theme of man (the microcosm) in relation to nature (the macrocosm). The most important are *Archidoxis* (c. 1524); the treatises on syphilis (c. 1529); *Opus Paragranum* (c. 1529); *Opus Paramirum* (c. 1530); *Philosophia Sagax* (c. 1536); and *Labyrinthus Medicorum* (1538).

Paracelsian philosophy was both traditional and new. Its medieval elements are traceable to alchemy and Kabbalism, which are branches of a trunk rooted in Hellenistic Neoplatonism, the Corpus Hermeticum, and Gnosticism. These occult lores shared the concept of creation through corruption; the axiom "That which is above is one with that which is below"; belief in a bisexual, homogeneous, hylozoic universe; a cyclic theory of time; and an animism approximating pantheism.

A mystery religion of life rather than merely of gold, medieval alchemy employed Semitic and Greco-Roman mythology as a screen against the unenlightened and as a vehicle of private communication for adepts. Although Paracelsus counted himself an adept, he abandoned the tradition of reserve and discarded most of the mythological symbolism. Unlike his predecessors, he wrote to clarify. He explained that alchemy's real desideratum was the secret of life.

Like Kabbalists and alchemists, Paracelsus believed in the theory that decay is the beginning of all birth. Nature emerges through separations: First, prime matter separates out of ultimate matter (also called *Yliaster* or *Mysterium Magnum*), which is eternal and paradoxically immaterial. "The first was with God ... that is *ultima materia*; this *ultima materia* He made into *prime matter* ... that is a seed and the seed is the element of water [fluid]." God spins ultimate matter out of himself. This yields, by separation, the prime matter of individual objects, a watery matrix, perpetually spawning nature, perpetually resolvable back into ultimate matter. Human creativeness in art, alchemy, or pharmacology repeats the primal act. The human demiurge, like God, separates rather than combines.

The Paracelsian theory of time resembles that of Plotinus. Time is qualitative change: growth, transition—even fate. Given the basic concept of cyclic generation and decay, Paracelsian time would be for the material cosmos a cycle of becoming. But there are two orders of time: force time (within) and growing time (without). Like the Paracelsian concept of "prime matter" in relation to "ultimate matter," this theory of time is essentially dualist.

"Above" and "below" are substantially the same: "Heaven is man and man is heaven, and all men together are the one heaven," but microcosm and macrocosm are contained by membranes or partitions.

Paracelsus rejected the concept of humors as governed by planets and substituted a chemical theory of humors as properties: salt, sweet, bitter, and sour. He retained the medieval alchemistic variant of the four elements and a quintessence, the fifth element, that is life. He tended to treat fire as less elementary than the combustible principle, sulfur. Medieval alchemy had stressed the sexual polarity of two elements, fire (identified with the male principle) and water (identified with the female principle), and contrasted flame with flow and sulfur with mercury. Paracelsus reinterpreted these as principles rather than as elements and added a third principle, salt. These are properties or states—combustible, fluid or vaporous, and solid; each confers on matter its structure, corporality, and function. As constituents of ultimate matter, these are absolutes; as components of nature, they are infinitely variable in all sensuously discernible properties. Every natural object has its own sulfur, salt, and mercury, as well as its own quintessence.

Absolute life comes from *Ens Seminis*, the cosmic protoplasm. *Ens Astrale* is to the microcosm (man) as the firmament is to the macrocosm (nature). It can sustain or poison from within, as a toxic atmosphere can poison sea water and fish. *Ens Veneni* is the poison from without. Nature lives by dying; life eats life. Man may eat the flesh of an animal whose food would poison him, but within every living body there is an alchemist that selects what is food for that body. *Ens Naturale* is the bodily harmony of the chemical humors. *Ens Spirituale* has its equivalent in what psychiatry calls the psyche. Against the common belief of his day, Paracelsus argued that madness was not demonic possession and that evil dreams were not intercourse with incubi or succubi. Mind produces diseases both in itself and its own body or in another mind or body through hypnosis, fetishism, or demonstrable ill will. Most diseases are positive evils, but there is *Ens Dei*, God's will, which no doctor can circumvent.

Although accused by Erasmus of dualist heresy because of the importance he gave primal matter and because he described illness as intrinsically evil, Paracelsus died in the Church of Rome, and his burial place became a shrine.

See also Avicenna; Erasmus, Desiderius; Galen; Gnosticism; Kabbalah; Macrocosm and Microcosm; Neoplatonism; Pantheism; Plotinus; Time.

Bibliography

WORKS BY PARACELSUS

Opera Omnia. 12 vols, edited by John Huser. Basel, 1589–1591. The original German text.

Opera Omnia. 3 vols, edited by F. Bitiskius. Geneva, 1658. In Latin.

Sämtliche Werke. 15 vols, edited by Karl Sudhoff and E. Matthiessen. Munich, 1922–1933. In German; the standard critical edition.

Four Treatises of Theophrastus von Hohenheim, edited by Henry Sigerist, C. Lilian Temkin, George Rosen, and Gregory Zilboorg. Baltimore: Johns Hopkins Press, 1941.

Selected Writings, edited by Jolande Jacobi; translated by Norbert Guterman. New York: Pantheon, 1951 and 1958. Contains an introduction by the editor. Excellent.

WORKS ON PARACELSUS

Browning, Robert. *Paracelsus.* London, 1835.

Dear, Peter. *Revolutionizing the Sciences: European Knowledge and Its Ambitions, 1500–1700.* Princeton, NJ: Princeton University Press, 2001.

Debus, Allen G. *The Chemical Philosophy: Paracelsian Science and Medicine in the Sixteenth and Seventeenth Centuries.* New York: Science History Publications, 1977.

Debus, Allen G. "The Paracelsian Compromise in Elizabethan England." *Ambix* 8 (June 1960): 71–97.

Donne, John. *Ignatius His Conclave.* London, 1613.

Koyre, Alexandre. "Paracelsus (1493–1541)." *Graduate Faculty Philosophy Journal* 24 (1) (2003): 169–208.

Pachter, Henry M. *Magic into Science.* New York: Schuman, 1951. Represents Paracelsus as a proto-Faust; readable.

Pagel, Walter. "Paracelsus and the Neoplatonic and Gnostic Tradition." *Ambix* 8 (October 1960): 125–166.

Pagel, Walter. *Paracelsus. An Introduction to Philosophical Medicine in the Era of the Renaissance.* New York: Karger, 1958. Excellent.

Pagel, Walter. "The Prime Matter of Paracelsus." *Ambix* 9 (October 1961):, 117–135.

Stillman, John Maxson. *Paracelsus.* London: Open Court, 1920. Emphasis on science.

Stoddart, Anna M. *The Life of Paracelsus.* London: Murray, 1911. Browning's interpretation.

Webster, Charles. *From Paracelsus to Newton: Magic and the Making of Modern Science.* Cambridge, U.K.: Cambridge University Press, 1982.

Weeks, Andrew. *Paracelsus: Speculative Theory and the Crisis of the Early Reformation.* Albany: State University of New York Press, 1997.

Linda Van Norden (1967)
Bibliography updated by Tamra Frei (2005)

PARACONSISTENT LOGICS

The driving thought of paraconsistency is that there are situations in which information, or legal, scientific, or philosophical principles (and so on) are inconsistent, but in which people want to draw conclusions in a sensible fashion. Clearly, if one uses a logical consequence relation in which contradictions imply everything—that is, in which $A, \neg A \vdash B$, for all A and B—this is not possible: a person would have to conclude everything (*triviality*). This motivates the definition of a paraconsistent logic. The principle of inference that contradictions entail everything is called *explosion* (or *ex falso quodlibet sequitur*). A paraconsistent logic is one in which explosion is not valid.

Paraconsistent logics are not new. As Aristotle (*An. Pr.* 63^b31–64^a16) points out, syllogistic is paraconsistent. The idea that explosion is a correct principle of inference seems to have arisen in the twelfth century, with the discovery of the following simple argument. Suppose that $\neg A$; then $\neg A \lor B$. But now suppose that A as well. Then B follows by the disjunctive syllogism (A, $\neg A \lor B \vdash B$). Explosion and the disjunctive syllogism had variable for-

tunes in later Medieval logic. A common move was to distinguish two notions of validity: one (*material*) for which they held; and one (*formal*) for which they do not. All this was forgotten after the Middle Ages. But since the early twentieth century, the hegemony of Frege/Russell (classical) logic, according to which explosion is valid, has ensured the orthodoxy of the principle.

Modern formal paraconsistent logics started to appear in the second half of the twentieth century. Amongst the earliest paraconsistent logics were those proposed by Stanisław Jaśkowski (1948) and Newton da Costa (1963). The paraconsistent possibilities of the relevant logic of Alan Anderson and Nuel Belnap (1960s) was also soon recognized. By the end of the twentieth century there were many paraconsistent logics with well-defined semantics and proof theories.

In the semantics of most paraconsistent logics, validity is defined in terms of the preservation of truth-in-an-interpretation. It must therefore be possible to have interpretations where A and $\neg A$ are both true. There are several ways of achieving this end. One is to take truth to be truth-at-a-world in a world-semantics for modal logic (as in Jaśkowski's system D_2, "discussive logic"). In this case, the inference of adjunction ($A, B \vdash A\&B$) will fail, giving rise to a nonadjunctive paraconsistent logic. Another possibility is to graft a non-truth-functional negation on to some positive logic (as in the da Costa C-systems). The truth value of $\neg A$ is not determined by that of A; both may then be true. This gives so-called "positive-plus" paraconsistent logics. A third possibility is to employ a many-valued logic in which some designated truth value, v, is a fixed point for negation. That is, if the value of A is v, the value of $\neg A$ is also v. v may be the value *both true and false*, as in Graham Priest's *LP*, or the value 0.5 where the semantics has the real numbers between 0 and 1 as truth values. The way that negation is handled in relevant logic also has the same effect.

In nearly all paraconsistent logics, there are ways of recapturing the full force of classical reasoning. Thus, in discursive logic, if the premises are conjoined then they have all of their classical consequences. Da Costa suggested augmenting the language with an operator, $°$, such that, intuitively, $A°$ expresses the consistency of A. The classical negation of A can then be expressed by $\neg A\&A°$. A different way was suggested by Diderik Batens. Consistency-ordering is defined on interpretations, such that classical interpretations (and only those) come out as the most consistent. A notion of validity is then defined according to which an inference is valid iff (meaning "if and only if") the conclusion holds in all those interpretations which are as consistent as possible, given only that the premises hold in them. This gives a nonmonotonic notion of consequence according to which the consequences of a consistent set of sentences are just their classical consequences. (Batens developed the idea into a whole family of nonmonotonic logics with interesting properties, Adaptive Logics.)

Paraconsistent logics have many applications. They can be used as the inference engine for a computational database, where the data may not be reliable, or used to analyze the reasoning of inconsistent theories in the history of science—such as the original infinitesimal calculus or Bohr's theory of the atom. (The inconsistency of each of these was acknowledged in their times.) The same also holds true for the inconsistent but nontrivial theories that paraconsistent logic makes possible, including various mathematical theories. One can be interested in these because they have an intrinsically elegant structure, are instrumentally useful, and are good approximations to the truth. None of this requires one to suppose that the inconsistent theories may be true.

The view that some contradictions are true is dialeth(e)ism (a di/aletheia being a true statement of the form $A\&\neg A$). Unless a dialetheist takes everything to be true (not an attractive view!), they also require a paraconsistent logic. Though there have been dialetheists—such as Hegel—in the history of European philosophy, dialetheism is a strongly heterodox view because it flies in the face of the Law of Noncontradiction. The construction of contemporary paraconsistent logics has given the view a new lease of life. In particular, beginning in the 1970s, it was advocated by Priest and Richard Sylvan (né Routley).

Modern dialetheists argue for their view by appealing to certain features of motion, inconsistent systems of norms, and various other considerations. A major appeal has always been to the paradoxes of self-reference, such as the Liar and Russell's paradox (and related phenomena such as Gödel's incompleteness theorem). The paradoxical arguments are what they appear to be: arguments establishing that certain contradictions are true. In particular, a dialetheist can subscribe to the principles which generate these paradoxes: the unrestricted T-schema for truth ("A" is true iff A) and the unrestricted comprehension principle for sets (for any condition, there is a set comprising all and only those things satisfying that condition). In particular, it is possible to construct inconsistent but nontrivial theories containing these principles. Not all paraconsistent logics are suitable for this enterprise, however. In this context, any logic which endorses

the principle of contraction ($A \rightarrow (A \rightarrow B) \vdash A \rightarrow B$) gives rise to triviality, in the form of Curry paradoxes. Such logics include the da Costa C logics and the stronger relevant logics.

See also Logic, History of; Logic, Non-Classical; Relevance (Relevant) Logics.

Bibliography

Brown, Bryson. "Paraconsistent Logic: Preservationist Variations." In *Handbook of the History of Logic*. Vol. 7, edited by Dov M. Gabbay and John Woods. Amsterdam, Holland: Elsevier, forthcoming.

Batens, Diderik. "Inconsistency-Adaptive Logics." In *Logic at Work: Essays Dedicated to the Memory of Helena Rasiowa*, edited by E. Ortowska, 445–472. Heidelberg, Germany: Physica Verlag, 1999.

Batens, Diderik, Chris Mortensen, Graham Priest, and Jean-Paul Van-Bendegem, eds. *Frontiers of Paraconsistent Logic*. Baldock, U.K.: Research Studies Press, 2000.

Carnielli, Walter, A., Marcelo E. Coniglio, and João Marcos. "Logics of Formal Inconsistency." In *Handbook of Philosophical Logic*. Vol. 12, edited by Dov M. Gabbay and Franz Guenthner. Dordrecht, Holland: Kluwer, forthcoming.

Mortensen, Chris. *Inconsistent Mathematics*. Dordrecht, Holland: Kluwer, 1995.

Priest, Graham. *In Contradiction: A Study of the Transconsistent*. 2nd ed. Dordrecht, Holland: Martinus Nijhoff, 1987. Oxford: Oxford University Press, forthcoming.

Priest, Graham. "Paraconsistent Logic." In *Handbook of Philosophical Logic*. 2nd ed., vol. 6, edited by Dov M. Gabbay and Franz Guenthner, 287–393. Dordrecht, Holland: Reidel, 2002.

Priest, Graham, Richard Routley, and Jean Norman, eds. *Paraconsistent Logic: Essays on the Inconsistent*. Munich, Germany: Philosophia Verlag, 1989.

Graham Priest (2005)

PARADIGM-CASE ARGUMENT

"Paradigm-case argument" is a form of argument against philosophical skepticism found in contemporary analytic philosophy. It counters doubt about whether any of some class of things exists by attempting to point out paradigm cases, clear and indisputable instances. A distinguishing feature of the argument is the contention that certain facts about language entail the existence of paradigm cases. This claim, however, has been disputed in recent years, and the future status of the argument depends upon whether it can be upheld.

The paradigm-case argument has been used against a wide range of skeptical positions. A typical example is doubt about our ability to perceive directly material objects. Such doubt can be raised by reflection upon the physiological and physical facts about perception. For example, since seeing involves the transmission of light waves to our eyes and these waves are what immediately affects our eyes, it may appear that we are mistaken in thinking that we see objects. If anything, we should say that we see light waves. The fact that it takes a certain amount of time for light to travel from an object to our eyes lends support to this. How can we see something unless we see it as it is at the present moment? While considerations such as these show how skepticism can arise, one striking fact about the paradigm-case argument is that if it is valid, the skeptic can be refuted directly without the necessity of examining in detail the reasons behind his position.

The first step in the argument is to make the skepticism bear on particular cases. If we cannot perceive material objects, then, presumably, we cannot see the table we are working on or the pen with which we write. Next, a situation is sketched in which, ordinarily, no one would hesitate to affirm just the opposite. If the light is excellent, our eyes open, our sight unimpaired, the table directly before us, and so on, then we should ordinarily have no qualms about stating that we see a table.

The argument would be weak if it relied merely on the fact that people would ordinarily have no doubts in such situations, for it does not follow from this that they state the truth. But the argument claims something more for the kind of situations it describes. It holds that they are indisputably examples of seeing a table because of their relationship to the meaning of the expression "seeing a table." Typically, this relationship is brought out by saying that such a situation is just what we call "seeing a table" or that it is just the sort of circumstances in which one might teach someone the meaning of the expression "seeing a table." Generalizing and taking the strongest interpretation of the force of these remarks, one might ask: "If this *is* just what we call *X*, then in saying that it is *X*, how can we fail to state the truth? If this *is* a situation in which we might teach the meaning of *X*, then how can it fail to be a case of *X*?" In denying that anyone ever sees a table, the skeptic seems to be placed in the position of refusing to apply the expression "seeing a table" to the very situation to which that expression refers.

If the skeptic concedes that the situation presented is an instance of that which he doubted to exist, then he admits defeat. But if, despite what has been said, he will not concede this, the final stage of the argument poses a dilemma. When the skeptic wonders whether we ever really see such things as tables, we naturally understand the words he uses in their usual sense. By "usual sense" is meant no more than what we should have understood by his words *see* and *table* if, instead, he were describing some scene he had witnessed. But how can his words be construed in this way when he refuses to use them of a typical situation in which their usual meaning might be taught and which is just what we ordinarily call "seeing a table"? On the other hand, if the skeptic claims some different or novel meaning for his words, the original shock of his skeptical conclusion is blunted. For in some special sense of the words, it may be true that we never see tables. In fact, what often happens is that the skeptical position maintains its plausibility only through an unnoticed fluctuation between the usual sense of the key expressions and some special sense. The paradigm-case argument may serve to bring out into the open the fact that an unusual meaning must be looked for.

FURTHER APPLICATIONS

Other examples of philosophical doubt to which the paradigm-case argument has been applied include skepticism about the validity of inductive reasoning, about man's free will, about the possibility of knowledge concerning empirical facts generally, and about the reality of the past. In many cases these skeptical positions are founded entirely on a priori considerations, and their stand is not merely that, as a matter of fact, there are no instances of some class of things, but that, as a matter of logical necessity, there could not be any. Philosophers who have argued that we can never genuinely know anything about the empirical world, for example, have almost invariably thought such knowledge a logical impossibility. Their reason is often the supposed impossibility of complete verification of any empirical assertion about the world. But this they take to be a necessary truth following from the fact that there are an infinite number of possible observations and investigations relevant to any such assertion. Similarly, the impossibility of justifying inductive reasoning (that which goes from examined cases to a general conclusion or from past instances to a prediction) has been held on the grounds that there is a logical obstacle in the way of all attempts at justification.

Against such a priori skepticism the argument need not produce an actual paradigm case. The mere fact that a hypothetical case can be described is sufficient. This in part accounts for the fact that philosophers who have employed the argument in practice do not bother to describe an actual occurrence. So, for example, one writer, in using the argument to refute skepticism about induction, asks us to imagine that "the observed confirmatory instances for the theory of gravitation were a million or ten million times as extensive as they now are" (Paul Edwards, "Bertrand Russell's Doubts about Induction," p. 65). By its very statement this is only a hypothetical case. But the skeptic about induction cannot admit that if this were to happen, we should *then* be justified in accepting the law of gravitation, because if justification were a logical impossibility, no paradigm case of justified inductive inference would even be conceivable.

But not all philosophical skepticism is completely a priori. Doubts about the human ability to choose among genuine alternatives is often supported, for example, by citing the success of the behavioral sciences and arguing that they will eventually be able to describe and predict human actions through causal laws. Here the philosopher appears to argue from empirical premises. But here, also, the descriptions of paradigm cases offered to the skeptic have usually been hypothetical. A writer, for example, who pointed to a marriage where there has been no pressure and the like placed on the two people as a paradigm case of choosing freely would not feel compelled to prove the existence of some actual marriage fitting this description.

The reason why a purely hypothetical instance can be given even where the skepticism is based on empirical premises is that there is a sense in which the skeptic does not deny the existence of paradigm cases. In this example he would not, for instance, dispute the frequent occurrence of the sort of marriage described. And he would be prepared to admit that in such cases the appearances are in favor of a free choice having been exercised. But, he thinks, the other considerations provided by his skeptical argument show that, in fact, it is doubtful or impossible that such an occurrence should be an instance of genuinely free choice. This is why the appeal to the connection between such situations and the meaning of, in this example, the expression "free choice" is the vital step in the paradigm-case argument. It is that which, if anything, shows that whatever the skeptical argument, these circumstances *must* be counted as instances of free choice.

BACKGROUND

The idea that philosophy cannot cast doubt on the applications ordinarily made of everyday expressions is not a new one. It can be seen, for example, in George Berkeley's refusal to draw skeptical consequences from his radical thesis that nothing exists apart from the mind. He did not conclude that we are mistaken in talking of material objects such as trees and tables; instead, he attempted to show how his thesis could be used to analyze the meaning of statements about these things. Everyday language succeeds in saying something true about the world; the only question for him was, *What* does it say?

But what is perhaps novel is the erection of this idea into an explicit philosophical argument. And this is largely the product of what has been called the "revolution in philosophy," which began in England shortly before World War II and which has subsequently dominated much of Anglo American philosophy. The possibility of defeating skepticism by reference to particular cases, however, was already present some time before this in the many essays on the subject, dating from the first decade of the twentieth century, by G. E. Moore.

G. E. MOORE. Moore thought of his opposition to skepticism in any form as a defense of common sense. The statements of common sense that he wished to defend were of two kinds: such context-free statements as "Earth has existed for many years" and such context-bound statements as "Here is a human hand" and "This is a pencil." Moore held that he knew with certainty the truth of statements of both kinds. Any skeptical argument, therefore, which entailed that he did not or could not know them must be mistaken. To his critics this has seemed a strange sort of defense of common sense, for how can one defend a position merely by reaffirming it? In answering this, some writers have suggested that Moore was implicitly using the paradigm-case argument. While it is difficult to interpret Moore's affirmation of context-free statements in this way, the suggestion is quite plausible, for example, when we find him attacking skepticism about the existence of material objects by holding up his hand and saying that it is quite certain that this is a human hand and that at least one material object therefore exists ("Proof of an External World," pp. 145–146).

Moore himself, however, apparently saw his procedure in a different light. He thought of it as a challenge to the skeptic: Which is more certain, the (usually esoteric) premises of your argument or the commonsense statements that you are compelled to deny? Moore also pointed out that whereas the skeptic has an argument that leads to the denial of some commonsense statement, a counterargument can be constructed using the commonsense statement as a premise and the denial of the skeptical reasons as a conclusion. The question then seems to resolve into who has the more certain premises. And in this conflict common sense surely seems to be on firmer ground. In an examination of four assumptions from which Bertrand Russell had drawn skeptical conclusions, for example, Moore ends by saying: "I cannot help answering: 'It seems to me more certain that I *do* know that this is a pencil and that you are conscious, than that any single one of these four assumptions is true, let alone all four'" ("Four Forms of Scepticism," p. 226). And at a much earlier time he wrote: "I think the fact that, if [David] Hume's principles were true, I could not know of the existence of this pencil is a *reductio ad absurdum* of those principles" (*Some Main Problems of Philosophy*, p. 120).

In this interpretation of his procedure, Moore defends common sense as the more certainly true view of the world. The paradigm-case argument, in contrast, appeals to language to show that skepticism conflicts with the facts about the use of expressions needed to state it. Although Moore pointed to the importance of particular cases, it is necessary to look at the ideas that have subsequently come to the forefront of Anglo American philosophy to see why a connection with language should be thought relevant.

WITTGENSTEIN. Of central importance are the views of Ludwig Wittgenstein, whose work has heavily influenced many of those who have used the paradigm-case argument. (It is, however, debatable whether Wittgenstein himself employed the argument.) One of his central contentions, in opposition to his own earlier work, the *Tractatus Logico-Philosophicus*, was that while rules can be formulated for language, it is a mistake to view the particular uses of language as deriving their correctness from being in accord with rules. Rather, the fact that those who speak the language agree that *this* is the correct thing to say here and *that* incorrect there shows what the rules are. If anything, this agreement in judgment about particular cases is primitive. So, in the notes he dictated to some of his students in 1933–1934 (subsequently known as the *Blue Book*), Wittgenstein said, "It is part of the grammar of the word 'chair' that *this* is what we call 'to sit on a chair.'" It would be a mistake to take it as a consequence of such remarks that if the users of a language agree in calling *this* an example of *X*, then, in the sense which the expression has in their language, this *must* be a case of *X*. Such a principle would indeed immediately yield the validity of the paradigm-case argument.

But there is an obvious objection that an example will illustrate. There was a time, perhaps, when all agreed in calling Earth flat, although it was not. They were in agreement, but they were all mistaken. This, however, is a

situation in which people were relying upon certain evidence that proved misleading. And in holding that there is a connection between the situations in which we should use a description and the meaning, or "grammar," of the description, Wittgenstein was probably thinking of circumstances in which we are not relying on evidence. It was one of his important ideas that where it makes sense to speak of having evidence that something is so, it must be (logically) possible to get beyond mere evidence.

Thus, while we may sometimes have evidence that someone is sitting in a chair (from, for example, a report that he is), Wittgenstein would argue that when we are standing in a well-lit room looking at the person so seated, it would be a mistake to suppose we then have mere evidence. This idea runs directly counter to long traditions in philosophy. For philosophers, even those who are not skeptics, have most often held that one gets beyond evidence only in a very small class of statements—in general, only first-person, singular, present-tense assertions about one's own mental life. It appears reasonably certain, however, that some such general claim as Wittgenstein's must be substantiated before the paradigm-case argument can be declared valid, because a paradigm case of, for example, a free choice must be one in which there is *more* than just good evidence that a free choice has been made. Otherwise, the skeptical reasons may be sufficient to show that the evidence is misleading.

Whether Wittgenstein's view, if correct, is sufficient to show the validity of the paradigm-case argument is another question. It will depend, for example, upon whether a situation in which we have got beyond mere evidence is also one in which we cannot be mistaken.

It is important to note that the idea that we must be able to get beyond evidence presupposes that we are dealing with a concept free from logical inconsistency. We cannot, for example, ever be confronted with a round square or a genuine trisection of an angle. But a priori skepticism is based on a "proof" that a certain concept could have no instantiation because there would be some inconsistency in supposing it did. The paradigm-case argument, if it is to be generally employed, may need a proof of its own that no expression in everyday use can turn out to designate a self-inconsistent idea. While this has sometimes been held, more needs to be said about it. It seems impossible that anyone should prove, for example, that the idea of a table is self-inconsistent, but it is not so implausible to suppose that someone might show that the idea of a time machine or of transmigration of souls, which are ordinary expressions in the sense intended, contain contradictions. And is it beyond doubt that the concept of a free choice, for example, is logically irreproachable? Moreover, if it were to be demonstrated independently that no expression in ordinary language can designate a self-inconsistent idea, this would be sufficient by itself to discredit any a priori skepticism concerned with such expressions and would render the subsequent use of a paradigm-case argument superfluous.

There is a further difficulty in supposing Wittgenstein's view—that what we say in particular circumstances is determinant of what we mean—to entail the validity of the paradigm-case argument. This arises from the fact that particular cases can be related to the meaning of an expression without necessarily being paradigm cases.

This may be brought out by an illustration. Suppose someone doubts the existence of elephants. Very likely the surest way to convince him of his mistake would be to show him the elephants at a zoo or circus. That we call *these* elephants shows something about the meaning of the word *elephant*. If the skeptic about elephants sees no connection between what he has been shown and the existence of elephants, we have grounds for suspecting that he does not know what the word *elephant* means. But the connection need not be that having seen these things, he must admit that elephants exist. All he must admit is that these things have the appearance of elephants (see Wittgenstein, *Philosophical Investigations*, paragraph 354). If he maintains, for example, "These certainly look like elephants, but I am sure that they are in reality camels with false noses and padding," he has acknowledged a connection between what he has been shown and the meaning of the word *elephant*. His skepticism, however, remains.

At this time it is an open question whether the important general ideas about the connection of language to particular cases that have fostered the use of the paradigm-case argument also entail its validity.

CRITICISM AND VARIATIONS

Critics of the paradigm-case argument have questioned the legitimacy of the move from "This is just what we call *X*" to "Thus, it is a genuine case of *X*." Some reasons for doubt about this transition have already been mentioned. It should be pointed out, however, that there are times when the transition is legitimate, although the paradigm-case argument can draw no comfort from this fact.

Suppose, for example, that someone doubted that there are any bachelors but admitted that there are unmarried males of marriageable age. We might naturally say to him, "But this is just what we call 'being a bachelor.'" Here, however, the doubter has no reply (other than to question whether this *is* how the word is used) because *this* refers to a description that logically entails "being a bachelor." In the paradigm-case argument, however, especially where the case is actually pointed out instead of described, no such entailment is normally claimed.

If there is not an entailment, however, then there seems room for the skeptic to maneuver. How can one hold that no matter what the skeptic's reasons may be, he must admit *this* as an instance of what he doubted to exist? Faced with such difficulties, some proponents of the paradigm-case argument have placed restrictions on its use. They have said that it is valid only for expressions designating concepts that must be taught ostensively—that is, taught through examples. Philosophers have often held, for example, that color words can be taught only in this fashion. The usual reason given is that the concept of a particular color is simple and that its meaning cannot be captured by a verbal definition. Hence, it must be taught by pointing out things that are of that color. When the paradigm-case argument is confined to such concepts, a special reason is supplied for why there must be indisputable instances. If there were not (or had never been) any red objects, how could the concept get into the language?

The appeal to what must be taught ostensively is frequently presented as if it were merely an elucidation of the force of the paradigm-case argument. But it seems, instead, to be a separate and distinct form of argument. There is, for example, no need to describe or point out particular circumstances. The conclusion that there are instances of, for example, red objects is drawn directly from the premise that the concept can be taught only ostensively. There would, perhaps, be point in calling this form of argument by a different name.

ARGUMENT FROM OSTENSIVE TEACHING. Whether such an argument is valid against a skeptic will depend upon several questions that have yet to be conclusively answered. First, are there any concepts that can be taught only ostensively? Is it logically impossible for someone to have the concept of, for example, redness without having obtained it through ostensive teaching? Second, even if a concept must be taught through such methods, must there be exemplifications of the concept? It seems possible, for example, to teach someone the meaning of "is red" by using objects that merely appear to be red as long as this fact is concealed from the student. Third, even if the answer in the above cases is affirmative, are the important concepts that give rise to skepticism of the required kind? Is the concept of choosing freely, for example, one that can be taught only by such methods?

Sometimes it is said that the paradigm-case argument need be confined only to those concepts that can be taught ostensively. When this is done, no conclusion can be immediately drawn about the existence of cases falling under the concept. The concept of a unicorn could be taught ostensively if only there were such a creature, but as things stand, it never has been. What, then, is the value of such a restriction? The idea seems to be that if a concept can be taught ostensively, then there must be conceivable circumstances, at any rate, in which something falls under the concept—those circumstances in which it could be taught in this fashion. Such an argument, in general, has force only against an a priori skeptic. But it is possible that the circumstances in which, it is claimed, the concept could be taught ostensively actually occur and that the skeptic may not wish to dispute their existence. It might be urged, for example, that the concept of acting freely can be taught ostensively in circumstances which the skeptic about freedom would have to admit do occur. Some of the same problems about ostensive teaching arise for this kind of argument as for the previous one.

EVALUATIVE CONCEPTS. Still another restriction on the use of the paradigm-case argument has been proposed by some writers. J. O. Urmson questions the legitimacy of applying it to evaluative expressions such as "good (inductive) reasons" ("Some Questions concerning Validity"). His point is that the use of evaluative expressions has a dimension that the use of purely classificatory expressions lacks. Evaluative expressions not only sort out things and situations but also signify approval or condemnation. The skeptic, therefore, may be willing to grant that there are differences between what we call, for example, "good inductive reasons" and "bad inductive reasons" and that he has said nothing to show that these differences are not exemplified. But he may question whether these differences support our approval of the one and our rejection of the other. Thus, to take Urmson's analogy, he may grant a difference between what we call "good apples" and what we call "bad apples" but urge that our standards are faulty. How can pointing out that *this* is just what we call a "good apple," he may ask, show that we would not do better to approve of some other kind?

TWO SORTS OF SKEPTICISM. Urmson's point, if valid, appears to have many consequences. The dispute concerning whether we can exercise genuine freedom of choice about our own actions does not seem on the surface to be a dispute involving evaluative concepts. Philosophers, however, have been particularly uneasy about the use of the paradigm-case argument in this area, in contrast, for example, to its employment against skepticism about the existence or perception of material objects. The explanation may be that there are two sorts of skepticism involved. It may be that the skeptic about human freedom is not, in fact, denying that many of the ordinary relevant expressions mark genuine distinctions but, rather, querying the purpose to which we put these distinctions. In contrast, the skeptic about the existence of material objects does appear to deny that there is, for example, a distinction between a material object and the mere appearance of one.

We contrast seeing material objects with seeing hallucinatory or imaginary objects. By describing circumstances in which we ordinarily are in no doubt about which member of these distinctions is present, the paradigm-case argument may be construed as pointing out that the everyday expressions do, after all, serve a function. The fact that we do make these contrasts in practice and, more importantly, that we generally agree in our judgments shows that some genuine distinction is being made. Moreover, the skeptic does not usually dispute the fact that we can independently reach agreement about particular cases. Thus, it might be said to him, "Whatever your arguments to show that we never see material objects, for example, after we have looked at them and debated them, there will still be that difference between what we have called 'a real object' and what we have called 'hallucinations,' 'illusions,' or 'imaginary objects.' We shall still need to mark that distinction and so return to our usual way of describing things."

While this seems quite powerful against, for example, skepticism about the perception of material objects, the same sort of explanation of the paradigm-case argument is not so convincing when tried out on disputes about evaluative terms or the existence of genuinely free choices. The trouble may be that although the skeptic's arguments cannot destroy the correctness of contrasting what we should call cases of freely choosing from those we should not, his argument may still destroy what we thought to be the point of making the distinction. To say that a choice was free often involves the ascription of responsibility and the possibility of praise and blame. We behave differently toward persons who have made a free choice than we do toward those who have been coerced. If we knew all our "choices" to be the product of prior conditioning or hereditary traits—a possibility that appears often to generate skepticism about our freedom—would we still be on solid ground in behaving differently toward those who have made a "free choice"? Although we could continue to make the same distinctions we do now as far as classification goes, we might think that to call certain choices "free" would have a hollow ring.

Whatever the ultimate verdict on the paradigm-case argument as a refutation of skepticism, there can be no doubt that its use in recent philosophy has generated very important questions about the relationship of language to the world.

See also A Priori and A Posteriori; Common Sense; Induction; Knowledge, A Priori; Moore, George Edward; Philosophy of Language; Russell, Bertrand Arthur William; Skepticism, History of; Wittgenstein, Ludwig Josef Johann.

Bibliography

BACKGROUND

Austin, J. L. "Other Minds." In *Essays on Logic and Language*, edited by Antony Flew. 2nd series. Oxford: Blackwell, 1953.

Chappell, V. C. "Malcolm on Moore." *Mind* 70 (1961): 417–425.

Malcolm, Norman. "George Edward Moore." In his *Knowledge and Certainty*. Englewood Cliffs, NJ: Prentice Hall, 1963.

Malcolm, Norman. "Moore and Ordinary Language." In *The Philosophy of G. E. Moore*, edited by Paul A. Schilpp. 2nd ed. New York, 1952.

Moore, George Edward. *Philosophical Papers*. New York: Macmillan, 1959. See especially "A Defence of Common Sense," "Proof of an External World," "Four Forms of Scepticism."

Moore, George Edward. *Some Main Problems of Philosophy*. London: Allen and Unwin, 1953. See especially Chs. 1, 5–6.

White, A. R. *G. E. Moore*. Oxford: Blackwell, 1958.

Wisdom, John. "Philosophical Perplexity." In his *Philosophy and Psycho-analysis*. Oxford: Blackwell, 1953.

Wittgenstein, Ludwig. *The Blue and Brown Books*. Oxford: Blackwell, 1958.

Wittgenstein, Ludwig. *Philosophical Investigations*. Translated by G. E. M. Anscombe. New York: Macmillan, 1953.

APPLICATIONS AND CRITICAL DISCUSSIONS

Alexander, H. G. "More about the Paradigm Case Argument." *Analysis* 18 (1958): 117–120.

Beattie, Catherine. "The Paradigm Case Argument: Its Use and Abuse in Education." *Journal of Philosophy of Education* 15 (1981): 77–86.

Black, Max. "Paradigm Cases and Evaluative Words." *Dialectica* 27 (1973): 262–272.

Black, Max. "Making Something Happen." In *Determinism and Freedom*, edited by Sidney Hook. New York: New York University Press, 1958. Application to freedom of the will and causation.

Bouwsma, O. K. "Descartes' Evil Genius." *Philosophical Review* 58 (1949): 141–151. Application to skepticism about the external world.

Butchvarov, Panayot. "Knowledge of Meanings and Knowledge of the World." *Philosophy* 39 (1964): 145–160.

Danto, Arthur C. "The Paradigm Case Argument and the Free-Will Problem." *Ethics* 69 (1959): 120–124. Critical.

Edwards, Paul. "Bertrand Russell's Doubts about Induction." In *Essays on Logic and Language*, edited by Antony Flew. 1st series. Oxford: Blackwell, 1951. Application to skepticism about induction and a sympathetic analysis.

Eveling, H. S., and G. O. M. Leith. "When to Use the Paradigm Case Argument." *Analysis* 18 (1958): 150–152.

Findlay, J. N. "Time: A Treatment of Some Puzzles." Ibid. Application to skepticism about the passage of time.

Flew, Antony. "'Farewell to the Paradigm-Case Argument': A Comment." *Analysis* 18 (1957): 34–40. Defense against criticism by Watkins.

Flew, Antony. "Philosophy and Language." In *Essays in Conceptual Analysis*, edited by Antony Flew. London: Macmillan, 1956. Sympathetic.

Hanfling, Oswald. "What's Wrong with the Paradigm Case Argument?" *PAS* 91 (1991): 21–38.

Harre, R. "Tautologies and the Paradigm Case Argument." *Analysis* 18 (1958): 94–96.

MacIntyre, A. C. "Determinism." *Mind* 66 (1957): 28–41. Contains criticism of application made to freedom of the will.

Mackie, J. L. *Contemporary Linguistic Philosophy—Its Strength and Weakness*. Dunedin, New Zealand: University of Otago, 1956.

Malcolm, Norman. "Moore and Ordinary Language." In *The Philosophy of Bertrand Russell*, edited by Paul A. Schilpp. Sympathetic analysis and several applications.

Nagel, Ernest. "Russell's Philosophy of Science." In *The Philosophy of Bertrand Russell*, edited by Paul A. Schilpp. Evanston, IL: Open Court, 1944. Application to several of Russell's views.

Passmore, John. *Philosophical Reasoning*. London: Duckworth, 1961. See Ch. 6 for a critical analysis.

Richman, Robert J. "On the Argument of the Paradigm Case." *Australasian Journal of Philosophy* 39 (1961): 75–81. Critical.

Richman, Robert J. "Still More on the Argument of the Paradigm Case." *Australasian Journal of Philosophy* 40 (1962): 204–207.

Sosa, E. "The Paradigm Case Argument: Necessary, Causal, or Normative." *Methodos* 15 (1963): 253–273.

Stebbing, L. Susan. *Philosophy and the Physicists*. London: Methuen, 1937. See Ch. 3 for application to skepticism about the properties of material objects.

Stroud, Barry. *The Significance of Philosophical Skepticism*. Oxford: Oxford University Press, 1984.

Urmson, J. O. "Some Questions concerning Validity." In *Essays in Conceptual Analysis*, edited by Antony Flew. London: Macmillan, 1956. Critical of application to evaluative concepts.

Watkins, J. W. N. "Farewell to the Paradigm-Case Argument." *Analysis* 18 (1957): 25–33. Critical.

Watkins, J. W. N. "A Reply to Professor Flew's Comment." *Analysis* 18 (1957): 41–42.

Will, F. L. "Will the Future Be Like the Past?" In *Essays on Logic and Language*, edited by Antony Flew. 2nd series. Oxford: Blackwell, 1953. Application to skepticism about induction.

Williams, C. J. F. "More on the Paradigm Case Argument." *Australasian Journal of Philosophy* 39 (1961): 276–278. Defense of the argument against criticisms of Richman.

Keith S. Donnellan (1967)
Bibliography updated by Benjamin Fiedor (2005)

PARADOXES

See *Logical Paradoxes; Zeno of Elea*

PARANORMAL PHENOMENA

See *Parapsychology; Precognition*

PARAPSYCHOLOGY

Parapsychology is the modern name for what used to be called psychical research. The word is usually used in a narrow sense, as scientifically based research, but sometimes it is used more broadly to cover the whole range of the occult. The term *psi* is often used as a briefer equivalent. Psi phenomena are paranormal, that is, beyond the range of what is considered to be part of the ordinary world.

The Society for Psychical Research (SPR) was established in England in 1882 and is given credit for organizing systematic research in the English-speaking Western world. Many of its founders were distinguished intellectuals who were themselves spiritualists and interested in immortality. The American Society for Psychical Research was founded soon after. Though some of the earlier researchers did scientific studies, they more often conducted other kinds of investigations of psi, investigating ostensible cases of dramatic psi, and frequently working with mediums.

THE MODERN SCIENTIFIC ERA

The modern scientific era in parapsychology is usually credited to Joseph Banks Rhine, who established the first university laboratory devoted exclusively to experimental research on psi. In 1957 Rhine and others organized the Parapsychological Association, which twenty years later became, over much opposition, an affiliate member of the American Association for the Advancement of Science. Some parapsychologists, however, insist that the pursuit of psi by scientific methods is ill advised and advocate a return to the more traditional types of psychical research.

Parapsychologists work primarily on a common core of phenomena that include telepathy (mind-mind), clairvoyance (mind-matter, now called remote viewing), psychokinesis (PK; mental action on matter), precognition and retrocognition (direct awareness of future or past mental or material states), and often survival issues (disembodied existence and reincarnation). More specialized topics might include hauntings and apparitions, séances, poltergeists, dowsing, psychic healing, and near-death and out-of-the-body experiences, but probably not astrology, the Bermuda Triangle, UFOs, past-life regression, and alien abductions.

Psi research is commonly defined as the study of things and processes that go beyond the commonly accepted ways of interaction in the world. Parapsychology is unusual in that what it studies is defined primarily in negative terms. For example, extrasensory perception (ESP) is defined in terms of gathering information not by sensory means. Moreover, parapsychologists typically admit that they lack agreement on what psi is or how it operates, and some parapsychologists prefer to speak of their field as the study of a limited range of "anomalies," refusing to make positive claims that psi is an actual power of some sort.

IMPLICATIONS OF PSI

Clearly, the existence of psi would have enormous implications for Western philosophy, not only by extending the range of commonly accepted ways of interacting with the world but also by reinforcing dualistic and idealistic worldviews that have hitherto supported their critiques of science on non-psi grounds, that is, on the alleged failure of the dominant materialist paradigm to allow proper room for consciousness, including qualia, volitions, intentions, and logical reasoning. If it were shown that psi exists, the foundations of modern Western metaphysics would be shaken, most would say, overthrown.

C. D. Broad (1953) formulated the issue in terms of what he called "the basic limiting principles" of Western thought, which he said were justified either by self-evidence or by overwhelming and uniformly favorable empirical evidence. These principles, abbreviated, are that causation always works forward by acting through a continuous chain of events linking cause and effect, that mind acts on matter only through its own brain, that mental activity is dependent on the brain, and that knowledge is acquired only through present sensations or communications. It is clear that psi would challenge all these principles and thus threaten the Western worldview.

Judged in terms of these limiting principles, psi is not only *para*normal but *anti*normal. Telepathy and clairvoyance imply that minds act directly on remote minds or material objects, bypassing the brain and violating the rule of continuous links in causation. PK would also violate that chain, providing mental action directly on remote objects, and both precognition and retrocognition would violate both forward causation and how knowledge is acquired. There is no question that psi is magical, judged by our basic limiting principles.

Some parapsychologists attempt to minimize the conflict between psi and the Western worldview by claiming that psi should be understood in terms of psychological laws rather than laws of physics by assimilating psi to such psychological connections as association or by pointing to altered states such as dream states or hypnosis that seem to facilitate psi production. They point out that psi fits in well with idealism, panpsychism, and typically Eastern philosophies that tend to understand nature in terms of mind rather than by understanding mind in terms of nature as in Western views. Also, some dualists point out that the mind-brain dualism itself violates the modern scientific paradigm and claim that ESP and PK (but not precognition) can be assimilated to mind-brain interaction, as an extended application of the powers that the mind uses to interact with its own brain (Dilley 1988).

PROBLEMS IN PSI RESEARCH

Parapsychologists are hampered in their research by the lack of a common body of theory as well as by not knowing how to produce psi on demand or predict how it will behave once it occurs. Without any firm basis for understanding psi, it is difficult to test alternative hypotheses. Few believe that psi can be controlled consciously, and some believe that psi is actually resistant to demonstration, sometimes called the *shyness effect*. Moreover, successful psi production seems to be related to belief in psi. Even when psi is produced successfully, investigators do not know for sure whether psi is coming from the subjects of an experiment, from the experimenter, from defects in the experimental design, or even from fraud. Skeptics point to an additional problem about psi that arouses their suspicion, that psi does not seem to affect ordinary experiments in physics laboratories or enable psychics to win steadily at casinos.

Critics of psi research claim that replication requirements demanded by modern science have not yet been met and that experimenters have not yet devised protocols that will guarantee positive results and can be obtained by independent investigators. Defenders of psi sometimes accept this charge, but reply that the unpredictability of psi prevents replication in the strong sense and that multiple demonstrations of psi by well-run experiments should constitute acceptable scientific evidence. Psi researchers continue to try to understand psi in the hopes of learning how to control it but progress has been disappointing, considering that more than a century has passed since the founding of the SPR.

Parapsychologists are unanimous that psi is incompatible with present materialism. They accept a wide range of metaphysical theories. There are a few, a vigorous minority, who think that psi can be reconciled with current science by massive revisions in the concepts of Western science. They point to various modifications proposed by physicists that could result in fitting psi into a revised physics. As has been already mentioned, some parapsychologists have turned to idealism, panpsychism, or various kinds of Eastern philosophy that better accommodate psi.

By far the more prevalent view is that psi should be understood in terms of metaphysical dualism, that ESP and PK are just extraordinary extensions of the powers that the mind uses to interact with its own brain. Opinions are divided whether telepathy is a third power, using unconscious levels of mind to connect conscious minds, or whether so-called telepathic phenomena can be reduced to ordinary mind-brain interactions. Henri Bergson once suggested that minds might be potentially omniscient and able to influence every object in the universe, but that brains limit the activity of psi to what is biologically and socially more useful. Both Broad and H. H. Price have made use of this model to explain why psi occurs only seldom.

CONTROVERSIES ABOUT PSI

Controversies over proper methods to be used in parapsychology also divide parapsychologists. Many parapsychologists believe that stories and anecdotes cannot be trusted and that the only reliable way to establish the existence of psi is by using the scientific method, while others believe that careful examination of anecdotes and other subjective reports can show the existence of psi and worry that the use of the scientific method stifles psi production.

Why cannot anecdotal evidence and the testimony of personal experience or the results of the kinds of investigations of early researchers be trusted? Such evidence has often turned out to be highly unreliable. Standards of evidence were often weak and many of even the strongest apparently evidential cases have been exposed as fraudulent or careless. It is commonly acknowledged that the history of psi research has been troubled by fraud, and some studies thought exceptionally thorough (such as those done by Samuel G. Soal) have been exposed as fraudulent. On the positive side, John Beloff (1993) presents a reasonably cautious survey of the case for psi, covering many important researchers and their subjects.

Those readers interested in the history of fraud should consult Paul Kurtz's *A Skeptic's Handbook of Parapsychology* (1985), which has ten chapters devoted to fraud, as well as George P. Hansen's "Deception by Subjects in Psi Research" (1990), which offers an extensive analysis of fraud. Faced with the problem of doubts about nonexperimental evidence, many parapsychologists have devoted themselves to gathering evidence for psi that will meet contemporary standards for scientific evidence and much has been accomplished since the 1990s.

THE CASE FOR PSI

Does psi exist? Opinions are widely variant. Popular opinion polls indicate widespread belief in psi in the general population. A poll of parapsychologists attending a Parapsychological Association meeting showed more than a 90 percent favorable response to the claim that psi exists, and more than an 80 percent favorable response to precognition. A poll of college faculty in 1979 produced a wide gap between humanities and arts faculty and psychologists. More than two-thirds of arts and humanities faculty answered affirmatively that psi was an established fact, a proportion similar to that of the general population, but only one-third of psychologists held that opinion. A poll of elite scientists in 1984 showed that only 4 percent thought that ESP was an established fact, with 25 percent thinking that ESP was a likely possibility. A large number expressed no opinion, but 10 percent thought that ESP was an impossibility.

There is no consensus on the existence of psi. Even some parapsychologists have become discouraged, either leaving the field or continuing to function as parapsychologists even though they do not believe in psi. Western philosophers and psychologists tend to reject psi, believing that a combination of fraud, careless investigation, gullibility, and wishful thinking (such as the wish for immortality) can account for the continued belief in psi.

On the contrary, psi believers sometimes claim that skeptics reject psi because psi powers are intrinsically threatening and that the existence of psi would overthrow the reigning paradigm in Western thought. More cautious people on both sides claim that there are interesting cases that suggest psi and that there is evidence that supports the existence of psi, but that the case for psi is not yet conclusive.

However true it might be that earlier investigations failed to meet modern experimental standards, parapsychologists overwhelmingly claim that the available evidence is virtually conclusive and have claimed to provide evidence that meets even the most scrupulous standards. However, it is fair to say that the best that those recent experimental findings have provided is evidence of a low level of psi, that psi cannot yet be demonstrated on demand, and that psi still cannot be produced reliably or consistently by independent investigators.

However, for the first time in the history of psi research, it is possible that psi researchers can produce the kind of evidence that will be regarded by knowledgeable skeptics as constituting scientific evidence. In particular, there are three major lines of ongoing research efforts that prove interesting and that have been analyzed carefully by skeptics: studies using the Ganzfeld procedure, remote viewing experiments, and experiments involving efforts to affect random number generators. Many of the results of these studies are discussed by K. Ramakrishnan Rao (2001). Some of the skeptics most conversant with psi research have been impressed with these results but still have reservations. Interested persons should consult Ray Hyman and Charles Honorton (1986), Daryl J. Bem and Honorton (1994), and Hyman (1989). James E. Alcock (1990) presents a number of reservations about the scientific case for psi in general, including specific criticisms of remote viewing and random number generation studies. There is agreement on both sides that they need to be at least open to persuasion and that continuing studies are needed, especially studies done in independent laboratories. It should also be pointed out that studies subsequent to those referred to earlier have not been conclusive.

Many parapsychologists would argue that there is convincing evidence for psi in studies that seem to provide evidence for survival of bodily death. The best candidates for evidence are cited in the literature on "cross-correspondences" gathered by members of the SPR almost a century ago, and studies of well over two thousand putative "reincarnation cases." Gardner Murphy (1979) does a careful analysis of cross-correspondences, and Stevenson (1987) cites some of the best cases for reincarnation. Hoyt L Edge et al. (1986) provide a careful presentation of issues related to survival. Paul Edwards (1996) offers one of the most comprehensive general attacks on reincarnation evidence, as well as on the character and competence of reincarnation scholars in general; however, be forewarned that he is known for his ad hominem attacks.

The cross-correspondences involved mediums whose trance writings and utterances were purported to be communicated by Frederic Myers, a classics scholar and one of the founders of the SPR, and by other deceased persons. The material lent itself to the interpretation that Myers was attempting to communicate to researchers, through different mediums who were separated by time and place, using bits of information and images that could be put together to provide a coherent set of references to the same classical myth. The case for survival was weakened by the fact that some of the participants were themselves classicists and might have inadvertently produced the data telepathically, and led some to prefer the "super-psi" hypothesis, so-named because the power of psi required to explain the phenomena surpasses any degree of psi that is reinforced by the experimental literature.

A recent development in survival research since the 1990s is the use of combination locks, set by believers who hope to use mediums to communicate the combinations that will open the locks. In one case so far, a lock has been opened by use of computer techniques, and survival researchers are putting their hopes on more sophisticated encryptions. As of 2005, no lock has been successfully opened by the proposed methods of disclosure.

SOURCES OF PSI

Generally, Western philosophers have been skeptical of psi, but there have been many who have vigorously defended it. Prominent among them are Henri Bergson, Charlie Dunbar Broad, C. J. Ducasse, James Hyslop, William James, C. W. K. Mundle, H. H. Price, Robert Almeder, Robert Brier, Stephen E. Braude, Hoyt L. Edge, and David Ray Griffin. There have also been some defenders among psychologists, prominently John Beloff, Irvin Child, Alan Gauld, Harvey J. Irwin, Gardner Murphy, William McDougall, and Charles Tart. Among the knowledgeable skeptical psychologists are James E. Alcock, Ray Hyman, and Charles E. M. Hansel, as well as Susan Blackmore and Richard Wiseman, who are former pro-psi proponents. The best-known anti-psi philosophers who have worked on the psi literature are Paul Edwards, Antony Flew, and Paul Kurtz. Also, the unclassifiable Martin Gardner is firmly among the unconvinced.

Besides the invaluable Proceedings of the SPR, there are a number of journals devoted entirely to psi phenomena, such as *Journal of Psychical Research, Journal of the American Society of Psychical Research, Journal of Parapsychology, European Journal of Parapsychology,* and *International Journal of Parapsychology,* all of which are reliable sources of the best in psi. Of note is the *Journal of Scientific Exploration,* which sometimes reports on psi topics and is generally pro-psi. The multidisciplinary *Journal of Consciousness Studies* sometimes gives coverage to psi and related issues. Two other journals deserve special mention: the nicely balanced but short-lived *Skeptical Zetetic* and the *Skeptical Inquirer,* which claims to maintain an open mind but is widely regarded as being openly hostile to psi in all of its forms. There are also journals, too numerous to mention, that are devoted to more limited phenomena usually included in parapsychology.

See also Bergson, Henri; Broad, Charlie Dunbar; Consciousness; Dualism in the Philosophy of Mind; Ducasse, Curt John; Idealism; Immortality; James, William; Materialism; Panpsychism; Philosophy of Mind; Precognition; Qualia; Reincarnation; Volition.

Bibliography

BOOKS AND ARTICLES ADVOCATING PSI

Almeder, Robert. *Death and Personal Survival: The Evidence for Life after Death.* Lanham, MD: Rowman & Littlefield, 1992.

Beloff, John. *Parapsychology: A Concise History.* New York: St. Martin's Press, 1993.

Beloff, John. *The Relentless Question: Reflections on the Paranormal.* Jefferson, NC: McFarland, 1990.

Bem, Daryl J., and C. Honorton. "Does Psi Exist? Replicable Evidence for an Anomalous Process of Information Transfer." *Psychological Bulletin* 115 (1) (1994): 4–18.

Broad, C. D. *Religion, Philosophy, and Psychical Research: Selected Essays.* London: Routledge, 1953.

Broad, C. D. *Lectures on Psychical Research: Incorporating the Perrott Lectures Given in Cambridge University in 1959 and 1960.* London: Routledge and Kegan Paul, 1962.

Dilley, Frank. "Mind-Brain Interaction and Psi." *Southern Journal of Philosophy* 26 (4) (January 1988): 469–480.

Edge, Hoyt L., et al. *Foundations of Parapsychology: Exploring the Boundaries of Human Capability.* Boston: Routledge, 1986.

Griffin, David Ray. *Parapsychology, Philosophy, and Spirituality: A Postmodern Exploration.* Albany: SUNY Press, 1997.

Irwin, H. J. *An Introduction to Parapsychology.* 2nd ed. Jefferson, NC: McFarland, 1994.

Murphy, Gardner. *Challenge of Psychical Research: A Primer of Parapsychology.* Westport, CT: Greenwood Press, 1979.

Rao, K. Ramakrishnan, ed. *Basic Research in Parapsychology.* 2nd ed. Jefferson, NC: McFarland, 2001.

Stevenson, Ian. *Children Who Remember Previous Lives: A Question of Reincarnation.* Charlottesville: University Press of Virginia, 1987.

Wolman, Benjamin E., ed. *Handbook of Parapsychology.* Jefferson, NC: McFarland, 1986.

BOOKS AND ARTICLES REJECTING PSI

Alcock, James E. *Science and Supernature: A Critical Appraisal of Parapsychology.* Buffalo, NY: Prometheus Books, 1990.

Edwards, Paul. *Reincarnation: A Critical Examination.* Amherst, NY: Prometheus Books, 1996.

Gardner, Martin. *Science: Good, Bad, and Bogus.* Buffalo, NY: Prometheus Books, 1981.

Hansel, C. E. M. *ESP and Parapsychology: A Critical Reevaluation.* Buffalo, NY: Prometheus Books, 1980.

Hansen, George P. "CSICOP and the Skeptics: An Overview." *Journal of the American Society for Psychical Research* 84 (January 1990): 25–80. Originally titled "Deception by Subjects in Psi Research."

Hyman, Ray. *The Elusive Quarry: A Scientific Appraisal of Psychical Research.* Buffalo, NY: Prometheus Books, 1989.

Hyman, Ray, and Charles Honorton. "A Joint Communiqué: The Psi Ganzfeld Controversy." *Journal of Parapsychology* 50 (1986): 351–364.

Kurtz, Paul, ed. *A Skeptic's Handbook of Parapsychology.* Buffalo, NY: Prometheus Books, 1985.

COLLECTIONS OF PHILOSOPHICAL ARTICLES ON PARAPSYCHOLOGY

Flew, Antony, ed. *Readings in the Philosophical Problems of Parapsychology.* Buffalo, NY: Prometheus Books, 1987.

French, Peter A., ed. *Philosophers in Wonderland: Philosophy and Psychical Research.* St. Paul, MN: Llewellyn, 1975.

Ludwig, Jan, ed. *Philosophy and Parapsychology.* Buffalo, NY: Prometheus Books, 1978.

Thakur, Shivesh C., ed. *Philosophy and Psychical Research.* London: Allen and Unwin, 1976.

Wheatley, James M. O., and Hoyt L. Edge, eds. *Philosophical Dimensions of Parapsychology.* Spring Field, IL: Charles C Thomas, 1976.

Frank B. Dilley (2005)

PARETO, VILFREDO
(1848–1923)

Vilfredo Pareto, the Italian economist, sociologist, and philosopher, was born in Paris, where his father, the Marchese di Pareto, a supporter of Mazzini, was living as a refugee. In 1858 the family returned to Italy, where Pareto received a mixed mathematical and classical secondary education. In 1870 he graduated with a degree in engineering from the Turin Istituto Politecnico. He embarked on a career with the Italian railways and soon became a director. He was deeply, though ambivalently, influenced by his father's involvement in radical politics.

Throughout his life Pareto believed in the superiority of liberal free trade, but his disillusionment with the economic protectionism of the Italian government developed into a fierce hatred of the political and social side of liberal ideology, which he thought had resulted in indefensible economic policies. This hatred led Pareto into intemperate attacks on the government, which retaliated by banning his lectures, and Pareto was eventually forced to abandon his career in government service. At about this time he became acquainted with the mathematical economist Léon Walras, professor at Lausanne. In 1893 Pareto was appointed lecturer at Lausanne, and he succeeded to Walras's chair the following year. He lived in Switzerland for the rest of his life, eschewing political activity until Benito Mussolini's advent to power in 1922. The Fascists acknowledged a large debt to Pareto's writings and conferred numerous honors on him, but since he died after only one year of the Fascist regime, his considered attitude to it must be a matter of conjecture.

LOGICAL AND NONLOGICAL CONDUCT

Pareto's social thought was largely conditioned by his reactions to contemporary political developments in Italy. He claimed to provide an impartial presentation and explanation of the facts of social existence without commitment to any particular sectional interest. In fact, however, his writings constitute a violently polemical defense of economic liberalism and political and social authoritarianism. This gulf between his professions and his practice is ironically in tune with his skepticism about the extent of men's understanding of their own behavior. In his economic writings, *Cours d'économie politique* (2 vols., Lausanne, 1896–1897) and *Manuel d'économie politique* (Paris, 1909), he tried to prove mathematically that the system of free trade provides maximum social benefit. In *Les systèmes socialistes,* (2 vols., Paris, 1902), he attempted to refute the claims of socialism that it provided a superior solution to economic problems. But if the logical case for economic liberalism was as overwhelming as it seemed to Pareto, he had to show why it was not generally practiced. This led him from economics to sociology and to the distinction between logical and nonlogical conduct, which constitutes one of his most distinctive contributions to sociological theory.

Pareto introduced this distinction in the course of a discussion of the nature of a scientific sociology. His conception of "logico-experimental" science was largely Baconian, and his methodological desiderata for a scientific sociology were that all its concepts should have strictly controlled empirical reference; that all its theories should be subject to rigorous experimental or observational control; and that all its inferences should follow with strict logic from the data. He set himself to show how these norms should be applied in the sociological investigation of the ideas and systems of thought current in a given society, which, because they bear "the image of social activity," are an important part of the sociologist's data. Pareto thought it important not to accept such ideas and theories at their holders' valuations but to ask two questions about them: (1) Are their explanatory claims justified by logico-experimental standards? (2) Why are they accepted, and what are the social consequences of this acceptance? The question of acceptance became particularly pressing for Pareto in the case of widely held theories that did not seem to measure up to logico-experimental criteria. He thus regarded the logical critique of sophistries as only a prolegomenon, although a necessary one, to the real problems of sociology.

Many of Pareto's own criticisms of sophistries, especially of those committed by his political opponents, are extremely cogent and witty. However, his general account of the distinction between sound explanation and sophistry is less satisfactory. He held that an action was logical if it was performed by the agent with the intention of achieving an empirically identifiable end, if it actually tended to result in the achievement of that end, and if the agent had sound logico-experimental grounds for expecting this end to result. He designated as nonlogical any action that failed to measure up to any of these diverse criteria, and proceeded to classify what seemed the most characteristic ways in which this failure could occur.

Pareto regarded economic activity directed at maximizing profit, clearheaded Machiavellian political activity, and scientific work as the three most important types of logical conduct. But he left largely unasked most of the fundamental philosophical questions to which such an account gives rise. In particular, unlike his contemporary Émile Durkheim, he did not investigate the possibility that established forms of social behavior are themselves presupposed by the concepts most fundamental to his account—concepts such as "empirical reference," "respect for logic," and "setting oneself an end." Pareto's important insight, however, contained in his idea of "nonlogical conduct," that there are many forms of activity concerning which it makes no sense to ask what reasons people have for performing them, could naturally have led to such an investigation, had Pareto been more of a philosopher and less of a brilliant political pamphleteer. His failure to press this line of inquiry impeded him from

maintaining a clear distinction between nonlogical and illogical actions, and what he claimed to be a dispassionate account of the nature of social life became a massive polemical indictment of alleged human folly. It is also one of the roots of his uncritical acceptance of science as the mother and guardian of logic, notwithstanding his repeated attacks on worshipers of "the Goddess Science."

RESIDUES AND DERIVATIONS

If the reasons offered by men for many of their own actions are not logically compelling, a different kind of explanation seems to be needed. To find this explanation Pareto undertook a wide-ranging, but unsystematic and biased, historical and comparative survey of human social behavior. In the course of it, he claimed to detect a contrast between kinds of conduct that constantly recur with very little variation and those that are highly diverse and changeable. The former he labeled "residues," the latter "derivations." The variable elements, or derivations, prove to be the theories with which people attempt to justify their residues. The alleged persistence of the same residue, even after the agent's abandonment of the derivation that had been supposed to justify it, gave Pareto an additional reason for claiming that the derivation was not the real explanation of the existence of the residue.

This theory has obvious affinities with Karl Marx's concept of "ideology," with Sigmund Freud's "rationalization" (although Pareto seems to have been ignorant of Freud's work), and with Durkheim's "collective sentiments." Unlike these writers, however, Pareto offered no systematic account of why men have recourse to derivations, contenting himself with the observation that among the residues is to be found a tendency of men "to paint a varnish of logic over their conduct."

The theory of residues is similarly incomplete. His most consistently held view seems to have been that the residues are constants and must be accepted as brute facts. At times he said that they were determined by certain congenital psychological "sentiments," although he failed clearly to distinguish these from the residues themselves. Nor did he explain how sentiments differ from the "interests" that he supposed to underlie logical economic activities. At other times he suggested that residues change as a result of social conditions. "A number of traits observable in the Jews of our time, and which are ordinarily ascribed to race," he wrote, "are mere manifestations of residues produced by long centuries of oppression." Moreover, in his Machiavellian advice to statesmen to reinforce in their subjects those residues that are politically advantageous to themselves, by means of propaganda in favor of suitable derivations, Pareto even implied that derivations could influence residues. Such difficulties stemmed largely from Pareto's failure to face the philosophical questions about the nature of logic that his theories should have led him to ask.

ELITES AND THE CYCLE OF HISTORY

The two classes of residues most important for Pareto's sociological theory were combinations and persistence of aggregates. Men dominated by combinations are the innovating, risk-taking experimenters, the "foxes," linked by Pareto with the economic class of speculators. At the other extreme are the "lions," dominated by persistence of aggregates, wedded to the status quo and willing to use force in its defense. These are to be found among the *rentier* class. Pareto thought that all societies are ruled by elites, composed of those naturally most able in the various forms of social activity. The balance between combinations and persistence of aggregates in the elites and the lower social strata respectively determines the general character of a society. Inconsistently with his insistence on the nonlogical character of value judgments, Pareto thought there was an objective distinction between healthy and decadent social states, a distinction strongly influenced by his own attachment to free trade and political authoritarianism. Elites must be enterprising and innovative but also ready to use force in defense of their authority. However, the latter propensity tends to hinder the "circulation of the elites," leading to an accumulation of ability among the masses. Alternatively, the former tendency may degenerate into a flabby humanitarianism that weakens authority. In either case, a revolution results, leading to government by new elites. Pareto's belief in the constant repetition of this process led him to a cyclical view of history.

See also Decision Theory; Durkheim, Émile; Freud, Sigmund; Marx, Karl; Philosophy of Economics; Sociology of Knowledge.

Bibliography

WORKS BY PARETO

Trattato di sociologia generale, 2 vols. Florence: Barbera, 1916. 2nd ed., 3 vols. Florence, 1923. Translated by A. Bongiorno and A. Livingston as *The Mind and Society,* 4 vols. London; Cape, 1935.

Sociological Writings. Translated by Derick Mirfin. New York: Praeger, 1966.

WORKS ON PARETO

Aron, Raymond. "Vilfredo Pareto." In *Main Currents in Sociological Thought,* Vol. 2. Translated by Richard Howard and Helen Weaver. New York: Basic, 1967.

Borkenau, Franz. *Pareto.* London: Chapman and Hall, 1936.

Bruni, Luigino. *Vilfredo Pareto and the Birth of Modern Microeconomics.* Cheltenham, U.K.: Edward Elgar, 2002.

Burnham, James. *The Machiavellians.* New York: John Day, 1943.

Curtis, C. P., and G. C. Homans. *An Introduction to Pareto: His Sociology.* New York: Knopf, 1934.

Parsons, Talcott. *The Structure of Social Action.* New York: McGraw-Hill, 1937.

Powers, Charles H. *Vilfredo Pareto.* Newbury Park, CA: Sage, 1987.

Sica, Alan. *Weber, Irrationality, and Social Order.* Berkeley: University of California Press, 1988.

Winch, Peter. "The Mind and Society." In *The Idea of a Social Science,* 2nd ed. Atlantic Highlands, NJ: Humanities Press, 1990.

Peter Winch (1967)
Bibliography updated by Philip Reed (2005)

PARFIT, DEREK
(1942–)

Derek Parfit is senior research fellow of All Souls College; a regular visiting professor at Harvard, New York University, and Rutgers; and a fellow of both the British Academy and the American Academy of Arts and Sciences.

Born in China and educated in England at the Dragon School and Eton, Parfit took his degree in modern history at Oxford University and later turned to philosophy. He is legendary as a mentor and for his acute monograph-length criticisms of manuscripts, as well as for his important contributions to ethics, practical reasoning, and metaphysics. Parfit is widely regarded as one of the most important contemporary philosophers.

Along with John Rawls's *A Theory of Justice,* Parfit's magnum opus, *Reasons and Persons,* helped turn ethics from a moribund and peripheral subject that largely focused on the meanings of moral terms into a vibrant and central philosophical topic. Brimming with ingenious examples, powerful arguments, and startling conclusions, it has significantly shaped the philosophical agenda, introducing into discussion a host of new topics, examples, and terminology.

In Part One, Parfit discusses the ways in which theories about morality and rationality can be self-defeating and also makes claims about rational irrationality, blameless wrongdoing, imperceptible harms and benefits, harmless torturers, and other mistakes in moral mathematics. Part Two defends a theory of individual rationality, the Critical Present-aim Theory, which rejects both purely desire-based instrumental theories and a purely self-interested or egoistic theory. Parfit offers a new outlook on the old question of whether morality must lose out in a conflict with prudence or rational egoism. Parfit notes that rational egoism is a hybrid position, neutral with respect to time but partial with respect to persons. Correspondingly, it can be challenged from one direction by morality, which is neutral with respect to both persons and time, and from the other direction by a present-aim theory, which is partial with respect to both persons and time. Parfit suggests that rational egoism rests on an unstable middle ground that requires a firm distinction between persons and time that is metaphysically dubious. Of additional interest are Parfit's insights regarding the rationality of attitudes to time and time's passage.

In Part Three, Parfit propounds a reductionist account of personal identity, somewhat like the Buddhist *no-self view*. Appealing to a dazzling array of so-called puzzle cases involving hypothetical fission, fusion, and branch lines of different *selves* or *person-stages*, Parfit challenges widely held beliefs about the nature and importance of personal identity. Most assume that there is a *deep, further fact* that constitutes personal identity, a fact that must be all or nothing and that matters greatly in rational and moral deliberations. On Parfit's view, while the logic of identity is all or nothing, the relations that constitute personal identity over time are matters of degree, and sometimes there may be no answer to the question of whether a future self will be me. What matters in survival are physical and psychological continuities with the *right* kind of cause, where the right kind of cause, he provocatively suggests, might be any cause.

Part Four presents a host of puzzles and paradoxes regarding future generations. The Non-Identity Problem is raised by the fact that any choice between two social or economic policies will affect who it is who will later live. Even if one's choice between two such policies would greatly lower the quality of life of future generations, this choice may not be worse for any of the people who would later live since if one had chosen the other policy, these people would never have existed. Parfit here challenges the deeply held view that moral arguments should appeal to the interests of all of the affected people. Parfit argues that it is hard to avoid what he calls the Repugnant Conclusion, or the view that compared with the existence of billions of people whose quality of life is very high, it would be in itself better if there existed some much larger number of people whose lives would be barely worth living. Parfit also presents the Mere Addition Paradox, in which various plausible assumptions are shown to lead to a contradiction. These arguments profoundly challenge deep beliefs about moral and practical reasoning.

At the time of the writing of this entry, Parfit was completing a second book *Climbing the Mountain* that will be about Kant's ethics, contractualism, and consequentialism. In discussing Kant's Formula of Humanity, Parfit argues that although one should not *regard* other people merely as a means, whether one is acting wrongly never depends on whether one is treating people merely as a means. Parfit defends Kant's claim that one must never treat people in ways to which they could not rationally consent. He then argues that if one revises Kant's Formula of Universal Law and appeals to a view about rationality and reasons that is not desire based but value based, Kant's formula can provide the best version of contractualism.

On the standard moral map, there are two main kinds of systematic moral theory. One kind is consequentialist, with utilitarian theories as the best-known examples. The other kind is Kantian theories and various forms of contractualism, which are often presented as the main systematic alternative to all forms of consequentialism. This map, Parfit argues, should be redrawn. Of the different ways of thinking about morality, it is Kantian and contractualist theories that do most to support consequentialism. Kantians, contractualists, and consequentialists ought to conclude that, in John Stuart Mill's metaphor, they have been climbing the same mountain on different sides.

Parfit also argues that Kantian and contractualist theories should take less ambitious forms. These theories should be presented not as accounts of wrongness or of moral reasoning but as claiming to describe a higher-level property that can make acts wrong, under which ordinary wrong-making properties can be subsumed. There are, moreover, several kinds of wrongness; and the most important questions are not about wrongness, but about reasons.

Parfit believes that the best way to respond to skepticism about the possibility of ethical progress is to make some. Perhaps as much as any philosopher in the last 100 years, he has done so.

See also Ethics; Kant, Immanuel; Metaphysics; Rawls, John; Thinking.

Bibliography

Rawls, J. *A Theory of Justice*. Cambridge, MA: Harvard University Press, 1971.

WORKS BY PARFIT

Reasons and Persons. Oxford: Oxford University Press, 1984.

"Overpopulation and the Quality of Life." In *Applied Ethics*, edited by Peter Singer. Pp. 145–154. Oxford: Oxford University Press, 1986.

"Equality or Priority?" Delivered as the Lindley Lecture at the University of Kansas, November 21, 1991. Copyright by the Department of Philosophy, University of Kansas, 1995. Reprinted in *The Ideal of Equality*, edited by Matthew Clayton and Andrew Williams, pp. 81–126 (New York: St. Martin's Press, 2000).

"The Unimportance of Identity." In *Identity*, edited by H. Harris, pp. 13–45. Oxford: Oxford University Press, 1995.

"Reasons and Motivation." *Proceedings of the Aristotelian Society* (supplement). 1997, pp. 99–130.

"Why Anything? Why This?" *The London Review of Books* (January 22; February 5, 1998): 24–27; 22–25.

"Experiences, Subjects, and Conceptual Schemes." *Philosophical Topics* 26 (1 and 2) (1999): 217–270.

"Rationality and Reasons." In *Exploring Practical Philosophy*, edited by Dan Egonsson, et al, pp. 17–39. Burlington, VT: Ashgate, 2001.

"Justifiability to Others." In *On What We Owe to Others*, edited by Philip Stratton-Lake, pp. 67–89. Oxford: Blackwell, 2004.

"Kant's Arguments for His Formula of Universal Law." In *The Egalitarian Conscience, Essays in Honor of G. A. Cohen*, edited by Christine Sypnowich, Oxford University Press (in press).

"Persons, Bodies, and Human Beings." In *Contemporary Debates in Metaphysics*, edited by John Hawthorne, Dean Zimmerman, and Theodore Sider. Oxford: Blackwell (in press).

Works about Parfit

Barry, B., et al. "Symposium on Derek Parfit's *Reasons and Persons*" *Ethics* 96 (1986): 703–872.

Dancy, J., ed. *Reading Parfit*. Oxford: Blackwell, 1997.

Temkin, L. "Intransitivity and the Mere Addition Paradox." *Philosophy and Public Affairs* 16 (2) (1987): 138–187.

Larry Temkin (2005)

PARKER, THEODORE

(1810–1860)

Theodore Parker, an American theologian and social reformer, was the grandson of Captain John Parker, who led the Lexington minutemen. Theodore Parker was born in Lexington, Massachusetts, and, except for scattered months of formal schooling during the winter, was almost entirely self-taught. Although unable to afford tuition, he was allowed to take the Harvard examinations, and in 1834 he was admitted to the Harvard Divinity School. He was ordained minister of a small parish in West Roxbury, Massachusetts, in 1837. In 1845, after he had become a controversial figure and commanded a large audience, his supporters created the 28th Congregational Society in Boston and later rented the Boston Music Hall, where Parker preached to one of the largest congregations in the country. He became equally famous as a scholar, preacher, theologian, and reformer. Parker died in Florence, Italy.

In his religious thought Parker's radicalism was partly instinctive and partly the result of environmental influences. In an autobiographical essay completed just before his death, Parker remembered how he had been taught as a boy to respect the voice of conscience as the "voice of God in the soul of man" and encouraged to develop a spirit of free inquiry "in all directions." His religious upbringing was extremely liberal, and when he entered upon his formal theological studies, he had not only rejected the doctrine of the Trinity but was already suspicious of the validity of miracles and the "infallible, verbal inspiration of the whole Bible." Profiting by the encouragement of the liberal Unitarian professors at Harvard, he began an intensive study of the Bible that ultimately led him to a knowledge of twenty languages and did much to confirm his earlier suspicions regarding biblical authority.

As a young minister Parker was a great admirer of William Ellery Channing and Ralph Waldo Emerson. He responded to Emerson's Divinity School Address with enthusiasm and was an anonymous contributor to the polemical pamphlet war that followed.

Parker's own religious philosophy was strongly influenced by Immanuel Kant and by the critical studies of such biblical scholars as Wilhelm Martin DeWette and theologians such as David Friedrich Strauss and Ferdinand Christian Baur. Academic study and his own religious experience convinced him that the foundation of religion was based on "great primal intuitions of nature that depend on no logical process of demonstration." The three most important were the intuition of God, the intuition of morality, and the intuition of immortality. Basing his theology on these facts of consciousness, Parker emphasized the infinite perfection of God and the perfectibility of man.

His ideas first received wide publicity in 1841, when he delivered an ordination sermon titled "The Transient and the Permanent in Christianity." In this sermon Parker contrasted the transiency of theology and Scripture with the permanence of the great moral truths of Christianity, truths that depended for their validity not on the authority of Christ but on the voice of God in the human heart. Parker spoke as a Unitarian minister, but the reception he received from organized Unitarianism was as wrathful as Channing's reception had been at the hands of the Calvinists twenty years earlier. As his more conservative followers faded away, Parker developed his radical ideas at greater length in a series of lectures he published in 1842 as *A Discourse of Matters Pertaining to Religion.* The following year he published his own edition and translation of DeWette's critical study of the Old Testament, *Beiträge zur Einleitung in das Alte Testament.*

Emerson referred to Parker as "our Savonarola," and Parker's essay on transcendentalism is one of the clearest expressions that we have of the American rejection of the empirical philosophy of the Enlightenment. Modern scholarship has established, however, that Parker's transcendentalism was not identical with Emerson's, for Parker relied less completely on intuition and more on the critical study of history and theology.

Parker's extraordinary capacity for sustained scholarly endeavor was almost matched by his capacity for action. The "Absolute Religion" he advocated required the application of religious truth to social problems, and Parker often preached on such subjects as crime, poverty, temperance, and prostitution. Long before the proponents of the social gospel, Parker recognized the power of organized evil in the world and sought to marshal religious sentiment against it. He was inevitably drawn into abolitionism. A friend of Wendell Phillips and William Lloyd Garrison, he helped to lead the resistance to the Fugitive Slave Law in Boston and was a supporter of John Brown before Harper's Ferry.

Parker traveled widely on lecture tours, making about one hundred appearances a year during the last decade of his life. His influence on the public mind was at its peak just before his death.

See also Channing, William Ellery; Consciousness; Emerson, Ralph Waldo; Enlightenment; Intuition; Kant, Immanuel; Neo-Kantianism; New England Transcendentalism; Religion and Morality; Strauss, David Friedrich.

Bibliography

Parker's work is collected in *Theodore Parker's Works,* edited by Frances P. Cobbe, 14 vols. (London, 1863–1870). A centenary edition was published by the American Unitarian Association, 15 vols. (Boston, 1907–1911). Henry Steele Commager has edited *Theodore Parker: An Anthology* (Boston: Beacon Press, 1960).

Biographical studies include Henry Steele Commager, *Theodore Parker, Yankee Crusader* (Boston: Little Brown, 1936), John Dirk, *The Critical Theology of Theodore Parker* (New York: Columbia University Press, 1948), and John Weiss, *Life and Correspondence of Theodore Parker,* 2 vols. (New York: Appleton, 1864).

Irving H. Bartlett (1967)

PARMENIDES OF ELEA
(born c. 515 BCE)

Parmenides of Elea, the most original and important philosopher before Socrates, was born c. 515 BCE. He changed the course of Greek cosmology and had an even more important effect upon metaphysics and epistemology. He was the first to focus attention on the central problem of Greek metaphysics—What is the nature of real being?—and he established a frame of reference within which the discussion was to be conducted. The closely related problem of knowledge, which to a great extent dominated philosophy in the fifth and fourth centuries, was raised at once by his contrast between the Way of Truth and the Way of Seeming. His influence can be found in Empedocles, Anaxagoras, and the atomists; it is strong in most of Plato's work, particularly in the vitally important dialogues *Parmenides, Theaetetus,* and *Sophist.*

Plato in his dialogue *Parmenides* describes a meeting in Athens of Parmenides, Zeno, and Socrates. Parmenides was then about 65, Zeno about 40, and Socrates "very young." Though the meeting is probably fictitious, there is no reason why the ages should be unrealistic. Since Socrates died in 399, when he was about 70, and since he was old enough in Plato's dialogue to talk philosophy with Parmenides, the meeting would have to be dated about 450, making Parmenides' birth about 515. An alternative dating (Diogenes Laërtius, *Lives* IX, 23, probably from Apollodorus's *Chronica*) puts his birth about 25 years earlier, but this can be explained away.

Plato's remark (*Sophist* 242D) that the Eleatic school stems from Xenophanes is not to be taken seriously. Parmenides founded the school in the Phocaean colony of Elea in southern Italy, and its only other noteworthy members were his pupils Zeno and Melissus (the tradition that the atomist Leucippus was from Elea is probably false).

WRITINGS

The work of Parmenides is not extant as a whole. Plato and Aristotle quote a line or two; from later writers, particularly Sextus Empiricus and Simplicius, about 150 lines can be recovered. Parmenides wrote in hexameter verse. All the fragments seem to come from a single work, which may have been called *On Nature*; it is unlikely to have been very long, and the fragments may amount to as much as a third of the whole. The survival of a long consecutive passage of more than sixty lines (Fr. 8) is of the greatest importance; it is the earliest example of an extended philosophical argument.

The poem begins with a description of the poet's journey to the home of a goddess, who welcomes him kindly and tells him that he is to learn "both the unshakeable heart of well-rounded Truth, and the beliefs of mortals, in which there is no true reliability" (Fr. 1). The rest of the poem consists of the speech of the goddess in which she fulfills these two promises.

The interpretation of Parmenides is thoroughly controversial, and a short article cannot do more than offer one possible account, with a brief mention of the more important and plausible variants. In the interests of brevity many expressions of doubt have been omitted.

THE PROEM

Sextus Empiricus (*Adversus Mathematicos,* VII, 111ff.) quotes 32 lines that he asserts to be the beginning of Parmenides' *On Nature* (Fr. 1). The poet describes his journey in a chariot, drawn by mares that know the way and escorted by the Daughters of the Sun. The Sun Maidens come from the Halls of Night and unveil themselves when they come into daylight. There is a gateway on the paths of Night and Day, with great doors of which the goddess Justice holds the key. The Sun Maidens persuade Justice to open the gates for themselves and Parmenides, and they pass through. "The goddess" welcomes him kindly as a mortal man in divine company, shakes his hand, and sets his mind at rest by telling him that it is right and just that he should have taken this road. He must now learn both the truth and the unreliable beliefs of mortals.

Although few examples of contemporary poetry have survived for comparison, it is safe to say that this proem is a mixture of tradition and innovation. The "journey" of the poet is a literary figure closely paralleled in an ode by Pindar (*Olympian* 6). There, as for Parmenides, the journey is an image of the course of the song; the poet rides in a chariot, a gate has to be opened, the team knows the way, and the road is notably direct. The route followed by Parmenides' chariot, although straight and swift, is impossible to chart. The details are vague. What is clear is that the whole journey is nowhere on earth, but in the heavens, and that it begins in the

realm of darkness and ends in the realm of light. This imagery is confirmed by other indications—the escort of Sun Maidens and their unveiling.

It can hardly be doubted that the journey symbolizes progress from ignorance to knowledge on a heroic or even cosmic scale. The epic verse form signifies a deliberately heroic context, for earlier philosophers probably wrote in prose (though Parmenides may also have chosen verse as being more memorable). Parmenides' journey in search of knowledge must recall Odysseus's journey to Hades (*Odyssey* XI) to get directions from Teiresias to guide him on his way home. The location of Parmenides' journey recalls the magic regions of this part of the *Odyssey,* where in one place dawn follows immediately upon nightfall because "the ways of night and day are close together" (X, 86) and where in another place there is no daylight at all, since Night envelops everything (XI, 19). There may also be reminiscences of the journey of Phaethon in the chariot of the Sun.

Sextus, after quoting Fragment 1, gives a detailed allegorical interpretation of it, and in this he has been followed by some modern scholars. But this is wrong; it is impossible to trace a consistent allegory, and in any case detailed allegory was a later invention.

The identity of the goddess is puzzling. The wording of the proem itself suggests that she is the same as the goddess Justice who holds the keys of the gates; in a later fragment, however, she speaks of Justice in the third person (possibly even in Fr. 1.28; certainly in Fr. 8.14). It may be that Parmenides left the identification intentionally vague. Simplicius does not mention the goddess at all but introduces his quotations as if the first person referred to Parmenides himself. The Neoplatonists appear to have called her "the nymph Hypsipyle" (that is, High Gate; Proclus, "Commentary on the *Parmenides*" Book IV, Ch. 34).

It is probably wrong to say that in his proem Parmenides is setting himself up as a mystic or that he is claiming to have received a divine revelation. If mysticism entails some privileged access to truth through nonrational means, then Parmenides was no mystic. The fragments show that he argued for his conclusions; his goddess tells him to use his reason to assess her words (Fr. 7.5). A single visionary experience is ruled out by the opening of the proem, in which the tenses show that the journey is a repeated one—perhaps repeated every time the poem is recited. Unless the claim of every poet to be inspired by the Muses is itself a claim to a divine revelation, this seems to be an inappropriate description of Parmenides' experience.

At the time of its composition, the proem was probably understood as a claim that the poet had something of great importance to say. The course of his divinely inspired song was a path that led to the light of knowledge. By making Justice responsible for opening the gate for him, he claimed that this was a right and proper path for him to follow and, therefore, a path that led to truth. By putting the whole of his doctrine into the mouth of a goddess, he claimed objectivity for it; it was not beyond criticism, since the goddess instructed him to judge it by reason, but it was not to be regarded as a merely personal statement by Parmenides.

THE THREE WAYS

The goddess begins by telling Parmenides what are the only possible ways of inquiry. She describes three ways, produces reasons for ruling out two of them, and insists on the remaining one as the only correct one.

First two ways are stated, each being defined by a conjunctive proposition. The first is "that it *is*, and cannot not be; this is the way of Persuasion, for she is the attendant of Truth." The second is "that it *is not*, and must necessarily not be, this I tell you is a way of total ignorance" (Fr. 2).

The literal meaning of Parmenides' Greek in these propositions is hard to see. The verb "to be" is used in the existential sense. He uses it in the third person present indicative without any subject expressed. Some interpreters say that there is no subject to be understood; however, without any subject the sentence is incomplete, and no doubt the impersonal subject "it" is to be regarded as contained in the verb, as it often is. What this "it" refers to has to be derived from the rest of the argument and will be discussed shortly.

Immediately after the statement of the first two ways, the second way is ruled out on the ground that it is impossible to know or to utter what does not exist: "Whatever is for thinking and saying *must* exist; for it can exist [literally, 'is for being'], whereas nothing cannot" (Fr. 6). The line of thought seems to be that the object of thought *can* exist, and since "nothing" cannot exist, the object of thought cannot be nothing. But it must either exist or be nothing; hence, it *must* exist. The basic premises then are that "nothing" is nonexistent (presumably regarded as tautological) and that the object of thought *can* exist (that is, it is possible to think of something).

Parmenides makes it quite plain, by the use of inferential particles, that there *is* an argument in this passage (though this has been denied) along the lines described.

It is therefore legitimate to fill in the basic proposition of the Way of Truth ("it is") from the grounds on which it is based. The unexpressed subject of this proposition must be "the object of thought or knowledge" (this is convincingly shown by G. E. L. Owen, "Eleatic Questions"). The Way of Truth will therefore show what can be said of a thing if it is to be a proper object of thought; the first step is to assert that it must *be*, that it should not *be* is unthinkable. Subsequently, the subject is referred to as *tò eóv* ("that which is," "what is real," "what exists").

After ruling out the second way, the goddess continues with a warning against a third way, the way followed by mortal men, who wander about senselessly, knowing nothing and getting nowhere. Their characteristic error is that they have made up their minds that "to be and not to be is the same and not the same" (Fr. 6). The third way can be identified with "the beliefs of mortals" mentioned at the end of the proem and discussed in detail in the main body of Parmenides' work, after the Way of Truth (this identification is often denied). Mortals treat existence and nonexistence as the same in that they attach them both to the same objects by supposing that things sometimes exist and sometimes do not (that is, that there is change) and by supposing that some things exist that contain less of being than others and therefore contain some nonexistence (that is, that there is difference). They treat them as not the same in that they suppose they have different meanings. The language in which the censured doctrine is expressed is reminiscent of Heraclitus, but Heraclitus is certainly not the only mortal who suffers from Parmenides' lash here.

The third way is ruled out by pointing to an alleged contradiction in it. It asserts that "things that are not, are" (Fr. 7). From the arguments of the recommended way, described later, it would appear that what is objectionable in the third way is its assumption of intermediate degrees of existence, of things that exist at one time but not another, at one place but not another, or in one way but not another. Ordinary habits of speech and the data of sense perception would lead a man along this path; the goddess gives a warning to "judge by *reason* the hard-hitting refutation that I have uttered."

THE WAY OF TRUTH

The Way of Truth has now been shown by elimination to be the right way. The long Fragment 8 proceeds to make deductions from the basic proposition that "it" (the object of thought and knowledge if the analysis given above is correct) "exists and must exist."

Its first property is that it is ungenerated and inde-structible. It cannot have come into being out of what does not exist since what does not exist is absolutely unthinkable and since there would, moreover, be no explanation of why it grew out of nothing at one time rather than another. There is no growth of what exists (and no decay either, but Parmenides offers no separate argument for that); hence, "either it is or it is not" (Fr. 8.16)—and that decision has already been made. It *is,* as a whole, entirely.

Since there is no growth or decay of what exists Parmenides argues that no distinctions can be made within it. There are no degrees of being—differences of density, for instance; the whole is full of continuous being. What exists is single, indivisible, and homogeneous. Here Parmenides apparently moves from the temporal continuity of being to its spatial uniformity; in the same way Melissus, his pupil, argues for the absence of a beginning or end in time and then assumes the absence of a beginning or end in space (Melissus, Frs. 3–4).

Next follows an assertion that since there is no generation or destruction, there is no motion or change in what exists. This argument is expanded by Melissus (Fr. 7). Any form of change or rearrangement implies the destruction of a state of affairs that exists and the generation of one that does not exist. Thus, Parmenides concludes that what exists "remains the same, in the same … held fast in the bonds of limit by the power of Necessity" (Fr. 8.29). It already is whatever it can be. Motion, as a species of change, is apparently denied by the same argument.

The last section of the Way of Truth is particularly difficult. Parmenides repeats his assertion that there is no not-being and there are no different degrees of being; what exists is equal to itself everywhere and reaches its limits everywhere. From this he concludes that it is "perfect from every angle, equally matched from the middle in every way, like the mass of a well-rounded ball" (Fr. 8.42–44). There is no agreement among modern scholars as to whether this is a literal assertion that what exists is a sphere (a view held by John Burnet and F. M. Cornford) or only a simile indicating that it is like a ball in some respect other than shape (a view held by H. Fränkel and Owen). The latter view seems more probable. Parmenides' stress lies on the qualitative completeness, or perfection, of what exists, not on its spatial extension. The point of the simile might be put like this: As a ball is equally poised about its center so that it would make no difference which direction you took if you examined it from the center outward, so what exists is all the same from any center.

THE WAY OF SEEING

Having completed her account "about truth," Parmenides' goddess fulfills her promise to describe mortal beliefs. Only about forty lines survive from this part of the poem. The fundamental difference from the Way of Truth is made clear at the outset: Mortals give names to two forms, and that is where they are wrong, for what exists is single. They assume the existence of two opposites, Fire and Night, probably characterized in terms of sensible opposites such as hot–cold, light–dark, light–heavy, soft–hard. Using these two forms as elements, the Way of Seeing apparently offered a detailed account of the origin of the stars, sun, moon, earth and all the things on the earth "as far as the parts of animals" (Simplicius, *In de Caelo* 559.25), some embryology, sense perception, and doubtless other things. The details are unimportant (though Parmenides is credited with the first assertion that the morning star is identical with the evening star, according to Diogenes Laërtius, *Lives* IX, 23); the interesting and puzzling thing is that he should have added a cosmogony to the Way of Truth at all. Modern scholars differ about his intention.

Eduard Zeller took the cosmogony to be an account of the beliefs of Parmenides' contemporaries; Burnet called it "a sketch of contemporary Pythagorean cosmology." However, there is no evidence for this. Such a review would seem to be pointless, and in antiquity the cosmogony was recognized as Parmenides' own. One can ignore the suggestion that it represents those of his early beliefs that were later superseded. The discussion now turns on this point: Is the Way of Seeing granted relative validity as a sort of second best, or is it wholly rejected? If it is wholly rejected, why did Parmenides write it?

Recently, the first view has been defended as follows by, for example, W. J. Verdenius, Gregory Vlastos, Hans Schwabl, and W. R. Chalmers. The goddess in the prologue promised that Parmenides would learn about mortal beliefs as well as truth and would hardly have done so if they had no validity at all. Unless the phenomenal world is granted some degree of reality, the philosopher himself, the learner of truth, appears to be condemned to nonexistence; however, the mind, described in physical terms in the Way of Seeing (Fr. 16), is the faculty that grasps what is real in the Way of Truth. Moreover, some of the language of the Way of Seeing deliberately echoes that of the Way of Truth. The two opposites, Fire and

Night, transgress the canons of truth by being distinguished from each other, but they are each described as self-identical and as containing no nonexistence, like the real being of the Way of Truth (Frs. 8.57–59, 9.4). Later writers in antiquity, notably Aristotle (*Metaphysics* A5, 986b27–34), took Parmenides to be yielding to the necessity of providing his own account of the phenomenal world. For reason, Aristotle said, there was just one being, but for sense perception more than one. Others have argued that the Way of Truth is the way an immortal looks at the world sub specie aeternitatis, whereas the Way of Seeming is the way mortals see the same world in time. Many variations on these themes have been suggested.

The contrary view, defended recently in differing forms by Owen, A. A. Long, and Leonardo Taran, has more justification in the text of Parmenides. The goddess makes it clear enough that the Way of Seeming is wholly unreliable (Frs. 1.30, 8.52) and that the Way of Truth leaves no room whatsoever for intermediate degrees of reality. The text itself contains a statement of the intention: "Thus no judgment of mortals can ever overtake you" (Fr. 8.61; the metaphor is from chariot racing). Although this is ambiguous, the likeliest sense is that Parmenides is equipped by the Way of Seeming to defeat any mortal opinion about the phenomenal world. All descriptions of the phenomenal world presuppose that difference is real, but the Way of Truth has shown that what exists is single and undifferentiated. The transition to the Way of Seeming is made by pointing to the fundamental mistake in assuming even the minimum of differentiation in reality—that is, in assuming that two forms of what exists can be distinguished (Fr. 8.53–54). Once this assumption is made, a plausible description of the phenomenal world can be offered, but anyone who has followed Parmenides thus far will recognize the fundamental fallacy in even the most plausible description. This explanation is more consistent with the later history of Eleaticism, for Zeno and Melissus showed no interest in positive cosmology.

PARMENIDES AND GREEK PHILOSOPHY

There is general agreement that Parmenides followed the Milesians, Heraclitus, and Pythagoras and preceded Empedocles, Anaxagoras, and the atomists (the thesis of K. Reinhardt that Heraclitus answered Parmenides has been generally rejected). Ancient tradition credits him with a Pythagorean teacher, Ameinias (Diogenes Laërtius, *Lives* IX, 21). It is often said that the rigorous deductive method of the Way of Truth was learned from the mathematicians, who at that time in Italy were likely to be Pythagoreans, but the truth is that too little is known of the mathematics of the time to allow this to be more than a guess.

In general, the relevance of Parmenides to earlier philosophy is fairly clear, though there is room for doubt about his attitude toward individual men. (Various scholars have found in the text attacks on Anaximander, Anaximenes, Heraclitus, and the Pythagorean school.) All previous systems had assumed the reality of change in the physical world and attempted to explain it. Thales, Anaximander, and Anaximenes held that the world evolved from a simpler state into a more complex one. Anaximander's view was that different substances ("the opposites") grew out of a primitive undifferentiated "indefinite"; Anaximenes gave a more precise description of the manner of differentiation and said that the original substance, air, turned into other substances by rarefaction and condensation. Heraclitus apparently abandoned the idea of an original simple state, asserting that everything in the world is always changing—"an ever-living fire." In somewhat less materialistic language the Pythagoreans produced a cosmogony based on the imposition of limit upon the unlimited. Parmenides' critique was equally damaging to all of these theories, since his argument, if accepted, condemned all difference as illusory.

It is often said that Parmenides' attack on the reality of the physical world depends on his confusion of two senses of the verb "to be"—the existential and copulative. It cannot logically be true that a subject *is* and at the same time *is not* (existentially); from this Parmenides is supposed to have concluded that it cannot be true that a subject *is* black and at the same time *is not* white and hence that all differentiation is impossible. The surviving text does not bear this out. Parmenides' premise (and his fundamental fallacy) was, rather, that "what is not" is absolutely unthinkable and unknowable. Every change would involve the passage of what is into what is not, and hence every attempt to describe a change would involve the use of an unintelligible expression, "what is not."

The argument of the Way of Truth is metaphysical and would apply to any subject matter whatsoever; it is false to suppose that it applied only to Pythagorean cosmogony or only to the materialist cosmogonies of the Ionians. But that Parmenides' primary intention was to criticize the earlier cosmogonists seems clear from the addition of the Way of Seeming to the Way of Truth. His own Real Being was certainly not a ball of matter, as Burnet and others thought. On the other hand, it was not something to which spatial terms were wholly inapplicable. It filled the whole of space and thus was in some sense a competitor of other accounts of the cosmos. The main effects of his work, too, were on cosmology.

The error of Parmenides' ways was not seen immediately, perhaps not until Plato's *Sophist*. Their immediate effect was to produce theories that attempted to save the natural world from unreality without transgressing Parmenides' logical canons. In brief, they produced theories of elements. Empedocles envisaged a cosmos made of the four elements that were later made standard by Aristotle—earth, water, air, and fire. He satisfied some of Parmenides' criteria by making his elements unchangeable and homogeneous. What he refused to accept from Parmenides was that difference was impossible without diminution of reality; his four elements were asserted to be different from one another yet equally real. He explained apparent change as the rearrangement in space of the unchanging elements. Anaxagoras went further to meet Parmenides by asserting that all natural substances, not just a privileged four, were elementary and unchangeable. The atomists responded in a different way; they accepted that no qualitative difference is possible but rescued the phenomenal world by asserting that "what is not" exists in the form of void—that is, as empty space separating pieces of real being from each other. (The equation of void with "what is not" is sometimes attributed to Parmenides himself, but it was probably first made by his follower Melissus, who explicitly denied its existence in his Fragment 7.)

Plato inherited from Parmenides the belief that the object of knowledge must exist and must be found by the mind and not by the senses. He agreed that the object of knowledge is not something abstracted from the data of sense perception but a being of a different and superior order. He differed, however, in that he allowed the sensible world to have an intermediate status, as the object of "belief," rather than no status at all (*Republic* 477B and elsewhere). He differed more significantly, too, in that he reimported plurality into the real and knowable by distinguishing different senses of "not-being" (*Sophist* 237B ff. and 257B ff.).

See also Anaxagoras of Clazomenae; Anaximenes; Aristotle; Atomism; Cosmology; Diogenes Laertius; Empedocles; Epistemology; Heraclitus of Ephesus; Leucippus and Democritus; Melissus of Samos; Metaphysics; Neoplatonism; Nothing; Plato; Pythagoras and Pythagoreanism; Quantum Mechanics; Sextus Empiricus; Simplicius; Socrates; Space; Thales of Miletus; Xenophanes of Colophon; Zeno of Elea.

Bibliography

Fragments and ancient testimonia are in *Fragmente der Vorsokratiker*, edited by H. Diels and W. Kranz, 10th ed. (Berlin, 1961), the standard collection. Fragments with English translation and commentary are in G. S. Kirk and J. E. Raven, *The Presocratic Philosophers* (Cambridge, U.K.: Cambridge University Press, 1957), but the commentary is rather inadequate. They are also found in Leonardo Taran, *Parmenides* (Princeton, NJ: Princeton University Press, 1965), and in Italian, with a long bibliography, in Mario Untersteiner, *Parmenide* (Florence: Nuova Italia, 1958).

The most important recent studies are H. Fränkel, "Parmenidesstudien," in his *Wege und Formen frühgriechischen Denkens* (Munich, 1955), and G. E. L. Owen, "Eleatic Questions," in *Classical Quarterly*, n.s., 10 (1960): 84–102.

Other studies are H. Diels, *Parmenides Lehrgedicht* (Berlin: G. Reimer, 1897); John Burnet, *Early Greek Philosophy* (London, 1892); K. Reinhardt, *Parmenides und die Geschichte der griechischen Philosophie* (Bonn, 1916); W. Kranz, "Über Aufbau und Bedeutung des Parmenideischen Gedichtes," in *Sitzungsberichte der Deutschen Akademie der Wissenschaften zu Berlin* 47 (1916): 1158–1176; Eduard Zeller, *Die Philosophie der Griechen*, 6th ed., Vol. I (Leipzig, 1919), Ch. 1; F. M. Cornford, "Parmenides' Two Ways," in *Classical Quarterly* 27 (1933): 97–111, and *Plato and Parmenides* (London: K. Paul, Trench, Trubner, 1939); G. Calogero, *Studi sul eleatismo* (Rome, 1932); and Harold Cherniss, *Aristotle's Criticism of Presocratic Philosophy* (Baltimore: Johns Hopkins Press, 1935).

Some more recent studies are W. J. Verdenius, *Parmenides: Some Comments* (Groningen, Netherlands, 1942); Olof Gigon, *Der Ursprung der griechischen Philosophie von Hesiod bis Parmenides* (Basel, 1945); Gregory Vlastos, "Parmenides' Theory of Knowledge," in *Transactions of the American Philological Association* 77 (1946): 66–77; Hans Schwabl, "Sein und Doxa bei Parmenides," in *Wiener Studien* 66 (1953): 50–75; C. M. Bowra, *Problems in Greek Poetry* (Oxford, 1953); Eric A. Havelock, "Parmenides and Odysseus," and Leonard Woodbury, "Parmenides on Names," in *Harvard Studies in Classical Philology* 63 (1958); W. R. Chalmers, "Parmenides and the Beliefs of Mortals," in *Phronesis* 5 (1960): 5–22; A. A. Long, "The Principles of Parmenides' Cosmogony," in *Phronesis* 8 (1963): 90–107; J. Mansfeld, *Die Offenbarung des Parmenides und die menschliche Welt* (Assen: Van Gorcum, 1964); and W. K. C. Guthrie, *A History of Greek Philosophy*, Vol. II (Cambridge, U.K.: Cambridge University Press, 1965).

David J. Furley (1967)

PARMENIDES OF ELEA [ADDENDUM]

David Furley's original entry remains an exemplary introduction to Parmenides' thought. Since its publication, philosophers have focused on the character of the routes of inquiry that the goddess lays out in the poem, suggesting different interpretations of the subjectless *is* (or *esti*), and of the nature of *to eon*, the subject of inquiry. In addition, scholars have continued to study the *Proem* (the opening lines of the poem) and the *Doxa* (the goddesses' statement of mortal opinion), but there is no consensus about either.

Newer studies emphasize the undoubted influences of Homer and Hesiod (fl. c. 800 BCE) as models for Parmenides' language and poetic images, while others recognize the continuity of Parmenides' thought with that of his predecessors. For example, Xenophanes of Colophon questions whether human knowledge is possible: In the absence of divine warrant or intercession, how can human beings of limited experience achieve genuine understanding? Parmenides' analysis of the unchanging nature of the object of genuine thought and inquiry, and his use of a goddess who nevertheless uses arguments and demands that her hearer evaluate her claims (DK 28 B7.5) can be seen as an attempt to defend the possibility of human knowledge and explore its limits. Some scholars suggest that this account of Parmenides is too rationalistic, but the consensus remains that he is part of a philosophical tradition that continues in Plato, Aristotle, and later Greek thought.

Reading Parmenides as exploring the nature of inquiry and the proper object of understanding and knowledge, many scholars are more willing to countenance forms of "to be" in Parmenides that are not primarily existential. Attention has been paid to predicative, veridical, and fused predicative-existential notions of being, and it is likely that some sort of hybrid account best captures Parmenides' meaning. What-is (*to eon*) must exist, but existence is not Parmenides' primary concern. Rather, the object of genuine thought must be or have an essence (predicative), and must be what is the case (veridical). What is not (or lacks an essence) cannot be real. As such it cannot be an object of understanding. Contrary to mortal thinkers, Parmenides denies that coming-to-be and other sorts of change are real or can be attributed to what is real. The arguments of fragment 8 show that only what is wholly of a single kind, unchangingly and perfectly what it is, can be real. Such an entity (*eon*) is a unity, admitting none of what is not, and so can be grasped completely by thought.

There is no doubt that Parmenides claims that what-is is one. The question is the sort of unity or monism to which Parmenides is committed. Some scholars challenge the interpretation (going back to Plato) that Parmenides advocated numerical monism in the same sense as Melissus of Samos, who asserted the reality of only one thing.

On the alternative account, although whatever there is must be one, more than one thing may be real. Stronger and weaker versions of this view have been taken. It can be argued that numerical pluralism is consistent with Parmenides' views of the unified nature of what-is, although Parmenides himself does not specify how many basic entities there are.

The role of the *Doxa* section of the poem remains a problem, especially if one follows many scholars in rejecting the view that mortals err by positing what does not exist or by supposing that there is a plurality of real things. There is no general agreement, and some modern interpretations accept the more traditional view, found in Furley's entry, that no cosmological account can be acceptable. Another suggestion is that, although the sensible world of change and becoming described in the *Doxa* is not the world of genuine reality, the cosmology of the *Doxa* nonetheless succeeds because it gives a true account and explanation of the unreal world of appearances. Or the *Doxa* might be intended as a lesson, offering a model cosmological account with a problem at its heart (the commitment to genuinely real opposite forms) that shows what must be avoided in an adequate account of how things are.

A further focus of study has been the positive importance of Parmenides' arguments for later philosophers (the later pre-Socratics and Sophists as well as Plato). This has led to a new appreciation of the Parmenidean basis for pluralistic and atomistic pre-Socratic theories and for the foundations of Plato's thought. In addition, scholars explore differences of theory and argument strategy among Parmenides, Zeno of Elea and Melissus, controverting the traditional interpretation that lumps them together as maintaining a single "Eleatic position."

See also Aristotle; Homer; Melissus of Samos; Plato; Pre-Socratic Philosophy; Sophists; Xenophanes of Colophon; Zeno of Elea.

Bibliography

Barnes, Jonathan. "Parmenides and the Eleatic One." *Archiv für Geschichte der Philosophie* 61 (1979): 1–21.

Caston, Victor, and Daniel W. Graham, eds. *Presocratic Philosophy: Essays in Honor of A. P. D. Mourelatos*. Burlington, VT: Ashgate, 2002

Coxon, A. H. *The Fragments of Parmenides*. Dover, NH: Van Gorcum, 1986.

Curd, Patricia. *The Legacy of Parmenides*. Rev. ed. Las Vegas, NV: Parmenides Publishing, 2004.

Gallop, David. *Parmenides of Elea: Fragments*. Toronto: University of Toronto Press, 1984.

Kahn, Charles H. "The Thesis of Parmenides." *Review of Metaphysics* 22 (1969/70): 700–724.

Lesher, J. H. "Parmenides' Critique of Thinking: The poludêris elenchos of Fragment 7." *Oxford Studies in Ancient Philosophy* 2 (1984): 1–30.

Long, A. A. "Parmenides on Thinking Being." In *Proceedings of the Boston Area Colloquium in Ancient Philosophy* 12, edited by J. J. Cleary and W.C. Wians. Lanham: University Press of America, 1996.

McKirahan, Richard. *Philosophy Before Socrates*. Indianapolis: Hackett, 1994.

Mourelatos, A. P. D., ed. *The Pre-Socratics: A Collection of Critical Essays*. Princeton, NJ: Princeton University Press, 1993.

Mourelatos, A. P. D. *The Route of Parmenides*. New Haven, CT: Yale University Press, 1971.

Schofield, M. "Did Parmenides Discover Eternity?" *Archiv für Geschichte der Philosophie* 52 (1970): 113–135

Solmsen, F. "The 'Eleatic One' in Melissus." *Mededelingen der Koninklijke*. Nederlandse Akademie van Wetenschappen, Afd. Letterkunds, Nieuwe Reeks 32/8 (1969): 221–233; reprinted in Solmsen, Kleine Schriften III, 137–149.

Patricia Curd (2005)

PASCAL, BLAISE
(1623–1662)

Blaise Pascal was a French mathematician, physicist, inventor, philosopher, and theologian. He was born in Clermont in Auvergne, the son of a minor noble who was a government official. Pascal's mother died in 1626. In 1631 the family moved to Paris but fled in 1638 because of the father's opposition to the fiscal regulations of Richelieu. The next year Pascal's younger sister, Jacqueline, successfully acted in a children's play performed for Richelieu and thus gained a pardon for her father, who then became the royal tax commissioner at Rouen.

MATHEMATICS AND PHYSICS

Pascal was a prodigy, privately educated by his father, who was an excellent mathematician. His father wanted his son to have a good humanistic background before he learned mathematics and science, but at the age of twelve, Pascal discovered by himself the principles of geometry. When his father realized this, he abandoned his original plan for his son's education and encouraged his mathematical development. While still a teenager, Pascal published important mathematical and scientific papers and was a young prodigy in the Parisian intellectual circles. His father and he became members of a scientific discussion group organized by Father Marin Mersenne. There he would have met a wide range of people, probably including Thomas Hobbes, Descartes, and others. At sixteen, Pascal wrote his first major work, *Essai pour les coniques* (published in 1640), which his sister reported was "considered so great an intellectual achievement that people said that they had seen nothing as mighty since the time of Archimedes." In 1642 Pascal invented the calculating machine, originally designed to help his father in his tax work. This machine was one of the first applied achievements of the "new science." Pascal's writings on the calculating machine from 1645 to 1652 indicate the inordinate difficulties of putting theory into practice, the wide divergence between the levels of metallurgical and mathematical skill, and the monumental importance of this early contribution to the industrial revolution.

For the rest of his life Pascal continued to make major mathematical contributions in probability theory, number theory, and geometry. Although he gave up serious concern with mathematical problems after his religious conversion in 1654, a notable analysis of the nature of the cycloid grew out of a night's insomnia in 1658. Pascal's important work in the philosophy of mathematics, *L'esprit géométrique*, was probably written in 1657 and 1658 as a preface to a textbook in geometry for the Jansenist school at Port-Royal.

THE VACUUM

In 1646 Pascal learned of Evangelista Torricelli's (1608–1647) experiment with a barometer, which involved placing a tube of mercury upside down in a bowl of mercury. Having successfully repeated the experiment, Pascal asked himself what kept some of the mercury suspended in the tube and what was in the space above the column of mercury in the tube. Many scientists believed that the pressure of the outside atmosphere was responsible for holding up the column of mercury, but they had no proof. All agreed that the space at the top of the tube contained some kind of rarefied and invisible matter; hence, no vacuum. In 1647 Pascal published *Experiences nouvelles touchant le vide*, a summary of a series of experiments with variously shaped and sized tubes and different liquids, in which he set forth the basic laws about how much water and how much mercury could be supported by air pressure and about how large a siphon had to be to function. He also sketched out the reasons why a genuine vacuum could and did exist above the column of mercury or other liquid supported in the barometer.

Father Estienne Noel, rector of the Collège de Clermont in Paris, challenged Pascal, insisting that nature abhors a vacuum and therefore would not allow one to exist; thus, the alleged empty space created in Pascal's experiments actually contained a special kind of matter. Pascal's reply, in which he gave the conditions for judging a hypothesis, is one of the clearest statements on scientific method made during the seventeenth century. Pascal asserted that a hypothesis could be disproved if one could elicit either a contradiction or a conclusion counter to fact from the affirmation of the hypothesis. However, if all the facts fit the hypothesis or follow from it, this merely shows the hypothesis is probable or possible. "In order to show that a hypothesis is evident, it does not suffice that all the phenomena follow from it; instead, if it leads to something contrary to a single one of the phenomena, that suffices to establish its falsity." Pascal showed that Noel's and Aristotle's hypothesis that there is no vacuum is false because conclusions contrary to experimentally established facts follow from it, whereas his own theory of a genuine vacuum is a possible or probable explanation of the facts in question.

In 1648 Pascal's brother-in-law performed the experiment of carrying a barometer up a mountain. This established the change in the level of the column of mercury. Pascal checked the results at various heights on a church tower in Paris. He then declared that these results established

> that Nature has no abhorrence of a vacuum, that she makes no effort to avoid it; that all the effects that are ascribed to this horror are due to the weight and pressure of air; … and that, due to not knowing this, people have deliberately invented that imaginary horror of a vacuum, in order to account for them.

Combining his ingeniously derived experimental data with a clear analysis of the possible explanatory hypotheses, Pascal arrived at one of the major achievements of seventeenth-century science. His theory of the vacuum and air pressure played an important role in the development of the mechanical theory of nature and the elimination of some of nature's alleged occult qualities and personal characteristics. The preface to the *Traité du vide* (which is all that has survived of the *Traité*) contains a defense of the new science and a discussion of the nature of scientific progress. In the study of nature, Pascal insisted that respect for authority should not take precedence over reasoning or experience (in theology, however, he maintained that it should). The secrets of nature, he said, are hidden from us, and although it is always active, we do not always discover its effects. In the course of time, through experience and understanding, we come to learn more about the natural world. Hence, as more data are accumulated, we should expect to find previously accepted hypotheses replaced by newer ones. Our conclusions about nature are always limited by the amount of experience gathered up to now. In time we seek for truths in terms of our experience and comprehension. What is sought for may be unchanging, but the results of the quest are the variable developments that constitute the history of science. Thus, there is no reason for preferring the ancient scientific views of Aristotle or anyone else to the latest achievements of scientific reasoning, based on the most recent data.

PASCAL AND JANSENISM

Pascal's mathematical and scientific accomplishments are among the most important of his time, but his religious and philosophical views have overshadowed them. His writings in religion and philosophy grew out of his involvement with the Jansenist movement. In 1646, after his father was injured, two Jansenists came to take care of him. The whole family, including Blaise, became interested in and involved with this Catholic reform movement, with his sister Jacqueline, becoming a nun at Port-Royal de Paris. From 1652 to 1654, Pascal turned away from religious interests, spending his time mainly with libertine friends who were gamblers, womanizers, and probably freethinkers. Pascal often visited his sister at Port-Royal, indicating to her that he had a great contempt for the world and people but that he did not feel drawn to God. However, after a traumatic experience crossing the Pont Neuf in Paris during a storm, Pascal had a religious conversion. He recorded this religious experience in *Le Mémorial* as "certitude, certitude, feeling, joy, peace." A year later, in 1655, with the encouragement of his sister, he made his first retreat at Port-Royal-des-Champs. Thereafter, Pascal objected vehemently to the philosophy of Descartes, unfavorably contrasting the God of the philosophers—namely, Descartes's God—with the God of Abraham, Isaac, and Jacob.

In January 1655 Pascal went to Port-Royal-des-Champs, the order of the two Port-Royal convents, for a two-week retreat. There a famous discussion with the Jansenist theologian, Isaac Le Maistre de Saci, took place, published in the *Entretien avec M. de Saci*. This text indicates that Pascal had already formulated many of the views later developed in the *Pensées*. During the next several months, Pascal often visited the two Port-Royal convents. On one of these visits Pascal met Antoine Arnauld, the leading Jansenist philosopher and theologian, who was about to be condemned by the Sorbonne for his views. In *Lettres provinciales*, a series of eighteen letters published in 1656 and 1657, Pascal defended Arnauld and satirized his Jesuit opponents and their theological and moral view. These letters, published under the pseudonym Louis de Montalte, were probably the cooperative work of Pascal, Arnauld, and Pierre Nicole, though they were principally by Pascal. One of the great French literary masterpieces, the *Lettres provinciales* mercilessly ridicules the casuistry of various Jesuit moralists for what Pascal considered their lax, inconsistent, and unchristian views and defends Jansenism against charges of heresy. The arguments of various sixteenth-century and seventeenth-century scholastics are torn apart, and the charges against the Jansenists rebutted in a dazzling display of wit, irony, abuse, argument, and literary brilliance. Nevertheless, the *Lettres provinciales* was placed on the Index in 1657, and shortly thereafter the Jansenist movement was condemned by the pope. In 1661 the schools at Port-Royal were closed, and the nuns and solitaires had to sign a submission to the church.

Until 1659 Pascal worked on a wide variety of subjects defending Jansenism, composing his *Écrits sur la grâce*, *De l'esprit géométrique*, *De l'art de persuader*, and the works on the cycloid and preparing his *Apologie de la religion chrétienne*, the unfinished work posthumously published as the *Pensées*. In 1659, seriously ill, Pascal practically stopped writing. In 1660 he was somewhat better and wrote his *Trois discours sur la condition des grands*. The next year, after the suppression of Jansenism and the death of Jacqueline, Pascal wrote his final work on Jansenism, *Écrit sur la signature du formulaire*, urging the Port-Royalists not to give in. He then withdrew from all further controversy. His last achievement, illustrating another side of his genius, was the invention of a large carriage with many seats and the inauguration of what was in effect the first bus line, carrying passengers from one part of Paris to another for a fixed fare. One of his motives was to gain money to give to the poor, because he had already disposed of almost all his worldly possessions. Much of his will is devoted to bequeathing portions of his bus revenues to various hospitals.

PHILOSOPHY OF MATHEMATICS AND SCIENCE

Pascal left unpublished his two most important philosophical works, the *Pensées* and *De l'esprit géométrique*. *De l'esprit géométrique* was first published in the eighteenth century. In it Pascal dealt with the problem of the method for discovering truths. The ideal method, he declared, would be one which defined all of the terms employed and demonstrated all propositions from already established truths, but this is impossible, because the basic terms to be defined presuppose others to explain their meaning, and the fundamental propositions to be proved presuppose still others. Thus, it is impossible to reach first terms and principles. Instead, we find primitive terms that admit of no further definitions that clarify them and principles that are so clear that nothing clearer can be found to aid in proving them. "From which it seems that men are naturally and unalterably powerless to deal with any science whatsoever in an absolutely perfected manner."

Given this state of affairs, geometrical procedure is the most perfect known to humankind—a balanced one in which those things that are clear and known to everyone are not defined and everything else is defined, and in which those propositions known by all are assumed and other propositions are derived from them. Pascal insisted that this did not mean either that human beings could know by natural means that the premises of geometry were really true or that the fundamental concepts were thoroughly understood. Rather, the geometrical method provided the greatest certitude attainable by use of our limited capacities. Essentially, it developed an axiomatic system in which, from primitive terms and axioms, a set of propositions could be logically derived. Such a set would be true if the axioms were true.

In the companion piece to *L'esprit géométrique*, *De l'art de persuader*, Pascal explained how we come to be convinced of first principles and of conclusions from them. Conclusions are explained via the geometrical method. The problem of first principles raises a basic point for Pascal's theory of knowledge that is developed in the *Pensées*. Our reason and understanding can only work out axiom systems. Because we cannot prove the first principles, we can always cast skeptical doubts upon their truths, no matter how certain they may appear to us at various times. We can overcome this constant tendency toward skepticism (which also occurs in scientific research, because we can never know the secrets of nature but only plausible and as yet unrefuted hypotheses about the world) only by recognizing that principles are gained through instinct and revelation. This recognition requires admitting the importance of feelings and of submission to God in the quest for truth.

RELIGION

Pascal left the *Pensées* unfinished, with many notes of varying sizes pinned together. The first editors copied all the materials exactly as Pascal left them but published only those portions that they felt were completed, organizing them as they saw fit. Later editors assumed that the

Pensées was a collection of fragments, left in a disordered state by their author, and that each editor could arrange the fragments as he wished. Victor Cousin in 1842 pointed out that only selections of the *Pensées*, often somewhat embellished by the various editors, existed in print, and he urged a definitive edition based on the manuscripts in the Bibliothèque Nationale. One of these, the *Recueil original*, consists of the fragments in Pascal's own handwriting, pasted on large sheets of paper. For the next century editors used this manuscript for varying presentations of the text. In the 1930s and 1940s Zacharie Tourneur and Louis Lafuma established that the *Recueil* was pasted together after Pascal's death and that another manuscript, a copy by one of Pascal's relatives, represented the actual state of the work as organized and partially completed by the author. This led to Lafuma's definitive edition in 1952, which radically changed the order of the fragments, finally presenting the development of the themes in the *Pensées* as Pascal had intended them to be read.

THE HUMAN CONDITION. In the Lafuma edition the initial sections, "Order," "Vanity," "Misery," "Boredom," and "Causes of Effects," all portray the human condition by showing humankind's ways of dealing with and reacting to the ordinary world. The sixth and seventh sections turn to the core of humankind's philosophical problem—how to find truth and happiness. If humans are miserable, vain creatures, unable by their own resources to find first truths from which to derive others, they have to realize that "we know truth not only by reason but more so by the heart. It is in this latter way that we know first principles, and it is in vain that reason, which plays no part in this, tries to combat them" (Lafuma 1952, p. 110; Brunschvicg, p. 292). The principles of geometry are known instinctively by the heart, and reason employs these principles to establish theorems. Both heart and reason yield results that are certain, but by different routes, and it would be ridiculous to require proofs of the heart's instincts and intuitions or intuitive knowledge of what is proved. The inability of reason to establish first principles serves to humiliate reason but not to undermine our certainty. The realization of the limitations of reason helps us, Pascal declared, to recognize our wretchedness, and the greatness of humankind is that people alone are capable of such a recognition.

The climax of this attempt to show the ultimate nonrational foundation of our knowledge of first principles comes in the next section, "Contradictions." In a famous passage on skepticism (131 and 434) Pascal began by pointing out that the strongest contention of the Pyrrhonists was that we have no assurance of the truth of any first principles apart from faith and revelation except that we feel them within us. This natural feeling is no convincing proof of their truth, because apart from faith we cannot tell whether humans were created by a good God, an evil demon, or by chance. The truth-value of the principles depends upon their source. Pascal then explored the depths of complete skepticism and showed that if one had no assurance or any principles, one could be certain of nothing; but at the same time one could not even become a complete skeptic.

What then will man do in this state? Will he doubt everything? Will he doubt whether he is awake? Whether he is being pinched, whether he is being burned, will he doubt that he doubts, will he doubt that he exists?

We cannot go so far as that; and I set it forth as a fact that there has never been a complete perfect Pyrrhonist. Nature sustains our feeble reason and prevents it from raving to that extent. …

What kind of a chimera then is man? What novelty, what monster, what chaos, what subject of contradictions, what prodigy? Judge of all things, imbecile worm of the earth, depository of truth, sink of uncertainty and error, glory and scum of the world.

Who will unravel this tangle? Certainly it surpasses dogmatism and Pyrrhonism; and all human philosophy. …

Nature confounds the Pyrrhonists and reason confounds the dogmatists. …

Know then, proud man, what a paradox you are to yourself. Humble yourself, weak reason. Silence yourself, foolish nature, learn that man infinitely surpasses man, and hear from your master your real state which you do not know.

Hear God.

The problem of knowledge thus becomes, for Pascal, a religious one. Only through submission to God and through acceptance of his revelation can we gain completely certain knowledge. The greatest achievements in science and mathematics rest on a fundamental uncertainty, because the basic principles employed, known through instinct and intuition, are open to question. Skeptical probing can only reveal the human predicament in its fullest and prepare us to submit and accept a religious foundation of knowledge.

The *Pensées* then proceeds to show how humans try to avoid recognizing their situation through diversion and philosophy. Philosophy can only lead us continually to skepticism, from which we are saved by our own intuitive knowledge of truth. We seek for happiness but cannot find it apart from religion. Pascal then tried to show in the famous wager argument (418 and 233) that it is not unreasonable to believe in God. God, he argued, is infinitely incomprehensible to us. But either God exists or he does not exist, and we are unable to tell which alternative is true. However, both our present lives and our possible future lives may well be greatly affected by the alternative we accept. Hence, Pascal contended, because eternal life and happiness is a possible result of one choice (if God does exist) and because nothing is lost if we are wrong about the other choice (if God does not exist and we choose to believe that he does), then the reasonable gamble, given what may be at stake, is to choose the theistic alternative. The person who remains an unbeliever is taking an infinitely unreasonable risk just because he or she does not know which alternative is true. Pascal's dialectic in his religious apologetics prods people to realize that there is not enough evidence to confirm the religious hypothesis and not enough to reject it. So, a person in his or her fallen state chooses on moral characters rather than philosophical ones.

Pascal is not just presenting the problem of human knowledge in philosophical terms. As he once explained to his fellow members at Port-Royal, what he was working on as the culminating statement of his views was "an apology for the Christian religion." The *Pensées* are either this apology or reflect a good deal of its content or design. The skeptical problems and the skeptical attitude are part of the apologetic project. But Pascal does not see skepticism as leading to religious knowledge or religious truth, but more as neutralizing man's rational impulses. Pascal was not following the route of Michel Eyquem De Montaigne, Pierre Charron, and Francois de La Mothe Le Vayer. He was using their skeptical weapons to combat the dogmatists and to make the skeptics aware of the religious dimension. Pascal did not see skepticism as leading to the relaxed, tranquil view of the ancient Pyrrhonists, but rather to a sharpened and heightened desperation. The desire to know could not be satisfied by human rational faculties but there was a necessity to know.

What Pascal contributes to the skeptical discussion is what José Maia Neto (1995) has called the "Christianization of Pyrrhonism." The Christianization of Pyrrhonism is seen in Pascal's description of people's state without God. This state, theologically, is what has happened to humankind in the Fall. Humans in this condition can find no security through reasoning or the use of their faculties, *and* they can unfortunately realize the desperation of their situation. They still have a glimmer or afterglow of the prelapsarian state of affairs but are unable to reach it. Pascal tried to show how belief can be achieved by curbing the passions, submitting to God, and using reason as a means of realizing that true religion is beyond reason and is known only through Jesus. We are suspended between two infinities, the infinitely small (the void) and the infinitely great (the Divine). Reason exposes our plight to us. Our desire for truth and happiness makes us see the futility of science, mathematics, and human philosophy as ways of finding the answers humans seeks.

THE CHRISTIAN RELIGION. The later sections of the *Pensées* are devoted to apologetics, arguing that the Christian religion is the true religion. From historical data, moral precepts, miracles, and the fulfillment of prophecies, Pascal argued that the Bible is the source of true religious knowledge. He contended that the Old Testament foretold Christ's coming and the Jewish rejection of him. Using the recently rediscovered Spanish antiSemitic classic by Raymundus Martinus, *Pugio Fidei*, Pascal took material from many Jewish sources to claim that "God used the blindness of the Jewish people for the benefit of the elect" (469 and 577) and that "if the Jews had been completely converted by Jesus Christ, we would not have had any but suspect witnesses. And if they had been exterminated, we would not have had any at all" (592 and 750). The apologetic argument, Pascal admitted, was not logically decisive but only persuasive. The real problem was to *be* a Christian, and here reason could not help. Humans could submit, but they still desperately required God's Grace.

> The prophecies, the miracles themselves, and the proofs of our religion are not of such a nature that it could be said they are absolutely convincing, but they are also of such a kind that it cannot be said that it would be unreasonable to believe them. Thus there is evidence and obscurity to enlighten some and confuse others, but the evidence is such that it surpasses or at least equals the evidence to the contrary, so that it is not reason that can determine men not to follow it, and thus this can only be as a result of lust or malice of heart…[so] that it appears that in those who follow it [religion], it is grace and not reason which makes them follow it, and that in

those who shun it, it is lust and not reason that makes them shun it. (835 and 564)

Pascal's views hardly constitute an organized system. Most of his works are fragmentary, and he apparently made no effort to put the fragments together. His career first as a mathematical prodigy, then as a student of physics and finally as a religious thinker made continuous intellectual development difficult. From the vantage point of his fideistic religious views his mathematical and scientific efforts appeared to him as of small significance. Throughout the *Pensées* Pascal tried to characterize the role and limits of mathematical and scientific achievements, in keeping with what he himself had accomplished. But his religious views were essentially antiphilosophical. Among philosophical views he found skepticism the most congenial insofar as it revealed most clearly "the misery of man without God" and prepared men for faith and grace.

Pascal's religious concerns have overshadowed his other contributions and as a result his impact has been mainly on thinkers concerned with religious subjects. In recent years Pascal has been studied seriously by existentialists because of his brilliant portrayal of the human condition, and he has often been compared with Kierkegaard, especially in terms of his antiphilosophical and fideistic statement of Christianity. Pascal's works on scientific method and the philosophy of mathematics have tended to be neglected, but in these areas he was one of the clearest and most advanced thinkers of his age. His many-sided genius and his unequaled command of the French language make him one of the most inspiring and thought-provoking of writers. Pascal fills a major place in the history of ideas both for his work in mathematics, physics, and philosophy of science and for his insights into human nature and his analysis of Christianity.

See also Epistemology; Jansenism; Philosophy of Religion; Philosophy of Science, History of.

Bibliography

WORKS BY PASCAL

Le manuscrit des pensées de Pascal (1662), edited by Louis Lafuma. Paris: Libraries Associés, 1962. A photoreproduction of the manuscript text with a preface by Jean Guitton.

Oeuvres completes, edited by Jean Mesnard. Paris: Desclée de Brouwer, 1992.

Oeuvres completes, edited by Louis Lafuma. Paris: Editions du Seuil, 1963. Preface by Henri Gouhier.

Oeuvres de Blaise Pascal: publiées suivant l'ordre chronologique, avec documents complémentaires, introductions et notes, edited by Léon Brunschvicg, P. Boutroux, and F. Gazier. 14 vols. Paris: Hachette et cie, 1904–1914.

Pensées sur la religion et sur quelques autres sujets. 3rd ed. Paris: Delmas, 1960.

English Translations

Great Shorter Works of Pascal. Translated and with an introduction by Émile Cailliet and John C. Blankenagel. Philadelphia: Westminster Press, 1948.

Pensées: The Provincial Letters. Translated by W. F. Trotter and Thomas McCrie. New York: Modern Library, 1941.

Pensées. Translated by W. F. Trotter. New York: E. P. Dutton, 1958. Introduction by T. S. Eliot.

Pensées. Translated with an introduction by Martin Turnell. London: Harvill, 1962.

The Physical Treatises of Pascal: The Equilibrium of Liquids and the Weight of the Mass of Air. Translated by I. H. B. Spiers and A. G. H. Spiers. Introduction and notes by Frederick Barry. New York: Columbia University Press, 1937.

WORKS ABOUT PASCAL

Abercrombie, Nigel. *Saint Augustine and French Classical Thought.* Oxford: Clarendon Press, 1938.

Bishop, Morris. *Pascal: The Life of Genius.* New York: Reynal and Hitchcock, 1936.

Bishop, Morris, and Sister Marie Louis Hubert. "Pascal Bibliography." In *A Critical Bibliography of French Literature.* Vol. 3, edited by Nathan Edelman. Syracuse, NY: Syracuse University Press, 1961.

Bremond, Henri. *Histoire littéraire du sentiment religieux en France.* 12 vols. Paris: Bloud et Gay, 1916–1933. See vol. 4 (1921) for Pascal.

Brunschvicg, Léon. *Descartes et Pascal, lecteurs de Montaigne.* New York: Brentano's, 1944.

Brunschvicg, Léon. *Le génie de Pascal.* Paris: Hachette, 1924.

Busson, Henri. *La pensée religieuse française de Charron à Pascal.* Paris: J. Vrin, 1933.

Busson, Henri. *La religion des classiques (1660–1685).* Paris: Presses Universitaires de France, 1948.

Cahiers de Royaumont. *Blaise Pascal, l'homme et l'oeuvre.* Paris: Editions de Minuit, 1956.

Cailliet, Émile. *Pascal: The Emergence of Genius.* 2nd ed. New York: Harper, 1961.

Chestov, Léon [Leo Isakovich Shestov]. *La nuit de Gethsémani; Essai sur la philosophie de Pascal.* Paris: Grasset, 1923.

Goldmann, Lucien. *Le Dieu caché.* Paris: Gallimard, 1955. Translated by Philip Thody as *The Hidden God: A Study of Tragic Vision in the Pensées of Pascal and the Tragedies of Racine.* New York: Humanities Press, 1964.

Humbert, Pierre. *Cet effrayant génie … : L'oeuvre scientifique de Blaise Pascal.* Paris: A. Michel, 1947.

Jovy, Ernest. *Études pascaliennes.* 9 vols. Paris: J. Vrin, 1927–1936.

Julien-Eymard d'Angers [Charles Cheshenau]. *Pascal et ses précurseurs.* Paris: Nouvelles Éditions latines, 1954.

Lafuma, Louis. *Histoire des Pensées de Pascal (1656–1952).* Paris: Éditions du Luxembourg, 1954.

Laporte, Jean. *Le Coeur et la raison selon Pascal.* Paris: Elzévir, 1950.

Maia Neto, Jose. *The Christianization of Pyrrhonism: Scepticism and Faith in Pascal, Kierkegaard, and Shestov.* Dordrecht, Netherlands: Kluwer, 1995.

Mesnard, Jean. *Pascal, l'homme et l'oeuvre.* Paris: Boivin, 1951. Translated by G. S. Fraser as *Pascal: His Life and Works.* London: Harvill, 1952.

Strowski, Fortunat. *Pascal et son temps.* 3 vols. Paris: Plon-Mourrit et cie, 1907.

WORKS ON JANSENISM

Abercrombie, Nigel. *The Origins of Jansenism.* Oxford: Clarendon Press, 1936.

Orcibal, Jean. *Les origines du Jansénisme.* 5 vols. Louvain: Bureaux de la Revue, 1947–1962.

Sainte-Beuve, Charles A. *Port-Royal.* 7 vols. Paris: Eugéne Renduel, 1840–1859. 3-vol. ed., Paris: Gallimard, 1953–1955.

Richard Popkin (1967, 2005)

PASTORE, VALENTINO ANNIBALE
(1868–1956)

Valentino Annibale Pastore, an Italian philosopher and logician, was born at Orbassano (Teramo), Italy. He educated himself in literary studies, and then obtained a degree in letters from the University of Turin, under Arturo Graf, with a thesis on *La vita delle forme letterarie* (The life of literary forms), which was published at Turin in 1892. Pastore then turned to philosophy and was influenced by Hegelianism through the teachings of Pasquale d'Ercole. At the same time he was influenced by such scientists as Friedrich Kiesow, A. Garbasso, and Giuseppe Peano. In 1903 he published in Turin his thesis in philosophy, *Sopra le teorie della scienza: logica, matematica, fisica* (On the theories of science: logic, mathematics, physics). In 1911 he began teaching theoretical philosophy at Turin, where he was full professor from 1921 until 1939 and where he instituted a laboratory of experimental logic.

Pastore's thesis was published in the same year in which Benedetto Croce's *La critica* appeared and in which irrationalism burst out in Italy in diverse forms—as a revolt against positivism, as a rebirth of idealism, as an expression of the "bankruptcy of science." Having been educated in an environment in which Hegelianism was not ignored but was linked with the point of view of classical positivism, Pastore became aware of the impossibility of separating the sciences (mathematical and natural) from philosophy, or of substituting the sciences for philosophy. In the first case, if philosophy were severed from the conditions that render it possible and nourish it, it would become empty and would wither; in the second case, the sciences themselves would eventually lose consciousness of their relationships, their fundamental rationale, and their methods and goals. Pastore therefore sought to assess the meaning of scientific knowledge and of its logical procedures.

Turning his attention to logical problems in particular, Pastore was at first drawn toward Bertrand Russell's thesis of the identity of logic and mathematics, as is shown in *Logica formale e dedotta dalla considerazione dei modelli meccanici* (Formal logic deduced by the consideration of mechanical models; Turin, 1906) and *Sillogismo e proporzione* (Syllogism and proportion; Turin, 1910). His principal work of this period, *Il problema della causalità, con particolare riguardo alla teoria del metodo sperimentale* (The problem of causality, with particular attention to the theory of experimental method; 2 vols., Turin, 1921), which deals with causality, shows his systematic effort to single out the mutual relationship between scientific investigation and philosophical research. Pastore examined three aspects of causality—experience, science, and philosophy—and distinguished and analyzed the idea of cause, the concept of the causal relation, and the principle of causality.

After 1922, Pastore's interests were still focused on scientific knowledge, but he clarified his conception of philosophy as the study of "pure thought," as "not of that which is common to all particular systems, by being inherent in each one, but of that which results from all the particular systems, even though not being inherent in each one." From this conception he evolved his idea of a "general logic" whose basis lies "outside of particular logical systems." Around 1936, assisted by Ludovico Geymonat, he investigated the "logic of strengthening" as a "theory of primal systems," that is, as a search for "the process of construction of the most elementary forms of thinking and of their relationships," by means of a distinction between logic as logicality (general presystematic logic) and logic as a particular system, joining, as he himself said, "the deduction of the discourse (D) with the logical intuition of the universe (U)." Pastore did not seek to reach a demonstration of intuitive principles, nor to propose an ontological intuition, but rather to establish the laws of the relationship between D and U, between the analysis of the discourse and a synthetic vision of the universe.

In the final phase of his work Pastore's concern with the sense of mystery became marked ("logic has always two allies at its side: sadness and mystery"). In the light of this concern he examined and discussed both the existentialist movements and the historical materialism of Karl Marx and V. I. Lenin.

See also Croce, Benedetto; Experience; Hegelianism; Irrationalism; Lenin, Vladimir Il'ich; Logic Machines; Marx, Karl; Peano, Giuseppe; Positivism; Russell, Bertrand Arthur William.

Bibliography

Additional works by Pastore are *Il solipsismo* (Turin, 1923); *La logica del potenziamento* (Naples, 1936); *Logica sperimentale* (Naples, 1939); *L'acrisia di Kant* (Padua: CEDAM, 1940); "Il mio pensiero filosofico," in *Filosofi italiani contemporanei,* edited by M. F. Sciacca (Como, 1944), pp. 333–349; *La filosofia di Lenin* (Milan: G. Bolla, 1946); and *La volontà dell'assurdo. Storia e crisi dell'esistenzialismo* (Milan: G. Bolla, 1948).

Works on Pastore are Carmelo Ottaviano, "La 'logica del potenziamento' della scuola di Torino," in *Logos* 17 (1934): 277–289; Francesco Crestano, "Intorno alla logica del potenziamento e alla logica dei comportamenti," in *Archivio di filosofia,* 5 (1935): 322–331 (and in *Idee e concetti,* Milan, 1939); and Filippo Selvaggi, *Dalla filosofia alla tecnica: La logica del potenziamento* (Rome: Apud aedes Universitatis Gregorianae, 1947), with bibliography.

Eugenio Garin (1967)
Translated by Robert M. Connolly

PATER, WALTER HORATIO
(1839–1894)

Walter Horatio Pater, an English essayist and critic, lived mainly in Oxford, where he read classics at Queens College and later became a fellow of Brasenose. He was a central figure of and inspiration for English fin de siècle art and art criticism and a profound influence on Oscar Wilde. He is of importance in philosophical aesthetics for his association with and championing of the *l'art pour l'art* doctrine of his age and for his insistence on "aesthetic criticism" of literature and the fine arts, stressing the subjective sensitivity of the critic and his power to paint evocative pictures of moments of intense experience in finely wrought, decorative prose. He is important in general philosophical history for his aphoristic but consistent statements that a relativist position was the only appropriate position for the modern temperament.

In the course of his career he proposed a highly personal conception of Platonism (*Plato and Platonism,* New York and London, 1893), playing down the immutable aspect of the theory of forms and emphasizing the imaginative sweep of Plato's more informal thinking. Pater maintained that moral values and moral standards were relative to the achievements and conditions of an age. Although he was formerly a Christian, he did not believe that Christian revelation had a privileged status, and he stressed the anthropological interpretation and psychological significance of all religious ritual. His tendency to ethical relativism, his inclination to praise goodness for its beauty, and his attitude toward religion as an aesthetically satisfying experience without final commitment made him many enemies in Oxford. The Paterian temperament was identified with aestheticism, or the hedonistic enjoyment of the intensely lived moment of beauty, the "exquisite passion," regardless of formal and moral standpoints. He was blamed for much of the moral eccentricity and artistic preciousness and pretentiousness of his followers, who deliberately courted decadence. However, he himself led a rather carefully balanced, withdrawn life, to which the famous sentence from the conclusion to *The Renaissance,* "To live always with this hard, gemlike flame, to maintain this ecstasy, is success in life," can be applied only with some difficulty.

In his *Imaginary Portraits* (London, 1887), Pater developed the genre of imaginative presentation of personalities embodying certain philosophies of life. His novel, *Marius the Epicurean* (London, 1885), regarded by many as his major work, is one such imaginary portrait on a large scale, picturing the religious development of a highly civilized, aesthetically sensitive agnostic at the time of Marcus Aurelius and probably indicating Pater's own attitude toward religion.

Pater's importance for English letters might be said to lie largely in his having cultivated the essay form to a high level of competence combined with elegance, making a fine art out of deliberate abstention from judgment, out of tentativeness and the impressionistic recording of subjective states of mind. His best criticism occurs in the collection *The Renaissance,* in his essay on Samuel Taylor Coleridge in *Appreciations* (London, 1889), and in the essay on style (appended to *Appreciations*).

Pater understood the "historical method" to be the attempt to understand artistic phenomena in relation to the conditions that produced them and to commend them to the sympathetic imagination of the reader. Unlike Matthew Arnold, who had contrasted personal and historical assessment with the "real" assessment of art, Pater did not believe in any fully objective standards but only in the completely honest account of personal impressions against the background of historical relativity. While ostensibly agreeing with Arnold that one must see the object "as it really is," he insisted that this can be done only on the basis of knowing one's own impressions "as they really are." The critic needs a certain kind of temperament, the power of being deeply moved by the presence of beautiful objects. Pater acknowledged no distinction here between beautiful things in and apart from art. Yet he offered some fine insights into the autonomy and interdependence of the various arts, especially in the implications of his much-quoted passage from the essay "The School of Giorgione" in *The Renaissance*: "All art aspires constantly towards the condition of music." In the preceding paragraph of the essay, Pater wrote that each art has "its own specific order of impressions, and an untranslatable charm." Yet each art form, as art, needs the complete fusion of matter and form that music exemplifies in its purity.

See also Aesthetic Judgment; Aesthetic Qualities; Aesthetics, History of; Arnold, Matthew; Coleridge, Samuel Taylor; Marcus Aurelius Antoninus; Plato; Platonism and the Platonic Tradition; Wilde, Oscar Fingal O'Flahertie Wills.

Bibliography

PRINCIPAL WORKS BY PATER

Essays from the "Guardian." London, 1897. Published uniformly, may be regarded as Vol. IX of the works.

Works, 8 vols. London, 1900–1901.

WORKS ON PATER

Benson, A. C. *Walter Pater.* London: Macmillan, 1906.

Cecil, Lord David. *Walter Pater.* Cambridge, U.K.: Cambridge University Press, 1955.

Eliot, T. S. "The Place of Pater." In *The Eighteen-Eighties,* edited by Walter de la Mare. Cambridge, U.K.: Cambridge University Press, 1930.

Gaunt, William. *The Aesthetic Adventure.* London: J. Cape, 1945.

Greenslet, Ferris. *Walter Pater.* London: William Heinemann, 1904.

Hough, Graham. *The Last Romantics.* London: Duckworth, 1949.

Iser, Wolfgang. *Walter Pater.* Tübingen: Niemeyer, 1960.

Eva Schaper (1967)

PATERNALISM

The term *paternalism* has long been in currency among moral and political philosophers, but its circulation became much wider, and its definitions much more precise, following the widely read debate over "the legal enforcement of morality" between Patrick Devlin (*The Enforcement of Morals,* 1965) and H. L. A. Hart (*Law, Liberty, and Morality,* 1963). Hart had endorsed the liberal doctrine of J. S. Mill, that the only legitimate reason for state interference with the liberty of one person is to prevent him from harming other persons. Mill was especially emphatic in denying that the actor's "own good, either physical or moral," is ever an adequate reason for interference or criminal prohibition ([1859], 1985, p. 9). What Mill denied in this passage is precisely what came to be called "legal paternalism" in the writings of his followers, including Hart nearly a century later. Thus, paternalism was regarded as a thoroughly unacceptable view by nineteenth-century liberals.

PHYSICAL AND MORAL

In his exchange with Devlin, however, Hart conceded that a certain amount of physical paternalism could be accepted by twentieth-century liberals, here departing from Mill who, he wrote, "carried his protests against paternalism to lengths that may now appear to us as fantastic" (Hart 1963, p. 32). He cited, for example, Mill's criticism of restrictions on the sale of drugs. Devlin then responded by drawing a distinction between "physical paternalism," which protects people from physical harm that could be caused by their own voluntary conduct, and "moral paternalism," which offers similar protection against "moral harm" of the actor's own causing. Devlin could see no consistent way in which the physical paternalist like Hart could avoid commitment to moral paternalism, for if it is the prevention of harm that justifies prohibition in the one case, why not use state power to prevent an equal amount of harm, though of a different kind, in the other case? Similarly, Devlin concluded, there is no relevant difference between criminalization meant to prevent moral harm and criminal prohibitions meant to "enforce the moral law as such." The view that "enforcement of morality," quite apart from harm prevention, is a valid reason for criminal prohibitions is widely called "legal moralism." It is anathema to liberals.

One way in which liberals sometimes defend themselves from Devlin's argument is by maintaining that Devlin's moves from physical to moral harm and from preventing moral harm to "enforcing the moral law" do not follow logically. One liberal critic, Joel Feinberg (1986), even goes so far as to deny, in the teeth of the immense combined authority of Plato and Aristotle to the contrary, that "moral harm" is a coherent concept.

HARD AND SOFT

A distinction is commonly made between hard (or strong) paternalism and soft (or weak) paternalism. Hard paternalism justifies the forcible prevention of some dangerous but self-regarding activities even when those activities are done in a fully voluntary (i.e., free and informed) way. Soft paternalism, on the other hand, permits individuals or the state to prevent self-regarding dangerous behavior only when it is substantially nonvoluntary or when temporary intervention is necessary to establish whether it is voluntary or not.

Most soft paternalists are liberals strongly opposed to paternalism. Most of them, when they think of the paternalism they oppose, think of what is here called hard paternalism. Therefore they would prefer to go by the name of soft antipaternalists. The term *hard antipaternalism* could be reserved for the totally uncompromising liberal who would oppose interference even with some choices known to be involuntary, and with temporary compulsory intervention that is only for the purpose of determining whether the intended conduct truly is voluntary, and even with the imposition of compulsory education about risks or state-administered tests to assess the dangerous actor's understanding of the risks, with licenses required for self-regarding dangerous behavior, like mountain climbing. Clarity would be improved if philosophers would speak of paternalism only when what is meant is hard paternalism, justifying prohibition even of wholly voluntary self-regarding conduct, when dangerous. Then soft and hard antipaternalism would be the names of a moderate and extreme liberalism, respectively.

The controversy over paternalism in the criminal law is genuine and difficult. Those who are strongly opposed to paternalism find it not only mistaken but arrogant and demeaning. It is very difficult to reconcile it with even a minimal conception of personal autonomy (rightful self-government) when it proclaims that state officials may rightfully intervene even against my protests to "correct" my choices, and this on the ground that they know what is good for me better than I do myself. But if we reject paternalism altogether, we seem to fly in the face both of common sense and of long-established customs and laws. The state, for example, does not accept "consent" as a justification for mayhem or homicide. Similarly, the law of contracts will not validate certain agreements even though they are voluntary on both sides—when, for example, they are usurious or bigamous. One would be hard put to accept these traditional state-created disabilities without abandoning one's opposition to paternalism. But if we continue our adherence to paternalism, we may discover that in other areas paternalism justifies too much, the flat-out prohibition, for example, of whiskey, cigarettes, and fried foods, which tend to be bad for people too, whether they know it or not.

MEDICAL CONTEXTS

Writers on medical ethics confront paternalism at every turn, often in human contexts that are less familiar to those whose interest is primarily focused on criminal law. Those characteristic social situations have led to some forms of ethical analysis supplementary to those that prevail among the critics and defenders of "legal paternalism." For example, not all of the moral problems raised by paternalism in medical settings are problems for legislators drafting mandatory rules or other governmental officials such as judges or police officers. Moreover, paternalism is not exclusively a criterion for the legitimacy of coercion. Sometimes what is at issue is some other practice that normally has high moral costs, most notably deception rather than coercion, as in false but comforting statements to frightened patients or the unacknowledged or mendacious use of placebos. Sometimes a medical provider may have to decide whether to tell a "white lie" to his patient, not for the sake of her health, but rather as a way of preventing her from experiencing intense despair in her final hours about a matter having no direct connection with medical treatment. In a hypothetical case invented by C. M. Culver and B. Gert (1976, p. 46), a woman on her deathbed asks her physician how her son is doing, and the doctor replies that he is doing well even though he knows that "the son has just been killed trying to escape from jail after having been indicted [a fact unknown to his mother] for multiple rape and murder." An opponent of (hard) paternalism would probably consider the doctor's mendacity to be a violation of the patient's autonomy. A medical paternalist would probably argue that the truthful alternative in this case would be cruel to the point of indecency. They might both be right.

PROS AND CONS

Problems involving paternalism in medical contexts are quite diverse. They include not only truth-telling cases but also suicide attempts, requests for euthanasia, and the use of human volunteers in dangerous experiments. The paternalist position in these conflicts is that protecting volunteers or patients from harm and promoting their benefit should take precedence over respecting their autonomy by permitting them to act freely on their well-informed choices in matters that are almost exclusively self-regarding.

T. L. Beauchamp (1977) and Beauchamp and J. F. Childress (1979) in their influential works rejected hard paternalism nearly categorically, emphasizing that to overturn the deliberate choices of adult human beings that affect only them, or only them clearly and directly, is to deny that their lives really belong to them. The apparent exceptions—cases in which commonsense morality would seem to justify interference with the patient's voluntary choice—invariably turn out to be cases in which that choice is not fully voluntary after all; that is, the patient or volunteer subject had not been adequately informed about the risks he would be accepting, or he was not perfectly free of coercive influences, or some other condition, such as infancy, drug intoxication, high fever, rage, or depression, had diminished his capacity to act rationally. To restrict his liberties in such circumstances, or to motivate him by telling him a lie, would be to interfere with actions that are not fully voluntary in the first place. To interfere with dangerous self-regarding but less-than-voluntary behavior can be justified by soft paternalism (that is by soft *and* hard antipaternalism). Another example illustrates the point. "If we see a normally calm person who we know has been experimenting with hard drugs, go into a sudden frenzy, and seize a butcher knife with the clear intention of cutting his own throat, then [of course!] we have the right to interfere. In so doing we will not be interfering with his real self or blocking his real will…. His drug-deluded self is not his 'real self,' and his frenzied desire is not his 'real choice,' so we may defend him against these internal threats to his autonomous self, which is quite another thing than throttling that autonomous self with external coercion" (Feinberg 1986, p. 14). Interference on this ground is no more paternalistic than interference designed to protect an individual from an attack by some berserk assailant. Paternalists have been quick to point out, however, that this example, and others like it, hardly fit the more usual examples of risky choice making.

Writing from the practical point of view, and a philosophical position more friendly to paternalism, Culver and Gert (1982), in response to Beauchamp, point out that many crucial questions remain for the soft antipaternalist analysis. Most of these stem from the vagueness of the distinction between voluntary and nonvoluntary. Culver and Gert remind us that voluntariness is usually a matter of degree with no conveniently placed bright lines to guide us. In this respect it resembles the concept of harm (which is also crucially involved in hard paternalists' calculations) and the degree of violation of a moral rule, like that forbidding telling lies, or that condemning coercion, and even the degree to which the overruled choices of, say, a patient, are purely self-regarding—another essential variable.

Culver and Gert, however, do not endorse the hard paternalistic position without limit. Rather, they hold that some (hard) paternalistic interventions are justified, and some are not, but reject the unqualified antipaternalism of Beauchamp and Childress, which denies that (hard) paternalistic prohibitions and interferences are ever justified, and the unqualified paternalism of many utilitarian writers, which holds that *all* paternalistic behavior is justified, except that which will be counterproductive in the long run.

See also Aristotle; Bioethics; Hart, Herbert Lionel Adolphus; Liberty; Mill, John Stuart; Plato.

Bibliography

Arneson, Richard. "Paternalism, Utility and Fairness." *Revue Internationale de Philosophie* 170: 409–423.

Beauchamp, T. L. "Paternalism and Bio-behavioral Control." *Monist* 60 (1977): 62–80.

Beauchamp, T. L., and J. F. Childress. *Principles of Biomedical Ethics.* New York: Oxford University Press, 1979.

Brennan, Samantha. "Paternalism and Rights." *Canadian Journal of Philosophy* 24 (1994).

Brock, D. "Paternalism and Promoting the Good." In *Paternalism,* edited by R. Sartorius. Minneapolis: University of Minnesota Press, 1983. This is one of the leading statements of a qualified utilitarian theory of paternalism.

Culver, C. M., and B. Gert. "Paternalistic Behavior." *Philosophy and Public Affairs* 6 (1976): 45–47.

Culver, C. M., and B. Gert. *Philosophy in Medicine.* New York: Oxford University Press, 1982.

Devlin, P. *The Enforcement of Morals.* London: Oxford University Press, 1965.

Dworkin, G. "Paternalism." *Monist* 56 (1972): 64–84. An influential early article that helped shape twenty years of discussion.

Dworkin, G. "Paternalism: Some Second Thoughts." In *Paternalism,* edited by R. Sartorius, 105–113. Minneapolis: University of Minnesota Press, 1983.

Dworkin, Gerald. "Moral Paternalism." *Law and Philosophy.* 2005.

Dworkin, Gerald. "Paternalism." *The Stanford Encyclopedia of Philosophy* (Winter 2002), edited by Edward N. Zalta.

Dworkin, Ronald. "Equality and The Good Life." In *Sovereign Virtue,* 268–270. Cambridge, MA: Harvard University Press, 2000.

Faden, R. R., and T. L. Beauchamp. *A History and Theory of Informed Consent.* New York: Oxford University Press, 1986. The definitive work on its subject.

Feinberg, J. *The Moral Limit of the Criminal Law.* Vol. 3: *Harm to Self.* New York: Oxford University Press, 1986.

Freeman, Samuel. "Liberalism, Inalienability, and Rights of Drug Use." In *Drugs and the Limits of Liberalism,* edited by Pablo DeGrieff. Ithaca, NY: Cornell University Press, 1999.

Goldman, Alan. "The Refutation of Medical Paternalism." *The Moral Foundations of Professional Ethics.* Towata: Rowman & Littlefield.

Hart, H. L. A. *Law, Liberty, and Morality.* London: Oxford University Press, 1963.

Husak, Douglas N. "Legal Paternalism." In *The Oxford Handbook of Practical Ethics,* edited by Hugh LaFollette. New York: Oxford University Press, 2003.

Kleinig, J. *Paternalism.* Totowa, NJ: Rowman and Allanheld, 1983.

Mill, J. S. *On Liberty* (1859). Indianapolis, 1985.

Sartorius, R., ed. *Paternalism.* Minneapolis: University of Minnesota Press, 1983. This excellent collection includes, in addition to the selections by Brock and Dworkin already cited, fifteen useful articles and a superb bibliography.

Shiffrin, Seana Valentine. "Paternalism, Unconscionability Doctrine, and Accommodation." *Philosophy and Public Affairs* 29 (Summer 2000): 205–250.

Sunstein, Cass, and Richard Thaler. "Libertarian Paternalism Is Not an Oxymoron." *University of Chicago Law Review* 70 (Fall 2003): 1166.

VanDe Veer, D. *Paternalistic Intervention: The Moral Bounds of Intervention.* Princeton, NJ: Princeton University Press, 1986.

Joel Feinberg (1996)
Bibliography updated by Gerald Dworkin (2005)

PATRIOTISM

The various current meanings of the term *patriotism* emerged during and after the early modern period. In the tradition of republicanism, patriotism is the citizens' commitment to or love for their shared political freedom and the institutions that sustain it. This commitment manifests itself in civic activity on behalf of the political commonwealth and its members. In this tradition, *patriotism* is often synonymous with *public spiritedness*. In the nineteenth century, patriotism was increasingly interpreted in a different, nationalist manner, and patriotism and nationalism are nowadays often equated.

An effective tool for mobilizing popular support for national policy, including military aggression and other forms of national aggrandizement, patriotism is often regarded as implying the glorification of war and imperialism. Opponents of such policies have also acted in the name of patriotism, however. Therefore, two preliminary questions require answers before any further discussion of the ethical implications of patriotism can proceed. First, the *patria*, the object of patriotic loyalty or activity, needs to be specified. According to some, this is the constellation of political institutions one finds oneself in. According to others, it is one's cultural or linguistic community (nation), one's country, the physical environment in which one was born or with which one identifies, or a combination of these. Accordingly, one can distinguish between different kinds of patriotism, such as "constitutional patriotism" and "nationalist patriotism." Second, while all agree that patriotism is a certain attitude, there is disagreement as to its precise nature. If it is an attitude of loyalty, what does loyalty require? Does patriotism require a certain sentiment, such as love or enthusiasm? Or should it primarily be understood as a social practice, and if so, what type of practice?

The belief in the superiority of one's own *patria* and a concomitant disdain for others is not a necessary element of the concept of patriotism. Nor does patriotism require that one refrain from criticizing one's *patria*. Indeed, criticism of governmental policy is often presented as patriotic since it aims at improving the *patria*.

The contemporary philosophical discussion of patriotism focuses on its relation to cosmopolitanism, as one aspect of the more general debate about particularism and universalism. Many authors in the republican tradition have argued emphatically that patriotism and cosmopolitanism are compatible, even that patriotism is a step toward cosmopolitanism, as it widens the individual's scope of concern beyond that of the family and so prepares one for the wider community of humankind. Others, however, especially defenders of patriotism in the nationalist tradition (as well as many defenders of cosmopolitanism), have seen an irreconcilable tension between (nationalist) patriotism and cosmopolitanism, on the grounds that cosmopolitanism would (rightly or wrongly, depending on which side one is on) prohibit favoring one's own national group over the rest of humankind.

Any defense of patriotism should address the question where justified special care or commitment ends and unjust parochialism begins. Thus, the philosophical debate over patriotism takes place in the context of the debate over "special obligations." Here the question is whether patriotism is prohibited (e.g., as necessarily jingoistic, as violating a moral standard of impartiality), permissible (and if so, under what conditions), or a duty (e.g., as a necessary condition for a well-functioning polity, or as a special obligation toward one's fellow citizens). Clearly, the specific answer one gives to this question depends on both one's particular conception of patriotism and one's underlying moral theory.

See also Loyalty; Nationalism.

Bibliography

Kleingeld, Pauline. "Kantian Patriotism." *Philosophy and Public Affairs* 29 (2000): 313–341.

Nussbaum, Martha C., et al. *For Love of Country: Debating the Limits of Patriotism*, edited by Joshua Cohen. Boston: Beacon Press, 1996.

Primoratz, Igor, ed. *Patriotism*. Amherst, NY: Humanity Books, 2002.

Viroli, Maurizio. *For Love of Country: An Essay on Patriotism and Nationalism*. Oxford: Clarendon Press, 1995.

Pauline Kleingeld (2005)

PATRISTIC PHILOSOPHY

"Patristic philosophy" is the term used to refer to the philosophical presuppositions, motifs, and structures in the writings of the early Christian apologists and Church Fathers. These writers were essentially theologians rather than philosophers, for their starting point lay in God and his self-revelation. Their use of philosophy can be divided into three periods: (1) the beginnings (roughly the first and second centuries CE), in which ideas derived from Platonism, Stoicism, and (to a lesser extent) Skepticism were employed chiefly for apologetic purposes, largely under the influence of Hellenistic Judaism; (2) the early Alexandrian period, during which Middle Platonism and Stoicism were dominant, especially in the thought of Clement and Origen; and (3) the development of Christian Neoplatonism, first under the influence of Porphyry and later under that of Proclus. The influence of Philo of Alexandria may have been felt during the first period and certainly was an important factor in the second.

BEGINNINGS

THE NEW TESTAMENT. In the New Testament, as in the Apocrypha (for example, in the Wisdom of Solomon), there are ideas that are at least latently philosophical. As early as Paul's first letter to the Corinthians (8:6), the Christian faith was being formulated with the use of prepositions that in Greek philosophy indicated causal relations. For Christians there was "one God the Father, from whom is everything and for whom are we, and one Lord Jesus Christ, through whom is everything and through whom are we." The Father was thus represented as the first and final causes (see Romans 11:36, a doxology), the Lord as the instrumental cause. Such an analysis was presumably derived from Hellenistic Judaism; Philo spoke thus concerning God and the Logos. In Romans 1:19–21 Paul discussed the primal knowledge of God's eternal power and deity, which he revealed by means of what he created. Men capable of receiving revelation knew God but turned away to worship the creation instead of the Creator (Romans 1:25; cf. Philo, *De Opifi-*

cio Mundi, Bk. 7). The theme of a revelation implicit in the structure of the created world is further developed in sermons ascribed to Paul in Acts 14:15–17 and 17:22–31 (the setting of the latter sermon contains reminiscences of the charges brought against Socrates and other philosophers at Athens), and in Colossians 1:15–20 the causal functions of Christ are further elaborated. The idea of the Logos, or creative Word of God, in John 1:1–14 is not necessarily philosophical either in its origin, which is probably not Philo, or in its expression. Later Christian theologians, however, interpreted it as philosophical, thus creating a bridge between Christianity and philosophy. These later theologians may perhaps have relied on Philo.

SECOND-CENTURY CHRISTIANITY. In the apocryphal *Preaching of Peter*, God is described by means of adjectives clearly philosophical in origin. God is uncontained, without needs, incomprehensible, eternal, imperishable, and invisible. These negative adjectives reflect ideas current not only in the Platonism of the time but also in Hellenistic Judaism. They are close to later Gnostic developments, and it has been suggested that both are derived from a rather fully developed doctrine of God current in early second-century Christianity. This view is confirmed by what Ignatius of Antioch (early second century) says of Christ as God and man: "the timeless, the invisible who for us was visible, the intangible, the impassible who for us was passible" (*Polycarpi* 3.2). Ignatius is obviously employing current language about God to describe Christ. About 140 the doctrine was more fully expressed in the *Apology* of Aristides (Ch. 1). God is the unmoved mover and ruler of the universe, for "everything that sets in motion is more powerful than what is moved, and what rules is more powerful than what is ruled." God is eternal, without beginning (what begins also ends) or end (what ends is destructible); he is therefore ungenerated, uncreated, immutable, and immortal. He has no defects or needs; he is not contained or measurable but contains all; he is immobile (he could not move from one place to another); and he is positively Wisdom and wholly Mind. According to Philo and others, God has no name, form, or parts.

A problem arose when such negative attributes were combined with traditional Jewish and Christian ideas about God as the Creator active in history. Basilides, a Christian Gnostic, tried to avoid any kind of analogical statement by arguing that the doctrine of emanation would make God spiderlike, whereas the doctrine of creation would make him anthropomorphic. Basilides claimed instead that originally there was absolutely nothing, and then the nonexistent God made, so to speak, a nonexistent universe out of the nonexistent. Like certain Middle Platonists, Basilides held that God was completely transcendent, since "the universe cannot speak of him or contain him in thought"; he cannot even be called ineffable.

Christian thinkers, however, were generally less audaciously speculative. The apologist Justin Martyr (c. 160) wrote an account of conversion from Platonic religious philosophy to Christian truth. Justin had experienced the teaching offered by Stoics, Peripatetics, Pythagoreans, and Platonists but had little insight into any but the last. While a novice in Platonism he encountered a Christian who— apparently with Peripatetic arguments—demolished his defenses of the innate immortality of the soul and its reminiscence of the eternal world. After his conversion Justin continued to quote from Plato's dialogues (which in his view were partly based on the Old Testament), although his position was now fully eclectic: "Whatever has been said well by anyone belongs to us" (*Apologies*, Bk. 2, Ch. 13). He criticized the Stoic doctrines about fate and the *ekpyrosis* (destruction of the cosmos by fire) but expressed his admiration not only for Heraclitus and Socrates but also for the first-century Stoic moralist Musonius Rufus. Justin's disciple Tatian was much less friendly to philosophers, although he tried to create a theology largely Platonic in inspiration. His incidental reference to "the God who suffered" suggests that at a crucial point he had to rely on paradox.

The writings of the later apologists show that philosophy continued to influence theology. In the *Legatio* of Athenagoras (c. 178), there is an important attempt to demonstrate the oneness of God and consequently an approach toward a doctrine of the Trinity. In another treatise the logical necessity of corporeal resurrection is upheld on grounds that are largely Peripatetic. About the same time, Theophilus of Antioch set forth the doctrine that God is known only through his activities, to which his attributes and appellations refer; God is without beginning because uncreated, immutable because immortal. The word *theos* is derived from verbs referring to his creative acts. His invisibility is explained by analogies to the soul, a pilot, the sun, and a king. God is not "contained" but is the locus of the universe. He is known only through his Logos, originally existing within him as reason (*endiathetos*), then expressed as word (*prophorikos*) at creation.

Philosophical ideas influenced not only the apologists but other Christians as well. Irenaeus of Lyons (c. 185) was no philosopher, but in five passages he accepted a description of God originally derived from Xenophanes, "seeing entirely, knowing entirely, hearing entirely" (Fr. 24 in *Fragmente der Vorsokratiker*, edited by H. Diels and W. Kranz, 10th ed., Berlin, 1961) and amplified it, ascribing it both to "religious men" and to "the Scriptures." In three instances he added the Platonic phrase "the source of all good things."

During the crucial second century, then, Christian theologians generally shared their doctrine of God with Platonists. Their doctrine of the Logos resembled that of the Stoics, although Christian theologians believed in one Logos (as in Philo) rather than many. They used Skeptical arguments against the pagan gods. Their ethical teaching was often close to that of the Roman Stoa as represented by Musonius (and Epictetus). Like non-Christians of various schools, they tended to believe that there had once been a unified religious philosophy, Oriental in origin, from which later philosophers had deviated. This first philosophy, it was thought, had been based on the inspiration of the divine Logos or on borrowing from Moses, or on both. The views of the Christian theologians were thus close to the kind of Hellenistic Judaism represented by Philo. Few writers took up the philosophical problems presented by the Incarnation; several of them do not even mention Jesus.

THE CHRISTIAN PLATONISTS OF ALEXANDRIA

In the cultural center of Alexandria, Christian philosophical theology came into its own, first in the writings of Clement of Alexandria (late second century) and later in the fuller treatment of Origen. The rather disdainful attitude of both writers toward "simpler believers" illustrates the tension between traditional and philosophical theology in their time. Philosophy was often viewed elsewhere as a seedbed of heresy; such was the case at Rome with Hippolytus and at Carthage with Tertullian, even though both these writers used philosophical definitions and arguments. Clement and Origen made use of the writings of Philo and other Hellenistic Jews, although both were directly acquainted with most of the works of Plato, some Middle Platonic writings, a few Aristotelian treatises, and a great deal of Stoic literature. Clement's learning was both broader and more superficial than Origen's. His philosophical ideas apparently developed away from the boldness of his semi-Gnostic *Hypotyposes* (now lost) toward the greater caution reflected in the *Stromata*, in which philosophy became the handmaid of a theology traditional in essence if not always in expression.

The principal points at which the influence of philosophy is obvious are the doctrine of transcendence of God and the ideal world, analysis of the divine nature of Christ, divine impassibility as a model for human conduct, and Platonic and Stoic ethical conceptions. Following Philo, Clement made use of the allegorical method in order to relate his theology to the Bible. He was the head of a private philosophical school, training pupils to become Christian Gnostics. In later times he was far less influential than Origen, head of an authorized church school first at Alexandria and later at Caesarea. The ideas of both teachers, however, continued to create theological ferment as late as the sixth century.

LATER PATRISTIC PHILOSOPHY

We can hardly view Eusebius of Caesarea as a philosopher, but in the writings of the Cappadocian Fathers (especially Gregory of Nazianzus and Gregory of Nyssa) technical philosophical arguments are frequently adapted for theological use, as they are throughout the patristic period. During the fourth century the attack upon Christianity by Porphyry was largely forgotten (a new attack was produced by the emperor Julian), and the logical rigor of his eclectic Neoplatonism was viewed as supporting theology. Extensive quotations from Porphyry and his master Plotinus appear in Eusebius's writings as well as in the later treatise *Against Julian* by Cyril of Alexandria. Toward the end of the fourth century, a faintly Christianized Neoplatonism appeared in the West in the commentary on Plato's *Timaeus* by a certain Calcidius, who relied primarily on Porphyry. Before being baptized, Marius Victorinus had translated one of Porphyry's works into Latin; he made frequent use of Porphyry's teaching in his later treatises *On the Trinity*. Both Ambrose and Augustine were deeply influenced by Porphyry, whose writings paved the way for Augustine's conversion. In the late fifth century the ideal world of the Neoplatonist Proclus was Christianized in the influential writings ascribed to Dionysius the Areopagite.

See also Apologists; Origen.

Bibliography

For critical textual editions, the following two series:

Corpus Scriptorum Ecclesiasticorum Latinorum. Vienna: Kommission zur Herausgabe des Corpus der lateinischen Kirchenväter, 1864–present.

Corpus Christianorum Series Latina. Turnhout, Belgium: Brepols Publishers, 1953–present.

For two series with translations of many complete works:

The Fathers of the Church. Washington, DC: Catholic University of America Press, 1947–present.

Roberts, Alexander, and James Donaldson, eds. *The AnteNicene Fathers: Translations of the Writings of the Fathers down to A.D. 325*. Buffalo: Christian Literature Publishing. Many of these translations have been superseded, but there is some material available in English only in these volumes.

For a one-volume sampler of texts in translation that will serve the interests of many readers:

Bettenson, Henry, ed. and tr. *The Early Christian Fathers*. London: Oxford University Press, 1956.

For general studies, see the following three works.

Wolfson, Harry Austryn. *Studies in the History of Philosophy and Religion*. Vol. I. Cambridge, MA: Harvard University Press, 1973.

Armstrong, A. H., ed. *The Cambridge History of Later Greek and Early Medieval Philosophy*. Cambridge, U.K.: Cambridge University Press, 1970.

Gersh, Stephen. *Middle Platonism and Neoplatonism: The Latin Tradition*. 2 vols. Notre Dame, IN: University of Notre Dame Press, 1986. Vol. II is more relevant to the subject.

For recent studies on individual figures or themes mentioned in the original article:

Barnard, Leslie W. *Athenagoras: A Study in Second Century Christian Apologetic*. Paris: Beauchesne, 1972.

Barnard, Leslie W. *Justin Martyr: His Life and Thought*. London: Cambridge University Press, 1967.

Cerrato, J. A. *Hippolytus between East and West: The Commentaries and the Provenance of the Corpus*. Oxford: Oxford University Press, 2002.

Cyril of Alexandria. *Letters*. 2 vols. Translated by John I. McEnerney. Washington, DC: Catholic University of America Press, 1987.

Cyril of Alexandria. *Select Letters*, edited and translated by Lionel R. Wickham. Oxford: Clarendon Press, 1983.

Goodenough, Erwin R. *The Theology of Justin Martyr: An Investigation into the Conceptions of Early Christian Literature and Its Hellenistic and Judaistic Influences*. Amsterdam: Philo Press, 1968.

Grant, Robert M. *Irenaeus of Lyons*. London: Routledge, 1997.

Hadot, Pierre. *Marius Victorinus: recherches sur sa vie et ses oeuvres*. Paris: Études augustiniennes, 1971.

Joly, Robert. *Christianisme et philosophie: études sur Justin et les apologistes grecs du deuxième siècle*. Bruxelles: Éditions de l'Université de Bruxelles, 1973.

Minns, Denis. *Irenaeus*. Washington, DC: Georgetown University Press, 1994.

Moorhead, John. *Ambrose: Church and Society in the Late Roman World*. London: Longman, 1999.

Morino, Claudio. *Church and State in the Teaching of St. Ambrose*. Translated by M. Joseph Costelloe. Washington, DC: Catholic University of America Press, 1969.

Osborn, Eric. *Irenaeus of Lyons*. New York: Cambridge University Press, 2001.

Osborne, Catherine. *Rethinking Early Greek Philosophy: Hippolytus of Rome and the Presocratics*. Ithaca, N.Y.: Cornell University Press, 1987.

Pelikan, Jaroslav. *Christianity and Classical Culture: The Metamorphosis of Natural Theology in the Christian*

Encounter with Hellenism. New Haven, CT: Yale University Press, 1993.

Ramsey, Boniface. Ambrose. London: Routledge, 1997.

Vallée, Gérard. A Study in AntiGnostic Polemics: Irenaeus, Hippolytus, and Epiphanius. Waterloo, Ont., Canada: Wilfrid University Press, 1981.

Wilken, Robert L. Judaism and the Early Christian Mind: A Study of Cyril of Alexandria's Exegesis and Theology. New Haven, CT: Yale University Press, 1971.

Robert M. Grant (1967)
Bibliography updated by William E. Mann (2005)

PATRIZI, FRANCESCO
(1529–1597)

Francesco Patrizi, also known as Patritius, was a vigorous defender of Platonism and an unremitting foe of Aristotelianism. He was versatile even for his time, being at once philosopher, mathematician, historian, soldier, and literary critic. Born in Dalmatia, he studied at Padua (Francesco Robertelli was a teacher-friend) and Venice. Having been an early and avid reader of Marsilio Ficino's *Theologia Platonica,* he turned from careers in business and in medicine to develop further his interest in Platonism.

After some years in France, Spain, and Cyprus in the service of various noblemen, Patrizi was in 1578 appointed by Duke Alfonso II as professor of Platonic philosophy at the University of Ferrara—which, with Florence and Pisa, was an important center of Platonism in Italy. In 1592 he was called to the University of Rome by Pope Clement VIII. He considered the privilege of expounding Platonism at Rome his crowning achievement, and he held that position until his death.

Although intellectual activity was his chief concern, Patrizi also showed interest in practical matters: He offered means for diverting a river threatening Ferrara, and presented plans for improving military strategy against the Turks and naval plans against the British.

In 1553 Patrizi's *Discorso* on types of poetic inspiration appeared, followed by his dialogues on history (1560). After visiting France, Spain, and Cyprus, he published *Discussiones Peripateticae* (1581), which violently attacked Aristotelianism. His achievement dates largely from his appointment at Ferrara, although correspondence with Telesio (1572) indicates an earlier interest in the study of nature. In *Della Poetica* (1586), he produced the first modern study of literary history, which also was an attack on Aristotle's *Poetics.* In 1587 there appeared several polemics defending his friend Orazio Ariosto against Torquato Tasso and Jacopo Mazzoni and upholding Patrizi's Platonic view of art as transcendental against their Aristotelian theory of poetry as imitation.

Patrizi's chief philosophical work, *Nova de Universis Philosophia* (1591), contained four parts: *Panaugia,* on light; *Panarchia,* on first principles; *Pampsychia,* on souls; and *Pancosmia,* on mathematics and natural science. Dedicated to Gregory XIV, who had been a fellow student at Padua, its aims were the linking of Christianity with the teachings of Zoroaster, Hermes, and Orpheus; the derivation of the world from God through emanation; and the insistence on a quantitative study of nature. His last work was *Paralleli Militari* (1594).

Patrizi's metaphysics of light is suggestive of Ibn Gabirol and Robert Grosseteste, and places him in the company of Geronimo Cardano and Bernardino Telesio. Defending the cognitive value of mathematics (as did Nicholas of Cusa), Patrizi helped to establish the subsequent priority of space over matter in the study of nature. His doctrines, fanciful yet impressive, failed (as did those of Giordano Bruno and Telesio), for want of an adequate method, to overthrow the well-entrenched Aristotelians. The decisive attack came only in the seventeenth century, when Galileo Galilei and others postulated a new physics of quantities that was related to astronomy and was based on experiments and calculations.

See also Aristotelianism; Bruno, Giordano; Ficino, Marsilio; Galileo Galilei; Grosseteste, Robert; Ibn Gabirol, Solomon ben Judah; Matter; Nicholas of Cusa; Platonism and the Platonic Tradition; Space; Telesio, Bernardino.

Bibliography

WORKS BY PATRIZI

Discorso. 1553.

Della Historia. Venice, 1560.

Discussiones Peripateticae. Basel, 1581.

Della Poetica. Ferrara: V. Baldini, Stampator Ducale, 1586.

Nova de Universis Philosophia. Ferrara, 1591.

Paralleli Militari. Rome: L. Zannetti, 1594.

WORKS ON PATRIZI

Brickman, B. *An Introduction to Francesco Patrizi's* Nova de Universis Philosophia. New York, 1941.

Kristeller, P. O. *Renaissance Thought: The Classic, Scholastic, and Humanistic Strains.* New York, 1961.

Robb, N. *Neoplatonism of the Italian Renaissance.* London: Allen and Unwin, 1935.

Salata, F. "Nel terzo centenario della morte di F. Patrizi." *Atti e memorie della Società Istriana di Archeologia e Storia Patria* 12 (1897): 455–484.

Jason L. Saunders (1967)

PAULER, AKOS
(1876–1933)

The Hungarian philosopher Akos Pauler, son of an archivist and historian and grandson of a professor of law, grew up in an intellectual and bookish environment. Even before he matriculated, he published his first article in the scholarly journal *Bölcseleti Folyoirat* in 1893. It was a defense of metaphysics against positivism—metaphysics starts from what is given and goes back to that without which the given cannot be thought. This is, in germ, Pauler's "reductive method" (as against induction and deduction), which became his main preoccupation in later life. However, influenced by his university professor Imre Pauer, he was first a positivist for about a decade. After obtaining his doctorate at Budapest in 1898, he spent a year at Leipzig and another at the Sorbonne. In 1902 Pauler became *Privatdozent* at Budapest and, in 1906, lecturer in ethics on the faculty of law at Pozsony (Bratislava). His departure from positivism seems to have started during this period, since his work on ethics published in 1907 at Budapest, *Az Etikai Megismerés*, is close to the Kantianism of Heinrich Rickert. In 1912 Pauler became professor of philosophy at Kolozsvár, and from 1915 he occupied the chair of philosophy at Budapest.

Most expositions of Pauler mention his division of philosophy into five parts—logic, ethics, metaphysics, aesthetics, and ideology—presented in the first seven paragraphs of his *Bevezetés a Filozofiaba* (Introduction to philosophy; Budapest, 1920; revised 3rd ed., Budapest, 1933). However, it will be sufficient to discuss only his logic and metaphysics.

For Pauler, logic is the most important part of philosophy, which is not surprising in view of his broad notions of logic, the scope and nature of which can be seen from his four "laws of logic"—the law of identity: "Everything is identical only with itself," from which follow the laws of contradiction and excluded middle; the law of connection: "Everything is connected with other things," which includes the law of sufficient reason; the law of classification: "Everything can be classified," which includes the *dictum de omni et nullo*; and the law of correlativity: "There is nothing relative without an absolute." Only the first three laws, in a slightly different version, are found in earlier works. The fourth law was added in the "Introduction to Philosophy."

Pauler's metaphysics is a combination of Aristotelian and Leibnizian elements, but by the end of his life it had moved toward Platonism and Neoplatonism. A substance is a center of self-activity based on intention or wish (*vágy*); the body is a manifestation of this activity. The interaction of substances not only proves their plurality but also provides the unity of the world. Since all change is from potentiality to actuality, the whole world process is a self-realization and self-liberation. All substances strive toward the first principle of their development, the principle of self-liberation, which is the Absolute. Moreover, substances exist insofar as they strive toward the Absolute. At first, God was described as something other than the Absolute, but Pauler later developed this Absolute into a theistic concept. He also introduced the Platonic *anamnesis* and the Augustinian *illuminatio* into his theory of knowledge.

Toward the end of his life he seems to have identified his reductive method with the Platonic dialectic, and his reductive method ultimately leads us to the notion of Good. He also criticized Aristotle for having misunderstood Plato. According to Pauler, Aristotle was mistaken in assuming that the Ideas are in the field of reality. They are, in fact, in the field of validity; that is, we do not come to them in the search for new entities, but in the search for those presuppositions without which we cannot think validly. We do this not by induction or deduction but by reduction.

See also Absolute, The; Aristotle; Logic, History of; Metaphysics; Neoplatonism; Platonism and the Platonic Tradition; Positivism.

Bibliography

There is a full bibliography of Pauler's published and unpublished works in *Pauler Akos Emlékkönyv* (Budapest, 1933), a special number (No. 6) of the publications of the Hungarian Philosophical Association that is devoted to Pauler.

See also J. Somogyi, "Die Philosophic Akos Paulers," in *Kantstudien* 30 (1925): 180–188, and C. Carbonara, "Akos von Pauler e la logica della filosofia dei valori," in *Logos* 3 (1931).

German translations of Pauler's works are *Grundlagen der Philosophie* (Berlin: W. de Gruyter, 1925) and *Logik* (Berlin and Leipzig: W. de Gruyter, 1929).

Julius Kovesi (1967)

PAULING, LINUS
(1901–1994)

Linus Pauling was a chemist, peace campaigner, and double Nobel Laureate who played a central role in two great unifying projects of twentieth-century science.

Born in Oregon, U.S.A., in 1901, Pauling worked his way through college, receiving a BS in chemistry from Oregon Agricultural College in 1922. There he read papers on valence by physical chemists G. N. Lewis and Irving Langmuir, sparking his interest in the theory of chemical structure and bonding. He moved to California Institute of Technology (Caltech) for doctoral work on X-ray studies of inorganic crystal structures and had published twelve papers by the time he graduated in 1925. In 1926 he traveled to Europe on a Guggenheim postdoctoral fellowship, visiting Munich and other centers of the new quantum mechanics. On his return from Europe, Pauling resumed his work on X-ray crystallography, developing what he later called his *chemical intuition* about possible crystal structures. He also set about applying quantum mechanics to chemistry. Simultaneously with physicist John Clarke Slater, he developed physicists Walter Heitler and Fritz London's 1927 work on the hydrogen molecule to explain the structure of polyatomic molecules. The resulting valence-bond approach to molecular quantum mechanics, which modeled observed molecular structures as *resonance hybrids* of classical structures, faced competition from the *molecular-orbital* approach. The early success of the valence-bond approach is largely due to Pauling's advocacy, his developing intuitive visual representations to accompany his theoretical work, and his publication of the enormously influential *Nature of the Chemical Bond* (1939), which brought together his many contributions to structural chemistry.

Despite this central role in unifying the sciences, Pauling was no reductionist. He regarded his application of quantum mechanics to chemistry as a synthesis of physical theory with independent principles of chemical structure.

Pauling's second great unifying project was the chemical understanding of biologically important molecules. From the 1930s onward, he applied the X-ray and electron-diffraction methods, used earlier on inorganic crystals, to the structure of peptides and proteins, including hemoglobin. Subsequently, Pauling studied the molecular basis of the immune system and identified the first molecular disease—sickle-cell anemia. Pauling's work was also influential in James Watson and Francis Crick's proposal of a double-helix structure for DNA in 1953, though Pauling denied having participated in a *race* to discover the structure of the molecule.

Pauling was a controversialist in science and in politics: Though he publicly defended Japanese internees, he supported U.S. entry in to the Second World War and was active scientifically in the war effort, earning a Presidential Medal of Merit in 1948. During the cold war, however, he became increasingly involved in campaigning for nuclear disarmament and for a test-ban treaty on both political and scientific grounds. This, and his defense of blacklisted scientists, led to interest from the Federal Bureau of Investigation and the denial of a passport in the early 1950s. A passport was forthcoming, however, when Pauling was awarded the 1954 Nobel Prize in Chemistry for his work on the chemical bond and his contributions to the understanding of the structure of proteins. His political campaigning also earned him a second Nobel Prize (in Peace) in 1962.

Pauling left Caltech in 1964, partly as a result of his high political profile, spending the next decade at the Santa Barbara Center for the Study of Democratic Institutions (1964–1967), the University of California at San Diego (1967–1969), and Stanford University (1969–1973). On retirement from there, he cofounded the Linus Pauling Institute of Science and Medicine in Palo Alto, California, from where he continued his popular, though scientifically controversial, advocacy of high doses of vitamin C to improve health and to slow down aging. He remained active in research until nearly the end of his life.

See also Chemistry, Philosophy of; Peace, War, and Philosophy; Quantum Mechanics; Social and Political Philosophy.

Bibliography

Hager, Thomas. *Force of Nature: The Life of Linus Pauling.* New York: Simon and Schuster, 1995.

Mason, Stephen. "The Science and Humanism of Linus Pauling (1901–1994)." *Chemical Society Reviews* (1997): 29–39.

Pauling, Linus. *The Nature of the Chemical Bond and the Structure of Molecules and Crystals; An Introduction to Modern Structural Chemistry.* 3rd ed. Ithaca, NY: Cornell University Press, 1960.

Pauling, Linus. "Fifty Years of Progress in Structural Chemistry and Molecular Biology." *Daedalus* 99 (4) (Fall 1970): 988–1014.

Robin Findlay Hendry (2005)

PAUL OF VENICE
(1369–1429)

Paolo Nicoletto Veneto joined the Hermits of St. Augustine as a boy and later taught at the Augustinian convent and the University of Padua for most of his life. The order's *Register* lists him at the *Studium* in Oxford from 1390 to 1393 where he studied theology but not logic, as often believed. Briefly, he served as prior general of the Augustinian order and later as ambassador to Cracow, Poland. In 1420, he was implicated in sedition against the Venetian Republic, was banished, and spent his last years in Siena and Perugia.

More than twenty works, extant in some 270 manuscripts, are attributed to him, but Paul's authorship of some of those works is questionable. His popular *Logica Parva* transmitted elementary Oxford logic to Italy. His *Lectura super librum Posteriorum Analyticorum* and *Summa Naturalium* were similarly important for conveying the Oxford style of scientific investigation to Italy. Judged by the number of manuscripts, other works had less influence, for example, *Lectura super librum de Anima*.

The *Logica Magna*, a gigantic work (200 folios) attributed to Paul, exists in only one manuscript and two fragments. This encyclopedic album covers most topics of scholastic logic that were disputed at Oxford in the last half of the fourteenth century. Its author undoubtedly took part in those debates that occurred while Paul was yet unborn or still a youth. With few exceptions, inconsistencies of doctrine, rules, and examples between *Logica Magna* and *Logica Parva*, as well as other factors, make it highly unlikely that they were written by the same person.

Logica Parva contains the core of scholastic logic that remained resilient against Humanist criticism well into the modern world. Focusing on logical form, it distinguishes between the logical signs (e.g., of affirmation/negation, of quantification, of conjunction, disjunction and implication) and nonlogical signs (ordinary nouns and verbs) of a language. Next, it gives inference rules (*consequentia*) keyed to the logical signs. Finally, it supports a truth-conditional concept of truth in which the truth of a sentence is decidable in virtue of its logical form. Material supposition serves as a quotational device within a meta language where any sentence of the object language can be quoted. Translation is understood as the substitution of one sentence for another in virtue of their common logical form and comparable nonlogical terms.

Paul of Venice organized and conveyed Oxford learning to Italy in the early fifteenth century. Humanists who urged a return to classical Latin usage and condemned the *barbari britanni* undoubtedly had works like his in mind, but few humanists read or understood them. Lorenzo Valla's *Dialectica* criticizes the *logica vetus* of Boethius but ignores the *logica moderna*. J. L. Vives rejects *sophismata* as a pedagogical method in *Adversus pseudo-*dialecticos* but retains Scholastic concepts under a neoclassical nomenclature in *De artibus*.

See also Augustinianism; Boethius, Anicius Manlius Severinus; Humanism; Logic, History of; Philosophy of Science, History of.

Bibliography

PRIMARY SOURCES

Logica Magna. Tractatus de suppositionibus, edited and translated by A. R. Perreiah. St. Bonaventure NY: Franciscan Institute, 1971.

Logica Magna. Part II, Fascicule 6: *Tractatus de Veritate et Falsitate Propositionis, Tractatus de SignificatoPropositionis*, edited by Francesco Del Punta, translated by Marilyn McCord Adams, 1978; Part I, Fascicule 1: *Tractatus de Terminis*, edited and translated by Norman Kretzmann, 1979; Part I, Fascicule 7: *Tractatus de scire et dubitare*, edited and translated by Patricia Clark, 1981; Part II, Fascicule 8: *Tractatus de Obligationibus*, edited and translated by E. Jennifer Ashworth, 1988; Part II, Fascicule 3: *Tractatus de Hypotheticis*, edited and translated by Alexander Broadie, 1990; Part II, Fascicule 4: *Capitula de Conditionali et de Rationali*, edited and translated by G. E. Hughes, 1990; Part I, Fascicule 8: *Tractatus de necessitate et contingentia futurorum*, edited and translated by C. J. F. Williams, 1991. Oxford: Oxford University Press.

MODERN EDITIONS

Ruello, F., ed. *Paulus Venetus, Super Primum Sententiarum Johannis de Ripa Lecturae Abbreviatio.* Firenze: Leo S. Olschki, 1980.

Perreiah, A. R. trans. *Paulus Venetus Logica Parva*, (an English translation of the 1472 edition with introductory essay and notes). Munich: Philosophia Verlag, 1984.

Perreiah, A. R., ed. *Paulus Venetus Logica Parva, First Critical Edition from the Manuscripts with Introduction and Commentary.* Leiden, NY: E. J. Brill, 2002. Bibliography, pp. 301–310.

SECONDARY SOURCES

Conti, Alessandro D. *Esistenza e Verita: Forme e strutture del reale in Paolo Veneto e nel pensiero filosofico del tardo medioevo.* Roma: Istituto Storico Italiano per il Medio Evo, 1996. Bibliography, pp. 301–316.

Perreiah, A. R. *Paul of Venice: A Bibliographical Guide.* Bowling Green, OH: Philosophy Documentation Center, 1986.

Alan R. Perreiah (2005)

PAULSEN, FRIEDRICH
(1846–1908)

Friedrich Paulsen, a German philosopher and educational theorist, was born in the village of Langenhorn, Schleswig-Holstein, to a farming family descended from generations of seamen of the North Frisian Islands. In his autobiography Paulsen described his early life in detail, attributing to it the firm moral character and concern for people that marked his later work in philosophy and education. After attending the Altona Gymnasium, he entered the university at Erlangen in 1867. The following year he went to the University of Berlin, where a reading of F. A. Lange's *History of Materialism* and participation in Adolf Trendelenburg's seminar on Aristotle induced him to abandon theology for philosophy. After studies in Berlin, Bonn, and Kiel, Paulsen taught at Berlin. The professorship of philosophy to which he later succeeded there was, due to his own interests and the needs of the university, expanded to include pedagogy.

Philosophy could not, for Paulsen, be detached from the moral and cultural issues of private and public life, and the needs of the general public determined both the language and the content of his teaching and writing. Although far from negligent of the critical problems of theoretical and practical philosophy, he always tested the validity of their solutions by common sense and the public well-being. His collection of essays and addresses *Zur Ethik und Politik* (1905) shows the range of his interests and his public concern. Although he was temperate and reasonable, his efforts to distinguish good from evil in contemporary political and social life subjected him to political attack and involved him in public controversy.

Although Paulsen influenced all levels of German education, his published works deal chiefly with German universities and preparatory schools. His *Geschichte des gelehrten Unterrichts auf den deutschen Schulen und Universitäten* (1885) pioneered in the history of higher education and aroused wide controversy, helping to effect a liberalization of preuniversity education.

Paulsen usually described his philosophical position as idealistic monism but sometimes described it as pantheism. Participating in the revival of Immanuel Kant and Aristotle in the second half of the nineteenth century, Paulsen found in both an epistemological realism, an emphasis upon practical reason over theoretical reason, and a teleological metaphysics. His own position was formulated in opposition to the two extremes of a rigid Christian orthodoxy and scientific materialism. Irrational supernaturalism and mechanistic naturalism are the enemies in his two textbooks, *System der Ethik* (1889) and *Einleitung in die Philosophie* (1892), and in his *Philosophia Militans* (Berlin, 1901). He rejected Christian supernaturalism because of its dualism in theoretical philosophy and its legalism and rigorism in practical philosophy. Materialism was discarded because its denial both

of human freedom and of the reality of purposes is offensive to man's ethical demands.

Paulsen's two textbooks were addressed not merely to students but to the thoughtful layman. Simply written with many concrete applications and references to contemporary ethical and social problems, they appeared in many editions in German and in translation and set a pattern for introductory textbooks and courses in philosophy for at least four decades. In them Paulsen formulated his method as (1) analysis of problems and the construction of possible solutions, (2) a survey of the historical development of philosophical thought on each problem, and (3) a choice of the solution most coherent with an inclusive world view.

This method brought Paulsen close to a pragmatic and personalistic viewpoint. In his ethics he supported a modern utilitarianism or eudaemonism that repudiated the hedonism of the British school, replacing it with the goal of human welfare and an objective perfection of the ends of life. The good life is thus grounded in the will, not in feeling. In determining the valid ends of conduct, the individual must be guided by the historical tradition, which may be trusted ultimately to destroy evil and to bring about the survival of the good. Book I of the *System*, devoted to such historical evaluation, is still a most useful introduction to the history of ethics. Paulsen stressed the distinctions between the ascetic ethical ideals of early Christianity and the humanism of classical Greece, but he regarded as necessary the modern effort to reconcile them.

Ethical thought involves the problems of evil, of freedom, and of God. Evil is justified in a monistic world, because by overcoming evil we find the way and the will to the good. Although human freedom is real, it is never a motiveless freedom of action. The psychological theory of freedom is correct in finding the ground of free action in the human will or in man's determining his conduct through deliberation and resolution. The metaphysical theory of freedom, which denies that there are causes of the will, must itself be denied. Morality, in its historical development of responsibility and a sense of duty, comes to require a higher will with a right to command and thus provides an argument for the existence of a deity who is also implicit in the evolutionary account of nature.

In such later ethical writings as the article "Ethik" in Paul Hinneberg's *Systematische Philosophie* (Berlin and Leipzig, 1907), Paulsen moved closer to G. W. F. Hegel by introducing an "objective will" as the manifestation in the social forms of life of a universal reason to which individual conscience is a cognitive response. Paulsen held that the principles of ethics are rational in the sense that they arise from the conditions of life. They need not determine one's metaphysics, but teleological ethics demands an evolutionary teleology in which the purpose of nature is fulfilled in human reason.

Paulsen's *Introduction to Philosophy* was devoted to metaphysical and epistemological questions. In it he is led to monism by the Lotzean argument from finite interaction, by E. Hartmann's vitalism and energism, and by a creative vitalistic interpretation of evolution. His solution to the mind-body problem is a theory of panpsychistic parallelism, showing the influence of Benedict de Spinoza and Gustav Theodor Fechner. Mind and body are distinct aspects of a unified "All-One," a mental process of which history and nature are the two series of "modifications." This identity is affirmed of God in relationship to nature and to history. Science is limited to the phenomenalistic aspect of nature. Although God enters into interaction with lesser spirits, the concept of personality must be purged of its human limitations before it can be ascribed to God, who is to be thought of rather as a superpersonal source of energy and reason in nature and man.

See also Aristotle; Fechner, Gustav Theodor; Hartmann, Eduard von; Hegel, Georg Wilhelm Friedrich; Kant, Immanuel; Lange, Friedrich Albert; Materialism; Neo-Kantianism; Panpsychism; Pantheism; Spinoza, Benedict (Baruch) de; Utilitarianism; Vitalism.

Bibliography

WORKS BY PAULSEN

Geschichte des gelehrten Unterrichts auf den deutschen Schulen und Universitäten vom Ausgang des Mittelalters bis zur Gegenwart. Leipzig, 1885. 3rd ed., 2 vols., Berlin, 1919–1920, translated by E. D. Perry as *The German Universities: Their Character and Historical Development.* New York: Macmillan, 1895.

System der Ethik mit einem Umriss des Staats und Gesellschaftslehre. Berlin, 1889. Translated from the 4th German edition by Frank Thilly as *A System of Ethics.* New York: Scribners, 1899.

Einleitung in die Philosophie. Berlin, 1892. Translated from the 3rd German edition by Frank Thilly as *Introduction to Philosophy,* New York: Holt, 1895.

Immanuel Kant: Sein Leben und seine Lehre. Stuttgart: Frommanns, 1899. Translated from the 3rd German edition by J. E. Creighton and A. Lefevre as *Immanuel Kant: His Life and Doctrine.* New York: Scribners, 1902. Paulsen's most important and influential historical study. Interprets Kant as a realist.

Philosophia Militans. Gegen Klerikalismus und Naturalismus. Berlin: Reuther and Reichard, 1901.

Zur Ethik und Politik: Gesammelte Vorträge und Aufsätze, 2 vols. Berlin, 1905.

Aus meinem Leben. Jugenderinnerungen. Jena: Diederichs, 1909. Translated by Theodor Lorenz as *Friedrich Paulsen: An Autobiography.* New York: Columbia University Press, 1938. Gives details of Paulsen's academic career and political influence as well as bibliographical data. Part II of this work, never published in German, was translated from Paulsen's manuscript.

WORKS ON PAULSEN

Schulte-Hibbert, B. *Die Philosophie Friedrich Paulsens.* Berlin, 1914.

Speck, Johannes. *Friedrich Paulsen. Sein Leben und sein Werk.* Langensalza, Germany, 1926.

Spranger, Eduard, ed. *Gesammelte pädagogische Abhandlungen.* Stuttgart: J.G. Cotta, 1912. Contains a complete bibliography.

L. E. Loemker (1967)

PAVLOV, IVAN PETROVICH
(1849–1936)

Ivan Petrovich Pavlov, the Russian physiologist and originator of conditioned-reflex method and theory, was born the eldest son of a priest in Riazan'. After home tutoring, church school, and theological seminary (where he read G. H. Lewes's *Physiology*), he entered the University of St. Petersburg, where I. F. Tsyon confirmed his physiological interests. At the Military Medical Academy, as assistant to Tsyon and later to S. P. Botkin, the experimental pharmacologist, he excelled in surgery and in experimental physiological research, which he continued in Botkin's laboratory after qualifying as an approved physician in 1879. In 1881 he married a fellow student, and despite desperate financial struggles, he received his MD in 1883 with a dissertation on the heart's innervation. With a traveling fellowship, he worked in Leipzig with Karl Ludwig and in Breslau with Rudolf Heidenhain; he returned to Botkin's laboratory in 1886 to continue research on nervous control of circulation and digestion. In 1888 he discovered the secretory nerves of the pancreas, and the following year he wrote on "sham feeding" and gastric "psychic secretion" (at sight of food).

In 1890 he became professor of pharmacology at the Military Medical Academy and director of the physiological department of the new Institute of Experimental Medicine donated by the prince of Oldenburg. In 1895 he was named professor of physiology at the Military Medical Academy, although the rector, Pashutin, delayed confirmation of the appointment till 1897. *The Work of the Digestive Glands* (1897), which reported the research that won Pavlov the Nobel Prize in physiology in 1904, was widely translated. Next he investigated salivary "psychic" secretion, devising a neat surgical technique to enable collection and measurement of the saliva of dogs. Reflex salivation was measured upon ingestion (natural stimulus) and sight ("psychic" stimulus) of food, and also upon application, to hungry dogs before feeding, of artificial ("conditioned") stimuli—visual, auditory, olfactory, and tactile. The "conditioned reflex"—a term coined by I. E. Tolochinov—was thus a simple unit of acquired behavior, as involuntary as salivation itself; its formation, persistence, and disappearance followed rules that Pavlov elucidated in meticulous experiment for more than thirty years, gradually constructing a neurophysiological theory of behavior and learning. Pavlov's work attracted pupils and collaborators, produced a plentiful literature, and continued without significant interruption through World War I and the Russian Revolution.

A reflex theory of behavior accorded well with Marxist dialectical materialism, and Pavlov's researches received governmental encouragement and financial support. Pavlov was never a Marxist or a communist; he resigned his professorship in 1924 in protest against anticlerical discrimination at the academy, but he continued to enjoy state support, including new laboratories, and official foreign-language publication; his research village, Koltushy, was even renamed Pavlovo. When conditioned-reflex theory was extended to human behavior, Pavlovian doctrine became the Soviet Union's official "psychology," basic to psychiatry, pedagogy, industrial research, and other fields ranging from criminal reeducation to space exploration.

Pavlov's collected lectures appeared in English, French, and German translations in the 1920s, with a further volume, *Conditioned Reflexes and Psychiatry*, in 1941. He observed that a conditioned reflex might comprise excitation (secretory or motor) or inhibition, both processes located in the cerebral cortex. Concentration and irradiation of excitation, enabling discrimination and generalization of response, followed laws of induction, conceived as resembling ionic polarization, with excitation and inhibition spreading wavelike over a largely unspecialized cortex. Specialization occurred in the analyzers, or cortical receptor areas (visual, auditory, etc.), which sorted stimulus signals and regulated responses.

Pavlov found that for permanence a conditioned reflex required reinforcement with the unconditioned stimulus. Disturbance of an already established temporal or spatial pattern of stimuli, including excessive require-

ment of discrimination, produced disordered responses in the three successive phases of (a) equalization of response to all stimuli, (b) paradoxical responses, and (c) ultraparadoxical responses, involving reversal of positive and inhibitory responses. Ultimate derangement ("neurosis") was behavioral breakdown in uncontrolled excitement or complete inhibition, depending upon the type of the nervous system. An increasing preponderance of inhibition was evident in the progression from (a) controlled activity, to (b) delayed activity, corresponding to deliberation or thought, to (c) hypnotic states with concentrated activity bounded by general inhibition, to (d) sleep considered as generalized inhibition. Nervous systems were classified as strong excitable, weak inhibitable, and two central "balanced" types, lively and stolid, analogous to the "Hippocratic temperaments," choleric, melancholic, sanguine, and phlegmatic, respectively. Conditioned reflexes were most stable in the two more inhibited types of dog (and probably of humans).

From 1928 until his death Pavlov surveyed human psychology and psychiatry, drawing bold analogies between psychiatric syndromes and the reactions of dogs to experimental laboratory situations. Manic-depressive psychosis was viewed as an excitation-inhibition disorder and paranoia as a pathologically persistent excitatory process in a circumscribed cortical area. Later work by others has shown the value of conditioning theory for a "how" explanation and for an empirical treatment for certain phobias and compulsions, but Pavlov's formulations, without direct experimental or adequate clinical basis, are subjective intuitions clothed in pseudophysiological vocabulary. His experimental observations were objective and sound, and his apparently prosaic method allowed repeatable exact measurement, although what else was being measured by measuring saliva remains unclear. When he wrote of "reflexes" of freedom and slavery in dogs and humans, or of an animal's "strong" or "weak" cortex, or of ripples of excitation or inhibition, he failed to recognize the subjective nature of his interpretations. Insight was hindered by his premature oversimplification and an increasingly militant materialist monism.

Pavlov's was the principal and most developed of the several physiopsychologies of his time. His priority was disputed by V. M. Bekhterev, a neurologist whose "reflexology" of "associated reflexes" was developed simultaneously although independently in the same academy; Pavlov undoubtedly published first, however. Pavlov yielded experimental priority to the American E. L. Thorndike and admitted the theoretical influence of I. M. Sechenov, a former professor of physiology in St. Petersburg, whom Pavlov styled "father of Russian physiology." Sechenov's *Reflexes of the Brain* (1863, in *Selected Physiological and Psychological Worts*, Moscow, 1952–1956) followed his studies in Berlin, where Wilhelm Griesinger taught a psychology of temperamental types and psychic reflexes that was philosophically based upon Arthur Schopenhauer and René Descartes (*Mental Pathology and Therapeutics*, Berlin, 1845 and 1861; translated by C. L. Robertson and J. Rutherford, London, 1867).

Pavlov's influence continues paramount in Russia. Elsewhere it is an important component in behavior theory and therapy, but with a strong admixture of Bekhterev and John B. Watson in practical techniques and a preponderance of C. L. Hull's learning theory in vocabulary.

See also Behaviorism; Descartes, René; Dialectical Materialism; Induction; Marxist Philosophy; Schopenhauer, Arthur.

Bibliography

WORKS BY PAVLOV

The Work of the Digestive Glands. Translated by W. H. Thompson. London, 1902.

Conditioned Reflexes; an Investigation of the Physiological Activity of the Cerebral Cortex. Translated and edited by G. V. Anrep. London: Oxford University Press, 1927; New York: Dover, 1960. The best English translation of the early papers.

Lectures on Conditioned Reflexes. Vol. I: *Twenty-five Years of Objective Study of the Higher Nervous Activity (Behavior) of Animals*. Translated and edited by W. Horsley Gantt, with G. Volborth. New York: International, 1928. Vol. II: *Conditioned Reflexes and Psychiatry*. Translated and edited by W. Horsley Gantt. New York: International, 1941.

Selected Work. Translated by S. Belsky, edited by J. Gibbons under the supervision of K. S. Koshtoyants. Moscow: Foreign Languages, 1955.

Experimental Psychology and Other Essays. New York: Philosophical Library, 1957; London, 1958. A reprint of *Lectures on Conditioned Reflexes*, omitting Pavlov's patriotic and political speeches.

Essays in Psychology and Psychiatry. New York, 1962. A selection from *Experimental Psychology and Other Essays* in paperback.

Psychopathology and Psychiatry; Selected Works. Compiled by Y. Popov and L. Rokhin, translated by D. Myshne and S. Belsky. Moscow: Foreign Languages, 1962.

Conditioned Reflexes, Lectures on Conditioned Reflexes, and *Selected Works* contain some of the same papers in different translations. *Lectures on Conditioned Reflexes* and *Selected Works* have some later "psychiatric" papers, and *Selected Works* has some early papers on circulation and digestion preceding Pavlov's work on conditioned reflexes. *Psychopathology and Psychiatry* is selected entirely from his "psychiatric" work.

WORKS ON PAVLOV

Asratyan, E. A. *I. P. Pavlov, His Life and Work*. English ed., Moscow: Foreign Languages, 1953. An early and approved biography.

Babkin, B. P. *Pavlov: A Biography*. Chicago: University of Chicago Press, 1949 and 1960; London: Gollancz, 1951.

Cuny, H. *Ivan Pavlov: The Man and His Theories*. London: Souvenir Press, 1964. Brief, semipopular outline of Pavlov's life and work.

Frolov, Y. P. *Pavlov and His School—The Theory of Conditioned Reflexes*. Translated by C. P. Dutt. New York: Oxford University Press, 1937.

Gray, J. A., ed. and tr. *Pavlov's Typology*. Oxford and New York: Pergamon Press, 1964. Includes a detailed authoritative survey of this field by B. M. Teplov.

Platonov, K. I. *The Word as a Physiological and Therapeutic Factor—The Theory and Practice of Psychotherapy according to I. P. Pavlov*. Translated by D. A. Myshne. Moscow: Foreign Languages, 1959. This work applying Pavlov's teachings openly acknowledges a debt to Bekhterev's.

Scientific Session on the Physiological Teachings of I. P. Pavlov. Moscow: Foreign Languages, 1951.

Simon, B., ed. *Psychology in the Soviet Union*. Stanford, CA: Stanford University Press, 1957.

Todes, P. *Ivan Pavlov: Exploring the Animal Machine*. New York: Oxford University Press, 2000.

Todes, P. *Pavlov's Physiology Factory: Experiment, Interpretation, Laboratory Enterprise*. Baltimore, MD: Johns Hopkins University Press, 2002.

Wells, H. K. *Pavlov and Freud*. 2 vols. New York: International, 1956–1960; reprinted 1962.

J. D. Uytman (1967)
Bibliography updated by Vladimir Marchenkov (2005)

PEACE, WAR, AND PHILOSOPHY

Speculation about war and peace as conditions of interstate relations has tended to divide thinkers into two groups—those who regard war as inevitable, perhaps even desirable, and those who consider it an evil capable of being replaced by lasting peace through good will or improved social arrangements. The first group is sometimes described as "realist" and the second as "idealist," but these terms have the drawback that such idealist philosophers (in the ontological sense) as Plato and Georg Wilhelm Friedrich Hegel often accept war as a permanent condition of human existence. It is therefore proposed here simply to call the first group "conservatives" and the second "abolitionists," though a wide spectrum of opinion clearly exists within each subdivision.

THE CONSERVATIVE TRADITION

THE GREEKS. Ancient Greek thought commonly accepted war between the city-states themselves and between Greeks and "barbarians" as part of the order of nature. The Greek gods were a warlike breed who had come to power after a brutal struggle with the Titans. Ares was one of their leading figures, but the goddess of peace, Irene, was merely a subordinate deity attendant on the great gods. A view of war widely prevalent in Greece was that of Heraclitus of Ephesus. War, Heraclitus taught, was the "father of all and king of all," and it was through war that the present condition of humankind, some men free and some enslaved, had evolved. If strife between the warring elements in nature were abolished, nothing could exist; "all things," according to Heraclitus, "come into being and pass away through strife."

It was not until the later phases of the war between Athens and Sparta (431–404 BCE) that a pacifist note unusual in the Greek world was struck in such works as Euripides' *The Trojan Women* (performed in 415 BCE) and Aristophanes' *Lysistrata* (411 BCE). Even so, the conclusion drawn by Plato from the Peloponnesian War was that the state must be organized for violent survival in an unruly world. Plato's *Republic* is, in effect, a design for a military community on the Spartan model. Plato does, however, distinguish between war among Greeks and war between Greeks and outsiders; the former, according to the *Republic*, is to be legally regulated whereas any excess is permissible in the latter.

CHRISTIANITY AND NATURAL LAW. The conservative acceptance of war as a fact of life was also basic to the intellectual attitudes of the Roman Republic and Empire and was sustained during the Middle Ages, when Catholic writers wrestled with the problem of the conditions on which ecclesiastical approval could be given to the wars of secular monarchs. St. Thomas Aquinas in *Summa Theologiae* (Question 40), while claiming that peace was the greatest aim toward which man should strive in fulfillment of his natural ends, nevertheless placed on monarchs the duty to defend the state. Similarly, Dante contended in *De Monarchia* that "peace was the target at which all shafts were sped" but that it was to be attained by the imposition of a world law, if necessary by force, issuing from a revived Roman Empire. The legacy of Christian teaching that had the most lasting influence, however, concerned the application of natural law, strongly tinged by Christian ethics, to the conduct of war.

The Spanish Jesuit theologian Francisco Suárez held that war is not intrinsically evil and that just wars may be waged. Suárez defined three conditions of legitimate war. It must be waged by lawful authority—that is, by the supreme sovereign; the cause of making war must be just, and other means of achieving justice must be lacking; and war must be conducted and peace imposed with moderation. A similar view was taken by Hugo Grotius, who held that far from war's being a breakdown of the law of nations, it is, in fact, a condition of life to which law is as applicable as it is to the conditions of peace. War, Grotius argued in his *De Iure Belli ac Pacis Libri Tres* (1625), should not be fought except for the enforcement of rights and, when fought, should be waged only within the bounds of law and good faith. This conception survives in the assumption behind such twentieth-century international organizations as the League of Nations and the United Nations that only wars fought on behalf of international interests, such as the maintenance of world peace, are just.

THE ADVENT OF NATIONALISM. In the era of European secular nationalism following the Renaissance the idea of war as a necessary or desirable institution strengthened. The Italian city-states of the Renaissance, whose diplomatic practice formed the model for the early European national states, were continually at war with one another; these were, however, limited conflicts that aroused no great indignation among philosophers. A typically acquiescent view of war was that of Sir Thomas More in his *Utopia* (1518). The Utopians have a pragmatic, not particularly heroic idea of war, which they regard as a normal event; war is to be fought as economically and safely as possible when one's lands are invaded or one's allies are oppressed.

A more profound view was that of the Florentine statesman and writer Niccolò Machiavelli. Like all conservatives, Machiavelli assumed that armed conflict was part of the human lot not because man was evil—Machiavelli was inclined to regard man as weak and stupid rather than evil—but because of the activity of malign fate (*fortuna*), which is always forcing man to arm himself against adversity. Machiavelli, unlike Heraclitus, held out no hope that war raised man to a higher plane; the prince is condemned to seek victory in war merely in order to survive in the hostile world. In peace a ruler should not sit with hands folded but should always be improving his state's military power against the day of adversity.

At the same time the formation of great national states in England and France was forcing men to speculate on the justification of government, especially since the acceptance of the papacy as the ultimate and sacred authority had been considerably weakened. The concept of a "state of nature" in which men exist without a common superior and in a state of internecine war was introduced to help explain the growth and functions of government. Thomas Hobbes explained in his *Leviathan* (1651) that war is not the act of fighting but the disposition *to fight* that exists where there is no common superior to ensure that violence shall not be permitted. Only through the establishment of a commonwealth—that is, a superior law-enforcing agency to which all men are subject—can peace and civilization be ensured. Hobbes did not regard the state of nature as a historical condition that had occurred in the past; he inferred that such would be man's state if the commonwealth did not exist.

John Locke differed from Hobbes in holding that there were natural rights in the state of nature that it was government's function, after its establishment, to protect; hence, war was not a universal condition in the state of nature but occurred only when force was exercised without right. For Locke there was an intrinsic difference between war waged for natural rights and war waged without this sanction. For Hobbes war in the state of nature, as well as war between sovereign states, could be neither right nor wrong since these categories exist only within the commonwealth. Benedict de Spinoza shared Hobbes's view of the inevitability of war where men are without a common government, but, like Locke, he could not reconcile himself to the total absence of morality or law in the state of nature. The Hobbesian argument has nevertheless been of immense importance in shaping modern Western man's attitude toward war and peace. It is that peace is the result of man's determination, deriving from fear of death and the wish for what Hobbes called "commodious living," to create an overriding government. Hobbes did not make clear whether he thought that man could sustain peace in his international relations, but it is clear that, unlike Locke, he considered that nothing short of a world state with a monopoly of power over the nations would suffice to ensure such peace.

Before the Napoleonic Wars, however, war, owing to its limited scale, could not be regarded as the decisive factor in the health or illness of nations. But with the Messianic fervor unleashed by the French Revolution, all Europe appeared to be caught up in revolt against the existing order, internal and external, and the expansion of national wealth showed for the first time the potentialities of nationalistic wars for good or evil. It was in the aftermath of the revolution that the more extreme conservative attitude toward war came into its own in certain countries and war began to be thought of as a positive principle of national regeneration. Germany in particular fostered these views, possibly because that country entered the struggle for national ascendancy somewhat late so that its militarism was proportionately more intense.

Hegel is well known for his conception of history as a struggle of opposites from which a synthesis emerges that transcends the two original conflicting forces. For Hegel the national state was the means by which the Idea realized itself in history. Since the Idea can materialize itself only if the state is allowed to live out its predetermined functions, it follows that the individual's life has no meaning except insofar as it serves the state's ends and that no principle is left by which the relations between states can be subject to moral criteria. Hegel had no patience with the notion of a league of nations for the establishment of permanent peace because he believed war was the catalyst through which history unfolded its purpose. Man must accept war or stagnate.

Arthur Schopenhauer rejected Hegel's idea of the state as the divine expression of justice. For him the state exists because there is injustice; the state is needed to protect man against the effects of his own egotism. In turn, man's egotism and his generally evil nature are a reflection of the dissonances of the Will that for Schopenhauer lies behind the world's realities. Under these conditions war is inevitable, but Schopenhauer, unlike Hegel, did not see war as a progressive factor in history but as a result of the immaturity and weakness of the masses and the love of luxury and power of their strong-willed leaders. Schopenhauer saw no hope of lasting peace.

THE MILITARISTS. Friedrich Nietzsche may be judged as an extreme representative of the romantic cult of war and as marking the transition to modern totalitarian militarism. Nietzsche was capable of deploring the wastefulness of war; however, in his fully mature writings, *Thus Spake Zarathustra* (1892) and *The Will to Power* (first published in 1901), he glorified war and the dangerous life. The phrase "a good war hallows every cause" (*Thus Spake Zarathustra*), may be taken as typical of this attitude. For Nietzsche's supermen war is a natural activity, the supreme witness to their superior quality; they should never succumb to the "slave morality" of Christianity, with its accent on humility, submissiveness, and turning the other cheek.

In the teaching of Heinrich von Treitschke the functions of the state were unlimited, as was the individual's duty to submit to its commands. The state's first duty was to maintain its power in its relations with other states and to maintain law within its own borders; its second duty was the conduct of war, the crucible in which the elements in a state's greatness are fused. The hope of a world state or permanent peace is vain; the Aryan race can only keep by the sword what it has won by the sword. Treitschke admitted that the cost of war had risen steeply and, hence, that wars should be shorter and less frequent. But this did not affect the basic axiom that war is the "one remedy for an ailing nation."

Treitschke's ideas were absorbed by the German military writer Friedrich von Bernhardi, who used them to foster the militantly nationalist mood in which Germany entered World War I. In *Germany and the Next War*, Bernhardi repeated the basic notions of Treitschke: War is the process by which the truly civilized nations express their strength and vitality, life is an unending struggle for survival, war is an instrument in biological evolution. And Bernhardi drew on other conservative writers: Heraclitus; Frederick the Great, whose writings represented war as bringing out man's finest qualities; and Karl von Clausewitz, who described the nation's place in the world as a function of the interplay between its national character and its military tradition.

The conservative-militarist tradition, with its racist overtones, was inherited by the German Nazi and Italian fascist writers of the interwar period, though these added little to the work of their forebears. More recently, the advent of nuclear weapons has made nonsense of the glorification of war, though belief in its inevitability is still not uncommon. Almost the only considerable section of contemporary opinion that believes that national survival after nuclear war is conceivable is that of the Chinese communists. Even they, however, are careful to insist that they would never initiate a nuclear war, and it is, moreover, a feature of all communist thought that the final global victory of communism will remove all cause of war. Communists therefore differ from the conservatives we have considered in that although they regard war as contingent (or perhaps inevitable) in a capitalist system, they have no doubt that permanent peace is attainable under communism.

THE ABOLITIONISTS

THE PREMODERN AGE. As we have seen, the ancient Greeks (and the same may be said of the writers of the Roman world) were not distinguished for protests against war, though the Stoics of the Roman Empire preached a cosmopolitanism that assumed the oneness of all humankind, making war between its members an affront. When Stoicism was embraced by the Roman emperors, however, it lost its pacifist element, and the same may be said for the early Christian doctrine of nonviolence. Also, during the Middle Ages the fact that the papacy was both the supreme fount of church doctrine and a temporal power of considerable military strength ruled out complete pacifism as a church doctrine.

The outstanding opponent of war during the Renaissance was the great humanist Desiderius Erasmus, though it is incorrect to speak of him as an absolute pacifist. In his *Anti-polemus, or the Plea of Reason, Religion and Humanity against War* (1510), Erasmus argued that every man's duty was to spare no pains to put an end to war. War was directly opposed to every purpose for which Erasmus conceived man to have been created; man is born not for destruction but for love, friendship, and service to his fellow men.

PROJECTS FOR EUROPEAN PEACE. During the seventeenth century speculation in Europe about the possibility of permanent peace began to develop, stimulated by growing international commerce and the desire to bind Europe together in a final effort to expel the Turks. This anti-Muslim aim had already figured prominently in the plan for the unification of Europe designed by Pierre Dubois in *De Recuperatione Terre Sancte* (1305–1307) and in the celebrated proposal for a federation of Christian princes that George of Poděbrad, king of Bohemia, had presented to his fellow monarchs in 1461. The seventeenth-century proposals were immensely varied, ranging from utterly Utopian ideas to some that might have achieved realization as limited international alliances. Some were limited to Western Europe, others included all Europe, and some embraced the whole Christian world. "The Grand Design" (1620–1635), probably compiled by the duke of Sully, the chief minister of Henry IV of France, and *Some Reasons for an European State* (1710) by John Bellers both proposed to divide Europe into provinces of roughly equal size under a common government. A few schemes, such as Emeric Cruce's *The New Cyneas, or Discourse of the Occasion and Means to Establish a General Peace and the Liberty of Commerce throughout the World* (1623), aimed at the formation of a single world state with all the races and religions under its jurisdiction. In these plans provision was generally made for some form of representative government. William Penn in *An Essay towards the Present and Future Peace of Europe* (1693) contemplated annual European parliaments; the Abbé de Saint-Pierre in *A Project for Settling an Everlasting Peace in Europe* (1713) preferred a perpetual congress in order to reflect the viewpoints of the states in his European federation; Cruce called for world assemblies. These confederations were chiefly advocated as defenses of peace, though other aims were also mentioned; Henry IV and the duke of Sully, for instance, had in mind, besides European peace, wars against the Muscovites and Turks and the weakening of the Hapsburgs as the preliminary steps to uniting Europe under French hegemony.

In the eighteenth century these peace plans were given a new lease of life with the French and German Enlightenment. Jean-Jacques Rousseau took the peace project of the Abbé de Saint-Pierre and applied it to the Europe of his own day in *A Project of Perpetual Peace* (1761), with the insistence that unless the proposed central authority was powerful enough to overawe all the constituent states, the proposal would fail. Rousseau recommended the plan to governments on the ground that a single European authority strong enough to enforce peace would also ensure internal stability in the constituent states. He admitted, however, that governments were probably too shortsighted to appreciate the merits of the plan. A similar project of European confederation was that of Immanuel Kant, titled *Eternal Peace* (1795). Kant's recipe is notable for its claim that the maintenance of peace requires the achievement of constitutional government by the states.

NINETEENTH-CENTURY PEACE MOVEMENTS. The nineteenth century was even more prolific in its plans for organizing the nations to ensure peace. In Europe and the United States there arose strong unofficial peace movements that urged the creation of agencies for the arbitration of interstate differences and the equitable settlement of political issues, together with the strengthening and codification of international law. In the atmosphere of harmony that followed the Congress of Vienna the Great Powers of Europe met regularly to deal with threats to peace, while such functional organizations as the European river commissions and the Universal Postal Union (1875) dealt quietly with matters of practical concern to the nations. The hope of a permanent international assembly that might develop into a world legislature was held out at the Hague conferences of 1899 and 1907, and it seemed likely that the growing stake of nations in peaceful intercourse would soon render war obsolete.

The English utilitarians, such as Jeremy Bentham, James Mill, and John Stuart Mill, provided much of the theoretical background of the peace movements. They contended that war was an anachronistic encumbrance on a free society, benefiting no one but aristocrats and professional soldiers. Richard Cobden voiced the commercial classes' distaste for war in his pamphlet *Russia*

(1836). Herbert Spencer, an extreme exponent of laissez-faire society, denounced war in his *Social Statics* (1851) as an outcome of excessive government authority; with the functions of government reduced and individual liberty restored, all reason for war would disappear. This liberal, economic case for peace culminated in the striking claim by Norman Angell in *The Great Illusion* (1908) that war had become so destructive of all economic values that nations would never again engage in it.

PACIFICISM AND INTERNATIONALISM. World War I disastrously falsified Angell's prophecy; nevertheless, it reinforced the conviction of liberal-minded people that war was an absolute evil and that the creation of expedients to keep the peace, such as the League of Nations and collective security, was the most urgent task of the twentieth century. A strong cleavage now became apparent between absolute pacifists—for example, H. M. Swanwick, Gerald Heard, Aldous Huxley—and those who supported "just" wars fought under the league's aegis—for example, Gilbert Murray, Lord Cecil of Chelwood, P. J. Noel-Baker. Few of the abolitionists, however, considered a world federation necessary to ensure permanent peace. John Dewey, for instance, argued in the 1920s that it would be sufficient for states to agree to declare war illegal and to prosecute countries that resorted to it as criminals.

The advent of World War II and the invention of nuclear weapons, followed by the failure of the great powers to act unanimously in the United Nations Security Council, raised the question whether the abolitionists' aim can be attained short of the total surrender of national sovereignty. One curious effect of the nuclear stalemate has been to drive many abolitionists into the somewhat conservative belief that peace must be kept by the maintenance of a military balance between the two world camps. Others, like John Strachey in *On the Prevention of War* (London, 1962), contend that the two superpowers must go beyond this and exercise a kind of condominium over the rest of the world.

The outstanding British philosopher Bertrand Russell continued to believe that the rational conviction of the utter futility of nuclear war can in itself maintain peace provided that the realities of thermonuclear war are widely enough publicized (*Common Sense and Nuclear Warfare*, London, 1959). As a long-term measure, however, Russell saw no alternative to a world state, which must in the first instance be imposed by one nation or group of nations; only after the world authority has been in power for a century or so will it feel confident enough to base its power on consent rather than force (*New Hopes for a Changing World,* London, 1951, p. 77). It is not clear, however, whether Russell really wished to pay the price of global despotism in return for peace; elsewhere, he wrote that a new war would be preferable to a universal communist empire (Robert E. Egner and Lester E. Denonn, eds., *The Basic Writings of Bertrand Russell,* London, 1961, p. 691). Here, in essence, is the issue facing the abolitionist in the nuclear age; whether war is a greater or lesser evil than the imposition on himself and his nation of hostile values which the present anarchic world, with its attendant threat of war, allows him to keep at a distance.

See also Bentham, Jeremy; Dante Alighieri; Dewey, John; Enlightenment; Erasmus, Desiderius; Grotius, Hugo; Hegel, Georg Wilhelm Friedrich; Heraclitus of Ephesus; Hobbes, Thomas; Just War Theory; Kant, Immanuel; Locke, John; Machiavelli, Niccolò; Mill, James; Mill, John Stuart; More, Thomas; Nationalism; Nietzsche, Friedrich; Pacifism; Plato; Renaissance; Rousseau, Jean-Jacques; Russell, Bertrand Arthur William; Schopenhauer, Arthur; Spinoza, Benedict (Baruch) de; Stoicism; Suárez, Francisco; Thomas Aquinas, St.; Violence.

Bibliography

The following are sources for some of the views discussed above.

CONSERVATIVES

Bernhardi, Friedrich von. *Germany and the Next War.* Translated by Allen H. Powles. London: E. Arnold, 1914.

Clausewitz, Karl von. *On War.* Translated by J. J. Graham. London: K. Paul, Trench, Trubner, 1940.

Guthrie, W. K. C. *A History of Greek Philosophy,* Vol. I. Cambridge, U.K.: Cambridge University Press, 1962. Ch. 7 contains quotations from Heraclitus.

Hegel, Georg Wilhelm Friedrich. *Hegel's Philosophy of Right.* Translated by T. M. Knox. Oxford: Clarendon Press, 1942. Especially pp. 209–223.

Hobbes, Thomas. *Leviathan.* Edited by Michael Oakeshott. Oxford: Blackwell, 1960. Especially Ch. 13.

Schopenhauer, Arthur. *The World as Will and Idea.* Translated by R. B. Haldane and J. Kemp, 3 vols. London, 1909. Especially Vol. III, Ch. 46.

Spinoza, Benedict de. *The Political Works.* Edited by A. G. Wernham. Oxford: Clarendon Press, 1958. Especially p. 23.

Thomas Aquinas. *Selected Political Writings.* Edited by A. Passerin d'Entrèves. Oxford: Blackwell, 1959. Especially pp. 159–161.

Treitschke, Heinrich von. *Politics.* Translated by Blanche Dugdale and Torbende Bille, 2 vols. London, 1916. Especially Vol. I, pp. 61–70.

ABOLITIONISTS

Dewey, John. *Characters and Events,* 2 vols. New York: Holt, 1929. Vol. II, p. 670.

Kant, Immanuel. *Eternal Peace.* Translated by W. Hastie. Boston, 1944.

Rousseau, Jean-Jacques. *A Project of Perpetual Peace.* Translated by Edith M. Nuttall. London: R. Cobden-Sanderson, 1927.

SECONDARY SOURCES

Adams, Robert P. *The Better Part of Valor: More, Erasmus, Colet and Vives, on Humanism, War, and Peace.* Seattle: University of Washington Press, 1962.

Aron, Raymond. *Paix et guerre entre les nations.* Paris: Calmann-Lévy, 1962. A sociological and historical inquiry into the conditions in international relations that make for war and peace, together with an assessment of proposals for maintaining international equilibrium.

Beales, A. C. F. *The History of Peace.* London, 1931. A survey of movements, predominantly unofficial, for the promotion of world peace since the creation of the first "peace societies" in 1815. The book includes some useful chapters on nineteenth-and early-twentieth-century ideas on the maintenance of peace.

Hemleben, S. J. *Plans for World Peace through Six Centuries.* Chicago: University of Chicago Press, 1943. A handy abstract of famous plans for the maintenance of peace since the late Middle Ages.

McDonald, L. C. *Western Political Theory in the Modern World.* New York, 1962. A useful survey of modern Western political ideas, including thinking on war and peace; the book deals with both secular trends and individual thinkers.

Meinecke, Friedrich. *Machiavellism: The Doctrine of Raison d'État and Its Place in Modern History.* Translated by Douglas Scott. London, 1957. A translation of *Die Idee der Staatsräson in der neueren Geschichte* (1924), a treatise on the perennial conflict between the power impulse in human nature and the search for a higher ethical rule in political relations.

Stawell, F. M. *The Growth of International Thought.* London: Butterworth, 1929. A concise history of pacifism and internationalism.

Vagts, Alfred. *A History of Militarism.* New York: Norton, 1937. Mainly a study of the ideas and practices of the eighteenth-and nineteenth-century European social movements that sought to make military men the dominant power in the state.

F. S. Northedge (1967)

PEACE, WAR, AND PHILOSOPHY [ADDENDUM]

The nuclear threat that preoccupied Bertrand Russell receded into the background during the Vietnam War. After that war's end in 1975, the risk of a nuclear confrontation between the superpowers again became a major concern.

This issue came in for sustained moral analysis in Douglas Lackey's *Moral Principles and Nuclear Weapons* (1984) and Steven P. Lee's *Morality, Prudence, and Nuclear Weapons* (1993). But considerable philosophical interest focused more narrowly on so-called paradoxes of nuclear deterrence. Herman Kahn had spoken of "rationality of irrationality" strategies in *On Thermonuclear War* (1960). The question was whether it is rational to threaten to do the irrational (wage all-out nuclear war). The strategy of Mutual Assured Destruction (MAD) seemed to presuppose that it is, since it rested on the threat of massive retaliation in the event of a major nuclear first-strike. The moral version of the paradox, explored by Gregory S. Kavka in *Moral Paradoxes of Nuclear Deterrence* (1987), concerns whether it is moral to threaten to do the immoral (wage all-out nuclear war). This interest, and concern with the nuclear issue generally, waned with the end of the cold war following the collapse of the Soviet Union in the early 1990s.

Meanwhile, the 1960s saw a resurgence of interest in the just war theory, with both religious and secular attention to the doctrine extending into the twenty-first century. The religious approach had both Roman Catholic and Protestant advocates. Theologian Paul Ramsey set the tone for the Protestant approach in *War and the Christian Conscience: How Shall Modern War Be Conducted Justly?* (1961) and *The Just War: Force and Political Responsibility* (1968). The American Catholic Bishops detailed the Catholic position in their 1983 pastoral letter, *The Challenge of Peace: God's Promise and Our Responsibility*. An influential secular contribution appeared with political scientist Michael Walzer's *Just and Unjust Wars* (1977), in which a Hobbesian approach to political theory was adapted to the moral assessment of war. Philosophers quickly took up the issue of just war, particularly after the 1991 Persian Gulf War in which the United States under President George H. W. Bush expressly invoked the just war theory in defense of the U.S.-led war to drive Iraq out of Kuwait.

Just war theorists include both conservatives and abolitionists. Some regard war as virtually inevitable. They seek to ensure that it is undertaken only when justified and that its destructiveness is minimized. Others believe that war may eventually be done away with, but in the meantime, they believe, the moral criteria justifying resort to war and its conduct must be followed.

Set apart from just war theorists are pacifists, who believe that war, at least in the modern world, cannot be justified morally. Duane L. Cady provides a conceptual analysis of pacifism in *From Warism to Pacifism: A Moral Continuum* (1989). While theoretically one could be a "just war pacifist," holding that the just war theory contains the correct criteria for morally assessing war but maintaining that those criteria are never in fact met, most pacifists believe that just war criteria are inadequate, and that even if they are satisfied, they do not suffice to justify war. In particular, they reject the resort to the principle of double effect that would justify the foreseeable killing of innocents so long as it is not intentional and other conditions are met.

With the resurgence of feminism in the 1960s, some feminist philosophers took up the issue of war. While rarely strict pacifists, they tended to be abolitionists and to argue that war is a manifestation of patriarchal society and can be done away with only with the transformation of that society into one of gender equality. In particular, many of them, such as Sara Ruddick in *Maternal Thinking: Toward a Politics of Peace* (1989), see the key to a new way of thinking about war and violence in the distinctive experiences of women, particularly in mothering and caregiving.

RIGHTS AND SOVEREIGNTY

As the modern nation-state system began forming in the seventeenth century, the notion of the equality of states and their right to be free of interference in their internal affairs by other states eventually became the recognized (though not always honored) norm. The treatment of persons within a state's own borders was generally considered its own business. Toward the end of the twentieth century, there was wider acceptance of the idea that states could violate the sovereignty of other states if necessary to prevent crimes such as genocide and massacres of individuals within those states' borders. In the 1990s, genocide in Rwanda and so-called ethnic cleansing in the former Yugoslavia commanded particular attention in this regard. This presented philosophers and experts on international law with a challenge to show either that, properly understood, international law already allows such actions or that it could be modified to make room for them.

Thus, the world government that Russell proposed presents a challenge to state sovereignty from one direction, threatening to eliminate the plurality of independent sovereign states. The idea of unilateral military intervention for humanitarian reasons presents a challenge from a different direction, retaining the plurality of states but making their sovereignty conditional upon their honoring of human rights.

Additionally, so-called low intensity conflicts and the rise of terrorism brought conceptual issues to the forefront. With the declared wars characteristic of the first half of the twentieth century receding into the past, even standard war itself, in the sense of vast armies arrayed against one another, may be phasing out. In its place, the twenty-first century is seeing terrorism, violence, guerrilla warfare, and flexible, far-reaching military actions, such as by the United States in Afghanistan and Iraq. Whether these represent new forms of war or a twenty-first-century substitute for war is a conceptual issue that philosophers and international lawyers have yet to decide. The challenge of peace, in any event, is to find nonviolent ways of dealing with the conflicts leading to these various forms of violence.

See also Feminist Philosophy; Just War Theory; Pacifism; Rights; Russell, Bertrand Arthur William; Sovereignty; Terrorism; Violence.

Bibliography

Cady, Duane L. *From Warism to Pacifism: A Moral Continuum.* Philadelphia: Temple University Press, 1989.

Chatterjee, Deen K., and Don E. Scheid, eds. *Ethics and Foreign Intervention.* Cambridge, U.K.: Cambridge University Press, 2003.

Cohen, Avner, and Steven Lee, eds. *Nuclear Weapons and the Future of Humanity: The Fundamental Questions.* Totowa, NJ: Rowman & Allenheld, 1986.

Christopher, Paul. *The Ethics of War & Peace: An Introduction to Legal and Moral Issues.* 3rd ed. Upper Saddle River, NJ: Pearson/Prentice Hall, 2004.

Elshtain, Jean Bethke, ed. *Just War Theory.* New York: New York University Press, 1992.

Elshtain, Jean Bethke, and Sheila Tobias, ed. *Women, Militarism, and War: Essays in History, Politics, and Social Theory.* Savage, MD: Rowman & Littlefield, 1990.

Gallie, W. B. *Philosophers of Peace and War: Kant, Clausewitz, Marx, Engels and Tolstoy.* Cambridge, U.K.: Cambridge University Press, 1978.

Gray, J. Glenn. *The Warriors: Reflections on Men in Battle.* New York: Harper & Row, 1967.

Holmes, Robert L. *On War and Morality.* Princeton, NJ: Princeton University Press, 1989.

Johnson, James Turner. *Morality and Contemporary Warfare.* New Haven, CT: Yale University Press, 1999.

Kahn, Herman. *On Thermonuclear War.* Princeton, NJ: Princeton University Press, 1960.

Kavka, Gregory S. *Moral Paradoxes of Nuclear Deterrence.* Cambridge, U.K.: Cambridge University Press, 1987.

Lackey, Douglas. *Moral Principles and Nuclear Weapons.* Totowa, NJ: Rowman & Allanheld, 1984.

Lee, Steven P. *Morality, Prudence, and Nuclear Weapons.* Cambridge, U.K.: Cambridge University Press, 1993.

Norman, Richard. *Ethics, Killing, and War.* Cambridge, U.K.: Cambridge University Press, 1995.

Ramsey, Paul. *The Just War: Force and Political Responsibility.* New York: Scribner, 1968.

Ramsey, Paul. *War and the Christian Conscience: How Shall Modern War Be Conducted Justly?* Durham, NC: Duke University Press, 1961.

Ruddick, Sara. *Maternal Thinking: Toward a Politics of Peace.* Boston: Beacon Press, 1989.

Sterba, James P., ed. *The Ethics of War and Nuclear Deterrence.* Belmont, CA: Wadsworth, 1985.

Walzer, Michael. *Just and Unjust Wars.* New York: Basic Books, 1977.

Wasserstrom, Richard A., ed. *War and Morality.* Belmont, CA: Wadsworth, 1970.

Robert L. Holmes (2005)

PEANO, GIUSEPPE
(1858–1932)

Giuseppe Peano, an Italian mathematician and logician, was a professor of mathematics at the University of Turin from 1890 to 1932 and also taught at the military academy in Turin from 1886 to 1901. In 1891 he founded the *Rivista di matematica,* which was later also published in French (*Revue de mathématique*) and in Interlingua (an international language developed from Latino sine flexione, an auxiliary language based on Latin), which Peano propounded in 1903. In 1898 Peano acquired a small printing establishment in Turin, and he soon became an accomplished printer; his skill seems to have been of help to him in the process of simplifying logico-mathematical symbolism.

Peano's contributions to mathematics include the first statement of vector calculus (*Elementi di calcolo geometrico,* Turin, 1891) and the first example of integration by successive approximations within the theory of ordinary differential equations; with the single hypothesis that the data were continuous he proved the existence of the integrals of such equations. He submitted to rigorous criticism the foundations of arithmetic, of projective geometry, and of the general theory of sets. Peano's postulates (1899) were a set of five postulates for the arithmetic of natural numbers that allowed arithmetic to be constructed as a hypothetical-deductive system. In 1882 Peano first arrived at the principle that rigorous language can be separated from ordinary language both within and without mathematics. As Bertrand Russell wrote, Peano's method "extended the region of mathematical precision backwards towards regions which had been given over to philosophical disagreement" ("My Mental Development," in *The Philosophy of Bertrand Russell,* Paul A. Schilpp, ed., Evanston, IL, 1951, p. 11).

In 1890 Peano introduced the use of iota and inverted iota to distinguish a one-member class from its member, which permitted him to overcome previous confusion between ∈ ("being a member of"), ⊃ ("contained in"), and = ("equal to"). In general, Peano showed the importance of distinguishing the properties of a class from those of the individuals of that class, a need shown, for example, by his "sophism" (actually, a paralogism): "Peter and Paul are apostles; the apostles are twelve; therefore Peter and Paul are twelve."

Peano's work in mathematical logic is to be found in his "Formulario completo," which includes, among other items, the well-known *Formulaire de mathématiques,* a compendium of mathematics derived from a set of postulates by means of a new notation. The "Formulario," in its encyclopedic, high-level approach, anticipated the thorough expositions of Bourbakism. In using a notation at least as rigorous as those of C. S. Peirce and Gottlob Frege, and more comprehensive and expedient than theirs, Peano's work marked a transition from the old algebra of logic to contemporary methods. His notation is still partially in use, mainly through its adoption by Russell and A. N. Whitehead in *Principia Mathematica.*

After 1913 Peano ceased to follow developments in symbolic logic. He regarded as artificial Russell's interpretation of numbers as classes of classes. Peano made several hints concerning the need for analyzing the relation of formal language to ordinary language, but he was not himself interested in undertaking such analysis. A philosophical interpretation of some of Peano's techniques is to be found in the work of his pupil Giovanni Vailati, who pointed out the general importance of Peano's discoveries concerning recursiveness, implicit definitions, and the theory of postulates. The "Formulario completo," however, still offers suggestions for research.

See also Computability Theory; Frege, Gottlob; Logic, History of: Modern Logic; Mathematics, Foundations of; Peirce, Charles Sanders; Russell, Bertrand Arthur William; Vailati, Giovanni; Whitehead, Alfred North.

Bibliography

WORKS BY PEANO

Opere scelte. 3 vols, edited by Ugo Cassina. Rome: Edizioni Cremonese, 1957–1959. Includes much of what is referred to as the "Formulario completo": The 5 vols. below, plus minor publications of 1888–1913.

Formulaire de mathématiques. Vol. I, Turin: Bocca Frères, Ch. Clausen, 1894; Vol. II, in 3 parts, Turin, 1897–1899; Vol. III, Paris, 1901.

Formulaire mathématique. Vol. IV. Turin, 1903.

Formulario mathematico. Vol. V. Turin, 1905–1908. In Latino sine flexione.

WORKS ON PEANO

Cassina, Ugo. "L'oeuvre philosophique de Giuseppe Peano." *Revue de métaphysique et de morale* 40 (4) (1933): 481–491.

Cassina, Ugo. "Vita et opera de Giuseppe Peano." *Schola et Vita* 7 (3) (1932): 117–148. In Interlingua.

Couturat, Louis. "La logique mathématique de M. Peano." *Revue de métaphysique et de morale* 7 (4) (1899): 616–646.

Jourdain, P. E. B. "Giuseppe Peano." *Quarterly Journal of Pure and Applied Mathematics* 43 (1912): 270–314.

Russell, Bertrand. *The Principles of Mathematics.* Cambridge, U.K.: Cambridge University Press, 1903.

Stamm, E. "Józef Peano." *Wiadomości Matematyczne* 36 (1933): 1–56.

Terracini, Alessandro, ed. *In memoria di Giuseppe Peano.* Cuneo, 1955. Essays by various authors.

Ferruccio Rossi-Landi (1967)

PEARSON, KARL
(1857–1936)

Karl Pearson, a British scientist and philosopher of science, was born in London. He studied mathematics at King's College, Cambridge, where he became acquainted with James Clerk Maxwell, Sir George Stokes, and Isaac Todhunter and developed an interest in history, religion, and philosophy. He became a fellow of his college in 1880 and also studied law at Heidelberg and Berlin. Although he was called to the bar in 1881, he never practiced law. In 1884, at the age of twenty-seven, he was appointed to the chair of applied mathematics and mechanics at University College, London, a post that he held until 1911. For part of this time he also held a lectureship in geometry at Gresham College, London, where he developed his ideas in the philosophy of science for a popular audience. Through his friend Francis Galton he became interested in statistical problems in the biological sciences, helped to lay the foundations of modern statistical theory and biometry, and, in 1901, with Galton and Weldon, founded the journal *Biometrika.* In 1896 he was elected a fellow of the Royal Society and in 1911 he was appointed to the new chair of eugenics at University College. Pearson was an enthusiastic socialist and humanist. He retired in 1933 and died three years later.

Pearson published many scientific papers, as well as essays on most of the subjects in which he was interested. His philosophical work is contained mainly in *The Grammar of Science* (1892) and *The Ethic of Freethought* (1888), a collection of essays and lectures. He is usually regarded as an important early figure in modern positivism, but his contribution in this field has perhaps been overrated. Much of his work derives from that of Ernst Mach.

He accepted and developed Mach's sensationalist, antimetaphysical standpoint, but he was not afraid to talk with approval of "a sound idealism" replacing "the crude materialism" of earlier physics. His concern was to emphasize the social background of science and to urge that good citizenship demanded the application of the scientific habit of mind to everyday living. He appears to have regarded this as a large part of the justification of scientific activity, but he also held that science "justifies itself in its methods." Like Mach he dwelt on "the unity of science," which depends upon its method rather than upon its material. This method, based as it is upon verification, rules out metaphysics. The metaphysician is a poet, who does no harm so long as he is recognized as such, but he is often taken to be something more. According to Pearson, an acceptable moral theory is more likely to develop from the experiments of the biologist than from the speculations of the philosopher.

He saw scientific laws as brief formulas representing complex relationships between many phenomena. Their "discovery" is the work of a creative but disciplined imagination; they are products of the human mind. Following Lloyd Morgan, he said that an external object is a construct; that is, "a combination of immediate with past or stored sense-impressions." He asserted, mysteriously and unsatisfactorily, that the distinction between real objects and imaginary ones is that only the real objects depend upon immediate sense impressions.

A fundamental distinction in his work is that between perception, the "physical association" of stored sense impressions, and conception, their "mental association." This appears to mean that perception is merely the copresentation of impressions, while conception is the "recognition" of relations. But the physical and the psychical differ only in degree, not in kind, because both physics and psychology deal with relations between sense impressions, although from different standpoints. On the whole, human brains work in the same way, and thus one receives the same sense impressions and forms the same constructs as another. This ensures the universal validity of science. The field of study of the various sciences is, in fact, immediate sense impressions; these are the phenomena that scientific laws relate, so that "the field of science is much more consciousness than an external world." The consciousness of others is established by an argument from analogy.

We tend to project our sense impressions and to regard them as existing externally to and independently of ourselves, but this is a mistake. The distinction between external and internal is arbitrary and no more than a practical convenience. It is based on distinguishing between classes of sense impressions, not between sense impressions and something else. We cannot assert the existence of causes of sense impressions, but Pearson wanted to leave open the possibility of such existents. He therefore used the term *sensation* in an unusual way: Sensation is "that of which the only knowable side is sense-impression." This is intended to express agnosticism about the causation of sense impressions while allowing him to say, "The outer world is for science a world of sensations, and sensation is known to us only as sense-impression."

Some scientific concepts are not of immediate sense impressions; for instance, atom and molecule. There are just two possibilities: Scientists may regard the atom as real and thus capable of being a direct sense impression, or as ideal and thus merely a "mental conception assisting them in formulating laws." In contrast, a metaphysical conception is of what is both real and independent of sense perception.

Pearson concluded that science is not explanatory but merely descriptive. For instance, Isaac Newton's law of gravitation is a description in the simplest possible terms of a wide range of phenomena; that is, of the "routine" of our perceptions. To talk of it as ruling nature is to confuse other senses of "law" with the scientific sense. Causal statements are records of regular sequences in past experience and cannot assert any necessity in them. Using Humean arguments, Pearson held that forces, because they are not discoverable in sense experience, cannot be regarded as causes. "Force" is but a name hiding our ignorance of the explanation of motion. The idea of necessity is appropriate only to relations between conceptions, not to relations between perceptions. Prediction and knowledge are possible only because we find repetition in our sense impressions. Even so, our knowledge is only probable and should, strictly speaking, be called "belief."

The whole of science involves the distinction between the perceptual and the conceptual. Scientific concepts generally are ideal limits of concepts originating in perception. This is especially obvious in the mathematical treatment of the world. Empirical space and time are "modes of perception." Space is "a mental expression for the fact that the perceptive faculty has separated coexisting sense impressions into groups of associated impressions"; time indicates "the progression of perceptions at a position in space." Neither space nor time is infinite or infinitely divisible, since each must be limited by our powers of perception and discrimination. Conceptual space and time, and the space and time of mathematics, are idealizations of their empirical counterparts and do not suffer from their limitations.

The aim of science is to construct conceptual models of the universe, devices to assist us in describing the correlation and sequence of phenomena. The failure to recognize this has led scientists to accept definitions of force, mass, atom, and—in the biological sciences—life that are riddled with metaphysical obscurities. Much of Pearson's philosophical writing consists in the empiricist elucidation of these fundamental concepts, in an attempt to remove these obscurities.

See also Belief; Mach, Ernst; Maxwell, James Clerk; Morgan, C. Lloyd; Newton, Isaac; Philosophy of Science, History of; Positivism; Scientific Method; Space; Time.

Bibliography

Pearson's main philosophical work is *The Grammar of Science* (London, 1892). The second edition (1900) contained two new chapters. The third (1911) contained only the first eight chapters (physical sciences) of the first two editions but had a new chapter on causation and a new final chapter on modern physical ideas, written largely by E. Cunningham. The Everyman edition (London, 1937) contains a more detailed account of the various editions.

Other works by Pearson are *The Ethic of Freethought, a Selection of Essays and Lectures* (London: Unwin, 1888; and London: A. and C. Black, 1901); *The Chances of Death and Other Studies in Evolution* (London: Arnold, 1897), a volume of essays and lectures; *National Life from the Standpoint of Science* (London: A. and C. Black, 1901); and *The Life, Letters and Labours of Francis Galton*, 3 vols. (Cambridge, U.K.: Cambridge University Press, 1914–1930).

Pearson edited and completed Isaac Todhunter, *A History of the Theory of Elasticity and of the Strength of Materials from Galilei to the Present Time*, 2 vols. Cambridge, U.K.: Cambridge University Press, 1886–1893), and W. K. Clifford, *Common Sense of the Exact Sciences* (New York: Appleton, 1885), for which he wrote the chapter "Position" and much of "Quantity" and "Motion."

Works on Pearson include V. I. Lenin, *Materialism and Empirio-Criticism*, translated by A. Finchberg (Moscow, 1937); G. M. Morant, *A Bibliography of the Statistical and Other Writings of Karl Pearson* (London: Biometrika Office, University College, 1939); E. S. Pearson, "Karl Pearson, an Appreciation of Some Aspects of His Life and Work," in *Biometrika* 27 (1936): 193–257, and 29 (1937): 161–248; C. S. Peirce, *Collected Papers* (Cambridge, MA: Harvard University Press, 1931–1958), passim, but especially Vol. VIII, which contains a long review of *The Grammar of Science*; and G. U. Yule and L. N. G. Filon, "Karl Pearson," in *Obituary Notices of Fellows of the Royal Society*, Vol. II (London, 1936–1938), pp. 73–110.

For reviews of *The Grammar of Science*, see those by C. G. K. (probably C. G. Knott) in *Nature* 46 (1892): 97–99, with replies by Pearson on pp. 199 and 247; by F. A. D. (of 2nd ed.) in *Nature* 62 (1900): 49–50; by E. A. Singer Jr. (of 2nd ed.) in *Philosophical Review* 9 (1900): 448–450; and an unsigned review in *Mind*, n.s., 1 (1892): 429–430.

There are numerous casual references to Pearson's views in books on the philosophy of science but few detailed discussions.

Peter Alexander (1967)

PECKHAM, JOHN
(c. 1225–1292)

John Peckham, or Pecham, the English philosopher and theologian, and defender of Augustinian doctrines, was born in Patcham, near Brighton, Sussex. Educated at the monastery at Lewes, he continued his studies at Oxford and Paris, and sometime during the 1250s he joined the Franciscan friars at Oxford. Subsequently he became a master of theology in Paris in 1269 and returned to Oxford in 1272. Peckham was provincial of the English Franciscans from 1275 to 1277 and then lectured at the papal court for two years. In 1279 he was appointed archbishop of Canterbury and held this office until his death.

Peckham's philosophical career represents a concentrated effort to counteract the growing allegiance to Aristotle through a return to the thought of Augustine. There seems little doubt that he was motivated to take this stand by the Lenten sermons of St. Bonaventure, who in the late 1260s had alerted his friars to the growth of heterodox Aristotelianism—which was apparent, for example, in the work of Siger of Brabant. Peckham did not reject all philosophy that stemmed from Greek and Arabic sources—as a matter of fact, he systematically used Aristotelian terminology—but his approach was a highly selective use of non-Christian philosophers to the extent that their works could be made to harmonize with the thought of Augustine. Among the disciples of Peckham who perpetuated this attitude were Matthew of Acquasparta, Roger Marston, and, later, Vital du Four.

Peckham's theory of knowledge shows the persistence of a special type of apriorism in the Franciscan school of this period. Clues to this apriorism are to be found in the *Summa* of Alexander of Hales, which taught that the human intellect is incapable of a satisfactory a posteriori analysis of the first principles or of the most basic "perceptibles," such as time and space. Similarly, Augustine said: "If we both see that which you say to be true, and both see that which I say to be true, where, I ask you, do we see it? Neither I in you, nor you in me, but both in the unchangeable Truth itself, which is above our minds" (*Confessions* XII.24). Peckham concludes that more is required for the operation of the intellect than mere sensation that "contacts" accidents but does not reach the essence of things.

Even granting the intellect's power of abstracting essences, Peckham says that the mind does this either knowingly or unknowingly. If knowingly, then the mind knows before abstracting, and hence it is useless to abstract. If unknowingly, then the mind is at the mercy of chance and can hardly be called an intellect at all. Consequently, the intellect is not a passive Aristotelian tabula rasa, but a beam moving outward and casting its light on things. However, this explanation is not sufficient because in matters of intellectual knowledge, certitude, and evidence, man must be assisted by a divine illumination—a divine active intellect—in addition to his own human active intellect. This assistance by divine illumination is not a direct vision of God or an infusion of ideas. Rather, it is an assistance over and above that given by God as the conserving cause of all that exists. Its purpose is to guarantee necessity and certitude (considered irrevocably unobtainable through sensation) for our knowledge.

In the realm of natural theology, there was one key axiom that pervaded Franciscan philosophical circles in Peckham's time—that creatures are entirely dependent upon the First Cause with regard both to the fact of existing and to their ability to act. From this it follows that whatever causal powers a creature may possess are ontologically delegated to it by the First Cause. The important corollary of this principle is that the First Cause can bypass the agency of the creature and intervene to produce the effect immediately. Peckham invokes this principle to some extent in the illumination theory of knowledge. He also uses it to defend the autonomous existibility of prime matter without any form against the contrary opinion of Thomas Aquinas.

Peckham also took rather strong exception to Thomas's opinion that no single thing ever has more than one form. All medieval philosophers were agreed that the First Cause was pure form and that prime matter was completely formless. Against Thomas, Peckham and his confreres held that in each thing there are many forms, or at least many grades of one form. The dispute soon fossilized into two schools—the Dominicans and the Franciscans—and as often as not their arguments generated more heat than light. In any case, Peckham held that in humanity there are several forms—vegetative, sensitive, and rational—in a gradated order that cooperates toward the good and unity of the being as a whole.

John Peckham's career represents a sincere effort to perpetuate and to update the doctrines of Augustine. He suffered much distress as archbishop of Canterbury when, as a stubborn defender of Augustine, he incurred the wrath of the equally stubborn Dominican defenders of Thomas.

Many of the points that were merely hinted at in Peckham's philosophy were taken up by his disciples and elaborated in full-length treatises. A final judgment of this English Franciscan must await the publication of many of his works that are still in manuscript.

See also Alexander of Hales; Aristotelianism; Aristotle; Augustine, St.; Augustinianism; Bonaventure, St.; Marston, Roger; Matthew of Acquasparta; Siger of Brabant; Thomas Aquinas, St.

Bibliography

WORKS BY PECKHAM

Tractatus Pauperis. Caps. 1–6, edited by A. Van den Wyngaert, Paris, 1925, 3–72; caps. 7–9, edited by F. Delorme, in *Studi Francescani,* series 3, 4 (1932): 47–62, 164–193; caps. 10, 16, edited by A. G. Little, in *British Society of Franciscan Studies* 2: 27–55, 63–87; caps. 11–14, edited by F. Delorme, in *Collectanea Franciscana* 14 (1944): 90–117; caps. 14, edited by F. Delorme, in *Fr. Richardi de Mediavilla Quaes. Disp. de Privileg. Martini Papae IV* 79–88, Quaracchi, 1925.

Tractatus de anima. Edited by G. Melani. Biblioteca di Studi Franciscani. Florence, 1948.

Perspectiva communis. Edited by D. Lindberg. Madison: University of Wisconsin Press, 1970.

Tractatus de perspectiva. Edited by D. Lindberg. St. Bonaventure, NY: Franciscan Institute, St. Bonaventure University, 1972.

De numeris misticis. Edited by B. Hughes. *Archivum Franciscanum Historicum* 78 (1985): 3–28, 333–383.

Quodlibeta Quatuor. Edited by G. Etzkorn and F. Delorme. Bibliotheca Franciscana Scholastica XXV. Grottaferrata, 1989.

Quaestiones Disputatae. Edited by G. Etzkorn, L. Oliger, H. Spettmann, I. Brady, and V. Potter. Bibliotheca Franciscana Scholastica XXVIII. Grottaferrata, 2002.

Tractatus de sphaera. Edited by B. MacLaren. PhD diss. Eastern Kentucky University.

WORKS ON PECKHAM

Boureau, A. *Théologie, science et censure au XIIIe siècle. Le cas de Jean Peckham.* Paris: Belles Lettres, 1999.

Callebaut, André. "Jean Peckham O.F.M. et l'augustinisme." *Archivum Franciscanum Historicum* 18 (1925): 441–472.

Crowley, Theodore. "John Peckham O.F.M., Archbishop of Canterbury, versus the New Aristotelianism." *Bulletin of the John Rylands Library* 33 (1951): 242–255.

Douie, Decima L. *Archbishop Pecham.* Oxford: Clarendon Press, 1952. Includes a good bibliography.

Ehrle, Franz. "J. Peckham über den Kampf des Augustinismus und Aristotelismus in der zweiten Hälfte des 13 Jahrhunderts." *Zeitschrift für katholosche Theologie* 13 (1889): 172–193.

Etzkorn, G. "John Pecham, O.F.M.: A Career of Controversy." In *Monks, Nuns and Friars in Mediaeval Society*, edited by E. King, J. Schaefer, and W. Wadley, 71–82. Sewanee, TN: University of the South, 1989.

Etzkorn, G. "Révision dans l'ordre des Quodlibets de Jean Pecham." *Bulletin de Philosophie Médiévale* 19 (1977): 65.

Spettmann, Hieronymus. "Die Psychologie des Johannes Pecham." In Vol. XX of *Beiträge zur Geschichte der Philosophie des Mittelaters*, 1–102. Münster, 1919.

Teetaert, A. "Peckham Jean." In *Dictionaire de Théologie Catholique*, XII/1, 1933, col. 100–140. One of the best overall articles on Peckham.

Girard J. Etzkorn (1967, 2005)

PEIRCE, CHARLES SANDERS

(1839–1914)

Charles Sanders Peirce, the American philosopher, physicist, and mathematician and the founder of pragmatism, was born in Cambridge, Massachusetts. His father, Benjamin Peirce, was the leading American mathematician of the time and Perkins professor of mathematics and astronomy at Harvard. Young Charles was born and bred a scientist, and from his earliest years he showed great promise in mathematics and the physical sciences. He attended Harvard, graduated in 1859, and subsequently studied at the Lawrence Scientific School, from which he received his degree in chemistry summa cum laude in 1863.

During the next fifteen years, Peirce simultaneously pursued several distinct careers. He worked as an astronomer at the Harvard Observatory, where he did pioneer work in photometric research. He also worked as a physicist for the U.S. Coast and Geodetic Survey, of which his father was superintendent, and achieved some distinction for his discovery of hitherto undetected errors in pendulum experiments used to determine the force of gravity. And he worked, more or less privately, at philosophy and logic, steadily publishing works on these sub-

jects from 1866 on. By 1879 he had achieved sufficient stature in these last two fields to be appointed lecturer in logic at the newly organized Johns Hopkins University in Baltimore, Maryland. He remained at Johns Hopkins from 1879 until 1884, meanwhile continuing to work for the Coast and Geodetic Survey—a connection that he sustained until 1891. In 1887, after having inherited some money, he retired to Milford, Pennsylvania, where he lived in relative isolation until his death. Peirce was twice married—in 1862 to Harriet Melusina Fay, whom he divorced in 1883, and in 1883 to Juliette Froissy, who survived him. He had no children.

PHILOSOPHICAL ORIENTATION

Peirce was a systematic philosopher of great breadth, and his writings cover almost all fields of philosophy. His greatest contributions were in the field of logic, but he wrote extensively on epistemology, scientific method, semiotics, metaphysics, cosmology, ontology, and mathematics, and less extensively on ethics, aesthetics, history, phenomenology, and religion. Since Peirce's views underwent considerable change as he grew older, it is not possible to speak of his philosophy as a single system: Rather, he formulated several systems, each of which represents a different phase in his development. These different systems, however, deal with the same problems and embody the same fundamental concept of philosophy.

Peirce came to philosophy as a student of Immanuel Kant, from whom he had acquired the architectonic theory of philosophy. In brief, this theory holds that the domain of knowledge can be so characterized that general assertions can be proven true of all possible knowledge; the theory also holds that it is the dependence of all knowledge upon logic that makes such a characterization possible. Accordingly, the doctrine holds that it is possible to derive from logic the fundamental categories and principles that form the basis of all that can ever be known. In formulating this theory, Kant assumed that logic was a completed, unchanging science. But Peirce was one of that group of men, including George Boole, Augustus De Morgan, Gottlob Frege, and others, who revolutionized logic and prepared the way for A. N. Whitehead and Bertrand Russell's *Principia Mathematica*. Hence, for Peirce, logic was a growing, changing subject, and as it changed, so, according to the architectonic theory, Peirce's philosophy had to change with it. Thus the major shifts in Peirce's system are correlated with his major discoveries in logic and reflect the modifications that he thought those discoveries entailed. In the following exposition, Peirce's work will therefore be dealt with chronologically, and each system will be treated in order.

THE FIRST SYSTEM, 1859–1861

Peirce's first system is a form of extreme post-Kantian idealism. The sources of this idealism are not known: Whether he evolved it himself or derived it from some other source, such as Emersonian transcendentalism, cannot now be determined. What is clear is that by 1857 he was seeking to combine the Transcendental Analytic with Platonic idealism.

CATEGORIES. From Kant's doctrine of the Transcendental Sciences, Peirce derived a threefold ontological classification of all there is into matter (the object of cosmology), mind (the object of psychology), and God (the object of theology). Peirce referred to these three categories as the It (the sense world), the Thou (the mental world), and the I (the abstract world), respectively; and it was from these pronouns that he subsequently derived the names Firstness, Secondness, and Thirdness, by which he usually called his categories.

Having divided all there is into these three categories, Peirce's problem was then to define the relations among them. Specifically, the problem of knowledge as it appears in the first system is how the ideas in the mind of God can be known by human minds. Peirce thought he had found the solution to this problem in the Kantian principle that all phenomena and all concepts—all that can be before the mind—are representations, for he understood this to imply that the ideas in the mind of God, which Peirce conceived as Platonic archetypes, are first given a material embodiment in the form of the objects of our experience and are then derived by us from those objects by abstraction. So Peirce took the Transcendental Analytic to be a description of this process: The synthesis in intuition is the synthesis of the divine idea (already present in an unconscious form within the soul) with "the matter of sensation" to form the empirical object which is also, by virtue of the divine idea, the transcendental object; and the concept is derived by abstraction from the object given in intuition. But when it came to explaining just how the Kantian categories served to effect so un-Kantian a synthesis as that demanded by his own semiotic idealism, Peirce found himself in grave difficulties, and after struggling with the problem for some time he was forced to conclude that the Kantian table of categories was simply inadequate.

TRANSITIONAL PERIOD: STUDY OF LOGIC

According to the architectonic principle, the inadequacy of the table of categories implies the inadequacy of Kant's logical classification of propositions. In 1862, therefore, Peirce began the serious study of logic, and he naturally turned to the Scholastics for instruction. Although he began his study in the belief that the fundamental problem was the classification of propositions, he soon learned from John Duns Scotus that the classification of arguments, or forms of inference, was more fundamental, since the significance of propositions depends upon the role they play in inference. He was therefore led to investigate the irreducible forms of inference, and so to study Kant's famous paper "The Mistaken Subtlety of the Four Syllogistic Figures," in which Kant argued that all inference is reducible to Barbara or to a combination of Barbara and immediate inference. In the "Memoranda concerning the Aristotelian Syllogism," which he published in 1866, Peirce showed that Kant's argument is invalid, for the syllogism by which the reduction of the second and third figures is made is itself in the figure from which the reduction is being made. Peirce therefore concluded that the first three figures are irreducible. Moreover, Peirce noted that if the first figure is defined as the deduction of a conclusion from a major and a minor premise, then the second figure can be described as the inference of the major from the minor and conclusion and the third figure as the inference of the minor from the major and conclusion. Accordingly, Peirce held that the first figure is purely deductive, the second figure inductive, and the third figure hypothetical.

For Peirce this discovery had great importance. His previous belief in the existence of synthetic a priori propositions had rested on the two doctrines, derived from Kant, that all thought involves inference and that all inference is in Barbara. Granting these doctrines, it is clear that the major premises must be innate in the mind. But with the discovery of the role of hypothesis and induction, all synthetic propositions can be regarded as inferred, and so the problem shifts to the process of synthetic inference and to scientific inquiry.

At about the same time that he discovered the irreducibility of the three figures, Peirce made another important discovery in logic—namely, that the copula can be interpreted as the sign relation. This view, which was probably derived from the scholastic theory of supposition, enabled him to regard all propositions as instances of a single fundamental relation, and the analysis was quickly extended to inferences also by treating the conclusion as a sign that is determined by the premises to represent the same state of affairs that they themselves represented. Such a result was thoroughly in line with Peirce's early semiotic idealism, and it meant that the fundamental logical relation from which the categories must be derived is signhood.

THE SECOND SYSTEM, 1866–1870

In 1867 Peirce published a paper titled "On a New List of Categories," in which he attempted to solve the problem of relating his three ontological categories of mind, matter, and God.

THE SIGN RELATION. Starting from Kant's position that knowledge occurs only when the manifold is reduced to the unity of a proposition, Peirce asked what that unity consisted in. Since he conceived the proposition in subject-predicate form, this is equivalent to asking how the predicate is applied to the subject. On the basis of the reduction of the copula to signhood, Peirce argued that the predicate is applied to the subject by being made to stand for the same object for which the subject stands. Thus a proposition would be impossible without reference to some object. But how does the predicate come to stand for this object? Only, Peirce held, by being interpreted as standing for it by some interpreting representation, or mind, so that no proposition is possible unless such an interpretant also exists. And how does the mind make this interpretation? Only, Peirce held, by the sign's representing its object in some respect, that is, by referring to some attribute of the object. Hence, propositions would be impossible if there were no pure abstract attributes embodied in the object to form the basis of comparison among them. So his argument, in essence, was that all synthesis involves the sign relation, that the sign relation consists in a sign standing for something to someone in some respect, and therefore that unless there are things, minds, and abstractions, there is no knowledge. But since the pure abstract attribute is the Platonic Form in the mind of God, what Peirce was really arguing is that without his three ontological categories signhood would be impossible.

Aspects of reference. In the "New List," Peirce did not present his categories directly as ontological classes; rather, he began with the problem of unifying the manifold by joining the predicate to the subject through the sign relation and then analyzed signhood into the three aspects of reference: reference to abstraction, reference to an object, and reference to an interpretant. These three aspects are then made the basis for a systematic classification of signs according to the prominence given to each reference, and this mode of classification is applied to terms, propositions, and arguments. In the case of arguments, Peirce rederived the division into hypothesis, induction, and deduction, thus presenting the three forms of syllogistic as consequences of his analysis of signs.

Logic, however, is not the only science of signs; indeed, it is but one of three, each of which studies a particular aspect of the subject. The first is speculative grammar, which studies the relation of signs to the abstraction; the second is logic, which investigates the relation of signs to their objects; and the third is speculative rhetoric, which investigates the reference of signs to their interpretants. Peirce could therefore derive his three ontological categories by abstraction from the three references of signs, but he had to show further how we can know the objects referred to and whether or not they are real. For these purposes he needed a theory of cognition and a theory of reality.

COGNITION. Peirce stated his new theories of cognition and reality in three articles published in 1868 in the *Journal of Speculative Philosophy*. These papers simply develop the implications of the "New List." Since the reference of a sign to its object is established by its being predicated of another sign which already refers to that object, and since the predication exists only because there is an interpreting sign that so interprets it, it is clear that the series of signs is doubly infinite. Peirce accepted this conclusion and asserted that there is neither a first nor a last cognition. While this doctrine appears bizarre, it has a clear purpose. What Peirce was trying to avoid was the classic dilemma of the empiricist who, having tracked cognition back to an original impression of sense, finds himself completely unable to prove the accuracy of that first impression.

Peirce held that if we examine what actually occurs in cognition, we find the process to be something like the following. In the flood of sensory stimuli that pours in upon us, we detect certain relations that lead us to segregate some stimuli and to interpret these as having a common referent. We do not know what the first such stimulus having that referent may have been, and the question is meaningless, since it is only after many stimuli have occurred that we note their relations. As experience progresses and we acquire more relevant stimuli, we further conceptualize this referent, and in time we acquire a progressively more and more complete and precise idea of it. But our knowledge is never fully complete, so that this process of learning and inquiry is endless. It is true that once we have a relatively detailed concept of the referent, we assume that the object antedated our experience of it and in fact caused that experience; epistemologically, however, it is the experience that comes first and the notion of the object that comes later. The object, then, is a hypothesis designed to give coherence to our experience, and this hypothesis is derived by hypothetical and inductive reasoning; hence, the process of cognition can be fully described by the three forms of inference. Moreover, it follows that the object must be as we conceive it, since it is only as we conceive it that it is postulated at all, and therefore there can be no such thing as an incognizable cause of cognition, for the postulate that an object exists is warranted only by the coherence it gives to experience. Accordingly, whatever is, is cognizable.

REALITY. The above theory of cognition leads at once to a theory of reality. The object is real, Peirce held, only if as the number of cognitions goes to infinity, the concept of the object tends to a limiting form. It follows, therefore, that although the object is not independent of being thought (since it is only as it is thought that it exists at all), it is nevertheless independent of the thought of any particular man and represents what would be agreed upon by an ideal community of investigators if inquiry were to go on forever.

Many empiricists would agree with Peirce that if the object is real, then if inquiry does go on forever, our hypotheses will converge to a final true description. But few would follow him in holding that the object is real because inquiry converges. What Peirce was attempting to do in this instance was to propound a doctrine that was at once phenomenalistic and realistic. To do this, he had to give a phenomenal definition of reality that would compromise neither the inexhaustibility of the real nor the particularity of the phenomenal, and the infinite series of cognitions seemed to do just that. But could Peirce prove that the infinite series is convergent? In 1868 he thought he could do this by means of an argument that purported to show that the concept of a universe in which induction and hypothesis would not lead to agreement was self-contradictory. When he subsequently discovered that this argument was fallacious, his theory of reality had to be substantially revised.

Universals. Peirce's theory that reality consists in the convergence of inquiry led to a further consequence. For it follows that the real object must be as we conceive it to be, and since, as the "New List" showed, the predicate of a judgment is always general, it further follows that univer-

sals are real. On this basis Peirce declared himself a scholastic realist of the moderate, or Scotist, school. The claim is misleading, for whereas the scholastic doctrine rests on the assertion that the universal in the mind and the individual out of the mind have a common nature, Peirce's argument rests on the fact that no cognition is wholly determinate—that is, that there is no true individual, and that therefore everything is to some degree general. Peirce's "realism" was thoroughly idealistic throughout.

THE THIRD SYSTEM, 1870–1884

By 1870 Peirce had propounded, in outline at least, an architectonic philosophy based upon the principles that all cognition involves the sign relation; that the sign relation involves three classes of referents; and that these referents are real and can be adequately known by scientific inquiry. But this theory depended upon logical doctrines that Peirce was forced to abandon when he discovered the logic of relations.

The logic of relations. The first work on the new logic had been done by Augustus De Morgan, but little progress was made with the subject until Peirce entered the field in 1870. It was in this area that Peirce made his greatest contributions to logic, and it is no exaggeration to say that it was he who created the modern logic of relations. Philosophically these new discoveries in logic had important consequences, for the logic of relations forced Peirce to abandon the subject-predicate theory of the proposition that underlies the "New List," and so required that he overhaul his basic position. Probably the most notable revisions directly attributable to the new logic are the doctrines of pragmatism and the doubt-belief theory of inquiry.

THE DOUBT-BELIEF THEORY OF INQUIRY. Peirce formulated the doubt-belief theory in 1873, but it was first published in a series of six papers in *Popular Science Monthly* in 1877 and 1878. These papers do not constitute a rejection of the earlier theory of cognition; rather, they elaborate the earlier theory and set it in the context of biological evolution.

Any organism that is to survive, Peirce held, must develop habits of behavior that are adequate to satisfy its needs. Such habits are rules of behavior that prescribe how we should act under given conditions in order to achieve a particular experiential result. Now such habits, when thoroughly adopted, Peirce called beliefs. Since to possess beliefs is to know how to satisfy one's wants, belief is a pleasant state: Doubt, or the absence of belief, is an unpleasant state, since one is then uncertain how to act and is unable to attain the desired goals. The organism will therefore seek to escape from doubt and to find belief. The process by which the organism goes from doubt to belief Peirce defined as inquiry. Clearly, there are various methods of inquiry, and the most satisfactory method will be that which leads most surely to the establishment of stable belief—that is, to beliefs that will stand in the long run.

PRAGMATISM. From the standpoint of the inquiring organism, a belief concerning a particular object is significant because it permits the organism to predict what experiences it will have if it acts toward the object in a given way. Recalling Kant's use of the term *pragmatic,* namely, "contingent belief, which yet forms the ground for the actual employment of means to certain actions, I entitle *pragmatic belief*" (*Critique of Pure Reason,* A 824, B 852), Peirce propounded what he called the pragmatic theory of meaning, which asserts that what the concept of an object means is simply the set of all habits involving that object. This doctrine involves a major change in Peirce's thinking, and one that is directly due to the logic of relations.

Prior to 1870, Peirce conceived the meaning of a term as the embodied abstraction that it connotes. The meaning of the concept of an object is therefore the same abstraction that is the essence of the object. But once relations were admitted as propositional constituents coordinate with quality, it became possible to conceive the object not only in terms of indwelling qualities but also in terms of relations among its states and with other objects—that is, in terms of its behavior. Accordingly, instead of regarding the behavior of the object as determined by its qualitative essence, the behavior itself may now be regarded as the essence. The meaning of the concept of an object may therefore be given by the set of laws completely specifying the behavior of the object under all conditions. These laws are conditional statements relating test conditions to phenomenal results, and such laws, considered as governing behavior, are habits relating action to experiential effects. Hence, the principle of pragmatism asserts that the concept of the object is synonymous with the set of all such conditionals. Since actual synonymy is asserted, it follows that the concept of a real object can be completely translated into phenomenal terms, but only, it should be noted, into dispositionally phenomenal terms—a point that was to cause Peirce considerable trouble.

Pragmatism: A theory of meaning. Pragmatism is Peirce's most famous philosophical doctrine, although it was made famous by William James rather than by Peirce. As Peirce defined it, pragmatism is purely a theory of meaning—not of truth. Moreover, it is a theory of meaning that combines two rather distinct emphases. First, Peirce intended pragmatism to be a principle of scientific definition. By permitting the translation of a concept into phenomenal results that are observable under stated test conditions, the principle legitimizes the use of theoretical constructs in science and thus does much to clarify the nature and status of scientific theory and proof. But when Peirce chose to call the doctrine pragmatism and insisted that the concept must be translatable into "practical effects," the choice of Kantian terminology was not accidental. Peirce was also stressing the utilitarian aspect of science and of all knowledge—that is, the fact that significance lies in the relation to ends desired. Peirce drew no distinction between these two aspects of pragmatism: For him they formed a single doctrine.

Scientific method. Taken together, pragmatism and the doubt-belief theory imply that the stable beliefs sought by inquiry are in fact the laws of science. The problem of finding the best method of inquiry therefore becomes that of the justification of scientific method, which in Peirce's terms means the justification of induction and hypothesis. Although Peirce formally presented this justification in terms of the operating characteristics of the procedures, he admitted that the relative frequency with which inductive and hypothetical inferences lead to the truth cannot be calculated; hence, our assurance that synthetic inference does ultimately lead to truth comes from the fact that inquiry will converge to a limiting result that is true by definition. Thus, in this instance Peirce admitted that the convergence of inquiry to a final opinion cannot be proven but must be assumed, and since his definition of reality rests upon the convergence of inquiry, this is equivalent to saying that the existence of the real is improvable and must be assumed. But even as an assumption the doctrine presents problems, for it amounts to saying that if inquiry were to go on forever it would converge, and thus involves fundamental questions concerning counterfactuals.

Counterfactuals. The problem of counterfactuals is central to Peirce's philosophy, and his failure to solve it was one of the chief reasons that his system of the 1870s had to be rejected. Pragmatism requires that the concept of a real object be wholly translatable into a set of conditionals relating test conditions to observations. But then it would seem that the concept of the real object is devoid of content: That is, if the concept of the real object is synonymous with the set of conditionals, each of which is purely phenomenal, then the assertion of reality adds nothing to which a nominalist might object. Peirce, however, did not regard the concept of reality as vacuous; he argued that the conditionals are asserted to be true always, whether actually under test or not. The real, therefore, is a permanent possibility of sensation—not merely a series of sensations. But this leads directly to the counterfactual problem, or the equivalent problem of real possibility. Peirce's theory requires that there be real possible sensations—an assertion that is not only unprovable but pragmatically meaningless, since possible sensations are pragmatically equivalent to actual sensations. Thus, far from proving phenomenalism realistic, Peirce found his position reduced to a subjectivism that was the exact antithesis of the scholastic realism he had hoped to establish.

THE FOURTH SYSTEM, 1885–1914

During the years he spent at Johns Hopkins, Peirce was extremely productive in the field of logic. He further developed and extended the calculus of relations and applied it to problems in mathematics. He also clarified and revised his theory of synthetic inference, began the study of the Cantor set theory, and in 1885, with the help of his student, O. H. Mitchell, discovered quantification—a discovery in which Frege had anticipated him by six years. These new developments in logic, together with the rather serious difficulties in his own philosophical position that had become apparent by the end of the 1870s, led Peirce to attempt a radical reformulation of his position in 1885. This reformulation involved a complete revision of the categories, the theory of cognition, and the theory of reality.

THE CATEGORIES. In the 1885 version of the categories, Peirce distinguished sharply between their formal and material aspects. Formally considered, the categories (Firstness, Secondness, and Thirdness) are simply three classes of relations—monadic, dyadic, and triadic. Moreover, Peirce held that these classes are irreducible and that all higher relations (quartic, quintic, etc.) are reducible to some combination of these three. The irreducibility of monadic and dyadic relations is generally admitted. The irreducibility of triadic relations is argued on the ground that all combinatorial relations are triadic, since they involve a relation between two elements and a resulting whole. Granting this, it follows that triadic relations are irreducible, because analysis could only resolve them into components and a combinatorial relation, and that com-

binatorial relation would itself be triadic. But once the notions of element and combination are given, relations of more than three correlates are easily generated, and so all higher relations may be regarded as being constructed from the three basic types.

Among triadic relations Peirce distinguished pure and degenerate species. A pure triadic relation is one in which no two of the correlates would be related without the third. His example of such a relation is signhood, for the sign relates object and interpretant, the interpretant relates sign and object, and the object, by establishing the identity of the extensional domain, relates sign and interpretant. Since Peirce held that all thought is in the form of signs, it follows that all thought is irreducibly triadic, which is another way of stating the Kantian doctrine that all thought is synthetic.

Since a monadic relation is a one-place predicate, the material aspect of Firstness must be qualitative, and Peirce therefore called it quality; what he meant by this term in 1885, however, was not the embodied abstraction that he had described in 1867. Quality now refers not to a concept but to a phenomenal suchness that is the immediate, nonconceptual given of sensation. In the 1885 version, not the concept red, but that suchness of an object that leads us to classify it as red, is a quality.

Peirce called the material aspect of Secondness *haecceity,* a term derived from Duns Scotus's *haecceitas,* meaning "thisness." As experienced, haecceity is known as shock or brute resistance: Peirce described it as an immediately given, nonconceptual experience of dyadic opposition or "upagainstness." The fact that the experience implies the dynamic interaction of two things, and is therefore dyadic in structure, permits it to qualify as the material aspect of Secondness. For Duns Scotus, haecceity was the principle of individuation, and Peirce accepted this meaning: Only individual things have haecceity. It was apparently the discovery of quantification theory that led Peirce to this formulation, for in the variable of quantification theory he found a sign capable of referring directly to an object without describing it, and "thisness" was intended as that property of the object by virtue of which such a reference can be made.

The material aspect of Thirdness is less clearly defined than that of the other two categories. Peirce described it as combination, or mediation, where the latter term signifies either connection or means-ends relations among things. Signhood may also be regarded as part of the material aspect of Thirdness, and so too may generality, since the general constitutes a connection among particulars. Clearly, what Peirce was describing in this instance has much less the character of the immediately given than is the case for the other two categories. The reason is that Peirce not only regarded all thought as triadic—he also regarded all pure triads as conceptual. The material aspect of Thirdness is therefore the experience of thought or rationality. One of Peirce's problems was to explain just how so immaterial a thing can be perceived.

COGNITION. The revision of the categories raised some important problems in regard to cognition. Not only did Peirce have the problem of demonstrating how Thirdness can be perceived, but he also had the problem of explaining how quality and haecceity could be perceived. For in his earlier writings on cognition, Peirce had explicitly denied the existence of first impressions of sense of precisely the sort that he now introduced as the material aspects of his first two categories. Moreover, a further set of problems relating to cognition arose from the doubt-belief theory itself. For in that theory, logic, both deductive and synthetic, is treated as a method whereby an inquiring organism seeks belief. The status of logic, therefore, is that of a useful but contingent means to a sought end—contingent both upon our seeking this particular end, which is a characteristic of the present evolutionary state, and upon our choosing the most efficient of the several available means. Thus, in the doubt-belief theory, logic loses that necessary relation to all possible knowledge that is asserted by the architectonic theory and required to prove the universality of the categories.

Classification of knowledge. Throughout the 1890s Peirce labored at the problem of reconstructing the architectonic theory. Since the architectonic theory presupposes a classification of knowledge into two classes—logic, and all other knowledge—Peirce's problem was to develop this classification so as to ensure the universality of the categories, while at the same time not contradicting his theory of inquiry. The final system of classification was not attained until 1902. In that system, Peirce divided knowledge into practical (or applied) and theoretical sciences, and then further subdivided the theoretical sciences into sciences of discovery and sciences of review (the latter merely summarizing the findings of the sciences of discovery). The major portion of the classification thus deals with the sciences of discovery. The classification is by presupposition.

The first science is mathematics, which Peirce regarded as presupposed by all others. Mathematics is divided into three branches: mathematics of logic, mathematics of discrete series, and mathematics of continua. It is to the mathematics of logic that Peirce assigned the threefold classification of relations that constitutes the formal aspect of the categories. Next after (and presupposing) mathematics comes philosophy, which Peirce divided into phenomenology, normative science, and metaphysics. Phenomenology, which here appeared in Peirce's writing for the first time, is defined as the study of all that can be before the mind, but in practice, it is devoted to proving that all phenomenal experience is resolvable into three factors, which are the material aspects of the three categories. Thus Peirce sought to show that his categories, in both their formal and material aspects, are presupposed by all other knowledge.

Normative science has three divisions: aesthetics, ethics, and logic. In this classification logic appears explicitly as the science of how we ought to reason in order to obtain our objectives—whatever they may be. Thus the contingent and utilitarian aspect of logic, first brought out by the doubt-belief theory, is here made central. But reasoning as we ought is only one aspect of acting as we ought, which is the proper subject of ethics: Hence, logic presupposes the science of ethics, or the science of how conduct should be regulated to attain our ends. But what our conduct ought to be depends on our aims, and these Peirce held to be the subject of aesthetics, which is the science of what is desirable in and of itself. Hence Peirce subscribed to an aesthetic theory of goodness and made the good and the beautiful coincide.

Following and presupposing philosophy is idioscopy, which Peirce subdivided into the physical and psychical sciences. Each division is further subdivided to yield what we would ordinarily regard as the physical, biological, and social sciences. All domains of science thus fall within the classification, and so depend upon the categories. The classification thus serves the purpose of preserving the architectonic while ensuring the normative role of logic.

Perception. Peirce's determination to preserve both the universality and phenomenal observability of the categories as well as the normative character of logic is evident in the theory of percepts and perceptual judgments that he propounded at this time. According to Peirce, physiology and psychology tell us that our percepts are synthesized from the myriad neural stimuli that assail us from without. Of these neural stimuli themselves and of the process of synthesis we are entirely unaware; the earliest step in cognition of which we are at all conscious is the percept. But we cannot really be said to know the percept; what we know is a perceptual judgment, which is a proposition telling us what the nonlinguistic percept was. The perceptual judgment, such as "red patch here now," is a hypothesis that explains the percept, but it is a peculiar hypothesis, since it is immediate and indubitable. Even if the perceptual judgment is immediately followed by a contradictory perceptual judgment, still that second perceptual judgment relates to a later percept, and it remains indubitable that my first and now forever vanished percept was truly red. Perceptual judgments, therefore, form the real starting point in knowledge and must be taken as the ultimate evidence statements.

Peirce described the processes of synthesis that precede and lead to the perceptual judgment as unconscious inference. Their inferential character is defended, here as in his earlier writings, by an argument that identifies the psychological processes of association with the forms of inferences. But since these processes are unconscious, they are beyond our control and thus are not subject to logical criticism—for logical criticism, being normative, is applicable only to voluntary and controllable behavior. On the other hand, conscious inferences, such as the processes whereby we derive knowledge from the perceptual judgments, are thoroughly subject to logical criticism. Accordingly, Peirce could hold both that there is no first impression of sense and that the object (percept) is given to us by a synthesis in intuition. He could further hold that our knowledge has a definite starting point in propositions that give direct reports of phenomenal observation and that whatever is asserted in those judgments of perception must be accepted as given. Thus, in the theory of percepts and perceptual judgments, Peirce tried to reconcile his denial of first impressions with his doctrine of direct phenomenal contact with the world.

On the basis of this theory, Peirce held that the material aspects of all three categories are empirically observable. Quality and haecceity are argued to be directly observable aspects of the percept. But so, too, according to Peirce, is Thirdness, for what is asserted in the perceptual judgment is necessarily true, and the perceptual judgment, being a proposition, has a predicate that is general. Since the generality is given in the perceptual judgment, and since criticism cannot go behind the perceptual judgment, this generality must be regarded as given in perception, and hence as being observable. Thus, by phenomenological analysis, all the categories can be shown to be present in experience.

REALITY. In the course of his study of the logic of relations, Peirce noted that the analysis of certain relations leads to an infinite regress. Thus the relation "in the relation R to" must itself be related to its subjects by the same relation, for example, "in the relation 'in the relation R to'

to," and so on. Such relations, which can be analyzed only into relations of the same sort, Peirce called continuous relations, since they fit the definition of the continuum as that of which every part is of the same nature as the whole. They are, according to Peirce's theory, pure triadic relations; therefore their irreducibility follows from the irreducibility of Thirdness. Moreover, since every relation must be related to its subjects by some such relation, Peirce drew the conclusion that all relations involve a continuous relation.

Continua. During the 1880s, Peirce had become acquainted with Georg Cantor's work on set theory, which bears directly on the problem of continuity. Recognizing at once the great importance of Cantor's work for both logic and mathematics, Peirce undertook the study of the foundations of mathematics and attempted to construct his own theory of cardinal and ordinal numbers. Peirce's papers on this subject are highly technical, and only the briefest summary of them can be given here. In developing his theory of cardinal numbers, Peirce discovered a form of the paradox of the greatest cardinal. His efforts to solve this paradox led him to the erroneous conclusion that the series of transfinite cardinals is only countably infinite and has an upper limit that is the power of the linear continuum. It follows that if the continuum consisted of discrete elements, then there would exist a greatest cardinal, and to avoid this conclusion he held the continuum to be a "potential" set consisting of possible points. Accordingly, although subsets of any multitude may be actualized from the continuum, nevertheless, not all of the possible points are actualizable, since if they were, we should have a greatest cardinal and hence a contradiction. Peirce believed that by such arguments he had established that whatever is truly continuous involves unactualized possibility; hence the problem of the existence of real possibility, which he had found insoluble in the 1870s, was now reduced to that of the reality of continuity. Peirce used the arguments of Zeno in an attempt to prove that space and time must be truly continuous in his (Peirce's) sense, and he went on to argue that continuous relations are truly continuous both intensively and extensively. In defining the continuum as that of which every part is the same sort as the whole, Peirce was brought to the conclusion that real relations, and so real laws, are in some sense continua.

Synechism. The doctrine that the world contains real continua Peirce called synechism. He regarded this as his most important philosophical doctrine and preferred to have his whole philosophy called by this name. He also asserted that it was a modern form of scholastic realism.

Scholastic or not, it is certainly realistic, for it holds that the external referents of true laws are real continua which, since they involve unactualized possibilities, contain real generality. To support this doctrine, Peirce had to define an ontology that would explain what those referents might be. Peirce was no stranger to such an enterprise. He began his work in philosophy in the 1850s, with the doctrine of the three ontological categories, and although he subsequently redefined the categories several times in less ontological fashion, he never forgot the question of what realities lay behind his categories. It is therefore not surprising that following the 1885 revision of the categories, Peirce returned to the problem of ontology, and this soon led him to propound an evolutionary cosmology.

EVOLUTIONARY COSMOLOGY. Peirce had several reasons for formulating an evolutionary cosmology in the 1890s. Not only did synechism require a clarification of his ontological commitments, but he was also impelled toward such a formulation by problems arising within the theory of cognition. First, the doubt-belief theory, by imbedding inquiry within an evolutionary context, made the utility of scientific method relative to a particular evolutionary adaptation, the permanence of which is by no means guaranteed and must therefore be investigated.

A second reason for Peirce's formulating an evolutionary cosmology in the 1890s springs from his doctrine of critical common sense. Like all students of scientific method, Peirce was perplexed by the problem of how we discover true hypotheses. Considering the infinity of possible false hypotheses, it is evident that not even Peirce's theory of synthetic inference could account for the remarkable frequency with which we do, in fact, find a true explanatory hypothesis. Utilizing the evolutionary doctrines current at the time (including the inheritance of acquired characteristics), Peirce argued that the human mind must possess some innate adaptation that enables us to guess the correct laws of nature more readily than pure chance would allow. Such an adaptation would mean that true hypotheses appear to us peculiarly simple and natural. According to Peirce, it follows, then, that judgments of common sense, conceived through the mechanism of the inheritance of acquired characteristics as quasi-instinctual beliefs that have been built up through centuries of experience, should have a greater probability of being true than have parvenu doctrines. But this probability is at best low, so that commonsense judgments cannot be accepted without critical analysis and careful test. Thus Peirce's doctrine of common sense is thoroughly critical: Common sense is to be regarded as a likely source of true hypotheses, but no hypothesis is to be accepted without empirical validation. But in terms of the doubt-belief theory, this doctrine leads to a serious problem. Should the course of evolution alter significantly, our innate adaptation, which has proven so useful in the past, would become positively harmful, since it would direct us to seek explanations in terms of an adaptation that no longer obtains. Accordingly, it becomes a question of considerable moment to inquire what the future course of evolution will be.

The continuous external referent. In the doubt-belief theory, Peirce had formulated the principle that a law, which he conceived as governing the behavior of an organism, is a habit. Now a habit, considered as a psychological entity, is a connection among feeling states and actions, and this connection, Peirce held, must consist in an actual substantive continuity among them. Peirce based this assertion on a variety of arguments, including the felt continuity of mental phenomena (the impossibility of memory without continuous connection between past and present) and certain arguments drawn from the behavior of protoplasm under stimulation. It was therefore Peirce's doctrine that habit, considered as a psychological entity, is a continuum corresponding to a law that is conceived as governing behavior. To find continuous external referents for all laws, Peirce asserted that the universe is itself a living organism possessed of feelings and habits and that our laws of nature describe the habits of the universe. Thus, after 1885, the subjective idealism of Peirce's early writings became an extreme form of objective idealism.

Knowledge, feeling, volition. From the position that the universe is an organism, it follows that all our experience of the external world must be describable as experience of some state or behavior of this organism. But the possible forms of experience are defined by the material aspects of the categories, while Peirce took the possible components of mind to be defined by the traditional division into knowledge, volition, and feeling. He had already identified knowledge with belief-habit and made it the correspondent of law, or Thirdness. He now identified feeling as the correspondent of Firstness and volition as the correspondent of Secondness. But the doctrine asserts more than mere correspondence, for Peirce seeks to account for the fact that all our experience can be classified by the categories, and his explanation for this fact is that what is for the cosmic organism feeling, volition, and belief is experienced by the individual as Firstness, Secondness, and Thirdness.

Chaos and order. The habits created through inquiry are, objectively viewed, laws of behavior. What then, according to Peirce, is doubt, or the absence of belief? In the state of doubt, there will be feeling, but no habit and no order—hence, objectively viewed, the state of doubt will appear as purely random or chance behavior. Thus, objective orderliness or randomness corresponds to states of the universe in which habit is either strong or weak. The irritation of doubt is redefined as an intense consciousness associated with states of unordered feeling; as order or habit increases, the intensity of consciousness declines until, in the case in which virtually complete regularity has been established, it is so low as to be all but undetectable. Mind that is so hidebound with habit we regard as dead matter.

When the doubt-belief theory is applied to the organic universe itself, the result is an evolutionary cosmology. In the beginning, Peirce held, there is nothing but an undifferentiated continuum of pure feeling wholly without order—a primal chaos. From this starting point, the universe evolves by means of the development of habits. We have here the typical Spencerian passage from homogeneity to heterogeneity, but without benefit of Herbert Spencer's mechanical model. In the course of time, the universe becomes ever more orderly—but at any given time its habits remain less than perfectly regular and there are still areas requiring the further fixation of belief.

This cosmology is the basis for Peirce's doctrine of tychism—that there is absolute chance in the universe. For as law is the objective manifestation of habit, so chance is the objective manifestation of lack of habit; hence the primal undifferentiated continuum of feeling is literally a world of pure chance. Evolution constantly diminishes the amount of objective chance in the universe, but only in the limit does it wholly disappear. At any given time, some chance remains, and the laws of nature are not yet wholly exact.

Pragmatism and universal evolution. The doubt-belief theory describes inquiry as an attempt to escape the irritation of doubt. But it is hardly proper to say that the universe seeks to escape from doubt, and some better motive is required. The state toward which the universe is evolving is, according to Peirce's theory, one of complete order. Since such a state involves the complete subjection of feeling and action to belief, Peirce regarded it as the realization of rationality in the concrete, or, in his terms, of "concrete reasonableness." But it is also a state of maximum beauty, for Peirce's aesthetic is a coherence theory of beauty. Accordingly, the normative theory of inquiry may be brought to bear in explaining the evolutionary process. The end sought is concrete reasonableness; the

means, supplied by ethics, is the regulation of conduct by this aim. In the area of inquiry, this implies the discovery of those laws necessary to regulate behavior. Thus pragmatism, or pragmaticism, as Peirce renamed his doctrine after 1905 in order to distinguish it from James's, also serves the cause of evolution, for in translating the concept into a set of habits we discover the practical effects of the object—that is, how our conduct is affected. It remains for scientific inquiry, then, to discover the truth or falsity of potential habits and hence to fix belief. Thus the course of universal evolution and our modes of inquiry must remain ever in harmony, for the objective logic of evolution is identical with the logic of discovery. All nature works by a common process to a common end, and the duty of the individual man is to aid that process by devoting himself to scientific inquiry.

See also Boole, George; Cantor, Georg; Categories; Chance; Common Sense; Counterfactuals; De Morgan, Augustus; Duns Scotus, John; Frege, Gottlob; Idealism; Induction; James, William; Kant, Immanuel; Logic, History of; Mathematics, Foundations of; Pragmatism; Realism; Russell, Bertrand Arthur William; Scientific Method; Scotism; Universals, A Historical Survey; Whitehead, Alfred North.

Bibliography

WORKS BY PEIRCE

The Collected Papers of Charles Sanders Peirce, Vols. I–VI, edited by Charles Hartshorne and Paul Weiss, Cambridge, MA: Harvard University Press, 1931–1935; Vols. VII–VIII, edited by Arthur Burks, Cambridge, MA: Harvard University Press, 1958. This is the basic published collection of Peirce's writings. (The usual method of citation to these volumes is by volume number, followed by a decimal point and the paragraph number—for example, 3.456.)

Charles S. Peirce's Letters to Lady Welby. Edited by Irwin Leib. New Haven, CT: Whitlock's, 1953. These letters, written between 1903 and 1911, are largely devoted to the theory of signs and contain some of Peirce's best writings on that subject.

WORKS ON PEIRCE

Buchler, Justus. *Charles Peirce's Empiricism.* New York: Harcourt Brace, 1939. An incisive study of Peirce's more empirical doctrines, with particular emphasis on pragmatism and common-sensism.

Feibleman, James. *An Introduction to Peirce's Philosophy, Interpreted as a System.* New York: Harper, 1946. A broad but superficial survey.

Gallie, W. B. *Peirce and Pragmatism.* London: Penguin, 1952. A thoughtful book devoted chiefly to Peirce's pragmatism.

Goudge, Thomas A. *The Thought of C. S. Peirce.* Toronto: University of Toronto Press, 1950. Goudge holds that Peirce's work contains two contradictory positions, which he calls naturalism and transcendentalism. The book is an exposition of this thesis and of its implications.

Lewis, Clarence I. *A Survey of Symbolic Logic.* Berkeley: University of California Press, 1918. Ch. 1, Sec. 7. This is still the best essay on Peirce's work in logic.

Moore, Edward C., and Richard S. Robin, eds. *Studies in the Philosophy of Charles Sanders Peirce, Second Series.* Amherst: University of Massachusetts Press, 1964.

Murphey, Murray G. *The Development of Peirce's Philosophy.* Cambridge, MA: Harvard University Press, 1961. An attempt to interpret Peirce's work chronologically and systematically through the architectonic principle.

Thompson, Manley. *The Pragmatic Philosophy of C. S. Peirce.* Chicago: University of Chicago Press, 1953. A thoughtful and systematic study of Peirce's pragmatism and related problems.

Weiss, Paul. "Charles Sanders Peirce." In *Dictionary of American Biography.* New York, 1934. Vol. XIV. A very fine biographical article on Peirce.

Wiener, Philip, and Frederic Harold Young, eds. *Studies in the Philosophy of Charles Sanders Peirce.* Cambridge, MA: Harvard University Press, 1952. This collection of essays on Peirce's philosophy is extremely uneven: it contains some excellent articles and some very poor ones. The papers by Savan, Thompson, Fisch and Cope, and Weiss are particularly good.

Murray G. Murphey (1967)

PEIRCE, CHARLES SANDERS [ADDENDUM]

Charles Sanders Peirce, one of America's most original philosophers, produced a body of work remarkable for its scope and enduring relevance. For many years Peirce's principal contributions to mainstream philosophy were in logic and philosophy of science, but changes in the philosophic terrain since 1967 have brought new areas of his thought to prominence. The resurgence of interest in pragmatism, due in large measure to its promotion by Richard Rorty, and the adoption of Peirce by the Frankfurt School as the philosopher who may hold the key to the problem of modernity, have brought attention to Peirce's unique brand of pragmatism and to his philosophy of signs. Outside of philosophy, the active interdisciplinary field of semiotics that began in Chicago with Charles Morris acknowledges Peirce as the founder of modern sign theory.

Peirce was a late child of the enlightenment, a staunch believer in the universal applicability of mathematics and in the continuous growth of knowledge through sustained inquiry. He was a diligent student of the history of science and understood that the advancement of knowledge is crucially linked to nondeductive (inductive and abductive) reasoning and shared experimental methods. He was convinced that a prerequisite for successful experimentation is an external world resistant to actions arising from misconceptions of it. These views led Peirce to an anti-Cartesian epistemology rooted in perceptual experience and committed to fallibilism and the repudiation of deductive foundationalism. Peirce generalized his view of the advancement of science to all forms of learning from experience, and he concluded that all meaningful conceptions are necessarily related to experiential expectations (conceived consequences). This is the epistemological motivation for his meaning-focused pragmatism (pragmaticism).

Sometimes Peirce is said to have equated truth with settled belief, but that applies only when belief is settled as the result of a steadfast application of scientific method. Other methods for overcoming doubt and settling belief, such as the a priori method or the methods of tenacity and authority, while not without some advantages, do not provide grounds for confidence that truth will be reached. Even the sustained application of scientific method can never issue in a guarantee that inquiry has "stormed the citadel of truth." Truth is always relative to propositions and is, therefore, grounded in the conventionality of symbolism (for propositions can only be expressed symbolically). The true represents the real precisely insofar as inquiry forces beliefs to yield to the dictates of an independent reality, but the "correspondence" of truth and reality that is hoped for at the end of inquiry is at best an ideal limit; we can never be certain that we have reached the truth. This is Peirce's fallibilism. It is typical of Peirce's philosophy that truth and reality are correlates in a triadic relation, where the mediating relate involves a community of inquirers (interpreters).

Peirce believed that the key to intelligence of any kind is sign action (which is always goal directed), and he formulated an elaborate semiotic theory to facilitate the analysis and classification of signs. Peirce's division of signs into icons, indexes, and symbols is his best-known semiotic bequest—although his distinction between tones, tokens, and types is also widely used—but these are only two of many triads that permeate his philosophy. Peirce held that minds are sign systems and thoughts are sign actions, and it is not too far-fetched to say that the mission of his semiotic is similar to that of modern-day cognitive science. Peirce's epistemological shift from a focus on ideas to signs marks him as a forerunner, if not a founder, of philosophy's so-called linguistic turn and, also, of the modern—and postmodern—emphasis on textualism. Peirce's triadic theory of signs distinguishes semiotics from semiology, a generally dyadic theory of signs stemming from the work of Ferdinand de Saussure. Recently there have been attempts to reconcile these two approaches.

Current interest in Peirce's thought extends over most of philosophy. Peirce's graphical logic (his existential graphs) is used as a basis for computational linguistics. The recent move away from logicism has led to renewed interest in Peirce's philosophy of logic, according to which logic is not the epistemic foundation for mathematics. The rehabilitation of systematic and speculative thought has attracted attention to Peirce's evolutionary cosmology, which holds that the principal constituents of the universe are chance, law, and habit formation. Peirce insisted that change is really operative in nature (his tychism), that continuity, in general, prevails (his synechism), and that love or sympathy has a real influence on the course of events (his agapism). He contributed America's most original and thoroughgoing phenomenology (his phaneroscopy), and he advanced unique views on religion and on the significance of sentiment and instinct. He stressed the importance of the existent and the individual while, at the same time, admiring the ideal and insisting that rationality is rooted in the social. Peirce's intellectual legacy is a rich system of thought that helps organize and unify a broad array of issues in modern philosophy.

See also Chance; Classical Foundationalism; Cognitive Science; Enlightenment; Logic, History of; Philosophy of Science, History of; Pragmatism; Rorty, Richard; Truth.

Bibliography

WORKS BY PEIRCE

The New Elements of Mathematics by Charles S. Peirce, 4 vols. Edited by C. Eisele. The Hague: Mouton, 1976.

Complete Published Works Including Selected Secondary Material (microfiche edition). Edited by K. L. Ketner et al. Greenwich, CT, 1977. A companion bibliography is also available: *A Comprehensive Bibliography of the Published Works of Charles Sanders Peirce with a Bibliography of Secondary Studies.* Edited by K. L. Ketner. Greenwich, CT: Johnson Associates, 1977. Rev. ed., Bowling Green, OH, 1986.

Writings of Charles S. Peirce: A Chronological Edition. Edited by the Peirce Edition Project. Bloomington: Indiana University Press, 1982–.

Historical Perspectives on Peirce's Logic of Science: A History of Science, 2 vols. Edited by C. Eisele. New York: Mouton, 1985.

Reasoning and the Logic of Things: The Cambridge Conferences Lectures of 1898. Edited by K. L. Ketner. Cambridge, MA: Harvard University Press, 1992.

The Essential Peirce: Selected Philosophical Writings, 2 vols. Edited by N. Houser and C. Kloesel. Bloomington: Indiana University Press, 1992–1998.

WORKS ON PEIRCE

Apel, K.-O. *Charles S. Peirce: From Pragmatism to Pragmaticism.* Translated by J. M. Krois. Amherst: University of Massachusetts Press, 1981.

Brent, J. *Charles Sanders Peirce: A Life.* Bloomington: Indiana University Press, 1993.

Burch, R. W. *A Peircean Reduction Thesis.* Lubbock: Texas Tech University Press, 1991.

Delaney, C. F. *Science, Knowledge, and Mind: A Study in the Philosophy of C. S. Peirce.* Notre Dame, IN: University of Notre Dame Press, 1993.

Eisele, C. *Studies in the Scientific and Mathematical Philosophy of Charles S. Peirce.* Edited by R. M. Martin. The Hague, 1979.

Esposito, J. L. *Evolutionary Metaphysics: The Development of Peirce's Theory of Categories.* Athens: Ohio University Press, 1980.

Fisch, M. H. *Peirce, Semeiotic, and Pragmatism.* Edited by K. L. Ketner and C. J. W. Kloesel. Bloomington: Indiana University Press, 1986.

Freeman, E., ed. *The Relevance of Charles Peirce.* La Salle, IL: Hegeler Institute, 1983.

Hausman, C. R. *Charles S. Peirce's Evolutionary Philosophy.* Cambridge, U.K.: Cambridge University Press, 1993.

Hookway, C. *Peirce.* London: Routledge and Kegan Paul, 1985.

Houser, N., D. D. Roberts, and J. Van Evra, eds. *Studies in the Logic of Charles S. Peirce.* Bloomington: Indiana University Press, 1996.

Ketner, K. L., ed. *Peirce and Contemporary Thought: Philosophical Inquiries.* New York: Fordham University Press, 1995.

Murphey, M. G. *The Development of Peirce's Philosophy.* Cambridge, MA: Harvard University Press, 1961.

Raposa, M. L. *Peirce's Philosophy of Religion.* Bloomington: Indiana University Press, 1989.

Roberts, D. D. *The Existential Graphs of Charles S. Peirce.* The Hague: Mouton, 1973.

Nathan Houser (1996)

PELAGIUS AND PELAGIANISM

Pelagius was a spiritual adviser to Christian aristocrats in Rome around the turn of the fifth century CE. In a commentary on the Pauline epistles, a treatise *On Nature*, and other writings, he sought to bolster Christian asceticism by opposing Manichaean determinism and affirming human capacity to progress toward moral perfection. His moral character and theological insights attracted followers who defended and developed his teachings.

Opposition to Pelagius and his followers began to intensify after Alaric's sack of Rome forced them to emigrate. In 411 one of Pelagius's protégées, Caelestius, sought ordination to the priesthood in Carthage and instead was condemned for his views on the nature and effect of Adam's sin. In his defense, Caelestius appealed to the teachings of a priest named Rufinus, whom Caelestius had heard oppose the notion of inherited sin. Pelagius himself traveled quickly through North Africa to Palestine where his teaching aroused Jerome's ire. In 415 Pelagius was called to defend himself before the bishop of Jerusalem and again before an episcopal synod at Diospolis, both of which acquitted him.

Indignant at these acquittals, Augustine—who had already written several anti-Pelagian treatises—led the literary and ecclesiastical attack on Pelagianism. Following conciliar, papal, and imperial condemnations in 418, Pelagius and Caelestius largely disappear from the historical record. Nineteen Italian bishops refused to subscribe to the papal proscription; among them was Julian of Eclanum, who wrote several lengthy polemical treatises, fragments of which survive embedded in Augustine's refutations. The judgment that Pelagian teachings were heretical was upheld by the ecumenical council at Ephesus in 431.

Modern scholarship has emphasized the importance of distinguishing between Pelagianism as a historical movement and Pelagianism as a theological system, the latter caricaturing the former. From the viewpoint of Christian orthodoxy, Pelagianism has often been construed as the heretical mirror image of Augustine's theology. Whereas Augustine defended established practices and doctrines such as infant baptism and original sin, Pelagianism controverted these and other traditions with novel heretical teachings that have been characterized as naturalistic, Stoic, and even godless. The theological tradition also canonized Augustine's characterization of Pelagians as *enemies of grace*, thereby implying that they deliberately denied grace, or at least reduced it to God's provision of the law and free will. Moreover, Pelagianism is accused of vainly overemphasizing the capacity of human free will. According to Augustine's full-blown predestinarian scheme, even the faith with which fallen human beings respond to God's gracious offer of salvation is itself a gift from God, given to some and withheld from others. As the opposite, Pelagianism implies an overconfidence that human nature is uncorrupt and possesses sufficient resources to attain moral perfection and eternal salvation solely by its own efforts without assistance from God's grace.

Like any caricature, this portrait of Pelagianism contains true features but distorts them by exaggerating some details and omitting others. The identification and subsequent scholarly analysis of additional Pelagian writings have revealed that Pelagian tenets are more nuanced than the prevailing stereotype suggests. Pelagius and his followers did not intentionally oppose Christian orthodoxy. Quite the contrary, they not only contrasted their teachings with the heresies of Arianism, Manichaeism, Origenism, and Jovinian, but also hurled countercharges of novelty and heterodoxy back at their opponents. As an historical movement, Pelagianism encompassed a diverse group of individuals who differed on a number of practical and theological issues but united in opposition to moral laxity and theological determinism. The defining characteristic of Pelagianism was not a negative denial of grace but, rather, the positive affirmation that it was possible (at least theoretically) for human beings to live sinlessly. If human beings *ought* to avoid sin—and most Pelagians considered this proposition a scriptural imperative—then human beings must be *able* to avoid sin.

Philosophical questions about freedom, responsibility, and justice were prominent in the Pelagian controversy but always in relation to theological concerns. For example, both Pelagius and Augustine strove to balance human free will and divine grace. Pelagius affirmed grace not only as God's creation of human free will and God's revelation through the law and through Christ, but also as the remission of sins in baptism and even as a constant help to free will, although Augustine dismissed the sincerity of the latter conception. Conversely, Augustine affirmed free will but apart from grace limited its scope in fallen humanity to choosing among evils. While Augustine accused his opponents of emphasizing free will to the extent that they denied any role for God's active grace, the Pelagians argued that Augustine's understanding of grace amounted to a determinism that eliminated free will.

The Pelagians defined sin as an act of will, not a substantial defect of nature; hence sin must be avoidable, and conversely that which cannot be avoided cannot be sin. Thus, when human beings choose to sin, they bear moral responsibility for their own actions and cannot blame God, the Devil, or even a vitiated nature. Consequently, the Pelagians understood the effect of Adam's sin as imitation of sinful habits rather than inheritance of a sinful nature, and most of them affirmed infant baptism, denying only that its function was to cleanse the newborn of inherited sin. Moreover, they argued that the inevitability and substantiality of original sin made God responsible for evil. For Julian, Augustine's teaching that the guilt of

Adam's sin was transmitted to each human being at conception also implied that marriage and reproduction were tainted by evil, therein betraying Augustine's lingering affinity with Manichaeism.

Finally, both sides in the Pelagian controversy refused to embrace theological positions that appeared to impugn divine justice. If sin were unavoidable, the Pelagians argued, it would be unjust for God to demand sinlessness and then to condemn human beings for sinning. Similarly, they saw injustice in the notion that God would condemn infants not for acts of their own volition but merely for inherited sin. Indeed, any god who would impute to one person the sins of another would be unjust. Augustine countered that a just God could not abide the suffering of infants unless these miseries were somehow deserved as a result of original sin, which rendered all humanity liable to God's just condemnation. Augustine posited that even God's sovereign choice to save some and not others, though an inscrutable mystery, could not be unjust.

See also Arius and Arianism; Augustine, St.; Augustinianism; Determinism, Theological; Freedom; Justice; Mani and Manichaeism; Origen; Philosophy of Religion; Religion; Responsibility, Moral and Legal.

Bibliography

WORKS BY PELAGIUS

De divina lege. In "Patrologia Latina." Vol. 30, cols. 106–116, edited by J. P. Migne, Paris: 1865 (included here among works falsely attributed to Jerome.

De natura. Fragments collected in "Pelagius' Schrift *De natura*: Rekonstruktion und Analyse." Winrich A. Löhr. *Recherches augustiniennes* 31 (1999): 235–294.

De virginitate. In *Sulpicii Severi Libri qui supersunt*, edited by C. Halm. "Corpus Scriptorum Ecclesiasticorum Latinorum," Vol. 1, 225–250. Vindobonae: C. Geroldi filium, 1866 (included here with the works of Sulpicius Severus).

De vita Christiana. In "Patrologia Latina." Vol. 40, cols. 1031–1046, edited by J. P. Migne, Paris: 1887 (here attributed to Augustine).

Epistola ad Celantiam. In *Sancti Eusebii Hieronymi Epistulae*, edited by Isidorus Hilberg. "Corpus Scriptorum Ecclesiasticorum Latinorum," Vol. 56.1, 329–356. Vindobonae: Verlag der Österreichischen Akademie der Wissenschaften, 1996 (here attributed to Jerome).

Epistola ad Demetriadem. In "Patrologia Latina." Vol. 30, cols. 16–46, edited by J. P. Migne, Paris: 1865 (included here among works falsely attributed to Jerome).

Expositiones XIII Epistularum Pauli. In *Pelagius's Expositions of Thirteen Epistles of St. Paul*, edited by Alexander Souter. Cambridge, U.K.: Cambridge University Press, 1922–1931 (Latin edition and commentary; 3 vols.).

Libellus fidei. In "Patrologia Latina." Vol. 48, cols. 488–491, edited by J. P. Migne. Paris: 1862.

OTHER PELAGIAN WRITINGS

Bohlin, Torgny. *Die Théologie des Pelagius und ihre Genesis.* Uppsala University Arsskrift 9. Uppsala: A.-B. Lundequist, 1957.

Caelestius. *Liber de 13 capitula.* Fragments collected in *Rom und Pelagius: Die theologische Position der Römischen Bishöfe im pelagianischen Streit in den Jahren 411–432*, edited by Otto Wermelinger, 297–299. Stuttgart: Anton Hiersemann, 1975.

Caspari, C. P., ed. *Briefe, Abhandlungen, und Predigten aus den zwei letzten Jahrhunderten des kirchlichen Alterthums und dem Anfang des Mittelalters.* (1890). Reprinted Brussels: Culture and Civilization, 1964 (Latin edition of six works by an anonymous Pelagian, with commentary).

Julian of Eclanum. *Ad Florum.* Fragments embedded in Augustine's *Contra Julianum opus imperfectum*, Books I–III, *Sancti Aureli Augustini Opera*, Sec. 8, Part. 4, edited by E. Kalinka and M. Zelzer. "Corpus Scriptorum Ecclesiasticorum Latinorum." Vol. 85.1. Vindobonae: Hoelder-Pichler-Tempsky, 1974; and Books IV–VI, "Patrologia Latina," Vol. 45, edited by J. P. Migne. Paris: 1865.

Julian of Eclanum. *Iuliani Aeclanensis. Expositio libri Iob; Tractatus prophetarum Osee, Iohel et Amos; accedunt operum deperditorum fragmenta post Albertum Bruckner denuo collecta aucta ordinate.* "Corpus Christianorum." Series Latina, Vol. 88, edited by Lucas De Coninck. Turnholt: Brepols, 1977 (Latin edition of two exegetical works and collected fragments of Julian's other writings).

Rufinus. *Liber de fide.* In *Rufini presbyteri Liber de fide: A Critical Text and Translation with Introduction and Commentary*, edited by Mary W. Miller. Washington, DC: Catholic University of America Press, 1964.

Fragments of Caelestius's *Definitiones* and Pelagius's *Pro libero arbitrio, Eclogarum*, and *Epistola ad Innocentium* are collected in "Patrologia Latina," Vol. 48, col. 255–698, edited by J. P. Migne. Paris: 1862 (also includes a discussion of Pelagianism).

SECONDARY STUDIES

Bonner, Gerald. *Augustine and Modern Research on Pelagianism.* Villanova: PA: Villanova University Press, 1972. Good overview of influential scholarship and its conclusions.

Bonner, Gerald. "Pelagianism and Augustine." *Augustinian Studies* 23 (1992): pp. 33–51, and 24 (1993): pp. 27–47. Updated summary and observations on trends in Pelagian research.

Brown, Peter. "The Patrons of Pelagius: The Roman Aristocracy between East and West." In *Religion and Society in the Age of St. Augustine.* London: Faber and Faber, 1972, pp. 208–226

Brown, Peter. "Pelagius and his Supporters: Aims and Environment." In *Religion and Society in the Age of St. Augustine.* London: Faber and Faber, 1972, pp. 183–207.

Clark, Elizabeth A. "From Origenism to Pelagianism." In *The Origenist Controversy: The Cultural Construction of an Early Christian Debate.* Princeton: Princeton University Press, 1992, pp. 194–244.

Evans, Robert F. *Pelagius: Inquiries and Reappraisals.* NY: Seabury Press, 1968. Highlights Jerome's role in the Pelagian controversy.

Ferguson, John. *Pelagius: A Historical and Theological Study.* Cambridge: W. Heffer & Sons, 1956.

Lamberigts, Mathijs. "Julian of Aeclanum: A Plea for a Good Creator." *Augustiniana* 38 (1988): 5–24.

Morris, John. "Pelagian Literature." *Journal of Theological Studies* 16 (1965): 26–60.

Nuvolone, Flavio G., and Aimé Solignac. "Pélage et pélagianisme." In *Dictionnaire de spiritualité, ascétique et mystique, doctrine et histoire*, Vol. 12B, cols. 2889–2942. Paris: Beauchesne, 1986. Excellent comprehensive survey of Pelagian literature and its authors and attribution, with extensive bibliography.

Plinval, Georges de. *Pélage. Ses écrits, sa vie et sa réforme.* Lausanne: Librairie Payot, 1943. Dated in its attribution of most extant Pelagian writings to Pelagius, but influenced Pelagian scholarship for decades.

Rees, B. R. *The Letters of Pelagius and His Followers.* Woodbridge, Suffolk: Boydell Press, 1991. Translations of a number of Pelagian letters and ascetic treatises.

Rees, B. R. *Pelagius: A Reluctant Heretic.* Woodbridge, Suffolk: The Boydell Press, 1988.

Michael R. Rackett (2005)

PERAS

See *Apeiron/Peras*

PERCEPTION

The term *perception* may be used generally for mental apprehension, but in philosophy it is now normally restricted to sense perception—to the discovery, by means of the senses, of the existence and properties of the external world. Philosophers have been concerned with the analysis of perception—that is, the study of its nature and of the processes involved in it—and with its epistemological value—that is, how far, if at all, it can be regarded as a source of knowledge about the world. Their answers to these closely interrelated questions have been formulated in various theories: the commonsense theory and other kinds of direct realism, the representative or causal theory, critical realism, the sense-datum theory, and phenomenalism. This entry will be devoted to the main features of perception that underlie the various theories and that have raised philosophical problems and controversy. It will discuss both the initial evidence that may be analyzed without recourse to scientific findings and the causal and psychological process revealed by scientific investigation.

INITIAL EVIDENCE AND ANALYSIS

REFLECTIVE EXAMINATION. As percipients we are all familiar with perception, and so the first evidence should come from reflection on our own experience. The following points may thus be made about perception.

First, it is awareness of the external world—of material objects, to use a technical term for physical objects in general, animals, plants, and human beings insofar as they are perceptible (their bodies, in fact). The main characteristics of such objects are that they are external, independent of the percipient, and public, meaning that many people can perceive them at once. Perception, in being the awareness of such objects, may be contrasted with imagery, bodily sensations, or having dreams.

Second, perception is, or seems to be, intuitive—immediate and normally undoubting, a direct face-to-face confrontation with the object in sight or a direct contact in touch. Nor are we normally conscious of any processes of reasoning or interpretation in it. On the rare occasions when we reason or we have doubts about what an object is, the reasoning or doubts are about the identity or character of something already perceived—for instance, a rectangular red object or something white on the hillside.

Third, perception is variable in quality and accuracy; we may fail to notice something, to see clearly, to hear distinctly, and so forth. Three types of variation may be involved: variations in attention, in what we notice or discriminate; variations in quality or distinctness (for instance, where there is nearsightedness or fog); and variations in liability to err—we may misidentify what we perceive or mistake its qualities.

Fourth, perception nevertheless normally gives us knowledge of material objects and properties. With a few fairly obvious tests, like touching and looking closely, or using the evidence of other percipients, we can establish certainty or else correct the first sight or hearing.

Fifth, perception often issues in some judgment or assertion (to others or perhaps only to oneself)—for example, "There is a green fly on the roses" or "Here's the milkman"—but it may not.

ILLUSIONS. Illusions, comprising illusions proper, hallucinations, and cases of the relativity of perception, have traditionally been the most important origin of the major problems of perception. The two main claims of the argument from illusion are (1) illusions show that perception is never absolutely certain, that tests are never final, and (2) the appearances we are aware of in illusions, especially hallucinations, cannot be identified with the real properties of objects and must therefore be private objects of awareness, or sensa (indeed, all perception involves awareness of sensa that in correct, or veridical, perception belong to the object or correspond to its properties).

The first claim was long thought to rule out perceiving as a source of knowledge; instead, one had to turn to pure reason, or rational intuition, which was held to provide mathematical knowledge. But, since the absolute certainty of mathematics came to be generally ascribed to its ultimately analytic, or even tautological, character, the tendency now would be to stress the negligibility of the possibility of error in tested perception and to use a different standard of certainty and knowledge concerning matters of fact, one that allows perceptual statements to qualify.

The second claim, concerning the existence of sensa, is vital in that almost all theories of perception either found their analyses on it (as does the sense-datum theory) or seek to controvert it or explain it away (as does commonsense realism). The seeds of this conflict already lie in the results of the reflective examination. Insofar as perceiving seems to vary in quality and accuracy, it is easy to say that in illusions we merely see the object looking different from what it is. But if perception is a direct intuitive confrontation, the illusory appearance must be a genuine existent, perceived as it really is, a sensum in fact; "looking different from what it is" must be interpreted as "presenting sensa different from the standard ones." In any case, some phenomena—for example, the integration of hallucinatory images with a perceived background—are difficult to explain without supposing awareness of private sensa in all perception, and almost all the phenomena require scientific and psychological findings for their full explanation, thus pointing beyond this initial evidence.

PERCEPTUAL CONSCIOUSNESS AND PERCEIVING. The occurrence of illusions may lead to ambiguity in the use of *perceive* and allied terms. Thus, in double vision a man may be conscious of two bottles where there is only one. Do we say "He perceived two bottles" or "He perceived one bottle"? Each alternative has been adopted philosophically, and to avoid ambiguity, it is safer to distinguish (1) "X is perceptually conscious of Y" from (2) "Y is present to X's senses (or light from it is acting on his sense organs)" and use "X perceives Y" only when both are meant.

This recommendation is claimed to have the further advantage of enabling us to discuss as perceptual consciousness the state of mind (or mental act) occurring in both veridical perceiving and illusions. Perceptual consciousness of, for example, a dagger might occur when only a stick was present or even, as in Macbeth's case, when nothing was there. The notion of such consciousness as a common factor in perceiving a real dagger, in having hallucinations of one, and in mistaking something else for one fits in best with dualist theories, such as the sense-datum theory (especially H. H. Price's version) or critical realism, since it suggests that the contents of such consciousness differ from the external object perceived. Direct realists are suspicious of it; for them having hallucinations is something (imagery, perhaps) quite different from normal perception, even if confused with it, whereas in illusions they want to stress that one is perceiving the real object present—seeing a stick *as* a dagger or the round table *as* elliptical.

But even if perceiving a round table as round or in perspective as elliptical is taken as immediate confrontation needing no further analysis, seeing a stick as a dagger (or a piece of wax as a tomato or a bush in a fog as a man) can hardly be equally simple and immediate. In such cases and in hallucinations one has to admit that one seems to see an object quite different from that present to the senses. This can fairly be described as perceptual consciousness of the (ostensible) object (dagger, wax, or man) and distinguished in analysis from actually perceiving an object (dagger, wax, or man). And in view of the subjective similarity it is but a short step to suppose that perceptual consciousness of X also occurs in perceiving X as X, the difference between illusory and veridical perception of an X lying not in this common consciousness but in whether X is present and acting on the sense organs. Any philosophy of perception should analyze this perceptual consciousness and explain how it may occur without the presence of the corresponding object.

ANALYSES OF PERCEPTUAL CONSCIOUSNESS. Three major analyses are integral parts of the theories of perception mentioned above. First is the traditional notion that perceiving—that is, perceptual consciousness—is the interpretation of sensations as properties of external objects. Second, the sense-datum theory claims that perceptual consciousness is taking for granted that the sense datum one is sensing belongs to a material object. Third, the analysis of the critical realists, though stated as an analysis of perceiving, amounts to saying that perceptual consciousness is taking an intuited datum or character complex to characterize an external object.

The essential difficulty in these three analyses is that they contradict introspective evidence by splitting up perceptual consciousness into the awareness of some private data, recognizable by analysis as such, and the act of interpreting them as, or taking them to be, objects or object properties. In experience there is no such core of sensing or intuiting data distinguishable from the consciousness of a material object, even if only subsequently; still less is there any passage of the mind from awareness of sensation as such to object perception. And if some critical realists are less liable to this difficulty because they do not treat their data or character complexes as existents readily distinguishable from material objects, they do this only at the expense of obscurity or disagreement as to what the data are. Attempts at a remedy must be postponed until the psychological processes in perception are considered.

A fourth analysis is the idealist claim that all perceiving is judging, which is really an analysis of perceptual consciousness but is easier to follow if stated in terms of perceiving. It is that perceiving (perceptual consciousness) consists in making a judgment, which has an implicit sensory basis, about the real existence of an object or property. Thus, perceiving a tomato on a plate or perceiving that the dog has hurt its leg are the sensorily grounded judgments "There is a tomato on a plate" or "The dog has hurt its leg." The "perceiving that" description of a perception (for example, "He saw that the dog was hurt") certainly seems to suggest judgment, though the form may be misleading and may only be for emphasis of the feature noticed. But the main reasons for this analysis are (a) that perceiving is true (veridical) or false (erroneous) and only judgments or assertions can be true or false and (b) that perception is more than just sense experience, for we identify and interpret what is given (that is, it involves inference from implicit data, and the conclusion of such an inference must be a judgment).

One may object that truth characterizes what is asserted, not the asserting—the judgments, in the sense of propositions, to which perceiving may lead, but not the act of perceiving itself. Perceiving may be proper, correct, clear, or accurate, but not true or false. Many other things we do may be done correctly and be liable to errors without being forms of judging, such as playing the piano, playing games, tying knots. False judgment is not the only form of error. Also, the idealist doctrine that all perceiving is judging is open to the general objection to the first three analyses above, particularly because the nature of the implicit data or sensory grounds is very obscure. Attempts to elucidate it—for example, Brand Blan-

shard's—turn them into sensa. Furthermore, the term *judgment* suggests something intellectual, explicit, and considered, with consciousness of the evidence for the assertion—conditions inappropriate to much perception. Also, we may correct a faulty judgment on learning the truth, but such knowledge does not enable us to correct illusory perceptions; we still see the mirage, and the railroad tracks still appear to meet in the distance.

Fifth, there is a causal analysis of perceptual consciousness—namely, that it is inferring that one's sensa are caused by an external object. This may be associated with representative realism but is not essential to it; representative realism's main thesis is that the sensa and the consciousness are externally caused by objects that the sensa "represent." One may accept this thesis along with any of the analyses of perceptual consciousness—the causal inference it involves is subsequent to the perceiving, and so is a claim about perception. The difficulties of supposing that perceptual consciousness *consists in* such an inference from effect to cause are that (a) we are not conscious of such an inference; (b) if we started only with private sensa, any inference to external causes would be too difficult and complex to be automatic and unconscious—it would *have* to be conscious; and (c) it leads to paradoxes, such as that children, being ignorant of the supposed causation of perception, cannot therefore perceive or be perceptually conscious of anything.

CONCEPTUAL ANALYSIS OF PERCEIVING. A rather different approach to perceiving is adopted by those who advocate conceptual analysis—that is, a close study of the ordinary meaning (or use) of expressions. This analysis is naturally associated with commonsense realism, for ordinary language tends to reflect ordinary views on perception or at least what once were such views. Such analysis, however, may well indicate features of perception that are not normally realized and so supplement or even correct reflective examination of an introspective kind.

Much attention along these lines has been directed to the categorization or classification of perceiving. Previous philosophers have referred to perception in various ways: as an act, even an operation, as a process, and as a mental state. None of these is satisfactory. "Act," at least as activity or operation, suggests listening or watching rather than just hearing or seeing; "state" and "process" suggest something long-term, and "process," like "activity," suggests something open to public observation—yet whereas one may observe X looking at Y one cannot observe X seeing Y. (One can perhaps claim that the best description of perception is "mental act," which would put perceiving in a special category with realizing, noticing, deciding and so on, but mental acts as such are suspect to these philosophers.) One suggestion is that perceiving is simply having an experience, but this neglects the active side of recognizing and identifying involved in it. A more popular suggestion is that perceiving is a skill or art, or, rather, since seeing X or hearing Y occur at a definite time, perceiving is the exercise of a skill.

Oddly enough, the evidence for this is not linguistic. We may speak of a skilled observer, one who can direct and coordinate a series of perceptions, but not a skilled perceiver; we do not say that X is an expert at the art of seeing or hearing things. Rather, this suggestion is based on the fact that perceiving can be improved by learning and experience, so that one recognizes things easily, avoids mistakes, or can make allowances for such factors as distance. Although this may occur to one on reflection, however, its full and precise extent has been established only by psychological investigation. As soon as one seeks out this and other psychological evidence about perceiving or even asks how one learns by and exploits experience in perceiving, one is carried far beyond language and conceptual analysis to a scientific study of the subject. Also, to maintain that perceiving is the exercise of a skill brings one back to the suggestion that it is an operation or activity.

More striking perhaps was the earlier claim of Gilbert Ryle that "perceiving" is an achievement verb, like "finding" or "winning," and indicates the scoring of an investigational success. This means that perceiving is not an activity or process, though it may be the successful termination of the activity of looking for something; it is instantaneous, not something that takes time or can be observed. Ryle's aim was to attack representative realism and its associated dualisms of mind and body, sensa and object, by claiming that (a) perceiving, usually thought to be a private mental activity because it is not an overt one, is not an activity at all and thus provides no evidence of a mental world and that (b) since it is not a process, perceiving is not the final stage or effect of a process, particularly not of the causal process from object to person. Hence, there is no need to suppose that science proves that perceiving is awareness of private sensa.

These are not very convincing arguments. As to the first, winning or scoring involves some activity such as kicking a ball. Likewise, perceiving involves experiences of colors or sounds and the psychological processes discussed below; these are normally claimed to be mental. The second is a non sequitur—instantaneous success may be the end and result of a causal process. Thus, scoring

and finding may be observed and may be the result of a process or series of activities; other conditions may also be required but do not rule out their being effects. More generally, if perceiving is an achievement, what are misperception, illusion, failure to see properly, a casual glance? An analysis of perceiving must take these into account and not apply only to veridical perception. Ryle also failed to show how perceiving is related to the causal processes representative realism emphasizes. Thus, if instantaneous, perceiving can no longer be the relation across time and space that direct realism would need to claim in view of the factually verified time lag, the time taken by the causal transmission from a distant object. Indeed, contrary to Ryle's intention, a dualist interpretation of his claim is possible. Perceptual consciousness is instantaneous; when it is also successful, that is, when its content corresponds to the properties of the object causing it, it is perceiving; when unsuccessful, it is misperception or illusion.

THE CAUSAL PROCESSES IN PERCEPTION

THE CAUSAL CHAINS. The causal processes involved in perception form causal chains from the external object to the percipient's brain. In sight a complex system of light waves, sometimes emitted by the object but normally a differential reflection of light from the object's surface, travels from the object to the percipient's eyes. This system is diversified in intensity and wavelength according to the shape, brightness, and color of the object surface and, on striking the eyes, is focused so that an image of the object is cast (upside down) on each retina. Each retina has a mosaic of more than 120 million receptors, which are activated by the light cast on them in this image. The light causes chemical changes in the receptors; these changes, in turn, cause electrical impulses to pass along the nerve fibers that lead from the receptors to one of the two visual receiving areas of the brain. The impulses set up activity there and in certain other association areas; this done, the person then sees the object. More than one million such fibers form the optic nerve from each eye, and each fiber consists of a succession of cells that are made to conduct by a chain reaction; the resultant impulses can be picked up and reproduced on a cathode-ray tube.

In hearing, a pattern of sound waves is emitted or reflected from the object and strikes the eardrum; this causes vibrations to be transmitted through a series of bones to the liquid filling in the inner ear, thereby setting up vibrations in the basilar membrane of the cochlea according to the frequency (waves per second, corresponding to pitch) and intensity of the sound. The receptors in the cochlea then transmit electrical impulses along the nerve fibers to another receiving area in the brain. (These impulses are not at the frequency of the incoming sound.)

In smell and taste there is a chemical stimulation of receptors in the nose and tongue by particles of the substance perceived, and the receptors, in turn, send neural impulses to another area of the brain. For touch, the brain is linked to receptors all over the skin, some of which respond to the pressure of direct contact with the object, some to heat, and some to cold (or, rather, to rate of change in skin temperature). Other receptors in the skin and the body respond to a wide range of stimuli by transmitting to the brain impulses that ultimately cause a sensation of pain. There are also other senses—for example, a kinesthetic sense by which receptors in the muscles send impulses to the brain so that the position of the limbs is sensed or unconscious adjustments are made to guide and make efficient voluntary movement. There are also receptors in the vestibule and semicircular canals behind the ear that assist balance and give us information about head position.

The chain process (object-[waves]-receptor-nerve impulses-brain activity) is a necessary condition of perception of an external object, for if it is interrupted by damage to the sense organ, no perception occurs. It is not a fully sufficient condition in that other areas of the brain must be suitably active so that the person is conscious and minimally attentive—that is, not wholly absorbed in thought. The interesting question is whether or how far the chain process is necessary and sufficient for perceptual consciousness of an object, granted conditions of consciousness and attention. At least the brain activity is clearly necessary, but theoretically one might insert stimulation at some point on the chain and thus cause experiences the same as those that would normally be attributed to the external object. This apparently happens naturally in illusions and hallucinations, including phantom limbs, and electrical stimulation of the appropriate areas of the brain may cause sensations of color, smell, or touch. (The sensations are not like the contents of perceptual consciousness of objects, but this difference may be due to the comparative crudity of the artificial stimulation by an electrode; also, activity in the association areas is necessary for normal perception.) Thus, it seems probable that suitable activity in the nervous system is a necessary and sufficient condition of perceptual consciousness, though it may be that some kind of external

stimulation, even one quite unlike the object perceived, is required to trigger it.

TIME LAG. Causal processes take time. In the case of distant objects this is marked. Thus, because sound waves travel much more slowly than light waves, the flash of some distant gunfire or explosion may be seen appreciably before the sound is heard. Even at its great speed light takes eight minutes to reach us from the sun and four years and four months from the nearest star. Consequently, we may well be "seeing" a star long after it has disintegrated, for the perceptual consciousness occurs at approximately the time of the arrival of the star's light on Earth. But as time is required for the sense organ to be activated and for the nerve impulses to travel to and spread in the brain, there is a slight but variable time lag in all perception; an accurate estimate is not possible but the delay is probably of the order of one-tenth of a second for nearby objects.

UNIFORMITY OF NERVE IMPULSES. One surprising fact is that the nerve impulses are of a similar type for all the senses. All that travels along any nerve from any receptor to the brain is a sequence of such impulses varying normally between 10 and 100 per second. The frequency variation is, in fact, a mark of intensity; the stronger the stimulus, the more impulses per second. Consequently, what distinguishes causation of an experience of sound from that of smell or an experience of a high pitched sound from that of a low one is not the impulse itself but the connections of the nerve fibers excited and conducting—where they start in the sense organ and where they end in the brain. (Though if one imagines a cross section across a bundle of nerve fibers, the pattern of some conducting and some not conducting can be regarded as a changing code.) Thus, excitation by nerve impulses of one tiny portion of the brain results in awareness of a loud shrill sound, excitation of another in awareness of a blue line. Various areas of the body are mapped in the brain, a group of receptors (or sometimes an individual receptor) in the skin and tissues corresponding to each point in the cerebral receiving area. Similarly, the retinal image is reproduced point by point in the brain, though with each half reproduced in a separate area, duplicated there, and distorted. Again, a strip of brain tissue is activated at different points according to the frequency of the sounds heard, as if it were a keyboard.

COMPLEXITIES. There are nevertheless many complexities in the system, only a few of which we can mention here. The nerve connections are intricate, with feedback fibers from the brain to the incoming sensory fibers and cross connections between the sensory fibers; in the grouping of receptors and in the brain there is summation—several nerves join one that conducts only when all or most of them do. (In fact, neurologists constantly use such terms as *selecting, integrating, summating,* and *coding.*)

Binocular vision involves retinal disparity (a slight difference in the images cast on the two retinas) and the operation of two visual receiving areas reached by crossed-over nerve fibers so connected that the left-hand receiving area receives the signals coming from the right half of each retina and the right-hand area receives those of the left half. As a result we somehow normally see one object with depth and solidity rather than two two-dimensional ones.

Constant small eye movements are necessary for vision, with a shifting of the retinal image and of the resultant pattern of impulses in the fibers of the optic nerve, yet the object is seen as steady.

Most of the impulses reaching the brain from the eye come from a small portion of the retina (the fovea) that has relatively many receptors giving great distinctness; for exact vision the image is focused on the fovea by eye movement.

Color vision is particularly complex, and its mechanism is disputed. All the colors we know can be produced by suitable mixtures of red (long-wave), green (medium-wave), and blue (short-wave) light. White light can be formed by an appropriate combination of three colors or even of two widely separated ones. (Light, or "spectral" colors, mix differently from paint colors.) The simplest theory is that there are receptors in the eye reacting to each primary light color (red, green, and blue) and the brain, by summating the three color inputs, is enabled to cause the final color sensation. Thus, grass looks green because it absorbs red and blue light but reflects green, and a buttercup is yellow because it absorbs blue but reflects green and red, which combine to produce yellow. There are many difficulties in this theory. For instance, no receptors for blue can be positively located in the eye, only for red and green ones; the light from a green surface actually contains a mixture of wave lengths, with green predominating; the light wave lengths cover the spectrum of all the colors of the rainbow; the brightness and purity of the color also affect its hue. A final theory must therefore be very complicated.

The auditory receiving area gets impulses from both ears. This enables us to locate the source of a sound. If a sound is to the left, then sound waves reaching the left ear differ in phase (that is, timing of the wave crests) and in intensity from those reaching the right ear. The brain apparently combines the different inputs so that the location is done unconsciously and we just hear the sound as if it came from a certain direction.

LIMITATIONS OF THE SENSES. Radiant energy is known to range from short cosmic rays to long radio waves, but the eye responds only to visual light, which is a narrow band occupying about one-seventieth of the whole range. Even then we cannot distinguish light of different polarizations, as bees and birds apparently can, or see very small objects or fine structures. Similarly, in hearing we can distinguish only waves between 20 and 20,000 cycles per second; dogs, cats and rats can hear higher notes. Our sense of smell is obviously very inefficient compared with that of most other animals. Hence, though we can extend our range of observation by microscopes, infrared or X-ray photographs, radiotelescopes, and so on, it is clear that our senses themselves are very limited as a direct source of knowledge of the external world.

THE CAUSAL ARGUMENT. The causal argument maintains that the existence and character of these causal processes refute direct realism and force the adoption of a dualist position. Perception of an external object cannot be the direct contact or immediate confrontation it seems to be, since it requires this causal chain from object to the percipient's brain and is prevented if that is interrupted— for instance, if the optic nerve is cut or one of the small bones in the ear does not move properly. In this sense directness or immediacy must mean no intermediary and no possibility of interruption. The causal chain suggests that perceptual consciousness and its objects are generated, or brought into being, by the causal process, presumably by its last stage, the brain activity. In other words, insofar as perceptual consciousness is intuitive, it is awareness of some content or object quite distinct from the external object.

This suggestion is supported by various points. First, the time lag—perceptual consciousness may occur after the external object has disappeared or moved, so its content cannot be identified with the object. Second, the possibility of perceptual consciousness without any external object at all or without one at all similar seems confirmed by the production of sensations by stimulation of the cerebral cortex and seems actualized in hallucinations.

Third, the enormous complexity involved shows that the subjective simplicity of perception is illusory, at least insofar as a relation to an external object is concerned. Fourth, illusions and the relativity of perception are often explicable in terms of the causal processes. Unless the contents of perceptual consciousness are generated and conditioned by the causal process, one has to attribute bizarre and contradictory properties to the external object. Fifth, the simplicity and uniformity of nervous impulses show that they cannot transmit all the various secondary qualities that make up objects as we know them. These qualities must thus characterize contents of consciousness generated by the causal process. (This point is supported by such other limitations as the purely mechanical transmission through the bones of the ear.) Hence, it follows from the fourth and fifth points that one must abandon the other assumption of direct realism—that even when we are not perceiving them, objects continue to exist with the exact qualities we normally observe in them.

There is a good deal of resistance to these conclusions. One obstacle is that they seem to require a self-refuting type of representative realism. This fear is unjustified. It must also be noted that granted the dualist conclusion that the causal process generates the sensory experience whose content is (numerically) different from the external object, the nature of that experience and its content is still open. It may be that the awareness is of sensa, or it may be a full-fledged perceptual consciousness of percepts or ostensible objects. One is not even forced to adopt a mind-body dualism, though it is normally thought that sensa or percepts are mental. One might claim that though apparently distinct objects, they are in fact only the contents of sense experience, not existing apart from the sensing of them (adverbial analysis), and that they and the brain activity are two aspects of the reaction of the organism or person as a whole. This would mean that sensa are only a correlated aspect of brain activity, not effects of it, though still conditioned by the rest of the chain. In this way one might bypass one of the notorious difficulties of ordinary dualism—the unique and obscure causal relation supposed to exist between material brain and immaterial mind.

Sometimes, however, the opposition takes the form of denying the relevance of the scientific evidence to philosophy; it tells us only what the causes of perceiving are, not what perceiving itself is. Philosophers must investigate the latter and leave the causal processes to the scientist. But scientists normally hold that these processes require the adoption of representative realism, thus giv-ing them philosophical relevance; also, those philosophers who wish to concentrate on the nature of perception alone usually come up with some answer (the sense-datum analysis or a view that perceiving is the exercise of a skill or an investigational success) that is compatible with or even supports a dualist interpretation of the causal processes. But, above all, to achieve full understanding of anything so vital as perception, one must consider its causes and conditions, particularly as their study has traditionally been claimed to transform our concepts of perceiving itself and of our knowledge of the external world.

THE PSYCHOLOGICAL PROCESSES

It is clear from experimental psychology that perceptual consciousness involves a whole range of adjustments and selective or quasi-interpretative processes. The main evidence for this lies in differences between what psychologists often call the phenomenal properties of an object (those we are perceptually conscious of) and its stimulus properties. In this context the stimulus is the pattern of light rays from the object striking the eye, of sound waves striking the ear, or of heat or pressure from touching the object. The stimulus properties are those that we should observe in the stimulus (such as shape, color, pitch) could we observe it directly and in itself. This is difficult to achieve, and in fact the evidence of cameras, tape recorders, and other instruments is used, plus knowledge of the nature of the object and reasoning from the laws of perspective or of physics generally. The difference between the two kinds of property is presumed to be the result of modifications by the percipient.

ATTENTION AND SELECTION. It is a simple fact of experience that the quality and accuracy of perception vary with our attention. We often look inattentively and fail to notice pronounced features of a scene, yet we may carefully observe and thus notice unexpected details—a mark on the wallpaper, a printer's error, a wrong note in a recorded symphony. From the evidence of other people, from photographs, and from other means there may be no doubt that these features appeared all the time in the stimulus properties even when we were unconscious of them. Besides confirming this, psychologists have shown how greatly what we do or do not notice depends on habits of attention or interests, on often unconscious "priming" or "set." A mother will hear her baby cry but not notice much louder noises; an architect may notice features of buildings, and a boy notices makes of cars, both being oblivious to much else. Thus, perceptual consciousness is very selective, and this selection is usually largely unconscious, though voluntary attention can greatly modify it. One special case of voluntary attention is of importance—"perceptual reduction" or "phenomenological observation," where we concentrate on the sensible qualities of what we perceive and not, as is usual, on the identification of the object concerned. An artist must do this when he has to paint a scene, and this kind of observation may reveal all sorts of previously unnoticed details of color, shape, and so on. It is open to question whether this kind of reduction reveals an element present in all perception—namely, sensing—or whether, and this is more plausible, it is simply a special kind of perception of external objects not found in normal perceiving.

ERRORS AND ENRICHMENT. Some errors in perception can be attributed to psychological factors—misidentifications because of careless observation, seeing what one expects to see rather than what is actually present, thinking that one hears the expected visitor coming when no one is there, and the like. These point to a common characteristic of perception and one apparent only when it goes wrong—the enrichment of perception by imagery and thought. Many psychological experiments have been concerned with this. For example, vague or ambiguous stimuli (pictures or sounds) are presented to different groups of people who see or hear them as definite objects or words, and the direction in which they are thus unconsciously supplemented or altered can be shown to be caused by suggestion or by the interests, emotional state, or physical state of the person. Another kind of case is the divergence between several eyewitnesses' accounts of an incident, which may all differ from a filmed record. Again, blind spots or other visual defects are often not apparent to the subject, who unconsciously fills in the gap (this happens to us all if we look with one eye, for there is a blind spot where the optic nerve leaves the retina). Extreme cases are hallucinations where the apparition is integrated with the background or casts shadows. Unnoticed supplementation by imagery, which is admittedly private and mental, seems strong evidence for the dualist claim that the contents of perceptual consciousness are similarly private and must be distinguished from object properties.

LEARNING AND CUES. Our perception is clearly affected by learning and experience. Identification and discrimination afford obvious examples; one can learn to identify objects seen or photographed from unusual angles, to detect animals in natural camouflage, to distinguish different birds' songs. Driving a car involves perceptions of distance and relative speeds, perceptions that are acquired by experience. Psychological investigation has shown the role of learning to be far greater than this. Perception of spatial relations generally depends to a large extent on learning (normally unconscious and in childhood) to harmonize sight and touch and to use various cues. This is shown by various experiments, such as those with distorted rooms or inverted spectacles, and by the evidence of blind men who recover their sight. Among the various cues used for perception of distance and of solidity are shadows, aerial and linear perspective, parallax (or relative movement), and the interposition of objects. These assist binocular vision and enable us to see depth even with one eye.

FIGURE-GROUND AND GESTALT. In perception our immediate consciousness is of an organized or structured whole. Some shape or feature stands out and is seen as the figure against a background, and if discrete units such as dots are presented, we see them as grouped or patterned in some way. This characteristic of experience has been particularly stressed by Gestalt psychologists, who produced much experimental evidence to show that we see wholes or structures (Gestalten, literally, "forms") and that perception develops by discriminating these in and from a background and not by synthesis of atomic elements or point sensations first perceived separately. Such organization of the visual field, though little affected by learning, is nevertheless largely the result of processes in the percipient himself. The clearest evidence of this comes from the reversals, or "alternating illusions," where the stimulus (picture or succession of sounds) is constant but is perceived differently at different times; thus, sometimes one pattern or shape stands out as the figure, sometimes another. Examples are the goblet that may appear as two faces in profile, Edwin Boring's wife–mother-in-law figure, Ludwig Wittgenstein's duck-rabbit, and the staircase that seems to be seen now from above, now from below.

PERCEPTION OF MOTION. Perception of motion was closely investigated by the Gestalt psychologists, who drew attention to the Phi phenomenon, which is the impression of movement between adjacent stationary stimuli that are activated in succession. This underlies the consciousness of movement on a motion picture or television screen and is used in illuminated advertisements in which if groups of lights are successively switched on for a brief time, one is perceptually conscious of a moving figure or even of words moving along. Intermittent illumination may also make moving objects appear stationary. Thus, when illuminated by the flashing light of a stroboscope, a moving crank in a machine may, if the flashing is properly adjusted, be seen as stationary and examined for defects; if there is a slight maladjustment of the flashing, it may seem to rotate slowly backward like the wheels of coaches in Western films. There is a clear distinction in these cases between the properties of the stimulus and the contents of consciousness. Figure-ground effects also occur in movement perception, such as when the moon seems to sail through the clouds or when one's stationary train seems to move if an adjacent one starts.

OBJECT CONSTANCY. The widespread phenomenon of object constancy in perception differs from the above in that the phenomenal properties of an object tend to remain constant or nearly so even though the stimulus properties vary considerably. Thus, when we look at a round object—for example, a dish—from an angle, it often still looks round and not elliptical, although by the laws of perspective the stimulus (light-ray pattern) or retinal image is elliptical, as would appear on a photograph taken from the percipient's viewpoint. (This causes complication in stating the argument from illusion and perspective realism.) Only if the angle is very marked does the dish look elliptical. ("Look" here refers to the sensible quality, not to what we judge to be the object's shape.) Similarly with size, brightness, and color—a man looks much the same size at ten yards' distance as at five even though the image cast on the retina is half as high in the former case; a white patch in the shade reflects less light than a dark one in bright sunlight, but it still looks white; a white patch in a yellowish light still looks white although it is reflecting yellowish light (one may be surprised by color photographs taken in the evening, for the camera cannot adapt itself to the yellower light).

In general, over a range of varied stimuli we tend to see something corresponding to the property of the object or at least some compromise between this and the stimulus property. Experiments show that this constancy depends not on knowledge of the object but on the visibility of its background, for if the background is cut off by a screen so that only the object is visible, constancy does not hold and the stimulus property is seen. It is as though we made unconscious allowance for distance, angle of sight, and illumination as revealed by the whole scene. But this is not a learned or intelligent adjustment; children and even chickens or fish apparently see things with constancy, though to some extent it can be counteracted by adopting a stimulus attitude (trying to see the stimulus property).

PHILOSOPHICAL SIGNIFICANCE. The existence of these many complex processes that underlie perceptual consciousness and affect its content reinforces the causal argument by making even more incredible the direct-realist notion of perceiving as a straightforward direct confrontation with the actual properties of objects. If perception were a simple intuitive awareness of such properties, there would be no place in it for variations in quality; for the effects of interests, priming, and learning; and for the use of cues for enrichment by or integration with supplementary imagery, for constancy adjustments (especially where they produce a compromise between object and stimulus properties), for changing figure-ground effects, or for the Phi phenomenon.

The range of these processes is far greater than that which would be compatible with the usual analyses of perceptual consciousness—namely, that it is the interpretation of sensations (or inference from implicit grounds) or the taking for granted that a sensed datum belongs to an object. These views were mainly influenced by the possibility of error in perception, particularly in identification, although they took some account of the use of cues and of the role of learning. But they seem inadequate to cover the part played by attention and unconscious selection or by such organization adjustments as figure-ground, grouping, object constancy, or the Phi phenomenon, whereas some of the imaginative supplementation goes far beyond what can be called interpreting a datum. It is sometimes claimed that these adjustments are interpretations. But this is implausible, for they seem little affected by learning and are not intelligent since lower animals make them. Nor can many of the illusions or adjustments be overcome by knowledge of the facts or by conscious interpretation; where some counteraction is possible, as in object constancy, it is very difficult, and for most people the presence or absence of screens in experiments is compelling in its effect.

The final objection to such analyses concerns the alleged pure sensory data; interpreting or taking for granted, insofar as we are aware of it, is of something we are conscious of as distinct and external and which is thus already the effect of many of these processes. Normally, however, perceptual consciousness seems intuitive—that is, without interpretation and quite unanalyzable; except in perceptual reduction its content almost always consists of ostensible objects. All the same, psychological evidence shows that there is a range of subjective processes. The only answer seems to be a genetic hypothesis, not an analysis into elements. Perceptual consciousness is introspectively a whole but must be supposed to be a product of a range of selective, supplementary, integrative or organizational, and quasi-interpretative processes acting on a supposed basic sentience. But—and this is the point—both processes and sentience are unconscious and so may plausibly be regarded as cerebral activities or adjustments of the nervous system. However, since we cannot as yet give any precise neurological statement of these processes, we have to describe them as if they were conscious, basing the description on the difference between the input to the senses and the finished product, but this product (perceptual consciousness) does not reveal within itself the processes that may be supposed to form it.

The suggestion that perceptual consciousness is the product of many unconscious processes is controversial, and any general conclusions about perception are bound to be personal. Hence, the main attention in this entry has been on the facts that have to be taken into account in any fully adequate view of perception, and the reader is also referred to the statement of the various theories here and in other related entries. In this way one has the material for assessing the general view here adopted—namely, that the causal and psychological processes essential to perception, as well as its liability to illusion, require abandonment of direct realism for a dualist position. One must distinguish perceptual consciousness, whose content or objects are subjective and private to the percipient, from perception that occurs when this perceptual consciousness is caused by an external object with properties corresponding to its content. But one must not confuse this dualism with the traditional representative realism, which is only a variant of it, some form of critical realism being superior; the sense-datum theory's dualism of sense data and objects (perceptual consciousness is not thus analyzable, and its content consists of ostensible material objects); or the Cartesian mind-body dualism (it is possible also to adapt this view of perception to a double-aspect account of mind and body).

See also Illusions; Phenomenalism; Primary and Secondary Qualities; Realism; Sensa.

Bibliography

GENERAL INTRODUCTIONS

Perception is discussed, though usually less extensively than in the related entries in this encyclopedia, by most introductory books on philosophy. For example, see Bertrand Russell, *Problems of Philosophy* (London: Williams and Norgate, 1912) and *Outline of Philosophy* (London: Allen and Unwin, 1927); Charles Harold Whiteley, *Introduction to Metaphysics* (London, 1955); John Hospers, *Introduction to Philosophical Analysis* (New York: Prentice-Hall, 1953; London: Routledge and Paul, 1956); and Arthur Pap, *Elements of Analytic Philosophy* (New York: Macmillan, 1949). A clear and useful outline with emphasis on the associated epistemological problems is A. J. Ayer's *The Problem of Knowledge* (London: Macmillan, 1956). A more detailed introductory treatment is given by R. J. Hirst, *The Problems of Perception* (London: Allen and Unwin, 1959), Chs. I–VI; the later chapters of this book develop a more advanced treatment of perceptual consciousness and the scientific evidence on the lines adumbrated here.

PERCEPTUAL CONSCIOUSNESS

For analyses of perception in the sense of perceptual consciousness, see H. H. Price, *Perception* (London: Methuen, 1954) on the sense-datum theory; Durant Drake and others, *Essays in Critical Realism* (London: Macmillan, 1920), and Roy Wood Sellars, *The Philosophy of Physical Realism* (New York: Macmillan, 1932), on critical realism; Brand Blanshard, *The Nature of Thought*, Vol. I (London: Allen and Unwin, 1939), on idealism; and Roderick M. Chisholm, *Perceiving: A Philosophical Study* (Ithaca, NY: Cornell University Press, 1957), which is a causal analysis with a general consideration of perceiving and epistemological questions. Roderick Firth, "Sense-Data and the Percept Theory," in *Mind* 58 (232) (1949): 434–465, and 59 (233) (1950): 35–36, is critical of any such analyses.

CONCEPTUAL ANALYSIS

For the approach by conceptual analysis see "On Seeing and Hearing" by Winston H. F. Barnes, "Identification and Existence" by Stuart Hampshire, and "Sensation" by Gilbert Ryle in *Contemporary British Philosophy*, Vol. III, edited by H. D. Lewis (London: Allen and Unwin, 1956); Gilbert Ryle, *The Concept of Mind* (London: Hutchinson, 1949), Ch. 7, and *Dilemmas* (Cambridge, U.K.: Cambridge University Press, 1954); Anthony M. Quinton, "The Problem of Perception," in *Mind* 64 (253) (1955): 28–51; and D. W. Hamlyn's discussion of psychological theories, *The Psychology of Perception* (London: Routledge and Paul, 1957). John Langshaw Austin's *Sense and Sensibilia* (Oxford: Clarendon Press, 1962) is an outstanding defense of common sense against the argument from illusion, but unfortunately he does not discuss the scientific evidence. Another direct-realist study is D. M. Armstrong's *Perception and the Physical World* (New York: Humanities Press, 1961).

SCIENTIFIC BACKGROUND

Useful elementary accounts of the causal and psychological processes are given in such textbooks as Ernest Ropiequet Hilgard, *Introduction to Psychology* (New York: Harcourt Brace, 1953); David Krech and Richard Stanley Crutchfield, *Elements of Psychology*, 3rd ed. (New York: Knopf, 1962); and Robert Sessions Woodworth and D. G. Marquis, *Psychology* (New York: Holt, 1947; London: Methuen, 1949). Rather more detail, with a philosophical discussion as well, is given in George McCreath Wyburn, Ralph William Pickford, and R. J. Hirst, *Human Senses and Perception* (Edinburgh: Oliver and Boyd, 1964). Two significant but unconventional psychological books that raise philosophical questions of interest to the advanced student are James Jerome Gibson, *The Perception of the Visual World* (Boston: Houghton Mifflin, 1950), and Friedrich August von Hayek,

The Sensory Order (Chicago: University of Chicago Press, 1952; London: Routledge, 1953).

INTERPRETATIONS OF SCIENTIFIC EVIDENCE

See the works by Price, Chisholm, Hirst and the critical realists mentioned above and Arthur O. Lovejoy, *The Revolt against Dualism* (La Salle, IL: Open Court, 1930), also a critical realist. C. D. Broad's *Perception, Physics and Reality* (Cambridge, U.K.: Cambridge University Press, 1914) and *Scientific Thought* (London: Kegan Paul, 1923), sense-datum analyses, are very technical at times. William Pepperell Montague, *The Ways of Knowing* (New York: Macmillan, 1925), gives a general comparison of the different realist (and other) views. See also the more sophisticated types of representative realism—namely, John Raymond Smythies, *Analysis of Perception* (London: Routledge and Paul, 1956), or Bertrand Russell, *Analysis of Matter* (London: Kegan Paul, 1927) and *Human Knowledge* (London: Allen and Unwin, 1948). Of Russell's two books, the first is often difficult, and the second is more for the general reader.

OTHER RECOMMENDED TITLES

Alston, William P. *The Reliability of Sense Perception*. Ithaca, NY: Cornell University Press, 1993.

Armstrong, D. M. *Belief, Truth, and Knowledge*. Cambridge, U.K.: Cambridge University Press, 1973.

Ayer, A. J. *The Foundations of Empirical Knowledge*. London: Macmillan, 1940.

BonJour, Laurence. *The Structure of Empirical Knowledge*. Cambridge, MA: Harvard University Press, 1985.

Brewer, Bill. *Perception and Reason*. Oxford: Clarendon Press, 2002.

Burnyeat, Myles. "Conflicting Appearances." *Proceedings of the British Academy* 65 (1979): 69–111.

Dancy, J., ed. *Perceptual Knowledge*. Oxford: Oxford University Press, 1988.

Dicker, Georges. *Perceptual Knowledge*. Dordrecht: Reidel, 1980.

Dretske, Fred. *Seeing and Knowing*. London: Routledge and Kegan Paul, 1969.

Fales, Evan. *A Defense of the Given*. Lanham, MD: Rowman & Littlefield, 1996.

Fumerton, Richard. *Metaphysical and Epistemological Problems of Perception*. Lincoln: University of Nebraska Press, 1985.

Goldman, Alvin. "Perceptual Knowledge and Discrimination." *Journal of Philosophy* 73 (1976): 771–791.

Grice, H. P. "The Causal Theory of Perception." *PAS*, Supp. 35 (1961): 121–168.

Jackson, Frank. *Perception: A Representative Theory*. Cambridge, U.K.: Cambridge University Press, 1977.

Perkins, M. *Sensing the World*. Indianapolis: Hackett, 1983.

Sellars, Wilfrid. *Science, Perception, and Reality*. Atascadero, CA: Ridgeview Press, 1991.

R. J. Hirst (1967)
Bibliography updated by Benjamin Fiedor (2005)

PERCEPTION, CONTEMPORARY VIEWS

Philosophical accounts of perception aim to give a coherent and systematic account of the nature of our sensory experiences. Philosophical accounts differ from scientific ones, which aim at explaining how the specific mechanisms of perception work. Philosophers are interested in general features that are common to anything that we might reasonably call perception, abstracting away from the specific mechanisms by which we perceive the world. Contemporary theorists of perception have proposed theories aimed at addressing a number of questions about perception, including the following: What accounts for the distinctive feel of our sensory experiences? Is perception a representational state with specific content (like desires and beliefs)? Is perception a "direct" awareness of the world? How does perception make possible beliefs and thoughts about the world? How do perceptions serve as reasons for belief, making possible knowledge of the world?

APPEARANCE, REALITY, AND PHENOMENAL CHARACTER

One main source of philosophical puzzlement that has persisted since ancient times is the distinction between appearance and reality. To see the distinction, consider an example in which you see a ripe tomato sitting on a well-lit table. Assuming your eyesight is good, the tomato will appear a certain way to you; for example, it may appear red and round. This is a case of what we will call veridical perception. The tomato appears red and round to you, and in reality it is that way. It is, of course, also possible to misperceive, in which case the way things appear will not match the way they are. For example, if the tomato is in unusual lighting, it might appear to be purple rather than red. Likewise, if you are wearing shape-distorting glasses, the tomato might appear to be tall and skinny rather than short and plump, as it really is. These are cases of illusion, which involve objects appearing to you to have properties other than the ones that they have in reality. A second kind of misperception, distinct from illusion, is hallucination. Hallucinations are experiences in which it appears to you as if an object with certain properties is present, when in reality you are not in perceptual contact with any such object. For example, it might appear to you as if there is a red and round tomato before you when in fact there is no object there at all.

One problem that the possibility of misperception raises is epistemic and has to do with whether we are able to know things about the world. Skeptics about knowledge of the external world have held that, in order for you to have knowledge of the world, you must be able to rule out the possibility that you are now misperceiving. But, these skeptics claim, there are certain possibilities of radical misperception that you cannot properly rule out—for example, you can't rule out the possibility that you are right now dreaming, or the possibility that you are really a brain in a vat being fed experiences as of the external world by an evil superscientist who is directly stimulating your brain. Defenders of the common sense idea that we have perceptual knowledge attempt to reply to the skeptic's challenge.

As we will see, the possibility of misperception also provides a challenge for metaphysical accounts of the nature of perceptual appearances. The challenge arises in part because giving a theory of the nature of appearances requires accounting for what is sometimes called the phenomenal character of experience, or, more simply, the phenomenology of experience. The phenomenal character of a cognitive episode is, in Thomas Nagel's famous phrase, "what it is like" to undergo it. A feature unique to conscious states is that there is something it is like to be in them. There is, for example, a way it is like for one to see a tomato.

The phenomenal character of perceptual experiences seems to be a crucial part of what distinguishes such experiences from other conscious mental events such as occurrent thoughts, desires, and beliefs. For example, what it is like for you to think about a tomato that is in front of you with your eyes closed will be very different from what it is like to open your eyes and *see* the tomato. Seeing a tomato has a sensory, visual phenomenology that merely thinking about a tomato lacks. Although nonperceptual mental states like beliefs and desires arguably have a phenomenal character (for example, there is presumably something it is like for you to think about mathematical sums while in a sensory-deprivation tank with no perceptual experience at all), the phenomenal character of perceptual awareness is distinctive.

It may be that not all perceptions are conscious and so have a phenomenal character. It is common in psychology to distinguish between unconscious and conscious perceptions, and there is a growing psychological literature suggesting that much of the perceptual information that guides our actions is not conscious. (A good introduction to the psychological evidence is in Melvin Goodale's *Sight Unseen*.) It is a question of considerable philosophical interest what unconscious perception is and how to distinguish it from conscious perception.

Nevertheless, we will focus here on theories of perception that seek to give an account of conscious perceptual experience.

There are several aspects of the phenomenal character of perceptual experience that philosophers have thought need to be reflected in a philosophical account of perception. First, there are differences in phenomenal character at the level of the different sense modalities. For example, what it is like to see a tomato is different from what it is like to taste, touch, or smell it. Each mode of perceptual awareness—vision, taste, touch, smell, and audition—has its own distinctive sensory phenomenal character.

Second, there are similarities and differences in phenomenal character at the level of experiences within a sensory modality. For example, a tomato might appear to be red, another might appear to be green, and a third might appear to be very similar in color to the red one. Philosophers are also interested in the way that experiences from different perspectives give rise to differences in phenomenal character, even when there is no change in the way objects appear to be. For example, looking at the tomato from different angles or from nearer or farther away yields differences in the appearances, even though all of these experiences are arguably veridical perceptions and there is no change in the way the object appears to be. When viewed from close up, the tomato in a meaningful sense "appears larger" than when one looks at it from afar. Or, to take another example, it may be that part of the surface of a tomato "appears white" owing to the way the light is reflecting off its surface, even though in another sense the tomato appears uniformly red. These observations suggest a distinction between what we will call constant and perspectival modes of appearance talk. In the constant mode, saying that "an object appears so-and-so" implies that if you are not subject to an illusion, then the object *is* so-and-so. But this is not the case in the perspectival mode; it can be the case that "an object appears so-and-so" and that you are not subject to an illusion, while *not* being the case that the object really is so-and-so. For example, when you see the highlight on the tomato, it is correct to say that patch of the tomato "appears white" in the perspectival sense of appearance talk, but also correct to say that it "appears (to be) red" in the constant mode.

Since what we want in an account of perceptual experience is an account of perceptual consciousness, a correct theory of sense perception must be phenomenally adequate; it must do justice to the phenomenal character of experience.

ARGUMENTS FROM ILLUSION

A problem that divides philosophers of perception is how to account for the phenomenal character of experience while at the same time explaining the possibility of misperception. To see how the problem arises, consider a theory of perceptual experience that some philosophers have dubbed Naive Realism. As its name suggests, Naive Realism tries to take what is seen as a prereflective account of perception and use it as a philosophical theory of perception. According to them, perceptual consciousness is, in its fundamental nature, a relation of direct awareness between a perceiver and public objects and their properties. Moreover, it is these properties and objects of which one is aware that explain the phenomenal character of experience. Consider again our case of a tomato's visually appearing to you to be red and round. What explains the phenomenology of such an experience? The Naive Realist thinks that common sense is clear about what explains this: It is the tomato itself and the qualities of it presented to awareness that constitute what it is like to see the tomato. To explain what it is like to have a perceptual experience, we simply need to describe the objects that appear to you and their properties of which you are aware.

One challenge for Naive Realism is to explain differences in the phenomenal character of appearances described in the perspectival mode. For example, we saw that in the perspectival mode it is correct to say that the tomato viewed from afar appears smaller than when viewed from close up. Yet in both viewings of the tomato, it seems reasonable to suppose that you veridically perceive the size of the tomato, a property of the tomato that does not change. (This is why it is correct to say in the constant mode that whether the tomato is viewed from up close or from afar it appears to be the same size, say, roughly the size of your closed fist.) It seems, then, that what explains the difference in phenomenal character of these two viewings is not a property of the tomato, as the Naive Realist supposes.

Perhaps an even more difficult problem for the Naive Realist arises from the possibility of misperception. When you see the ripe tomato and your experience is veridical, you are in a perceptual state that we can describe by saying that "it appears to you as if there is something red and round before you." But it seems entirely possible for the very same type of state described in this way (complete with its distinctive phenomenal character) to occur as part of illusory or hallucinatory experience. For example, if you were wearing shape- and color-distorting glasses, it might be that what is in reality a tall, oblong, purple thing

looks to you just like a plump, red tomato. This illusory experience might have the same phenomenal character as your veridical perception of a red, round tomato. The problem for the Naive Realist is that it *cannot be* in this case that the real color and shape properties of the thing you are seeing are what explain what it is like to see the object. The thing you are seeing is tall and purple, whereas your experience is as of something red and round.

The possibility of hallucination raises an exactly similar problem for Naive Realists. Consider a case in which you have a hallucination of a tomato when there is not one anywhere nearby. To fill out the case a bit, we might imagine that a futuristic superscientist stimulates your visual cortex in just the same way that it is stimulated when you see a tomato and thereby produces in you an experience that is every bit as vivid as a veridical perception of a tomato. If this were the case, it obviously can't be true that what explains the phenomenal character of your experience is a direct awareness of a real tomato that is red and round. In the case as described, there is not even a tomato there!

Although we have been focusing on specific visual examples involving seeing tomatoes, there is nothing special about our choice of examples. For *any* veridical perception that we could describe as one in which "it perceptually appears to you as if such-and-such is the case," it seems possible for you to be in a state with the very same phenomenal character that is an illusion or a hallucination. The problem for the Naive Realist is that they don't have the resources to explain the phenomenal character of these states, since their account at best only explains the phenomenal character of veridical perceptions.

The considerations here are related to a family of arguments that were commonly referred to in the twentieth century as "the argument from illusion." As might be apparent from our discussion, we can actually distinguish among arguments from perspective, illusion, and hallucination, depending on which of these phenomena is under consideration. Further on we will consider how different theorists propose to answer these problems, including responses on behalf of those who want to defend Naive Realism from the objections.

SENSE-DATA THEORY

One historically important answer to the problems of perspective, illusion, and hallucination is that of the Sense-Data Theory. The theory is not as commonly held among contemporary theorists as it was among philosophers in the early twentieth century (such as G. E. Moore, H. H. Price, and C. D. Broad), but it still has a few defenders today (for example, Howard Robinson). According to Sense-Data Theorists, perception involves an immediate awareness of mental "Sense-Data," which are taken to be objects such that awareness of them fully determines their existence and nature.

Its proponents offer the Sense-Data Theory as the best explanation of the perspectival character of appearances, and of the possibility of misperception. Consider again our example of seeing the tomato. We saw that one challenge to Naive Realists is to answer questions about the perspectival character of appearances like this one: Why is it that looking at a tomato up close results in an experience that can be described in the perspectival mode as one in which the tomato appears larger than it does when you are standing far away from it? The Sense-Data Theorist will answer that this is because in the former case you are aware of a sense datum that *really is* larger than the sense datum you are aware of when you look at the tomato from afar. An advocate of the arguments from illusion and hallucination against Naive Realist might also ask this question: How is it, then, that a state with a single phenomenal character—for example, a state in which it seems to you as if there is a red, round tomato before you—could occur either in a veridical perception or in a hallucination or in an illusion? The Sense-Data Theorist's answer is that the veridical perception, illusion, and hallucination all involve your being directly aware of sense data with the same properties, for example, sense data that are red and round.

According to the Sense-Data Theory, one is aware of objects and properties in the world only indirectly, in virtue of a more direct awareness of sense data and their properties. One challenge for the Sense-Data Theorist is to explain how sense data must be related to the world in order for one to perceive the world (albeit indirectly). For example, a Sense-Data Theorist owes us an answer to the following question: What makes it the case when you veridically perceive a tomato that being directly aware of a red, round sense datum counts as perceiving the real-world tomato? One possible reply would be that in order to perceive the tomato, you must be aware of a sense datum that has properties that resemble (or are isomorphic to) the properties of the tomato in the world. But this cannot be quite right. You can perceive a tomato even when your experience is a radical illusion such that you misperceive all of the tomatoes properties.

For example, if you look at the tomato through shape and color distorting lenses, the sense datum of which you

are aware will not match the tomato in any of its shape or color properties (for example, the sense datum might be purple and tall while the tomato is short and red). But it might still be true that you see the tomato, even though you misperceive its properties. A second reply on behalf of the Sense-Data Theorist might be that you see the tomato if and only if the tomato causes the sense data of which you are aware. This proposal faces the problem that there are many different causes of the sense datum that don't count as things that you see. For example, the image on your retina is one of the causes of your perceptual experience (and its properties even seem to resemble the qualities of the sense data of which you are aware). But you do not see the images on your retina. Only eye doctors who are looking inside your eyes see retinal images. It seems that an object must cause an experience in the "right way" in order for the subject to perceive the object. It is a difficult problem, though, to say what this right way is.

Sense-data theories have been subject to many other objections. Arguments from illusion to the existence of sense-data theories have been criticized on grounds that they illicitly rely on a general principle of the following form: If it appears to you as if something has a certain property, then you are aware of something that really does have that property. Relying on this claim is sometimes referred to as the "sense-datum fallacy." The assumption has been thought to lead to absurd conclusions, like the conclusion that when an antique vase appears ancient and cracked to me, there is a sense datum that really is ancient and cracked. However, this conclusion might be blocked by restricting the properties mentioned in the principle to perceptible properties, such as color and shape. Moreover, the arguments from illusion, hallucination, and perspective should perhaps best be thought of as inferences to the best explanation. On this way of construing the arguments, the Sense-Data Theorist claims that postulating sense data offers the best explanation of the possibility of phenomenally identical illusions and hallucinations, and offers the best account of the perspectival nature of experience.

Other common objections to Sense-Data Theory allege that the view leads to skepticism, setting up a problematic epistemic "veil of perception" between the world and us, or that sense data are not scientifically respectable because they do not seem to be the sorts of things that fit easily into a physical picture of the world. In recent years, perhaps the most common objection to sense-data theories arises from a point about the phenomenal character of experience. Philosophers such as Gilbert Harman (1990/1997) and Michael Tye (1995) have claimed that there is a tension between Sense-Data Theory and what is sometimes metaphorically referred to as the "transparent" or "diaphanous" nature of experience. The idea that experience is transparent is the idea that perception, and in particular visual perception, seems on the face of it to be a direct presentation of objects and properties as they are in themselves, and does not seem to involve an awareness of subjective properties and objects that represent objects in the world, as the Sense-Data Theory suggests. In perception, it is argued, we seem to be aware only of public properties and objects. For example, philosophers who think experience is transparent will say that when you see the tomato and reflect on your experience, the only properties that you will seem to be aware of are the public properties of the tomato. As rendered by the transparency metaphor, experience doesn't seem to be an opaque object that we know to be related in some way to the external world, as we might expect if the Sense-Data Theory were true; rather, experience seems "transparent," and the world and its properties (metaphorically speaking) *shine* through it.

INTENTIONALIST THEORIES

Philosophers such as Gilbert Harman (1990/1997), Michael Tye (1995), and Fred Dretske (1995), have suggested that by treating experience as an intentional state we can account for the transparency of experience while agreeing with the Sense-Data Theorist that there is a common kind of state involved in veridical perception that could also occur in illusion or hallucination. Intentional states are those with representational contents that can be correct or incorrect. A familiar example is belief. To believe that there is a tomato on the table, for example, is to be in a state that has a representational content—namely the content *There is a tomato on the table*. This content can be correct or incorrect depending on whether there is in fact a tomato on the table.

Intentionalists claim that experience is like belief in being a state that represents the world as being some way or other, and they hold that the representational content of experience fully explains its phenomenal character. (Sometimes this claim of Intentionalists is put in terms of what is called a "supervenience claim": phenomenal properties supervene on intentional content, i.e., there can be no change in phenomenal qualities without a change in the intentional content of experience.) When it appears to you as if there is a tomato before you, for instance, you are in a state that represents certain properties typical of tomatoes (for example, being round, red, and so on). According to Intentionalists, the way in which

the world is represented explains the phenomenal character of the experience. Moreover, the same experience could occur in a misperception. The experience is correct if there really is a tomato with those properties before me. It is illusory if there is an object there, but it isn't red or round. The experience is hallucinatory if there is no object there at all.

Intentionalists accommodate the transparency of perceptual experience by claiming that, even though perceptual experience involves a state that represents, introspection is open only to the properties and objects represented by the experience, all of which are taken by Intentionalist theorists to be external properties and objects. The way objects are represented in perceptual experiences is consequently not like the way in which objects are represented when one looks at a photograph of them. When one looks at a photograph of one's grandmother, one is aware of some of the features on the film in virtue of which the photograph represents Grandma (for example, the colors and shapes on the surface of the film). Perceptual experience is more like conceptual thought, at least thoughts that do not employ mental imagery. When one thinks about one's grandmother (supposing one doesn't use a bit of mental imagery to do so), one is not aware of the properties in virtue of which one's thought is about one's grandmother. One is simply aware of the represented object, one's grandmother. Likewise, according to Intentionalists, when one *sees* one's grandmother, one is not aware of the properties in virtue of which one's experience is representing grandmother; one is only aware of what is represented—Grandmother and her properties.

Some early versions of Intentionalism claimed that perception is not merely *similar* to belief, it is in fact a kind of belief. (This was, for example, David Armstrong's view in his book *Perception and the Physical World* [1961]) However, such a view faces serious objections. A noncontroversial way of showing that experiences are not beliefs is to note that experiences are not revisable in light of counterevidence in the way that beliefs are. For example, one might believe that one's current experience is illusory or hallucinatory. If one has good enough reason to believe this, one can fail to believe the evidence of one's senses, even though the perceptual experience, complete with its phenomenal character, will remain intact.

A related question that arises for those who hold that perception is not a kind of belief is whether experience is like belief insofar as it essentially involves a deployment of concepts. Some philosophers of perception have propounded Conceptualism, the view that every sensory element of perception involves an exercise of concepts by the perceiver. Conceptualism is often held on the ground that the only way that a state can serve as a reason for belief is if the state is conceptual through and through. Conceptualism is defended in this way by Bill Brewer (1999) and John McDowell (1994), although both argue for the position in the context of defending Disjunctivism (a view explained below) rather than Intentionalism. Some theorists object to Conceptualism on the grounds that animals or small children can perceive the world even though they lack concepts that would allow them to form beliefs about the world. Others object to Conceptualism on the grounds that the fine-grained phenomenal character of experience suggests that experience has "nonconceptual content." These philosophers suggest that the complexity and specificity of the properties and objects that you see in a single glance outstrip your conceptual capacity to form conceptual thoughts about these objects and properties.

Several potential objections to Intentionalist theories have been raised in the philosophical literature. One challenge for Intentionalists is the same as a challenge raised above for Sense-Data Theorists, namely to give an account as to how an object must be related to perceptual experience in order for the experience to be a perception of the object. It has seemed to most Intentionalists that the answer to this question involves an object's causing the experience in "the right sort of way." (For example, your experience as of a tomato must be caused in the right way by a tomato in order for you to see a tomato.) But it is difficult to say what this "right sort of way" is.

Quite a few philosophers have objected that Intentionalism lacks the resources to explain what is distinctively sensory about the phenomenal character of experiences. This general objection is pressed in a variety of ways. Some philosophers (such as Christopher Peacocke 2001) have challenged Intentionalists to provide an account of facts about appearances described in the perspectival mode, such as the way the tomato appears smaller when one moves further away from it. Other theorists attack the alleged transparency of experience by citing examples of what they claim are experiences that do not seem to be about public objects or properties. In some examples of perceptual experience, these philosophers claim, we seem to be aware of objects or properties that are essentially private and depend on our awareness of them. Proposed examples include experiences involving afterimages, double vision, blurred vision, and the "inner light show" that one experiences when one shuts one's eyes tightly.

Still other philosophers have objected that Intentionalists cannot explain the difference in phenomenal character between perception and other intentional states such as thinking. Earlier it was suggested that the phenomenal character of seeing a tomato is very different from merely thinking about the tomato. But both seem to be intentional states, and it seems that they might have the very same content—for example, the content *There is a red and round tomato on the table*. A challenge for the Intentionalist is to explain the difference between these two states. Some Intentionalists have suggested that the difference can be explained because perceptual experience is nonconceptual and plays a distinctive role in relation to beliefs and desires. A related challenge for Intentionalists is to distinguish between the phenomenal character of experiences in different modalities. For example, one can both feel the roundness of a tomato and also see the roundness. These states both represent the same property, the roundness of the tomato, so the Intentionalist might seem to be committed to thinking that the phenomenal character is the same. But of course the phenomenal character of the states is quite different.

Those who find the foregoing objections to Intentionalism compelling might still hold on to the idea that perception is an intentional state and that the content of the state *in part* explains the phenomenal character of experience. They will hold, however, that something in addition to the intentional content is required in order to account for the distinctively sensory phenomenal character of experience. Some philosophers (for example, Timothy Crane 1992) have suggested that in order to explain the phenomenal character of experience fully, we need to appeal not only to intentional contents but also to *modes of presentation* of those contents. For example, to explain the phenomenal character of your seeing the tomato we need to mention not only that you are in a state with the content that there is a red tomato before you, but also that this content is presented *visually*, rather than, say, tactilely. Others, such as Ned Block, suggest that we need to appeal to nonintentional properties of experience, sometimes called "qualia" in order to fully account for the phenomenal character of experience. This alternative is, in fact, consistent with the Sense-Data Theory. It is possible to develop a view according to which the perception of the tomato has an intentional content (for example, the content *There is something red and round before you*) that partly explains the phenomenal character of the experience, while also arguing for the need to postulate an awareness of a mental sense datum with certain properties in order to give a complete explanation of the phenomenal character of experience. (This seems to be a view held by Christopher Peacocke in his book *Sense and Content*, though he speaks of awareness of "visual fields" rather than sense data.)

DISJUNCTIVISM

In recent years there has been a resurgence of attempts to defend Naive Realism by giving what is called a disjunctive account of experiences. Disjunctivists challenge the claim that for any veridical perceptual state of a subject (seeing a ripe tomato, for example), an event of the very same kind, individuated by its phenomenal character, could occur in a misperception. As stated earlier, one can describe the state of seeing the tomato as one in which "it appears to you as if there is something red and round before you," and this state can occur either in veridical perception, illusion, or hallucination. According to Disjunctivists, the state that we describe in this way is not a unified kind. The most that can be said about it is that this it is *either* (1) a state in which you are veridically perceiving a red and round tomato (in which case you are directly aware of the tomato and its properties) *or* (2) a state in which you are having a hallucination or an illusion that is indistinguishable from a veridical perception as of a tomato.

One might complain that so far, this is no theory at all, but at best a promise of one. The theory does not tell us anything, for example, about the phenomenal character of hallucinatory experiences. Disjunctivists, one might think, owe us an account of the phenomenal character of the "bad" side of the disjunct that involves hallucinatory experience. Many Disjunctivists resist the call to give a robust account of the phenomenal character of hallucinatory experience. For instance, Michael Martin, in "The Limits of Self Awareness" 2004, gives a purely epistemic characterization of hallucination. According to him, the most that can be said about the nature of hallucination is that it is indistinguishable from a genuine perception. For example, in the case where an advanced neuroscientist stimulates your visual cortex in exactly the way it is stimulated when you veridically perceive a tomato, Martin will say that the most fundamental thing we can say to explain the nature of this state is that this is a state such that you can't know purely on the basis of the experience that it isn't a genuine perception of a tomato. Many theorists, though, will think that the obvious explanation as to *why* your hallucination of a tomato can't be distinguished from a veridical perception is that the hallucination has a phenomenal character of a kind that requires a substantive metaphysical explanation—for example, the sort of

explanation that Sense-Data Theorists and Intentionalists give.

Other Disjunctivists have made some tentative proposals for what accounts for the phenomenal character of hallucinatory states. Harold Langsam (1997), for example, says that it is possible to develop a theory according to which it is the physical regions of space around the subject where the object appears to be that are the relata of hallucination, and William Alston (1999) has suggested in passing that hallucination may involve an awareness of mental images. Such theorists face what might seem to be embarrassing questions that challenge their theoretical disunity. Given that their account of hallucinatory states fully explains the phenomenal character of experience, why not apply that same explanation to the case of veridical perception? Isn't it explanatory profligacy to rely on a disjunctive account when a unified one is available?

In response, Disjunctivists might counter that the explanatory cost of having an ununified view is well worth paying because alternative accounts of perception are subject to fatal flaws. In fact, a typical strategy of Disjunctivists has been to try to show that alternative theories of perception face insurmountable difficulties, leading to skepticism or making it mysterious how it is possible to think about the external world, or failing to do justice to the phenomenal character of experience.

See also Alston, William P.; Armstrong, David M.; Broad, Charlie Dunbar; Dretske, Fred; Harman, Gilbert; Illusions; McDowell, John; Moore, George Edward; Nagel, Thomas; Realism; Sensa.

Bibliography

Alston, William P. "Back to the Theory of Appearing." *Philosophical Perspectives* 13 (1999): 181–203

Armstrong, D. M. *Perception and the Physical World*. London: Routledge, 1961.

Block, Ned. "Mental Paint and Mental Latex." *Philosophical Issues* 7 (1996): 19–49.

Brewer, Bill. *Perception and Reason*. Oxford: Oxford University Press, 1999.

Crane, Tim. *The Contents of Experience*. New York: Cambridge University Press, 1992.

Dretske, Fred I. *Naturalizing the Mind*. Cambridge, MA: MIT Press, 1995.

Foster, John. *The Nature of Perception*. New York: Oxford University Press, 2000.

Goodale, Melvin, David Milner, and A. D. Milner. *Sight Unseen: An Exploration of Conscious and Unconscious Vision*. Oxford: Oxford University Press, 2004.

Harman, Gilbert. "The Intrinsic Quality of Experience." In *The Nature of Consciousness: Philosophical Debates*, edited by N.

J. Block, O. J. Flanagan, and G. Guzeldere. Cambridge, MA: MIT Press, 1997. First published in 1990.

Jackson, Frank. *Perception: A Representative Theory.* Cambridge, U.K.: Cambridge University Press, 1977.

Johnston, Mark. "The Obscure Object of Hallucination." *Philosophical Studies* 120 (2004): 113—183.

Langsam, Harold. "The Theory of Appearing Defended." *Philosophical Studies* 87 (1997): 33–59.

Martin, Michael G. F. "The Limits of Self-Awareness." *Philosophical Studies.* 120 (2004): 37–89.

McDowell, John. *Mind and World.* Cambridge, MA: Harvard University Press, 1994.

Peacocke, Christopher. "Does Perception Have a Nonconceptual Content?" *Journal of Philosophy* 98 (2001): 239–264.

Robinson, Howard. *Perception.* London; New York: Routledge, 1994.

Shoemaker, Sydney. "Introspection and Phenomenal Character." *Philosophical Topics* 28 (2000): 247–273.

Smith, A. D. *The Problem of Perception.* Cambridge, MA: Harvard University Press, 2002.

Swartz, Robert J. *Perceiving, Sensing, and Knowing.* Garden City, NY: Anchor Books, 1965.

Tye, Michael. *Ten Problems of Consciousness: A Representational Theory of the Phenomenal Mind, Representation, and Mind.* Cambridge, MA: MIT Press, 1995.

Michael Pace (2005)

PERCEPTUAL CERTAINTY

See *Illusions*

PERCEPTUAL CONSCIOUSNESS

See *Perception*

PERFECTION

The concept of "perfection" has two closely allied and often overlapping meanings. First, it means "completeness," "wholeness," or "integrity": *X* is perfect when he (or it) is free from all deficiencies. Second, it means the achievement of an end or a goal. This meaning emerges most clearly from the connection between the Greek words *teleios* ("perfect") and *telos* ("end" or "goal"). An entity is perfect (to use Aristotelian terms) when it has achieved its goal by actualizing its potentialities and realizing its specific form. Bringing these two meanings together, one would say that a thing is complete or entire when it has fulfilled its nature and thereby reached its

"end." The concept is best examined first under its religious, and second under its moral, aspect.

DIVINE PERFECTION

It has not always been believed that God (or, more generally, "the divine") is perfect. Thus, the deities of the Homeric pantheon were both ontologically and morally deficient. They differed from men only in being "deathless" (*athanatoi*). But in Christian theology the perfection of God has always been affirmed by orthodox writers. In St. Anselm's celebrated definition, God is *id quo nihil maius cogitari possit* ("that than which nothing greater can be conceived"). St. Thomas Aquinas later maintained that since God is self-existent, he must be infinite (or limitless) in intelligence, goodness, and power. He also claimed, in the fourth of his five Ways, to prove the existence of God as absolute perfection from the limited degrees of perfection in creatures. Thomists hold that by the "analogy of proportionality" we can attribute to God "in a more eminent way" (*eminentiori modo*) every "pure" perfection that exists in creatures (that is, every perfection that is capable of preexisting in an infinitely spiritual degree).

Those who hold this view of God's infinity must face two questions that have continually perplexed Christian philosophers. First, can we intelligibly assert that all perfections coexist infinitely in a single being? Thus, can God be both infinitely just and infinitely merciful? Second, if God is both infinitely powerful and infinitely good, how can we explain the presence of evil in the world?

MORAL PERFECTION

Ever since men began to reflect on the moral life, they have been aware of some perfect ideal of character and conduct toward which they must strive. Thus, in the Greco-Roman world the Stoics wrote copiously of the "perfect" (*teleios*) man. In their view perfection consisted in the subjugation of the passions to reason (*logos*) in a state of "self-sufficiency" (*autarkeia*). Sometimes they regarded moral virtue as the imitation of divine perfection, and sometimes they held out a human figure (especially Socrates) as the model of excellence; but more often they wrote abstractly of their ideal "wise man."

There can be no doubt that Jesus required moral perfection of those who would follow him. Thus, in the Sermon on the Mount, he told his disciples, "You, therefore, must be perfect, as your heavenly Father is perfect" (Matthew 5:48). In saying this Jesus reaffirmed the Old Testament, in which the Jews, as the people of the covenant, are required to be perfect (or "holy") by obedience to the law (*Torah*) which embodies God's will and reflects his character. The above-mentioned verses (Matthew 5:38–47) show that love, especially love of one's enemies, is the element in divine perfection that disciples are to imitate. Jesus' moral perfectionism was further expressed in his demands for complete inward purity (Matthew 5:21–22, 27–28) and self-renunciation (Mark 8:34–38).

Inevitably, theologians have affirmed that moral perfection is the goal of the Christian life. In the New Testament epistles perfection has three main characteristics. First, the norm of perfection is Christ himself, as the Incarnation of God. Second, the essence of perfection is love—the divine love revealed in Christ and made available to believers through the Spirit. Thus, St. Paul, having listed several virtues, wrote, "And above all these put on love, which is the bond of perfectness" (Colossians 3:14). Third, perfection is corporate. Thus, the author of Ephesians looks forward to the time when "we all attain to the unity of the faith and of the knowledge of the Son of God, to perfect manhood, to the measure of the stature of the fulness of Christ" (4:13). Postbiblical theologians (for example, St. Augustine and Thomas Aquinas) continued to give primacy to love, by which all the natural virtues are supernaturally perfected.

Two comments on this Christian scheme are relevant. First, as early as St. Ambrose there emerged a distinction between the basic "precepts" according to which all Christians were expected to live and the "counsels of perfection" that only a few ("the religious") could follow. This distinction, which persisted throughout the Middle Ages, was based on such texts as Matthew 19:16–22 and could be plausibly represented as an attempt to combine adherence to Christ's absolute demands with a realistic attitude toward the spiritual capacities of the average Christian in a secular occupation. But it was rejected by the Reformers, and with special vehemence by Martin Luther.

Second, although some Christians have held that it is possible to achieve perfection (that is, sinlessness) in this life, the majority have held that the strength of original sin makes this impossible. Moreover, many biblical texts (particularly I John 1:8–10) imply the Lutheran view that all Christians remain throughout their mortal lives *simul justi et peccatores* ("at the same time justified and sinners"). From a purely philosophical standpoint Immanuel Kant held that since the moral law requires holiness, and since we cannot achieve it in this life, we must postulate another life in which an infinite progress

toward it will be possible (*Critique of Practical Reason*, translated by T. K. Abbott, London, 1909, p. 218).

Finally, if we take human perfection in its widest sense to mean an ideal that satisfies man's deepest needs or fulfills his "true" being, we can see clear points of similarity between Christian and non-Christian systems. Thus, although humanists, Buddhists, and Christians have in common many virtues that they regard as normative, they put them in differing contexts. These virtues are practiced by the humanist as self-sufficient ends, by the Buddhist as means of entrance to nirvana, and by the Christian as both the outcome of present faith in God and a preparation for a future vision of him "face to face."

See also Anselm, St.; Augustine, St.; Degrees of Perfection, Argument for the Existence of God; Thomas Aquinas, St.; Virtue and Vice.

Bibliography
Flew, R. N. *The Idea of Perfection in Christian Theology.* Oxford: Oxford University Press, 1934.

Kirk, Kenneth E. *The Vision of God.* London: Longmans, Green, 1931.

Niebuhr, Reinhold. *An Interpretation of Christian Ethics.* London: Harper, 1935. An important examination of Jesus' perfectionism and the problems that it raises.

Saunders, Kenneth. *The Ideals of East and West.* Cambridge, U.K.: Cambridge University Press, 1934.

H. P. Owen (1967)

PERFECTION, DEGREES OF

See *Degrees of Perfection, Argument for the Existence of God*

PERFORMATIVE THEORY OF TRUTH

Until relatively recently, it was taken for granted by all philosophers who wrote on the subject of truth, regardless of their differences on other matters, that words such as *true* and *false* were descriptive expressions. This presupposition has been challenged by P. F. Strawson, who developed the theory that "true" is primarily used as a performative expression. A performative utterance may be understood by considering a paradigm case: "I promise." To say "I promise" is not to make a statement about my promising but simply to promise. To use a performative expression is not to make a statement but to perform an action. Strawson, in his essay "Truth," holds that to say that a statement is true is not to make a statement about a statement but to perform the act of agreeing with, accepting, or endorsing a statement. When one says "It's true that it's raining," one asserts no more than "It's raining." The function of "It's true that" is to agree with, accept, or endorse the statement that it's raining.

Strawson's performative analysis of "true" was conceived as a supplement to F. P. Ramsey's assertive redundancy, or "No Truth," theory of truth. Ramsey claimed that to say that a proposition is true means no more than to assert the proposition itself. "It is true that Caesar was murdered" means no more than "Caesar was murdered." "It is false that Caesar was murdered" means no more than "Caesar was not murdered." According to this view, "true" has no independent assertive meaning, and the traditional notion of truth as a property or relation is misguided. Ramsey suggested that "true" is used for purposes of emphasis or style, or to indicate the position of a statement in an argument.

CRITICISM OF SEMANTIC THEORY

Strawson set himself the positive task of explaining the use of "true" in ordinary language and criticizing the metalinguistic or semantic theory of truth, which has an affinity with Ramsey's view. Philosophers such as Rudolf Carnap, who hold the metalinguistic position, agree with Ramsey that to say that an assertion is true is not to make a further assertion. However, these philosophers claim that truth is a metalinguistic property of sentences, which means that to say that a statement is true is to make a statement about a sentence of a given language. According to this thesis, the statement that it's true that it's raining should, strictly speaking, be written: "'It's raining' is true in English."

Strawson argues that translation practice shows the metalinguistic thesis to be false. He points out that a translator would not handle a truth declaration as if it were a sentence description. Consider the manner in which a translator would handle a case where it is perfectly clear that one really is speaking about an English sentence:

(1) "It's raining" is a grammatical English sentence.

Suppose a translator wanted to translate (1) into a different language. He would retain the constituent "It's raining" in its original English, in order to show that (1) is a description of an English sentence. But consider

(2) It's true that it's raining.

There would be no hesitation in translating the whole statement, including the constituent "It's raining." This shows that (2) is not, as the metalinguistic thesis claims, a description of an English sentence. Hence, "true" is not a metalinguistic predicate.

Philosophers who maintain that "true" is a descriptive expression have been misled by grammatical form. "True" is a grammatical predicate, but it is not used to talk about anything. Strawson compares "true" with "Ditto." A makes an assertion. B says "Ditto." Insofar as B talks about or asserts anything, he talks about or asserts what A talked about or asserted. A's assertion is the occasion for the use of "Ditto," but because "Ditto" is not composed of a grammatical subject and predicate, one is not tempted to think that in uttering "Ditto" B is making an additional statement.

The parallel with "Ditto" illuminates the tie between statements and "true." The making of a statement is the occasion for, but not the subject of, a truth declaration. "True" has no statement-making role. To say that a statement is true is to perform the act of agreeing with, accepting, endorsing, admitting, confirming, or granting that statement. Such expressions as "I grant …," "I confirm …," and "Yes" are perfectly capable of substituting for "The statement is true."

EXPRESSIVE USE OF "TRUE"

While Strawson emphasizes the performative role of "true," he also calls attention to another kind of use, which he calls expressive. This use is often found in sentences beginning "So, it's true that …," "Is it true that …," and "If it's true that …." In these utterances, "true" functions like the adverb "really," to express surprise, doubt, astonishment, or disbelief. However, "true" has only an expressive function in these utterances. It does not contribute, in either its expressive or its performative role, to the assertive meaning of what is said. Thus Strawson's thesis remains compatible with Ramsey's view. "True" does not change the assertive meaning of a statement. It has no statement-making role.

RESOLUTION OF "LIAR" PARADOX

The performative analysis of a truth declaration enabled Strawson to offer an original resolution of a well-known paradox that arises when one says:

(3) What I am now saying is false.

If (3) is true, then it is false; and if it is false, then it is true. Hence, we arrive at a paradox whose resolution has been one of the achievements of the metalinguistic analysis of "true." According to this analysis, (3) is read in the following manner:

(3a) The object-language statement I am making now is false.

Since (3a) no longer refers to itself, the contradictory consequences disappear. Strawson dispenses with the metalinguistic solution and dissolves the paradox in a manner consistent with his own analysis of "true." To utter (3) is like saying "Ditto" when no one has spoken. It is not to make a statement but, rather, to produce a pointless utterance. Since (3) is not a statement, it is not a statement that implies its own denial. Hence, the paradox disappears without the necessity for metalinguistic machinery.

OBJECTIONS TO STRAWSON'S ANALYSIS

Strawson does not distinguish a truth declaration from such expressions as "I grant …," "I accept …," "I concede …," "I admit …," "I insist …," "Yes …," or "Ditto." It should be noted, however, that there are differences between using these expressions and saying that a statement is true. Expressions such as "I grant …," "I concede …," "I accept …," "I admit …," and "I insist …" suggest a "me versus you" background. They underline the act performed as *mine*. This is not the role of "That's true." Moreover, one should distinguish between expressions like "Yes," which simply register bare assent, and "The statement is true." If asked whether I agree with Smith's statement, I may say, "Yes, but my opinion isn't worth very much; I haven't studied the evidence." However, to say "His statement is *true*, but my opinion isn't worth very much; I haven't studied the evidence" sounds unnatural. "True," unlike "Yes," has the force of adequate evidence.

GEACH'S CRITICISM. P. T. Geach offered the following criticism of Strawson's analysis of "true" ("Ascriptivism," p. 233). Consider arguments of this pattern.

If x is true, then p;
x is true;
Ergo p.

Strawson claims that the second premise, "x is true," should be analyzed as an agreeing performance. However, it cannot be claimed that in the hypothetical premise "If x is true, then p," the constituent "x is true" is an agreeing performance. If I say, "If x is true, then p," I am not agreeing with or accepting x. Hence, the explanation of "true" in the hypothetical premise must differ from its explanation in the second categorical premise. However, if the explanation of "true" changes from one premise to another, the argument would be invalid, since the fallacy of equivocation has been committed. However, the argument is clearly valid. Hence, Strawson's analysis of "true," which implies that a different explanation is required for occurrences of "true" in hypothetical and categorical statements, must be wrong.

Geach's criticism, however, appears to rest on a misunderstanding of the behavior of performatives in logical arguments. Take a clear case of a performative, "I promise to help you." Now consider the following argument.

If I promise to help you, then I'm a fool; I promise to help you; *Ergo* I'm a fool.

There is a performative occurrence of "I promise" in the second premise, but not in the first. When I say, "If I promise to help you, then I'm a fool," I am not promising to help you. Hence, the use of "I promise" in the first hypothetical premise requires an explanation that differs from the explanation of "I promise" in the second hypothetical premise, yet the argument remains perfectly valid. A fallacy of equivocation is not committed simply because an expression has a performative use in one premise of a logical argument and a nonperformative use in another.

Occurrences of "true" in hypotheticals do not fit a performative analysis, but it must be remembered that while Strawson emphasizes the performative use, he does not claim that this is the whole story. The nonperformative use of "true" in hypothetical statements may be considered to fall under what Strawson calls the expressive use. What is the difference between the following statements?

(4) If Khrushchev's statement is true, there are no missile bases in Cuba.

(5) Khrushchev's statement implies there are no missile bases in Cuba.

While (4) and (5) have the same assertive meaning, (4) suggests that Khrushchev's statement is in doubt. Hence "true" in (4) contributes only to the expressive quality of the statement. Since "true" in (4) has only an expressive function, but not a statement-making role, (4) does not constitute an exception to Strawson's analysis.

"BLIND" USES OF "TRUE." An interesting challenge to Strawson's position is found in "blind" uses of "true." This use of "true" is exemplified when a person applies "true" to a statement without knowing what the statement is. For example, suppose a man says, "Everything the pope says is true." Presumably he does not know every statement the pope has made. It cannot, therefore, be claimed that he is making the statements made by the pope. One cannot substitute the pope's statements for "Everything the pope says is true" without a change in meaning. Hence, "Everything the pope says is true" does not, as Strawson claims, have the same assertive meaning as the pope's statements. The notion, which Strawson takes over from Ramsey, that a truth declaration has the same assertive meaning as the statement dubbed true, does not hold for blind uses of "true."

It may be argued that the speaker is blindly endorsing all the pope's statements. In that case, "Everything the pope says is true" would be analyzed as a performative use of "true" which falls outside the range of Ramsey's thesis. But this analysis could not be maintained for blind uses like "I hope that what Jones says will be true." The speaker is plainly not endorsing what Jones will say. Moreover, since "true" in this case does not function like the adverb "really," it cannot be maintained that "I hope that what Jones will say is true" exemplifies an expressive use of "true" either. Hence, neither Strawson's nor Ramsey's position seems to hold up for blind uses of "true."

Strawson, however, has analyzed blind uses of "true" in what he takes to be a Ramsey-like method. In his later paper, "A Problem about Truth—A Reply to Mr. Warnock," Strawson shifts from his original position and grants that "at least part of what anyone does who says that a statement is true is to make a statement about a statement" (p. 69). This is a departure from his earlier view that "true" has no statement-making role. For the blind truth declaration "Everything the pope says is true," Strawson would offer the following Ramsey-like paraphrase: "Things are as the pope says they are." According to Strawson, this paraphrase is a statement about the pope's statements, but it also conforms to the spirit of Ramsey's view. Presumably, Strawson considers this analysis to be a Ramsey-like analysis because "true" is eliminated from the paraphrase. It must be remembered, however, that Ramsey held "true" to be eliminable because "true" is a "superfluous addition" to a statement ("Facts and Propositions," p. 17). Hence, one can always substitute P for "P is true" without loss of assertive meaning. While Strawson has eliminated "true" from "Everything the pope says is true" in the paraphrase "Things are as the pope says they are," he has not fulfilled Ramsey's claim that "true" is superfluous. A philosopher who holds the correspondence theory of truth can also eliminate "true" by substituting "Everything the pope says corresponds to the facts" for "Everything the pope says is true." However, this surely would not be a Ramsey-type elimi-

nation. Since "true" is not a superfluous addition to a blind truth declaration, it does not seem that blind uses can be paraphrased in the spirit of Ramsey.

See also Carnap, Rudolf; Paradigm-Case Argument; Performative Utterances; Pragmatism; Ramsey, Frank Plumpton; Semantics, History of; Strawson, Peter Frederick; Truth.

Bibliography

Austin, J. L. *How to Do Things with Words*. Cambridge, MA: Harvard University Press, 1962.

Bach, Kent, and R. M. Harnish. "How Performatives Really Work." *Linguistics and Philosophy* 15 (1992): 93–110.

Ezorsky, Gertrude. "Truth in Context." *Journal of Philosophy* 60 (5) (February 28, 1963).

Geach, P. T. "Ascriptivism." *Philosophical Review* 69 (April 1960).

Horwich, P., ed. *Theories of Truth*. New York: Dartmouth, 1994.

Kincade, J. "On the Performatory Theory of Truth." *Mind* 67 (1958).

Kirkham, Richard. *Theories of Truth: A Critical Introduction*. Cambridge, MA: MIT Press, 1992.

Miller, S. R. "Performatives." *Philosophical Studies* 45 (1984): 247–260.

Ramsey, F. P. "Facts and Propositions." *PAS*, Supp. 7 (1927). Reprinted in *Truth*, edited by George Pitcher, 16. Contemporary Perspectives in Philosophy Series. Englewood Cliffs, NJ: Prentice-Hall, 1964.

Recanati, F. *Meaning and Force: The Pragmatics and Philosophy of Performative Utterances*. Cambridge, U.K.: Cambridge University Press, 1987.

Searle, J. "How Performatives Work." *Linguistics and Philosophy* 12 (1989): 535–558.

Searle, J. "Meaning and Speech Acts." *Philosophical Review* 71 (1962).

Sinnott-Armstrong, Walter. "The Truth of Performatives." *International Journal of Philosophical Studies* 2 (1) (1994): 99–107.

Strawson, P. F. "A Problem about Truth—A Reply to Mr. Warnock." In *Truth*, edited by George Pitcher, 68 (see above).

Strawson, P. F. "Truth." *Analysis* 9 (6) (1949). Reprinted in *Philosophy and Analysis*, edited by Margaret MacDonald, 260. Oxford, 1955.

Strawson, P. F., and J. L. Austin. "Truth." *PAS*, Supp. 24 (1950).

Walsh, W. H. "A Note on Truth." *Mind* 61 (1952).

Warnock, G. J. "A Problem about Truth." In *Truth*, edited by George Pitcher, 54 (see above).

White, Michael. "A Suggestion Regarding the Semantical Analysis of Performatives." *Dialectica* 30 (1976): 117–134.

Ziff, Paul. *Semantic Analysis*, 118. Ithaca, NY: Cornell University Press, 1960.

Gertrude Ezorsky (1967)
Bibliography updated by Benjamin Fiedor (2005)

PERFORMATIVE UTTERANCES

At the beginning of *How to Do Things with Words* (1962), John Langshaw Austin challenged the common assumption that "the business of [a declarative sentence] can only be to 'describe' some state of affairs, or to 'state some fact'" (p. 1). Obviously, that is not the business of interrogative and imperative sentences, but Austin argued that even certain declarative sentences are typically used to do something other than make statements. For example, an employer can fire someone by saying "You're fired," and an employee can quit by saying "I quit." In uttering such a sentence, one is not merely saying what one is doing, one is actually doing it. Such a sentence has a remarkable property: To utter it is (typically) to perform an act of the very sort named by its main verb.

It does seem remarkable that you can do something just by saying what you are doing. Most types of acts are not like that. You cannot stand on your head by saying that you are standing on your head, and you cannot convince someone that you love them by saying that you are convincing them that you love them. Yet in the right circumstances you can fire someone or quit a job just by uttering the right sort of sentence. How is this possible, and what sorts of acts can be performed in this way? Does this phenomenon of *performativity* require a special explanation, perhaps involving some kind of convention, or it is just a special case of something more general?

EXPLICIT PERFORMATIVE UTTERANCES

Austin (1961) dubbed *performative* such verbs as "promise," "apologize," "request," "fire," and "quit." Performative sentences are generally in the first-person singular with their main, performative verb in the simple present tense, active voice. So, for example, you can promise to attend by saying "I promise to attend" (but not by saying "I promised to attend" or "She promises to attend"), and you can apologize by saying "I apologize" (but not by saying "I apologized" or "She apologizes"). The word "hereby" may be inserted before the performative verb, thereby indicating that this utterance is the vehicle of the performance of the act named by the verb. Some performative sentences are in the first-person plural ("We guarantee your safety"), the second-person singular or plural ("You are advised to get vaccinated"), or the impersonal passive ("Smoking is prohibited)." Occasionally the performative verb is in the present progressive, as in "I'm warning you to stay away" and "I'm asking you for the last time to clean up your room." Because utterances of performative sentences are characteristically performances of acts of the very sort named by their main verbs, Austin called them "explicit performative utterances," or simply "performatives."

Notice that such acts as promising, apologizing, and requesting, which Austin called "illocutionary acts," can be performed without using a performative sentence, hence without making explicit what one is doing. For example, one can promise by saying "You can count on me to … ," apologize by saying "I'm sorry," and request by saying "I'd like you to …" This raises the question whether performativity, although involving the use of a special sort of sentence, requires a special explanation. In this regard note also that performative sentences do not have to be used performatively and obviously are not so used when they are embedded in larger linguistic contexts. For example, saying "If I promise to take you to the play, will you quit nagging me?" is not to make a promise, and saying "I apologize only if I feel guilty" is not to apologize.

PERFORMATIVES AND CONVENTIONS

It is generally accepted that linguistic meaning is a matter of convention. So to that extent every utterance is conventional, insofar it is made with linguistic means. However, it might seem, as it did to Austin, that performatives are conventional in a more specific way and that this explains their performativity. If so, then, for example, an utterance of "I promise to …" amounts to a promise because, and only because, there is a convention, or what John Searle (1969) called a "constitutive rule," to the effect that an utterance of such a sentence counts as a promise. That is, roughly, it counts as such only because it is generally recognized to count as such. This view seems plausible as regards certain institution-bound performatives, where a specific form of words is designated, and often required, for the performance of an act of a certain sort. For instance, uttering the words "I pronounce you husband and wife" counts (in the requisite circumstances) as the act of marrying a couple; uttering "The jury finds the defendant guilty" counts as finding the defendant guilty (convicting the defendant); and uttering "(I) double" counts as doubling in bridge. Indeed, in institutional contexts there are often designated expressions that, though not performative in form, have the same effect, such as an umpire's "Out," a legislator's "Nay," or a judge's "Overruled." Of course, these specialized performatives and other designated forms of words have to be uttered by the appropriate person in the appropriate circumstances, but the relevant convention provides for this. Not just anyone can adjourn a meeting, sentence a convicted criminal, or christen a ship, and not just under any circumstances (with his "doctrine of the Infelicities" Austin classified the various ways in which such utterances can go wrong as "flaws," "hitches," and "abuses" [1962, pp. 12–38]). So it does seem that in institutional cases performativity is a matter of convention: A certain person's uttering a certain form of words in a certain context plays a certain official role because, and only because, it is generally recognized as so doing.

However, as P. F. Strawson (1964) contended, Austin was overly impressed with institution-bound cases. In such cases there are specific, socially recognized circumstances in which a person with specific, socially recognized authority may perform an act of a certain sort by uttering words of a certain form in order to effect, or officially affect, institutional states of affairs (see Bach and Harnish 1979, ch. 6). Ordinary performative utterances, on the other hand, are not bound to particular institutional contexts. Like most illocutionary acts, Strawson argued, they involve an intention not to conform to an institutional convention but to communicate something to an audience. An utterance counts as a promise, an apology, or a request because, and only because, the speaker intends it to count as such and the audience, recognizing that intention, regards it as such. To be sure, it is only under certain circumstances that a speaker will make such an utterance with such an intention and his audience will so regard it, but this is not in virtue of any convention.

It might be suggested, as it was by Jerrold Katz (1977), that performativity is explained not by social conventions but by linguistic ones. Perhaps there is some distinctive feature of the meaning of performative verbs that explains how one can perform an act of the very sort named by the verb by uttering a performative sentence containing that verb. However, this suggestion loses its plausibility when one takes into account a range of linguistic data beyond the simple performatives considered so far. In particular, there are what Bruce Fraser (1975) called "hedged performatives," which philosophers have largely overlooked, such as "I can promise you . . . ," "I must ask you . . . ," and "I would like to invite you . . ." Utterances of such sentences standardly have performative effect, but the meanings of the sentences themselves are not inherently performative. This is clear because without contradicting myself I could say "I can promise you, but I won't," "I must ask you, but if I did, my wife would never forgive me," or "I would like to invite you,

but I can't." In each of these cases I would not be performing an act of the type in question but would merely be telling you that I am able to promise, that I am required to ask you, or that I would like to invite you. In addition, there are other sorts of sentences that, unlike hedged performatives, do not even contain performative verbs but which are standardly used in the same kind of way: "It would be nice if you . . ." to request, "Why don't you . . . ?" to advise, "Do you know . . . ?" to ask for information, "I'm sorry" to apologize, and "I wouldn't do that" to warn. Clearly these standard uses are not predictable from their linguistic meanings alone.

The variety of forms of sentences that are standardly used to perform acts of the same types as those accomplished by explicit performative utterances suggests that performativity is not a matter of convention, whether social or linguistic. Performativity requires no special explanation. Rather, its explanation belongs to the general theory of speech acts (see Searle 1989 and Bach and Harnish 1992 for two contrasting accounts). Performative sentences are just one kind among various kinds of sentences that are standardly used to perform types of illocutionary acts not predictable from their meanings alone (see Bach and Harnish 1979, ch. 10). Performativity is a pragmatic phenomenon not a semantic one, a matter of language use rather than linguistic meaning. The standardization of performative and other forms of sentences for uses not predictable from their meanings does not show that they are governed by special conventions but merely that there is a practice of using sentences of certain forms in certain ways. The claim that they are conventional falsely entails that an utterance of a certain form of words would not have the force it has unless it is generally recognized to count as such. The claim that they are merely standardized for these special uses requires something less. Standardization merely streamlines the inference the hearer must make to identify the speech act being performed; it creates the illusion of conventionality where there is really but a pragmatic regularity. (For further discussion of these issues, see Reimer 1995, Bach 1995, and Harnish 1997).

PERFORMATIVES AND STATEMENTS

When introducing the notion of performatives, Austin contrasted them with utterances like "I state that … ," "I claim that … ," and "I predict that …" These explicit *constatives* are like utterances of ordinary declarative sentences in that they "describe some state of affairs, or to state some fact," which Austin denied that performatives do. Yet he came to realize that explicit constatives are relevantly similar to explicit performatives: Their main verbs also make explicit the type of act being performed. After all, an assertion or a prediction is made with "I assert …" or "I predict …" in just the same way that a promise or a request is made with "I promise…" or "I request …" Accordingly, what makes explicit performatives distinctive is not what the speaker does but that the speaker makes explicit what he or she is doing.

Austin also came to realize that what can be done explicitly without a performative can also be done without making explicit the type of act being performed. In the latter part of *How to Do Things with Words* he developed the distinction between *locutionary* and *illocutionary* acts, which effectively superseded the distinction between constative and performative utterances. Locutionary acts are acts of saying something, and illocutionary acts are performed in the act of saying something. This distinction applies not only to promises, requests, and apologies, but also to statements and the like (Austin retained the term "constative" for them).

For example, in uttering "I promise to be there" and thereby explicitly saying that one promises to be there or in uttering merely "I will be there" and thereby just saying that one will be there, one can promise to be there. Similarly, in uttering "I state that Mars has two moons" and thereby explicitly saying that one states that Mars has two moons or in uttering merely "Mars has two moons" and thereby just saying that Mars has two moons, one can state that Mars has two moons. Note that stating is distinct from saying. In the right circumstances, one might say that Mars has two moons but state, albeit figuratively, that a certain belligerent person has two obsequious functionaries. In general, a speaker need not make explicit what he or she is doing in order to do it. Explicit performatives do have a distinctive self-referential character, but that does not mean that their illocutionary force requires special explanation. Indeed, if the successful "performance of an illocutionary act involves the securing of uptake" (Austin 1962, p. 116), then if anything it should be easier for an explicit performative to succeed, precisely because the speaker is saying what he or she is doing.

One remaining question concerns whether performatives are statements too (see Bach 1975), contrary to Austin's insistence that making explicit "is not the same as stating or describing" (1962, p. 61). When he introduced the category of explicit performative utterances, he claimed that even though they are utterances of declarative sentences, they are not cases of making statements and are not descriptive. However, this does not seem right, for the simple reason that the verbs in performative sentences can be modified, as in "I gladly promise … ," "I sincerely apologize … ," and "I reluctantly request …" This strongly suggests that a speaker of such a sentence would be making a statement. The speaker would be describing himself or herself, as promising gladly, apologizing sincerely, or requesting reluctantly.

Performatives have even been described as "self-verifying" (originally by Lemmon 1962 and more recently by Johansson 2003). Clearly they are self-referential, in that if one utters a performative sentence and uses it performatively, one is making explicit what one is thereby doing. But to describe them as self-verifying is to claim that they make themselves true. This seems right, but notice that a performative is not self-verifying in the way that an utterance of, for example, "I am speaking" or "I am alive" is self-verifying. It is not the bare fact of the utterance that, given its content, makes it true. Suppose I utter "I hereby apologize" and thereby apologize. It is true that I am thereby apologizing, but what makes this true is that I am using the sentence to perform the illocutionary act of apologizing. In that way, it is self-verifying.

Does this self-referential, self-verifying character help explain performativity, is it just a curious feature of explicit performative utterances, or what? As Searle (1989) has argued, the performativity of performative utterances does not depend on their being self-verifying. That gets things backwards: they are self-verifying statements because of their performativity. However, as Kent Bach and Robert Harnish (1992) have argued, their character as statements plays a key role in the speaker's being able to communicate to his audience what he is doing, precisely because he is using a performative to make explicit what he is doing.

See also Austin, John Langshaw; Pragmatics.

Bibliography

Austin, J. L. *How to Do Things with Words*. Cambridge, MA: Harvard University Press, 1962.

Austin, J. L. "Performative Utterances." In his *Collected Papers*, edited by J. O. Urmson and G. J. Warnock. Oxford: Oxford University Press, 1961.

Bach, Kent. "Conventionalization vs. Standardization." *Linguistics and Philosophy* 18 (1995): 677–686.

Bach, Kent. "Performatives Are Statements Too." *Philosophical Studies* 28 (1975): 229–236.

Bach, Kent, and Robert M. Harnish. "How Performatives Really Work." *Linguistics and Philosophy* 15 (1992): 93–110.

Bach, Kent, and Robert M. Harnish. *Linguistic Communication and Speech Acts*. Cambridge, MA: MIT Press, 1979.

Fraser, Bruce. "Hedged Performatives." In *Syntax and Semantics*. Vol. 3, edited by Peter Cole and Jerry Morgan. New York: Academic Press, 1975.

Ginet, Carl. "Performativity." *Linguistics and Philosophy* 3 (1979): 245–265.

Grice, H. P. "Meaning." *Philosophical Review* 66 (1957): 377–388.

Harnish, Robert. M. "Performatives and Standardization: A Progress Report." *Linguistische Berichte* 8 (1997): 161–175.

Johansson, Ingvar. "Performatives and Antiperformatives." *Linguistics and Philosophy* 26 (2003): 661–702.

Katz, Jerrold J. *Propositional Structure and Illocutionary Force.* New York: Crowell, 1977.

Lemmon, E. J. "Sentences Verifiable by their Use." *Analysis* 12 (1962): 86–89.

Recanati, François. *Meaning and Force: The Pragmatics of Performative Utterances.* Cambridge, U.K.: Cambridge University Press, 1987.

Reimer, Marga. "Performative Utterances: A Reply to Bach and Harnish." *Linguistics and Philosophy* 18 (1995): 655–675.

Searle, John R. "How Performatives Work." *Linguistics and Philosophy* 12 (1989): 535–558.

Searle, John R. *Speech Acts: An Essay in the Philosophy of Language.* Cambridge, U.K.: Cambridge University Press, 1969.

Searle, John R. "A Taxonomy of Illocutionary Acts." In *Language, Mind, and Knowledge*, edited by Keith Gunderson. Minneapolis: University of Minnesota Press, 1975.

Strawson, P. F. "Intention and Convention in Speech Acts." *Philosophical Review* 73 (1964): 439–460.

Kent Bach (2005)

PERGAMUM, SCHOOL OF

See *Neoplatonism*

PERIPATETICS

The original meaning of the word *peripatos* was "a covered walking place." The house that Theophrastus provided for the school of Aristotle contained such a *peripatos*. This yielded a proper name for the school itself—the Peripatos—and its members came to be known as "those from the Peripatos" or "Peripatetics." This derivation should be preferred to that previously current, according to which the term "Peripatetic" referred to a method of teaching while walking about, known to have been used by Protagoras, for example, and assumed to have been adopted by Aristotle. Although this view goes back to Hermippus at the end of the third century BCE, it is now generally regarded as a mistaken inference, based on nothing more than the name itself.

The history of the Peripatetics can be divided into two periods—that immediately following the death of Aristotle and that following the revival of interest in Aristotelian studies resulting from the edition of the treatises by Andronicus of Rhodes in the time of Marcus Tullius Cicero or a little later. When Theophrastus became president of the school in the year before Aristotle's death, he continued to show an interest in virtually the whole range of Aristotelian studies. But whereas it is now generally supposed that Aristotle retained a keen interest in metaphysical questions to the end of his life, it was the shift of emphasis away from Platonic otherworldliness to the phenomena of the world around us, a subject also found in Aristotle, which seems to have attracted Theophrastus most. Strato, Theophrastus's successor, made important developments in physical theory, transforming Aristotle's doctrine into a fairly full-blooded materialism. But after Strato's death about 269 BCE, his successors became almost exclusively concerned with questions about the content of the good life and the way to reach it, with questions of rhetoric, and with the distinctively Hellenistic interest in anecdote, gossip, and scandal. Many of the specifically Aristotelian doctrines were abandoned, and the school had become very much the same as a number of others in Athens by the end of the second century BCE.

The reasons for this disintegration are uncertain. It may be that the concentration of interest upon empirical questions discouraged speculation. Empiricism as such, however, has interested philosophers intensely at other periods of history. Some have supposed that the disintegration was part of a philosophic failure of nerve characteristic of the Hellenistic age as a whole. But this view of the Hellenistic age is probably incorrect, and in any case such a failure of nerve clearly applied less to Stoics, Epicureans, and Skeptics of the period than it did to the Peripatetics. Thus, their fate would remain unexplained.

It may be that the history of the Aristotelian writings had something to do with what happened to the Peripatetics. According to the well-known story, on Theophrastus' death his copies of Aristotle's writings went to Neleus of Scepsis in the Troad (Asia Minor). In one extreme view this meant that the Peripatetics in Athens thereafter had access only to the published works of Aristotle—namely, the dialogues. In fact, there seem to have been copies of at least some of the treatises available in Alexandria, in Rhodes, and probably in Athens throughout the Hellenistic period. They do not appear to have been much studied in the Peripatos, however, where knowledge of Aristotle came primarily from the writings of Theophrastus when not from the dialogues. Indeed, in a sense the school of Aristotle might more correctly be called the school of Theophrastus. The weakness of its links with Aristotle's own thought may explain its relative failure in philosophy.

Andronicus of Rhodes wrote a special study on the order of Aristotle's works and published an edition of the treatises in the order in which they have survived to us. His edition is the source of all subsequent ones. Andronicus is sometimes dated as early as 70 BCE, but as Cicero never refers to his edition, it may not have been published until after Cicero's death in 43 BCE. Andronicus initiated a revival in Aristotelian studies, and the Peripatos flourished at least down to the time of Alexander of Aphrodisias (about 200 CE). Among those influenced by this revival were the geographer Ptolemy and the physician Galen. Alexander wrote important commentaries on the main Aristotelian treatises, and the tradition of writing such commentaries continued into the Byzantine period through such scholars as Themistius, Ammonius, and Simplicius, who must be classed as Platonists rather than as Aristotelians. All the commentators treated Aristotle's writings as a systematic corpus, and from the start all were influenced in varying degrees by both Stoic and Platonist doctrines.

The general approach, apart from certain unintended distortions, was intensely conservative. From time to time modifications of interest were proposed, however. The successor of Andronicus, Boëthius of Sidon (who is not to be confused with the earlier Stoic of the same name), rejected the doctrine that the universal is prior by nature to the particular and would not grant to form the title of primary substance. In so doing, he took a big step in the direction of medieval nominalism. The pseudo-Aristotelian treatise *De Mundo* is often regarded as a product of this period. It culminates in a theology in which a transcendent deity maintains order in the cosmos by the exercise of an undefined power, and in a general way the work has affinities with both Stoic writers like Posidonius and Neoplatonists. It seems, however, to imitate the Aristotle of the dialogues rather than the treatises, and it may antedate the edition of Andronicus.

See also Alexander of Aphrodisias; Aristotelianism; Aristotle; Cicero, Marcus Tullius; Empiricism; Epicureanism and the Epicurean School; Galen; Hellenistic Thought; Neoplatonism; Platonism and the Platonic Tradition; Posidonius; Protagoras of Abdera; Simplicius; Stoicism; Strato and Stratonism; Themistius; Theophrastus.

Bibliography

The earlier Peripatetics, fragments and testimonia, are in *Die Schule des Aristoteles*, edited by F. Wehrli, 10 parts (Basel, 1944–1959). See also P. Moraux, *Les listes anciennes des ouvrages d'Aristote* (Louvain, Belgium, 1951); I. Düring, *Aristotle in the Ancient Biographical Tradition* (Goteborg, Sweden, 1957), Part III, Chs. XVII and XVIII, and Part IV; and C. O. Brink, "Peripatos," in *Realencyclopädie der classischen Altertumswissenschaft*, edited by A. Pauly and G. Wissowa, Supp. Vol. VII (Stuttgart, 1940). See also the Aristotelian commentators in *Commentaria in Aristotelem Graeca*, 23 vols. and 3 supp. vols. (Berlin, 1882–1909). *De Mundo* is translated by D. J. Furley with Aristotle's *On Sophistical Refutations*; translated by E. S. Forster (Cambridge, MA, and London, 1955).

G. B. Kerferd (1967)

PERRY, RALPH BARTON
(1876–1957)

Ralph Barton Perry, the American realist philosopher, was born in Poultney, Vermont. He attended Princeton University, where he received his B.A. in 1896; he received his M.A. from Harvard in 1897 and his Ph.D. in 1899. For a brief period he taught at Williams and Smith colleges. From 1902 to 1946 he taught at Harvard, where, after 1930, he was the Edgar Pierce professor of philosophy. He was Hyde lecturer at various French universities during the year 1921–1922. In 1920 he was elected president of the eastern division of the American Philosophical Association, and he served as Gifford lecturer from 1946 to 1948.

Perry was the author of some two hundred essays and two dozen books, in addition to countless lectures and letters to newspapers, and he was considered the chief living authority on William James. Perry believed that a comprehensiveness of view is philosophy's contribution to human wisdom; in his own work he willingly risked inaccuracy to range over every province of science, art, philosophy, and religion. He insisted on the merit of this venture, insofar as it was an attempt to achieve systematic unity in a field that would otherwise be divided between experts who were unaware of one another's achievements.

REACTION AGAINST IDEALISM

As an early polemicist against idealism, Perry claimed that the relationship of the world to the mind is an accidental or subordinate aspect of the world. He argued that the relationship of knowing the world is not like the relationship of owning an object. An object owned becomes in a sense a part of the owner, whereas the world, although it lends itself to being known, does not thereby become entirely a part of the knower. It is not exhaustively defined by the relationship of being known. This claim became one of the basic tenets of what Perry and five other young American philosophers formulated as New Realism in their cooperative volume *New Realism* (1912). They argued that the world is real and independent of mind, and that it is directly present or "immanent" to the mind in knowledge and consciousness. Together these tenets formed their "cardinal principle"—the "independence of the immanent."

In his article "The Ego-centric Predicament" (1910), Perry had shown how this "predicament" had been used illicitly to argue for idealism. The idealist argument begins with the predicament that "it is impossible for me to discover anything which is, when I discover it, undiscovered by me," and concludes that "it is impossible to discover anything that is not thought." The idealist, Perry claimed, has confused the statement that "everything which is known, is *known*" with the claim that "everything which *is*, is known." Perry maintained that the predicament was simply methodological: the extent to which knowledge conditions any situation in which it is present cannot be discovered by the simple and conclusive method of direct elimination.

Perry did not deny that this predicament presents a real difficulty, but he did deny that it argues either for idealism or realism. He never suggested what could be done to overcome the difficulty, but he did not think there were other than methodological implications in it. Instead, Perry argued that the objects of knowledge and experience are independent of egocentricity. "Independence" here refers not to a particular kind of relation but rather to the absence of one. Perry defined it as nondependence. The independent object may be related or not, provided that it is not related in the way the dependent object is. The independent object can be related to consciousness, or mind, but not be dependent on that relationship for its existence.

However, as Perry developed his position (in *Present Philosophical Tendencies,* 1925), it turned out that independent objects of knowledge are not the real independent objects of the commonsense world but "neutral entities" indifferent to both the subjective and the physical (or objective) relations in experience. They do not exist in any place; they exist only in the logical sense, as either a class or members of a class. They are therefore preeminently independent of consciousness. The propositions of logic and mathematics are typical of such enti-

ties, and Perry contended that analysis of such propositions reveals neither a knowing relation nor reference to a knower.

In taking this position, Perry had adopted James's neutral monism, and although he eventually abandoned it, he continued to describe his own philosophy as, among other things, "neutralism." Perry's move away from neutral monism and New Realism is best seen in his two works on value theory, *General Theory of Value* (1926) and *Realms of Value* (1954). The first work sets forth Perry's theory of the generic nature of value, while the second details the varieties and types of this value as they appear in the major human institutions, or "realms of value."

THEORY OF VALUE

Believing that value was neither unanalyzable nor purely emotive, Perry formulated his well-known definition, "Any object, whatever it be, acquires value when any interest, whatever it be, is taken in it." Value is that which attaches to any object of any interest. Interest is defined as that which is characteristic of the motor-affective life, namely, instinct, desire, feeling, will, and all their states, acts, and attitudes. A thing is an object of interest when its being expected induces actions that anticipate its realization or nonrealization. Interested action is thus actively selective, tentative, instrumental, prospective, and fallible.

According to Perry, this theory did not conflict with the "independence of the immanent," because the latter, being restricted to knowledge, did not demand that values be conceived as independent. Yet Perry's theory included a cognitive element in all value or interest. Cognition gives the interest its object, Perry said, and the character of the object of interest is essentially the same as that of the object of cognition. The "mediating judgment" in interest and cognition is expectation and belief, and without belief there would be no basis for truth and error. All interest is characterized by expectancy, but it differs from cognition in that it also includes being for or against, favoring or disfavoring, the expected. Since both interest and cognition have this element of expecting something and being prepared to cope with it, expectancy is the key to understanding both.

Because expectancy looks forward and does not disclose itself except through a train of subsequent events, the object of interest and of cognition can be conceived of only as an ideal or "problematic" object, possessing the ambiguity or dual possibility of truth and error. This object is "internal" to the act or cognition and must be distinguished from its "external" referent, that which confirms or fails to confirm the expectation of the problematic object. Expectation is the meaning of an object.

Perry pointed out that during the process by which a sensory stimulus leads to an eventual sense perception, not only muscles and nerves, but attitudes, meanings, and interpretations are oriented toward the stimulus. Thus, when the ear is assailed by a stimulus, the organism listens toward the source and acts, or prepares to act, both upon that source and upon its context. At this point a conversion takes place: one hears the sound there and then perceives it as a bell having further characteristics. Thus, a stimulus touches off a reaction, and then the stimulus is superseded by thought, which now has an object, although the original stimulus has ceased to exist. The stimulus has been converted into an object; the sound has been converted into a bell, or in other words, into what it means, what is expected of it. This is the "perceptual object," that part of the total surrounding field to which the organism alerts itself, embracing what is expected of the sensory object.

This object is characterized both by meaning—that is, by what the organism expects of it—and by being part of the surroundings. When Perry went on to describe its status further, his monistic bias became apparent. He maintained that if the ideal object is not somehow present in nature, it would be impossible to affirm that nature is as it is "represented" in the finished product of scientific inquiry. If the logical and mathematical structures of knowledge are to be true of nature, they must be *in* nature; the laws of nature reign in the realm of nature and not in the realm of natural science, which discovers them.

MORAL VALUE. Having offered his theory of value, Perry went on to show in what sense we can say one value is "better" or "worse" than another. This too, he thought, called for a definition—that is, a descriptive account of the meaning of "better" and "worse." For Perry, that meant a description of those conditions that would enable us to say with justification that one object of an interest was better (or worse) than another.

The key to this problem of value was integration or harmony of interests. To integrate or harmonize interests is to remove from them such qualities as independence, irrelevance, dissimilarity, opposition, indifference, antagonism, or incompatibility. Harmony in place of conflict is Perry's *summum bonum*. Morality takes the conflict of interests as its point of departure. What Perry called the moralization of life—the harmonizing of interests for the sake of the interests harmonized—is effected through "reflective agreement" between the personal and the social will. "Harmonious happiness" is justified by its provision for the several interests that it harmonizes. Ought and obligation, then, are not moral ultimates but are justified by the good end.

That Perry's moral criterion was an absolute in an otherwise nonabsolutistic theory did not occur to him. However, he did assert that the criterion must agree with human nature and the circumstances of human life in such a way that men can adopt it and be governed by it. It must also possess qualifications for being accepted in lieu of other standards. Perry thought his concept of harmony, in its appeal to each knower's will, did possess universality because it embraced all interests—that is, that it was to some extent applicable to everybody's interest.

The adequacy of Perry's theory rests therefore on his assumption that for all men "better" signifies a greater inclusiveness and harmony of values. Perry was by no means unaware of the need for social arrangements that would render the interests of individuals mutually innocent and cooperative. Almost half of his books were devoted to some aspect of this problem, and they were often written in response to the problems facing his country at the time. He brought to all of them his standard of harmonious happiness, or reflective agreement, a "creed of inclusiveness" that excluded only hatred and personal aggrandizement.

See also Ethics, History of; Idealism; James, William; Monism and Pluralism; New Realism; Realism; Value and Valuation.

Bibliography

WORKS BY PERRY

"The Ego-centric Predicament." In *The Development of American Philosophy*, edited by W. G. Muelder and L. Sears. Boston and New York: Houghton Mifflin, 1940. Reprinted from original article in *Journal of Philosophy* 7 (1) (1910): 5–14.

"A Realistic Theory of Independence." In *The New Realism*, by E. B. Holt et al., 99–151. New York: Macmillan, 1912.

The Present Conflict of Ideals; A Study of the Philosophical Background of the World War. New York: Longmans, Green, 1918.

Present Philosophical Tendencies; A Critical Survey of Naturalism, Idealism, Pragmatism and Realism Together with a Synopsis of the Philosophy of William James. New York, 1925.

General Theory of Value; Its Meaning and Basic Principles Construed in Terms of Interest. New York: Longmans, Green, 1926; reissued in 1950.

Philosophy of the Recent Past; An Outline of European and American Philosophy since 1860. New York and Chicago: Scribners, 1926.

"Realism in Retrospect." In *Contemporary American Philosophy,* edited by G. P. Adams and W. P. Montague, Vol. II, 187–209. New York: Macmillan, 1930.

The Thought and Character of William James, as Revealed in Unpublished Correspondence and Notes, Together with His Published Writings, 2 vols. Boston: Little Brown, 1935. A Pulitzer Prize biography.

Our Side Is Right. Cambridge, MA: Harvard University Press, 1942.

Puritanism and Democracy. New York: Vanguard Press, 1944. Best single statement of Perry's social and political philosophy.

The Citizen Decides: A Guide to Responsible Thinking in Time of Crisis. Bloomington: Indiana University Press, 1951.

Realms of Value; A Critique of Human Civilization. Cambridge, MA: Harvard University Press, 1954.

WORKS ON PERRY

Boman, Lars. *Criticism and Construction in the Philosophy of the American New Realism.* Stockholm, 1955. Mainly an exposition of Perry and other New Realists that utilizes the tools of modern philosophical analysis.

Harlow, Victor. *A Bibliography and Genetic Study of American Realism.* Oklahoma City: Harlow, 1931.

Hill, Thomas English. *Contemporary Theories of Knowledge.* New York: Ronald Press, 1961. Critical discussion of Perry as a "polemical" New Realist.

Thomas Robischon (1967)

PERSISTENCE

Smith is reading an open book that was shut this morning. At least it certainly seems like the same book he placed closed on his nightstand and opened to read this evening. But, then again, nothing can be both shut and not shut, Smith's book being included among those things that cannot violate G.W. Leibniz's law. So, no matter that common sense dictates that Smith's shut book did not blink out of existence to be instantaneously replaced by an open book, perhaps it is a different book after all.

Very roughly, that is the start of the problem of persistence—an initial worry about how an object can persist through a change in its properties. It is a problem that may seem easily dismissed until we identify its source in some of our basic metaphysical commitments and recognize the costs that accompany any way of addressing it. The understanding of the problem of persistence expressed below was developed alongside and informed by Sally Haslanger's work (Haslanger 2003).

THE INITIAL WORRY

We can sharpen the initial worry about books and other ordinary objects that persist through change by noting that it emerges from the conjunction of three core metaphysical theses.

THREE CORE METAPHYSICAL THESES

CONSISTENCY: Nothing can have incompatible properties.
CHANGE: Change involves incompatible properties.
PERSISTENCE: Objects persist through change.

The core theses express firmly held intuitions that most metaphysicians would agree are central to a coherent theory of how ordinary things—books, rocks, Smith, and even ourselves—exist and persist in the world. But, a commitment to any two of the theses seems to implicitly deny the remainder. Suppose PERSISTENCE and CHANGE are true, that some objects persist through change that involves incompatible properties. For instance, consider the book that Smith removed from his nightstand to read that was shut, and though open now, remains the same book. If we also assume CONSISTENCY is true, then nothing can have the incompatible properties of being shut and being open (given that a book is open if, and only if, it is not shut). Thus, it seems that the shut book from Smith's nightstand must be distinct from the open book in his hands. But that denies that the book persisted in the first place.

A careful reader will note that the contradiction was not precisely forced; nevertheless there is a significant tension that at least threatens contradiction. One strategy for responding to this worry is to bypass it by rejecting CONSISTENCY, PERSISTENCE, or CHANGE. A second strategy is to resolve the tension by first identifying its source and then clarifying or modifying our ideas to remove that source.

DISMISSING THE INITIAL WORRY

There are three options in pursuing the straightforward strategy of dismissing the initial worry about persistence by denying one of the core theses, none of which is promising. First, we might contend that something can both have and not have a property (forfeiting CONSISTENCY). However, such a move entails rejecting the law of noncontradiction, Aristotle's "most certain of all principles" according to which "the same attribute cannot at the same time belong and not belong to the same subject in the same respect" (Barnes 1984. Aristotle's *Metaphysics* IV.3.1005b1.17). But, countenancing contradictions to find a noncontradictory account of persistence makes no sense (though someone like Donald Baxter, 2001, might disagree). Indeed, such a drastic step may allow for something to both have and not have the property of persisting.

Second, we might adopt the position that change either does not happen or does not involve incompatible properties (forfeiting CHANGE). Here, we could deny change altogether, perhaps accepting Parmenides's picture of a static, monolithic reality in which "what is is ungenerable and imperishable, a whole of a single kind, and unshaking and complete" (Curd 1998, p. 68). Or, we could hold that change occurs without involving incompatible properties. But change just does involve either something being *F* and something becoming not-*F*, or something being not-*F* and something becoming *F*. Sacrificing our minimal metaphysical commitments about how change works amounts to change nihilism. This strategy avoids contradiction at a very high metaphysical cost.

Finally, we could argue that nothing persists (forfeiting **PERSISTENCE**). Heraclitus told us: "You could not step twice into the same rivers; for other waters are ever flowing on to you" (EpistemeLinks.com 2005, Heraclitus of Ephesus, *On the Universe*, fragment 41). We might go along with him, agreeing that: "Nothing endures but change," giving us a metaphysics that does not include persisting objects, but merely flowing processes (EpistemeLinks.com 2005, Diogenes Laertius, *Lives of Eminent Philosophers*, Bk. IX, sec. 8). Such persistence nihilism is again a move at odds with strong intuitions and a range of metaphysical theories.

Thus, the strategy of dismissing one of the core theses leaves us without an intuitively tenable account of how ordinary things—Smith, books, rocks—exist and persist in the world. This motivates the search for an account of persistence that genuinely addresses the worry by reconciling the core theses.

FINDING THE SOURCE

The second way of dealing with the initial worry is to get much clearer about the source of the problem and then seek remedies by revising our ideas in a way that avoids the problem by attacking the source directly. Our understanding of **CONSISTENCY** needs to remain intact unless we allow contradictions, which is off the table here. However, **CHANGE** and **PERSISTENCE** leave room for interpretation. For instance, they leave open what counts as persistence, change, and incompatible properties being involved in change.

Modifying our understandings of these phenomena can ease the tension among the core theses. In our everyday understanding of the world, we assume that persisting objects survive the gain and loss of some simply instantiated properties. The following three aspects of this understanding are central to grasping why philosophical issues arise with persistence.

CHANGE AS ALTERATION. An object alters by gaining or losing properties. More precisely, an object alters if, and only if, it is numerically identical to objects that have different properties at different times. In our everyday understanding of the world, objects change by altering, and plenty of ordinary objects alter. Smith's book that was shut and Smith's book that is open is a single book that has the properties of being shut and open at different times. When Smith opened his book, the shut book did not wink out of existence exactly when an open book happened to blink into existence right into his hands. Rather, Smith's book was shut and then open—it altered as Smith turned to his bookmarked page.

PERSISTENCE AS SURVIVAL. An object survives if it has more than a momentary existence. More precisely, an object survives if, and only if, it is numerically identical to something that exists at a different time. In our everyday understanding of the world, objects persist by surviving, and plenty of ordinary objects survive. Consider the book Smith placed on his nightstand last evening that went untouched until this evening, and the book he removed from his nightstand this evening. The book that Smith put down last evening is the very same book that he picked up this evening. Although a day older, it is numerically identical to the book Smith read the prior evening—it survived the day spent on his nightstand.

INVOLVING INCOMPATIBLE PROPERTIES AS JUST HAVING INCOMPATIBLE PROPERTIES. An object just has a property if, and only if, it simply instantiates (*Fx*) that property. That is, an object just has a property if, and only if, no extrinsic facts are relevant to the truth of the proposition that the object has that property. In our everyday understanding, ordinary objects just have incompatible properties sometimes, regardless of how the rest of the world is. David Lewis brings out the intuitiveness of this when he writes: "When I sit I'm bent, when I stand I'm straight. When I change my shape, that isn't a matter of my changing relationships to other things, or my relationship to other changing things. I do the changing, all by myself. Or so it seems" (Lewis 1999, p. 187).

Like Lewis being straight, with respect to Smith's book, we tacitly hold that nothing beyond his book matters to its being shut—that there is a primitive, non-relational bond between the book and the property of being shut. If it is not open, Smith's book just has the property of being shut, regardless of its relation to the nightstand it rests upon at 7:00 a.m. We can capture these key aspects of our everyday understanding in terms of how objects persist through change with three additional theses.

THREE EVERYDAY METAPHYSICAL THESES

<u>ALTERATION</u>: If an object changes, then the object existing before the change and the numerically identical object existing after the change are the proper subjects of the incompatible properties involved in the change.

<u>SURVIVAL</u>: If an object persists through change, then the object existing before the change is numerically identical to the one existing after the change.

<u>ATEMPORAL INSTANTIATION</u>: If an object is the proper subject of a property, then (i) the object has that property, and (ii) facts about time and tense are irrelevant to the truth of the proposition that the object has that property.

<u>ALTERATION</u> constrains how things change. <u>SURVIVAL</u> constrains how things persist. <u>ATEMPORAL INSTANTIATION</u> constrains how incompatible properties are involved in change. Making our everyday understanding explicit is useful because it allows us to see that: (1) This understanding conjoined with the three core theses forces a contradiction; and (2) reconciling the core theses requires denying or revising some part of our everyday understanding. The following argument demonstrates both points. In it, we suppose that Smith opens the book that had been resting shut on his nightstand.

AN ARGUMENT AGAINST OUR EVERYDAY UNDERSTANDING

What follows are three assumptions about the book that capture the three core metaphysical theses: (1) It is not the case that the book is shut and the book is open (captures <u>CONSISTENCY</u>); (2) the book persists through change (captures <u>PERSISTENCE</u>); (3) the book changes in a way that involves the incompatible properties of being shut and being open (captures <u>CHANGE</u>).

The following steps draw on the three everyday metaphysical theses: (4) The book existing before the change is numerically identical to the book existing after the change (<u>SURVIVAL</u> and step two); (5) the book is the proper subject of being shut and being open (<u>ALTERATION</u>, steps three and four); (6) the book is shut and the book is open (<u>ATEMPORAL INSTANTIATION</u> and step five). From these six steps, a contradiction arises as steps (1) and (6) cannot both be true. One can conclude, then, that given the truth of the core metaphysical theses, something within the everyday metaphysical theses is false.

This argument can be run for any ordinary object that persists through change. Thus, to address, rather than dismiss, the initial worry, one of the three everyday theses must be revised or forfeited. The problem is to do so while striking a balance between respecting our intu-

itions and achieving philosophical success. Such is the strategy of three broad approaches to persistence below. Each blocks step (6) in its own way and thereby achieves a consistent view. But, given the nature of the problem demonstrated above, each solution will obviously face trade-offs in terms of intuitive appeal.

ADDRESSING THE WORRY

Perdurantism, exdurantism, and endurantism are each accounts of persistence that retain a commitment to the core metaphysical theses, but give up part of our everyday understanding of how things such as Smith, books, and rocks persist and change in our world. The first two accounts are built on a metaphysics of temporal parts, whereas the third depends on a metaphysics of enduring things.

METAPHYSICS OF TEMPORAL PARTS AND PERSISTENCE Ordinary objects have spatial parts. Perhaps they also have modal parts, dependent parts, abstract parts, or logical parts, among others. The metaphysics of temporal parts (MTP) leaves that open. The particular claim MTP makes is that objects have temporal parts. These temporal parts, time slices, or stages exist only at a moment. So, on a view consistent with MTP, multiple momentary book stages could exist—a shut-book stage, a distinct open-book stage, and so on. Perdurantism and exdurantism rely on the temporal stages of MTP to explain the persistence of ordinary objects.

Perdurantism Perdurantists take change over time to be analogous to change over space. Just as color changes across the surface of a canvas when different spatial parts of the canvas have incompatible colors, so the color of a lemon changes across the time as it ripens when different temporal parts—a distinct green stage and a distinct yellow stage—have incompatible colors. In both cases, change consists in distinct parts of an object having incompatible properties.

On this view, ordinary objects are space-time worms composed of distinct momentary stages. So, just like a taut rope extends through space, it also extends through time. For, as a fusion of its temporal stages, it has parts in the past, present, and future. An object that is a space-time worm is only partially present at any one moment because its different stages exist at different times.

The perdurantist ontology makes the three core and two everyday metaphysical theses co-realizable. An object changes when distinct stages of a single space-time worm just have the incompatible properties involved in change

(CHANGE and ATEMPORAL INSTANTIATION). It survives a change in virtue of the space-time worm that exists at the times that its distinct stages exist (PERSISTENCE and SURVIVAL). And, because distinct stages bear the incompatible properties rather than a single object, there is no one thing that has incompatible properties (CONSISTENCY).

For instance, Smith's book changes because its stages just have the incompatible properties of being shut and being open. The book survives this change because it is numerically identical to the space-time worm constituted by its stages. Finally, no contradiction arises because distinct stages of the book have the incompatible properties, rather than Smith's book as a whole.

However, perdurantism requires us to sacrifice change as alteration. ALTERATION entails that change occurs only if one and the same thing has a property and then lacks the property. It entails that the book changes only if it and something numerically identical to it have the incompatible properties of being open and shut. But, perdurantists hold that distinct proper parts of a space-time worm book bear the incompatible properties—the shut-book stage and the open-book stage. So, there is no one thing that has incompatible properties—indeed that is how perdurantism avoids contradiction. By blocking step (5) in the argument above, perdurantists also block (6). Yet, in gaining a coherent account of persistence, perdurantists accept an account on which change is merely a succession of momentary stages that have incompatible properties.

Exdurantism Exdurantists or stage theorists take identity over time to be analogous to identity between possible worlds. To see this, assume that an actual sill-length window swag could be a floor-length swag in virtue of a floor-length counterpart in some possible world. Analogously, exdurantists assume that Smith's now open book was shut in virtue of a closed book counterpart resting on his nightstand in the past. In both cases, distinct objects (the sill-length swag and its floor-length counterpart, the present open book and its earlier shut counterpart) have incompatible properties.

On this view, an ordinary object is a single momentary stage that extends through space, but not through time, and that has temporal counterpart stages. Any object that is a single stage is wholly present at exactly and only the moment it exists.

The exdurantist ontology makes the three core and one everyday metaphysical theses co-realizable. An object changes when it and a counterpart stage just have the incompatible properties involved in change (CHANGE and ATEMPORAL INSTANTIATION). It persists when it and its temporal counterpart exist at different times (PERSISTENCE). And, because distinct stages bear the incompatible properties rather than a single object, there is no one thing that has incompatible properties (CONSISTENCY).

For instance, the change in Smith's book involves incompatible properties because his book just has the property of being open and a counterpart stage just has the property of being shut. Smith's book persists through this change in virtue of standing in a counterpart relation to a stage from a different time in the actual world. Finally, because no single thing is open and is shut (rather, distinct stages are), no contradiction arises.

Notice that according to exdurantism, the object that changes and persists just has one of the incompatible properties—Smith's book, the entire book, just is open. In contrast, according to perdurantism the object that changes and persists never just has either of the incompatible properties—Smith's book is never just open or shut. Exdurantism thus fares a bit better intuitively on this point, for when we look at Smith and see him reading an open book, we think his book is open, not some other object that is merely part of his book.

However, exdurantism pays for this metaphysical perk elsewhere. Exdurance precludes the possibility of persistence as survival, for no ordinary objects survive. SURVIVAL entails that a persisting object exist both before and after it changes. It entails that if Smith's book persists, then the shut book on the nightstand is numerically identical to the open book in Smith's hands. But, exdurantists maintain that no book is numerically identical to both the earlier open stage and the later shut stage. At best, a persisting object continues (in some sense) in virtue of a succession of distinct momentary stages bearing the relevant counterpart relations to each other. But, an earlier and a later stage in such a succession are no more one and the same object than the first and third links in a five-link chain are one and the same link. Thus, given the ontology in which ordinary objects are all momentary stages, nothing exists that could survive change.

Moreover, because it shares the strategy of using MTP to explain persistence with perdurantism, exdurantism also forfeits ALTERATION. As above, there is no one object that loses one property and gains another. Instead, distinct objects bear the incompatible properties—Smith's open book and a shut stage to which it stands in a counterpart relation. But, the costs of exdurantism do return a benefit—giving up both SURVIVAL and ALTERATION blocks both (4) and (5) without which (6) does not follow. Of course, to recoup these costs, exdurantists may try to retain some form of ALTERATION or SURVIVAL by revising our notion of existence. They could hold momentary stages derivatively exist across time in virtue of counterpart relations to other stages that exist at different times. Clearly, the burden of proof would fall on an exdurantist to prove that derivative existence *just is* existence.

To sum up, both perdurantists and exdurantists endorse MTP. They maintain a commitment to the three core theses by using temporal parts to bypass the contradiction that arises by simply predicating incompatible properties to a single object. Both approaches conflict with change as alteration—so neither can hold simply that the book is open and the book is shut, rather distinct stages have these properties. Ultimately, though, the views differ in metaphysical costs. Perdurantists may maintain that persisting objects survive change because they attribute incompatible properties to different parts of a single space-time worm. Exdurantists must deny SURVIVAL because they attribute incompatible properties to distinct ordinary objects.

METAPHYSICS OF ENDURING THINGS AND PERSISTENCE According to the metaphysics of enduring things (MET), some objects endure. To claim that some objects endure is to claim that in some cases a numerically identical object is wholly present at different times. This claim states the minimal metaphysical commitments that distinguish the ontologies of MET from MTP.

MET and MTP agree that ordinary objects have spatial parts, and that they may have modal parts, dependent parts, abstract parts, or logical parts, among others. MET also leaves open whether any objects have temporal parts.

However, although it permits stages, MET requires the existence of some objects that fall outside the ontologies of perdurantists or exdurantists. For, an enduring object is wholly present at different times and neither a space-time worm nor a single momentary stage can be wholly present at different times.

Endurantism relies on MET's enduring objects to explain how ordinary objects can be altered and survive change. These objects are the key resource that perdurantism and exdurantism lack by being grounded in MTP.

Endurantism Endurantists hold that ordinary objects persist through change by enduring. In doing so, they take identity over time to be numerical identity between objects wholly present at different times. They take change over time to be the instantiation of incompatible properties by numerically identical objects at different times. So, arguably they hold the most intuitive understanding of change over time as a phenomenon that

is nothing more than one and the same object gaining and losing properties across time.

On a basic endurantist view, ordinary objects are enduring things. For example, an endurantist would hold that as an ordinary object, a book is not constituted by stages because it is wholly present at different moments. Thus, an ordinary, enduring book would be distinct from any sort of space-time worm or single momentary stage or counterpart stage that may or may not also exist.

The endurantist ontology makes the three core and two everyday metaphysical theses co-realizable. An object changes by altering because, in some sense, it has the incompatible properties involved in change (CHANGE and ALTERATION). It survives a change in virtue of the single enduring object that has those properties in some sense at different times (PERSISTENCE and SURVIVAL). Finally, although a wholly present ordinary object in some sense has incompatible properties, it does not just have those properties. Rather, facts external to an ordinary object concerning time or tense mediate the instantiation of incompatible properties. There are a variety of ways to mediate the instantiation. For instance, given a pair of incompatible properties and an object that has them in some sense, an endurantist could hold that the object has one property now and had the other property earlier. With various forms of mediated instantiation, the endurantist avoids contradiction (CONSISTENCY).

For instance, Smith's book changes because it has incompatible properties in some sense—his book is open but that very book was shut. Smith's book survives this change in virtue of being numerically identical to the book at the time it is open and the book at the time it was shut. Finally, because no single thing is open and is shut (rather, the book is open and was shut), the position remains consistent.

The important move of adopting temporally mediated property instantiation—instantiation mediated by time or tense—allows endurantists to hold that an ordinary object can be wholly present both before and after a change in spite of its having incompatible properties. This is why the view allows for the survival and alteration of objects so easily.

However, endurantism faces its own metaphysical cost—it requires us to give up the idea that an object just has the properties in virtue of which it changes. ATEMPORAL INSTANTIATION entails that there be a primitive bond unmediated by time or tense between the object and the relevant properties. Perdurantists and exdurantists preserve this bond because on their views distinct objects just have the incompatible properties. MTP allows them to say, without contradiction, that one book stage just is open and a distinct book stage just is shut (*Fx* and *not-Fy*). In contrast, without stages as a resource, to preserve that bond the endurantist would have to say that the book just is open and that the book just is shut (*Fx* and *not-Fx*)—a flat contradiction. Instead, the view of change involving objects just having incompatible properties is replaced by one in which objects have incompatible properties in some sense mediated by time or tense (*F* is *x* and *F* was *not-x*). This is how endurantism directly blocks step (6) in the argument above.

In contrast to the sacrifices of the MTP theorists that include losing robust notions of survival and alteration, giving up primitive instantiation in favor of mediated instantiation may be appealing. But there are repercussions.

First, temporal concerns intuitively seem irrelevant to whether an object has those intrinsic properties in virtue of which it can change. Smith's green eyes, the position of his nightstand, and, likewise, the time of day all seem to be matters outside of the metaphysical status of Smith's book in terms of whether it is open or shut.

Second, those concerned about Bradley's regress may worry about relying on mediated property instantiation to explain persistence. Some take the position that primitive bonds are required to block the regress. The endurantist strategy rules out the possibility of such bonds holding between persisting objects and the properties involved in change.

Third, it obscures how the properties involved in change are incompatible. An enduring object has the properties of being *F* and not being *F* involved in change in a way that does not generate contradiction because, in some sense, they can be co-instantiated. For instance, if Smith's book is shut-in-the-morning and open-in-the-evening, this looks no more problematic than Smith's book being rectangular and red. Thus, with any kind of mediated instantiation, the endurantist will need to explain the incompatibility of the relevant properties. For, without incompatibility between the properties, change itself becomes questionable.

Various strands of endurantism handle these worries more or less well, depending in large part on how they mediate property instantiation. Possible methods include: time indexed properties (*x* is *F-at-t*), time relative predicate relations (*x* is-at-*t* *F*), relations with times as arguments (*x* is *F* at *t*), adverbial accounts (*x* is *F* t-*ly*), temporal context sensitivity (obtains at *t* (*x* is *F*)), and tense (*x* was *F*).

CONCLUSION

Perdurantism, exdurantism, and endurantism share the virtue of allowing us to maintain a commitment to the core theses of CONSISTENCY, PERSISTENCE, and CHANGE. Each does so by offering an account of persistence through change on which no single object just has the incompatible properties involved in change—whether it is because distinct objects just have those properties or a single object has them in a mediated way. Though they differ in particular metaphysical costs and benefits, this common feature is why they succeed in addressing rather than dismissing the initial worries with persistence.

At this point, the real problem with persistence is not deciding whether things persist—but rather explaining how they persist. The challenge today is to choose well among the metaphysical costs of reconciling the core theses so as to yield a coherent, useful theory that still respects our intuitions. The heart of the current persistence debate revolves around which view does the best job. Thus, it is worth remarking very briefly on three metaphysical concerns that provide, or seem to provide, reasons for favoring one approach to persistence over another.

First is the metaphysics of time. Eternalism, presentism, and the growing block view are among the main alternative accounts of the nature of time. Their different commitments regarding the reality of times make these views incompatible. The eternalist claims that all times exist, the presentist argues that only the present exists, and the growing block theorist holds that the past and the present exist, but not the future. The truth of eternalism or presentism or the growing block view would help choose between accounts of persistence if, as some have suggested, MTP entails either eternalism or the growing block view, or MET entails presentism. However, recent work on persistence suggests that MTP or MET can incorporate eternalism, presentism, or the growing block view, though perhaps not with equal ease.

Second is a concern with how propositions about the past, present, and future have truth values. At issue, is whether the *is* of predication is irreducibly tensed (serious tensing) or the *is* is timeless (surface tensing) in the logical structure of propositions. Some have thought this issue will help decide among approaches to persistence because they believe that endurantists must use serious tensing. However, though endurantists must use some form of mediated property instantiation, it need not be a form that depends on tensing.

Third is an issue about how temporary intrinsic properties must be instantiated. Intuitively, an intrinsic property of an object is one that the object has simply by virtue of being itself. Temporary intrinsics are intrinsic properties that an object has only temporarily. Above, being bent and being straight are temporary intrinsic properties of Lewis. Real change occurs when an object has, in some sense, incompatible temporary intrinsic properties at different times. Thus, any tenable account of persistence will need to explain how objects have temporary intrinsic properties.

Now, many hold the view that there must be a primitive bond between an object and its temporary intrinsic properties, that objects just have them. If so, then endurantism is not a viable account of persistence. For, endurantism achieves consistency only by insisting on some form of mediated property instantiation. However, among the many forms of mediated property instantiation, some mesh better than others with our intuitions and theoretical commitments regarding temporary intrinsics. So there is room for endurantists to come up with a reasonable account of temporary intrinsics when they devise an alternative to **ATEMPORAL INSTANTIATION**.

See also Aristotle; Identity; Lewis, David; Metaphysics; Parmenides of Elea; Time.

Bibliography

Armstrong, David. "Identity Through Time." In *Time and Cause*, edited by P. van Inwagen. Dordrecht: Reidel, 1980.

Balashov, Yuri. "Enduring and Perduring Objects in Minkowski Space-Time." *Philosophical Studies* 99 (2000): 129–166.

Barnes, Jonathan. *The Complete Works of Aristotle: The Revised Oxford Translation*. Princeton, NJ: Princeton University Press, 1984.

Baxter, Donald. "Loose Identity and Becoming Something Else." *Noûs* 35 (2001): 592–601.

Bradley, F. H. *Appearance and Reality*, 2nd ed. Oxford: Oxford University Press, 1897.

Brogaard, Berit. "Presentist Four-Dimensionalism." *Monist* 83 (2000): 341–356.

Carter, William and H.S. Hestevold. "On Passage and Persistence." *American Philosophical Quarterly* 31(1994): 269–283.

Cartwright, Richard. "Scattered Objects." In *Analysis and Metaphysics*, edited by Keith Lehrer. Dordrecht: D. Reidel, 1975.

Chisholm, Roderick. "Identity Through Time." In *Language, Belief, and Metaphysics*, edited by H. Keifer and M. Munitz. Albany: State University of New York Press, 1970.

Craig, William Lane. "McTaggart's Paradox and the Problem of Temporary Intrinsics." *Analysis* 58 (1998): 122–127.

Curd, Patricia. *Legacy of Parmenides: Eleatic Monism and Later Presocratic Thought*. Princeton, NJ: Princeton University Press, 1998.

EpistemeLinks.com. "Quotations for philosopher Heraclitus," www.epistemelinks.com/Main/Quotations.aspx?PhilCode= Hera, 2005.

Forbes, Graham. "Is there a Problem about Persistence?" *Aristotelian Society* 61 (1987): 137–155.

Gallois, André. *Occasions of Identity: The Metaphysics of Persistence, Change, and Sameness*. New York: Oxford University Press, 1998.

Haslanger, Sally. "Humean Supervenience and Enduring Things." *Australasian Journal of Philosophy* 72 (1994): 339–359.

Haslanger, Sally. "Persistence through Time." In *The Oxford Handbook of Metaphysics*, edited by Michael J. Loux and Dean W. Zimmerman. Oxford: Oxford University Press, 2003.

Haslanger, Sally. "Persistence, Change, and Explanation." *Philosophical Studies* 56 (1989): 1–28.

Hawley, Katherine. *How Things Persist*. Oxford: Oxford University Press, 2001.

Hawley, Katherine. "Persistence and Non-Supervenient Relations." *Mind* 108 (1999): 53–67.

Heller, Mark. "Varieties of Four-Dimensionalism." *Australasian Journal of Philosophy* 71 (1993): 47–59.

Hinchliff, Mark. "The Puzzle of Change." In *Philosophical Perspectives, 10, Metaphysics*, edited by James Tomberlin. Cambridge, MA: Blackwell, 1996.

Hirsch, Eli. *The Concept of Identity*. Oxford: Oxford University Press, 1982.

Johnston, Mark. "Is There a Problem about Persistence?" *Aristotelian Society* 61 (1987): 107–135.

Lewis, David. *On the Plurality of Worlds*. Oxford: Basil Blackwell, 1986.

Lewis, David. "Rearrangement of Particles: Reply to Lowe." In *Papers in Metaphysics and Epistemology*. Cambridge, U.K.: Cambridge University Press, 1999.

Lewis, David. "Tensing the Copula." *Mind* 111 (2002): 1–13.

Lewis, David. "Zimmerman and the Spinning Sphere." *Australasian Journal of Philosophy* 77 (1999): 209–212.

Lombard, Lawrence. "On the Alleged Incompatibility of Presentism and Temporal Parts." *Philosophia* 27 (1999): 253–260.

Lowe, E. J. "Lewis on Perdurance versus Endurance." *Analysis* 47 (1987): 152–154.

Lowe, E. J. "The Problem of Intrinsic Change: Rejoinder to Lewis." *Analysis* 48 (1988): 72–77.

Lowe, E. J. "Substantial Change and Spatiotemporal Coincidence." *Ratio* 16 (2003): 140–160.

Ludlow, Peter. *Semantics, Time, and Tense*. Cambridge, MA: MIT Press, 1999.

Markosian, Ned. "A Defense of Presentism." In *Oxford Studies in Metaphysics*, edited by Dean Zimmerman. Oxford: Oxford University Press, 2003.

Markosian, Ned. "The 3D/4D Controversy and Non-Present Objects." *Philosophical Papers* 23 (1994): 243–249.

McTaggart, J. M. E. *The Nature of Existence*, vol. 2. Cambridge, U.K.: Cambridge University Press, 1927.

Mellor, D. H. *Real Time*. Cambridge, U.K.: Cambridge University Press, 1981.

Merricks, Trenton. "Endurance and Indiscernibility." *Journal of Philosophy* 91 (1994): 165–184.

Merricks, Trenton. "Persistence, Parts, and Presentism." *Noûs* 33 (1999): 421–438.

Myro, George. "Identity and Time." In *The Philosophical Grounds of Rationality*, edited by Richard Grandy and Richard Warner. New York: Clarendon Press, 1986.

Oaklander, L. Nathan. "Temporal Passage and Temporal Parts." *Noûs* 26 (1992): 79–84.

Oderberg, David. *The Metaphysics of Identity over Time.* London; New York: Macmillan, 1993.

Parsons, Josh. "Must a Four-Dimensionalist Believe in Temporal Parts?" *The Monist* 83 (2000): 399–418.

Prior, A. N. *Papers on Time and Tense.* London: Oxford University Press, 1968.

Prior, A. N. *Past, Present and Future.* Oxford: Clarendon Press, 1967.

Prior, A. N. "Thank Goodness That's Over." *Philosophy* 34 (1959): 12–17.

Quine, W. V. O. "Identity, Ostension, and Hypostasis." In *From a Logical Point of View*, 2nd ed. Evanston: Harper and Row, 1963.

Sider, Theodore. "Presentism and Ontological Commitment." *Journal of Philosophy* 96 (1999): 325–347.

Sider, Theodore. *Four-Dimensionalism: An Ontology of Persistence and Time.* Oxford: Oxford University Press, 2001.

Simons, Peter. "Continuants and Occurrents." *Proceedings of the Aristotelian Society* 74 (2000): 59–75.

Simons, Peter. "How to Exist at Time When You Have No Temporal Parts." *The Monist* 83 (2000): 419–436.

Taylor, Richard. "Spatial and Temporal Analogies and the Concept of Identity." *Journal of Philosophy* 52 (1955): 599–612.

Thomson, Judith Jarvis. "Parthood and Identity across Time." *Journal of Philosophy* 80 (1983): 201–220.

van Inwagen, Peter. "Four-Dimensional Objects." *Noûs* 24 (1990): 245–255.

van Inwagen, Peter. "Temporal Parts and Identity across Time." *Monist* 83 (2000): 437–459.

Varzi, Achille. "Perdurantism, Universalism, and Quantifiers." *Australasian Journal of Philosophy* 81 (2003): 208–215.

Wasserman, Ryan. "The Argument from Temporary Intrinsics." *Australasian Journal of Philosophy* 81(2003): 413–419.

Zimmerman, Dean W. "One Really Big Liquid Sphere: Reply to Lewis." *Australasian Journal of Philosophy* 77 (1999): 213–215.

Zimmerman, Dean W. "Temporary Intrinsics and Presentism." In *Metaphysics: The Big Questions.* Cambridge, MA: Blackwell, 1998.

Zimmerman, Dean W. "Temporal Parts and Supervenient Causation: The Incompatibility of Two Humean Doctrines." *Australasian Journal of Philosophy* 76 (1998): 265–288.

Roxanne Marie Kurtz (2005)

PERSONAL IDENTITY

One of the commonest of daily experiences is that of recognizing our friends. A less common, though still fairly familiar, experience is the decision that a certain person is or is not the person he claims to be. The problem of personal identity is that of clarifying the principles behind these indispensable processes of reidentification. To reidentify someone is to say or imply that in spite of a lapse of time and the changes it may have wrought, the person before us now is the same as the person we knew before. When are we justified in saying such a thing, and when are we not?

THE BASIC PROBLEMS

Some philosophers have said that we are never justified, because sameness and change are, in themselves, incompatible. They have argued that it is almost paradoxical to say that something has changed and yet is still the same. There is nothing special about the case of persons in this connection, of course, except that we might, as persons ourselves, be expected to be more concerned about this case or to have access to some of the facts needed to deal with it. One set of such facts is the private set of thoughts, feelings, and images that each of us has, and such philosophers as David Hume have emphasized how constant and rapid are the changes in them with which our identity has to contend. The problem generated by this alleged paradox will be referred to as the problem of the unity of a person through change or, more briefly, as the problem of unity.

Most discussions of personal identity, however, have taken it for granted that sameness and change are, at least, often compatible and have concentrated on the conditions under which reidentification of persons can take place. What enables us to say, in spite of the changes wrought by time, that person *A*, before us now, *is* the person *B* whom we formerly knew and that person *C*, also before us now, is not?

The problem of the conditions for reidentifying persons should be distinguished from the problem of individuating persons. To individuate among a class of beings is to pick out one from another; to reidentify a member of a class of beings is to recognize him as the same as someone known at an earlier time. It is, of course, unlikely that these two notions can be kept separate, since, on the one hand, one has to be able to pick out a being from among his contemporaries before one is able to identify him with a past member of his class (which, in turn, had to be picked out) and since, on the other hand, it is hard to see how a being that exists in our world of time and change can be picked out, at least in the deeper sense of being recognized, without being picked out as a being with a certain history. It is not accidental that the word *identify* can sometimes mean the one procedure and sometimes the other. This article will be concerned directly only with the problem of the reidentification of persons, which will be called the problem of criteria.

It has had two main competing answers. One is that the criterion of the identity of a person is the identity of the body that he has—that it is either a necessary or a sufficient condition of saying correctly that this person before us is Smith that the body this person before us has is the body that Smith had. The other answer is that the criterion of the identity of a person is the set of memories he has—that it is either a necessary or a sufficient condition of saying correctly that this person before us is Smith that he should have memories of doing Smith's actions or of having Smith's experiences.

It is clear that in practice we settle problems of identification in both ways. But we can still ask of each one whether it is necessary or sufficient; we can ask whether each is independent of the other; and we can ask whether one is more fundamental than the other. It is in connection with these questions that we find what are usually called puzzle cases. These are stories, sometimes true but usually imaginary, which are thought to contain prima facie conflicts between the two criteria. In deciding how the conflict is to be resolved, it is thought that we show the order of priority of the two criteria. For instance, there are the cases of ostensible "bodily transfer," like that of the cobbler and the prince mentioned by John Locke. In this story what physically seems to be a cobbler wakes one morning with all the apparent memories of a prince, with no knowledge of shoe mending, and with disgust at his present sordid surroundings. We might make the story harder by imagining that at the same time what looks like the prince wakes up in the royal palace with cobbler memories. In a story like this, persons seem to recall actions and events associated with a body other than the one they now have. Should we say that they are the persons their supposed memories suggest they are or the persons they physically seem to be? To decide this entails deciding on the relative importance of the two criteria of identity.

RELATED ISSUES

The two problems I have distinguished are bound to and do overlap in the literature. The difficulty and importance of the question of personal identity, however, are greatly increased by the fact that it lies at the point of intersection of several major lines of philosophical inquiry.

INFLUENCE OF DUALISM. The problem of personal identity has traditionally been raised in a dualist context. Those who have discussed it have been greatly influenced by the picture of a person as composed of two entities—body and mind—which are only contingently related to each other. This has restricted the problem of unity so that it has become the problem of how one can be justified in attributing unity to the mind. This looks much harder than the problem in its more comprehensive form, since the thoughts, feelings, and images a person has are far less stable than is his body and since it is, to say the least, not easy to find what Hume calls "the bond that unites" them. Failing to find it, a philosopher may resort to a doctrine of spiritual substance and say that within each person there is some central component that preserves his identity because it never changes as his thoughts and feelings do; the philosopher must then decide whether this component can be detected by introspection or is unknowable. If he rejects this doctrine, as Hume did, he may give way to complete skepticism about identity.

SELF-KNOWLEDGE. The second issue with which the problem is involved is the relation between the knowledge a person has of himself and the knowledge that others have of him. There are a great many facts about a person that others can learn, it is often said, only by inference but to which he himself seems to have direct and privileged access. The usual examples are facts about his present thoughts, feelings, and intentions. But it looks as though something similar may be true about the past. Although others may have to ascertain whether I am a certain previously known person or did a certain past action by reference to external records or to my observable appearance, I seem to know this directly, in memory. This bears on the puzzle stories. It seems absurd, if we imagine ourselves as one of the participants in these tales, to suggest that someone else might know better than we who we are. If this is really absurd, the puzzles have to be settled in favor of memory; if it is not, we have to explain our natural tendency to want to settle them this way.

IMMORTALITY. A third connected issue is the possibility of survival. If the unity of a person is necessarily connected with the continuance of his body through time, then it is logically impossible for a person to survive the death of his body. If bodily identity is a necessary criterion of personal identity, then even if it could be shown that some nonphysical characteristics of a person continued after his bodily death, the person himself would not have been shown to have survived any more than (to use

Antony Flew's example) he would have been if it had been possible to preserve his appendix in a bottle. On the other hand, if bodily identity is not a necessary criterion of personal identity, perhaps bodily death is merely one major event in a person's history and not the end of him. And if the fundamental criterion of identity is memory, it would seem to follow that a person might be known, at least to himself, to have survived death because he continued to have memories in his disembodied state.

MORAL CONSIDERATIONS. The concept of a person has moral connections. Problems of reidentification arise in practice largely when we have to decide questions of right or responsibility, such as right to inheritances or responsibility for crimes. Identity is a necessary though not a sufficient condition of someone's being accorded rights or being made to shoulder penalties. This applies in the afterlife, too. Only if beings who exist after our death can be identified with us can they rightly be held heirs to our merit or blame. A theory of personal identity must take this fact properly into account.

THE "SELF"

One result of these wider connections has been an unfortunate technical restriction on the language in which personal identity has come to be discussed. It has been referred to as the problem of the self. This word is sometimes used to mean the whole series of a person's inner mental states and sometimes, more restrictedly, the spiritual substance to which the philosopher says they belong. The use of the word *self,* however, has the effect of confining the question to the unity of the mind and of preventing the answer from relying on the temporal persistence of the body. This has made the unity problem seem intractable, especially when the fleetingness of mental images, feelings, and the like is contrasted with the temporal persistence their owner needs in order even to engage in the relatively lengthy processes of dreaming, reasoning, or scrutinizing the external world. This article therefore avoids a terminology that has ruled out one line of solution ab initio by making it impossible to endow the owner of mental processes with physical characteristics.

By far the most important classical discussions are those of Locke and Hume, and it is therefore useful to begin consideration of the problem of personal identity by reference to their attempts to solve it.

LOCKE

INCOMPLETENESS OF THE CONCEPT OF IDENTITY. Locke began his discussion of identity in Chapter 27 of the *Essay concerning Human Understanding* by pointing out a vital fact that others, including Hume, have since neglected. The concept of identity has to be joined to some substantive notion like that of a tree or a person in order to have any use at all. What makes us say that a given entity is the same depends on what sort of entity it is. This implies an answer to the unity problem—an entity of any sort can remain the same throughout its changes provided that the changes that take place in it are characteristic of entities of that sort and are allowed for in their concept. Over the years a tree can double its size and remain the same tree since this sort of change is characteristic of trees and is allowed for in the concept of a tree. It cannot, however, sprout wings and fly or burn to ashes and still remain a tree, for changes of these kinds are not allowed for. This being so, no hidden substance is necessary for the retention of its identity since there is no need of the unchanging character that this is said to provide. The same is true, presumably, of persons, and all that seems to remain is the much harder question of what changes are allowed for in this concept—the problem of the criteria of identity. Locke characteristically failed, however, to follow through the implications of his own insight. Although he saw the inutility of the concept of substance, he still retained it and led himself into some confusions.

These confusions are partly engendered by his apparent assumption that is it possible to find one single criterion of identity for each sort of being. Our concepts are not as tidy as this. When the assumption is brought to bear on the very untidy concept of a person, the result is a distortion of the concept's logical character. This takes the form of a supposed distinction between "person" and "man."

"MAN" AND "PERSON." A man, according to Locke, is a certain sort of living organism whose identity depends on its biological organization. On the other hand, he defined a person as "a thinking intelligent being, that has reason and reflection, and can consider itself as itself, the same thinking thing, in different times and places; which it does only by that consciousness which is inseparable from thinking and essential to it." Further, "as far as this consciousness can be extended backwards to any past action or thought, so far reaches the identity of that person." To sever the two notions in this way is a radical departure from ordinary usage, in which the two words are often interchangeable. Locke admitted this, without, however, seeing that the admission conceded that his account must be inaccurate as a description of the two "ideas." Of course, there is a point in the division; behind it lies the recognition that there are two criteria of identity for persons. This Locke tried to accommodate to his belief that for each sort of entity there is one criterion only, by arguing that there are two distinct concepts, each of which has its own unique criterion, rather than one concept with two criteria. But Locke was not trying merely to be tidy; more important is the motive supplied in his claim that "person" is what he called a "forensic" term. A person is a morally responsible agent. It is clear that to establish by physical evidence that the man before us in the dock is the one who did the deed is not sufficient to show that he should suffer the penalty (though it is surely sufficient to show that no one else should, unless he instigated or compelled the deed). Locke wanted to mark this fact by a special restriction on the notion of a person, so that to state that someone is the same person who did the deed is to imply accountability without room for more (or much more) dispute. He thought it obvious that what makes people accountable for their actions is their ability to recognize them as their own. This seems to mean two things: first, an awareness of what one is doing when one is doing it and, second, an ability to remember having done it. Hence, he said that the criterion for the identity of persons, as distinct from men, is consciousness, a concept intended to embrace both awareness and memory. The fact that the same *man* is before us does not mean that the same person is, since the *man* may not be conscious of having done the deed in question and if the *man* is not conscious of having done it, then the *person* did *not* do it. Here Locke brought in the puzzle cases:

> Should the soul of a prince, carrying with it the consciousness of the prince's past life, enter and inform the body of a cobbler, as soon as deserted by his own soul, everyone sees he would be the same *person* with the prince, accountable only for the prince's actions…. Had I the same consciousness that I saw the ark and Noah's flood, as that I saw an overflowing of the Thames last winter, I could no more doubt that I who write this now, that saw the Thames overflowed last winter, and that viewed the flood at the general deluge, was the same *self* … than that I who write this am the same *myself* now whilst I write … that I was yesterday.

Locke was misconstruing the facts to which he draws our attention. Even granting that only persons are accountable, persons are still men (for men are accountable). We may be morally right in making the memory of crimes a condition for punishment, but memory does not thereby become the sole criterion of identity, for physical

presence at the crime is also a condition of responsibility for it. Both the criteria are used together, and the most Locke has shown is that the satisfaction of only one is not, for moral purposes, enough; he has not shown that each serves a different concept. One is tempted to sever them only because of the puzzle stories. These, however, do not represent the conditions under which our concepts have been evolved but, rather, imaginary new conditions that might force us into the decision to change them. As things now stand, we have one complex concept, represented variously by words like "person," "man," or "human being" and embedded in the specific notions of cobbler, prince, beggar, or thief. This concept has two complementary criteria of identity. If we allow ourselves to be forced to say that there are two concepts, each with one criterion, we are saying that our criteria here and now allow us to hold that the memory of a crime, even without physical presence, is enough to establish responsibility for it.

There is a possible Lockean reply to this. It is to say that when a person remembers his deeds but clearly does not have the body that performed those deeds, the deeds can nevertheless still be his because he may have done them in a previous body and have inherited another since. The same person will then no longer be the same man. This cannot be evaluated until we have considered the puzzle cases at some length. For the present let us turn to Locke's attempt to make memory the single necessary and sufficient criterion of personal identity. If this attempt is successful, his treatment of the puzzles is made highly plausible; if not, it becomes highly suspect.

IDENTITY AS MEMORY. That there is a big difficulty in the problem of identity as memory was clear to Joseph Butler and has recently been very skillfully argued by Antony Flew. Locke wished to say that Smith is the same person who did or witnessed X if, and only if, Smith has the memory of doing or witnessing X. But this is unclear. The verb *remember* and its cognates have a strong and a weak sense. In the strong sense, to say that someone remembers something is to imply the correctness of his recollection (at least in all but minor details). To say in this idiom that someone's recollection is erroneous is to say that he does not really remember, but only seems to. In the weak sense, to say someone remembers something is merely to say that he sincerely claims to remember it (in the strong sense). In the weak sense, memories can be mistaken. Now, it is clear that even though we do pay special attention to what people claim to remember when settling questions of identity, the fact that someone claims to remember doing or witnessing something does not show that he did it or witnessed it. Even though sincere, he might be mistaken. Thus, to say that Smith is the same person if he has the memory of X must, it seems, mean that he has to remember X in the strong sense of "remember." But here a twofold difficulty arises.

How are we to decide between a genuine and an apparent memory in any given case? The candidate's inner conviction is unreliable. We seem to have to resort to more than the memory claims themselves. And the critical evidence would seem to have to be evidence of the person's physical presence at the scenes he describes. This suggests that the memory criterion is not self-sufficient, as Locke says it is, for in order to know that it is satisfied on a given occasion, we seem to have to use the bodily criterion first.

Apart from this it is much too stringent to restrict personal identity to cases where a person can actually recall his past actions or experiences. People forget. Therefore, we must alter our wording. Smith, we have to say, is the same person who did or witnessed X if, and only if, he could remember it. But what does "could" mean here? Taken in a practical sense, it seems too strong, for this would imply that if Smith did do or witness X, there is some actual set of procedures that, if we applied them, would enable him to recall it. But this may not be so; even psychoanalysts fail. If, on the other hand, "could" is not given this sort of sense, it is hard to see what its use here contributes, unless it is merely another way of saying that Smith is the one who did or witnessed X if, and only if, he is the person to whom the application of procedures designed to induce recollection is appropriate. Unfortunately, this is either straightforwardly untrue (since before we discovered who did or saw X, it would be appropriate to apply such procedures to all likely candidates, not just to Smith) or merely a concealed way of saying that Smith is actually the person who did it, so that *no one other than he could* remember it. Thus, the concept of memory seems, in this argument, to presuppose that of personal identity, rather than the reverse.

These arguments show that Locke was mistaken in trying to define personal identity in terms of memory because such a definition is necessarily circular. In at least this sense Butler was correct when he said that memory presupposes, and does not constitute, personal identity. Some philosophers have gone on to say that memory is not a criterion of identity for persons at all, since, they say, we cannot know whether someone's apparent memories are real without knowing by physical means that he is the person who was involved in the events he recalls. But this, it will be argued later, is also a self-defeating

move. For the present it can be seen that Locke was undoubtedly wrong in holding that memory could be the *sole* criterion of identity for persons.

SPIRITUAL SUBSTANCE. A great deal of the argument of Locke's chapter is designed to reconcile his preference for memory with his doctrine of spiritual substance. The doctrine of spiritual substance is inherited from his view that some doctrine of substance is necessary to account for the fact that the qualities of an object cohere. This is presumably intended to account for their exhibiting a permanent ownership through time, as well as their belonging together in one region of space. Yet Locke denied that we have any knowledge of what substance is like, since our knowledge is restricted to the qualities of things. In the case of persons the doctrine is one of spiritual rather than material substance (whatever the difference between two unknowns may be). But it is clear that nothing whose character is totally unknown can be detectable by the senses or by introspection, so that the doctrine of substance, as Locke held it, cannot provide any answer to the problem of criteria. No one could be said to be applying a concept on the basis of facts to which he has no access. An intractable problem now arises. Granting for the moment that memory is the sole criterion of identity, what is the relation between this fact and that of the existence of the underlying substance? Is it not possible that the application of the memory criterion might lead us to ascribe identity when this was not metaphysically backed by the continuance of one substance? If this should happen, would we have made a mistake?

The most straightforward answer is the paradoxical one of saying that the memory criterion is merely a guide for making identity judgments and that their ultimate metaphysical justification must forever elude us—which would mean that we could never be more than roughly sure we were punishing the right people for crimes. Locke sought to soften this by two devices. One was to sever "substance" and "person" in the same way that he severed "man" and "person" and to insist that only persons are bearers of responsibility, the concept of substance being obscure and irrelevant. The difficulty with this is that it leaves the doctrine of substance without any connection to those entities whose unity it was supposed to explain. The other device was to say that it is the "more probable opinion" that the consciousness that makes for personal identity is "annexed to" one immaterial substance rather than a plurality and to found the faith in its not being otherwise on the goodness of the Deity "who, as far as the happiness or misery of any of his sensible creatures is concerned in it, will not, by a fatal error of theirs, transfer from one to another that consciousness which draws reward or punishment with it."

But these are no more than devices and have to be used only if we represent the identity of persons as composed of one kind of fact yet recognized through another. For Locke himself, in his early comments on the varying criteria of identity for objects of different kinds, has provided us with a demonstration of the total inutility of the doctrines of substance. We do not need them to account for our ascriptions of identity through change; these rest upon our noticing characteristic patterns of sequence in things. But these patterns do not just supply the criteria for ascribing continuance. They are also the reasons for our doing so at all. In other words, the answer to the unity question lies in the same facts that yield the answer to the criteria question. The invention of substance was intended to explain a practice whose explanation Locke had himself provided in another way. That he did not draw the moral and altogether abandon this invention may in part be the result of his having inherited it from others and in part the result of the incompleteness of his account of the criteria of personal identity.

In Locke, then, we find: one answer to the unity problem in terms of substance and another in terms of the objects' characteristic patterns of change, which renders the first answer unnecessary; a clear recognition of the connection between problems of practical identification and moral responsibility, which is exaggerated to the point of caricature by the separation of the concepts of a person and a man; an unambiguous claim for the priority of the memory criterion of identity for persons, which seems on superficial examination to lead to circularities; and an introduction of the puzzle cases to force a decision in favor of the last claim. With the lessons of Locke's insights and errors behind us, we turn to Hume.

HUME

In Hume's famous section on personal identity (*Treatise of Human Nature*, Book I, Part IV, Sec. 6), we find a treatment of the topic that is, as would be expected, more polished and consistent than that of Locke. But since it is also radically defective, its very tidiness makes it less fertile. It has had a baffling effect on generations of readers because of Hume's ability to destroy metaphysical palliative solutions to problems without uncovering the confusions that give rise to them. This, in turn, issues in a paralyzing skepticism that rendered Hume even less capable than Locke of reaching a clear understanding of the conceptual structure he examines.

Hume began by attacking the spiritual-substance solution to the problem of unity, as it appears in the claim that there is a unique and simple "self" that each person is able to detect within himself. He argued with effective simplicity that he was unable to detect it in himself. He was accordingly forced to conclude that the belief in personal identity, since it lacks this justification, is erroneous. People are "nothing but a bundle or collection of different perceptions" in a constant state of change—for perceptions are all that Hume *could* detect in himself. In this situation all that a philosopher can do is examine how it is that men (himself included) "suppose ourselves possessed of an invariable and uninterrupted existence through the whole course of our lives." This psychological objective Hume tried to attain by uncovering a basic conceptual confusion that he claimed we all fall into. We fail, he said, to distinguish properly between two things—the "idea of an object, that remains invariable and uninterrupted thro' a supposed variation of time" (which is the prototype of identity) and the "idea of several different objects existing in succession, and connected together by a close relation" (which is as good an example as any other of diversity). We confuse these two ideas because of the mental laziness that makes us content with their superficial similarity. Strictly ("to an accurate view"), change destroys identity, but we are easily beguiled into overlooking that change has occurred. Once launched upon this convenient path of error, the mind is led further and further along it by certain recurring facts—it is easier for us to overlook than notice gradual changes, changes that are characteristic of certain objects, and changes that occur according to certain smooth and regular patterns, and so we choose to overlook them. Everyone is prone to this error, which therefore acquires the dubious sanction of custom. Sooner or later, however, philosophers arrive on the scene and notice the recurrent paradox in which men have thus involved their thinking. They see both that we do ascribe identity to changing things and that we have no apparent ground for doing this. The result is that since they cannot *find* such a ground, they *invent* one. Hence, the metaphysical fancies of substance and the self. But these are hollow solutions; there is no discernible bond uniting a person, though there are sufficient interrelationships between his thoughts, feelings, and memories to explain why we erroneously ascribe unity to him. Hume had no consolation to offer us in this alleged predicament other than his usual one: Even though philosophical constructions cannot justify custom, philosophical criticism cannot dislodge it. For philosophical reasonings have power only in the study, not at the backgammon table.

SAMENESS AND CHANGE. Given the premise that Hume shared with the philosophers of substance, his conclusions follow only too clearly. This premise is that there is indeed a paradox in ascribing both change and identity to the same subject, since to ascribe change is to deny that we *have* the same subject. To agree to this is to deny that there can be any genuine solution to the problem of unity and to show that even a substance solution is at best a palliative—and a misleading one. But this is a very odd premise to concede without a battle. It has the extreme, language-destroying consequence that no predicates that cannot be simultaneously ascribed to one subject can be ascribed to a subject at two different times. If it is a mere matter of custom that we violate this principle, at least the custom is indispensable. Surely, much argument is needed to show that the custom is paradoxical and the principle necessary. And there is very little argument in Hume to this effect. His account of the fundamental confusion he claimed to have detected is made plausible only by its vagueness. It looks reasonable to say there is a contrast between one continuing object and a succession of related objects, but this is so only if "object" is tacitly replaced by the same noun in each case. There is a contrast between one continuing note and a succession of related notes (and who would confuse one with the other?) but not between one continuing tune and a succession of related notes. It is by means of the second sort of arrangement, not the first, that we incorporate change into our language. In order to understand the unreality of the contrast that Hume was foisting upon himself, one has merely to recall Locke's principle that "same" is an incomplete term that functions only in conjunction with substantives. There are some conjunctions that would yield the contrast—"same note" and "succession of different notes" is obviously one. It is equally obvious that "same tune" and "succession of different notes" is not one. Thus, Hume was wrong to look for the source of the contrast, when it does exist, in the concepts of identity and diversity considered alone. The concepts do not operate alone and yield his conflict only in those cases where they are joined with the right substantives. In most cases it does not exist, because most substantive concepts (including that of a person) are designed to incorporate changes.

There is, of course, one sense of the words *same* and *identical* in which sameness and change are incompatible. This is the sense of "same" in which, if applied to two distinct things, it means "alike" and, if applied to one thing at different times, it means "unaltered." This we might call the comparative sense of the word. It is to be distinguished from the numerical sense, in which two things said to be the same are said not to be two, but one. Clearly, one thing cannot be said to be both changed and the same if the comparative sense is intended, but this is not the sense we intend when we wonder whether we are entitled to consider someone the same throughout changes. Once this is noted, we can easily see that there is no need to assume that "to an accurate view" an object has to be the same in the comparative sense to remain the same in the numerical sense. If this is missed, a sense of paradox will be only too easy to sustain.

On the other hand, our concepts do not allow all kinds of change indiscriminately. How much is allowed depends on the concept in question. A man can change in more ways before he is destroyed than a chair can. To know what alterations are and are not allowed is to know, among other things, what the criteria of identity are for the class of entities grouped under the concept in question. These matters may not always be easy to settle precisely. We may not be in a position to say whether we have the same things on certain occasions. When the roof is removed, does the house still exist, or are we left with something else? If the walls are torn down and rebuilt, do we have the same house or another? Sometimes the only answer at such a point is a decision on the scope of the concept. But for general purposes usage over the years has provided us with rough and ready conventions that (this is a truism) language-users know.

Hume was aware of this fact, but the logic of his position forced him to misrepresent it. Instead of presenting us with some general indications of the sorts of change that tend to be allowed under concepts (changes that are gradual, small, functionally absorbable into the whole, and so on), he claimed to present us with the factors which, in his view, beguile us most regularly into the habit of ignoring the changes taking place in objects right under our noses. But these factors (which do not at all conceal the changing character of our world from us) are the same ones that appear without this disguise in a correct account of the situation. It is from a detailed knowledge of the very facts he outlined that we derive the criteria for those very identity judgments that he declared to be always unjustified. This is not the first or last time a philosopher has drawn our attention to facts supposed to support one theory when they in fact support another.

Similar considerations apply to what Hume said about the creation of substance doctrines. It is probably true that philosophers have invented these in order to answer the unity problem, and it is, of course, a merit in Hume that he saw that there is no independent evidence for the truth of such doctrines. But he did not see that the primary objection to them is not that they cannot be shown to be true, but that they are unnecessary. They are invoked to soften a paradox that does not exist. There is no contradiction between saying a thing or person has changed and remains that same thing or person if the changes are characteristic of that sort of thing or of persons. If there is no paradox here, there is no need of any metaphysical postulate to conceal it. If Hume had seen this, he would not have tried to render more palatable the skepticism to which he was led by rejecting the doctrine of substance, for such skepticism could arise only if the doctrine were thought to be both false *and* necessary. But it is only false. The substantialists do not vindicate the ordinary language-user, and Hume does not convict him. Both have misdescribed what he is doing.

PERSONS. In the specific comments that Hume made about the identity of persons, he was clearly working, as was Locke, in the restricted framework in which "person" means "mind." Only thus can we read his statement that people are nothing but bundles of perceptions. The restriction makes him exaggerate for skeptical purposes the discontinuity he claimed to have discovered in the life histories of persons—a discontinuity that does not exist if we include the history of each person's body as well as that of his mind.

But this error hides a deeper one. There is a curious unreality about Hume's discussion of whether we can observe any real bond between the perceptions of a person. This question cannot, of course, be raised unless we can already distinguish between one person and another. Hume, that is to say, was asking whether there is any uniting bond among those perceptions that belong to one person. But why should this question puzzle him if he can already distinguish between those perceptions that belong to one person and those that belong to another? It is at least likely that those features of persons that enable us to distinguish one from another (to individuate) at any one time should also enable us to reidentify people after lapses of time. Yet these features are, and have to be, largely physical ones. For each of us can have (or perceive) only his own perceptions, and without the recognition of the bodies of others, there would be no question of the ownership of perceptions other than one's own ever arising (or, therefore, of the ownership of one's own). In asking his question, Hume was assuming that the perceptions persons are alleged to consist of are somehow known to be in parallel strings, so that the only question remaining is what unites those perceptions that belong on any one string. But if, as he saw, there is no clear psychical factor uniting them, it might still be true

that whatever determines their belonging to a particular string also serves to join them together along it. And this, after all, is part of what the body does. His puzzle arises in the form that baffled him only if we first differentiate persons from one another on the basis of their bodies and then, forgetting that we have done it this way, look for some substitute for this principle among the contents of the mind. The principle that the question throws into doubt has to be assumed for the question to be raised.

In Hume, therefore, we find a dismissal of metaphysical construction and an awareness of the general characteristics of the complex facts out of which we forge our criteria of identity. These, however, are rendered completely sterile by the skeptical use to which Hume had to put them. The skepticism is, in turn, the result of a rationalistic oversimplification of the notion of identity that prevented Hume from discovering the muddle at the heart of the unity puzzle and of the dualistic framework of thought within which he worked.

SOME INTERIM CONCLUSIONS

We can now draw some conclusions from this investigation of the two main classical discussions of self-identity. The first is that the problem of the unity of persons is a spurious problem that rests upon two errors concerning the idea of identity. One of the errors is the failure to take enough note of the distinction between comparative and numerical identity. The other is the failure to note that the concept of numerical identity works in harness with substantive class concepts that provide those who know how to employ them with rules for making correct identity judgments on entities within their classes.

The second conclusion is that the concept of spiritual substance is not only unverifiable (as Hume saw) but also unnecessary (as Locke saw and Hume did not).

The third conclusion is that the unity problem has acquired a specious appearance of difficulty because of a tacit restriction placed by philosophers on the concept of a person. Since only the psychical components of the person are considered, a picture of change and discontinuity is conjured up that makes the fictitious contrast between identity and change seem even more alarming.

This leads naturally into the fourth conclusion—that it is salutary to remind ourselves that our actual concept of a person is of a psychophysical being. Hence, talk of the criteria of identity for purely psychical beings is not talk of the concept of a person that we actually have. How far they would differ has yet to be decided, but we must at least begin by asking what the actual criteria for embodied human beings are. Here we must bear in mind the apparent circularity of the view that memory is the sole criterion for the identity of human beings. The examination of Locke suggested that in order to apply it some covert reference to the identity of the body has to be made. We must first examine this suggestion with some care.

We shall begin by trying to clarify further the notion of a criterion. It will then be argued that the bodily criterion of identity is in certain important ways more fundamental than the memory criterion in present discourse, although memory is still properly called a criterion in spite of Locke's failure. It could not, however, be the sole criterion. We shall finally consider the puzzles and argue that although they present us with some difficult conceptual decisions, they would not *necessitate* a change of convention in favor of memory, although this is a *possible* response to them. An attempt will be made to show that the response, if made, is innocuous, so that the puzzles are devoid of the wide implications philosophers have thought them to have.

CRITERIA

Thus far, two things have been meant in calling bodily identity and memory criteria of personal identity. One is that it is by reference to one or the other of these facts about people that questions of identity are usually settled. The other is that practical knowledge of how to settle these questions in these ways is a necessary part of having the concept of a person. More needs to be said than this.

There are two areas where the notion of a criterion has been of special concern in recent philosophy. One is the problem of the knowledge of the mental life of other persons. It has been said by some, following Ludwig Wittgenstein, that we can have this knowledge because people's behavior is able to supply us with criteria for saying correctly that they have certain mental states. The other is the problem of the relationship between judgments of fact and evaluative judgments. It has been said by J. O. Urmson, R. M. Hare, and others that certain facts about things or people serve as criteria for evaluating them as good or bad. In both these cases the relationship the word *criterion* names is thought to be tighter than an inductive one and yet looser than a deductive one. In this discussion the word will not be used in this sense, since the relationship between bodily identity and memory, on the one hand, and personal identity, on the other, seems to be closer than this; it seems, in fact, to be straightforwardly deductive. In the discussion of Locke we saw that saying someone remembers something in the strong

sense entails that it forms a part of his life history. It is now claimed that if a person before us has the body that Smith used to have, it follows that he is Smith.

Two comments are necessary. First, this does not commit us to any view about how we know that the criteria are satisfied. To explain how we discover that this man really remembers or really has Smith's body, it might be necessary to use the notion of a criterion in some other, weaker sense—to say, for example, that a certain accumulation of evidence left no more room for reasonable doubt on the matter. But this is another issue. Second, an objection has to be countered. It might be objected that if the relationship between memory or bodily identity and personal identity is deductive, then the criteria are sterile and unusable. For, the argument might go, if either of these facts entailed that this was the same person, we would have to know independently who it was before we could be sure the criterion was satisfied. (This is the objection mentioned in the case of Locke.) This is not a genuine difficulty, but it is instructive. The reason for introducing it can only be the doctrine that if one proposition, *P*, entails another, *Q*, then it is impossible to know *P* without first knowing *Q*. But this is only a dogma that has to be tested against the facts, which do not bear it out.

The difficulty can teach us, however, that the standard objection to Locke is too simple. Even though the fact that memory entails personal identity prevents us from defining one in terms of the other without a circle, it is still possible that we may sometimes know that a person remembers without having previously checked on his identity. If this were not so, then memory could not serve as a criterion, for it is an additional part of the notion of a criterion, as all philosophers have used the term, that it can be applied. I shall shortly argue that this knowledge is possible.

BODILY IDENTITY. Some philosophers have said that the bodily criterion is not a criterion at all because there are some occasions in which we find human bodies that are not persons—that is, dead bodies or bodies that are biologically alive but incapable of exhibiting personality. But my thesis is that bodily identity is a sufficient criterion for reidentifying persons and by hypothesis these are not persons. If we are asking whether *X* before us, who is a person, is the same as Smith whom we once knew, who was a person, it is a sufficient condition of an affirmative answer to know that *X*'s body is Smith's body.

A more serious-looking argument against bodily identity comes from the puzzles. It might be said that when we use the bodily criterion, we are covertly assuming that there has not been any bodily transfer. This raises an important point of method: How are the puzzles to be treated? We shall treat them as cases of proposed conceptual innovation, as if those who invent them do so to make us imagine circumstances that would force us to change our conceptual habits and rely on one criterion alone, even though we now use two. I have argued that in using two criteria, we have not faced the sorts of problems the puzzles present. If this is right, then no proviso against them can be embodied in our present thinking, even covertly. (If anyone considers that such contingencies *are* already provided for, then what is said below about the puzzles can probably be transposed into the key needed to examine his view of what sort of provision we make.)

There are several ways in which the bodily criterion is more fundamental than the memory criterion. In the present thesis these statements should seem like truisms.

Although both criteria are sufficient, only bodily identity is necessary. "This is the person who fired the shot" is entailed equally by "This person has the body of the person who fired the shot" and "This person remembers firing the shot"; but although the third statement entails the first statement, it does not entail the second.

The bodily criterion is more extensive. It is a matter of chance that men remember the tracts of their lives that they do remember rather than those that they do not, and we can apply the memory criterion only when there are memories to use. But in a clear sense the bodily criterion can always be used, for the body is present whenever the person is.

The bodily criterion is more varied. There are more ways in which we can determine whether a person is physically the same as someone than there are ways of determining whether his recollections are genuine. There are blood tests, fingerprints, photographs, the testimony of witnesses, and much else. Of course, a candidate's memory claims can be used to support this evidence, just as physical evidence can be used to support memory claims. The resort to physical tests when the memory claims are in doubt, however, is much more nearly inevitable than the resort to memory claims when physical evidence is inconclusive, since there are so many ways of adding to the physical evidence and it is free from the nagging thought that there is more than one way of coming by information about the past.

These examples are enough to show that we should regard overconfident readings of the puzzle cases with some suspicion, since the normal order of priority between our criteria is not what these readings suggest that it is.

MEMORY. It has already been suggested that even though Locke was mistaken in thinking that he could define personal identity in terms of memory, it does not follow that he was wrong to think of memory as a genuine criterion of personal identity. It might be possible to know that someone remembered without first ascertaining in another way who he is. But if this is possible, it has to coexist with the fact that when men's memory claims are in doubt, decision hinges for the most part on physical tests.

One way of trying to relate these two is to say that when we accept a memory claim unchecked, as we often do, we are relying on an inductive connection between the memory claims of a person and the events he refers to. We have found, that is, that this man's memory claims are usually true or, perhaps, that most people's are usually true. We now accept his word on this basis. Sydney Shoemaker has argued persuasively that this is too simple. He has claimed that it is a logical truth that memory claims are usually true, not an inductive one. Following are his arguments: (1) If someone frequently said with sincerity that he remembered events that did not occur, we would be justified in concluding that he did not know how to use the word *remember*. (2) If a child learning the language were to behave in this way with the word *remember* or one of its cognates, we would tell him that he had not learned how to use it. (3) If we were translating an unknown language and were inclined to translate certain expressions in it as memory expressions, our decision whether to do so would have to hinge in part upon the truth or falsity of the statements beginning with those expressions; if they were generally false, we could not translate them in this way.

If these arguments are accepted, it should probably be added that in order to understand memory claims at all, we must be able to recognize cases of genuine memory, so that there must be *some* such cases and also that just as lies and false promises must be in the minority to succeed, so must insincere or mistaken memory claims. These arguments appear enough to refute any generalized skepticism about memory, unless the skeptic is prepared to deny that our language has those features on which these arguments depend—that its users are generally successful in communicating by means of it and that it is learned and not instinctive. We shall not investigate how far it is correct to regard something established by this sort of argument as a "necessary truth." Although the arguments do depend upon features of language that might be argued to be contingent ones, it is still clear that the conclusions are not straightforwardly inductive, and for this reason I shall allow the label to stick.

It is, then, a necessary truth that memory claims are usually true, from which it follows that they can usually be relied upon in practice. But this does not tell us whether any given memory claim is true. The situation here is, rather, that we are justified in accepting someone's memory claims unless there is some reason to doubt them. Only when there is such a reason do we need to check them. It is this that enables memory to serve as a criterion of identity.

But this is a far cry from Locke's theory that memory is the sole criterion. The very facts that show it to be a criterion at all show that it could not be the only one. We must be able to use the distinction between true and false memory claims (even to learn memory language), and this means we must have at our disposal a way or ways of checking the claims that are made. This implies, of course, that we must be able to discover whether the speaker was, indeed, present at that which he describes. Thus, the availability of the bodily criterion of identity is a necessary condition of our having made the distinction between genuine and false memories, even though it often must, from our previous arguments, be in order not to resort to it but to accept memory claims at their face value. Memory is thus a criterion of identity, but it is absurd to suggest it could be the only one, for without the ability to use another we would lack the ability to use it.

This bears out the view that the bodily criterion is more fundamental. There are arguments in Shoemaker, however, which suggest that just as the memory criterion depends on the bodily criterion in the way we have seen, a similar dependence exists the other way. There is a dependence the other way, but it is not a parallel one. The dependence is one found in all cognitive procedures. Unless people had memories, they could not know past facts. If they did not know past facts, they could not know past facts about themselves or other persons, for we have to depend on either our own recollections or those of other witnesses to learn about the past of a human body. At some point memory testimony has to be accepted without further question, and to accept someone's testimony is to accept that he was indeed a witness to some past event. This is true and supplies us with one more argument to show that memory claims must usually be correct, but it does not establish parity between the two criteria because it does not show that in dealing with a problem of reidentification, it is impossible in theory to dispense with the memory claims of the candidate himself. This is possible, however, and is one of the reasons for the greater importance of the bodily criterion.

In spite of this many philosophers have accorded memory greater weight than the bodily criterion. This seems to be a result of what I shall call the "internality" of memory. In remembering, a person seems to have direct, rather than inferential, access to his own past, to know past facts about himself from the inside. This view of memory is reinforced by the fact that most people would admit to having quasi-perceptual experiences in the form of mental imagery when they remember. Most readers unhesitatingly follow the writers of bodily-transfer stories in assuming them to be intelligible—for how could someone who had systematic recollections of this kind be proved wrong about his own identity by outsiders?

This attitude is not shaken as much as it should be by the fact that in ordinary unsystematic cases we frequently find that even the most vivid recollections are illusory. This is presumably because of the traditional picture of memory as some sort of introspective contemplation of imagery. But what brings memory into the public arena and enables us to use it as a criterion of identity is not this or that sort of private experience but the claims made as a result of it. Indeed, the memory claims of those who deny having memory images are as negotiable in common speech as those of the rest of us. If someone were to claim that he remembered an event and if we were able to determine that he had indeed witnessed it, could give us correct information about it, and could not have come by this information through later research or hearsay, there could be no doubt that he did remember it. The presence or absence, vividness or faintness, of his private images would be of no interest.

It is nevertheless characteristic that when people remember, they have images. If it were not, it is hard to see how the traditional picture of memory could have gained currency. It is true that memory claims are corrigible public claims to knowledge about the past and true that those who make them usually seem to have memory images. It is the first claim that explains why memory has the status it has as a criterion of personal identity. It is the second claim that helps us to understand why some have thought it more fundamental a criterion than it is. For although the subject's unique possession of his images does not confer immunity on the claims he makes, it may have much to do with the fact that he makes them. And it is easy to imagine cases where someone has such experiences and makes the memory claims that they characteristically engender only to find out afterward that these claims are unfounded. This is common enough. It is an easy extension of this to imagine situations in which the events described by such a person did in fact take place, but in the presence of a human body other than the one he has. We then have a typical philosopher's puzzle case. In such a situation characteristic image-laden experiences might take place, and the customary memory claims might be uttered, yet the contextual conditions surrounding correct memory claims would not exist. To allow in some such cases that the speaker really does remember is to change the meaning of this word, but the characteristic intimacy and feeling of conviction that such inner experiences engender might hide this fact from those imagining such examples.

BODILY TRANSFER

It is now time to look at the puzzles. There are, however, a great variety of these, and without deliberate restriction it is impossible to produce any example of the intricate conceptual decisions involved in them. We shall accordingly leave aside puzzle stories of persons who seem to vanish and reappear or who seem to be reincarnations of someone dead and keep to the case of apparent bodily transfer. What is said here is probably comparable to what could be said in these other cases.

Let us take a story in which the servants in a royal palace waken a person who looks as if he is the prince but who evinces complete bewilderment at his surroundings, utters memory claims befitting a cobbler, is astonished on looking into the mirror, and so on. At the same time a man who looks as if he is the cobbler produces princely reactions and memory claims and demands to be returned to the royal palace. What should we say?

B. A. O. Williams has pointed out that the puzzle cases are harder to state in detail than is usually thought. Are we really able to imagine a person with the cobbler's memories (which will include some acquired skills and personality traits) and the prince's body? I shall ignore this complication, though in fact it tends to support what I shall argue to be the best solution.

The first thing to notice about such a puzzle is that it is puzzling. We are torn two ways over it, as we would expect to be if we have two criteria in apparent conflict. On reflection, however, it is more puzzling because if what I have said above is correct, the bodily criterion is the more fundamental of the two, so that the priorities in present practice would lead one to expect that the puzzle should be settled in its favor. Yet those such as Locke, who invent these stories, take it for granted that our tempta-

tions are to settle it in favor of memory. And as far as their judgment of the temptations of most readers goes, they seem to be right. Any answer to the puzzle must take both sides of this paradox into account and try to reconcile them.

PRIORITY OF BODILY CRITERION. Let us first consider the recommendation that our cobbler-prince episode should make us abandon the bodily criterion in favor of the memory criterion.

Put in this bald way, the proposal is absurd. We have already seen reason to say that memory could not be the sole criterion for the identity of persons because using it requires the availability of another. But this, although true, is far too brusque a reaction to the puzzle, which could be used to argue a more modest proposal—to *weaken* the bodily criterion in certain circumstances.

The advocate of bodily transfer could begin his case by making certain admissions and could then say that they do not destroy the case for it. The admissions would be these.

First, in order to set up any case at all, we have to have someone who now makes memory claims that fit a body other than the one he now has. This requires that he should be reidentifiable as the same throughout the period during which he utters the claims. The claims have to be systematic in the circumstances, so the period has to be considerable. For such reidentification the criterion of bodily identity would be necessary.

Second, in order to set up any case at all, we have to know that there was actually a person in the past about whose life these memory claims seem to be accurate reports and that all the claims fit the life history of the *same* person in the past, who *was* the person the claimant now says he *is*. This can be known only if in the past we were able to reidentify that person over the period of his life. This requires the past availability of the bodily criterion.

But when these admissions are made, the advocate of bodily transfer need go no further; he can hold his ground here and say that bodily transfer is still possible. If we had a case where the memory claims of the man who seemed to be the cobbler systematically fitted the past of the prince and vice versa, these claims could be checked up on in detail. And they would be found, ex hypothesi, to fit a past human body; the only difference from normal would be that the body that they fitted was not the body uttering them. Yet the past of the body uttering them would itself be taken care of by a systematic set of memory claims now uttered by that body which they did fit. In such circumstances it surely would be wholly natural to say that the two men had exchanged bodies.

In spite of much recent writing on the puzzles, there seems to be no satisfactory demonstration that the change in convention that would follow on our saying a transfer had occurred would lead to absurdities. It is therefore a possibility. If we make this decision, we would be forced to so weaken the bodily criterion that we were entitled to infer from its being the same body to its being the same person only if there were no (systematic) memory claims which pointed to its being another person. This would place the two criteria in a position of relative parity, for the memory criterion would hold in normal circumstances subject to bodily checks and the bodily criterion would hold except in those abnormal cases where there were detailed and systematic memory claims that conflicted with the normal reading of the bodily evidence.

Having allowed this, we must now emphasize two things. One is that other readings of these cases could be made, as will shortly be argued. The other is that even the adoption of the bodily-transfer reading of them does not have the exciting implications most have thought.

We have already seen that it lends no support to the view that memory either is or ever could be the sole criterion of identity for persons.

It also does nothing to support the suggestion that people could exist with no bodies at all or to give concrete meaning to the common picture of bodily transfer as someone's *going out of* one body *into* another.

Transfer cases, even if allowed, could only be exceptional. If they were not, we would have a world in which the procedures for applying memory concepts would be much more complex than they now are, and virtually impossible to learn. I do not think we could come to learn memory language if the basic use of the word *remember* were one in which it could refer not only to the past of the body uttering it but also to the past of another body (which, in turn, it could be allowed to "fit" only if it were certain that there were no other systematic memory claims to fit the same period available from that body itself). A concept as epistemologically fundamental as that of memory has to be more easily come by than it would be in this sort of world. But granted that it is simpler and has been learned in more straightforward ways, as at present, then it could be stretched to subsequently cover the exceptional cases.

The conclusion is, therefore, that although the logical possibility of bodily transfer has to be admitted, the implications are small and the wisdom of this particular change in our conventions is not self-evident.

ABANDONING THE MEMORY CRITERION. We shall now consider the reverse suggestion—that in the face of such a puzzle we abandon the memory criterion and keep the bodily criterion.

It is not immediately obvious what could be meant by this. If it means that we should ignore the memory claims of candidates for reidentification, this is something we could do in any case; the point at issue is the status of those claims when they are considered. If it means that we should reject memory claims that clash with the bodily facts, then this is something we do already and no change in conventions is implied in it. It must mean that we disallow the inference from "He remembers X" to "X formed part of his life history." But the difficulty here is that in order even to gather the bodily facts, we need to learn about the pasts of others, we have to use either our own memories or those of witnesses, and checks on one set of memories, as we saw earlier, require reliance on other sets. So a change of convention here must allow for the continuance of this reliance.

It seems possible to allow for it in only one way—to continue to say that memory claims are generally correct accounts of past actions or events but to add that these actions or events may have formed part of the life of a person other than the one now making memory claims about them. People, in other words, would be allowed to recall events in the lives of others. Two comments may be made here.

For reasons that would parallel those in the previous section, it seems that cases where people *did* recall events in the lives of others would have to be rare.

Suppose that in spite of his protestations X was just admitted to be the prince because he has the prince's body. He now says, "But I remember mending the shoes last night." Suppose X finally gives in and concedes that he must be the prince although it is still agreed on all sides that the cobbler did mend the shoes last night. X cannot just say, "Oh, I really remember the cobbler's mending the shoes, not myself." This will not do because it fails to distinguish between the new, special case in which one person remembers the deeds of another without having done them (or even having been present) and the familiar case in which one person remembers another's deeds through having witnessed those deeds. It is the second case that would be conveyed by a sentence like "I remember the cobbler's mending the shoes." I am not sure how far this difficulty could be removed by verbal adjustment, but it is at the minimum an inconvenience under the new convention.

The conclusion is as before.

DENIAL THAT ONE CRITERION IS SATISFIED. There would thus seem to be two possible alternative conceptual changes that we could make, each of which would weaken a familiar inference and each of which would be awkward, though not demonstrably impossible. As a matter of fact, however, we already have at our disposal a much simpler device for dealing with such puzzles. Instead of pretending to abandon or to alter one criterion, we can refuse to allow that one of them is satisfied. This need not be thought of as merely a temporary device. If we were to come across odd examples of pieces of iron that did not obey the lodestone but seemed otherwise to satisfy tests for being iron, we could postpone conceptual change for some time by insisting either that the tests had not been properly administered or that it was not really a lodestone. Such moves would become irrational only if maintained in the face of repeated examples. It is hard to admit that the point of irrationality could ever be reached in the present case.

There are clearly only two moves of this sort here. We can deny that it is really the same body, on the grounds that the memory claims it utters fit another, or we can deny that it is really the case that the speaker remembers, because it was not the body before us that was present. Note that neither move involves denying a criterion as the term is being used here. It merely involves refusing to accept that one criterion is satisfied in those cases where accepting that both were satisfied would land us in direct contradiction. There seem to be insuperable obstacles in adopting the first move. For one thing, it would require us, in the case of human bodies, to adopt standards of reidentification that differ from those we accept in the case of all other physical objects. (And if we disregarded this and insisted on behavioral or memory criteria for the identity of human bodies, we would destroy the distinction between a human body and a person.) For another, we would find ourselves led straight into an absurdity. Note again that we are retaining the bodily criterion while making this move. If what is known to be spatiotemporally continuous with the prince's body utters cobblerlike memory claims and if for this reason we say that it is not really the prince's body, we are not able to go on to say that it is, instead, the cobbler's body; for, by hypothesis, it is not spatiotemporally continuous with the cobbler's body and is therefore *not* the same physical object as that body. Thus, it is nobody's body at all, which is absurd.

Hence, we are not able to make the move of denying that it is the body it seems to be. But there is nothing to prevent us from making the other move—of saying that unless the bodily facts at least coincide with the memory claims a person utters, then these claims are false, however closely they fit the past of someone else. This would merely be the determined application to special cases of a procedure we now follow.

We could not, of course, stop there, for we would have to explain how the person came to forget his own past and have so much accurate information about another's. Heroic hypotheses of retrocognitive clairvoyance would have to be brought forward to deal with such strange things. Such hypotheses would have to explain how it was that a person could have information about someone else's past in a manner so phenomenologically similar to the way in which he normally remembered his own. But no greater heroism would be called for here than would be called for by accepting that one person could exchange bodies or memories with another—for the second idea would require much the same sort of hypothesis as the one I have mentioned, and the first would make it puzzling that people should remember their own pasts. Of course, each would introduce a difficult conceptual change.

PUZZLE CASES BECOMING COMMON. But would we not be forced into a conceptual change if such cases became common? For once, the complexities of our problem make it easier to deal with and enable us to give a negative answer. This can be understood from two sides. It has already been argued that either of the possible conceptual changes would require that the cases of bodily transfer or memory exchange be rare; otherwise, we would not have the memory concepts we do have. Yet in order even to state the problem, we must use memory concepts. From the other side, we have to remember that if we were to adopt the device recommended, then in cases like the one in our story we would say of the characters not that they remembered but that they "retrocognized." If such a convention were adopted, however, it would become the appropriate language for the persons to use in such situations. For what makes our problem is what makes the memory criterion possible—the occurrence of memory claims. These are made in public memory language. If the public language changed so that the inappropriateness of a standardly worded memory claim for such circumstances became generally recognized, then the persons themselves, on discovering that the bodily facts did not fit, would not say that they remembered but that they "retrocognized." Thus, by the time the cases became common, they would cease to exist in the logically puzzling form, because they would cease to be heralded by claims to remember. Pieces of iron do not talk; people are different, and the very data of the puzzles would change if the cases occurred frequently.

PRIMACY OF MEMORY. The solution has now to contend with the fact that we do feel a genuine compulsion to read these puzzle stories in some way that favors memory and to say that the claimant himself must know who he is better than others ever could. There are two reasons for this compulsion. One derives from the internality of memory, the other from psychophysical dualism.

On the internality of memory it is enough to repeat that although it is people's public memory claims that relate to decisions about their identity, such claims seem to be made for the most part when people have had characteristic image-laden experiences. Many philosophers consider these to be more closely related to the logic of remembering than they really are, and since the privacy of imagery places reports of it in an epistemologically privileged position, this privilege is erroneously thought to extend to memory claims—overlooking the fact that memory claims are not reports of imagery. When a person imagines himself being involved in a puzzle story, he supplies himself with vivid and systematic imagery to occasion memory claims that do not fit his present body, and he forgets that the persistence and vividness of the memory could not override the impact of the public physical checks that are a necessary part of the conventions governing memory claims.

As for the theoretical dualism that lies behind so many arguments about personal identity, it has here been argued that however we read them, the puzzles do nothing to support dualism. But the investigation of them has been conditioned in many cases by dualist preconceptions.

Shoemaker correctly remarked that the concept of bodily transfer is compatible with a behavioristic view of the mind, for one might mean, when saying that the cobbler and prince had exchanged bodies, that in the case of each person his distinctive behavior patterns (including his memory claims and behavior) were to be found in a body other than the one in which they used to be found. This is true, but if this solution to the puzzles were urged upon us in conjunction with an overtly behaviorist view of personality, it seems plain that there would be no special obviousness in or compulsion toward this solution as opposed to the others, even though it would still be a possible one. The reason that we all feel some degree of compulsion toward accepting the bodily-transfer solution is that dualist preconceptions intrude themselves when we investigate the stories. It is taken for granted that we have an independently clear concept, with recognized criteria of identity, of a soul, spirit, or mind, which can be thought of as having a purely contingent relationship to the body, which it may abandon in favor of another body. (Locke's phraseology in introducing the puzzle is to the point: "Should the soul of a prince … enter and inform the body of a cobbler…".) The only available criterion for such a purely psychical being is presumably memory, but we have already seen that it cannot be self-sufficient in the way it would have to be for us to conceive such an entity independently. Yet this is necessary to justify otherwise vacuous talk about such an entity's entering one body, leaving another, and the rest. Anyone feeling impelled to read the puzzles in favor of memory is probably making covert use of this illegitimate picture.

An important objection could now be raised. It might be said that even though much reflection has been infused with a dualist theory, this is a linguistic fact of life that philosophers must accept without complaint, for all language-users, not just philosophers, tend to be dualists. Thus, all language-users, if faced with the puzzles, would tend to opt for the memory solution. If so, how can a philosopher cavil at this solution? For what we *should* say is usually to be determined by a decision as to what we *would* say.

This raises the difficult general question of how to react to a misleading theory that has filtered into ordinary discourse. In the present case we could argue as follows. Philosophers such as Gilbert Ryle have exposed many errors and confusions in traditional dualism. But they have spoiled their own case by representing themselves as champions of the common man against the professional philosopher. It is easy enough to show that nonphilosophers are dualists, too. However, the common man is a dualist in the same sense in which the philosopher is one—when he interprets his own thinking about mental qualities and conduct. What the antidualist arguments show is that laymen misconstrue in their interpretative moments the utterances and thoughts that they engage in in their day-to-day existence. (We could say that all of us are occasionally philosophers, when we think about our ordinary mental concepts, but most of us are bad philosophers because we misinterpret them.) These common theoretical misconstructions, though inconsistent with our daily use of such concepts, are usually harmless because of the merciful logical dispensation that allows us to make good sense with our concepts while talking nonsense about them. Occasionally, however, the prolonged continuance of the misguided theory can infect the practice. One such occasion is the present one, where the tacit appeal to the illegitimate concept of an independently identifiable psychical entity exerts a compulsion upon the reader of a puzzle story to interpret that story as a case of bodily transfer. Here it seems legitimate to replace bad theory by better and to argue against taking this solution for granted. The memory solution the dualist reading implies is at best one competitor among others, and one is led to think it is required only by our use of concepts on more normal occasions if one has misunderstood those occasions.

CONCLUSIONS

Of the two problems distinguished at the outset, this article has tried to show that the first, the unity problem, is spurious, since the paradox on which it rests is only apparent. The criteria problem admits of no such clear-cut solution, since it is clear on examination that both the bodily criterion and the memory criterion are ineluctable components of our concept of a person. The bodily criterion is more fundamental, but the memory criterion is, in its own way, indispensable because of the basic epistemological status of memory itself. This is one of the many facets of the irreducibly psychophysical nature of persons. One important result of this conclusion is that it is absurd to consider memory as the sole necessary or sufficient condition of identity. Thus, it would not even seem possible to construct a coherent concept of an independently identifiable bodiless person of whose identity memory would be the sole criterion. It would seem to follow that disembodied survival is logically absurd. It is impossible to decide here whether the doctrine of bodily resurrection fares better. Our examination shows that the puzzle stories can at most embody situations in which the relationships between the two criteria could be altered by conceptual decision. They could not embody situations in which either could be abandoned in favor of the other.

See also Butler, Joseph; Dualism in the Philosophy of Mind; Hare, Richard M.; Hume, David; Identity; Immortality; Locke, John; Memory; Persons; Reincarnation; Self; Self-Knowledge; Shoemaker, Sydney; Williams, Bernard.

Bibliography

The literature devoted explicitly to the problem of personal identity is fairly small, but the amount that is devoted to related questions is immense. These works were made direct use of in the article: John Locke, *Essay concerning Human Understanding*, edited by Campbell Fraser (Oxford: Clarendon Press, 1894), Book 2, Ch. 27; David Hume, *A Treatise of Human Nature*, edited by L. A. Selby-Bigge (Oxford: Clarendon Press, 1896), Book I, Part 4, Sec. 6; Joseph Butler, "Of Personal Identity," appendix to *The Analogy of Religion*, edited by W. E. Gladstone (Oxford, 1897), Vol. I, pp. 385ff.; Antony Flew, "Locke and the Problem of Personal Identity," *Philosophy* 26 (1951): 53–68; Terence Penelhum, "Hume on Personal Identity," *Philosophical Review* 64 (1955): 571–589, and "Personal Identity, Memory, and Survival," *Journal of Philosophy*, 56 (1959): 882–903; B. A. O. Williams, "Personal Identity and Individuation," *PAS* 57 (1956–1957): 229ff.; Sydney Shoemaker, "Personal Identity and Memory," *Journal of Philosophy* 56 (1959): 868–882.

The most important classical discussion that is not discussed in this article is Thomas Reid, *Essays on the Intellectual Powers of Man* (Edinburgh, 1785), Essay III, especially Chs. 4 and 6. Reid has some admirable criticisms of Locke, but he is too wedded to the concept of substance to see that Locke's departures from common conceptual practice are not remedied by the use of it.

Another classic discussion is Immanuel Kant, *Critique of Pure Reason*, translated by Norman Kemp Smith (London: Macmillan, 1929), pp. 341ff.

There are some recent books whose discussions repay close study. See C. D. Broad, *The Mind and Its Place in Nature* (London, 1937), Sec. E, pp. 553ff. For stimulating arguments in favor of the notion of a substantial self, see C. A. Campbell, *On Selfhood and Godhood* (London: Allen and Unwin, 1957). Risierei Frondizi, *The Nature of the Self* (New Haven, CT: Yale University Press, 1953), contains interesting discussions of Locke and Hume, but its positive discussion seems to be vitiated by the restrictions of the terminology in its title. P. A. Minkus, *Philosophy of the Person* (Oxford: Blackwell, 1960), is obscure to a degree but has the only extended discussion of Reid. See also Sydney Shoemaker, *Self-Knowledge and Self-Identity* (Ithaca, NY: Cornell University Press, 1963), and his entry "Memory" in this encyclopedia.

The following articles take positions that radically differ from the arguments of the present article. H. P. Grice, "Personal Identity," *Mind* 50 (1941): 330–350, argues that the "self" is a logical construction consisting of experiences linked conceptually by memory. An authoritative presentation of the Kantian thesis that perceptual acts require a persisting subject or owner is found in H. J. Paton, "Self-Identity," in his *In Defence of Reason* (London, 1951). J. R. Jones, "The Self in Sensory Cognition," *Mind* 58 (1949): 40–61, attempts to dispense with the notion of a subject of perceptual acts. This paper generated an exchange on the concept of the self between its author and Antony Flew; see Antony Flew, "Selves," *Mind* 58 (1949): 355–358, and J. R. Jones, "Selves: A Reply to Mr. Flew," *Mind* 59 (1950): 233–236. This article has not been able to deal with the detail of the arguments presented in these papers but would hold that each in its own way is handicapped by the restrictions placed on the discussion of personal identity by Hume and by the use of the terminology of the "self." On the perplexities surrounding the notion of a purely mental subject, rather than the psychophysical person, as the owner of mental acts and events, see Ch. 6 of Gilbert Ryle's *The Concept of the*

Mind (London: Hutchinson, 1949), and Ch. 3 of P. F. Strawson's *Individuals* (London: Methuen, 1959). Both of these books have strongly influenced this article.

Other helpful recent treatments are C. B. Martin, *Religious Belief* (Ithaca, NY: Cornell University Press, 1959), Ch. 6, and A. M. Quinton, "The Soul," *Journal of Philosophy* 59 (1962): 393–409.

Terence Penelhum (1967)

PERSONAL IDENTITY [ADDENDUM]

At the center of the debate about personal identity since the 1970s has been the work of Derek Parfit, whose ideas, first published in his article "Personal Identity" (1971) and then extended and elaborated in his monumental *Reasons and Persons* (1984, part 3), revitalized and to some extent transformed the topic. The following discussion explains how this has come about and relates Parfit's ideas to those of other influential writers on personal identity from the 1960s on, in particular Bernard Arthur Owen Williams (1973), Sydney Shoemaker (1970, 1985, 1999), Robert Nozick (1981), Roderick M. Chisholm (1976), David Wiggins (1967, 1980, 1996), and Richard G. Swinburne (1973–1974). Since the 1990s the debate about personal identity has come to be focused on the correctness of the animalist view, the view that we are animals and that our identity conditions are entirely biological. This view is defended by a number of authors including Paul F. Snowdon (1991), Peter van Inwagen (1990), and Eric T. Olson (1997). Once again, a knowledge of Parfit's views is essential to understanding the arrival of animalism on the philosophical scene and assessing the plausibility of the animalist's position.

THE REDUPLICATION ARGUMENT

The starting point for the development of Parfit's ideas was provided by Williams in "Personal Identity and Individuation" (1973), in which he puts forward his famous reduplication argument, intended as an objection to any account of personal identity that entailed the possibility of reincarnation. Any such account, he argues, would have to make personal identity consist in psychological links between the later reincarnation claimant and the original person. But no such account could rule out the possibility of a situation in which there were two equally good "candidates" for identity with an earlier person, two people bearing just the same psychological links to the earlier person. But since two people cannot be identical with one person, no such account can provide a sufficient condition of personal identity.

A consensus quickly emerged, however, among other writers on personal identity, that the significance of Williams's argument was greater than he had seen. Though Williams himself remained recalcitrant, others saw that his argument consequently challenged, not just any account of personal identity that allowed for such possibilities as reincarnation, which involves a radical separation of personal identity from bodily identity, but any account of personal identity that proposed as a sufficient condition of personal identity a conceivably duplicable relation—that is, a relation that could conceivably take a one-many form. The result of this was to focus attention on the principle underlying Williams's argument, called the "only x and y rule" by Wiggins (1967, 1980) in his discussion of the reduplication argument, which emphasized the generality of the argument. The correct formulation of this principle is difficult, but roughly speaking it asserts that the question whether later x is the same person as earlier y can depend only on facts about x and y and the relationship between them, and no facts about any other individuals can be relevant to whether x is y. Otherwise put, what this principle asserts is that whether later x is identical with earlier y can depend only on the intrinsic relationship between them; it cannot be determined extrinsically.

RESPONSES TO THE REDUPLICATION ARGUMENT

One way to respond to the reduplication argument while retaining the only x and y rule is to question the logic of the argument. According to Williams in a reduplication situation the rival candidates for identity with the original person must be new existents, identical neither with him or her nor with one another. But it is possible, as argued by several writers, including John Perry (1972) and David Lewis (1976), to reject this description of the reduplication situation. It must be accepted that the post-fission rivals are distinct people, but it is possible, according to these philosophers, to reject the view that they are new existents; rather, they have existed all along, but have only become spatially distinct with the fission. There are various versions of this view. Their common element is the multiple occupancy thesis, that what makes it the case that two people existing at one time are two may be facts about what is the case at other times. This implies that we cannot know for certain how many people exist at a certain time without knowing the future.

This response to Williams allows the retention of an account of personal identity, which allows the possibility of reincarnation, while accepting the only x and y rule. However, a simpler, and more popular, response to Williams is simply to reject the only x and y rule and to elaborate an account of personal identity that explicitly packs into its sufficient condition the constraint that x is identical with y only if there is no third candidate z who can be considered a better or equally good candidate for identity with y. Such an account of personal identity, in terms of psychological continuity, is elaborated by Shoemaker in "Persons and Their Pasts" (1970), in which he also fashions the important concept of quasi memory as a way of responding to the objection that a vicious circle must be involved in explaining personal identity in terms of, possibly among other things, memory. Another sophisticated development of the best candidate approach is contained in Nozick's *Philosophical Explanations* (1981).

IDENTITY AND SURVIVAL

But the straightforward rejection of the only x and y rule is implausible, unless some account of its attractiveness is given. It is at this point that Parfit's ideas become relevant. In response to Williams's argument Parfit (1971, 1984) proposes that identity does not matter in survival. What does matter is a relation of psychological connectedness-cum-continuity that does conform to the only x and y rule, but it seems plausible that identity obeys the only x and y rule only because we mistakenly identify this relation with identity.

The contention that identity does not matter in survival, which is Parfit's most discussed claim, is one component of the reductionist view of personal identity he recommends, according to which facts about personal identity are not facts over and above other facts, as facts about nations are not facts over and above facts about people and their relations. Another component is that there need be no answer to a question of personal identity: Personal identity may in some cases be indeterminate. In addition, Parfit holds that there are no facts about personal identity other than facts about mental states, their relations to one another, and their relations to physical bodies and the happenings therein. Persons are not "separately existing" entities, and a complete description of reality could be wholly impersonal.

Of these three components of the reductionist view the first is the most obscure. What Parfit means by it, however, is that we do not have among our basic concerns a desire for our own continued existence and well-being.

Insofar as we are concerned about these our concern is derivative from a concern for those future people (in the actual world, contingently, ourselves) linked by certain relations of psychological continuity and connectedness to ourselves as we are now. It is because we do not appreciate that this is the structure of our basic concerns that we are tempted to think that the only x and y rule is correct. The contention that personal identity may be indeterminate is a more straightforward claim. What Parfit has in mind is that in at least some of the puzzle cases described in the literature on personal identity our concepts, suited as they are in the first place to our actual circumstances, have no determinate application. Whether such indeterminacy is to be regarded as due merely to vagueness in language or to vagueness in the world is, however, a debatable point (for the argument that it must be regarded as due merely to vagueness in language, see Evans 1978). Parfit's third contention, that facts about personal identity are nothing over and above facts about the relations of mental states, indicates the Humean influence on his views.

RESPONSES TO PARFIT

Opponents of the reductionist view are described by Parfit as nonreductionists or as proponents of the simple view. According to this view personal identity is an unanalyzable datum. One such nonreductionist is Chisholm (1976), whose work is perhaps the most careful working out of such a view in the literature. Chisholm defends the simple view as the development of the views on personal identity by Bishop Butler (1897) and Thomas Reid (1941). Personal identity is what it is and not another thing, and it is identity in a strict and philosophical sense. Another philosopher who defends the simple view, and does so in conscious opposition to Parfit, is Swinburne (1973–1974). Swinburne emphasizes in particular the difficulty of making sense of the idea that one's own personal identity may be indeterminate and in doing so draws on arguments from Williams (1970).

These philosophers reject the whole Parfitian reductionist package. But the elements of the package are, arguably, separable. Or, at least, so some philosophers think. Thus, Shoemaker (1985) rejects the Parfitian claim that persons are reducible to their experiences in any sort of Humean way but accepts both that identity does not matter in survival and that personal identity can be indeterminate. Again, Lewis (1976) rejects Parfit's claim that identity does not matter in survival and the best candidate approach that it supports, while accepting that personal identity can be indeterminate.

Parfit's reductionist thesis about personal identity is not easy to assess or respond to. But, just as no philosopher writing on personal identity can afford to ignore the work of John Locke or David Hume, the same is true for Parfit. It can now be said that no other philosopher of the last century has had such an impact on the debate about personal identity. And Parfit's influence continues to affect the twenty-first-century debate, most notably by indicating how there is philosophical space for the animalist position.

ANIMALISM

The animalist thesis is that we—you and I and any other readers of this entry—are animals of a certain kind, that is, human beings, members of the species Homo sapiens. The thesis is not that all persons are animals. The possibility of persons that are not animals, but gods, angels, or inorganic robots is allowed. But the animalist does insist that we are human animals and as such have the persistence conditions of human animals. The second claim made by the animalist is that such persistence conditions involve no form of psychological continuity whatsoever and are entirely biological (a compromise position defended by Wiggins [1996] and McDowell [1997] is that we are animals, but our persistence conditions are neither wholly psychological nor wholly biological).

According to the animalist, then, things of different kinds can be persons, and the persistence conditions of an entity that is a person will depend on the kind of person it is. Hence, there are no necessary and sufficient conditions for personal identity as such, as sought for by the proponents of the psychological continuity approach. In that sense, there is no problem of personal identity. *Person* does not name a sort of substance but is merely a functional term, like *genius* or *prophet*, and is applicable to any thing with certain capacities (thought and reflective self-consciousness).

The main objection to the animalist thesis is that it does not accord with the intuition that transplantation of a cerebrum from one head to another with consequent transference of psychology (as in Shoemaker's Brown-Brownson case [1970]) will preserve the identity of the person. It is the transplant intuition that makes plausible—independently of a dualist metaphysics—psychological continuity accounts of personal identity.

The animalist, however, has a response to this argument. And it is at this point that Parfit's ideas become relevant. The transplant intuition is mistaken, the animalist can say (Olson 1997), and only seems to be attractive to us because the cerebrum recipient (Brownson) is the Parfitian survivor of the cerebrum donor (Brown) (for example, stands to the former in those relations of psychological continuity and connectedness that constitute what matters in survival), and we mistakenly believe that identity is what matters in survival. So we are led to believe that the cerebrum recipient is the same person as the cerebrum donor. Indeed, it may even be correct to say that the cerebrum recipient is the same person as the cerebrum donor, because we may use the phrase *same person* in ordinary speech not to express strict identity but to only imply Parfitian survival (Olson 1997).

DIFFICULTIES FOR ANIMALISM

The animalists can explain away the attractiveness of the transplant intuition in this way, of course, only if they endorse Parfit's thesis that identity is not what matters in survival. Moreover, since Parfit's thesis is controversial, the animalists must either endorse Parfit's own argument for it, or substitute another if they are to employ it with intellectual integrity. However, Parfit's own argument for his thesis, which appeals to cases of reduplication, involves rejection of the only x and y rule and the acceptance of a best candidate account of personal identity. But it seems difficult to accept that for natural biological organisms like human beings the only x and y rule must be rejected and a best candidate account endorsed.

However this may be, animalism has thus brought us back to the debate over the reduplication argument initiated by Williams (1973) and further explored by Lewis (1976) and Shoemaker (1970).

Shoemaker (1999) also points out that to reject the transplant in the way just described the animalist must in fact make a more radical divide between what matters and personal identity than Parfit himself. For it is consistent with Parfit's thesis that if a future person is my Parfitian survivor then he is literally identical with me unless fission or fusion or some other circumstance obtains, which precludes literal identity on logical grounds. But to explain the transplant intuition away by appeal to the distinction between what matters and personal identity, the animalist must reject this proposition. Again, the animalist must reject the proposition that if I exist at a future time I am then one of my present self's Parfitian survivors.

THE TOO MANY MINDS OBJECTION

These are difficulties for the animalists. However, their contention is that their opponents have still greater difficulties. The chief positive argument for their position given by animalists is the Too Many Minds Objection or, as Olson (1997) calls it, the Problem of the Thinking Animal (see also Snowdon 1991).

The basic structure of the Too Many Minds Objection is straightforward. If I am not a human animal, then as I sit here writing this so does another thinking intelligent being with reason and reflection. For human animals are surely thinking things and if the human animal I presently coincide with (but am not identical with) lacks what it takes to think, then so do I (we share our brain, nervous system, and whole past history since I can satisfy Locke's definition of a person). So, if animalism is false, there are at least two rational beings within my skin, a person and an animal, and I am never alone. But the animal I share my skin with is not a person—there are not two persons here (so Locke's definition is wrong). However, since it shares the entire material basis for my thinking, it shares my thoughts, so it thinks that it is a person. But then how do I know that I am the person and not the animal thinking wrongly that I am a person (no doubt I have my reasons, but so does my animal, and since it is not a person, they must be insufficient)?

The defense of the animalist position is thus that to reject it involves an absurdly inflated ontology (I am never alone) and an outrageous skepticism (I cannot ever know that I am a person). And, if that were not enough, its rejection also undermines the formulation of the very problem its opponents seek to solve, since human animals are rational, intelligent beings, that is, Lockean persons, and yet must be denied to be persons in the sense the debate concerns. So whatever answer the opponent of animalism gives to the question of personal identity, it cannot be an answer to the Lockean question it was originally advertised as an answer to. In fact, there can be no answer to that question.

Three responses to this argument exist. The first is to say that we are human animals, but that our persistence conditions are partly psychological, so that the transplant intuition can be endorsed (Wiggins 1996, McDowell 1997). The second response is to deny that human animals can think (Shoemaker 1999) because a certain sort of persistence condition is necessary for being a thinker. The third response is to accept that human animals think and that we are never alone, but to deny that this involves the absurdities or the loss of the problem of personal identity that the animalist suggests. The concept of a person relevant to the debate, it has to be said, is not that which Locke explicitly defines, but that of the self, the object of first-person reference, and a distinction is needed between the concept of the thinker of "I"-thoughts (which applies both to the person and the animal, and the object of self-reference (which applies only to the person) (Noonan 1998).

CONCLUSION

Which, if any, of these responses to the Too Many Minds Objection can be accepted is a matter of current controversy. But even if they are all rejected, the animalist still faces challenges.

One of the most powerful is that the animalist's position is itself vulnerable to the Too Many Minds Objection. One way of arguing this is to defend (with Shoemaker 1999) the contention that the animalist must recognize something that coincides throughout its life with the animal, but outlasts it, the entity Shoemaker calls its "corpse to be." Another way of arguing that the animalist faces the Too Many Minds Objection is to suggest that he or she cannot, but must, accommodate indeterminacy in human personal identity over time without acknowledging coinciding thinkers unless he or she can hold that such indeterminacy is in the world rather than in language.

Whether or not these ways of arguing for the vulnerability of animalism to the Too Many Minds Objection are ultimately acceptable, it is clear that at the beginning of the twenty-first century the debate over personal identity is as lively and unsettled as ever. It is also becoming evident that its final resolution must turn on wider issues of ontology and philosophical logic.

See also Philosophy of Mind.

Bibliography

Butler, Joseph. *The Analogy of Religion: Natural and Revealed.* London: Henry G. Bohn, 1897.

Chisholm, Roderick M. *Person and Object: A Metaphysical Study.* La Salle, IL: Open Court, 1976.

Evans, Gareth. "Vague Objects." *Analysis* 38 (1978): 208.

Lewis, David. "Survival and Identity." In *The Identities of Persons,* edited by Amélie Oksenberg Rorty, 17–40. Berkeley: University of California Press, 1976.

McDowell, John. "Reductionism and the First Person." In *Reading Parfit,* edited by Jonathan Dancy, 230–250. Malden, MA: Blackwell, 1997.

Noonan, Harold. "Animalism versus Lockeanism: A Current Controversy." *Philosophical Quarterly* 48 (1998): 302–318.

Nozick, Robert. *Philosophical Explanations.* Cambridge, MA: Harvard University Press, 1981.

Olson, Eric T. *The Human Animal: Personal Identity without Psychology.* New York: Oxford University Press, 1997.

Parfit, Derek. "Personal Identity." *Philosophical Review* 80 (1971): 3–27.

Parfit, Derek. *Reasons and Persons.* Oxford, U.K.: Clarendon Press, 1984.

Perry, John. "Can the Self Divide?" *Journal of Philosophy* 69 (1972): 463–488.

Reid, Thomas. *Essays on the Intellectual Powers of Man*, edited by A. D. Woozley. London: Macmillan, 1941.

Shoemaker, Sydney. "Critical Notice of Reasons and Persons." *Mind* 94 (375) (1985): 443–453.

Shoemaker, Sydney. "Eric Olson: The Human Animal." *Noûs* 33 (1999): 496–504.

Shoemaker, Sydney. "Persons and Their Pasts." *American Philosophical Quarterly* 7 (4) (1970): 269–285.

Snowdon, Paul F. "Personal Identity and Brain Transplants." In *Human Beings*, edited by David Cockburn. New York: Cambridge University Press, 1991.

Swinburne, Richard G. "Personal Identity." *Proceedings of the Aristotelian Society* 74 (1973–1974): 231–247.

Van Inwagen, Peter. *Material Beings*. Ithaca, NY: Cornell University Press, 1990.

Wiggins, David. *Identity and Spatio-temporal Continuity*. Oxford, U.K.: Blackwell, 1967.

Wiggins, David. "Replies." In *Essays for David Wiggins: Identity, Truth, and Value*, edited by Sabina Lovibond and S. G. Williams. Cambridge, MA: Blackwell, 1996.

Wiggins, David. *Sameness and Substance*. Cambridge, MA: Harvard University Press, 1980.

Williams, Bernard Arthur Owen. "Personal Identity and Individuation." In *Problems of the Self: Philosophical Papers, 1956–1972*. Cambridge, U.K.: Cambridge University Press, 1973. Originally appeared in the journal *Proceedings of the Aristotelian Society* in 1956–1957.

Williams, Bernard Arthur Owen. "The Self and the Future." *Philosophical Review* 79(1970): 161–80.

Harold W. Noonan (1996, 2005)

PERSONALISM

"Personalism" is a philosophical perspective or system for which person is the ontological ultimate and for which personality is thus the fundamental explanatory principle. Explicitly developed in the twentieth century, personalism in its historical antecedents and its dominant themes has close affiliations with and affinities to other (mainly idealist) systems that are not strictly personalist. This article will concentrate on American personalism, although the movement is not only American; there are and have been advocates of personalism or closely related positions in Europe, Great Britain, Latin America, and the Orient.

BACKGROUND OF THE TERM

The term *person* comes from the Latin word *persona*, meaning mask and/or actor. It came to refer to a role and to a man's dignity in relation to other men. This usage is reinforced by theological language for which *persona* is the Latin equivalent of the Greek *hypostasis* (standing under) and for which both *persona* and *hypostasis* are closely related to *ousia* (substance). These associations foreshadow the ultimacy that personalism attaches to personality, both in value (a person is identified with his dignity) and in being (person is substance). On this basis we can understand the importance that personalists have attached to Ancius Manlius Severinus Boethius's definition of person as an individual substance of a rational nature (*Persona est naturae rationabilis individua substantia*). The effect of the modern critique of the concept of substance on the definition of person will be considered later.

In comparison with *persona*, the term *personalism* is relatively recent. Walt Whitman and Bronson Alcott both used the term in the 1860s; early in the twentieth century it was adopted and applied more systematically. In France, Charles Renouvier wrote *Le personnalisme* in 1903; in Germany, William Stern developed critical personalism in *Person und Sache* (1906). In the United States, Mary Whiton Calkins began to use the term in 1907 and Borden Parker Bowne adopted it the following year. Bowne said of himself, "I am a Personalist, the first of the clan in any thorough-going sense." About this time, personal idealism established itself in England. Shortly thereafter, Neo-Scholastic (and hence, more realistic) versions of personalism emerged, especially in France.

HISTORICAL ANTECEDENTS

The historical antecedents of these personalistic philosophies are so pervasive and for the most part so well-known that they need not be discussed in detail here. A. C. Knudson supplies abundant historical background in *The Philosophy of Personalism* (1927). In general, personalism has been decisively influenced by both the Greek metaphysical and the biblical religious motifs of the dominant Western theological tradition. With the notable exception of J. M. E. McTaggart's atheistic personalism, personalism in virtually all its forms has been integrally connected with theism. Nevertheless, it has usually considered itself a system defensible on philosophical grounds and not one based merely on theological presuppositions.

Recognition of the dominant historical influences on personalism would not, therefore, be complete without mention of several modern philosophers. Following René Descartes, the primacy and indubitableness of personal experience and its identification as mental substance have exercised a decisive influence on nearly all forms of personalism. The Cartesian principle is apparent in Edgar Sheffield Brightman's definition: "A person ... is a complex unity of consciousness, which identifies itself with its past self in memory, determines itself by its freedom, is purposive and value-seeking, private yet communicating, and potentially rational" (in *A History of Philosophical Systems,* edited by V. Ferm, p. 341).

Gottfried Wilhelm Leibniz is sometimes spoken of as the founder of personalism. His doctrine that all reality is composed of monads (psychic entities) without remainder and that monads are essentially centers of activity has been particularly influential on idealistic personalists of pluralistic and panpsychistic types.

The influence of George Berkeley converged with that of Leibniz in providing an impetus to idealistic personalism. Material substance is reinterpreted as the "language" of the Divine Person. Further reinforcement for this theme is found in Immanuel Kant's doctrines of the phenomenality of the sense world and the primacy of the practical reason. It is only in the personal world of the practical (moral) reason that one has access to the noumenal. This Kantian direction has had enormous influence on what might be called ethical personalism.

G. W. F. Hegel was the single most important influence in the development of absolute idealism (absolutistic personalism). His emphasis on dialectical movement toward wholeness, on the concrete universal, and on the ultimacy of spirit has had a decided influence on other forms of idealistic personalism, notably that of Brightman.

One thinker who does not compare with the foregoing figures in eminence deserves to be mentioned because of his influence on such American personalists as Bowne and G. T. Ladd. He is Hermann Lotze, whose main work is *Mikrokosmus* (1856–1858).

TYPES OF PERSONALISM

In characterizing more precisely the systematic position of personalism, it will be helpful to distinguish two major forms: realistic personalism and idealistic personalism. The former can best be understood in the context of supernaturalism or traditional metaphysical realism, and the latter in terms of metaphysical idealism.

REALISTIC PERSONALISM. For realistic personalists, personality is the fundamental being. That is, ultimate reality is a spiritual, supernatural being. There is also, however, a natural order of nonmental being, which although created by God is not intrinsically spiritual or personal. Many Neo-Scholastics, for example J. Maritain, E. Gilson, and E. Mounier, identify themselves as personalists in the realistic sense. In fact, realistic personalism has been developing with remarkable vitality both in Europe and America in conjunction with the resurgence of Catholic theological thought. There are, however, some realistic personalists who do not stand in the scholastic tradition; among them may be mentioned N. Berdyaev, J. B. Pratt, D. C. Macintosh, Georgia Harkness, and A. C. Garnett.

IDEALISTIC PERSONALISM. Excluding Platonism and Kantianism, there are three main types of idealism: absolute idealism, panpsychistic idealism, and personal (pluralistic) idealism. Although there are no neat lines of demarcation separating these types, oversimplification can in this case be illuminating.

(1) Absolute idealism (or absolutistic personalism) is the view that reality is one absolute mind, spirit, or person. All finite beings, however otherwise designated (for example, as physical things, logical entities, or human beings), literally participate in this absolute being; they *are* ontologically by virtue of their being manifestations or activities of the absolute mind. Since this is so distinctive a philosophical tradition, it receives full treatment elsewhere. Representative thinkers who have either had influence on or association with other personalistic positions are Edward Caird, T. H. Green, Josiah Royce, A. E. Taylor, Mary W. Calkins, and W. E. Hocking. With reservations, C. A. Campbell, Brand Blanshard, Paul Tillich, and Gabriel Marcel may also be included here.

Absolute idealism has not commended itself to personal idealism, which, in opposing complete immanence or monism, is closer to realistic personalism and related theistic positions.

(2) For panpsychistic idealism, Leibniz's monadology is the paradigm. Reality is a hierarchy of psychic beings (monads) determined by the degree of consciousness possessed by any monad. The supreme monad (God) has created all other monads in preestablished harmony. Panpsychism has been developed in various ways by James Ward, F. R. Tennant, H. W. Carr, A. N. Whitehead, and Charles Hartshorne.

In many respects, panpsychistic idealism may be considered to be continuous with personal idealism. Although personal idealists do not deny the possibility that there are more grades of self or mind than the human and the divine, they tend to believe that panpsychists have not adequately resolved the tension between pluralistic and monistic strains in their position.

(3) Personal idealism is usually considered the most typical form of personalism. It is idealistic: all reality is

personal. It is pluralistic: reality is a society of persons. It is theistic: God is the ultimate person and, as such, is the ground of all being and the creator of finite persons. Henceforth *personalism* will be used to mean personal idealism.

SYSTEMATIC THEMES

Among the first generation of American exponents of personalism the most significant were George Holmes Howison (1834–1916) and Borden Parker Bowne (1847–1910).

In the 1860s Howison was a member of the St. Louis Philosophical Society. The discussion of Hegelian idealism, to which this group devoted so much of its time, led Howison to reject what he considered the submerging of the finite individual in the Absolute.

His basic metaphysical position is stated categorically: "All existence is either (1) the existence of *minds,* or (2) the existence of *the items and order of their experience*; all the existences known as 'material' consisting in certain of these experiences, with an order organized by the self-active forms of consciousness that in their unity constitute the substantial being of a mind, in distinction from its phenomenal life" (in J. W. Buckham and G. M. Stratton, eds., *George Holmes Howison,* p. 128). Howison's unswerving pluralism led him not only to reject pantheism but also to deny creation. "These many minds … have no origin at all—no source in *time* whatever. There is nothing at all, prior to them, out of which their being arises… . They simply *are,* and together constitute the eternal order" (ibid., p. 129). Howison's "eternal republic" is reminiscent of Royce's community.

Bowne taught philosophy at Boston University from 1876 until his death. Berkeley, Kant, and Lotze were the major influences on his thought. Like Howison, Bowne was a pluralistic idealist, but unlike Howison, he was explicitly theistic. The Divine Person is not only the creator of finite selves or persons but is also the "world ground," whose "self-directing intelligent agency" shows itself in the order and continuity of the phenomenal world.

Bowne's famous chapter in *Personalism* on "The Failure of Impersonalism" expresses his basic polemic against Hegelian absolutism, Herbert Spencer's evolutionism, associationism, and materialism. At the same time, he fought just as hard against fundamentalism and dogmatic supernaturalism. Through his influence on many generations of students at the Boston University School of Theology, he contributed decisively to liberalizing the leadership of the Methodist Church.

Three of Bowne's students were the leading exponents of personalism in the period following World War I. Albert C. Knudson (1873–1953) continued the personalist tradition in theological context at Boston University School of Theology. Ralph Tyler Flewelling (1871–1960) developed the School of Philosophy of the University of Southern California and also founded and edited the journal the *Personalist.*

Edgar Sheffield Brightman (1884–1953), the most important of Bowne's students, taught at Boston University from 1919 until his death. Brightman, a creative and original thinker, developed a comprehensive and coherent personalistic system.

Brightman espoused an epistemological dualism of "the shining present" (or "situation-experienced") and "the illuminating absent" (or "situation-believed-in"). Immediate experience is the inescapable starting point, but experience always refers beyond itself (self-transcendence). The possibility of reference is found in the activity of the mind in knowing; the adequacy of reference is determined by the criterion of coherence. Maximum coherence in interpreting experience is maximum truth. In his emphasis on the tentativeness and testing of hypotheses, Brightman is empirical; in his emphasis on system and inclusive order, he is rationalistic.

In metaphysics, Brightman maintained that "everything that exists [or subsists] is in, of, or for a mind on some level." He defined personalism as "the hypothesis that all being is either a personal experient (a complex unity of consciousness) or some phase or aspect of one or more such experients" (*Person and Reality,* p. 135). The natural world is understood as an order within or as a function of the mind of God. Finite persons are created by the uncreated Person. Human persons are, therefore, centers of intrinsic value.

Brightman might be called a value empiricist. His *Moral Laws* (1933), which has not received the attention it deserves, works out an impressive ethical theory. In his philosophy of religion values have a central place. The value dimension of human experience provides the evidence of a religious dimension of reality. Hence, generically, God is the source and conserver of values.

The most distinctive aspect of Brightman's thought is his revision of the traditional idea of God. He argued that if we are to take personality seriously as the basic explanatory model, then we must accept a temporalist view of God. If God is personal, he is omnitemporal, not timeless. Brightman also argued that the traditional conception of divine omnipotence could not be maintained without seriously qualifying the divine goodness. His penetrating consideration of evil, suffering, and death led him to conclude that the will of God is limited by nonrational conditions (the Given) within the divine nature that are neither created nor approved by that will. God maintains constant and growing—although never complete—control of the Given. Some personalists, including L. Harold DeWolf, prefer to follow Bowne's more traditional view of God's eternity and omnipotence. Others, like Peter A. Bertocci, find in Brightman's revisions the conditions of an intelligible and cogent theism.

CURRENT DEVELOPMENTS

In recent years, personalism may seem to have been eclipsed by the rise of existential and analytic philosophies. However, many of the doctrines and motifs of personalism have been or are being appropriated and elaborated by other positions. Existentialism and the phenomenological movement have turned to the exploration of personal existence in ways that will be gratifying to most personalists. This movement should be particularly fruitful for personalists since it grapples in new ways with the relation of the body to the person, a problem that has caused a long-standing ambiguity in personalistic thought. Both realistic and idealistic personalists have stumbled over this problem. Phenomenological investigations may therefore provide an impetus for new conceptions of personality.

The analytic concentration on language also contributes to an improved understanding of personal symbolizing and communication, and the renewed interest in philosophy of mind, stimulated by recent psychological theories, again provides material that is important in the development of personalist thought. Personalists would seem to have an advantage in being willing to risk a systematic conception of the total person that would combine surface experience (sense) and depth dimension (value).

Among the large number of Brightman's students who have been developing various facets of personalistic thought, the best known is Bertocci, Brightman's successor as Borden Parker Bowne professor of philosophy at Boston University. Other contemporary personalists also continue to demonstrate that personalism can be a viable alternative among persistent philosophical perspectives.

See also Absolute, The; Berdyaev, Nikolai Aleksandrovich; Berkeley, George; Blanshard, Brand; Bowne, Borden Parker; Brightman, Edgar Sheffield; Caird, Edward; Descartes, René; Existentialism; Gilson, Étienne Henry; God, Concepts of; Green, Thomas Hill; Hegel, Georg Wilhelm Friedrich; Hocking, William Ernest; Howison, George Holmes; Idealism; Kant, Immanuel; Leibniz, Gottfried Wilhelm; Lotze, Rudolf Hermann; Marcel, Gabriel; Maritain, Jacques; McTaggart, John McTaggart Ellis; Mounier, Emmanuel; Panpsychism; Platonism and the Platonic Tradition; Renouvier, Charles Bernard; Royce, Josiah; Taylor, Alfred Edward; Tennant, Frederick Robert; Tillich, Paul; Whitehead, Alfred North.

Bibliography

GENERAL WORKS

Brightman, E. S. "Personalism (Including Personal Idealism)." In *A History of Philosophical Systems,* edited by V. Ferm, 340–352. New York: Philosophical Library, 1950.

Flewelling, R. T. "Personalism." In *Twentieth Century Philosophy,* edited by D. D. Runes, 323–341. New York: Greenwood, 1968.

Knudson, A. C. *The Philosophy of Personalism.* New York: Abingdon Press, 1927.

AMERICA

Beck, Robert N. *The Meaning of Americanism.* New York: Philosophical Library, 1956.

Bertocci, P. A. *Introduction to the Philosophy of Religion.* New York: Prentice-Hall, 1951.

Bertocci, P. A., and R. M. Millard. *Personality and the Good.* New York: David McKay, 1963.

Bowne, B. P. *Metaphysics.* New York, 1898.

Bowne, B. P. *Personalism.* Boston, 1908.

Bowne, B. P. *Theism.* New York, 1902.

Brightman, E. S. *Person and Reality.* New York: David McKay, 1958. Edited after Brightman's death by P. A. Bertocci; contains a selected bibliography of Brightman's writings compiled by J. E. Newhall.

Brightman, E. S. *A Philosophy of Religion.* New York: Prentice-Hall, 1940.

Buckham, J. W. *The Inner World.* New York: Harper, 1941.

Buckham, J. W., and G. M. Stratton, eds. *George Holmes Howison, Philosopher and Teacher.* Berkeley: University of California Press, 1934.

Čapek, Milič. *The Philosophical Impact of Contemporary Physics.* Princeton, NJ: Van Nostrand, 1961.

DeWolf, L. H. *The Religious Revolt against Reason.* New York: Harper, 1949.

Flewelling, R. T. *Creative Personality.* New York: Macmillan, 1926.

Flewelling, R. T. *The Person or the Significance of Man.* Los Angeles, 1952.

Howison, G. H. *The Limits of Evolution.* New York: Macmillan, 1901.

Muelder, W. G. *Foundations of the Responsible Society.* New York: Abingdon Press, 1959.

Munk, Arthur W. *History and God.* New York: Ronald Press, 1952.

White, H. V. *Truth and the Person in Christian Theology.* New York: Oxford University Press, 1963.

Closely related positions are developed in the works of J. E. Boodin, J. S. Moore, D. S. Robinson, J. S. Bixler, and C. Hartshorne.

ENGLAND

Carr, H. W. *Cogitans Cogitata.* London: Favil Press, 1930.

Carr, H. W. *The Unique Status of Man.* London, 1928.

Oman, J. *Grace and Personality.* Cambridge, U.K., 1917.

Sturt, H., ed. *Personal Idealism.* New York: Macmillan, 1902.

Webb, C. C. J. *God and Personality.* London, 1919.

Note also the writings of H. Rashdall, W. R. Sorley, and F. C. S. Schiller.

GERMANY

Eucken, Rudolf. *Die Einheit des Geisteslebens in Bewusstsein und Tat der Menschheit.* Leipzig, 1888.

Lotze, H. *Mikrokosmus.* Leipzig, 1856–1858.

Stern, William. *Person und Sache.* Leipzig, 1906.

Note also the writings of Max Scheler.

FRANCE

Brunner, A. *La personne incarnée.* Paris: Beauchesne, 1947.

Lahbari, M. A. *De l'être à la personne: Essai de personnalisme réaliste.* Paris, 1954.

Maritain, J. *The Person and the Common Good.* London: Bles, 1948.

Mounier, E. *A Personalist Manifesto.* Paris, 1936.

Mounier, E. *Le personnalisme.* Paris: Presses Universitaires de France, 1950.

Nedoncelle, M. *Vers une philosophie de l'amour et de la personne.* Paris, 1957.

Ravaisson, F. *De l'habitude.* Paris, 1933.

Renouvier, C. *Le personnalisme.* Paris, 1903.

Note also the writings of Henri Bergson.

ADDITIONAL WORKS

Berdyaev, N. *The Destiny of Man.* Translated by N. Duddington. London: Centenary, 1937.

Buber, Martin. *I and Thou.* Edinburgh: Clark, 1937.

Romero, Francisco. *La filosofia de la persona.* Buenos Aires: Talleres Gráficos de la Editorial Radio Revista, 1938.

Stefanini, L. *Personalismo filosofico.* Rome, 1954.

John H. Lavely (1967)

PERSONS

INTRODUCTION

This entry is on personhood and the general philosophical question that will be treated is: What is a person? Common use of the term *person* makes reference to adult human beings. Typical examples of sentences in which this term is used are: "Descartes is the person most responsible for inaugurating the Modern Period in Western thought"; "No person can be President of the United States unless he/she was born in the United States"; and "Human fetuses may be considered persons." As the controversial last example should make clear, the term person is not used exclusively to refer to adult human beings. In much of the literature on persons, the term is used in a non-species-specific way. Many authors take *human being* to be a term of biology and leave the definition to science. Given that, here is a restatement of the initial question: What must a being be like to be a person?

There are many categories into which the term person fits. People refer to social persons, moral persons, metaphysical persons, legal persons, religious persons, and so on. While no one category of personhood can be considered the correct category, philosophers have tended to concentrate on either the metaphysical or the moral aspects of personhood. After a few words on the other categories, the metaphysical and moral notions of person will be the primary focus of the present entry.

The principal use of the concept of a person in the Christian community is that of God's personhood. This comes out most clearly in the tradition where the Holy Trinity is referred to as "three persons in one God." Although the concept of the Holy Trinity defies comprehension for many, one of the ideas spawned by this is that there is some way humans are like God, which is that they are both persons. Aquinas affirms that the term person applies to God as well as to human beings, though it does not apply in the same way. His definition of person is "a subsistent individual of a rational nature" (Aquinas 1945, p. 290). As applied to humans, Aquinas takes his lead from the use of person as one who is dignified, of high standing (in the community). He says that each individual of a rational nature is a person. However, since the dignity of God is greater than every other dignity, therefore, person applies preeminently to God. It is perhaps obvious that Aquinas is applying cultural as well as metaphysical attributes in his definition of the term.

As used in the legal sense, person refers to any being, object, or organization that has standing before the law. Perhaps the most enlightening example in the literature of law is that corporations are persons in the legal sense. This is because corporations have legal rights and responsibilities (some have also argued that corporations should be considered moral persons with moral rights and responsibilities). Legal rights would include equal protection, freedom of the press, due process, and so on, all of which can certainly be applied to corporations. Some legal findings have not, however, extended full personhood to corporations, denying the following: pleading the Fifth Amendment in order to avoid self-incrimination, and Fourth Amendment rights of protection of persons.

Other interesting cases in the *legal persons* category are those of the fetus and the newborn. While these beings are protected under the law and, therefore, may be claimed to be legal persons, many philosophers have taken the position that fetuses are not persons in the moral sense of this term. Michael Tooley (1983) has argued that late-term fetuses and even newborns are not persons in the moral sense of this term. Tooley takes the side of caution here with newborns and says that since our knowledge of their development is limited, we need to agree on some cut-off point or other; he settles for a week, after which we can with clear conscience consider the newborn a person.

The social person is not so clearly defined, it seems, as persons of the other categories. The general framework for someone being a person in the social sense is for that being/person to be recognized as a person by those who are recognized as persons within the social community. Here, thoughts run to some of the ideas of Richard Rorty (1979, 1982), who takes the view that persons will be decided upon and not discovered. This is a provocative, and for some a rather radical, view, leaning toward relativism (though this is denied by Rorty) because if someone or some group in a society is judged by the society to be nonpersons, and if personhood is a matter of decision and not discovery, then said someone or the members of said group are, in fact, simply not persons. Ultimately, Rorty's position is that the concept of personhood is something that has been, and is still being, worked out in the *conversation* that is the history of the world.

METAPHYSICAL CONSIDERATIONS

This section is devoted to the metaphysical aspects of the concept of personhood.

CONDITIONS FOR PERSONHOOD. Over the centuries, necessary and sufficient conditions for personhood have been laid out by various philosophers. John Locke is usually the starting place for any serious philosophical study of the concept of personhood because he seems to be the first to make explicit what he meant by the term. He writes that a person "is a thinking intelligent Being, that has reason and reflection, and can consider it self as it self, the same thinking thing in different times and places; which it does by that consciousness, which is inseparable from thinking, and as it seems to me essential

to it." (Locke 1975, p. 335) Although Locke is here working on the idea of personal identity, there are at least three important concepts he introduces that would seem indispensable conditions of personhood proper, namely, reason, a first-person perspective, and consciousness. These characteristics of personhood arise in virtually all of the literature on the topic.

There is also the sense in which Locke uses person as a legal (forensic) term that may be useful to consider. Again, Locke is working on the issue of personal identity; however, what he says is important for thinking about persons in both the metaphysical and moral senses of the term. He writes:

> *Person*, as I take it, is the name for this *self*. Where-ever a Man finds, what he calls *himself*, there I think another may say is the same *Person*. It is a Forensick Term appropriating Actions and their Merit; and so belongs only to intelligent Agents capable of a Law, and Happiness and Misery. This personality extends it *self* beyond present Existence to what is past, only by consciousness, whereby it becomes concerned and accountable.

> (LOCKE 1975, P. 346)

While it can easily be seen that Locke is here referring to concern and accountability in the legal sense, the reference to happiness and misery may naturally lead one to contemplate what it means to be a person in the moral sense of the term. The section "Moral Considerations" herein will be devoted to this discussion.

P. F. STRAWSON'S THEORY OF PERSON. What was at one time *the* dominant paradigm on persons is the British philosopher P. F. Strawson's theory. While there are moral overtones, his is primarily a metaphysical theory. He gives the following definition: "the concept of a type of entity such that *both* predicates ascribing states of consciousness *and* predicates ascribing corporeal characteristics, a physical situation, etc., are equally applicable to a single individual of that single type" (Strawson 1963, pp. 101–102).

Strawson argues that a person is not some sort of compound of two different kinds of substance: (1) a pure consciousness/ego, and (2) a corporeal entity. These exist together in one being, according to Strawson. He is doubtful that there could even be such a thing as a pure consciousness existing on its own, devoid of any connection with a "physical situation." When he says that a person is not an "animated body" or an "embodied anima," he is here speaking to the idea that person refers to an individual who must be analyzed as a unified individual of whom both types of predicates can be ascribed.

The predicates referred to here are as follows: *M-predicates*, on the one hand, are applicable to material bodies, to which there is no question of applying states of consciousness. Examples are: "is in the park," "is blue," "is flat." *P-predicates*, on the other hand, are all other predicates ascribed to persons. These are various, says Strawson. His examples are: "is smiling," "is going for a walk," "is in pain," "thinking hard," "believes in God" (Strawson 1963, pp. 104).

It is interesting to note that some P-predicates imply the having of consciousness by the subject of reference. Strawson's example is *posted a letter*. One consequence of this is that, theoretically, there are ways to tell when to ascribe P-predicates to others as well as to oneself. That is, there will often be indicators of the presence of P-predicates. What are they? One cannot just argue from one's own case. Strawson holds that one can ascribe a P-predicate to oneself only if one can apply it to others. On many occasions, one ascribes P-predicates to others on the basis of observing their behavior. He is not saying that others' behavior is a *sign* that P-predicates may be ascribed but, rather, that the criteria of observed behavior is logically adequate for the ascription of P-predicates. Further, some P-predicates one ascribes to oneself are not ascribed by using self-observation. This would seem to call into question the adequacy of Strawson's criteria for ascribing P-predicates in which he says that the same criteria for ascribing P-predicates to others must be/is adequate for ascribing P-predicates to oneself.

His conclusion on this point is that the character of P-predicates is such that one uses behavior criteria for ascribing to others and both behavior and nonbehavior criteria for ascribing to oneself. For him, to have the concept of a person is to be a "self-ascriber" as well as an "other-ascriber" of P-predicates.

THE CONSTITUTION VIEW. Lynne Rudder Baker is a leading proponent of this theory of personhood. In her closely argued book *Persons and Bodies* (2000), Baker tells us that while persons are constituted by their body, a person and a person's body are not identical. Her definition of *constitution* amounts to this: Where x constitutes y at time t, x, and y must be spatially coincident; x must be in a circumstance where y's primary-kind property can be realized (where a primary-kind property is the property or characteristic an individual has by virtue of the kind of thing it is; for example: Secretariat's primary-kind property is that of being a horse); it is necessary that if any-

thing (z) has some property at t that is z's primary-kind property and if z is in a favorable circumstance to have y's primary-kind property, then there is some individual u such that u has y's primary-kind property at t and u is spatially coincident with z at t; it is possible that: x exists at t and there is no individual w such that w at t has y's primary-kind property and is spatially coincident with x; y being immaterial implies that x is immaterial. Recall here that Baker is setting up her definition of what it means to be a person and hence has in mind (at least) what is usually taken as a clear example of a person, to wit, the adult human being, with a physical body.

A principal theme in Baker is that of the nonidentity of the person and the person's body. She draws an analogy between a thing and that of which it is constituted, and a person and that which a person is constituted, by using the example of Michelangelo's work of art *David* and the material of which it is constituted. Baker claims that the marble (called Piece) is not identical with *David*. Part of the argument runs as follows: If *David* and Piece are identical, then there is no property had by one and not had by the other. Piece has the property of being able to exist in a world without art whereas *David* (having as its primary-kind property that of being a statue, a work of art) does not have this property. Hence, constitution does not entail identity. (This is a very lean version of Baker's argument and the reader is advised to study the longer work for important details.)

This much said, Baker goes on to distinguish the person from the person's body (as that of which the person is constituted). Her argument hinges on the fact that the body (*qua* body) fails to possess what can be called the person-making property, that is, possession of a *first-person perspective*. The first-person perspective quite simply is the perspective by which one is/becomes conscious of oneself as oneself. Baker distinguishes two grades of the first-person perspective. An example of the *weak grade* would be referenced by someone uttering "I am 6 foot, 2 inches tall." The person (P) who utters this sentence is thought to have the ability to distinguish P from others. However, this is only half of what a full-on first-person perspective can be, according to Baker. If P utters the sentence "I wish I were 6 foot, 2 inches tall," this indicates that P sees not only that P is distinct from others, but also that P sees P as P. Following Castañeda, Baker uses the asterisk/star on the pronoun indicating first-person perspective to indicate as much. Hence, the sentence uttered would be written as "I wish I* were 6 foot, 2 inches tall."

To restate the important conclusion, the upshot of all of this is that since a person's body cannot take the first-person perspective, and since a person is a being who does or has the capacity to take the first-person perspective, a person's body and a person are not identical.

According to Baker, the first-person perspective underlies all versions of what it means to be a person, which rely on self-consciousness as the person-making characteristic. One example of a self-consciousness-based theory of personhood is one that Tooley (1983) writes about. On his interpretation, a being is self-consciousness to the extent that it is in possession of a concept of a self as a continuing subject of experiences and other mental states, is such an entity itself, and believes that it is itself such an entity. Tooley's important analysis of this, and other concepts, will be treated in the next section because Tooley's program revolves around the concept of person-hood in the moral sense.

OTHER SUGGESTED CONDITIONS FOR PERSON-HOOD. One of the most widely considered conditions for personhood is freedom of the will. A unique and pivotal contribution to this subject comes from Harry Frankfurt (1971), who argues that freedom of the will, in the guise of what he calls "second-order volitions," is a sufficient condition for personhood.

Consider an individual who smokes a pipe and is addicted to pipe smoking. A "first-order desire" here might be the bare desire for the sensation of filling one's lungs with smoke from the tobacco burning inside the pipe bowl. There may also be other, associated first-order desires, such as the desire for sensing the aroma present when one is filling the bowl; the feeling and taste of the pipe stem on one's lips, teeth and tongue; and so on. This bare, first-order desire to smoke can take the propositional form "R desires to *x*."

A "second-order desire" is to be construed as a desire referring to the first-order desire. For example, where R desires to smoke but also has the desire to not desire to smoke (say, for health reasons), the desire to not desire to smoke is a second-order desire. In a situation where R experiences both desires but is moved by and acts on the second-order desire, Frankfurt says that R's second-order desire is the *effective* desire. Frankfurt understands this as R wanting R's second-order desire to be R's will. In this case, where the second-order desire comes to be R's will, Frankfurt terms this a "second-order *volition*," which he says is a sufficient condition for personhood. In Frankfurt's terms, a "wanton" (W) is someone who doesn't care about W's will, which is clearly not the case for R. Wan-

tons have first-order desires but are not persons because they have no second-order volitions (albeit it is possible that they have second-order desires). Freedom of the will amounts simply to making one's second-order volition(s) one's will.

A chief benefit, according to Frankfurt, of this interpretation of freedom of the will is that it implies moral responsibility for the actions that R takes when acting on R's second-order volitions. Where R has the will R wants to have, and acts on this will, R is taken to be morally responsible for the actions R commits.

Another important contributor to the literature on persons is Daniel Dennett, who makes a distinction between metaphysical persons ("roughly, the notion of an intelligent, conscious, feeling agent") and moral persons ("roughly, the notion of an agent who is accountable, who has both rights and responsibilities") (Dennett 1976, p. 176). Though Dennett focuses for the most part on the conditions for metaphysical personhood, he does say that the concept of a person is "inescapably normative." Shy of drawing the conclusion that *the* set of necessary and sufficient conditions for personhood will never be fully articulated, he does lend some voice to a few of the conditions he considers necessary.

The six conditions Dennett delineates are: consciousness (being the subject of intentional predicates); rationality; being the object of a certain attitude (having a *personal* attitude taken toward one); the ability to reciprocate this attitude; verbal communication; self-consciousness. According to Dennett, to be rational is just to be Intentional, and to be Intentional is just to be the object of a certain attitude. These three conditions, says Dennett, are themselves necessary, though not sufficient, for the ability to reciprocate the personal attitude, which is itself necessary but not sufficient for the capacity for verbal communication, which is itself a necessary, though not sufficient, condition for self-consciousness, which is itself a necessary condition for moral personhood.

Some would say Dennett's last word is overly skeptical. Not only does he not believe the set of sufficient conditions for personhood will ever be known, and not only are the chosen conditions in some sense arbitrary, and not only is it sometimes impossible to recognize just who are persons, when problems of moral responsibility arise, "we cannot even tell in our own cases if we are persons."

MORAL CONSIDERATIONS

This section is devoted to the moral aspects of the concept of personhood. One important aspect of the topic of personhood is the use of person in a moral sense. The central question, that is, What is a person? can be translated into the question, What must a being be like to have moral rights (and moral responsibilities)? Setting off "and moral responsibilities" in parentheses here is meant to highlight the problem of assigning moral responsibilities to such beings as human infants; many, if not all, nonhuman animals; and perhaps those humans who are, say, in the late stages of Alzheimer's disease. While there are many who argue that these *persons* have moral rights, there is scant literature proclaiming their having moral responsibilities. This suggests a further question about moral personhood, to wit, whether a person can be the bearer of rights but not responsibilities.

MICHAEL TOOLEY'S THEORY. Tooley writes: "The question of what beings it is seriously wrong to destroy is one of the central questions of ethics." The question covers human as well as nonhuman beings. It applies to human fetuses, newborns, the mentally/cognitively challenged, the criminally insane, sociopaths, and those in the throes of diseases that impair brain activity. It also covers dogs, cats, giraffes, dolphins, whales, chimpanzees, gorillas, trout, sharks, trees, birds, and alligators. The question is distinctly *not* kind-, type-, or species-specific.

While the final goal in Tooley's work on the concept of personhood appears to be discovering whether abortion and infanticide are morally permissible, his work is distinctively metaphysical. He seems to believe that a person may be defined as a being who possesses at least moral rights (and perhaps moral responsibilities), and he sees that the analysis of these concepts requires laying out the concepts closely associated with these. However, Tooley has certain other questions in mind as he analyzes various conditions for personhood. Take the example of *rationality* as a suggested condition for personhood. He asks whether a being could rightly be thought a person who lacked the capacity for rationality. On the heels of this is the pointed question about whether it would be seriously wrong to destroy a being who was rational (staying with the example). It is this question that places his work squarely in the area of the moral aspects of personhood rather than the metaphysical. Or, if one prefers, any analysis of the moral aspects of personhood will automatically require metaphysical analysis as well.

Tooley runs through many of the suggested conditions for personhood, analyzing them in terms of whether they are necessary and/or sufficient conditions. Four of these suggestions are that a person is: (1) a subject of nonmomentary interests; (2) an entity that possesses rationality; (3) an entity that is capable of action; (4) an entity that possesses self-consciousness.

A brief sketch of Tooley's treatment of these conditions is as follows: As a subject of nonmomentary interests, an individual will have the capacity for a host of desires, the total set being in some sense "unified." While Tooley is not identifying interests with desires, he is making the case that desires may be inferred from interests. This is as it should be when interpreting interests in such a way that the subject can be said to *be interested*, as in "Don is interested in astronomy." However, it is more difficult to make sense of the idea of interests here when the meaning of *interest* has to do with what is in an individual's benefit, as characterized by the sentence "As an astronomer, it would be in Don's interest to study mathematics." While the former meaning of interest, allowing the inference to desires, would not seem to have the relevant moral sense, Tooley brings in moral significance by associating this concept of interest with the representation of the item of interest in consciousness. In the end, Tooley says that persons may be identified with "entities that have desires that are interrelated in such a way that the entities can be viewed as subjects of nonmomentary interests."

As to whether a being in possession of rationality is a person, Tooley takes the view that the relevant sort of rationality to be discussed has to do with what is called *agency*, where an agent is an enduring substance of a mental nature, with the capacity for deliberative reason-based action. Rightly claiming that there is little disagreement that this sort of rationality is insufficient for personhood, he argues that neither is it necessary. Though Tooley does not believe it plausible that rationality necessitates personhood, he does allow that any being who is rational and possesses nonmomentary interests is a person. Even the addition of a relevant form of free will, or the capacity for rational deliberation, is not enough to make rationality itself a necessary condition for personhood.

Tooley's third suggested condition for personhood is that of having the capacity for action. The name for anyone capable of action is *agent*, and Tooley claims there is little disagreement whether being an agent is a sufficient condition for being a person; it is. It is not, however, a necessary condition, according to Tooley. One important concern he brings up here is that if agency involves what is called a libertarian free will, then if universal determinism should turn out to be true, even normal adult human beings would not be persons. Tooley's reasoning on this is that even if it should be the case that all events are determined, that fact would not lead to the conclusion that it is not seriously wrong to destroy a normal adult human being. But now, on an account of agency that does not necessarily involve the possession of free will, Tooley presumes that the agent will possess nonmomentary interests. Since these sorts of interests have already been argued to be unnecessary to confer personhood, adding these to agency will not have the result of necessitating personhood on an agent so characterized.

The last suggested condition for personhood analyzed by Tooley is self-consciousness, which he argues is neither necessary nor sufficient for personhood. It is not necessary because there could be an individual who was aware of a continuing self but not in possession of this awareness *qua* individual continuing self. Self-consciousness is not a sufficient condition, according to Tooley, because it is conceivable that some individual may well be self-conscious but not be a subject of either momentary or continuing interests. For all this, however, it appears that Tooley would agree with the general consensus that it would be seriously wrong to destroy such an individual.

OTHER AREAS, OTHER CONCERNS. The area of medical ethics has produced by far the greatest amount of work on the concept of personhood. And within this field, the question of the status of the fetus has generated the most debate. The issue here is whether or not a fetus is a person in the moral sense of that term, that is, whether the fetus has a right to life. As is clear, this is but one issue in the abortion debate; yet it has generated as many books and papers as any topic in contemporary moral philosophy. The question of the moral status of the fetus characteristically revolves around discussions as to whether the fetus possesses any of the suggested conditions for personhood. Early term fetuses, whose brains have not developed sufficiently for, say, consciousness and rationality, are widely agreed to be nonpersons (with the notable exception that the religious contingent—specifically Roman Catholics—will not accept this conclusion, arguing that a fetus is a person from the moment of conception). A great controversy still surrounds mid- and late-term fetuses because it is simply unclear what their capacities are, and it appears an important question whether these individuals are more or less like nonhuman animals usually denied personhood.

Another interesting debate centers on the fetus being a *potential* person. The issue is whether a being who is going to be a person in the natural course of events should be treated as a person prior to becoming what it will be. One of the considerations that makes this question so significant is that there seems to be little relevant difference between a very-late-term fetus and a newborn infant. If such a fetus is not a person, that is, fails to possess self-consciousness, rationality, free will, and so on, then it would appear that the newborn is not, either. But this conclusion is one very few people have been willing to draw. (Tooley's work on potential personhood, in *Abortion and Infanticide*, is crucial reading.) A significant point made by some people on this topic is that the infant, upon birth, becomes a member of the specific community into which it is born whereas the fetus is not yet a member. It is somehow thought that having seen, held, and fed the infant are *attachment factors* leading to the community seeing the infant as a person. Such is not the case with even a late-term fetus.

Another question one can ask is whether people who commit heinous crimes lose their status as persons in the moral sense. This sort of case brings out clearly a distinction between the legal and moral senses of the concept of personhood. Under the law, a murderer/rapist can, in certain circumstances, retain the right to life (that is, not be sentenced to death). One argument many opponents of the death penalty have used is the following: premise 1: the individual sentenced to death under the law has a moral right to life, premise 2: no law can abridge a moral right, conclusion: the death penalty violates an individual's moral right to life. It is easy to see how this argument might be run if one accepts the conditions for personhood outlined above, to wit, self-consciousness, rationality, the ability for complex communication, free will, and so on. The committing of atrocious crimes would not appear incompatible with the agent possessing these characteristics.

However, if other necessary conditions are added to the list, such as the concern for others and respect for persons, it is more difficult to see how anyone could commit such crimes and at the same time maintain this person also had respect for others. Where the moral sense of person is defined as "a being with moral rights and responsibilities," the way would be open to argue that the death penalty *is* morally permissible. From this perspective, the conditions of personhood have significant practical impact.

Finally, the issue of animal rights has become one of the most widely debated issues of our time. Opponents argue, to a person, that nonhuman animals are nonpersons, though no one this writer is aware of argues that therefore we can treat nonhuman animals anyway we want (such as causing unnecessary pain). Proponents *sometimes* argue that many nonhuman animals display characteristics matching a fair number of the suggested conditions for personhood. For example, some will say the neighbor's dog is conscious, displays rational behavior, can engage in fairly complex communication, and has a large measure of free will. This is to say that these animals possess very important characteristics thought to be relevant for designating adult humans as persons. Unless people will assent to some form of speciesism, they say, people must admit that these animals need to be treated as persons. This is at least sufficient, it is believed, to make it seriously wrong to harm the animal.

An interesting topic in animal rights, where the concern is whether nonhuman animals are, or should be, considered persons, is the question whether persons, in the moral sense, are beings who do have both moral rights as well as moral responsibilities. It is never argued that the neighbor's dog has moral responsibilities. This being the case, proponents of animal rights are never proponents of animal responsibilities. Even if there are cases where a person seemingly has a right without there existing a corresponding responsibility, it remains an open question whether these cases speak to the essential issues regarding the questions of personhood.

See also Abortion; Baker, Lynne Rudder; Dennett, Daniel C.; Frankfurt, Harry; Locke, John; Rights; Strawson, Peter F.; Thomas Aquinas, St.

Bibliography

Adams, E. M. "The Concept of a Person." *Southern Journal of Philosophy*, XXII(4), 1985: 403–412.

Aquinas, Thomas. *The Summa Theologica*, Piana text. In *The Basic Writings of Saint Thomas Aquinas*, edited by Anton C. Pegis. New York: Random House, 1945.

Armstrong, Susan, and Richard G. Botzler, eds. *Animal Ethics Reader*. New York: Routledge, 2003.

Baker, Lynne Rudder. *Persons and Bodies: A Constitution View*. Cambridge, UK, Cambridge University Press, 2000.

Beauchamp, Tom L. "The Failure of Theories of Personhood." *Kennedy Institute of Ethics Journal* 9 (4) (1999): 309–324.

Becker, Gerhold K., ed. *The Moral Status of Persons*. Atlanta: Rodopi Press, 2000.

Becker, Lawrence C. "Human Being: The Boundaries of the Concept." *Philosophy and Public Affairs* 4 (4) (1975): 334–359.

Bertocci, Peter. "The Essence of a Person." *Monist* 61 (1978): 28–41.

Brandt, Richard. "The Morality of Abortion." *Monist* 56 (1972): 503–526.

Burke, Michael B. "Copper Statues and Pieces of Copper: A Challenge to the Standard Account." *Analysis* 52 (1) (1992): 12–17.

Callahan, Daniel. *Abortion: Law, Choice and Morality*. New York: Macmillan, 1970.

Callahan, Sydney. "The Moral Duty to the Unborn and Its Significance." In *The Silent Subject*, edited by Brad Stern. Westport, CT: Greenwood, 1996.

Carter, W. R. "Once and Future Persons." *American Philosophical Quarterly* 17 (1) (1980).

Castañeda, Hector-Neri. "He: A Study in the Logic of Self-Consciousness." *Ratio* 8 (1966): 130–157.

Chisolm, Roderick M. *Person and Object: A Metaphysical Study*. LaSalle, IL: Open Court, 1976.

Dennett, Daniel. "Conditions of Personhood." In *Identities of Persons*, edited by A. O. Rorty. Berkeley: University of California Press, 1976.

Duska, Ronald "On Confusing Human Beings and Persons." *Proceedings of the American Catholic Philosophical Association*, LIX (1984): 158–165.

English, Jane. "Abortion and the Concept of a Person." *Canadian Journal of Philosophy* 5 (2) (1975): 233–243.

FitzPatrick, William J. "Totipotency and the Moral Status of Embryos: New Problems for an Old Argument." *Journal of Social Philosophy* 35 (1) (2004): 108–122.

Fletcher, Joseph. *Humanhood: Essays in Biomedical Ethics*. Amherst, NY: Prometheus Books, 1979.

Frankfurt, Harry. "Freedom of the Will and the Concept of a Person." *Journal of Philosophy*, LXVIII (1) (1971): 5–20.

French, Peter. "The Corporation as a Moral Person." *American Philosophical Quarterly* 16 (1979): 207–215.

French, Peter. "Kinds and Persons." *Philosophy and Phenomenological Research* 44 (2) (1983): 241–254.

Garrett, Jan-Edward. "Persons, Kinds, and Corporations: An Aristotelian View." *Philosophy and Phenomenological Research* 49 (1988): 361–381.

Goodman, Michael F., ed. *What Is a Person?* Clifton, NJ: Humana Press, 1988.

Kitcher, Patricia. "Natural Kinds and Unnatural Persons." *Philosophy* 54 (1979): 541–547.

Langford, Glenn. "Persons as Necessarily Social." *Journal for the Theory of Social Behavior* 8 (1978): 263–283.

Lewis, David. "Counterparts of Persons and Bodies." *Philosophical Papers*. Vol. 1, 47–54. New York: Oxford University Press, 1983.

Locke, John. *An Essay concerning Human Understanding*, edited by P. H. Nidditch. Oxford, U.K.: Oxford University Press, 1975.

Lomasky, Loren E. "Being a Person—Does It Matter?" *Philosophical Topics* 12 (3) (1982): 139–152.

Meldon, A. I. *Rights and Persons*. Berkeley: University of California Press, 1977.

Morris, Herbert. "Persons and Punishment." *Monist* 52 (4) (1968): 475–501.

Noonan, John T. Jr. "An Almost Absolute Value in History." In *The Morality of Abortion*, edited by John T. Noonan Jr. Cambridge, MA: Harvard University Press, 1970.

Parfit, Derek. *Reasons and Persons*. Oxford, U.K.: Clarendon Press, 1984.

Regan, Tom. *The Case for Animal Rights*. Berkeley: University of California Press, 1983.

Rorty, Richard. *Philosophy and the Mirror of Nature*. Princeton, NJ: Princeton University Press, 1979.

Rorty, Richard. "The World Well Lost." In *Consequences of Pragmatism*. Minneapolis: University of Minnesota Press, 1982, 3–18.

Rosenkrantz, Gary S. "Reflections on the Ontological Status of Persons." *Philosophy and Phenomenological Research* 65 (2) (2002): 389–393.

Scott, G. E. *Moral Personhood: An Essay in the Philosophy of Moral Psychology*. Albany: State University of New York Press, 1990.

Singer, Peter. *Animal Liberation: A New Ethics for Our Treatment of Animals*. London: Cape, 1976.

Singer, Peter. *Practical Ethics*. Cambridge, U.K.: Cambridge University Press, 1979.

Strawson, P. F. *Individuals: An Essay in Descriptive Metaphysics*. Garden City, NY: Doubleday, 1963.

Tooley, Michael. *Abortion and Infanticide*. Oxford, U.K.: Clarendon Press, 1983.

Weiss, Roslyn. "The Perils of Personhood." *Ethics* 89 (1978): 66–75.

Werhane, Patricia H. *Persons, Rights, and Corporations*. Englewood Cliffs, NJ: Prentice Hall, 1985.

Young, Frederic C. "On Dennett's Conditions of Personhood." *Auslegung* 6 (1979): 161–177.

Michael F. Goodman (2005)

PERSPECTIVE REALISM

See *Realism*

PESSIMISM AND OPTIMISM

"Pessimism" and its opposite, "optimism," are only secondarily philosophical theories or convictions; primarily they are personal opinions or attitudes, often widely prevalent, about the relative evil or goodness of the world or of men's experience of the world. As such they vary with the temperaments and value experiences of individuals, and with cultural situations far more than with philosophical traditions.

Both pessimism and optimism in the above sense may be reactions to experiences that vary in scope and content. Four types of reactions or judgments may be distinguished: (1) psychological or anthropological (involving judgments about the dominance of evil or good in one's own experience or in human experience generally); (2) physicalistic (judging the physical world to be dominantly evil or good); (3) historicistic (based on appraisals of the evil or goodness of a historical or cultural period or of the forces and institutions that determine history); and

(4) universal, or cosmic (involving judgments about the dominance of evil or good in the universe as a whole).

Since the issue of the goodness or evil of human life involves belief in beneficent or malevolent forces upon which man's well-being is dependent, optimism and pessimism are prominent aspects of religious beliefs, and these beliefs may involve many or all of the above types of judgments.

Philosophical pessimism and optimism result from the critical analysis and clarification of judgments of the dominance of good or evil, an evaluation of the experiences upon which these judgments are based, and the presentation of reasons to justify or refute such statements. There is widespread doubt whether the terms *optimism* and *pessimism* are sufficiently precise for philosophical purposes and also whether optimistic and pessimistic beliefs are philosophically justifiable. This article will be concerned chiefly with philosophical formulations and arguments for optimism and pessimism with some reference to their manifestations in religion.

Optimistic and pessimistic attitudes and theories are much older than the terms used to describe them. The term *optimisme* was first used in the Jesuit journal *Mémoires de Trévoux* in 1737 to designate Gottfried Wilhelm Leibniz's doctrine (which appears in his *Théodicée* and in other of his philosophical writings) that this is the best of all possible worlds. Leibniz himself used the term *optimum* in a technical sense that applied to the unique maximal or minimal instance of an infinite class of possibilities, and he held that this principle of the optimum was applied by God in the creation of the world. *Optimisme* was admitted by the French Academy to its dictionary in 1762. The first known appearance of the term *optimism* in English was in 1759, also in reference to the system of Leibniz. *Pessimism* came into general use only in the nineteenth century, although its first known appearance in English was in 1795 in one of Samuel Taylor Coleridge's letters.

The superlative form of the Latin adjectives *optimus* and *pessimus* is not generally justified by any form of philosophical optimism or pessimism. It is true that Leibniz defended an optimal position in the formula "the best of all possible worlds," but this use of the superlative did not prevent his acknowledging the existence of much evil—indeed, the necessity of evil in all finite existence. Similarly, Arthur Schopenhauer affirmed that this is the worst of all possible worlds, but his chief philosophic concern was with finding a way of salvation from the evil of the world through art, a morality of sympathy, and philosophic and religious contemplation. The most thoroughgoing philosophical pessimist of the nineteenth century, Eduard von Hartmann, held that this is the best of all possible worlds; yet evil necessarily outweighs good in it, and it would be better if there were no world at all.

The philosophical issues might better have been served by the comparative forms "meliorism" and "pejorism" ("betterism" and "worsism"). Although the verb forms "meliorate" and "pejorate" did appear in the sixteenth and seventeenth centuries, respectively, "pejorism" has found no acceptance, while "meliorism" has been used, following William James, to express the view that although the world is a mixture of good and evil, it can be bettered by man's moral efforts to improve it.

RELIGIOUS AND PHILOSOPHICAL ISSUES

Optimism and pessimism are thus relative terms; the former theory undertakes to give philosophical reasons for assuming that in whatever horizon or context is involved, good preponderates over evil, while the latter theory attempts to show that evil preponderates over good. The arguments in each case may be efforts to generalize from experiences of good and evil, or they may, and usually do, also involve a priori factors, basic definitions, and theological or metaphysical doctrines.

EMPIRICISM AND RATIONALISM. A primary consideration in discussing optimism and pessimism is the definition and criteria of good and evil. Empiricists have generally adopted a hedonistic definition of good, and hedonism has frequently ended in pessimism: The universe seems not to be constituted to provide man with more pleasure than pain. But it has proved difficult to reduce normative judgments of value to the psychological measures of pleasure and pain, joy and sorrow, or satisfaction and dissatisfaction. Other criteria are also involved—for example, the conservation or destruction of life, the progress or decay of cultural institutions and values, human freedom and bondage (in various senses), and the just control of power.

While empiricism shows an inclination toward pessimism (and skepticism), rationalism operates with normative principles that have an affinity with affirmations of the identity of reality and goodness. Nevertheless, exponents of hedonism are driven to recognize qualitative distinctions between pleasures and pains and the complex interplay of pleasures and pains that makes possible greater goods, while beneath the most rational and optimistic systems of modern thought lurks the shadow of fear, if not of despair. Leibniz wrote during a period of devastating European wars and intended his thought to serve as the foundation for a European culture that would protect Europe against the threat of a new barbarism. Voltaire, Edward Gibbon, and Pierre Maupertuis expressed the same fears, and in America, Benjamin Franklin, Thomas Jefferson, Alexander Hamilton, and John Adams had forebodings of the dangers of revolution and the collapse into barbarism that might follow a failure to establish a sound political order.

RELIGION. Religion involves both optimistic and pessimistic aspects. Since the essence of religion is salvation from evil, an optimistic element is essential to it; yet not all individuals or groups are saved. The magical component in religion is optimistic, since it promises success in the achievement of desired values; yet the failure of religious rites or prayers is common enough to support pessimism. Salvation is postponed to a future life, and the present world is viewed as a vale of tears, or as the historical conflict between good and evil, or as a source of desires to be resisted, or as an illusory order that possesses no substance. Yet in all religion there is also a joyous world-affirming element that expresses itself in community life and mystical or prophetic exaltation. Eschatological religions combine pessimism about a temporal world that is destined to end with joyous optimism about the new life that will follow.

METAPHYSICS. If hedonistic criteria of good and evil are a common source of pessimism, those systems of thought that hold to an ultimate identity of existence and value are the mainstay of optimism. Two philosophical convictions in particular have supported optimistic convictions in Western thought. One rests upon the Platonic and Aristotelian ideal of the perfectibility of man. It regards all the powers of man as capable of control and harmonization (without great resistance from senses and impulses). The other is metaphysical but has the same sources. Regarding the universe as a hierarchy of being and goodness, ordered from infinite perfection though all levels of particularization to the total formlessness of matter, or mere potentiality, it finds all evil and error to consist in a negation or privation of being.

Other traditions also have a bearing upon optimism and pessimism. Efforts to interpret the universe as normatively indifferent (traditional materialism, for example) usually end in pessimism. Dualisms of various kinds, on the other hand, whether they distinguish between cosmic powers of good and evil or between a real order of value and a phenomenal order of fact, tend to end in optimism.

SCIENCE. Finally, natural science has presented considerations that affect the problem of optimism and pessimism. Fires, earthquakes, floods, storms, diseases, and, ultimately, death have always been regarded as evil because they interfere with human purposes and hopes. But the theory of natural selection and the second law of thermodynamics, which has been held to imply an end to the universe at a finite time in the future, have put the issue of the destructiveness of natural powers, animate and inanimate, on a more objective basis by casting serious doubts upon the possibility and the goodness of evolution and progress.

HISTORY OF PESSIMISM AND OPTIMISM

RELIGIOUS PESSIMISM. Religion is relevant to the problem of optimism and pessimism insofar as it offers salvation to men, evokes attitudes of world-affirmation and world-renunciation, and involves beliefs about the place of man and his hopes in the world. In this sense Schopenhauer was justified in calling religion the metaphysics of the people. Most religions combine a certain joyous response to divine grace with a sense of anguish and guilt at man's failures. Most advanced religions reflect a deeply rooted intuition of natural and historical evils and of the human limitations to which man is subject.

Indian thought. When the Brahmanic tradition in India emerged from the earlier Vedic religious forms, it partly concealed an underlying pessimism with the doctrine of maya—namely, that the world in which man suffers is a world of illusion, and release follows from recognizing this and the supplementary truth that man's true nature is one with the Brahman. This Brahmanic tradition was supplemented by a popular polytheistic religion that combined an easy tolerance of the diversity of natural delights and griefs with a singleness of purpose in carrying out those disciplines (whether physical, moral, intellectual, or mystical) that assure the self of its ultimate release and redemption. The fatalistic doctrine of the eternal cycle of rebirth, together with the doctrine of karma, intensifies a mood of pessimism, since this cosmic law of justice sentences most men to relive the deceptions of life again and again.

This element of pessimism implicit in Hinduism became the driving force of Buddhism in its various forms. The fourfold truth revealed to Gautama under the bo tree begins with the misery of human existence, caused by desire, and offers as salvation only the renunciation of desire and the attainment of that state of negation which is the highest bliss.

Western religions. As the Eastern religions show, the religious source of pessimism is to be found in the emergence of man's self-consciousness at a level at which he feels his isolation and estrangement in a world in which sickness, suffering, and death interfere with, and ultimately nullify, his hopes for a desired future. This mood showed itself in early Babylonian and Egyptian literature, as well as in the Hebrew Scriptures and in the Greek conception of life as being lived in the shadow of a fate (*moira*) from which death itself fails to offer a complete escape. Homer, although generally healthy-minded, judged that "there is nothing more wretched than man, of all things that breathe and are" (*Iliad* XXIV, 446ff.), and Sophocles wrote, in *Oedipus at Colonus,* "Not to be born is the most to be desired; but having seen the light, the next best is to go whence one came as soon as may be." In the Old Testament, the books of Job and Ecclesiastes reflect the same struggle with the meaninglessness of life.

However, the Judeo-Christian tradition is generally regarded as being optimistic. It applied a theistic view of Providence first to the history of a "chosen people" and then more universally to the moral interpretation of human history and of divine justice. The meaning of history is the redemption of God's people and, more generally, the Kingdom of God or the Reign of Grace. Moreover, although the Hebrews had only a vague conception of life after death, Christianity offered the assurance of a blessed life—an assurance based neither upon a concept of strict justice, as in karma, nor upon works, but on divine Grace.

However, much Christian eschatology has condemned the present world to destruction and the people in it to judgment and condemnation. The division of people into saints and sinners has often comforted those conscious of their sainthood but has not generally strengthened the ideal of a great community of love. Doctrines of original sin and predestination of the damned, of apocalyptic horrors terminating history, and of the complete alienation of man from the world (the despair of life) have been a part of the Christian tradition and have been revived in our own time, when the consciousness of guilt and of alienation has been reinforced by the secular study of modern man.

Thus, most religion, in different contexts, emphasizes both good and evil in man, the universe, and history.

ANCIENT PHILOSOPHICAL VIEWS. The Greeks, whose thought turned about the polarities of matter and form, impulse and reason, power and justice, freedom and order, and the transient and the permanent in experience, came to conclusions that have influenced all later discussions of the problem of good and evil in Western culture. When Friedrich Nietzsche condemned Socrates for making the Apollonian mood supreme in Greek art and thought, he attributed to him a type of serene intellectualistic optimism that has formed much of Western culture, particularly through its elaboration and systematization by Plato and Aristotle, who by ultimately identifying existence and value and supporting the ideal of rational perfectibility provided the philosophical grounds for Western optimism. But Plato was not so one-sidedly optimistic as Neoplatonism later became. The *Republic,* for instance, recognizes the possibility for man and society to attain justice and happiness, but it imposes harsh conditions for their attainment and is pessimistic about their ever being achieved by more than a select few.

In Hellenistic and Roman thought the nature of evil was a persistent problem that was shared by Epicureans, Stoics, Skeptics, and eclectics. Skepticism is often regarded as the intellectualistic counterpart of pessimism, but it has also often been the basis for an optimistic fideism. Although Epicureans and Stoics answered the question of the nature of evil differently, both the qualified hedonism of the one and the rejection of all external goods and emphasis upon self-sufficiency of the other tended to support a cultured tranquillity of contented, sometimes even grateful, acceptance. Both denied the evil of death, and the Stoics denied the evil of pain as well. While the Stoics relied upon determinism, and the Epicureans upon indeterminism, both denied that the gods were in any way connected with, or cognizant of, man's good. From Plutarch's *De Stoicorum Repugnantiis* (first century CE) to Vanini's *Amphitheatrum Aeternae Providentiae* (1615), the Stoics were charged with attributing evil to divine Providence, while the Epicureans grounded their conception of the contentment of the wise man upon his freedom from interference by the gods.

The decline and fall of Rome brought to consciousness a new dimension of pessimism—the despair evoked by the collapse of a historical order that had claimed eternity and universality. The relativity of good and evil to historical change provided the individual with a mode of adjustment to the evils of social and institutional decline. St. Augustine's great adaptation of Platonism to a Christian solution to this problem has been the source not only of most later religious optimism, but also of the great theodicies of the West, from the medieval and Renaissance Platonists to Leibniz and G. W. F. Hegel.

EARLY MODERN VIEWS. The Middle Ages have often been regarded as having been clouded with pessimism (they provided Hegel with the cultural type that he described as "the unhappy consciousness"), while the Renaissance and seventeenth century have been regarded as comparatively optimistic, culminating in baroque exuberance. But recent scholarship views the medieval and Renaissance periods as a cultural continuity moving toward "modernity." In the face of a deep concern for the physical, social, and moral evils of Europe, intellects in both periods were engaged in a concerted effort to lay a rational Christian foundation for human happiness and harmony. While the political and social conditions varied, and the ideal of transformation changed from an eschatological revolution to continuous progress, Greek and Roman intellectual traditions continued to limit the philosophical effort to synthesize science, moral rationalism, and religious faith. Science and technology, nationalism, new ideals of individual freedom and toleration, and contact with new lands and cultures shifted and enlarged the scope of inquiry and intensified the problems, but the differences between Peter Abelard, Thomas Aquinas, John Duns Scotus, and William of Ockham on the one hand, and René Descartes, Benedict de Spinoza, Francis Bacon, and John Locke on the other are far more superficial than the continuity of their problems and their tradition.

Seventeenth-century discussions of the dominance of good or evil were affected by the new perspectives on human life that evolved in the Renaissance—notably, the emphasis upon individualism; the conflict about the nature of human freedom; the problem of the control of political power, which resulted from the collapse of the medieval synthesis and the multiplication of small states; and the ideal of a rule of reason, strengthened by the successful combination of mathematics and experimentation in the scientific mastery of nature.

Developments in psychology. The discussion of optimism and pessimism was affected by two developments in psychological thought: Galen's doctrine of the four humors was applied to man's reactions to good and evil, and there was a wide recognition of the role of the affections and appetites in human life. A comparison of Albrecht Dürer's famous engraving of Melancholia (1514) with Robert Burton's *Anatomy of Melancholy* (1621) is revealing. In Dürer's time the dominance of the melancholy humor was held to be the source of contemplation and therefore of mathematical and other forms of learning; Burton treated melancholia as pathological and analyzed its types, causes, and cures. Unfortunately, there is no work analogous to Burton's erudite essay that deals with the dominance of the opposing humor, the sanguinary. But the use of the humors to explain pessimism and optimism initiated a long tradition of distinctions that includes the Earl of Shaftesbury's and Jean-Jacques Rousseau's theories of the natural affections, the *Weltschmerz* and *Weltfreude* of the German romantics, and after Schopenhauer, the psychoanalytic classifications of Sigmund Freud and Alfred Adler and the psychological typologies of worldviews by William James, Wilhelm Dilthey, Max Scheler, and others.

A closely related trend was the growing recognition of the role of the affections in determining human attitudes and conduct. The third book of Luis Vives's work on the mind (*De Anima et Vita Libri Tres,* 1538) was an important source for later attempts by such thinkers as Descartes, Spinoza, and Thomas Hobbes to explain human actions in terms of feeling and desires. In Hobbes the result was a pessimistic theory of human nature; in Michel Eyquem de Montaigne, Blaise Pascal, and thinkers of the libertine tradition, it was a relativization of human ends that undermined the absoluteness of goods and evils; but in the thinking of Vives himself and in the rationalistic tradition of the seventeenth century (for example, Descartes, Spinoza, and Leibniz), an idealistic optimism resulted from the doctrine that the affections are docile and readily moldable into socially constructive attitudes.

Politics and history. The problem of power (particularly political power) and its responsiveness to reason was a second noteworthy development affecting the estimation of good and evil. Machiavelli had formulated the fundamental theory of a *raison d'état* in a way that provided pragmatic support for the principle of the divine right of rulers. The series of disastrous wars that swept over Europe, however, intensified a mood of eschatological expectation and heightened the fear or hope of revolution and an overthrow of the existing order. The transfer of the eschatological hope from an afterlife to the temporal world, and the resulting faith in human progress, were the result primarily of the increase of scientific and technological knowledge and the wider expansion of faith in reason. Hobbes entirely restricted his realistic definition of justice as the power of the strongest to the limits of the present historical order, thus secularizing St. Augustine's pessimistic appraisal of the City of Man and providing a modern ancestry for pessimistic interpretations of history.

Rationalism. From the metaphysical point of view, however, the rationalistic tradition of the seventeenth century may be regarded as optimistic; it constituted an effort to bring the real into harmony with the ideal or the normative. This effort concentrated on the law of nature and on the individual's relation to the absolute source of power and wisdom. In Descartes, human passions are regarded as supporting the ideal of *generosité* and *honnêteté*; in Spinoza, actuality is generalized into possibility, and passive affections are shown to be imperfect but corrigible through active affections; in Leibniz, truths of fact are held to be grounded in truths of reason, if we could only completely analyze the former. This optimistic doctrine of reality is supported in these thinkers by the conviction that evil is finitude or limitation and that as our ideas move from confusedness, indistinctness, and inadequacy toward clarity, distinctness, and adequacy, the goodness of the world and of our life is brought to light in an absolutely convincing way. Not all thinkers, of course, accepted this optimistic metaphysical resolution of the problem. Pascal was driven by his perception of the finiteness of man and the terror in which this finiteness involves him to a philosophy in which the heart, not the intellect, provides knowledge about ultimate reality. Pierre Bayle had recourse to a combination of skepticism and Manichaean dualism, while Locke was attracted on the one hand to libertinism, pluralism, and toleration, and on the other hand to arguments for faith in a determining divine Providence.

LEIBNIZ AND THE ENLIGHTENMENT. Gottfried Wilhelm Leibniz (1646–1716) is generally regarded as the outstanding modern philosophical optimist. His *Théodicée* (1710) is a prolonged argument for the rationality of Christian faith, the reasonableness of creation, and the view that this is the best of all possible worlds. The argument of this work is supported by a large body of writings that aimed at a *philosophia perennis* (a synthesis of the truth in all of the classical systems of thought) as well as a harmonious ordering of scientific, philosophical, and theological truth. This philosophical system, in turn, was intended to serve as the ethical basis for the great Leibnizian projects for engaging the leaders of Europe in the restoration of peace through the advancement of science and technology, the reform of the law, the perfection of logical and mathematical tools of learning and a universal encyclopedia, the reuniting of the churches, and the Christian conquest of the pagan parts of the world. Thus, Leibniz's optimism, although grounded on one of the most remarkable philosophical systems of Western thought, was also ideological; it aimed at concerted action in a variety of related fields, and in this sense it presupposed a deep sensitivity to the existing evils that were to be overcome.

In general, Leibniz's argument is that the man of good will (*homo honestatis*) should find his greatest happiness ("toute la joie dont un mortel est capable") in the recognition that in spite of its glaring evils this is the best of all possible worlds, because its creation involved the fullest possible realization of the divine attributes. He should also recognize that there prevails in the world a divine harmony that requires evil not only for the full manifestation of the infinite greatness of the world's Creator but also in order that this evil may contribute to a greater good than would otherwise be possible. The conception of evil involved in this argument combines three theories: the privative theory (supported by Leibniz's essentialist metaphysics) that the complete notion or law of every individual monadic series is a finite combination (erected by God) of its own simple perfections; a legalistic moral theory somewhat inconsistent with this, according to which justice requires retribution for man's sins and compensation for man's suffering; and an aesthetic theory that finds limited evil necessary (like the dark parts of a painting) for the perception of a more complete and inclusive good. Leibniz's defense of God is brilliant, and the many editions through which his *Théodicée* passed in the original French and in Latin and German translations produced an extensive following on the Continent and even in England, where it may have influenced the optimistic thought of Lord Bolingbroke, Alexander Pope, and others. Yet his argument is defective, most notably in his failure successfully to reconcile human freedom and responsibility with the determinism of the divine creation, and in his general inclination to explain what is in terms of what ought to be. Many readers have agreed with Jean Guitton (*Pascal et Leibniz,* Paris, 1951, p. 121) that "one would have to change very little to transform this supreme joy (in the supreme goodness of things) into a radical despair."

Deism. The optimism of the eighteenth century, influenced by Leibniz's defense of God rather than by his more subtle metaphysics, was deistic, and much of its thought followed the five creedal points of Lord Herbert of Cherbury, who asserted an instinctive faith in the law of nature that dictates belief in one God, a divine order of justice, a moral imperative, individual immortality subject to a system of rewards and punishments, and a condemnation of "enthusiasm" as divisive and disruptive of true religion. The spirit of deism was activistic, sometimes revolutionary, and intent upon scientific progress and the dissipation of superstition. In this sense it was optimistic.

Maupertuis. The eighteenth century was also the breeding ground of modern pessimism. Voltaire's shocked reaction to the Lisbon earthquake and his satirical attack on the Leibnizian formula in *Candide* stimulated the change in mood, but even more significant was the influence of Pierre-Louis Moreau de Maupertuis (1698–1759), to whom both the utilitarian Jeremy Bentham and the philosophical pessimist Eduard von Hartmann were indebted for their conception of a "balance of pain and pleasure." In his *Essai de philosophie morale* (1749), Maupertuis proposed a measure of good and evil in terms of *plaisir* and *peine.* (The French terms, their English equivalents *pleasure* and *pain,* and the German words *Lust* and *Unlust* have somewhat different psychological connotations that must here be ignored.) Maupertuis defined these terms functionally: *Plaisir* is any "perception" that the soul prefers to experience rather than not to experience; *peine* is the opposite. An examination of life in terms of moments of pleasure and pain, Maupertuis concluded, shows in a frightening way how preponderant pain is. Life is a constant wish to change one's perceptions in order to achieve fulfillment and to see the intervening times destroyed (*anéantir*). But if God were to abolish these intervening periods from even the longest life, only a few hours would remain. "In the usual life the sum of evil is greater than the sum of well-being."

KANT. If the optimism of the Enlightenment found the goodness of creation revealed both in nature and in historical progress, the decline of this tradition and the growth of a new pessimism grounded in the romantic movement may be traced in the thought of Immanuel Kant. The *Versuch einiger Betrachungen über den Optimismus,* written in 1759, argued for the Leibnizian "best of all possible worlds" in two steps: first, there must be one possible world that is the best, and second, it is necessary that this existing world is that best of all possible worlds. Kant urged the faith that each human being, recognizing "that the whole is the best and everything is good for the sake of the whole," should find his small place in this world. But in his critical period, after 1781, he found the fact of evil decisive in invalidating the Teleological Argument and recognized a "radical evil" in man that prevents him from exercising the good will and doing his duty. In the short paper of 1785, *Muthmasslicher Anfang der Menschengeschichte,* Kant could only advise maintaining one's courage in the face of life's tribulations.

ROMANTICISM AND IDEALISM. The shift in attitude noted above deepened into the pronounced pessimism of the romantics, many of whose writings reflect a feeling of overwhelming anguish at man's situation in the world. Johann Wolfgang von Goethe's early works (especially the *Sorrows of Young Werther*) reveal this *Weltschmerz,* as do the works of Heinrich Heine, Lord Byron, and Giacomo Leopardi. However, the German idealist philosophers struggled against it through various forms of voluntarism—a voluntarism that encompassed the cosmos in Johann Gottlieb Fichte, was involved in history through great individuals in Hegel, and developed into a theory of emerging personal creativity in the context of chaos in Schelling's philosophy of freedom. Thus, Eduard von Hartmann and Olga Plümacher were unjust to the influence of this *Weltschmerz* when they excluded it from consideration as a form of philosophical pessimism. In a real sense it anticipated, and was the historical forerunner of, the twentieth-century irrationalist philosophies and philosophies of despair.

SCHOPENHAUER AND VON HARTMANN. The greatest philosophical protagonist of the pessimistic tradition is, of course, Arthur Schopenhauer (1788–1860), who gave expression to it in the context of the Kantian distinction between a phenomenal nature and a real intelligible world in which the moral will and an interpersonal society of willing beings are primary. Schopenhauer interpreted the realm of phenomena as "illusory" and as the result of human conceptualization; the real world is irrational will-to-live, known intuitively through man's perception of his own nature. To discover this world is to recognize the ultimate and inescapable evil of existence.

Man's life, Schopenhauer held, is permanently condemned to be in bondage to the will-to-live. As the Indian thinkers discovered, the essential nature of every human life is desire, and this desire is never stilled, since even its satisfaction results in increased desire or ennui. The world as will, therefore, is unmitigated evil; good is illusory, but man, by his very nature as an intelligent, feeling animal, and facing inevitable death, is driven beyond this illusion to discover his own plight. This is therefore the worst of all possible worlds, since there is no good in it. The only escape is through renouncing will, but only the great artists, thinkers, and prophets are capable of doing this—and only in a finite and impermanent degree. There is, however, an ethics involved in this pessimism; it is the ethics of sympathy and amelioration of the suffering of one's fellows.

Von Hartmann. Eduard von Hartmann found Schopenhauer's pessimism to be the ultimate expression of a romantic *Weltschmerz* in which a sense of guilt over the quest for pleasure was implicit. Although he adhered

generally to Schopenhauer's metaphysics (supplementing the will, however, with a parallel order of ideas, both will and ideas having their seat in the unconscious), he modified his own theory of conflict in nature by stressing the purposiveness of every individualized act of will. He also rejected the Darwinian theory of change through struggle and survival in favor of a theory of evolutionary creativity in which new forms arise in the germplasm of the old. In contrast to Schopenhauer's pessimism, von Hartmann claimed that his was a "powerful, energetic pessimism, filled with the joy of action," whose historical antecedent is to be found in Kant, not Maupertuis. This is not the worst of all possible worlds; the logical element (that is, the ideas) ensures that the world is a best possible world. Yet it would be better if there were no world at all, and this is in truth the end to which the universal will, spatialized, and individualized through the particularizations of intellect, is driving—the total negation of all will through the fulfillment of its purposes.

Although von Hartmann argued that his metaphysical system of the unconscious would be valid without his pessimism, it is apparent that the converse is not the case: his pessimism rests directly upon his metaphysics of the unconscious. Yet he supported his pessimism by a comprehensive examination of empirical arguments from neurology, psychology, and the history of culture. The optimistic illusion takes form in three stages: the belief first, that happiness is attainable in the present world; second, that there will be a future otherworldly life in which the good will be attained; and third, that the surplus of happiness will be achieved sometime in this world's future history. The transition from each stage of optimism to the next already involves a surrender of hope. Von Hartmann's refutation of optimism is not merely negative but consists of a constructive argument for three corresponding levels of pessimism, which he labeled empirical, transcendental, and metaphysical respectively. Transcendental pessimism involves the denial of life after death, a conclusion von Hartmann undertook to prove through a metaphysical argument for the inseparability of body and mind. Metaphysical pessimism is supported a priori by the inevitability of misery in a world of will individuated by ideas and by the total lack of feeling of the will after all existents have ceased to be. It is also shown, however, by the finiteness and ultimate failure of all the values of human life—particularly the ethical, religious, and aesthetic values.

It is in his argument for empirical or eudemonistic pessimism that von Hartmann showed his greatest skill in penetrating human motives and the interaction between pleasure and displeasure in human action. Twelve arguments, cumulative in force, were offered for the preponderance of pain over pleasure. On the simplest level, the growing fatigue induced by nervous processes diminishes the effort to retain pleasures, and as the fatigue grows, it increases the resistance to pleasure. Moreover, most pleasure is merely the negative kind that results from the cessation of positive unpleasantness or pain; thus, it can in no way equal the unpleasantness that it terminates. Displeasure coerces consciousness in a way that pleasure cannot, since pleasure must consciously be sought and discovered and occurs only when there is conscious motivation or desire for it. In shared experiences of pleasure the sense of solidarity and sympathy may momentarily intensify that pleasure, but this intense pleasure is correspondingly sooner exhausted than unintensified pleasure. In shared suffering or displeasure this sympathetic response may also occur, but it is overbalanced by callous and egoistic reactions. Moreover, history shows that as cultures advance in sensitivity and refinement, this overbalance of suffering increases proportionally. Such arguments, von Hartmann held, conclusively establish an excess of *Unlust* that confirms eudemonistic pessimism.

In his late work on the history and foundation of pessimism (2nd ed., 1892), von Hartmann modified his theory through an analysis of the different measures of value (*Wertmassstäbe*), of which pleasure is only one, the others being purposiveness, beauty, morality, and religiosity. These independent measures of value in themselves point to an optimistic view of life. Thus, he now called his thought a "eudemonological pessimism" but a "teleologico-evolutionary optimism"; yet the new measures are themselves not unmixed with the subjective feeling dimension, so that we must conclude that the overall balance of pleasure in the world is negative.

Von Hartmann's influence. Unlike Schopenhauer's pessimism, which was slow in gaining acceptance, von Hartmann's *Die Philosophie des Unbewussten* (Berlin, 1869; 9th ed. translated by W. C. Coupland as *The Philosophy of the Unconscious*, 3 vols., London, 1884) met with an immediate favorable response because of the changing intellectual and cultural mood of the last half of the century. The worst effects of the industrial revolution had become too conspicuous to be overlooked; colonialism involved nations in guilt; utopian reforms frequently ended in disillusionment; socialism shifted from its philanthropic to its "scientific" stage (von Hartmann himself was one of the early critics of social democracy); Darwinism intensified the perception of suffering and struggle in animate nature; and the romantic mood collapsed into a new naturalism according to which man was held in bondage to social forces and unconscious powers beyond his control. Novelists such as Charles Dickens, whose early works radiated Mr. Pickwick's cheerful vision of life, turned to the wretchedness of life and the irreducible evil of actual educational, penal, and political systems. Nathaniel Hawthorne and Herman Melville in America and Thomas Hardy in England reflected different aspects of this pessimistic movement, which mounted in strength until it developed into the fin de siècle mood of disillusionment, mortification, and decadence described and criticized by Cesare Lombroso, Max Nordau, and others.

Several of von Hartmann's followers carried his pessimism to the limit of nihilism. Julius Bahnsen (1830–1881) analyzed the "dominance of the offended spirit" (*das angekränkelte Gemüth*) that is split by hate, malcontent, and horror, and Philipp Mainländer (pseudonym of Philipp Batz, 1841–1876) pushed pessimism to its ultimate conclusion in total annihilation. In his *Philosophie der Erlösung* (2 vols., Berlin, 1876–1886) Mainländer held that the will to annihilation (*Vernichtungswille*) is included in the nature of every individual being, inorganic as well as organic, and that the ethics of the individual is egoistic and implies virginity and suicide as means of world salvation (that is, annihilation).

Von Hartmann's pessimism, although more critical and balanced than Schopenhauer's, also received extensive philosophical criticism. James Sully in England, Johannes Volkelt, Johannes Rehmke, Hermann Lotze, and Gustav Fechner in Germany, the spiritualists in France, and William James and others in America replied in terms of a more positive voluntarism or a more positive theory of value, thus laying the basis for a restoration of constructive liberalism in the twentieth century.

NIETZSCHE. The influence of Schopenhauer upon Friedrich Nietzsche was described by the latter in detail and is well known. He agreed with Schopenhauer's view that life is filled with suffering and a preponderance of evil, but rejected his ethics of resignation and of sympathy that was based upon it, as he also came to reject the metaphysical doctrine of will upon which it rested. Instead, Nietzsche's doctrine of the Dionysian man, or the superman, demanded a vigorous affirmation of life and power that would transcend both the "weakness doctrines of optimism" and tragedy as "the art of metaphysical comfort." In his "Versuch einer Selbstkritik" (1886; English translation in *The Philosophy of Nietzsche*, Modern Library edition, New York, pp. 934–946) Nietzsche corrected his earlier romantic reliance upon the ideal of "a pessimism of strength" that he found in Greek tragedy (*The Birth of Tragedy*), replacing it with an affirmation of man's powers of joyous creativity—the "laughter of Zarathustra." Although Nietzsche's ideal of a life "beyond good and evil" is ambiguous and easy to misread, he clearly transcended traditional conceptions of pessimism and optimism, pressing from the conceptual to the realm of personal living and valuing. His superman is a mixture of the rejection of accepted contemporary values, a rigorous discipline of the self in loneliness, and the joy of creativity and the hope of a new aristocracy of creative individuals.

Nietzsche's criticism of modern culture as nihilistic is beyond pessimism in the same sense that his ethics is beyond good and evil. Abstract theories of the balance of good and evil fall far short of reflecting the plight and the opportunity of modern man, upon whose will to power the civilization of the future must rest.

SANTAYANA AND FREUD. Two thinkers who differed greatly in their theoretical and practical approaches to human problems, George Santayana and Sigmund Freud, developed pessimistic theories that were similar in important respects to the pessimism of Schopenhauer. (Freud arrived at his pessimism independently and did not read Schopenhauer until late in life.)

Santayana found in metaphysical matter what Schopenhauer found in will—the ultimate ground of all permanence, power, and life and therefore the ultimate ground of the tragedy that is involved in man's efforts to live the life of reason and spirit. Through concrete personal vision Santayana transcended the old debate between optimism and pessimism. Unlike Nietzsche, he found his personal resolution of the problem of evil not in the egocentric ideal of the superman but in an ideal of stoic acceptance and self-sufficiency.

In Freud's work the libido and, later, the id play a role similar to that of the will in Schopenhauer's system. The failure to gratify the impulses emanating from the id produces basic dislocations in the "libido economy" and thus leads to suffering and illness. In *Das Unbehagen in der Kultur* (Vienna, 1930 [1929]; translated by Joan Riviere as *Civilization and Its Discontents,* London, 1930) Freud traces human suffering to three sources—the superior power of nature, the decay and death of our own bodies, and the shortcomings of social relations and institutions. Of these, the first two are insurmountable, and the third inevitably results in unhappiness and alienation from man's culture. Moral judgments are merely "the effort to support illusions with argument." The illusory world of subjective imagination and thought sometimes offers successful sublimations and corrections, but the ultimate way to soundness can be found only (if at all) by a return to the natural and cultural roots of our being through psychoanalytical techniques. In an earlier work, *Die Zukunft einer Illusion* (Vienna, 1927; translated by W. D. Robson-Scott as *The Future of an Illusion,* London and New York, 1928), Freud held out much hope for this ideal through the elimination of religion, which he saw as likely to accompany the progress of science.

THE TWENTIETH CENTURY. In the twentieth century, with its dislocation and destruction of human life and values, the tremendous potentialities of its technological advances, its moral and cultural uncertainties, and its rifts in the texture of human society, the problem of optimism and pessimism shifted from an attempt to determine the relative goodness and badness of the world to an attempt to face the plight of modern man—his situation and his powers and resources for achieving good. This is a shift from conceptual modes of assessing the goodness of man, nature, and the universe to cautious nominalistic and phenomenological analysis of the individual.

It is true that a moralistic optimism has found strong defense and influence through the work of William James and John Dewey, while Alfred North Whitehead and others have offered metaphysical support of rationality, creativity, and the discovery of values in general. On the other hand, Bertrand Russell, in "A Free Man's Worship" (1903), gave moving expression to a naturalistic pessimism that regards man's existence in an indifferent universe as brief and without meaning, yet exhorts him to resist these natural powers with all the force of a living and vigorous faith in himself and in the powers of man. More commonly, the prevailing temper is to ignore the natural order as being neutral toward good and evil, and to show concern rather for the human person as a self-conscious being cast in a given historical situation. Man's natural environment, which John Dewey (in agreement with Hegel) found to be an aspect of the situation in which man is to achieve his freedom, is now taken by many as an aspect of the situation into which man is "thrown," but which he transcends in his capacity as insular self-consciousness, will, decision maker, or confronter of the divine.

Existentialism is the final expression of the inverted romantic spirit that began with Schopenhauer. Rousseau's attack on civilization is broadened and shifted: it is not just civilization that debases man; the entire situation in which *Dasein* finds itself forces upon it a sense of aloneness, alienation, and despair. But this is not pessimism; conceptual theory is irrelevant. The person's response must be "existential," taking the form of a blind affirmation of will or a surrender to a confrontation (whether with Christ or communism). Such a response is beyond optimism as well. According to the existentialist, no theory of the goodness of the world is relevant, but only unreasoning hope. Although the works of Martin Heidegger and Jean-Paul Sartre are replete with themes that evoke reactions of pessimism and optimism, they significantly avoid raising the old issues concerning the relative predominance of good and evil in the world. Gabriel Marcel has eloquently made the distinction between optimism and hope in *Homo Viator* (Paris, 1944, Ch. 2). The more completely irrationalistic followers of the existentialist movement (Jean Genêt, for example) push this rejection of the traditional philosophical issue further into an ultimate reversal of good and evil and a doctrine of redemption through evil.

Although optimism and pessimism are terms that are useful in expressing fundamental human attitudes toward the universe or toward certain aspects of it, they have an ambiguity and relativity that makes them useless for a valid philosophical analysis. The question of the relative amounts of good or evil in human life and its environment is too involved to be resolved with existing philosophical tools. The dominant movements in contemporary philosophy prefer to describe and analyze the human situation more carefully in order to achieve greater understanding of the elements involved in it. That this must be done in cooperation with psychology and the natural and social sciences seems obvious; yet there are distinctively philosophical issues involved (some of which are very old) that are receiving more fruitful analysis with recent philosophical techniques. Until the basic concepts involved in a philosophical anthropology have received such analysis, the terms *optimism* and *pessimism* might wisely be avoided.

Among analytic philosophies, the empirical and positivistic trend that brushes aside all metaphysical and ethical issues as unphilosophical offers little help in this undertaking, although the old issue of a pleasure-pain balance may be regarded as an important attempt to meet analytical and empirical requirements of method. On the other hand, contemporary linguistic analysis is seeking firm ground for some of the ethical and axiological terms upon which discussions of good and evil must be based. But the analytic movement has been cautious in moving toward the metaphysical decisions upon which the resolution of these complex problems depend. It may be con-

jectured that when the present interest in analytic and phenomenological exploration develops into a bolder metaphysical phase, the terms *optimism* and *pessimism* may survive as descriptions of dominant human attitudes, but they may be superseded as philosophical theories by more adequate and more complex conceptual formulations of the meaning of human life and history.

See also Abelard, Peter; Adler, Alfred; Analysis, Philosophical; Aristotle; Augustine, St.; Bacon, Francis; Bayle, Pierre; Bolingbroke, Henry St. John; Brahman; Buddhism; Coleridge, Samuel Taylor; Darwinism; Descartes, René; Determinism and Indeterminism; Dewey, John; Dilthey, Wilhelm; Duns Scotus, John; Empiricism; Enlightenment; Evil, The Problem of; Existentialism; Fechner, Gustav Theodor; Fichte, Johann Gottlieb; Franklin, Benjamin; Freud, Sigmund; Galen; Gibbon, Edward; Goethe, Johann Wolfgang von; Hartmann, Eduard von; Hedonism; Hegel, Georg Wilhelm Friedrich; Heidegger, Martin; Herbert of Cherbury; Hobbes, Thomas; Homer; Idealism; James, William; Jefferson, Thomas; Kant, Immanuel; Leibniz, Gottfried Wilhelm; Leopardi, Count Giacomo; Life, Meaning and Value of; Locke, John; Lotze, Rudolf Hermann; Machiavelli, Niccolò; Maupertuis, Pierre-Louis Moreau de; Montaigne, Michel Eyquem de; Nietzsche, Friedrich; Nihilism; Pascal, Blaise; Plato; Platonism and the Platonic Tradition; Pope, Alexander; Rationalism; Rehmke, Johannes; Renaissance; Romanticism; Rousseau, Jean-Jacques; Russell, Bertrand Arthur William; Santayana, George; Sartre, Jean-Paul; Scheler, Max; Schopenhauer, Arthur; Skepticism, History of; Socrates; Spinoza, Benedict (Baruch) de; Teleological Argument for the Existence of God; Thomas Aquinas, St.; Vives, Juan Luis; Voltaire, François-Marie Arouet de; Whitehead, Alfred North; William of Ockham.

Bibliography

HISTORY OF PESSIMISM AND OPTIMISM

Billisch, Friedrich. *Das Problem des Übels in der Philosophie des Abendlandes*, 3 vols. Vienna: A. Sexl, 1959.

Diels, Hermann. *Der antike Pessimismus.* Berlin, 1921.

Hartmann, Eduard von. *Zur Geschichte und Begründung des Pessimismus*, 2nd ed. Leipzig, 1892.

Plümacher, Olga. *Der Pessimismus in Vergangenheit und Gegenwart. Geschichtliches und Kritisches.* Heidelberg, 1884.

Siwek, Paul. "Optimism in Philosophy" and "Pessimism in Philosophy," in *New Scholasticism* 23 (1948): 239–297, 417–439.

Sully, James. *Pessimism: A History and a Criticism.* London: n.p., 1877.

Tsanoff, Radoslav A. *The Nature of Evil.* New York: Macmillan, 1931.

Vyverberg, Henry. *Historical Pessimism in the French Enlightenment.* Cambridge, MA: Harvard University Press, 1958.

NINETEENTH-CENTURY VIEWS

Bailey, Robert B. *Sociology Faces Pessimism: A Study of European Sociological Thought amidst a Fading Optimism.* The Hague: Nijhoff, 1958.

Caro, Elme Marie. *Le pessimisme au XIXe siècle: Leopardi—Schopenhauer—Hartmann.* Paris: Hachette, 1878.

Copleston, Frederick. *Arthur Schopenhauer: Philosopher of Pessimism.* London, 1946.

Dorner, August. *Pessimismus: Nietzsche und Naturalismus, mit besonderer Beziehung auf die Religion.* Leipzig: F. Eckardt, 1911.

Gass, Wilhelm. *Optimismus und Pessimismus.* Berlin: G. Reimer, 1876.

Nordau, Max. *Entartung.* Berlin: C. Duncker, 1892. Translated from the second German edition as *Degeneration.* New York: Appleton, 1895.

Petraschek, Karl. *Die Logik des Unbewussten.* Munich, 1920. Vol. II especially.

Petraschek, Karl. *Die Rechtsphilosophie des Pessimismus.* Munich, 1929.

CONTEMPORARY ISSUES

Marcel, Gabriel. *Homo Viator.* Paris: Aubier, 1945. Translated by Emma Craufurd as *Homo Viator.* Chicago, 1951.

Marcuse, Ludwig. *Pessimismus: ein Stadium der Reife.* Hamburg: Rowohlt, 1953.

Unamuno, Miguel de. *Des sentimiento trágico de la vida en los hombres y en los pueblos.* Madrid, 1913. Translated by J. E. Crawford Flitch as *The Tragic Sense of Life in Men and in Peoples.* London, 1921.

L. E. Loemker (1967)

PESTALOZZI, JOHANN HEINRICH
(1746–1827)

Johann Heinrich Pestalozzi was a Swiss educator whose views profoundly affected the history and philosophy of education. Pestalozzi's father, a clergyman in Zürich, then the most lively center of awakening German culture and literature, died when his son was six years old. Pestalozzi's profound piety, the desire to love and to be loved, his compassion for suffering—and his extreme sensitivity and awkwardness in dealing with the practical affairs of life—were due largely to the exclusive upbringing of his pious mother.

After graduating from the Collegium Humanitatis (a secondary school), he turned to agriculture and experimented at his newly acquired farm, the Neuhof, with a school for the children of the neighboring farmers that was to combine elementary education with practical work. The Neuhof enterprise was a failure, financially as well as educationally, but it brought him the insights that determined his later educational, social, and religious theory and practice. These insights are jotted down in aphoristic style in *Die Abendstunde eines Einsiedlers* (Evening hour of a hermit; 1780), one of those astounding works of sudden illumination which we sometimes find in the lives of men of rare genius.

As a young man, Pestalozzi sympathized with a liberal student movement which was considered subversive by the patrician government of Zürich. He also sympathized actively with the Swiss and French revolutions at the end of the eighteenth century but was soon disappointed in the development of both.

In 1789 he took over the education of the desolate children of the town of Stans, which had been the scene of a battle between the French and the Swiss and had been badly ransacked by the French victors. Later he founded schools at Burgdorf and Münchenbuchsee, and finally at Iverdon on the shore of the Lake of Neuchâtel, attracting increasingly the attention of reform-minded men and women all over Europe. "Pestalozzianism," as a method of education that emphasized the importance of individual differences and the stimulation of the child's self-activity as against mere rote learning, was transferred also to the United States and resulted, about 1860, in a thorough reorganization of its elementary schools.

Like John Amos Comenius (whom he mentions, without being influenced by him), Pestalozzi was able to fuse his Christ-centered piety with a romantic concept of nature. First impressed by Jean-Jacques Rousseau, whose ideas he later rejected, he used the term *nature* as synonymous with all that is genuine, authentic, and free from artificiality. He regarded it as the function of education, as of all other social activities, to find the "organic" or "elemental" principles by which the inherent talent of every person could be developed to his fullest individuality, or to his "truth." His concept of truth, therefore, does not aim at logical universality; rather, it is, to use a modern term, *existential.*

A person can be educated toward maturity only if he has been allowed to sense in his earliest infancy and under the care of his mother and his family the vital element in all human relations, altruistic love. And he can safely pass over to his next developmental stage only if he has fully mastered the experiences and tasks of the preceding stage, if the whole of his personality has been formed by the "education of the heart, the hand and the mind," if the things he has learned have become really his own and have aroused a sense of commitment, and if, finally, he discovers the vertical line, his personal relation to God, without which all relations between man and man, man and nature, and man and knowledge remain empty and meaningless.

According to Pestalozzi, it is the curse of modern civilization that its hasty and primarily verbal education does not give man enough time for the process of *Anschauung*, a term perhaps best translated as "internalized apperception," or as dwelling on the meaning and challenge of an impression. Thus modern civilization leads a person more and more away from his deeper self into a tangle of self-perceptions, of useless, if not dangerous, knowledge, and of false ambitions, which will make him unhappy.

As in many similar cases, Pestalozzi's fame as an educator has prevented the scholarly world from recognizing the full scope and depth of his interests. Besides a few and often inadequate accounts, little attention has been paid to Pestalozzi as a man of passionate concern for social justice and for new forms of religious education which were intentionally prevented by corrupt ecclesiastical institutions.

Nor has his essay "Meine Nachforschungen über den Gang der Natur in der Entwicklung des Menschengeschlechtes" (On the path of nature in the history of mankind) received sufficient attention, although it is profounder and more realistic than the contemplations on human progress by the Marquis de Condorcet, Anne Robert Jacques Turgot, and other philosophers of the Enlightenment. According to Pestalozzi, the development of the human race is reflected in the life of every person. Each of us has in himself the primitive, the social, and the ethical human. Injustice, therefore, will remain, although we may profit from the experiences of earlier generations. But the state of moral freedom will be achieved by only a few chosen individuals, and they (in this sentence he refers to his own life) will hardly find a niche in the house of humankind.

See also Philosophy of Education, History of.

Bibliography

WORKS BY PESTALOZZI

German Editions

Sämtliche Werke, edited by A. Buchenau et al. Berlin: W. de Gruyter, 1927–. Critical edition, not yet completed.

Gesammelte Werke in zehn Bänden, edited by Emilie Bosshart et al. Zürich, 1944–1947.

Werke, edited by Paul Baumgartner. Zürich: Rotapfel, 1944–1949.

Translations

Leonard and Gertrude. Translated by Eva Channing. Boston, 1885.

How Gertrude Teaches Her Children, edited by Ebenezer Cooke, and translated by L. E. Holland and Francis Turner. London, 1894.

Pestalozzi's Main Writings, edited by J. A. Green. New York, 1912.

WORKS ON PESTALOZZI AND SELECTIONS

Anderson, L. F., ed. *Pestalozzi*. New York: McGraw-Hill, 1931.

Gutek, Gerald Lee. *Pestalozzi and Education*. New York: Random House, 1968.

Silber, Käte. *Pestalozzi: The Man and His Work*. 3rd ed. New York: Schocken Books, 1973.

Ulich, Robert. *History of Educational Thought*, 258–270. New York: American Book, 1950.

Ulich, Robert. *Three Thousand Years of Educational Wisdom*, 480–507. Cambridge, MA, 1959.

Robert Ulich (1967)
Bibliography updated by Michael J. Farmer (2005)

PETER AUREOL
(c. 1275/1280–1322)

Peter Aureol (or Petrus Aureolus, Petrus Aureoli, Peter Oriole, etc.), the French Franciscan philosopher and theologian called "Doctor Facundus," was born near Gourdon, Lot, between 1275 and 1280 and died in 1322. He entered the Franciscan order before 1300, probably at Gourdon, and was assigned to the province of Aquitaine. In 1304, Peter was at Paris, but whether he studied under John Duns Scotus is uncertain. His first work was *Tractatus de Paupertate* (1311). In 1312 he was lector at the *studium generale* at Bologna, where he composed his only purely philosophical work, the unfinished *Tractatus de Principiis Naturae* in four books. From 1314 to 1315, as lector at Toulouse, he wrote the original and influential tract *De Conceptione B. M. V.* and the *Repercussorium* against certain opponents of the tract. From 1313 to 1316, probably also at Toulouse, he composed his extensive *Scriptum Super I Sententiarum*, dedicated to John XXII. At the Chapter General of Naples in 1316, Peter was nominated to lecture on the *Sentences* at Paris. The newly elected general of the order, Michael of Cesena, who had just finished his own *Sentences* at Paris, gave his consent as required although Peter openly opposed him. Peter lectured at Paris from 1316 to 1318; his *Reportata*, formerly called "the first redaction," is now believed to belong to this period. In a letter dated July 14, 1318, John XXII asked the chancellor of Paris to grant Peter the licentiate.

Peter is later mentioned (November 13, 1318) as among the master regents. For the next two years he taught Scripture at Paris while composing his often-published *Compendium Sensus Litteralis Totius Scripturae* (1319). At the end of 1320, Peter became provincial of Aquitaine but was nominated archbishop of Aix and consecrated by the pope himself in 1321. He died either at Avignon or at Aix.

Although Peter's doctrines have never been thoroughly studied, he has long been regarded as a highly critical thinker who often discarded as useless philosophical theories of his time—for example, he rejected contemporary opinions on the cosmic influence of the intelligences. In particular, he criticized many theories of Thomas Wylton and Hervaeus Natalis. He often attacked Duns Scotus, yet he also frequently followed and defended him.

Peter's own philosophical system is characterized by skeptical and empirical traits. In epistemology he supported a form of conceptualism—a doctrine midway between the realism of the great Scholastics and the nominalism of William of Ockham—in which the intelligible species is not merely the *medium quo* but itself the immediate object of our knowledge. Universal concepts have some psychic reality but no objective foundation; any principle of individuation is thus rendered superfluous. Knowledge of the individual, because of its high degree of clarity and truth, is to be preferred to knowledge of the universal. In keeping with the principle of economy often called Ockham's razor, the constitutive elements of beings are to be limited, so that without extremely cogent reasons we should not accept a plurality of "realities" in a thing. In other philosophical fields Peter had many theories of his own. He defended the existence of neutral propositions, neither true nor false, and this led him to think that God cannot know with certainty future contingent events. Peter emphasized that man's knowledge of God is largely dependent upon the psychological dispositions of the individual; moreover, ontologically there is no common ground of being between men and God. In cosmology Peter had his own opinions on the plurality of forms, the notion of an infinite, the subjectivity of time, and the meaning of movement. He thus bears witness to the fact that there was no dogmatic uniformity in medieval Scholasticism.

See also Duns Scotus, John; Empiricism; Epistemology, History of; Medieval Philosophy; Skepticism, History of; Universals, A Historical Survey; William of Ockham.

Bibliography

Peter's *Tractatus de Paupertate* was edited in *Firmamenta Trium Ordinum B. P. N. Francisci* (Paris, 1511), Part IV, folio 116r–129r. The *Tractatus de Principiis Naturae* is preserved only in manuscript. *De Conceptione B. M. V.* and the *Repercussorium* were edited at Quaracchi, Italy, in 1904. The *Sententiarum* was edited in Rome in 1516; the critical edition by E. M. Buytaert, in 2 vols. (to date), (St. Bonaventure, NY, 1953–1956), includes the prologue and Book 1 (Distinctions 1–8), and the difficult question of the double redaction of the *Sentences* is discussed in the introduction. The *Reportata* was edited in 2 vols. (Rome, 1596–1605). The *Compendium* was edited by P. Seeboeck (Quaracchi, 1896). Peter's other works include *Compendiosa Expositio Evangelis Joannis*, Friedrich Stegmüller, ed., in *Franziskanische Studien* 33 (1951): 207–219; *Recommendatio et Divisio S. Scripturae*; *Commentariorum in Isiam*; one *Quodlibet* (1320) of 16 questions (edited Rome, 1605); and unedited questions and sermons.

SECONDARY SOURCES

Barth, T. Article on Peter in *Lexikon für Theologie und Kirche*. 2nd ed., Vol. VII (1963), p. 350.

Beumer, J. "Der Augustinismus in der theologische Erkenntnislehre des P. A." *Franziskanische Studien* 36 (1954): 137–171.

Gilson, Étienne. *History of Christian Philosophy in the Middle Ages*, 476–480, 777–779. New York: Random House, 1955.

Maier, Anneliese. Article on Peter in *Enciclopedia cattolica*. Vol. II (1949), 409–411.

Maier, Anneliese. "Literarhistorische Notizen über P. A." *Gregorianum* 29 (1948): 213–229.

Pelster, Franz. "Estudios sobre la transmisión manuscrita de algunas obras de P. A." *Estudios eclesiasticos* 9 (1930): 462–479, and 10 (1931): 449–474.

Pelster, Franz. "Zur ersten Polemik gegen Aureoli." *Franciscan Studies* 15 (1955): 30–47.

Pelster, Franz. "Zur Überlieferung des Quodlibet und anderer Schriften des P. A." *Franciscan Studies* 14 (1954): 392–411.

Stegmüller, Friedrich. *Repertorium Biblicum*. Vol. IV, notes 6415–6422.

Stegmüller, Friedrich. *Repertorium Comment. in Sententiae Petri Lombardi*. 2 vols. Würzburg, 1947. Vol. I, notes 314–318, 657–663.

Teetaert, A. "Pierre Auriol." In *Dictionnaire de théologie catholique*. Vol. XII. Paris, 1935. Cols. 1810–1881.

A. Emmen, O.F.M. (1967)

PETER AUREOL [ADDENDUM]

Peter Aureol (Petrus Aureolus, Petrus Aureoli, Peter Auriol, Peter Oriole), French Franciscan philosopher and theologian called "Doctor Facundus," was born near Gourdon, Lot. He entered the Franciscan order before 1300 and was assigned to the province of Aquitaine. In 1304, Aureol was at Paris, but whether he studied under

John Duns Scotus there is uncertain. His first work was *Tractatus de Paupertate* (1311). In 1312 he was lector at the studium generale at Bologna where he composed his only purely philosophical work, the unfinished *Tractatus de Principiis Naturae*. From 1314 to 1316, as lector at Toulouse, he wrote the original and influential tract *De Conceptione B. M. V.* and the *Repercussorium* against certain opponents of the tract. Probably in his Bologna and Toulouse period, Aureol was composing his extensive *Scriptum super Primum Sententiarum*; the work was substantially completed by late 1316 and dedicated to Pope John XXII. At the Chapter General of Naples in 1316, Aureol was nominated to lecture on the *Sentences* at Paris. The newly elected general of the order, Michael of Cesena, who had just finished his own *Sentences* at Paris, gave his consent as required, even though Aureol had openly opposed him.

Aureol lectured at Paris from 1316 to 1318; several extant commentaries on books I–IV of the *Sentences* are probably related to the lectures held in this period, but the relationship between the various versions is still not entirely clear [see, though, Nielsen (2002) and Schabel (2000)]. In a letter dated July 14, 1318, John XXII asked the chancellor of Paris to grant Aureol the licentiate. Aureol is later mentioned (November 13, 1318) as among the regent masters. For the next two years, he taught Scripture at Paris while composing his often-published *Compendium Sensus Litteralis Totius Scripturae* (1319) and holding at least one Quodlibetal disputation (1320). At the end of 1320, Aureol became provincial of Aquitaine but was nominated archbishop of Aix-en-Provence and was consecrated by the pope himself in 1321. He died either at Avignon or Aix.

Aureol is a perceptive critic of the views of earlier thinkers, frequently using the thought of Thomas Aquinas, Henry of Ghent, and Duns Scotus, to name but a few, as a springboard for arriving at his own opinion on the matter at hand. Aureol's views are often innovative, and some of them provoked heated reaction from contemporaries such as Hervaeus Natalis and Thomas Wylton, as well as important later thinkers such as William of Ockham, Gregory of Rimini, and John Capreolus. Aureol's thought influenced the scholastic discussion into the seventeenth century.

Aureol holds that there is no principle of individuation since only individuals exist in extramental reality. This is the foundation of Aureol's conceptualism inasmuch as it entails that all universality is a product of mental activity. Thus, Aureol rejects both the strict realism of Plato and the more moderate realism of the thir-

teenth century. Nevertheless, Aureol insists that our universal concepts have direct foundations in the really existing individuals in the world. All individuals have certain essential features; these features are proper to the individual (they are in no way universal), yet essential features in individuals of the same natural kind (e.g., rationality in each human being) are so similar that they cause any intellect to form the same universal concept. Which universal concept an individual someone actually forms (e.g., genus or species) depends on how closely that person wills to focus the intellect on the object of cognition. Concepts for Aureol are the products of intellectual acts, and, in one of his most idiosyncratic views, he argues that this product is numerically identical with the object of cognition, merely in another *mode of being* which Aureol calls *apparent* or *intentional* being (the being the object has in virtue of its being perceived). Aureol argues along similar lines for sense perception, and behind these views is his belief in the fundamental activity of cognitive powers: They place the object of cognition in another mode of being.

Aureol wants to ensure that his philosophical and theological explanations do not jeopardize human free will, and this comes to light in his ideas on predestination and particularly on future contingents and divine foreknowledge. In the latter areas, Aureol holds that future-tensed propositions can be neither determinately true nor determinately false but have to be neutral with regard to truth–value because otherwise everything would be determined and there would be no free will. Moreover, since for Aureol immutability is equivalent to necessity, if God knows in a determinate fashion future events as future, this knowledge will be subject to God's immutability, and hence it, and the events it describes, would be necessary. Thus, Aureol claims that God understands the future, not as future, but *indistantly* and as abstracted from all time. Aureol's view was revived at the University of Leuven in the fifteenth century and created a European-wide debate of such gravity that in 1474 the pope condemned aspects of the view.

In his epistemology, Aureol stresses the psychological experience of perception. Thus, in his interpretation of the important later-medieval distinction between intuitive and abstractive cognition, the difference between these two ways in which cognitive faculties form representations is phenomenological: Intuitive cognition appears as clear and immediate (like sight) while abstractive cognition appears discursive and mediate (like imagination). This same emphasis on psychology is found in Aureol's ideas on the foundation of knowledge, propositions known through themselves (*propositiones per se notae*): For Aureol, these propositions are characterized by being known suddenly (i.e., imperceptibly quickly) and without the aid of a teacher.

In metaphysics, Aureol adopts Duns Scotus's view that the concept of being is univocal between God and creatures and between substance and accident, but he modifies it to avoid some of the problems he sees with Duns Scotus's ideas. For Aureol, the concept of being is a totally indeterminate concept having no explicit content of its own; any intellectual acquaintance, no matter how weak, can be the basis for the formation of the concept of being. This position in turn had consequences for Aureol's view of metaphysics as a science since he holds that the subject of metaphysics is being as such. Aureol's pronounced voluntarism is in line with the Franciscan tradition, as is his view that theology is a practical (as opposed to a speculative) science, but his description of theology as *declarative* (as opposed to deductive or scientific) is quite unusual. Aureol also has distinctive views on the categories (especially on relations), on the ontology of accidents, and on infinity.

See also Capreolus, John; Duns Scotus, John; Epistemology; Gregory of Rimini; Henry of Ghent; Hervaeus Natalis; Metaphysics; Plato; Phenomenological Psychology; Thomas Aquinas, St.; William of Ockham.

Bibliography

WORKS

Tractatus de Paupertate (1311) was printed in *Firmamenta Trium Ordinum B. P. N. Francisci*, Part IV, Paris, 1511, fols. 116r–129r. *Tractatus de Principiis Naturae* (1312) is preserved only in manuscript. *De Conceptione B. M. V.* and the *Repercussorium* (1314–1316) were printed at Quaracchi, Italy, 1904 (*Bibliotheca Franciscana Scholastica medii aevi*, 3). *Scriptum super Primum Sententiarum* (1316) was printed in Rome, 1596; E. M. Buytaert published two volumes of a superior edition comprising the Prologue and Book 1 (Distinctions 1–8), St. Bonaventure, NY: 1952–1956. *Compendium Sensus Litteralis Totius Scripturae* (1319) was edited by P. Seeboeck in Quaracchi, 1896. Versions of books II–IV of *Sentences* commentary, along with *Quodlibet* (1320) of sixteen questions, were published in two volumes in Rome, 1605. Other works include *Compendiosa Expositio Evangelis Joannis*, edited by Friedrich Stegmüller, in *Franziskanische Studien*, Vol. 33, 1951, 207–219; *Recommendatio et Divisio S. Scripturae*; and unedited questions and sermons.

SECONDARY SOURCES

Bolyard, Charles. "Knowing Naturaliter: Auriol's Propositional Foundations." *Vivarium* 38 (2000): 162–76.

Friedman, Russell L. "Peter Auriol on Intentions and Essential Predication." In *Medieval Analyses in Language and Cognition: Acts of the Symposium. The Copenhagen School of Medieval Philosophy*, edited by Sten Ebbesen and Russell L. Friedman, 415–430. Copenhagen: Royal Danish Academy of Sciences and Letters, 1999.

Friedman, Russell L., admin. "The Peter Auriol Home Page." Available from http://www.igl.ku.dk/~russ/auriol.html. (This site includes information on Auriol's life and works, as well as extensive bibliography and text editions).

Halverson, James L. *Peter Aureol on Predestination: A Challenge to Late Medieval Thought*. Leiden: E. J. Brill, 1998.

Nielsen, Lauge Olaf. "Peter Auriol's Way with Words. The Genesis of Peter Auriol's Commentaries on Peter Lombard's First and Fourth Books of the *Sentences*." In *Mediaeval Commentaries on the* Sentences *of Peter Lombard*, edited by G. R. Evans 149–219. Leiden: E. J. Brill, 2002.

Pickavé, Martin. "Metaphysics as First Science: The Case of Peter Auriol." *Documenti e studi sulla tradizione filosofica medievale* 15 (2004): 487–516.

Schabel, Chris. *Theology at Paris 1316–1345. Peter Auriol and the Problem of Divine Foreknowledge and Future Contingents*. Aldershot, U.K.: Ashgate, 2000.

Tachau, Katherine H. *Vision and Certitude in the Age of Ockham: Optics, Epistemology, and the Foundation of Semantics, 1250–1345*. Leiden: E. J. Brill, 1988.

A. Emmen and Russell L. Friedman (2005)

PETER DAMIAN
(1007–1072)

Peter Damian, one of the greatest churchmen of the eleventh century, was born in Ravenna. After studying and teaching the liberal arts in several Italian cities, he joined a community of hermits at Fonte Avellana, near Gubbio, in Umbria (c. 1035), and became prior about 1040. He was soon called from the monastic life, however, to become an active leader in the growing movement of ecclesiastical reform. He became cardinal bishop of Ostia in 1057 and was sent on papal missions to Milan (1059), France and Florence (1063), Germany (1069), and Ravenna (1072). He died at Faenza.

Damian's attitude toward the humanistic culture of his time was ambiguous. Although he was a fine Latin stylist in both prose and verse, and a master of argument, he nevertheless belittled both grammar and dialectic. He argued, for example, that the study of grammar had begun badly when the devil taught Adam and Eve to decline *deus* in the plural (Genesis 3:5, "Ye shall be as gods"). As for dialectic, it could be nothing more than the "handmaid" (*ancilla*) of theology, and its usefulness even in that office was strictly limited.

The ascetic tradition of disdain for the world (*contemptus saeculi*), stemming from early Christian opposition to the naturalism and hedonism of pagan culture, dominated Damian's life and his pastoral care of others. His hostility to literary and logical studies was rooted in the conviction that the true purpose of human existence is to be found in the contemplation of God. Because he believed that religious communities should be nurseries of contemplatives, he was especially critical of the pursuit of secular studies by monks.

The intellectual conflicts of the age confirmed Damian in his opposition to dialectic. Theologians skilled in elementary Aristotelian logic were applying their analytical methods to major Christian doctrines, with more or less destructive results. While some defenders of orthodoxy responded to this challenge by attempting to formulate a rational apologetic for Catholic dogma, others (including Damian) were convinced that the pretensions of the dialecticians must be countered by unequivocal condemnation.

Peter Damian's most radical critique of human reason appeared in his major theological work, *De Divina Omnipotentia*. Here he argues not only that Christian dogma, being based on divine revelation, is beyond the range of rational demonstration but also that the norms of human rationality need not apply to the content of dogma. Indeed, his fundamental theological principle excluded any reasonable assurance that human experience as a whole could be orderly and intelligible. For Damian, the entire created order depends simply on the omnipotent will of God, which can even alter the course of past history.

See also Aristotelianism; Asceticism; Hedonism; Logic, History of: Medieval (European) Logic; Naturalism; Reason.

Bibliography

WORKS BY PETER DAMIAN

Opera omnia. In *Patrologia Latina*, edited by J.-P. Migne. Vols. 144 and 145. Paris: Vivès, 1867.

Selected Writings on the Spiritual Life. Translated by P. McNulty. London: Farber and Farber, 1959.

Book of Gomorrah. Translated by J. P. Payer. Waterloo, ON: Wilfrid Laurier University Press, 1982.

Letters. Vols. 1–4, translated by O. J. Blum; Vol. 5, translated by O. J. Blum and I. V. Resnick. Washington, DC: Catholic University of America Press, 1989–2004.

WORKS ON PETER DAMIAN

Endres, J. A. *Petrus Damiani und die Weltliche Wissenschaft.* Munich, 1910.

Gaskin, Richard. "Peter Damian on Divine Power and the Contingency of the Past." *British Journal for the History of Philosophy* 5 (1997): 229–247.

Holopainen, Toivo J. *Dialectic and Theology in the 11th Century.* Leiden: Brill, 1996.

Jestice, Phyllis G. "Peter Damian against the Reformers." In *The Joy of Learning and the Love of God. Studies in Honor of Jean Leclercq*, edited by E. R. Elder, 67–94. Kalamazoo, MI: Cistercian, 1995.

Eugene R. Fairweather (1967)
Bibliography updated by Jonathan J. Sanford (2005)

PETER LOMBARD
(c. 1095–1160)

Peter Lombard, the theologian and bishop of Paris, was born at Lumellogno, Lombardy. He was elected bishop in 1159 and died the next year in Paris.

Born of a Longobard family (hence his "surname"), Peter probably studied at Bologna. He went to France about 1134, first to Rheims and then to Paris, where he soon became a teacher at the school of Notre Dame. By 1142 he was known as a "celebrated theologian," and in the same year Gerhoh of Reichersberg mentions his gloss on St. Paul, which had been preceded by a commentary on the Psalms (both works were soon adopted as the standard Scripture gloss). His fame rests chiefly on his *Book of Sentences* (*Libri Quatuor Sententiarum*), finished in 1157 or 1158.

THE "SENTENCES"

The fruit of Peter Lombard's patristic studies, scholastic lectures, and long familiarity with theological literature and problems was the *Book of Sentences*. After a classical prologue, it treats of the Trinity and the divine attributes, of creation and sin, of the Incarnation and the life of grace and virtues, of the sacraments and Last Things. It seems to have received certain retouching and additions at the hands of the author before it was published in final form. Since it surpassed all other *summae* of the twelfth century in clarity of thought and didactic practicality, as well as in the range of its subject matter, it soon acquired great popularity. After 1222, when Alexander of Hales used it as the basis of his own theological course, it obtained official standing at Paris and other medieval universities; all candidates in theology were required to comment on it as preparation for the doctorate.

The work is basically a compilation, with numerous citations of the "sentences" of the Fathers and generous and often literal borrowings from near contemporaries: Anselm of Laon, Peter Abelard's *Theology*, the anonymous *Summa Sententiarum*, Hugh of St. Victor's *De*

Sacramentis Fidei Christianae, the *Decretum* of Gratian, and the *Glossa Ordinaria.* Not all Peter Lombard's opinions found acceptance: Lists of his positions not commonly accepted abound in medieval manuscripts. However, this did not lessen the work's influence in shaping scholastic method and thought for four or more centuries. Scholastic theology flourished within the framework of the *Sentences* but also suffered from the defects and limitations of this work. Because Peter Lombard failed to treat certain questions, such as the nature and constitution of the church, the role of Christ's resurrection in the economy of salvation, and certain other aspects of Christology, these subjects were not developed in the scholastic period.

THE SCHOLASTIC METHOD

Despite his overt criticism of dialectics, Peter Lombard was largely responsible for introducing the scholastic method into the schools. Anselm of Laon (d. 1117) and his school had begun a more systematic approach to the questions of theology as a result of the growth of dialectics in the eleventh century. This approach was perfected by Peter Abelard, whose *Theologia Scholarium* is a reasoned study of theological doctrine, and whose *Sic et Non* is a vast assemblage of scriptural, patristic, and canonical material used in arguing for and against specific questions. In the prologue of the latter work, Abelard proposed principles for the reconciliation of opposing texts by semantic analysis, the authentication of texts, possible changes of opinion on the part of an author, and so on. Although critical of Abelard on many doctrinal positions, Peter Lombard was thoroughly influenced by his method of contrasting authorities and arguments, interpreting their meaning, analyzing words, and drawing conclusions. As this method passed to the great Scholastics of the thirteenth through fifteenth centuries, it eventually led to the neglect of Scripture as the core of theological studies. Roger Bacon was to complain in 1267 that a "fourth sin" of contemporary theologians was their use of a *Summa magistralis,* the *Sentences,* in place of the Bible as the text of the faculty of theology.

DOCTRINES

To dismiss Peter Lombard, as some authors have done, as primarily an unoriginal compiler almost completely lacking any philosophical foundations, and of historical importance only through the popularity his work attained, is not exactly a just judgment. Certainly Peter did not possess the deep speculative mind of, for example, his contemporary Gilbert of Poitiers or the dialectical

keenness of Abelard. He made no pretense of being a philosopher, whatever he may have known of philosophical tradition. Rather, his work seems consciously to exclude the speculations of philosophy and to be primarily, if not exclusively, a work of theology based on Scripture and the doctrines of the Church Fathers. Peter Lombard was undoubtedly a compiler, yet a compiler who was master of his sources and of his own thought. Often enough, his doctrinal importance emerges only when his teachings are examined against the background of his times.

On the nature of God, for example, Peter Lombard is much more precise than the anonymous *Summa Sententiarum.* While the latter is inclined to speak of the divine essence or substance, the *Sentences,* following Augustine, makes it clear that, properly speaking, "substance" should not be predicated of the divine nature because it carries the connotation of accidents; rather, "essence," in the sense of absolute and total "beingness," or subsistent "being" (*esse*), is the proper name of God. From this Peter Lombard deduces the corollary that immutability is primary among the divine attributes. From God's immutability follows his simplicity, in marked contrast to the multiplicity which in one form or another characterizes all created beings. If other attributes are predicated of God—that he is strong or wise or just—these imply no division, composition, or distinction which would militate against his absolute self-identity. Hence, while God knows all things in one perfect, unchanging act of knowledge, things do not thereby exist in God in such a way that they share his essence. Here, however, Peter Lombard provides but the barest minimum on a question that was to receive much attention in the late thirteenth and early fourteenth centuries, the being of intelligibles.

When the creation of the world is considered in the first pages of Book II, Peter seems to react against the loquacity and daring speculation of some contemporary theologians in explaining Genesis; to all appearances, he deliberately avoids the teachings of the School of Chartres and follows Augustine's exegesis of the hexaemeron (through the *Glossa Ordinaria*), the *Summa Sententiarum,* and Hugh of St. Victor. His thought hesitates between the literal interpretation of the six days and the possibility of a simultaneous creation; although inclined to hold to the letter of the Scripture, Peter Lombard leaves the way open to the position that creation was a single act and that matter later developed according to the capacities implanted in it. Far less attention is given to the nature of man and the soul than to the purpose of man's creation and his dignity as the image of God. With a certain vehemence Peter insists on creation rather than emanation or traducianism to explain the origin of the soul. The powers of soul on the levels of sense, reason, and free will are considered almost exclusively in their relation to divine grace.

The same disregard for philosophical questions characterizes Peter's moral doctrine, which is based far less on simply rational standards of human nature or of law than on man's natural dignity as the image of God, the supernatural gift of grace, and the indwelling of the Spirit. Unlike Abelard, whose moral doctrine is man-centered in the Aristotelian tradition, Peter Lombard proposes an ethic based on God, with likeness to God as the goal of ethics and human life. If, as a theologian, he emphasizes man's absolute need of grace for virtuous acts, he lays equal stress on man's ability, under grace, to do good despite the weaknesses of human nature. The result is a moral doctrine that is far more positive than negative in character, an ethic of dignity.

See also Abelard, Peter; Alexander of Hales; Aristotelianism; Augustine, St.; Bacon, Roger; Chartres, School of; Dialectic; Gilbert of Poitiers; Medieval Philosophy; Patristic Philosophy; Saint Victor, School of.

Bibliography

WORKS BY PETER LOMBARD

"Gloss on the Psalms" (c. 1135–1137) may be found in *Patrologia Latina*, edited by J. P. Migne (Paris, 1844–1864), Vol. 191, pp. 55–1296; "Gloss on the Epistles of St. Paul" (1139–1141), ibid., pp. 1297–1696 and Vol. 192, pp. 9–520. Some twenty-nine sermons published under the name of Hildebert of Lavardin are contained in *Patrologia Latina*, Vol. 171, pp. 339–964. The *Libri Sententiarum* is available in many old editions; a critical edition was published at Quaracchi (Florence) in 1916, and a new edition was prepared by Editiones Collegii S. Bonaventure, Rome, in 1971–1981.

WORKS ON PETER LOMBARD

Among the important articles in *Miscellanea Lombardiana* (Novara: Istituto Geografico De Agostini, 1957) are L. Ott, "Pietro Lombardo: Personalità e opera," pp. 11–23; S. Vanni Rovighi, "Pier Lombardo e la filosofia medioevale," pp. 25–32; R. Busa, "La filosofia di Pier Lombardo," pp. 33–44; Stanley J. Curtis, "Peter Lombard, a Pioneer in Educational Method," pp. 265–273; and A. Gambaro, "Piero Lombardo e la civiltà del suo secolo," pp. 391–402.

Many articles of interest also appeared in the now defunct review *Pier Lombardo* between 1957 and 1962. Among them are E. Bertola, "La dottrina della creazione nel *Liber Sententiarum* di Piero Lombardo" 1 (1) (1957): 27–44; E. Bertola, "La dottrina lombardiana dell'anima nella storia delle dottrine psicologiche del XII secolo" 3 (1) (1959): 3–18. G. De Lorenzi, "La filosofia di Pier Lombardo nei

Quattro Libri delle Sentenze" 4 (1960): 19–34; C. Fabro, "Attualità di Pietro Lombardo," ibid., 61–73; and I. Brady, "A New Edition of the Book of Sentences" 5 (3 and 4) (1961): 1–8. The Brady article is a sort of prospectus of the forthcoming Quaracchi edition of the *Sentences*. All of *Miscellanea* and *Pier Lombardo* are of interest.

See also P. Delhaye, *Pierre Lombard, sa vie, ses oeuvres, sa morale* (Montreal and Paris, 1961).

Ignatius Brady, O.F.M. (1967)

PETER LOMBARD [ADDENDUM]

Although Father Ignatius C. Brady's entry from the first edition remains authoritative, significant progress has since been made in research on Peter Lombard. Most importantly, the new edition of the *Book of Sentences* to which Brady referred has become available in two volumes (Brady 1971–1981). Each of the two volumes contains an introduction, with detailed treatment of Lombard's life and works.

Brady's original entry requires two factual corrections. The first concerns the *Summa Sententiarum*, an important source of the *Book of Sentences*. This *Summa Sententiarum* has been identified as the work of Otto of Lucca—an identification that Brady himself accepted in a later publication (see Gastaldelli 1980, Brady 1986). Secondly, due to Lombard's indebtedness to the *Summa Sententiarum*, it now appears likely that he studied at Lucca, rather than at Bologna.

Brady spoke of the need to study Lombard against the background of his times, so that it might become possible to understand the superiority of the *Book of Sentences* by comparison with similar twelfth-century works. This task is addressed by Colish (1994).

The *Book of Sentences* was one of the most influential texts in medieval philosophy and theology. For recent research on the tradition of commentaries on the *Sentences*, see Evans (2002). Finally, for a concise introduction to the *Sentences*, see Rosemann (2004).

See also Medieval Philosophy.

Bibliography

Brady, Ignatius C., ed. *Magistri Petri Lombardi Sententiae in IV libris distinctae.* 2 vols. Grottaferrata, Italy: Editiones Collegii S. Bonaventurae Ad Claras Aquas, 1971–1981.

Brady, Ignatius. "Pierre Lombard." In *Dictionnaire de spiritualité*, vol. 12, *1604–1612*, edited by Marcel Viller. Paris: Beauchesne, 1986.

Colish, Marcia L. *Peter Lombard*. 2 vols. Leiden, Netherlands: E. J. Brill, 1994

Evans, G. R., ed. *Mediaeval Commentaries on the Sentences of Peter Lombard: Current Research*. vol. 1. Leiden, Netherlands: E. J. Brill, 2002.

Gastaldelli, Ferruccio. "La Summa Sententiarum di Ottone da Lucca. Conclusione di un dibattito secolare." *Salesianum* 42 (1980): 537–546.

Rosemann, Philipp W. *Peter Lombard*. New York: Oxford University Press, 2004.

Philipp W. Rosemann (2005)

PETER OF SPAIN

(13th century)

Many medieval authors are referred to by the name of Peter of Spain. One Peter of Spain is the author of a standard textbook on logic, *Tractatus* (Tracts), a work that became widely known as *Summule logicales* (Sum of logic) by *magistri Petri Hispani* and that would enjoy great renown in Europe for centuries to come. This work is typical of the manuals that gradually started to emerge within the context of twelfth- and thirteenth-century teaching practices.

With regard to the identity of this Peter of Spain, matters are rather complicated. Already in the Middle Ages there existed two traditions. One ascribed the *Tractatus* to a member of the Dominican Order (Black Friars), the other to the Portuguese secular priest who in 1276 became pope under the name of John XXI. The latter identification was favored until the latest research, done in the late 1990s, showed that most likely the author of the *Tractatus* was not John XXI but a Spanish Dominican, whose identity still remains unknown.

The *Tractatus* are believed to have been written between 1230 and 1245. Another work that has been attributed to the same author is on syncategorematic words (*Syncategoreumata*), probably written some time between 1235 and 1245. Besides these two introductory tracts on logic, there are other works written by a Peter of Spain, namely, a famous medical work titled *Thesaurus pauperum* and fourteen other works on medicine. A Peter of Spain also wrote *Scientia libri de anima* and commentaries on Aristotle's *De anima*, *De morte et vita*, and *De sensu et sensato*, as well as commentaries on works by Dionysius the Pseudo-Areopagite. In the manuscripts all these works are ascribed to Pope John XXI. In the late twelfth century another Peter of Spain (in modern times called Petrus Hispanus non-papa) compiled a textbook on grammar, *Summa "Absoluta cuiuslibet"*.

The author of the tracts on logic appears to be particularly interested in matters of ontology, in dealing with which he takes a realistic approach. Every common noun signifies a universal nature and can stand for anything sharing that nature. In sentences of the form A is B, in which A and B are common nouns, the copula *is* signifies some composition that includes the extremes (subject and predicate) A and B, and always expresses a qualified mode of being (*esse quodammodo*). Such a composition usually applies to a state of affairs possessing being in the absolute sense (*esse simpliciter*), as in "Man is an animal," but if the subject refers to a fictitious entity, for example, in "A chimera is a nonbeing," being should be understood as being in a qualified sense (*ens quodammodo*).

In the first example the expression *man*, in line with Peter's ontological stand, stands for the universal nature of manhood. Therefore, the expression is necessarily true, even if no man exists. Logical necessity, then, is based on ontological necessity, or, in other words, the necessity of propositions is founded on the necessity of the things spoken about. Necessity is associated with different types of things, like the relationships between certain concepts (such as genera and species) signifying them. Another type of necessity is found in mathematical entities. In logical argument it is important to distinguish sharply between (timeless) necessary being and being-at-a-certain-time. So an inference like "A man is necessarily an animal; therefore Socrates (who is a man) is necessarily an animal" is not valid, because a transition is made from necessary being to a being at a certain time. For Peter, the notion of necessity ultimately refers to a necessary state of affairs in reality, something that is, and must always be, the case.

Peter's account of the use of the consequential "if," in which he explains consequence in terms of causality, shows a similar connection between language and the domain of reality. Like the majority of his contemporaries, Peter has to deal with the famous question "whether from the impossible anything follows" (*utrum ex impossibili sequatur quidlibet*). According to him, the notion of impossibility can be taken in two ways, namely, either (1) absolute impossibility, which amounts to being-nothing, or (2) an impossible state of affairs, the objective content, that is, of expressions containing incompatible concepts, like in "A man is an ass." Indeed, from the latter type of impossibility something (but not anything) can follow, for example, the true conclusion "Therefore a man is an animal." From absolute impossibilities, such as the one present in "You know that you are a stone," nothing can be correctly inferred, and so anything follows. To be able to make a correct inference, the antecedent should be a "something" (*res*), not a "nothing."

See also Aristotelianism; Medieval Philosophy.

Bibliography

WORKS BY PETER OF SPAIN

Syncategoreumata. First Critical Edition with an Introduction and Indexes by L.M. de Rijk. Translated by Joke Spruyt. Leiden, Netherlands: Brill, 1992.

Tractatus: Called afterwards Summule logicales. First Critical Edition from the Manuscripts with an Introduction by L.M. de Rijk, Assen: Van Gorcum, 1972.

WORKS ABOUT PETER OF SPAIN

d'Ors, Angel. "Petrus Hispanus O.P., Auctor Summularum." *Vivarium* 35 (1) (1997): 21–71.

d'Ors, Angel. "Petrus Hispanus O.P., Auctor Summularum (II): Further Documents and Problems." *Vivarium* 39 (2) (2001): 209–254.

d'Ors, Angel. "Petrus Hispanus O.P., Auctor Summularum (III) 'Petrus Alfonsi' or 'Petrus Ferrandi'?" *Vivarium* 41 (2) (2003): 249–303.

de Rijk, L. M. "On the Genuine Text of Peter of Spain's *Summule logicales* I. General Problems concerning Possible Interpolations in the Manuscripts." *Vivarium* 6 (1) (1968): 1–34.

Spruyt, Joke, trans. *Peter of Spain on Composition and Negation*. Nijmegen, Netherlands: Ingenium, 1989.

Spruyt, Joke. "Thirteenth-Century Discussions on Modal Terms." *Vivarium* 32 (2) (1994): 196–226.

Spruyt, Joke. "Thirteenth-Century Positions on the Rule 'Ex impossibili sequitur quidlibet.'" In *Argumentationstheorie*, edited by Klaus Jacobi, 161–193. Leiden, Netherlands: Brill, 1993.

Joke Spruyt (2005)

PETRARCH
(1304–1374)

Petrarch, or Francesco Petrarca, the Italian humanist, poet, and scholar, was born in Arezzo into an exiled Florentine family. He was taken to Avignon in 1312, and there he spent most of his life until 1353, except for a period as a student of law at Montpellier and Bologna and several long journeys to Italy. After 1353 he lived in Italy, mainly in Milan, Venice, and Padua; he died in Arquà near Padua. Petrarch held several ecclesiastical benefices and also enjoyed the patronage of the Colonna and the Visconti.

Petrarch's fame rests first on his Italian poems and second on his work as a scholar and Latin writer. His Latin writings include poems, orations, invectives, historical works, a large body of letters, and a few moral treatises. Among the treatises we may mention especially *De Remediis Utriusque Fortunae* (On the remedies of good and bad fortune; 1366), *De Secreto Conflictu Curarum Mearum*, better known as *Secretum* (On the secret conflict of my worries; completed before 1358), *De Vita Solitaria* (On the solitary life; 1356), and *De Sui Ipsius et Multorum Ignorantia* (On his own and many other people's ignorance; 1367).

Petrarch was no philosopher in the technical sense, and even his treatises on moral subjects are loosely written and lack a firm structure or method. Much of his thought consists of tendencies and aspirations rather than of developed ideas or doctrines, and it is inextricably linked with his learning, reading, tastes, and feelings. Nevertheless, it would be wrong to underestimate Petrarch's impact on the history of Western thought. He was the first great representative of Renaissance humanism, if not its founder; as a poet, scholar, and personality, he had a vast reputation during his lifetime and for several subsequent centuries. In many ways he set the pattern for the taste, outlook, and range of interests that determined the thought of Renaissance humanism down to the sixteenth century. Petrarch was regarded, by himself and by his contemporaries, not only as a poet, orator, and historian but also as a moral philosopher, and many of his attitudes were to receive from some of his successors the intellectual and philosophical substance which they seem to lack in Petrarch's own work.

One important aspect of Petrarch's thought that was to be developed by many later humanists was his hostility toward Scholasticism—that is, the university learning of the later Middle Ages. He attacked astrology as well as logic and jurisprudence and dedicated entire works to criticizing the physicians and the Aristotelian philosophers. These attacks, though sweeping and suggestive, are highly personal and subjective and rarely enter into specific issues or arguments. When Petrarch rejects the authority of Aristotle or of his Arabic commentator Averroes, he does so from personal dislike, not from objective grounds; when he criticizes such theories as the eternity of the world, the attainment of perfect happiness during the present life, or the so-called theory of the double truth (that is, of the separate validity of Aristotelian philosophy and of Christian theology), his main argument is that these doctrines are contrary to the Christian religion.

Yet the positive value that Petrarch opposed to medieval science was neither a new science nor mere religious faith but the study of classical antiquity. All his life

Petrarch was an avid reader of the ancient Latin writers; he copied, collected, and annotated their works and tried to correct their texts and appropriate their style and ideas. He felt a strong nostalgia for the political greatness of the Roman Republic and Empire, and the hope to restore this greatness was the central political idea that guided him in his dealings with the pope and the emperor, with the Roman revolutionary Cola di Rienzo, and with the various Italian governments of his time.

Of the ancient Latin writers, Cicero and Seneca were among Petrarch's favorites. His polemic against dialectic and other branches of scholastic learning and his emphasis on moral problems seem to be modeled after the more moderate skepticism which Seneca expresses in his *Moral Epistles* with reference to the subtle dialectic of the older Stoics. To Seneca, Petrarch owes his taste for moral declamation and the Stoic notions that appear in his writings—the conflict between virtue and fortune, the contrast between reason and the four basic passions, and the close link between virtue and happiness. Even greater is Petrarch's enthusiasm for Cicero, to whom he owes the form of the dialogue and much of his information on Greek philosophy. We might even say that Petrarch and other humanists owe to their imitation of Cicero and Seneca not only the elegance of their style, but also the elusive and at times superficial manner of their reasoning.

Petrarch could not fail to notice the numerous references to Greek sources in the writings of his favorite Roman authors. He made an attempt to learn Greek, and although he did not progress far enough to read the ancient Greek writers in the original, his awareness of Greek philosophy and literature did affect his outlook and orientation. He owned a Greek manuscript of Plato and read the *Timaeus* and *Phaedo*, which were available to him in Latin translations. He also gathered information on Plato in Cicero and other Roman authors and cited some Platonic doctrines. However, more important than these occasional references to specific theories is Petrarch's general conviction that Plato was the greatest of all philosophers, greater than Aristotle, who had been the chief authority of the later medieval thinkers. "Plato is praised by the greater men, whereas Aristotle is praised by the greater number." In his *Triumph of Fame*, Petrarch places Plato before Aristotle, and his lines appear to be a conscious correction of the praise Dante had given to the "master of those who know." Petrarch's Platonism was a program rather than a doctrine, but it pointed the way to later humanist translations of Plato and to the Platonist thought of the Florentine Academy.

Petrarch assigned second place to Aristotle, but he was far from holding him in contempt. He knew especially Aristotle's *Ethics,* and he repeatedly suggested that the original Aristotle may be superior to his medieval translators and commentators. Petrarch thus pointed the way to a new attitude toward Aristotle that was to take shape in the fifteenth and sixteenth centuries. Aristotle was to be studied in the original Greek text and in the company of other Greek philosophers and writers; his medieval Latin translations were to be replaced by new humanist translations, and his medieval Arabic and Latin commentators were to give way to the ancient Greek commentators and to those modern Renaissance interpreters who were able to read and understand Aristotle in his original text. Thus, Petrarch was the prophet of Renaissance Aristotelianism, as he had been of Renaissance Platonism.

Although Petrarch opposed the classical authors to the medieval tradition, he was by no means completely detached from his immediate past. Christian faith and piety occupy a central position in his thought and writings, and there is no reason to doubt his sincerity. Whenever a conflict between religion and ancient philosophy might arise, he is ready to stand by the teachings of the former. The *Secretum,* in which Petrarch subjects his most intimate feelings and actions to religious scrutiny, is a thoroughly Christian work, and his treatise *De Remediis Utriusque Fortunae* is equally Christian, even specifically medieval. His treatise *De Otio Religioso* (On the leisure of the monks) belongs to the ascetic tradition, and even Petrarch's polemic against Scholasticism in the name of a genuine and simple religion continues or resumes that strand of medieval religious thought which found expression in Peter Damian and St. Bernard. In his treatise on his ignorance, Petrarch goes so far as to oppose his own piety to the supposedly irreligious views of his scholastic opponents. This shows that it was at least possible to reject Scholasticism and remain a convinced Christian, and to reconcile classical learning with religious faith.

In accordance with this attitude, Petrarch liked to read the early Christian writers, especially the Church Fathers, along with the pagan classics but without the company of the scholastic theologians. His favorite Christian author was St. Augustine, who occupies a position of unique importance in his thought and work. Aside from numerous quotations scattered in Petrarch's writings, it is sufficient to mention two notable instances. Petrarch's *Secretum* takes the form of a dialogue between the author and St. Augustine, who thus assumes the role of a spiritual guide or of the author's conscience. And in the famous letter in which Petrarch describes climbing Mont Ventoux, he expresses his feelings by a quotation on which his eyes chanced to fall in his copy of Augustine's *Confessions:* "And men go to admire the high mountains, the vast floods of the sea, the huge streams of the rivers, the circumference of the ocean, and the revolutions of the stars—and desert themselves" (*Confessions x,* 8, 15).

Besides these and a few other general attitudes, there is at least one theoretical problem on which Petrarch formulates views akin to those of many later humanists. He keeps asserting that man and his problems should be the main object and concern of thought and philosophy. This is also the justification he gives for his emphasis on moral philosophy, and when he criticizes the scholastic science of his Aristotelian opponents, it is chiefly on the grounds that they raise useless questions and forget the most important problem, the human soul. This is also the gist of the words with which Petrarch describes his feelings when he had reached the top of Mont Ventoux. The words are Petrarch's, and they express his own ideas, but they are characteristically interwoven with quotations from Augustine and Seneca.

Petrarch expresses for the first time that emphasis on man which was to receive eloquent developments in the treatises of later humanists and to be given a metaphysical and cosmological foundation in the works of Marsilio Ficino and Giovanni Pico della Mirandola. This is the reason that the humanists were to adopt the name "humanities" (*studia humanitatis*) for their studies—to indicate their significance for man and his problems. Yet behind Petrarch's tendency to set moral doctrine against natural science, there are also echoes of Seneca and St. Augustine and of Cicero's statement that Socrates had brought philosophy down from heaven to Earth. When Petrarch speaks of man and his soul, he refers at the same time to the blessed life and eternal salvation, adding a distinctly Christian overtone to his moral and human preoccupation. He thus comes to link the knowledge of man and the knowledge of God in a distinctly Augustinian fashion and also to discuss an important problem of scholastic philosophy that had its root in Augustine: the question of whether the will or the intellect is superior. In discussing this scholastic problem, Petrarch follows the Augustinian tradition, as other humanists and Platonists were to do after him, in deciding the question in favor of the will.

Petrarch, the great poet, writer, and scholar, is clearly an ambiguous and transitional figure when judged by his role in the history of philosophical thought. His thought consists in aspirations rather than developed ideas, but these aspirations were developed by later thinkers and were eventually transformed into more elaborate ideas. His intellectual program may be summed up in the formula that he uses once in the treatise on his ignorance: Platonic wisdom, Christian dogma, Ciceronian eloquence. His classical culture, his Christian faith, and his attack against Scholasticism all have a personal, and in a way modern, quality. At the same time everything he says is pervaded by his classical sources and often by residual traces of medieval thought. In this respect, as in many others, Petrarch is a typical representative of his age and of the humanist movement. He did not merely anticipate later Renaissance developments because he was unusually talented or perceptive; he also had an active share in bringing them about, because of the enormous prestige he enjoyed among his contemporaries and immediate successors.

See also Aristotelianism; Aristotle; Augustine, St.; Augustinianism; Averroes; Bernard of Clairvaux, St.; Cicero, Marcus Tullius; Dante Alighieri; Dialectic; Dogma; Florentine Academy; Humanism; Medieval Philosophy; Patristic Philosophy; Peter Damian; Pico della Mirandola, Count Giovanni; Plato; Platonism and the Platonic Tradition; Renaissance; Seneca, Lucius Annaeus; Stoicism.

Bibliography

WORKS BY PETRARCH

Petrarch's Italian poems have been printed in numerous editions and translations; see also Roberto Weiss, *Un inedito Petrarchesco* (Rome, 1950). Of the *Edizione nazionale* of his collected works only six volumes have appeared, containing his poem *Africa,* a part of his letters—*Le familiari,* edited by V. Rossi and U. Bosco, 4 vols. (Florence: Sansoni, 1933–1942)—and the *Rerum Memorandarum Libri,* edited by Giuseppe Billanovich (Florence: Sansoni, 1943). See also K. Burdach, *Aus Petrarcas aeltestem deutschen Schuelerkreise* (Berlin, 1929); *Petrarcas "Buch ohne Namen" und die päpstliche Kurie,* edited by P. Piur (Halle, Germany: Niemeyer, 1925); and *Petrarcas Briefwechsel mit deutschen Zeitgenossen,* edited by P. Piur (Berlin: Weidmann, 1933).

The collection of *Prose,* edited by G. Martellotti et al. (Milan and Naples, 1955), contains the *Secretum, De Vita Solitaria,* and selections from the invectives and other treatises. *Le traité De Sui Ipsius et Multorum Ignorantia,* edited by L. M. Capelli (Paris, 1906), is the only complete modern edition of this important treatise. For many other Latin works of Petrarch the old edition of his works, *Opera* (Basel, 1581), must still be used. See also *Scritti inediti,* edited by A. Hortis (Trieste, 1874).

English translations are available for the *Secret,* translated by William H. Draper (London, 1911); *The Life of Solitude,* translated by Jacob Zeitlin (Urbana, IL, 1924); *On His Own Ignorance,* translated by H. Nachod, who added the letter on the ascent of Mont Ventoux and excellent notes, in *The Renaissance Philosophy of Man*, edited by Ernst Cassirer, Paul Oskar Kristeller, and John H. Randall Jr. (Chicago: University of Chicago Press, 1948), pp. 36–133; the *Testament*, translated by Theodor E. Mommsen (Ithaca, NY, 1957); and for many letters—*Petrarch, the First Modern Scholar and Man of Letters*, 2nd ed., translated by James Harvey Robinson (New York, 1907), *Petrarch's Letters to Classical Authors*, translated by Mario E. Cosenza (Chicago: University of Chicago Press, 1910), and *Petrarch at Vaucluse*, translated by Ernest H. Wilkins (Chicago: University of Chicago Press, 1958).

WORKS ON PETRARCH

From the vast literature on Petrarch only a few works can be mentioned; for a bibliography, see N. Sapegno, *Il trecento* (Milan, 1948). For Petrarch's life and works see Edward H. R. Tatham, *Francesco Petrarca*, 2 vols. (London, 1925–1926); U. Bosco, *Petrarca* (Turin, 1946); Morris Bishop, *Petrarch and His World* (Bloomington: Indiana University Press, 1963); and, above all, numerous books and articles by Ernest H. Wilkins: *Studies in the Life and Works of Petrarch* (Cambridge, MA: Mediaeval Academy of America, 1955), *Petrarch's Eight Years in Milan* (Cambridge, MA: Mediaeval Academy of America, 1958), *Petrarch's Later Years* (Cambridge, MA: Mediaeval Academy of America, 1959), *Petrarch's Correspondence* (Padua, 1960), and *Life of Petrarch* (Chicago: University of Chicago, 1961).

For Petrarch as a scholar see Pierre de Nolhac, *Pétrarque et l'humanisme*, 2 vols., 2nd ed. (Paris, 1907), and "de Patrum et Medii Aevi Scriptorum Codicibus in Bibliotheca Petrarcae Olim Collectis," in *Revue des bibliothèques* 2 (1892): 241–279; numerous studies by Giuseppe Billanovich, especially *Petrarca letterato*, Vol. I, *Lo scrittoio del Petrarca* (Rome, 1947), and "Petrarch and the Textual Tradition of Livy," in *Journal of the Warburg and Courtauld Institutes* 14 (1951): 137–208. See also J. H. Whitfield, *Petrarch and the Renascence* (Oxford: Blackwell, 1943).

For Petrarch's political thought see Theodor E. Mommsen, *Medieval and Renaissance Studies*, edited by Eugene F. Rice (Ithaca, NY: Cornell University Press, 1959); Aldo S. Bernardo, *Petrarch, Scipio and the Africa* (Baltimore: Johns Hopkins Press, 1962); Jules Alan Wein, *Petrarch's Politics* (unpublished thesis, Columbia University, 1960); and Mario E. Cosenza, *Petrarch and the Revolution of Cola di Rienzo* (Chicago, 1913).

For Petrarch's religious and philosophical ideas see Armando Carlini, *Il pensiero filosofico religioso di Francesco Petrarca* (Iesi, Italy, 1904); Elena Razzoli, *Agostinismo e religiosità del Petrarca* (Milan, 1937); P. P. Gerosa, *L'umanesimo agostiniano del Petrarca* (Turin, 1927); K. Heitmann, *Fortuna und Virtus* (Cologne, 1958); William Granger Ryan, *Humanism and Religion in Petrarch* (unpublished thesis, Columbia University, 1950); and N. Iliescu, *Il canzoniere petrarchesco e Sant'Agostino* (Rome, 1962).

Paul Oskar Kristeller (1967)

PETRONIEVIĆ, BRANISLAV
(1875–1954)

Branislav Petronievič, a Yugoslav philosopher and paleontologist, was born in Sovljak, Serbia. He taught as a professor of philosophy at the University of Belgrade and was a member of the Serbian Academy of Science and Arts. In paleontology, Petronievič was the first to distinguish between the genera *Archaeopteryx* and *Archaeornis*; he also discovered new characteristics of the genera *Tritylodon* and *Moeritherium*.

Petronievič systematically treated many problems, both in pure philosophy and in scientific methodology. He considered himself a "born metaphysician" and devoted himself to constructing his own metaphysical system. But, although original, it grew out of the nineteenth-century empirical metaphysics of Hermann Lotze, Eduard von Hartmann, and Petronievič's teacher, Johannes Volkelt.

Petronievič's epistemological theory of empiriorationalism claimed that all contents of consciousness are absolutely real in the same sense as things per se. Thus there can be no absolute or immanent or transcendental illusion. Petronievič rejected phenomenalism also, specifically Immanuel Kant's. He claimed that an analysis of directly given empirical contents of consciousness shows that there are qualitatively simple evidences of experience, the "givenness of something"—the givenness of simple sensuous qualities as basic correlates of the laws of thought. Thought and being are identical, and apodictic knowledge of being itself is possible.

In his main philosophical work, *Principien der Metaphysik*, Petronievič claimed that the basic task of metaphysics is to explain the structure of the "world of multitude, diversity, and change" as the "pre-evidence" of the directly given empirical and transcendental reality. According to Petronievič, the world is a manifold of "discrete points of being" and of quality, of will, and so on. The world as a manifold is possible only because the real points of being are separated by real "acts of negation," which determine the qualities of being and without which being would be absolutely homogeneous. Petronievič regarded the principle of negation as "the absolute principle of the world," of both being and thought; only on the basis of this principle can the diversity and multiplicity of the world be deduced and explained. On similar grounds Petronievič considered the principle of sufficient reason the fundamental law of true knowledge.

Petronievič synthesized Benedict de Spinoza's monism and Gottfried Wilhelm Leibniz's monadological pluralism in his monopluralism. His original and profound "hypermetaphysical" teachings on the origin and development of the qualitative and quantitative manifoldness of the world have yet to be studied and evaluated. His views on real space and real time, which he regarded as discreta rather than abstract continua, deserve special attention. He constructed a new geometry of real discrete space.

Petronievićs view was essentially idealistic, since he held that absolutely unconscious atoms are impossible and that the soul, which is immortal, is a conscious monad.

Petronievićs upheld an ethical theory of transcendental optimism and free will. He devoted a number of studies to aesthetics, particularly in the work of the Yugoslav poet Petar II Petrović-Njegoš and of Lev Tolstoy.

Among his most notable contributions to the logical foundations of mathematics are his work on typical geometries, on the problem of the finitude or infinitude of space, the three-bodies problem, on differential quotients, and on mathematical induction. In psychology he developed theories about the observation of the transparent and on the depth and observation of compound colors. In the history of science his most notable works were on the methodology of Isaac Newton's discovery of the law of gravitation, on Johann Gottfried Galle's and Urbain-Jean-Joseph Leverrier's discovery of Neptune, and on Dmitri Mendeleev's discovery of the periodic system of elements.

See also Consciousness; Geometry; Hartmann, Eduard von; Idealism; Kant, Immanuel; Leibniz, Gottfried Wilhelm; Lotze, Rudolf Hermann; Mathematics, Foundations of; Monism and Pluralism; Newton, Isaac; Phenomenalism; Spinoza, Benedict (Baruch) de; Tolstoy, Lev (Leo) Nikolaevich.

Bibliography

WORKS BY PETRONIEVIĆ
Der ontologische Beweis für das Dasein des Absoluten. Leipzig, 1897.
Der Satz vom Grunde. Belgrade: Staatsdruckerei, 1898.
Prinzipien der Erkenntnislehre. Berlin, 1900.
Prinzipien der Metaphysik, 2 vols. Heidelberg, 1904–1911.
Die typischen Geometrien und das Unendliche. Heidelberg, 1907.
L'évolution universelle. Paris, 1921.
Résumé des travaux philosophiques et scientifiques de Branislav Petronievićs. Academie Royal Serbe, Bulletin de l'Academie des Lettres, No. 2. Belgrade, 1937.

WORKS ON PETRONIEVIĆ
Spomenica Branislav Petronijevićs. SAN No. 13. Belgrade, 1957. Articles on Petronievićs by various authors.

Bogdan Šešić (1967)

PETROVIĆ-NJEGOŠ, PETAR
(1813–1851)

Petar Petrović-Njegoš, Prince Petar II of Montenegro, was born in the village of Njegusi near Cetinje. As the government of Montenegro was then a theocracy, Njegoš, who ruled from 1830 to 1851, had to act as high priest, much against his own views and wishes. He was religious by conviction, but opposed to any religious fanaticism or formalities. By setting up a number of civil and cultural institutions, he transformed Montenegro from a tribal to a modern state.

Njegoš was one of the greatest Yugoslav poets. His principal works are *Slobodijada* (Ode to liberty), *Gorski Vijenac* (The mountain wreath), *Luča Mikrokozma* (The ray of the microcosm), *Šćepan Mali* (Schepan the small), and a number of minor poems, the best of which is the reflective poem *Misao* (The thought). His main themes were man's destiny, marked by struggle and suffering, and freedom, which he understood as partly the struggle for national liberty. The elaboration of these themes led Njegoš to many philosophical thoughts and meditations. Being predominantly a poet, he presented these thoughts in poetic images and visions. The philosophical conception implicit in these images is a Platonic dualism. God and matter are coeternal. Mind and body are opposed principles both ontologically and axiologically. Mind originates in heaven, whereas body belongs to the "realm of decay." The body is "the physical shackles of the soul"; passions "lay man below the beast," whereas mind makes him "equal to immortals." In *Luča Mikrokozma* Njegoš interpreted the union of mind and body as a consequence of sin and the Fall. The first man, Adam, was once pure spirit, but he joined Satan in his rebellion against God, although he soon repented. He was then "clad in a body" and cast upon Earth, which was created by God as a place of expiation after man's sin. Thus, Njegoš's Adam, unlike John Milton's or the Adam of official church doctrine, sinned prior to his bodily creation.

Luča Mikrokozma can be seen as providing metaphysical and religious reasons for the inevitability of suffering. *Gorski Vijenac* is a mighty hymn to the national struggle for liberation and to the struggle against evil in general. To justify this struggle Njegoš elaborated a dynamic and basically dialectical conception of the world. The world is made up of opposed and dangerous forces at permanent war. Through this struggle, order emerges out of chaotic disorder, and spiritual power triumphs over great confusion. Struggle and suffering are not mere evils but have a positive, creative aspect as well. The spark appears only after the flint is struck hard, and the soul that has endured temptations "nourishes the body with internal fire." Heroism is the master of evil, and human life has an aim only if it contributes to the realization of liberty, honor, and dignity. Njegoš's ethics were essentially derived from his people and, in turn, had a powerful influence on them in all the trying moments of their history.

See also Dialectic; Dualism in the Philosophy of Mind; Milton, John; Mind-Body Problem; Platonism and the Platonic Tradition.

Bibliography

WORKS BY PETROVIĆ-NJEGOŠ
Cjelokupna Djela, 9 vols. Belgrade, 1951–1955.

WORKS ON PETROVIĆ-NJEGOŠ
Djilas, Milovan. *Legenda o Njegošu.* Belgrade, 1952.
Latković, Vido. *Petar II Petrović Njegoš.* Belgrade, 1963.
Petronijević, Branislav. *Filozofija u "Gorskom Vijencu" i "Luči Mikrokozma."* Belgrade, 1924.
Šmaus, A. *Njegoševa "Luča Mikrokozma."* Belgrade, 1927.
Velimirović, Nikolaj. *Religija Njegoševa.* Belgrade, 1921.

Vuko Pavićević (1967)

PETZOLDT, JOSEPH
(1862–1929)

Joseph Petzoldt, a German empiriocritical philosopher, was born at Altenburg and taught mathematics and natural science at a Gymnasium in Spandau. In 1904 he became *Privatdozent* at the Technische Hochschule in Berlin-Charlottenburg, and in 1922 he was named associate professor. For a number of years he was chairman of the Gesellschaft für positivistische Philosophie.

Petzoldt was indebted to Ernst Mach's positivism, to the immanence philosophy of Wilhelm Schuppe, and above all to the empiriocriticism of Richard Avenarius. Petzoldt presented Avenarius's difficult philosophy in a popular form and developed it independently. For example, he offered a psychological explanation of the "narrowness," and therewith the unity, of consciousness; he tried to demonstrate the unlimited validity of psychophysical parallelism; and he analyzed ethical and aesthetic values and proposed a theory of the ethical and aesthetic permanence, or maximum stability, of humankind. According to this theory, all evolutionary processes end in states of permanence. Hence, human evolution is also heading toward a state of complete stability and toward the marking out of defining forms of permanence, that is, of invariably repeatable, fixed components of mental acts. The most basic feature of all the goals of our thought and creative work is permanence or durability—the realization of ever recurrent, repeatedly used ways of acting and the establishment of enduring forms amidst the profusion of particular configurations. An example of this is the tendency of thought toward stability, the striving for a stable conceptual system.

Petzoldt called his philosophy a "relativistic positivism." According to this view, both causality and substantiality are untenable and unnecessary categories, and the difference between the mental and the physical reduces to a difference in the "mode of interpretation." Petzoldt, like Avenarius, held that the concept of cause should be replaced by the mathematical concept to functional dependence, or uniqueness of coordination. According to Petzoldt, the causal relation is fully exhausted in a "law of uniqueness," which holds that for every process, the elements that exclusively determine it should be specified. Because there is thus nothing in the real world corresponding to the "animistic" concept of cause, this concept should be eliminated. The demand for a causal explanation that goes beyond the complete and simplest description of processes rests on misunderstandings; such an explanation is in principle unrealizable and is therefore meaningless.

The concept of substance, according to Petzoldt, originates from a need for stability in thinking. There are no absolute substances but only relatively constant complexes of sensory qualities. Since all properties hold good only relative to a subject, the idea of an absolute, nonrelative being should be discarded, and with it the category of substance. There is no "world-in-itself"; there is only a "world-for-us," whose elements are sensations, even though "things" are to be thought of as "continuing to exist" even when we do not perceive them. The world-for-us is apprehended as being mental insofar as it is perceived and as being physical insofar as it is known as a correlation of elements. That which is ultimately "given" is thus neither mental nor physical, neither immaterial nor material, neither "internal" nor "external," neither thing-in-itself nor phenomenon. These antitheses are merely relatively valid limiting concepts, intelligible only in their interrelation: they are formed only subsequent to, and on the basis of, the primordial unitary experience. Petzoldt's conception resembled Bertrand Russell's neutral monism.

Petzoldt's philosophy culminated in an evolutionary naturalism. "Man is not a permanence type, but an organism in a state of very active development; yet, like all other organisms and like self-developing systems generally, he is headed toward a form of permanence" (*Einführung in die Philosophie der reinen Erfahrung* [Introduction to the philosophy of pure experience], Vol. 2, p. 3). Just as organic evolution tends toward the production of permanence states and "man's brain approaches more and more a form of permanence," the spiritual and intellectual evolution of man likewise tends to permanence states. We strive for the completion of science, for the perfection of social institutions and customs by a progressive adjustment of national and social differences, and for the fulfillment of art through "emphasis on the typical and essential in the phenomena."

The goal of ethics is that in all that we do and think we help to realize the future permanence state that flows from the nature of man and his environment (p. 206). This is the state of maximum utilization of powers, and hence of maximum stability, toward which all evolution strives. Each of us must risk everything "in order to perfect his personality in accordance with the nature and extent of his abilities and to place himself entirely at the service of human society" (p. 212).

See also Avenarius, Richard; Ethics, History of; Evolutionary Theory; Mach, Ernst; Positivism; Schuppe, Ernst Julius Wilhelm.

Bibliography

Works by Petzoldt include *Maxima, Minima und Oekonomie* (Altenburg, 1891); *Einführung in die Philosophic der reinen Erfahrung*, 2 vols. (Leipzig, 1900–1904); *Das Weltproblem vom Standpunkte des relativistischen Positivismus aus historisch-kritisch dargestellt* (Leipzig, 1906); *Die Stellung der Relativitütstheorie in der geistigen Entwicklung der Menschheit* (Dresden, 1921); and *Das natürliche Höhenziel der menschheitlichen Entwicklung* (Leipzig, 1927).

An article on Petzoldt is by Christian Herrmann, "Nachruf: Joseph Petzoldt," in *Kant-Studien* 34 (1929): 508–510.

Franz Austeda (1967)
Translated by Albert E. Blumberg

PFÄNDER, ALEXANDER
(1871–1941)

Alexander Pfänder, a German philosopher and phenomenologist, was born in Iserlohn. In 1891 he began his studies at the University of Munich, where he came under the influence of Theodor Lipps. With the publication of the *Phänomenologie des Wollens: Eine psychologische Analyse* (Phenomenology of willing: a psychological analysis; 1900) he joined the philosophical faculty in Munich, where he remained for the rest of his life. In 1904 he came into contact with Edmund Husserl. Though the two of them had much in common in their phenomenological orientation and accordingly had great respect for each other, Pfänder was the leader of the phenomenological circle in Munich, which was distinct from the one that Husserl led in Göttingen and later in Freiburg. Under Pfänder's influence, the Munich phenomenologists were especially wary of the transcendental turn and its concomitant idealism that Husserl put forward in his *Ideas Pertaining to a Pure Phenomenology and Phenomenological Philosophy* (1913). In Pfänder's later years, in which he suffered from protracted ill health, he worked toward the development of an understanding psychology and elaborated on his concept of phenomenology and phenomenological philosophy in his lectures. His most outstanding contributions, however, are to be found in his specialized treatment of volitional, emotional, and intellectual phenomena.

Pfänder had embarked on phenomenological investigations already in the late nineteenth century, before the publication of Husserl's *Logical Investigations* (1900–1901). The fruit of these investigations, namely *Phenomenology of Willing*, is thus a noteworthy achievement as a phenomenological work that came about independently of Husserl. Here, Pfänder is concerned with volitional phenomena in particular, but the work encompasses important considerations of method. The method that Pfänder employs is explicitly a descriptive one and thereby excludes any attempt to explain the phenomena under consideration in terms of cause and effect. At the same time this descriptive method avoids the sort of metaphysical speculation about willing such as what had been put forward by Arthur Schopenhauer in the nineteenth century. It is also important to note that Pfänder's phenomenology is not an introspective endeavor of the sort in which Lipps was engaged. His insistence that introspection is in fact retrospection is rather reminiscent of Franz Brentano, as is Pfänder's description of phenomena by means of an analysis into elements. His emphasis on the experienced ego throughout his analyses, however, is no doubt an aspect of his phenomenology that he drew from Lipps.

According to Pfänder volition always involves not only a presentation of the willed object but also an attention relief in which the object is made prominent against the background of others. Moreover, "willing" is used in a broad sense to designate striving, but also in a narrower sense that is closer to the one of ordinary language. While he does not dismiss the possibility of pleasure as the goal of willing, he does not find this to be the case in all instances of willing. Moreover, his analyses of willing are guided by the observation that one can will only that which one believes to be possible. Accordingly, the experience of the volitional sphere involves considerations of other aspects of consciousness.

In 1913 and 1916 Pfänder turned his attention to the emotional rather than the volitional sphere of mental life, albeit with the conviction that the two are closely related. The articles that he published in these years for Husserl's phenomenological *Yearbook* are particularly concerned with sentiments (*Gesinnungen*) insofar as they are directed toward persons, places, animals, and so on, either positively or negatively, as when one speaks of someone being "well disposed" or "ill disposed" toward this or that. When there occurs a stirring of sentiment, this is an actual as opposed to a virtual or habitual sentiment. In each case the sentiment is something between a subject and an object and involves a centrifugal direction and streaming from the subject to the object. Moreover, the sentiment is either friendly or hostile toward the object in question. Sentiments can also be divided into genuine and spurious ones. The latter are exemplified by how one is disposed toward the characters in a theatrical performance. The rich array of analyses Pfänder employs in his investigations of sentiments was meant to be a contribution to the foundation of ethics and pedagogy.

Pfänder's *Logik* (Logic; 1921) should not be read as a logic textbook and certainly not as a logic in the technical sense that prevails in the current understanding of this term. Still, this work is of considerable interest as a philosophy of logic. Though his analyses of volitional and emotional phenomena are by and large focused on the acts of willing and feelings, *Logic* is primarily concerned with the correlates of intellectual acts. Pfänder calls these correlates thoughts (*Gedanken*), which are comparable to the meanings (*Bedeutungen*) that Husserl identifies as the subject matter of pure logic in the *Logical Investigations*, except that Pfänder conceives of thoughts as products of thinking. Moreover, Pfänder acknowledges not only special correlates of thinking but also a host of other objective correlates that are produced in a social context. In this sense *Logic*, like the works of other Munich phenomenologists (especially Adolf Reinach), opens up a new domain in the objective sphere for phenomenological investigation. Logic, Pfänder maintains, is particularly concerned with a class of thoughts known as judgments (*Urteile*). These are peculiar insofar as they involve a claim to truth and refer to states of affairs (*Sachverhalte*),

which are made focal in Pfänder's reflections on rules of inference as well as on the laws of identity, noncontradiction, the excluded middle, and sufficient reason.

See also Husserl, Edmund; Lipps, Theodor; Phenomenology.

Bibliography

Spiegelberg, Herbert, in collaboration with Karl Schuhmann. *The Phenomenological Movement: A Historical Introduction*, 3rd ed. The Hague: Nijhoff, 1982, pp. 170–191.

WORKS BY PFÄNDER

Phänomenologie des Wollens: Eine psychologische Analyse. Leipzig: Barth, 1900.

"Zur Psychologie der Gesinnungen." *Jahrbuch für Philosophie und phänomenologische Forschung* 1 (1913): 325–404; 3 (1916): 1–125.

Logik, 3rd ed. Tübingen: Max Niemeyer, 1963.

WORKS ON PFÄNDER

Spiegelberg, Herbert, and Eberhard Avé-Lallement, eds. *Pfänder-Studien*. The Hague: Nijhoff, 1982.

Robin D. Rollinger (2005)

PHANTASIA

The Greek word *phantasia* is usually translated "imagination." However, in Greek thought the word always retains a connection with the verb *phainomai*, "I appear." It can be used to refer both to the psychological capacity to receive, interpret, and even produce appearances and to those appearances themselves.

Plato has little to say about *phantasia* as such, although in *Sophist* 264a he describes it as "a blend of perception and judgement (*doxa*)." Elsewhere, in *Timaeus* 70eff., in a strange passage that locates parts of the soul in particular parts of the body, he describes the liver as functioning like a mirror that reflects images coming from the rational part of the soul, suggesting a link between imagination, dreams, and inspired prophecy.

Aristotle gives *phantasia* a specific place in his psychology, between perception and thought. In *De anima* 3.3 he offers an account of *phantasia* that includes mental images, dreams, and hallucinations. For Aristotle *phantasia* is based on sense-perception and plays a crucial role in animal movement and desire, as he explains in *De anima* 3.9 and in the *De motu animalium*.

In Hellenistic philosophy the term *phantasia* is most commonly used to refer not to the capacity to receive or interpret appearances but to those appearances themselves. Both the Epicureans and the Stoics use the word to refer to the impressions we receive through our senses. The Stoics developed a distinctive theory of the *kataleptike phantasia* or "cognitive impression," an impression that was self-evidently certain and therefore, they believed, offered, the criterion of truth and a secure basis for knowledge.

In later Greek thought the concept of *phantasia* is developed in a number of different ways. Literary critics, such as Longinus in *On the Sublime* 15.1, used it of a writer's capacity to visualize what he is describing and to recreate such visualization in the audience. In the second century CE, Philostratus, rather unusually, contrasts *phantasia* with *mimesis*, distinguishing between the ability of a sculptor like Phidias to portray gods he had never seen and the technique of copying, or imitation, employed by lesser artists. The link between imagination, dreams, and inspired prophecy suggested in Plato's *Timaeus* was developed by a number of later thinkers such as Plutarch (*De Pythiae oraculis* 397c, *De defectu oraculorum* 431bff.), Synesius (*De insomniis* chs. 4, 5, and 6) and Iamblichus (*De mysteriis* 3.2.3 and 3.14).

The Neoplatonists took over Aristotle's concept of *phantasia* along with the rest of his psychology but developed it in ways of their own. Plotinus in *Ennead* 4.3.30–31 suggests that there are two "image-making powers," one that receives images from sense-perception, and one that receives images from the intellect. The idea that imagination can receive images from the intellect is used by later Neoplatonists in connection with mathematics. Proclus, for example, in his commentary on Euclid, expounds the idea that when we are doing geometry, the figures about which we are thinking are "projections" in the imagination of innate intelligible principles.

See also Aristotle; Epicureanism and the Epicurean School; Imagination; Plato; Plotinus; Proclus; Stoicism.

Bibliography

Blumenthal, H. J. *Aristotle and Neoplatonism in Late Antiquity: Interpretations of the* De anima. London: Duckworth, 1996. See especially chapter 10.

Bundy, Murray Wright. *The Theory of Imagination in Classical and Medieval Thought.* Urbana: University of Illinois Press, 1927.

Cocking, J. M. *Imagination A Study in the History of Ideas,* edited by Penelope Murray. London: Routledge, 1991.

O'Meara, Dominic J. *Pythagoras Revived: Mathematics and Philosophy in Late Antiquity.* Oxford: Clarendon Press, 1989.

Watson, Gerard. *Phantasia in Classical Thought.* Galway: Galway University Press, 1988.

Anne Sheppard (2005)

PHENOMENALISM

Most philosophers have been led by the argument from illusion, by the causal argument, or by the introspective analysis advocated in the sense-datum theory to conclude that our immediate awareness in perception is not, as direct, or commonsense, realism claims, of material objects (of distinct, external physical entities perceptible by different persons at once) but of sensa (private, transitory, probably mental existents that may also be called sensations, sense data, ideas, representations, or impressions). Once this position is adopted, a serious difficulty arises concerning the nature and status of material objects. Representative realism claims that they exist external to us and cause the sensa or representations that correspond to them. The notorious difficulty of this view is that if all our direct awareness is concerned with the alleged effects, or sensa, how do we ever find out that material objects exist as their causes or what characteristics they possess? The theory seems to make material objects unobserved, and indeed unintelligible, causes of our perception. Although representative realism, especially in modern versions, tries to deal with this difficulty, it is still widely felt to be unsatisfactory. Therefore, alternative attempts have been made to deal with the problem of the nature of material objects. One such approach, which may loosely be called phenomenalist, is to reduce material objects to sensa, that is, to explain them as consisting solely of sensa or as being primarily groups or patterns of them. This approach results in slightly varying views, and when the term *phenomenalism* is used, reference is very often intended only to what we here call linguistic phenomenalism.

To introduce these variants of phenomenalism, we may consider one central problem that faces any attempt to reduce material objects to sensa, namely, the fragmentariness of perception. Any material object is believed to exist for long periods when it is not observed—for example, the furniture in an empty room, the beams in the roof, and so on—and some objects, such as rocks in Antarctica or under the ocean, may never have been observed. Yet when they are not observed, material objects cause no sensa, have no sensa belonging to them or constituting them. Hence, if material objects are reduced to actual sensa and consist only of them, they must cease to exist when unobserved, and those never observed must never have existed. Worse still, the material objects in a room must apparently come into and go out of existence as one looks at or away from them—the blinking of a human eye can destroy or create them. This seems such an intolerable paradox that George Berkeley, though tempted to say that material objects are simply collections of ideas, had to introduce God as their continuing basis or cause. True phenomenalism, however, can no more allow unobserved divine causes than unobserved material ones.

PROBLEM OF FRAGMENTARINESS

Several approaches to the problem of fragmentariness may be taken.

HUME. One might accept fragmentary existence, though saying it is no insuperable paradox: Objects are no more than groups or patterns of sensa, but owing to the regularity with which the same or similar series of sensa occur, we imaginatively fill in the gaps and falsely suppose that continuously enduring objects exist. This was David Hume's official view. One may say that just as a tune may bridge various pauses when no sound occurs and thus be a pattern of sounds with intervening gaps, so an object may be a group or pattern of sensa and gaps. Nevertheless, the theory is incredible and is only on the fringe of the phenomenalist group of theories. For one thing, it is difficult to see why sensa recur in groups or patterns if nothing exists in between; the existence of some continuant basis or focus of them seems a far simpler and more plausible hypothesis than what would be a series of unexplained coincidences.

SENSIBILIA. Hume himself toyed with the supposition that impressions might exist unobserved—that the gaps might be filled with unsensed sensa—and if H. H. Price is right, Hume should have developed this as his official theory. Such a development was explicitly formulated by Bertrand Russell in his *Mysticism and Logic*, where he gave the name "sensibilia" (singular, sensibile) to these "objects that have the same metaphysical and physical status as sense-data without necessarily being data to any mind." Russell regarded sensibilia as the ultimate constituents of matter; thus, objects consist of systems of sensed sensibilia (that is, sensa) and unsensed ones.

However, he soon abandoned this position, which seems untenable on two main grounds. First, it cannot explain the causal processes in perceiving. How does the sensing of sensibilia bring sensa into being? The evidence of the causal processes and of the conditioning of perception by the state of the nervous system and sense organs suggests that sensa are "generated," that is, brought into being, by events in the brain; this seems incompatible with the view that they existed as sensibilia before they were sensed. Second, what evidence is there of the exis-

tence or the nature of sensibilia? One cannot observe that such entities fill gaps between actual sensa; they are just as obscure and hypothetical as the unobserved material objects of representative realism and, in fact, introduce the very difficulty that they were intended to avoid.

FACTUAL PHENOMENALISM. Factual phenomenalism attempts to fill the gap between actual sensa with possible ones by defining material objects as groups of actual and possible sensa. This view was originated by J. S. Mill, who held that matter consists of "groups of permanent possibilities of sensation." Unfortunately, this theory also leaves quite obscure what possible sensa could be and adds the further implausibility that the gap-filling entities are purely possibilities and not actualities at all. If taken strictly, this should mean that nothing actually fills the gaps. To say that something, for instance, an accident, is possible implies that it is not actual, though it might be claimed that a possible X is an actual Y; for instance, the possible winner of a race is an actual horse, in which case once again matter will consist largely of unknown and unobservable entities. The view is also open to many of the objections to phenomenalism stated below.

LINGUISTIC PHENOMENALISM. Linguistic phenomenalism sees the basic problem before it in a different light, as one not of stating the constituents of matter but of elucidating the concept of a material object, of defining it in terms of sensa; and it seeks to achieve this not by formal definition but by a "definition in use," that is, by providing translations of statements about material objects into equivalent sets of statements about sensa. Thus, it is intended to show that what is meant by talking about tables, chairs, or similar objects can be expressed solely by talking about sensa; sometimes this is expressed by saying that material objects are logical constructions out of sensa. The underlying position is, in essence, that of Hume—that all we know to exist are sensa occurring in various patterns or sequences—but one main difference lies in the claim that these regular relationships between sensa are not something to be supplemented by imagination but are actually what we indirectly refer to by talking of material objects. Such objects are in fact coordinating concepts, devices that enable us to group and correlate our sense experiences, to identify and to refer to patterns in them.

The other main difference from Hume's position is in the linguistic presentation, the attempt to elucidate the concept by translation into a set of equivalent statements. This is in accordance with the linguistic approach contemporary with the heyday of phenomenalism, and it was held that statements about material objects and statements about sensa are simply two different ways of describing the same set of facts (facts that really concern sense experiences, their patterns and sequences). However, the sets of sensum statements not only are translations but also have a special form. Insofar as the object is observed, they are all categorical, but when it is unobserved, they are hypothetical. Thus, "I see a book on the table" is equivalent to "I have sensa *XYZ*," where *XYZ* might stand for "of a rectangular, red, solid-seeming shape on a flat brown expanse." However, "There is a book on the table in the next room" is equivalent to "If you were in the next room, you would have sensa *XYZ*." This introduces the notion of possibility that was not in Hume and that factual phenomenalism expresses so implausibly. It has the great advantage of expressing the possibility of sensa in the hypothetical form of the statement without suggesting that possible sensa are somehow constituents, perhaps the sole ones, of actual objects. Also of interest is that this approach was anticipated but not developed by Berkeley (*Principles*, Secs. 3 and 58), and occurs in places in J. S. Mill.

The result is an ingenious theory that transforms the problem of producing a viable alternative to representative realism. If successful, it would be an enormous theoretical economy; it would enable the facts of experience to be accounted for solely in terms of one type of existent, sensa, without any need to go beyond them and postulate other orders of material existence behind them. Indeed, it could further claim to be neutral between the sense-datum and adverbial analyses of sensing, for one could, as Alfred Jules Ayer did, translate material-object statements into statements about "sense contents," a term used to describe how we sense but not to refer to separate entities.

This version of phenomenalism achieved great popularity from about 1930 to 1950, particularly because it was associated with (1) logical positivism and operationalism, the meaning of material-object statements being held to lie in their mode of verification, that is, in the sensum statements that verify them; (2) Russell's analysis of abstract terms, for instance, that space is not an entity but a logical construction out of observations and measurements; (3) a way of dealing with unobserved entities in physics, namely, that electron statements are equivalent to, are logical constructions out of, sets of statements about physicists' observations. However, in the last two cases the data for the construction are prima-facie observations of material objects, and the construction is thus at a different level. Furthermore, the third case gains plausibility from the fact that electrons are

agreed to be unobservable; but no such unobservability belongs to tables and chairs.

DIFFICULTIES IN PHENOMENALISM

Because of its merits, linguistic phenomenalism became the dominant version of phenomenalism (so much so that the qualification "linguistic" may seem pedantic). All the same, many difficulties soon appeared in it and defied ingenious, almost desperately ingenious, attempts to deal with them. Further, the theory presupposed that our direct awareness is entirely of private sensa; consequently, it has suffered from the recent revival in direct realism. Without questioning that presupposition, we shall now consider the general difficulties in the theory.

LACK OF EQUIVALENCE. The original aim of linguistic phenomenalism was to give a fully equivalent translation of a material-object statement into sets of sensum statements, thus proving that it meant no more than is meant by a series of such statements. For various reasons this seems impossible. In the first place, according to the basic supposition of the sense-datum theory that is shared by phenomenalism, there is a different sensum for every different look, sound, feel, or other appearance of a material object. When a dish looks elliptical, one sensum belonging to it is obtained; when it looks round, another one is obtained; when it is felt, yet another; and so on. When one considers all the different points of view from which the dish can be seen and can look different, and then adds all the variations possible for the other senses and for other conditions of lighting and such, it would seem that the number of sensa belonging to the dish, and therefore the number of sensum statements necessary to produce a full analysis or translation of "There is a dish on the table," would be very great. Sometimes it is said that the number would be infinite because the different points of view are infinite in number; but this is dubious, for owing to object constancy, a slight change in point of view would not necessarily mean a different sensum.

At any rate, the list of sensum statements would have to be far longer than can be achieved in practice. Furthermore, if the analysis is really to be adequate, it must be systematic: The sets of sensum statements must be so ordered as to show something of the patterns or correlations that justify the material-object concept; but far from doing this, phenomenalists usually give up after one or two of the sensum statements have been formulated.

Equivalence has also been denied on the ground of difference in form. The original material-object statement is a categorical one, clearly stating that something actually exists. However, the translation is a series of hypothetical statements, and even when the apodoses of these describe experiences, their normal function seems to be either to avoid asserting actual existence (or occurrence) or to convey something quite different, such as a promise or a warning—"If you touch that, you will get burned." Indeed, "If you go to the next room, you will see a book on the table" may function as a request or a suggestion that the person go there. Worse still, in the counterfactual statements that form the translation offered about past events, actual existence is denied by implication. Thus, "Pterodactyls lived in the Mesozoic era" would probably be translated "If an observer had been present in the Mesozoic era, he would have had pterodactyl-like sensa." However, there was no observer at that time—in fact, no human beings at all—and no sensa as we know them. Thus, the assertion of actual existence is replaced in the alleged translation by assertions about what might have happened but did not.

Another bar to the claim of equivalence is that there is not full mutual entailment of original and translation. On the one hand, there might be some illusion or hallucination in which the sensum statements would be true and the material-object statement false: All the red booklike sensa might be present, and yet the object might be a box covered and shaped to look and feel like a book. This can, no doubt, be ruled out in practice by getting enough sensa, especially those resulting from such tests as opening the book, but it is doubtful how far results of such tests are really part of the meaning of the material-object statement and are therefore true features of the translation. On the other hand, the material-object statement might be true and the sensory ones false. There might be a book on the table, and yet you might not get sensa of it—the light might fail, you might be taken ill suddenly or be careless and inattentive, the book might be covered by other objects, and so on. There is a large range of conditions that would have to be stated to ensure the truth of the sensum statement. This is particularly true if the object is a small one: "There is a needle in this haystack." If you looked, would you get the needlelike sensa?

IMPURITY OF ANALYSIS. A troublesome practical difficulty facing phenomenalists is that it is impossible to specify more than a few sensa without recourse to material-object language (and not always then). Since in considering a book, the formula "sensa of a rectangular, red, solid-seeming shape on a flat brown expanse" would not differentiate the book from, say, a chocolate box, the temptation is to say "a red, rectangular, booklike sensum." But then one no longer has a translation, and the analysis

is impure; it is like saying that in French *cheval* means an animal of a *cheval*-like nature. Most phenomenalists succumb to this temptation and blame it on the poverty of language, which was designed for speaking about material objects; they say, not very convincingly, that they could invent a proper terminology for describing sensa accurately but that it would take too long.

Another type of impurity in phenomenalistic analyses lies in the protases of the hypotheticals, where reference is normally made to observers and landmarks, for example, "If you go to the next room, you will get sensa *XYZ*." Even if only your body is a material object, you are at least not a sensum; and similarly, the room is physical and material. Thus, such a hypothetical statement is not a pure sensum statement. Even giving directions by compass points, for example, "If you look north …," would seem to involve some dependence on material objects, such as the sun or a compass. Ayer suggested an ingenious way out of this difficulty: Instead of mentioning the observer and others, you describe the available sensa of the room or location, thus getting "Given sensa *ABC*, then sensa *XYZ* are obtainable," where *ABC* are "interior-of-roomlike sensa" and *XYZ* are "booklike sensa." (This also slightly mitigates the difficulty about standing conditions mentioned with respect to mutual entailment: If roomlike visual data are given, at least there is light enough to see large objects.) But once again, specifying the roomlike data without mentioning the room, though perhaps theoretically possible, presents great practical difficulties that no one has tried to surmount. Nevertheless, this second impurity problem has at least been reduced to the first one.

PUBLICITY AND PERSISTENCE OF OBJECTS. In view of the great difficulties facing any attempt at a fully equivalent and pure translation, the phenomenalist may modify his aims. He may say that by producing a few sentences of the translation and by using such short cuts as "booklike sensa" he can show the form a full analysis would take; he can give a schema or blueprint of it sufficient to show that a material-object statement really means no more than a set of sensum statements and to reveal the kind of relation between sensa that justifies the material-object concept. Others would argue that this is to abandon the real aim of phenomenalism: Unless one produces a fully equivalent translation, one cannot be sure that there is not some characteristic of material objects that cannot be rendered in terms of sensa. This objection is supported by drawing attention to several features of the ordinary concept of a material object that seem particularly resistant to phenomenalist analysis.

The first of these are the publicity of material objects (the fact that many people can perceive them at once) and their persistence or relative durability. Sensa are private and transitory, so how can statements about them convey the meaning of statements about objects? A phenomenalist answer would be that all we mean or are entitled to mean by saying that an object is perceived by two people at the same time is that they simultaneously sense similar sensa. This can be formulated as: Observer A has sensa XYZ at time t; observer B has sensa $X'Y'Z'$ also at time t; and both sets of sensa are located similarly with respect to other background sensa. The analysis can be supported by saying that when B senses visual and tactile data describable as data of his touching the object, then A gets visual data describable as data of B touching it. As to the persistence of objects, all this amounts to is that sequences of similar data recur. In development of this point, Hume claimed that it involves constancy (recurrence of the same data each time you look) and coherence (sequences of data changing in an orderly manner); Ayer, however, put most emphasis on the recurrence of reversible series of data, as when you look round the room and then back again.

But these answers are inadequate for the following reasons.

(1) They make the analysis impure by reference to observers: The whole point in the publicity of material objects is that two observers have similar sensa, as opposed to a case of double vision, where one person has two sets of sensa; in the persistence of material objects it is that one observer has the recurrent or reversible series of sensa. (Actually, the best evidence of persistence would be that A sees the object during the gaps in B's observation of it, for which mention of observers is clearly essential.)

(2) A more fundamental objection is that the assertion of the publicity and persistence of material objects is meant to convey more than the assertion of sets of sensa: One is maintaining, first, that a public object exists as the focus of two persons' perceptions and, second, that such an object continues to exist during the gaps between series of perceptions. ("Focus" here means either a common object of both perceptions, as in direct realism, or the common cause of the different sensa, as in representative realism.) It might be objected that this is simply putting forward an alternative to phenomenalism, but it seems fair to say that something like this realist claim is what we mean by a material object. Without the notion of focus or continuant, the agreement of different people's sensa or the recurrent sequences of one person's sensa are incredible series of coincidences. Why, for example, are such agreements so common in perception of objects but so rare in pains or dreams or imagery? Surely because there is something besides the sense experiences responsible for the agreement, namely, a common object or cause.

(3) Furthermore, the fragmentariness of our perception of an object is closely correlated with our own actions, as are Ayer's reversible series. If sensa of a table are replaced by sensa of the view outside the window, we must have moved our head and have looked out of the window; if we get sensa of the interior of the room after an hour's gap, we must have dozed off or have gone out and returned. This seems to show that the sensa are caused by continuing objects, the room and furniture; since the fragmentariness of our observation of these objects is explained by our actions, we do not have to assume that the objects are fragmentary as well—indeed, if they were, we should find them and their sensa appearing and disappearing without any action on our part, like the Cheshire Cat in *Alice in Wonderland*.

CAUSAL PROPERTIES AND PROCESSES. Any material object is thought to possess and to exercise many causal properties (its various powers to affect other objects by heat, propulsion, impact, pressure, chemical or electrical properties), and the concept of such an object may be claimed to involve them. They are so important that for many philosophers (for example, Price) they form the main stumbling block to the acceptance of phenomenalism, at least of the factual kind. Not only are these causal properties regularly exercised when the object is unobserved (fire still boils the water when the cook is not looking, beams still support the floor and roof even when quite hidden, and so on) but the properties and processes involved in the causation of perception—the events in the eyes and nerves of percipients—are also rarely if ever observed, and then only by scientists with special equipment. Thus, one may often perceive or experience the effects of unobserved causal properties; hence, actual sensa may be causally dependent on what are only possible ones—which is absurd.

Followers of linguistic phenomenalism may claim to avoid this. The observed movement of the hands of a clock caused by unseen works inside it, for example, is not a case of actual sensa due to possible ones. What one should say, rather, is that sensa of hands moving are sensed, and if one were to get sensa of the back of a clock with the cover removed, one would get sensa of cog wheels and shafts moving; or, more generally, given sensa of the effect, then if certain other sensa occur, sensa of the cause would also occur—S_e, and if S_x, then S_c. It must be noted that such an analysis presupposes the Humean, or regularity, view of causation, in which all that a causal relation amounts to is that the "effect" has been observed regularly to follow the "cause" (C causes E means whenever C, then E)—any conviction that the effect is brought about by some force in the cause that compels it to happen is mere superstition or is to be explained psychologically as the projection of our feeling of expectancy. However, this analysis will not satisfy those who maintain other theories of causation.

But even granting the regularity view, there is a special difficulty for phenomenalism. Presumably the "ifs" in the phenomenalist analyses are equivalent to "whenever" and themselves state regularities; whenever the floor board is taken up, one sees the beams supporting the floor. Hence, if causal relationship means no more than regularity or constant conjunction, the formula "S_e, and if S_x, then S_c" amounts to "S_e, and whenever S_x, then S_c" or "S_e, and S_x causes S_c." However, this expresses a causal relationship different from the original one; it concerns X and C rather than C and E, and, more important, expresses a relation between sensa, suggesting that one lot of sensa causes another. Indeed, this last conclusion must follow if nothing but sensory experiences exist. Thus, "The beam supports the floor" becomes "If (whenever) you have under-floor sensa, you have beam sensa," and hence, "Under-floor sensa cause beam sensa"—which is far from the original. (This point applies with greater force to the causation of perceptions; the causal properties of the percipient's nervous system must be expressed in terms of the sensa of some other person entirely—namely, the physiologist, who can observe them.)

It has been objected that all this is unfair; the causal language belongs only to material-object language, and causal relations are between material objects and events, while in the sensum language and analysis they are expressed as equivalent correlations. However, according to the regularity view of causation there is no reason why the relevant sensa, which are events and are regularly correlated, should not be causally connected. Hence, the difficulty illustrated by "under-floor sensa cause beam sensa" still stands; it suggests that causal connections are more than relations of sensa, and thus that phenomenalism is false.

Quite apart from this special difficulty, the proposed analyses of causal properties are open to the general difficulties of the phenomenalist account of the existence of objects. There is a similar impurity, particularly with respect to the causation of sense experiences, analysis of which involves reference to different observers. Equivalent translation is even more clearly ruled out: Since causal properties involve other objects as well as the object analyzed, they are more complex than such simple, sensible ones as color or shape and thus require a longer and more intricate set of sensum statements for their analysis. They also produce their effect only when a whole range of standing conditions holds, for instance, the spring will not drive the clock if the bearings are clogged with dirt. All these conditions would have to be specified for the mutual entailment of a causal material-object statement and a set of sensum statements.

See also Perception; Sensa.

Bibliography

STATEMENTS AND DEFENSES

In addition to Hume's own writings, of special interest are attempts to modernize and improve on Hume: Henry Habberley Price, *Hume's Theory of the External World* (Oxford: Clarendon Press, 1940), and Alfred Jules Ayer, *The Foundations of Empirical Knowledge* (New York: Macmillan, 1940).

On sensibilism, see Bertrand Russell, *Mysticism and Logic* (London: Allen and Unwin, 1918), and Price's *Hume's Theory of the External World*. Russell's theory developed from the phenomenalistic views he put forward in *Our Knowledge of the External World* (London: Allen and Unwin, 1914), which were criticized by C. D. Broad in "Phenomenalism," in *PAS* 15 (1914–1915): 227–251.

Factual phenomenalism is expounded by John Stuart Mill in *An Examination of Sir William Hamilton's Philosophy* (London, 1872), Ch. 11 and appendix to Ch. 12. H. H. Price, *Perception* (London: Methuen, 1932), is sympathetic, though Price finally abandons factual phenomenalism. For allied views, see Karl Pearson, *The Grammar of Science*, 3rd ed. (London: A. and C. Black, 1911), or Ernst Mach, *Contributions to the Analysis of Sensations* (Chicago, 1897; London, 1900).

Linguistic phenomenalism, including criticisms of earlier variations, may be found in A. J. Ayer, *The Foundations of Empirical Knowledge* (see above), and "Phenomenalism," in *PAS* 47 (1946–1947): 163–196, reprinted in his *Philosophical Essays* (London: Macmillan, 1952); however, his views in *The Problem of Knowledge* (London: Macmillan, 1956) involve some recantation. Also useful is D. G. C. MacNabb, "Phenomenalism," in *PAS* 41 (1940–1941): 67–90. Compare the sophisticated version by Clarence Irving Lewis in his *Analysis of Knowledge and Valuation* (La Salle, IL: Open

Court, 1947)—comments on this in Roderick M. Chisholm, "The Problem of Empiricism," in *Journal of Philosophy* 45 (19) (1948): 512–517; a reply by Lewis, ibid., 517–524—and Roderick Firth, "Radical Empiricism and Perceptual Relativity," in *Philosophical Review* 59 (1950): 164–183 and 319–331.

GENERAL CRITICISMS AND DISCUSSIONS

Introductory surveys are given by John Hospers, *Introduction to Philosophical Analysis* (New York: Prentice-Hall, 1953; London: Routledge and Paul, 1956), and Charles Harold Whiteley, *Introduction to Metaphysics* (London, 1955). There is a general discussion by A. C. Ewing, R. I. Aaron, and D. G. C. MacNabb in the symposium "The Causal Argument for Physical Objects," in *PAS*, Supp. 19 (1945): 32–100.

More advanced and definitely critical are Rodney Julian Hirst, *The Problems of Perception* (London: Allen and Unwin, 1959); Alfred Cyril Ewing, *Idealism, a Critical Survey* (London: Methuen, 1934); David Malet Armstrong, *Perception and the Physical World* (London: Routledge and Kegan Paul, 1961); J. J. C. Smart, *Philosophy and Scientific Realism* (New York: Humanities Press, 1963); Wilfrid Sellars, *Science, Perception and Reality* (New York: Humanities Press, 1963), Ch. 3; Richard Bevan Braithwaite, "Propositions about Material Objects," in *PAS* 38 (1937–1938): 269–290; R. I. Aaron, "How May Phenomenalism Be Refuted?" in *PAS* 39 (1938–1939): 167–184; George Frederick Stout, "Phenomenalism," ibid., 1–18; Isaiah Berlin, "Empirical Propositions and Hypothetical Statements," in *Mind* 59 (235) (1950): 289–312; W. F. R. Hardie, "The Paradox of Phenomenalism," in *PAS* 46 (1945–1946): 127–154; and Paul Marhenke, "Phenomenalism," in *Philosophical Analysis*, edited by Max Black (Ithaca, NY: Cornell University Press, 1950).

OTHER RECOMMENDED TITLES

Adams, Robert Merrihew. "Phenomenalism and Corporeal Substance in Leibniz." *Midwest Studies in Philosophy* 8 (1983): 217–258.

Ayer, A. J. *Language, Truth and Logic*. 2nd ed. New York: Dover, 1946.

Brandom, Robert. "Pragmatism, Phenomenalism, and Truth Talk." *Midwest Studies in Philosophy* 12 (1988): 75–93.

Fumerton, Richard. *Metaphysical and Epistemological Problems of Perception*. Lincoln: University of Nebraska Press, 1985.

Graff, Delia. "Phenomenal Continua and the Sorites." *Mind* 110 (2001): 905–935.

Jolley, Nicholas. "Leibniz and Phenomenalism." *Studia Leibnitiana* 18 (1986): 38–51.

Kamooneh, Kaveh. "Hume: A Supernaturalist and a Phenomenalist." *Philosophical Inquiry* 24 (2002): 95–102.

Moser, Paul K. "Beyond Realism and Idealism." *Philosophia* 23 (1994): 271–288.

Sosa, Ernest. "Epistemology Today: A Perspective in Retrospect." *Philosophical Studies* 40 (1981): 309–332.

Tye, Michael. "Phenomenal Consciousness: The Explanatory Gap as a Cognitive Illusion." *Mind* 108 (1999): 705–725.

Tye, Michael. "A Theory of Phenomenal Concepts." In *Minds and Persons: Royal Institute of Philosophy Supplement: 53*, edited by Anthony O'Hear. Cambridge, U.K.: Cambridge University Press, 2003.

Van Cleve, James. "C. I. Lewis' Defense of Phenomenalism." *Philosophy and Phenomenological Research* 41 (1981): 325–332.

Williamson, Timothy. *Identity and Discrimination*. Cambridge, MA: Blackwell, 1990.

R. J. Hirst (1967)
Bibliography updated by Benjamin Fiedor (2005)

PHENOMENOLOGICAL PSYCHOLOGY

"Phenomenological psychology" departs from empirical psychology by suspending naturalistic assumptions about human consciousness and by adopting a unique method, namely the phenomenological reduction, as a means of access to consciousness. Furthermore, its aim as a science is to reveal essential features of consciousness, eidetic structures, that hold for consciousness in general. Within the reduction, the focus can either be mundane, that is, directed to the mental as a region within itself, or transcendental, that is, directed to consciousness as the unique region within which all other forms of objectivity are constituted. When phenomenological psychology proceeds as an eidetic science, any results it may obtain will hold for any possible existing consciousness, but it cannot make any assertions about which of the possibilities it identifies are instantiated factually, since it must suspend all judgments about empirical facts. Phenomenological psychology reveals that mental life is intentional and at bottom temporal, and that it constitutes itself as a complicated, yet unified web of intentional relationships. This has led it to be closely associated with Gestalt theories. The task of phenomenological psychology is to reveal the various strata of mental life including both its active and passive elements, to exhibit the essential relationships among them, and to show how the complex and abstract levels are constituted out of simpler and more basic simple elements of consciousness.

In his contribution on phenomenology composed for the *Encyclopaedia Britannica* in 1928, Edmund Husserl introduced phenomenological psychology as a propaedeutic to transcendental phenomenology in general. Through the investigation of pure subjective consciousness, its forms and genesis, along with those of its correlative intentional objects, phenomenological psychology can provide the material for transcendental phenomenology. Phenomenological psychology makes clear that the starting point for phenomenology is consciousness as it presents itself to pure reflection. However, transcendental phenomenology proceeds one step further by bracketing out any necessary relationship to consciousness as a worldly phenomenon belonging to humans or any other animate beings, and by investigating the very nature of consciousness in general. Transcendental phenomenology is thus nothing other than a consequence of the universal epoché that belongs to the meaning of the transcendental question concerning the ultimate basis for cognition and its objects in general. From this perspective, the instantiation of consciousness in human and other animals is merely one example that can provide the point of departure for a change in attitude that leads to the notion of a pure transcendental consciousness in which all intentionalities, including the intention of oneself as an existing individual consciousness, are constituted.

See also Consciousness in Phenomenology; Husserl, Edmund.

Bibliography

Husserl, E. "Philosophie als strenge Wissenschaft." *Husserliana,* Vol. XXV, edited by T. Nenon and H.-R. Sepp. Dordrecht: Kluwer Academic, 1987. Translated by Q. Lauer as "Philosophy as a Rigorous Science" in *Phenomenology and the Crisis of Philosophy.* New York: Harper, 1965. Introduces his rejection of naturalistic approaches to the study of consciousness.

Husserl, E. *Phänomenologische Psychologie. Husserliana.* Vol. IX, edited by W. Biemel. The Hague, 1962. Translated by J. Scanlon as *Phenomenological Psychology.* The Hague: Nijhoff, 1977. Provides detailed analyses illustrating Husserl's general methodology and many specific results. Contains all four drafts of Husserl's article for the *Encyclopaedia Britannica,* and the subsequent Amsterdam lecture, which was based upon that article.

Gurwitsch, A. "Husserl's Conception of Phenomenological Psychology." *Review of Metaphysics* 19 (1965–1966): 689–727.

Kockelmans, J. J. *Edmund Husserl's Phenomenology.* West Lafayette, IN: Purdue University Press, 1994. An introduction to Husserl's mature thinking through a careful and extensive commentary on the *Encyclopaedia* article.

Thomas Nenon (1996)

PHENOMENOLOGY

"Phenomenology" is a term that has been used in as many widely varying senses in modern philosophy as has the term that names the subject matter of this science, "phenomena."

Johann Heinrich Lambert, a German philosopher contemporary with Immanuel Kant, first spoke of a discipline that he called "phenomenology" in his *Neues Organon* (Leipzig, 1764). He took "phenomenon" to refer to the illusory features of human experience and hence defined phenomenology as the "theory of illusion." Kant himself used "phenomenology" only twice, but he gave a new and broader sense to "phenomenon" that, in turn, resulted in a redefinition of "phenomenology." Kant distinguished objects and events as they appear in our experience from objects and events as they are in themselves, independently of the forms imposed on them by our cognitive faculties. The former he called "phenomena"; the latter, "noumena," or "things-in-themselves." All we can ever know, Kant thought, are phenomena.

The next generation of philosophers, notably G. W. F. Hegel, was at great pains to show that this was a mistake. Hegel's first major work, *Phenomenology of the Spirit* (1807), traced the development of Spirit (or Mind) through various stages, in which it apprehends itself as phenomenon, to the point of full development, where it is aware of itself as it is in itself—as noumenon. Phenomenology is the science in which we come to know mind as it is in itself through the study of the ways in which it appears to us.

In the middle of the nineteenth century, the definition of "phenomenon" was further extended until it became synonymous with "fact" or "whatever is observed to be the case." As a consequence, "phenomenology" acquired the meaning that it possesses most frequently in contemporary uses—a purely descriptive study of any given subject matter. In this sense, Sir William Hamilton, in his *Lectures on Metaphysics* (1858), spoke of phenomenology as a purely descriptive study of mind. Similar was Eduard von Hartmann's use of the word in the title of his book *Phenomenology of Moral Consciousness* (1878), which had as its task a complete description of moral consciousness. When the American philosopher C. S. Peirce used the term *phenomenology,* he had in mind not only a descriptive study of all that is observed to be real but also of whatever is before the mind—perceptions of the real, illusory perceptions, imaginations, or dreams. It was the task of phenomenology to develop a list of categories embracing whatever can be included in the widest possible meaning of "to be." Peirce introduced this sense of the term in 1902.

The changes described so far are all due to extensions of the meaning of "phenomenon," but phenomenology, the science of phenomena in these different senses, remained one field of study among others, having a relation to philosophy as a whole comparable to those of logic, ethics, and aesthetics. Frequently it was recommended as a descriptive study that was to precede any attempt to provide explanations of the phenomena. But since Edmund Husserl employed the term in the early 1900s, it has become the name of a way of doing philosophy—by using the phenomenological method. For the phenomenologists, who regard their method as the only correct way of proceeding in philosophy, phenomenology is therefore the best and perhaps the only legitimate way of philosophizing today. For other philosophers, phenomenology is one school or movement in philosophy today. At the same time, however, the older sense of the term persists. "Phenomenology" is therefore used in two distinct senses. In its wider sense it refers to any descriptive study of a given subject. In the narrower sense it is the name of a philosophical movement. This entry will deal with phenomenology in the second sense.

THE MOVEMENT AND ITS ORIGINS

"Phenomenology" became the name of a school of philosophy whose first members were found in several German universities in the years before World War I, notably at Göttingen and Munich. Between 1913 and 1930 this group published a series of volumes of phenomenological studies titled *Jahrbuch für Philosophie und phänomenologische Forschung*, whose editor in chief was Husserl, the most original and most influential thinker of the group. Most of the better-known members of the phenomenological movement—Moritz Geiger, Alexander Pfänder, Max Scheler, and Oscar Becker—were coeditors, at least for a time. Martin Heidegger was another coeditor, but he cannot be counted among the phenomenologists without serious qualifications. Other major figures in the movement were Adolf Reinach and Hedwig Conrad-Martius.

The contributions to the *Jahrbuch* ranged from Husserl's writings about the foundations of phenomenology, to essays in the philosophy of mind and Scheler's major work on ethics, to pieces on the nature of analytic judgments and the paradoxes in set theory. As the interests of the various phenomenologists differed, so did their conceptions of phenomenology. These disagreements emerged only gradually, as Husserl developed the theory of the phenomenological method further and encountered a progressively more critical reception among his fellow phenomenologists. At the outset, there was general agreement that phenomenology was to be descriptive and that it was to describe phenomena by means of direct awareness (*Anschauung*). It is best to

begin to clarify these terms by showing what they could, but do not, mean.

DESCRIPTION

The terms *descriptive*, *phenomenon*, and *direct awareness* all suggest that phenomenology is here used in its wider sense as a purely descriptive science of observable phenomena. But this wider sense of the term does not include what for the phenomenologists is the most important feature of phenomenology—that it is a nonempirical science. From the very beginnings of the phenomenological movement, when the conception of phenomenology was otherwise still quite vague, there was general agreement that phenomenology does not describe empirically observable matters of fact. Insisting on this, the early phenomenologists took a stand in opposition to philosophical views then in vogue.

Kant had distinguished three kinds of statements: empirical statements, statements true by definition (which he called "analytic"), and a third kind that he called "synthetic a priori." After being temporarily eclipsed by the German idealism of the early nineteenth century, Kant found many vigorous adherents in the later decades of that century. But there were also many philosophers who found Kant's account of the third type of statement—the statements that are neither empirical nor analytic—profoundly unsatisfactory and who, instead of attempting to supply an alternative account, rejected the tripartite classification altogether. This was done, for instance, by the German positivists Ernst Mach and Richard Avenarius, who insisted that there are no nonempirical statements that are not analytic. Of equal, if not greater, importance were those philosophers who regarded all statements as empirical. Analytic statements seemed to them clearly to rest on "the artful manipulation of language" (Mill's phrase), and they thought it therefore implausible that the statements of logic and/or mathematics should be analytic, that they should be true, and, more important, that they should be applicable to objects of everyday experience and science merely by virtue of an arbitrary choice of definitions. Accordingly, John Stuart Mill in England and Christoph Sigwart in Germany, among others, sought to show that statements in logic and mathematics are no less empirical than statements in the sciences.

In the case of logic, the most plausible argument for such a view begins with the observation that logic deals with correct and incorrect thinking. Thinking is a mental or psychological activity and must, therefore, be studied in psychology just as any other mental or psychological activity. It seems to follow, then, that logic is either a special field within empirical psychology or a practical discipline whose theoretical foundations are supplied by empirical psychology. In the former case, the relation of logic to psychology is comparable to that of learning theory or abnormal psychology to psychology as a whole. In the latter view, logic is related to psychology as surveying is to geometry or accounting to arithmetic.

OPPOSITION TO PSYCHOLOGISM. The phenomenologists were not the first to question the identification of logical with psychological statements—a view they called "psychologism." But while some other philosophers had approached the issue by distinguishing logic from psychology in terms of the distinction between theoretical and practical disciplines, the phenomenologists attacked the identification of logical with psychological statements on the grounds that the latter are empirical statements and the former are not. The most sustained and painstaking critique of psychologism is contained in the first volume of Husserl's *Logische Untersuchungen* (Logical Investigations; Halle, 1900–1901), and the arguments in that book served as a first rallying point for phenomenologists.

Husserl's attack on psychologism had a special edge to it because his *Philosophie der Arithmetik* (Philosophy of Arithmetic; Vol. I, Halle, 1891; the projected second volume was never published) had been a frankly psychologistic account of arithmetic. His change of heart was in part occasioned by a controversy with the German mathematician and philosopher of mathematics Gottlob Frege, in which Frege had insisted that a sharp line be drawn between psychological statements, on the one hand, and logical and/or mathematical ones, on the other.

Husserl devoted an entire book to the detailed examination and refutation of every variety of psychologistic doctrine, taking careful account of each view and trying to show its inadequacy. Underlying all his arguments, however, were a few general principles to which he appealed again and again in the course of his discussion:

(1) Psychology deals with facts; therefore its statements are empirical. It has not, until now, produced any precise scientific laws, and its generalizations are vague. The rules of logic, on the other hand, are precise. Hence, psychological generalizations can neither be identical with logical laws nor be premises from which they may be derived.

(2) Empirical statements are probable, at best, for there is always a real possibility that further evidence will show them to be false. Logical truths are necessary truths. A logical principle such as *modus ponens* ("Given that 'If *p*, then *q*' is true and that '*p*' is true, '*q*' is true") is not probable; it is necessarily valid.

(3) Closely connected with (1) and (2) is the argument that empirical generalizations rest on induction; they are derived from a number of individual cases. This is not true of logical rules.

Both (2) and (3) are supported by pointing out that where there is a conflict between a logical principle and an empirical generalization, the logical principle will always emerge victorious because necessary truth is not to be refuted by a probable statement and logical truth cannot be shown to be false by an inductive generalization.

(4) The empirical generalizations of psychology produce, at best, causal laws, and logical principles are not causal laws. Premises and conclusions of an argument are not related as cause and effect; the truth of a conclusion is not the effect of the truth of the premises. Causal relations hold between events, and events happen at definite times in definite places. But the premises of an argument do not "happen," nor does the conclusion; they are either true or false. In a valid argument the truth of the conclusion "follows" from the premises; it is not the effect of events called premises.

(5) Empirical laws imply matters of fact; logical rules do not. Since empirical laws are, presumably, derived from the observation of particulars, the existence of such particulars in some place and at some time can be inferred from the truth of the empirical law. *Modus ponens*, on the other hand, does not imply that there exists, in a particular place and at a particular time, a pair of statements of the form "If *p*, then *q*" and "*p*." Nor are any corresponding facts implied by any other logical law. This point is sometimes stated in a phrase, borrowed from Gottfried Wilhelm Leibniz, that empirical laws are true only for this actual world; logical laws are true "for all possible worlds."

The upshot of these arguments is that logical and empirical statements differ in kind. Logical statements are precise, necessarily true, and not derived inductively from particulars. They are, or give rise to, logical rules, not causal laws, and they do not imply matters of fact. Empirical statements, on the other hand, are vague, probably (but not necessarily) true, and based on inductive generalizations. They are, or give rise to, causal laws and imply the existence of matters of fact. Quite clearly, in the refutation of psychologism, the decisive argument, for Husserl, consisted in showing that there are two kinds of statements: empirical and nonempirical. Phenomenological statements are to be nonempirical.

To deny that phenomenological statements are empirical is to deny that their truth or falsity depends on sensory observation. But if not on sensory observation, on what does their truth depend? Some philosophers might be inclined to say that phenomenological statements are analytic. Insofar as only those statements are analytic that are true by virtue of explicit definition of terms, phenomenologists deny that their statements are analytic. We shall have abundant evidence that they are right in this, for phenomenological statements are not true by virtue of stipulation of meaning. But insofar as "analytic" is used in some other sense, it is not helpful either to assert or to deny that phenomenological statements are analytic; the meaning of the term *analytic* is much debated in contemporary philosophy and has therefore become extremely obscure. It is more profitable to ask the phenomenologists about the truth conditions of their statements. Their preliminary answer to this question consists in introducing the term *phenomenon* by saying that phenomenological statements are true if they accurately describe phenomena. This answer, however, remains merely a verbal maneuver unless *phenomenon* can be shown to have a clear and definite meaning.

PHENOMENA

We have seen that *phenomenon* is a technical philosophical term that different philosophers have used in very different senses. The phenomenologists sometimes say that "phenomenon" is their name for whatever appears to us in "immediate experience." By "immediate experience" they do not mean sensory observations that have not been interpreted or classified under general concepts ("raw sense data"). Like many other contemporary philosophers, the phenomenologists are not at all sure that there are for us any sensory observations that are not interpreted or classified under general concepts. The appeal to phenomena or to immediate experience is therefore not an appeal to simple, uninterpreted data of sensory experience. Furthermore, the appeal to phenomena does not presuppose the existence of a special class of objects called "phenomena." The phenomenologists do not claim to have discovered that besides all the kinds of entities found in this world (physical objects, thoughts,

numbers, feelings, poems, etc.) there is one other class, phenomena. Any object is a phenomenon if looked at or considered in a particular way. This particular way of looking at all kinds of objects is recommended in the slogan "Zu den Sachen!"

Literally translated, this slogan means "To the things!" where "things" must be taken in the widest possible sense to embrace all possible kinds of objects. Like other slogans, moreover, this one gains its force from having more than one meaning. If a German says to someone, "Zur Sache!" he is exhorting him, as we would say, "to get down to business." "Zu den Sachen!" admonishes one to get down to the proper business of the philosopher by examining and describing all kinds of objects in the particular way that reveals them as phenomena.

This explication of "phenomenon" is, so far, circular. To clarify what is meant by that term, we must therefore explain what alternative ways of doing philosophy are excluded by telling us to examine and describe phenomena. We must explain the polemical import of the slogan "Zu den Sachen!" Once this is done, we must pursue the concept of phenomenon further by attempting to clarify the nature of the examination and description that shows all kinds of objects as phenomena.

OPPOSITION TO REDUCTIONISM. The polemical import of "Zu den Sachen!" is readily made clear. In it the phenomenologists expressed their opposition to all reductionism, or, as Reinach called them, "nothing-but philosophies." Such philosophies are couched in sentences like "Logical laws are nothing but psychological laws," "Moral laws are nothing but the expressions of the mores of a given society," and "Aesthetic judgments are nothing but expressions of personal taste." To oppose all views of this sort would seem dogmatic. Some "nothing-but" statements may be false, but perhaps others are true; and one would think that each would have to be examined on its merits rather than be rejected summarily as an example of reductionism. However, the phenomenologists did not attack these "nothing-but" views on the grounds that they are false but on the grounds that the philosophers who held them, held them for the wrong kinds of reasons.

Psychologism, which is just one example of reductionism, did not assert that logical laws are nothing but psychological laws in the light of a thorough examination of the nature of logical laws that proved that they are identical with psychological ones. If someone challenged the psychologistic philosopher's views, he was not invited to examine for himself the nature of logical laws and to discover that they did not differ from those in psychology. Instead, he was given an argument from which it followed that logical laws "must" be psychological ones. Psychologistic assertions about logical and psychological laws do not result from an examination of laws in logic and psychology but are the logical consequences of certain more general assumptions. These assumptions themselves are not examined but are taken as self-evident.

Reductionism as attacked by the phenomenologist is the outcome of accepting certain statements that have not been examined carefully. If the implications of these assumptions are shown to conflict with facts about the world, the reductionist does not, the phenomenologists say, reexamine his original assumptions. Instead, he redefines the terms used to describe the facts about the world in such a way that the contradictions between these descriptions of facts and the implications of the original assumptions disappear. The redefinitions necessitated by the conflict between assumptions and facts are expressed in the "nothing-but" statements.

Opposition to phenomenalism. An example of a specific reductionist view attacked by the phenomenologists will clarify the process. David Hume's empiricism was attacked for its phenomenalism, that is, for its view that physical objects, as well as human beings, are no more than collections of their observable properties. ("Phenomenology" must not be confused with "phenomenalism.") "Observable properties" in this context refers exclusively to sensory qualities like shape, color, sound, etc. This view of Hume's did not issue from a careful examination of the nature of physical objects. Instead, it was a product of his psychological theories about the origin and meaning of concepts and words. Hume held that all concepts are either derived directly from sensory experience or are complex collections of such concepts. He regarded it as a consequence of this view that all concepts refer either to sensory qualities like shape, color, and sound or to complex collections of these. He also thought that all nouns are the names of concepts. It follows from this that all nouns naming physical objects refer to concepts that can be completely analyzed into simple concepts referring to sensory qualities. Hence physical objects—what is named by physical object nouns—are no more than complex collections of sensory qualities. However, this view is not supported by a careful examination of physical objects themselves but follows from, and hence "must" be true in the light of, Hume's psychology and views on the meanings of words.

Opposition to psychological atomism. Another target of the antireductionist polemic was the then popular attempt by philosophical psychologists like Wilhelm Wundt to define consciousness as a set of contents—sensations, feelings, affects—on which operations—association and apperception—are performed. This view was not the product of careful examination and description of the series of phenomena that we call consciousness but was a logical consequence of more general assumptions about the world. It missed, the phenomenologists maintained, the essential characteristic of consciousness that they, following Franz Brentano, called "intentionality."

Opposition to scientism. Also objectionable was the so-called scientism of the positivists Mach and Avenarius. Scientism regarded scientific statements as premises in philosophical arguments such that the truth of statements in philosophy depends on the truth of scientific statements. This view was a direct consequence of two assumptions: that all statements are either empirical or analytic, and that all empirical statements are, at least ideally, statements in science. Given these assumptions, there is a choice between restricting philosophy to the practice of logic, in which statements are often thought to be analytic, or saying that philosophical truths are empirical. If we choose the latter alternative, philosophical statements "must" have scientific premises.

But this conclusion, phenomenologists held, was drawn without paying careful attention to actual and possible functions of philosophy, which, they held, is independent of science. In this they were not motivated by any hostility toward science; on the contrary, their aim was to establish philosophy as a "rigorous science" by means of the phenomenological method. Husserl had discussed this aim at some length in his article "Philosophie als strenge Wissenschaft" ("Philosophy as Rigorous Science," in *Logos*, Vol. I, 1910–1911, 289–341). This phenomenological and rigorously scientific philosophy was expected to provide the foundations for the existing sciences by providing clear explications of the concepts that the sciences use but do not themselves explicate. For instance, the definition of number, in which Reinach was interested, was considered a task for phenomenology. Husserl was concerned with clarifying epistemological terms such as *meaning* and *truth*. So conceived, phenomenology had to be independent of the existing sciences because it was to explicate the concepts and procedures presupposed by them. To consider philosophy a branch or subsidiary of existing science was one more example of "nothing-but" philosophy.

Presuppositionless inquiry. Here it must be asked whether philosophers must not make certain assumptions. We cannot, it would seem, show that all statements are true by reference to the truth of other statements; some we must merely assume to be true. But phenomenologists are unconvinced by this sort of argumentation. Statements in phenomenology are not true because certain other statements are true; they are true because they describe the phenomena correctly. In order to achieve true description, the phenomenologist must resist the temptation to make assumptions and, afterward, to define his terms in such a way as to make the descriptions of facts consistent with the assumptions and what must be inferred from them. The phenomenologist does not frame theories; he merely examines and then describes phenomena as they present themselves to his unprejudiced view. Having no theoretical commitment and only one practical one—to examine all phenomena carefully and to take none of them as familiar or understood until they have been carefully explicated and described—the phenomenologist says that his science is descriptive and that it is presuppositionless.

This obviously does not mean that at any given time the phenomenologist may not be operating with certain unexamined assumptions—this can always happen. The claim of presuppositionlessness expresses the resolution to eschew all unexamined assumptions and the belief that such assumptions are unnecessary; No statement must be taken as true without examination. Phenomenology does not need any true but unexamined premises; the truth of all its premises can be tested by examining the phenomena.

This sheds some light on the second, affirmative sense of the slogan "Zu den Sachen!"—an exhortation to examine phenomena and to make them the sole touchstone of the truth of philosophical statements. But the precise import of this exhortation remains unclear until the meaning of "phenomenon" has been explicated, so this is a pressing question. It is also a question fraught with particular difficulties. Phenomena, as was stated, are those aspects of objects of every kind that are revealed by a particular way of looking at objects. The phenomenal aspects of objects are not revealed by ordinary empirical observation but only by looking at them as phenomena. The meaning of "phenomenon," on the other hand, cannot merely be stipulated in analytic statements. Hence, explications of "phenomenon" must result from using the phenomenological method and must be couched in phenomenological statements. But what these statements are cannot be made clear until it is clear what a phenomenon is, nor do we know what the phenomenological method is until we know what a phenomenon is.

"METHODOLOGICAL CIRCLE." The entire phenomenological enterprise is involved in a circle that can be called the "methodological circle." This methodological circle does not differ formally from the circle involved in any kind of logical investigation where the rules of inference, for instance, which the completed investigation hopes to formulate and justify must be employed during the course of the investigation itself so that its result, the logical rules, is the product of the application of the rules to themselves. The existence of this circle does not prove that logic is an impossible or unjustifiable discipline, nor does its presence in phenomenology support an analogous argument against it.

The occurrence of this circle should, however, put one on his guard against taking for completed analyses statements made by phenomenologists that are, in fact, merely gropings toward and anticipations of what phenomenology, its method, and the completed theory of method will be like in some indefinitely remote future. Phenomenology does not exist as a set of doctrines but at best as a method—and this method is to be developed by applying phenomenology to itself. Hence, even the phenomenological method is still in the process of being clarified, properly described, and elaborated; it is, at least to date, quite incomplete.

Husserl liked to refer to himself as a "perpetual beginner," an expression that meant several things to him. In one of its senses, it expressed what was just said about phenomenology: It is a method that can only be progressively developed by applying it to itself. Accordingly, most of Husserl's published works are discussions of the phenomenological method. This has sometimes been taken as a symptom of an excessive fondness for writing manifestoes, but discussions of phenomenological method are not of the nature of manifestoes prior to doing phenomenology, nor are they propaedeutics. Only while doing phenomenology can we clarify its method. To write about it was, in Husserl's case, to do phenomenology.

THE INTUITION OF ESSENCES

The preceding discussion has brought to light three properties of phenomenological statements:

(1) Phenomenological statements are nonempirical.

(2) Phenomenological statements are descriptive.

(3) Phenomenological statements describe phenomena.

These leave the task of making clear what phenomena are, a matter of disagreement among phenomenologists:

Most of the schisms within the phenomenological movement originate in disagreements about the set of conditions necessary for anything to be a phenomenon. We shall examine a variety of conditions proposed, beginning with the most simple and proceeding to more complex sets as the simpler ones turn out to be incomplete. The criterion of completeness for this set of necessary conditions is that any set of conditions required for anything to be a phenomenon must at least be consistent with the first requirement for phenomenological statements—that they be nonempirical. Hence, the set of conditions laid down for anything to be a phenomenon must clearly rule out any possibility that phenomena can be described in empirical statements.

The simplest specification of phenomenon, given by some early phenomenologists, contains only two conditions:

(1) Phenomena are essences.

(2) Phenomena are intuited.

The reason for identifying phenomena with essences is instructive. As we saw, it was claimed that there are some entities by virtue of which statements in phenomenology are said to be true or false. These entities (or phenomena) are not particular observable objects by reference to which empirical statements are confirmed or disconfirmed. Instead, the phenomenologists say, they are the necessary and invariant features of objects. Phenomenology explicates those features of any given object without which it could not truly be said to be the object that it is. These most general, necessary, and invariant features of objects have been called "essences" by other philosophers, and, following that terminological tradition, the phenomenologists also talk about essences.

Many philosophers in the past have held that statements about essences are empirical statements, arrived at by comparison of many examples of a type of object and extracting from the descriptions of all these examples the common features by means of some kind of generalization. Such a process has often been called abstraction. Abstract statements, since they are logically dependent on empirical descriptions of particular cases, are themselves empirical statements. Phenomenological statements, on the other hand, are, for the reasons given, not empirical statements. Hence, phenomenological statements are not reached by abstraction. They are, phenomenologists say, derived from a scrutiny of particular cases by seeing, intuition, or intuition of essences (*Wesensschau*).

The identification of phenomena as essences brings us one step closer to the goal of clarifying the particular

way of looking at objects that reveals objects as phenomena. It turns out to be a species of intuition. Phenomenology is a form of intuitionism and has, accordingly, acquired the ill repute of all intuitionisms of being no more than a veiled refusal to provide evidence for one's philosophical statements. But sometimes such a refusal can be justified. Intuitionism is objectionable only if the philosopher is not willing to argue either about the nature of his intuition or about the justification for appealing to it in this case—if his appeal to intuition is merely intended to terminate philosophical debate. The phenomenologists' appeal to intuition is not of this kind. Hence more can, and must, be said about intuition.

Intuition seems to be a psychological term. Its German counterpart, *Anschauung*, often means no more than "seeing." The objects of seeing, in its ordinary sense, are empirical objects. Essences are not empirical objects, so they cannot be seen in any ordinary sense of that term. Hence, intuition must be seeing of some extraordinary kind. One might suggest that the phenomenologists claim to have discovered one more human cognitive faculty than had been known before, but such a discovery of an actual human faculty would have to be couched in empirical statements. Phenomenologists do not make empirical statements, so they cannot claim—nor do they—to discover previously unknown cognitive faculties.

The point of introducing intuition is not psychological but epistemological. To appeal to intuition is not to make a psychological statement about the causal origins of certain statements but an epistemological one about the sort of evidence that will be relevant to them. To say that we know essences by intuition is to say, negatively, that the truth or falsity of statements about essences is not dependent on the truth about empirical statements.

The appeal to intuition makes another positive, epistemological point: Our acquaintance with essences possesses an epistemological feature also possessed by our sensory acquaintance with empirical objects. This logical feature is sometimes described by saying that what we see is described in self-validating statements. A statement, "*P*," about particular objects is self-validating if the strongest evidence that we can adduce for it is a statement like "I have seen that *P*" or "I have observed that *P*." We cannot, therefore, claim that "*P*" is true because there is some other true statement, "*Q*," from which "*P*" can be inferred and that is not equivalent to "*P*." Statements about essences are self-validating in the same sense. Given any statement, "*E*," of the form "_____ is the essence of _____," we cannot claim that "*E*" is true because there is some other true statement, "*F*," which is not equivalent to "*E*" and from which we can infer "*E*." Of course, some statements about the existence of particular objects may be deducible from other statements, and it is similarly true that some statements about essences may be deducible from other statements. But such a deduction does not provide stronger evidence for statements about empirical existence or about essences than do self-validating statements.

Phenomenological statements are not derived by means of abstraction from particular statements, since, if they were so derived, they would not be self-validating. But they are not the only self-validating statements; empirical statements are also self-validating. An adequate account of phenomena must state more than that phenomena are revealed in the intuition of essences; it must specify this intuition to clarify in what respects it differs from the simple seeing of objects of sensory observation.

BRACKETING EXISTENCE: FREE IMAGINATIVE VARIATION OF EXAMPLES

In the light of the problem about the meaning of intuition, the reason for introducing a further condition defining "phenomenon" becomes clearer. This condition is not accepted by all phenomenologists but was regarded as necessary by Husserl, Pfänder, Reinach, and Scheler. We are in a position, they said, to describe objects as phenomena only after we have "bracketed existence" or "suspended our belief in the existence of objects." Husserl calls this the "phenomenological epoche" or the "phenomenological reduction." *Epoche* was borrowed from the Skeptics, but Husserl's use of it differed from theirs.

These references to "bracketing" or "suspending belief in existence," together with the talk about essences, led to the view that phenomenology is a kind of essentialism and, as such, is diametrically opposed to existentialism. There is no room here to bring out all the confusions that produced this fairly common interpretation; suffice it to say that the phenomenological epoche is not achieved by resolving to make no more statements about existence or what exists. To bracket existence is not to eliminate existence in general or existing entities in particular from the list of possible objects for phenomenological study.

In the light of Husserl's repeated insistence on the close similarities between his phenomenology and René Descartes's methodical doubt, the phrase "suspending belief in the existence of objects" is often taken as a description of Cartesian doubt. But this is a misunderstanding, for Husserl insisted on distinguishing suspending belief in existence from doubting existence. This distinction cannot, therefore, be simply ignored.

Suppose a young woman states that she has direct evidence that she is terribly attractive to red-haired men. Her statement is not derived from a psychological law about the preferences of red-haired men or from a physiological one about their exceptional susceptibility to her figure and coloring. Her statement, a direct inductive generalization, is the result of her own experiences with red-haired men and tells us something about many or all of the members of the class of red-haired men. Besides all being red-haired and male, they have one further property: They cannot resist the charms of this young woman. In order to substantiate such a statement, she would have to cite cases of a number of red-haired men who at various times, under various circumstances, have given indubitable proof of their devotion. Two things are important here: that the red-haired men really exist and that their devotion to her is real. The truth of the inductive generalization depends at least on those two conditions. On the other hand, if the generalizations are correct, it follows that there exist (or existed) several red-haired men in this particular condition. If, however, the red-haired men do not exist or if their attachment is a figment of this young woman's imagination, then the general statement is false (unless evidence of a different kind can be found).

The story of this young woman was told in order to exemplify the relation of empirical generalizations to particular empirical statements—of "I am irresistible to red-haired men" to, for instance, "A red-haired matinee idol in New York committed suicide over me," and of both of these to the facts of the case. These relations were exemplified with an imaginary example, for it is quite unimportant that I do not know any young woman of this description. Where a description serves as an example in this sense (*example* is an ambiguous word), it is quite irrelevant whether the object described exists or not. If, on the contrary, I am interested in making a general statement about objects observed, it makes all the difference in the world whether the particular objects covered in my generalization exist and exist as described.

This is one sense of "bracketing existence." When existence has been bracketed in this sense, the descriptions of objects or situations do not serve as premises for an inductive generalization (or an abstraction), but as examples. But "example" is used in several senses. Sometimes it is used to designate one instance of an empirical generalization, but this is not the sense used here. At other times, examples serve a merely pedagogical function. I might have told my story about the young woman merely to provide a concrete illustration of abstract truth about empirical generalizations, in order to make the abstract statement easier to understand. In a third sense—"example" is used in phenomenology in this sense—the example both serves as an illustration and has evidential functions. In that case, the truth of the statement about empirical generalizations depends on the accuracy of the description of the example. I claim that my general statement is true because the description of the particular example is accurate, but how do I know whether a description is accurate so that it can have evidential force as an example? Since we have bracketed existence, I cannot say that the description is accurate because the case described has actually been observed to exist in a particular place and at a particular time, for examples need not be actual existents.

In order to understand this sense of bracketing existence, we must be able to answer two questions: (1) When can the description of an example rightly be said to be accurate? (2) How is a phenomenological statement to be derived from an example?

In this context Husserl talked about a procedure that he called "free imaginative variation," comparable to what Anglo American philosophers call the method of "counter-examples." Here we describe an example and then transform the description by adding or deleting one of the predicates contained in the description. With each addition or deletion, we ask whether the amended description can still be said to describe an example of the same kind of object as that which the example originally described was said to exemplify. Sometimes we shall have to say that if we add this predicate to the description or take that one away, what is then described is an example of a different kind of object from that exemplified by the original example. At other times the additions or deletions will not affect the essential features of the kind of object exemplified by the different examples.

In this way we discover the necessary and invariant features of a given kind of thing that the example must possess in order to be an example of that kind of thing. We also discover which features are accidental and hence irrelevant to the question whether this object, as described, is or is not an example of a certain kind of thing. What we discover is what phenomenologists call the "essence" of objects.

For example, let us suppose that we meet someone who does not have the usual five senses but only three: sight, touch, and hearing. We might be perplexed, but we

should still call him a person. The same would hold if he had three more senses than normal persons. But suppose we met someone who looked like a person but seemed to be deaf and blind, and without any tactile, olfactory, or gustatory sensations. He would still be regarded as a person, although as a seriously defective one. But suppose further that we find that this creature looks like a human being except that it has no sense organs at all. Would he nonetheless be called a person? No. An animal? No. A plant? Not really. We have no word in our language for such a being. We would not know what to say about it.

Here we have varied in imagination an example of a person with reference to one predicate, "possessing sense organs." We find that in order for anything to be a person, it must have sense organs of some kind; there is an essential (necessary and invariant) relation between "person" and "possessing sense organs." The results of free imaginative variation are statements of such essential connections. Since statements about phenomena are one kind of statement about essences (and vice versa), the statements resulting from this procedure are phenomenological statements.

"EPISTEMOLOGICAL CIRCLE." Phenomenological statements are made while existence is and remains bracketed. If true, they are so not because they describe something that we have directly observed. Nor are they true because they are warranted by a series of observations of particular objects or events. Hence, they do not imply the past or present existence of particular objects in just the way in which empirical generalizations imply it. All that is asserted in the phenomenological statement is that if any being is an example of a person, then it must have sense organs. We are, therefore, making an assertion about the necessary relations of properties: Whatever has the property of being a person must also possess the property of having sense organs.

This is the method of free imaginative variation. It would seem to provide an answer to the second question raised earlier—how a phenomenological statement is to be derived from an example. But the same procedure can also be said to provide an answer to the first question, how we decide whether an example is described accurately—whether the description contains all the essential predicates so that the thing described may rightly be said to be an example of a certain kind of object. For, once we have made clear the invariant features of the sort of thing exemplified, we are in a position to say whether the example contains all those necessary features. But to use free imaginative variation to answer both questions is, of course, circular; we derive the phenomenological statement from any given example by means of free imaginative variation and then confirm that the original example was accurately described because it possesses the invariant features expressed in the phenomenological statement. It would seem that we need an independent criterion for deciding the accuracy of the description of any given example, but there is no discussion of such an independent test in the writings of the phenomenologists. The phenomenological method appears, therefore, to be circular in a second sense that might be called the "epistemological circle."

Phenomenology, as we saw, is circular because it clarifies its own method while using it (the methodological circle); it is also circular, we see now, because it confirms its statements by reference to examples and then attests the accuracy of the descriptions of these examples by reference to the statements derived from them (the epistemological circle). We must now show that what we claimed earlier for the methodological circle—that its presence cannot be construed as an argument against phenomenology—is true for the epistemological circle as well. This will be argued for by an examination of a second sense of "bracketing existence." In this second sense, "bracketing existence" refers to the transition from nonreflective to reflective thinking.

BRACKETING EXISTENCE: PHENOMENOLOGY AND REFLECTION

In free imaginative variation we ask ourselves about any given property of an example, "Is this a necessary feature for being a such and such? Is that?" For our answer we do not appeal to empirical observation. Neither do we give an answer simply by deciding to regard some particular feature as essential. We do not define our terms arbitrarily; instead, with each variation, we ask ourselves whether the example described could still be recognizable as an example of the same sort of thing as that exemplified before. We ask ourselves what features an object must have in order to be recognized as an example of a certain kind of object. What we discover are necessary conditions for recognizing a certain kind of thing.

But recognition presupposes previous acquaintance. I cannot recognize someone whom I meet for the first time, unless I have seen pictures of him or have been given his description or perhaps dreamed of him before. But if we can recognize only what we know already, then we must already know the necessary features of the objects that we are able to recognize. In that case, there would seem to be no need to bracket existence and to

vary the examples freely in imagination in order to discover their essential features, since the entire procedure presupposes that we know these essential features all along.

The resolution of this difficulty comes when we consider that the word *know* has two radically different senses, which some English philosophers have called, respectively, "knowing how" and "knowing that." The latter refers to knowledge expressed in statements. To "know that" something is the case is to be able to put what is known into words. I can show that I know a person by describing his looks; however, it is of course also possible that I should know a person and yet be quite unable to give any sort of adequate description of his looks. It is often very difficult to give a good description of those persons whom we know very well. I know them, not in the sense that I can describe them but that I could recognize them anywhere. I can pick them out of a crowd without hesitation. I can identify them by their voice or their walk, although I might be hard put either to describe in words or to imitate them. This second kind of knowledge is "knowing how"; in the example, I know how to recognize a person.

These two kinds of knowledge are independent of each other. It is not a necessary condition for being able to do something, such as recognize someone, that I should be able to *say* that he is a person of a certain description. Conversely, it is not necessary that I should be able to do a certain kind of action, such as ride a bicycle, in order to be able to give a detailed and accurate description of riding a bicycle. It is, furthermore, possible that for certain kinds of knowing how there is no corresponding knowledge that.

Of some performances I can say: This time I did it right; last time I did it badly. Therefore, I possess criteria for proper performance. If asked what these criteria are, I may not be able to put them into words, but I know them in the sense that I use them and, in many cases, I can, upon reflection, state what they are. I have then, by means of reflection, produced knowledge that _____ corresponding to the knowledge how _____ which I possessed all along. This is what happens when I vary an example freely in imagination: I am always able to discriminate between the thing that I would recognize as a certain object and the thing that I would either take as a different kind of object or about which I would not know what to say. But only upon reflection can I verbalize the criteria implicit in such a recognition by stating the essential features of any given kind of object.

REFLECTIVE THINKING. When I vary examples freely in imagination, I reflect about the criteria implicit in my ability to recognize examples of the given sort of object; I now put into words the criteria that previously were merely implicit in my performances. This description of the two sides of the process called "bracketing existence" accords perfectly with Husserl's explanations of it. Phenomenology, he stated, is a reflective enterprise. In its reflection it brings to light what was previously "anonymous" or "latent" in our "performances" (Leistungen). But phenomenological reflection is a very special kind of reflection. In phenomenology we do not reflect about facts ("Did I see right? Was that really Jones lying in the gutter?") or about specific actions ("Should I have lectured Jones on the evils of drink?"). Phenomenological reflection does not produce any factual statements, nor does it employ factual statements as premises or as the starting points of reflection. In phenomenology we reflect about examples, in the sense explained; the result of such a reflection is not a factual statement or an empirical generalization but a statement about the necessary conditions for any object's being an example of the sort of thing considered in our reflection.

"Bracketing existence" and the other phrases applied in this context are used ambiguously. Why did Husserl fail to distinguish these two senses? We have already uncovered one source of this ambiguity by showing that we can employ the method of free imaginative variation of an arbitrarily chosen example in order to clarify the essential feature of any object only if we reflect about the example. Hence, treating a given case merely as an example (bracketing in the first sense) presupposes that we have made the transition from nonreflective to reflective thinking (bracketing in the second sense). Although the two kinds of bracketing are distinct, they must occur together.

But there is a second source of the ambiguous use of all these phrases. "Bracketing existence" and "suspending our belief in the existence" of an object seem to be particularly apt in describing important features of the transition from nonreflective to reflective thinking. Reflection involves questioning—more specifically, questioning something that I believed before or regarded as properly done. When I reflect, I ask, "Was that really Jones in the gutter?" or "Should I have helped him up?" Such questioning requires awareness that there are questions to be asked in this situation and that they are not pointless. Before I can reflectively question my earlier belief that it was Jones whom I saw lying in the gutter, I must be open to the possibility that it was not Jones. Hence, as I begin to reflect, I suspend my belief in the existence of Jones in

that condition in that place, or I put his existence in brackets. "Bracketing" in this sense means that I become aware of the possibility that something which I believed to exist does not exist as I thought it did, that a statement which I considered true is not, or that some act which I considered right when I did it might have been wrong. Once I have become aware of that possibility, I am ready to reflect.

The insight that phenomenological statements are the product of reflection resolves the methodological and the epistemological circles. The methodological circle arises because the method must be used to clarify what the method itself consists of. It seems, therefore, that we can use the method only if we know what it consists of, but we can know what it consists of only if we have already used it. Therefore it would seem that we can never get started. But since phenomenology is reflective, it does not presuppose knowledge that the phenomenological method consists of certain procedures; it only presupposes that we know how to use it (to reflect about the essential features of arbitrarily chosen examples), even if we cannot describe it. Such a description is not a necessary condition for using the method, so there is no problem here.

The epistemological circle is resolved in a similar manner. In the method of free imaginative variation, it seemed that we could know that a given phenomenological statement, "P," is true only if we know that the description, "E" of the corresponding example is accurate. But we can know that "E" is accurate only if we know that "P" is true. Hence, it would seem that we cannot know either that "P" is true or that "E" is accurate. But phenomenological reflection begins with my being able to recognize the example described in "E." I know that I describe the example accurately to the extent that I recognize the object in my description of it. Both the accuracy of "E" and the truth of "P" are tested by the criteria implicit in my ability to recognize the object. Hence, there is no difficulty in this case either.

NONEMPIRICAL STATUS OF PHENOMENA. In the search for a complete definition of phenomenon we have now discovered three conditions defining phenomena: (1) phenomena are essences, (2) phenomena are intuited, (3) phenomena are revealed by bracketing existence. The third requirement is twofold: Phenomena are known only upon reflection of a specific sort, namely, reflection about the essential features of arbitrarily chosen examples. Once again the question must be raised whether this definition of phenomena is complete. The criterion of completeness used earlier was that a definition of "phenomenon" is complete only if it is consistent with the first of the three requirements for phenomenological statements—that they are nonempirical. We must ask, therefore, whether phenomena as defined can be described in empirical statements or whether our definition has ruled out that possibility.

It may seem obvious that the definition of phenomenon is complete by this criterion because it seems impossible that phenomena as defined—as being revealed only by bracketing existence—could be described in empirical statements, for statements about phenomena are not statements about single, observed particulars or about series of such single, observed particulars. They are, rather, statements about the necessary relations between the properties of some example of a certain kind of thing in which we do not consider whether the description of our example refers to an actually existing object.

But can we really conclude from this fact, namely, that no observation of actually existent objects is consulted in phenomenological reflection, that the truth of phenomenological statements is independent of the truth of empirical observation statements? We must distinguish between the description of the process by which we arrive at phenomenological statements and the logical conditions that these statements must fulfill in order to be true. The former merely describes how I discover certain statements, but it reveals nothing about the truth conditions of my statements. It is said, for instance, that some Greek geometers discovered certain statements about plane figures by measuring and weighing actual plane figures of tin. They arrived at their statements by means of observations; they were able to make certain statements in geometry after observing actual physical objects, but their statements are no more empirically true (or false) than are the same statements when they appear as theorems in Euclid's *Elements*.

This example presents a case in which statements whose truth or falsity is independent of empirical observation are discovered through empirical observations. It is possible that statements about phenomena constitute a converse case where empirical statements are discovered without explicitly consulting observation of sensory particulars. For instance, it was stated in the preceding section that the phenomenologist does not necessarily consult actual observations when he describes phenomena; his example may be purely imaginary. But it is possible that the statements that he is thus able to make are nevertheless empirical statements. All that was said was that the making of a phenomenological statement is not immediately preceded by observations of existent objects.

Perhaps, however, this is not necessary, since we know the necessary conditions for anything to be an example of a certain kind of thing because we have observed examples of this kind of thing many times and have, as it were, performed an unconscious induction all along. If this is true, then phenomenological statements may still be empirical statements. That they are not empirical statements has not been proved by stating that they are not discovered by means of explicit and deliberate observation of existing objects. The description of "bracketing existence" and of the subsequent reflection has revealed something about the method of discovering statements in phenomenology, but it has not shown that the statement so discovered may not nevertheless be empirical in the sense of being either verifiable by reference to observations of particulars or confirmable or at least refutable by reference to such observations.

There is reason to suspect that the phenomenologists who required that existence be bracketed in phenomenology thought that this requirement assured them that the statements so discovered would not be empirical in any of the senses mentioned. But, as has been shown, they have no such assurance. Hence, they can have no assurance that what is discovered once we have bracketed existence is a phenomenon, in the sense of being the referent of a nonempirical statement. We need further argument to show that bracketing existence does reveal phenomena in the required sense, in all or at least in some cases. Some of the phenomenologists, notably Husserl, have brought forward a number of considerations that provide the arguments needed here. These considerations can best be approached by considering intentionality.

INTENTIONALITY

It was said earlier that reflection undertaken after we have bracketed existence yields, if successful, descriptions of activities that we perform with ease in everyday life but are not able at the same time to describe. Concerning such activities we also know when they miscarry, when they are performed incorrectly or in an improper context, or when someone mistakes such an activity for a different one. We possess criteria for correct and appropriate performance and identification of such activities but are, ordinarily, unable to formulate them. Reflection subject to bracketing of existence yields formulations of these criteria. The phenomenologists regarded all statements resulting from such reflection as nonempirical, but there is no ground for thinking that this is true. These phenomenologists also believed that all the activities that are reflectively described and clarified after bracketing existence are intentional activities. This view can also be shown to be open to objections, but from these two doubtful assertions we can extract a more defensible characterization of phenomena than the one reached so far. So far three necessary conditions for phenomena have been listed: (1) They must be essences that are (2) intuited (3) as the result of the exemplary reflection that requires bracketing existence. We now add a fourth condition, namely, that statements about phenomena must be limited to statements about intentional acts.

The noun *intentionality* does not refer to a thing (as does, for instance, *sodality*) but to the state of an entity— the state of being intentional. Although Husserl used *intentional* in all kinds of contexts, in its primary sense it is an adjective modifying "act"; being intentional is a characteristic of acts. In this employment, "intentional" has an ordinary meaning as a synonym for "deliberate" or "done on purpose," and a philosophical meaning different from, although related to, its ordinary, nonphilosophical meaning. The philosophical use of the term dates back to scholastic philosophy. Later, it completely disappeared from the philosophical vocabulary until it was reintroduced in 1874 by the Austrian philosopher Franz Brentano. Husserl, a student of Brentano's, gives credit to Brentano for reintroducing intentionality into philosophical discussion but adds that intentionality became a fruitful philosophical concept only in phenomenology.

Intentional acts have four aspects, and there are four distinct questions we can ask about them. The sentence "Luther thought that the devil was in his cell" is the complete description of an intentional act. We can ask who is performing an intentional act, and the answer consists of a proper name ("Luther"). It could also be a personal pronoun ("I" or "we") or a definite description ("the father of the Reformation"). We can, in the second place, ask what this person is doing, and the answer will consist of the inflected form of a verb ("thinks," "thought"). The third question concerns the intentional object of the act, what the act is about. In the example, Luther is thinking about the devil. Finally, we can ask in what manner or under what description the intentional object is object of the act; in the example, what is Luther thinking about the devil? "The devil is in my cell."

The intentional act, having four elements, is a tetradic relation. So, for instance, is the relation described in the sentence "I place the book on the table." Here also there are four elements: the subject or agent (myself), my action (placing), what I place (the book), and the table on which I place it. There is, however, an important difference between the two cases. The second statement is false unless there is a table on which I place the book. If the statement as a whole is true, the final of the four terms in the tetradic relation must also exist. It would be self-contradictory to say "I place the book on the table … but there is no table."

We can therefore infer the existence of the table from the truth of the statement "I place the book on the table." This is not so in the case of intentional acts. If it is true that Luther thought that the devil was in his cell, it is not therefore true that the devil exists, let alone that he was in Luther's cell. Luther might have had hallucinations; he might have been the victim of religious madness; or he might have been drunk. All three of these are situations in which we are inclined to see things that are not there or to believe that things exist which in fact do not. Nor can we conclude from the truth of the original sentence that the devil does not exist or was not in Luther's cell. The same holds of whatever is thought or believed to be the case. A belief that my wallet was stolen or that there are leprechauns does not allow the inference that there was a thief who stole my wallet or that there are leprechauns. The same is true of perceiving, of hoping, expecting, doubting, fearing, and all similar activities. The truth of a statement describing someone's intentional act does not allow the inference of either the existence or the nonexistence of what the act is about. This distinguishes intentional acts and their four elements from genuine tetradic relations, where the existence of all four elements can be inferred from the truth of a description of the relation.

THE NONINFERENCE CRITERION. The usual discussion of Husserl's doctrine of intentionality presents intentionality as (1) the defining characteristic of consciousness in the ordinary sense of that term, which (2) consists in the fact that all consciousness is consciousness of something. The first point is false; the latter is true but trivial. It merely asserts that to be conscious is to be related to something. But I am also related to something if, for instance, I own property. In that case I am the owner of something. But being the owner of something is not an intentional act because the existence of the object owned can be inferred from the fact that I own it. The existence or nonexistence of the object of the intentional act, however, cannot be inferred from the true description of that act. (We shall call this the "noninference criterion"). This, rather than merely being related to an object, is the property of intentional acts that distinguishes them from all other kinds of tetradic relations. Hence, it is a defining characteristic.

Two examples will show that intentionality is not the exclusive property of consciousness. Consider the sentences "Luther threw an inkwell in order to injure the devil" and "The rat pushes the lever in order to obtain food." Both sentences express tetradic relations: the agent (Luther, the rat), what he does (throwing, pushing), what he does it with (the inkwell, the lever), and the object of the activity (injuring the devil, obtaining food). It may be said that these are not intentional acts because the object in each case is not what the act is about but is, rather, an aim or a purpose. The acts described in these two sentences are intentional in the ordinary sense of being purposive, but according to the noninference criterion, they are also intentional in the philosophical sense because we cannot infer from the first sentence that the devil was injured and hence we cannot infer that the devil exists or does not exist, nor can we infer from the second that food was obtained by pushing the lever.

The acts described in the two sentences are not acts of consciousness or mental acts in the traditional sense. Throwing and pushing have traditionally been regarded as physical acts, but they differ according to the purpose served. When throwing something at a person in order to injure, one throws differently (much harder, for instance) than when one throws someone a cigarette in order to be helpful. Although physical, both of these acts are intentional in the philosophical sense. Hence intentionality is not, as Brentano thought and Husserl thought at certain times, the defining characteristic of consciousness in the ordinary sense. Husserl became aware of this and redefined "consciousness," in his later writings, by extending the term beyond its ordinary meaning to apply not only to mental acts but also to all kinds of activities, even to those usually regarded as physical, as long as they are intentional. Here intentionality became the defining characteristic of consciousness because this was how consciousness was defined. Husserl would perhaps not have wanted to apply "consciousness" to the behavior of animals, but his views on this point are not well known.

Inference. The verb "to infer" is used in a variety of senses in English, so it must be made clear in what sense it is used in the formulation of the noninference criterion. Suppose I see my foot as it sticks out unshod from my trouser leg and I say, "There's my foot." If someone asks me why I think that my foot is there (exists), I answer, "Because I see it" (or "Because I see something that looks like my foot"). In a loose sense of *infer*, I may be said to infer the existence of my foot from the fact that I see it. In this sense of *infer*, therefore, the correct description of an intentional act ("I see what looks like my foot") allows me to infer the existence of what I see (my foot). But this is inference in a loose sense. The conclusion does not follow necessarily from the premises. It is possible that the premise should be true and the conclusion false, as happens, for instance, when I am having hallucinations. There I see what looks like my foot, but the foot is not there. Common examples of this are the so-called phantom feelings—an amputee feels his foot long after it has been amputated. It is true that he feels his foot, but it is false that his foot is there. But if I say that I know my foot is under the table because I feel it, the inference (in the loose sense) is correct.

The sense of "to infer" used in the noninference criterion is stricter. In this sense we say that something is inferred from a premise or set of premises if the falsity of the conclusion is incompatible with the truth of the premise(s). In this sense it was said earlier that we can infer from the truth of "I place the book on the table" that there is a table. It would be self-contradictory to say "I place the book on the table … but there is no table" and to claim that both parts of this compound statement are true. It is in this stringent sense of "to infer" that the noninference criterion denies that we can infer the existence of the object of the intentional act from a true description of the act itself. The noninference criterion does not deny that feeling my foot, for instance, is often sufficient ground for saying that my foot is there. But it does deny that my foot must exist necessarily if I feel it. Intentional acts differ from other tetradic relations in that it is not inconsistent in the case of intentional acts to deny the existence of the final term of the four-term relation and to assert that the relation is described truly, but it is inconsistent to do this in the case of all nonintentional four-term relations.

Criterion is nonempirical. It is now easy to show that a statement of the noninference criterion is a nonempirical statement in the sense that no empirical statement can show it to be false. In this sense mathematical statements are nonempirical—no measurement of angles or lines in a triangle can show that geometrical statements about triangles are false. If there does appear to be a conflict between actual measurements and measurements predicted on the basis of certain geometrical propositions, we do not reject the geometrical proposition underlying our prediction; rather, we conclude that the measurements are false. The reason for this is, of course, that the procedures used in measuring presuppose the truth of the pertinent statements in geometry. In order to show that the statement of the noninference criterion is false, there must be at least one intentional act in which the existence of what the act is about or aims at follows with necessity from a true description of the act. But philosophers agree that no necessary relations are observed, or can be inferred from observations, so no statement about a necessary relation can be an empirical statement. Hence, the case needed to refute the noninference criterion cannot be described in empirical statements. It follows that the statement of the noninference criterion, not being refutable by means of an empirical statement, is not itself an empirical statement.

INTENTIONALITY AS A PHENOMENON. The statement of the noninference criterion satisfies the fourth condition laid down for phenomena: It is a statement about intentional acts. It is easy to show that it also satisfies the other three conditions for phenomena: (1) The preceding analysis consisted of reflection subject to bracketing of existence. (2) It brought to light certain essential features of intentional acts. (3) The truth of the statements rests on intuition, in the sense discussed earlier. Intentionality is, therefore, not only one mark of phenomena but is also itself a phenomenon. It has also been shown that the description of this phenomenon contains at least one nonempirical statement, namely, the noninference criterion. There is, then, at least one statement about phenomena, as now defined, that is nonempirical. This suggests that the four conditions for phenomena constitute a complete definition. However, the four conditions for phenomena are not sufficient for a complete definition, so a fifth condition must be added—that, with respect to intentional acts, phenomena serve as criteria of coherence.

CRITERIA OF COHERENCE

Intentional acts are of two kinds; they are either purposive or about something. Purposive acts may be said to be adequate to their intentional object if the means chosen accomplish their purpose. Acts that are about some intentional object may be said to be adequate if what is believed or asserted about an object is really true, if what is questioned is questionable, if what is doubted is doubtful. Whether a given purpose is pursued correctly by using certain means depends on the nature of the purpose and of the means chosen, and on the way the means are used. Whether Luther throws the inkwell correctly at the devil depends on the weight of the inkwell, the distance between him and the devil, and how he throws. There are correct and incorrect ways of throwing inkwells or anything else. Which ways are correct and which are not is a matter of empirical fact, to be discovered by empirical study. Hence, rules about correct performance

of this kind of intentional act are empirical rules. Similarly, it is in many cases an empirical question whether my beliefs are true, whether what I question is questionable, or whether what I doubt is doubtful. It can be shown that at least some of these rules satisfy all four defining conditions for phenomena; hence, they can be regarded as statements about phenomena, as defined so far. This, in turn, shows that the four conditions laid down do not constitute a complete definition of "phenomenon," for phenomena, under this definition, are capable of being described in empirical statements. We need a fifth condition.

The following consideration will yield the required fifth condition for a complete definition of "phenomenon." Before we can ask whether any given intentional act is correctly performed—whether it is adequate to its intentional object—we must be certain that what we are asking about is a genuine intentional act. Since intentional acts have four elements—the subject (or agent), the action, the intentional object, and either the means used or what is asserted about the intentional object—we need certain rules to determine which subject can be combined with what actions, which intentional objects, and which means or assertions to form coherent intentional acts. Not just any member of each of these four classes of elements can be combined with any other to form a coherent and intelligible intentional act.

COHERENCE AND INTELLIGIBILITY. The meanings of "coherent" and "intelligible" are best indicated by examples of their opposites, intentional acts that are incoherent or unintelligible. Purposive acts are not coherent and not intelligible (they "make no sense"), for instance, where the action and the means used are inappropriate to the intentional object. Someone might have said to Luther that it made no sense to throw anything at the devil because the devil is not a person but merely a symbol of evil. Not being a person, the devil has no body—and hence no location—and therefore cannot be made the target of any physical missile. A different case of an incoherent purposive act is that in which the means are inappropriate to the action. "Killing a person with kindness" is a metaphorical expression precisely because it literally makes no sense; the means chosen for killing a person are utterly inappropriate. They are not inappropriate merely in the sense that someone might try to use kindness as a murder weapon and discover that it does not do the job. It is not at all clear how one would proceed literally to try to kill someone with kindness. "Killing a person with kindness" is therefore not an intelligible or coherent intentional act. Similar incoherences can be found in the other relations among the four elements of intentional acts.

Corresponding incoherences appear in intentional acts that are about something. If what I believe about something is utterly inappropriate to its intentional object, such as "The Pythagorean theorem is mellifluous and sweet-smelling," there is no way of telling or even of finding out whether the statement is true. Asserting this sentence is not an intelligible intentional act, and hence the assertion is neither true nor false. Similar incoherences can occur between the action (for instance, "I predict") and its intentional object (for instance, some past event) or what is being predicted (that something happened yesterday).

So far the notions of coherence and incoherence, of intelligibility and unintelligibility, have been exhibited within single intentional acts. Husserl pointed out that there is also coherence and intelligibility of series of acts.

Suppose that Luther, rage suffusing his face, threw an inkwell at the devil with all his might and the very next moment rushed up to him, saying, "My dear fellow, I am so sorry. How very clumsy of me. Here, let me help you." This would be very surprising because the first action seemed clearly intended to injure, the second to placate. The change between the two is unmistakable and can be described by saying that the second act has a different intentional object from the first. As juxtaposed, the two acts make no sense because they seem to be members of two incompatible series of acts. The first act seems part of a series intended to enrage or injure the devil, and the second seems part of a different series aimed at mollifying the devil. The first action clearly leads to the expectation of another angry action. The second one disappoints that expectation, so the two actions make no sense, although each by itself makes sense. As single acts they are intelligible or coherent, but they do not make sense when they come in the above order. No one can understand what Luther is up to. We know what a man is up to if we understand a sequence of his actions and have correct expectations about what he is going to do next. If our expectations are disappointed, we may conclude that the agent has changed his mind or that we did not understand him to begin with. We understand or do not understand what someone is up to if his purposive actions form a coherent or incoherent series, respectively.

All this is true irrespective of whether the series of acts is performed well or badly. Hence, there are two sets of rules governing series of acts that correspond to the two sorts of rules governing individual acts: those which govern the coherence of act series and those which govern the adequacy of the act series to its collective purpose. What a man is up to in a series of acts can be inferred only from the sequence of acts performed. But not all sequences of acts are coherent. There are, therefore, rules about intentional acts determining the conditions for coherence of any series of intentional acts. Only if a series is coherent corresponding to the rules governing coherence can the question whether the actions and the means chosen are adequate to the aim pursued in the whole series be answered in the light of the relevant facts. Empirical statements about the adequacy of actions and means to their collective end are to be distinguished from statements about the coherence of such collections of acts.

It is not necessary to cite more examples to show that a series of acts which are about something are coherent or incoherent, intelligible or unintelligible, in analogous ways. A single act of belief, assertion, or questioning may be perfectly coherent and intelligible by itself but may be entirely out of context with what precedes or follows, and it is not understood what this person, in this act, is talking about, what he is trying to say.

HORIZON. Husserl used the term *horizon* to refer to the relations of coherence and incoherence of intentional acts. *Horizon* was not intended to refer to the place where sky and earth meet but to the edge of the perceptual field, which moves and changes with movements of the head or of the entire body. The horizon metaphor suggests that as the edge of the perceptual field (the horizon) leads us to expect a continuation of what lies before us, so any given intentional act suggests further acts that would be continuous or coherent with it. What is said in one act or done in one purposive action leads one to expect a second assertion or a second action continuous with the first. The second statement is continuous with the first if it is about the same object as the first; if in the second action one is up to the same thing as in the first, the two are continuous. I know what you are talking about or what you are up to when I know what sort of thing you will say or do next.

The horizon metaphor also implies that these relations between intentional acts are necessary conditions for any act being intentional, just as it is a necessary condition for the existence of a perceptual field that it have a horizon. Something is an act of asserting, for instance, if and only if I can repeat what I said in another way; if I can amplify, clarify, explain what I said; or if I can confuse, muddle up, and utterly obfuscate what my assertions are about. It is impossible that an intentional act should be without horizons, that is, unrelated to any other intentional act.

Criteria of coherence. As the horizons of the perceptual field are to some degree indefinite, so are the horizons of intentional acts. I cannot infer from any given assertion or activity of yours that you will next assert one particular statement or do some particular action and no other. When I see a church steeple on the horizon, I know that, when I come closer, I will not see a hippopotamus at its base. But there is definitely a point in coming closer to discover what the church or the building that resembled a church from a distance looks like.

Similarly, there is a point in listening to you to find out what your next statement is going to be or in watching what you are going to do. If I understand what you are talking about or what you are up to, I have some idea of what you are going to say or do next. I know the minimum conditions for your next statement and action; I know the limits beyond which your next action will not be continuous with the last or your next statement will not be about the same object as the last. Horizons are the necessary conditions for any series of assertions or activities to be intelligible. Different kinds of intentional acts have different kinds of horizons. Linguistic acts are related in terms of their meaning; purposive activities, by reference to the purpose. It is the task of phenomenology to clarify the different sorts of horizons (conditions for intelligibility) and to put into words what the horizons of individual examples of each kind of act are. Husserl called the clarification and formulation of horizons "intentional analysis." The results of such intentional analyses are statements of the criteria for the coherence of intentional act series.

Having understood what Husserl meant by "horizon" and that there are criteria for the coherence of single acts corresponding to the horizons in act series, we have found the fifth condition defining "phenomenon." Statements about phenomena must, besides satisfying the first four conditions, be about the criteria of coherence of single intentional acts or of sequences of intentional acts. When we look at any object as a phenomenon, we are trying to discover the criteria for coherence of those intentional acts in which the object (or its name or description) can figure.

ARE PHENOMENOLOGICAL STATEMENTS A PRIORI?

Traditionally philosophers have called statements "a priori" if they are (1) nonempirical and (2) necessarily true. Phenomenologists have always held that their statements

are a priori. The two parts of this claim must be examined separately.

It has been shown that phenomenologists agree that their statements are nonempirical, although they disagree about the description of phenomena. Some phenomenologists were content to describe them as essences intuited, but others regarded this as insufficient and added that phenomenological descriptions must be preceded by bracketing existence. But bracketing existence also turned out to be an inadequate guarantee that phenomenological statements are nonempirical. Therefore some members of the phenomenological movement, notably Husserl, added further requirements for statements about phenomena. The preceding discussion can be summarized by stating the five conditions that any statement must satisfy if it is to be a statement about phenomena:

(1) It must be about essences.

(2) It must be self-validating (intuitive).

(3) It must be the result of bracketing existence.

(4) It must be about intentional acts.

(5) It must lay down the criteria of coherence (or intelligibility) of intentional acts.

We must now, once again, ask: Are statements of this kind nonempirical?

THE SENSES OF *EMPIRICAL.* The above question is not easy to answer because the term *empirical* has several meanings. We must examine some of them.

Statements asserting particular matters of fact, such as "There is a fire burning in the fireplace," are true if observation shows them to be true and false if observation shows them to be false (for instance, that the fire has gone out). They are empirical because one observation will show them to be true or false.

General statements, such as "Continuous nervous tension produces high blood pressure," are neither confirmed nor refuted by one observation or even by a few observations but only by a series of carefully controlled observations. This case concerns generalizations about observable connections.

There is a further sense of "empirical" that applies to statements about objects which are in principle nonobservable, such as "ideal gases" or "perfectly elastic bodies." Such entities cannot be observed because they do not exist, and hence we cannot frame empirical statements about them in either the particular or the general sense of "empirical." These entities, which cannot be described in observation statements, are instead defined in a series of statements constituting a scientific theory. From such a theory statements can be deduced that can be tested by reference to direct experience. If observation shows the deduced statements to be false, we must reject the theory, and hence our theoretical statements about the unobservable entities are indirectly refuted by observation. These statements are therefore, in this indirect way, empirical because observations can serve to show them to be false.

PHENOMENOLOGICAL STATEMENTS. Phenomenological statements, as described in the preceding sections, are not empirical in the first two senses of the term. They are not empirical in the first sense because they are never statements about individual existing intentional acts but only about the criteria governing types of acts; only particular statements are empirical in the first sense. Empirical in the second sense are generalizations derived by induction from a series of observations of particulars. Such inductive generalizations presuppose that we know what particulars belong to the class of objects to be observed. If we want to make a generalization about the relation between nervous tension and high blood pressure, we must have a very precise idea of what must count as examples of nervous tension and what blood pressure counts as "high" blood pressure. Similarly, we cannot inductively arrive at statements about intentional acts unless we are already able to differentiate a coherent intentional act from an incoherent collection of each of the four kinds of elements of intentional acts.

The same applies to generalizations about coherent series of intentional acts. Nothing said by the phenomenologists should exclude the possibility of framing empirical (in the general sense) statements about intentional acts. All that is argued is that the criteria of coherence of individual acts as well as of series of acts are presupposed and therefore are not established by such inductive generalizations. Therefore, statements formulating these criteria cannot themselves be empirical generalizations.

It is undoubtedly a task for phenomenology to differentiate the different senses of "empirical," that is, to describe the different kinds of intentional acts involved in what we call experience and the criteria of coherence belonging to each kind of act. Oddly enough, the phenomenologists so far have barely begun to undertake such an examination, and hence their conviction that statements about phenomena, as now defined, are nonempirical is not supported by adequate phenomenological analyses. This important shortcoming in the theory of the phenomenological method is all the more serious because there are good reasons for thinking that there is one perfectly good sense of the words *experience* and *empirical* in which statements about phenomena, as defined, are empirical.

EMPIRICAL PHENOMENA STATEMENTS. In a scientific theory, the terms are defined in relation to one another in such a way that if we alter the definition of one term, the definitions of some of the other terms are also changed. The effect of such a set of interrelated definitions is to limit the contexts in which these terms may be applied. A set of phenomenological statements has a similar function; it limits the contexts in which given intentional acts may be performed. The limits imposed on these intentional acts in the phenomenological statements are interrelated as the definitions in a theory are. If we alter the limits of one intentional act, those of other acts are also changed. History and ethnology provide many examples of such changes.

Among the Trobriand Islanders, for instance, successful gardening requires the use of magic. Before seedlings are planted, a spell must be spoken over them. It is very important that the magician's mouth be as close as possible to the seedlings, for otherwise some of the power of the spell will be dissipated. The power of the spell resides not in the sound waves produced by the magician but in the meaning of the terms used, something that we would not regard as a physical phenomenon. Yet the power of the magical words is here treated as if it were a physical force that varies with the distance from the object it affects. It is clear that the Trobriander does not draw a distinction between the physical and the mental, so it makes perfect sense for him to say something that makes no sense to us—that the spell must be spoken as close as possible to the seedlings in order to be effective. He imposes different limits on his intentional acts—what makes literal sense to him is to us at best symptomatic of the confusions of the "primitive" mind—and these various limits are interrelated. We can formulate them in a set of phenomenological statements that we regard as false and he regards as true. This example shows the analogy between the limitations imposed on theoretical terms by their implicit definitions in a scientific theory and the mutual limitations imposed on intentional acts and expressed in phenomenological statements.

Statements in a scientific theory limit the application of the terms. If the limits imposed allow the use of the terms in false factual statements, these limits must be altered; the theory is invalid. In analogous ways phenomenological statements may be invalidated by experience. Phenomenological statements express the limits imposed on intentional acts, and if these limits are such that we cannot distinguish true factual statements from false ones, the limits must be altered; the phenomenological statements are invalid.

In order to make true generalizations about gardening and distinguish them from false ones, we need a clear notion of causation. Causal relations as discussed in science exist only between spatiotemporally contiguous events, and this implies that only spatiotemporally located events can be either causes or effects. A clear notion of causal relations, therefore, presupposes a clear distinction between events that are and those that are not spatiotemporally located, or between physical and mental events. Where such a distinction is not drawn, no clear understanding of causal relations is possible. The Trobriander does not differentiate physical events from mental events (and forces); hence he cannot clearly differentiate causal relations from noncausal relations. As a result, he cannot make general statements about gardening that are always true or always false as tested by the information available to us. They may, of course, be always true (or false) tested by what he knows. His generalizations are about classes containing very heterogeneous types of relations, both causal and noncausal. Statements about the causal are true under very different conditions from statements about the noncausal, so his generalizations are sometimes true and sometimes false, and he does not have the vocabulary necessary to reformulate them in such a way that they are always true or always false. This shows that the Trobriander's lack of scientific information about biology is not accidental. It is impossible for him to do natural science because his language lacks the requisite distinctions. Scientific statements cannot be made in his language, which is clear proof that it is inadequate and that the phenomenological statements describing his linguistic acts as well as the nonlinguistic ones, such as those associated with garden magic, are therefore invalid.

This argument as stated is not conclusive, but it can be strengthened to make a rather formidable case for holding that the phenomenologists are mistaken in their claim that their statements about phenomena are nonempirical in all senses of that term. This conclusion shows that the question asked at the very outset—what are the truth conditions of phenomenological statements—remains unanswered. In the preceding a good deal has been said about these truth conditions, but it has

been shown that that answer is incomplete. The phenomenologists' account of their method not only lacks a complete theory of experience in its different forms but also a complete theory of truth, at least as that term applies to the statements in phenomenology.

THE SENSES OF "NECESSARY." The second aspect of a priori statements is their necessity. A priori statements are necessary because they are nonempirical; if they are true at all, they are true independently of facts about the world. Even if all the statements about this world that are now true were false, and if, therefore, our world were very different from what it is now the a priori statements would still be true. They are true whatever happens to be the case in the world. Hence we may say that, if true at all, they must be true regardless of any facts. For this reason the term *necessary* has often been explicated as "true for all possible worlds." A different world from ours is one whose description requires factual statements to be true that are false of our world. Since necessary statements are true whatever factual statements may or may not be true, they are true for all possible worlds. A statement is necessary, therefore, to the extent that its truth is logically independent of the truth or falsity of empirical statements. It follows that there are different senses of "necessity" to correspond to the different senses of "empirical." There are, therefore, also different senses of "a priori." Hence, phenomenological statements are clearly a priori insofar as they are not empirical in the first two senses of that term. But phenomenological statements are empirical in a third sense and are therefore not a priori in that sense of "a priori" that contrasts with this third sense of "empirical."

NECESSARY PHENOMENA STATEMENTS. In the sense explained, statements are necessary if they are *true* necessarily. But if statements about phenomena are a priori—necessarily true *and* nonempirical—they are necessary in a second sense: Their truth is a necessary condition for any empirical statement to be capable of being either true or false. An empirical statement can be either true or false only if it is meaningful, and that depends on the coherence of the intentional act and of the intentional act series in which it is asserted. But as was seen, the coherence of such acts and act series is presupposed by any question about the adequacy of intentional acts to their intentional objects. Hence the statements that lay down the criteria for coherence of all kinds of intentional acts, including acts of asserting, must be true if we are to be able to decide whether any given intentional act is adequate to its intentional object—for instance, whether an assertion is true or a purposive action is successful. Insofar as phenomenological statements are a priori, they are, therefore, necessary in this second sense; they are presuppositions for the adequacy or inadequacy of any intentional act to its intentional object. The truth of phenomenological statements is logically prior to the truth or falsity of all empirical statements and to the correctness of all purposive actions.

CONTEMPORARY PHENOMENOLOGY

Political events in Europe and the shifting winds of doctrine caused the phenomenological movement to lose much of its original momentum after Husserl's death in 1938. The best-known twentieth-century philosophers who used the term *phenomenology* in descriptions of their own work were Martin Heidegger in Germany and Jean-Paul Sartre and Maurice Merleau-Ponty in France. All three used the term *phenomenology* in appreciably different senses from the phenomenologists previously discussed.

HEIDEGGER. Heidegger was a student of Husserl's and at one time was a coeditor of the *Jahrbuch*. In that journal (Vol. 8, 1927) appeared his first major work, *Sein und Zeit* (translated by J. Macquarrie and E. Robinson as *Being and Time*, New York, 1962). The phenomenologists so far discussed all agreed that it is the task of phenomenology reflectively to bring to light the criteria implicit in the intentional acts we perform in everyday life, in which we act in, get to know about, and learn to master that everyday world which Husserl christened the *Lebenswelt* ("world in which we live"). The emphasis here is on putting into words what is commonly and familiarly done without one's knowing how to describe accurately what he is doing. Heidegger also regarded phenomenology as a sort of reflection but not a reflection designed to put into words what is familiar in performance.

On the contrary, Heidegger's brand of phenomenology tried to open the way back to what had, he thought, become completely unfamiliar, what he calls *Sein* (being). He recognized that "being" had become a philosophically empty word. Hence we cannot gain a better understanding of being by reflecting only about the world insofar as it is familiar to us, for in that world "being" has become almost meaningless; there are very few contexts in which it makes sense to talk about "being." Thus, reflection about the criteria of intelligibility, which we use now, will not reveal much about being. Rather than reflect on these criteria, Heidegger proposes to ask why "being" has become almost meaningless to us. But since a question is

intelligible only to the extent that we can specify the sort of answer we expect, and since an answer to Heidegger's question would require a language in which "being" is meaningful, even an intelligible formulation of his question involves him in the attempt to re-create a very different language, in which "being," far from being an empty word, is the richest and most important concept. This language, he believed, is the language used by the pre-Socratic philosophers. Heidegger's phenomenology thus led him into an enterprise utterly unfamiliar to the other phenomenologists, the attempt to develop a new philosophical language by re-creating that of the pre-Socratic philosophers.

SARTRE. Sartre's major work, *L'être et le néant* (Paris, 1943; translated by H. E. Barnes as *Being and Nothingness*, New York, 1957), bears the subtitle *An Essay in Phenomenological Ontology*. The work does not, however, contain any explicit discussion of phenomenology, nor did Sartre explain his conception of phenomenology at length in any other work. More than once he differentiated phenomenology from science by saying that phenomenology makes statements about essences; science, about facts. In one long essay, "La transcendence de l'égo" (*Recherches Philosophiques*, Vol. 6, 1936–1937; translated by F. Williams and R. Kirkpatrick and published in book form as *The Transcendence of the Ego*, New York, 1958), he takes sharp issue with Husserl's transcendental phenomenology, particularly with the claim that in phenomenology we discover that there is a transcendental ego.

It would seem, then, that Sartre was a phenomenologist who, like many others, adopts the descriptive approach to essences but refuses to follow Husserl in his later developments of the theory of the phenomenological method. But Sartre differs radically insofar as he was not averse to constructing philosophical theories. His major work is an example of constructive philosophy in precisely that sense in which phenomenologists attacked it in their polemic against reductionism. Sartre's conception of phenomenology is no clearer if we look at his actual practice of the method than if we consider his sparse statements about it. If Sartre practiced phenomenology at all, the term as used by him and as applicable to his procedures has a different meaning from the one explicated in this discussion.

MERLEAU-PONTY. Merleau-Ponty's major work bears the title *Phénoménologie de la perception* (Paris, 1945; translated by Colin Smith as *Phenomenology of Perception*, London, 1962). Unlike Sartre, he includes an introduction devoted to a clarification of "phenomenology."

The clear and explicit result of this discussion is that Merleau-Ponty has interpreted the notion of phenomenology in a sense rather different from that subscribed to wholly or partly by members of the phenomenological movement, as well as from that used by either Heidegger or Sartre.

These three philosophers used "phenomenology" in appreciably different ways from those in which it has been used by the phenomenologists discussed. To be sure, there were also radical and profound disagreements among the latter about the nature and presuppositions of the phenomenological method, but they regarded these differences as different results arrived at by applying the same method. In this sense these philosophers—Husserl, Pfänder, Geiger, Becker, and Reinach, among others—can be regarded as belonging to one school of philosophy. All of them shared certain common views at the outset, and they believed that they were using the same method. But Heidegger, Sartre, and Merleau-Ponty began doing their respective brands of phenomenology by explaining what they considered phenomenology to be and how their conception differed from that of Husserl. They did not begin with the same common views, as did the earlier phenomenologists; and they did not regard their method as identical with that of Husserl and the other phenomenologists. For this reason they do not belong to the same school of philosophy.

See also Binswanger, Ludwig; Brentano, Franz; Existentialism; Existential Psychoanalysis; Heidegger, Martin; Intentionality; Life, Meaning and Value of; Psychologism; Sartre, Jean-Paul; Scheler, Max; Time, Consciousness of.

Bibliography

ORIGINAL WORKS IN GERMAN

Husserl, Edmund. *Husserliana*. Vol. I: *Cartesianische Meditationen*. The Hague: Nijhoff, 1950. The shortest, though not always easy, introduction to Husserl's mature conception of phenomenology.

Husserl, Edmund. *Husserliana*. Vol. VI: *Die Krisis der europaischen Wissenschaften und die transcendentale Phänomenologie*. The Hague: Nijhoff, 1954. A very late work of Husserl's; introduces the important notion of the *Lebenswelt*, the world of everyday life.

Husserl, Edmund. *Husserliana*. Vols. VII and VIII: *Erste Philosophie*. The Hague: Nijhoff, 1956–1959. Husserl's lectures on the history of philosophy and phenomenology; more accessible than many of his other writings.

Husserl, Edmund et al., eds. *Jahrbuch für Philosophie und phänomenologische Forschung*. 11 vols. Halle: Niemeyer, 1913–1930. Contains representative writings of all the major phenomenologists.

Reinach, Adolf. "Über Phänomenologie." In his *Gesammelte Schriften*, edited by Hedwig Conrad-Martius. Munich, 1921. A brief and very lucid statement of an early conception of phenomenology.

ORIGINAL WORKS IN TRANSLATION

Husserl, Edmund. *Cartesian Meditations*. Translated by Dorion Cairns. The Hague: Nijhoff, 1960.

Husserl, Edmund. *The Idea of Phenomenology*. Translated by William P. Alston and George Nakhnikian. The Hague: Nijhoff, 1964. Translates a series of lectures given in 1907 in which the transcendental-phenomenological reduction is introduced.

Husserl, Edmund. *Ideas*. Translated by W. R. Boyce Gibson. New York: Macmillan, 1931; New York: Collier, 1963.

Husserl, Edmund. "Phenomenology." Translated by C. V. Solomon. In *Encyclopaedia Britannica*, 14th ed., Vol. XVII, 699–702. 1927.

Husserl, Edmund. *Phenomenology and the Crisis of Philosophy: Philosophy as Science and Philosophy and the Crisis of European Man*. Translated with notes and introduction by Quentin Lauer. New York: Harper, 1965. Contains a long essay, published in 1910, in which Husserl provides an expanded version of his earlier polemics against psychologism. This book also translates portions of Husserl's late work, *Krisis*.

BOOKS ON PHENOMENOLOGY

Bachelard, Suzanne. *La logique de Husserl*. Paris, 1951. A lucid and detailed discussion of Husserl's *Formale und Transcendentale Logik* (1929).

Berger, Gaston. *Le cogito dans la philosophie de Husserl*. Paris: Aubier, 1941. One of the earliest and still one of the best monographs on one aspect of Husserl's thought.

Brand, Gerd. *Welt, Ich und Zeit*. The Hague: Nijhoff, 1955. Attempts a summary of Husserlian phenomenology on the basis of unpublished manuscripts. Rather general but often illuminating.

Brentano, F. *Psychology from an Empirical Standpoint*. Translated by A. C. Rancurello, D. B. Terrel, and L. L. McAlister; edited by L. L. McAlister. London: Routledge, 1969.

Cooper, D. E. *Heidegger*. London: Claridge Press, 1996.

Derrida, Jacques. *Speech and Phenomena*. Translated by Gayatri Chakravorty Spivak. Baltimore: Johns Hopkins Press, 1976.

Dreyfus, H. L. *Being-in-the-World: A Commentary on Heidegger's* Being and Time, *Division I*. Cambridge, MA: MIT Press, 1991.

Farber, Marvin, ed. *Philosophical Essays in Memory of Edmund Husserl*. Cambridge, MA: Harvard University Press for University of Buffalo, 1940. A collection of stimulating and sometimes informative essays on different aspects of Husserl's work.

Heidegger, M. *Being and Time*. Translated by J. Macquarrie and E. Robinson. London: SCM Press, 1962.

Merleau-Ponty, M. *Phenomenology of Perception*. Translated by C. Smith. London: Routledge and Kegan Paul, 1981.

Mohanty, J. N. *Edmund Husserl's Theory of Meaning*. The Hague: Nijhoff, 1964. An interesting discussion of Husserl's early work in the light of the treatment given the same questions by Bertrand Russell, G. E. Moore, and others.

ENCYCLOPEDIA OF PHILOSOPHY
2nd edition

Mohanty, J. N. *Transcendental Phenomenology: An Analytic Account*. Oxford: Blackwell, 1989.

Moran, D. *Introduction to Phenomenology*. London: Routledge, 2000.

Schrag, C. O. *Experience and Being*. Evanston, IL: Northwestern University Press, 1969.

Smith, B., and D. W. Smith, eds. *The Cambridge Companion to Husserl*. Cambridge, U.K.: Cambridge University Press, 1995.

Smith, D. W. *Husserl and Intentionality: A Study of Mind, Meaning, and Language*. Dordrecht: Reidel, 1982.

Sokolowski, R. *Introduction to Phenomenology*. Cambridge, U.K.: Cambridge University Press, 2000.

Spiegelberg, Herbert. *The Phenomenological Movement*. 2 vols. The Hague: Nijhoff, 1960; 3rd ed., The Hague: Kluwer Academic, 1982. Discusses phenomenology in general as well as individual contributors to the movement. Extremely informative.

ARTICLES ON PHENOMENOLOGY

Ayer, A. J., and Charles Taylor. "Phenomenology and Linguistic Analysis." *PAS*, Supp. 33 (1959).

Boehm, Rudolf. "Basic Reflection on Husserl's Phenomenological Reduction." *International Philosophical Quarterly* 5 (1965): 183–202.

Downes, Chauncey. "On Husserl's Approach to Necessary Truth." *Monist* 19 (1965): 87–106.

Findlay, J. N. "Phenomenology." In *Encyclopaedia Britannica*, 1965 ed.

Ryle, Gilbert. "Phenomenology." *PAS*, Supp. 11 (1932).

Smith, D. W. "Phenomenology." Stanford Encyclopedia of Philosophy. Available from http://www.plato.stanford.com.

Spiegelberg, Herbert. "Toward a Phenomenology of Experience." *American Philosophical Quarterly* 1 (1964): 1–8.

Richard Schmitt (1967)
Bibliography updated by Benjamin Fiedor (2005)

PHENOMENOLOGY [ADDENDUM]

The development of "phenomenology" is a consequence of the interpretation of the texts of the major figures, especially Edmund Husserl, and of independent phenomenological research. Quite often, the two projects have gone hand in hand. One major factor in the development of phenomenology during the period under review has been the ongoing publication of the Nachlass of the major figures (*Husserliana*, Martin Heidegger's *Gesamtausgabe*, as well as Maurice Merleau-Ponty's lectures). Another is the continuing conversation with analytic philosophy in the English-speaking countries, with structuralism and deconstructionism in France, and with hermeneutics, critical theory, and the tradition of German idealism in Germany.

One major starting point in the conversation with analytic philosophy has been Dagfinn Føllesdal's (1969) paper, which argues that Husserl's concept of Noema is a generalization of the Fregean notion of *Sinn*. Both the Sinn and the Noema are abstract entities, to be distinguished from the object toward which an intentional act may be directed. While the historical claim underlying this thesis—namely, that Gottlob Frege's was a major influence on the development of Husserl's thinking around the turn of the twentieth century—has been challenged (e.g., by Jitendra N. Mohanty), the systematic thesis of Føllesdal (as opposed to Aron Gurwitsch's thesis, that the Noema is the perceived object qua perceived and the object intended is but a system of noemata), has been influential.

Jaakko Hintikka developed another aspect of Husserl's theory of intentionality by construing the Noema as a function from possible worlds to individuals in those worlds. The resources of the semantics of Frege and of possible worlds have been pulled together to interpret Husserl in the work of David Smith and Ronald McIntyre. Mohanty and Frederick Seebohm have cautioned against reducing the intentional thesis of Husserl to an extensional thesis of possible worlds and have emphasized the need for a theory of constitution of possible worlds, if the latter are not to be posited in a naively ontological thesis. Still others, notably R. Sokolowski and Daniel Bell, have questioned the validity of ascribing to Husserl a Fregean-type theory. Sokolowski takes the Husserlian Noema to be identical with the object (with the proviso "as intended"), and Bell reads Husserlian Gegenstand to be a component of the intentional act and so quite unlike the Fregean reference.

From another perspective, John Searle has found the Husserlian intentionality thesis useful for his own work but goes beyond Husserl by appropriating, from Heidegger via Hubert Dreyfus, the idea of Background of skills and practices, and more recently by developing a theory of we-intentionality that is irreducible to I-intentionalities (reminiscent of the Hegelian *Geist* as well as of a thesis advanced by David Carr). This last discussion connects with the way phenomenology has related itself to cognitive science. Jerry Fodor's methodological solipsism has been related by Dreyfus to Husserl's, while Searle's emphasis on Background clearly falls on the Heideggerean side of the divide.

The tension between Husserlian phenomenology and hermeneutics lies in that the former is concerned with consciousness, its contents and structures, the latter with the individual's ontological relatedness to his world and to others. This issue becomes, Is interpretation to be construed as the gift of a transcendental ego, or is it to be construed as an ontological feature of the mode of being of *Dasein*? Hans-Georg Gadamer's theory of interpretation develops the latter alternative, while Paul Ricoeur comes closest to mediating between Husserlian thinking, especially of the *Logical Investigations,* and an ontologically construed hermeneutics. We must also recall Ricoeur's work on metaphor, in which, going beyond the traditional rhetorical and semantic theories of analytic philosophy, Ricoeur integrates them in such a manner as permits the poetic and disclosive dimension of language to emerge. Ricoeur's researches have also sought to mediate between time (the most radical subjectivity) and narrative (by which reality is redescribed, as by metaphors) and reestablish a certain reciprocity between them.

The most influential critique of classical phenomenology is offered by Jacques Derrida. While it is more common to look upon Derrida's work as refuting Husserl's transcendental phenomenology, it is also possible to maintain that Derrida's work is a further radicalization of Husserl's genetic phenomenology, an alleged result of which is the demonstration that constitution involves a perpetual deferral and difference, also that a radicalization of Husserl's concept of horizonal character of intentionality would call into question all fixity and univocity of meanings, and that possibilities of nonfulfillment of intention are necessarily inherent in all intentionality. But those who ascribe to Husserl a metaphysics of presence fall into the opposite trap of reifying "absence." As Sokolowski has shown, Husserl's thinking rather exhibits a mutual involvement of presence and absence.

Of those from analytic philosophy who have pursued some kind of phenomenology, mention must be made of Castañeda's rich phenomenology of indexical reference and of "I" thought. In the latter context, he distinguishes between the ground floor of empirical I-guise and successive phases of transcendental I-guises, among all of which there is a sameness that is yet not strict identity.

In the United States there is a continuing tendency, inaugurated by Dreyfus and Richard Rorty, to see in Heidegger a pragmatist philosopher, whereby clearly Heidegger's ontological concern with the meaning of being and the historical concern with the historicity of understanding of Being are either underplayed or sought to be altogether set aside. While it was at first usual to look upon Heidegger as an antiscience thinker, now—largely owing to the work of C. F. von Weizsäcker, J. Kockelmans, and Patrick Heelan—one has come to realize that Heidegger's

thinking could form the basis for an understanding and appreciation of science and technology. In general, phenomenological thinking about science has exhibited three distinct features: First, following Husserl in the *Crisis,* some have attempted to reestablish the proper connection between science and lifeworld. The most important work on this front is due to J. Mittelstrass. Second, following also Husserl's work in the *Crisis,* but more inspired by Heideggerean thought about historicity of *Dasein* as also by Thomas Kuhn's work on history of science, some have looked upon science as a historical accomplishment marked by epochal changes, epistemological breaks, shifts of paradigm—thereby rejecting the prevailing obsession with the logical structure of scientific theories and also the reigning prejudice in favor of a naively realistic and positivist theory of science. But within phenomenology itself, this time following Husserl's original concern, there is also a continuing concern with the nature and structure of logic and mathematics as theories and with the origin of such theories, their relation to practice and also to the lifeworld, on the one hand, and the transcendental, thinking ego on the other.

Heelan has developed the view, using the conceptual resources of Husserl, Heidegger, and Merleau-Ponty, that scientific observation, like all perception, is hermeneutical. Hermeneutical phenomenology of science focuses, in his view, not so much on theory as on experimental phenomena. Heelan defends a sort of realism called by him hermeneutic or horizonal realism as opposed to the instrumentalism of some phenomenologists. Thus, according to Heelan, in particle physics many phenomena have actual existence only within the context of the measurement processes. Kockelmans emphasizes what he regards as the ontological aspect of science: he draws attention to the role of "objectifying thematization," which lies at the root of every scientific activity. In this latter concept he brings together Husserl's idea of "thematization" and Heidegger's idea that a certain fundamental understanding of being makes possible science, philosophy, and technology. Although Kockelmans accepts the Kuhnian thesis of epochs in the history of science, he nevertheless holds that history of science is guided by an ideal of reason and that each new paradigm is necessarily a historical synthesis.

From its inception phenomenology had a special relation of love and hate toward psychology; at a later phase, it developed a special interest in history. With regard to psychology, there has been a long tradition of original work in what is known as phenomenological psychology. To the period under review belong some works of Medard Boss, Aron Gurwitsch, Hermann Minkowski, and Ricoeur. Boss has applied his Heideggerean conception of *Daseinsanalytik* to such contexts as sexual perversion, dream, and psychosomatic illness. Drawing upon his work on lived space and lived time, Minkowski studies how these can undergo modifications in psychoses, schizophrenia, manic-depression and hallucinations. Gurwitsch's *Marginal Consciousness,* posthumously published, continues the work done in *The Field of Consciousness.* However, for research in descriptive psychology, possibly the most important results are to be found in Edward Casey's two books on imagining and remembering. This research has opened out new fields of investigation. For example, in his work on remembering, Casey explores a number of neglected, nonrepresentational forms of remembering, including body memory and place memory, reminiscing and commemorating.

In the phenomenology of history, a brief reference may be made to the important work done by Ricoeur, who seeks to mediate between lived time and cosmic time. The past is irrevocably gone, and our access to it across the historical distance is made possible by creative imagination. Here fiction, by its quasi-historical character, comes to our help. History is not a totality, an absolute mediation. Nevertheless, there is a search for meaning, which is open-ended without a Hegelian *Aufhebung.* The idea of one history is a Kantian-type regulative idea.

See also Being; Cognitive Science; Critical Theory; Deconstruction; Derrida, Jacques; Frege, Gottlob; Gadamer, Hans-Georg; Heidegger, Martin; Hermeneutics; Husserl, Edmund; Indexicals; Intentionality; Kuhn, Thomas; Merleau-Ponty, Maurice; Modality, Philosophy and Metaphysics of; Phenomenological Psychology; Phenomenology; Ricoeur, Paul; Solipsism.

Bibliography

Bell, D. *Husserl.* London: Routledge, 1990.

Casey, E. S. *Imagining: A Phenomenological Study.* Bloomington: Indiana University Press, 1976.

Casey, E. S. *Remembering: A Phenomenological Study.* Bloomington: Indiana University Press, 1987.

Castañeda, H.-N. *Thinking, Language, and Experience.* Minneapolis: University of Minnesota Press, 1989.

Derrida, J. *Speech and Phenomena.* Translated by D. Allison. Evanston, IL: Northwestern University Press, 1973.

Dreyfus, H., ed. *Husserl, Intentionality, and Cognitive Science.* Cambridge, MA: MIT Press, 1982.

Føllesdal, D. "Husserl's Notion of Noema." *Journal of Philosophy* 66 (1969): 680–687.

Gurwitsch, A. *Marginal Consciousness,* edited by L. Embree. Athens: Ohio University Press, 1985.

Gurwitsch, A. *Studies in Phenomenology and Psychology.* Evanston, IL: Northwestern University Press, 1966.

Heelan, P. *Space Perception and the Philosophy of Science.* Berkeley: University of California Press, 1983.

Hintikka, J. *The Intentions of Intentionality and Other New Models for Modalities.* Dordrecht: Reidel, 1975.

Kockelmans, J. *Ideas for a Hermeneutic Phenomenology of the Natural Sciences.* Dordrecht: Kluwer Academic, 1993.

Kockelmans, J., ed. *Phenomenological Psychology: The Dutch School.* Dordrecht: Nijhoff, 1987.

Mittelstrass, J. *Die Möglichkeit von Wissenschaft.* Frankfurt am Main: Suhrkamp, 1974.

Mohanty, J. N. *Husserl and Frege.* Bloomington: Indiana University Press, 1982.

Mohanty, J. N. *The Possibility of Transcendental Philosophy.* Dordrecht: Nijhoff, 1985.

Ricoeur, P. *Time and Narrative.* Translated by K. Blarney and D. Pellauer. Chicago, 1988.

Searle, J. *Intentionality.* New York: Cambridge University Press, 1983.

Smith, D., and R. McIntyre. *Husserl and Intentionality.* Dordrecht: Reidel, 1982.

Sokolowski, R. "Husserl and Frege." *Journal of Philosophy* 84 (1987): 523–528.

von Weizsäcker, C. F. *Zeit und Wissen.* Munich: Hanser, 1992.

Jitendra N. Mohanty (1996)

PHILODEMUS
(c. 110–c. 40 BCE)

Philodemus of Gadara was an Epicurean philosopher and epigrammatic poet of the first century BCE. Born in Gadara in Palestine, he was taught philosophy in Athens by the head of the Epicurean school Zeno of Sidon (c.150–70s BCE) and by Demetrius Lacon, Zeno's younger contemporary. In the 80s or 70s he moved to Italy and earned the patronage of Lucius Calpurnius Piso Caesoninus, father-in-law of Julius Caesar. He seems to have spent part of his life at Herculaneum in Campania, probably in Piso's villa, and to have formed around him an Epicurean community of pupils and friends. His writings constitute the largest surviving portion of the library of the villa, which was buried beneath the mud and ashes when Vesuvius erupted in 79 CE and was partly excavated in the mid-eighteenth century. Thirty-seven distinct works are known or conjectured to be his and are contained in carbonized papyrus rolls in various states of fragmentation and corruption. However, it has been possible to gain considerable knowledge of Philodemus's methods and views. He emerges as a prolific writer with a wide range of interests who advances a conception of Epicurean orthodoxy first defined by Zeno and exhibits the intellectualism characteristic of the school of Athens. He was respected in educated Roman circles: Cicero speaks well of him, and he seems acquainted with both Vergil and Horace.

About thirty of his poems are preserved in the *Palatine Anthology*, and additional evidence suggests that he may have written hundreds. It is controversial whether there are relations between Philodemus's poetic output, his poetic theory, and his philosophical commitments. Except for a poetic invitation to Piso to participate in a festival in Epicurus's honor, his elegant epigrams make no mention of Epicureanism. Most of them concern love, and several contain autobiographical elements. They can be read as illustrating Philodemus's thesis that poetry as such does not benefit but only entertains.

In *On Poems*, he develops and defends his views, arguing both against literary theorists who held that a good poem be morally useful (Heraclides of Pontus, Neoptolemus of Parium, and an unnamed Stoic philosopher) and against formalists (notably, Crates of Mallos) who judged a poem only by reference to its form and aesthetic quality. He considers poetry an imitative art appreciated by reason, which requires careful composition in order to present clearly certain thoughts and move the listener. What makes a poem good is appropriate thoughts expressed in appropriate diction; changing the arrangement of words can destroy the poetic goodness of a verse. However, *On the Good King According to Homer* shows how to derive benefit from the poetry of Homer, especially how to extract both warning and advice from Homer's portrayal of different rulers. *On Music*, too, dissociates moral profit from artistic form. Music as such has no mimetic character. It is sound, an irrational element that causes pleasure to the ear. It affects the soul only via poetry, texts, or thought, which, however, are external to the musical art. *On Rhetoric* suggests a comparable approach to sophistic or epideictic rhetoric. Refuting Epicurean rivals who deny that rhetoric is an art, Philodemus holds that while forensic and political rhetoric are not arts, epideictic or sophistic rhetoric is. It consists mainly in the transmissible method of using the one naturally correct language to write clear and persuasive compositions, and the criteria pertaining to it are independent of its utility.

Philodemus gained credit for his historical work as well. The *Arrangement of the Philosophers*, especially the two books on the Academics and the Stoics, contains biographical and doxographical material and, occasionally, summaries of philosophical doctrines. The *Works on the Records of Epicurus and Some Others* relates the early history of the Epicurean school whereas the treatise *On Epicurus* eulogizes the founder and alludes to rituals of the Epicurean communities. The polemical treatises *On the Stoics* and *Against the …* should also be mentioned. Historical information about the theological doctrines of philosophers from the Presocratics to the Stoic Diogenes of Babylon is found in Philodemus's theological work *On Piety*, which offers a powerful defense of Epicurus's piety and reflects Zeno of Sidon's interpretation of Epicurus's views about the nature of the gods and our concepts and knowledge of them. *On the Gods* discusses our fear of the gods whereas *On the Way of Life of the Gods* treats aspects and attributes of divine existence. Both in theology and in other areas, Philodemus endorses the epistemological positions of his school, some of which may have been mentioned in a work on perception. *On Signs* confirms that he is also committed to the Epicurean methodology developed and defended against Stoic criticisms by Philodemus's teachers in Athens—in particular, the similarity method (a method of sign-inference based on analogy and induction) and the related procedure of comparative assessment (*epilogismos*). Two other works, one of which is subtitled *From the Lectures of Zeno*, make remarks about scientific methodology.

Philodemus engages in both theoretical and practical ethics, often in connection with moral psychology. *On Choices and Avoidances* rehearses canonical theses such as the cardinal principles of Epicurus's doctrine, the criteria of moral choice, the so-called fourfold medicine (*tetrapharmakos*), and the relation between the virtues and pleasure. *On Frank Speech* is the central piece of the ensemble *On Characters and Ways of Life*, to which *On Gratitude* and *On Conversation* also belong. It discusses frank speech (*parrhesia*), the principal educational method of late Epicurean schools and a major tool of moral and psychological therapy, and it reflects the views of Zeno on whose lectures the treatise is based.

Another major work is *On Vices and the Opposite Virtues and the People in whom they occur and the Situations in which they are found*. There survive the extant remains of three books that analyze and treat, respectively, the vices of flattery, arrogance, and greed, as well as other vices of professional administrators and money makers. The fragmentary contents of *On Wealth* are thematically related to this last topic.

The books *On Folly, On Lack of Proper Measure, On Erotic Love*, and, possibly, *On Envy* belong to the multivolume project *On the Passions*. We know very little about them whereas a good deal survives of *On Anger*, which describes the nature and consequences of anger and draws a distinction between violent rage and natural anger. Philodemus condemns the former but allows room for the latter, steering what might seem a middle course between the Peripatetic approval of rightful anger and the Stoic aim of eradicating the emotion altogether. *On Death* is conceptually related to the group *On the Passions* and may have belonged there. The surviving text addresses the question of whether the moment of death is always *physically* painful, and also examines cases in which death may cause great *emotional* pain, such as dying prematurely, ingloriously, or unjustly and leaving behind grieving friends. Philodemus's analyses and arguments, and his concession that it is sometimes natural to feel *bites* of sorrow, constitute significant contributions to moral psychology. Moreover, his methods of treating the emotions occupy an important place in the therapeutics of the Hellenistic era.

See also Cicero, Marcus Tullius; Epicureanism and the Epicurean School; Epistemology; Ethics; Hellenistic Thought; Peripatetics; Stoicism.

Bibliography

Armstrong, David, Jeffrey Fish, Patricia A. Johnston, and Marilyn. B. Skinner. *Vergil, Philodemus, and the Augustans.* Austin: University of Texas Press, 2004.

Blank, David. "Philodemus on the Technicity of Rhetoric." In *Philodemus and Poetry*, edited by Dirk Obbink, 178–188. Oxford: Oxford University Press, 1995.

De Lacy, Philip H., and Estella A. De Lacy. *Philodemus: On Methods of Inference.* Naples: Bibliopolis, 1978.

Gigante, Marcello. *Philodemus in Italy. The Books from Herculaneum.* Translated by Dirk Obbink. Ann Arbor: University of Michigan Press, 2002.

Indelli, Giovanni. *Filodemo, L'ira.* Naples: Bibliopolis, 1988.

Indelli, Giovanni, and Voula Tsouna-McKirahan. *Philodemus, On Choices and Avoidances.* Naples: Bibliopolis, 1995.

Janko, Richard. *Philodemus. On Poems Book I.* Oxford: Oxford University Press, 2000.

Konstan, David, Diskin Clay, Clarence E. Glad, et al. *Philodemus. On Frank Criticism. Introduction, Translation, and Notes.* Society of Biblical Literature. Atlanta, GA: Scholars Press, 1998.

Obbink, Dirk, ed. *Philodemus and Poetry.* Oxford: Oxford University Press, 1995.

Obbink, Dirk. *Philodemus, On Piety Part I.* Oxford: Oxford University Press, 1996.

Schofield, Malcolm. "*Epilogismos*: An Appraisal." In *Rationality in Greek Thought*, edited by Michael Frede and Gisela Striker, 221–237. Oxford: Oxford University Press, 1996.

Sider, David. *The Epigrams of Philodemos.* New York: Oxford University Press, 1997.

Sedley, David N. "On Signs." In *Science and Speculation*, edited by Jonathan Barnes. Jacques Brunschwig, Myles Burnyeat, and Malcolm Schofield, 239–272. Cambridge, U.K.: Cambridge University Press, 1982.

Sedley, David N. "Philodemus and the Decentralisation of Philosophy." *Cronache Ercolanesi* 33 (2003): 31–41.

Tsouna, Voula. "Philodemus the Therapy of Vice." *Oxford Studies in Ancient Philosophy* 21 (2001): 233–258.

Voula Tsouna (2005)

PHILO JUDAEUS
(fl. 20 BCE–40 CE)

Philo Judaeus, the Jewish Hellenistic philosopher, was the son of a wealthy and prominent Alexandrian family. Philo was well educated in both Judaism and Greek philosophy. Little is known about the actual events of his life except that in 40 CE the Jewish community of Alexandria sent him as the head of a delegation to Emperor Caligula to seek redress from the wrongs which the Gentile population inflicted upon the Jews. His *Legacy to Gaius* tells the story of this mission. Although he also wrote moral and philosophic treatises on problems then current, the main bulk of his writings are philosophic discourses on certain topics of the Hebrew Scripture. In content they are, on the one hand, an attempt to interpret the scriptural teachings in terms of Greek philosophy and, on the other, an attempt to revise Greek philosophy in the light of those scriptural traditions.

The scriptural teachings with which Philo set out to revise Greek philosophy contained certain definite conceptions of the nature of God and his relation to the world but only vague allusions to the structure and composition of the world. In dealing with the latter, therefore, he felt free to select from the various views of Greek philosophers whichever seemed to him the most reasonable, although occasionally he supported the selection by a scriptural citation. In dealing with the conception of God, however, he approached Greek philosophic views critically, rejecting those that were diametrically opposed to his scriptural traditions and interpreting or modifying those which were plastic enough to lend themselves to remolding.

GOD, PLATONIC IDEAS, CREATION

Of the various conceptions of God in Greek philosophy, Philo found that the most compatible with scriptural teaching was Plato's conception, in the *Timaeus,* of a God who had existed from eternity without a world and then, after he had brought the world into existence, continued to exist as an incorporeal being over and above the corporeal world. But to Plato, in the *Timaeus,* besides the eternal God, there were also eternal ideas. Philo had no objection to the existence of ideas as such, for he held that there was a scriptural tradition for the existence of ideas. But he could not accept the eternity of the ideas, for, according to his scriptural belief, God alone is eternal. By a method of harmonization that had been used in Judaism in reconciling inconsistencies in Scripture, Philo reconciled the *Timaeus* with the scriptural tradition by endowing the ideas with a twofold stage of existence: First, from eternity they existed as thoughts of God; then, prior to the creation of the world they were created by God as real beings. He may have found support for the need of such a harmonization in the many conflicting statements about the ideas in Plato's dialogues.

The ideas, which in Plato are always spoken of as a mere aggregation, are integrated by Philo into what he terms "an intelligible world," an expression that does not occur in extant Greek philosophic writings before him. Then, following a statement by Aristotle that the "thinking soul" (that is, nous), "is the place of forms" (that is, ideas), Philo places the intelligible world of ideas in a nous, which, under the influence of scriptural vocabulary, he surnamed Logos. Accordingly, he speaks also of the Logos as having the aforementioned two stages of existence.

For the same reason that he could not accept the view that the ideas are eternal, Philo also could not accept the view commonly held by contemporary students of Plato that the preexistent matter out of which, in the *Timaeus,* the world was created was eternal. But as a philosopher he did not like to reject altogether the reputable Platonic conception of a preexistent matter. And so here, too, he solved the difficulty by the method of harmonization. There was indeed a preexistent matter, but that preexistent matter was created. There were thus to him two creations, the creation of the preexistent matter out of nothing and the creation of the world out of that preexistent matter. For this too, it can be shown, he may have found support in certain texts of Plato.

In the *Timaeus*, Plato describes the creation of the world as an act that God "willed" ($\dot{\epsilon}\beta o\nu\lambda\acute{\eta}\theta\eta$), and similarly the indestructibility of the world is described by him as being due to the "will" ($\beta o\acute{\nu}\lambda\sigma\iota\varsigma$) of God. Presumably, by will in its application to God, Plato here means the necessary expression of God's nature, so that the creation of the world, and of this particular world of ours, was an act that could not be otherwise; and similarly the indestructibility of the world is something that cannot be otherwise. Philo, however, following the scriptural conception of God as an all-powerful free agent, takes the will by which God created the world to mean that had God

willed, he could have either not created the world or created another kind of world. And similarly, if it be his will, he can destroy the world, although, on the basis of a scriptural verse, Philo believed that God would not destroy it.

LAWS OF NATURE, MIRACLES, PROVIDENCE

The scriptural conception of God as an all-powerful free agent is extended by Philo to the governance of the world. Finding scriptural support for the belief in causality and in the existence of certain laws of nature current among Greek philosophers, except the Epicureans, Philo conceived of God's governance of the world as being effected by intermediary causes and by laws of nature which God had implanted in the world at the time of its creation. He even tried his hand at classifying the laws of nature that happen to be mentioned by various Greek philosophers. But in opposition to the Greek philosophers, to whom these laws of nature were inexorable, he maintained that God has the power to infringe upon the laws of his own making and create what are known as miracles. These miracles, however, are not created arbitrarily. They are always created with design and wisdom for the good of deserving individuals or deserving groups of individuals or humankind as a whole, for, to Philo, God governs by direct supervision not only the world as a whole but also the individual human beings within the world.

To express this particular departure of his from the generality of Greek philosophers, Philo gave a new meaning to the Greek term $\pi\rho\acute{o}\nu o\iota\alpha$, "providence." To those Greek philosophers who made use of this term it meant universal providence, that is, the unalterable operation of the inexorable laws of nature whereby the continuity and uniformity of the various natural processes in the world are preserved. To Philo it means individual providence, that is, the suspension of the laws of nature by the will and wisdom and goodness of God for the sake of human beings whose life or welfare is threatened by the ordinary operation of those laws of nature. With this conception of individual providence, Philo takes up the discussion of the human soul.

SOUL AND WILL

On the whole, Philo's conception of the soul is made up of statements derived from various dialogues of Plato. He distinguishes between irrational souls, which are created together with the bodies of both men and animals, and rational souls, which were created at the creation of the world, prior to the creation of bodies. Of these preexistent rational souls, some remain bodiless but others become invested with bodies. The former are identified by Philo with the angels of Scripture. Having in mind certain passages in Plato where such unbodied souls are identified with the popular Greek religious notions of demons and heroes, but knowing that Plato himself and also Aristotle and the Stoics dismissed these popular notions as mere myths, Philo says that the angels of Moses are what philosophers call demons and heroes, but he warns the reader not to take the existence of angels as mere myths. With regard to the preexistent rational souls that become embodied, he says, following Plato, that they are equal in number to the stars and are to be placed in newly born human beings whose bodies are already endowed with irrational souls. Again following Plato, Philo says that the irrational souls die with the bodies, whereas the rational souls are immortal. But he differs from Plato in his conception of the immortality of the soul. To Plato, the soul is immortal by nature and is also indestructible by nature. To Philo, immortality is a grace with which the soul was endowed by the will and power of God, and consequently it can be destroyed by the will and power of God if it has proved itself unworthy of the grace bestowed upon it.

A similar revision was also introduced by Philo into the Greek philosophic conception of the human will. In Greek philosophy, a distinction is made between voluntary and involuntary acts. But since all the Greek philosophers, except the Epicureans, believed in causality and in the inexorability of the laws of nature, for them the human will, to which they ascribed the so-called voluntary acts, is itself determined by causes and is subject to those inexorable laws of nature which govern the universe, including man, who is part of it. To all of them, except the Epicureans, no human act was free in the sense that it could be otherwise. The term *voluntary* was used by them only as a description of an act which is performed with knowledge and without external compulsion. To all of them, therefore, there was no free will except in the sense of what may be called relative free will. To Philo, however, just as God in his exercise of individual providence may see fit to infringe upon the laws of nature and create miracles, so has he also seen fit to endow man with the miraculous power to infringe upon the laws of his own nature, so that by the mere exercise of his will man may choose to act contrary to all the forces in his nature. This conception of free will is what may be called absolute free will.

KNOWLEDGE

Philo also revised the philosophic conception of human knowledge, including the philosophic conceptions of man's knowledge of God. Human knowledge, like all other events in the world, including human actions, is, according to Philo, under the direct supervision of God. Like all other events in the world, which are to Philo either natural, in the sense that they are operated by God through the laws of nature which he has implanted in the world, or supernatural, in the sense that they are miraculously created by God in infringement upon those laws of nature, so also human knowledge is either natural or supernatural, called by Philo "prophetic," that is, divinely revealed.

Under natural knowledge, Philo deals with all those various types of knowledge from sensation to ratiocination that are dealt with by Greek philosophers, especially Plato and the Stoics. He presents prophetic knowledge as a substitute for that type of knowledge that in Greek philosophy is placed above the various senso-ratiocinative types of knowledge and is described as recollection by Plato, as the primary immediate principles by Aristotle, and as the primary conceptions by the Stoics. Like all miracles, prophetic knowledge is part of God's exercise of his providence over individuals, groups of individuals, or humankind in general. An example of prophetic knowledge due to God's exercise of his providence over individuals is Philo's account of his own experience: Often, in the course of his investigation of certain philosophic problems, after all the ordinary processes of reasoning had failed him, he attained the desired knowledge miraculously by divine inspiration. An example of prophetic knowledge due to God's exercise of his providence over a group of individuals, as well as over humankind in general, is Philo's recounting of the revelation of the law of Moses.

HUMAN KNOWLEDGE OF GOD

Corresponding to the two kinds of human knowledge are two ways by which, according to Philo, man may arrive at a knowledge of God—an indirect ratiocinative way and a direct divinely revealed way. Philo describes the indirect way as the knowledge of the existence of God which the "world teaches" us, and he deals with the various proofs for the existence of God advanced by Greek philosophers. Most acceptable to him is the Platonic form of the cosmological proof in the *Timaeus*, inasmuch as it is based on the premise of a created world. He modifies the Aristotelian form of the cosmological proof so as to establish the existence of a prime mover, not of the motion of the world but of its existence. He similarly modifies the Stoic proof from the human mind to establish the existence not of a corporeal God immanent in the world but of an incorporeal God above the world.

In his discussion of the direct way of knowing God, however, Philo makes no mention of the Stoic proof of the innateness of the idea of God. His own direct way of knowing God he describes as a "clear vision of the Uncreated One." But as he goes on to explain it, this direct way of knowing God is only another version of the various indirect ways of knowing him and is similarly based upon the contemplation of the world. The difference between the indirect and direct ways is this: In the case of the various indirect ways, both the knowledge of the world and of the existence of God derived therefrom are attained laboriously by the slow process of observation and logical reasoning; in the case of the direct way, both the knowledge of the world and of the existence of God derived therefrom are flashed upon the mind suddenly and simultaneously by divine inspiration.

But the knowledge of God that may be gained by either of these two ways is, according to Philo, only a knowledge of his existence, not a knowledge of his essence; for as Philo maintains, "it is wholly impossible that God according to his essence should be known to any creature." God is thus said by him to be "unnamable" ἀκατόνομαστος), "ineffable" ἄρρητος), and "incomprehensible" ἀκατάληπτος). This distinction between the knowability of God's existence and the unknowability of his essence does not occur in Greek philosophy prior to Philo. In fact, in none of the extant Greek philosophic literature prior to Philo do the terms *unnamable, ineffable,* and *incomprehensible,* in the sense of incomprehensible by the mind, occur as predications of God. Moreover, it can be shown that both Plato and Aristotle held that God was knowable and describable according to his essence. Philo was thus the first to introduce this view into the history of philosophy, and he had arrived at it neither by Scripture alone nor by philosophy alone. He had arrived at it by a combination of the scriptural teaching of the unlikeness of God to anything else and the philosophic teaching that the essence of a thing is known through the definition of the thing in terms of genus and specific difference, which means that the essence of a thing is known only through its likeness to other things in genus and species. Since God is unlike anything else, he is, as Philo says, "the most generic being" (τὸ γενικώτατον), that is, the *summum genus,* and hence he cannot be defined and cannot be known.

As a corollary of this conception of the unknowability and ineffability of God, it would have to follow that one could not properly speak of God except in negative terms, that is, in terms which describe his unlikeness to other things. But still Scripture repeatedly uses positive terms as descriptions of God. All such terms, explains Philo, whatever their external grammatical form, whether adjectives or verbs, are to be taken as having the meaning of what Aristotle calls property, and the various terms by which God is described are to be taken as mere verbal variations of the property of God to act, in which he is unlike all other beings. For to act is the unique property of God; the property of all created beings is to suffer action.

THEOCRATIC GOVERNMENT

Philo widened the meaning of the conception of natural law in its application to laws governing human society. To Greek philosophers, with the exception of the Sophists, this application of the conception of natural law (or, as they would say, law in accordance with nature) meant that certain laws enacted by philosophers in accordance with what they described as reason or virtue were also in a limited sense in accordance with nature, that is to say, in the mere sense that they were in accordance with certain impulses, capacities, rational desires which exist in people by nature. The Greek philosophers assumed, however, that no law enacted for the government of humans, even when enacted by philosophers in accordance with reason and virtue, can be regarded as natural law in the sense of its being fully in harmony with the eternal and all-embracing laws of nature by which the world is governed. Philo agrees with the philosophers as to the limited sense in which enacted human law may be regarded as natural law but argues that a law revealed by God, who is the creator of the world (as, to Philo, the law of Moses was), is fully in harmony with the laws of nature, which God himself has implanted in the world for its governance. To Philo, therefore, natural law came to mean a divinely revealed law.

This widened conception of natural law led Philo to answer the question raised by Greek philosophers as to what was the best form of government. To both Plato and Aristotle no form of government based upon fixed law can be the best form of government, and Plato explicitly maintains that the best form of government is that of wise rulers who are truly possessed of science, whether they rule according to law or without law and whether they rule with or without the consent of the governed.

Against this, Philo argues that the best form of government is that based upon fixed law, not indeed upon manmade fixed law, but upon a divinely revealed fixed law. In a state governed by such a divinely revealed law, every individual has his primary allegiance to God and to the law revealed by God. Whatever human authority exists, whether secular, governing the relation of person to person, or religious, governing the relation of humanity to God, that authority is derived from the law and functions only as an instrument of the application of the law and its interpretation. Such a state, whatever its external form of government, is really ruled by God, and Philo came near coining the term *theocracy* as a description of it; the term was actually so coined and used later, by Flavius Josephus. But Philo preferred to describe it by the term *democracy,* which he uses not in its ordinary sense, as a description of a special form of government in contradistinction to that of monarchy and aristocracy, but rather as a description of a special principle of government, namely, the principle of equality before the law, which to him may be adopted and practiced by any form of government.

VIRTUE

In the course of his attempt to analyze the laws of Moses in terms of Greek philosophy, Philo injects himself into the controversy between the Peripatetics and the Stoics over the definition of virtue. Guided by scriptural tradition, he sides with Aristotle in defining virtue as a mean between two vices; hence, in opposition to the Stoics, he maintains that virtue is not the extirpation of all the emotions, that some emotions are good, that there is a difference of degree of importance between various virtues and various vices, and that the generality of human beings are neither completely virtuous nor completely wicked but are in a state which is intermediate between these two extremes and are always subject to improvement. He maintains, however, that by the grace of God some exceptional persons may be born with a thoroughly sinless nature.

Following Plato and Aristotle, both of whom include under the virtue of justice certain other virtues which they consider akin to justice, but guided also by scriptural tradition, Philo includes under justice two virtues that are entirely new and are never mentioned in any of the lists of virtues recorded under the names of Greek philosophers. Thus, on the basis of the scriptural verse (Genesis 15:6) that "Abraham had faith ($\dot{\epsilon}\pi\dot{\iota}\sigma\tau\epsilon\upsilon\sigma\epsilon\nu$) in God and it was counted to him for justice ($\delta\iota\kappa\alpha\iota\sigma\sigma\dot{\upsilon}\nu\eta\nu$)," Philo includes "faith" ($\pi\dot{\iota}\sigma\tau\iota\varsigma$), which he takes to mean faith in

the revealed teachings of Scripture, as a virtue under what the philosophers call the virtue of justice. Similarly, because the Hebrew term *ṣedakah* in Scripture is translated in the Septuagint both by $\delta\iota\kappa\alpha\iota\sigma\sigma\dot{\upsilon}\nu\eta$, "justice" (Genesis 18:19) and by $\dot{\epsilon}\lambda\epsilon\eta\mu\sigma\sigma\dot{\upsilon}\nu\eta$, "mercy," "alms" (Deuteronomy 6:25, 24:13), Philo includes "humanity" ($\phi\iota\lambda\alpha\nu\theta\rho\omega\pi\dot{\iota}\alpha$), in the sense of giving help to those who are in need of it, as a virtue under the philosophic virtue of justice. But on the basis of Scripture only, without any support from philosophy, he describes also "repentance" ($\mu\epsilon\tau\dot{\alpha}\nuo\iota\alpha$) as a virtue. In Greek philosophy, repentance is regarded as a weakness rather than as a virtue.

His scripturally based conception of free will as absolute led Philo to give a new meaning to the voluntariness of virtue and the voluntariness of the emotion of desire as used in Greek philosophy. Both Aristotle and the Stoics, using the term *voluntary* in the relative sense of free will, agree that virtue is voluntary, but they disagree as to the voluntariness of the emotions. To Aristotle, all emotions are involuntary, except the emotions of desire and anger, the latter of which by the time of Philo was subsumed under desire; to the Stoics, all emotions are voluntary. Philo, however, using the term *voluntary* in its revised sense of absolute free will, maintains that in this revised sense the term *voluntary* is to be applied, as in Aristotle, to virtue and to the emotion of desire.

Philo similarly gave a new meaning to the philosophic advice that virtue is to be practiced for its own sake. To Plato, Aristotle, and the Stoics, this advice was meant to serve as a principle of guidance to those who, like themselves, did not believe in individual providence and were not impressed by the explanations offered in the popular Greek religious theodicies as to why virtue is not always rewarded and vice not always punished. The reason underlying this advice was that since there is no certainty as to what external goods or evils would follow the practice of either virtue or vice, it is preferable for man to take his chance on the practice of virtue. This reasoning was presumably based on the common human experience that it is easier for one to induce in himself a feeling of happiness in the misery that may follow a life of virtue than it is to induce in himself a feeling of happiness in the misery, and sometimes even in the joy, that may follow a life of vice.

To Philo, however, the advice to practice virtue for its own sake is based upon his belief that providence is individual; that, despite common observation to the contrary, no virtue goes unrewarded; that acts of virtue are of graded merits; and that the reward is always in accordance with the merit of the act. With all this in the back of his mind, Philo's advice to practice virtue for its own sake (which he expresses in a different context by the statement that man is to serve God out of love and not out of expectation of a reward) means that such a practice of virtue is of the highest degree of merit, and the reward for it, which ultimately is of a spiritual nature in the hereafter, will be in accordance with its merit.

PHILOSOPHY OF HISTORY

Finally, Philo's belief in God as a free agent who acts by will and design in the world as a whole, as well as in the life of individual human beings, has led him to a theo-teleological philosophy of history. Alluding to passages in Polybius's *Histories,* in which the rise and fall of cities, nations, and countries are explained by analogy to the Stoic conception of cosmic history as a cyclical process which goes on infinitely, by necessity and for no purpose, Philo describes the cyclical changes in human history as being guided by "the divine Logos" according to a preconceived plan and toward a goal which is to be reached in the course of time. The preconceived plan and goal is that ultimately "the whole world may become, as it were, one city and enjoy the best of polities, a democracy." His description of the ultimate best of polities is an elaboration of the Messianic prophecies of Isaiah and Micah as to what will come to pass in the end of days.

This is a brief synopsis of Philo's revision of Greek philosophic conceptions of the nature of God and his relation to the world and man. The historical significance of Philo is that his revision became the foundation of the common philosophy of the three religions with cognate Scriptures—Judaism, Christianity, and Islam. This triple religious philosophy, which originated with Philo, reigned supreme as a homogeneous, if not a completely unified, system of thought until the seventeenth century, when it was overthrown by Benedict de Spinoza, for the philosophy of Spinoza, properly understood, is primarily a criticism of the common elements in this triple religious philosophy.

See also Aristotelianism; Aristotle; Emotion; Epicureanism and the Epicurean School; Hellenistic Thought; Jewish Philosophy; Logos; Love; Plato; Platonism and the Platonic Tradition; Spinoza, Benedict (Baruch) de; Stoicism; Virtue and Vice.

Bibliography

The present article is based upon H. A. Wolfson, *Religious Philosophy: A Group of Essays* (Cambridge, MA: Belknap Press of Harvard University Press, 1961), and *Philo: Foundations of Religious Philosophy in Judaism, Christianity*

and Islam, 3rd ed., rev., 2 vols. (Cambridge, MA: Harvard University Press, 1962).

Philo's writings have been translated in the Loeb Classical Library: *Philo,* translated by F. H. Colson and G. H. Whitaker, 10 vols., and 2 supp. vols. translated by Ralph Marcus (Cambridge, MA, and London, 1929–1962). *Selections from Philo,* edited with an introduction by Hans Lewy, are available in paperback in *Three Jewish Philosophers,* edited by Hans Lewy, Alexander Altmann, and Isaak Heinemann (New York: Meridian, 1960).

Works on Philo written from various points of view and of interest to students of philosophy are N. Bentwich, *Philo-Judaeus of Alexandria* (Philadelphia: Jewish Publication Society of America, 1910); Émile Bréhier, *Les idées philosophiques et religieuses de Philon d'Alexandrie,* 2nd ed., rev. (Paris, 1925); J. Daniélou, *Philon d'Alexandrie* (Paris, 1958); J. Drummond, *Philo Judaeus,* 2 vols. (London, 1888); E. R. Goodenough, *By Light, Light; the Mystic Gospel of Hellenistic Judaism* (New Haven, CT: Yale University Press, 1935); Isaak Heinemann, *Philons griechische und jüdische Bildung* (Breslau, 1932); E. Herriot, *Philon le juif* (Paris, 1898); C. Siegfried, *Philon von Alexandria* (Jena, Germany, 1875); M. Stein, *Pilon ha-Alexandroni* (Warsaw, 1937); and W. Völker, *Fortschritt und Vollendung bei Philon von Alexandrien* (Leipzig, 1938). See also H. L. Goodhart and E. R. Goodenough, "A General Bibliography of Philo," in E. R. Goodenough, *The Politics of Philo Judaeus* (New Haven, CT: Yale University Press, 1938), pp. 125–348.

Harry A. Wolfson (1967)

PHILO JUDAEUS [ADDENDUM]

The original entry on Philo Judaeus was written by Harry Wolfson, one of the preeminent scholars of medieval religious philosophy. A major premise of his general work is that Philo's philosophical project stands as the foundation for the religious philosophizing common to the three monotheistic cultures: Judaism, Christianity, and Islam. Though Philo, a Hellenized Alexandrian Jew of the first century CE, had little impact upon his own people, he had a manifest impact upon the church fathers, and according to Wolfson his "attempt to interpret the scriptural teachings in terms of Greek philosophy" was common philosophical coin until Spinoza, another Jew, in the seventeenth century tore down Philo's harmonizing project.

Philo scholarship was abundant throughout the last few decades of the twentieth century. There originated an annual conference, *The Studia Philonica Annual.* Much recent work has emphasized the Greek (Alexandrian) milieu that incubated Philo and his philosophy. Philo almost certainly knew no Hebrew and was familiar (only) with the Septuagint version of scripture. Further, his project of teasing out the inherent philosophicality of scripture took the form of allegory—a method adopted from the Stoic method of allegorical exegesis of Homer—that reached final form in the work of Crates of Mallos in the second century BCE. "Armed with Greek allegorical exegesis," writes David Winston, "which seeks out the hidden meanings that lie beneath the surface of any particular text, and given the Middle Platonist and Neo-Pythagorean penchant to read back new doctrines into the works of a venerable figure of the past, Philo was fully prepared to do battle for his ancestral tradition" (1981, p. 6). This passage by Winston describes the tool, and the philosophical prejudices, that motivated Philo to reveal the deepest truths of Scripture. As Maimonides adapted Aristotelian categories for purposes all his own, so Philo is to be understood "as essentially adapting contemporary Alexandrian Platonism, which was itself heavily influenced by Stoicism and Pythagoreanism, to his own exegetical purposes" (Dillon 1977, p. 182). Caught between two cultures, Philo stands as the first monotheistic thinker to find a manifest use for Greek philosophy for explicating his own religious tradition.

See also Aristotelianism; Homer; Maimonides; Platonism and the Platonic Tradition; Pythagoras and Pythagoreanism; Spinoza, Benedict (Baruch) de; Stoicism.

Bibliography

WORKS BY PHILO JUDAEUS

Philo of Alexandria On the Creation of the Cosmos according to Moses: Translation and Commentary. Translated by David T. Runia. Philo of Alexandria Commentary Series 1. Leiden, Netherlands: Brill, 2001.

Philo of Alexandria: The Contemplative Life, the Giants, and Selections. Translated by David Winston. New York: Paulist Press, 1981.

WORKS ON PHILO JUDAEUS AND HIS PHILOSOPHICAL BACKGROUND

Chadwick, Henry. "Philo and the Beginnings of Christian Thought." In *The Cambridge History of Later Greek and Early Medieval Philosophy,*" edited by A. H. Armstrong, 135–157. Cambridge, U.K.: Cambridge University Press, 1967.

Dillon, John. *The Middle Platonists,* 139–183. London: Duckworth, 1977.

Hay, David M., ed. *Both Literal and Allegorical: Studies in Philo of Alexandria's Questions and Answers on Genesis and Exodus.* Brown Judaic Series 232. Atlanta: 1991.

Hay, David M. "Philo's References to Other Allegorists." *Studia Philonica* 6 (1979–80): 41–75.

Hengel, Martin. *Judaism and Hellenism.* 2 vols. Philadelphia: Fortress, 1974.

Mendelson, Alan. *Philo's Jewish Identity.* Brown Judaic Series 161. Atlanta: 1988.

Nadler, Steven. "Spinoza and Philo: The Alleged Mysticism in the *Ethics.*" In *Hellenistic and Early Modern Philosophy,* edited by J. Miller and B. Inwood, 232–250. Cambridge, U.K.: Cambridge University Press, 2003.

Runia, David. *Exegesis and Scripture: Studies on Philo of Alexandria.* Variorum Collected Studies Series. London: 1990.

Runia, David. *Philo and the Church Fathers: A Collection of Papers.* Vigiliae Christianae Supplements 32. Leiden, Netherlands: Brill, 1995.

Runia, David. *Philo in Early Christian Literature: A Survey.* Compendia Rerum ad Novum Testamentum III Vol. 3. Assen-Minneapolis: 1993.

Runia, David. *Philo of Alexandria: An Annotated Bibliography 1937–86.* With R. Radice. Supplements to Vigiliae Christianae 8. Leiden, Netherlands: Brill, 1988. 2nd edition, Leiden, Netherlands: Brill, 1992.

Runia, David. *Philo of Alexandria: An Annotated Bibliography 1987–96.* Supplements to Vigiliae Christianae. Leiden, Netherlands: Brill, 2000.

Runia, David T. *Philo of Alexandria and the* Timaeus *of Plato.* PhD diss. Free University of Amsterdam. 2 vols. Amsterdam, 1983. Rev. ed., *Philo of Alexandria and the* Timaeus *of Plato,* Philosophia Antiqua 44. Leiden, Netherlands: Brill, 1986.

Sandmel, Samuel. *Philo of Alexandria: An Introduction.* New York: Oxford University Press, 1979.

Sterling, Gregory E., ed. *The Ancestral Tradition: Hellenistic Philosophy in Second Temple Judaism. Essays of David Winston.* Studia Philonica Monographs 4, Brown Judaic Series 331. Providence, RI: 2001.

Winston, David. "Aspects of Philo's Linguistic Theory." *The Studia Philonica Annual* 3 (1991): 109–125.

Winston, David. "Judaism and Hellenism: Hidden Tensions in Philo's Thought." *The Studia Philonica Annual* 2 (1990): 1–19.

Winston, David. *Logos and Mystical Theology in Philo of Alexandria.* Cincinnati, OH: Hebrew Union College Press, 1985.

Winston, David. "Philo and the Hellenistic Jewish Encounter." *The Studia Philonica Annual* 7 (1995): 124–142.

Winston, David. "Philo's Mysticism." *The Studia Philonica Annual* 8 (1996): 74–82.

Winston, David. "Philo's *Nachleben* in Judaism." *The Studia Philonica Annual* 6 (1994): 103–110.

Winston, David. "Plato's Conception of the Divine Nature." In *Neoplatonism and Jewish Thought,* edited by L. E. Goodman, 21–42. Albany: State University of New York Press, 1992.

Winston, David, and John Dillon. *Two Treatises of Philo of Alexandria: A Commentary on De Gigantibus and Quod Deus Sit Immutabilis.* Brown Judaic Series 25. Chico, CA: Scholars Press, 1983.

Daniel H. Frank (2005)

PHILOLAUS OF CROTON
(c. 470–385 BCE)

Philolaus of Croton (a Greek city in southern Italy) was a philosopher/scientist in the Pythagorean tradition. He was a contemporary of Socrates, being born c. 470 BCE, twenty years after Pythagoras died, and living until c. 385. On his first trip to Italy, Plato may have met an aged Philolaus; he mentions him as a teacher of the Thebans Simmias and Cebes in the *Phaedo*. A large body of pseudo-Pythagorean writings appeared in the first century BCE, and a number of these were forged in Philolaus's name, because he was one of the three most famous early Pythagoreans (along with Pythagoras himself and Archytas). Some fifteen fragments and a number of testimonia survive from these forged works. Philolaus, in fact, wrote one book, *On Nature*, which was probably the first book in the Pythagorean tradition (Pythagoras wrote nothing). Approximately eleven genuine fragments of that book have survived along with a number of testimonia. Aristotle discusses Pythagorean philosophy extensively but does not assign this philosophy to Pythagoras himself but rather to the "people called Pythagoreans," whom he treats as slightly older contemporaries of the atomists. This dating fits Philolaus exactly, and the agreement between the philosophy described by Aristotle and the fragments of Philolaus's book shows that Philolaus was the primary source for Aristotle's account.

Philolaus argued that the nature of the cosmos as a whole and of all things in it was to be explained in terms of two types of elements, unlimiteds and limiters. The unlimiteds include the material elements favored by his predecessors in the pre-Socratic tradition, such as earth, air, fire, and water but also continua such as space and time. Philolaus is emphatic, however, that such principles are not adequate to explain the cosmos because (1) limits, such as shapes, are also part of the cosmos humans can observe, and (2) such limiting features cannot have arisen from what is unlimited. Philolaus's cosmogony illustrates the role of these principles; the first thing to emerge was the central fire, which is a combination of the unlimited, fire, and the limiter, center. This central fire then draws in other unlimiteds such as time, void, and breath, which will be combined with limits to produce the cosmos known to humans.

Philolaus introduces harmony as an essential third principle, which specifies the way in which limiters and unlimiteds are combined. The central example is the musical scale in which the unlimited continuum of sound is limited by specific notes; harmony insures that these notes do not have a haphazard order, however, but are "fitted together" in accordance with whole number ratios. This idea depends on the earlier Greek discovery that, if a person plucks two strings, one of which is twice the length of the other, we will hear the interval of the octave between the two sounds, so that the octave corresponds to the ratio 2: 1. Similarly, the fifth will correspond to the ratio 3: 2 and the fourth to the ratio 4: 3. Philolaus appears to regard the cosmos as a whole as structured according to the ratios that determine diatonic scale. Plato may be influenced by Philolaus in using this same scale to construct the world soul in the *Timaeus*.

By specifying the "formula" according to which limiters and unlimiteds combine, numbers also define the essence of a given thing and thus play an important epistemological role for Philolaus: "And indeed all things that are known have number. For it is not possible that anything whatsoever be understood or known without this" (Fr. 4). On the one hand, Aristotle is clearly right that numbers are not separate from things in this system, as they were later in Plato; Philolaus and his successor Archytas were interested in the numbers of things, not in numbers separated from things. On the other hand, Aristotle's suggestion that the Pythagoreans thought that things just were numbers or that they were made of numbers is not supported by the fragments of Philolaus, where it is clear that things are made of limiters and unlimiteds. According to Philolaus, our senses reveal a world composed of unlimiteds and limiters (e.g., stuffs and shapes), but on further examination the phenomena point to the numerical ratios that govern them. It is doubtful that Philolaus had explicitly addressed the metaphysical status of these ratios. Aristotle may have thought that if numbers reveal the essence of things, then things are, in an important sense, numbers; but this is Aristotelian interpretation. Philolaus prefers to say that things are composed of limiters and unlimiteds and known through the numerical ratios in accordance with which the limiters and unlimiteds are combined.

Philolaus is the first person to move the earth from the center of the universe and make it a planet, and Copernicus saw Philolaus as an important predecessor. The earth does not orbit around the sun in Philolaus's system, however; the fixed stars, five planets, sun, moon, earth, and an enigmatic counter-earth all orbit around the central fire. The system may have some origins in a religious cosmology in which the central fire is identified with Tartarus, a region under the earth where the guilty are punished in Greek mythology. Aristotle suggests that the counter-earth was introduced to satisfy the *a priori* requirement that there be ten heavenly bodies around the central fire, because the Pythagoreans regarded ten as the perfect number. On the other hand, there is clear evidence that Philolaus intended the system to explain astronomical phenomena as well as satisfying *a priori* or religious requirements. The system can explain basic phenomena and is the first to include the five known planets in correct order, although it cannot account for such things as the apparent retrograde motion of planets. Philolaus clearly responded to objections to his system, which were based on the phenomena, arguing that the motion of the earth around the central fire did not produce a parallax effect, because the distance from the earth to the central fire was small in comparison to the distance between the earth and the planets. Similarly human beings never see the central fire or counter-earth, because the side of the earth on which they live is always turned away from the center, the earth rotating once on its axis during each orbit of the central-fire.

Philolaus argued that in each area of inquiry it was necessary to begin by identifying the minimum number of principles required to explain the phenomena. Limiters, unlimiteds, and harmony are the basic metaphysical principles; bile, blood, and phlegm explain disease; intellect, sensation, nutrition/growth, and generation are the basic psychic faculties. Philolaus drew an analogy between the birth of the cosmos and the birth of a human being, arguing that the embryo is initially hot and draws in cooling breath immediately upon birth, just as the cosmos begins with the central fire drawing in breath from the unlimited. It may be that he regarded the soul as a harmony of physical opposites, a view that Plato, perhaps in criticism of Philolaus, shows in the *Phaedo* to be inconsistent with a belief in an immortal soul.

In the *Philebus*, "the method of the men before our time," which Plato adapts to address problems in his own metaphysics, is clearly the metaphysical system of Philolaus, which thus had a significant impact on Plato's later metaphysics. Some have argued that Philolaus's metaphysics must go back to Pythagoras, but Aristotle clearly dates it to the time of Philolaus, and the system itself—with its emphasis on the necessity of limiters in addition to unlimiteds makes most sense, if it arose after Pythagoras—at a time when Parmenides had championed the role of limit in explaining reality.

See also Archytas of Tarentum; Pythagoras and Pythagoreanism.

Bibliography

TEXTS AND COMMENTARY

Huffman, C. A. *Philolaus of Croton: Pythagorean and Presocratic*. Cambridge, U.K.: Cambridge University Press, 1993.

DISCUSSIONS

Barnes, J. *The Presocratic Philosophers*. London: Routledge, 1982.

Burkert, W. *Lore and Science in Ancient Pythagoreanism*. Translated by E. Minar. Cambridge, MA: Harvard University Press, 1972.

Kahn, Charles H. *Pythagoras and the Pythagoreans*. Indianapolis: Hackett, 2001.

Kingsley, Peter. *Ancient Philosophy, Mystery and Magic*. Oxford: Clarendon, 1995.

Meinwald, Constance Chu. "Plato's Pythagoreanism." *Ancient Philosophy* 22 (1) (2002): 87–101.

Schibli, H. S. "On 'The One' in Philolaus, Fragment 7." *The Classical Quarterly*, n.s., 46 (1) (1996): 114–130.

Sedley, David. "The Dramatis Personae of Plato's *Phaedo*." In *Philosophical Dialogues: Plato, Hume, Wittgenstein*, edited by T. J. Smiley, 3–26. Oxford: Oxford University Press, 1995.

Carl A. Huffman (2005)

PHILO OF LARISSA
(159/8–84/3 BCE)

Philo of Larissa was a student of Clitomachus (187/6–110/9 BCE), whom he succeeded as head of the Academy in 110/09 BCE. In 88 BCE Philo transferred his activities from Athens to Rome, where Marcus Tullius Cicero, among others, studied under him. Present-day evidence does not allow one to say for certain whether Philo was the last head of the Academy or was succeeded by his student, Antiochus of Ascalon.

Philo taught rhetoric as well as philosophy, and an extended analogy of his between the way in which philosophy cares for the soul and the way in which medicine cares for the body has been preserved. But he seems to have been chiefly interested in epistemology, then the dominant concern of the Academy, and scholars are best informed about his views in this area.

It is likely that Philo first upheld Clitomachus's version of Academic skepticism, which endorsed the two theses for which Academics had argued in the their controversy with the Stoa since the time of Arcesilaus, who was head of the Academy in the mid-third century BCE. These are that nothing can be known—or a conclusion that amounts to this in the context of the debate with the Stoa—and that, in consequence, one should suspend judgment about all matters. As head of the school, however, he defended a mitigated form of skepticism that continued to embrace the thesis that nothing can be known, but now permitted assent to probable impressions, among them the impression that nothing can be known. The account of probability on which this view depends (*probabile* is Cicero's Latin for the Greek *pithanon*, meaning "persuasive") had been developed by Carneades (214/3–129/8 B.C.E.), Clitomachus's teacher, as an alternative to cognitive impressions that the Stoics had made the foundation of their epistemology and that supposedly afforded an absolutely secure guarantee of truth. This position had been anticipated by Metrodorus of Stratonicea, another pupil of Carneades, and seems to have been the position to which Aenesidemus, the one-time Academic who revived the Pyrrhonian school of skepticism in the first century BCE, objected.

In Rome, however, Philo came to hold that knowledge is possible. He did this not by renouncing the Academy's arguments against the Stoa, but by reinterpreting them. He now took them to show, not that knowledge is impossible, but that knowledge is impossible on the Stoic conception of knowledge, which is therefore mistaken. The fault lay with their insistence on a foundation of impressions that could not be false, a condition that the Academy had long argued could not be met and that Philo now held need not be met. And he maintained that his Academic predecessors had never intended to show anything else by their arguments. These new views were opposed by Academics who remained attached to skepticism and Antiochus, who had become convinced that knowledge is possible precisely because the Stoic conditions could be satisfied.

None of Philo's writings have survived. Though he probably wrote other works on epistemology and ethics, the only books we know of are the so-called "Roman Books," in which Philo set out his late views on knowledge and the history of the Academy.

See also Ancient Skepticism; Antiochus of Ascalon; Arcesilaus; Carneades; Cicero, Marcus Tullius; Stoicism.

Bibliography

Barnes, Jonathan. "Antiochus of Ascalon." In *Philosophia Togata: Essays on Philosophy and Roman Society*, edited by Miriam Griffin and Jonathan Barnes. New York: Oxford University Press, 1989.

Brittain, Charles. *Philo of Larissa: The Last of the Academic Sceptics*. New York: Oxford University Press, 2001.

Striker, Gisela. "Academics Fighting Academics." In *Assent and Argument: Studies in Cicero's Academic Books*, edited by Brad Inwood and Jaap Mansfeld. Leiden, Netherlands: Brill, 1997.

James Allen (2005)

PHILO OF MEGARA
(c. 400s BCE)

Very little is known about the life of Philo of Megara, or Philo Dialecticus. Since he was a pupil of Diodorus Cronus at the same time as Zeno of Citium, the founder of the Stoa (cf. Diogenes Laertius, DL 7.16), he was very probably active in Athens in the last decade of the 4th century BCE. He was not, as is assumed in the older literature, a member of the Megarian school of philosophy, but belonged to a separate sect, the Dialecticians. Hence there is no reason to make Megara his birthplace. From the titles of two lost treatises by the Stoic Chrysippus that were directed against Philo, we learn that Philo wrote *On Signs* (DL 7.191) and *On Moods (of Argument)* (DL 7.194). He also wrote a dialogue called the *Menexenus*, in which the five daughters of the Dialectician Diodorus Cronus, all of them also Dialecticians, were made to appear. It is possible that the theory of signs referred to in Pseudo-Galen's *Historia philosopha* c. 9 as belonging to the "dialecticians" goes back to Philo's treatise. The logical terminology in this report is in accordance with that used by the Dialecticians, and the epistemological terminology does not yet show Stoic influence. Signs are here defined as a special class of conditionals, namely sound conditionals with a true antecedent revealing the consequent. We are on safer ground with two other claims attributed to Philo, one concerning implication, the other the definition of modal concepts.

Philo argued that a conditional is true if and only if it is not the case that its antecedent is true and its consequent false (cf. Sextus Empiricus, SE *Adv. Math.* 8.113–114). Hence Philo seems to have given for the first time a truth-functional definition of the conditional. Against this claim, Diodorus Cronus held that a conditional is true if and only if it was not possible and is not possible that its antecedent is true and its consequent false (cf. SE, *Adv. Math.* 8.115–117). Thus the conditional "If it is day, I am talking," which proves to be true, according to Philo, provided that I am talking while it is day, will be false according to Diodorus. Although Sextus Empiricus in his report on this dispute has the consequent "follow" from the antecedent, it is not clear whether Philo and/or Diodorus want to make their criteria for the truth of the conditional a sufficient condition for the validity of an argument. It would have rather bizarre consequences in both cases: For Philo, any true propositions would entail each other, and for Diodorus, any true propositions about the past would entail each other.

Philo defines the possible as that "which, by the intrinsic nature of the proposition, is receptive of truth"; he defines the necessary as that "which, since it is true, by its own nature, is never receptive of falsehood". Similarly, the non-necessary is defined as that "which by its own nature is receptive of falsehood" and the impossible as that "which according to its own nature could never receive truth" (cf. Boethius, *De interpretatione* ii, 234). Here again he disagrees with Diodorus, who defines the possible as that "which either is or will be (true)." For Diodorus there can thus be no unrealized possibilities, whereas this is possible with Philo. Philo's modal logic, like that of Aristotle, seems to be based on an essentialist epistemology.

See also Chrysippus; Diodorus Cronus; Zeno of Citum.

Bibliography

WORKS BY PHILO OF MEGARA

The testimonia on Philo are to be found together with the material on Diodorus Cronus in vol. 1 of G. Giannantoni, *Socratis et Socraticorum reliquiae*. Naples: Bibliopolis, 1990, pp. 414–435. For a possibly Philonian theory of signs see: H. Diels. *Doxographi Graeci*. Berlin: Reimer, 1879, p. 605 (Pseudo-Galen, *Historia philosopha* c. 9).

WORKS ABOUT PHILO OF MEGARA

Kneale, W., and M. Kneale. *The Development of Logic*. Oxford: Clarendon, 1962 (pp. 122, 125f., 128–134).

Ebert, Theodor. "The Origin of the Stoic Theory of Signs in Sextus Empiricus." *Oxford Studies in Ancient Philosophy* 5 (1987): 83–126.

Theodor Ebert (2005)

PHILOPONUS, JOHN
(490–570)

John Philoponus of Alexandria, a sixth-century philosopher and theologian, is best known for his radical attempts to refute fundamental tenets of contemporary Aristotelian–Neoplatonic school philosophy. His main historical significance lies in the fact that he anticipated by centuries the early modern emancipation of natural philosophy from Aristotelian dogmatism. Philoponus (literally *Lover of Work*), or John the Grammarian, as he called himself, is commonly labeled a Christian Neoplatonist, but this epithet is misleading. Philoponus was a Christian, most likely by birth, and he received the standard philosophical training available at Alexandria in his day. Thus, his philosophical orientation was not a matter of choice, and his fierce rationalism, which he employed also as a tool to resolve controversial questions that divided Christianity, bears no resemblance to the genuine Christian Neoplatonism of Pseudo-Dionysius, the Areopagite (c. 500). Roughly 100 years after his death, the Third Council of Constantinople (680–681) condemned his theological doctrines as heresy and thereby curtailed the overall philosophical influence he could have had in later centuries.

Almost everything about Philoponus's life remains a matter of hypothesis. He was born presumably around 490 CE, but it is not known where (Kaster 1988); in the early sixth century, he studied in Alexandria, reading philosophy under Ammonius, Son of Hermias (c. 440–520), who had been a pupil of Proclus at Athens. In the early 520s, Philoponus taught both grammar and philosophy at Alexandria; some of his early commentaries on Aristotle are based on Ammonius's lectures, but in the process of multiple revisions, Philoponus added explanations, observations, and criticisms of his own. In the late 520s, early 530s, around the time of Justinian's eviction of the pagan philosophers in Athens (c. 529), Philoponus turns to writing polemical commentaries (on Proclus and Aristotle), which no longer aim at elucidation but at refutation, especially of the pagan doctrine of eternalism. These works provoked immediate condemnation of by Simplicius of Cilicia, a contemporary member of the Athenian School, the last great pagan mind of antiquity and expert commentator on Aristotle.

Although Philoponus was one of the most powerful and independent thinkers of his time, he never succeeded Ammonius as professor of philosophy. The reasons for this are unclear; although unknown external, personal or political circumstances may have played a role, a likely explanation is that Philoponus had reached a point where his fundamental disagreement with the philosophical establishment compromised his ability to continue the pedagogical tradition of the school. Leadership of the philosophical school remained in pagan hands well into the second half of the sixth century. Philoponus's later writings, from the 540s onward, deal with contemporary issues of theological controversy. He expounded his theological views with philosophical rigor, whether rejecting the orthodox belief in the divine–human duality of the nature of Christ (miaphysitism) or defending the substantial distinctness of the hypostases of the Trinity (tritheism). Philoponus must have died around 570.

Philoponus' *œuvre*, which bears witness to his interests in grammar, philosophy, psychology, medicine, mathematics, astronomy, and theology, may be divided into three related yet distinct parts (Scholten 1996): (1)

The commentaries on Aristotle (*Categories, Prior and Posterior Analytics, Physics, On Generation and Corruption, Meteorology*, and *On the Soul*); (2) the treatises of the critical period, notably, the two monumental polemical treatises *On the Eternity of World against Proclus* (shortly after 529) and the influential *On the Eternity of World Against Aristotle* (early 530s, extant only in fragments); and (3) a number of works on theological doctrine, some of which are only extant in Syriac translation; most important of the last group is a still-extant commentary on the biblical creation myth (*On the Making of the World*, written between 546 and 560) which also targets the naïve Christian cosmography of Cosmas Indicopleustes.

In his philosophical works, one can roughly distinguish between two kinds of criticism: on the one hand, the grappling with implausible Aristotelian theories, mostly physical, and on the other hand, outright repudiation of fundamental cosmological doctrines. Aristotle's definition of light as an incorporeal and instantaneous transition from the potentiality (*dunamis*) of a medium to be transparent to the actuality (*energeia*) of transparency fails to account for the laws of optics and for the calefactory property of the sun. Philoponus proposes to interpret light as an *incorporeal activity* rather than a state, capable of warming bodies and comparable to the soul in animals. Later, in the *Meteorology* commentary, which may be the transcript of his last lecture series on Aristotle, he argues materialistically that light and heat are consequences of the fiery nature of the sun, and that heat is generated when the rays emanating from the sun are refracted and warm the air through friction.

The *Physics* commentary contains one of his most celebrated achievements, the theory of the impetus, which is commonly regarded as a decisive step from an Aristotelian dynamics toward a modern theory based on the notion of inertia. To what extent Philoponus was influenced by previous philosophical or theological authors is a matter of controversy (Fladerer 2003). His own discussion, at any rate, commences with the expression of dissatisfaction with Aristotle's explanation that a projectile continues to move on account of the air's turbulence generated by the projectile itself. Philoponus proposes instead that a projectile moves on account of a kinetic force that is impressed on it by the mover and that exhausts itself in the course of the movement. In short, the medium contributes nothing to a projectile's motion; rather, it impedes it. Moreover, Philoponus holds that there is nothing to prevent motion from taking place in the void.

Occasionally, Philoponus resorts not only to thought experiments but also to pertinent observations that resemble physical experimentation. Aristotle's verdict that the speed of a falling body is proportional to its weight and indirectly proportional to the density of the medium is challenged by the same kind of empirical evidence that Galileo mustered centuries later.

Philoponus is critical of Aristotle's conception of space. He substitutes Aristotle's definition of the *place* of a body (the inner surface of that which contains it) with a conception of three-dimensional extension, its volume. Likewise, the most fundamental level of physical reality is not some mysterious *prime matter* but three-dimensional, indeterminate, and unqualified *corporeal extension*, a concept reminiscent of Descartes's *res extensa*.

The issue at stake in the two polemics against Proclus and Aristotle is the question of the contingency of the world. The earlier work obliterates a pamphlet of eighteen arguments for the eternity of the world written in the previous century by the powerful Neoplatonist Proclus. The lost *Against Aristotle* tackled influential arguments for eternity in *On the Heavens I* and *Physics VIII*. In both cases, Philoponus succeeds in pointing out numerous contradictions, inconsistencies, fallacies, and improbable assumptions. One clear casualty is Aristotle's peculiar postulate of an incorruptible celestial element (ether). The observable irregularities in the heavens, their complexity and changes in color, undermine the thesis of the radical ontological difference between the celestial and sublunary regions. Dissecting the text in unprecedented ways, Philoponus even paves the way for influential demonstrative arguments for noneternity. Although Philoponus concedes that in nature nothing comes to be from nothing, he offers the first *philosophical* defense of the Christian belief that God created the world *ex nihilo*. In the late theological treatise *On the Making of the World*, Philoponus suggests in passing that the celestial bodies were set to spin by a powerful impetus at the time of their creation and that they now continue to move not on account of their own nature but by the will of God.

It is impossible to gauge how Philoponus's ideas resonated with Christians during his lifetime. He was read and admired by Syrian and, to some extent, Islamic philosophers, but the anathema of 681 severely hampered the further propagation of his theological and philosophical work. As Simplicius before them, later thinkers like Thomas Aquinas (1224–1274) and Zabarella (1533–1589) roundly rejected Philoponus. Eventually, the arguments against eternity persuaded Bonaventure

(1217–1274) and Gersonides (1288–1344), and the theory of the impetus was reaffirmed by Buridan (1295–1356) and Oresme (1325–1382). In the sixteenth century, the first editions as well as numerous translations (into Latin) of the commentaries and the treatise against Proclus began to appear in print. In particular, Philoponus's criticism of Aristotle in the *Physics* commentary was widely discussed and persuaded such diverse thinkers as Gianfrancesco Pico della Mirandola (1469–1533) and Galileo Galilei (1564–1642).

See also Aristotelianism; Bonaventure, St.; Buridan, Jean; Galileo Galilei; Gersonides; Impetus; Neoplatonism; Oresme, Nicholas; Pico della Mirandola, Gianfrancesco; Proclus; Pseudo-Dionysius; Simplicius; Thomas Aquinas, St.; Zabarella, Jacopo.

Bibliography

MAJOR WORKS

On the Use and Construction of the Astrolabe, edited by H. Hase. Bonn: Weber, 1839 (ibid., Rheinisches Museum für Philologie 6, 1839, 127–171). Reprinted and translated into French by Alain P. Segonds, *Jean Philopon, traité de l'astrolabe*. Paris: Librairie Alain Brieux, 1981. Translated into English by H. W. Green in *The Astrolabes of the World*. Vols. 1 & 2. Robert T. Gunther. Oxford: University Press, 1932; Reprinted, London: Holland Press, 1976, pp. 61–81.

Commentary on Aristotle's Physics. In *Commentaria in Aristotelem Graeca*, XVI–XVII, edited by H. Vitelli. Berlin: Reimer, 1887–1888. Philoponus's most important commentary in which he challenges Aristotle's tenets on time, space, void, matter, and dynamics; there are signs of revision. Partial translations: *Philoponus, On Aristotle's Physics 2*, by A. R. Lacey. London: Duckworth, 1993; *Philoponus, On Aristotle's Physics 3*, by M. Edwards. London: Duckworth, 1994; *Philoponus, On Aristotle's Physics 5–8*, by Paul Lettinck. London: Duckworth 1993–1994; *Philoponus, Corollaries on Place and Void*, by David Furley. London: Duckworth, 1991.

On the Making of the World (*De opificio mundi*), edited by Wilhelm Reichardt. Leipzig: Teubner, 1897. Greek text and German translation by Clemens Scholten. *De opificio mundi = Über die Erschaffung der Welt*. Freiburg, New York: Herder, 1997. A theological–philosophical commentary on the Creation story in the book of Genesis, written probably 557–560.

On the Eternity of the World against Proclus (*De aeternitate mundi contra Proclum*), edited by Hugo Rabe. Leipzig: Teubner, 1899. Reprinted, Hildesheim: Olms, 1984. Translated by Helen S. Lang and Anthony D. Macro. *De aeternitate mundi. English and Greek*. Berkeley: University of California Press, 2001. A detailed criticism of Proclus's eighteen arguments in favor of the eternity of the world.

On the Eternity of the World against Aristotle (*De aeternitate mundi contra Aristotelem*). Not extant; fragments reconstructed and translated by Christian Wildberg. *Philoponus, Against Aristotle on the Eternity of the World*.
London: Duckworth, 1987. A refutation of Aristotle's doctrines of the fifth element and the eternity of motion and time consisting of at least eight books.

FURTHER READING

Fladerer, Ludwig. "Johannes Philoponos, Gregor von Nyssa und die Genese der Impetustheorie." In *Hommages à Carl Deroux V*, edited by Pol Defosse. Collection Latomus 279 (2003): 138–151.

Haas, Frans A. J. de. *John Philoponus' New Definition of Prime Matter: Aspects of its Background in Neoplatonism and the Ancient Commentary Tradition*. Leiden, New York: E. J. Brill, 1997.

Kaster, Robert A. *Guardians of Language. The Grammarian and Society in Late Antiquity*, 334–338. Berkeley: University of California Press, 1988.

Sambursky, Samuel. *The Physical World of Late Antiquity*, 154–175. London: Routledge and Kegan Paul, 1962.

Scholten, Clemens. *Antike Naturphilosophie und christliche Kosmologie in der Schrift "De opificio mundi" des Johannes Philoponos*. Berlin: De Gruyter, 1996.

Sorabji, Richard R. K. *Matter, Space, and Motion*, 227–248. London: Duckworth, 1988.

Sorabji, Richard R. K., ed. *Philoponus and the Rejection of Aristotelian Science*. London: Duckworth, 1987.

Sorabji, Richard R. K. *Time, Creation and the Continuum*, 193–231. London: Duckworth, 1983.

Verrycken, Koenraad. "The Development of Philoponus' Thought and Its Chronology." In *Aristotle Transformed*, edited by Richard R. K. Sorabji, 233–274. London: Duckworth, 1990.

Wildberg, Christian. "Impetus Theory and the Hermeneutics of Science in Simplicius and Philoponus." *Hyperboreus* 5 (1999): 107–124.

Wildberg, Christian. *John Philoponus' Criticism of Aristotle's Theory of Aether*. Berlin: De Gruyter, 1988.

Christian Wildberg (2005)

PHILOSOPHICAL ANTHROPOLOGY

Modern philosophical anthropology originated in the 1920s. During the 1940s it became the representative branch of German philosophy. It arose with, and has absorbed, *Lebensphilosophie*, existentialism, and phenomenology, although it is not identical with them. It has affinities with pragmatism and the sociology of knowledge. Although it is historically based on certain German traditions, it is also indebted to, and largely anticipated by, the eighteenth-century "science of human nature." It combines the critical traditions of the Enlightenment with an emphasis on dogmatic certitude.

HISTORICAL BACKGROUND

Following Bernhard Groethuysen, philosophical anthropology is often conceived as embracing all previous philosophy, insofar as previous philosophy dealt with man's place in the world. But this wide conception blurs the distinctive features of philosophical anthropology. Its history is best restricted to those authors and ideas whose impact is either admitted or can be traced in the literature of modern philosophical anthropology.

The impact of Søren Kierkegaard, Karl Marx, and Friedrich Nietzsche is pervasive. Other generally acknowledged forerunners are Blaise Pascal, Johann Gottfried Herder, Johann Wolfgang von Goethe, Immanuel Kant, G. W. F. Hegel, and Ludwig Feuerbach. Pascal's influence is discernible in philosophical anthropology's conception of man as self-contradictory and mysterious, capable of surpassing his natural limits in quest of authenticity. Pascal's distinction between the organic *esprit de finesse* and the abstract and lifeless *esprit géométrique* was accentuated by Kant's distinction between the phenomenal world of the senses, with its quest for happiness (in the sense of egotistic pleasure), and the noumenal world of the thing-in-itself, between a world of determinate law and a world of transcendental choice. These concepts reveal themselves in the philosophical anthropologists' assumption of an unbridgeable gap between value and reason, between the ideal and the practical. Kant's basic questions—"What can I know? What ought I to do? What may I hope?"—are universally accepted in philosophical anthropology.

Herder was the first German author to correlate biology and the philosophy of man. From him stems the conception of man as a deficient being who must compensate for his lack of natural tools and weapons by the creative use of weapons and technology. Hegel's theory of alienation and its Marxist version have become a vital element in philosophical anthropology's comprehension and critique of society. Feuerbach formulated the claim that man can be used as the common denominator of philosophy, the true *ens realissimum*, embracing reason, will, and emotion. He held that philosophical anthropology was to take the place of theology; and indeed, contemporary philosophical anthropology may be regarded as secularized theology. Feuerbach conceived of God as a projection and objectification of the human spirit, reflecting the categorial structure of the human mind and its conceptual tools. This, as well as the corresponding Hegelian view of the divine spirit as being reflected in human history, is one of the recurring themes of cultural philosophical anthropology.

In a specifically German version and modified by the methodology of the practitioners of the *Geisteswissenschaften*, the "science of human nature," which stemmed from Thomas Hobbes, John Locke, and the Earl of Shaftesbury and reached its culmination in the eighteenth century, is the principal root of philosophical anthropology. David Hume's *Treatise of Human Nature* provided a program for philosophical anthropology. "There is no question of importance whose decision is not comprised in the science of man…. In pretending to explain the principles of human nature we in effect propose a complete system of the sciences" (Everyman ed., Vol. I, p. 5). Philosophical anthropology took up Hume's empiricism with regard to the moral sciences, as well as his conception of religion.

Adam Smith's spectator theory of the moral sentiments was an early statement of the excentric position of man. The "Newtonian-Baconian" school of Scottish and French social thought of the eighteenth century (Francis Hutcheson, Adam Ferguson, John Millar, Dugald Stewart, Pierre-Louis Moreau de Maupertuis, Denis Diderot, and Jean Le Rond d'Alembert), which culminated in John Stuart Mill's sociology, was a direct precursor of philosophical anthropology in its aim of putting the study of man on an empirical biological basis. This school sought to elucidate and bridge the gap between man's distinctive nature and the sociocultural order in "the belief that it was natural for man to make an order of life different from that in which the race was nurtured earlier, that it was in the nature of his equipment that he should react intelligently and creatively to the situations in which he found himself" (G. Bryson, *Man and Society*, Princeton, NJ, 1945, p. 173).

The more widely recognized forerunners of philosophical anthropology—Herder, Christian Garve, and Wilhelm von Humboldt—were directly influenced by the Scottish and French anthropologists and Encyclopedists, who had undermined Cartesian dualism. Thus, at the end of the eighteenth century, there was a wide acceptance of certain propositions concerning man's creative powers, his individuality, and his sociability. The Scottish and French precursors, however, had intended to develop more rigorous methods of investigation than those used by contemporary philosophical anthropologists.

SUBJECT MATTER, ATTITUDE, AND GOAL

Like existentialism and *Lebensphilosophie*, philosophical anthropology studies man's existence, his experiences, and his anxieties, combining the subjectivism of existentialism with the cultural objectivism of *Lebensphilosophie.* It uses the phenomenological methods of *Verstehen* and reduction. Philosophical anthropology shares with existentialism, phenomenology, and *Lebensphilosophie* a critique of society. Yet these currents are not identical; Heidegger and Karl Jaspers, for example, refuse to be identified with philosophical anthropology, despite their great impact on it.

Philosophical anthropology seeks to interpret philosophically the facts that the sciences have discovered concerning the nature of man and of the human condition. It presupposes a developed body of scientific thought, and accordingly, in its program it aspires to a new, scientifically grounded metaphysics. It seeks to elucidate the basic qualities that make man what he is and distinguish him from other beings. It combines, and mediates between, what Kant designated as physiological and pragmatic anthropology.

Physiological anthropology studies man's natural limitations; pragmatic anthropology deals with man's potentialities, with what he, as a free agent, makes of himself, or is able and ought to make of himself. Thus, philosophical anthropology studies both man as a creature and man as the creator of cultural values—man as seen by a scientific observer and man as interpreted by himself (*Aussen-* and *Innenansicht*). Accordingly, most philosophical anthropologists wish to combine scientific methods with an imaginative philosophical approach.

Philosophical anthropology seeks to correlate the various anthropologies that have developed with the specialization of the sciences. Max Scheler distinguished between scientific, philosophical, and theological anthropologies, or interpretations of the fundamental structure of human activities, which know nothing of one another. In order to stem what its followers describe as anarchy of thought and the "loss of the center," philosophical anthropology offers itself as a coordinating discipline. With the dissolution of traditional beliefs in guidance by gods, by kings and feudal leaders, by God, or by nature, there is today a general lack of direction. Man is now, as he was for Protagoras, the only possible measure. By coordinating and interpreting fragmented knowledge, philosophical anthropology aims at a new understanding of man's essential qualities and potentialities. It aims to accomplish this by the development of suitable methods, by a factual elucidation of the perplexities inherent in human institutions, and by borderline research (coordinating different branches of the sciences) used as a basis for a new "map of knowledge."

Since philosophical anthropology arose as an interpretation of various scientific disciplines, it has practitioners in many fields. Although there are only a few academic chairs of philosophical anthropology (Göttingen, Nijmegen), the number of professed philosophical anthropologists is large, chiefly in the German-speaking countries, but also in the Netherlands, Spanish-speaking countries, the United States, and France. Modern French humanism, whether existentialist, religious, or Marxist, is both historically and analytically allied with philosophical anthropology. Many philosophical anthropologists stress that they are theological, historical, political, juristic, biological, phenomenological, or cultural philosophical anthropologists. Much so-called philosophical anthropology is best treated under metaphysics, ontology, theory of value, epistemology, theology, philosophy of science or of history, or under the related contemporary philosophies. This entry will discuss only the distinctive features.

Philosophical anthropology embraces most of the social sciences. Some leading practitioners, such as Arnold Gehlen, emphasize the concept of action, rather than man, as the distinguishing feature of philosophical anthropology, and define it as a new empirical discipline, *Handlungswissenschaft* (similar to "behavioral science" and the "theory of action"), as distinct from the natural sciences and the *Geisteswissenschaften.*

Philosophical anthropology is an attempt to construct a scientific discipline out of man's traditional effort to understand and liberate himself. At the same time, however, it is pervaded by the same antiscientific currents that mark existentialism, *Lebensphilosophie,* and phenomenology. But it is its dialogue with science that gives philosophical anthropology its peculiar character.

THE CRISIS OF SCIENCE

Philosophical anthropologists see a "crisis of science," a crisis first brought into view by three "humiliations of man." First, the humiliation of Copernican astronomy removed man's habitat, the earth, from the center of the universe; second, Charles Darwin's biological evolutionism "shamed and degraded" man; and third, the historical schools revealed the relativity of religious and national cultural values. The crisis in science has been brought to a head by modern developments in depth psychology, post-Euclidean mathematics, and the indeterminacy principle in nuclear physics. From the scientific point of view, these developments represent advances rather than a crisis. However, German philosophers since Kant have conceived of science as being fixed in a rigid mathematicomechanical determinism. According to philosophical anthropologists, this basic concept has broken down. There is a wide consensus among Continental thinkers that nineteenth-century materialism has been overcome and that the methods of the *Geisteswissenschaften* and phenomenology have been vindicated.

These methods seek the meaning immanent in events and in the works of man rather than the causal nexus between events. They aim to interpret other minds (both individual and collective), their peculiar intentions and tendencies, and the institutions through which their ideas have found expression. They investigate the conscious and unconscious actions of human beings and the structure of interpersonal (social and cultural) relationships. These methods are descriptive, interpretative, organic, and concrete, rather than explanatory, mechanical, and abstract, as in the natural sciences. This distinction of two methodologies—causal explanation on the one hand and *Verstehen* and phenomenological reduction on the other—takes up the emphasis of what is known in English as the Germano-Coleridgean school on, in the words of J. S. Mill, a philosophy of society in the form of a philosophy of history seeking a philosophy of human culture.

THEORY OF KNOWLEDGE

The crisis of science, according to philosophical anthropologists, evinces a deep crisis in the theory of knowledge—a crisis that makes imperative the adoption of pragmatic theories of truth. Traditional epistemology, they claim, was occupied with only one of the functions of consciousness. It failed to take into account what Pascal called the *logique du coeur* or *esprit de finesse,* which was akin to Samuel Taylor Coleridge's "imagination" and John Henry Newman's "illative reason." And consciousness itself is only a part of the forces that shape human reasons. For philosophical anthropologists, as for sociologists of knowledge, knowledge is determined by dispositions and by outside factors. Erich Rothacker claims that all knowledge is based on the particular ways of thought (*dogmatische Denkformen*) of national and sectional cultures, which determine both the questions asked and the answers given. Questions and answers have no validity apart from their appropriateness to the cultural environment (*Umwelt*). On the other hand, Scheler sought to establish an objective scale of values that would take into account nonrational elements. He distinguished in an ascending order the strata of vitality, intellectuality, and holiness (*Herrschaftswissen, Leistungswissen,* and *Heilswissen*). Despite his epistemological relativism,

Rothacker has applied a similar scheme of "lower" and "higher" values in his psychological theory. Although most philosophical anthropologists profess value relativism, implicit value scales may be discerned underlying their methodological views and cultural criticism.

METHODOLOGY

Philosophical anthropology rejects the Cartesian dualism of body and soul: Man is not part animal and part spirit but a being *sui generis,* distinct from animals in physical condition and in aspirations. This attitude, together with philosophical anthropology's theological roots, may account for a nearly universal (although currently weakening) rejection of Charles Darwin and Sigmund Freud for allegedly appealing to the forces of primitivism and animality in man. At the same time, many philosophical anthropologists reject modern intellectualism; their rejection of rationality, like that of many existentialists and *Lebensphilosophs,* has its roots in the romantic reaction to the Enlightenment and the French Revolution. In its suspicion of *Verwissenschaftlichung* ("scientism"), philosophical anthropology perpetuates the traditional German attacks on *Reflexionsphilosophie,* in which the nonrational aspects of reality are alleged to be ignored.

Philosophical anthropology's conception of method was formulated by Wilhelm Dilthey and Edmund Husserl. Husserl's nonempirical phenomenological approach to philosophical questions was claimed to be presuppositionless, wholly scientific, and logically prior to the natural sciences. It is concerned with meanings, an intuitive comprehension of directly experienced essences, and it involves a distinct method for "analyzing" (or rather, interpreting) facts, qualities, relationships, and the basic categories of human nature and culture—a method of analysis different from that which results in an explanatory theory. However, such thinkers as the biologist Adolf Portmann and the psychologist Karl Jaspers attempt to combine the scientific and interpretative approaches.

Ludwig Binswanger, for example, does not exclude the methods of natural science, but raises two objections to reveal their inherent limitations. One is that all abstractions are transpositions and simplifications of reality. The other is that the registration of stimuli in experimental psychology restricts the field of investigation so as to make the perception of meaningful wholes impossible; it precludes the essential selective and synthesizing activities.

Helmuth Plessner sees philosophical anthropology as the paradigm of borderline research. Although there is still a methodological gap between the physical and the social sciences, there has been spectacular progress toward methodological and substantive unification of physics, chemistry, and mineralogy, and of physiology and biochemistry. This progress supplies a model for philosophical anthropology. In its physical concerns, philosophical anthropology should correlate the work of medicine, zoology, chemistry, and physics, and in its nonphysical concerns, it should correlate the work of psychology, psychoanalysis, psychiatry, and the cultural sciences.

The physical and nonphysical concerns correspond to the traditional divisions of body and soul and of empiricism and subjective idealism. The division between body and soul emphasizes the ineluctable natural limitations of man and the determined aspects of his nature, and thus ignores his freedom and historicity, while the division between empiricism and subjective idealism has traditionally lost itself in metaphysical speculation. Philosophical anthropology tries to avoid both extremes; it sees man as essentially *homo absconditus,* inscrutable, an open question. Man must formulate his destiny so that he is not held rigidly in one role but safeguards his creative freedom. The direction in which this freedom permits man to fulfill himself is not amenable to scientific discovery, and thus science is devalued. Man's choices depend on his philosophical understanding of his own position in the world.

An infinite variety of choices is open to man. What distinguishes man's nature is not how he chooses, but that he does choose—that he is not determined by his biological and physiological constitution but is formed in the light of cultural values he himself has created and internalized. Philosophical anthropology's contribution to the study of cultures is its emphasis on the creative element in the unfolding of the various conceptions of man's position in the world. Therefore, man's self-understanding, or self-image, is a central theme of philosophical anthropology.

THE SELF-IMAGE OF MAN

Formerly, man was threatened not primarily by man, but by nature. Through science, nearly all natural phenomena have been or can be brought under man's control. Man is threatened neither by nature nor by the God who made nature, but by his own use of nature. Man's enemy is man, manmade structures, or the God who made man.

Again, even in coming to know nature, man (or his scientific representatives) meets himself rather than nature. Man no longer seeks nature as such, but nature as

we question it for specific scientific purposes and in the specific contexts of axiomatic frameworks that we ourselves have determined.

Thus, man is inescapably confronted by man. We have reason to ask, What is this man? But what causes us to ask questions about the form in which man's subjective image of himself appears in his consciousness?

Man's subjective image determines what he makes of himself. Animals are as nature has created them, but man must complete his character; nature has supplied only the rudiments of it. Man must form his own personality, and he does so according to his image of what he can and should be. Scheler has delineated a historical typology of Western man's self-images, or "reality-worlds."

Man first saw himself as *homo religiosus,* a view based on the Judeo-Christian legacy of supernaturalism and its ensuing feelings of awe and of inherited guilt. The next stage was *homo sapiens,* rational man in harmony with the divine plan. Since the Enlightenment, this image has been largely superseded by the naturalistic, pragmatic image of *homo faber*—man as the most highly developed animal, the maker of tools (including language), who uses a particularly high proportion of his animal energy in cerebral activities. Body and soul are regarded as a functional unity. Human being and development are explained by the primary urges of animal nature—the desire for progeny and the desire for food, possessions, and wealth. Machiavellianism, Marxism, racism, Darwinism, and Freudianism, it is claimed, are based on this interpretation of man.

These three self-images of man have in common a belief in the unity of human history and in a meaningful evolution toward higher organization. The images of *homo dionysiacus* and *homo creator* break with this tradition and herald a new orientation of anthropological thought. In the image of man as *homo dionysiacus,* man sees decadence as immanent in human nature and history. Typical exponents of this view are Arthur Schopenhauer, Nietzsche, and neoromantics like Ludwig Klages, Oswald Spengler, and Leo Frobenius. Man is seen as the "deserter" or the faux pas of life; as a megalomaniac species of rapacious ape; as an infantile ape with a disorganized system of inner secretions; or as essentially deficient in vital powers and dependent for survival on technical means. Man's power of thought is an artificial surrogate for missing or weak instincts, and his "freedom to choose" is a euphemism for his lack of direction. Human social institutions are pitiful crutches for assuring the survival of a biologically doomed race. Reason is regarded as separate from the soul, which belongs to the vital sphere of the body. Reason is the destructive, "demoniac" struggle with, and submergence of, the healthy activity of the soul.

The image of man as *homo creator* is likewise derived from Nietzsche, and also from Feuerbach. But the Nietzschean superman has been transformed into a stricter philosophical conception by Nicolai Hartmann, Max Scheler, and the Sartrean existentialists. Scheler called this view a "postulatory atheism of high responsibility." Man has no ontological knowledge of an ultimate being. Contrary to Kant's postulate of the ethical need for a God, in the new view there must be no God—for the sake of human responsibility and liberty. Only in a mechanical, nonteleological world is there the possibility of a free moral being. Where there is a planning, all-powerful God, there is no freedom for man responsibly to work out his destiny. Nietzsche's phrase "God is dead" expresses the ultimate moral responsibility of man; the predicates of God (predestination and Providence) are to be related to individual man.

Man's awareness of his own self-images illuminates the whole range of his genuine potentialities so that his choice of an authentic form of life is not restricted by narrowness of view.

THE MAJOR BRANCHES

Philosophical anthropology shares with French humanism a particular critical analysis of society, but before this analysis can be presented, it is necessary to make a survey of the important branches of philosophical anthropology and of their results.

BIOLOGICAL PHILOSOPHICAL ANTHROPOLOGY.
The reaction to determinism in the physical sciences has given rise to biological philosophical anthropology, or bioanthropology. Bioanthropology scrutinizes biological theories philosophically, primarily to correlate man's creative achievements and attitudes with his physiological organization. Man's cultural role—his character as a symbol-making being capable of abstraction, forethought, language, and intersubjective communication—is depicted as an irreducible function of his physiological constitution.

Among many important practitioners of bioanthropology are the biologists F. J. J. Buytendijk and Adolf Portmann and the philosopher Arnold Gehlen. Important starting points of bioanthropological thought have been Walter Garstang's concept of paidomorphosis and Jakob von Uexküll's concept of milieu (*Umwelt*), which was developed earlier, in philosophical terms, by Edmund Husserl. Paidomorphosis emphasizes the embryonic qualities that are preserved in man but lost in adult animals, as well as man's retarded extrauterine development. Gehlen has used the concept of man as a fetal ape to account for man's cultural achievements which, he claims, are conditioned by man's helpless status in the world. Devoid of instincts and of natural weapons and tools, man has been compelled to compensate for his shortcomings by active responses to the challenges of his environment and of his physiological urges. Man defends himself by his actions, whose scope, direction, and intensity, in contrast to instinctive reactions, are within his discretion. He transforms the natural environment into a system of action (*Handlungskreis*), the responses to which are perpetuated in institutions and language. Man's cultural environment is thus both a physiological condition of his survival and a distinctive criterion of his nature.

Uexküll. From his investigations into animal physiology, Uexküll derived a theory of the specific environmental determination of human life. Each species of animal lives in its own *Umwelt*; its consciousness of sense data is strictly limited by its innate capacities of perception. The range of these capacities corresponds to the teleology immanent in the "life plan" of different animals and is strictly limited to the life plan's specific tasks. Uexküll started from Kant's theory that the categories of the understanding determine the perception and conception of the data of the senses. It was Uexküll's teleological interpretation that distinguished his work from that of Western contemporaries who independently developed the sociology of animals. In the German romantic tradition, Uexküll was concerned with fighting the "mechanistic," positivistic conception of science that he saw represented in biochemistry and behaviorism.

Buytendijk. Buytendijk's physiological and psychological investigations have been undertaken in close contact with such phenomenologically oriented thinkers as Scheler, Plessner, Viktor von Weizsäcker, and V. E. von Gebsattel. Like Uexküll, Buytendijk rejects Cartesian dualism and its mechanical interpretation of bodily processes; unlike Uexküll, he rejects the hypothesis that man is determined by his *Umwelt*. Through his detailed comparisons of animal and human physiology and psychology, Buytendijk has sought to work out man's unique condition as expressed in his capacity for abstraction and symbolization (the ability to create signs representing what is bodily absent), and in his capacity for the logical correlation of signs. For Buytendijk, biology is a historical science that must be understood in motivational, teleological terms. He conceives of motives and processes as value-related and spontaneous, derived from the built-in planning capacity of a self-structuring organism. Parallels with *verstehende* sociology are obvious, but Buytendijk's impressive ability to rest his philosophical views on a biological basis cannot conceal the fact that he held his views prior to his scientific illustration and testing of them.

Portmann. Adolf Portmann's work represents the culmination of bioanthropology. It aims at an integration of biological with psychological, sociological, and anthropological thought. According to Portmann, human biology has turned into anthropology, because the life of man, despite superficial similarities to animal life, is something sui generis. Portmann emphasizes the uniqueness of human action, language, foresight, and upright carriage, and of the human growth rhythm—duration of pregnancy, bodily proportions, extrauterine babyhood, and late formation of the female pelvis. These qualities, he claims, arise from a characteristic interpenetration of the hereditary process and teleological, sociocultural processes. Man's individuality (which continues to grow while the body decays) and man's sociability combine to establish his undetermined "openness," in contrast to determination of the animal by his *Umwelt*.

Portmann's central concept is "internality," the fact that individuals are centers of purposeful activity who use the external shell of the body as a means of self-expression and of communication with other individuals. Portmann does not claim that the affirmation of man's individuality and sociability provides the "meaning of life." Although specific mysteries of man's biological structure have been solved, he claims, the "basic fact" for philosophical anthropology continues to be man's "mysteriousness." Man has no built-in evolutionary mechanism leading to an equilibrium; there is only a creative variability (*Disponibilität*) of the human situation. Man's spontaneous individuality creates new self-images; his sociability spreads and maintains them.

Portmann has sought, however, to advance beyond the limits of functional morphology to a vantage point that will illuminate the hierarchy of values—a vantage point whose need has increased in view of the tremendous potential power of biotechnical advances to influence and change the human condition, and perhaps human nature. However, as in the biophilosophies of Henri Bergson, Pierre Teilhard de Chardin, and Julian Huxley, it is easier to discern the philosophical basis of Portmann's biological hypotheses than it is to discover any positive contribution that biology has made to his philosophical thought. He first developed his conception of man as functional unit as a philosophical hypothesis.

"Openness" has been a theme of philosophical anthropology since the time of Herder and Kant.

In general, it must be said that no substantive lesson is to be drawn from either functional or analytical biology, except that it is of man's essence to create structured and meaningful systems of action. The biological foundation of man's creativity entails no concrete guide to what man ought to do. Nothing would appear to follow from the fact that creativity has biological roots except that man cannot permit himself to be altogether determined by any given environment. He must transcend it creatively, and he must be guided by ideas and leitmotifs rather than by instincts, by decisions rather than by reactions to stimuli. But the questions of what decisions man will take and what ideas he will adopt are not answered by bioanthropology, which emphasizes the malleability of human nature as a basic fact. Any insight into the potential content of human achievement must therefore be based on the plurality of the cultures that have unfolded in history. Bioanthropology thus leads into cultural philosophical anthropology.

CULTURAL PHILOSOPHICAL ANTHROPOLOGY. Like American cultural anthropology, cultural philosophical anthropology is concerned with man and his works, with culture history and culture sociology, and with historical morphology and the philosophy of history. It is interested primarily in developed societies—"high cultures" that have created a style of their own beyond the biological and trivial uniformities of the tribal state. Like German sociology, it emphasizes the multiformity rather than the uniformity of human nature, and the history rather than the theory of cultures. Like Portmann's bioanthropology, it finds an ultimate mystery in man—the mystery of archetypes and racial dispositions.

Cultural anthropology combines Dilthey's historicism with the phenomenological method. Man comes to know and liberate himself through history. A comparative study of societies elucidates the human situation and the human predicament. But this study results in the same merely formal characteristics elaborated by bioanthropology—the adaptability of the human mind, the need for a "sane" worldview, sociability with its ensuing problems, a common growth rhythm, and common basic physiological urges.

Arnold Gehlen and Erich Rothacker are the most representative cultural philosophical anthropologists, while Werner Sombart is the most opinionated. Gehlen and Rothacker present integrated theoretical systems that have an ultimately psychological basis. Their psychologies, like that of Dilthey, are essentially descriptive and interpretative, and their psychological interpretations mirror their cultural philosophies.

Rothacker has classified cultural factors in a scale by "laws of polarity." He seeks to understand individual cultures by a process of "reduction" to "national souls" (attitudes and dispositions that generate *Weltanschauungen*) and to myths. These ur-experiences are not further reducible; they are embodied in the racial inheritance. Therefore, although people do create and develop the *Umwelt* of their national cultures, the possibilities that are thereby realized are ultimately determined. Rothacker's historicist relativism is less free from ethnocentrism than one might be led to expect by the emphasis of philosophical anthropology on the openness of man.

Gehlen's psychology is rooted in the archaic stage of cultural development. The values of this stage serve as criteria for the evaluation of late cultures, which accordingly appear as falls from grace.

In Sombart's anthropology ethnocentric traits are also emphasized. Thus, man's irreconcilable diversity rather than his potential openness is seen as distinguishing the human situation.

Ernst Cassirer, on the other hand, sought to discover the basic function of human cultural achievements (language, myth, religion, art, science, history) behind their innumerable forms and to trace them to a common origin in man's symbol-making power—the power to build up an "ideal world" of his own.

PSYCHOLOGICAL PHILOSOPHICAL ANTHROPOLOGY. Bioanthropology and cultural philosophical anthropology are the most important branches of philosophical anthropology. Among other branches, only psychological philosophical anthropology and theological philosophical anthropology require separate mention.

Psychological philosophical anthropology is the most successful post-Freudian development in psychiatry on the Continent and, through existential psychoanalysis, is exerting considerable influence in the English-speaking world. The outstanding figures in this movement are Ludwig Binswanger, Erwin Straus, and Medard Boss. Erich Fromm seeks to incorporate his psychology within philosophical anthropology, and Rollo May in the United States and R. D. Laing in Britain follow similar lines. Their common belief is that traditional experimental psychology requires the assistance of philosophical thought to arrive at satisfactory results. Some psychological philosophical anthropologists oppose the empirical hypotheses and inductive statistical methods of experimental

psychology; most of them combine experimental methods with a specific philosophical or phenomenological approach.

Since psychological philosophical anthropology deals with individual cases, it lends itself to concrete and descriptive investigations. Analyses have been made of laughter and weeping, fantasy, shame, resentment, pleasure, love, and fear. These analyses do not consist in mere registration of stimuli but in selective and synthesizing acts of interpretation by phenomenological "reduction" to an intuition of essential qualities. Plessner has traced the capacity for laughter and weeping to man's "excentricity," his ability to transcend his innate nature and to observe, judge, and respond to situations. Human moods (*Stimmungen*) are typically described as obstacles to the achievement of authenticity. The irrational elements in moods undermine the continuity of character, which is man's potential ability to give meaning and direction to his life. Accidental attitudes that arise from the challenge of situations thus deprive man of his right to make responsible choices; they tie him to an impoverished, one-sided anthropology.

Binswanger developed existential analysis from Freud's psychoanalysis. He describes Freud's positivist, "utilitarian" anthropology as one-sided and negative. Its culture concept, he claims, concentrates negatively on the taming of natural urges rather than positively on a teleological image of man's potentiality. Freud's "somatographic" or "somatomorphic" conception of existence stresses the scientific analysis of sleep, dream, passion, and sensuality while, according to Binswanger, it neglects the historical and cultural aspects of existence, such as religion, art, ethics, and myth, all of which are as important as science. In Binswanger's view psychological investigation should be directed toward the self-transcending, exercise of man's liberty to make authentic choices. The psychologist's task is to illuminate the "inner life history" of the patient, his self-structuring in the light of his inner motivation. Self-structuring is equivalent to character or to the response that the individual makes to the challenge of the world around him. St. Augustine, to whom we owe the beginnings of autobiography, is a case in point. Illness prevented him from carrying out his ambition to become an orator. He transcended his natural disability by turning toward the spiritual world and thus arrived at his essential "real being." He could have reacted otherwise—by resentment or frustration, by neurosis or suicide. These and other potentialities held out to Augustine the temptation to restrict his character by the impoverishment inherent in giving in to an irresponsible choice—a choice suggested by the logic of the situation. Augustine chose an autonomous life that preserved his access to a full range of human values. Psychosis is explained as an "abortive encounter" with existence, or a form of existential misdirection. Diagnosis of a psychosis therefore depends on a valid interpretation of what constitutes an authentic existence. An authentic existence, according to Binswanger, consists in a life in keeping with a legitimate cultural (religious or national) tradition; in a dialogue with other beings (the "Thou"); or in the ability to act in character in the face of situational challenges.

However, the first of these criteria depends on values that are subject to unresolved doubt; the other two are so devoid of specific content that they hardly invite contradiction. Existential analysis, even more than psychoanalysis, obliterates the line between the normal and the abnormal and reduces psychological problems to questions of *Weltanschauung*.

Viktor von Weizsäcker, V. E. von Gebsattel, Erwin Straus, and Harald Schultz-Hencke have carried out structural analyses of inhibited character types and, in particular, of sexual perversions. Health is defined as openness to all potentialities of life, and obsessional urges are therefore interpreted as disturbed worldviews that enslave the individual in rigid, one-sided, compulsive attitudes and interfere with his social "I-Thou" relationships. Sexual perversions, in particular, have been construed by Gebsattel as obsessional urges that preclude a lasting I-Thou relationship based on mutual freedom, and as thus being incapable of providing ultimate satisfaction. Medard Boss, however, arguing from an equally existential basis, stoutly rejects this view. Gebsattel's apotheosis of the procreative element in love, however, points to the close affinity of philosophical anthropology with "secularized theology."

THEOLOGICAL PHILOSOPHICAL ANTHROPOLOGY. Theological anthropology emphasizes the Biblical conception of man in a dialogue with God. Martin Buber, Emil Brunner, and Dietrich Bonhoeffer are remarkable representatives of this movement, although their work is best studied in its theological context. However, the openness of man and his individuality and sociability are dominant themes of their work. The human difficulty of making the right choices is paralleled by the theological conception of man as simultaneously just and sinning.

A merely intellectual and logical exposition of God's message, in their view, is not enough for an understanding of God's revelation. An emphatic existential I-Thou relationship between man and God, based on the *logique du coeur,* is required. What matters is not that something is true, but how it can be made to come true. Belief in God has been explained by theological philosophical anthropologists, following Feuerbach, in terms of the self-understanding and the creative self-image of man.

The need for a postscientific interpretation of the Creed that is appropriate to a "mature" humanity and avoids theological sophistry has become a leading motif of theological anthropology, and this makes it difficult to distinguish between its tenets and those of secular philosophical anthropologies.

CRITIQUE OF SOCIETY

Philosophical anthropology shares with contemporary French humanism the conception that there is a crisis of the sciences that reflects a radical crisis of European society. It rejects contemporary bourgeois society, from either a romantic or a Marxist viewpoint, for the alleged dehumanizing tendencies it has developed in the process of rationalization following the breakup of feudal and religious institutions.

The rise of scientific rationalism is not regarded as a process of liberation from the shackles of superstition, conventions, and fallacies, but as a process that has deprived Western man of his "center of gravity" and has alienated him from his authentic nature through the replacement of value by "means-end" relationships, by neutral experiment, and by mechanico-mathematical abstraction. In the view of philosophical anthropologists, the "age of transition," or "age of crisis," which heralded the acceptance of utilitarianism in the English-speaking world, is still unresolved. Man's salvation from alienation is not seen as a continuous process of improvement or of piecemeal social engineering but as a radical challenge that is less concerned with practical reform than with a utopian rejection of the modern world.

The central theoretical insights of philosophical anthropology consist in an affirmation of the individuality and sociability of man as ultimate values. This theory would seem to suggest a social organization that combines an optimum of free choice with the minimum encroachment on individual liberty that is compatible with a viable social coexistence. This is in fact the utilitarian image of man that has prevailed since the early nineteenth century in the English-speaking world, where this image of man has been internalized to such an extent that the discussion of ultimate metaphysical questions has predominantly given way to the discussion of means to assure the accepted end of mutual accommodation and individual discretion. By contrast, on the Continent, and especially in Germany, the romantic reaction to the French Revolution precluded the acceptance of the philosophy of the Enlightenment. No commonly accepted concept of society was developed to counterbalance an unbridled individualism except the radical panaceas of nationalism and totalitarianism. By emphasizing the importance of both individuality and sociability, philosophical anthropology is returning to the type of position that gave birth to utilitarianism, and it may therefore be a step toward a utilitarian view of the world. Although most of its representatives present ethnocentric or nihilistic conclusions, these are not inevitable consequences of philosophical anthropology's affirmation of the creativity and sociability of man.

(See "Philosophical Anthropology" in the index for articles on philosophers who have especially concerned themselves with the topic.)

See also Alembert, Jean Le Rond d'; Augustine, St.; Bergson, Henri; Binswanger, Ludwig; Bonhoeffer, Dietrich; Brunner, Emil; Buber, Martin; Cartesianism; Cassirer, Ernst; Coleridge, Samuel Taylor; Darwinism; Determinism, A Historical Survey; Diderot, Denis; Dilthey, Wilhelm; Encyclopédie; Enlightenment; Existentialism; Ferguson, Adam; Feuerbach, Ludwig Andreas; Freud, Sigmund; Garve, Christian; Gehlen, Arnold; Geisteswissenschaften; Goethe, Johann Wolfgang von; Hartmann, Nicolai; Hegel, Georg Wilhelm Friedrich; Heidegger, Martin; Herder, Johann Gottfried; Historicism; Hobbes, Thomas; Humanism; Humboldt, Wilhelm von; Hume, David; Husserl, Edmund; Hutcheson, Francis; Idealism; Jaspers, Karl; Kant, Immanuel; Kierkegaard, Søren Aabye; Klages, Ludwig; Locke, John; Marxist Philosophy; Marx, Karl; Maupertuis, Pierre-Louis Moreau de; Mill, John Stuart; Newman, John Henry; Nietzsche, Friedrich; Pascal, Blaise; Plessner, Helmut; Racism; Scheler, Max; Schopenhauer, Arthur; Shaftesbury, Third Earl of (Anthony Ashley Cooper); Smith, Adam; Sombart, Werner; Spengler, Oswald; Stewart, Dugald; Teilhard de Chardin, Pierre; Utopias and Utopianism.

Bibliography

GENERAL AND HISTORICAL

Bryson, Gladys. *Man and Society.* Princeton, NJ: Princeton University Press, 1945.

Groethuysen, Bernhard. *Philosophische Anthropologie: Handbuch der Philosophie,* Part III, 1–207. Munich and Berlin, 1928.

Häberlin, Paul. *Der Mensch: Eine philosophische Anthropologie.* Zürich: Schweizer Spiegel, 1941.

Landmann, Michael. *De Homine,* 543–614. Freiburg and Munich, 1962. A comprehensive bibliography.

Landmann, Michael. *Philosophische Anthropologie.* Berlin, 1955.

Landsberg, P. L. *Einleitung in die philosophische Anthropologie.* Frankfurt, 1949.

Lipps, Hans. *Die Wirklichkeit des Menschen.* Frankfurt, 1954.

Litt, Theodor. *Die Selbsterkenntnis des Menschen.* Leipzig, 1938.

Löwith, Karl. *Das Individuum in der Rolle des Mitmenschen.* Munich, 1928.

Pappé, H. O. "On Philosophical Anthropology." *Australasian Journal of Philosophy* 39 (1961): 47–64.

Pfänder, Alexander. *Die Seele des Menschen.* Halle, 1933.

BIOLOGICAL PHILOSOPHICAL ANTHROPOLOGY

Buytendijk, F. J. J. *Allgemeine Theorie der menschlichen Haltung und Bewegung.* Berlin, 1956.

Buytendijk, F. J. J. *Mensch und Tier.* Hamburg, 1958.

Portmann, Adolf. *Die Biologie und das neue Menschenbild.* Bern, 1942.

Portmann, Adolf. *Zoologie und das neue Bild des Menschen.* Hamburg, 1956.

Pringle, J. W. S. *The Two Biologies.* Oxford: Clarendon Press, 1963.

PSYCHOLOGICAL PHILOSOPHICAL ANTHROPOLOGY

Bally, Gustav. *Der normale Mensch.* Zürich, 1952.

Boss, Medard. *Psychoanalyse und Daseinsanalyse.* Bern, 1957. Translated by Ludwig B. Lefebre as *Psychoanalysis and Daseins-analysis.* New York and London, 1963.

Gebsattel, V. E. von. *Prolegomena einer medizinischen Anthropologie.* Berlin: Springer, 1954.

Laing, R. D. *The Divided Self: A Study of Sanity and Madness.* London: Tavistock, 1960.

May, Rollo, ed. *Existence.* New York, 1958.

Schultz-Hencke, Harald. *Der gehemmte Mensch.* Leipzig: G. Thieme, 1940.

Strasser, Stefan. "Phenomenological Trends in European Psychology." *Philosophy and Phenomenological Research* 18 (1957): 18–34.

Weizsäcker, Viktor von. *Der kranke Mensch: Eine Einführung in die medizinische Anthropologie.* Stuttgart, 1951.

THEOLOGICAL PHILOSOPHICAL ANTHROPOLOGY

Kuhlmann, Gerhardt. *Theologische Anthropologie im Abriss.* Tübingen, 1935.

Loewenich, Walther von. *Menschsein und Christsein bei Augustin, Luther und J. Burckhardt.* Gütersloh, Germany, 1948.

Michel, Ernst. *Ehe: Eine Anthropologie der Geschlechtsgemeinschaft.* Stuttgart, 1948.

Rosenstock-Huessy, Eugen. *The Christian Future.* New York: Scribners, 1946.

H. O. Pappé (1967)

PHILOSOPHY

Defining *philosophy* is itself a philosophical problem. Perhaps a great many philosophers would agree that whatever else philosophy is, it is the critical, normally systematic study of an unlimited range of ideas and issues. But this characterization says nothing about what sorts of ideas or issues are important in philosophy or about its distinctive methods of studying them. Doing this will require some account of the special fields of the subject, its methods, its connections with other disciplines, its place in the academy, and its role in human culture. The task is large. Philosophy pursues questions in every dimension of human life, and its techniques apply to problems in any field of study or endeavor. It may be described in many ways. It is a reasoned pursuit of fundamental truths, a quest for understanding, a study of principles of conduct. It seeks to establish standards of evidence, to provide rational methods of resolving conflicts, and to create techniques for evaluating ideas and arguments. Philosophy may examine concepts and views drawn from science, art, religion, politics, or any other realm.

The best way to clarify these broad characterizations of philosophy is to describe its principal subfields (all of which are addressed in more detail in entries in this Encyclopedia devoted to them alone). It is appropriate to start with what might be called *traditional* subfields of philosophy, most commonly taken to be epistemology, ethics, logic, metaphysics, and the history of philosophy. These remain central in philosophical research; and although they are by no means its exclusive focus, they are intimately connected with virtually every other field of philosophical research and are widely treated as core areas in the teaching of the subject.

FIVE TRADITIONALLY CENTRAL SUBFIELDS OF PHILOSOPHY

EPISTEMOLOGY. Epistemology concerns the nature and scope of knowledge and justification. What does it mean to know (the truth), and what is the nature of truth? What sorts of things can be known, and can we be justified in our beliefs about what goes beyond the evidence of our senses, such as the inner lives of others or events of the distant past? Is there knowledge beyond the reach of science? What are the limits of self-knowledge? Can there be genuine moral knowledge? Quite apart from the depth, modality, or subject matter of knowledge, we may also ask: What are its basic sources? They have been widely thought to be perception, memory, introspection,

and reason (understood as a kind of reflection). But what of testimony? And can any substantive knowledge, say in mathematics, be utterly independent of experience in the way a priori (reason-based) knowledge is sometimes held to be?

A major epistemological problem connected with all of these sources is the status of skepticism. Skepticism has many forms, depending on the kind of knowledge or justification it represents as unattainable. What is commonly called Humean skepticism (deriving from David Hume's writings on causation and inductive inference) challenges the belief that any inductive arguments (*probable arguments*, in Hume's terminology) can ground knowledge. Cartesian skepticism, powerfully stated in Descartes's *Meditations*, challenges the belief that we have knowledge at all. Quite apart from whether there can be knowledge or justified belief, there is the question of the structure that a body of knowledge or of justified beliefs must have. Must it, for instance, contain beliefs possessing a kind of axiomatic status, or can it consist of elements that all lack that status or, indeed, are in no way privileged relative to other elements? Traditional *foundationalists*, such as Descartes, have held a view of the first kind; moderate foundationalists (represented by a large proportion of epistemologists since the middle of the twentieth century) hold that foundational cognitions are necessary in a body of knowledge or justified belief but need only be in a certain way noninferentially justified as opposed to indefeasibly justified; and coherentists and other nonfoundationalists have posited various ways aimed at accounting for knowledge and justification without appeal to foundational elements.

ETHICS. Ethics is the philosophical study of morality, particularly conceived as a set of standards of right and wrong conduct. Its most theoretical branch (commonly called *metaethics*) concerns the meanings or, more broadly, the logic, of our moral concepts—such as right action, obligation, and justice—the kinds of evidence we have for propositions about the corresponding subject matter, and the sorts of properties that apparently underlie the application of the concepts. On some major ethical views, such as J. S. Mill's utilitarianism, our obligations derive from our potential contributions to enhancing what is good. For this reason, among others, the concept of the good and the distinction between intrinsic and instrumental goodness are also major concerns of ethical inquiry. On other major ethical views, such as Immanuel Kant's, moral obligatoriness is a property possessed by acts themselves by virtue of their falling under nonconsequentialist principles, for instance, a principle that, quite apart from the consequences of lying, prohibits it.

Normative ethics is commonly contrasted with metaethics and is concerned to formulate and assess principles meant to guide moral decisions, whether in private or public life. A major question it raises is what moral specific obligations we have. Another is what moral rights persons as such have and, related to this, what legal rights a just society must accord its citizens. Still another is what constitutes a valid excuse for wrongdoing. Any moral philosopher may be concerned with the broad question of how moral disagreements may be rationally settled, and here we have a question that has both metaethical and normative aspects.

LOGIC. Logic is concerned to provide sound methods for distinguishing valid from invalid arguments or, on a wider conception, good from bad arguments in terms of criteria for determining how much support the conclusion receives from the premise(s). Arguments may be considered ordered sequences of propositions in which some—the premise(s)—are conceived as supporting another—the conclusion. A standard example is the following syllogism, which has a very common form: its premises are that *all human beings are mortal* and that *Socrates is mortal*; its conclusion is that *Socrates is a human being*. Deductive logic is concerned with appraising arguments in relation to the question whether the premises *entail* (or logically imply) the conclusion, as with the syllogism just presented. Inductive logic is concerned with appraising arguments in relation to probabilistic support. From premises about the factors that cause influenza, medical experts may conclude that millions of people will be infected during the next flu season. Inductive logic addresses the problem of how we may tell what probability this conclusion has given those premises. More generally, logic helps us to assess how well our premises support our conclusions, to see what we are committed to accepting when we hold a view, and to avoid adopting positions for which we lack supporting reasons. As applied to everyday thinking, the use of logic also helps us to find arguments where we might otherwise simply see a set of loosely related statements, to discover assumptions we did not know we were making, and to formulate the minimum claims we must establish if we are to prove (or inductively support) our point.

METAPHYSICS. Metaphysics seeks basic criteria for determining what sorts of things are real. Criteria of this kind are the special concern of ontology, which is central in metaphysics. Among major ontological questions are these: Are there mental, physical, and abstract things (such as numbers)? Or is there just the physical and the spiritual? Might there be merely matter and energy? Are persons highly complex physical systems, or do they have properties not reducible to anything physical? How much can a person—or other kind of thing—change and remain the very person or thing it is? In the case of persons, this question is central for the problem of personal identity, which, in turn, is crucial for understanding the possibility of nonembodied life. Another question about persons is whether they can be free in a sense not possible for lower animals and whether their freedom is possible if the world should be a deterministic system, that is, one in which every event is entailed by a universal law of nature and some simultaneous or antecedent event. What constitutes a law of nature, and, in particular, what constitutes a causal law, are themselves major questions in metaphysics. Metaphysics has also been traditionally taken to include cosmology, which is concerned with the nature of the universe as a whole and pursues such questions as whether it must have a beginning in time, whether it can be infinite, and whether it must have been created and, if so, by what kind of being or in what way. The nature of time is itself an important metaphysical question.

HISTORY OF PHILOSOPHY. The history of philosophy might be thought to be a branch of the discipline of history rather than of philosophy, much in the way the history of science is a branch of history and not itself a branch of science. This conception would be quite inadequate to the standard conception of the history of philosophy in the field of philosophy. On that conception the history of philosophy is a genuine subfield of philosophy: It is the historical and *philosophical* study of the history of the subject. It commonly includes more in the way of philosophical interpretation and—sometimes—philosophical appraisal of major texts than historiographic studies of either a single philosopher or whole periods in the history of the subject. This is in part because the interpretation—and certainly the proper appraisal—of a philosopher is itself a philosophical problem, often involving epistemological or metaphysical theorizing. A study of a single philosophical work important in the history of philosophy may thus count as a contribution to the history of philosophy and not just to the study of its author.

The history of philosophy, then, examines major philosophers, the influence of one philosopher on another (say, Aristotle on Aquinas, Husserl on Heidegger, or Frege on Russell) or entire periods in the development of philosophy, such as the Ancient, Medieval, Modern, Nineteenth Century, and Twentieth Century periods. It seeks to understand great figures, their influence on others, and their importance for perennial and contemporary issues. The history of philosophy in a single nation is often separately studied, as in the case of American Philosophy. So are major movements within a nation, such as German Idealism, as well as international movements with a substantial history, such as Existentialism, Logical Positivism, and Phenomenology.

From the wide scope of many of the questions pursued in these philosophical fields, it should be clear that philosophy has a kind of generality possessed by no other field. Metaphysics, for instance, concerns the basic categories encompassing *everything* that exists, and epistemology concerns standards of evidence that apply in *any* kind of thinking. It will also be evident that every other discipline presupposes answers to certain philosophical questions. All of the sciences, for example, presuppose that facts about the past can yield knowledge or justified beliefs about the future. Finally, it should be apparent that, although there are distinctively philosophical questions, no subject matter is (in all its aspects) beyond the reach of philosophical inquiry. Any subject matter can raise philosophical questions: about (for instance) the kinds of entities it concerns, its epistemological presuppositions, and its connection with other subjects.

OTHER MAJOR SUBFIELDS OF PHILOSOPHY

Many branches of philosophy have grown from the traditional core areas just described. What follows is a sketch of a number of the major ones. Comprehensiveness is not possible here, but a wider conception can be formed by reading the entries devoted to the subfields that will be described.

PHILOSOPHY OF MIND. This subfield has emerged largely from metaphysical concerns with mental phenomena. The philosophy of mind addresses not only the possible relations of the mental to the physical (for instance, to brain processes) but to the many concepts having an essential mental element: belief, desire, intention, emotion, feeling, sensation, passion, will, personality, and others. To what extent are any of these concepts explicable in terms of behavioral tendencies? Quite apart from that, what is the relation between mental properties and physical ones? Are the former dependent on the latter, and if so, what kind of dependence is in question? Could two biological beings, for instance, be alike in all

their physical properties and still differ in their mental ones? A number of major questions in the philosophy of mind cluster in the area of *action theory*: What differentiates actions, such as raising an arm, from mere body movements, such as the rising of an arm? A common answer has been that actions but not bodily movements must be caused by such mental events as volitions. But must mental elements, such as intentions, beliefs, and emotions enter into adequate explanations of our actions, or can actions be explained by appeal to ordinary physical events? And is a kind of mental causation, or at least the absence of a certain kind of deterministic causation, required for our actions to be *free*?

PHILOSOPHY OF RELIGION. Another traditional concern of metaphysics is to understand the concept of God, including special attributes such as being all-knowing (omniscient), all-powerful (omnipotent), and wholly good (omnibenevolent). Does omnipotence, for instance, entail the ability to alter the laws of logic? Both metaphysics and epistemology have been concerned to assess the various grounds offered to justify one or another form of theism (these include the famous cosmological and ontological arguments, among others treated in this encyclopedia). The philosophy of religion—also called *philosophical theology*—systematically examines these topics and many related subjects, such as the relation between faith and reason, the nature of religious language, the relation of religion and morality, and the question of how a God who is wholly good could allow the kind and amount of evil the world apparently contains. Here the philosophy of religion overlaps the theory of value, a branch of ethics. It is common for a major question to cross philosophical fields in this way, and the same holds for the relation between theology and ethics, for instance in relation to the question whether the rightness of actions could be equivalent to divine commandedness.

PHILOSOPHY OF SCIENCE. This is probably the largest subfield, generated in substantial part by epistemology and in part by metaphysics. Philosophy of science has been commonly divided into philosophy of the natural sciences and philosophy of the social sciences. It has recently been divided further, into philosophy of physics, of biology, of psychology, of economics, and of other sciences. Philosophy of science clarifies both the quest for scientific knowledge and the results yielded by that quest. It does this by exploring the logic of scientific evidence; the nature of scientific laws, explanations, and theories; the nature of the theoretical entities posited in explaining observable phenomena; and the possible connections among the various branches of science. How, for instance, is psychology related to brain biology, and biology to chemistry? And how are the social sciences related to the natural sciences? Are they methodologically like the latter but incapable of discovering universal as opposed to statistical laws? Must they work with mentalistic concepts such as belief and desire? Does explanation have the same form across the several sciences?

SUBFIELDS OF ETHICS. From ethics, too, have come major subfields. *Political philosophy* concerns the justification—and limits—of governmental control of individuals; the meaning of equality before the law; the basis of economic freedom; and many other problems concerning government. It also examines the nature and possible arguments for various competing forms of political organization, such as laissez-faire capitalism, welfare democracy (capitalistic and socialistic), anarchism, communism, and fascism. *Social philosophy*, often taught in combination with political philosophy (which it overlaps), treats moral problems with large-scale social dimensions. Among these are the ethics of journalism and the media, the basis of compulsory education, the possible grounds for preferential treatment of minorities, the justice of taxation, and the appropriate limits, if any, on free expression in the arts. The *philosophy of law* explores such topics as what law is, what kinds of laws there are—for instance, only positive (enacted) law or also, as Thomas Aquinas held, natural law—and how law is or should be related to morality. It also examines the sorts of principles that should govern punishment and criminal justice in general (ethical questions about law do not exhaust the philosophical questions about it but have been among those central in the philosophy of law). *Medical ethics* addresses many problems arising in medical practice and medical science. Among these are standards applying to physician–patient relationships; moral questions raised by special procedures, such as abortion and ceasing of life-support for terminal patients; and ethical standards for medical research, for instance, genetic engineering and experimentation using human subjects. *Business ethics* addresses such questions as the place of business in society, how moral obligations may conflict with the profit motive, and how these conflicts may be resolved. Other topics often pursued are the nature and scope of the social responsibilities of corporations, their rights in a free society, and their relations to other kinds of organizations.

PHILOSOPHY OF ART (AESTHETICS). This is one of the oldest subfields. It concerns the nature of art, including both the performing arts and literature, painting, and sculpture. Major questions in aesthetics include how artistic creations are to be interpreted and evaluated and how the arts are related to one another, to natural beauty, and to morality, religion, science, and other important elements of human life. Aesthetics also deals with epistemological questions concerning the kinds of evidence we can have about an artwork and—sometimes—the kinds it can give us about the world, particularly about human beings. There is also a metaphysics of the aesthetic: What kind of property is beauty in a painting, power in a symphony, or unity in a poem, and is a poem a physical entity existing where it is written or remembered, or is it something more abstract of which these mental and physical entities are in some sense vehicles?

PHILOSOPHY OF LANGUAGE. This field has close ties to both epistemology and metaphysics and, in the latter connection, to the philosophy of mind. It treats a broad spectrum of questions about language: the nature of meaning, the relations between words and things, the various theories of language learning, and the distinction between literal and figurative uses of language. A major concern in the field is the theory of reference: What, for instance, is required for us to succeed in referring to Socrates by using that name when we have never met him nor even read anything written by him? And if our thoughts are mental and *in* the mind, how can their content be about external objects? A question connected with all of these problems is the relation between the linguistic and the conceptual. To what extent, for instance, is it possible to have concepts at all without linguistic terms to express them, and is thought itself possible apart from language? Since language is crucial in nearly all human activity, the philosophy of language bears on our understanding both of other academic fields and of much of what we ordinarily do.

OTHER IMPORTANT SUBFIELDS. There are many other subfields of philosophy, and it is in the nature of philosophy as critical inquiry to develop new subfields when new directions in the quest for knowledge, or in any other area of human activity, raises new intellectual problems. There is no limit to the number of variety of possible subfields of philosophy. Among the subfields not yet mentioned, but often a focus or research or teaching (at least as a part of other courses), are Philosophy of Logic, Philosophy of History, Philosophy of Mathematics, Philosophy of Medicine, Philosophy of Education, Philosophy of Feminism, Philosophy of Linguistics, Philosophy of Criticism, Philosophy of Culture, Philosophy of Film, and Philosophy of Sport.

PHILOSOPHICAL METHODS

The *Dialogues of Plato* made famous what might be called the *Socratic method* in philosophy. It is the dialectical method, pursued by Socrates as represented by Plato in the *Dialogues*, in which ideas are set out, explored in relation to their meaning and implications, and assessed by such criteria as consistency and plausibility in relation to various standards, sometimes including common sense. In both Plato and Aristotle, we find early examples of what may plausibly be called *conceptual analysis*. Aristotle provides a particularly good example of how this may be conceived. In his *Nicomachean Ethics*, for instance, he seeks to give an account of the concept (or anyway of *a* concept) of virtue. He saw himself as clarifying the essence of the phenomenon of virtue; but if this essentialist view is understood in terms of his philosophical practice, it seems consistent with construing some of what he did as a kind of conceptual analysis. He is guided by the use of the relevant Greek terms in what we may suppose was educated parlance; yet he is not talking merely about linguistic usage. This is not to assimilate his kind of conceptual analysis to a Platonic kind on which concepts are to be understood by intellectual apprehension of them as abstract entities accessible to reflection. Indeed, if there are times when his analytic technique recalls Plato, there are others when his attention to usage and to what is said brings to mind some moments in the later work of Ludwig Wittgenstein.

A major question here, on which there is persisting difference of judgment among philosophers, is the extent to which these intellective procedures (whether Aristotelian or Platonic) are genuinely different from *linguistic analysis*. A related question is the degree of the authority of linguistic usage in determining the content of a concept. As important as dialectical method and conceptual analysis are in philosophy, however, neither can be described as *the* method of philosophy. It may be that every major philosopher has used at least one of them at some point; but even supposing (what is certainly controversial) that philosophy cannot be competently pursued on a large scale without some measure of at least the latter, there are other methods of inquiry that should be considered philosophical.

An important route to understanding philosophy and, especially, philosophical method, is a comparison of philosophical method with scientific method. From at least the middle of the twentieth century, and in at least

much of the Western philosophical tradition, there has been a (sometimes tacit) belief in scientific method as the paradigm of an objective, rational method of seeking truth. There has been an associated belief, or presupposition, that philosophy must, in methodology as well as doctrine, take account of the progress of science. This is not to say that the (or a) method of science, or some interpretation of scientific method, has become the dominant *philosophical* method. But there is a widely held assumption—which we might call the *assumption of the philosophical primacy of scientific method*—that scientific method is the primary model of the rational pursuit of truth, in a sense implying both that our philosophical method, if not itself scientific, should bear an appropriate resemblance to scientific method and that our philosophical results are probably mistaken if they are at odds with, or even unable to account for the possibility of, well-established scientific findings. It will help to describe this primacy assumption in the three major areas of concern in this entry: epistemology, metaphysics, and methodology.

EPISTEMOLOGY. Where scientific method currently has the primacy that has been mentioned, then, first of all, we might expect the assumption of its primacy to have an antirationalist thrust. For despite the rationalist point that a priori truths do not compete with scientific statements in explanation or theorizing, such truths are also traditionally conceived as beyond refutation by scientific procedures and as knowable by a nonscientific method (a kind of reflection). The second point is positive: The influence of scientific method as a model of rational belief formation has given impetus to the view that much of what we know is discovered by inference to the best explanation (a kind of inductive inference), and much of what we understand is understood in terms of underlying theoretical states or entities. Thus, even self-knowledge can be taken to be not only constituted by corrigible belief (roughly, belief whose justification can be defeated) but, often at least, to comprise beliefs arrived at by unconscious (or at least unnoticed) inference from appropriate data. The fallibilism that comes with a deep appreciation of scientific method has similar implications in other areas of apparent human knowledge.

METAPHYSICS. In metaphysics, the assumption of the philosophical primacy of scientific method implies a tendency to take science as the arbiter of the real. The obvious point here is that we should tend to countenance as real whatever our best confirmed scientific theories posit as such, or at least posit as explanatorily basic. (Granted, it is not always clear what this is even if we can decide what our best-confirmed theories are). But there is a further implication. We must also countenance as real whatever must be posited to understand science itself, for instance properties, numbers, or sets. And, in part on the basis of assuming Occam's Razor (roughly, the principle that in providing explanations we should not posit more entities or types of entities than necessary), many philosophers think we need countenance nothing else.

One good illustration of the point here is the effort to support realism in ethics by arguing (against both noncognitivist and epiphenomenalist views in metaethics) that moral properties have causal and explanatory power and hence can play an explanatory role substantially similar to the role of theoretical entities in the sciences. Moral realists need not be causalists, however; they all agree in holding the cognitivist metaethical view that moral claims have truth value (hence are true or false), but rationalists among them may deny that moral properties—even if in some way grounded in nonmoral properties, such as lying, beating, and killing, that have causal power—are themselves causal properties. Most philosophers would grant, however, that whether or not genuine properties *must* have causal power, whatever does have that power is real.

METHODOLOGY. If what has been said about the metaphysical implications of the assumption of the primacy of scientific method is correct, it should be easy to understand some of the methodological implications for philosophy. For in a way, the second metaphysical implication is methodological: Its basis is largely a commitment to scientific method as so well established, and so near to being self-evidently essential in the search for truth, that we should countenance whatever realities must be posited to account for its success and need *not* countenance any others. A further methodological implication is a tendency to solve philosophical problems, so far as possible, by construing them in a way that lends itself to scientific treatment. The mind–body problem is a good case in point, and eliminative materialism (which claims that explanations of behavior do not ultimately depend on appeals to the mental) illustrates how what seems unnecessary for scientific treatment of a problem may be ontologically discountenanced. Where the assumption of the philosophical primacy of scientific method is at its most influential, philosophical method is conceived as only locally autonomous: Scientific method and the results of its application are the basic determinants of both our standards of rationality and our inventory of reality.

Quite apart from the role in their thinking of scientific method as a model for philosophical inquiry, it may be that philosophers naturally tend to take one or the other of two central philosophical domains, epistemology or metaphysics, or some account developed therein, as primary, as *first philosophy*, in a suggestive but now uncommon terminology. If we give priority to epistemology, we tend to produce an ontology that posits the sorts of objects about which our epistemology says we can have knowledge or justified belief. If we give metaphysics priority, we tend to produce an account of justified belief which allows knowledge or justified belief about the sorts of things our ontology countenances as real. One's philosophical method affects both one's epistemology and metaphysics and one's sense of the relation between them. If our method is dominated by a priori reflection, we are likely to be rationalists in epistemology and realists in metaphysics, at least to the extent of countenancing whatever abstract objects must be posited to ground a priori knowledge. If our method is dominated by observation and experiment, or even by the idea that philosophical claims are ultimately responsible to observation and experiment, we are likely to tend toward empiricism in epistemology and, in metaphysics, to seek an ontology that countenances as real only what is either experience-able or necessary to account for our knowledge of what we experience.

Like epistemology or metaphysics, philosophical method can be primary in shaping a philosophical outlook. It is doubtful that it can wholly determine such an outlook; for apart from certain epistemological and metaphysical commitments, one cannot develop or even use a method. Similarly, one cannot develop an epistemology without making at least tentative metaphysical commitments or construct a metaphysics without making at least tentative epistemological commitments. Philosophers seem to accept as apparently axiomatic that what is knowable is in some sense real; and though, as many philosophers would regard as a lesson of skepticism, it is not self-evident that what is real is knowable, many philosophers cannot easily give up the conviction, or the quest to establish, that this is so. If this apparent asymmetry concerning the knowable and the real is genuine, then taken together with the primacy of our experience in our relations to others and the world, it may explain why epistemology tends, in at least many philosophers, to contribute even more than metaphysics to determining their overall views.

If philosophical method is to be clarified by the comparison with scientific method and not obscured by assimilation to the latter, it is essential that we distinguish scientific method from something of which it is an immensely impressive special case: *theoretical method*. The former is empirical and, broadly speaking, experimental. The latter is the more general method of building and rebuilding theories in relation to data: raising questions, hypothesizing, comparing and evaluating hypotheses in relation to data, revising theories in the light of the comparisons and evaluations, and adopting theories through assessing competing accounts of the same or similar problems. This distinction has not always been recognized or fully appreciated. For one thing, given the influence of empiricism (an influence to which few in modern philosophy are entirely immune), some thinkers tend to see scientific method as the only kind of theoretical method, at least outside logic and mathematics. But theoretical method is not the property of empiricism; rationalists can also use it, and so can both nonphilosophers and philosophers who are uncommitted with respect to, say, empiricism, rationalism, and pragmatism.

What is here called the theoretical method is very old—as ancient as systematic philosophy itself. It is illustrated in the Socratic attempt to refine definitions by revising them in response to examples and counterexamples; and it, or some major element in it, figures in all of the general philosophical methods considered here. However, the assumption of the primacy of scientific method and with it the often tacit view that scientific method is the only rational theoretical method outside logic and mathematics, is far from obvious.

Consider metaphysics: Properties and propositions, for example, far from being banished, are indispensable for many philosophers, including many who are scientifically oriented. Quite properly, this is in part because of what is required to understand science. But it may be in metaphysics, philosophy of language, and philosophy of mind that we find the greatest impetus toward preserving these common targets of Occam's Razor. Consider epistemology: There is to date no consensus that the traditional domain of the a priori has been accounted for on scientific or, especially, empiricist lines. If only a limited number of philosophers are willing to defend the view that there are synthetic a priori propositions (roughly, substantive propositions, such as basic moral principles, knowable on the basis of reflection on their content), increasingly, many philosophers are alive to the possibility that there may be. This is not to say that the analytic–synthetic distinction has been adequately clarified or is even important in many of the ways it has been thought to be. The suggestion is only that the categories of the analytic and the a priori are less and less widely thought to have been shown unintelligible or empty or even equivalent.

THE AUTONOMY OF PHILOSOPHY

Given what has been said in this entry, it should be plain that philosophy is a distinctive area of inquiry. Even if its concerns overlap those of various other disciplines, it has its own problems and at least some of its own methods. But distinctiveness is not the same as autonomy, which, as applied to a field of inquiry, implies a kind of independence of other such fields. Is philosophy autonomous in this sense? Positively, a rationalistic perspective can provide a stronger basis for the autonomy of philosophy than can an account of philosophy based on assuming the philosophical primacy of scientific method. The reference here is to *hard autonomy*—the kind grounded in a distinctive conceptual and methodological status. This is quite different from *soft autonomy*—the sociological and institutional independence of the discipline manifest chiefly in its generally having its own academic departments.

Soft autonomy is sustainable even if one's philosophical perspective is that of *naturalism*, which, in a strong form, might be described in rough terms as the view that nature is the whole of reality, and the only basic truths are truths of nature. On a form of this view associated with W. V. Quine, philosophy is continuous with natural science. This implies that there is no radical difference in the kinds of claims they can justify or in their standards of evidence: Indeed, epistemology itself is taken to be a kind of psychological inquiry into our cognitive standards and practices. The recently developed field of cognitive science, moreover, may from this perspective be viewed as a kind of naturalized philosophy of mind though its range may include more than problems addressed in that subfield of philosophy. This naturalistic approach to philosophy does not imply that there are no philosophical questions appropriately answered by reflection rather than through scientific inquiry, but the status of the answers is empirical rather than a priori; they are ultimately responsible to observation, as are scientific hypotheses, if in a less direct way. By contrast, on the traditional view that at least some major philosophical theses are a priori, it is clear why they are accountable to distinctively philosophical standards and need not be judged by the evidence drawn from sensory observation or scientific experiments.

To be sure, on the view that philosophy is simply more general than science or asks questions different in subject matter from those of the special sciences, a de facto autonomy may be sustained, an autonomy that is more than sociological and less than conceptual. But on that view, philosophy does not stand apart from science in the same way nor does it possess autonomous standards of assessment, particularly in normative matters. If, as has been common in the history of philosophy, it is seen as an autonomous cultural resource, as a normative critical enterprise responsible to its own standards, it would seem desirable that philosophy stand apart from science in the suggested way. But distinctness is not opposition nor does distinctness entail competition. Moreover, supposing the hard autonomy thesis is mistaken, soft autonomy may be retained with renewed emphasis. If (in ways to be sketched below) philosophy is, or at least should be, a cultural resource, then whatever philosophers think about hard autonomy, they have reasons to preserve the soft, sociological autonomy of the discipline.

PHILOSOPHY IN RELATION TO OTHER DISCIPLINES

There are many other disciplines, and here it is possible only to indicate how philosophy is related to some of the major ones. The place to begin is with the idea that philosophy is in a sense the *metadiscipline*, the one whose proper business includes accounting for the structure, methodology, and, indeed, the implicit metaphysics and epistemology, of the other disciplines.

For understanding other disciplines, philosophy is indispensable. Many important questions about a field, such as the nature of its concepts and its relation to other disciplines, do not belong to that discipline, are not usually pursued in it, and are philosophical in nature. Philosophy of science, for instance, is needed to supplement the understanding of the natural and social sciences, which may be derived from scientific work itself. Philosophy of literature and philosophy of history are of similar value in understanding the humanities, and philosophy of art is important in understanding the arts. Philosophy is, moreover, essential in assessing the various standards of evidence used by other disciplines. Since all fields of knowledge employ reasoning and must set standards of evidence, logic and epistemology have a general bearing on all of these fields.

Normative disciplines and their subfields—those subfields that overlap normative ethics or properly propose broadly ethical standards—deserve special comment. These include (among others) law, theology, and aesthetics.

LAW. The field of law generates many philosophical questions. One concerns the very nature of law, which some have held to imply a connection with morality and others have taken to be entirely a matter of institutional realities, such as a structure of promulgations and enforcements. On either view, philosophy bears directly on important questions of what relation the law *should* have to morality. It also bears on the relevant standards of evidence. What, for instance, constitutes proof of guilt, and what should determine who counts as a reasonable person in relation to standards of negligence and due care? The topics of moral and legal responsibility, including the problem of diminished capacity and partial blameworthiness, are also areas in which philosophical and legal concerns overlap.

THEOLOGY. Theology is another field that overlaps philosophy. Philosophy of religion concerns not only the problem of adequately characterizing the divine nature but the related question of the rationality conditions for religious faith. Another major question pursued in both philosophy and theology is the relation between ethics and religion. Both areas of inquiry are connected with understanding the nature of evil—whether moral, as with wrongdoing, or natural, as in the case of death from floods—and how evil is possible (in various kinds and degrees) in a world under a god who is all-knowing, all-powerful, and wholly good. Historically, philosophy has influenced theology, just as theology has influenced philosophy. Although it is widely thought that either can be pursued in abstraction from the other, philosophical assumptions are both inevitably presupposed and commonly discussed in the field of religion.

AESTHETICS. Philosophy of art has been mentioned; aesthetics also includes the theory of natural beauty and related questions concerning aesthetics value. Although it should be granted that practitioners of the arts need not know even the rudiments of the philosophy of their art, this is rarely, if ever, so for professional critics and interpreters of the arts. Even if it is possible for critics, philosophy provides a way of conceiving the work and products of the artist that helps critics to appreciate it and to see its place in the culture to which it belongs. Literature in particular may either raise philosophical questions in its own creative works or invite their philosophical interpretation. Philosophy itself constructs mininarratives as central examples, uses dialogue—implicitly or explicitly—and not infrequently relies on metaphors and other literary devices. It is a literary medium from the vantage point of which other kinds of literature can be viewed in relation to kindred standards of coherence, plausibility, clarity, and profundity.

The relation of philosophy to the professions should also be considered here. Its bearing on law has been noted. Not all of the professions can be mentioned, but it is appropriate to say something briefly about medicine, journalism and communication, and the broad field of business and economics.

MEDICINE AND OTHER HEALTH PROFESSIONS. The very notion of health is normative, particularly in the case of mental health. In this connection, ethics is clearly pertinent; so is philosophy of mind, with its emphasis on understanding the human person. Philosophy of science may yield a better understanding of—and even a greater capacity for—the integration of medical research with medical practice. Philosophy of religion can lead to a better understanding of many patients and of various other people with whom physicians work closely. Aesthetics and the history of philosophy may enhance the common ground practitioners can find with patients or colleagues who are from other cultures or have unusual orientations or views. Philosophy of medicine and medical ethics are obviously of direct relevance.

JOURNALISM AND COMMUNICATION. Journalists face a number of challenges on which philosophy bears. One is determining what is important enough to need coverage. Another is what constitutes objectivity in reporting on events and balance in editorializing. A third is ascertaining the quality of evidence on a given issue; this may be crucial in deciding whether to trust a source or to rely on an anonymous one. A comparative and, in some cases, a historical perspective is highly desirable (and arguably obligatory) in journalism; in achieving perspectives of these kinds, philosophical reflection is useful and sometimes indispensable. There are also more specific ways in which philosophy bears on journalism and communication: Philosophy of language, for example, should enhance understanding of communication, and philosophy of science should cast light on some of the technical subjects with which many people in journalism and communication must deal. Beyond this, political and social philosophy can deepen understanding of society and social institutions. For journalists with special interests, aesthetics, philosophy of law, and philosophy of religion are highly pertinent to the questions they face.

BUSINESS. For many people in business and (applied) economics, the bearing of philosophy on the world of commerce seems at best tenuous. But what we have seen

about business ethics alone should belie that impression. A sound ethical perspective is essential for producing a sound code of ethics; philosophical training is valuable in providing a clear, adequately comprehensive, and defensible code. Economic justice, as with employment policy and fair competition, is a major concern that is clarified by work in ethics. So are the nature and responsibilities of corporations, unions, and political parties. Moreover, if cost-benefit analysis is to be mastered, the understanding and assessment of probabilities is essential. These topics are treated by inductive logic and epistemology.

THE PLACE OF PHILOSOPHY IN THE ACADEMY

Some of what should be brought out here is implicit in what has been said: That philosophy is a basic and comprehensive field of knowledge and, as such, has a place in higher education should now be evident. Philosophy also contributes to the capacity for problem solving in any field. In this respect its value is interdisciplinary and subject matter neutral.

CRITICAL THINKING. The first thing to note in this connection is that the study of philosophy helps to develop both the capacity and the inclination to do critical thinking. Logic is the most general philosophical field that develops this ability. Ethics alone is quite general. Studies in the subject should show how philosophical reflection is applicable to moral problems of many kinds. Courses in ethics commonly aim both at giving students a better understanding of moral problems and at helping them develop a reasonable moral outlook from which to approach the moral problems that confront them in their own lives. No other discipline treats these problems in the same comprehensive and systematic ways. Indeed, scientists and others often explicitly hold that such problems are outside their professional domain. Epistemology may be cited as the only discipline that examines standards of evidence and criteria of rational belief systematically and in ways applicable to any subject matter whatsoever. A similar point holds for many other topics that are treated in depth by philosophy and are important for critical thinking; they include definition, knowledge, explanation, causation, justification, communication, meaning, and truth.

NORMATIVE ISSUES. Philosophy provides a unique and systematic approach to normative issues—those concerning what ought or ought not to be, what is right or wrong, what is intrinsically desirable or undesirable, and so on—as opposed to what is as a matter of fact simply the case.

What are the basic moral rights of persons? What moral obligations do people in a society have to one another? What constitutes justice in the distribution of goods and in the determination of punishment? Inquiries in such areas as ethics, political philosophy, philosophy of law, and aesthetics treat normative questions in depth. Courses in these fields usually examine several theories proposed by philosophers in answering these questions, and typically, students in them are encouraged to formulate and defend their own answers to the questions using the methods and concepts introduced in the courses. Given the importance that moral, social, aesthetic, and other value questions have in human life, the contribution philosophy can make in a balanced curriculum is incalculable. It might be thought that these questions do or can receive adequate treatment in the social sciences or perhaps in literature and history. These other disciplines, however, do not, and do not claim to, deal with normative questions in the way philosophy does; and many of the important normative problems philosophers study are not raised in other fields.

INTERDISCIPLINARY PERSPECTIVE. An important function of philosophy is to foster interdisciplinary perspective. For instance, although scientific explanation is, in one form or another, common to all the sciences, conceptual questions about its nature and comparative questions about its logic in the different sciences belong to the philosophy of science. Some of these questions have been treated by scientists but rarely with the comprehensiveness and generality required for a synoptic understanding of the topic. Every discipline generates some essentially philosophical questions about itself, and many questions about relations among different disciplines are also philosophical. Both kinds of questions are examined in such areas as philosophy of science, philosophy of art, philosophy of law, philosophy of history, and philosophy of language. Philosophy also critically examines methods of inquiry, both in science and in everyday life. Its approach in this is usually conceptual, evaluative, and comparative; and typically the philosophical study of these topics differs from other approaches in the techniques used, in the questions pursued, and in the scope of the theories produced in answering these questions. Both in exploring the interrelations among other disciplines and in examining their methods of inquiry, philosophy fulfills a unique and important role as a metadiscipline. It provides a kind of understanding of the other disciplines—particularly of their presuppositions, standards of evidence, and modes of explanation—which other fields of study neither attempt nor are able to provide.

WRITING AND EFFECTIVE COMMUNICATION. A major aim of higher education is to contribute to the quality of discourse in and beyond its institutions of learning. The study of philosophy generally requires analytical writing, critical reading, and formulating intellectual problems and proposed solutions to them. For these reasons, work in philosophy can greatly improve writing and communication skills. Even if writing is taught virtually throughout the curriculum, philosophy can play a major and distinctive part in the task. No other discipline emphasizes, in the same ways, either verbal argumentation or conceptual analysis. Few other disciplines emphasize, to the same degree, students' producing their own theories or critical assessments as opposed to exposition of existing material. In addition, clarity, accurate interpretation, due consideration for others' positions, and the importance of using concrete examples are also stressed in competent teaching of the writing that philosophy requires. These qualities of philosophical training in writing and speaking make the study of philosophy especially valuable in preprofessional pursuits as well as for those seeking a more general education.

THE CULTURAL SIGNIFICANCE OF PHILOSOPHY

INTELLECTUAL HISTORY AND CROSS-CULTURAL VISION. In its historical and cross-cultural investigations, philosophy provides a sense of intellectual history and contributes to one's understanding of one's own culture in relation to other cultures. Most philosophy departments and institutes have programs of research and teaching that address at least ancient, modern, and contemporary philosophy. Many departments offer courses in philosophies produced by cultures other than their own. Studies in these areas help people to locate themselves historically and culturally, to work out a reasonable system of values, and to achieve an understanding of alternatives among values, cultural patterns, and intellectual traditions.

EXAMINATION OF WORLD VIEWS. A presupposition of higher education is that most reflective people seek a coherent view of the world that makes sense of their experience, guides them in certain major decisions, and gives them at least tentative answers to some of the perennial problems concerning human life and its place in the universe. The study of philosophy helps one to formulate and assess such views, whether they are drawn from the history of thought in a particular part of the world from comparative cross-cultural studies, from popular interpretations of current science, or from the one's own—perhaps quite unarticulated—reactions to one's experience. Among the (partial) world views commonly examined in philosophy are materialism, which construes everything there is, including persons, as essentially physical; dualism, which takes minds and hence persons to be radically different from purely physical entities; and, of course, theism in many of its forms. Often, sociopolitical orientations, such as liberal democracy and Marxian socialism, are associated with world views. In examining these positions and world views, the approach of philosophy is holistic, conceptual, and evaluative. Moreover, whatever world view philosophers may hold, in teaching philosophy, they normally make it their business to present forcefully arguments for *and* against their own positions. Their most characteristic concern in this kind of endeavor is to develop a framework for making rational decisions on world views and sociopolitical orientations, not to inculcate any particular one.

ARTICULATION AND CRITIQUE OF PUBLIC POLICY. A huge number of public policy issues are *mainly* moral, and most of them have significant parts that are moral. Normative ethics thus has special bearing on their proper resolution. Abortion and prostitution are mainly moral issues; this is because the chief disagreements are generally over moral rights and principles rather than over nonmoral facts. Distribution of wealth and the structure of the health care system are largely moral issues; but nonmoral factual questions, such as what effects one or another system has, are relatively more important for these issues than for the former two. Moral philosophy speaks directly to problems of public policy. For one thing, they involve questions of justice and of human rights. It is a major task of moral philosophy to develop an adequate theory of justice and a related theory of moral rights. These theories attempt to answer such questions as whether justice requires an equal distribution of wealth; whether everyone has a right to material well-being; whether punishment, as distinct from rehabilitation, is morally justified; and what moral obligations rich nations have to help poor nations. The abortion issue is of particular concern here. This is because a major aspect of it concerns the metaphysical question (also debated in theological contexts) of what constitutes a human person. The issue cannot be adequately understood, then, without a degree of both ethical and metaphysical sophistication.

Philosophers, like others, are divided on these questions, but on one important point they are largely agreed: that there *are* ways of distinguishing good from bad reasoning on moral questions and that some answers to these questions are better than others. In any case, it should be clear that philosophical reflection may help in clarifying issues, evaluating or constructing arguments on each side, determining the full range of policy options, framing definitions (particularly in drafting legislation), deducing consequences from a position so that we can see what it commits us to, eliciting and criticizing basic assumptions, and evaluating a moral issue in the light of the best theories and principles available in moral philosophy.

THE PHILOSOPHER. Philosophy is so broad and complex that no one is an expert in all of its fields. This does not entail that there is nothing of a general kind that can be said about what constitutes a philosopher. The simplest thing to say is that any philosopher will have a high level of competence in at least one of the subfields described here. That will imply using at least one method sketched above or a substantially similar method; it will also imply having a sense of some of the other subfields of philosophy. It does not imply taking any particular view or reflecting on any particular problem. Philosophical training and dialectic are, however, sources of intellectual versatility. In this and other ways, philosophy can add to the depth, scope, and acuity of the wise, much as wisdom can add to the powers of discernment and judgment of the philosopher.

It is widely known that, etymologically, philosophy is the love of wisdom. There is also a strong association—perhaps partly derived from the emphasis on practical wisdom in both Plato and Aristotle—of philosophical reflection with wisdom. In part for these reasons, some people have assumed that a philosopher must be wise, particularly in practical matters. If wisdom in a domain (such as human relations) is taken to be knowledge and soundness of judgment in that domain, it is true that philosophical reflection has high potential for leading to a degree of wisdom, at least in some important domains. It is certainly true that wisdom is a characteristic of many philosophers and inclines many who have it to appreciate one or another philosophical problem. But philosophical competence is no guarantee of wisdom, and wisdom of many kinds is possible for nonphilosophers.

Perhaps the most positive point to be made here is that philosophical competence in a subject-matter area will reveal at least a substantial proportion of the truths and some of the conceptual resources that are needed by a person who has wisdom in that domain. Much depends on the area in question: The more *conceptual* or normative it is, the greater the bearing of philosophy. Philosophical competence brought to the field of law, for example, can go a long way: Major questions in the law concern evidence, conceptual distinctions, and such normative notions as justice and blameworthiness. These are areas in which epistemology and ethics have much to contribute. The connection of philosophy to computer science may be less close; but even apart from the importance of logic in this field, there are ethical questions of, for instance, privacy and intellectual property rights, for which competence in ethics is of great value.

Quite apart from whether philosophers are characteristically wise, their cultural role includes criticism of major elements in their culture, particularly those that are intellectual, ethical, aesthetic, religious, or political. Certain important kinds of philosophical criticism are in a certain way neutral: The charge of inconsistency or incoherence is morally neutral; the point that an argument is invalid is logical and leaves open whether the argument's constituent propositions are true. A not uncommon view among philosophers has been that, qua philosophers, they should remain neutral in this way, abstaining from moral and political positions. On this view, taking these positions is appropriate for philosophers in their role as citizens but not in their role as professional philosophers.

A less restrictive view is that philosophers as a group, as represented by, for instance, the American Philosophical Association, should not take moral or political positions in official resolutions; and a still less restrictive position would apply this restriction to political but not moral issues. Nonetheless, just as there are philosophical works that systematically defend normative ethical views, there are some defending normative political positions. Why, it may be asked, should philosophers who have well-developed normative political positions not put them forward for the general public as philosophically well grounded? Publication itself may be regarded as a step in this direction, particularly if the style of the work and the medium of publication lend themselves to wide reading by the general public. Moreover, as electronic publication becomes more widespread and more readily accessible to the general public, the distinction between what is published for a professional audience and what is addressed to a wide public audience may become harder to draw.

Disagreement among philosophers about the proper cultural role of philosophy is likely to continue, and they can quite reasonably hold different views on the kinds of public moral or political positions appropriate for wide dissemination by philosophers as individuals as opposed to philosophers acting institutionally or as a corporate body. But we may safely say that, particularly with the declining influence of positivism from the middle of the twentieth century to the present time, few philosophers now believe that taking normative positions in ethics, politics, and elsewhere is not properly philosophical. One way to put a major part of this point is to say that philosophers as such may be prescriptive as well as descriptive. Indeed, even counseling people to avoid slipshod reasoning is prescriptive. Moreover, quite apart from any explicit prescriptions, criticisms of reasoning or counterexamples to proposed ideas are implicitly prescriptive: Plainly, one should not rely on bad reasoning or maintain an idea to which there are clear counterexamples. As a critical enterprise, philosophy is implicitly normative. As appraising major guiding ideas in human life, it is implicitly prescriptive.

CONCLUSION

Philosophy is the systematic and critical study of ideas and issues, a reasoned pursuit of fundamental truths, a quest for a comprehensive understanding of the world, a study of principles of conduct, and much more. Every domain of human existence raises questions to which its techniques and theories apply, and its methods are applicable in the study of any subject or the pursuit of any vocation. Its inquiries encompass the critical study of knowledge and reality, of value and obligation, of religion and science, of language and literature, of art and the professions. In the academy, philosophical studies enhance the capacity for problem solving, the ability to understand and express ideas, and the power to frame cogent arguments. In the culture in which it is practiced, philosophy can be a critical voice, a defender of ideals, a creator of visions.

Philosophy also develops understanding and enjoyment of things whose absence impoverishes many lives: aesthetic experience, communication with many different kinds of people, discussion of current issues, the discerning observation of human behavior, and intellectual zest in the pursuit of knowledge. For individuals in or outside the academy, the study of philosophy provides a major route to developing a well-reasoned vision of the good life and an ability to communicate this vision, defend it, and where necessary modify it. A well-reasoned vision of what human life ought to be yields an ordered set of long-term goals and a sense of the significance of life; it provides, often, the steady intellectual stimulation of comparing a theory of human experience with the constantly changing, ever-surprising panorama that our experience is; and it anchors our relations with others in a framework that enables us to conceive human conduct with some measure of clarity and understanding.

Bibliography

This entry contains many proper names, as well as many terms common in philosophy, that have entries devoted to them in this encyclopedia. Readers seeking an overall perspective on the nature of philosophy are urged to consider entries on these philosophers or philosophically important terms. One may also find much of relevance to understanding what philosophy is by consulting the entries on special fields, say epistemology, ethics, metaphysics, and the philosophy *of* subfields, such as philosophy of mind, of religion, or of science. Also recommended are the philosophy entries in the first edition of this work (1967) and its supplement (1996). Some of the material in this entry is drawn (with permission) from parts of two documents (of which the author was principal writer) published by the American Philosophical Association with the idea of clarifying the nature of the field and its academic study: "The Role of Philosophy Programs in Higher Education." *Proceedings and Addresses of the American Philosophical Association* 53 (3) (1980): 363–370; and "Philosophy: A Brief Guide for Undergraduates." *Proceedings and Addresses of the American Philosophical Association* 56 (2) (1982): i–xviii. Some material is also based on the author's "Realism, Rationality, and Philosophical Method," written with a similar purpose and appearing in *Proceedings and Addresses of the American Philosophical Association* 61 (1987): 65–74.

Robert Audi (2005)

PHILOSOPHY, HISTORIOGRAPHY OF

See *History and Historiography of Philosophy*

PHILOSOPHY BIBLIOGRAPHIES

See *"Philosophy Bibliographies" in Vol. 10*

PHILOSOPHY DICTIONARIES AND ENCYCLOPEDIAS

See *"Philosophy Dictionaries and Encyclopedias" in Vol. 10*

PHILOSOPHY JOURNALS

See *"Philosophy Journals" in Vol. 10*

PHILOSOPHY OF BIOLOGY

Biology refers both to the systematic investigation of living things, and to the body of knowledge that is the product of that investigation. Throughout biology's history, however, some important questions debated by biologists have not been so much about the organisms being studied, but about the nature of life, the proper way to investigate it and the form biological knowledge should take. When inquiry shifts from questions about living things to questions about proper and improper ways of asking, or answering, or adjudicating, such questions, it shifts to a philosophical level. One need not, of course, be trained in a department of philosophy to contribute to such an inquiry. Indeed many of the most significant contributions to the subject have been made by people trained in the sciences. Nevertheless such contributions are to the subject designated as philosophy of biology.

One assumption implicit in the very name is that the biological sciences are distinctive enough from other sciences that a general inquiry into the nature of science will not suffice. It was common among logical empiricists to suppose it would—in texts written in that tradition one often finds the biological and social sciences dealt with in chapters late in general books in philosophy of science (Braithwaite 1953, Hempel 1966, Nagel 1961). Two early challenges to this assumption were *The Ascent of Life* by Thomas Goudge (1961) and *The Biological Way of Thought* by Morton Beckner (1959).

These two early contributors were followed by a number of introductions to philosophy of biology written in the 1970s and 1980s, most of which were focused narrowly on evolution and genetics, and a standard set of associated philosophical questions (Hull 1974, Ruse 1973, Rosenberg 1985, Sober 2000). But in 1982 an NEH Summer Institute in Philosophy of Biology organized by Richard Burian and Marjorie Grene attracted a group of philosophers ready to focus more or less exclusively on the biological sciences. In 1984 *Philosophy of Science* devoted a "special issue" to the philosophy of biology; shortly thereafter Michael Ruse played a pivotal role in organizing both a journal (*Biology and Philosophy*) and a society (International Society for History, Philosophy, and Social Studies of Biology) devoted exclusively to the biological sciences. Since that time, the scope of research has broadened dramatically, with important contributions focusing on the biomedical sciences, physiology, cell biology, neurobiology, and developmental biology (Amundson 2005; Bechtel and Richardson 1993; Fox Keller 2000; Oyama, Griffiths, and Gray 2001; Robert 2004; Schaffner 1993; Sterelny and Griffiths 1999). And it is now common in general introductions to philosophy of science to have two chapters on philosophy of biology (for example, Salmon et al. 1992; Machamer and Silberstein 2002). In addition, there has been a tendency to integrate advances in the history of biology into these philosophical discussions.

This entry focuses on issues associated with three related biological domains: genetics, evolution, and development. Some of the most interesting recent philosophical work is focused on developmental biology and its relationship to the other two domains just mentioned. But important work is also being done on areas such as ecology, ethology, and neurobiology: each raises its own special philosophical questions.

DARWIN, MENDEL AND A PARTIAL SYNTHESIS

Two publications in the mid-nineteenth century— Charles Darwin's *On the Origin of Species* and Gregor Mendel's "Experiments in Plant Hybridization"—were to have a lasting impact on the structure of the scientific study of life, an impact still evident in the way philosophers think about biology as a science. Darwin self-consciously characterized the theory of evolution by natural selection presented in his book as one that would provide a theoretical unity to the study of life. As he put it in a letter to the philosopher Sir John Herschel:

> … I find so many young and middle-aged truly good workers in different branches, either partially or wholly accepting my views, *because they find that they can thus group and understand many scattered facts.* This has occurred with those who have chiefly or almost exclusively studied morphology, geographical Distribution, systematic Botany, simple geology & palaeontology.

(BURKHARDT 1994, PP. 135–136)

Darwin argued that central to explanations in all these domains were a set of "laws," which modern scholars identify as the principles at the core of the theory of evolution by natural selection:

Variation. The characteristics of the individual members of a species vary to a greater or lesser degree.

Inheritance. Some of that variation is heritable, transmitted from parents to off-spring.

Geometric increase. Populations tend to increase at a geometric rate.

Struggle for existence. Given limited resources, predation, disease, and so on, the tendency to geometric increase is checked, leading to a struggle for survival.

Differential survival. Individuals with advantageous variations tend on average to survive longer and leave more off-spring.

Differential reproduction. The offspring of parents with advantageous variations tend to have the same advantageous variations.

Darwin used the term "Natural Selection" to refer to the last two principles: "I have called this principle, by which each slight variation, if useful, is preserved, by the term Natural Selection…" (Darwin 1859/1964, pp. 117, 127) And, since the above theory neither provides for the introduction of new variation nor for the divergence within species that actually leads to speciation, he followed the presentation of his theory with lengthy discussions of divergence of character and laws of variation. Crucially, he saw divergence leading to new species and higher taxa as simply long run extrapolations of the same processes that lead to the production of varieties within a species; and he decoupled the causes of new variation from the adaptive needs of the organism.

Modern presentations of the theory often reduce it to a combination of the production of heritable variation and the differential perpetuation of variation. Many philosophical problems emerge from this reduction, and a number of philosophers have been urging a formulation of the theory more in tune with Darwin's.

In 1866, just seven years after Darwin's *Origin*, a scientifically trained monk published the results of nine years of careful experimentation. Mendel's work was revolutionary both in its methods and its conclusions. Trained at the University of Vienna in experimental physics and statistics as well as botany (where he learned about recent developments in agricultural plant hybridization), Mendel realized that the combination of experimental controls and statistical analysis could be used to solve the puzzles of plant hybridization. In the varieties of pea plants with which he experimented, he established that a number of factors were inherited independently, that if one crossed plants with alternate forms of a factor (for example, green and yellow peas) all their offspring would appear like one or the other (the dominant form), and that the next generation of plants would reveal a ratio of the forms of approximately three dominant to one recessive. Further experimental analysis would reveal that the "dominant" plants were a predictable mixture of pure dominants and plants with a dominant and a recessive factor.

But he went beyond just outlining his experiments and providing plausible inductive inferences from them. In the last section of his paper he suggested an underlying causal mechanism that could account for the observed regularities that he had reduced to a mathematical law of the development of hybrids.

Largely ignored for the remainder of the nineteenth century, the basic idea was developed in quite different ways by many researchers from different disciplinary backgrounds in the first decade of the twentieth century. Scholars have from then until now referred to this theory of inheritance as Mendelian genetics, and the regularities he uncovered experimentally as "Mendel's laws." And because this theory had essentially two distinct components—one related to inheritance, and one related to development—it in theory provided a way of unifying branches of the study of life that Darwin admitted he had not. A number of key steps taken between 1905 and 1920 isolated Mendel's "factors" (genes) to chromosomes and paved the way for generalizing Mendel's principles of inheritance in a mathematical form that would allow their investigation in large populations that do not breed under strictly controlled experimental conditions. This permitted the integration of Mendelian genetics with Darwinism, and it is no surprise that the leading figures in creating this synthesis—J. B. S. Haldane, Ronald Fisher, and Sewall Wright—all had a passion for both mathematics and natural history (Provine 1971, Plutynski 2004, Sarkar 1992). And all had, by quite different routes, fallen under the spell of Darwin's theory of evolutionary descent driven primarily by natural selection.

The basic idea behind their synthesis was remarkably simple: think of populations of organisms in terms of the frequencies of the genes associated with the various traits found in those populations, and think of evolution in terms of gradual changes in those frequencies, under such influences as the migration of organisms in and out of the population, randomly occurring genetic mutations, genetic recombinations of various kinds and, above all, natural selection. Mathematical models were developed which permitted one to predict changes in the genetic make up of future populations given information (or, more often, assumptions) about these variables, the number of alleles of genes for given traits and assumptions about the relative fitnesses of different combinations of

these alleles, know as "genotypes." The crucial step in developing these models was, of course, that each of these potential influences on gene frequencies was treated as a quantitative variable—including fitness.

It should be noted that all of these people—and the founder of experimental population genetics, Thomas Hunt Morgan, should be added—treat "genetics" as the study of the transmission of genes in reproduction. Indeed, even in the twenty-first century a synonym for Mendelian genetics is transmission genetics. The Evolutionary Synthesis did not include the study of development or developmental genetics, except for the use of embryological evidence in constructing evolutionary phylogenies. We will come back to this omission later.

Concluding the preface of *Evolution: The Modern Synthesis*, Julian Huxley declared: "The need today is for concerted attack and synthesis" (Huxley 1942, p. 8). That Synthesis was in the making when he wrote (the key publications by Theodosius Dobzhansky, Ernst Mayr, and George Simpson were published between 1937 and 1944), and by the 1959 centenary of the publication of Darwin's *Origin* it was declaring itself triumphant. Most of the philosophical issues related to evolutionary biology under discussion in the 2000s are a direct consequence of the form that the "Synthetic" theory takes This entry mentions five that are critical and discusses four of them in detail.

1) The concept of chance in evolutionary theory and the theory's probabilistic nature.

2) Fitness and selection.

3) Units and levels of selection.

4) The nature selection/adaptation explanations.

5) The ontological status of species and the epistemological status of species concepts.

THE ROLE OF CHANCE. Chance is a contrastive concept; to say that some outcome is chance is typically to deny that it resulted from some cause or other. In evolutionary theory "chance" plays a key role both in discussing the generation of variation and the perpetuation of variation (a distinction owed to John Beatty; see also Sober 1984, ch. 4). Consider the following variation grid, created by considering whether the contribution to fitness of a variation does or does not play a role in either the generation or the perpetuation of that variation:

	Variations	
	Generation	Perpetuation
Fitness Biased	Lamarck	Darwin
Not Fitness Biased	Darwin Neutralism	Lamarck Neutralism

The uniquely Darwinian position is that the generation of variation is chance in that it is not biased by fitness differences (as it is for Lamarckian theories), but the perpetuation of variation typically is biased by fitness differences. Neutralism, to be discussed shortly, will claim that a significant amount of evolutionary change is due to randomly generated variation that is perpetuated by chance as well.

But now consider the following discussion of chance and selection:

> In Darwin's scheme of things, recall, chance events and natural selection were consecutive rather than alternative stages of the evolutionary process. There was no question as to which was more important at a particular stage. But now that we have the concept of random drift taking over where random variation leaves off, we are faced with just such a question. That is, given chance variations, are further changes in the frequencies of those variations more a matter of chance or more a matter of natural selection?

(BEATTY 1984, P. 196)

In the first two sentences, as often, the generation of variation is characterized as a "chance" process because selection plays no role at that stage—the generation of variations is not biased by the adaptive requirements of the organism. The concept of "random variation" is often used by neo-Darwinians as a synonym for "chance variation" in precisely this sense, as in the following from a product of Morgan's "fruit fly lab" and one of the architects of the evolutionary synthesis:

> … mutation is a random process with respect to the adaptive needs of the species. Therefore, mutation alone, uncontrolled by natural selection, would result in the breakdown and eventual extinction of life, not in the adaptive or progressive evolution.

(DOBZHANSKY 1970, P. 65)

The generation of variations is a "chance" process in the sense that the probability assignments are not biased by "adaptive needs" or "fitness."

The remainder of the quotation from Beatty concerns the perpetuation of variations, and in particular

how to distinguish variations perpetuated by selection from those perpetuated by another process known as "random drift," in which traits that are selectively neutral may become fixed in a population simply as a result of what statisticians call "errors of sampling." Suppose, for example, that a pair of bats get blown to an island far away from their colony. They mate, and their offspring mate, and a number of genes become fixed in the growing populations simply because they were present in the founding pair, not because they are favored by selection. In the above quoted paper Beatty argues that "it is conceptually difficult to distinguish natural selection from random drift" (Beatty 1984, p. 196). As the entry discusses, this problem arises from a standard way of characterizing "fitness."

Genetic drift plays a critical role in one primary challenge to the neo-Darwinian synthesis, "neutralism," and the concept of chance is often used to draw the contrast. In the following quote, one prominent champion of the neutral theory of molecular evolution characterizes his position:

> … the great majority of evolutionary changes at the molecular (DNA) level do not result from Darwinian natural selection acting on advantageous mutants but, rather, from random fixation of selectively neutral or very nearly neutral mutants through random genetic drift, which is caused by random sampling of gametes in finite populations.

(KIMURA 1992, P. 225)

Here genetic drift refers to a process whereby a selectively neutral allele becomes fixed in a population as a result of a "random (chance) sampling of gametes." This is a rival to neo-Darwinism only because of Kimura's claim that this produces a majority of the evolutionary changes at the molecular level. The contrast between "chance" and "fitness biased" processes is used by Kimura to distinguish means of perpetuating certain variations. We are contrasting two sampling processes.

There is currently a lively debate about whether to characterize this contrast by reference to differences in the sampling processes (Millstein 2002, 2005) or by reference to the expected outcomes of sampling (Brandon and Carson 1996, Brandon 2005). On Millstein's view it is realistically possible for the outcomes to be identical, and thus she seeks to defend a view according to which selection is defined as discriminate sampling (based on selectively relevant differences) and drift as indiscriminate sampling. Both samplings are "probabilistic," of course, but that in no way obviates the above contrast.

FITNESS AND SELECTION. All parties to this dispute are now realizing that wider issues about the nature of probability, explanation, mathematical abstraction, and causation are likely at stake in such disagreements. As one case in point, at least part of the dispute over differentiating drift from selection derives from the tendency to characterize natural selection so that it is indistinguishable from random drift (Brandon 1990, Lennox 1992, Lennox and Wilson 1994).

If we think of selection as a discriminative or biased sampling process, that natural raises the question of the basis of the biasing. Typically, the answer is that it is differences in fitness, the values assigned to different genotypes in the models of population genetics, which some readers will think of as different degrees of adaptation to the relevantly characterized environment.

But as noted above, it is not uncommon to find characterizations of the fitness of a genotype in terms of its relative contribution to the gene pool of future generations—the genotype contributing the larger percentage being the fitter. The expression "survival of the fittest" has essentially been eliminated from any serious presentation of Darwinian selection theory but the concept of "fitness" plays a prominent, and problematic, role. In the mathematical models used in population genetics "fitness" is represented by the variable W. Here is a rather standard textbook presentation of the relevant concepts:

> In the neo-Darwinian approach to natural selection that incorporates consideration of genetics, fitness is attributed to particular genotypes. The genotype that leaves the most descendants is ascribed the fitness value $W = 1$, and all other genotypes have fitnesses, relative to this, that are less than 1. … Fitness measures the relative evolutionary advantage of one genotype over another, but it is often important also to measure the relative penalties incurred by different genotypes subject to natural selection. This relative penalty is the corollary of fitness and is referred to by the term selection coefficient. It is given the symbol s and is simply calculated by subtracting the fitness from 1, so that: $s = 1 - W$.

(SKELTON 1993, P. 164)

In this passage evolutionary advantage is equated with reproductive success and fitness is treated indifferently as a quantitative measure of both. But since, as we have seen, natural populations can evolve (via drift) in the absence of natural selection, and since balancing selection may prevent a population from evolving, it is clear that establishing, by measuring different reproduc-

tive rates among its members, that the genetic makeup of a population has changed does not establish that natural selection was the source of that change; nor does the fact that no change has been measured establish that natural selection is not operative.

The most widely accepted solution to this problem is to argue that fitness measures a reproductive propensity of organisms (Brandon 1978, Mills and Beatty 1979, Richardson and Burian 1992). Brandon tends to equate fitness in this sense with "adaptedness," and to contrast it with "realized fitness"—differences in realized fitness are explained by differential adaptation to a common selective environment. This suggests that fitness is in some sense relational, enhancing chances of reproducing relative to an environment (Lennox 1992, Lennox and Wilson 1994). In any case, as Millstein has insisted, characterizing fitness as a reproductive propensity raises the question of how to understand this propensity and its organic basis (Millstein 2003).

UNITS AND LEVELS OF SELECTION. A number of challenges to Darwinian selection theory have emerged since the mid-twentieth century. Those challenges can be placed into two broad categories: (1) proposed limitations on natural selection as the primary cause of evolutionary change; and (2) expansions of the scope of natural selection to include new "targets" and "levels." It will be noted that in neither case is it obvious that the theory itself requires modification in the face of such challenges—in principle these might be nothing more than challenges to the theory's range of application. However, if it turned out that most evolutionary change could be explained without recourse to natural selection, this would be grounds for arguing that evolutionary biology was no longer Darwinian (see Godfrey-Smith in Orzack and Sober 2001.)

Darwin conceived of natural selection as almost exclusively an interaction between individual organisms and their organic and inorganic environments. Taking that as our starting point, we can see two challenges to Darwinism today with respect to the units of selection. One comes from those defending a strong form of genic selectionism, such as G. C. Williams (1966, 1992) and Richard Dawkins (1976, 1982), who argue that selection is always and only targeting genes. Here is a clear statement:

> These complications [those introduced by organism/environment interactions] are best handled by regarding individual [organismic] selection, not as a level of selection in addition

to that of the gene, but as the primary mechanism of selection at the genic level.

(WILLIAMS 1992, P. 16)

Dawkins' preferred mode for making the same point is to refer to organisms—or interactors, to use language introduced by David Hull—as the vehicles of their genes (the replicators), in fact vehicles constructed by the genome for its own perpetuation. Neither Williams nor Dawkins deny that there is interaction between phenotype and environment that plays a role in the differential perpetuation of genes. Their argument is that those interactors are part of the "genic selection mechanism," as Williams worded it above.

This view has been extensively challenged by philosophers of biology on both methodological and conceptual grounds (Brandon 1996, ch. 8; Mitchell 2003, ch. 4; Moss 2003, ch. 1; Sober 1984, chs. 3, 7; Sterelny and Griffiths 1999, chs. 4–5), though there are, among philosophers, also enthusiastic supporters (Dennett 1995). In all the give and take, it is seldom noticed how odd it is that defenders of this view claim to be carrying the Darwinian flag (Gayon 1998 and Gould 2003 are exceptions). Yet it is certainly not a position that Darwin would recognize—and not merely because he lacked a coherent theory of the units of inheritance. It is not a Darwinian view because for Darwin it was differences in the abilities of organisms at various stages of development to respond to the challenges of life that had causal primacy in the explanation of evolutionary change. Gene selectionism was explicitly challenged on these grounds by key figures in the Synthesis (for example, Ernst Mayr).

The Darwinian view of the units of selection also has challenges from the opposite direction. In the 1970s a number of biologists working in the fields of paleontology and systematics challenged the Neo-Darwinian dogma that you could account for "macro-evolution" by simple, long-term extrapolation from the processes modeled by population genetics. (The case was enhanced by parallel and contemporaneous developments in embryology and functional morphology that are discussed in the last section of this entry.) Stephen Jay Gould (2003), in a chapter titled "Species as Individuals in the Hierarchical Theory of Selection" combines two conceptually distinct theses: first, the thesis defended by Michael Ghiselin (1997) and championed and refined by David Hull (2001), that species are in a robust sense of the term "individuals"; and second, that there may well be selection among groups of organisms, *qua* groups. This approach brings us to the brink of problem (5) on the list,

how to understand the species category and species as taxa, questions discussed only briefly.

Gould exemplifies one approach to group selection—the unit of selection is always the individual, but there are individuals other than individual organisms that are subject to selection. A very different result emerges if one assumes that groups of organisms such as demes, kin-groups, or species, though not individuals, are nevertheless possible units of selection. Adding to the conceptual complexity, some researchers propose that "group selection" be restricted to the process whereby group-level traits provide advantages to one group over another, in which case there are strict conditions delimiting cases of group selection, while others focus solely on group level effects. Thus a debate analogous to that earlier discussed regarding the definitions of "fitness" emerges here—by group selection do we mean a distinct level of causal interaction, or merely a tendency within certain populations for some well defined groups to displace others over time? (For further discussion, see Sterelny and Griffiths 1999, 151–179; Hull 2001, 49–90.) It is now common to characterize "selection," "interactor," and "replicator" abstractly and to specify the conditions under which an entity is properly identified as a unit of selection. This allows one to leave it an open and essentially empirical question whether, under the right conditions a particular "unit" could be subject to selection. With the modular picture of development that is emerging, the "developmental module" will likely be added to the list.

SELECTION, ADAPTATION, AND TELEOLOGY. Perhaps the central promise of Darwinism, and the reason it was rightly seen as a challenge to the Argument from Design for a benevolent creator, was that it provides a scientific explanation for both phylogenic continuity and adaptive differentiation by means of the same principles. The nature of "selection explanations" is a topic to which much philosophical attention has been devoted in recent years (Allen, Bekoff, and Lauder 1998; Sober 1984). How does one account for the apparently teleological character of explanation by natural selection?

The appearance of teleology is certainly present in Darwinian explanations, and has been since Darwin spoke of natural selection working solely for the good of each being. The appearance of teleology stems from the ease with which both evolutionary biology and common sense take it for granted that animals and plants have the adaptations they do because of some benefit or advantage to the organism provided by those adaptations. But in what sense can the adaptive advantage be the cause of the presence of the adaptation?

Some insist it cannot (Ghiselin 1997). Others argue that such explanations are actually masked appeals to the past effects of selection (see the papers in Allen, Bekoff, and Lauder, section 3). This entry sketches a case that shows selective explanations of adaptations are robustly teleological (see Lennox 1992, 1993; and the papers in Allen, Bekoff, and Lauder 1998, section 1).

Are the functions performed by confirmed adaptations a central and irreducible feature of explanations of the presence of those adaptations? If the answer is yes, the explanations are teleological. Take the following example. In research combining painstaking field work and laboratory experimentation, John Endler demonstrated that the color patterns of males in certain Caribbean guppy populations resulted from a balance of mate selection and predator selection. For example, he demonstrated that a group of males with a color pattern that matched that of the bottoms of the streams and ponds they populated except for bright red spots have that pattern because a common predator in those populations, a prawn, is color blind for red. Thus red spots did not put their possessors at a selective disadvantage, and were attractors for mates\ (Endler 1983).

Their pattern of coloration was a complex adaptation serving the functions of predator avoidance and mate attraction—and it is an adaptation, as that term is used in Darwinism, only if it is a product of natural selection (Williams 1966, Brandon 1985, Burian 1983). In order for it to be a product of natural selection, there must be an array of color variation available in the genetic/developmental resources of the species wider that this particular pattern but including this pattern. Which factors are critical, then, in producing differential survival and reproduction of guppies with this particular pattern in a shared homogeneous environment? The answer would seem to be the *value*-consequences this pattern has compared to others available in promoting viability and reproduction. In popular parlance (and the parlance favored by Darwin), this color pattern is good for the male guppies that have it, and for their male offspring (Binswanger 1990, Brandon 1985, Lennox 1992). This is a robust version of "consequence etiology" accounts of selection explanations (Bekoff, Allen, and Lauder 1998, section 1), which stresses that selection ranges over value differences which are causally relevant to one among a number of color patterns having a higher fitness value. Selection explanations are, then, a particular kind of teleological explanation, an explanation in which that for the

sake of which a trait is possessed, its valuable consequences (avoiding predation, attracting mates), account for the trait's differential perpetuation and maintenance in the population.

SPECIES AND TAXONOMY. Darwin at one point in the *Origin* says that he considers the term "species" one that is given arbitrarily, for convenience. He based that comment on a review of the taxonomic work of his day, and a similar review today would have the same result. Equally competent taxonomists will disagree about whether to rank a group of similar organisms as members of the same species or as members of two distinct species. This issue takes on philosophical import because speciation—the "origin of species," to use Darwin's language—is taken to be the key step in the evolution of life. One would hope to have a clear way of deciding, at least in principle, when that step has been completed! But every attempt to give a clear account of what makes a taxonomic unit a member of the species category runs up against rather compelling problems. Surrounding this topic, which has generated an enormous literature, are both epistemological issues regarding the basis for our species concepts and ontological issues about the nature of species. Interested readers should consult the work of Marc Ereshefsky (1992, a collection of essays defending various views of the species category) or Kim Sterelny and Paul Griffiths (1999, chapter 9; a readable and current overview of the issues).

GENES

In standard texts in the philosophy of biology in the 1970s and 1980s (as well as in most of the more technical journal articles) genetics played a key role in the discussion of two philosophical topics: reductionism, and the structure of evolutionary theory (Hull 1974, ch. 1; Schaffner 1969; Ruse (1973), ch. 10; Rosenberg 1985, ch. 4). The discussion began by importing a theory of reduction that had been developed with physical theories in mind, and asking whether, on such models, there had been a reduction of Mendelian or transmission genetics to the molecular level. This model, developed most clearly by Ernst Nagel (1961), imagined two theories formalized with axioms and laws. Reduction would require that the laws of one theory be, in some clear sense, deducible from the fundamental laws of the other, as, with appropriate corrections, Kepler's planetary laws could be from those of Newtonian celestial mechanics. Typically, this would also require that the key concepts in the two theories be interdefinable. This model was developed into a "general reduction/replacement model" by Kenneth Schaffner (1969) in a paper in which he argued for the potentially application of such a model to the case of genetics.

David Hull (1974) pointed out that a critical problem in the way of achieving this goal was that the two theories had essentially different goals and domains—hereditary transmission of differences versus genetic input into the biochemistry of development. This suggested to him not only the impossibility of a reduction, but its irrelevance to biology. All parties to this discussion concluded that one needed a much more elaborate account of both biological theory structure and explanation to even try to answer the question.

A number of recent discussions have stressed that understanding both biological investigation and explanation in terms of mechanisms and their operations provides a more realistic picture of fields such as neurobiology and molecular biology (see Machamer, Darden, and Craver 2000; Waters 1994, 2000). It may also provide a more tractable notion of "reduction" in terms of "underlying mechanisms." Detailed histories of the development of genetics played a very important role in this discussion, and thus it was one important area driving the integration of history and philosophy of biology. A fine review of that topic, as well as a carefully hedged defense of genic reductionism which takes into account the complex, interlevel nature of typical biological theories, can be found in Schaffner 1993, chapter 9 (and see Waters 1994 for a somewhat different defense).

One of the puzzles that emerges from reviewing the literature on genetics and reduction is that Hull's point, mentioned above, about the fundamentally different aims of molecular genetics and transmission genetics only really gets serious consideration once developmental biology comes to the fore in the 1990s (see Waters 1994 and the papers in Beurton, Falk, and Rheinberger 2000). This is still very much a discussion in process, so the entry touches on some of the philosophical and historical questions being raised about different uses of the gene concept (or, alternatively, different gene concepts) in evolutionary and developmental contexts.

The traditional gene concept associated with Mendelian genetics that formed the basis of evolutionary biology was important because it was the basis of heritable differences in populations. Genes, or more precisely alleles, were the sources of heritable variation in populations, and thus provide "the material basis for evolution." In the context of developmental biology, however, the focus of research has always been on the genes as sources of deep relationships among species within and even across phyla. Here is a succinct expression of the difference:

> In the Modern Synthesis of population genetics and evolution, genes become manifest by differences in alleles that are active in conferring differential reproductive success in adult individuals. The gene is though to act as a particulate, atomic unit. In current syntheses of evolution and developmental genetics, important genes are manifest by their similarities across distantly related phyla, and they are active in the construction of embryos. These developmental genes are thought to act in a context-dependent network.

> (SCOTT GILBERT, IN BEURTON, FALK, AND RHEINBERGER 2000, P. 178)

In a defense of genic selectionism George Williams argues that genes should be understood as units of information.

> Only DNA provides the durable archive for most of the earth's organisms. This constraint should not blind us to the fact that it is information we are concerned with, and that DNA is the medium, not the message. A gene is not a DNA molecule; it is the transcribable information coded by the molecule.

> (WILLIAMS 1992, P. 11)

Williams praises philosophers for adopting the distinction between replicators and interactors discussed earlier, but he is critical of them for regarding "replicators as material objects and miss[ing] the codex concept" (Williams 1992, p. 12). Notice that what this approach does is allow nominal acceptance of advances in our understanding of cellular mechanisms at the molecular level while continuing to treat the gene as an "atomic" unit differentiated by reference to phenotypic differences. That is, development can continue to be "black boxed" by taking the gene to be any selectively relevant bit of the "codex" for the organism. In principle it should allow Williams to take on board a suggestion made by Sterelny and Griffiths; on grounds that lots of things get replicated in reproductive cycles "gene selectionism should be generalized to 'replicator selectionism'"(Sterelny and Griffiths 1999, p. 69).

However, taking this approach also raises a new set of concerns, namely those involved with the application of concepts from information theory in the characterization of genes and gene action. This way of talking became extremely popular after the "breaking of the genetic code" in the 1960s. Complementary strands of this "double helix" consist of only four bases, two purines (Adenine [A] and Thymine [T]) and two pyramidines (Guanine [G] and Cytosine [C]); and since proteins consist of polypeptide chains made from only twenty different amino acids, if DNA is to contain the "instructions" for synthesizing all the possible proteins, the simplest possible "code" would be one in which three bases combined to specify each amino acid. The bases came to be represented as the "letters" of the genetic "alphabet"; they combine into syllables, words and "reading frames"—the book of life! The coded script is "transcribed" and "translated"; there is an "encoding" and "decoding" process; and with the discovery of the complexities of DNA transcription, it is not surprising that terms like "editing" and "proofreading" got added. It is not inevitable that these metaphors should lead researchers to present the genome as both the architect and the blueprint for building an organism—but it was natural. (For a compelling story of the history, see Keller 2000.)

Are there problems with it? A number of philosophers of biology think so, and they are discussed in this entry in two parts. The entry first discusses those problems that are not specific to developmental biology, and then discusses the philosophical debates around Developmental Systems Theory and "evo-devo."

The aforementioned quotation from George Williams (1992) establishes that some evolutionary biologists want to take the information metaphor one step further, and allow it to float free from its source in the discovery of the relationship between DNA sequence and amino acid differences. Genes are units of information, pure and simple. The value of doing this is that it allows one to avoid the troubling fact that the causal complexity of the processes involved in biological development make it quite meaningless to talk about some relatively short and self-contained DNA sequence as a gene for anything other than an amino acid, perhaps.

What could "information" be, in this case? It seems not to be information in the sense of mathematical information theory. One suggestion is to see it from a "teleosemantic" point of view; that is, genes are something akin to units of "meaning," their meaning being what they are present for, the phenotypic trait whose selection insures the replication of that gene (Sterelny and Griffiths 1999, pp. 82–92). Critics have argued that this simply severs completely the causal connection between DNA sequences and phenotypic traits. And it looks as if the original impulse for gene selectionism gets lost. It looks like the interactor—whether it is a colony, an animal, or a gamete—is the only serious causal determinant of differential reproduction. "A purely functional notion of a gene, untied to anything constant at the molecular level, is not a definition suitable for gene selection theory, whatever its other uses might be" (Sterelny and Griffiths 1999, p. 90).

A very different defense of the language of information in biology would in fact tie it very tightly to the detailed machinery of molecular biology, and therefore takes seriously the role of the analogies based on this language in the development of molecular genetics, such as treating DNA as a "reading frame" made up of triplet units, which then allows one to see certain mutations as analogous to "frame shifts" that create nonsense (Maynard Smith 2000, p. 184). But even here, the sense of "information" that seems relevant to the analogy is again a semantic notion tied to meaning and intentionality, not that of the 'signals', 'channels', and 'sources' of "information theory." And thus all the problems associated with that notion are still present. (See the replies to Maynard Smith in Godfrey-Smith 2000; Sarkar 2000.) There is consensus here, however, that the language associated with codes and information storage and retrieval was extremely important in the development of molecular biology. Insofar as there is disagreement, it is over whether these metaphors have outlived their usefulness and are now in fact the source of significant misunderstanding.

THE CHALLENGE OF DEVELOPMENT

Much recent philosophy of biology has focused on the process of development. There are at least two reasons for this. First, the model of the gene described in the previous section is deeply problematic, and one response was the philosophical defense of a developmentalist alternative based on the work of Susan Oyama, known as Developmental Systems Theory or DST. In an important and productive exchange on "the developmentalist challenge" to this sort of "genetic primacy," Ken Schaffner (1998) identified eleven theses of DST, and focused on four with which he thinks serious researchers in biomedical molecular genetics would, in one form or another, agree. The basic idea is that development is a product of a complex time series of interactions among many cellular and extra-cellular factors, among which "genes" (and the quotation marks are important) are just one. As a consequence, DST denies what I have called "information theoretic determinism." In so far as the information metaphor has value (this is currently much disputed), it is applicable only to the developing system—genes carry information, if at all, only as aspects of developmental systems.

Another obvious consequence of DST is the rejection of various common themes of behavioral genetics (Lewontin 1995). Schaffner's approach to these DST theses is to compare them with work done on a "simple model system," one of the organisms at the center of human genome research, the nematode worm *C. elegans*. This worm became a model organism due to Sidney Brenner adopting it to investigate the development, from zygote to mature adult, of an entire nervous system (and behavior). It was ideal for many reasons, not the least of which was its simplicity—a nervous system containing only 302 neurons forming roughly 5,000 synapses. Schaffner compares the DST theses about genes, development and behavior with the results of the massive, worldwide research assault on *C. elegans* to see how they hold up. This entry cannot follow the details, but one can see from his eloquent conclusion that at least some of the DST argument is acceptable to him:

> Characterizing simple "genes for" behaviors is, accordingly, a drastic oversimplification of the connection between genes and behavior, *even when we have the (virtually) complete molecular story*. The melody of behavior represents no solo performance—it is the outcome of an extraordinarily complex orchestra—and one with no conductor.
>
> (SCHAFFNER 1998, P. 247)

This paper was the target for responses from philosophers of biology and biologists more or less sympathetic to DST (Gilbert and Jorgensen 1998, Wimsatt 1998) and Schaffner was given the last word in reply. This selection of papers constitutes the best introduction to the DST reply to gene-centered research (see Waters 2005).

Independently of philosophical discussion of DST, there are compelling reasons for philosophers to be interested in evolutionary developmental biology, or "Evo-devo." Given the long history of both developmental biology and evolutionary biology, and the long history of their interactions, one might wonder why the goal of integration has appeared on the horizon only in the twenty-first century. The answer is a complex of historical, philosophical, and biological components.

According to one historical narrative (Beurton, Falk, and Rheinberger 2000; Burian 2005), the rapid development of new investigative techniques in molecular biology, driven in part by the medical and agricultural potential of the methods of genetic modification, and the field of "genomics" that evolved along with the Human Genome Project, provided the means for investigating development at the molecular level. This gave rise to a number of quite revolutionary discoveries; this entry notes only two: (1) The "Hox" regulatory genes encode a special sort of protein with a stretch of amino acids known as a "homeodomain." These proteins attach to quite specific segments of DNA, regulating the expression of a series of genes. These proteins act in concert and have "modular" effects on such things as organ formation, body segmentation and bilateral duplication of body parts (a clear introduction can be found in Burian 2005, chs. 11 and 12). (2) Molecular genetics is providing a highly complex, "interactive" picture of gene regulation. It will be noted that in the description of the Hox genes it became clear that certain proteins were responsible for their regulation. In fact all sorts of signals, some coming from within the cell and some from the extracellular environment, play a role in gene expression. This is now so widely accepted that philosophers and historians refer to it as "the interactionist consensus." According to this picture, genes are one of many interacting factors all of which must play their roles in order to give rise to an organism—the study of this interactive process is termed "epigenetics," though it is unclear to what extent its practitioners understand development as a truly epigenetic process (Robert 2004, ch. 1).

On this view, the integration of evolutionary and developmental biology will be—is being—effected by the long overdue integration of molecular genetics, and the molecular understanding of development, into evolutionary studies. At least one advocate of this view (Burian 2005) has stressed the modularity of this view of development, and the implication of the semi-autonomy of these developmental modules (body segmentation and bilateralism, organ systems, limb structure, and so on) for the way evolution can possibly work.

There is another way of viewing the history, being developed in different ways by Alan Love and Jason Robert (Love 2003, Robert 2004). Love focuses on what the proponents of Evo-devo claim their investigations can do that the current evolutionary "synthesis" cannot. Many proponents of this field put the explanation of evolutionary novelties such as feathers, tetrapod limbs, or jaws as the central contribution of development to evolution. While they are happy to concede to population genetics and ecological genetics the explanation of gradual evolutionary changes in traits associated with one or a few Mendelian genes, they argue that the explanation of the appearance of novelties at particular phylogenetic junctures requires an understanding of the network of changes in the organization of developmental resources needed to produce the novel structure, and an understanding of its functional morphology. The history of work on evolutionary novelties focuses attention on a number of research programs in developmental biology, functional morphology and paleontology, all focused on understanding the first appearance of novel structures and behaviors—and all more or less ignored by the evolutionary synthesis.

Jason Robert argues for the primacy of the organism as it develops from zygote to maturity, and thus for a seriously "top down" or "whole to part" view of developmental causation. This allows us to see the analytic tools that allow us to understand the details of the developmental mechanisms as a first step, with true understanding of development coming when we have an integrated understanding of how those mechanisms interact. Pretty much everyone looking at this rapidly developing area of biology agrees with the following sentiment from Burian:

> During the next few decades, I believe, biologists will highlight the roles played in constructing organisms by dynamic regulatory systems above the level of the genome. The result will be a nonvitalist but much more holistic, vision of the organism, one that places the integration of the organism at the focus of attention. In short, our new understanding of the apparatus regulating gene expression has undermined classical genetic determinism.

(BURIAN 2005, P. 243)

As Robert as pointed out, this prediction for the future sounds remarkably like a return to the "organismic" biologists, such as E. S. Russell, writing in the 1920s and 1930s, against the then rising tide of a population genetic centered evolutionary synthesis (Robert 2004). There are, of course, critics of this viewpoint. While the aforementioned text indicated that Schaffner's review of *C. elegans* research encouraged him to accept, at least in a modified form, some of the theses of "the developmentalist challenge" to genetic determinism, the modifications were significant. And some would likely say he has gone too far, arguing that what we have in this new molecular understanding of development is a vindication of reductionism (Waters 1994, 2004, 2005; Rosenberg 1985, discussed in Robert 2004, pp. 12–15).

Evo-devo once again brings into focus the question of the unity of biology as a science. As stressed earlier, one thing that the evolutionary synthesis provided for philosophers of biology was an image of how the biological sciences could be unified that was decidedly unlike the standard models based on the physical sciences. The attempt to unify evolutionary biology and developmental biology may complicate that image considerably. The fields omitted from the synthesis share key concepts (for example, gene, homology) with evolutionary biology, but appear to deploy them in very different ways. Moreover, the methods of investigation in functional morphology, developmental biology and population genetics or ecology are extremely different. The central problems and questions to be answered are very different, because the basic research agendas of the fields are very different. A field that focuses on "the production of the tetrapod limb" and a field that thinks of populations as gene pools of heritable variation being sampled by selection do not appear to look at organisms in the same way (Amundson, in Orzack and Sober 2001; Love 2003). As this proposed "synthesis" or "integration" takes place, philosophers of biology can both test their models of theoretical unification against the accomplishment of evo-devo, and can provide its advocates with ideas about adequacy conditions for a successful integration. One thing appears certain at this point: evo-devo specialists who have explicitly written on this topic see a special set of problems that will require an integration of concepts and techniques from evolutionary biology and developmental biology; they do not imagine one field being gradually "reduced" to another.

What, then, are the logical and conceptual prerequisites for such an integrated investigation? If we look back to where we started in this entry, it will be recalled that the "integration" of Darwinism with the Mendelian genetics of populations, required the concepts of "fitness" and "selection" to be reshaped into a mathematical form; and what began as a cytologically and developmentally based genetics eventually "black-boxed" development in the interests of focusing on the transmission of genetic "information" from one generation to the next. These changes, in the interests of integration or synthesis, gave rise to a host of philosophical problems. Perhaps, with philosophers and historians inextricably involved with this new synthesis, at least some problems can be avoided.

See also Darwin, Charles Robert; Evolutionary Theory (Natural Selection); Special Sciences.

Bibliography

Allen, Collin, Mark Bekoff, and George Lauder, eds. *Nature's Purposes: Analyses of Function and Design in Biology.* Cambridge, MA: MIT Press, 1998.

Amundson, Ronald. *The Changing Role of the Embryo in Evolutionary Thought*. Cambridge, U.K.: Cambridge University Press, 2005.

Ayala, Francisco. *Population Genetics: A Primer*. San Francisco: Benjamin Cummings, 1982.

Ayala, Francisco. "Teleological Explanations in Evolutionary Biology." In *Nature's Purposes: Analyses of Function and Design in Biology*, edited by Collin Allen, Mark Bekoff, and George Lauder. Cambridge, MA: MIT Press, 1998.

Beatty, John. "Chance and Natural Selection." *Philosophy of Science* (Special Issue: Philosophy of Biology) 51 (2) (1984): 183–211.

Bechtel, William, and Robert Richardson. *Discovering Complexity*. Princeton, NJ: Princeton University Press, 1993.

Beckner, Morton. *The Biological Way of Thought*. New York: Columbia University Press, 1959.

Beurton, Peter, Raphael Falk, and Hans-Jörg Rheinberger, eds. *The Concept of the Gene in Development and Evolution*. Cambridge, U.K.: Cambridge University Press, 2000.

Binswanger, Harry. *The Biological Basis of Teleological Concepts*. Los Angeles: ARI Press, 1990.

Braithwaite, Richard B. *Scientific Explanation*. Cambridge, U.K.: Cambridge University Press, 1953.

Brandon, Robert. *Adaptation and Environment*. Princeton, NJ: Princeton University Press, 1990.

Brandon, Robert. "Adaptation Explanations: Are Adaptations for the Good of Replicators or Interactors?" In *Evolution at a Crossroads*, edited by Bruce Weber and David Depew. Cambridge, MA: MIT Press, 1985.

Brandon, Robert. *Concepts and Methods in Evolutionary Biology*. Cambridge, U.K.: Cambridge University Press, 1996.

Brandon, Robert. "The Difference between Drift and Selection: A Reply to Millstein." *Biology and Philosophy* 20 (1) (2005): 153–170.

Brandon, Robert, and Richard Burian, eds. *Genes, Organism, Populations: Controversies over the Units of Selection*. Cambridge, MA: MIT Press, 1984.

Brandon, Robert, and Scott Carson. "The Indeterministic Character of Evolutionary Theory: No 'No Hidden Variables' Proof but No Room for Determinism Either." *Philosophy of Science* 63 (3) (1996): 315–337.

Burkhardt, Frederick, et al. *The Correspondence of Charles Darwin*. Vol. 9. Cambridge, U.K.: Cambridge University Press, 1994.

Burian, Richard. "Adaptation." In *Dimensions of Darwinism*, edited by Marjorie Grene. Cambridge, U.K.: Cambridge University Press, 1983.

Burian, Richard. *The Epistemology of Development, Evolution, and Genetics: Selected Essays*. Cambridge, U.K.: Cambridge University Press, 2005.

Darden, Lindley, and J. Cain. "Selection Type Theories." *Philosophy of Science* 56 (1989) 106–129.

Darwin, Charles. *On the Origin of Species: A Facsimile of the First Edition* (1859). Cambridge, MA: Harvard University Press, 1964.

Dawkins, Richard. *The Extended Genotype*. Oxford: Oxford University Press, 1982.

Dawkins, Richard. *The Selfish Gene*. Oxford: Oxford University Press, 1976.

Dennett, Daniel. *Darwin's Dangerous Idea*. New York: Simon & Shuster, 1995.

Depew, David, and Bruce Weber. *Darwinism Evolving*. Cambridge, MA: MIT Press, 1995.

Dobzhansky, Theodosius. *Genetics of the Evolutionary Process*. New York: Columbia University Press, 1970.

Endler, John. "Natural and Sexual Selection on Color Patterns in Poeciliid Fishes." *Environmental Biology of Fishes* 9 (2) (1983): 173–190.

Ereshefsky, Marc. *The Units of Evolution: Essays on the Nature of Species*. Cambridge, MA: MIT Press, 1992.

Gayon, Jean. *Darwinism's Struggle for Survival*. Cambridge, U.K.: Cambridge University Press, 1998.

Ghiselin, Michael. *Metaphysics and the Origin of Species*. Albany, NY: Student University of New York Press, 1997.

Gilbert, Scott, and Erik Jorgensen. "Wormwholes: A Commentary on K. F. Schaffner's 'Genes, Behavior, and Developmental Emergentism.'" *Philosophy of Science* 65 (2) (1998): 259–266.

Godfrey-Smith, Peter. "Information, Arbitrariness, and Selection: Comments on Maynard Smith." *Philosophy of Science* 67 (2) (2000): 202–207.

Godfrey-Smith, Peter. "Three Kinds of Adaptationism." In *Adaptationism and Optimality*, edited by Steven Orzack and Elliott Sober. Cambridge, U.K.: Cambridge University Press, 2001.

Goudge, Thomas. *The Ascent of Life*. Toronto: University of Toronto Press, 1961.

Gould, Stephen Jay. *The Structure of Evolutionary Theory*. Cambridge, MA: Harvard University Press, 2003.

Griffiths, Paul, and Robin Knight. "What Is the Developmentalist Challenge?" *Philosophy of Science* 65 (2) (1998): 253–258.

Hempel, Carl. *The Philosophy of Natural Science*. Englewood Cliffs, NJ: Prentice-Hall, 1966.

Hull, David. *The Philosophy of Biological Science*. Englewood Cliffs, NJ: Prentice-Hall, 1974.

Hull, David. *Science and Selection: Essays on Biological Evolution and the Philosophy of Science*. Cambridge, U.K.: Cambridge University Press, 2001.

Hull, David, and Michael Ruse, eds. *The Philosophy of Biology*. Oxford: Oxford University Press, 1998.

Huxley, Julian. *Evolution: The Modern Synthesis*. London: George, Allen and Unwin, 1942.

Keller, Evelyn Fox. *The Century of the Gene*. Cambridge, MA: Harvard University Press, 2000.

Keller, Evelyn Fox, and Elisabeth Lloyd, eds. *Keywords in Evolutionary Biology*. Cambridge, MA: Harvard University Press, 1992.

Kellert, Stephen, Helen Longino, and Kenneth Waters, eds. *Scientific Pluralism*. Minneapolis: University of Minnesota Press, 2005.

Kimura, Motoo. "Neutralism." In *Keywords in Evolutionary Biology*, edited by Evelyn Fox Keller and Elisabeth Lloyd. Cambridge, MA: Harvard University Press, 1992.

Lennox, James G. "Darwin *Was* a Teleologist." *Biology and Philosophy* 8 (4) (1993): 408–421.

Lennox, James G. "Philosophy of Biology." In *Introduction to the Philosophy of Science*, edited by Merrilee Salmon et al. Englewood Cliffs, NJ: Prentice-Hall, 1992.

Lennox, James G. "Teleology." In *Keywords in Evolutionary Biology*, edited by Evelyn Fox Keller and Elisabeth Lloyd. Cambridge, MA: Harvard University Press, 1992.

Lennox, James G. "Teleology by Another Name: A Reply to Ghiselin." *Biology and Philosophy* 9 (4) (1994): 493–495.

Lennox, James G., and Bradley Wilson. "Natural Selection and the Struggle for Existence." *Studies in History and Philosophy of Science* 25 (1) (1994): 65–80.

Lewontin, Richard. *Human Diversity*. New York: Scientific American Library, 1995.

Love, Alan. "Evolutionary Morphology, Innovation, and the Synthesis of Evolutionary and Developmental Biology." *Biology and Philosophy* 18 (3) (2003): 309–345.

Machamer, Peter, Lindley Darden, and Carl Craver. "Thinking about Mechanisms." *Philosophy of Science* 67 (1) 2000: 1–25.

Machamer, Peter, and Michael Silberstein. *The Blackwell Guide to the Philosophy of Science*. Oxford: Blackwell Publishers, 2002.

Maynard Smith, John. "The Concept of Information in Biology." *Philosophy of Science* 67 (2) (2000): 177–194.

Millikan, Ruth Garrett. "In Defense of Proper Functions." In *Nature's Purposes: Analyses of Function and Design in Biology*, edited by Collin Allen, Mark Bekoff, and George Lauder. Cambridge, MA: MIT Press, 1998.

Millstein, Roberta. "Are Random Drift and Natural Selection Conceptually Distinct?" *Biology and Philosophy* 17 (2002): 33–53.

Millstein, Roberta. "Selection vs. Drift: A Response to Brandon's Reply." *Biology and Philosophy* 20 (1) (2005): 171–175.

Mitchell, Sandra. *Biological Complexity and Integrative Pluralism*. Cambridge, U.K.: Cambridge University Press, 2003.

Mitchell, Sandra. "Functions, Fitness, and Disposition." In *Nature's Purposes: Analyses of Function and Design in Biology*, edited by Collin Allen, Mark Bekoff, and George Lauder. Cambridge, MA: MIT Press, 1998.

Moss, Lenny. *What Genes Can't Do*. Cambridge, MA: MIT Press, 2003.

Nagel, Ernst. *The Structure of Science*. New York: Harcourt, Brace and World, 1961.

Orzack, Steven, and Elliott Sober, eds. *Adaptationism and Optimality*. Cambridge, U.K.: Cambridge University Press, 2001.

Oyama, Susan, Paul Griffiths, and Russell Gray. *Cycles of Contingency: Developmental Systems and Evolution*. Cambridge, MA: MIT Press, 2001.

Plutynski, Anya. "Explanation in Classical Population Genetics." *Philosophy of Science* (Proceedings of the 2002 Biennial Meeting of the Philosophy of Science Association) 71 (5) (2004): 1,201–1,214.

Provine, William. *The Origins of Theoretical Population Genetics*. Chicago: University of Chicago Press, 1971.

Robert, Jason. *Embryology, Epigenesis, and Evolution: Taking Development Seriously*. Cambridge, U.K.: Cambridge University Press, 2004.

Rosenberg, Alexander. *The Structure of Biological Science*. Cambridge, U.K.: Cambridge University Press. 1985.

Ruse, Michael. *The Philosophy of Biology*. London: Hutchinson and Company, 1973.

Salmon, Merrilee, et al. *Introduction to the Philosophy of Science*. Englewood Cliffs, NJ: Prentice-Hall, 1992.

Sarkar, Sahotra, ed. *The Founders of Evolutionary Genetics: A Centenary Reappraisal*. Dordrecht: Kluwer Academic Publishers, 1992.

Sarkar, Sahotra. *Genetics and Reductionism*. New York: Cambridge University Press, 1998.

Sarkar, Sahotra. "Information in Genetics and Developmental Biology: Comments on Maynard Smith." *Philosophy of Science* 67 (2) (2000): 208–213.

Schaffner, Kenneth. *Discovery and Explanation in Biology and Medicine*. Chicago: University of Chicago Press. 1993.

Schaffner, Kenneth. "Genes, Behavior, and Developmental Emergentism: One Process, Indivisible?" *Philosophy of Science* 65 (2) (1998): 209–252.

Skelton, Peter. *Evolution: A Biological and Palaeontological Approach*. Harlow, U.K.: Pearson Education Ltd., 1993.

Sober, Elliott. *The Nature of Selection*. Cambridge, MA: MIT Press, 1984.

Sober, Elliott. *The Philosophy of Biology*. 2nd ed. Boulder, CO: Westview Press, 2000.

Sterelny, Kim, and Paul Griffiths. *Sex and Death: An Introduction to the Philosophy of Biology*. Chicago: University of Chicago Press, 1999.

Waters, Kenneth. "Genes Made Molecular." *Philosophy of Science* 61 (2) (1994): 163–185.

Waters, Kenneth. "Molecules Made Biological." *Revue Internationale de Philosophie* 4 (214) (2000): 539–564.

Waters, Kenneth. "A Pluralist Interpretation of Gene-centered Biology." In *Scientific Pluralism*, edited by Stephen Kellert, Helen Longino, and Kenneth Waters. Minneapolis: University of Minnesota Press, 2005.

Williams, George C. *Adaptation and Natural Selection: A Critique of Some Current Evolutionary Thought*. Princeton, NJ: Princeton University Press, 1966.

Williams, George C. *Natural Selection: Domains, Levels, and Challenges*. Oxford: Oxford University Press, 1992.

Wilson, David Sloan. "Individual Selection and the Concept of Structured Demes." In *Genes, Organism, Populations: Controversies over the Units of Selection*, edited by Robert Brandon and Richard Burian. Cambridge, MA: MIT Press, 1984.

Wimsatt, William. "Simple Systems and Phylogenetic Diversity." *Philosophy of Science* 65 (2) (1998): 267–275.

Wright, Larry "Functions." In *Nature's Purposes: Analyses of Function and Design in Biology*, edited by Collin Allen, Mark Bekoff, and George Lauder. Cambridge, MA: MIT Press, 1998.

Wright, Larry. *Teleological Explanation*. Berkeley: University of California Press, 1976.

James Lennox (2005)

PHILOSOPHY OF ECONOMICS

Why would philosophers be interested in economics? There are at least two answers. First, lessons from economics bear directly on moral and political philosophy, as well as on theorizing about rationality. Second, economics provides a case study of some of the most challenging problems in the philosophy of science.

ECONOMICS AS MORAL PHILOSOPHY

What is the ethical basis of economics? If economics is grounded in a theory of the right, what kind of theory is it? Is it a theory of the right grounded in a utilitarian conception of the greatest good for the greatest number, or a Kantian conception of the sovereignty of individual economic agents? Or, if economics is grounded in a theory of value, is the value to be understood in utilitarian or contractarian terms (as an aggregate, or as a matter of mutual advantage)?

PLATO. Alfred North Whitehead described philosophy as a series of footnotes to Plato. What about economics? Plato's *Republic* describes the emergence of a society not by social contract or by conquest but spontaneously, through the workings of the market. "The barest notion of a state must include four or five men" (Book II, 369D). People need food, shelter, and clothing, but "all things are produced more plentifully and easily and of a better quality when one man does one thing" (Book II, 370B). People thus start to specialize in farming, carpentry, and weaving. It quickly becomes obvious, though, that "more than four citizens will be required, for the husbandman will not make his own plough ... Neither will the builder make his tools—and he too needs many; and in like manner the weaver and shoemaker" (Book II, 370C). Commercial society thus emerges as an unplanned consequence of the transparent advantages of the division of labor.

ADAM SMITH. In more substantial ways, economics is a footnote to yet another philosopher, born some twenty centuries later. It was Adam Smith, professor of logic and of moral sciences at the University of Glasgow, whose work led more or less directly to the rise of economics as a separate academic discipline. The first three chapters of Smith's *Wealth of Nations* (1981 [1776]) explain the role that division of labor plays in a prosperous society, culminating in a brilliant critique of protectionist trade policy. Using the manufacture of pins as an example, Smith notes that a solitary worker could scarcely make one pin per day, but in a pin-making factory employing ten workers, "one man draws out the wire, another straights it, a third cuts it, a fourth points it, a fifth grinds it at the top for receiving the head ... ; and the important business of making a pin is, in this manner, divided into about eight-

een distinct operations ... Those ten persons, therefore, could make among them upwards of forty-eight thousand pins a day" (p. 15).

Smith then explains how the division of labor is facilitated by the propensity to truck and barter. We do not build factories for our own personal consumption. We specialize to that degree only when we have opportunities to serve large communities. Smith's next insight is that the extent of specialization is limited by the size of the market. A rural carpenter specializes in anything made of wood; a carpenter in a large city specializes in residential house construction; a carpenter serving national and international markets can specialize in making childproof doorknobs. The wealth of nations depends on economic agents being able to reach far beyond their small circle of friends. The farther they can reach, the larger the markets they can reach both as producers and as consumers, the greater will be the division of labor, and the richer they and everyone with whom they trade will be. Because economic agents work with suppliers, distributors, and customers on a global scale, they can produce thousands of pins a day, rather than a small handful at best.

The homage Smith pays, then, is not so much to the self-interest of butchers and bakers as to the division of labor that enables artisans to continuously be renewing, reinventing, and extending the limits of their craft. These opening chapters of *Wealth of Nations* are perhaps the most insightful part of the most insightful work of economics ever written.

Smith's most pointed argument on behalf of a lightly regulated economy, though, is probably to be found in his less famous work, *The Theory of Moral Sentiments* (1976 [1759]). There, Smith argues that a "man of public spirit" will not be a fanatical reformer but instead "will respect the established powers and privileges even of individuals, and still more those of the great orders and societies ... When he cannot conquer the rooted prejudices of the people by reason and persuasion, he will not attempt to subdue them by force" (p. 223). By contrast, a "man of system," "is apt to be very wise in his own conceit, and is often so enamored with the supposed beauty of his own ideal plan of government that he cannot suffer the smallest deviation from any part of it. He goes on to establish it completely and in all its parts, without any regard either to the great interests, or to the strong prejudices which may oppose it. He seems to imagine that he can arrange the different members of a great society with as much ease as the hand arranges the different pieces upon a chess board. He does not consider that the pieces upon the chessboard have no other principle of motion besides that which the hand impresses upon them; but that in the great "chess board" of human society, every single piece has a principle of motion of its own, altogether different from that which the legislature might choose to impress upon it" (1976 [1759], p. 234).

SMITH'S LEGACY. Smith anticipates Marx in expressing reservations about the alienating aspects of repetitive labor in a factory setting. Smith also comes close to anticipating James Buchanan and Gordon Tullock's insight (1962) that legislators respond to incentives as much as anyone else does—that legislators are not philosopher-kings, above the fray, but instead make their moves on a chess board of society, like everyone else. None of the pieces gets to decide where all the other pieces will be at a given moment. Political order, like economic order, biological order, or any other complex order, will take its shape not because any particular designer intended it to take that shape, but simply because that is what happened when the pieces came together, all with plans of their own. The insight of Smith, Buchanan and Tullock, and others, is that our world is strategic—all the way up. Even a country's most powerful politicians can do no more than hope to exert some influence. It is hard to incorporate this insight into moral and political philosophizing. What would it be like to develop a theory of how to live, and how to pursue social change, in a world where no one is in charge?

Alexander Rosenberg (1988) observes that the products of natural selection are exquisitely functional and almost unimaginably complex, despite no one being in charge. Unplanned economies likewise are functional, indeed typically more functional than centrally planned ones. How is this possible? Friedrich Hayek (1994) argues that a free economy economizes on rationality, morality, and knowledge in a way that a central plan cannot. Central planning models assume central planners will know what they need to know, and will use such knowledge wisely, and for purposes other than their own. Starting with such assumptions, advocates of central planning aim to invest planners with enough power (to implement the "right" decisions) that other agents with less benign plans will be unable to interfere. Unfortunately, giving central planners that much power to do the right thing also gives them that much power to do the wrong thing: to repay debts to their most powerful supporters, to cover up mistakes, to eliminate enemies (anyone who criticizes them), and so on. According to Hayek, there is a fatal conceit involved in thinking that economies would work better if, per impossible, central planners were in charge.

To Ludwig von Mises (the other main protagonist in the "Socialist Calculation Debate," along with Hayek), economics is a value-free, a priori science, more or less like mathematics. But Daniel Hausman and Michael McPherson (1996) plausibly conclude that, "economics remains partly a moral science. It can't be done without moral presuppositions, and it's hard to do it well without addressing moral issues intelligently. Similarly, moral philosophy can't be done without beliefs about human interactions, and it's hard to do it well without knowledge of the kind that economists seek" (p. 8). For example, Hausman and McPherson ask whether market competition results in firms with moral scruples being driven into bankruptcy. They give several reasons to think the answer is no, but their main point is simply that the question matters, and matters in economics, not only in moral philosophy. It bears whether there is any point in being in favor of the market competition that economists study.

Extending Hausman and McPherson's point, and relating it back to Adam Smith, if a firm would need to dominate a small town market in order to do a profitable volume of business, it may find itself needing to cater to the interests of a "lowest common denominator." Or at least, the firm that survives to serve that small market in the long run will be the one that best serves the majority of clients in that small market. By contrast, if a firm can operate on a global scale (advertising on the Internet, perhaps), then capturing even 1 percent of the market can be hugely profitable. In this way, globalization makes possible a proliferation of specialized firms catering to especially discerning clientele, raising free-range poultry, growing organic broccoli, auctioning nineteenth-century German marbles, manufacturing parachutes out of recycled newspaper, or whatever entrepreneurs think of next. (Israel Kirzner, a student of Mises, criticizes how standard equilibrium models treat entrepreneurial innovation. As Kirzner sees it, standard models treat innovations as exogenous shocks, when in fact entrepreneurial innovation is a central driving force in all but the most repressive states, which is why real economies are *always* in disequilibrium.)

ECONOMICS AS SCIENCE

Lionel Robbins (1935) defined economics as "the science which studies human behavior as a relationship between ends and scarce means which have alternative uses" (p. 16). It is amazing how much can be derived from a premise that economic agents put scarce resources to their most efficient use. But is the premise true? Milton Friedman (1984) seems to say it makes little difference; the unrealism of a theory's assumptions are unimportant, so long as the theory's predictions are correct. Hausman describes Friedman's essay as the most influential work on economic methodology of the twentieth century. Analogously, Hausman says, Ptolemy's astronomy is still used for navigational purposes. Is Hausman right? The idea is theory-laden, and more technical than it appears. It is true that the Copernican revolution did not require us to make any radical changes in our ways of navigating, but is that like saying our navigational methods are premised on the earth being at the center of the universe? Probably not, but Hausman's main point still stands: We do not need to know the rock-bottom truths of astronomy, astrophysics, or anything else in order to have theories that track relevant facts well enough to enable us to navigate. Likewise, in economics, the statement that economic agents are pursuing their own self-interest is close enough to the mark for many purposes, and accordingly has, for many purposes, a lot of explanatory and predictive power. We better understand much of what we see around us when we grasp that self-interest is a more or less ubiquitous motive. Yet, we also see every day that people are motivated by things other than self-interest: by benevolence, vengefulness, and also (as Hobbes observed) by pigheaded, self-destructive vainglory.

THE SCIENTIFIC ATTITUDE. One of the biggest methodological blunders we could make would be to retreat from this messy empirical reality to the empty platitude that people do whatever they do, and this is all we really mean when we say all action is self-interested. When we give up the willingness to let our generalization be tested (and sometimes disconfirmed) by reality, we also give up the generalization's relevance as a tool for understanding reality. As a sometimes disconfirmed generalization, the postulate of self-interest lets us know when to regard a behavior as surprising, worthy of scientific curiosity, and so on. We may find that seemingly altruistic behavior turns out to be, in some previously unnoticed way, self-interested after all. But so long as we avoid the trap of assuming this *must* be the case, no matter what, we leave ourselves open to learning something new. (The new direction of progress may not be economics per se. New directions tend to evolve into new sciences. Just as moral philosophy helped spawn economics, economics can help spawn new disciplines or subdisciplines.) Meanwhile, so long as we understand the postulate of self-interest as a simplification of reality, one that abstracts from messy empirical details, the postulate will be useful.

Karl Popper sought to distinguish between science and nonscience. The real issue is about scientific attitude—whether a theory's proponents treat the theory as something to scrutinize rather than to zealously defend. In any case, it is hard to confirm an economic theory, or any other kind of theory. We give theory a chance to fail, and are impressed by and more confident in it as it survives repeated testing. But as scientists we acknowledge that surviving a test does not put us in a position to be supremely confident. Real science does not work that way; its fruits are not indubitable certainties.

What are the limits of a general theory's ability to help us understand? Daniel Little suggests, "The abstract analysis of the firm based on rational agents arriving at efficient outcomes must be supplemented with more detailed analysis of the specific circumstances and arrangements within which the firm took shape" (1995, p. 6). This is not a throwaway line but is in fact rather disturbing. It suggests there are severe albeit vague limits on the prospects for general explanation.

In the same way, one might see the history of philosophy as pointing to a similar conclusion. Namely, the search for general explanations, general theories, even general definitions, has a history of butting up against recalcitrant limits. There is a point to analyzing knowledge as justified true belief; yet, we now know of cases where this analysis is not good enough. It seems that no matter how much we tweak a theory or a definition, perfection is not an option. When cartographers try to map a three-dimensional terrain by projecting it onto two dimensions, there is no such thing as a representation of the terrain without distortion. A Mercator projection makes Greenland look as large as Africa, and anything we do to correct this distortion of relative size will distort something else in the process. This is an example of a problem for which a perfect solution simply does not exist, and theorists in all sorts of philosophical disciplines, confident though they may be that there is an objective truth about the three dimensional terrain out there, and that their job as theorists is to provide an accurate map of that objective reality, are finding themselves facing the reality that, as a rule rather than as an exception, there are no perfectly accurate theories. Our theorizing needs to be supplemented by knowledge of the local terrain. There is no denying our need for practical wisdom, or as Little puts it, for "detailed analysis of specific circumstances and arrangements" (1995, p. 6).

ECONOMICS AS AN EXPERIMENTAL SCIENCE. Experimental economics starts with the idea that economic hypotheses are testable in replicable ways in laboratory settings. What is an experiment? What is a theory? What would count as testing a theory? When we test a theory, are we trying to prove it, or disprove it? Are the meanings of economic concepts exhausted by their verification conditions, or are economic theories important and meaningful apart from any efforts we make or could make empirically to test them?

For example, Hausman says, "one might argue that preferences and beliefs are in some sense unobservable" (1984, p. 15). But inferential bases for the ascription of preferences can rather unambiguously be observed in laboratory settings. Experimental subjects can be given opportunities to buy and sell "widgets" that are stripped of all properties other than resale value—the widgets are nothing more than entries on a computer-kept ledger. Experimenters specify those resale values (that is, how much money subjects will be paid for any widgets they possess at the end of the experiment). Thus, much information that is hidden outside the laboratory can be known and controlled in a laboratory setting, enabling researchers to draw reasonably well-grounded inferences about subjects' motives and strategies.

For example, if we interpret subjects as being in a prisoner's dilemma situation, such that declining to cooperate is a dominant strategy, and then we see subjects cooperating instead, we are free to hypothesize that the situation is not really a prisoner's dilemma, retreating to a view that by definition subjects will act to maximize their payoff, and therefore by definition subjects will decline to cooperate in a genuine prisoner's dilemma. In a laboratory setting, we can do better than that. We can specify all the payoffs and communicate them unambiguously to experimental subjects. We can train them over a sequence of trial runs to make sure they understand their situation. Then we can observe and learn. If subjects do not behave as our theories predict, or if 60 percent behave as predicted and 40 percent do not, then so be it. There is no such thing as being in a situation where there is exactly one theory that fits the observed facts. It is a truism in philosophy of science that any given set of observations will be compatible with an infinite number of theoretical explanations.

Nevertheless, what we learn to accept in the laboratory is that subjects do not consistently act to maximize their monetary payoff. They show inclinations to cooperate, to trust, to be "fair," and so on, that go beyond anything it is reasonable for us to try to explain in terms of the hypothesis that subjects are acting to maximize their monetary payoff. We can even design the experiment so

as to yield fine-grained information about why subjects decline to cooperate, when they do. For example, we can suppose that the two main reasons not to cooperate in a prisoner's dilemma are greed (the preference to get the good for free when one expects others to cooperate in producing the good) and fear (the preference not to cooperate when one expects others not to). In the field, it may be impossible to tell the difference between greed and fear, since all we observe is whether subjects are cooperating. Laboratory experiments, though, can be designed to tell the difference. That is, we can go beyond the hypothesis that everyone will defect when defection is a dominant strategy to test the hypothesis that when people defect, it is because they are afraid their partners will defect, not because they hope to exploit partners who cooperate. In the laboratory there is much defection, but also much cooperation, and much more cooperation when fear is eliminated as a motive for defection, even when the motive to free ride is left untouched, indeed, even when defecting remains a dominant strategy (see Mark, Schmidtz, and Walker 1989). Perhaps this takes us from economics proper into fields such a psychology, sociology, and so on. But economists probably should find move encouraging, inasmuch as it indicates that their simplest behavioral postulates, in virtue of being disconfirmable (and sometimes disconfirmed), are at the same time fruitful and interesting.

ENVIRONMENTAL ECONOMICS AND ENVIRONMENTAL PHILOSOPHY. Environmental economists are presumed to be advocates of conservationist "wise use" policies, where environmental philosophers are presumed to be advocates of preservationist "no use at all" policies regarding scarce environmental assets. Perhaps the picture never was this simple, but in any case it is changing. Philosophers like Bryan Norton (1991) and Mark Sagoff (2004) are, in various ways, going beyond simple dichotomies in search of new policy paradigms that make sense from both long-term environmental and medium-term economic perspectives.

THE PSYCHOLOGICAL AND INSTITUTIONAL PREREQUISITES OF MARKET ECONOMIES. Since the fall of the Soviet Union, and the subsequently mixed results of formerly communist countries in establishing market economies, wiser and humbler economists have been exploring the idea that market economies cannot be invented, manufactured, or decreed but must instead be treated as organically evolving systems that grow over time. Citizens of the former Soviet Union, it seems, do not understand instinctively how to behave as market agents. If they grow up in a world where the only examples of entrepreneurship involve bribery and theft, then they will think of entrepreneurs as a species of predator and will not grasp the concept of mutual advantage in the way that owners of small businesses in free countries do.

ECONOMICS OF CULTURE. Economists likewise have begun to turn their attention to the intertwined evolution of economy and culture. Explosions of cultural innovation seem to occur in cities that are at the same time undergoing explosive growth as worldwide commercial centers.

BEYOND HOMO ECONOMICUS. As noted earlier, the postulate of self-interest is most illuminating when treated as a testable empirical hypothesis, so that when behavior fails to conform, it will not simply be ignored but will instead be seen as of scientific interest. One of many cases in point is the "ultimatum" game. Two subjects are assigned the task of dividing a fixed amount of money. The first subject, Proposer, makes a proposal about how to divide the money. The second subject, Responder, has two options: reject the proposal, in which case neither subject gets anything; or accept the proposal, in which case the subjects split the money as proposed. The game is not repeated, so a Responder who is rational as per the Homo economicus model ought to accept any proposal that offers Responder a positive payoff. A bit more tenuously, Proposer, expecting Responder to be rational as per the Homo economicus model, ought to offer responder the smallest possible positive payoff. In fact, neither of these predictions is born out in the laboratory. Proposers most commonly offer to split the money fifty-fifty. Cristina Bicchieri (2005) reports that in a variety of trials and conditions, including in different cultures, responders tend to reject offers below 20 percent of the total, even when the stakes are substantial relative to prevailing wage rates in the subjects' community.

NEUROECONOMICS. Kevin McCabe tested a variation of the ultimatum game while recording subjects' brain activity with functional MRI (Kevin McCabe, et al, 2001). In some trials, subjects were informed that their partner was a computer program playing a fixed probabilistic strategy; these were paired with trials where subjects were informed that their partner was another human subject. Roughly half the subjects chose not to cooperate with human partners. Their brain activity was similar in the computer partner and human partner trials. Subjects who did cooperate, roughly half the total, showed markedly greater brain activity in the prefrontal cortex.

The implication: subjects who cooperate are not treating trials with human partners as situations calling simply for payoff calculation. The prefrontal cortex is thought to be the part of the brain dealing with social situations, not with arithmetic calculation. Cooperators evidently are treating the transaction not only as an economic exchange but also as a social exchange, calling for empathetic understanding of the motivations of another agent. It is too early to say where this line of research is leading, but it suggests we may hope some day for a unified explanation of departures from the postulate of self-interest, including the above-reported departures from dominant strategy in the prisoner's dilemma. That is, subjects who do not conform to the predictions of Homo economicus models may be departing from the models in virtue of perceiving the situation as calling not for calculation of their possible payoffs, but instead for something else, such as an exchange of tokens of mutual respect. In any case, our sensitivity to economic motives is a variable. What gets us to focus on the economic bottom line—the numbers—rather than on friendships, grudges, self-esteem, status, and so on, is interestingly complex.

See also Decision Theory; Game Theory; Philosophy of Social Sciences.

Bibliography

ECONOMICS AS MORAL PHILOSOPHY

Buchanan, James, and Gordon Tullock. *The Calculus of Consent: Logical Foundations of Constitutional Democracy.* Ann Arbor: University of Michigan Press, 1962.

Coase, Ronald. *Essays on Economics and Economists.* Chicago: University of Chicago Press, 1994.

Gauthier, David. *Morals By Agreement.* New York: Oxford University Press, 1986.

Griswold, Charles. *Adam Smith and the Virtues of Enlightenment.* New York: Cambridge University Press, 1999.

Hausman, Daniel M., and Michael S. McPherson. *Economic Analysis and Moral Philosophy.* Cambridge, U.K.: Cambridge University Press, 1996.

Hayek, F. A. *Road to Serfdom.* Chicago: University of Chicago Press, 1994.

Kirzner, Israel. *Competition and Entrepreneurship.* Chicago: University of Chicago Press, 1973.

Mises, Ludwig. "Economic Calculation in the Socialist Commonwealth." In *Collectivist Economic Planning: Critical Studies of the Possibilities of Socialism,* edited by F. A. Hayek, 87–130. London: Routledge & Kegan Paul, 1935.

Plato. *Republic and Other Works.* Translated by B. Jowett. New York: Anchor Books, 1973.

Rosenberg, Alexander. *Philosophy of Social Science.* Boulder, CO: Westview Press, 1988.

Sen, Amartya Kumar. *On Ethics and Economics.* Oxford, U.K.: Blackwell, 1987.

Smith, Adam. *An Inquiry into the Nature and Causes of the Wealth of Nations* [1776], edited by R. H. Campbell and A. S. Skinner. 2 vols. Indianapolis: Liberty Fund, 1981.

Smith, Adam. *The Theory of Moral Sentiments* [1759], edited by D. D. Raphael and A. L. Macfie. Indianapolis: Liberty Fund, 1976.

ECONOMICS AS SCIENCE

Friedman, Milton. "The Methodology of Positive Economics." In *Philosophy of Economics*, edited by Daniel M. Hausman, 210–244. New York: Cambridge University Press, 1984.

Hausman, Daniel M., ed. *The Philosophy of Economics*. New York: Cambridge University Press, 1984.

Little, Daniel, ed. *On the Reliability of Economic Models: Essays in the Philosophy of Economics*. Boston: Kluwer, 1995.

Little, Daniel. *Varieties of Social Explanation*. Boulder, CO: Westview, 1991.

McCloskey, Deirdre. *The Rhetoric of Economics*. 2nd ed. Madison: University of Wisconsin Press, 1998.

Robbins, Lionel. *An Essay on the Nature and Significance of Economic Science*. 2nd ed. London: Macmillan, 1935.

EXPERIMENTAL ECONOMICS

Mark, Isaac R., D. Schmidtz, and James M. Walker. "The Assurance Problem in a Laboratory Market." *Public Choice* 62 (1989): 217–236.

Smith, Vernon. "Constructivist and Ecological Rationality in Economics." Nobel Prize lecture, December 8, 2002.

ENVIRONMENTAL ECONOMICS AND PHILOSOPHY

Norton, Bryan. *Toward Unity among Environmentalists*. New York: Oxford University Press, 1991.

Sagoff, Mark. *Price, Principle, and the Environment*. New York: Cambridge University Press, 2004.

Schmidtz, David. "When Preservationism Doesn't Preserve." *Environmental Values* 6 (1997) 327–339.

PSYCHOLOGICAL AND INSTITUTIONAL PREREQUISITES OF MARKET ECONOMIES

Brennan, Geoffrey, and Philip Pettit. *The Economy of Esteem: An Essay on Civil and Political Society*. Oxford: Oxford University Press, 2004.

Fukuyama, Francis. *Trust: The Social Virtues and the Creation of Prosperity*. New York: Free Press, 1996.

North, Douglass. *Institutions, Institutional Change and Economic Performance*. New York: Cambridge University Press, 1990.

ECONOMICS OF CULTURE

Appiah, Kwame Anthony. *In My Father's House: Africa in the Philosophy of Culture*. New York: Oxford University Press, 1992.

Cowen, Tyler. *Creative Destruction: How Globalization Is Changing the World's Cultures*. Princeton, NJ: Princeton University Press, 2002.

Cowen, Tyler. *In Praise of Commercial Culture*. Cambridge, MA: Harvard University Press, 1998.

BEYOND HOMO ECONOMICUS

Bicchieri, Cristina, *The Grammar of Society: The Nature and Dynamics of Social Norms*. New York: Cambridge University Press, 2005.

Guth, W., R. Schmittberger, and B. Schwarze. "An Experimental Analysis of Ultimatum Games." *Journal of Economic Behavior and Organization* 3 (1982): 367–388.

Henrich, Joseph, Robert Boyd, Samuel Bowles, Colin Camerer, Ernst Fehr, Herbert Gintis, and Richar McElreath. "In Search of Homo Economicus: Behavioral Experiments in 15 Small-Scale Societies," *American Economic Review*, 91 (2001): 73–79.

Kahneman, Daniel, and Amos Tversky. "Choices, Values, and Frames." *American Psychologist* 39 (1984): 341–350.

Schmidtz, David. *Rational Choice and Moral Agency*. Princeton, NJ: Princeton University Press, 1995.

Simon, Herbert. *Models of Bounded Rationality and Other Topics in Economics*. Cambridge, MA: MIT Press, 1982.

NEUROECONOMICS

McCabe, Kevin, Daniel Houser, Lee Ryan, Vernon Smith, and Theodore Trouard. "A Functional Imaging Study of Cooperation in Two-Person Reciprocal Exchange." *Proceedings Of the National Academy of Science* 98 (2001): 11832–11835.

David Schmidtz (2005)

PHILOSOPHY OF EDUCATION, EPISTEMOLOGICAL ISSUES IN

Epistemological issues have always enjoyed a central place (along with metaphysical, moral, and social/political issues) in philosophical thinking about education. In the entry "Philosophy of Education, History of" in this encyclopedia, Kingsley Price skillfully treats the entire history of the subject, from the Presocratics to John Dewey. This entry covers the intervening decades, focusing on epistemological issues.

By the time of Dewey's death in 1952, philosophy in the English-speaking world was becoming increasing dominated by the analytic movement, which emphasized as methodological matters the importance of clarity, careful analysis, rigorous argumentation, and detailed attention to language, and philosophy of education was no exception to this general trend. The key figures in the development of analytic philosophy of education were Israel Scheffler in the United States, and Richard Peters and Paul Hirst in the United Kingdom. While their work exemplified two different strands of analytic philosophy—Peters and Hirst worked in the 'ordinary language' tradition of analytic philosophy, which emphasized the explication of meanings as manifested in ordinary language, while Scheffler's brand of analysis took more serious account of logic and its associated formal techniques, and was more inclined to overrule ordinary language when theoretical improvement could be so gained—both sought to bring a level of clarity and sophistication to an area of philosophy that did not always enjoy these, and to integrate philosophy of education with general philosophy. The following discusses some central epistemological issues in philosophy of education.

EPISTEMIC AIMS OF EDUCATION

What is the fundamental epistemic aim of education? For educators, is the highest aim that of *truth* and the bringing about of true belief in students? Or is it, rather, *rationality* and the fostering of rational (or perhaps *justified*) belief? Perhaps that aim is the more encompassing one of *knowledge*, which includes and integrates both of the previous possibilities? Or could the aim be that of enhancing student *understanding*? Each of these has its advocates and deserves brief explication.

TRUTH. The most important contemporary advocate of truth as the fundamental epistemic aim of education is Alvin Goldman (1999). On his *'veritistic'* view, the fundamental epistemic aim of education is the production of true belief in students, along with the development of student ability to discover new (to them) truths by way of inquiry.

Goldman's view has much to recommend it, although it faces some difficulties as well. First, not all modes of transmitting truths to students—brainwashing, indoctrination, deception, and the like—are educationally acceptable, despite their efficacy in producing true belief. Second, from the educational point of view it matters not only *that* students believe truths, but also *on what basis* they believe them: Mindless or otherwise unjustified true belief is not typically the intended aim of educational activities, despite the truth of the relevant student belief. Third, the general failure to enjoy 'direct access' to truth suggests that the relevant educational aim is not true belief, but rather student ability to estimate or judge the truth competently (Scheffler 1965, p. 54). These difficulties suggest that the fundamental epistemic aim of education is not true belief but rather *rational* belief.

RATIONALITY/CRITICAL THINKING. The great majority of historically significant philosophers of education have endorsed the fostering of student rationality, or its educational cognate *critical thinking*, as the (or at least a) basic epistemic aim of education. On this view, educational efforts ought to strive to foster the abilities and dis-positions conducive to rational student belief, the latter conceived as belief properly based on *good reasons*. Accordingly, educational activities are epistemically successful just to the extent that they result in enhanced student ability to evaluate candidate reasons for belief fairly and competently, and strengthened student disposition both to so evaluate and to believe accordingly. The dispositional or 'critical spirit' element of the view connects epistemic matters with matters of *character*, and the view as a whole is justified in terms of an appeal to the moral duty to treat students with *respect as persons*: Treating students with respect requires educating them in ways intended to foster critical thinking and thereby their autonomy, independence of judgment, and ability to shape—as far as possible—their own minds and lives (Siegel 1988, 1997; Bailin and Siegel 2003).

Although versions of this view enjoy considerable support from both philosophers (historical and contemporary) and educators, it faces the important objection that rationality and critical thinking are arguably best thought of not as ends in themselves, but rather instrumentally, as *means* to the end of true belief: Why think that the former are epistemically valuable, other than as an effective route to truth (Goldman 1999)? This raises two questions: Can rationality/critical thinking be thought to be valuable other than instrumentally, as a means to truth? Can the virtues of both these putative epistemic ends of education be suitably combined (Siegel 2005b)?

KNOWLEDGE. Taking the fundamental epistemic aim of education to be knowledge has the advantage that, suitably understood in its 'strong' sense, that aim includes both truth and rationality/justification. This better captures the sense in which educators are concerned with the fundamental epistemic aim *of education*, since, from the educational point of view, mere true student belief is less adequate than true belief that is justified, rational, or otherwise based on good reasons; and justified or rational but nevertheless false belief is less adequate than such belief that is also true. This view, that knowledge (in the 'strong' sense that includes both truth and rational justification as conditions of knowledge) is the fundamental epistemic aim of education, is defended by several contemporary authors (Scheffler 1960, 1965, 1989; Adler 2003; Siegel 2005b). It appears to capture the strengths of both the previous views and to meet the objections to them outlined above.

UNDERSTANDING. The way in which all these putative epistemological aims of education involve student *under-*

standing is less than crystal clear, and a plausible case has been made by Catherine Z. Elgin, furthering a philosophical approach pioneered by Nelson Goodman, that it is the latter—rather than truth, rationality or knowledge—that deserves to be regarded as the fundamental epistemic aim of education (Elgin 1999a, 1999b). Whether or not understanding can be integrated successfully with the other main proposed epistemic aims of education, can be shown to be less fundamental than those others, or deserves pride of place as the fundamental such aim, remains the subject of ongoing debate.

TESTIMONY, TRUST, AND TEACHING

Should students believe what their teachers tell them? Arguably, they should, and recent work on the epistemology of testimony suggests as much (Goldman 1999). But student belief in the otherwise unsupported testimonial pronouncements of their teachers conflicts with the view that critical thinking is an important aim of education, since such belief seems clearly enough not to be belief based on reasons subjected to critical scrutiny by the believer/student. Live issues concerning the epistemology of testimony are helpfully illuminated by the educational case. This is obviously not the place to tackle the broad question of the epistemology of testimony. But the educational case concerning testimony in the classroom setting deserves brief comment.

First, it is important to be clear about the sort of student under consideration. Very young children/students cannot evaluate the testimonial pronouncements of their teachers; they lack the cognitive capacity to do so. Such capacity develops gradually; before it is substantially achieved, trust in their teachers' pronouncements seems unproblematic. But how long is the period during which students enjoy such a holiday from the ordinary demands of responsible oversight of their cognitive lives? This is, at least in part, an empirical matter concerning the facts of psychological/cognitive development. Once such development has taken place and students are able to monitor and evaluate the epistemic standing of their beliefs, do those testimony-based beliefs enjoy positive justificatory status if the only thing the student can say in their defense is "my teacher said so"? Here the *reductionist* (who, like David Hume, holds that testimony-based beliefs are justified only if that justification can be reduced to testimony-independent good reasons to trust the speaker's testimony on a given occasion) and the *antireductionist* (who, like Thomas Reid, holds that testimony is itself a basic source of justification) will divide in the predictable way. But the latter will have to explain why the aim of fostering critical thinking (discussed above) can or should be abandoned in the case of teacher testimonial pronouncements, and how so abandoning it can be reconciled with the duty to treat students with respect as persons. It is not meant here to suggest that the antireductionist is doomed to failure. But the educational case does provide a sharp test case of epistemological views concerning testimony.

It should also be noted that the case in which students have nothing to justify their belief in the testimonial pronouncements of their teachers other than the pronouncements themselves is arguably relatively rare and certainly not typical. Just as believers typically have considerable evidence for the general reliability of testimony, so that their trust in testimonial pronouncements is accompanied by testimony-independent evidence that sanctions such trust (Adler 2002), so, too, do students typically have such evidence concerning their teachers' pronouncements. For even when students begin a class with no testimony-independent reason for believing what their teacher tells them, as the class proceeds and students observe their teacher lecture, explain, answer questions, and extemporize, such observation itself provides testimony-independent reason for trusting the teacher's testimonial pronouncements concerning the subject matter at hand (Siegel 2005b).

INDOCTRINATION, TEACHING, AND BELIEF

Questions concerning the places of testimony and trust in the classroom lead naturally to questions concerning teaching and indoctrination. During the decades in which the analytic approach dominated the field, philosophers of education devoted considerable effort to the analysis of the concept of indoctrination (Snook 1972, Spiecker and Straughan 1991, Siegel 1988). The theories of indoctrination developed then divided into three broad types, which located indoctrination in either the *aim* or *intention* of the teacher/indoctrinator (namely, to get students to believe matters independently of the evidence for them), the *method* employed in transmitting the relevant beliefs (that is, in a way that precludes student questioning or demand for reasons), or the character or *content* of the doctrines transmitted (that is, content that does not admit of rational support or that is believed independently of such support). These three ways of understanding indoctrination have in common that (successful) indoctrination results in beliefs that students do not, will not, and/or cannot subject to critical scrutiny. That is, indoctrination, when successful, results in student acquisition of both specific beliefs and of habits or dispositions to believe independently of the evidential status of the indoctrinated beliefs. In this way indoctrination appears to be incompatible with most of the epistemic aims of education canvassed above, most obviously that concerning the fostering of rationality/critical thinking.

However, the seemingly obvious view that educators should eschew indoctrination in favor of more respectable epistemic educational practices is not so quickly established. First, can education be nonindoctrinating, either in principle or in practice, or is indoctrination inevitable? One might think it unavoidable since, as was suggested above, at least at early stages of development, students do not in fact have the cognitive capacity to challenge, evaluate, or critically consider that which they are taught. If it is for this reason unavoidable, is indoctrination as a consequence not necessarily or always a bad thing, something to be avoided by responsible educators? After all, if students are incapable of subjecting teacher testimonial pronouncements to critical scrutiny until after a certain cognitive-developmental stage is reached, language and concepts acquired, and an appropriate level of reasoning ability attained, it is hard to see how teachers can help bring students to the point at which they can exercise their critical abilities except by indoctrinating them. The alternative view, namely, that indoctrination is avoidable, requires a distinction between indoctrination and nonindoctrinating belief inculcation, but such a distinction is often thought to be controversial (Siegel 1988, 2005b).

Second, (why) should we value educational processes that result in student ability to subject candidate beliefs to critical scrutiny? Philosophers of education who differ in their answers to the question of the fundamental epistemic aim of education will differ in their answers to this one. Veritists will answer that we should value such processes because that ability will increase student acquisition of true belief. Advocates of critical thinking will answer, rather, that we should value them because student acquisition of rational/justified belief will be enhanced, and, moreover, that desirable dispositions will be fostered. Advocates of knowledge (in the strong sense) will embrace both these answers. Those who think indoctrination inevitable may well deny that we should value such processes at all (and may deny that there are, in fact, any such processes).

OPEN-MINDEDNESS, BELIEF, AND COMMITMENT

A further epistemic good related to critical thinking, often regarded as a basic educational aim, is that of *open-mindedness*: Roughly, the ability to regard one's beliefs as fallible and subject to rational rejection or revision in light of evidence and critical reflection (Hare 1979, 1985). But how can open-mindedness be reconciled with the aim of fostering student knowledge or rationality, given that the latter involve student *belief*? That is, how can students be expected both to believe those belief-candidates that reasons and evidence indicate are worthy of belief, and at the same time to remain open-minded about those very beliefs? This tension is insightfully addressed by Jonathan Adler (2004), who urges that open-mindedness be conceived as a meta-attitude toward one's beliefs rather than as a weakening of one's degree of belief or a weakened commitment toward the beliefs themselves, and that it be understood in terms of our general interest in attaining knowledge; he relates these matters to other fundamental issues concerning tolerance, autonomy, and authority that have long animated philosophers of education.

FURTHER TOPICS

There is a range of further issues concerning epistemological dimensions of education that should be mentioned, even though they cannot be addressed in detail here. They include the following issues.

FURTHER ISSUES CONCERNING CRITICAL THINKING. Partly because of its enduring status as a favored educational ideal, considerable philosophical energy has been expended on issues concerning critical thinking other than those already addressed. A particularly animated discussion involves the question of its *generalizability*: Is critical thinking generalizable—that is, applicable to a broad range of topics, domains, and issues—or is it rather *subject-specific*, such that critical thinking in one domain or discipline is importantly different from critical thinking in other areas? A range of views on the question can be found in *The Generalizability of Critical Thinking* (Norris 1992). A further issue is the place of *domain-specific knowledge* in critical thinking; here William Hare (1995) is particularly helpful. The relation between critical and creative thinking has also attracted considerable attention, with some arguing that these are fundamentally distinct and others arguing against such a sharp distinction. The topic has been insightfully treated in a series of works by Sharon Bailin, who challenges the distinction; see Bailin and Siegel 2003 and references therein.

CURRICULUM. It seems obvious enough that the curriculum should contain that knowledge/information thought to be most important for students to have, but the value and epistemological status of particular sorts of curricular content is controversial. Should a given subject, say mathematics, enjoy pride of place in the curriculum because it is in some sense intellectually central, or is its place secured by virtue of its practical importance or in some other way? More broadly, do particular content areas—science, language and literature, history, and the like—deserve their place in the curriculum because they constitute distinct "forms of knowledge" that are in some sense epistemologically fundamental, intrinsically important, and therefore the stuff of which all "liberally educated" students should be familiar (Hirst 1974)? Can this "forms of knowledge" view of traditional school subjects be sustained (Phillips 1987, pp. 120–136)? Moreover, does this idea of "liberal education" overemphasize the traditional and theoretical to the detriment of the practical, and/or does it reflect a culturally biased "Eurocentric" view of reason, knowledge, and education's character and priorities (Siegel 1997, Bailin and Siegel 2003)?

TEACHING AND LEARNING. How should teaching and learning be conceived and the former conducted? The issues here are many and complex and depend for their resolution on psychological matters as well as on philosophy of mind and other areas of philosophy, yet they are rightly thought to be epistemological (in part) in so far as teaching is thought to involve knowledge transmission and the development of the ability to acquire knowledge, and learning is thought to involve such acquisition. (Passmore 1980, Pearson 1989, Hare 1993).

"GROUP EPISTEMOLOGIES" AND FEMINIST, MULTICULTURALIST, AND POSTMODERNIST CHALLENGES TO IDEALS OF REASON IN EDUCATION. By the 1970s analytic philosophy began to lose its dominant position in the field and, again, philosophy of education followed the trend established in the parent discipline. The rise of Feminism, Multiculturalism, and Postmodernism brought with them important challenges to traditional views concerning the universality and neutrality of 'reason' and rationality and, indeed, to the nature of knowledge itself. While space precludes serious attention to these challenges here, or even a clear articulation of the issues, they are an important part of the contemporary scene in the philosophy of education. (For further discus-

sion and references, see Bailin and Siegel 2003; Siegel 1997, 2004, 2005).

See also Dewey, John; Feminist Epistemology; Multiculturalism; Philosophy of Education, Ethical and Political Issues In; Philosophy of Education, History of; Postmodernism.

Bibliography

Adler, Jonathan E. *Belief's Own Ethics.* Cambridge, MA: MIT Press, 2002.

Adler, Jonathan E. "Knowledge, Truth, and Learning." In *A Companion to the Philosophy of Education*, edited by Randall Curren. Oxford: Blackwell, 2003, p. 285–304.

Adler, Jonathan E. "Reconciling Open-mindedness and Belief." *Theory and Research in Education* 2 (2) (2004): 127–142.

Bailin, Sharon, and Harvey Siegel. "Critical Thinking." In *The Blackwell Guide to the Philosophy of Education*, edited by Nigel Blake, Paul Smeyers, Richard Smith, and Paul Standish. Oxford: Blackwell, 2003, p. 181–193.

Elgin, Catherine Z. "Education and the Advancement of Understanding." In *Proceedings of the 20th World Congress of Philosophy*. Vol. 3, edited by David M. Steiner. Philosophy Documentation Center, 1999a, p. 131–140.

Elgin, Catherine Z. "Epistemology's Ends, Pedagogy's Prospects." *Facta Philosophica* 1 (1999b): 39–54.

Goldman, Alvin I. *Knowledge in a Social World.* Oxford: Oxford University Press, 1999.

Hare, William. "Content and Criticism: The Aims of Schooling" *Journal of Philosophy of Education* 29 (1) (1995): 47–60.

Hare, William. *In Defence of Open-mindedness.* Kingston: McGill-Queen's University Press, 1985.

Hare, William. *Open-mindedness and Education.* Kingston: McGill-Queen's University Press, 1979.

Hare, William. *What Makes a Good Teacher? Reflections on Some Characteristics Central to the Educational Enterprise.* London, ON: Althouse, 1993.

Hirst, Paul H. *Knowledge and the Curriculum: A Collection of Philosophical Papers.* London: Routledge & Kegan Paul, 1974.

Hirst, Paul H., and R. S. Peters. *The Logic of Education.* London: Routledge & Kegan Paul, 1970.

Norris, Stephen P., ed. *The Generalizability of Critical Thinking: Multiple Perspectives on an Educational Ideal.* New York: Teachers College Press, 1992.

Passmore, John. *The Philosophy of Teaching.* Cambridge, MA: Harvard University Press, 1980.

Pearson, Allen T. *The Teacher: Theory and Practice in Teacher Education.* New York: Routledge, 1989.

Phillips, D. C. *Philosophy, Science, and Social Inquiry: Contemporary Methodological Controversies in Social Science and Related Applied Fields of Research.* Oxford: Pergamon Press, 1987.

Scheffler, Israel. *Conditions of Knowledge: An Introduction to Epistemology and Education.* Glenview, IL: Scott, Foresman, 1965.

Scheffler, Israel. *The Language of Education*. Springfield, IL: Charles C. Thomas, 1960.

Scheffler, Israel. *Reason and Teaching*. 2nd ed. Indianapolis, IN: Hackett, 1989.

Siegel, Harvey. *Educating Reason: Rationality, Critical Thinking, and Education*. London: Routledge, 1988.

Siegel, Harvey. "Epistemology and Education: An Incomplete Guide to the Social-Epistemological Issues." *Epistéme* 1 (2) (2004): 129–137.

Siegel, Harvey. "Israel Scheffler." In *Fifty Modern Thinkers in Education: From Piaget to the Present*, edited by Joy A. Palmer. London: Routledge, 2001, 142–148.

Siegel, Harvey. *Rationality Redeemed? Further Dialogues on an Educational Ideal*. New York: Routledge, 1997.

Siegel, Harvey. "Truth, Thinking, Testimony, and Trust: Alvin Goldman on Epistemology and Education." *Philosophy and Phenomenological Research* (2005).

Snook, I. A., ed. *Concepts of Indoctrination: Philosophical Essays*. London: Routledge & Kegan Paul, 1972.

Spiecker, Ben, and Roger Straughan. *Freedom and Indoctrination in Education: International Perspectives*. London: Cassell, 1991.

Harvey Siegel (2005)

PHILOSOPHY OF EDUCATION, ETHICAL AND POLITICAL ISSUES IN

Education is the promotion of learning and development. Educational activities include attending to explanations, lectures, or demonstrations, but it does not follow that teaching or direct instruction is the whole or the essence of education. Education also involves the communication of care and the transmission of elements of at least one culture, but these, too, are only part of what constitutes education. Additionally, education is a form of governance; *to educate* has always meant "to rear, bring up, instruct, train, discipline, develop," but its Latin root, *ēdu-cāre*, is related to *ēducĕre* (from *ē*, "out," and *dūcĕre*, "to lead"), a term of governance. The terms *pedagogy* and *pedagogue* (schoolteacher) derive similarly from the Greek *paidagôgos*, a term of governance (from *paidion*, "child," and *agô*, "to lead") referring to the household slave who supervised the children and led them out into the city from one teacher and place of learning to another. The modern term *governess*, signifying a woman employed to educate the children of a household, is similarly and conspicuously a term of governance.

As a form of governance, education requires justification, and it entails responsibilities, aims, a manner of going about its business, and substance or a communi-cated content. These are the fundamental aspects of governance, and the philosophy of education can be organized by categories corresponding to them: the authority to educate (justification), the adequate and equitable provision of education (responsibilities), the aims of education (aims), pedagogy and educational ethics (manner), and curriculum (substance or content).

On this account of the divisions of philosophy of education, it becomes evident that an ethic of governance would provide a unifying normative structure. The most obvious and durable illustration of this is an ethic of respsect for persons as self-determining agents. Ethics of this kind have dominated philosophy from the time of Socrates, and they have implications for each of the five named aspects of governance and for each of the five corresponding divisions of philosophy of education. The primary aim and responsibility of educators is to promote autonomy or effective self-determination, and to do so equitably, displaying equal respect within their sphere of educational authority. The scope of the educational authority they possess, the manner in which they exercise that authority, and the content of the education they provide will in turn be limited and shaped by the character of this responsibility. They endeavor to cultivate the intellectual and moral virtues essential to good judgment, to nurture capabilities that will provide the basis of lives worth living, and to enable each student to understand the circumstances of his or her own life and the possibilities that lie before him or her. While promoting autonomy or effective self-determination in such ways, educators teach in a manner respectful of their students and the values inherent in the subjects they teach.

An influential alternative to such an ethic of respect is the ethic of care championed by Nel Noddings (1992) and others. Considered as an ethic of education, it assigns great importance to caring for students. It proposes the development of caring in students as the central purpose or aim of education and sets forth a conception of curriculum based not on the diverse forms of disciplinary knowledge but on the diverse forms of human developmental potentials and diverse "centers of care" or objects of potential interest and devoted attachment. Advocates of this view are less clear about its implications for matters of educational justice and authority, but in addressing the latter, they begin from the presumption that care and control are incompatible. They concede that an ethic of care does not constitute a comprehensive moral point of view, but the debate, which originated not in moral theory but in the psychology of moral development, has been framed as an opposition and subsequent reconciliation between justice and care.

An alternative would be to hold that the literature of care offers not a competing ethic or ethical theory, but a cluster of important empirical observations about the fundamental place in human development and well-being of being cared for, coming to care about and for oneself, and forming attachments. These tenets have been acknowledged by liberal theorists who regard a deontological ethic of respect as morally fundamental. Examples include the attention to continuity and quality of relationships in schools in the work of Randall Curren (2000, 2003) and conceptions of teaching and the curriculum as providing potential objects of attachment and fulfillment, as discussed in the work of Kenneth Strike (2003) and Harry Brighouse (2005).

Within the educational framework established by an ethical-political orientation, there are roles to be played by guiding norms of other sorts, such as epistemic rationality, craftsmanship, and artistry. If self-determination is enhanced by knowledge and understanding, then curricula must communicate, and teachers display respect for, the epistemic norms pertaining to knowledge and understanding. If the promotion of autonomy or meaningful choice among satisfying lives requires that students have opportunities to experience and develop competence in pursuits that are fulfilling and allow them to make their way in the world, then curricula must communicate, and teachers display respect for, the norms of craft and artistry proper to such pursuits.

Attempts have been made to undermine the distinction between epistemic and moral-political norms that is assumed here. Postmodernists and some varieties of feminists and neo-Marxists hold that the norms of epistemic rationality, at least in their familiar forms, are aspects of systems of oppression and have no objective standing. Such views have had many defenders within the philosophy of education in recent years, but the moral principles they appear to rely on are no more radical than those of the dominant liberal-democratic tradition, which has itself always been at least latently egalitarian. What distinguishes these contemporary critical stances is the assumptions of fact they employ, their salutary attention to previously neglected forms of inequality and disrespect, and—more problematically—their epistemic and metaphysical doctrines.

Although many of the ethical and political issues in philosophy of education were addressed by R. S. Peters and others in, and opposed to, the analytical philosophy of education movement of the 1960s and 1970s, philo-

sophical exploration of them has become more common since the 1980s. This growth of interest in such issues includes debates about parental choice in schooling, public support for religious schools, moral education, inclusion of students with disabilities in regular classrooms, accountability and high-stakes testing, affirmative action in university admissions, and the limits of academic freedom.

EDUCATIONAL AUTHORITY

The question of how to apportion authority over education between parents and public authorities has become important since the early 1980s, as parents in the United States have challenged public school curricula and have increasingly chosen home schooling, usually on religious grounds. What role should parental wishes and rights play in determining the content of public education? When it comes to regulating private, religious, and home schooling, how are parents' interests in the faith and character of their children to be balanced against the protection of children's interests and the need to prepare them for citizenship in a multicultural society? Is it acceptable to exempt religious schools from laws that protect girls and women from discrimination on the basis of sex?

William Galston and other defenders of wide parental discretion argue that parents can be trusted more than government authorities to know and protect their children's interests, that parents have a strong and legitimate interest in transmitting their values to their children, and that it is in the interest of children to be educated in the "thick" cultural traditions that faith communities can provide but that public institutions constrained by requirements of neutrality cannot. James Dwyer (1998) and others have argued in response that it is incoherent to attribute to parents an individual liberty that entails a right to control or predetermine the life course of another person, even a child. Amy Gutmann (1987), Eamonn Callan (1997), Stephen Macedo (2000, 2002), and others have argued that respect for reasonable pluralism cannot be secured by unlimited accommodation of the wishes of parents whose own cultural communities are intolerant. Civic virtues of respectful and reasoned engagement with the views and values of others must be educationally nurtured if a political culture of tolerance and mutual respect is to survive, and it follows from this that educational policy must favor, if not absolutely insist upon, universal standards of civic education. Dwyer, Brighouse, Meira Levinson (1999) and others argue that liberal respect for children as persons in their own right requires policies that ensure that all children enjoy an education that introduces them to a variety of cultural and ethical traditions and enables them to think critically about the circumstances and conduct of their own lives.

A related debate over school choice and privatization has taken on significance as schemes to promote parental choice among schools (for example, providing government vouchers redeemable for all or part of tuition) have spread to many parts of the world. Defenders of such schemes have argued that they are necessary to eliminate the differential impact of ability to pay on the freedom of parents to practice their religions, but also that a free market in educational services would promote efficiency and superior educational results. The debate is fraught with empirical speculation on all sides, but Colin Crouch (2003) has made a strong case for the view that privatization would abandon the idea that education is a right of citizenship, and others have addressed the ethical and political principles involved in ways that set the empirical issues aside. Curren has examined the grounds on which a public system of schools might be considered necessary, and he and Brighouse have arrived at similar requirements of justice for any system of education to be deemed acceptable (Curren 2000, Brighouse 2000). Both argue that some choice schemes might satisfy those requirements, that responsibility lies with the state to ensure that those requirements are met, and that public authority over education must be retained at least to the extent necessary to fulfill that responsibility.

A third debate concerns the professional authority of educators themselves. The authority to teach is typically granted through processes of certification and selective employment. But once teachers are employed, by what means are they, schools, and those who supervise them to be held accountable for their performance? Debate has focused on the promise and perils of high-stakes testing as a mechanism of accountability, and there is clearly much of ethical significance at stake. To what extent do extensive testing regimes undermine student motivation to learn? To what extent do they limit the exercise of sound professional judgment and thereby undermine good teaching?

EDUCATIONAL RESPONSIBILITIES

How are educational adequacy and equity to be understood? One debate concerns the kind of educational equality to be achieved and the degree to which equality is a requirement of justice. The major divide has been between those who argue that schooling is to be distributed so as to promote equality of opportunity to live well

and those who defend one or another threshold of educational adequacy. Best known among the latter views is Gutmann's argument that in order for the rights of citizenship to be meaningful, every citizen must be provided an education sufficient to make possible *effective* participation in democratic processes (Gutmann 1987).

Another area of lively debate concerns the diversity of students served by schools. The main topics have been religious diversity and the free exercise of religion, gender equity, racial justice and antiracist education, the rights of linguistic minorities, and justice for students with disabilities.

As regards higher education, the focus has been on access or who gains admission. The issue of whether the use of standardized admissions tests such as the SAT (Scholastic Assessment Test) is racially discriminatory has been examined in detail by Robert Fullinwider and Judith Lichtenberg (2004), and countless philosophers have contributed to the debate over the merits of affirmative action in admissions as a way to promote racial and gender equity.

All such views are dismissed as insufficiently transformative, socially and politically, by Paulo Freire and other advocates of revolutionary pedagogies. Because they view the content of conventional schooling as inherently exclusionary and oppressive in ways that sustain unjust regimes, they hold that justice demands forms of teaching that liberate oppressed populations by promoting critical consciousness and action.

EDUCATIONAL AIMS

Does the aim of educating children for their own good conflict with the aim of educating them for the common good? Is the point of transmitting culture to sustain the culture, to benefit the child, or both? Is the point of civic education to stabilize governments that may be corrupt, to prepare citizens to be vigilant in discouraging government corruption, or both? Is the point of education to promote a thriving economy, to enable the child to earn a living, or both? For example, if the economy needs more engineers, how far can schools go in developing the required science curriculum in a preprofessional direction without violating the spirit of a "general" education? What makes the potential for conflict more than conjectural is the existence of other models of the science curriculum. Instruction in science might aim for a broad humanistic and historical understanding of science or an appreciation of the relationships between science, technology, and society; and such aims would not require the

ENCYCLOPEDIA OF PHILOSOPHY
2nd edition

emphasis on mastery of equations and their application that is characteristic of preprofessional instruction.

The hope of reconciling education's worthy aims has rested largely with the enterprise of identifying a highest aim. The dominant choice through much of the Western tradition has been fostering good judgment in matters both public and private; but the dominant choice in recent decades has been autonomy. Although its meaning is often not well defined, *autonomy* seems to signify much the same thing as practically applied good judgment. The coherence and adequacy of the concept of autonomy have been questioned, usually on the grounds that it ignores the social context of personal identity, choice, and efficacy. Defenders of autonomy argue that the metaphysical assumptions of autonomy are not what critics suppose.

PEDAGOGY, DISCIPLINE, AND THE ETHICS OF TEACHING

The landscape of pedagogy has been dominated by different versions of the contrast between pedagogies of content delivery and pedagogies of critical thinking, some more politically charged than others. Friere frames this as a contrast between the "banking" and "problem solving" models, others as a contrast between transmission and construction(ism), and still others as a contrast between teaching that does or does not promote active learning and critical thinking. Defenders of problem solving, constructionist, and critical-thinking pedagogies all offer ethical and emancipatory rationales.

The matter of how coercive classroom management should be has been discussed in connection with pedagogy, classroom dialogue, and theories of motivation and basic psychological needs. A key issue is whether the organization of work and social life in the classroom creates the opportunities for all students to satisfy their basic psychological needs in acceptable ways. If it does, then problems of classroom management will be small, and if it does not, then it will be both more necessary and less just to penalize unwanted conduct.

While most work on the ethics of teaching addresses specific issues, Strike (2003) offers a general account that incorporates ideals of promoting growth, exemplifying civic virtues, and teaching one's subject with integrity or in a way that is true to its inherent virtues. Work on the ethics of higher education has addressed issues of academic freedom, tenure, institutional neutrality, university-business partnerships, sexual harassment, diversity, research ethics, ethical issues in student-life policies, athletics, and the professional responsibilities of faculty and administrators.

THE SUBSTANCE OF SCHOOLING

Discussion of the content of education has often taken the idea of an education in the liberal arts as its point of departure, and multicultural calls to broaden the "canon" or textual basis of liberal education have proliferated. The purpose of a multicultural curriculum is variously described as providing a more accurate view of the world, promoting the self-esteem of those not born into the culturally dominant class or race, correcting the self-perceptions of those who do belong to the dominant class or race, or promoting intercultural or interracial understanding, harmony, mutual respect, or global citizenship. A more radical strand of critique, advanced by Walter Feinberg (1983) and others, holds that the function of schooling is to reproduce social and economic inequality and that school curricula are systems of exclusionary knowledge codes, which mediate that function.

In recent years the major debates about moral education have revolved around three kinds of models and how to move beyond them. Cultural-transmission models call for initiating children into the prevailing moral order by immersing them in a school culture that replicates and teaches it through rituals, moralistic literature, and the like. These models are faulted primarily for their lack of progressivism. Romantic or child liberationist models trust children to spontaneously develop moral sensibilities and commitments but are faulted for their empirical shortcomings. Intellectualist or neo-Kantian models have attempted to sidestep debates over the content of morality and moral education by focusing on the form of morality and moral reasoning. Lawrence Kohlberg's cognitive-developmental variant of this model has been widely influential and widely criticized for ignoring the motivational aspect of moral development and for promoting an ethic of justice that is at odds with the patterns of female moral development, which are said to pertain more to care and inclusion. Alternative models include an ethics of care that emphasizes the nurturing of natural sympathy, neo-Aristotelian approaches that defend roles for both habituation and critical reason, and mixed developmental approaches that consider the moral sentiments, social and community factors, and identity formation together with the cognitive aspects of moral development.

See also Affirmative Action; Authority; Ethics, History of; Feminist Epistemology; Multiculturalism; Philosophy of Education, History of; Rationality; Respect; Socrates.

Bibliography

Brighouse, Harry. *On Education*. London: Routledge, 2005.

Brighouse, Harry. *School Choice and Social Justice*. Oxford: Oxford University Press, 2000.

Callan, Eamonn. *Creating Citizens: Political Education and Liberal Democracy*. Oxford: Oxford University Press, 1997.

Carr, David, and Jan Steutel, eds. *Virtue Theory and Moral Education*. London: Routledge, 1999.

Curren, Randall. *Aristotle on the Necessity of Public Education*. Lanham, MD: Rowman & Littlefield, 2000.

Curren, Randall, ed. *A Companion to the Philosophy of Education*. Oxford: Blackwell, 2003.

Crouch, Colin. *Commercialization or Citizenship: Education Policy and the future of Public Services*. London: Fabian Society, 2003.

Dwyer, James. *Religious Schools v. Children's Rights*. New York: Cornell University Press, 1998.

Feinberg, Walter. *Understanding Education*. Cambridge, U.K.: Cambridge University Press, 1983.

Fenner, David, ed. *Ethics in Education*. New York: Garland, 1999.

Friere, Paulo. *The Pedagogy of the Oppressed*. New York: Seabury, 1970.

French, Peter. *Ethics and College Sports*. Lanham, MD: Rowman & Littlefield, 2004.

Fullinwider, Robert, ed. *Public Education in a Multicultural Society*. Cambridge, U.K.: Cambridge University Press, 1996.

Fullinwider, Robert, and Judith Lichtenberg. *Leveling the Playing Field: Justice, Politics, and College Admissions*. Lanham, MD: Rowman & Littlefield, 2004.

Gutmann, Amy. *Democratic Education*. Princeton, NJ: Princeton University Press, 1987.

Hirst, Paul, and Patricia White, eds. *Philosophy of Education: Major Themes in the Analytic Tradition*. Vol. 3, *Society and Education*. London: Routledge, 1998.

Katz, Michael S., Nel Noddings, and Kenneth Strike, eds. *Justice and Caring: The Search for Common Ground in Education*. New York: Teachers College Press, 1999.

Levinson, Meira. *The Demands of Liberal Education*. Oxford: Oxford University Press, 1999.

Macedo, Stephen. *Diversity and Distrust: Civic Education in a Multicultural Society*. Cambridge, MA: Harvard University Press, 2000.

Macedo, Stephen, and Yael Tamir, eds. *Moral and Political Education*. New York: New York University Press, 2002.

McDonough, Kevin, and Walter Feinberg, eds. *Citizenship and Education in Liberal Democratic Societies*. Oxford: Oxford University Press, 2003.

Noddings, Nel. *The Challenge to Care in Schools*. New York: Teachers College Press, 1992.

Nussbaum, Martha. *Cultivating Humanity: A Classical Defense of Reform in Liberal Education*. Cambridge, MA: Harvard University Press, 1997.

Peters, R. S. *Ethics and Education*. London: George Allen & Unwin Ltd., 1966.

Pritchard, Michael. *Reasonable Children: Moral Education and Moral Learning*. Lawrence: Kansas University Press, 1996.

Sellars, Mortimer. *An Ethical Education*. Oxford: Berg Publishers, 1994.

Simon, Robert. *Neutrality and the Academic Ethic*. Lanham, MD: Rowman & Littlefield, 1994.

Strike, Kenneth. "The Ethics of Teaching." In *A Companion to the Philosophy of Education*, edited by Randall Curren. Oxford: Blackwell, 2003.

Wolfe, Alan, ed. *School Choice: The Moral Debate*. Princeton, NJ: Princeton University Press, 2003.

Randall Curren (2005)

PHILOSOPHY OF EDUCATION, HISTORY OF

There was probably a time when human culture was transmitted spontaneously from one generation to another. The young of the species cannot survive to maturity unless they assimilate some beliefs about the world, some attitudes toward it, and some skill in solving the practical problems it presents; and the only source from which they can derive this minimal wisdom is the culture of their elders. The tendency to imitate offers a ready-made mechanism for inheritance, and in primitive communities, where benign surroundings allowed a leisurely and spontaneous association with children or where a harsh environment spared no time from the effort to keep soul and body together, the education of the young must have proceeded without much thought or care. In societies that were a little more advanced, the need for instruction in tribal ceremonies and the apprenticeship of sons to fathers and of daughters to mothers may have covered spontaneous education with a thin veil of deliberateness. Still, in uncivilized communities generally, culture must have been passed on without the agency of persons especially devoted to that purpose.

Through time, beliefs accumulate, attitudes grow more diversified, skills become more numerous and more complex. This increase in the volume of culture must have rendered obsolete the deliberate spontaneity of its transmission. Mastering what there was to know required special and enduring effort; teaching others to master it demanded more than a casual supervision of their lives. A culture thus enhanced could find lodgment only in a special class of persons—those who were able to encompass it. And this class—seers, priests, and scholars—must have become its chief dispenser to succeeding generations.

BEGINNINGS IN GREECE

There are two important consequences of the concentration of culture in the hands of a specialized class. Conscious of their possession, scholars naturally came to ask how it might be improved and purified; and this question led to the beginning of research. Second, because they were held responsible for instruction, both scholars and laymen came to expect that some good purpose should be served by their teaching—that it not only should preserve and extend culture but that teaching should serve some other purpose as well.

The earliest records show that the first of these effects, the beginning of research, began to appear in Europe near the beginning of the sixth century BCE. For a long time, no doubt, the learned had looked upon the things of sensory experience as irreducible constituents of the world and, relying upon ancient religious belief, had explained the origin and changes of those things by reference to the gods who presided over them. Now, however, a torrent of speculation deprived sensory things of their irreducible reality and the gods of their explanatory force. Water, pure matter, air, fire—each was advanced as the ultimate stuff of things by some. Other thinkers preferred a substance which possessed all the qualities of sensory things and that was broken into many small bits. Some regarded sensory things as nothing but atoms moving in the void; others resolved their hitherto independent reality into numbers or mathematical structures. And others, still, saw their independence disappear into the absolute unity that was the only reality. Almost all saw the things of ordinary sensory experience as resulting from natural forces working upon the elements or somehow breaking up the unity. The more ancient wisdom was improved by pointing out that the world was really something different from what it seemed to the senses and by disallowing any explanatory value to myth.

SOPHISTS. The second effect of the concentration of culture, the desire to serve a higher purpose, began to appear about the middle of the fifth century BCE. The diversity of opinions concerning the nature of things, their origin and change, and related topics, led in some minds to a profound skepticism. Gorgias (c. 480–380 BCE) argued that nothing exists; that if something did, no one could know it; and that if one could know it, he could communicate his knowledge to no one else. Protagoras (c. 490–c. 421 BCE) held that man is the measure of all things. Each concluded that belief is properly an individual concern and that what is good and right is similarly dependent upon individual interests. They did not draw the conclusion that one might do as he pleased, however; they urged, rather, that conformity to custom and convention furthers the interest of the individual person more than flouting does. They and their fellow Sophists moved through the cities of Hellas, giving instruction in the

practical arts, in the humane and literary subjects, in rhetoric, in law and politics, and in the more theoretical considerations out of which their natural and egoistic principles grew. They asked a fee for their instruction, and that procedure was an innovation. But an even greater novelty was their view of their own function as teachers—a view of the transmission of culture not for its own sake merely, or for *ad hoc* purposes, but in order to help their pupils achieve the comprehensive goal of a practically successful life at home, in the court, or in the legislative assembly.

SOCRATES. Socrates (c. 470–399 BCE), to judge from Plato's presentation of him, was even more conscious of his mission as a teacher than were the Sophists. He shared their skepticism toward physical and cosmological theories, but unlike them he refused to leave unchallenged any dogmatic trust in conventional morality. In his hands rhetoric became dialectic; and in his teaching the purpose to which the pupils of the Sophists put the former—the persuasion of others to whatever view the speaker finds most useful—became the discovery of truth, in the dialectical search for which all barriers of personal prejudice and social dogma must give way. He was convinced that the human mind could discover the truth about the physical world and about the life of man in it, although he was equally certain that no one had yet achieved this knowledge. His mission as a teacher, he thought, was to free his pupil's mind from confusion and dogma in order that it should be able to find and recognize the truth—especially the truth about the good or virtue. Confusion and dogma would disappear upon examination of the unclear and unfounded ideas that constituted them. Thus, although Socrates' purpose was positive, his teaching often shows a primarily negative aspect. The skepticism and conventionality of the Sophists brought an objective of prudence to their education; but the skepticism and rationality of Socrates gave to his instruction the purpose of a life of virtue whose discovery required a clarification of the ideas involved in ordinary discourse.

PLATO. Plato (427–347 BCE), influenced by the Sophists as well as by the speculative scientists and metaphysicians and inspired by the instruction of Socrates, gave us the first fully developed philosophy of education—that is, the first explicit, philosophical justification of a theory of education. In his *Republic,* on the basis of observation, he ascribed to all human beings, but in varying degrees, three distinct abilities: the ability to reason, which seeks the good life, the ability for appetition, which is connected with the body and is somewhat wayward, and the ability to enforce the decisions of reason about what is good against the inclination of appetites. He ascribed to all states, on a similar basis, three functions: that of legislation, that of economic production and distribution, and that of armed enforcement of law and foreign policy.

Plato recommended that education be employed as the chief method of reforming both the individual's character and the state. In a just character each of the three abilities is exercised to the height of its power: Reason recognizes what is good, the appetites freely conform, and the ability to enforce the decisions of reason assures that conformity. In a just state each adult citizen performs that function for which he is best fitted: The highly rational engage in legislation, the predominantly spirited (Plato's name for the ability to enforce reason's decisions about the good) enforce it, and the chiefly appetitive operate the economy. Justice consists in a harmony that results when each part of a thing performs the function proper to it and refrains from interfering with the function of any other part. Reform in individual character and in the state is movement toward personal and social justice.

A system of universal, compulsory, public education from birth to maturity ought to be instituted to bring about this individual and social improvement. All should be taught to read, to write, to count, to appreciate the traditional poetry and drama (highly censored for the young), and to engage in gymnastic exercise. Some should learn the military art, and others should study the sciences and dialectic—the search for the fundamental principle that explains all reality and value. Each student should be tested to discover which ability dominates his soul and should be sent into the state to perform the function appropriate to it when he reaches the limit of his development, which the testing reveals. Thus, each class in the state would be recruited from those best fitted to perform its function. Such a system of education would produce individuals whose souls are as just as their abilities allow and a state whose parts or classes are similarly harmonious.

Plato's philosophical justification of his theory of education consists of three parts. First, he shows that the just state or republic and the just individual are good. For every class of things, there is a Form, or Idea, existing in a supernatural realm, resemblance to which determines the class. The resemblance between a member of the class and its Form is its goodness. The Form for the class of states is that pattern into which the three constituent classes fall when each performs its proper function. The Form for the class of human beings is that pattern into which the parts of the soul fall when each is properly

developed. Thus, insofar as a person is just, he is also good, for he resembles the Form of humanity. And insofar as the state is just, it is also good, for it resembles the Form of states. The goodness of a just character and of a just state warrants Plato's recommending them to our efforts.

Besides this ethical support for his recommendations Plato provides a metaphysical explanation for the facts upon which he rests them—the facts of human nature and of society. Every particular falls into some class, and the class is made what it is by virtue of the Form copied by all the members of that class. If we ask, then, why every human being should possess the three abilities (reason, appetite, and spirit) and why every state should perform the three functions (legislation, economic production and distribution, and law enforcement), the answer is that they cannot fail to possess and perform them since exactly that is required by their Forms.

Plato's epistemology gives a third support to his theory of education. First, his contention that we can know only the Forms in their logical connections, coupled with the view that the entire realm of becoming is a copy of that of the Forms, leads to the conclusion that even though knowledge is not an infallible guide to the course of nature it is more useful than mere opinion. In this way he argues that knowledge is useful in the pursuit of justice. He holds, second, that the only method appropriate to acquiring knowledge is that of purely rational inference. Assuming that the method of learning is identical with that of discovering truth, he argues that instruction should follow the path of deduction wherever that is possible.

Plato's philosophy of education resembles in some respects the thought of the metaphysicians and physicists of the fifth and sixth centuries; with them it shares the faith that the human mind can achieve knowledge of what exists. It resembles the thought of the Sophists in its insistence that the world of ordinary sensory experience cannot be known. But of their reliance on conventional morality, it shows no trace at all. Rather, Plato shares with Socrates the conviction that virtue can be known and that it is the business of education to reform conventional morality in its direction.

DEFINITION OF "PHILOSOPHY OF EDUCATION." Plato's work, especially in the *Republic*, serves as a paradigm of a definition of the phrase "philosophy of education." He sets forth an educational theory—that is, a view about the facts of human nature and society on which are based recommendations about the curriculum, the methods, and the administration of education, regarded as means to the ultimate goal of just and good citizens living in a just and good society. His ethical theory justifies this goal; his metaphysical theory supports the recommendations ancillary to the goal; and his epistemology explains the effectiveness of some of the teaching methods he advocates as well as our capacity to perceive truth generally. "Philosophy of education" means any body of thought like this one—any body of thought that includes a theory of education, an ethics that justifies the goal that the theory adopts, a metaphysics that explains the psychological and sociological parts of the theory of education, and an epistemology that explains why certain methods of teaching and learning are effective and demonstrates our ability to know the truth of any thought whatsoever.

Many philosophies of education do not contain reference to all the subjects with which Plato was concerned. Nonetheless, his reflections on education fix the meaning of the phrase by constituting a model, resemblance to which (at least to some degree and in some respect) allows any body of thought to be called philosophy of education.

HELLENISTIC THOUGHT. After Plato's work, nothing very novel was added to philosophy of education for some seven centuries. There is extant some work of Aristotle's (384–322 BCE), but it is fragmentary and a part of a theory of education rather than a philosophical treatment of such a theory. Epicurus (341–270 BCE) and his followers Zeno of Citium (336?–265? BCE) and the Stoics advocated a tranquility in life—the Epicureans through cultivation of quiet pleasures easily obtained, the Stoics through willing acceptance of the lot for which one is necessarily determined and (among the later members of the school) through a love for all humankind viewed as a brotherhood. But Epicureans and Stoics, as far as we know, themselves developed neither a theory nor a philosophy of education. In the first century CE, Quintilian (c. 35–c. 95) published his *Institutio Oratoria* (*The Training of an Orator*). Quintilian recommends that in his training an orator be given appropriate objectives toward which he can direct his native but unformed impulses. The life of the orator, he dimly suggests, is good because it meets the Stoic requirements of indifference to external circumstance and utility to fellow citizens. His book harks back to the humanistic curriculum of the educator and orator Isocrates (436–338 BCE) and to the Sophists. It was of much influence in later antiquity and again, after its rediscovery, on humanistic education in the Renaissance, but it embodies a theory of education rather than

philosophical reflection upon education. Other authors, for example, Plutarch (c. 46–120 CE) and Quintus Septimius Florens Tertullian (c. 160–c. 220), comment on education, but not in a philosophical way.

Although the literature of the Hellenistic age shows little that is new in philosophy of education, two ideas of great importance for change in that philosophy were, nonetheless, gradually coming to dominate men's minds. One is the idea that a chief factor in the good life is obedience to law; the other, that a necessary ingredient in that same life is the happiness of a love that unites all those who obey the law as well as each of them to the lawgiver himself. The Christian ideal of the brotherhood of men under God, their creator, is the expression these ideas assumed, and the movement of Christianity, although influenced by Plato, not to mention Plotinus (205–270), produced a new philosophy of education.

MIDDLE AGES

AUGUSTINE. The new philosophy is the work of St. Augustine (354–430). Human nature, according to his view, must be described in terms of substance and faculties influenced by historical forces. Every human being is a combination of body and soul; the soul possesses the faculties of knowing, feeling, and willing. The first enables us to know whatever we sense and remember to have sensed, certain abstract principles which the mind carries within itself, and the world of sensible things as they are ordered by those principles. The faculty of feeling enables us to desire and to feel emotions which center on desires. The faculty of willing enables us to choose from among differing desires those we want to realize—an ability which exercises itself freely and which, when exercised correctly, employs rules of choice that flow from divine commands.

Human nature cannot be accounted for in terms of substance and faculties alone, however. A historical force always determines how these faculties operate. Before the Fall, Adam and Eve used their faculties in the right way—especially their faculty of desire, directing its operation upon what they ought to desire, centering their love on God and on one another in communion with him, and choosing freely to obey his commands whenever the clamor of bodily appetite opposed itself to the right. But from their original sin, of which the Fall was a natural consequence, flows the force which determines their descendants to act as sinfully as they—to choose freely to disobey God's command by selecting egoistic and carnal desires for realization. Human nature must be painted in terms of substance and faculties corrupted by early events in human history.

Human society is constituted by the direction of the activities of its members toward a single goal, but, like the human soul, it cannot be understood merely in terms of this abstract function. The unity of purpose that in principle constitutes the family, the city, the empire, and the community of humans and angels is disrupted by inherited self-seeking. Another historical force determines two other communities—the city of earth and the city of God—each of which is reflected in the four just mentioned. The advent of Christ signifies God's wish to enable men, despite their sinfulness, to merit salvation. The city of earth is made up of those who refuse to believe in Christ's mission and to repent; its members will not be saved. The city of God is composed of those who believe in that mission and feel genuine repentance; its members will enter upon eternal communion with God after the day of judgment.

The ultimate objective of education grows out of the corruption of human nature and God's concern over it. Like the ultimate objective of the church, that of education is conversion and repentance. On the elementary level the curriculum should be the seven liberal arts—a program of studies prefigured by Plato's curriculum; on the advanced level it should consist in philosophy and theology. The method appropriate to the lower level involves censorship and the prevention of idleness in order to stifle sinful desires. The liberal arts should be taught in an authoritative manner because not all who seek elementary instruction are sufficiently rational to know the truth and since no more than belief is required for salvation. On the higher level, authority gives way to proof since those who advance thus far are able to achieve knowledge. The liberal arts, coupled with religious worship and instruction, ensure correct belief about the nature and order of the universe and about God's relation to man; philosophy and theology show the more able—those destined for the hierarchy of the church—why those beliefs are true.

Augustine's philosophical reflections upon his theory of education stem from his conception of God. He advances, first, a theory of language according to which every word means what it names, and every sentence, the combination of things named by its component words. He concludes that since on this theory no one can tell someone else what he does not already know, each man must learn for himself by consulting things as they are illuminated in a light of divine origin. Teaching is not informing; it is reminding others or ourselves of the knowledge supplied by God.

Second, from the concept of God flows the justification of the objective of education. The goodness of each created thing consists in its resemblance to the idea held before God's mind as the pattern for its creation; this idea is its exemplar. The exemplar for men is the obedience to God's commands and love for him and for one another in him that gave perfection to life before the Fall. To be happy is to possess what one wants at the time of wanting it; since God is the only eternal thing, he is the only dependable object of desire. To be happy is to illustrate the exemplar for man, and conversion, the objective for education, consists in achieving that condition.

Augustine finds in God, also, a metaphysical explanation of human nature and society. In the first moment God created everything either in actuality or in potentiality. All history—each person's repentance or failure to repent, each society's deeds, both good and bad—is the unfolding of what was first merely potential; what happens is what must happen because of the initial creation and God's all-comprehending providence. Human nature and society must be corrupt; hence, conversion must be the ultimate purpose of education.

Later medieval thought. During the centuries that followed the death of Augustine the interest in another world became so dominant that education diminished in importance, and reflection upon it very nearly ceased. Attention was centered on the otherworldly results of repentance or its failure at the expense of training for terrestrial existence; and so dogmatic was the assurance of the need for conversion that any effort to justify this objective appeared useless if not impious. The clergy, then Europe's teacher, offered a meager training to those working toward holy orders and some understanding of religious ritual to the laity. But the transmission of culture diminished greatly. The widespread acceptance of the otherworldly objective of education stifled philosophical reflection upon it. Comment on education is found in the writings of the Venerable Bede (673?–735), of Alcuin (735–804), and of Hrabanus Maurus in the early ninth century; but they are at most casual and at least unphilosophical. Thomas Aquinas (1224?–1274) devoted some systematic attention to the philosophy of education, but his chief contribution to it concerns not the objective of training but the nature of teaching—a discussion which continues the thought of Augustine on that subject.

RENAISSANCE. With the Renaissance came a revival of interest in ancient learning and a recognition of value in terrestrial life. In accord with this change of outlook some writers assigned to education an egoistic and prudential purpose like that of the Sophists. Reformationist thought—at least in Martin Luther's case—demanded universal, compulsory, state-controlled education in order that religion should be national and God's word available directly to all. Ignatius Loyola (1491–1556), through the Society of Jesus, established a widespread system of schools and universities; and in 1599 the society established a plan of education for them (*ratio studiorum*) that exercised much influence on Catholic education. But Reformationist and Counter-Reformationist literature reveals much more polemic and dogma than philosophical reflection upon education.

MODERN PERIOD

COMENIUS. In the seventeenth century, philosophical reflection upon education began anew, and its history from that time to the present is that of the gradual secularization and naturalization of the Christian objective assigned to education by Augustine. The work of John Amos Comenius (1592–1670) begins this process. (In particular, see his *The Great Didactic* and *The Way of Light*.)

Like Augustine, Comenius holds that human nature is corrupted by inherited sin, but he also asserts that it is capable of absolute perfection. The soul contains the possibilities of erudition (perfect knowledge), of virtue (adherence to the rules of right conduct), and of piety (love of God, the author of humankind). Like Augustine, Comenius viewed history as a decline from innocence, but he held, nonetheless, that there is a zigzag pattern in history, leading to an age of perfect terrestrial existence before the last judgment devoid of international strife and ruled over by Christ. In this last age the possibilities in the human soul realize themselves in perfect knowledge, virtue, and piety, and all societies unite in a single international brotherhood. The reward for striving after this perfection is immortal blessedness. Comenius held that a system of public, universal, state-supported schools, from childhood to maturity, should further the full actualization of the soul's possibilities and assist history toward its goal. The curriculum should constitute a cyclical development from the simple and abstract elements of science, art, language, literature, and religion to their complex and concrete forms. The methods of instruction should consist in the uniform application to the young of the human species of principles observed in the development of the young of other species, both plant and animal.

Comenius's philosophical reflection on his theory of education centers, like Augustine's, around the notion of God. God made humankind in his own image, and, because God is perfect, humans may become so as well. To achieve perfect knowledge is to make perfectly clear to ourselves the things our sensations reveal and to order them according to innate principles which reason brings to light. To perfect conduct is to identify the rule of one's will with a command of God, and to perfect piety is to love God in one's obedience to him. Human nature and human history find a metaphysical explanation in divine providence, which manifests itself through the opposed forces of light and darkness. The business of education is to perfect individuals in the three ways mentioned. It also makes the personal life of each human being perfectly Christian and aids history in its progress toward final social perfection.

LOCKE. Late in the seventeenth century, not long after Comenius, John Locke (1632–1704) published *Some Thoughts concerning Education*. In this book, in *An Essay concerning Human Understanding*, and in *Second Treatise of Civil Government*, he carried further the secularization of the objective of education started by Comenius. With Augustine and Comenius, Locke held that man is free, but in opposition to them he denied that man is inherently sinful by virtue of his racial history. Each person is a mental substance joined to a bodily substance, as Augustine asserted; mental activity, however, can be described wholly without reference to substance, in terms of two faculties, understanding and will. The faculty of understanding enables man both to know and to desire, but what man knows is determined by the ideas his environment allows to enter his mind, and what he desires is determined by the objectives his environment supplies to a few native instincts. The second faculty is the will, and its exercise consists in choosing desires for realization where they conflict.

Society in the state of nature is based on a natural division of labor and on the need to care for offspring. In that state the original "common" of the world was largely transformed into private property, and the function of primitive society was to enforce natural law, or the law of God according to which private property ought to be respected. Disputes inevitably arose, and, since everyone possessed the power to enforce the law of nature, they often could not be settled amicably. Political society came into existence as a guarantee against such disputes. It is based upon a contract or agreement between the community and others according to which each member of the community agrees not to exercise his power to enforce natural law provided that the others who constitute the government will exercise it for him. It follows that the exercise of governmental power is legitimate only where it protects private-property rights. A government of the kind instituted after the Glorious Revolution, having popular representation, Parliamentary determination of the sovereign, majority rule, and separation of legislative from executive power, Locke held, is best suited for achieving this objective because it can most efficiently check unnecessary governmental activity.

The purpose of education is to produce people who will advance the happiness of the community. They must be of good character and properly disposed toward learning. Good character consists in the habits of acting virtuously, prudently, and with good breeding. The proper disposition toward learning is not possession of it but an esteem for it and the habit of acquiring it when the need arises. These habits and dispositions can best be acquired by a tutorial education at home, by a method of pitting one instinctual desire against another in order to establish them, and by presentation of clear and distinct ideas to the pupil in the order and connection possessed by their objects. In both moral and intellectual training one should appeal to the interests of the child, bring him to learn for himself, and give public approbation to his success. The child who will benefit from such instruction and who will contribute to the happiness of the community is the son of landed gentry, who can look forward to a place in government. The poor should be given sufficient education to make them religious and self-supporting.

The production and maintenance of a good society is the chief objective of Locke's theory of education. Such a society is one in which men find pleasure or happiness in the performance of duty, and Locke's ethical reflection endeavors to justify this conception of the good life. Duty is obedience to natural law as embodied in civil law concerning the protection of private property. Like all moral principles, it can be known with certainty to be valid; it can be demonstrated from the ideas of God, of his creature man, and of the relation between them. The moral and intellectual training of the gentleman will cause him to find his pleasure in doing his duty; the exercise of this duty through government as well as through more informal social controls will spread a similar happiness throughout all levels of society.

Locke's theory of knowledge led him to conclude that we can be perfectly certain of any proposition whose truth we can intuit, demonstrate, or perceive through our senses or through our memory of such perception. Since the validity of duty can be demonstrated, we can know that it is right to perform it; and in this way, his emphasis on moral education is justified. Since the theory holds that we can know very little of the sensible world—only what we remember having perceived through our senses or are now perceiving through them—the de-emphasis of intellectual pursuits is also justified. We must accept many propositions about nature on faith or as merely probable; hence, we do not need to busy the heads of the young with any detailed consideration of them.

ROUSSEAU. Jean-Jacques Rousseau (1712–1778) advanced three distinct philosophies of education; in the most influential of the three he varied the social theme found in Locke's thought. In his discussion of a new constitution for Poland he advocated a highly nationalistic program on the ground that where a nation's institutions are in good health, education should support and renew them. In Émile, he set forth a program appropriate to women, holding that their education should give them charm, ability for household management, and thorough-going dependence on their husbands in matters not pertaining to the home. But the major part of Émile deals with the education of gentlemen, embodies a theory of education that has exerted much influence upon educational practice, and assigns to education a social ideal quite as secular and political as Locke's but applied in an altogether different way.

Rousseau described human nature, as did Locke, as independent of historical influences and as initially perfectly innocent. A human being is a substance with faculties—those of pleasure and pain, of sense, of reason, of desire and emotion, and of will. These faculties emerge clearly at different stages in the life of the individual according to a general pattern, and the personality is more or less stable according as the newly emerged faculty is made to harmonize with the exercise of others already established. Despite the general pattern, each individual differs from others and must achieve stability through a procedure adapted to his own case.

In the early history of humankind there was no society. Men were independent and therefore equal. With improvement in techniques of hunting, fishing, and farming, they acquired property; with property, they acquired families, differentiation of economic function, interdependence, and inequality. As society became more complex, greed, ambition, and deliberate selfishness entered the soul; in time, men developed government and law in order to protect the property of the wealthy against one another's greed and against the greed of the poor.

Inequality is fixed in the structure of eighteenth-century society and is due for removal by revolutionary action.

Rousseau presented detailed recommendations for educating gentlemen to live happily in these circumstances. They differ for each stage of development, but he urged that in all the child must learn for himself through personal observation of and active participation in the world of nature and society. A tutor who devotes his entire career to one pupil should attend to the pupil's individual interests and instruct him by rousing those interests into activity. The young man who completed this education would have enjoyed to the full each of the stages in his development and would be possessed of a strong body and stable mind. This stability would consist in his possessing no desire for whose realization he did not also possess the requisite power. It would make him neither learned nor urbane, but it would lead him to adopt a rural life in which he could survive the social storm Rousseau anticipated.

Rousseau advanced three criteria for knowledge: sensory experience of the consequences of action, the dictates of the heart, and practical utility. The first he transformed into a method of instruction—the method of letting the child experience for himself the consequences of acting upon his ideas in order to learn what is true about nature and society. The second he employed to warrant his inclusion in education of a considerable amount of simple religious doctrine. The third he relied upon to exclude from education a great deal of philosophy and other literature that he found devoid of practical consequence.

Rousseau's metaphysical reflection led him to hold that all of nature, including men's bodies and their actions, is governed by law but that since duty often requires one to act in ways other than those determined by this law, there is a supernatural realm in which duty presides. To act according to duty is to use the right rule for selecting one desire from among many as a basis for action, and since this selection and realization runs counter to nature, we must be exercising free will when we act rightly.

Rousseau's thought about morality concluded with the view that the good life is one in which there is neither the shallowness of desires that have been multiplied to match excess in power nor the discontent of an excess of power over desires but the happiness which occurs when power to fulfill desires equals the desires one harbors and is exercised to realize only those which are in accord with duty—a view not unlike Locke's. Duty Rousseau understood in terms of the general will. This is the welfare of the nation as opposed to the corporate will, or the welfare of a smaller group, and to the particular will, or the welfare of the individual.

It is our duty to act for the general will where that is possible. But in the major nations of Europe all institutions have been subverted to the service of corporate and particular wills. The social contract (which is, whatever the historical account of it may be, the agreement to act in accord with duty rather than for some lesser goal) has been betrayed by those in authority. Consequently, the ideal of duty cannot serve as the purpose of education generally. The realization or preservation of one's own will must be put in its place. In this way Rousseau justified the individualistic effort at internal peace that informs the theory of education with which he was most concerned.

PESTALOZZI. The educational proposals of Johann Heinrich Pestalozzi (1746–1827), unlike those of Rousseau, whom he greatly admired, bear no trace of direct revolutionary inclinations. But he had a warm sympathy for the downtrodden, and he advocated education for all as a condition of social reform. By his example and his books he contributed greatly to the common-school movement in Europe and America. The influence of Rousseau on his thought is evident chiefly in Pestalozzi's insistence on treating children in ways appropriate to the process of development through which they all must pass.

This process exhibits three stages. The contents of the child's mind are at first blurred and indistinct. Next, objects stand out in consciousness characterized by explicit forms and qualities. Last, these objects are understood as examples of general concepts; they are, to use Pestalozzi's word, defined. Throughout the process the person is himself active in securing and clarifying images and in transforming them into ideas that contain knowledge. Each child should be dealt with in accord with the place he occupies in this threefold process, and a major part of teaching consists in enabling him to work out for himself his own knowledge or definition of things.

Knowledge always contains three elements: the number of things known, the form they exhibit, and the language that embodies them. Pestalozzi concluded that learning must start with the elements into which each of these may be analyzed. The elements of number are units, and arithmetic (operations with units) must be mastered in order to understand number. Form Pestalozzi seems to have thought of as visual and tactual; its elements, consequently, are lines, angles, curves, etc. The student must understand these elements before he can understand form. The elements of language are ultimately letters, and the mastery of language depends on mastering their spoken and written forms.

Pestalozzi set forth detailed methods for teaching the elements of number, form, and language. They grew out of those he thought natural to a mother's dealings with her children. In the family situation a mother can know in what stage of development each of her children finds himself; she can teach him to count, to draw, and so on, through use and observation of ordinary materials in the context of the economic employment, such as spinning and weaving, in which the family engages; and she can assure herself that he comes to perceive objects clearly and to define them for himself according as his stage of growth permits. These methods, directed toward enabling each child to acquire knowledge based on his own perception (*Anschauung*) of things, Pestalozzi thought could be employed in a school situation. The schools he operated in Switzerland, taking the Swiss village family as their model, attracted imitators from many parts of Europe and America.

Besides knowledge of things, teaching should bring children to a knowledge of skills which exhibit their physical or motor capacities as knowing does their intellectual abilities; and Pestalozzi thought that the performance of deeds could be analyzed into elements just as knowledge could. He was convinced that learning how to do things required the mastery of elementary motions, just as coming to know required the mastery of the elements of number, form, and language. The teaching of morality and religion—more important than that of knowledge and skill—involved transferring the child's feelings of dependence on the mother to other persons in society and to God. But Pestalozzi's treatment of the development of the motor and moral capacities is not so detailed and clear as his discussion of the education of the intellect although he insisted upon the inseparable unity of the three capacities.

The direct influence of Pestalozzi on philosophy of education is negligible. He was not interested in it. Still, his schools and his writings on the theory of education strongly influenced some who were.

FROEBEL. Pestalozzi's younger contemporary Friedrich Froebel (1782–1852) spent several years working in one of Pestalozzi's schools. Froebel was also much given to philosophical reflection, upon which, he thought, the theory and practice of schools depended—especially that of the kindergarten, which he invented almost single-handed.

Froebel's speculations found the goal of education in the full and integrated development of all the powers of the individual and in the internal harmony, as well as the harmonious relations with society, nature, and God, that this development assures. This goal cannot be imposed upon the student; he must achieve it for himself through activities expressive of the powers he harbors. One who has accomplished the goal exhibits a steadiness and solidity of character that gives him integrity in all situations and the intellectual habits (not a store of remembered facts) that enable him to acquire knowledge when necessary.

The process by which this goal may be reached, the process of education, consists in the unfolding of what is present in infancy. Each person is like a plant, and as a plant develops toward a given stage of maturity, so the life of each human being consists in the filling out, through increase of varied detail, of a pattern present from the start. This process is also one of increasing clarity of self-expression and culminates in a clear consciousness of the self. The development of the individual is altogether continuous, and the stages of infancy, childhood, boyhood, youth, and maturity into which it is divided are characterized not by the emergence of novelties, as Rousseau had suggested, but by an increase of clarity in consciousness of the tendencies present in all.

Froebel worked out methods of education in accord with this view of individual development. The methods applicable in the earlier stages should merely enable spontaneous expression of the pupil's self; methods applicable to the later stages should supervise and direct that development. His treatment of the stage of childhood amounts to the nearly single-handed invention of the kindergarten—an institution that spread quickly, especially throughout the United States. His treatment of boyhood involved considerable innovation in the methods, materials, and curriculum of elementary schools.

In the first stage, the infant should be nurtured and cared for. In the second, the senses and language develop, and the child's tendencies toward this development should be permitted free expression. Play is the most important method for this expression. Froebel invented various apparatus (called "gifts") to serve as educative toys; introduced activities (called "occupations"), such as drawing and clay modeling, which, along with the gifts, develop sense perception; emphasized song and spontaneous conversation to develop language and prescribed games, often played in a circle (to which figure he attached cosmic if obscure significance), to develop the sociality inherent in the child.

The stage of boyhood should be developed by instruction. The boy is becoming self-conscious; in order to develop steadiness of character, he should participate in the administration of the school through school government. The study of nature, stories, learning in groups, family work, making things—all these further steadiness of character and habits of intellectual readiness. Froebel insisted that instruction, the direction of development, should not aim at the practically useful but at that self-consciousness of integrated and developed powers which is the proper objective of individual and social evolution. About the stages of youth and maturity Froebel had little comment.

Froebel saw education—the early, spontaneous, and the later, but directed, unfolding of the essential powers of each individual—in a metaphysical setting, tinged with mysticism, obscurantism, and incoherence and indebted heavily to the absolute idealism of his day. The Absolute embraces everything and is continually evolving as force in nature and as mind in man. This cosmic evolution proceeds from action to reaction to equilibrium, from simple to complex, from unconsciousness to self-consciousness. Froebel identifies the Absolute with God and its evolution with his creation. Everything has a purpose that unifies it and that binds it into larger organic wholes, by virtue of evolution or creation. The evolution of the Absolute is reflected in miniature in that of humanity. The human race has developed through five stages, and the life of each individual reflects this racial and cosmic evolution. Education, Froebel thought, ought to enable this process to fulfill itself in each person without hindrance. It ought to be the minister to individuals of a cosmic and racial evolution.

The best life for man is the fullest realization of a consistent will—the consciousness of the best self that he can develop. This self-consciousness is awareness of purposes inherent in him; in becoming aware of them, man becomes free. Evil is the distortion by some external factor of a tendency native to the self; all tendencies are naturally good if allowed to develop into self-conscious, harmonious freedom. Although some education should direct, the fundamental early education is chiefly negative; that is, preventive of external obstruction to the development of natural tendencies.

Froebel's metaphysical and ethical doctrines inspired him to activity that had enormous practical effect upon the schools directly, and while the chief influence on his thought lies in the practical work of Pestalozzi, Immanuel Kant (1724–1804) influenced it indirectly, at least through the pervasive effect of his theories on German thought in general.

KANT. The impact on educational theory of the work of Pestalozzi and Froebel was an emphasis on developing individuality in the student, and this impact may be traced to the thought of Rousseau. In the work of Kant a greater optimism than Rousseau's gave a less individualistic objective to education.

Kant conceived of human nature in terms of three faculties: cognition, which organizes sensory elements into the orderly world of experience; desire, which exercises itself in an instinctive effort at lawless, egoistic domination over others; and will, which selects desires for realization according to a rule. Human society grows out of the exercise of these faculties. The instinctual desire for domination leads to conflict between individuals; the faculty of cognition yields knowledge about how this conflict can be avoided—by association in republics; and the will leads to actual societies of this kind for mutual protection. But between republics conflict breaks out anew; and in order to avoid it, these states tend to unite in a peaceful international community. This community is the natural result of the unimpeded development of human faculties; and since we must believe that all things develop their capacities fully, we must believe that it stands at the end of historical progress.

It is the ultimate objective of education not to advance the welfare of individual students, but to promote the realization of the peaceful international state as the embodiment of human perfection. Accordingly, teachers should not regard the economic or other success of their charges but should center attention upon the fullest possible development of their faculties. This development can be assured by supplying to the cognitive faculty the general truths it should use to organize sensory elements into nature as we experience it, by rigorously disciplining the faculty of desire in order to eliminate the instinct for lawless behavior, and by enabling the will freely to use the right rules in organizing the remaining desires. The result of such instruction will be a perfected character and intellect, which, through the progress of generations, will assist history to realize the educational ideal.

Kant's ethical theory supplies a criterion for the kind of conduct which makes the international state possible. It is conduct which embodies rules that can be generalized without absurdity—rules which fit into the famous "categorical imperative." "Break your promise when you wish to" is not such a rule; for if instead of applying it to your own desires alone, you try to imagine all persons using it in selecting some for realization, the notion of a promise completely disappears. The rule degenerates into the nonsensical "Break a promise which no one ever takes to be a promise when you wish to." "Always keep your promise" is a necessary moral rule, and like all rules which fit the categorical imperative it is so because we cannot imagine the generalization of its opposite without imagining something rationally absurd. In the international state the character of each person will be so perfected that each will act upon such a rule when it is necessary to make a moral choice. Thus, the state will be both realized and preserved. Kant's philosophy of morals, in this way, clarifies part of the notion of an ideal social order which education should subserve.

Kant's metaphysics makes a great deal of the distinction between two realms—the realm of things we can experience, or phenomena, and the realm of things which transcend experience, or noumena. Following Rousseau, Kant held that human beings dwell in both realms and that in the former their desires and actions are determined by natural laws, whereas in the latter they are governed by right rules or duties. To act rightly requires that a person freely employ a right rule and that he not act in a way determined by a law of nature. Hence, whenever one acts rightly he acts as a free citizen of the noumenal world—he freely applies a rule to his desires to decide which one to act upon. This proposition of Kant's ethical theory illumines his method of training the will; that is, his method of preventing the growth of habit and of requiring that children freely adopt a rule in some hypothetical situation of choice.

Kant's views about history provide a goal for his theory of education, and his ethical and metaphysical theories explain part of that ideal and the method proposed for arriving at it.

FICHTE. Rousseau's despair of achieving the national welfare led him to advocate the cultivation of individual self-sufficiency; and while it was no part of their theories, the effect of the work of Pestalozzi and of Froebel was to further attention to the individual student in the practice of education. Kant's enthusiasm for international well-being led him to advocate a future achievement for the entire race through the fostering of universal faculties rather than through the development of individuality. Enthusiasm for national existence as opposed both to individuality and to internationalism brought Johann Gottlieb Fichte (1762–1814) to advocate an objective more like the one Rousseau would have recommended if he had been more hopeful about the national institutions of his day.

Addressing the German people during the subjection of Prussia to Napoleon Bonaparte, Fichte urged that education be used to unite all Germans in a state that, through purity of race and character, would lead the world. Education was the only independent action allowed by the French; if all German children were separated from their parents, reared in a partially self-governing community in which each individual might learn directly the responsibilities of citizenship, taught through the energizing force of interest rather than by reward and punishment, and thus prepared for an adult life of wholehearted and unswerving duty, this possibility of independent action could be turned to the advantage of all Germany. It would lead to the creation of a reformed and unified German state, devoted to the right, and worthy (unlike others) of world dominance. This nationalistic objective of his somewhat fanciful proposals Fichte might have supported by his view that the best state is highly authoritarian—one in which the fulfillment of each man's duty to work is made possible by the state's provision of the opportunity and compensation for work and the complete control of the economy required by that guarantee. This socialistic ideal, in turn, he might have supported by his view that the physical world must be understood as the means and medium by use of which and in which duty becomes embodied in fact. This view is consonant with his metaphysical idealism, according to which the ego posits itself and its objects for the purpose of doing what it ought—a position Fichte developed out of his criticism of Kant's doctrine concerning noumena.

HERBART. Like Fichte, Johann Friedrich Herbart (1776–1841) gave much thought to the doctrine of noumena; but unlike him, he arrived at a kind of realism, to be described later, opposed to the metaphysical idealism Fichte, G. W. F. Hegel, and others made current in the Germany of his day. He relied upon it to advance an objective of education which assigns importance both to individuality and to sociality—both to being a person of the best possible sort and to being a citizen of the best possible society.

There are five criteria, the "moral ideas," all of which must be exhibited by a person with the best possible character and a society of the best possible sort. Applied to a person, the first two of these ideas are relations between his will and other aspects of his character, while the last three are relations between his will and other persons.

When one knows what he wills and approves of it, he is "inwardly free," and inward freedom is the only freedom men enjoy. When one's will is strong, directed toward many things, or "many-sided," and constituted by inclinations toward objectives systematically ordered by the teleological relations they bear to one another, he possesses "perfection." When one directs his will toward enabling the wills of others to be realized, for the sake of that realization rather than for his own benefit, he is "benevolent." The remaining two ideas apply not to wills alone but to the embodiment in action of one person's will with respect to others. When several persons deliberately live according to a principle or law, thus preventing conflict, each individual acts "rightly"; and when a person willfully benefits or harms another, the idea of "equity" or "requital" requires that a corresponding benefit or injury be visited upon the doer of the deed.

A society—a political state or group of any kind—to which the five moral ideas apply is one in which law prevails because of the general relinquishment of rights whose exercise leads to conflict; one in which there is a system of rewards which makes requital to each citizen for that relinquishment; one in which an administrative system exhibits benevolence by assuring to all the greatest satisfaction of will; one in which many interests or wills, both individual and collective, find coherent realization or perfection in a cultural system; and one in which the society, being "inwardly free," knows its own will and approves of it—a trait that requires a soul for society not unlike that of the individual person.

Assuming that if the individuals in a group acquire the moral ideas the group will also, Herbart holds that the immediate objective of education is to produce individuals who exhibit them; and the production of such persons consists in the appropriate use of truths of psychology. These truths describe the relations of ideas or representations, and Herbart is distinguished in the history of psychology as having been among the first to have endeavored to state those relations in a rigorous, mathematical way. He regarded the propositions of his psychology as based on introspection and as justified by metaphysical reflection. Released from its technical form, his psychology may be stated, in part, as follows.

Each idea, Herbart held, endeavors to preserve itself and succeeds in that endeavor to some degree, that is, *is* itself, more or less. The degree of its success depends upon its relations to other ideas, and these are of three kinds: of opposition, of mere dissimilarity, and of similarity. Red and blue (not-red) are opposed to each other, and short of some third idea that combines them, such as the idea of a substance red on one surface and blue on another, they cannot both be present in the same consciousness. Red and circular are merely dissimilar; consequently, they may both present themselves either in combination in a red circle or in simple juxtaposition or may be present separately. A red rose and a red apple are similar ideas; consequently, one may come to be attached to the other. The effort of each idea to preserve itself—an effort which cannot be completely canceled—succeeds insofar as we are conscious of the idea. The greater the success, the greater is the clarity of our awareness of it; the less the success, the dimmer our consciousness of it. But the degree of the success of any idea depends upon the aid and attack it sustains from others; so that the clarity or obscurity of any idea—its place with respect to the threshold that separates conscious from unconscious ideas (a piece of psychological apparatus made current by Herbart)—depends upon the context of other ideas in which it occurs. Where they oppose it and are stronger than it is, it disappears into unconsciousness and becomes an unconscious impulse, striving to emerge into consciousness the moment it is not prevented by the occurrence there of its stronger opposites. Where the context includes merely dissimilar ideas, it may remain in consciousness, but not for long. The flux of experience will soon bring ideas into consciousness that will drive it down into the dark through opposition or keep it in the light by uniting with it through similarity. Where other ideas are similar, they come to its aid, forming a strong union that, so long as it remains, draws to itself its similars, inward from new sensory perceptions and upward from the storehouse of unconscious old sensations. Such a union of ideas is an "apperceptive mass" or "circle of thought"—another piece of psychological apparatus Herbart helped to make current. The psychology upon which Herbart based his educational procedures informs us that new pieces of information can be mastered only insofar as they become united with some apperceptive mass of ideas and that insofar as they are not so united, they are transformed into unconscious strivings, able to present themselves to consciousness only when a lack of their opposites there allows it or the presence of their similars there draws them up into it.

A person consists of ideas that dwell on two levels. On the level of consciousness he is a succession of ideas, each of which originates either in physiological activity or in sensation and quickly unites with some apperceptive mass or is pressed down into unconsciousness by the success of others striving to occupy consciousness. On the level of unconsciousness are all the ideas whose weakness or whose lack of similarity to those in consciousness chains them in that dark domain. On the level of consciousness the succession of ideas is punctuated by acts of attention. These are simply ideas in which we are, more or less, completely "absorbed." Some, like loud sounds, are involuntary; others, like highly discriminated shades of color or purposefully held thoughts, are voluntary. As objects of attention these ideas are isolated, but they either quickly become unconscious or acquire "meaning" and connection by drawing up into consciousness those "circles of thought," or apperceptive masses of similar ideas, in whose context they acquire significance. An idea attended to much or clearly, together with its circle of thought, is an interest—a desire to bring into existence that which it represents in some future time. The apperceptive mass to which the idea belongs, together with the relations of that mass to others, presents a framework for its suppression, its mere entertainment, or its realization and makes it a desire rather than a free-floating fancy—a part of the person rather than a casual caprice. An act of will is a desire together with the intention that what it refers to should occur. The ego is the central point of the person—the present idea from which memories radiate into the past, interests (desires, acts of will, etc.) into the future, and to which entire apperceptive masses are drawn from the domain of the unconscious or forced down into it.

Ideas, thus arranged and centered, exhaust the person as an introspectible entity. They result from the exercise of no faculties (Herbart seems both to have used this concept and to have declared it nonsignificant), for the soul possesses none. To think of something, to desire it, to will it, to have a feeling toward it—all this is nothing but, in different ways, to be conscious of an idea as connected with others.

Herbart's view of the nature of a person provided him with a method of education which became widespread both in theory and in practice. Education, he held, is instruction, and instruction should consist in four steps. (His followers made them five, prefixing "preparation" for it to "presentation" of an idea.) First, the idea or information to be learned must be "presented" to the student's clear attention; second, the idea thus presented must be allowed to draw up from the student's unconsciousness all ideas whatsoever whose similarity attracts them to it; third, through comparison most of these associations should be eliminated in favor of those which give the idea its proper meaningfulness in a circle of thought; last, to strengthen the idea's bonds in that circle, the student should be brought to "apply" the idea to new situations. This procedure, based upon the flux of ideas from

the center of attention into the apperceptive mass to which they belong, gives the student mastery over new information; and mastery, or the ability to reproduce ideas, is the purpose of instruction.

To instruct a person is to construct him; since feelings, desires, etc., are all ideas, providing the student with ideas is providing him with all the materials of personality. But the instructor, by arranging the conditions in which the student acquires new ideas, determines not merely the materials out of which he is formed but also the organization or form those materials assume. And a person, as we have seen, is simply ideas organized in a certain way.

But education is not merely the construction of a person; it is also the effort to construct one who exhibits the five moral ideas. Herbart refers to this aim as the production of "character," and he deals chiefly with the production of "perfection," or "many-sidedness." If the child's attention is called to many things in his own experience, and if the store of this experience is supplemented vicariously through communication with other persons—a communication based on sympathy with them—his interests will naturally become numerous, and by control of the natural mechanism of apperception, well organized and strong. Perfection of will or character, tinged with an inevitable individuality, is a necessary ingredient in the objective of education, but it is also essential to sensible choices in adult life.

Herbart advanced a metaphysical view as a ground for his psychology. Reality is neither mental, as the prevalent idealism held, nor physical in the sense of being extended in space and time. Its characteristics are quite unknowable except for those of being independent of our minds and composed of perfectly simple entities (*Realen*), not unlike the monads of Gottfried Wilhelm Leibniz. These simple reals conflict with one another from time to time, and on such occasions, there occurs an effort on the part of each to preserve itself from destruction. In a body, this act of self-preservation is its state; in a soul, such an act of self-preservation is an idea that represents, so far as that is possible, the attacking entity. Being simple, the soul cannot engage in more than one act at once; hence the struggle of ideas against one another and the inevitable fall into unconsciousness or into the unity of some apperceptive mass.

The ethical theory by which Herbart justified the five moral ideas as the standard for personal and social existence is one which holds that moral judgments are a species of aesthetic judgments. As such, they neither need nor can be given justification. The human taste prefers persons and societies that live up well to the five ideas, but the validity of the standard by which they are measured is still nothing different in kind from the taste we enjoy for music, painting, and the natural landscape.

J. S. MILL. In determining the objective for education, John Stuart Mill (1806–1873) disregarded several distinctions emphasized by his predecessors. He ignored the distinction between national and international well-being, speaking of society without qualification, and he argued that individual and social interests might be identified. But his work resembles that of Herbart in some ways: He endeavored to make use of psychology to achieve his educational objective, and the psychology he employed, although it regarded the elements of the mind in a different way, attributed relations to them—those of association—not altogether unlike those Herbart thought he had found.

Mill conceived of a human being in terms of a body and mind, but although they occur in his thought he scarcely makes use of the ideas of substance and of faculty in understanding human nature. The body, with the help of external things, determines what our sensations are like, and it harbors physiological structures which cause us to find activities and things of certain kinds instinctually pleasant or painful. The mind is a series of sensations and ideas with attendant feelings and emotions, held together by connections of an associative kind. Conscious elements are connected in these ways when they have been associated in past experience in certain circumstances. Under these conditions, when one element recurs in consciousness it brings its associates with it. The conditions of association are never repeated from one person to another; hence, every human being is unique.

In his *Utilitarianism* Mill holds that the best society is one in which there is the greatest amount of happiness for the greatest number of people. He understands happiness as constituted by pleasure properly proportioned between higher and lower activities, individual self-realization, and fulfillment of duty.

The chief purpose of education is to bring individuals closer to this social ideal. Careful attention to the content of the curriculum can develop the proper proportion between higher and lower desires and consequently between higher and lower pleasures. The method of instruction can ensure individual self-realization by making room for free discussion and personal discovery of truth. The most difficult task is so to associate egoistic pleasures with fulfillment of duties as to connect them in all subsequent experience. The success of this effort will be a person who finds pleasure in doing what he ought even though doing so involves personal sacrifice. Compulsory elementary education for all and higher education for those who can benefit from it will go a long way toward a society in which happiness is at its maximum.

Mill supported his theory of education by providing a justification of the utilitarian ideal by a theory of meaning according to which free discussion of the consequences of our ideas is the best way to make their meaning clear and by a theory of knowledge according to which we can, by using his famous canons of empirical inquiry, come to be perfectly certain about the sequences of things in nature whose use enables the development of that type of character which will advance the good society.

SPENCER. Herbert Spencer (1820–1903) advanced as the objective for education a life for the individual suffused with pleasure and as full as possible. Its fullness consists in the satisfaction of five kinds of interests, listed here in order of decreasing importance: those pertaining to one's own preservation directly, to it indirectly as does making one's living to begetting and rearing a family, to political and social affairs, and to aesthetic enjoyments. The only knowledge that enables the adequate satisfaction of these interests is scientific, and education of the intellect should be concerned to propagate it rather than knowledge of the classics. Moral education should consist in allowing the natural consequences of mistakes to strengthen knowledge of how to satisfy these interests, and physical education should provide a body that would further their satisfaction. Each individual is charged with finding his own happiness, and the function of government should be merely that of preventing others from infringing upon his pursuit of it. Consequently, education itself should be privately sought and conducted rather than socially compelled and supported.

Spencer held the metaphysical view that reality is unknowable, that it manifests itself in the individual life as phenomena—some vivid and some faint—and that it is expressed in the cosmic dimension as evolution—as change from homogeneous to heterogeneous conditions through differentiation and integration. In evolution survival goes to the fittest; and the fittest are those who find the phenomenon of vivid pleasure associated with the useful and utility in those actions that bring about or constitute "complete living." Education should assist in realizing this end that, in any case, evolution marks out for man.

DEWEY. In the work of John Dewey (1859–1952), the most influential of the twentieth-century philosophers of education, Mill's ideal for education is somewhat simplified and his doctrine of the meaning of ideas, together with Spencer's emphasis on the utility of knowledge, transformed into a criterion for distinguishing knowledge from belief. As we have seen, Mill thought that happiness consists of three distinct factors—pleasure, duty, and self-realization—and he held that education should promote the greatest amount of happiness for the largest number of people. In the place of pleasure Dewey put activity that is satisfactory to the person acting; in the place of duty, the most satisfactory activity; and in the place of self-realization, the fact that the most satisfactory activity is that which the individual most genuinely prefers. The best life, Dewey held, is one in which the most genuinely satisfactory activity is most widespread throughout society. This view depends on his view of human nature.

Human nature cannot be understood in terms of substance and faculty, for there are no such things. Consequently, there can be no single set of activities that characterize all human life, as traditional philosophers and psychologists have supposed. All human beings begin life as biological organisms, filled with unformed energy or impulse, ready to assume whatever direction experience assigns; and since each environment generates a different experience of the world—a different set of patterns of response to it—human beings vary as much as do their environments. The habits that impulse takes on sometimes cease to provide a satisfactory release for it, and in these situations intelligence enters into life to solve the problems thus created. We form hypotheses as to how impulses can be reorganized, look forward to the consequences in action, select those whose anticipation makes us prefer them, act to secure them, and thus test the hypothesis from which they were inferred. Intelligence is the master habit of readjusting others when they break down, and while it characterizes human beings, it does so in no specific way since its possession brings with it no special knowledge but only the ability to acquire any knowledge whatever by finding it in the consequences of action.

Dewey thought of society in terms of group habits. A nation is composed of political parties, religious institutions, courts, etc., and each of these is a complex habit of acting in which many people take part. A society is a set of group habits or institutions that fit together. A good society is one which, by virtue of the ways in which its subordinate institutions fit together, enables growth in satisfaction for its citizens.

Education, according to Dewey, is the process of imposing on the impulse of infants the society or the set of group habits into which the infants are born; it is the perpetuation of society. But it is also a good deal more. For since one of the habits to be imposed upon impulse is that of acting intelligently, education must also foster the reform of society toward an ever better condition. To perpetuate intelligence is to begin its use, and the schools are thus the basis for social progress.

Since there is no single set of abilities running throughout human nature, there is no single curriculum which all should undergo. Rather, the schools should teach everything that anyone is interested in learning. Since a child can learn nothing without using his intelligence, and since this comes into play only when some habit breaks down, he should be inspired with interest in the subject matter he should learn and then made to feel some problem in not actuating that interest or habit. This method requires individual attention to discover particular interests and capabilities. Since the child learns best when he is working with others, he should be given a certain measure of participation in school affairs. In the light of these strictures on curriculum, method, and administration Dewey hoped to produce a child highly endowed with intelligence and disposed to reform society in the direction of the ideal of continually growing satisfactions.

Dewey's ethical ideal was advanced as a justification for this pedagogical objective. To be morally good is to be a set of consequences, deliberately intended and capable of satisfying impulse better than would any other set to which it is preferred; it is a preferred activity. To say that such activity satisfies impulse better than does some other which is rejected is to say that it makes possible more satisfactions in oneself and others than does the other—that it contains the possibility of greater growth. Democracy is a better society than any other because it permits more satisfaction of impulse on the part of more people than does any other. And the intelligent person leads a better individual life than does one who acts from some other habit, such as superstition, because his life contains the opportunity for more satisfactions than does that of one who is hemmed in by dogma. The criterion of growth shows that the objective of education ought to be the democratic society and the intelligent man.

Dewey's theory of knowledge lends support to the reformist tendency in education. The truth of a proposition is its utility, and to know something is to be aware of how to use the known proposition to secure some desirable consequence. Consequently, any genuine teaching will result, if successful, in someone's knowing how to bring about a better condition of things than existed earlier. Knowledge is knowing how to do what is useful—a view that may have resulted from Dewey's consideration of Spencer and Mill. This theory of knowledge helps to give the pragmatic flavor to Dewey's philosophy of education.

Dewey's metaphysical reflection helps in the same direction. Traditional metaphysics, such as Plato's, has erred in supposing that truth is a passive apprehension of the real and that its object is eternally separated from the vicissitudes of experience. Traditional metaphysical reflection has forgotten that to mean something is to act to secure certain consequences, and it has therefore overlooked the truth that knowing what is real consists in meaning it or in acting in a certain way to bring about certain consequences. What is real is a set of experiences, each of which is meant by some agent and all of which are connected together in one thing or event by his activity. Dewey used this notion of what is real to justify his method of learning by doing, his view of the curriculum as whatever interests of each student enable him to organize into a unity on his own, and of method as the procedure for arousing interest in organizing or reorganizing the elements of a subject matter.

In Plato's philosophy of education the supernatural realm of the Forms, by lending validity to the just person and the just state, supported the program of education. In St. Augustine's work the educational ideal was organized wholly around God and the theological view of his relation to things; a similar description applies to Thomas Aquinas's thought about education. Comenius also centered his philosophy of education around religious and theological doctrines, but his insistence on the future perfection of human life on earth and on the observation of nature in the search for effective teaching methods marks a beginning in the process of naturalizing the wholehearted supernatural Christian ideal of his predecessors.

Locke found a basis for the goal of education in God's will, but the national welfare, which God's law or the law of nature promotes, and the analysis of it partly in terms of pleasure are additional worldly conditions whose emphasis constitutes a different facet of the disintegration of the supernatural ideal. Rousseau held that God exists, but the chief justification of his objective for education—an internally peaceful life apart from society—lies not in God's having ordained it but in the notion of the general will and its absence from national institutions. Froebel, a follower of Pestalozzi and of Rousseau, made much use of religious language, but by identifying God and the Absolute he removed philosophy of education still further than did Rousseau from a religious center.

Kant held that we cannot avoid belief in God, although he also held that the belief can have no experiential content; but this position effects his educational goal in no way. The chief moral component of that goal is the categorical imperative—a notion Kant wished to conceive wholly in logical terms. The peaceful international state is not justified by being God's will but by being the result of a social life which embodies duty and which constitutes the perfect realization of our intellectual and moral powers. Fichte found the ideal for education in a national existence that would assure Germany of a position of world importance, and Herbart held that individuals and societies that are morally worthwhile are those that satisfy the aesthetic demands of human beings. Spencer made no use of religious propositions in his philosophy of education; nor did Mill, although he regarded great religions as great works of the imagination. Dewey's ideal of a society, containing the possibility of most growth in satisfaction, is completely devoid of religious affiliation. He would probably have said that interest in achieving it can become religious—that, indeed, it should—but by "religious" he would have meant little more than enthusiastic.

The history of philosophy of education reflects a movement evident in other phases of thought—a successive contribution on the part of antiquity to the Christian ideal for transmitting culture from one generation to another and then a gradual elimination from that ideal of supernatural and Christian elements. Of course, at no time has there been a wholehearted and single-minded devotion to any ideal, and there are many who do not accept naturalism today. Nonetheless, one way of understanding the history of philosophy of education is to regard the attitude of philosophers toward the justification and explanation of educational theory as having been expressed first in Plato's classic supernaturalism, next in Augustine's Christian supernaturalism, and then as undergoing a gradual alteration into the wholly non-Christian and naturalistic view represented by John Dewey.

See also Philosophy of Education, Contemporary Issues; Philosophy of Education: Epistemological Issues in; Philosophy of Education: Ethical and Political Issues in.

Bibliography

INDIVIDUAL WORKS

Augustine. "De Ordine." In *Ancient Christian Writers; The Works of the Fathers in Translation*, edited by Johannes Quasten and Joseph C. Plumpe. Vol. V, *Lord's Sermon on the Mount*. Westminster, MD, 1950.

Augustine. "The Teacher." In *Ancient Christian Writers; The Works of the Fathers in Translation*, edited by Johannes Quasten and Joseph C. Plumpe. Vol. XI. *Greatness of the Soul [and] The Teacher*. Westminster, MD, 1950.

Comenius, John Amos. *The Great Didactic*. Translated by M. W. Keatinge. London, 1896.

Comenius, John Amos. *The Way of Light*. Translated by E. T. Campagnac. London, 1938.

Dewey, John. *Democracy and Education*. New York: Macmillan, 1916.

Fichte, Johann Gottlieb. *Addresses to the German Nation*. Translated by R. H. Jones and G. H. Turnbull. Liverpool, 1922.

Froebel, Friedrich. *The Education of Man*. Translated by W. N. Hailmann. New York, 1887.

Herbart, Johann Friedrich. *Outlines of Educational Doctrine*. Translated by Alexis F. Lange. London, 1901.

Herbart, Johann Friedrich. *Science of Education, Its General Principles Deduced from Its Aim*. Translated by Henry M. Felkin and Emmie Felkin. Boston, 1893.

Herbart, Johann Friedrich. *A Text-book in Psychology*. Translated by Margaret K. Smith. New York, 1894.

Kant, Immanuel. "Lecture Notes on Pedagogy." In *The Educational Theory of Immanuel Kant*, edited and translated by Edward Franklin Buchner. Philadelphia, 1908. Also translated by Annette Churton as *Education*. Ann Arbor, MI, 1960.

Kant, Immanuel. "The Natural Principle of the Political Order Considered in Connection with the Idea of a Universal Cosmopolitan History." In *Kant's Principles of Politics*, edited and translated by W. Hastie. Edinburgh, 1891.

Kant, Immanuel. "Perpetual Peace." In *Kant's Principles of Politics*, edited by W. Hastie. Edinburgh, 1891.

Locke, John. *Second Treatise of Civil Government*.

Locke, John, "Some Thoughts concerning Education." In *Locke on Education*, edited by R. H. Quick. London, 1913.

Mill, John Stuart. "On Genius." *Monthly Repository* 6 (1832): 649–659. Partly reprinted in Kingsley Price, *Education and Philosophical Thought*, 449–459. Boston, 1962.

Mill, John Stuart. *On Liberty*.

Mill, John Stuart. *Utilitarianism*.

Pestalozzi, Heinrich. *How Gertrude Teaches Her Children*. Translated by L. E. Holland and F. C. Turner. London, 1894.

Plato. *Republic*. In *Dialogues of Plato*. Translated by Benjamin Jowett, 4th ed. Oxford, 1953.

Quintilian. *Institutio Oratoria*. Translated by H. E. Butler as *The Training of an Orator*. 4 vols. New York, 1920–1922. Loeb Classical Library.

Rousseau, Jean-Jacques. "Considerations concerning the Government of Poland and Its Projected Reform." Edited and translated by Kingsley Price in Ch. IV of *Education and Philosophical Thought*. Boston, 1962.

Rousseau, Jean-Jacques. *A Discourse upon the Origin and Foundation of the Inequality among Mankind*. London, 1761.

Spencer, Herbert. *Education, Intellectual, Moral and Physical*. London, 1861; rev. ed., 1883.

HISTORICAL SURVEYS

Boyd, William. *The History of Western Education*. London, 1952.

Eby, Frederick. *The Development of Modern Education*. New York: Prentice-Hall, 1952.

Laurie, S. S. *Studies in the History of Educational Opinion from the Renaissance*. Cambridge, U.K.: Cambridge University Press, 1903.

Windelband, Wilhelm. *A History of Philosophy*. Translated by James H. Tufts. New York, 1950.

CONTEMPORARY LITERATURE

Adler, Mortimer J., and Milton Mayer. *The Revolution in Education*. Chicago: University of Chicago Press, 1958.

Bode, Boyd Henry. *Progressive Education at the Crossroads*. New York and Chicago: Newson, 1938.

Brameld, Theodore Burghard Hurt. *Patterns of Educational Philosophy; A Democratic Interpretation*. Yonkers-on-Hudson, NY: World Book, 1950.

Broudy, Harry S. *Building a Philosophy of Education*. 2nd ed. Englewood Cliffs, NJ: Prentice-Hall, 1961.

Brubacher, John S. *Modern Philosophies of Education*. New York: McGraw-Hill, 1939; 3rd ed., 1963.

Dewey, John. *Experience and Education*. New York: Macmillan, 1938.

Henry, Nelson B., ed. *National Society for the Study of Education Forty-first Yearbook*. Chicago, 1941. Pt. I, *Philosophies of Education*.

Henry, Nelson B., ed. *National Society for the Study of Education Fifty-fourth Yearbook*. Chicago, 1955. Pt. I, *Modern Philosophies and Education*.

Hutchins, Robert M. *Education for Freedom*. Baton Rouge: Louisiana State University Press, 1943.

Kilpatrick, W. H. *The Philosophy of Education*. New York, 1951.

Maritain, Jacques. *Education at the Crossroads*. New Haven, CT: Yale University Press, 1943.

Morris, Van Cleve. *Existentialism in Education; What It Means*. New York: Harper and Row, 1966.

Nunn, Thomas Percy. *Education: Its Data and First Principles*, 3rd ed., rev. New York and London, 1962.

O'Connor, D. J. *Introduction to the Philosophy of Education*. New York: Philosophical Library, 1957.

Peters, R. S. *Authority, Responsibility and Education*. London, 1959.

Phenix, Philip H. *Philosophy of Education*. New York, 1958.

Price, Kingsley. *Education and Philosophical Thought*. Boston: Allyn and Bacon, 1962.

Reid, L. A. *Philosophy and Education*. London, 1962.

Scheffler, Israel. *The Language of Education*. Springfield, IL, 1960.

Smith, B. Othanel, and Robert H. Ennis, eds. *Language and Concepts in Education*. Chicago, 1961.

Ulich, Robert. *Philosophy of Education*. New York, 1961.

Walton, John, and James L. Kuethe, eds. *The Discipline of Education*. Madison: University of Wisconsin Press, 1963.

Kingsley Price (1967)

PHILOSOPHY OF FILM

In one way, the philosophy of film is almost as old as the technology of film; in another way, it is a phenomenon that only emerges fully a century after the earliest screenings of films in 1895. Philosophizing about film has been with us for around a century in the form of the lively debates about the nature of the new medium that sprang up in the wake of its invention. As early as 1907 Henri Bergson had adopted the *cinematographic illusion* as a key metaphor of the scientific, and classical philosophical, conception of time and movement. And in 1916 we see the publication of the first extended philosophical treatise on film, as medium and art form, with the publication of Hugo Münsterberg's (1863–1916) *The Photoplay: A Psychological Study* (2002). So the two-way traffic between film and philosophy—the new medium as a source of philosophical insight and the application of philosophy to the problems thrown up by it—begins.

The publication of Münsterberg's study inaugurated the tradition of *film theory*—reflection on the nature of the medium of film, philosophical in all but name, but typically written by filmmakers, writers, art historians, and cultural critics rather than philosophers per se. Film theorists were preoccupied with the ontology of cinema and with the nature of representation and expression in film, and discussion of these matters typically revolved around the concept of *medium specificity*—the notion, in Münsterberg's words, that the new technology constituted a "specific form of artistic endeavor" (Münsterberg 2002, p. 65) with specific properties and potentials, which demarcated it from the established arts. Münsterberg contrasted film—the *photoplay*—with the stage play, and argued that the key to the power of film was its ability to express human intentional states, such as attention, memory, imagination, and emotions. "The close-up," wrote Münsterberg of one of the key techniques of film, "has objectified in our world of perception our mental act of attention and by it has furnished art with a means which far transcends the power of any theater stage" (Münsterberg 2002, p. 87). This principle of contrast with established art forms, which was ubiquitous in discussions of film through at least its first half century, arose from the desire to demonstrate that film was not merely a technological curiosity, a fairground novelty, or a means of recording and reproduction that might serve to disseminate paintings or plays, but, precisely, a legitimate art form on a par with any of the established arts.

This emphasis on the specificity of film was a legacy of philosophical aesthetics and especially the attempts from the eighteenth century onward to establish a *system of the arts*. Two of the most significant theorists, for example, filmmaker Sergei Eisenstein (1898–1948); and Rudolf Arnheim (1904–, who would become best known as a psychologist of art, made significant allusions to G. E. Lessing's (1729–1781) *Laocoön: An Essay on the Limits of Painting and Poetry* (1766). Lessing had argued that poetry and painting each have their characteristic domains of representation—the temporal and the spatial—and corresponding limits to what they can effectively represent. In his 1938 essay "A New *Laocoön*," Arnheim follows Lessing's example by arguing that theater and cinema, similarly, need to be understood as distinct media with distinct essential features and thus different aesthetic advantages and deficits. Without denying the existence of 'composite' artistic forms—such as opera, in which drama and music are combined—Arnheim argues that, ultimately, theatre is the art of dialogue, while cinema is the art of the moving visual image. Formulating his ideas in the wake of the introduction of the *talkie* in the late 1920s, Arnheim argued that the addition of speech to the movies was a kind of contamination or corruption of the medium proper.

Eisenstein developed the notion of *montage*, which he regarded as the definitive feature of the art of film, through both his filmmaking practice and his theoretical writings, as well as in dialogue with other major filmmakers and theorists of the period—including Lev Kuleshov (1899–1970), V. I. Pudovkin (1893–1953), Dziga Vertov (1896–1954), and Béla Balázs (1884–1949). Initially referring narrowly to the editing of shots, Eisenstein widened the reference of montage to include any technique that involved the interaction of more basic elements: In this sense, one can speak of montage within a shot or between whole sections of a film as much as the montage between two shots literally cut together.

Eisenstein's essay on the *Laocoön* makes reference to Lessing's work in a manner quite different from Arnheim. Where Arnheim draws an analogy between painting and poetry, on the one hand, and cinema and theater, on the other, for Eisenstein, it is the substance of Lessing's claims about painting and poetry and the relationship of cinema to these two forms that is at stake. Cinema—or more particularly, montage—synthesizes the temporality of poetry with the spatiality of painting. Eisenstein ranges widely and generously across literature, painting, theater, and music, and where Arnheim and Münsterberg are concerned to distinguish the characteristics of theater and cinema, Eisenstein more often than not discerns protocinematic techniques in these other art forms. The specificity of cinema thus emerges for Eisenstein more in terms of the realization and culmination of techniques evident in older media and art forms rather than in the addition of a new medium of art, which stands alongside the traditional forms.

Münsterberg, Eisenstein, and Arnheim were all rooted in the era of *silent* cinema. André Bazin (1918–1958) is widely regarded as the first major theorist of the sound era, and while he, like his precursors, was concerned with the specificity of cinema and often explored the nature of cinema by comparative examination of other media, his perspective on film marks a departure from those theories emerging from the silent era. In "The Ontology of the Photographic Image" (1945), Bazin argues that what is distinctive of and crucial to film is its ability to *capture* the phenomenal world, in the most literal sense; a film is like a fingerprint of reality. Bazin does not wish to deny that films are, like all works of art, the products of those who design them. Greta Garbo (1905–1990) may have been carefully groomed and lit for the camera, but it is still, in a strong sense, the real Garbo that we see in the film. Thus, in contrast to Münsterberg's focus on the rendering of intentional states in films, the distinctive capacity of film as an art for Bazin lies in the way in which human intentionality is bypassed at a certain vital moment in the production of a film, allowing reality to impress itself upon the film unmediated by human intentions or interests.

In *Image and Mind*, Gregory Currie terms this dimension of film and photography "natural counterfactual dependence," which contrasts with the "intentional counterfactual dependence" of painting (Currie 1995, p. 55): The properties of a photograph or a film depend directly on visible properties of the scene before the camera whereas the properties of a painting of the same scene are "mediated by the beliefs of the artist" (Currie 1995, p. 54). And this facet of film is something that filmmakers can facilitate, as in the practice of location shooting where the artifice of studio set construction and the control that such artifice brings with it is foregone in favor of the relative unruliness of real spaces. Such techniques bring out the special kind of realism that (on this account) is inherent in the medium as such.

CONTEMPORARY PHILOSOPHY OF FILM AND THE PROBLEM OF SPECIFICITY

Given the existence of a rich tradition of film theory—the surface of which is only scratched here—in what sense is it true to say, that the philosophy of film only coalesced as a field of debate a century after the invention of the medium? Following Bergson, there have been other important contributions by professional philosophers, including Maurice Merleau-Ponty (1908–1961), Bazin's contemporary and an influence upon him. The American philosopher Stanley Cavell has made a distinctive contribution (to which we will return) by developing and elaborating an ontology of cinema incorporating Bazin's key insights. And there have been other isolated philosophical essays on film. But it is not until the 1990s that a continuous debate about film emerges among professional philosophers, eventually establishing itself as a subdomain within aesthetics and the philosophy of art—a field of debate sufficiently developed to warrant a separate entry in this encyclopedia. Two rather divergent areas of debate have emerged that, for good or ill, generally fall in line with the division between modern analytic and Continental philosophy. In relation to the latter, there is a substantial literature around the work of Gilles Deleuze. Alongside the literature on and by Deleuze stands work by other contemporary Continental philosophers, such as Jean-François Lyotard, Paul Virilio (1932–) and Slavoj Žižek (1949–). Through much of this work, the influence of psychoanalysis is evident.

Deleuze's approach to cinema, as advanced in his two-volume *Cinema* (1992), is based on a fundamental revaluation of Bergson's remarks on the relationship between cinema, movement, and time. In *Creative Evolution* (1907), Bergson argued that both classical philosophical and modern scientific conceptions of movement in fact eliminated movement as an authentic phenomenon by representing motion as a series of immobile instants strung together. The mechanism of cinema realized this conception in literal terms: a succession of still frames which, when projected in sufficiently quick succession, generate an impression or illusion of movement. Deleuze argues, however, that the cinema also enables, and is a part of, the recognition of movement as an irreducible phenomenon. And as cinema evolves over the course of the twentieth century, it provides us not only with an image of movement but one of time—in the Bergsonian sense of *duration* of time as a continuous, experiential whole.

The conception of the *philosophy of film*, and of philosophy more broadly embodied by Deleuze's approach to cinema, is—at least on its own understanding—in marked contrast to more widely accepted notions of philosophy. Rejecting the idea that the philosophy of film *reflects on* the phenomenon of film, Deleuze argues instead that the philosophy of film—like philosophy more generally—is a creative activity and in this sense is parallel to the activity of filmmaking rather than standing above or outside it. Where filmmakers create through the medium of cinema, in the form of sequences of movement and duration, philosophers create concepts. Deleuze is thus eager not only to play up the creative character of philosophy as he understands it but to emphasize the conceptual value of filmmaking.

The growing literature on cinema within Anglo-American aesthetics comprises the second major branch of contemporary philosophy of film. The main intellectual reference points here are analytic philosophy of mind and language, cognitive psychology, and Wittgenstein. The two contemporary conversations on the philosophy of film are largely separate even if the participants in each can hear the other conversation and occasionally might even talk to each other. There are certainly points of connection: Deleuze's claim that the cinema provides us with an image of movement resonates with the debate in analytic philosophy of film concerning the sense in which the motion we see in a film is real (rather than merely illusory) while his claim that the postwar era witnesses the flourishing of a cinema that privileges time rather than movement echoes the claim within Anglo-American film theory that much art cinema liberates time and space from their traditional subordination to the demands of narrative.

Among the philosophers who have helped to establish the analytic strand of the philosophy of film, none have contributed more than Noël Carroll (1947–); and among the many orthodoxies that Carroll has challenged is the very idea of medium specificity.

In "Forget the Medium!" (2003), Carroll questions both the coherence of the concept *the* medium of film as well as the prescriptivism that typically follows on from the positing of specific qualities that are thought to be distinctive of the medium. He points out that if we think of the medium in terms of the tools and materials of an artistic practice, few, if any, art forms will be defined by a single, fixed medium of expression (and, more radically, he suggests that some art forms may not have *a medium* at all). *Painting* really encompasses a whole range of possible means of marking a surface in order to create a visual design, just as the creation of music encompasses a vast array of instruments for shaping sound. We can, however, understand why earlier film theorists may have focused on the idea of a new medium since the technology of film ushered in a type of depiction that was different in kind, and not merely in degree, from anything that preceded it: moving, photographic depiction. The developments in the basic technology of film were, for the first thirty years of cinema, all refinements of this technology, and so it could appear to have an underlying stability and unity that made it apt to think of in terms of a single medium.

Later technological developments, however, begin to strain the concept of a single and stable medium—Arnheim's alarm at the coming of synchronous sound was shared by many filmmakers and theorists of the time. The advent of television and video raises equally difficult questions—if film is a unique and distinctive medium, should we posit still another new medium of the electronic moving image? And still another one for the digital moving image? Many have answered these questions in the affirmative, erecting boundaries between the various types of moving image. The emergence of new moving image technologies has often led to attempts at distinguishing the specificity of each of these media—such specificity usually taking account not only of the material nature of the technology but of its institutional and social deployment: Thus, television is said to have its own specificity, distinct from that of film, not only because of the electronic basis of broadcasting but the corporate nature of most television output; its continuous *flow*; and the small-screen, domestic context of television viewing. Video, in turn, has been defined dialectically against television, focussing on the portability, immediacy, capacity for instant replay and live feedback, and nonnarrative experimentation characterizing video art and activist video.

Carroll, however, contends that the positing of a succession of media *specificities* only compounds the error of thinking of film as a medium and proposes, instead, that we engage in some conceptual pruning and relandscaping. In place of the medium of film, we should think in terms of the *art form of the moving image*. This superordinate category captures what was new when cinema first emerged and what continues to mark works of this type off from paintings, photographs, operas, novels, and so forth, but it does so without tying it to any particular technology.

From another angle, the emergence of computer-generated imagery as a pervasive feature of mainstream narrative filmmaking has led some theorists to argue that there really was something importantly distinctive about the prototypical live action, photographic film characteristic of the first century of cinema but that that distinctiveness is now disappearing. As the computerized rendering of moving picture settings and characters becomes commonplace—whether through the modification of a live action source or through digital creation from the ground up—the Bazinian idea of film as an imprint of reality is weakened. As we watch *The Lord of the Rings*, we really cannot be sure which parts of the image were created through the act of photographic recording (of a set, a real location, a performer) and which were generated digitally; all we can be confident of is that the film as a whole represents a blending of these methods. As a consequence, according to Lev Manovich (1960–) in *The Language of New Media*: "cinema can no longer be clearly distinguished from animation." Far from being distinct from painting, by virtue of the direct causal relationship between image and referent, cinema in the digital age has become, instead, "a subgenre of painting" (Manovich, p. 295). Manovich's view of digital media forms the mirror image of and complement to the realist ontology of film favored by Currie, for whom both animation and abstract film are, at best, marginal instances of film.

OTHER DEBATES

So we find in contemporary philosophy of film a continued debate about the very idea of *film*, as a unified phenomenon and coherent field of study. However, there are a multitude of other debates underway, intersecting at various angles with arguments about the ontology of the medium. The themes and questions being addressed include the following:

(1) *The perception of moving images.* What do we see when we look at a moving photographic image? Do we see a representation? Or is such a moving image *transparent*, in the sense that we see the objects depicted through the moving image, as Kendall Walton (1939–) has argued? Do we *imagine seeing* that which is depicted, or do we engage in *perceptual imagining*, as Currie contends, in which we imagine that certain things are true, based on the moving images we see, but we do not imagine seeing those things? To what extent is our ability to comprehend moving pictures dependent on certain natural perceptual capacities and to what extent on learned conventions?

(2) *Identification, emotional response and ethics.* In what sense and to what extent might we be said to *identify* with the characters, or the camera, when we watch a film? Do we typically empathize or sympathize with characters? Are we subject, in any sense, to an *illusion*? Are our emotional responses to film largely irrational and paradoxical, or is there a kind of rationality to them? Do these emotions have a sig-

nificant relationship to the ethical value of cinema—its ability, in small or large ways, either to corrupt or to educate? Does the medium of film, or particular forms of filmmaking, embody ideological values and beliefs, such as those bearing on gender or ethnic identity?

(3) *Authorship, intention, and expression.* Given the collective basis of almost all film production, can a film be *authored* in just the same way as a poem or a painting? Does the fact of multiple authorship affect the expressive capacities of film, relative to other art forms, or the way in which we interpret and appreciate films?.

(4) *Fiction and nonfiction.* How does the psychology of watching fiction differ from the psychology of watching documentaries? Does a filmic fiction share more with a novel than a documentary film; does a documentary share more with written history or reportage than it does with a fiction film? Is there a sense in which all films have a documentary dimension?.

FILM AS PHILOSOPHY

One important question that has become a focus of debate asks: To what extent might film be a vehicle of philosophy as opposed to its subject? Can film serve as a distinct medium through which the act of philosophy might be undertaken as opposed to a phenomenon to which philosophy is applied? Can film philosophize? Eisenstein was one of the most forthright and ambitious defenders of the idea that film might act *as* philosophy, with plans for a film version of Karl Marx's *Das Kapital* and a host of arguments in support of *intellectual cinema*. But Eisenstein was not alone. According to Deleuze, the cinema creates new concepts by its own distinctive means. And Cavell has argued that certain key cinematic genres, such as the "Comedy of Remarriage" discussed in *Pursuits of Happiness* (1981), give expression to the philosophical problem of skepticism, insofar as they dramatize, within the intimate arena of romance, the difficulty of knowing the thoughts and feelings of others. Moreover, in the hands of some writers, the *film as philosophy* thesis is very much akin to the treatment of literature as a kind of philosophy, a proposal advanced most explicitly by Martha Nussbaum.

To a considerable degree, the plausibility of the proposal depends on the conception of philosophy that is assumed within it; so the debate is ultimately driven onto the terrain of metaphilosophy. On the one hand, to the extent that one conceives of philosophy as a professional discipline whose central goals are the posing of questions and the making of arguments in a reasonably robust and formalized sense, then the idea that film might act as an effective medium for such goals looks strained. On the other hand, to the extent that one thinks of philosophy more broadly as a form of self-conscious reflection on any aspect of life that we usually accept unthinkingly, then film—along with art in general—looks much more promising as a means of engaging in such reflection and thus as a form that philosophy might take.

Among the proponents of the film as philosophy thesis are Stephen Mulhall (1962–) and Thomas Wartenberg. Where Cavell focusses on *classical Hollywood* films (especially screwball comedies and melodramas), Mulhall has developed and extended Cavell's approach to encompass contemporary Hollywood filmmaking through studies of the *Alien* tetralogy and the *Mission: Impossible* films. For Mulhall the series of *Alien* films embody philosophical reflection not only on the overt themes of the films, such as human embodiment and the process of reproduction, but on various aspects of the nature of commercial filmmaking itself, including stardom, authorship, and sequeldom. Mulhall is emphatic about the strength of his claims, stating that certain films should be seen "as thinking seriously and systematically about [philosophical views and arguments] in just the ways that philosophers do" (Mulhall 2002, p. 2).

Wartenberg has emphasized the various ways in which films might make genuine contributions to philosophy even if they cannot be construed as making arguments in any conventional sense, including the creation of thought experiments that challenge habitual assumptions and the provision of illustrations that are integral to a philosophical claim, and thus cannot be discarded without damage to the claim in question. Wartenberg has argued that the first *Matrix* film engages us philosophically by creating a thought experiment resembling René Descartes's image of the evil demon, challenging our confidence in the knowledge we gain from sense experience. In other work Wartenberg has emphasized the insights that films may proffer on the terrain of social, political, and moral philosophy. Other authors have made parallel claims about the philosophical significance of various art and avant-garde films, but what unites Cavell, Mulhall, and Wartenberg and makes them distinctive is their emphasis on popular filmmaking, the type of filmmaking that might seem the least congenial—and thus offering the greatest challenge—to the film as philosophy hypothesis.

Counterarguments to these proposals stress the special nature of philosophical knowledge (in normative, if not descriptive terms); the central role of explicit reasoning and argument within it; and the distinctness of philosophy from cognition, self-reflection, and knowledge considered more generally. Paisley Livingston (1951–) has argued that proponents of the *bold* version of the thesis, for whom films can make original philosophical contributions exploiting the specific properties of the medium, are faced with a disabling dilemma: If the contribution can be paraphrased, then any uniqueness premised on medium specificity disappears; if it cannot be paraphrased, then it is difficult to see how a contribution is being made to philosophy proper, when conceived as a discursive discipline. Murray Smith (1962–) has made the complementary point that the *nonparaphrasability* of art is one of its most significant values, and one that brings it into tension with the widely accepted philosophical goals of clarity and explicitness.

Wherever one stands on this issue, and on the question of specificity, the emergence of a debate on the idea of film as philosophy, alongside the diversity of other questions and debates described here, testifies to the seriousness with which the moving image is now taken by philosophers and the consolidation of the philosophy of film at the outset of cinema's second century.

See also Aesthetic Qualities; Art, Expression in; Art, Formalism in; Art, Interpretation of; Art, Ontology of; Art, Performance in; Art, Representation in; Cavell, Stanley; Continental Philosophy; Deleuze, Gilles; Descartes, René; Lyotard, Jean François; Marx, Karl; Nussbaum, Martha; Visual Arts, Theory of the.

Bibliography

Allen, Richard. "Looking at Motion Pictures." In *Film Theory and Philosophy*, edited by Richard Allen and Murray Smith, 76–94. Oxford: Clarendon Press, 1997.

Allen, Richard, and Murray Smith. *Film Theory and Philosophy*. Oxford: Clarendon Press, 1997.

Arnheim, Rudolf. *Film as Art* [1933]. London: Faber, 1983.

Arnheim, Rudolf. "A New *Laocoön*: Artistic Composites and the Talking Film." In *Film as Art*, 164–189. London: Faber, 1983.

Bazin, André. "The Ontology of the Photographic Image." In *What Is Cinema?* Translated by H. Gray, 9–16. Berkeley: University of California, 1967.

Bergson, Henri. *Creative Evolution*. Translated by Arthur Mitchell. New York: Modern Library, 1944.

Carroll, Noël. *The Philosophy of Horror; or, Paradoxes of the Heart*. New York: Routledge, 1990.

Carroll, Noel. "Forget the Medium !" In *Engaging the Moving Image*, 1–9. New Haven, CT: Yale University Press, 2003.

Cavell, Stanley. *Pursuits of Happiness: The Hollywood Comedy of Remarriage*. Cambridge, MA: Harvard University Press, 1981.

Cavell, Stanley. *The World Viewed: Reflections on the Ontology of Film*, 2nd ed. Cambridge, MA: Harvard University Press, 1979.

Cubitt, Sean. *Videography: Video Media as Art and Culture*. New York, 1993.

Currie, Gregory. *Image and Mind: Film, Philosophy, and Cognitive Science*, Cambridge, U.K.: Cambridge University Press, 1995.

Deleuze, Gilles. *Cinema 1–2*. Translated by Hugh Tomlinson and Barbara Habberjam. London: Athlone Press, 1992.

Eisenstein, Sergei. *Selected Works 1: Writings 1922–1934*. Translated and edited by Richard Taylor, London: British Film Institute, 1988.

Eisenstein, Sergei. *Selected Works 2: Towards a Theory of Montage. 1937–40*. Translated by Michael Glenny, edited by Michael Glenny and Richard Taylor. London: British Film Institute, 1991.

Freeland, Cynthia. "Feminist Frameworks for Horror Films." In *Post-Theory: Reconstructing Film Studies*, edited by David Bordwell and Noel Carroll, 195–218. Madison: University of Wisconsin Press, 1996.

Gaut, Berys. "Film Authorship and Collaboration." In *Film Theory and Philosophy*, edited by in Richard Allen and Michael Smith, 149–172. Oxford: Clarendon Press, 1997.

Livingston, Paisley. "Cinematic Authorship." In *Film Theory and Philosophy*, edited by in Richard Allen and Michael Smith, 132–148. Oxford: Clarendon Press, 1997.

Livingston, Paisley. "Theses on Cinema as Philosophy." *Journal of Aesthetics and Art Criticism*. Spec. issue on film as philosophy (January 2006): 1–8.

Manovich, Lev. *The Language of New Media*. Cambridge, MA: MIT Press, 2001.

Mulhall, Stephen. *On Film*. London: Routledge, 2001.

Münsterberg, Hugo. *The Photoplay: A Psychological Study, and Other Writings*, edited by Allan Langdale. New York: Routledge, 2002.

Nussbaum, Martha. *Love's Knowledge*. New York: Oxford University Press, 1990.

Plantinga, Carl. *Rhetoric and Representation in Nonfiction Film*. New York: Cambridge University Press, 1997.

Smith, Murray. *Engaging Characters: Fiction, Emotion, and the Cinema*. Oxford: Clarendon Press, 1995.

Smith, Murray. "Film Art, Argument, and Ambiguity." *Journal of Aesthetics and Art Criticism*. Spec. issue on film as philosophy (January 2006): 26–35.

Walton, Kendall. "Transparent Pictures: On the Nature of Photographic Realism." *Critical Inquiry* 11 (1984): 246–277.

Wartenberg, Thomas E. "Philosophy Screened: Experiencing *The Matrix*." In *The Philosophy of Film: Introductory Text and Readings*, edited by Thomas E. Wartenberg and Angela Curran, 270–83. Malden, U.K.: Blackwell, 2005.

Wartenberg, Thomas E. *Unlikely Couples: Movie Romance as Social Criticism*. Boulder, CO: Westview Press, 1999.

Wilson, George M. *Narration in Light: Studies in Cinematic Point of View*. Baltimore, MD: Johns Hopkins University Press, 1986.

Murray Smith (2005)

PHILOSOPHY OF HISTORY

The term "philosophy of history" probably covers a larger variety of endeavors than similar terms such as "philosophy of law" or "philosophy of science." It is hard to bring under one definition the many philosophical questions and responses that are concerned with history. One reason for this, which has long been acknowledged, is that the English term "history," like its cognates in many Western languages (*histoire, Geschichte*), is normally used to refer to two distinct, though related, things. On the one hand it refers to the temporal progression of large-scale human events, primarily but not exclusively in the past; on the other hand, "history" refers to the discipline or inquiry in which knowledge of the human past is acquired or sought. Thus "philosophy of history" can mean philosophical reflection on the historical process itself, or it can mean philosophical reflection on the knowledge we have of the historical process. Philosophers have done both sorts of things, and this has led to a distinction between "substantive" (or sometimes "speculative") and "critical" (or "analytical") philosophy of history. The first is usually considered part of metaphysics, perhaps analogous to the "philosophy of nature," whereas the second is seen as epistemology, as in the "philosophy of science." While this distinction has been useful, it becomes blurred when we find some philosophers doing a mixture of both, and others, while certainly reflecting philosophically on history, doing neither. This entry begins with the standard distinction, only to see it lose some of its usefulness in the course of the exposition.

1. "SUBSTANTIVE" PHILOSOPHY OF HISTORY: PHILOSOPHICAL REFLECTION ON THE HISTORICAL PROCESS

The term "philosophy of history" originates with Voltaire in the 1760s, but it is most closely associated with German philosophers of the Enlightenment and post-Enlightenment periods: Kant, Herder, Hegel, and Marx. Hegel's "Lectures on the Philosophy of History," delivered in the 1820s and published shortly after his death, have dominated the discussion. The lectures represent Hegel at the height of his influence, and their relatively brief (less than a hundred pages) introduction is as clear and straightforward as it is comprehensive. Soon translated into other languages (e.g., English in 1857), it is probably the most widely read of Hegel's works. So great was Hegel's impact that his approach to history became paradigmatic not only for many who followed his lead, but also for those who later attacked the very project of the philosophy of history. What is more, philosophers who reflected on history before Hegel are often thought to have been engaged in the same kind of inquiry he was. But this is anachronistic, and misleading. The substantive philosophy of history is often described, in keeping with Hegel, as the search for the meaning and purpose of world history, and for the force that drives history toward its goal. While this describes many instances of reflection on the historical process, it is a simplification and is not necessarily an apt description of philosophical thought about history prior to Hegel. The most general description of the substantive philosophy of history is that the philosopher tries to "make sense" of the historical process, usually in the face of evidence to the contrary. But the "sense" that the philosopher seeks varies considerably: sometimes it is rational sense, sometimes moral sense, sometimes religious sense.

Philosophical reflection on the historical process seems to originate in early Christian philosophy, which is in turn indebted to the Jewish conception of time. The Hebrew scriptures introduce historical time into a world dominated by cyclical and ahistorical conceptions of time. Indian, Persian, and Greek thought are based on unchanging patterns and eternal recurrence, in which individual events, both natural and human, get whatever significance they have from reflecting, imitating, or instantiating these timeless forms. The sequence of individual events is not "going anywhere." Their essence, what gives them their being, lies outside of time altogether. In spite of the compelling historical accounts left by Herodotus and Thucydides, for Greek philosophers even political arrangements—constitutions such as aristocracy, monarchy, democracy—are portrayed, in the classical texts of Plato and Aristotle, for example, as following cyclical patterns of rise, fall and repetition.

By contrast, for the ancient Jews, human events—both political and religious—get their significance not from a "vertical" and imitative relation to eternal patterns, but from a "horizontal" relation backward and forward to other events in real time: backwards to creation, Adam's fall, God's covenant with his people, its captivity, exile, rulers, and heroes, and so on; forward to the redemption of God's people with the coming of the Messiah. Time is the story of a people's progress from creation through perils, dangers, and risks to final salvation. Christianity takes up this historical conception of time and intensifies it, first by affirming the coming of the Messiah as a central, real historical event, in the *middle* of history, as it were, pointing ahead to a final salvation in

the second coming; and second, by extending the promise of salvation to all mankind through a progressive spread and universal triumph of Christianity. Creation, the fall, incarnation, and last judgment are unique, unrepeatable occurrences, and individual events and deeds, both human and divine, are arrayed along a line of time that extends from beginning to end. Given this conception, events are coming from somewhere and are going somewhere in time. Origin and destiny give meaning to human events and actions.

This conception of historical time is not itself a philosophy of history but a cultural and religious worldview. Philosophical reflection begins when this conception generates problems, as it did in the age of Augustine. This philosopher struggled with problems of good and evil, freedom and divine justice, responsibility and punishment. History entered the picture when these concepts were projected onto the stage of the large-scale social events of his own time. The conversion of the Roman Empire under Constantine (323 CE) was seen by early Christian theologians as the vindication of their religion and the harbinger of its eventual triumph throughout the world. During Augustine's time (354–430) the empire was under attack by barbarians, Rome itself had been invaded, and the empire seemed in danger of destruction. Pagans took this as a sign that Christianity was responsible for the demise of the empire, and Christians wondered why God seemed to be punishing Rome rather than rewarding it for its conversion and crowning it with glory. Here it was historical developments, rather than just evil deeds and events, that seemed at odds with religious doctrine, and this constituted the problem Augustine felt the need to solve, addressing both pagan and Christian audiences.

In response, Augustine denied that salvation and divine justice were to be sought in human secular history or its political or even religious institutions. Instead, they were to be found in the City of God, whose citizens have their real life outside secular time. Augustine had already considered the notion of time as limited by eternity in trying to reconcile free will and God's foreknowledge. Augustine's response to the problem of history was to seek the meaning and purpose of history not in history itself, but rather outside of time altogether. In Augustine's thought, the Platonic conception of the timeless realm triumphs over the religious view of history handed down from Judaism and Christianity. As often occurs in the history of Christian thought, Greek philosophy comes to the rescue of the religious worldview. At the same time Augustine inaugurates the tradition of Christian apologetics, later called theodicy: justifying God's ways to humans. Because of the presuppositions that frame Augustine's whole discussion, his project might best be called a theology of history.

Two things should be noted about history as Augustine conceives it: First, as we have noted, its purpose and goal lie not in historical time but outside and beyond it; second, in spite of Augustine's emphasis on human freedom, the driving force behind historical change, what links human events to their ultimate purpose, is the divine will. These two features of history remained more or less constant in the Christian tradition until the time of the enlightenment. Jacques Bénigne Bossuet's *Discourse on Universal History* (1681) still shares in this conception. He sees the world in apparent moral disorder, with the authority of the church being challenged, but assures his readers of the guidance of divine providence and the ultimate salvation of the faithful.

Giambattista Vico, in the *New Science* (1725–1730), also appeals to the idea of providence, but his approach to history is more novel and more modern, because he thinks of providence as embodied in rational, developmental laws rather than acts of divine intervention. He also believes that providence uses narrow human self-interest and self-love to further its own higher ends, a concept usually seen as foreshadowing Hegel's idea of the cunning of reason. Vico is also known for dignifying historical knowledge, in the face of both ancient and modern disdain for it when compared to our knowledge of nature. Because human beings make history through their own acts, Vico believes, they are capable of knowing it. Because God creates nature, only he can truly know it. In this Vico challenges his contemporaries, the Cartesian defenders of the new mathematical science of nature as the paradigm for all knowledge.

In the French Enlightenment, humans take center stage and their reason makes them capable of shaping their own destinies. Human events come under calculation and control. The future is no longer something to be prophesied or predicted, but something to be produced. The legitimacy of rulers can be questioned, and the people can overthrow them. History begins to look like a progress from a past of darkness and superstition into the light of reason and human self-determination. The purpose and goal of history now lies not outside and beyond it, but within it at some attainable point in the future. It is the result of human rather than divine agency, and it is now conceived not as salvation but as emancipation.

Even though Voltaire introduces the term "philosophy of history" it is possible to argue that his view of his-

tory, shared by the enlightenment *philosophes* and the revolutionaries of the eighteenth century, was not so much a philosophical reflection on history but again, like the religion of the Jews and early Christians, an emerging political and cultural worldview. The philosophy of history begins, as before, when this worldview generates problems. The late enlightenment period produced a vast new literature of discovery and travel, which led among other things to the beginnings of history as something like an academic discipline with critical methods and justifiable assertions. While this trend was not completed until the nineteenth century, even its beginnings allowed for a new distinction between our warranted knowledge of the past and our beliefs about history's overall direction and goal.

Thus Kant's forays into the philosophy of history tend to raise critical questions about what the enlightenment philosophers never doubted. A late text (1798) bears the title "An old question raised again: is the human race constantly progressing?" But even his earlier essay, "Idea for a Universal History from a Cosmopolitan Point of View" (1784), his major contribution to the philosophy of history, argues only for the limited thesis that the course of past history "permits us to hope" for "a steady and progressive though slow evolution" toward a better state for mankind (1963, p. 11). Kant wants to share the enlightenment point of view, just as he wants to endorse the claims of natural theology, but his critical reason forces him to limit its pretensions. As should be expected when reading Kant, of course, in no way is the idea of divine providence taken for granted. Progress in history, should it be found, would be toward "the achievement of a universal civic society which administers laws among men" (p. 16), which is "the most difficult and the last [problem] to be solved by mankind" (p. 17). He discusses at some lengths the difficulties of such an achievement, asserting as he does elsewhere that it would require solving "the problem of a lawful external relation among states" (p. 18). This is the greatest difficulty of all, because we can see the same antagonism among states as among individuals, which has led again and again to war. But after "devastations, revolutions, and even complete exhaustion," nature brings states to the realization that they must move "from the lawless condition of savages into a league of nations" (p. 19).

By the time he reaches this point the status of Kant's discourse on history should be clear to the reader. He is not making claims about the actual course of history; rather, he is outlining the ideal conditions under which alone, he thinks, history could exhibit any progress.

Because these conditions are in his day far from having been realized, Kant's claims are clearly prescriptive and moral in character. Thus he can assure practicing historians that he is making no attempt to displace their work, because he is propounding an Idea of world history based upon an *a priori* principle (p. 25), an "[I]dea of how the course of the world must be if it is to lead to certain rational ends" (p. 24).

By using the term "Idea," a *terminus technicus* from the *Critique of Pure Reason*, which the translators signal by means of capitalization, Kant indicates a rational concept whose empirical reality not only is not, but, according to the *Critique, cannot* be exhibited in experience. But, like human freedom itself, neither can its possibility be empirically denied. Thus the course of history does not provide evidence that the "civic union of the human race" will ever be achieved, but neither does it prove that it never will be. Its realization must at least be regarded as possible, and the Idea that we have of it may help bring it to pass (p. 24). Kant is telling us not where history is going but where it *ought* to be going. Only in this minimal sense can philosophy help "make sense" of history, namely by articulating the "cosmopolitan standpoint" from which alone it can be freed from its apparent moral chaos. And by showing that its moral realization is at least possible, it "permits us to hope" for a better future. Kant's concept of hope is usually associated with his philosophy of religion and refers to the individual's hope for salvation in the world to come. But here he rationally justifies hope for a better future for mankind on earth.

In *Idea for a Universal History*, the concepts of a universal civic society, or league of nations, and of history as progressing toward it, legitimize certain political choices. They are Ideas capable of guiding our action in the social sphere. Kant is anticipating the project of expanding his ethical principles, with such notions as a kingdom of ends, into a political theory. Ethics and politics alike belong to Kant's practical philosophy, not his theoretical philosophy. Their central concern is not with what is the case but with what we ought to do. And the same is true of his philosophy of history.

Johann Gottfried von Herder, a younger contemporary of Kant's, is another German philosopher who reacts critically to the enlightenment's views of history. In his *Ideen zur Philosophie der Geschichte der Menschheit* (1784–1791), he undertakes a universal history, and for him, as for Voltaire, this means expanding the traditional scope of history to include non-European peoples. But Herder takes this insight in a different direction. While the thinkers of the French Enlightenment sought proof of the universality of human reason, Herder by contrast is struck by the diversity and particularity of human nature, embodied in distinct peoples and cultures. Rejecting the Enlightenment's emphasis on reason, legislation and science, Herder sees human nature in the expressions of feeling, such as art, music, poetry, and custom.

The Enlightenment philosophers saw the growth of scientific rationality expanding to the political realm and imagined a future in which reason triumphed over the dark forces of superstition and emotion. Herder, with his emphasis on diversity and culture, was less convinced that history was moving in any unified direction, much less a progressive one. True, his devout Protestantism kept him from embracing the complete cultural relativism that many would later draw from his work. But in contrast to Kant, whose sympathies still lie with the Enlightenment, Herder becomes one of the first great figures of the Romantic movement that grew up in opposition to it.

It is against this background of the Enlightenment and its German critics that Hegel's classic text must be understood. He begins by distinguishing a "philosophische Weltgeschichte" from history proper; philosophy, he says, has "thoughts of its own," *a priori* thoughts, to bring to the study of history (1988, p. 10). But the "only" thought that philosophy brings to the study of history is that of reason—"that reason rules the world," and thus that world history like everything else can be seen as a rational or reasonable (*vernünftig*) affair (p. 12). Reason not only sets the goal for history but also governs the realization of that goal. Hegel did not invent this idea, he reminds us; the idea that reason rules the world is that of Anaxagoras, and it has also been expressed in the idea of divine providence. This too suggests a rational plan, God's plan, but providence is usually portrayed as being hidden from us. Unwilling to settle for pious ignorance, Hegel believes that the rationality of providence can be known and explained. If we take seriously the idea of providence, the demonstration of its rationality would amount to a theodicy or "justification of God" (p. 18).

The embodiment of reason is spirit (*Geist*), both in individuals and in peoples, whose nature is to be conscious and self-conscious, and whose actualization is to be autonomous and self-sufficient, that is, to be free. But this actualization is a temporal process, and that process is history. Spirit actualizes itself and achieves freedom through history, drawing its energy from human passions and intentions; but the result of this process is often at odds with the actual intentions of the individuals and peoples involved. It is here that Hegel's speaks of the "cunning of reason" (p. 35), because reason achieves ends of its own by using the ends of others. In history, it is only when individuals and peoples organize themselves into states that freedom can finally be truly actualized. It is here, in law, the ethical life of the community and political order, not in the mere absence of constraint, that the "positive reality and satisfaction of freedom" are to be found (p. 41).

The actual course of history can be seen as the display of human perfectibility leading toward the realization of freedom. This pathway is not a smooth one, however, but consists in the spirit's "hard and endless struggle against itself." Spirit hides its own nature from itself, and is even "proud and full of enjoyment in this self-estrangement" (p. 59). Individuals and peoples struggle against each other, and many morally good and virtuous people suffer unjustly. But history moves on a different plane, and here the acts of individuals, especially those of the great figures of history, are not to be judged by moral standards. It is the spirit of peoples, not individuals, that are the agents of history, but these, "progressing in a necessary series of stages, are themselves only phases of the one universal Spirit: through them, that World Spirit elevates and completes itself in history, into a self-comprehending *totality*" (p. 82). The self-comprehension of world spirit is philosophy itself.

In several places Hegel presents in the broadest outlines the necessary stages through which the world spirit has passed on its path toward the realization of freedom. In the ancient "oriental" world only one—the emperor or tyrant—is free. In the Greek and Roman worlds only *some* persons are free. It was first the "Germanic peoples, through Christianity, who came to the awareness that every human is free by virtue of being human" (p. 21). The realization of freedom is the goal that gives meaning to what happens in history, and this realization takes place within history itself, not beyond it. Moreover, it has occurred or is occurring in "our world," "our time" (Hegel 1956, p.524).

Karl Marx is usually seen as a continuation of the classical period of the philosophy of history. Marx admitted some indebtedness to Hegel, but thought of himself as the anti-Hegel, whose idealism "stands on its head" and "must be turned right side up again." More important, Marx rejected not only Hegel, and Hegel's philosophy of history, but academic philosophy as a whole, wanting to be read and understood strictly as a social theorist and reformer. Yet it seems beyond doubt that Marx expounds a philosophy of history in the "classical" sense. Even understood as a blueprint for reform or revolution, his work is founded on and cannot be understood apart from

an account of history. This account is summarized neatly by his collaborator, Friedrich Engels, in his preface to the 1888 English edition of the *Communist Manifesto*, in which he states what he calls the "fundamental proposition of Marxism." "In every historical epoch," Engels writes, "the prevailing mode of economic production and exchange and the social organization necessarily following from it" form the basis of that epoch. "Consequently the whole history of mankind ... has been a history of class struggles, contests between exploiting and exploited, ruling and oppressed classes." The outcome of this history is that "nowadays, a stage has been reached" where the emancipation of the exploited and oppressed class—the proletariat—from the exploiting and ruling class—the bourgoisie—would entail "at the same time, and once and for all, emancipating society at large from all exploitation, oppression, class distinctions, and class struggles" (Marx and Engels 1998, p. 48). The notion of history as class struggle recalls Hegel's description of the spirit's "hard and endless struggle against itself," its "self-estrangement" in which it "must overcome itself as its own truly hostile hindrance" (Hegel 1988, p. 59). In the background of these descriptions is Hegel's famous account in his *Phenomenology of Spirit* of the struggle between master and servant, an account that can be interpreted in economic and material terms, and which is certainly an account of exploitation and oppression. As Marx admits, this is the origin of a "dialectic" account of the movement of history, which Marx appropriates for his own purposes.

Different as they are from each other to their adherents, Hegel and Marx both reveal their indebtedness to the Enlightenment. For both, it is human affairs and strivings, not divine actions, that drive history, and its purpose or culmination, conceived not as salvation but emancipation, lies within history, not outside or beyond it. Yet unlike the Enlightenment idea of progress, their conception seems to require an end of history. Hegel often speaks as if it has already arrived, and Marx projects it into the near future. Both are unclear what happens after that.

This was but one of many conceptual problems that led to widespread criticism of Hegel's and Marx's philosophies of history and to a general mistrust of the whole project. The idea of attributing a purpose or goal to history as a whole became suspect. Hegel's speculative idealism fell on hard times, and his philosophy of history was seen as the worst manifestation of its extravagant pretensions. It was also read by many, rightly or wrongly, as a glorification of the Prussian monarchy as the culmination of history. Marx's apparent belief in an inevitable outcome of history was not widely accepted by philosophers, even those sympathetic to his proposed political and social reforms; only the official orthodoxy of the Soviet Union and other communist states took it seriously. Sweeping treatments of history as a whole and the rise and fall of civilizations, such as Oswald Spengler's *Decline of the West* (1918–1922) and Arnold Toynbee's *A Study of History* (1934–1954), were reviewed in the popular press, but not taken seriously by academic philosophers.

The criticism of the philosophy of history reached a high point in the years following World War II and came from different directions. Karl Loewith (*Meaning in History*, 1949) argued that the classical philosophy of history was a secularized version of the Christian story of salvation, that is, religion in disguise. Karl Popper (*The Poverty of Historicism*, 1957) denounced it as pseudoscience. Both studies linked it to the development of twentieth-century totalitarianism. Positivists and analytic philosophers rejected it as an incoherent and unrealizable philosophical project.

Something resembling the classical philosophy of history stayed alive, in milder form, in European and North American Marxism. With the discovery and publication of Marx's early writings in the early 1930s and after, a fuller picture emerged of Marx the thinker, different from the Marx of Soviet propaganda. In particular, the full sense of Marx's indebtedness to Hegel, and his connection to the young, "left" Hegelians became clearer, something that had already been argued by Georg Lukacs in his *History and Class Consciousness* (1923). Marx also influenced the work of many historians, especially in Britain and France. Thus in Western eyes Marx took his place belatedly as a "respectable" philosopher in the Hegelian and post-Hegelian tradition, a development Marx himself would probably not have welcomed. This in turn led to a new assessment of Hegel himself in light of his influence on Marx.

Thus a tendency developed in the 1930s and after to read Hegel through the eyes of Marx and vice versa. This happened in France under the influence of Alexandre Kojeve and Jean Hyppolite, and in Germany through the "Frankfurt School" of Herbert Marcuse, Max Horkheimer, and Theodore Adorno. In this tradition Hegel and Marx were read not so much as making metaphysical or quasi-scientific claims about the direction or outcome of history as offering blueprints for political action and social analysis. Like Kant, they were outlining the conditions under which history *could* make sense, rather than asserting that it does.

Western Marxism remained strong in Europe and later in America through the Cold War period, but by the 1980s French philosophers began to turn away. The "grand narratives" of both Marxism and the capitalist idea of progress were seen by such thinkers as Jean-Francois Lyotard and Michel Foucault as belonging to a period of "modernity" that was coming to an end and giving way to a "postmodern" age. These and other philosophers, who came to be identified with the "postmoderns" label, thought of themselves as continuing the attack on the substantive philosophy of history that had begun a century before, but broadening it to include the Enlightenment idea of human progress, linked to science and technology, still held by many in the West. Defenders of the Enlightenment project, such as Jürgen Habermas, feared that this wholesale rejection of the Enlightenment was a new kind of antirationalism and a rejection of important human values. The postmoderns tend to see in any overarching or "totalizing" set of values the specter of oppression.

These debates have generally not been interpreted as continuations of the classical philosophy of history, but both sides can be seen as thinking about history and its direction in broad terms. And both sides share the ultimate value of emancipation as the key to progress in history. Though the explicit pursuit of questions in the style of the classical philosophy of history is rare, there have been recent examples. The collapse of the Soviet Union, and the trend away from dictatorships and toward democracies in Latin America and elsewhere in the 1990s, inspired Francis Fukuyama (*The End of History and the Last Man*, 1992), to revive Hegel's idea of the End of History. The march toward freedom announced by Hegel, he argued, long discredited by the atrocities of the twentieth century, could now be seen to be back on track. Fukuyama's thesis did not attract many adherents; was soon thought, like Hegel's, to be refuted by events; and was treated by many as an artifact of its time. The same, of course, could be said of the grandiose claims of Hegel and Marx—or indeed of any other philosopher.

The persistence and recurrence of philosophical reflections on the course of history as a whole, as in the case of the debates about modernity and of Fukuyama's book, indicate that the substantive philosophy of history may not have completely disappeared. Perhaps the need to make sense of history, and the continued existence of cultural worldviews about history, such as the idea of progress, will always push philosophers to look at history as a whole in search of its meaning and purpose—or to deny that it has any.

2. "CRITICAL" PHILOSOPHY OF HISTORY: PHILOSOPHICAL REFLECTION ON HISTORICAL KNOWLEDGE

Serious discussion of questions about historical knowledge began in the nineteenth century, when the substantive philosophy of history had passed its peak in Hegel and history had established itself as a serious discipline in the academy. Prior to the late Enlightenment period, history was generally conceived as a literary genre more valued for the moral and practical lessons it could derive from past events than for its accuracy in portraying them. In some ways the substantive philosophy of history, looking for purpose and meaning in the whole of history, was simply a more sweeping and more pretentious version of ordinary historical discourse. By the middle of the nineteenth century, important new historical studies of antiquity and the middle ages had appeared. Beginning in Germany, history had acquired the dignity and trappings of a *Wissenschaft*, complete with critical methods for evaluating sources and justifying its assertions. The great historian Leopold von Ranke, one of the leading figures of the "historical school" in Germany, was explicitly repudiating the idea of history as edifying moral discourse when he famously claimed that the purpose of his historical work was simply to show the past "as it really was" (*zeigen, wie es eigentlich gewesen*).

For philosophers from Descartes through Kant, mathematics and mathematical natural science had served as the paradigm case of knowledge of the real world. How did the newly flourishing knowledge of the historical past fit in? Some philosophers, such as John Stuart Mill and those in the "positivist" tradition inaugurated by Auguste Comte, argued for the unity of all knowledge and tried to assimilate history to science. Just as physics formulated the laws of nature, and explained events by their means, the science of society would seek out social laws; history was just a case of applying these laws to the past.

Led by the neo-Kantians (e.g., Wilhelm Windelband, Heinrich Rickert,) and by Wilhelm Dilthey, German philosophers questioned this understanding of historical knowledge, focusing on the fact that its object is not natural occurrences but human actions. With history in mind, they began to work out the idea of *Geisteswissenschaften* or sciences of the human spirit, in contrast to the sciences of nature. Not only is the object of history

different from that of the natural sciences, they maintained, its aim is also different: it is concerned with individual events and courses of events for their own sake, not in order to derive general laws from them (it is "idiographic" rather than "nomothetic"). Moreover, because human actions are at the center of historical concern, to give an account is often to understand the subjective thoughts, feelings, and intentions of the persons involved rather than to relate external events to their external causes ("understanding" rather than "explanation"). For some philosophers, this made it inevitable that the historian's value judgments would enter into the account of events and actions, and that the "objectivity" so prized in natural science was neither attainable nor desirable.

This opposition between "positivists" and what we might call the "humanists" on the status of historical knowledge, begun in the nineteenth century, continued to shape the epistemology of history well into the twentieth century. Those positivists who accepted the humanists' description of historical knowledge could not consider history to be a genuine science. Those humanists who wanted to defend history as offering genuine knowledge of the past had to contend that the natural sciences did not offer the only model for what qualifies as knowledge. Among the latter, two notable attempts to characterize historical knowledge are those of Benedetto Croce and R. G. Collingwood (1999). Both argued that historical understanding of the past requires moving from action as an external event (e.g., Caesar leading his army across the Rubicon) to the reconstruction of the "inside" of the event: the experience or thought of the agent that motivated it.

Some of the issues that concerned philosophers of history were reflected in the work of historians as well. With the rise of the social sciences in the twentieth century (sociology, anthropology, political science), many historians coveted a place among them, arguing that history had to be "objective" and "value-free." If that meant ignoring the subjective motivations of historical agents, so be it. They borrowed quantitative methods from the social sciences and applied them to the study of the past. Leading the way were the historians of the Annales school in France, beginning in the 1930s. Its best-known theoretician, Fernand Braudel, argued that history should shift its focus from the "surface" ripples of political history to the deeper-lying and slower-moving currents of social, economic, and geographical change. The move toward social history had a large impact on the discipline, and it was partly motivated by the desire to make history more "objective"—but only partly. Braudel's view reflected something closer to the substantive than to the critical philosophy of history, namely a belief about what the historical process really is.

Among philosophers, the positivist conception of historical knowledge was revived in the 1940s, under the aegis of the unity-of-science movement in analytical philosophy, by Carl G. Hempel. The focus was on the idea of *historical explanation*: Does history merely describe events, or does it try to explain them? And if it explains them, how does its mode of explanation compare with explanation in natural science?

Hempel argued that history does attempt to explain events, not merely describe them, and it does so according to a pattern no different from that found in the natural sciences: it brings events under general laws that allow us to show how they follow from their antecedents. Given such a law, the event to be explained should be logically deducible from its antecedents. Critics such as William Dray (1989) objected to Hempel's "covering law theory" (as Dray called it) on several grounds. Dray did not dispute the claim that history often tries to explain events, but, following Collingwood, he argued that a satisfying historical explanation often consists of reconstructing the reasons behind an action rather than finding its external causes. Further, it is hard to find general laws, of the kind that would be comparable to physical laws, being articulated in historical work.

Hempel conceded that historical accounts bear little surface resemblance to scientific explanations, that they seem to offer merely probabilistic rather than deductive explanations, and that their accounts are often just "sketches" of more complete explanations. But in doing so, he revealed the strongly prescriptive character of his account—a character it shared with much of the epistemology of his day. The implication was that if history could not live up to the standard of natural science, it could not qualify as genuine knowledge. Dray's larger objection to Hempel's approach was that philosophers should pay attention to what historians actually do, and to the wide variety of conceptual strategies in their work, rather than prescribing standards derived from abstract logical analysis or reducing their work to an imitation of a different, and equally idealized, endeavor. In this he was a harbinger of a trend in analytic epistemology that eventually extended even to the philosophy of natural science itself.

Nevertheless, the discussion of history among analytic philosophers in the 1950s was dominated by the theme of causal explanation, and above all by the contrast with the natural sciences. Hempel's proposal set the tone.

Even those such as Dray, who argued for the autonomy of historical knowledge, shared this preoccupation. Thus the confrontation of "positivists" with "humanists" continued. At the same time, the discussion extended to other, related topics.

One distinction that was much discussed in this literature was that between history and chronicle. It was agreed that history had to do more than just list facts. As Morton White put it schematically in his *Foundations of Historical Knowledge* (1965):

> The chronicler is likely to tell us: "The king of England died, and then the queen of England died, and then the prince of England died, and then the princess of England died"… But a corresponding history may read: "The king of England died, so the queen of England grieved. Her grief led to her death. Her death led the prince to worry, and he worried to the point of suicide. His death made the princess lonely, and she died of that loneliness.…" (1965, p. 223)

A chronicle simply lists a series of events in the order in which they happened, but according to White, "a history contains causal statements" (p. 223). But what kind of causation do emotions have? Even they seem to have the teleological character of reasons. The distinction between chronicle and history raises further problems. The chronicle involves more than a simple statement of facts. The historian has *selected*, from all the possible facts there are, some that are relevant to the story that is to be told. The problem of selection relates to the problem of historical objectivity, because even if facts are established by careful critical methods, the decision of which ones to look for, and which to include in a historical account, may derive from the interests and values of the historian.

Another problem, related to explanation, had to do with the nature of the *explanandum* in historical accounts. What do historians explain? The distinction between explanation and understanding, or between explanation by causes vs. explanation by reasons, may be relevant to the discussion of individual persons and their actions. But in history the focus is more often on large-scale entities such as nations, peoples, and classes, and on events such as wars, revolutions, and economic crises. We often impute actions or mental states to states or groups, as when we say that "Congress decided," "Japan was offended," "organized labor was fed up," and the like. To what extent are these expressions just shorthand for references to the actions or feelings of individuals? If these large-scale entities do not themselves act and feel, are they subject to causal explanation, and if so what kind? Are there social laws governing the behavior of such entities and the occurrence of such events, which can be discovered independently of reference to the individuals that make them up, as methodological holists believe? Or must everything be traced, at least implicitly, to individuals? These are questions, of course, that arise in the social sciences generally and are not peculiar to history.

Positivism, reductionism, and the unity-of-science movement gradually lost their hold on analytic philosophy, largely under the influence of the later Wittgenstein, and philosophy of science was itself transformed. Arthur Danto, whose *Analytical Philosophy of History* appeared in 1965, later wrote an essay called "The Decline and Fall of the Analytical Philosophy of History" (1995). Danto claimed that Hempel's project was one of the many casualties of Thomas Kuhn's *The Structure of Scientific Revolutions* (1962). In an ironic reversal of fortune, worthy of a good novel, the attempt to absorb the philosophy of history into the philosophy of science was upended when science was reconceived as an essentially historical phenomenon and the philosophy of science became a branch of the philosophy of history—or at least of history proper. Epistemology was now devoted to describing what scientists actually did, rather than producing idealized and prescriptive accounts, and this meant following their work historically.

Danto was too hard on himself, however, when he described himself retrospectively as pursuing a Hempelian program. His *Analytical Philosophy of History* was actually itself part of a revolution going on the philosophy of history in the 1960s. The model for the philosophical understanding of history was shifting from *science* to *literature*. The old idea of history as a literary genre was revived. While Danto continued to think of history as explaining events causally, his account of how it does this drew heavily on the concept of *storytelling* or *narrative*. The concept of narrative had been used before in analytic philosophy, to distinguish between chronicle and history, but Danto's sophisticated treatment of it was explicitly modeled on literary narratives such as novels. At the heart of Danto's account is the idea that in a historical narrative, as in a good story, events are selected and described retrospectively with reference to later events. Thus the temporal character of events, and the temporal position of the narrator in relation to them, determines the structure of a historical account.

But Danto was not alone in looking to the literary model. W. B. Gallie had published a book called *Philosophy and Historical Understanding* (1964) whose premise was that "history belongs to the genus 'story.'" With the

work of Louis Mink in the early 1970s (later collected in *Historical Understanding*, 1987), the trend was well under way to look at narrative as a "cognitive instrument" and history as "mode of comprehension" (these are Mink's terms) based on narrative. Some analytic philosophers (e.g., Maurice Mandelbaum and Leon Goldstein) objected to the emphasis on narrative for favoring the literary presentation of history over the hard work of discovery, evaluation of sources and critical hypothesis that lies behind it. History, they said, is a disciplined inquiry whose goal is knowledge. Narrative is merely the way—indeed only one way—its results are "written up" for public consumption. But Mink's idea is that narrative is more than just literary presentation. It constitutes a conceptual framework for dealing with human events, utterly distinct from scientific explanation, which is entirely appropriate to history. Danto later calls narrative the "metaphysics of everyday life" (Danto 1985, p. xiv).

In literary theory, of course, the study of narrative had a long tradition and had produced a number of classic studies in the English-speaking world. The rise of French structuralist literary theory in the 1960s had also involved considerable focus on narrative, drawing on the earlier work of theorists from Eastern Europe such as Roman Jakobson and Vladimir Propp. But literary theory and the philosophy of history had little contact until the appearance of Hayden White's *Metahistory* in 1973. Drawing on the literary theories of Northrup Frye, Roland Barthes, and others, White produced a theory of narrative in general that he then applied to history by examining the work of both classical historians (Ranke, Michelet) and philosophers of history (Hegel, Marx). White (1973) argues that their work is guided by the same plot structures—romance, comedy, tragedy, and satire—that govern the production of literary texts. White's book was widely influential but also highly controversial, especially among historians, because White seemed to be portraying their work as guided by literary motives, or motifs, rather than by the project of telling the truth about the past.

By this time the study of narrative was burgeoning on all sides, with a lot of emphasis on the fact that narrative or storytelling is a cross-cultural and cross-disciplinary phenomenon sui generis, turning up not only in history and fiction, but also in films, folktales, medical case histories, psychotherapy, medieval altar paintings and tapestries, comic strips, court testimony, and so on. Some theorists proposed a new discipline, to be called "narratology," which would seek out the common features of narrative in all its manifestations. Under the broadening influence of both Hayden White (1973) and structuralist and poststructuralist theories of literature, the works of historians were studied as examples of narrative form.

At a time when many historians, as noted earlier, were trying to escape traditional approaches by shifting the focus of history away from human actions, there was much difference of opinion on whether narrative was essential to history at all. *Annales* historians in France, and quantitative historians ("cliometricians") elsewhere, disdained traditional historical language and thought narrative dispensable. Those who followed the trend toward the history of "*mentalites,*" or social attitudes and thought patterns, implicitly agreed. The point was made that histories have not always told stories. White, by contrast, argued that even such standard examples of nonnarrative history as Burkhard's *Civilization of the Renaissance in Italy* and Huizinga's *Waning of the Middle Ages*, were implicit or truncated literary narratives. Paul Ricoeur in *Time and Narrative* (1983) made a similar claim about Braudel's *The Mediterranean and the Mediterranean World*, the example *par excellence* of the *Annales* school's nonnarrative approach, arguing that large-scale "quasi-persons" turned up in "quasi-plots" in Braudel's work, a kind of narrative in disguise.

3. POSTMODERN SKEPTICISM AND ITS CRITICS

To the outside observer it might seem that with this shift to the discussion of narrative, the epistemological questions that originally motivated the "critical" philosophy of history were gradually fading from view. In the work of Danto, Mink, and Gallie, the concept of narrative had evolved, partly in reaction to the positivist program of Hempel, within the world of analytical philosophy, and it was undoubtedly part of the critical or epistemological reflection on historical knowledge. Even though these thinkers increasingly took literature as their model for understanding history, they were still interested in history's cognitive role. But when this tradition collided with structuralism in Hayden White's work, and with the larger, more literary world of narratology, the problem of knowledge seemed to lose its interest. The focus had shifted from history as knowledge to the historical text as literary artifact (as White called it). While this development is sometimes called the "linguistic turn" in the philosophy of history, it is more properly called the turn to the text. Literary analysis had apparently replaced epistemology.

This is only partly true, however, as there was more to the structuralist and poststructuralist treatment of history than just literary interest. Their analysis contained a profoundly skeptical view of history as a claim to knowledge. They were inclined to see narrative structure as an *a priori* cultural form *imposed* on the real world, an alien structure that by its very nature distorted or misrepresented the messy and chaotic character of human life and action. Their model was fiction, and they saw narrative originating in the literary imagination or the archetypical plot structures embedded in culture. As for history, which pretends to represent the past as it really was, here narrative inevitably achieves the opposite effect, according to them. At best it dresses up reality, reflecting our need for satisfying coherence, and, if we really believe it, derives from wishful thinking. Far from reflecting reality, it escapes from it. At worst, narrative in its role as the "voice of authority" seeks to put across a moral view of the world in the interests of power and manipulation. This skeptical view was increasingly expressed in the writings of Hayden White, after *Metahistory*, and to some extent in those of Mink as well.

There is some irony in this development. The turn to narrative had begun as an attempt to defend the autonomy of history against the claim that it had to be transformed into science in order to be genuine knowledge. It was another chapter in the ongoing battle of the humanists against the positivists. For the humanists, narrative, like "understanding," as opposed to "explanation," was supposed to be capable of telling us about the past as it really was—human actions and intentions—whereas scientific reduction was the alien framework imposed from outside. Now the narrativists seemed to join the positivists in believing that the literary form of traditional history stands in the way of its epistemic pretensions. As we have seen, the antinarrative historians of the *Annales* school, and many other social and economic historians, agreed with them. The only difference was that the poststructuralists, unlike the positivists and the working historians, held no brief for the epistemic pretensions of the sciences and social sciences either. All was linguistic construction, all was imposed on reality—if indeed it makes any sense to speak of a "reality" outside our constructions.

Thus epistemology had not completely disappeared from the narrative treatment of history; there was still a concern for its epistemic status. But the consensus among the most influential poststructuralist or postmodern theorists (the latter term came to prevail) was that it had none. Many of the issues associated with the critical philosophy of history—objectivity, the role of evidence, the nature of explanation—were simply not treated at all. To that extent the project of the critical philosophy of history had been transformed, if not eclipsed.

One theorist who had a lot to say about historical knowledge was Michel Foucault, whose work gradually took on enormous importance from the late 1960s on, first in France and then elsewhere. Foucault's early work was in the history of medicine and psychiatry, but it engaged fundamental social and philosophical issues such as the normal vs. the abnormal and reason vs. insanity. His middle works (*The Order of Things* [1970], *The Archaeology of Knowledge* [1972]) dealt more broadly with knowledge in the human sciences. In keeping with the "linguistic turn," his focus was on forms of discourse, and his treatment took the form of contrasting widely divergent historical examples of scientific theory. His thoughts on history came through primarily in his defense of his own approach against more traditional treatments. He contrasted his own method, which he called "archaeological," with what he called the "history of ideas." He opposed the latter not only because he wanted to look beyond the surface level of ideas to the "discursive practices" that lay behind them; but also because the traditional historical approach tended to view the science of the past as a deficient form of knowledge striving toward the present. Rather than being a teleological continuum, according to Foucault, history manifests discrete breaks between radically different periods, which cannot properly be compared at all as if their sciences were all trying to do the same thing. Foucault was clearly criticizing traditional historians for imposing a teleological structure on the past; but he was doing so by arguing for an alternative conception of historical reality. Thus his work perhaps belongs as much to the substantive as to the critical philosophy of history. And while it differs in some ways from the more literary approach to history of other contemporary trends, it is like them in treating historical knowledge as conceptual construction. The question of its truth does not arise.

This did not sit well with many historians, who were still toiling away, reading documents, sifting and evaluating evidence, attempting to tell the truth, and to distinguish it from falsity, about the past. Historians on the whole had never had a great deal of patience with the philosophy of history; now many were further alienated, if not openly hostile. It is true that White, Barthes, and others had opened the hostilities by portraying professional history, in effect, as a powerful establishment managing the past for political purposes. Now many historians argued that, on the contrary, by questioning the idea of historical truth, the postmoderns were fostering an "anything goes" attitude that opened the doors to Stalinist-style rewriting of history, Holocaust denial, and other falsifications. Postmodern theory provided no way of dis-

tinguishing between history and fiction, in the view of its critics. Some historians, it is true, were intrigued by skeptical doubts about history's capacity to know the past. Robert Novick noted (*That Noble Dream*, 1988) that even the respected American historian Charles Beard, in the 1930s, had called historical objectivity a "noble dream" that could never be fulfilled; and Novick went on to argue, with the help of postmodern theories, for an even stronger skepticism about the past. As could be expected, his 1988 book stirred much controversy among professional historians.

But historians were not the only ones who were unhappy with the postmodern turn. Philosophers in the analytic tradition (McCullagh, Bunzl) were prompted by the controversy over Novick's book to mount arguments against the skeptical relativism it represented. While generally admitting the role of culture and language in shaping our approach to the past, these authors adduce some of the standard arguments about the self-refuting character of skepticism and defend the place of evidence and critical judgment in distinguishing better from worse historical accounts. Paul Ricoeur (1984–1988), a continental philosopher who also drew heavily on the analytical philosophy of history, attempted to soften the excesses of postmodernism by reconnecting narrative texts with their roots in human experience. Ricoeur believed that narrative, in both fictional and historical form, "humanizes" the experience of time, bringing order and measure to human existence. He argued that history and fiction draw on each other and often intersect in important ways. But he did not agree with the tendency of his French contemporaries to reduce history to fiction, or to blur the distinction between them. In writing about history, he devoted careful attention to the restraining and guiding role of document and evidence in historical discourse. He also believed that narrative texts build on structures that are already present in ordinary experience, transforming them, and then affecting and enriching ordinary experience in their turn.

Other philosophers of history countered the views of White and the postmoderns by arguing against the idea that narrative is an alien framework imposed on a nonnarrative reality. What reality is meant? Human reality, which history is about, is the temporal flow of experiences and actions that engage persons in their social context. While it may not always have the crafted contours of a novel's plot, neither is it a chaotic absence of order or a meaningless one thing after another. According to this argument, human experience, and especially human action, are ordered in a manner that foreshadows the structures of narrative itself. Events are experienced as temporal configurations with beginnings, middles, and ends; actions project an end and organize the means for achieving it. The agent grasps a sequence of events together in a temporal order much as a narrator organizes the events of a story; it is as if the agent is constructing and telling himself a story and then acting it out. On this view the narrative we find in historical writings—and in fictional writings too—is not a merely literary device at odds with the human world, it is something more like an extension of human existence by other means.

According to this "continuity theory" (as some have called it), narrative structures constitute "the metaphysics of everyday life," as Danto called it, and offer the key to understanding not only experience and action, but also the self who acts (1985, p. xiv). The self can be seen as constructing itself by implicitly or explicitly telling, and of course also revising, its life story. This theory can be extended from individual to social life, where it becomes relevant to history. Communities, large and small, may be said to constitute themselves in the stories they tell themselves about themselves. Here historical consciousness and historical writing have their place. Written history can be seen as the collective memory that permits a society to hold itself together and plan its future.

Critics of the continuity theory have argued that it does not succeed in answering the skepticism of the postmoderns, which was seemingly its intention. It counters the theory that historical narrative is in principle incapable of portraying the past by arguing against the radical discontinuity between narrative and the real world. But even if it succeeds in demonstrating the protonarrative character of everyday action and experience, and in extending this to the social level, it does not account for the differences between these protonarrative structures and fully formed narratives we find in novels and histories. As regards historical knowledge, this theory, according to its critics, fails to provide a positive account of how narrative can succeed in arriving at historical truth and distinguishing it from falsehood.

4. HISTORICITY, HISTORICISM AND THE HISTORICIZATION OF PHILOSOPHY

These criticisms inadvertently reveal something about the discussion of narrative and history, especially when it draws on continental philosophy for its inspiration, that once again raises questions about how to classify it as philosophy of history. We already found that the focus on historical narratives as literary texts, under the influence of White and the structuralists, moved away from traditional epistemological questions without completely abandoning them. Historical knowledge took a back seat to the literary properties of historical writing. Some of the attempts we have been discussing, designed to counter the influence of poststructuralism on the philosophy of history, similarly defy the standard classification. This is because they draw heavily on the phenomenological and hermeneutical tradition going back to Husserl and Heidegger. These philosophers reflect on history in a way that is indeed related to traditional epistemological and even metaphysical concerns, but not in the way associated with the standard distinction between the substantive and the critical. In this tradition, the key concept is "historicity."

"*Geschichtlichkeit*," sometimes translated as "historicality," is a term used by Husserl and Heidegger in the 1920s and 1930s in their phenomenological descriptions of consciousness and human existence. The importance of this notion attests to the influence on both philosophers of Dilthey, who had died in 1911 but whose posthumously published work was still studied intensely. We have encountered Dilthey as the philosopher of the *Geisteswissenschaften*, whose project of working out a "critique of historical reason" made him an important contributor to the epistemological debates about history. But he also believed that historical knowledge is rooted in certain features of human existence. "We are historical beings before we become observers of history," he wrote, "and only because we are the former do we become the latter." (Dilthey 2002, p. 297)

Husserl and Heidegger, following Dilthey's lead, expand in slightly different ways on what it means to be a "historical being." The phenomenological concept of "world" is central for both: The human world is not merely a container for human beings but a complex of meanings. Past and future are part of that world, and both philosophers devote extensive analysis to temporality. Human experience is not confined to the present but consists of a temporal grasp, holding on to the past and anticipating or projecting its future. The self is not simply a substance that persists through time, but a self-constituting unity of temporal interrelations. These are all essential, ontological features of human existence: it is not as if the human being existed first and then just happened to come up against the world, the past, the future. An existence without these would not be a human existence at all.

The same can be said of the social dimension of existence—Husserl speaks of intersubjectivity and Heidegger of being-with-others. Taking this dimension into account, we can see that past and future take on broader meanings. The social past—history—has meaning for us and figures in our lives prior to and independently of explicit historical representation and disciplined inquiry. Husserl asserts in his late works that all human activity, even that of a science such as mathematics, has to be understood historically. According to Heidegger, we appropriate our history in an act of self-interpretation, and it becomes part of the future we project for ourselves. Our history is part of our self-understanding and in that sense part of our being. Like the world and others, history is an essential feature of our existence, not something added on or something we could be without.

Though the term "narrative" is not used in these early treatments of the concept of historicity, the idea is implicit in it. Dilthey did compare self-understanding to the composition of an implicit autobiography. The German term *Geschichte*, like the French *histoire*, can mean both "history" and "story," and both senses of the term are often implied." Husserl writes that "the ego constitutes itself for itself, so to speak, in the unity of a *Geschichte*," suggesting that the temporal synthesis of past, present and future, in which the self takes shape, is like telling the story of one's life (Husserl 1999, p. 75). It is easy to see in these concepts the prefiguration of the narrative conception of human time that later theorists apply to history in the larger, social sense.

How does the discussion of historicity fit into the philosophy of history? Clearly it qualifies as philosophical reflection on history, but it does not correspond to the standard categories with which we began. It does have some bearing on the understanding of history as a discipline, in the sense that it seeks the roots of historical knowledge in human existence. It addresses the question of why we seek to know about the past at all. It suggests that the past is more than just an object of curiosity for us, because it corresponds to a dimension of our being. Knowing about the past is knowing where we have come from and thus who we are. History as a disciplined, critical inquiry, as it has developed in the academy, is thus just an extension and intensification of the project of self-knowledge. But while this addresses the nature of historical inquiry, it is not raising the traditional epistemological questions about whether genuine knowledge of the past is possible, how or whether objectivity can be achieved, etc. It is interested in historical inquiry as a human activity, and seeks to understand its significance within human existence as a whole.

If these questions are not epistemological, it may be argued that they are metaphysical. Understanding human nature, after all, has always been a central metaphysical endeavor. This does not mean, however, that these questions are part of the substantive philosophy of history. The latter has traditionally set out to understand the whole process of human history, and this is different from the focus on what is essential to individual human existence. We find few pronouncements in the phenomenological, hermeneutical or narrativist literature about the meaning and purpose of history as a whole.

The concept of historicity became an issue in the French structuralist attack on the phenomenological tradition in the 1960s. The anthropologist Claude Levi-Strauss argued that many of the non-Western societies he studied were "peoples without history" in the sense that they devalue temporal change. The primary purpose of social organization in these societies is to prevent change or contain it as much as possible within an interpretive framework in which its significance can be denied. Their sense of themselves as individuals and as societies is not derived from a consciousness of the difference between past, present and future. Unlike Western societies, they have no interest in their past origins, nor do they ponder their future destiny; in this sense they are not characterized by historicity at all. Levi-Strauss famously attacked Jean-Paul Sartre for making historicity essential to humanity and by implication excluding "peoples without history" from the human race. Either they are somehow less than human, or they are relegated as "primitive peoples" to some remote prehistory, even though they still exist in the present. Levi-Strauss's attack foreshadows the postmodern view that the emphasis on history is a "Eurocentric," and thus provincial and limited, conception.

A related trend in twentieth-century philosophy might be seen as an extension of the notion of historicity, though it does not necessarily follow from it. If human existence is through-and-through historical, then all human endeavor is dependent on and limited to its historical position, including the search for truth. Truths thought to be timeless turn out to be nothing more than reflections of their historical age. Historical relativism of this sort is sometimes called "historicism" (though that term has also been used in a different sense—notably by Karl Popper, who used it to mean "historical determinism"). We have already encountered skeptical relativism about historical knowledge itself, and we have noted that some philosophers are skeptics about scientific knowledge as well. But to attribute the relativity of all knowledge to history in particular is a special form of skepticism. Like all skepticism, this form has self-referential problems, because the alleged relativity would extend to the relativist thesis itself.

But some philosophers have not flinched at this prospect, propounding the radical historicization even of philosophy. Thus the later Heidegger, and more recently Richard Rorty, view philosophy itself as a large-scale episode in Western history that is nearing or has reached its end. Perhaps this is the ultimate inversion of Hegel's grand design for the philosophy of history: He thought history had come to an end by being fully comprehended in thought. Philosophy ultimately triumphs over history. For Heidegger and Rorty, it is philosophy that has come to an end, and the triumph belongs to history.

See also Adorno, Theodor Wiesengrund; Anaxagoras of Clazomenae; Aristotle; Augustine, St.; Barthes, Roland; Bossuet, Jacques Bénigne; Collingwood, Robin George; Comte, Auguste; Continental Philosophy; Croce, Benedetto; Danto, Arthur; Determinism in History; Dilthey, Wilhelm; Engels, Friedrich; Enlightenment; Foucault, Michel; Geisteswissenschaften; Habermas, Jürgen; Hegel, Georg Wilhelm Friedrich; Heidegger, Martin; Hempel, Carl Gustav; Herder, Johann Gottfried; Historicism; Horkheimer, Max; Husserl, Edmund; Hyppolite, Jean; Kant, Immanuel; Kuhn, Thomas; Lukács, Georg; Lyotard, Jean François; Marx, Karl; Marxist Philosophy; Mill, John Stuart; Plato; Popper, Karl Raimund; Positivism; Progress, The Idea of; Rickert, Heinrich; Ricoeur, Paul; Romanticism; Rorty, Richard; Sartre, Jean-Paul; Spengler, Oswald; Structuralism and Post-structuralism; Thucydides; Toynbee, Arnold Joseph; Vico, Giambattista; Voltaire, François-Marie Arouet de; Windelband, Wilhelm.

Bibliography

Augustine, Saint, Bishop of Hippo. *The City of God against the Pagans*, edited and translated by R. W. Dyson. New York: Cambridge University Press, 1998.

Carr, David. *Time, Narrative, and History*. Bloomington: Indiana University Press, 1986.

Collingwood, R. G. *The Principle of History: And Other Writings in Philosophy of History*, edited by William H. Dray and W. J. van der Dussen. New York: Oxford University Press, 1999.

Danto, Arthur. *Narration and Knowledge: Including the Integral Text of Analytical Philosophy of History*. New York: Columbia University Press, 1985.

Dilthey, Wilhelm. *The Formation of the Historical World in the Human Sciences*. Vol. 3: *Selected Works*, edited by Rudolf A. Makkreel and Frithjof Rodi. Princeton and Oxford: Princeton University Press, 2002.

Dray, William H. *On History and Philosophers of History*. Leiden, Netherlands: Brill, 1989.

Fukuyama, Francis. *The End of History and the Last Man*. New York: Harper Collins, 1992.

Hegel, Georg Wilhelm Friedrich. *Introduction to the Philosophy of History*. Translated by Leo Rauch. Indianapolis and Cambridge: Hackett, 1988.

Hegel, Georg Wilhelm Friedrich. *The Philosophy of History*. Translated by J. Sibree. New York: Dover, 1956.

Husserl, Edmund. *Cartesian Meditations*. Translated by Dorion Cairns. Dordrecht/Boston/London: Kluwer Academic Publishers, 1999.

Kant, Immanuel. *On History*, edited and translated by Lewis White Beck. New York: Macmillan, 1963.

Lemon, M. C. *Philosophy of History: A Guide for Students*. London: Routledge, 2003.

Löwith, Karl. *Meaning in History*. Chicago: University of Chicago Press, 1949.

Lyotard, Jean-François. *The Postmodern Condition: A Report on Knowledge*. Translated by Geoff Bennington and Brian Massumi. Minneapolis: University of Minnesota Press, 1984.

Marx, Karl, and Friedrich Engels. *The Communist Manifesto*. Edited by David McLellan. Oxford: Oxford University Press, 1998.

Mink, Louis. *Historical Understanding*, edited by Brian Fay, Eugene O. Golob, and Richard T. Vann. Ithaca, NY: Cornell University Press, 1987.

Novick, Peter. *That Noble Dream: The "Objectivity Question" and the American Historical Profession*. Cambridge, U.K.: Cambridge University Press, 1988.

Popper, Karl. *The Poverty of Historicism*. London: Routledge, 1957.

Ricoeur, Paul. *Time and Narrative*. 3 vols. Translated by Kathleen McLaughlin and David Pellauer. Chicago: University of Chicago Press, 1984–1988.

White, Hayden. *Metahistory*. Baltimore, MD: Johns Hopkins University Press, 1973.

White, Morton. *Foundations of Historical Knowledge*. New York: Harper and Row, 1965.

ANTHOLOGIES

Ankersmit, Frank, and Hans Kellner, eds. *A New Philosophy of History*. Chicago: University of Chicago Press, 1995.

Burns, Robert, and Hugh Rayment-Packard, eds. *Philosophies of History: From Enlightenment to Postmodernity*. Oxford, U.K.: Blackwell Publishers, 2000.

Dray, William H., ed. *Philosophical Analysis and History*. New York: Harper and Row, 1966.

Fay, Brian, Philip Pomper, and Richard T. Vann, eds. *History and Theory: Contemporary Readings*. Oxford, U.K.: Blackwell Publishers, 1998.

Roberts, Geoffrey, ed. *The History and Narrative Reader*. London: Routledge, 2001.

David Carr (2005)

PHILOSOPHY OF LANGUAGE

What, if anything, can philosophy teach us about language? It is a feature of English that its adjectives come before its nouns, as in *green table*. This syntactic fact distinguishes English from French. In English there is a difference in sound between words that begin with a b and ones that begin with a p. This phonological fact distinguishes English from other languages. Some Arabic languages, for example, have trill sounds. This phonetic feature distinguishes these Arabic languages from English. Are any of these linguistic features philosophically interesting?

It is doubtful whether any philosopher seriously believes that, qua philosopher, they have anything interesting to say about the syntactic, phonetic, and phonological features of languages in general or of English in particular. Why, then, should it be any different for all of the other features of language? For example, that in English a relative pronoun proceeds the noun phrase it modifies or that English declarative sentences are of the subject-verb-object variety, are interesting facts about English syntax, but why should any of this be of philosophical interest?

Many theorists claim that philosophers of language are interested in answering questions of the sort: What need someone know in order to understand his or her language? Do they need to know the sorts of facts just mentioned? In some sense of *know*, they must. Someone who speaks English, normally, can recognize another as a non-English speaker, as a nonnative English speaker, or not a perfectly fluent English speaker simply by virtue of the fact that this speaker employs syntactic structures or phonemes that are not a part of English, or fails to recognize differences between distinct phonemes of English. For example, if someone failed to recognize a difference between an articulation of the words *bit* and *bet*, this would constitute partial evidence that the individual in question does not (fully) grasp English. But why is this philosophical? It is not! Still, philosophy does matter to language. Why anyone should think so is a complicated matter; one that an answer to will be sketched in the sections that follow.

COMMUNICATIVE ABILITIES

It is uncontroversial that linguistic expressions carry meaning. Right now, you are looking at ink marks on a piece of paper. These marks are in English, they have meaning, and should you know these meanings, you can figure out what they say. We spend a lot of our lives exercising our communicative abilities; abilities to produce utterances (spoken, written, felt, etc.) that others can interpret; and, abilities to interpret utterances that others have produced. These abilities in assigning meanings to expressions—simple and complex—are required in order to ask for help, read traffic signs, interest others, surf the net, read newspapers, write e-mails, watch movies, comfort others, listen to lectures, order food, read a bus schedule, buy wine, quarrel, and make jokes.

One of the central topics in philosophy of language today is to provide an explicit and systematic account of whatever knowledge we have of the meanings of the expressions of our language that enables us to communicate with it. Surrounding these projects are a number of subtle philosophical issues.

WHAT IS MEANING?

What is the meaning of an expression? Traditional scholarly books and articles all weigh in with one analysis or another about the nature of meaning. Some posit that the meaning of an expression is what it applies to (*apple* means the set of apples), the idea that we associate with it (*God* means, say, the idea of a benevolent omnipotent omniscient being), or the characteristic behavior that its uses evince (*Fire!* means run for safety), and so on.

Criticisms run that this or that analysis cannot be right, because if meaning were this, then two expressions that differ in meaning would turn out to be synonymous, or that a meaningful expression would turn out to be, on the proposed analyses, meaningless. For example, a critic of the view that the meaning of an expression is what it applies to might argue that even though the two sentences "Cicero was Roman" and "Tully was Roman" are not synonymous as the referents of *Cicero* and *Tully* are the same. A critic of the view that the meaning of an expression is the idea(s) we associated with it might argue that even though someone can associate the idea of warm weather with the word *grass*, the idea of warm weather is still not part of its meaning. Anyone who denies this should visit Ireland in January.

Though neither argument is definitive (after all, paraphrasing Ludwig Wittgenstein, theories do not get refuted; they just become no longer interesting to defend), they still illustrate how theories of meaning can be, and often are, evaluated. In traditional criticisms, intuitions about what we believe expressions to mean are dominate. The question of what the relationship is between theories (the sole aim of which is to provide an analysis of an important concept) and theories (the aim of which is to explain various phenomena) is left open by this to and fro (for more on the analysis of the concept of meaning, see William P. Alston's *Philosophy of Language*).

A major shift in the philosophical study of meaning took place about fifty years ago with the abandonment of efforts to analyze the concept of meaning (Quine 1953). But, if it is not an analysis of the concept of meaning that philosophers are after, what, then, warrants evaluations of various claims about what meaning is?

Whatever meaning is, it is relatively uncontroversial what knowledge of it enables us to do: It enables us to understand language. Because we know what the expressions of our language mean, we understand English. In rejecting an account we are saying in effect that this cannot be what we know that enables to understand English, because if it were we need not understand English. Thus, if you were taught the referent of every English word, you would not understand an English interlocutor. On this account, being asked, "Was Cicero the same man as Tully?," should produce bewilderment. On the referential theory, it is analogous to being asked whether bachelors are unmarried men. But if it is not knowledge of the referent of an expression that enables one to understand it, what does enable one to understand it?

The picture that understanding a word is learning to associate an idea with it goes back at least to the early empiricist Thomas Hobbes. It is a bad theory, for suppose you were told, "Though grass covers Ireland in January, it is not warm there then." Were your understanding of the word *grass* to include the idea of warmth, you should find this comment linguistically confused, much like being told "Though John is a bachelor, he has a wife!" But if understanding consists neither in knowing the referents of your words, nor the ideas you associate with them, what then might you know that would enable you to understand English?

The picture that dominated theories of meaning throughout most of the last century is (various versions of) linguistic behaviorism (Skinner 1957). Linguistic competence with an expression is knowing how to behave appropriately when confronted with its uses. For example, suppose you are told "Go get a coke!" In virtue of understanding English, what should you do? Should you automatically get a coke? Presumably not, for that would render linguistically competent English speakers all very active. Perhaps you need only know what you are supposed to do. But what are you supposed to do when someone asks you for a coke? Good manners might require that you should do something when asked, but understanding English requires nothing of you. These various critical points are intended to establish that no particular behavior is associated with language understanding, and so they scream out for clarification from anyone who wants to be a behaviorist about linguistic competence, clarification that was never forthcoming (Chomsky 1959).

MEANING IS RELATIONAL, EXTRINSIC, VAGUE, AND CONVENTIONAL

Beginning with a banality such as understanding a language requires knowing the meanings of its expressions, as philosophers well know, is a necessary precaution against a rampant background of skepticism in some philosophical quarters about the notion of meaning. Some of this skepticism generates from the consideration that whatever is alleged to carry meaning does not do so inherently. For instance, there is nothing about English words that requires "Snow is white" to mean that snow is white. In another language, they might mean grass is green, and so it follows that whatever words mean depends partly on the language from which these words originate. But this sort of relativity should not compromise the reality of what words mean. After all, no one is inherently a father. The relational property of fatherhood depends on a relationship to someone else—a child. Likewise, whether or not a string of words means that snow is white depends on this string's relationship to a specific language.

This issue concerning the meaning of words should not be confused with reservations about the reality or truth of conventions. Being married, like fatherhood, is a relational property. But unlike fatherhood, marriage is not grounded in biology. It is, so to speak, a matter of convention or social arrangement who is married to whom. But, extant conventions might easily have been different. Everyone who is currently married might just as easily not have been without suffering any substantial change to their being—rather, only a change in convention. It is a mistake, however, to infer from this possibility that there really is no such thing as marriage. Likewise, if it is a matter of convention that *dog* means dog and not cat, then it does not follow that there should be a dispute over what *dog* means.

The reality of meaning is equally left uncompromised by considerations about vagueness or borderline cases. Two words translate or paraphrase each other just in case they share the same meaning. In many instances, we are simply unsure whether two words translate or paraphrase each other; and there is no higher source to which we can appeal to settle our doubts. In short, that meaning is relational, extrinsic, vague, or conventional does not compromise its reality.

LANGUAGE AND USE OF LANGUAGE: SEMANTICS AND PRAGMATICS

Of course, linguistic meaning is not our only employment of the concept of meaning. We sometimes speak of another's action as meaningful, as when identifying purpose as our aim. In seeking the meaning for which Bill burned down his house, however, it need not be assumed that Bill's act of burning down his house is meaningful in the same way as the English sentence "Bill burned down his house" is. For one, it is not conventional meaning we seek in another's act, but rather the underlying intentions. For what reason did Bill carry out his sorry deed?

Similarly, people use words with intent. John might assert "Snow is white" because he wants to alert his listeners to the fact that English is his native tongue. No one would conclude on this basis that the words "Snow is white" mean that English is John's language. We can see clearly that with these speech acts, the notion of meaning enters twice. First, in choosing a vehicle to express our message, words whose conventional meaning best conveys that message are employed. And, secondly, in interpreting a linguistic act, an attributed meaning can and often does exceed this conventional meaning.

An audience can exploit context and individual histories in order to discern an agent's purpose or message. Why did he tell me, "I love you," when he knows that I am fully aware of it? Does he mean to reassure me? Or, does he dread losing me, and so, means by his words for me to feel guilt about our imminent separation? Such exegetical issues concern us all whenever we try to size up what others mean by their particular use of words. With conventional linguistic meaning, speakers rely on a prior comprehension in order to convey successfully a message; with these other sorts of meaning, speakers hope—wittingly or not—to exploit presumed shared beliefs and expectations in discerning nonconventional meaningful aspects of linguistic acts.

In summary: When theorizing about meaning, it is crucial to distinguish between language and the use of language. Languages, such as English, exist independently (in a sense that requires clarification) of what anyone happens to do with them. If these sentences together in this order had never been assembled, it would have made no difference to the existence of English. English words and sentences would have meant whatever they do. Speakers simply exploit the meanings of these words in their writings, and a reader exploits those same meanings

in order to understand what is written. For an example, consider sentence (1): Some American musicians are scared of a small Norwegian troll.

Most likely, (1) has never before been written. That, of course, does not prevent it from meaning whatever it does in English. It has its meaning independently of ever having been uttered or thought about. So far our discussion has been primarily concerned with the meaning that sentences have in English (by virtue of being English sentences)—that is, their conventional or literal meaning. The study of the literal meaning of words and sentences is often called semantics.

Conventional meaning, however, is as we have seen not the be all and end all of communication. We often (maybe always) use sentences to communicate contents quite different from their conventional meaning, as observed in the following conversation. Sam asks Chris in sentence (2): Can you help Alex with his paper tonight? Chris in sentence (3) responds: I'm driving into New York to see Jill. By uttering (3), Chris can succeed in telling Sam that she cannot help Alex with her paper that night. Of course, that's not the literal meaning of sentence (3). The literal meaning of that sentence is that Chris is driving into New York to see Jill. But by uttering (3), Chris can succeed in communicating to Sam more than the literal meaning of the sentence she uttered. The study of how words and sentences can be used to communicate contents that go beyond their literal meaning is often called pragmatics. The goal of pragmatics is to study the various mechanisms that speakers exploit to communicate content that goes beyond literal meaning (for more on the distinction between pragmatics and semantics, see H.P. Grice's *Studies in the Ways of Words*). But in ascribing conventional meaning, one can incur theoretical costs.

REPRESENTATIONAL AND COMPOSITIONAL MEANING (SEMANTIC) THEORIES

Philosophers of language and linguists talk about the vehicles that carry meaning as both representational and compositional. Representations represent—so the sentence "Bill Clinton is tall" represents Bill Clinton as tall; however, the sentence "The president of the United States in 1999 is tall" also is true of Bill Clinton, and also represents him as tall, but it does so in a different manner. But it differs not only inasmuch as it uses a different vehicle. The Italian sentence "*Il presidente degli Stati Unitii in 1999 e' alto*" represents Bill Clinton as tall in exactly the same way that "The president of the United States in 1999 is tall" does, even though these two vehicles of representation are distinct. With these two sentences, however, the vehicles are synonymous—they carry the same meaning, whereas the first two are not synonymous, though both vehicles happen to be true in the same circumstances.

Suppose, for instance, that someone else had been president in 1999; then, the latter two sentences with definite descriptions might be false, but the first sentence with a proper name would still be true. So, whatever meaning is, it would appear to be more fine-grained than a mere symbol-object relationship. If words were merely tags for objects, no two co-tags would differ in meaning. It would seem that vehicles denote objects under representational guises, and these guises are part of what that expression means.

There has been much written about the nature of this guise, yet little of it has been clear. Whatever guises are, we have seen that they must be more fine-grained than the objects to which expressions apply because expressions with the same referent can differ in meaning, but guises must also be more coarsely-grained than the ideas speakers associate with expressions. Two people might use the same expression but associate different ideas with it; for you, *snow* might connote misery but for a skier it might connote joy.

Synonymous sentences in the same or distinct languages are supposed to share guises; those that are non-synonymous do not, even if the sentences happen to be about the same objects, events, or state of affairs. Like the shadows in Plato's cave allegory, guises suggest existing somewhere in between linguistic items and idiosyncratic ideas associated with expressions by individual speakers, on the one hand, and the objects to which they are conventionally attached, on the other.

Guises are what determine whether a linguistic item is about one thing and not another; they are the concepts that enable us to understand the linguistic items we use. The definite descriptions *the forty-second president of the United States* and *the husband of Hilary Clinton* pick out the same person, Bill Clinton, but they do so in different ways. The ways in which they pick him out are another way to think about the guises associated with expressions. The former expression picks out Bill Clinton partly by virtue of his having the property of being the forty-second president of the United States; and the latter expression picks him out partly by virtue of his being Hilary Clinton's husband. Thus, these two expressions each represent the same individual, but they do in different ways—under different guises.

But there is more to the concept of a guise than is evidenced by representational powers. Natural languages are essentially productive and systematic. They exhibit productivity in that there are no obvious upper bounds on the number of creative linguistic acts that can be performed through speech. Novel sentences can be formed by conjoining any two meaningful indicative sentences—as in, "John left, but Mary stayed"—or by prefacing any meaningful indicative sentence with a psychological verb—as in, "Carl believes that Martha is ill" or "Carl fears that Martha is ill."

Because humans lack magical abilities, this capacity to produce and comprehend novel linguistic acts requires explanation. The standard explanation is that speakers of a natural language must have learned rules that enable them to determine the meaning of a complex expression strictly on the basis of its significant parts. The existence of such compositional rules explains our capacity with productive representational systems—by assuming that any unbounded representational system is compositional, we have an explanation for mastery over productive representational systems (for further discussion of compositionality, see Jerry Fodor's and Ernie Lepore's *Compositionality Papers*).

The property of compositionality can also be invoked in order to explain the following feature: It is a distinctive feature of English that when a grammatical sentence of the form "A R's B" is meaningful, then if "B R's A" is grammatical, not only is it also meaningful, but its parts are presumed to make the exact same meaningful contribution that they do in the original configuration. This aspect of a representational system is referred to as its systematicity.

The existence of a set of compositional rules accounts for systematicity as well as productivity. Compositionality requires that meaningful expressions compose in systematic ways to produce meaningful complexes. The expressions *the red shoe*, *the table*, and *fell on* mean what they mean regardless of whether they are configured to read "The red shoe fell on the table," or "The table fell on the red shoe." To be more specific: reconsider (1). Its literal meaning and, indeed, the literal meaning of any English sentence, depends on two factors: A) the meaning of the words (i.e., *some, American, musicians, are* and *troll*; and B) the way in which these words are assembled. Put together as in (4), what results is a sentence entirely different in meaning from (1): (4) Some Norwegian musicians are scared of a small American troll.

From these apparently obvious facts we can derive the idea that languages have compositional meaning theories. The idea is that the literal meaning of a sentence (its literal or conventional content) is the result of the (literal/conventional) meaning of its parts (the words in it) and the manner in which these parts are put together (their mode of composition).

Furthermore, as we have already noted, in addition to the systematicity of our sentences, speakers are also able to understand and produce indefinitely many sentences—sentences neither they nor anyone else in their community has ever uttered before. This shows that their knowledge of language must be productive; it must extend beyond a fixed lexicon of predefined static elements, and must include a generative system that actively composes linguistic knowledge so as to describe arbitrarily complex structures. The hallmark of productivity in language is recursion. Recursive patterns of complementation, as in (5), and recursive patterns of modification, as in (6) and (7), allow phrases to be nested indefinitely many times within a single sentence: (5) Chris thinks that Kim thought that Robin wanted Sandy to leave; (6) Chris bought a gorgeous new French three-quart covered copper saucepan; (7) Chris is writing a book that describes inventors that have built machines that changed the world that we live in.

Speakers' capacity to formulate and recognize an open-ended array of possible sentences shows how acute a problem it is to coordinate meaning across speakers. When we learn the meanings of expressions of our native language, we must generalize from the finite record of our previous experience to an infinity of other expressions and situations. If we thereby arrive at a common understanding of the meanings of these expressions, it must be because language is structured by substantive and inherent constraints that we are able to exploit. More generally, if our discoveries in the theory of meaning are to help explain how speakers can use language meaningfully, we should expect that the generative mechanisms we postulate as theorists will be compatible with the psychological mechanisms that underlie speakers' abilities.

There are many ways to implement this idea of a compositional meaning theory. One that has been prominent in the philosophical literature is that a theory of meaning for a natural language, L, should consist of a finite set of axioms specifying the meaning of the words and the rules for how they can be composed. These axioms would then permit the derivation of theorems that specify the meaning of complex expressions (such as *some American musicians*) and sentences, such as (1)–(7).

So understood, a semantic theory is a formal theory from which we can derive the meaning of an infinity of English sentences. The reason why (1)–(7) mean what they mean in English is that their meanings are encoded, so to speak, in the basic axioms of a correct meaning theory for English.

A straightforward way, then, for a philosopher of language to explain productivity and systematicity is to assume that the meanings of particular sentences can be calculated by inference from general facts about meaning in the language. For example, consider the compositional meaning theory presented in (8)–(10): (8) *Snow* is a noun phrase and refers to the stuff snow; (9) *White* is an adjective phrase and refers to the property whiteness; and (10) If N is a noun phrase and refers to the stuff S and A is an adjective phrase and refers to the property P, then N is A is a sentence and is true if, and only if, S is P.

From this theory, we can derive (11) as a logical consequence: "Snow is white" is true if, and only if, snow is white. Why should we think of (11) as a characterization of the meaning of the English sentence "Snow is white?" We can because it links up this sentence with a condition in the world stated in objective terms—in this case, the condition that snow is white. As theorists of meaning, we can utilize this kind of theory, which Donald Davidson calls an interpretive truth-theory, to provide a general account of how sentences link up with conditions in the world (Davidson 1967, 2001; Lepore and Ludwig 2005).

We use atomic formulas to axiomatize the meanings for elementary structures in the language and use conditional formulas to describe the meaning of complex structures in the language as a function of the semantics of their constituents. We then reason logically from the axioms to associate particular sentences with particular conditions in the world. As in (8)–(10), this inference will be compositional, in that the conclusions we derive will be inferred through a logical derivation that mirrors the syntactic/grammatical derivation of the sentence.

There are two ways to view interpretive truth-theories such as (8)–(10). We can exploit an interpretive truth-theory to formulate a theory of meaning for a new language. For example, we could be pursuing translation. In this case, we are interested in systematically articulating translations of sentences in the object language in terms of sentences in our own; we understand these translations to be derived by inference from the axioms of the theory. Another way to view interpretive truth-theories (and other sorts of compositional theories of meaning), such as (8)–(10), is as ingredients of the speakers' psychology. On this view, we regard the axioms of a theory of meaning as generalizations that native speakers know tacitly about their own language. When speakers formulate or recognize particular utterances, they reason tacitly from this implicit theory to derive conclusions about specific new sentences. On this understanding, interpretive truth-theories offer an explanation of how speaker knowledge of meaning and inference underlie linguistic competence.

FORMALISM IN PHILOSOPHY OF LANGUAGE

The view we just described invites an analogy between the semantics of natural languages and the semantics of the artificial languages of formal logic. The analogy goes back to Gottlob Frege (1879), who took logic to clarify the features of natural language essential for correct mathematical thought and communication. The work of Richard Montague (1974) took the analogy further. Montague explicitly advocated an exact parallel between the semantic analysis of English—what ordinary speakers actually know about their language—and the semantics of intensional higher-order logic. In fact, many techniques originally developed for giving semantics to logical languages turn out to be extremely useful in carrying out semantic analysis.

INDIRECT SPEECH ACTS

Interpreting a dream partly involves assigning it meaning, but does this imply that dreams are representational in the way that language is? In one sense, they are obviously so. This is the sense in which we might say of any image that it is representational. An image of a horse is of a horse, and not of sheep. But this is a notion of representation irrelevant to our current concerns in the philosophy of language, because it appeals to a natural (and not a conventional) relation between an image and its corresponding object. If dreams are supposed to be representational in the same sense in which photographs or other sorts of images are, then talk of a compositional theory of interpretation or meaning of dreams is not anything like the sort of theory that one invokes for systems of representations such as natural language. For one, photographic images are neither productive nor systematic, nor are they even fine-grained in the way in which linguistic representational systems are. An image of Bill Clinton is an image of the president of the United States, and nothing short of an election can pull them apart. More famously, an image of John giving Bill a toy is indistinguishable from an image of Bill receiving a toy from John, though these inseparable acts are distinct. It is clear that the sort of systematicity that occurs so naturally within bona fide linguistic representational systems cannot be applied to images with the same ease.

We return now to our earlier contrast between literal/conventional meaning and meaning in purpose or what we might call agent meaning. When the subject is employing so-called indirect speech acts, then what one means by one's words must take into consideration background factors. So, for example, suppose Janet says, "It's raining outside." Her words mean that it is raining outside, but she herself might mean for her audience to bring their umbrellas. When Janet spoke she intended her audience to come to believe what she was trying to get across. In order for her words to have meant that her audience is to take their umbrellas, she must have intended her audience to recognize her ulterior motive.

Speaker meaning in contrast to literal/conventional meaning, then, requires (at least) two sorts of intentions, one about what a speaker is trying to get their audience to believe by their utterance and another about getting them to recognize what he or she is trying to do. More specifically, what a speaker means by their words depends on what they intend their audience to come to believe, and what he or she intends them to recognize him or her as intending them to come to believe. Both component intentions, tacitly or not, must accompany an utterance in order for the speaker to mean something by what they say. By Janet's utterance of "It's raining," she means for her listener to bring their umbrella just in case she intends them to come to believe this and she intends them to recognize that she intends them to come to believe this. She intends for them to come to believe they are to bring their umbrella, and she intends them to recognize that she intends them to come to believe they are to bring their umbrella.

Implicit in our discussion is, of course, the assumption that speaker meaning can exceed word meaning. For you to bring your umbrella is not what Janet's words "It's raining" literally/conventionally mean, nor is it implied by anything that these words literally/conventionally mean. Speaker meaning is determined by word meaning alone just in case it is either expressed or implied by what the words used mean; conversely, it is not determined by literal meaning alone if it is neither expressed nor implied by what the speaker's words literally mean. A simple test separates the former distinction from the latter. If we try to deny speaker meaning determined by word meaning, then we end up making inconsistent claims. Because Janet can consistently assert that it is raining outside without intending for you to bring any umbrella, what she means is neither expressed nor implied by what her words mean (Grice 1989).

Inquiries about speaker meaning not determined by word meaning are about nonlinguistic motives, beliefs, desires, wishes, fears, hopes, and other psychological states that provoke verbal expression. Speaking is an action; it is what we do with meaningful words. This requires reasons, and reasons not entirely about what our words mean. Linguistic and nonlinguistic psychological states both come into play.

SENTENCES MEANING AND UNDERSTANDING

To sum up: One chief goal of philosophy of language is to show how speaker knowledge of a natural language allows speakers to use utterances of sentences from their language meaningfully. As we have seen, one rough and tentative answer has been: If speakers know a recursive compositional meaning theory for their language, then they can use its rules and axioms to calculate interpretive truth conditions for arbitrarily complex novel sentences. But we have also seen that even if speakers can infer the truth conditions of sentences from their language on the basis of (tacitly) employing a compositional meaning theory for their language, such knowledge alone cannot account for all of what goes on in communication. Communication invariably takes us further than the literal/conventional meaning of our words. How do we go further in a communicative exchange than what our words literally mean?

A preliminary, approximate answer is this: We begin by idealizing the information mutually available to us in a conversation as our common ground (Stalnaker 1973). The common ground settles questions about whose answers are uncontroversial, in that interlocutors know the answers, know that they know the answers, and so forth. Meanwhile, the common ground leaves open a set of possibilities about which there is not yet agreement: Maybe there is a matter of fact that could turn out (for all that the interlocutors know) to be one of various ways, or maybe the interlocutors actually do know how it turns out but do not realize that the knowledge is shared—so it could be that the others know, and it could be that they do not—and so forth. We might represent these possibilities in the common ground as a set of possible worlds (situations).

Let the set of possible worlds in which a given sentence is true represent the proposition associated with the sentence. If we adopt this picture, then we can formalize the effect that asserting a formula has on the common ground. When interlocutor A asserts a formula f, he or she introduces into the conversation the information that f is true. Suppose that f expresses the proposition that p. Before A asserts f, the common ground is some set of worlds C. After, the common ground must also take into account f. This formula f restricts the live possibilities by requiring the worlds that are in the common ground to make true the further proposition that p. So, the change that occurs when A asserts f is that the common ground goes from C to C together with the proposition that p. This concise model forms the basis of a range of research characterizing the relationship between truth-conditional semantics (literal/conventional meaning) and conversational pragmatics in formal terms (van Benthem and ter Meulen 1997).

This idealization obviously has its limits. And it is easy to come up with strange puzzles when one moves (perhaps inadvertently) beyond the limits of these idealizations. Before considering one such puzzle, we digress to discuss perhaps one of the most important results from one of the most important research programs in the philosophy of language in the last half-century.

SAUL KRIPKE AND HILARY PUTNAM ON TWIN EARTH

Imagine a planet exactly like Earth, except that where Earth has water, this other planet, Twin Earth, has another mysterious substance, say, XYZ. To human senses, this substance seems exactly the same as water; nevertheless, it has a fundamentally different chemical structure. Imagine further that it is still the year 1700, and chemical structure has yet to be discovered. Still, we judge that the English word *water*, on Earth, means water, whereas the Twin English word *water*, on Twin Earth, means XYZ. Moreover, if an earthling were suddenly teleported to Twin Earth, they would still speak English, and their word *water* would still mean water—this despite the fact that they might have exactly the same dispositions as Twin Earthers have to accept or reject statements about their new surroundings. In short, the unfortunate earthling would think they were surrounded by lots of water, and would be completely wrong.

What moral should we draw from Putnam's (1975) Twin Earth thought experiments? Should we conclude that when you look at how a speaker is disposed to respond to English sentences, *water* can be interpreted equally well as water, XYZ, or even the disjunction of the two? These interpretations are different, and they assign distinct truth values to English sentences in meaningful (but ultimately inaccessible) situations. In fact, though, when we say *water* in English means water, according to Kripke, we are applying a standard based on our recognition that English speakers intend to pick out a particular kind of stuff in their own environment.

As a community, English speakers have encountered this stuff and named it *water*. And as a community, English speakers work together to ensure first that the community maintains the referential connection between the word *water* and that stuff, and only secondarily, that the individuals in the community can themselves identify examples of the stuff in particular situations. When as observers we recognize that *water* means water, we are not summarizing the epistemic abilities of particular speakers. Rather, we are summarizing social commitments and causal connections in the community that have worked across speakers to hook the word *water* up with the stuff, and keep it that way. What philosophers of language do, ultimately, is to explain how speakers can use language to refer in shared ways to shared aspects of the world.

Kripke (1972) motivates his account with an analogy between words for kinds, such as *water*, and proper names, such as *Richard Feynman*. In the case of proper names, we can point to the social practices that initially fix the reference of a name and transmit that reference within the community. A baby boy is born. His parents call him by a certain name. They talk about him to their friends. Others meet him. The name spreads from link to link much like a chain. To use another example: Let us say that a speaker on the far end of a similar type of chain, who hears about Richard Feynman, may be referring to him even though they cannot remember from whom they first heard his name. They know Feynman is a famous physicist. A certain passage of communication reaching ultimately to the man himself does reach the speaker. The speaker is then referring to Feynman even though he or she cannot identify him uniquely. He or she does not know what a Feynman diagram is and does not know what the Feynman theory of pair production and annihilation is. Not only that, the speaker would have trouble distinguishing between Gell-Mann and Feynman (Kripke 1980).

The result is that we can judge a speaker's reference with a proper name independently of sentences that the speaker would accept or reject. In the case of common nouns such as *water*, the word has had its reference since time immemorial. Nevertheless, new speakers still link themselves into chains of reference that participate in and preserve the connection between *water* and water. So analogously, we take an English speaker's word *water* to refer to water, independently of sentences the speaker would accept or reject.

Most philosophers of language find the Kripke/Putnam views about the meanings of names and so-called natural kind terms satisfying; it offers a close fit to an intuitive understanding of ourselves. It seems that we really do commit to use our words with the same reference as our community. And when others make claims about the world, it seems that we really do assess and dispute those claims with respect to the common standard in the community.

For example, on the Kripke/Putnam view, we inevitably focus on certain aspects of an agent's verbal behavior and not others when we assign meanings to their utterances. We do so because we locate the theory of meaning as part of a broader science of the mind, which combines a theory of language with a theory of action (including an account of our intentions and social relationships) and a theory of perception (including an account of the limits and failings of our observation). The theory of meaning in itself explains only so much—and, not surprisingly, just because we understand the meaning of someone's sentences, we do not ipso facto understand them.

Crucially, this new view predicts that some statements are necessarily true solely in virtue of the meanings of the words involved. We have already seen that it is a fact about meaning that *Richard Feynman* names Richard Feynman, or that *water* names water. We can go further. *Hesperus* names the planet Venus, *Phosphorus* names the planet Venus, *is* names the identity relation. So sentence (12) follows, just as a matter of meaning alone: (12) Phosphorus is identical to Hesperus. Given that *Hesperus* and *Phosphorus* are both names for the planet Venus, (12) must be true. There is no way that that planet could have failed to be that planet. Like sentence (12), the other facts that follow from the meanings of our language are necessarily true.

However, on the Kripke/Putnam account, facts about meaning turn out not to be knowable a priori. We discover them. To illustrate, imagine that, early on, the ancient Greeks were in an epistemic situation that left it open whether the bright object that sometimes appeared in the morning sky was the same as the bright object that sometimes appeared in the evening sky. They could not distinguish themselves from their doubles on a Twin Earth where the morning star and the evening star actually were distinct objects (alien satellites, we might suppose). These Twin Earthers would speak a language in which (12) translates into a false sentence—indeed, a necessarily false sentence. For the ancient Greeks, however, the translation of (12) was necessarily true. Eventually, the ancient Greeks advanced their science, and improved their epistemic situation. They realized that, in our case, there is only one celestial object. At the same time, then, they discovered that (12) is necessarily true.

When we reflect on the generality of Twin Earth thought experiments, it is clear that facts about meaning are knowable a posteriori. We can imagine being quite wrong about what our world is like. In these imaginary situations, our empirical errors extend to errors we make about what our words mean. And, of course, we can also imagine disagreeing with others about what the world is like. Though we are committed to use our words with the shared reference of our community, we must be prepared to resolve our dispute by giving up facts that we think are necessarily true—facts that we think characterize the meanings of our words and the contents of our thoughts. With this model of how proper names and common nouns attach to the world before us, we are now ready to return to the puzzles alluded to above in connection with assertion.

ASSERTION

Why would a speaker ever assert an identity statement like (12)? The trigger for a puzzle comes from arguments that sentence (12) must be true. If this is so, then consider what happens when A asserts C. We update the common ground C by intersecting it with the set of all possible worlds (situations)—the proposition expressed by Hesperus is Phosphorus—leaving exactly the same set C. A, therefore, on this model, has done nothing; the interlocutors' information has not changed at all! But obviously this result is absurd. What has gone wrong?

In fact, in assuming that assertions update the context with the proposition they express, we have implicitly assumed that the participants in the conversation have certain and complete knowledge of their language. For example, interlocutors can calculate that Hesperus is Phosphorus expresses a necessarily true proposition only if they can calculate that Hesperus names Venus and Phosphorus names Venus. Of course, under such circumstances, they do not learn anything from the sentence. It is easy to see how this assumption could go unnoticed.

In discussion, we typically assume the reference of our terms—precisely what matters in the "Hesperus is Phosphorus" case—is not at issue. However, consider how to formalize uses of sentences in more realistic situations (as we do so, we must be careful to respect the intuitions of Kripke's and Putnam's thought experiments

[Stalnaker 1978]). Suppose an interlocutor B does not know that Hesperus is Phosphorus. What that really means is that B cannot distinguish between two possible situations. In the first, there is only one heavenly body out there, and B's community speaks a language English₁ where both Hesperus and Phosphorus are names for that body. In the second, there are two distinct heavenly bodies, and B speaks a language English₂ where Hesperus is a name for one of them and Phosphorus is a name for the other. Because these possibilities are open for B, they must both also be represented in the common ground.

Now, we need a correspondingly expressive notion of assertion. When interlocutor A says something, A is committed that it is true according to the standards for reference that prevail in the community. Any assertion that A makes should turn out to be true in the language A speaks. What we have just seen is that any point of evaluation w in the common ground could potentially have its own language English_w with relevant differences from English as spoken in the real world. Adapting Stalnaker's (1978) terminology, we can associate any utterance u with a diagonal proposition; this proposition is true at a point w if the proposition that u expresses in English_w is true in w.

In the case of Hesperus being Phosphorus, the effect of A's assertion is to intersect the common ground with this diagonal proposition. Concretely, we retain in the common ground worlds of the first kind, where English₁ is spoken, Hesperus and Phosphorus are necessarily the same and A's assertion is necessarily true. However, we discard from the common ground worlds of the second kind, where English₂ is spoken, Hesperus and Phosphorus are necessarily different and A's assertion is necessarily false (there is substantially more to be said about the relationship between utterance meaning and the information that interlocutors convey).

METHODOLOGICAL ISSUES

We have seen that many important philosophical issues have to be settled in advance before a theorist can construct a compositional meaning theory for, say, English in order to account for linguistic competence with English. For example, the theorist is required to be guided by some idea of what counts as getting it right. If the goal is to get a set of axioms from which the theorist can infer the literal meaning of all possible English sentences, he or she needs to have some idea of how to determine that a particular theory implies the correct literal meanings. Here are four interrelated philosophical topics devoted to such methodological issues:

- Semantics-Pragmatics Distinction: Within the totality of communicated content (all the information communicated by an utterance) it is difficult to distinguish between the literal content and that which is generated through various pragmatic mechanisms (it has proved exceedingly difficult to distinguish between semantic content and pragmatic content). Any theory of meaning must incorporate criteria that distinguish different kinds of content and tells us how to classify content. Many debates in philosophy of language are based, in part, on different ways of drawing the semantics—pragmatics distinction.

- Role of Appeals to Intuitions: Most arguments in philosophy of language appeal to intuitions. We appeal to intuitions about what was said about grammaticality, about inferential connections, and sometimes about what would be true in other possible worlds. No position in the philosophy of language can be defended without various appeals to intuitions. That raises two questions: Why should we think intuitions provide us with reliable evidence? What kinds of intuitions should we rely on?

- The Nature of Meaning: How a philosopher of language goes about constructing a theory of meaning will depend on what he thinks meaning is. Are meanings entities? Is meaning reducible to something else? Do we even need to appeal to meaning or can we leave it out of theory of communication? The meanings of sentences are often referred to as propositions. What are propositions? These foundational issues have dominated discussion in philosophy of language for centuries.

- The Nature of Languages: There is an ongoing philosophical debate about what languages are, what kind of objects they are. Some think they are abstract objects, some think they are social/public objects, some think they are psychological structures, some think natural languages such as English should play an important theoretical role, some think they are superfluous in a serious meaning theory.

WIDER PHILOSOPHICAL IMPLICATIONS

To the noninitiated, research in the philosophy of language can seem technical and without deep philosophical implications. However, any such perception is simply the result of ignorance. Debates in the philosophy of language have wide-reaching implications for all branches of

philosophy and research in those other branches inevitably make assumptions about issues that belong under the rubric *philosophy of language*. Indeed, it is not possible to do serious work in any branch of philosophy today without a solid training in the philosophy of language.

The list of such important connections between the philosophy of language and the rest of philosophy could be made very, very long indeed. Limitations of space require we restrict attention to a few topics—epistemology will be one of them. Some of the most discussed contemporary positions in contemporary epistemology draw in a very direct way on views from the philosophy of language.

David Lewis (1996) claims that the epistemological skeptic (i.e., someone who argues that knowledge is impossible) can be refuted once the correct theory of meaning for *know* is adopted. According to Lewis, the correct theory for *know* is one that assigns it a context sensitive meaning, much as with the expressions *I*, *you*, and *here*. Obviously, once someone claims that the meaning of an expression is context sensitive, they become accountable to the philosophy of language. The theory of meaning for context sensitive expressions such as *I* is well-evidenced, and so, if *know* is like them it will have to stand up to certain qualifying tests all such expressions satisfy.

Putnam (1982) argues that his theory of meaning and reference implies that the skeptic's central argument is incoherent. His argument is based on a philosophical position on the nature of meaning. To the extent that his theory of meaning stands up to the scrutiny of the philosopher of language, skepticism may be refuted.

Kripke (1972) argues, as we saw above, that his theory of proper names refutes the traditional view (going back at least to Immanuel Kant) that necessary truths can only be knowable a priori and contingent truths only a posteriori. According to Kripke, it follows from the theories of meaning for proper names and natural kind terms such as *gold* and *tiger* that we can discover necessary truths empirically (many scientific discoveries turn out to be discoveries of necessary truths), and it turns out that we can gain knowledge of contingent facts a priori.

Some of the most discussed contemporary positions in contemporary metaphysics also draw in a very direct way on views from the philosophy of language. Kripke (1972) argues that his theory of reference implies that mental states cannot be physical states (i.e., that materialism is false).

Some of the most discussed contemporary positions in contemporary value theory draw in a very direct way on views from the philosophy of language also. One of the central strands in contemporary ethics is called expressivism. This is the view that sentences containing moral terms (e.g., *good*, *bad*, *should* and so on) cannot be true or false. They serve simply to express attitudes. Expressivism is a view about the meaning of words (Ayer 1946).

See also Artificial and Natural Languages; Conditionals; Content, Mental; Contextualism; Davidson, Donald; Frege, Gottlob; Hobbes, Thomas; Intuition; Kant, Immanuel; Kripke, Saul; Language; Lewis, David; Meaning; Montague, Richard; Phonology; Plato; Pragmatics; Propositions; Putnam, Hilary; Reference; Rule Following; Semantics; Semantics, History of; Sense; Syntactical and Semantical Categories; Syntax; Vagueness; Wittgenstein, Ludwig Josef Johann.

Bibliography

Alston, W. *Philosophy of Language.* Englewood, NJ: Prentice Hall, 1964.

Ayer, A.J. *Language, Truth, and Logic* (1936), 2nd ed. London: Gollancz, 1946.

Benthem, Johan van and Alice ter Meulen, eds. *The Handbook of Logic and Language.* Cambridge, MA: MIT Press, 1997.

Chomsky, Noam. "A Review of B. F. Skinner's Verbal Behavior." *Language* 35 (1959): 26–58.

Davidson, Donald. *Inquiries into Truth and Interpretation.* 2nd ed. Oxford: Clarendon Press, 2001.

Davidson, Donald. "Truth and meaning." *Synthese* 17 (1967): 304–323.

Fodor, Jerry A. and Ernie Lepore. *The Compositionality Papers.* Oxford: Oxford University Press, 2002.

Frege, Gottlob. *Begriffsschrift, eine der arithmetischen nachgebildete formelsprache des reinen denkens.* Halle: L. Nebert, 1879.

Grice, H.P. *Studies in the Way of Words.* Cambridge, MA: Harvard University Press, 1989.

Kripke, Saul A. *Naming and Necessity.* Cambridge MA: Harvard University Press, 1980.

Kripke, Saul A. *Naming and Necessity.* In *Semantics of Natural Language,* edited by D. Davidson and G. Harman. Reidel, 1972.

Lepore, Ernest and Kirk Ludwig. *Donald Davidson: Meaning, Truth, Language, and Reality.* Oxford: Oxford University Press, 2005.

Lewis, David. "Elusive Knowledge." *Papers in Metaphysics and Epistemology* (1996): 549–567.

Ludlow, Peter. *Readings in the Philosophy of Language.* Cambridge, MA: MIT Press, 1997.

Montague, Richard. "English as a Formal Language." In *Linguaggi nella società e nella tecnica.* Milan: Edizioni di Comunità, 1970.

Montague, Richard. *Formal Philosophy: Selected Papers of Richard Montague*, edited and with an introduction by Richmond H. Thomason. New Haven, CT; London: Yale University Press, 1974.

Montague, Richard. "The Proper Treatment of Quantification in Ordinary English." In *Approaches to Natural Language,* edited by K. J. J. Hintikka, J. M. E. Moravcsik, and P. Suppes. Dordrecht: Reidel, 1973.

Putnam, Hilary. "The Meaning of 'Meaning.'" In *Philosophical Papers II: Mind, Language, and Reality.* Cambridge, U.K.: Cambridge University Press, 1975.

Putnam, Hilary. *Reason, Truth, and History.* Cambridge, U.K.: Cambridge University Press, 1982.

Quine, W.V.O. "Two Dogmas of Empiricism." In *From a Logical Point of View.* Cambridge, MA: Harvard University Press, 1953.

Skinner, B. F. *Verbal Behavior.* New York: Appleton-Century-Crofts, 1957.

Stalnaker, Robert. "Assertion." In *Syntax and Semantics 9,* edited by Peter Cole. New York: Academic Press, 1978.

Stalnaker, Robert. *Context and Content.* Oxford: Oxford University Press, 1999.

Stalnaker, Robert. "Presuppositions." *Journal of Philosophical Logic* 2 (4) (1973): 447–457.

Ernest Lepore (2005)

PHILOSOPHY OF LANGUAGE IN CONTINENTAL PHILOSOPHY

The task of the philosophy of language within the tradition of continental European philosophy has been to overcome the idea of language as an instrument or as a means at the disposal of human beings. Although it has proved possible retrospectively to see Georg Wilhelm Friedrich Hegel (1770–1831) as a resource for this task, Johann Georg Hamann (1730–1788) and Wilhelm von Humboldt (1767–1835) both contributed more. Hamman was the first to give centrality to language and Humboldt, with his formulation that language is an *energeia* not an *ergon*, an activity not a work, opened the door to a more dynamic approach to it. However, it was not until the second half of the twentieth century that these insights were fully explored and decisively surpassed.

MARTIN HEIDEGGER

Martin Heidegger's attempt to go beyond the instrumentalist and expression theories of language is most pronounced in his later thought, especially in *On the Way to Language.* His formulation, *Die Sprache spricht* (language speaks) is an effort to displace the centrality of the human subject in accounts of language: It is not primarily the human being, but language, that speaks. The human being speaks only in response to language. This insight arose when he shifted his focus from everyday speech, which is explored at length in *Being and Time* as part of his account of everyday existence, to the poetic word. Already in 1936, in "The Origin of the Work of Art" (2002 [1950]), Heidegger claimed that it was not the human being, as in *Being and Time*, but art and most specifically poetry, that brings beings into the open and gives to human beings their outlook on themselves. This led directly, some ten years later, to the famous formulation of his *Letter on "Humanism"* (1998 [1947]) that "language is the house of Being" (p. 239). It announces not only the sense in which humans inhabit language, but also the sense in which the human being belongs to the historical destiny of Being and is called to respond to it. The implications of this account emerge not only in his readings of the poetry of, for example, Friedrich Hölderlin, Stefan George, Rainer Maria Rilke, and Georg Trakl—readings that are directed to undergoing an experience with language such that language transforms people—but also in his reading of the history of philosophy, where thinkers are understood to be saying the word of Being for their time. The words of Being function, somewhat like the work of art, to found a world.

Heidegger's approach to language is directed against the tendency to understand language in terms of something else, such as activity, spirit, or world view. That is why the focus falls on experiencing language. It is Heidegger's view that language shows itself as language only when language comes to be infused with silence. Language comes to be infused with silence mundanely when language fails people so that they are lost for words. For Heidegger, the thinker experiences something similar at a more profound level at the end of European and North American metaphysics. At that time the thinker lacks a word for Being and so can no longer accomplish the philosophical task of naming Being, for example, as *idea*, *energeia*, *subjectum*, or will. Indeed, for Heidegger it is only the lack of a word for Being in our epoch that gives rise to the insight that naming Being was the philosopher's task. However, this is not a negative experience. It is in the experience of language that Heidegger positions his thought as no longer metaphysical, albeit it is not yet beyond European and North American metaphysics. That Heidegger's clearest accounts of this experience arise in the course of his readings of Hölderlin and George show the extent to which his own self-understanding was moulded by the dialogue between poetry and thinking.

MAURICE MERLEAU-PONTY

Like Heidegger, Maurice Merleau-Ponty in *Phenomenology of Perception* (1962 [1945]) distinguished a creative or speaking speech that formulates for the first time, which he called *parole parlante*, from ordinary or spoken speech, *parole parlée*. What unites all of Merleau-Ponty's texts on language is a concern for the creative aspect of language, its capacity to say what has never been said, which he explored as an antidote to the dream of some philosophers to develop a transparent, algorithmic, language. However, unlike Heidegger, Merleau-Ponty's approach to language was from the outset already informed by psychology, and by the late 1940s he had begun to incorporate developments in linguistics. This tendency culminates in "Indirect Language and the Voices of Silence," which begins with Ferdinand de Saussure's insight that meaning is a function of the differences between words, their divergence from each other. Words do not directly signify anything; they are not tied to a preestablished signification. There is thus an "instructive spontaneity" of speech that leads Merleau-Ponty to the insight that people do not speak of Being so much as Being speaks in them, a formulation with clear Heideggerian echoes. The vitality of speech is also apparent when in a conversation one can no longer tell, as Merleau-Ponty famously puts it, what comes from one's dialogue partner and what is one's own contribution.

HANS-GEORG GADAMER

Dialogue is also at the core of Hans-Georg Gadamer's account of language. In his philosophical hermeneutics, which he developed in most detail in *Truth and Method* (1989 [1960]), he highlighted how in dialogue one seeks to reach an understanding with a living person or a text about some topic. However, underlying the effort to reach agreement was an already existing agreement because every dialogue presupposes a community of language as the element in which the dialogue takes place. Hence he conceived the task of a hermeneutical reflection on language not as that of investigating how each language in spite of its differences from other languages could say everything it wants to say, which he characterized as a concern of the philosophy of language and linguistics. His question was rather how to make sense of the intimacy of thought and language because language is not a prison, which is evident because one can readily come to understand a foreign language. Gadamer's answer was to reject accounts of language that relied on conventionalism and preschematization in favor of an account that emphasized its generative and creative power. This led

Gadamer to formulate the idea of the virtuality of language, by which he meant its inexhaustibility, its capacity to exceed what has already been said. Gadamer's account of the infinite resources of language can be seen as an attempt to resist Heidegger's account of the breakdown of the function of language within European and North American metaphysics, but he shared with Heidegger the conviction that language has people in its grip, that it speaks people more than people speak it. As evidence for this view he cited that the time when a text was written can be more precisely determined by its linguistic usage than from its author.

JACQUES DERRIDA

At the heart of Jacques Derrida's understanding of language is his identification of European and North American metaphysics with logocentrism, such that the alleged primacy of presence within European and North American metaphysics is reflected in the alleged transparency of speech and the speaker's mastery over it. By contrast, writing, even before it reaches its destination, is organized around the absence, and possible death of the sender or the addressee, or both. Derrida's deconstruction of logocentrism is sometimes mistakenly understood as a championing of writing to compensate for its previous reduction to the status of a mere supplement to speech, for example, as when Plato presented it as an aid to memory. Nevertheless, Derrida's interest is not so much in what is normally understood by writing as in what he calls arche-writing or protowriting, which is the condition of all forms of language, indeed of all organized systems. Derrida's use of the word "writing" in this contest is strategic: It is intended to reverse the priority of speech over writing, but only as a prelude to passing beyond the opposition between them both.

As Derrida explained in *Of Grammatology* (1976), the inflation of the sign *language* is the inflation of the sign itself. He presented this as a symptom of the historical epoch in which what had finally been gathered under the name *language* came to be summarized as *writing*. Derrida thus does not advocate grammatology in the sense of a science of writing, but, engaging in his own form of grammatology in the sense of a provisional science of textuality, he finds that both linguistics and psychoanalysis fail to recognize the resistance of language to pure ideality, and thus fail to escape logocentrism. However, once made thematic, this tension need not be regarded negatively. By shifting the focus to textuality Derrida draws attention to the way that one can find, for example within the language of Saussure and Sigmund

Freud, both the symptoms of the logocentrism of European and North American metaphysics and the trace of what it represses. Derrida performs a similar operation on Heidegger, from whom he had initially drawn the basic outline of his account of European and North American metaphysics. In this way, Derrida continued Heidegger's project of overcoming the conception of language as instrument or medium, but without relying on poetic language to accomplish the task, as had been the case with Heidegger, Merleau-Ponty, and Gadamer.

See also Derrida, Jacques; Gadamer, Hans-Georg; Heidegger, Martin; Hermeneutics; Merleau-Ponty, Maurice.

Bibliography

Derrida, Jacques. *De la grammatologie.* Paris: Minuit, 1976. Translated by G. Spivak as *Of Grammatology* (Baltimore, MD: Johns Hopkins University Press, 1976).

Gadamer, Hans-Georg. *Wahrheit und Methode.* Tübingen, Germany: J.C.B. Mohr, 1960. Translated by Joel Weinsheimer and Donald G. Marshall as *Truth and Method* (New York: Continuum, 1989).

Heidegger, Martin. *Sein und Zeit.* Halle: Niemeyer, 1927. Translated by Joan Stambaugh as *Being and Time* (Albany: SUNY Press, 1996).

Heidegger, Martin. *Brief über den Humanismus.* Bern, Switzerland: A. Franke, 1947. Translated as "Letter on 'Humanism,'" in *Pathmarks* (Cambridge, U.K.: Cambridge University Press, 1998).

Heidegger, Martin. "Der Ursprung des Kunstwerkes." In *Holzwege.* Frankfurt, 1950. Translated by Julian Young and Kenneth Haynes as "The Origin of the Work of Art," in *Off the Beaten Track* (Cambridge, U.K.: Cambridge University Press, 2002).

Heidegger, Martin. *Unterwegs zur Sprache.* Pfullingen, Germany: Neske, 1959. Translated by Peter Hertz as *On the Way to Language* (New York: Harper and Row, 1971).

Merleau-Ponty, Maurice. *Phénoménologie de la perception.* Paris: Gallimard, 1945. Translated by C. Smith as *Phenomenology of Perception* (London: Routledge, 1962).

Merleau-Ponty, Maurice. "Le langage indirect et les voix du silence." In *Signes.* Paris: Northwestern University Press, 1960. Translated by R. C. McCleary as "Indirect Language and the Voices of Silence." In *Signs* (Evanston, IL: Northwestern University Press, 1964).

Robert Bernasconi (2005)

PHILOSOPHY OF LANGUAGE IN INDIA

The earliest Indian thinking about language, found in Vedas (Arapura and Raja 1990), is speculative, but later discussions involve sophisticated arguments among various schools of thought. These discussions, which concern speech units (Sanskrit *śabda*, "sound, speech element, word") and associated meanings (*artha*), share certain themes. One is epistemological. Sounds are evanescent; an instant after they are pronounced they disappear. Consequently, the question arises: How can one rightly speak of complex units like words (*pada*) and sentences (*vākya*) as perceptible entities? Similarly, though one speaks of actions and things involved in them, it is also arguable that acts and things which are thought to be perceived as wholes actually are not so; there is a stream of instants, none of which lasts long enough to enable a qualified cognition of complex external entities. How, then, can one maintain that speech units signify actual actions and things? The second point concerns theory and procedure. Indian scholars operate with constructs in order to account for facts and behavior. This approach was evident already at an early period (ca. 7th c. BCE), when Vedic scholars posited constructed analyzed texts (*padapāṭha*) from which the Vedic texts as continuously recited (*saṁhitāṭha*) were derived by rules.

Indian thinkers accept certain means of acquiring knowledge, referred to as *pramāṇa* (a derivate of *pra-mā* [3rd sg. pres. *pramimīte*], apprehend"). At least two *pramāṇa*s are generally accepted: direct perception (*pratyakṣ*) and inference (*anumāna*). A third, verbal transmission (*śabda āgana*), is accepted by others, including Patañjali's yoga system. A means of knowing through similarity of one thing to another (*upamāna*) makes up a set of four *pramāṇa*s adopted by a major school of logicians, Nyāya. Not all thinkers, however, accept *śabda/āgama* as a separate *pramāṇa*; some account for knowledge acquired verbally through inference.

MEANINGFUL UNITS AND SYMBOLS

Systematic speech sounds—vowels (*a*, *ā*, *i*, *ī*, etc.) and consonants (*k*, *kh*, *g*, *gh*, *ṅ*, etc.) are distinguished from mere sounds (*dhvani*) such as the noise made by a drum. Classes of larger units are also recognized, the major ones being nominal forms (*nāman*), verbs (*ākhyāta*), preverbs (*upasarga*), and particles (*nipāta*); for example, *gauḥ* (nom. sg.), "cow, ox," *gacchati* (3rd sing. pres.), "goes, is going," *upa* in *upa gacchati*, "approaches," and *vā*, "or," respectively.

At an early stage, represented in pre-Pāṇinian texts and alluded to in later works like Patañjali's great mid-second-century BCE commentary (*Mahābhāṣya*) on Pāṇini's c. fifth-century BCE grammar, verbs and nouns were defined semantically. In one view, verbs signify varieties of being (*bhāva*): something comes into being (*jāyate*, "is born"), continues to be (*asti*, "is"), undergoes change while remaining the same entity (*vipariṇamate*, "changes"), increases (*vardhate*, "grows"), decreases (*apakṣīyate*, "diminishes"), and ceases to be (*vinaśyati*, "perishes"). Some scholars reduce these to three stages, with the second encompassing the third, fourth, and fifth. Alternatively, verbs are considered to signify particular actions (*kriyā*, *karman*), the most general action being signified by *kṛ*, "do." This definition is supported by usage: (1) *devadattaḥ pacati*, "Devadatta is cooking," is an appropriate answer to (2) *kiṁ karoti devadattaḥ*, "What is Devadatta doing?" These two views are superseded by considering that whatever a verbal base (*dhātu*) signifies—now spoken of as *kriyā* or *bhāva*—is conceived of as involving continuity in time, always associated with some time. As a consequence, not only terms such as *kṛ* (*karoti*), "do," *pac* (*pacati*), "cook," and *vraj* (*vrajati*), "go," but also ones like *as* (*asti*), "be," *ās* (*āste*), "be seated," and *sthā* (*tiṣṭhati*), "come to a stand, be in place," are now part of a single class of units signifying *kriyā/bhāva*. The canonical statement of this position, which can be seen already in the *Mahābhāṣya*, appears in Bhartṛhari's mid-fifth-century *Vākyapadīya* (3.8.1): whatever is always spoken of as something to be brought to accomplishment, whether it is already accomplished or not, is referred to as *kriyā* ("action") by virtue of its taking on a sequential status.

Contrasting with such semantic definitions, there is a formal approach, epitomized by the grammarian Pāṇini, who assigns to his class of units called *dhātu* verb bases listed in an appendix to the main corpus of rules and to items derived from both verbs and nominal forms (Cardona 1997).

There is a conception of units under which words are groups of sounds and larger units are groups of words. This view is represented in the section of Kauṭilya's Arthaśāstra (disputed date but not later than the third century CE) that deals with writing edicts (2.1.13–14) and in other works. It is already reflected in an argument Kātyāyana (third century BCE) mentions when he speaks of a group of sounds (*varṇasaṅghāta*) as being meaningful (*arthavat*). The same view is presupposed in the Ṛgvedaprātiśākhya (2.2), which describes the continuous recitation of a text (*saṁhitā*) as consisting in one's continuously putting together the last sounds of words (*padāntān*) with the initial sounds (*padādibhiḥ*) of following words, without any temporal separation (*kālāvyavadhānena*). Pāṇini himself (1.4.109: *paraḥ sannikarṣaḥ saṁhitā*) states that the maximum drawing together (*paraḥ sannikarṣaḥ*) of sounds is called *saṁhitā*. One may consider that such a procedure accepts that sounds do actually come together to form larger units, but it is also possible that this is an artifact necessary for the proper description by rules of what is found in a language.

From an argument presented by Kātyāyana and Patañjali, it is clear they were aware that one cannot speak of physical sounds truly co-occurring in immediate succession, for example, gauḥ, "cow" = g-au-ḥ. For speech does not produce two sounds simultaneously, since sounds (varṇānām [gen. pl.]) have the property of disappearing immediately upon being pronounced (uccaritapradhvaṁsitvāt [abl. sg.], Kātyāyana's vārttika 10 on 1.4.109: … uccaritapradhvaṁsitvāca varṇānām). As Patañjali explains: when g is pronounced, there is no au or ḥ; when au is pronounced, there is no g or ḥ; and when ḥ is pronounced, there is g or au.

If there is no physical composite unit such as gauḥ, the question arises: What is it that it is understood to signify? Two approaches were taken on this issue. One involves memory. It is assumed that when a sound is perceived, this experience leaves in one a lasting trace (saṁskāra, vāsanā); the last sound uttered in a given stretch produces a cognition accompanied by the traces left from preceding cognitions of sounds, and this final cognition is what produces an understanding of meanings of words and the sentences they make up. Alternatively, sounds are considered merely to manifest (vyañj) actual meaning bearers. These signifiers are posited elements called sphoṭa, distinct from physical sounds but manifested (vyaṅgya, "to be manifested") by them. Three major sphoṭa types are assumed: sentence (vākyasphoṭa), word (padasphoṭa), and subword meaningful elements (varṇasphoṭa) such as bases and affixes.

The first of these views was proposed at least by the time of the Mīmāṃsaka commentator Śabara (second century) and was accepted by adherents of different schools. The sphoṭa theory was first expounded fully by the grammarian-philosopher Bhartṛhari and remained basically the position of grammarians. Each of these positions was subjected to criticisms. Arguments against the first revolve about the nature of memory, what is recalled, and in what manner; the main argument against the sphoṭa position is that it requires positing units which one can do without.

WORD-MEANING RELATIONS

Speakers and hearers communicate and understand messages by means of words and sentences of a language they share. It is therefore universally accepted that a relation (sambandha) holds between words (śabda, pada) and

meanings (artha) and that this relation can be a direct or indirect one, respectively called śakti ("capacity") or abhidhā ("signifying") and lakṣaṇā ("secondary meaning relation, metaphor"). A term that directly signifies (vācaka) a meaning is qualified as śakta ("capable") and its meaning as śakya, the object of this capacity. For example, gaṅgā directly refers to a flow of water, the river Gaṅgā. By lakṣaṇā, the same term can refer to the banks of the river. Thinkers of different schools engaged in arguments concerning both the nature of what is signified and the relations that link words and their meanings.

Concerning what words signify, at one extreme there is the view that terms like ghaṭa, "clay pot," aśva, "horse," pac, "cook, bake," refer to actual external entities, including actions one can witness. Other positions start from the observation that what one can actually perceive is not such an external thing (vastu) or action (kriyā): The latter is a stream of moments (kṣaṇa) that are beyond direct perception, and the former also can be broken down into such moments. The putative wholes treated as having identity are mental constructs (vikalpa).

One view consequent on this observation, adopted by certain Buddhistic thinkers, is that signification applies negatively, being a removal or differentiation (apoha) of all that is not the momentary entity in question, which is thus differentiated (apoḍha, "removed") from all others. The relation between a word—itself a construct—and its significand is then one of cause (kāraṇa) and effect (kārya): Words have mental constructs as their sources and bring about a comprehension of mental constructs. Although they accept that words and their meanings are related as signifier and significand (vācyavācakabhāvasambandha), Pāṇinian grammarians such as Bhartṛhari—with earlier precedents—also consider the cause and effect relation acceptable and conceive of the significands as word-meanings (śabdārtha) that are mental (bauddha) and not necessarily external objects (vastu).

In this connection, grammarians speak of a vivakṣā, a desire to speak about things in a particular manner. For example, it is in the nature of things that a sword (asi) serves as a means of cutting; one says, for example, (3) devadattḥ asinā chinatti, "Devadatta is cutting with a sword," using the instrumental asinā to refer to a sword as a means. If a sword is quite sharp, one may also appropriately say (4) asiḥ sādhu chinatti," the sword (asiḥ, nom. sg.) cuts well (sādhu)," speaking of a sword as an agent of cutting in the same way that (3) refers to Devadatta as an agent. In order to account for such usages, Pāṇini orders a group of rules that assign direct participants in the accomplishment of actions (*kāraka*) to particular categories in such a manner that the participant in question is eligible to be assigned both to the category of participants called *karaṇa*, "instrument," by virtue of being the means (*sādhakatama*, "which is means more than any other") of accomplishing an act and, by a later rule, to the category of agents (*kartṛ*) by virtue of being an independent (*svatantra*) participant. Since a sword cannot be spoken of as an independent participant in the act of cutting without one's simultaneously considering it a means used by someone, this involves a conflict (*vipratiṣedha*), and Pāṇini provides explicitly that in case of such conflicts, what is provided for by a subsequently stated rule takes precedence over the provision of a preceding rule (see Cardona 1974). In connection with such situations, Patañjali notes that this involves what he calls *laukikī vivakṣā*, "communal desire to speak"; that is, it is not a matter of individual preference but of the way a community of speakers (*loka*, "world") expresses itself.

There is also the point of view that words have a natural relation of fitness (*yogyatā*) with their meanings, comparable to the fitness of different sense faculties with respect to what is perceived. Moreover, words and their meanings are commonly identified with each other.

However one conceives of the relation, each generation acquires a knowledge of words related to their meanings by observing how people interact. For example, a child witnesses an interaction between his father (F) and his grandfather (G): G says (5) *gām ānaya*, "bring the cow," to F, who then brings a cow, but F brings a horse when G says to him (6) *aśvam ānaya*. The child learns therefrom that *gām* and *aśvam* respectively designate a cow and a horse. This is an instance of reasoning from concurrent presence (*anvaya*) and absence (*vyatireka*): (a) $x \rightarrow y$, (b) $\bar{x} \rightarrow \bar{y}$. If both hold, then x which precedes y is its cause. Thus, if a given meaning is understood when a given term or member of a set of terms is used and not understood when this is not used, then the comprehension of the meaning in question is said to be caused by the term, to which this meaning is attributed.

Assuming that words designate positive significands, in ordinary usage one thinks of the term *go*, "cow," as referring to something that one can see and speak of repeatedly, using the same term. Moreover, in order to account for the repeated cognition of a cow each time one is seen, which can be verbalized saying (7) *iyaṁ gauḥ*, "this is a cow," it is assumed that each cow belongs to a class characterized by a class property (*jāti*, "generic property") that inheres in every member: *gotva* ("the property of being a cow").

If one assumes that a word-meaning relation is learned between an instance of the term *go* and a particular cow and also assumes that when another instance of *go* is used it too can refer to this particular cow, then the reasoning procedure shown above is violated, since one now has y in the absence of x. To assume that a separate relation is grasped between each instance of *go* and each individual (*vyakti*) cow has the consequence that no speaker can acquire the knowledge of such an infinite number of relations. Various solutions are proposed to remedy the situation (see Deshpande 1992 and Scharf 1996). One view, espoused by Mīmāṁsakas, is that the primary word-meaning relation is between a term and the class property (*jāti*). A sentence such as (5) is used, however, with the intention (*tātparya*) that someone bring a cow, not a class property. This is accounted for by assuming that in such an utterance *gām* signifies not only a class property, through a primary relation (*śakti*), but also a particular cow, through the secondary relation called *lakṣaṇā*. An alternative to this position is adopted by grammarians and logicians of the Nyāya school: A term like *go* signifies an individual (*vyakti*) qualified (*viśiṣṭa*) by its class property.

There are other instances where *lakṣaṇā* is said to operate. Consider (8) *kuntān praveśaya*, "have the javelins (*kuntān* [acc. pl.]) come in (*praveśaya*)." *Praveśaya* is a form (2nd sg. imper.) of a causative verb whose noncausal is *praviś* (3rd sg. pres. *praviśati*) "enter." Javelins cannot enter a room of themselves, so they cannot be caused to perform this act in the same way that one can cause people to enter a room. In order to make sense of the intent (*tātparya*) of a speaker who uses (8), it is accepted that *kunta* here bears a secondary relation with the men who bear javelins. In the same vein, consider (9) *gaṅgāyaṁ matsyāḥ*, "there are fish in the Gaṅga," and (10) *gaṅgāyaṁ ghoṣaḥ*, "there is a dairy colony on the Gaṅga." Assuming that *gaṅgāyām* (loc. sg. fem.) is used to refer to a locus in or on which something is located, (9) makes immediate sense, but (10) is hard to understand: fish can live in a river but a village of dairymen cannot be located physically in or on a body of flowing water. It is assumed, then, that in (10) *gaṅā*, which bears a primary word-meaning relation with a river, now bears a secondary relation with its bank (*tīra*).

(10) involves an assumed semantic incompatibility such that it is not possible for the primary meanings of *gaṅgāyām* and *ghoṣaḥ* to be related. However, it is not sufficient to say that what prompts one to understand a sec-

ondary meaning here is solely the impossibility of the referents being connected (*anvayānupapatti*). For this could be resolved also under the assumption that *ghoṣa* has a secondary relation with fish, so that (10) is understood to say what (9) says. Yet this is not the case: A person who hears (10) understands it to say that a dairy colony is located on the edge of the Gaṅga. Accordingly, the major reason prompting a secondary word-meaning relation is considered to be the impossibility of reconciling the primary meaning of a term with the intention (*tātparya*) of a speaker.

Understanding (8) and (10) in the way shown involves setting aside the primary meanings of *kunta* and *gaṅgā*. Consider now (11) *arko' staṁ gataḥ*, "the sun (*arkaḥ*) has set (*gataḥ*, "gone," *astam*, "home")." This can have its literal meaning. Without rejecting this meaning, moreover, there are several possible meanings that can be suggested (*vyaṅgya*, "to be made manifest"), depending on contexts and the persons uttering (11). For example, a go-between saying this to a woman who is to meet a lover suggests it is time to set out, but a servant saying this to a Brahmin means to imply that it is time for his master to perform the evening prayer. Another function of words is therefore considered, called *vyañjanā* (usually translated "suggestion"). This is principally accepted by theoreticians of poetics, though later Pāṇinian grammarians accept it, mainly because under the theory that a meaning bearer is a *sphoṭa*, which is manifested (*vyaṅgya*) by physical sounds.

SENTENCE AND SENTENCE MEANING

Adherents of various schools of thought in ancient and medieval India adopted different views concerning sentences and their meanings. One position—most systematically elaborated and defended first by Bhartṛhari—is that the true unit of communication is an atomic (*akhaṇḍa*) sentence (*vākya*), associated with an equally atomic sentential meaning, considered to be the object of a single flash of knowledge, hence referred to as *pratibhā* ("flash"). This thesis can be justified in so far as actual communication involves whole utterances, but it encounters the problems mentioned earlier in connection with words and their meanings: it is not possible for one to acquire a knowledge of all relations between all possible atomic sentences and their meanings. Moreover, a grammarian's aim is to give a generalized description of all possible sentences in terms of their structures, both formal and semantic, which is impossible if this thesis is taken strictly. Hence, Pāṇinians agree that at least one lower level—of words—must be accepted in terms of

both language learning and description. They maintain, however, that words and their constituent bases, affixes, and so forth are constructs posited in order to account for whole utterances.

Under another view, held by some Mīmāṁsakas, there are no sentences qua distinct meaningful units. The sentential meaning of any stretch one calls a sentence is now accounted for indirectly, through the meanings of individual words. A parallel is drawn with the effect produced by utterances such as (12) *putras te jātaḥ*, "You've had a son" (*putraḥ* [nom. sg.], "son," *jātaḥ* [pptcple. nom. sg. m.], "born," *te* [dat. sg.], "to you") or (13) *garbhiṇī te duhitā*, "Your (*te* [gen. sg.]) daughter (*duhitā*) is pregnant (*garbhiṇī*)." Each of the words of these sentences signifies its particular meaning. These word meanings are then related to each other in accordance with the speaker's intention (*tātparya*) to convey a message and the hearer's semantic expectation (*ākāṅkṣā*) that each meaning has to be linked to other meanings of words in the utterances. The effects are happiness on the part of a man who learns he has had a son and sadness on the part of a man who learns his unmarried daughter is pregnant. Similarly, the words of all utterances denote only their individual meanings, which are then related to each other. An intermediate position is taken by logicians of the Nyāya system, who consider that the meaning of an utterance is apprehended through the intermediary of related words: The first word is first cognized as shown earlier, with the consequent memory of the word-meaning relation and a memory trace of the word and its meaning, then this process is repeated until, with the perception of the last word, a cumulative memory trace results of all the words and their meanings related to each other.

Whatever position one takes, two requirements apply to sentences. First, constituents must be in proximity (*āsatti*): each word following the first word of a sentence is uttered immediately after the preceding word, without the intervention of any term that is not syntactically related to the others. Secondly, there must be semantic expectancy (*ākāṅkṣā*), so that a hearer expects that the meaning signified by a word such as *gām* in (5) is connected with an action, since it contains an object-signifying suffix, and *ānaya* requires an object. As shown, the intention of a speaker (*tātparya*) also comes into play. Another requirement must be met if one is mainly interested in an utterance's serving as a means of conveying true knowledge: semantic compatibility (*yogyatā*, "the property of being connectible"). For example, each word of (14) *agninā puṣpāṇi siñcati*, "... is irrigating (*siñcati*) flowers (*puṣpāṇi* [acc. pl.]) with fire (*agninā* [instr. sg.]))," conveys a meaning that is immediately understood. (14) cannot, however, convey a meaning acceptable in our world, where the act of irrigating requires a liquid (*dravadravya*) as a means. Accordingly, Naiyāyikas would deny that (14) has the status of *pramāṇa*. One might go so far as to deny that (14) produces a verbal cognition (*śabdabodha*). Against this, the following is pointed out. Upon hearing (14), a person would respond by asking how one can speak of irrigating with something that is not a liquid? The hearer has indeed related the meanings of the words in the well-formed utterance (14) according to their syntax, but the resulting sentence meaning is not acceptable in the world as we experience it.

Adherents of different schools differ also concerning the ways in which verbal cognitions (*śabdabodha*) are portrayed. Pāṇinian grammarians, logicians of the Nyāya school, and Mīmāṃsakas of the Bhāṭṭa school can agree that (15) *devadattaḥ kaṭaṃ karoti*, "Devadatta is making (*karoti* [3rd sg. pres.]), a mat (*kaṭam* [acc. sg.])," speaks of a given man making a mat. On the other hand, they give different paraphrases reflecting what they consider to be the *śabdabodha* prompted by this sentence, reflecting the preoccupations and theoretical premises of different schools of thought (see Cardona 1975 and Matilal 1985). Pāṇini accounts for the structure of Sanskrit through a set of derivational rules starting from semantics, and this is most efficently done under the assumption that the principal meaning of (15) is the action. Naiyāyikas are principally interested in the values of utterances as conveyors of valid knowledge, and within this system they operate with subjects and predications, so that the main qualificand in (15) is the person referred to by *devadattaḥ*. Mīmāṃsakas deal chiefly with the exegesis of Vedic utterances related to ritual performance, and in this context the principal meaning of an utterance is the act of bringing about a result.

CONCLUSION

These different interests and the fact that adherents of these systems and others either accepted the authority of Pāṇinian grammar or reacted to it led to ongoing arguments and counterarguments, with successive refinements over millennia, making India a center for the intense study of language and the philosophy of language.

See also Brahman; Knowledge in Indian Philosophy; Liberation in Indian Philosophy; Logic, History of: Logic and Inference in Indian Philosophy; Mind and Mental States in Indian Philosophy; Truth and Falsity in Indian Philosophy; Universal Properties in Indian Philosophy.

Bibliography

Aklujkar, Ashok. 1990. "Bhartṛhari: Trikāṇḍī or Vākyapadīya, with Vṛtti on Books 1 and 2." In *The Philosophy of the Grammarians*, edited by Harold G. Coward and K. Kunjunni Raja, 172–174. Princeton, NJ: Princeton University Press, 1990.

Arapura, John G., and K. Kunjunni Raja. "Philosophical Elements in Vedic Literature." In *The Philosophy of the Grammarians*, edited by Harold G. Coward and K. Kunjunni Raja, 101–106. Princeton, NJ: Princeton University Press, 1990.

Biardeau, Madeleine. *Théorie de la connaisance et philosophie de la parole dans le brahmanisme classique.* Paris: Mouton, 1964.

Cardona, George. "Pāṇini's *kārakas*: Agency, Animation and Identity." *Journal of Indian Philosophy* 2 (1974): 231–306.

Cardona, George. *Pāṇini: His Work and Its Traditions.* Vol. 1, *Background and Introduction.* 2nd ed. Delhi: Motilal Banarsidass, 1997.

Cardona, George. "Paraphrase and Sentence Analysis: Some Indian Views." *Journal of Indian Philosophy* 3 (1975): 259–281.

Coward, Harold G., and K. Kunjunni Raja, eds. *The Philosophy of the Grammarians.* Vol. 5 of *Encyclopedia of Indian Philosophies.* Princeton, NJ: Princeton University Press, 1990.

Coward, Harold G., and K. Kunjunni Raja. "Introduction to the Philosophy of the Grammarians," In *The Philosophy of the Grammarians*, edited by Harold G. Coward and K. Kunjunni Raja, 1–97. Princeton, NJ: Princeton University Press, 1990.

Deshpande, Madhav M., trans. *The Meaning of Nouns: Semantic Theory in Classical and Medieval India = Nāmārthanirṇaya of Kauṇḍabhaṭa.* Translated and annotated. Dordrecht and Boston: Kluwer, 1992.

Ganguli, Hemanta Kumar. *Philosophy of Logical Construction: An Examination of Logical Atomism and Logical Positivism in the Light of the Philosophies of Bhartṛhari, Dharmakīrti and Prajñākaragupta.* Calcutta: Sanskrit Pustak Bhandar, 1963.

Matilal, Bimal K. *Logic, Language and Reality: An Introduction to Indian Philosophical Studies.* Delhi: Motilal Banarsidass, 1985.

Raja, K. Kunjunni. *Indian Theories of Meaning.* 2nd ed. Adyar, Madras: Adyar Library and Research Centre, 1969.

Ruegg, David Seyfort. *Contributions à l'histoire de la philosophie linguistique indienne.* Paris: Boccard, 1959.

Scharf, Peter M. *The Denotation of Generic Terms in Ancient Indian Philosophy: Grammar, Nyāya and Mīmāṃ.* Philadelphia: American Philosophical Society, 1996.

George Cardona (2005)

PHILOSOPHY OF LAW, HISTORY OF

The problems of authority, law and order, obligation, and self-interest first became central topics of speculation in the thought of the Sophists (late fifth and early fourth centuries BCE). The most famous Sophists all stressed the distinction between nature (*physis*) and convention (*nomos*), and they put laws in the latter category. They generally attributed law to human invention and justified obedience to law only to the extent that it promoted one's own advantage. Laws were artificial, arrived at by consent; the majority of acts that were just according to the law were contrary to nature; the advantages laid down by the law were chains upon nature, but those laid down by nature were free. In the time of the Sophists notions of law, justice, religion, custom, and morality were largely undifferentiated; yet in this same period some of the crucial problems of legal philosophy were first formulated, and attempts were made at a formal definition of law. Thus, Xenophon (*Memorabilia* I, 2) reported that Alcibiades, who associated with both Critias and Socrates, remarked to Pericles that no one can really deserve praise unless he knows what a law is. Pericles replied that laws are what is approved and enacted by the majority in assembly, whereby they declare what ought and what ought not to be done. He admitted that if obedience is obtained by mere compulsion, it is force and not law, even though the law was enacted by the sovereign power in the state. Xenophon also reported an alleged conversation between Socrates and the Sophist Hippias in which both maintained an identity between law, or what is lawful, and justice, or what is right, while admitting that laws may be changed or annulled (ibid. IV, 4). Socrates claimed that there are "unwritten laws," uniformly observed in every country, which cannot conceivably be products of human invention. They are made by the gods for all men, and when men transgress them, nature penalizes the breach.

Socrates and the Sophists, as presented in Plato's dialogues, disagreed concerning human nature. The Sophists conceived of man as egoistically motivated and antisocial, whereas for Socrates, as for Plato and Aristotle, man was a social being with other-regarding as well as self-regarding motives, who finds fulfillment in social life. By contrast, the Sophist Callicles, in Plato's *Gorgias*, holds that man is no exception to the law of nature, according to which the stronger rules; manmade laws and social institutions violate human nature. The less radical Sophists, although they could not identify law with some feature of reality, still accepted its practical usefulness.

PLATO AND ARISTOTLE

PLATO. There is hardly any problem of legal philosophy not touched upon by Plato. He wrote during the decline of the Greek polis, when law and morality could appear as mere conventions imposed by shifting majorities in their own interest and the harmony between the legal order and the order of the universe could not easily be maintained. Plato sought to restore, as far as possible, the traditional analogy between justice and the ordered cosmos. Justice, or right action, cannot be identified with mere obedience to laws, nor can a truly moral life be reduced to conformity with a conventional catalog of duties. Duties involve a knowledge of what is good for man, and this bears an intimate relation to human nature. The question "What is justice?" dominates Plato's *Republic*. Plato conceived of justice as that trait of human character which coordinates and limits to their proper spheres the various elements of the human psyche, in order to permit the whole man to function well. In order to understand the operation of justice in the human soul, Plato examined human nature writ large, the city-state. The state functions well when it is governed by those who know the art of government, and the practice of this art requires a positive insight into the Good. In a just society every citizen performs the role of which he is best capable for the good of the whole. Similarly, in the moral economy of the individual's life, justice prevails when reason rules and the appetites and lower passions are relegated to their proper spheres. A just social order is achieved to the extent to which reason and rational principles govern the lives of its members.

Plato's emphasis on reason found its way into his definition of law. Law is reasoned thought (*logismos*) embodied in the decrees of the state (*Laws* 644D). Plato rejected the view that the authority of law rests on the mere will of the governing power. The *Laws* contains a detailed discussion of many branches of law and is an attempt at a formulation of a systematic code to govern the whole of social life. In contrast with the ideal polis of the *Republic*, in which there would be little need for legislation, in the *Laws* Plato accepted "law and order, which are second best" (*Laws* 875D).

ARISTOTLE. Aristotle, who discussed law in numerous contexts, nowhere gave a formal definition of it. He wrote variously that law is "a sort of order, and good law is good order" (*Politics* 1326a), "reason unaffected by desire" (ibid. 1287a), and "the mean" (ibid. 1287b). However, these must be taken not as definitions but as characterizations of law motivated by the point Aristotle was making in the given context.

Following Plato, Aristotle rejected the Sophistic view that law is mere convention. In a genuine community—as distinguished from an alliance, in which law is only a covenant—the law concerns itself with the moral virtue of the citizenry (*Politics* 1280b). Aristotle sharply distinguished between the constitution (*politeia*) and laws (*nomoi*); the constitution concerns the organization of offices within the state, whereas the laws are "those according to which the officers should administer the state, and proceed against offenders" (ibid. 1289a). The constitution of a state may tend to democracy, although the laws are administered in an oligarchical spirit and vice versa (ibid. 1292b). Legislation should aim at the common good of the citizens, and justice—what is equal—should be determined by the standard of the common good (ibid. 1283a). Yet Aristotle recognized that the law is often the expression of the will of a particular class, and he stressed the role of the middle class as a stabilizing factor.

In his discussion of the forms of government in Book III of the *Politics*, Aristotle took up the Platonic problem of rule by the best man versus rule according to laws. A society of equals by its very nature excludes the arbitrary rule of one man. In any case, even the best man cannot dispense with the general principles contained in laws; and legal training helps to make better officers of government. Furthermore, administrators, like all men, are subject to passion, and it is thus preferable to be judged by the impersonal yardstick of the laws. This in no way conflicts with the need to change the law through legislation when it has been found by experience to be socially inadequate. But not all law is the product of legislation; customary law is in fact more important than the written law.

Aristotle's discussion of the judicial process foreshadows many modern notions. Although it is better to have written laws than to rely completely on discretion, "some matters can be covered by the laws and others cannot" (ibid. 1287b20). General rules are insufficient to decide particular cases (ibid. 1286a26), although "well-drawn laws should themselves define all the points they possibly can and leave as few as may be to the decision of the judges" (*Rhetoric* 1354a32). Aristotle seems to have had two considerations in mind. First, judicial decision making is practical—it involves deliberation—and as such cannot be completely determined in advance. Second, the resolution of disputed issues of fact in a particular case, on which the decision depends, cannot be settled in advance by legislation. This stress on the insufficiency of general rules connects with Aristotle's influential discussion of equity (*epieikeia*). Equity is just, "but not legally just but a correction of legal justice" (*Nicomachean Ethics* 1137b10). Aristotle sometimes seems to suggest that equity comes into play when there are gaps in the law, so that it consists in the judge's acting as the lawgiver would act if he were present. Yet he also seems to suggest that equity corrects the harshness of the law when adherence to the written law would work an injustice. Principles of equity are thus closely related to the unwritten universal laws "based on nature," a "natural justice" binding on all men, even those who have no association or covenant with each other. Nevertheless, what is naturally just may vary from society to society.

The locus classicus of Aristotle's discussion of justice is Book V of the *Nicomachean Ethics*. Generically, justice has to do with one's relations to others, and there is a sense of "justice" that refers to the complete moral virtue of the member of the community in such dealings. There is also a sense in which "justice" refers to a particular virtue involving the fair dealings of individuals in matters handled by private law. Two kinds of rights fall under this special virtue: rights in division (where each individual claims his fair share of goods, honors, and so on) and rights in redress (for wrongs done by one individual to another, such as failure to fulfill a contract).

ROME

STOICS. The Stoics, who conceived of the universe as a single, organic substance, exercised a lasting influence on legal thought. Nature, which exhibits structure and order, and man both partake of intelligence, or reason (*logos*). An animal is directed by a primary impulse toward self-preservation that adapts it to its environment. In man, reason is the "engineer of impulse," and man's actions may be evaluated only within the framework of the whole of nature. The criterion of moral action is consistency with the all-determining law of nature (*koinos logos*). This conception of a law of nature that is the ultimate standard of human laws and institutions was combined with Aristotelian and Christian notions to form the long-standing natural-law tradition of medieval legal philosophy. Another important Stoic contribution was the belief in the equality of all men in a universal commonwealth and a rejection of Aristotle's doctrine of slavery.

CICERO AND SENECA. The writings of Marcus Tullius Cicero (106–43 BCE) were important in transmitting classical legal thought to the medieval world. Although he was a professional arguer of legal cases, Cicero's philosophical treatment of law in his *De Legibus* disclaims any interest in "clients' questions" or the "law of eaves and house-walls." His legal philosophy was essentially Stoic; he denied that the positive law of a community (written or customary), even when universally accepted, is the standard of what is just. Nor is mere utility the standard: "Justice is one; it binds all human society, and is based on one law, which is right reason applied to command and prohibition" (*De Legibus* I, 15). An unjust statute is not a true law. Law and morality are logically connected, and only that which conforms to the law of nature is genuine law. This view exercised a lasting influence on natural-law thinking and reappeared in the thought of Thomas Aquinas.

Like Cicero, Lucius Annaeus Seneca (c. 4 BCE–65 CE) aided in transmitting Stoic notions to later thinkers. He reiterated the conception of the equality of all men under natural law, but perhaps more important was his conception of a golden age of human innocence, a prepolitical state of nature. Legal institutions became necessary as human nature became corrupted.

ROMAN LAW. The influence of Stoicism may be traced in pronouncements of the Roman jurists. It is disputed whether these were any more than remarks designed to ornament legal texts, but they nevertheless influenced the thought of later ages. The jurists distinguished three kinds of law: *jus naturale*, *jus gentium*, and *jus civile*. In practice, the last originally referred to the law of the city of Rome, but ultimately it was applied to any body of laws of a given community. The *jus gentium* first meant the law applied to strangers, to whom the *jus civile* was not applicable, and was later extended to those legal practices common to all societies. Gaius (mid-second century), who systematized the Roman law in his *Institutes*, identified the *jus naturale* and *jus gentium* as universal principles of law agreeable to natural reason and equity. Thus, law was not a mere expression of human will or institution but that which is rationally apprehended and obeyed. The *jus gentium* was not an ideal law by which the positive law was judged but the rational core of existing legal institutions.

Ulpian (c. 170–228) distinguished *jus naturale* from *jus gentium* by stating that *jus naturale* is not peculiar to human beings but is taught by nature to all animals. Thus, among animals there is an institution similar to human marriage. Slavery and its attendant rules are products of the *jus gentium*, for by the *jus naturale* all men were born free. It is not clear, however, that Ulpian

regarded slavery as bad. To him we owe the oft-repeated definition of justice: "the constant wish to give each his due" (*Digest* I, 1, 10). Following Celsus (c. 67–c. 130), he defined law (*jus*) as "the art of the good and the equitable" (ibid. I, 1, 1). Again, it does not seem that Ulpian thought of the *jus naturale* as an ideal law opposed to the *jus civile* or to the *jus gentium*. It has been suggested that behind Ulpian's thought was a conception of a natural state antecedent to the conditions of organized society.

The doctrines of the Roman jurists owe their lasting influence to their incorporation into the *Corpus Juris Civilis* of Justinian (sixth century), principally in the section called the *Digest*. The compilers of Justinian's *Institutes* (a section of the *Corpus Juris*) seem to have distinguished the *jus naturale* from the *jus gentium* and seem to have regarded the former as a set of immutable divine laws by which the positive law may be morally evaluated (*Institutes* I, 2, 11; III, 1, 11). The *Corpus Juris* also preserved statements of the Roman jurists concerning the source of the authority to make and unmake the laws constituting the civil law. According to a number of these statements, this authority resides in the consent of the people; however, the statement that "what pleases the prince has the force of law" (*Digest* I, 4, 1) was probably a more accurate view of the facts. Justinian seems to have combined these views theoretically in his reference to a (nonexistent) "ancient law" by which the Roman people transferred all their powers to the emperor (*Codex* I, 17, 1, 7).

EARLY MIDDLE AGES

To the legal thought of the Stoics and the Roman philosophers and jurists the Church Fathers added a distinctively Christian element. The law of nature was no longer the impersonal rationality of the universe but was integrated into a theology of a personal, creative deity. The relationship among the Mosaic law, the Gospels, and natural law emerged as a specific problem; the notion of *jus divinum* (divine law) as a distinct type of law, along with the three recognized by the jurists, was crystallized. The notion of the fall of man from a state of perfection (which may be compared with the view of Seneca) played an important role. Thus, according to St. Ambrose (340–397) the Mosaic law—a law of sin and death (see Romans 8:2)—was given because man failed to obey the law of nature. The fact that many legal institutions, such as slavery and private property, deviate from this ideal law does not necessarily imply that they are unjust or illegitimate; for the natural law is adapted to man only in a condition of innocence.

Of the Church Fathers, St. Augustine (354–430) was perhaps the most original and complex: Only one point in his thought will be noted here. Cicero maintained that nothing can be nobler than the law of a state (*De Legibus* I, 14) and that if a state has no law, it cannot truly be considered a state (ibid. II, 12). The law of the state must therefore embody justice, for without *justitia* there is no *jus*. Augustine considered this position in *The City of God*, Book XIX. According to Augustine, since Rome had no justice, Cicero's position has the inconvenient consequence that Rome was no state at all. We must therefore seek another definition of "state" (*populus*) in which justice is not an essential element. Augustine stressed the notion of order—"a harmonious multitude"—with the suggestion that legal order need not be moral or just. There are passages in Augustine, however, which seem to uphold a more orthodox natural-law position. In any event the terms of his discussions are somewhat different; his main points of contrast are divine and human law, rather than *jus naturale* and *jus civile*.

The sources of the natural-law theories that were to dominate Western legal philosophy for many centuries were the writings of the Greek and Roman philosophers and poets, Justinian's *Corpus Juris Civilis*, and the Church Fathers. Isidore of Seville (c. 560–636), an encyclopedist and an important transmitter of Roman thought to later writers, concisely expressed the natural-lawyer's ideal regarding positive law: "Law shall be virtuous, just, possible to nature, according to the custom of the country, suitable to place and time, necessary, useful; clearly expressed, lest by its obscurity it lead to misunderstanding; framed for no private benefit, but for the common good" (*Etymologies* V, 21).

MIDDLE AGES AND RENAISSANCE

CIVILIANS AND CANONISTS. In the revived study of Roman law in the twelfth century, associated with the glossators, legal philosophy received a fresh stimulus. Of special interest are the attempts at reconciling differences among the Roman jurists on the definition of law and the classification of its branches. In the main, the civilians were in the broad tradition of natural-law thinking; *jus* flows from *justitia*, although it must always fall short of perfect justice, which is God's alone. Irnerius (c. 1050–c. 1130) thus claimed that statutes ought to be interpreted in the light of equity. Strict law requires that all agreements be kept, but equity allows exceptions to the rule. This equity, according to Azo (c. 1150–c. 1230), must be written, rather than a principle found in the judge's heart.

The middle of the twelfth century also saw the systematization of the canon law. In the *Decretum* of Gratian a high degree of jurisprudential competence was brought to this task. The tripartite division of law of the Roman lawyers was verbally accepted, but the leading conceptions were Augustine's *jus divinum* and *jus humana*. Natural law was identified with the former, while the distinctive feature of the latter (covering both *jus gentium* and *jus civile*) was custom. Natural law is contained in the Mosaic law and the Gospels; the command to do unto others what we would have them do unto us is its fundamental principle. Natural law relates to man's rational nature and is immutable; the *mistica*, the cultic regulations found in Scripture, are part of the natural law only in their moral aspect. The commentators on Gratian further divided natural law so as to include not only commands and prohibitions but also *demonstrationes*, which point to what is good for humankind, such as possession of all things in common. In man's fallen condition custom has legitimately modified the *demonstrationes* in permitting private property and slavery. The other branches of natural law may not be abrogated and are the standards by which even the ecclesiastical law must be judged. Gratian (if not all his commentators) seems to have generally maintained a clear distinction between natural (divine) law and canon law.

AQUINAS. The rediscovery of Aristotle in the thirteenth century greatly influenced the further development of legal philosophy. The culmination of the natural-law tradition is the theory of Thomas Aquinas (c. 1224–1274), who integrated Stoic, Christian, and Aristotelian elements within a comprehensive philosophic system. Laws are standards of conduct that have a binding, or obligatory, character. This can be understood only if laws have some kind of rational origin. Combining this view with a teleological conception of nature and social order, Aquinas regarded legal control as purposive. Laws, he concluded, are ordinances of reason promulgated for the common good by the legitimate sovereign. Four types of law may be distinguished: eternal law, an expression of God's rational ordering of the universe; divine law, which guides man toward his supernatural end; natural law, which guides man toward his natural end; and human law, which regulates through the prospect of punishment the affairs of men in a given community in the light of that community's special requirements. Crucial to the concept of natural law are the notions of natural inclinations and right reason. "All those things to which man has a natural inclination are naturally apprehended by reason as being good and consequently as objects of pursuit, and their contraries as evil, and objects of avoidance" (*Summa Theologiae* I–II, 94). The relationship between inclination and reason, accounting for the apprehension of the natural law, has been variously interpreted. The precepts of natural law have as their common foundation the principle "Do good and avoid evil." Natural law is a standard to which human law must conform, and Aquinas employed Aristotle's conception of practical reasoning in explaining the derivation of human law from natural law by the legislator, thus accounting for differences between legal systems and for the possibility that rational men should disagree as to what human laws ought to be. He affirmed the long-standing view that an unjust law is no law; but although an unjust law is not binding in conscience, considerations of utility may require one to obey it. Aquinas allowed that such "laws" may be said to possess a "legal" character insofar as they are promulgated under the color of law by the legitimate prince.

Aquinas discussed in detail and with great acuity all of the problems treated by his predecessors. His influence may be traced in the English writers John Fortescue (c. 1394–c. 1476), Thomas Hooker (c. 1586–1647), and Christopher St. Germain (1460–1540). According to St. Germain, natural law is nothing other than the common-lawyer's notion of "reasonableness." More recent Thomist thinkers, such as François Gény (1861–1959) and Jean Dabin, have advanced novel ideals within the Thomistic tradition.

OCKHAM. Some medieval writers seem to have espoused a protopositivism in their emphasis on the primacy of the will; this is characteristic of the Augustinian-Franciscan tradition. Thus, William of Ockham (c. 1285–1349) regarded the divine will as the norm of morality. "By the very fact that God wills something it is right for it to be done." Nevertheless, it is doubtful that Ockham would have affirmed that what the sovereign commands is just. His position is somewhat unclear, however, for he—like all medieval writers—continued to use the rhetoric of natural law in his *Dialogus*: In one of its senses *jus naturale* is composed of universal rules of conduct dictated by natural reason. A right, such as the immutable right of private property, is a dictate of right reason.

RISE OF ABSOLUTISM. A tendency to combine natural-law doctrines with a theory of royal absolutism began in the fourteenth century. A group of civilians, known as the postglossators, undertook to forge a workable system of law out of the older Roman law, which they regarded as the *jus commune* of Europe. The technically trained administrators in the rising nation-states, they were naturally concerned with fundamental problems of legal theory. Bartolus of Sassoferrato (1314–1357) maintained that the ruler is not bound by the laws, although it is

"equitable" that he should voluntarily submit to them. The *jus gentium*, however, is immutable. Lucas de Penna (1320–1390) discussed jurisprudential questions in detail. Law is the articulation of the ethical virtue of justice, and reason is the foundation of law. At the same time he maintained, as did many civilians, that the prince's lordship rests on divine authority. The ruler is responsible to God alone and not to the people; law is not the expression of the will of the community. Nonetheless, although the prince is unfettered by the laws, bad laws (those that contradict divine law) have no binding force. It is not clear, in Lucas's view, whether the obligation to obey law derives primarily from the rationality of law or from the divine grant of authority to the ruler.

LATER RENAISSANCE

BODIN. Jean Bodin (1530–1596), the great exponent of unlimited sovereignty under natural law whose views were apparently influenced by the fourteenth-century civilians, like them appears to have had difficulty in adapting Christian legal thought to the conditions of the secular nation-state. In his *Six Books of the Commonwealth* Bodin was emphatic that "law is nothing else than the command of the sovereign in his exercise of sovereign power." But although the prince "has no power to exceed the law of nature," which is decreed by God, it seems plain that Bodin no longer thought of right reason as linking natural and positive law. Bodin's endorsement of the command theory also appears in his treatment of custom. The relative weights of positive law and custom had long been debated by the medieval lawyers, but Bodin was one of the first to hold that custom owes its legal authority to the sufferance of the ruler. In this he anticipated the idea of tacit command expressed by Thomas Hobbes and John Austin.

INTERNATIONAL LAW. The emergence of nation-states also brought the problem of the rational foundation of international law to the forefront of legal thinking. This development may be seen in the writings of the Spanish Thomists Francisco de Vitoria (1492/1493–1546) and Francisco Suárez (1548–1617) and of Hugo Grotius (1583–1645), a Dutch Protestant jurist with broad humanistic leanings. According to Vitoria, the *jus gentium* either belongs to or is derivable from the natural law and consists in prescriptions for the common good in the widest sense, namely, for the international community. Rights and obligations are thus conferred upon nations acting through their rulers.

The conception of a law of nations was developed in great detail by Suárez. Although his *De Legibus* is Thomistic in many respects, Suárez explicitly stated that Aquinas's account of law is inadequate. Suárez began by distinguishing laws in the prescriptive sense from laws of nature in the descriptive sense, which are laws only metaphorically. (Many positivists trace the origin of natural-law thinking to the tendency to confuse these two types of law.) With regard to prescriptive laws, Suárez defined a law (*lex*) as "the act of a just and right will by which the superior wills to oblige the inferior to this or that" or as "a common, just and stable precept, which has been sufficiently promulgated" (*De Legibus* I, 12). The reference to stability is notable: Laws generally survive both the lawgiver and the populace living when they are enacted, and they are valid until abrogated. Such considerations have led recent writers to reject the identification of laws with mere acts of will; but although Suárez rejected the voluntaristic notion of natural law associated with the Ockhamists, he held that the civil law is enacted "more by the will than by reason." It is not derived from natural law by logical inference but by "determination," and hence is, in a sense, arbitrary (ibid. II, 20). Most medieval writers tended to use *lex* and *jus* interchangeably; Suárez, however, defined the latter as "a certain moral power which every man has, either over his own property or with respect to what is due to him" (ibid. I, 2). Although Aquinas briefly discussed *jus naturale* as contrasted with *jus positivum* (*Summa Theologiae* II–II, 57), the concept of a "natural right" was almost entirely absent from his thought. It is clearly present in Suárez, who, in the style of John Locke (1632–1704) and the Enlightenment philosophers, formulated a list of natural rights. Nevertheless, the individualism of these writers is not present in Suárez. His attitude was quite remote from eighteenth-century natural-law and natural-right theorists, who thought that a perfect system of law could be deduced from the natural law.

Despite Grotius's tendency to underestimate his predecessors, his *De Jure Belli ac Pacis* (1625) clearly showed the influence of such writers as Vitoria and Suárez. He developed their notion of a "just war," a topic that was still discussed by Hans Kelsen (1881–1973) and other twentieth-century theorists concerned with the problem of sanctions in international law. Just wars presuppose the existence of laws governing relations between sovereign states; such laws have their origin in natural law and in treaties, which in turn presuppose precepts of the law of nature. The denial of the existence of natural law supposes that men are egoistically motivated, accepting law as a "second best." However, following Aristotle and

the Scholastics, Grotius held that man is social, altruistic, and rational. Therein lies the origin of law, which would be binding whether or not God exists. This statement has been regarded by historians as epoch making; they claim that Grotius separated jurisprudence from theology. More important, perhaps, is the tendency in Grotius and others who followed him to identify natural law with certain rational principles of social organization, and thus to loosen its tie with the Stoic metaphysical conception of the law of nature.

SEVENTEENTH TO LATE NINETEENTH CENTURIES

HOBBES AND MONTESQUIEU. Thomas Hobbes (1588–1679) was perhaps the most important of the seventeenth-century legal philosophers. His break with the tradition of natural law provoked much controversy. Hobbes employed the terminology of "natural right," "laws of nature," and "right reason." But the first was for him simply "the liberty each man hath to use his own power as he will himself, for the preservation of his own nature; that is to say, of his own life" (*Leviathan* 14); the second are principles of self-interest, which are often identified with the third. There is no right reason in nature (*Elements of Law* II, 10, 8). The natural condition of humankind is one of perpetual war, in which common standards of conduct are absent. There is no right or wrong, justice or injustice, mine or thine in this situation. The crucial steps in Hobbes's theory are the identifications of society with politically organized society and of justice with positive law. Laws are the commands of the sovereign; it is in reference to such commands that the members of a society evaluate the rightness or justness of their behavior. An "unjust law" is an absurdity; nor can there be legal limitations on the exercise of sovereign power. No writer has put forward a positivistic conception of law with greater style and forcefulness than Hobbes. Difficulties in his position emerge from his concession that although the sovereign cannot commit an injustice, he may commit iniquity; the idea of injury to God in the state of nature; and the treatment of conscience in *De Cive*. Hobbes solved the problem of the source of the obligation to obey the sovereign's command by his "social contract" doctrine, the interpretation of which is still discussed by scholars. His unfinished *Dialogue between a Philosopher and a Student of the Common Laws of England* examines various doctrines of the English law as put forward by Sir Edward Coke, and it is notable for its critical examination of Coke's statement that reason is the life of the law.

The *Second Treatise of Civil Government* by Locke, primarily an attack on Robert Filmer's "divine right" theory, contains certain implied criticisms of Hobbes. Its interest for legal philosophy lies in its use of a version of the social contract to treat the question of the obligation to obey the law, its conception of limitations on sovereign power, and its individualistic view of natural inalienable rights, particularly rights in property. Locke's influence was enormous, and his view of natural rights had a profound effect on the development of law in the United States.

A new approach to the understanding of law and its institutions was put forward by Baron de Montesquieu (1689–1755). He, too, spoke the language of natural law and defined laws as "necessary relations arising from the nature of things" (*The Spirit of the Laws* I, 1). But his special importance lies in his attempt to study legal institutions by a comparative historical method, stressing the environmental factors that affect the development of law. This suggestion had been anticipated by Bodin, and Giambattista Vico (1668–1744) had also applied a historical method to the study of Roman law, but Vico's work had little immediate influence. Montesquieu's doctrine of the separation of powers had an extraordinary influence. His sharp separation of judicial from legislative and executive power reinforced the conception that the judge is a mere mouthpiece of the law and that judges merely declare the existing law but never make it. In 1790, in his *Reflections on the Revolution in France*, Edmund Burke turned the historical approach to a practical political use when he protested against proceeding a priori in the "science of constructing a commonwealth."

KANTIANISM. Immanuel Kant (1724–1804) contributed to legal philosophy as he did to other branches of philosophy. The keynote of his legal philosophy was inspired by Jean-Jacques Rousseau (1712–1778), who set as the problem of his *Social Contract* the reconciliation of social coercion and individual freedom. Kant's legal philosophy may be called a philosophy of justice in which the concept of freedom plays a central role. Kant sought a systematic understanding of the principles underlying all positive laws that would enable us to decide whether these laws are in accordance with moral principles. Positive law "proceeds from the will of a legislator," and any viable legal system will take into account the particular conditions of the given society. With these conditions the theory of law has no concern. The theory is an application of the results of moral philosophy to the conditions of "men considered merely as men." This endeavor covers both the domain of law (*Recht*) and the domain of ethics; the principle that right action is action in conformity with universalizable maxims holds for both juridical and moral laws. A law (*Gesetz*) is a formula expressing "the necessity" of an action. Juridical and moral laws are distinguished in that the former regulate external conduct irrespective of its motives. (But this does not mean that a judge should necessarily ignore the lawbreaker's motives when passing sentence upon him.) Any man, as a morally free agent, is entitled to express his freedom in activity so long as it does not interfere with the similar freedom that others possess. This is the principle underlying all legislation and "right." Juridical law also involves the authority to compel conformity and to punish violations. The necessary and sufficient condition for legal punishment is that the juridical law has been broken. It must be recognized, however, that the domain of such law is restricted by the limits of compulsion. While it is morally wrong to save one's own life by killing another, even where this is the only expedient, it can never be made legally wrong to kill in such a case. The principle of law receives content in Kant's application of it to particular private rights in external things and in his analysis of the methods for acquiring such rights.

Kant's influence on jurisprudence, after being somewhat eclipsed by Hegelianism, reemerged at the end of the nineteenth century. One of the most important neo-Kantians was Rudolf Stammler (1856–1938), who invented, but eventually discarded, the phrase "natural law with variable content." Accepting the Kantian distinction between "form" and "matter," he attempted to discern the form of all laws. He defined law as "exceptionless binding volition." Just law is an ideal involving principles of respect and cooperation.

UTILITARIANISM AND POSITIVISM. While Kant and his followers may be said to have fostered a variety of natural-law thinking (although different from the Stoic and Thomistic types), Jeremy Bentham (1748–1832) and his followers (notably John Stuart Mill) claim to have rejected such thinking entirely. Of the influences on Bentham, two may be briefly noted. David Hume (1711–1776) argued that moral distinctions are not derived from reason; passion, or sentiment, is the ultimate foundation of moral judgment. Justice is grounded in utility. Second, the Italian criminologist Cesare Beccaria (1738–1794), in his *Of Crimes and Punishments* (1764), subjected the existing institutions of criminal law and methods of punishment to relentless criticism. His standard of judgment was whether "the greatest happiness of the greatest number" was maximized. Bentham acknowledged his debt to Beccaria, and this "principle of utility" was the base of Bentham's voluminous projected "codes." He did not, however, define the nature of law by reference to utility. In his *The Limits of Jurisprudence Defined* (published in 1945) he defined a law as the expression of "the will of a sovereign in a state." Bentham's views, which were well suited to deal with the problems engendered by the industrial revolution in England, were of immense importance in effecting legal reform. In 1832, the year of his death, the Reform Act was passed, largely as a result of the work of his followers. Mill's *On Liberty* (1859) is an attempt to treat the limits of legal coercion by the state along modified utilitarian lines.

In legal philosophy Bentham's influence affected the English-speaking world especially through the thought of John Austin (1790–1859), the seminal figure in English and American legal positivism and analytic jurisprudence. Austin tried to find a clear demarcation of the boundaries of positive law, which would be antecedent to a "general jurisprudence" comprising the analyses of such "principles, notions, and distinctions" as duty, right, and punishment, which are found in every legal system; these analyses in turn were to be employed in "particular jurisprudence," the systematic exposition of some given body of law. Austin began by distinguishing "law properly so called" and "law improperly so called." The former is always "a species of command," an expression of a wish or desire, analytically connected with the ideas of duty, liability to punishment (or sanction), and superiority. The last notion led Austin to his famous and influential analysis of "sovereignty"; "laws strictly so called" (positive laws) are the commands of political superiors to political inferiors. From this it follows that international law is merely "positive international morality" rather than law in a strict sense. (Some writers, viewing this as an unfortunate and perhaps dangerous consequence, were led to various revisions of Austinianism.) Austin's "separation" of law and morality is often taken as the hallmark of legal positivism. "The existence of law is one thing; its merit or demerit is another," he wrote in *The Province of Jurisprudence Determined* (V, note). Yet Austin was a utilitarian; in distinguishing between the law that is and the law that ought to be, he did not mean that law is not subject to rational moral criticism grounded in utility, which he took to be the index to the law of God. At this point Austin was influenced by such "theological utilitarians" as William Paley.

Austin's views were subjected to vigorous discussion both without and within the traditions of positivism and analytical jurisprudence. And as the disciplines of history, anthropology, and ethnology assumed an increasing importance during the nineteenth century, rival approaches to the understanding of law developed. Thus, Sir Henry Maine (1822–1888), who formulated the historical law that legal development is a movement from status to contract, argued in his *Early History of Institutions* (London, 1875) that the command-sovereignty theory of law has no application in a primitive community, where law is largely customary and the political "sovereign," who has the power of life or death over his subjects, never makes law. The Austinian view can be saved only by maintaining the fiction that what the "sovereign" permits, he commands. Nonetheless, Austin had many followers at the turn of the twentieth century, such as T. E. Holland (1835–1926) and J. W. Salmond (1862–1924), who attempted to preserve the imperative and coercion aspects of his theory while introducing revisions.

The role of the courts was increasingly emphasized. In the United States, John Chipman Gray (1839–1915) wrote *The Nature and Sources of the Law* (New York, 1909; 2nd ed., New York, 1921), one of the most important American contributions to the subject. Acknowledging his debt to Austin, Gray defined law as "the rules which the courts [of the State] lay down for the determination of legal rights and duties." This required him to construe statutes, judicial precedents, custom, expert opinion, and morality as sources of law rather than as law. All law is judge-made. The machinery of the state stands in the background and provides the coercive element, which does not enter into the definition of "law." Gray's influence may be traced in the realist movement in the United States.

HEGELIANISM AND THE HISTORICAL SCHOOL. While England was largely under the sway of the utilitarians, Kantianism, Hegelianism, the historical school, and legal positivism flourished in Germany, both singly and in various combinations. In his *Philosophy of Right*, G. W. F. Hegel (1770–1831) developed some Kantian themes in his own characteristic way. Law and social-political institutions belong to the realm of "objective spirit," in which interpersonal relationships, reflecting an underlying freedom, receive their concrete manifestations. In attempting to show the rightness and the rationality of various legal relationships and institutions in given moments of the development of "spirit," and in seeing them as natural growths, Hegel formulated a theory of law and the state that was easily combined with various historical, functional, and institutional approaches to legal phenomena.

Friedrich Karl von Savigny (1779–1861) is often regarded as the founder of the historical school. His *Of the Vocation of Our Age for Legislation and Jurisprudence* (1814) was published before Hegel's work and was probably influenced by Johann Gottlieb Fichte (but not by Fichte's *Grundlage des Naturrechts*, 1796), whose notion of the "folk-spirit" was widely known. Law, like language, originates spontaneously in the common consciousness of a people, who constitute an organic being. Both the legislator and the jurist may articulate this law, but they no more invent or make it than does the grammarian who codifies a natural language. Savigny believed that to accept his conception of law was to reject the older notions of natural law; nevertheless, it is often claimed that Savigny's conception was merely a new kind of natural law standing above, and judging, the positive law.

Otto von Gierke (1844–1921), the author of *Das deutsche Genossenschaftsrecht*, clearly fits into the tradition of the historical school. Gray, in *The Nature and Sources of the Law*, subjected the theories of Savigny and his American follower, James C. Carter (1827–1905), to severe criticism. It should be noted that Maine's views have nothing in common with those of Savigny; in Maine's work the metaphysics of the *Volksgeist* is entirely absent.

LATE NINETEENTH CENTURY TO MID-TWENTIETH CENTURY

JHERING AND GERMAN POSITIVISM. Rudolf von Jhering (1818–1892), eminent both as a historian of law and as a legal theorist, rejected both Hegel and Savigny: Hegel, for holding the law to be an expression of the general will and for failing to see how utilitarian factors and interests determine the existence of law; Savigny, for regarding law as a spontaneous expression of subconscious forces and for failing to see the role of the conscious struggle for protection of interests. However, Jhering shared the broad cultural orientation of many of the Hegelians, and he was grateful to Savigny for having overthrown the doctrine of "immutable" natural law. Jhering's contribution was to insist that legal phenomena cannot be comprehended without a systematic understanding of the purposes that give rise to them, the study of the ends grounded in social life without which there would be no legal rules. Without purpose there is no will.

At the same time there are strong strains of positivism in Jhering: Law is defined as "the sum of the rules of constraint which obtain in a state" (*Der Zweck im Recht*, p. 320). In this respect he was close to the German positivists, who emphasized the imperative character of

law. Karl Binding (1841–1920), an influential positivist, defined law as "only the clarified legal volition [*Rechtswille*] of a source of law [*Rechtsquelle*]" (*Die Normen und ihre Uebertretung*, p. 68). In this period the slogan of German positivism, "All law is positive law," emerged. Yet Jhering opposed many of the claims of the analytical positivists; his essay "Scherz und Ernst in der Jurisprudenz" (Leipzig, 1885) ridiculed their "heaven of jurisprudential concepts."

SOCIOLOGICAL AND ALLIED THEORIES. Jhering's work foreshadowed many of the dominant tendencies of twentieth-century legal philosophy. Hermann Kantorowicz regarded Jhering as the fountainhead of both the "sociological" and "free-law" schools. The former term covers too wide a group of writers to be surveyed here, some of whom were concerned solely with empirical work, while others combined empirical work with a philosophical outlook. Proponents of the jurisprudence of interests (*Interessenjurisprudenz*) eschewed Jhering's inquiries into the metaphysical and moral bases of purposes, claiming that he did not sufficiently attend to the conflict of interest behind laws; law reflects dominant interest. (Similar analyses were made in the United States; for example, the "pressure-group" theory of politics advanced by A. F. Bentley [1870–1957] in *The Process of Government*, Chicago, 1908.) Much attention was devoted to the analysis of the judicial process and the role that the "balancing" of interests plays in it. As Philipp Heck, one of its leading exponents, remarked: "The new movement of 'Interessenjurisprudenz' is based on the realization that the judge cannot satisfactorily deal with the needs of life by mere logical construction" (*Begriffsbildung und Interessenjurisprudenz*, p. 4).

This sentiment was endorsed by the closely allied "free-law" movement. According to this group, "legal logic" and the "jurisprudence of conceptions" are inadequate for achieving practicable and just decisions. The judge not only perforce frequently goes beyond the statute law, but he also often ought to go beyond it. The "free-law" writers undertook the normative task of supplying guidelines for the exercise of judicial discretion, and the judicial function was assimilated to the legislative function. The focus on such problems reflected the enormous change, occasioned by the industrialization of Western society, in the functions of the state. No longer did the nation-state exist merely to keep the peace or protect preexisting rights; rather, it played a positive role in promoting social and individual welfare. The philosophy of law thus became increasingly concerned with the detailed working out of the foundations of legal policy.

The "free-law" theorist Eugen Ehrlich (1862–1922), who influenced such American theorists as Karl N. Llewellyn (1893–1962) and other representatives of legal realist tendencies, summarized his *Grundlegung der Soziologie des Rechts* as follows: "At the present as well as at any other time, the center of gravity of legal development lies not in legislation, not in juristic science, nor in judicial decision, but in society itself." He rejected the positivistic tenet that only norms posited by the state are legal norms, for in any society there is always more law than is expressed in legal propositions. The "inner order" of an association is the basic form of law. Ehrlich also engaged in empirical study of the "legal facts" (*Rechtstatsachen*) and "living law" of various communities in the Austro-Hungarian Empire. Ehrlich may thus be said to have considered custom as law in its own right. However, many positivists would argue that he was not able to account for the normative character of custom.

MARXISM. The Marxist stress on economic interests was often combined with the sociological and free-law views. Central to the Marxist position are the notions of "class" (usually defined in terms of legal relationship to property and the means of production) and "class interest," which leads to the analysis of the role of law in different societies with differing class structures. Addressing their critics, Karl Marx and Friedrich Engels wrote: "Your law [*Recht*] is but the will of your class exalted into statutes [*Gesetz*], a will which acquires its content from the material conditions of existence of your class" (*Communist Manifesto*, 1848). This suggests that law is merely part of the ideological superstructure and has no effect on the material organization of society. It raises the question of whether law exists in all societies—for instance, in primitive society or in the "classless" society arising after the triumph of socialism—and the further question of the nature and function of law in the transitional period from capitalism to socialism. The issue of "revolutionary legality" or "socialist legality" was treated by V. I. Lenin, E. Pashukanis, and Andrei Vishinsky. An important Marxist study of the relationship between law and the economy is that of the Austrian socialist Karl Renner (*Die Rechtsinstitute des Privatrechts und ihre soziale Funktion*, 1929).

PURE THEORY AND RELATIVISM. Although the sociological approaches to law have many practitioners, the most controversial and perhaps the most influential twentieth-century view was that of Hans Kelsen, a leading exponent of legal positivism. Influenced by the epistemology of the neo-Kantians, Kelsen distinguished sharply between the "is" and the "ought," and consequently between the natural sciences and disciplines, such as legal science, which study "normative" phenomena. Legal science is a descriptive science—prescriptive and valuational questions cannot be scientific—and Kelsen's "pure theory" aimed at providing the conceptual tools for studying any given legal system irrespective of its content. The theory is "pure" in that it is divorced from any ideological or sociological elements; it attempts to treat a legal system simply as a system of norms. Kelsen's view was thus similar to the analytical jurisprudence of Austin, but Kelsen regarded legal norms as "de-psychologized commands." In order to understand an act of will as a norm-creating act, we must already employ a norm that serves as a "schema of interpretation." The jurist who seeks to understand legal phenomena must ultimately presuppose a basic norm (*Grundnorm*), which is not itself a positive legal norm. Legal systems are sets of coercive norms arranged in hierarchical fashion; lower norms are the "concretizations" of higher norms. In Kelsen's analysis the "dualisms" of state and law and public and private law disappear, and the relationship between international law and national legal systems is seen in a fresh light.

Unlike Kelsen, Gustav Radbruch (1878–1949) did not found a school. His position, which he called relativism, has many affinities with that of Kelsen; but Radbruch maintained that law, which is a cultural phenomenon, can be understood only in relation to the values that men strive to realize through it. He attempted to analyze these values in relation to legal institutions, showing the "antinomies" among these values that led to his relativism. World War II raised the question in the minds of many legal philosophers whether the separation of law and morals of legal positivism, which was popular in Germany, contributed to the rise of Nazism. Concern over this problem seems to have caused Radbruch to move away from his earlier relativism toward a kind of natural-law position.

REALISM AND OTHER RECENT TRENDS. In the United States, until the mid-twentieth century, legal philosophy had largely been the province of lawyers rather than of professional philosophers. This may account for its sociological and realistic tone. The erudite Roscoe Pound (1870–1964) was its most prolific writer. Pound recognized the influence of Josef Kohler (1849–1919) and his notion of jural postulates and, especially, of Jhering. The pragmatism of William James also contributed to the development of his views. In an early article, "Mechanical Jurisprudence" (*Columbia Law Review* 8 [1908]: 605–610), Pound argued for an understanding of the interests that the law seeks to protect. Introducing a distinction between "law in books" and "law in action," he maintained the need for a close study of the actual operation of legal institutions. On both scores his influence in the United States has been momentous, but it is difficult to summarize his position; he is often associated with a "social engineering" approach to law. Law contains both precepts and ideal elements. Among precepts Pound distinguished rules, principles, conceptions, doctrines, and standards. It is pointless to isolate some canonical form to which all laws are reducible. The ideal element consists of received ideals "of the end of law, and hence of what legal precepts should be and how they should be applied." Pound offered an elaborate, although tentative, survey of the individual, public, and social interests secured by law. This list was criticized and amended by Pound's Australian disciple Julius Stone (*The Province and Function of Law*, 1946). In his later years Pound moved toward a kind of natural-law thinking, arguing for a more intimate connection between law and morality; he abjured the realist tendencies, which had been influenced by his earlier thought, as "give it up" philosophies.

It is exceedingly difficult to characterize the legal realists; they disclaim a common doctrine but recognize an interest in a common set of problems. With J. C. Gray, the spiritual godfather of American legal realism was Justice Oliver Wendell Holmes Jr. (1841–1935). In his seminal essay "The Path of the Law" (*Harvard Law Review* 10 [1896]: 457–478), he advocated viewing law as the "bad man" would, in terms of the practicable remedies afforded individuals through the medium of the courts. Holmes presented in that article his famous definition of law as "the prophecies of what the courts will do in fact." It may be argued, however, that this definition, while perhaps adequate from the advocate's viewpoint, can hardly apply to the judge. When the judge asks what the law is on some matter, he is not trying to predict what he will decide.

Joseph W. Bingham was one of the first realists. In "What Is the Law?" (*Michigan Law Review* 11 [1912]: 1–25 and 109–121), Bingham argued that legal rules, like scientific laws, have no independent existence, being simply mental constructs that conveniently summarize particular facts. Laws are really judicial decisions, and the so-called rules or principles are among the (mentally) causative factors behind the decision. This nominalism and behaviorism, which characterized much of early realist writing, was criticized by Morris R. Cohen (1880–1947), until recently one of the few academic philosophers in the United States concerned with legal philosophy. "Behavior analysis" was advocated by Karl N.

Llewellyn, who extended it beyond judicial behavior to "official" behavior (*Jurisprudence*, Chicago, 1962; collected papers).

The so-called myth of legal certainty was attacked by Jerome Frank (1889–1957) in his *Law and the Modern Mind* (New York, 1930), which explained the genesis of the myth in Freudian terms. In the sixth edition (New York, 1949) Frank was somewhat friendlier toward natural-law thinking, characterizing his change of attitude as going from an earlier "rule-skepticism" to "fact-skepticism" (*Courts on Trial*, Princeton, NJ, 1949). Other important realists include Thurman Arnold, Leon Green, Felix Cohen, Walter Nelles, Herman Oliphant, and Fred Rodell. Both positivism and realism were attacked by Lon L. Fuller (*Law in Quest of Itself*, Chicago, 1940), a leading American exponent of non-Thomistic natural-law thinking (*The Morality of Law*, New Haven, CT, 1964). The revival of natural-law doctrines is one of the most interesting features of current legal thought. Recent contributions and criticisms may be found in the journal *Natural Law Forum*.

The Scandinavian countries are a center of legal philosophy, and many of their leading writers are realists. They are more consciously philosophical than their American counterparts. The leading spirit was Axel Hägerström (1868–1939), who rejected metaphysical presuppositions in legal philosophy and insisted on an understanding of legal phenomena in empirical terms. Many legal concepts can be understood only as survivals of "mythical" or "magical" thought patterns, which should ideally be eliminated. Vilhelm Lunstedt (*Legal Thinking Revised*, Stockholm, 1956) was most radical in his rejection of metaphysics. Values are expressions of emotion and should be excluded from legal science. The "method of social welfare" should be substituted for the "method of justice." Alf Ross (*On Law and Justice*, London, 1958) argued that the first method is as "chimerical" as the second and presents an analysis of legal policy-making as a kind of rational technology. Laws, Ross argued, are directives to courts. The concept "valid law" as used by jurists and legal philosophers cannot be explicated in purely behavioristic terms; inner psychological attitudes must also be included. A similar view is presented by Karl Olivecrona (*Law as Fact*, London, 1939), who wrote important realist analyses of legal language and severely criticized command theories of law, such as Austin's. In *Inquiries into the Nature of Law and Morals* (translated by C. D. Broad, Cambridge, U.K., 1953), Hägerström argued that Kelsen's "pure theory" never escapes the "will" element either, and hence falls subject to all the criticisms that may be leveled against the command theories.

In the mid-twentieth century, the most influential legal philosopher in the English-speaking world was H. L. A. Hart. In his *Concept of Law* (Oxford, 1961) he developed a view of law as consisting of a "union of primary and secondary rules." The former are rules imposing duties; the latter are rules of recognition, change, and adjudication. The first of the secondary rules (those for recognizing the rules of a system) seems to be crucial to his account of all three. His position was in many respects similar to that of Kelsen. He gave an interesting analysis, allied to Ross's account, of what it means to say that a rule exists. Hart saw the relationship between law and morals as contingent, in contrast with the Thomistic view of a logical connection between the two; this led him to an interpretation of natural law not unlike that presented by some Renaissance writers. In a number of important articles Hart focused on the nature of definition in jurisprudence, the analysis of psychological concepts in the law, legal responsibility, and the principles of punishment.

See also Aristotelianism; Aristotle; Augustine, St.; Austin, John; Beccaria, Cesare Bonesana; Bentham, Jeremy; Bodin, Jean; Burke, Edmund; Celsus; Cicero, Marcus Tullius; Cohen, Morris Raphael; Engels, Friedrich; Enlightenment; Fichte, Johann Gottlieb; Filmer, Robert; Grotius, Hugo; Hegel, Georg Wilhelm Friedrich; Hägerström, Axel; Hart, Herbert Lionel Adolphus; Hegelianism; Hippias of Elis; Historical School of Jurisprudence; Hobbes, Thomas; Hume, David; James, William; Justice; Kant, Immanuel; Kelsen, Hans; Legal Positivism; Lenin, Vladimir Il'ich; Locke, John; Marx, Karl; Marxist Philosophy; Medieval Philosophy; Mill, John Stuart; Montesquieu, Baron de; Natural Law; Neo-Kantianism; Patristic Philosophy; Plato; Positivism; Pragmatism; Radbruch, Gustav; Realism; Renaissance; Rousseau, Jean-Jacques; Savigny, Friedrich Karl von; Seneca, Lucius Annaeus; Socrates; Sophists; Stammler, Rudolf; Stoicism; Suárez, Francisco; Thomas Aquinas, St.; Thomism; Utilitarianism; Vico, Giambattista; Vitoria, Francisco de; William of Ockham; Xenophon.

Bibliography

Ago, Roberto. "Positive Law and International Law." *American Journal of International Law* 51 (1957): 691–733.

Allen, C. K. *Law in the Making*, 7th ed. Oxford: Clarendon Press, 1964.

Berolzheimer, Fritz. *System der Rechts- und Wirtschaftsphilosophie*, 5 vols. Munich: Beck, 1904–1907. Vol. II translated by R. S. Jastrow as *The World's Legal Philosophies*. Boston: Boston Book, 1912.

Bodenheimer, Edgar. *Jurisprudence*. Cambridge, MA: Harvard University Press, 1962.

Cairns, Huntington. *Legal Philosophy from Plato to Hegel*. Baltimore: Johns Hopkins Press, 1949.

Carlyle, R. W., and A. J. Carlyle. *A History of Mediaeval Political Theory in the West*, 6 vols. Edinburgh and London: Blackwood, 1903–1936.

Cohen, M. R. *Law and the Social Order*. New York: Harcourt Brace, 1933.

Cohen, M. R. *Reason and Law*. Glencoe, IL: Free Press, 1950.

Davitt, T. E. *The Nature of Law*. St. Louis: Herder, 1951.

Del Vecchio, Giorgio. *Justice*. Translated by Lady Guthrie. Edinburgh: Edinburgh University Press, 1952.

Dias, R. W. M. *Bibliography of Jurisprudence*. London: Butterworths, 1964.

Ebenstein, William. *The Pure Theory of Law*. Madison, WI, 1945.

Ehrlich, Eugen. *Grundlegung der Soziologie des Rechts*. Munich, 1913. Translated by Walter L. Moll as *Fundamental Principles of the Sociology of Law*. Cambridge, MA: Harvard University Press, 1936.

Entrèves, A. P. d'. *Natural Law*. London: Hutchinson, 1951.

Friedman, Wolfgang. *Legal Theory*, 4th ed. London: Stevens, 1960.

Friedrich, C. J. *The Philosophy of Law in Historical Perspective*, 2nd ed. Chicago: University of Chicago Press, 1963.

Gierke, Otto von. *Das deutsche Genossenschaftsrecht*, 4 vols. Berlin: Weidmann, 1868–1913. Partially translated by F. W. Maitland as *Political Theories of the Middle Age*. Cambridge, U.K.: Cambridge University Press, 1900. Also partially translated by Ernest Barker as *Natural Law and the Theory of Society*. Cambridge, U.K.: Cambridge University Press, 1934.

Gurvitch, Georges. *Sociology of Law*. New York: Philosophical Library and Alliance Book, 1942.

Hall, Jerome. *Studies in Jurisprudence and Criminal Theory*. New York: Oceana, 1958.

Hamburger, Max. *The Awakening of Western Legal Thought*. Translated by B. Miall. London, 1942.

Hart, H. L. A. "Philosophy of Law and Jurisprudence in Britain (1945–1952)." *American Journal of Comparative Law* 2 (1953): 355–364.

Heck, Philipp. *Begriffsbildung und Interessenjurisprudenz*. Tübingen, 1952.

Jaeger, Werner. "In Praise of Law." In *Interpretations of Modern Legal Philosophies*, edited by P. L. Sayre. New York: Oxford University Press, 1947.

Jennings, W. I., ed. *Modern Theories of Law*. London: Oxford University Press, H. Milford, 1933.

Jhering, Rudolf von. *Die Normen und ihre Uebertretung*. Leipzig, 1872.

Jhering, Rudolf von. *Der Zweck im Recht*, Vol. I. Leipzig: Breitkopf and Härtel, 1877. Translated by I. Husik as *Law as a Means to an End*. Boston: Boston Book, 1913.

Jolowicz, H. F. *Lectures on Jurisprudence*. London: University of London, Athlone Press, 1963.

Jones, J. W. *Historical Introduction to the Theory of Law*. Oxford: Clarendon Press, 1940.

Kantorowicz, Hermann. *The Definition of Law.* Cambridge, U.K.: Cambridge University Press, 1958.

Kelsen, Hans. *What Is Justice?* Berkeley: University of California Press, 1957.

Kocourek, Albert. "The Century of Analytical Jurisprudence since John Austin." In *Law: A Century of Progress,* edited by A. Reppy. New York: New York University Press, 1937.

Lloyd, Dennis. *Introduction to Jurisprudence.* London: Stevens, 1959.

Lottin, O. *Le droit naturel chez saint Thomas d'Aquin et ses prédécesseurs.* Bruges, 1931.

Macdonnell, J., and E. W. D. Manson, eds. *Great Jurists of the World.* London: Murray, 1913. Biographical.

Morris, C. "Four Eighteenth Century Theories of Jurisprudence." *Vanderbilt Law Review* 14 (1960): 101–116.

Paton, G. W. *A Text-Book of Jurisprudence,* 2nd ed. Oxford: Clarendon Press, 1951.

Patterson, E. W. *Jurisprudence.* New York: Foundation Press, 1953.

Pollock, Frederick. *Jurisprudence and Legal Essays.* London: Macmillan, 1961.

Pound, Roscoe. *Jurisprudence,* 5 vols. St. Paul, MN: West, 1959. A collection of much of his work.

Renner, Karl. *Die Rechtsinstitute des Privatrechts und ihre soziale Funktion.* Tübingen: Mohr, 1929. Translated by A. Schwarzschild as *The Institutions of Private Law and Their Social Function.* London, 1949.

Rommen, Heinrich. *Die ewige Wiederkehr des Naturrechts.* Leipzig, 1936. Translated by T. R. Hanley as *The Natural Law.* St. Louis, 1947.

Spencer, A. W., ed. *Modern French Legal Philosophy.* New York, 1921.

Stone, Julius. *The Province and Function of Law.* Sydney: Associated General Publications, 1946.

Ullmann, Walter. *The Medieval Idea of Law.* London, 1946.

Verdross, A. *Abendländische Rechtsphilosophie.* Vienna: Springer, 1958.

Villey, M. *Leçons d'histoire de la philosophie du droit.* Paris: Dalloz, 1957.

Vinogradoff, Paul. *Outlines of Historical Jurisprudence,* 2 vols. London: Oxford University Press, 1910–1922.

M. P. Golding (1967)

The article below reproduces some portions and revises other portions of the previous article.

PHILOSOPHY OF LAW, HISTORY OF [ADDENDUM]

The problems of authority, law and order, obligation, and self-interest first became central topics of speculation in the thought of the Sophists, in the late fifth and early fourth centuries BCE. The most famous Sophists stressed the distinction between nature (*physis*) and convention (*nomos*), and they put laws in the latter category. They generally attributed law to human invention and justified obedience to law only to the extent that it promoted one's own advantage. Laws were artificial, arrived at by consent; most acts that were just according to the law were contrary to nature; the advantages laid down by the law were chains upon nature, but those laid down by nature were free.

In the time of the Sophists notions of law, justice, religion, custom, and morality were largely undifferentiated; yet in this same period some of the crucial problems of legal philosophy were first formulated, and attempts were made at a formal definition of law. Thus, Xenophon (*Memorabilia* I, 2) reported that Alcibiades, who associated with both Critias and Socrates, remarked to Pericles that no one can really deserve praise unless he knows what a law is. Pericles replied that laws are what is approved and enacted by the majority in an assembly, whereby they declare what ought and what ought not to be done. He admitted that if obedience is obtained by mere compulsion, it is force and not law, even though the law be enacted by the sovereign power in the state. Xenophon also recounted an purported conversation between Socrates and the Sophist Hippias in which both maintained an identity between law—or what is lawful—and justice—or what is right—while admitting that laws may be changed or annulled (*Memorabilia* IV, 4).

Socrates claimed that there are "unwritten laws," uniformly observed in every country, that cannot conceivably be products of human invention. They are made by the gods for all men, and when men transgress them, nature penalizes the breach.

Socrates and the Sophists, as presented in Plato's dialogues, disagreed concerning human nature. The Sophists conceived of humans as egoistically motivated and antisocial, whereas for Socrates, as for Plato and Aristotle, people are a social beings, other-regarding as well as self-regarding, who find fulfillment in social life. By contrast, the Sophist Callicles, in Plato's *Gorgias*, holds that we are no exception to the law of nature, according to which the stronger rules; man-made laws and social institutions violate human nature. The less radical Sophists, although they could not identify law with some feature of reality, still accepted its practical usefulness.

PLATO AND ARISTOTLE

PLATO. There is hardly any problem of legal philosophy not touched upon by Plato. He wrote during the decline of the Greek polis, when law and morality could appear as mere conventions imposed by shifting majorities in their own interest and the harmony between the legal order and the order of the universe could not easily be maintained. Plato sought to restore, as far as possible, the traditional analogy between justice and the ordered cosmos. Justice, or right action, cannot be identified with mere obedience to laws, nor can a truly moral life be reduced to conformity with a conventional catalogue of duties. Duties involve a knowledge of what is good for human beings, and such knowledge bears an intimate relation to human nature.

The question "What is justice?" dominates Plato's *Republic*. Plato conceived of justice as that trait of human character that coordinates and limits to their proper spheres the various elements of the human psyche. In order to understand the operation of justice in the human soul, Plato examined human nature writ large: the city-state. The state functions well when it is governed by those who know the art of government, and the practice of this art requires a positive insight into the Good. In a just society every citizen performs the role to which he or she is best suited for the good of the whole. Similarly, in the moral economy of the individual's life, justice prevails when reason rules and the appetites and lower passions are relegated to their proper spheres. A just social order is achieved to the extent to which reason and rational principles govern the lives of its members.

Plato's emphasis on reason found its way into his definition of law. Law is reasoned thought (*logismos*) embodied in the decrees of the state (*Laws* 644D). Plato rejected the view that the authority of law rests on the mere will of the governing power. The *Laws* contains a detailed discussion of many branches of law and is an attempt at a formulation of a systematic code to govern the whole of social life. In contrast with the ideal polis of the *Republic*, in which there would be little need for legislation, in the *Laws* Plato accepted "law and order, which are second best" (*Laws* 875D).

ARISTOTLE. Aristotle, who discussed law in numerous contexts, nowhere gave a formal definition of it. He wrote variously that law is "a sort of order, and good law is good order" (*Politics* 1326a), "reason unaffected by desire" (*Politics* 1287a), and "the mean" (*Politics* 1287b). However, these must be taken not as definitions but as characterizations of law motivated by the point Aristotle was making in the given context.

Following Plato, Aristotle rejected the Sophistic view that law is mere convention. In a genuine community—as distinguished from an alliance, in which law is only a covenant—the law concerns itself with the moral virtue of the citizenry (*Politics* 1280b). Aristotle sharply distinguished between the constitution (*politeia*) and laws (*nomoi*); the constitution concerns the organization of offices within the state, whereas the laws are "those according to which the officers should administer the state, and proceed against offenders" (*Politics* 1289a). The constitution of a state may tend to democracy, although the laws are administered in an oligarchical spirit and vice versa (*Politics*1292b). Legislation should aim at the common good of the citizens, and justice—what is equal—should be determined by the standard of the common good (*Politics*1283a). Yet Aristotle recognized that the law is often the expression of the will of a particular class, and he stressed the role of the middle class as a stabilizing factor.

In his discussion of the forms of government in Book III of the *Politics*, Aristotle took up the Platonic problem of rule by the best man versus rule according to laws. A society of equals by its very nature excludes the arbitrary rule of one individual. In any case, even the best person cannot dispense with the general principles contained in laws; and legal training helps to make better government officials. Furthermore, administrators, like all people, are subject to passion, and it is thus preferable to be judged by the impersonal yardstick of the laws. The importance of the rule of law in no way conflicts with the need to change the law through legislation when it has been found by experience to be socially inadequate. But not all law is the product of legislation; customary law is in fact more important than the written law.

Aristotle's discussion of the judicial process foreshadows many modern notions. Although it is better to have written laws than to rely completely on discretion, "some matters can be covered by the laws and others cannot" (*Politics*1287b20). General rules are insufficient to decide particular cases (*Politics*1286a26), although "well-drawn laws should themselves define all the points they possibly can and leave as few as may be to the decision of the judges" (*Rhetoric* 1354a32). Aristotle seems to have had two considerations in mind. First, judicial decision-making is practical—it involves deliberation—and as such cannot be completely determined in advance. Second, the resolution of disputed issues of fact that determine the outcome of a particular case cannot be settled in advance by legislation. This stress on the insufficiency of general rules connects with Aristotle's influential discussion of equity (*epieikeia*). Equity is just, "but not legally just but a correction of legal justice" (*Nicomachean Ethics* 1137b10).

Aristotle sometimes seems to suggest that equity comes into play when there are gaps in the law, so that it consists in the judge's acting as the lawgiver would act if he were present. Yet he also seems to suggest that equity corrects the harshness of the law when adherence to the written law would work an injustice. Principles of equity are thus closely related to the unwritten universal laws "based on nature," a "natural justice" binding on all persons, even those who have no association or covenant with one another. Nevertheless, what is naturally just may vary from society to society.

The *locus classicus* of Aristotle's discussion of justice is Book V of the *Nicomachean Ethics*. Generically, justice has to do with one's relations to others, and there is a sense of justice that refers to the complete moral virtue of the member of the community in such dealings. There is also a sense in which "justice" refers to a particular virtue involving the fair dealings of individuals in matters handled by private law. Two kinds of rights fall under this special virtue: rights in division (where each individual claims his fair share of goods, honors, and so on) and rights in redress (for wrongs done by one individual to another, such as failure to fulfill a contract).

ROME

STOICS. The Stoics, who conceived of the universe as a single, organic substance, exercised a lasting influence on legal thought. In their view, nature, which exhibits structure and order, and man both partake of intelligence, or reason (*logos*). An animal is directed by a primary impulse toward self-preservation, which adapts it to its environment. In humans, reason is the "engineer of impulse," and our actions may be evaluated only within the framework of the whole of nature. The criterion of moral action is consistency with the all-determining law of nature (*koinos logos*). This conception of a law of nature that is the ultimate standard of human laws and institutions was combined with Aristotelian and Christian notions to form the long-standing natural-law tradition of medieval legal philosophy. Another important Stoic contribution was the belief in the equality of all people in a universal commonwealth and a rejection of Aristotle's doctrine of slavery.

CICERO AND SENECA. The writings of Cicero (106–43 BCE) were important in transmitting classical legal thought to the medieval world. Although Cicero was a professional arguer of legal cases, his philosophical treatment of law in his *De Legibus* disclaims any interest in "clients' questions" or the "law of eaves and house-walls." His legal philosophy was essentially Stoic; he denied that the positive law of a community (written or customary),

even when universally accepted, is the standard of what is just. Nor is mere utility the standard: "Justice is one; it binds all human society, and is based on one law, which is right reason applied to command and prohibition" (*De Legibus* I, 15). An unjust statute is not a true law. Law and morality are logically connected, and only that which conforms to the law of nature is genuine law. This view exercised a lasting influence on natural-law thinking and reappeared in the thought of Thomas Aquinas.

Like Cicero, Seneca (c. 4 BCE–65 CE) aided in transmitting Stoic notions to later thinkers. He reiterated the conception of the equality of all persons under natural law, but perhaps more important was his conception of a golden age of human innocence, a prepolitical state of nature. Legal institutions became necessary as human nature became corrupted.

ROMAN LAW. The influence of Stoicism may be traced in pronouncements of the Roman jurists. It is disputed whether these were any more than remarks designed to ornament legal texts, but they nevertheless influenced the thought of later ages. The jurists distinguished three kinds of law: *jus naturale, jus gentium,* and *jus civile*. In practice, the last originally referred to the law of the city of Rome, but ultimately it was applied to any body of laws of a given community. The *jus gentium* first meant the law applied to strangers, to whom the *jus civile* was not applicable, and was later extended to those legal practices common to all societies. Gaius (mid-second century), who systematized the Roman law in his *Institutes*, identified the *jus naturale* and *jus gentium* as universal principles of law agreeable to natural reason and equity. Thus, law was not a mere expression of human will or institution but that which is rationally apprehended and obeyed. The *jus gentium* was not an ideal law by which the positive law was judged but the rational core of existing legal institutions.

Ulpian (c. 170–228) distinguished *jus naturale* from *jus gentium* by stating that *jus naturale* is not peculiar to human beings but is taught by nature to all animals. Thus, among animals there is an institution similar to human marriage. Slavery and its attendant rules are products of the *jus gentium*, for by the *jus naturale* all people were born free. It is not clear, however, that Ulpian regarded slavery as bad. To him we owe the oft-repeated definition of justice: "the constant wish to give each his due" (*Digest* I, 1, 10). Following Celsus (c. 67–c. 130), he defined law (*jus*) as "the art of the good and the equitable" (*ibid.* I, 1, 1). Again, it does not seem that Ulpian thought of the *jus naturale* as an ideal law opposed to the

ENCYCLOPEDIA OF PHILOSOPHY
2nd edition

jus civile or to the *jus gentium*. It has been suggested that behind Ulpian's thought was a conception of a natural state antecedent to the conditions of organized society.

The doctrines of the Roman jurists owe their lasting influence to their incorporation into the *Corpus Juris Civilis* of Justinian (sixth century), principally in the section called the *Digest*. The compilers of Justinian's *Institutes* (a section of the *Corpus Juris*) seem to have distinguished the *jus naturale* from the *jus gentium* and seem to have regarded the former as a set of immutable divine laws by which the positive law may be morally evaluated (*Institutes* I, 2, 11; III, 1, 11). The *Corpus Juris* also preserved statements of the Roman jurists concerning the source of the authority to make and unmake the laws constituting the civil law. According to a number of these statements, this authority resides in the consent of the people; however, the statement that "what pleases the prince has the force of law" (*Digest* I, 4, 1) was probably a more accurate view of the facts. Justinian seems to have combined these views theoretically in his reference to a (nonexistent) "ancient law" by which the Roman people transferred all their powers to the emperor (*Codex* I, 17, 1, 7).

EARLY MIDDLE AGES

To the legal thought of the Stoics and the Roman philosophers and jurists the Church Fathers added a distinctively Christian element. The law of nature was no longer the impersonal rationality of the universe but was integrated into a theology of a personal, creative deity. The relationship among the Mosaic law, the Gospels, and natural law emerged as a specific problem; the notion of *jus divinum* (divine law) as a distinct type of law, along with the three recognized by the jurists, was crystallized. The notion of the fall of man from a state of perfection (which may be compared with the view of Seneca) played an important role. Thus, according to St. Ambrose (340–397) the Mosaic law—a law of sin and death (see Romans 8.2)—was given because humans failed to obey the law of nature. The fact that many legal institutions, such as slavery and private property, deviate from this ideal law does not necessarily imply that they are unjust or illegitimate; for the natural law is adapted to us only in a condition of innocence.

Of the Church Fathers, St. Augustine (354–430) was perhaps the most original and complex: Only one point in his thought will be noted here. Cicero maintained that nothing can be nobler than the law of a state (*De Legibus* I, 14) and that if a state has no law, it cannot truly be considered a state (*ibid.* II, 12). The law of the state must therefore embody justice, for without *justitia* there is no

jus. Augustine considered this position in *The City of God*, Book XIX. According to Augustine, since Rome had no justice, Cicero's position has the inconvenient consequence that Rome was no state at all. We must therefore seek another definition of "state" (*populus*) in which justice is not an essential element. Augustine stressed the notion of order—"a harmonious multitude"—with the suggestion that legal order need not be moral or just. There are passages in Augustine, however, which seem to uphold a more orthodox natural-law position. In any event, the terms of his discussions are somewhat different; his main points of contrast are divine and human law rather than *jus naturale* and *jus civile*.

The sources of the natural-law theories which were to dominate Western legal philosophy for many centuries were the writings of the Greek and Roman philosophers and poets, Justinian's *Corpus Juris Civilis*, and the Church Fathers. Isidore of Seville (c. 560–636), an encyclopedist and an important transmitter of Roman thought to later writers, concisely expressed the natural-lawyer's ideal regarding positive law: "Law shall be virtuous, just, possible to nature, according to the custom of the country, suitable to place and time, necessary, useful; clearly expressed, lest by its obscurity it lead to misunderstanding; framed for no private benefit, but for the common good" (*Etymologies* V, 21).

MIDDLE AGES AND RENAISSANCE

CIVILIANS AND CANONISTS. The revived study of Roman law in the twelfth century, associated with the glossators, gave a fresh stimulus to legal philosophy. Of special interest are the attempts at reconciling differences among the Roman jurists on the definition of law and the classification of its branches. In the main, the civilians were in the broad tradition of natural-law thinking; *jus* flows from *justitia*, although it must always fall short of perfect justice, which is God's alone. Irnerius (c. 1050–c. 1130) thus claimed that statutes ought to be interpreted in the light of equity. Strict law requires that all agreements be kept, but equity allows exceptions to the rule. This equity, according to Azo (c. 1150–c. 1230), is a principle that must be written, not merely lodged in the judge's heart.

The middle of the twelfth century also saw the systematization of the canon law. In the *Decretum* of Gratian a high degree of jurisprudential competence was brought to this task. The tripartite division of law of the Roman lawyers was accepted, but the leading conceptions were Augustine's *jus divinum* and *jus humana*. Natural law was identified with the former, whereas the distinctive feature of the latter (covering both *jus gentium* and *jus civile*) was custom. Natural law is contained in the Mosaic law and the Gospels; the command to do unto others what we would have them do unto us is its fundamental principle. Natural law relates to our rational nature and is immutable; the *mistica*, the cultic regulations found in scripture, are part of the natural law only in their moral aspect.

The commentators on Gratian further divided natural law so as to include not only commands and prohibitions but also *demonstrationes*, which point to what is good for all humans, such as possession of all things in common. In our fallen condition custom has legitimately modified the *demonstrationes* in permitting private property and slavery. The other branches of natural law may not be abrogated and are the standards by which even the ecclesiastical law must be judged. Gratian (if not all his commentators) seems to have generally maintained a clear distinction between natural (divine) law and canon law.

AQUINAS. The rediscovery of Aristotle in the thirteenth century greatly influenced the further development of legal philosophy. The culmination of the natural-law tradition is the theory of Thomas Aquinas (1224–1274), who integrated Stoic, Christian, and Aristotelian elements within a comprehensive philosophic system. Laws are standards of conduct that have a binding, or obligatory, character. This idea can be understood only if laws have some kind of rational origin. Combining this view with a teleological conception of nature and social order, Aquinas regarded legal control as purposive. Laws, he concluded, are ordinances of reason promulgated for the common good by the legitimate sovereign.

According to Aquinas, four types of law may be distinguished: eternal law, an expression of God's rational ordering of the universe; divine law, which guides us toward our supernatural end; natural law, which guides us toward our natural end; and human law, which regulates through the prospect of punishment the affairs of people in a given community in the light of that community's special requirements. Crucial to the concept of natural law are the notions of natural inclinations and right reason. "All those things to which man has a natural inclination are naturally apprehended by reason as being good and consequently as objects of pursuit, and their contraries as evil, and objects of avoidance" (*Summa Theologiae* I–II, 94). The relationship between inclination and reason, accounting for the apprehension of the natural law, has been variously interpreted. The precepts of natural law have as their common foundation the principle "Do good and avoid evil." Natural law is a standard to which human law must conform, and Aquinas employed Aristotle's conception of practical reasoning in explaining the derivation of human law from natural law by the legislator, thus accounting for differences between legal systems and for the possibility that rational men should disagree as to what human laws ought to be. He affirmed the long-standing view that an unjust law is no law; but although an unjust law is not binding in conscience, considerations of utility may require one to obey it. Aquinas allowed that such "laws" may be said to possess a "legal" character insofar as they are promulgated under the color of law by the legitimate prince.

Aquinas discussed in detail and with great acuity all of the problems treated by his predecessors. His influence may be traced in the English writers John Fortescue (c. 1394–1476), Thomas Hooker (c. 1586–1647), and Christopher St. Germain (1460–1540). According to St. Germain, natural law is nothing other than the common-lawyer's notion of "reasonableness." Among late-twentieth century Thomist scholars, the works of John Finnis have been especially influential.

OCKHAM. Some medieval writers seem to have espoused a protopositivism in their emphasis on the primacy of the will; this is characteristic of the Augustinian-Franciscan tradition. Thus, William of Ockham (c. 1285–1349) regarded the divine will as the norm of morality. "By the very fact that God wills something it is right for it to be done." Nevertheless, it is doubtful that Ockham would have affirmed that what the sovereign commands is just. His position is somewhat unclear, however, for he—like all medieval writers—continued to use the rhetoric of natural law in his *Dialogus*: in one of its senses, *jus naturale* is composed of universal rules of conduct dictated by natural reason. A right, such as the immutable right of private property, is a dictate of right reason.

THE RISE OF ABSOLUTISM. A tendency to combine natural-law doctrines with a theory of royal absolutism began in the fourteenth century. A group of civilians known as the postglossators undertook to forge a workable system of law out of the older Roman law, which they regarded as the *jus commune* of Europe. The technically trained administrators in the rising nation-states, they were naturally concerned with fundamental problems of legal theory. Bartolus of Sassoferrato (1314–1357) maintained that the ruler is not bound by the laws, although it is "equitable" that he should voluntarily submit to them. The *jus gentium*, however, is immutable. Lucas de Penna (1320–1390) discussed jurisprudential questions in detail. Law is the articulation of the ethical virtue of justice, and reason is the foundation of law. At the same time, he maintained, as did many civilians, that the prince's lordship rests on divine authority. The ruler is responsible to God alone and not to the people; law is not the expression of the will of the community. Nonetheless, although the prince is unfettered by the laws, bad laws (those that contradict divine law) have no binding force. It is not clear, in Lucas's view, whether the obligation to obey law derives primarily from the rationality of law or from the divine grant of authority to the ruler.

LATER RENAISSANCE

BODIN. Jean Bodin (1530–1596) was a great exponent of unlimited sovereignty under natural law whose views were apparently influenced by the fourteenth-century civilians. Like them, he appears to have had difficulty in adapting Christian legal thought to the conditions of the secular nation-state. In his *Six Books of the Commonwealth*, Bodin was emphatic that "law is nothing else than the command of the sovereign in his exercise of sovereign power." But although the prince "has no power to exceed the law of nature," which is decreed by God, it seems plain that Bodin no longer thought of right reason as linking natural and positive law. Bodin's endorsement of the command theory also appears in his treatment of custom. The relative weights of positive law and custom had long been debated by the medieval lawyers, but Bodin was one of the first to hold that custom owes its legal authority to the sufferance of the ruler. In this he anticipated the idea of tacit command expressed by Thomas Hobbes and John Austin.

INTERNATIONAL LAW. The emergence of nation-states also brought the problem of the rational foundation of international law to the forefront of legal thinking. This development may be seen in the writings of the Spanish Thomists Francisco de Vitoria (c. 1492–1546) and Francisco Suárez (1548–1617) and of Hugo Grotius (1583–1645), a Dutch Protestant jurist with broad humanistic leanings. According to Vitoria, the *jus gentium* either belongs to or is derivable from the natural law and consists in prescriptions for the common good in the widest sense—namely, for the international community. Rights and obligations are thus conferred upon nations acting through their rulers.

The conception of a law of nations was developed in great detail by Suárez. Although his *De Legibus* is Thomistic in many respects, Suárez explicitly stated that Aquinas's account of law is inadequate. Suárez began by distinguishing laws in the prescriptive sense from laws of nature in the descriptive sense, which are laws only metaphorically. (Many positivists trace the origin of natural-law thinking to the tendency to confuse these two types of law.) With regard to prescriptive laws, Suárez defined a law (*lex*) as "the act of a just and right will by which the superior wills to oblige the inferior to this or that" or as "a common, just and stable precept, which has been sufficiently promulgated" (*De Legibus* I, 12). The reference to stability is notable: Laws generally survive both the lawgiver and the populace living when they are enacted, and they are valid until abrogated. Such considerations have led recent writers to reject the identification of laws with mere acts of will; but although Suárez rejected the voluntaristic notion of natural law associated with the Ockhamists, he held that the civil law is enacted "more by the will than by reason." It is not derived from natural law by logical inference but by "determination," and hence is, in a sense, arbitrary (*De Legibus* II, 20).

Most medieval writers tended to use *lex* and *jus* interchangeably; Suárez, however, defined the latter as "a certain moral power which every man has, either over his own property or with respect to what is due to him" (*De Legibus* I, 2). Although Aquinas briefly discussed *jus naturale* as contrasted with *jus positivum* (*Summa Theologiae* II–II, 57), the concept of a "natural right" was almost entirely absent from his thought. It is clearly present in Suárez, who, in the style of Locke and the Enlightenment philosophers, formulated a list of natural rights. Nevertheless, the individualism of these writers is not present in Suárez. His attitude was quite remote from eighteenth-century natural-law and natural-right theorists, who thought that a perfect system of law could be deduced from the natural law.

Despite Grotius's tendency to underestimate his predecessors, his *De Jure Belli ac Pacis* (1625) clearly showed the influence of such writers as Vitoria and Suárez. He developed their notion of a "just war," a topic still discussed by theorists concerned with the problem of sanctions in international law. Just wars presuppose the existence of laws governing relations between sovereign states; such laws have their origin in natural law and in treaties, which in turn presuppose precepts of the law of nature. The denial of the existence of natural law supposes that people are egoistically motivated, accepting law as a "second best." However, following Aristotle and the Scholastics, Grotius held that humans are social, altruistic, and rational. Therein lies the origin of law, which would be binding whether or not God exists. This statement has been regarded by historians as epoch-making;

they claim that Grotius separated jurisprudence from theology. More important, perhaps, is the tendency in Grotius and others who followed him to identify natural law with certain rational principles of social organization and thus to loosen its tie with the Stoic metaphysical conception of the law of nature.

THE SEVENTEENTH TO LATE-NINETEENTH CENTURIES

HOBBES AND MONTESQUIEU. Thomas Hobbes (1588–1679) was perhaps the most important of the seventeenth-century legal philosophers. His break with the tradition of natural law provoked much controversy. Hobbes employed the terminology of "natural right," "laws of nature," and "right reason." But the first was for him simply "the liberty each man hath to use his own power as he will himself, for the preservation of his own nature; that is to say, of his own life" (*Leviathan* 14); the second are principles of self-interest, which are often identified with the third. There is no right reason in nature (*Elements of Law* II, 10, 8). The natural condition of mankind is one of perpetual war, in which common standards of conduct are absent. There is no right or wrong, justice or injustice, mine or thine in this situation. The crucial steps in Hobbes's theory are the identifications of society with politically organized society and of justice with positive law. Laws are the commands of the sovereign; it is in reference to such commands that the members of a society evaluate the rightness or justness of their behavior. An "unjust law" is an absurdity; nor can there be legal limitations on the exercise of sovereign power.

No writer has put forward a positivistic conception of law with greater style and forcefulness than Hobbes. Difficulties in his position emerge from three areas: his concession that, although the sovereign cannot commit an injustice, he may commit iniquity; the idea of injury to God in the state of nature; and the treatment of conscience in *De Cive*. Hobbes solved the problem of the source of the obligation to obey the sovereign's command by his "social contract" doctrine, the interpretation of which is still discussed by scholars. His unfinished *Dialogue Between a Philosopher and a Student of the Common Laws of England* examines various doctrines of the English law as put forward by Sir Edward Coke, and it is notable for its critical examination of Coke's statement that reason is the life of the law.

The *Second Treatise of Civil Government* by John Locke (1632–1704), primarily an attack on Robert Filmer's "divine right" theory, contains certain implied criticisms of Hobbes. Its interest for legal philosophy lies in its use of a version of the social contract to treat the question of the obligation to obey the law, its conception of limitations on sovereign power, and its individualistic view of natural inalienable rights, particularly rights in property. Locke's influence was enormous, and his view of natural rights had a profound effect on the development of law in the United States.

A new approach to the understanding of law and its institutions was put forward by Montesquieu (1689–1755). He, too, spoke the language of natural law and defined laws as "necessary relations arising from the nature of things" (*The Spirit of the Laws* I, 1). But his special importance lies in his attempt to study legal institutions by a comparative historical method, stressing the environmental factors that affect the development of law. This suggestion had been anticipated by Bodin, and Giambattista Vico (1668–1744) had also applied a historical method to the study of Roman law, but Vico's work had little immediate influence. Montesquieu's doctrine of the separation of powers had an extraordinary influence. His sharp separation of judicial from legislative and executive power reinforced the conception that the judge is a mere mouthpiece of the law and that judges merely declare the existing law but never make it. In 1790, in his *Reflections on the Revolution in France*, Edmund Burke turned the historical approach to a practical political use when he protested against proceeding a priori in the "science of constructing a commonwealth."

KANTIANISM. Immanuel Kant (1724–1804) contributed to legal philosophy and other branches of philosophy. The keynote of his legal philosophy was inspired by Jean-Jacques Rousseau (1712–1778), who set as the problem of his *Social Contract* the reconciliation of social coercion and individual freedom. Kant's legal philosophy was a philosophy of justice in which the concept of freedom plays a central role. Kant sought a systematic understanding of the principles underlying all positive laws, one that would enable us to decide whether these laws are in accordance with moral principles. Kant held that positive law "proceeds from the will of a legislator," and any viable legal system will take into account the particular conditions of the given society: With these conditions the theory of law has no concern. The theory is an application of the results of moral philosophy to the conditions of "men considered merely as men." This endeavor covers both the domain of law (*Recht*) and the domain of ethics; the principle that right action is action in conformity with universalizable maxims holds for both juridical and moral laws.

A law (*Gesetz*) is a formula expressing "the necessity" of an action. Juridical and moral laws are distinguished in that the former regulate external conduct irrespective of its motives. (But this does not mean that a judge should necessarily ignore the lawbreaker's motives when passing sentence upon him.) Any person, as a morally free agent, is entitled to express his freedom in activity so long as it does not interfere with the similar freedom that others possess. This is the principle underlying all legislation and "right." Juridical law also involves the authority to compel conformity and to punish violations. The necessary and sufficient condition for legal punishment is that the juridical law has been broken. It must be recognized, however, that the domain of such law is restricted by the limits of compulsion. While it is morally wrong to save one's own life by killing another, even where this is the only expedient, it can never be made legally wrong to kill in such a case. The principle of law receives content in Kant's application of it to particular private rights in external things and in his analysis of the methods for acquiring such rights.

Kant's influence on jurisprudence, after being somewhat eclipsed by Hegelianism, reemerged at the end of the nineteenth century. One of the most important Neo-Kantians was Rudolf Stammler (1856–1938), who invented but eventually discarded the phrase "natural law with variable content." Accepting the Kantian distinction between "form" and "matter," he attempted to discern the form of all laws. He defined law as "exceptionless binding volition." Just law is an ideal involving principles of respect and cooperation.

UTILITARIANISM AND POSITIVISM. Although Kant and his followers may be said to have inspired a variety of natural-law philosophies (although different from the Stoic and Thomistic types), Jeremy Bentham (1748–1832) and his followers (notably John Stuart Mill) claim to have rejected such thinking entirely. Of the influences on Bentham, two may be briefly noted. David Hume (1711–1776) argued that moral distinctions are not derived from reason; passion, or sentiment, is the ultimate foundation of moral judgment, and justice is grounded in utility. Second, the Italian criminologist Cesare Beccaria (1738–1794), in his *Of Crimes and Punishments* (1764), subjected the existing institutions of criminal law and methods of punishment to relentless criticism. His standard of judgment was whether "the greatest happiness of the greatest number" was maximized. Bentham acknowledged his debt to Beccaria, and this "principle of utility" was the base of Bentham's voluminous projected "codes." He did not, however, define the nature of law by reference to utility. In his *The Limits of Jurisprudence Defined* (published in 1945) he defined a law as the expression of "the will of a sovereign in a state." Bentham's views, which were well suited to deal with the problems engendered by the Industrial Revolution in England, were of immense importance in effecting legal reform. In 1832, the year of his death, the Reform Act was passed, largely as a result of the work of his followers. Mill's *On Liberty* (1859) is an attempt to treat the limits of legal coercion by the state along modified utilitarian lines.

In legal philosophy Bentham's influence affected the English-speaking world especially through the thought of John Austin (1790–1859), a seminal figure in English and American legal positivism and analytic jurisprudence. Austin tried to find a clear demarcation of the boundaries of positive law, which would be antecedent to a "general jurisprudence" comprising the analyses of such "principles, notions, and distinctions" as duty, right, and punishment, which are found in every legal system; these analyses in turn were to be employed in "particular jurisprudence," the systematic exposition of some given body of law.

Austin began by distinguishing "law properly so called" and "law improperly so called." The former is always "a species of command," an expression of a wish or desire, analytically connected with the ideas of duty, liability to punishment (or sanction), and superiority. The last notion led Austin to his famous and influential analysis of "sovereignty": "laws strictly so called" (positive laws) are the commands of political superiors to political inferiors. From this it follows that international law is merely "positive international morality" rather than law in a strict sense. (Some writers, viewing this as an unfortunate and perhaps dangerous consequence, were led to various revisions of Austinianism.) Austin's "separation" of law and morality is often taken as the hallmark of legal positivism. "The existence of law is one thing; its merit or demerit is another," he wrote in *The Province of Jurisprudence Determined* (V, note). Yet Austin was a utilitarian; in distinguishing between the law that is and the law that ought to be, he did not mean that law is not subject to rational moral criticism grounded in utility, which he took to be the index to the law of God. At this point Austin was influenced by such "theological utilitarians" as William Paley.

Austin's views were subjected to vigorous discussion both without and within the traditions of positivism and analytical jurisprudence. And as the disciplines of history, anthropology, and ethnology assumed an increasing importance during the nineteenth century, rival approaches to the understanding of law developed. Thus, Sir Henry Maine (1822–1888), who formulated the historical law that legal development is a movement from status to contract, argued in his *Early History of Institutions* that the command-sovereignty theory of law has no application in a primitive community, where law is largely customary and the political "sovereign," who has the power of life or death over his subjects, never makes law. The Austinian view can be saved only by maintaining the fiction that what the "sovereign" permits, he commands. Nonetheless, Austin had many followers at the turn of the twentieth century, such as T. E. Holland (1835–1926) and J. W. Salmond (1862–1924), who attempted to preserve the imperative and coercion aspects of his theory while introducing revisions.

The role of the courts was increasingly emphasized. In the United States, John Chipman Gray (1839–1915) wrote *The Nature and Sources of the Law*, one of the most important American contributions to the subject. Acknowledging his debt to Austin, Gray defined law as "the rules which the courts [of the State] lay down for the determination of legal rights and duties." This required him to construe statutes, judicial precedents, custom, expert opinion, and morality as sources of law rather than as law itself. All law, on this view, is judge-made. The machinery of the state stands in the background and provides the coercive element, which does not enter into the definition of "law." Gray influenced the realist movement in the United States.

HEGELIANISM AND THE HISTORICAL SCHOOL. While England was largely under the sway of the utilitarians, other trends flourished in Germany: Kantianism, Hegelianism, the historical school, and legal positivism. In his *Philosophy of Right*, G. W. F. Hegel (1770–1831) developed some Kantian themes in his own characteristic way. In his view, law and social-political institutions belong to the realm of "objective spirit," in which interpersonal relationships, reflecting an underlying freedom, receive their concrete manifestations. In attempting to show the rightness and the rationality of various legal relationships and institutions in given moments of the development of "spirit," and in seeing them as natural growths, Hegel formulated a theory of law and the state that was easily combined with various historical, functional, and institutional approaches to legal phenomena.

Friedrich Karl von Savigny (1779–1861) is often regarded as the founder of the historical school. His *Of the Vocation of Our Age for Legislation and Jurisprudence* (1814) was published before Hegel's work and was probably influenced by Fichte (but not by Fichte's *Grundlage des Naturrechts*, 1796), whose notion of the "folk-spirit" was widely known. Law, like language, originates spontaneously in the common consciousness of a people, who constitute an organic being. Both the legislator and the jurist may articulate this law, but they no more invent or make it than does the grammarian who codifies a natural language. Savigny believed that to accept his conception of law was to reject the older notions of natural law; nevertheless, it is often claimed that Savigny's conception was merely a new kind of natural law standing above, and judging, the positive law.

THE LATE-NINETEENTH AND TWENTIETH CENTURIES

JHERING AND GERMAN POSITIVISM. Rudolf von Jhering (1818–1892), eminent both as a historian of law and as a legal theorist, rejected both Hegel and Savigny: Hegel, for holding the law to be an expression of the general will and for failing to see how utilitarian factors and interests determine the existence of law; Savigny, for regarding law as a spontaneous expression of subconscious forces and for failing to see the role of the conscious struggle for protection of interests. However, Jhering shared the broad cultural orientation of many of the Hegelians, and he was grateful to Savigny for having overthrown the doctrine of "immutable" natural law. Jhering's contribution was to insist that legal phenomena cannot be comprehended without a systematic understanding of the purposes that give rise to them, the ends grounded in social life without which there would be no legal rules. Without purpose there is no will.

At the same time there are strong strains of positivism in Jhering: Law is defined as "the sum of the rules of constraint which obtain in a state" (*Der Zweck im Recht*, p. 320). In this respect he was close to the German positivists, who emphasized the imperative character of law. Karl Binding (1841–1920), an influential positivist, defined law as "only the clarified legal volition [*Rechtswille*] of a source of law [*Rechtsquelle*]" (*Die Normen und ihre Ueber-tretung*, p. 68). This period saw the emergence of the slogan of German positivism: "All law is positive law." Yet Jhering opposed many of the claims of the analytical positivists; his essay "Scherz und Ernst in der Jurisprudenz" ridiculed their "heaven of jurisprudential concepts."

SOCIOLOGICAL AND ALLIED THEORIES. Jhering's work foreshadowed many of the dominant tendencies of twentieth-century legal philosophy. Hermann Kantorow-icz regarded Jhering as the fountainhead of both the "sociological" and "free-law" schools. The former term covers too wide a group of writers to be surveyed here, some of whom were concerned solely with empirical work, whereas others combined empirical work with a philosophical outlook. Proponents of the jurisprudence of interests (*Interessenjurisprudenz*) eschewed Jhering's inquiries into the metaphysical and moral bases of purposes, claiming that he did not sufficiently attend to the conflict of interest behind laws; law reflects dominant interest. (Similar analyses were made in the United States; for example, the "pressure-group" theory of politics advanced by A. F. Bentley [1870–1957] in *The Process of Government*). Much attention was devoted to the analysis of the judicial process and the role that the "balancing" of interests plays in it. As Philipp Heck, one of its leading exponents, remarked: "The new movement of 'Inter-essenjurisprudenz' is based on the realization that the judge cannot satisfactorily deal with the needs of life by mere logical construction" (*Begriffsbildung und Inter-essenjurisprudenz*, p. 4).

This sentiment was endorsed by the closely allied "free-law" movement. According to this group, "legal logic" and the "jurisprudence of conceptions" are inadequate for achieving practicable and just decisions. The judge not only perforce frequently goes beyond the statute law, but he also often ought to go beyond it. The "free-law" writers undertook the normative task of supplying guidelines for the exercise of judicial discretion, and the judicial function was assimilated to the legislative function. The focus on such problems reflected the enormous change, occasioned by the industrialization of Western society, in the functions of the state. No longer did the nation-state exist merely to keep the peace or protect preexisting rights; rather, it played a positive role in promoting social and individual welfare.

The philosophy of law thus became increasingly concerned with the detailed working out of the foundations of legal policy. The "free-law" theorist Eugen Ehrlich (1862–1922), who influenced such American theorists as Karl N. Llewellyn (1893–1962) and other representatives of legal realist tendencies, rejected the positivistic tenet that only norms posited by the state are legal norms, for in any society there is always more law than is expressed in legal propositions. The "inner order" of an association is the basic form of law. Ehrlich also engaged in empirical study of the "legal facts" (*Rechtstatsachen*) and "living law" of various communities in the Austro-Hungarian empire. Ehrlich may thus be said to have considered cus-

tom as law in its own right. However, many positivists would argue that he was not able to account for the normative character of custom.

MARXISM. The Marxist stress on economic interests was often combined with the sociological and free-law views. Central to the Marxist position are the notions of "class" (usually defined in terms of legal relationship to property and the means of production) and "class interest," which lead to the analysis of the role of law in different societies with differing class structures. Addressing their critics in *The Communist Manifesto* (1848), Marx and Engels wrote: "Your law is but the will of your class exalted into statutes, a will which acquires its content from the material conditions of existence of your class" (p. 24). This suggests that law is merely part of the ideological superstructure and has no effect on the material organization of society. It raises the question of whether law exists in all societies—for instance, in primitive society or in the "classless" society arising after the triumph of socialism—and the further question of the nature and function of law in the transitional period from capitalism to socialism. The issue of "revolutionary legality" or "socialist legality" was treated by Lenin, E. Pashukanis, and Andrei Vishinsky. An important Marxist study of the relationship between law and the economy is that of the Austrian socialist Karl Renner (*Die Rechtsinstitute des Privatrechts und ihre soziale Funktion*, 1929).

PURE THEORY AND RELATIVISM. Although the sociological approaches to law had many practitioners, a more controversial and perhaps more influential twentieth-century view was that of Hans Kelsen, a leading exponent of legal positivism. Influenced by the epistemology of the Neo-Kantians, Kelsen distinguished sharply between the "is" and the "ought," and consequently between the natural sciences and disciplines, such as legal science, which study "normative" phenomena. Legal science is a descriptive science—prescriptive and valuational questions cannot be scientific—and Kelsen's "pure theory" aimed at providing the conceptual tools for studying any given legal system irrespective of its content. The theory is "pure" because it is divorced from any ideological or sociological elements; it attempts to treat a legal system simply as a system of norms. Kelsen's view was thus similar to the analytical jurisprudence of Austin, but Kelsen regarded legal norms as "de-psychologized commands." In order to understand an act of will as a norm-creating act, we must already employ a norm which serves as a "schema of interpretation." The jurist who seeks to understand legal phenomena must ultimately presuppose a basic norm (*Grundnorm*), which is not itself a positive legal norm. Legal systems are sets of coercive norms arranged in hierarchical fashion; lower norms are the "concretizations" of higher norms. In Kelsen's analysis the "dualisms" of state and law and public and private law disappear, and the relationship between international law and national legal systems is seen in a fresh light.

Unlike Kelsen, Gustav Radbruch (1878–1949) did not found a school. His position, which he called relativism, has many affinities with that of Kelsen; but Radbruch maintained that law, which is a cultural phenomenon, can be understood only in relation to the values that men strive to realize through it. He attempted to analyze these values in relation to legal institutions, showing the "antinomies" among these values that led to his relativism. World War II raised the question in the minds of many legal philosophers whether the legal positivism that was popular in Germany, with its separation of law and morals, contributed to the rise of Nazism. Concern over this problem seems to have caused Radbruch to move away from his earlier relativism toward a kind of natural-law position.

REALISM. In the United States, legal philosophy had largely been the province of lawyers rather than of professional philosophers. This may account for its sociological and realistic tone. The erudite Roscoe Pound (1870–1964) was the most prolific writer on this subject. Pound recognized the influence of Josef Kohler (1849–1919) and his notion of jural postulates and, especially, of Jhering. The pragmatism of William James also contributed to the development of his views. In an early article, "Mechanical Jurisprudence," Pound argued for an understanding of the interests that the law seeks to protect. Introducing a distinction between "law in books" and "law in action," he maintained the need for a close study of the actual operation of legal institutions.

On both scores his influence in the United States has been momentous, but it is difficult to summarize his position; he is often associated with a "social engineering" approach to law. Law contains both precepts and ideal elements. Among precepts Pound distinguished rules, principles, conceptions, doctrines, and standards. It is pointless to isolate some canonical form to which all laws are reducible. The ideal element consists of received ideals "of the end of law, and hence of what legal precepts should be and how they should be applied." Pound offered an elaborate, although tentative, survey of the individual, public, and social interests secured by law. This list was criticized and amended by Pound's Aus-

tralian disciple Julius Stone (*The Province and Function of Law*, 1946). In his later years Pound moved toward a kind of natural-law thinking, arguing for a more intimate connection between law and morality; he abjured the realist tendencies, which had been influenced by his earlier thought, as "give it up" philosophies.

It is difficult to characterize the legal realists; they disclaimed a common doctrine but recognized an interest in a common set of problems. Along with J. C. Gray, the spiritual godfather of American legal realism was Justice Oliver Wendell Holmes, Jr. (1841–1935). In his seminal essay "The Path of the Law," he advocated viewing law as the "bad man" would, in terms of the practicable remedies afforded individuals through the medium of the courts. Holmes presented in that article his famous definition of law as "the prophecies of what the courts will do in fact." It may be argued, however, that this definition, while perhaps adequate from the advocate's viewpoint, can hardly apply to the judge. When the judge asks what the law is on some matter, he is not trying to predict what he will decide.

Joseph W. Bingham was one of the first realists. In "What Is the Law?" Bingham argued that legal rules, like scientific laws, have no independent existence, being simply mental constructs that conveniently summarize particular facts. Laws are really judicial decisions, and the so-called rules or principles are among the (mentally) causative factors behind the decision. This nominalism and behaviorism, which characterized much of early realist writing, was criticized by Morris R. Cohen (1880–1947). "Behavior analysis" was advocated by Karl N. Llewellyn, who extended it beyond judicial behavior to "official" behavior (*Jurisprudence*, Chicago, 1962; collected papers).

The so-called myth of legal certainty was attacked by Jerome Frank (1889–1957) in his *Law and the Modern Mind*, which explained the genesis of the myth in Freudian terms. In the sixth edition Frank was somewhat friendlier toward natural-law thinking, characterizing his change of attitude as going from an earlier "rule-skepticism" to "fact-skepticism." Other important realists are Thurman Arnold, Leon Green, Felix Cohen, Walter Nelles, Herman Oliphant, and Fred Rodell. Both positivism and realism were attacked by the Harvard legal philosopher Lon L. Fuller (1902–1978), a leading American exponent of non-Thomistic natural-law thinking.

The Scandinavian countries were a center of legal philosophy, and many of their leading writers have been realists. They have been more consciously philosophical than their American counterparts. The leading spirit was

Axel Hägerström (1868–1939), who rejected metaphysical presuppositions in legal philosophy and insisted on an understanding of legal phenomena in empirical terms. Many legal concepts can be understood only as survivals of "mythical" or "magical" thought patterns, which should ideally be eliminated. Vilhelm Lunstedt (*Legal Thinking Revised*, Stockholm, 1956) was most radical in his rejection of metaphysics. Values are expressions of emotion and should be excluded from legal science. The "method of social welfare" should be substituted for the "method of justice." Alf Ross (*On Law and Justice*, London, 1958) argued that the first method is as "chimerical" as the second and presents an analysis of legal policy-making as a kind of rational technology. Laws, Ross argued, are directives to courts. The concept "valid law" as used by jurists and legal philosophers cannot be explicated in purely behavioristic terms; inner psychological attitudes must also be included. A similar view was presented by Karl Olivecrona (*Law as Fact*, London, 1939), who wrote important realist analyses of legal language and severely criticized command theories of law, such as Austin's. In *Inquiries Into the Nature of Law and Morals* (translated by C. D. Broad, Cambridge, 1953), Hägerström argued that Kelsen's "pure theory" never escapes the "will" element either, and hence it falls subject to all the criticisms that may be leveled against the command theories.

CRITICAL LEGAL STUDIES. The critical legal studies (CLS) movement, associated with the work of Duncan Kennedy, among many others, borrowed much from legal realism. CLS scholars shared the rule-skepticism of the realists and their rejection of legal formalism. Both groups emphasized the role played by extra-legal factors in shaping the law. For CLS scholars, however, the realists did not go far enough in developing a "critique" of the ideological bias concealed within legal doctrines. A central preoccupation of the critical scholars was the indeterminacy and vagueness of the law. CLS writers attempted to "deconstruct" the law by exposing its inconsistencies and tracing them to the conflicting social and economic forces responsible for shaping it.

H. L. A. HART AND POSITIVISM. One of the most influential legal theorists of the last half of the twentieth century, H. L. A. Hart (1907–1992), in his *Concept of Law*, developed the view that the law is a union of "primary" and "secondary" rules. Primary rules impose duties; secondary rules specify how primary rules may be changed, interpreted, and recognized as valid. A rule of recognition specifies what is to count as law in a given system. In a

series of works beginning with *Taking Rights Seriously*, Ronald Dworkin attacked Hart's theory, maintaining that when courts reason about "hard" cases, they invoke standards or principles that cannot be captured by a Hartian rule of recognition. Principles (such as "no man should profit from his own wrongdoing") are part of the law, Dworkin argued, and so Hart's positivism is descriptively inaccurate. In *Law's Empire*, Dworkin argued that law is an "interpretive" concept, so that a judge facing a difficult case must seek to identify the best "constructive interpretation" of the legal doctrine of his community, viewing the legal materials normatively, in their "best light." Law is the product of an interpretation that best sums up the legal texts and principles of a given community into a coherent and attractive whole.

Hart's work spurred debate among legal positivists regarding the proper understanding of Hart's rule of recognition. Hart maintained that moral norms are not necessarily a part of the criteria for the validity of law. But could there be legal systems that *do* incorporate moral criteria of legal validity? "Exclusive" legal positivists, such as Joseph Raz, responded in the negative; "inclusive" positivists, such as Jules Coleman, answered affirmatively.

LATE-TWENTIETH-CENTURY DEVELOPMENTS. A resurgence of interest in natural law characterized the end of the twentieth century, with works by Robert George (*In Defense of Natural Law*) and especially John Finnis, beginning with his *Natural Law and Natural Rights*. Several other prominent jurisprudential "schools" also emerged in the last decades of the twentieth century. Among these were feminist jurisprudence and the law and economics movement. Work by Catherine MacKinnon and other feminist lawyers sought to expose the patriarchal assumptions underlying purportedly neutral legal doctrine; and scholars led by scholar and judge Richard Posner argued that an economic analysis of the formation and function of legal rules and doctrines provides the best explanation for existing law.

See also Aristotelianism; Aristotle; Augustine, St.; Austin, John; Beccaria, Cesare Bonesana; Bentham, Jeremy; Bodin, Jean; Burke, Edmund; Celsus; Cicero, Marcus Tullius; Cohen, Morris Raphael; Dworkin, Ronald; Engels, Friedrich; Enlightenment; Fichte, Johann Gottlieb; Filmer, Robert; Grotius, Hugo; Hägerström, Axel; Hart, Herbert Lionel Adolphus; Hegel, Georg Wilhelm Friedrich; Hegelianism; Hobbes, Thomas; Hume, David; James, William; Just War Theory; Kant, Immanuel; Kelsen, Hans; Legal Positivism; Lenin, Vladimir Il'ich; Locke, John; Marx, Karl; Marxist Philosophy; Mill, John Stuart; Montesquieu, Baron de; Natural Law; Neo-Kantianism; Ockhamism; Paley, William; Patristic Philosophy; Plato; Positivism; Posner, Richard; Radbruch, Gustav; Realism; Rousseau, Jean-Jacques; Savigny, Friedrich Karl von; Seneca, Lucius Annaeus; Social Contract; Socrates; Sophists; Stammler, Rudolf; Stoicism; Suárez, Francisco; Thomas Aquinas, St.; Thomism; Utilitarianism; Vico, Giambattista; Vitoria, Francisco de; William of Ockham; Xenophon.

Bibliography

Christie, George C., and Patrick H. Martin. *Jurisprudence: Text and Readings on the Philosophy of Law*. 2nd ed. St. Paul: West, 1995.

Coase, Ronald. "The Problem of Social Cost." *Journal of Law and Economics* 3 (1960): 1–44.

Cohen, M. R. *Law and the Social Order*. Hamden: Archon Books, 1967.

Coleman, Jules. "Negative and Positive Positivism," *Journal of Legal Studies* 11 (1982): 139–164.

Coleman, Jules. and Scott Shapiro, eds. *The Oxford Handbook of Jurisprudence and Legal Philosophy*. Oxford: Oxford University Press, 2002.

Del Vecchio, Giorgio. *Justice*. Translated by Lady Guthrie. Edinburgh: University Press, 1956.

D'Entreves, A. P. *Natural Law*. London: Hutchinson, 1977.

Duxbury, Neil. *Patterns of American Jurisprudence*. Oxford: Clarendon Press, 1995.

Dworkin, Ronald. *Law's Empire*. Cambridge, MA: Harvard University Press, 1986.

Dworkin, Ronald. *Taking Rights Seriously*. Cambridge, MA: Harvard University Press, 1977.

Ehrlich, Eugen. *Fundamental Principles of the Sociology of Law*. Translated by Walter L. Moll. New York: Arno Press, 1975.

Finnis, John. *Aquinas: Moral, Political, and Legal Theory*. New York: Oxford University Press, 1998.

Finnis, John. *Natural Law and Natural Rights*. Oxford: Clarendon Press, 1980.

Friedrich, C. J. *The Philosophy of Law in Historical Perspective*. 2nd ed. Chicago: University of Chicago Press, 1965.

Gierke, Otto von. *Das deutsche Genossenschaftsrecht*. Vols. 1–4. Berlin: Weidmannsche Verlagsbuchhandlung, 1868–1913. Partially translated by Ernest Barker as *Natural Law and the Theory of Society*. Cambridge, U.K.: Cambridge University Press, 1958.

George, Robert P. *Natural Law Theory: Contemporary Essays*. Oxford: Clarendon Press, 1992.

Golding, Martin, and William Edmundson, eds. *Philosophy of Law and Legal Theory*. Oxford: Blackwell, 2005.

Hall, Jerome. *Studies in Jurisprudence and Criminal Theory*. New York: Oceana, 1958.

Hamburger, Max. *The Awakening of Western Legal Thought*. Translated by B. Miall. Westport: Greenwood Press, 1970.

Hart, H. L. A. *The Concept of Law*. 2nd ed. New York: Oxford University Press, 1994.

Hart, H. L. A. *Essays in Jurisprudence and Philosophy*. Oxford: Clarendon Press, 1983.

Hart, H. L. A. "Philosophy of Law and Jurisprudence in Britain (1945–1952)." *American Journal of Comparative Law* 2 (1953): 355–364.

Hayman, Robert L., Jr., et al. *Jurisprudence Classical and Contemporary: From Natural Law to Postmodernism*. 2nd ed. St. Paul: West, 2002.

Jhering, Rudolf von. *Law as a Means to an End*. Translated by I. Husik. New York: A. M. Kelley, 1968.

Jones, J. W. *Historical Introduction to the Theory of Law*. Westport: Greenwood Press, 1970.

Kairys, David. *The Politics of Law*. New York: Pantheon Books, 1982.

Kelly, J. M. *A Short History of Western Legal Theory*. Oxford: Oxford University Press, 1992.

Kennedy, Duncan. "Form and Substance in Private Law Adjudication." *Harvard Law Review* 89 (1976): 1685–1778.

King, Peter J., *Utilitarian Jurisprudence in America: The Influence of Bentham and Austin on American Legal Thought in the Nineteenth Century*. New York: Garland, 1986.

Kocourek, Albert. "The Century of Analytical Jurisprudence Since John Austin." In *Law: A Century of Progress*, edited by A Reppy. New York: New York University Press, 1937.

Lobban, Michael. *The Common Law and English Jurisprudence, 1760–1850*. Oxford: Clarendon press, 1991.

Mackinnon, Catharine A. *Toward a Feminist Theory of the State*. Cambridge, MA: Harvard University Press, 1989.

Maine, Henry S. *Ancient Law*. Boston: Beacon Press, 1963.

Minow, Martha. *Making All the Difference*. Ithaca: Cornell University Press, 1991.

Morison, W. L. *John Austin*. Stanford: Stanford University Press, 1982.

Morris, C. "Four Eighteenth-Century Theories of Jurisprudence." *Vanderbilt Law Review* 14 (1960): 101–116.

Patterson, Dennis, ed. *A Companion to Philosophy of Law and Legal Theory*. Oxford: Blackwell, 1996.

Pollock, Frederick. *Jurisprudence and Legal Essays*. Westport: Greenwood Press, 1978.

Posner, Richard A. *Economic Analysis of the Law*. 6th ed. New York: Aspen, 2002.

Postema, Gerald. *Bentham and the Common Law Tradition*. Oxford: Clarendon, 1986.

Pound, Roscoe. *Jurisprudence*. 5 vols. St. Paul: West, 1959.

Raz, Joseph. *The Authority of Law*. Oxford: Oxford University Press, 1979.

Raz, Joseph. *The Concept of a Legal System*. Oxford: Clarendon, 1970.

Rhode, Deborah. *Justice and Gender*. Cambridge, MA: Harvard University Press, 1991.

Rommen, Heinrich. *The Natural Law*. Translated by T. R. Hanley. Indianapolis: Liberty Fund, 1998.

Shuchman, Philip. *Cohen and Cohen's Readings in Jurisprudence and Legal Philosophy*. 2nd ed. Boston: Little, Brown, 1979.

Smith, Patricia. *Feminist Jurisprudence*. New York: Oxford University Press, 1993.

Somek, Alexander. "German Legal Philosophy and Theory in the Nineteenth and Twentieth Centuries." In *A Companion* to *Philosophy of Law and Legal Theory*, edited by Dennis Patterson. Oxford: Blackwell, 1996.

Stone, Julius. *The Province and Function of Law*. London: Stevens Press, 1961.

Tushnett, Mark. "Critical Legal Studies: A Political History." *Yale Law Journal* 100 (1991): 1515–1544.

Ullmann, Walter, *The Mediaeval Idea of Law*. New York: Barnes and Noble, 1969.

Unger, Roberto Magabeira, *The Critical Legal Studies Movement*. Cambridge, MA: Harvard University Press, 1983.

Villey, M. *Leçons d'histoire de la philosophie du droit*. Paris: Dalloz, 1957.

Vinogradoff, Paul. *Outlines of Historical Jurisprudence*. 2 vols. New York: AMS Press, 1971.

M. P. Golding (1967)
Updated by David M. Adams (2005)

PHILOSOPHY OF LAW, PROBLEMS OF

The existence of legal systems, even the most rudimentary, has afforded the opportunity for a variety of academic disciplines. Of these some are, or purport to be, empirical: They include the historical study of particular legal systems or specific legal doctrines and rules, and sociological studies of the ways in which the content and the efficacy of law and the forms and procedures of law-making and law-applying both influence and are influenced by their economic and social setting, and serve social needs or specific social functions. But since law in most societies soon reaches a very high degree of complexity, its administration requires the special training of judges and professional lawyers. This in turn has created the need for a specific form of legal science concerned with the systematic or dogmatic exposition of the law and its specific methods and procedures. For this purpose the law is divided into distinct branches (such as crime, tort, and contract), and general classifications and organizing concepts are introduced to collect common elements in the situations and relationships created by the law (such as rights, duties, obligations, legal personality, ownership, and possession) or elements common to many separate legal rules (such as act and intention).

No very firm boundaries divide the problems confronting these various disciplines from the problems of the philosophy of law. This is especially true of the conceptual schemes of classification, definition, and division introduced by the academic study of the law for the purpose of exposition and teaching; but even some historical and sociological statements about law are sufficiently general and abstract to need the attention of the philosophical critic. Little, however, is to be gained from elab-

orating the traditional distinctions between the philosophy of law, jurisprudence (general and particular), and legal theory, although importance has often been attributed to them. Instead, as with other branches of philosophy, it is more important to distinguish as belonging to the philosophy of law certain groups of questions which remain to be answered even when a high degree of competence or mastery of particular legal systems and of the empirical and dogmatic studies mentioned above has been gained. Three such groups may be distinguished: problems of definition and analysis, problems of legal reasoning, and problems of the criticism of law. This division is, however, not uncontroversial; and objections to it are considered in the last section of the article.

PROBLEMS OF DEFINITION AND ANALYSIS

THE DEFINITION OF LAW. All the obscurities and prejudices that in other areas of philosophy surround the notions of definition and of meaning have contributed to the endlessly debated problems of the definition of law. In early arguments the search for the definition of law was assumed to be the task of identifying and describing the "essence" or "nature" of law, and thus the uniquely correct definition of law by reference to which the propriety of the use, however well established, of the expressions "law" and "legal system" could be tested. It is frequently difficult to distinguish from this search for the essence of law a more modest conception of definition that, while treating the task as one of identifying and describing the standards actually accepted for the use of these expressions, assumes that there is only one "true," "strict," or "proper" use of them and that this use can be described in terms of a single set of necessary and sufficient conditions. A wide range of different considerations has shown how unrealistic or how sterile this assumption is in the case of law and has compelled its surrender. Among these considerations is the realization that although there are central clear instances to which the expressions "law" and "legal system" have undisputed application, there are also cases, such as international law and primitive law, which have certain features of the central case but lack others. Also, there is the realization that the justification for applying general expressions to a range of different cases often lies not in their conformity to a set of necessary and sufficient conditions but in the analogies that link them or their varying relationships to some single element.

Lexical definitions and deviant cases. The foregoing are difficulties of definition commonly met in many areas of philosophy, but the definition of law has peculiar difficulties of its own. Thus, the assumption that the definition of law either has been or should be lexical, that is, concerned with the characterization or elucidation of *any* actual usage, has been challenged on several grounds. Thus it is often asserted that in the case of law, the area of indeterminacy of actual usage is too great and relates to too many important and disputed issues, and that what is needed is not a characterization or elucidation of usage but a reasoned case for the inclusion in or exclusion from the scope of the expressions "law" and "legal system" of various deviations from routine and undisputed examples. These deviant cases include not only international law and primitive law but also certain elements found in developed municipal legal systems, such as rules to which the usual sanctions are not attached and rules that run counter to fundamental principles of morality and justice.

Pragmatic definitions. In the above circumstances some theorists disclaim as necessarily deceptive any aim to provide an analysis or definition of law which is a neutral description or elucidation of usage; instead, they speak of the task of definition as "stipulative," "pragmatic," or "constructive," that is, as designed to provide a scheme or model for the demarcation and classification of an area of study. The criterion of adequacy of such pragmatic definitions is not conformity to or the capacity to explain any actual usage but the capacity to advance the theorists' specific aims, which may differ widely. Thus, a definition of law to be used for the instruction or assistance of lawyers concerned primarily with the outcome of litigation or court proceedings will differ from the definition used to demarcate and unify the fruitful area of historical study and will also differ from the definition to be used by the social critic concerned with identifying the extent to which human interests are advanced or frustrated by modes of social organization and control.

Structural problems. Neither the legitimacy of pragmatic definitions nor their utility for deliberately chosen objectives need be disputed. But it is clear that they avoid rather than resolve many of the long-standing perplexities that have motivated requests for the definition of law and have made it a philosophical problem. The factors that have generated these perplexities may be summarized as follows: Notwithstanding the considerable area of indeterminacy in their use, the expressions "law," "a law," "legal system," and a wide range of derivative and interrelated expressions ("legislation," "courts of law," "the application of law," "legal adjudication") are sufficiently determinate to make possible general agreement in judgments about their application to particular instances. But

reflection on what is thus identified by the common usage of such terms shows that the area they cover is one of great internal complexity; laws differ radically both in content and in the ways in which they are created, yet despite this heterogeneity they are interrelated in various complex ways so as to constitute a characteristic structure or system. Many requests for the definition of law have been stimulated by the desire to obtain a coherent view of this structure and an understanding of the ways in which elements apparently so diverse and unified. These are problems, therefore, of the structure of law.

Coercion and morality. Reflection on the operations of a legal system discloses problems of another sort, for it is clear that law as a mode of influence on human behavior is intimately related to and in many ways dependent upon the use or threat of force on the one hand and on morality and justice on the other. Yet law is also, at points, distinct from both, so no obvious account of these connections appears acceptable: They appear to be not merely contingent, and since they sometimes fail, the statement of these connections does not appear to be any easily comprehensible species of necessary truth. Such tensions create demands for some stable and coherent definition of the relationships between law, coercion, and morality; but definitions of law have only in part been designed to make these important areas of human experience more intelligible. Practical and indeed political issues have long been intertwined with theoretical ones; and as is evident from the long history of the doctrines of natural law and legal positivism, the advocacy of a submissive or a critical attitude to law, or even of obedience or disobedience, has often been presented in the form of a persuasive definition of the relationship between law and morality on the one hand and between law and mere force on the other.

THE ANALYSIS OF LEGAL CONCEPTS. Although legal rules are of many different types and may be classified from many different points of view, they have many common constituents; and although the law creates for both individuals and groups a great variety of different situations and relationships, some of these are constantly recurrent and of obvious importance for the conduct of social life. Both lawyers and laypeople have frequent occasion to refer to these common elements and situations, and for this purpose they use classifications and organizing concepts expressed in a vocabulary which has bred many problems of analysis. These problems arise in part because this vocabulary has a more or less established use apart from law, and the points of convergence and divergence between legal and nonlegal usage is not always immediately obvious or easily explicable. It is also the case that the ways in which common elements in law or legal situations are classified by different theorists in part reflect and derive from divergent conceptions of law in general. Therefore, although different writers use such expressions as "rights" and "duty" in referring to the same legal situations, they select different elements or aspects from these situations. A third factor calling for clarification is the fact that many of the commonest notions used in referring to legal phenomena can be explicated only when certain distinctive ways in which language functions in conjunction with practical rules have been understood. These problems of analysis are illustrated in the case of the concepts of (1) legal obligation or duty, (2) a legal transaction, and (3) intention. (Certain distinctions once made between the notions of a legal obligation and a legal duty are no longer of importance and will be disregarded.)

Legal obligations or duties. The situation in which an individual has a legal duty to do or to abstain from some action is the commonest and most fundamental of all legal phenomena; the reference to duty or its absence is involved in the definition of such other legal concepts as those of a right, a power, a legal transaction, or a legal personality. Whenever the law of an effective legal system provides for the punishment of those who act or fail to act in certain ways, the word *duty* applies. Thus, to take a simple example, if the law requires under penalty that persons of a certain age shall report for military service, then such persons have, or are "under," a legal duty to do so. This much is undisputed, however much theorists may dispute over the analysis of "duty" or its application to situations created not by the criminal law but by the law relating to torts or to contract.

However, even the above simple situation can be viewed from two very different standpoints that give rise to apparently conflicting analyses of duty. From one of these (the predictive standpoint), reporting for military service is classified as a duty simply because failure to report renders likely certain forms of suffering at the hands of officials. From the other standpoint (the normative standpoint), reporting for military service is classified as a duty because, owing to the existence of the law, it is an action that may be rightly or justifiably demanded of those concerned; and failure to report is significant not merely because it renders future suffering likely but also because punishment is legally justified even if it does not always follow disobedience.

From Jeremy Bentham onward the predictive analysis of duty as a chance or likelihood of suffering in the event

of disobedience to the law has been advocated by important writers for a variety of theoretical and practical reasons. On the one hand it has seemed to free the idea of legal duty from metaphysical obscurities and irrelevant associations with morals, and on the other to provide a realistic guide to life under law. It isolates what for some people is the only important fact about the operation of a legal system and what for all people is at least one important fact: the occasions and ways in which the law works adversely to their interests. This is of paramount importance not only to the malefactor but also to the critic and reformer of the law concerned to balance against the benefits which law brings its costs in terms of human suffering.

By contrast, the normative point of view, without identifying moral and legal duty or insisting on any common content, stresses certain common formal features that both moral and legal duty possess in virtue of their both being aspects of rule-guided conduct. This is the point of view of those who, although they may not regard the law as the final arbiter of conduct, nevertheless generally accept the existence of legal rule as a guide to conduct and as legally justifying demands for conformity, punishment, enforced compensation, or other forms of coercion. Attention to these features of the idea of duty is essential for understanding the ways in which law is conceived of and operative in social life.

Although theorists have often attributed exclusive correctness to these different standpoints, there are various ways in which they may be illuminatingly combined. Thus, the normative account might be said to give correctly the meaning of such statements as that a person has a legal duty to do a certain action, while the predictive account emphasizes that very frequently the point or purpose of making such statements is to warn that suffering is likely to follow disobedience. Such a distinction between the meaning of a statement and what is implied or intended by its assertion in different contexts is of considerable importance in many areas of legal philosophy.

Legal transactions. The enactment of a law, the making of a contract, and the transfer by words, written or spoken, of ownership or other rights are examples of legal transactions which are made possible by the existence of certain types of legal rules and are definable in terms of such rules. To some thinkers, such transactions (acts in the law, or juristic acts) have appeared mysterious—some have even called them magical—because their effect is to change the legal position of individuals or to make or eliminate laws. Since, in most modern systems of law, such changes are usually effected by the use of words, written or spoken, there seems to be a species of legal alchemy. It is not obvious how the mere use of expressions like "it is hereby enacted …," "I hereby bequeath …," or "the parties hereby agree …" can produce changes. In fact, the general form of this phenomenon is not exclusively legal, although it has only comparatively recently been clearly isolated and analyzed. The words of an ordinary promise or those used in a christening ceremony in giving a name to a child are obvious analogues to the legal cases. Lawyers have sometimes marked off this distinctive function of language as the use of "operative words," and under this category have distinguished, for example, the words used in a lease to create a tenancy from the merely descriptive language of the preliminary recital of the facts concerning the parties and their agreement.

For words (or in certain cases gestures, as in voting or other forms of behavior) to have such operative effect, there must exist legal rules providing that if the words (or gestures) are used in appropriate circumstances by appropriately qualified persons, the general law or the legal position of individuals is to be taken as changed. Such rules may be conceived from one point of view as giving to the language used a certain kind of force or effect which is in a broad sense their meaning; from another point of view they may be conceived as conferring on individuals the legal power to make such legal changes. In Continental jurisprudence such rules are usually referred to as "norms of competence" to distinguish them from simpler legal rules that merely impose duties with or without correlative rights.

As the expressions "acts-in-the-law" and "operative words" suggest, there are important resemblances between the execution of legal transactions and more obvious cases of human actions. These points of resemblance are of especial importance in understanding what has often seemed problematic—the relevance of the mental or psychological states of the parties concerned to the constitution or validity of such transactions. In many cases the relevant rules provide that a transaction shall be invalid or at least liable to be set aside at the option of various persons if the person purporting to effect it was insane, mistaken in regard to certain matters, or subjected to duress or undue influence. There is here an important analogy with the ways in which similar psychological facts (mens rea) may, in accordance with the principles of the criminal law, excuse a person from criminal responsibility for his action. In both spheres there are exceptions: In the criminal law there are certain cases of "strict" liability where no element of knowledge or intention need be proved; and in certain types of legal transaction, proof that a person attached a special meaning to the words he used or was mistaken in some respect in using them would not invalidate the transaction, at least as against those who have relied upon it in good faith.

Attention to these analogies between valid legal transactions and responsible action and the mental conditions that in the one case invalidate and in the other excuse from responsibility illuminates many obscure theoretical disputes concerning the nature of legal transactions such as contract. Thus, according to one principal theory (the "will" theory) a contract is essentially a complex psychological fact—something that comes into being when there is a meeting of minds (consensus ad idem) that jointly "will" or "intend" a certain set of mutual rights and duties to come into existence. The words used are, according to this theory, merely evidence of this consensus. The rival theory (the "objective" theory) insists that what makes a contract is not a psychological phenomenon but the actual use of words of offer and acceptance, and that except in special cases the law simply gives effect to the ordinary meaning of the language used by the parties and is not concerned with their actual states of mind. Plainly, each side to this dispute fastens on something important but exaggerates it. It is indeed true that, like an ordinary promise, a legal contract is not made by psychological facts. A contract, like a promise, is "made" not by the existence of mental states but by words (or in some cases deeds). If it is verbally made, it is made by the operative use of language, and there are many legal rules inconsistent with the idea that a consensus ad idem is required. On the other hand, just because the operative use of language is a kind of action, the law may—and in most civilized legal systems does—extend to it a doctrine of responsibility or validity under which certain mental elements are made relevant. Thus a contract, although made by words, may be vitiated or made void or "voidable" if a party is insane, mistaken in certain ways, or under duress. The truths latent among the errors of the "will" theory and the "objective" theory can therefore be brought together in an analysis that makes explicit the analogy between valid transactions made by the operative use of language and responsible actions.

Intention. The fact that the law often treats certain mental states or psychological conditions as essential elements both in the validity of legal transactions and in criminal responsibility has thrust upon lawyers the task of distinguishing between and analyzing such notions as "will," "intention," and "motive." These are concepts that have long puzzled philosophers not primarily concerned with the law, and their application in the law creates further specific problems. These arise in various ways: There are divergencies between the legal and nonlegal use of these notions which are not always obvious or easily understood; the law, because of difficulties of proof or as a matter of social policy, may often adopt what are called external or objective standards, which treat certain forms of outward behavior as conclusive evidence of the existence of mental states or impute to an individual the mental state that the average man behaving in a given way would have had. Although statutes occasionally use such expressions as "maliciously," "knowingly," or "with intent," for the most part the expressions "intentionally" and "voluntarily" are not the language of legal rules but are used in the exposition of such rules in summarizing the various ways in which either criminal charges or civil claims may fail if something is done—for instance, accidentally, by mistake, or under duress.

The problems that arise in these ways may be illustrated in the case of intention. Legal theorists have recognized intention as the mental element of central importance to the law. Thus, an intention to do the act forbidden by law is in Anglo American law normally the sufficient mental element for criminal responsibility and also is normally, although not always, necessary for responsibility. So if a man intends to do the act forbidden by law, other factors having to do with his powers of self-control are usually irrelevant, although sometimes duress and sometimes provocation or deficient ability to control conduct, caused by mental disorder, may become relevant. In fact, three distinct applications of the notion of intention are important in the law, and it is necessary to distinguish in any analysis of this concept (1) the idea of intentionally doing something forbidden by law; (2) doing something with a further intention; and (3) the intention to do a future act. The first of these is in issue when, if a man is found to have wounded or killed another, the question is asked whether he did it intentionally or unintentionally. The second is raised when the law, as in the case of burglary defined as "breaking into premises at night with the intention of committing a felony," attaches special importance or more severe penalties to an action if it is done for some further purpose, even though the latter is not executed. The third application of intention can be seen in those cases where an act is criminal if it is accompanied by a certain intention—for instance, incurring a debt with the intention never to pay.

Of these three applications the first is of chief importance in the law, but even here the law only approximates to the nonlegal concept and disregards certain elements in its ordinary usage. For in the law the question whether a man did something intentionally or not is almost wholly a question concerning his knowledge or belief at the time of his action. Hence, in most cases when an action falling under a certain description (such as wounding a police officer) is made a crime, the law is satisfied, insofar as any matter of intention is concerned, if the accused knew or believed that his action would cause injury to his victim and that his victim was in fact a police officer. This almost exclusively cognitive approach is one distinctive way in which the law diverges from the ordinary idea of intentionally doing something, for in ordinary thought not all the foreseen consequences of conduct are regarded as intended.

A rationale of this divergence can be provided, however. Although apart from the law a man will be held to have done something intentionally only if the outcome is something aimed at or for the sake of which he acted, this element which the law generally disregards is not relevant to the main question with which the law is concerned in determining a man's legal responsibility for bringing about a certain state of affairs. The crucial question at this stage in a criminal proceeding is whether a man whose outward conduct and its consequences fall within the definition of a crime had at the time he acted a choice whether these consequences were or were not to occur. If he did, and if he chose that insofar as he had influence over events they would occur, then for the law it is irrelevant that he merely foresaw that they would occur and that it was not his purpose to bring them about. The law at the stage of assessing a man's responsibility is interested only in his conscious control over the outcome, and discards those elements in the ordinary concept of intention which are irrelevant to the conception of control. But when the stage of conviction in a criminal proceeding is past, and the question becomes how severely the criminal is to be punished, the matter previously neglected often becomes relevant. Distinctions may be drawn at this stage between the individual who acted for a certain purpose and one who acted merely foreseeing that certain consequences would come about.

The second and third applications of the notion of intention (doing something with a further intent and the intention to do a future action) are closer to nonlegal usage, and in the law, as elsewhere, certain problems of distinguishing motive and intention arise in such cases.

PROBLEMS OF LEGAL REASONING

Since the early twentieth century, the critical study of the forms of reasoning by which courts decide cases has been a principal concern of writers on jurisprudence, especially in America. From this study there has emerged a great variety of theories regarding the actual or proper place in the process of adjudication of what has been termed, often ambiguously, "logic." Most of these theories are skeptical and are designed to show that despite appearances, deductive and inductive reasoning play only a subordinate role. Contrasts are drawn between "logic" and "experience" (as in O. W. Holmes Jr.'s famous dictum that "the life of the law has not been logic; it has been experience") or between "deductivism" or "formalism" on the one hand and "creative choice" or "intuitions of fitness" on the other. In general, such theories tend to insist that the latter members of these contrasted sets of expressions more adequately characterize the process of legal adjudication, despite its appearance of logical method and form. According to some variants of these theories, although logic in the sense of deductive and inductive reasoning plays little part, there are other processes of legal reasoning or rational criteria which courts do and should follow in deciding cases. According to more extreme variants, the decisions of courts are essentially arbitrary.

LEGISLATION AND PRECEDENT. In Anglo American jurisprudence the character of legal reasoning has been discussed chiefly with reference to the use by the courts of two "sources" of law: (1) the general rules made by legislative bodies (or by other rule-making agencies to which legislative powers have been delegated) and (2) particular precedents or past decisions of courts which are treated as material from which legal rules may be extracted although, unlike legislative rules, there is no authoritative or uniquely correct formulation of the rules so extracted. Conventional accounts of the reasoning involved in the application of legislative rules to particular cases have often pictured it as exclusively a matter of deductive inference. The court's decision is represented as the conclusion of a syllogism in which the major premise consists of the rule and the minor premise consists of the statement of the facts which are agreed or established in the case. Similarly, conventional accounts of the use of precedents by courts speak of the courts' extraction of a rule from past cases as inductive reasoning and the application of that rule to the case in hand as deductive reasoning.

In their attack on these conventional accounts of judicial reasoning, skeptical writers have revealed much that is of great importance both to the understanding and to the criticism of methods of legal adjudication. There are undoubtedly crucially important phases in the use of legal rules and precedents to decide cases which do not

consist merely of logical operations and which have long been obscured by the traditional terminology adopted both by the courts themselves in deciding cases and by jurists in describing the activities of courts. Unfortunately, the general claim that logic has little or no part to play in the judicial process is, in spite of its simple and monolithic appearance, both obscure and ambiguous; it embraces a number of different and sometimes conflicting contentions that must be separately investigated. The most important of these issues are identified and discussed below. There are, however, two preliminary issues of peculiar concern to philosophers and logicians which demand attention in any serious attempt to characterize the forms of legal reasonings.

Deductive reasoning. It has been contended that the application of legal rules to particular cases cannot be regarded as a syllogism or any other kind of deductive inference, on the grounds that neither general legal rules nor particular statements of law (such as those ascribing rights or duties to individuals) can be characterized as either true or false and thus cannot be logically related either among themselves or to statements of fact; hence, they cannot figure as premises or conclusions of a deductive argument. This view depends on a restrictive definition, in terms of truth and falsehood, of the notion of a valid deductive inference and of logical relations such as consistency and contradiction. This would exclude from the scope of deductive inference not only legal rules or statements of law but also commands and many other sentential forms which are commonly regarded as susceptible of logical relations and as constituents of valid deductive arguments. Although considerable technical complexities are involved, several more general definitions of the idea of valid deductive inference that render the notion applicable to inferences the constituents of which are not characterized as either true or false have now been worked out by logicians. In what follows, as in most of contemporary jurisprudential literature, the general acceptability of this more generalized definition of valid inference is assumed.

Inductive reasoning. Considerable obscurity surrounds the claim made by more conventional jurisprudential writers that inductive reasoning is involved in the judicial use of precedents. Reference to induction is usually made in this connection to point a contrast with the allegedly deductive reasoning involved in the application of legislative rules to particular cases. "Instead of starting with a general rule the judge must turn to the relevant cases, discover the general rule implicit in them .... The outstanding difference between the two methods is the source of the major premise—the deductive method assumes it whereas the inductive sets out to discover it from particular instances" (G. W. Paton, *A Textbook of Jurisprudence,* 2nd ed., Oxford, 1951, pp. 171–172).

It is of course true that courts constantly refer to past cases both to discover rules and to justify their acceptance of them as valid. The past cases are said to be "authority" for the rules "extracted" from them. Plainly, one necessary condition must be satisfied if past cases are in this way to justify logically the acceptance of a rule: The past case must be an instance of the rule in the sense that the decision in the case could be deduced from a statement of the rule together with a statement of the facts of the case. The reasoning insofar as the satisfaction of this necessary condition is concerned is in fact an inverse application of deductive reasoning. But this condition is, of course, only one necessary condition and not a sufficient condition of the court's acceptance of a rule on the basis of past cases, since for any given precedent there are logically an indefinite number of alternative general rules which can satisfy the condition. The selection, therefore, of one rule from among these alternatives as the rule for which the precedent is taken to be authority must depend on the use of other criteria limiting the choice, and these other criteria are not matters of logic but substantive matters which may vary from system to system or from time to time in the same system. Thus, some theories of the judicial use of precedent insist that the rule for which a precedent is authority must be indicated either explicitly or implicitly by the court through its choice of facts to be treated as "material" to a case. Other theories insist that the rule for which a precedent is authority is the rule which a later court considering the precedent would select from the logically possible alternatives after weighing the usual moral and social factors.

Although many legal writers still speak of the extraction of general rules from precedents, some would claim that the reasoning involved in their use of precedents is essentially reasoning from case to case "by example": A court decides the present case in the same way as a past case if the latter "sufficiently" resembles the former in "relevant" respects, and thus makes use of the past case as a precedent without first extracting from it and formulating any general rule. Nevertheless, the more conventional accounts, according to which courts use past cases to discover and justify their acceptance of general rules, are sufficiently widespread and plausible to make the use of the term *induction* in this connection worth discussing.

The use of *induction* to refer to the inverse application of deduction involved in finding that a past case is the instance of a general rule may be misleading: It suggests stronger analogies than exist with the modes of probabilistic inference used in the sciences when general propositions of fact or statements about unobserved particulars are inferred from or regarded as confirmed by observed particulars. *Induction* may also invite confusion with the form of deductive inference known as perfect induction, or with real or alleged methods of discovering generalizations sometimes referred to as intuitive induction.

It is, however, true that the inverse application of deduction involved in the use of precedents is also an important part of scientific procedure, where it is known as hypothetic inference or hypotheticodeductive reasoning. Hence, there are certain interesting analogies between the interplay of observation and theory involved in the progressive refining of a scientific hypothesis to avoid its falsification by contrary instances and the way in which a court may refine a general rule both to make it consistent with a wide range of different cases and to avoid a formulation which would have unjust or undesirable consequences.

Notwithstanding these analogies, the crucial difference remains between the search for general propositions of fact rendered probable by confirming instances but still falsifiable by future experience, and rules to be used in the decision of cases. An empirical science of the judicial process is of course possible: It would consist of factual generalization about the decisions of courts and might be an important predictive tool. However, it is important to distinguish the general propositions of such an empirical science from the rules formulated and used by courts.

DESCRIPTIVE AND PRESCRIPTIVE THEORIES. The claim that logic plays only a subordinate part in the decision of cases is sometimes intended as a corrective to misleading descriptions of the judicial process, but sometimes it is intended as a criticism of the methods used by courts, which are stigmatized as "excessively logical," "formal," "mechanical," or "automatic." Descriptions of the methods actually used by courts must be distinguished from prescriptions of alternative methods and must be separately assessed. It is, however, notable that in many discussions of legal reasoning these two are often confused, perhaps because the effort to correct conventional misdescriptions of the judicial process and the effort to correct the process itself have been inspired by the realization of the same important but often neglected fact: the relative indeterminacy of legal rules and precedents.

This indeterminacy springs from the fact that it is impossible in framing general rules to anticipate and provide for every possible combination of circumstances which the future may bring. For any rule, however precisely formulated, there will always be some factual situations in which the question whether the situations fall within the scope of the general classificatory terms of the rule cannot be settled by appeal to linguistic rules or conventions or to canons of statutory interpretation, or even by reference to the manifest or assumed purposes of the legislature. In such cases the rules may be found either vague or ambiguous. A similar indeterminacy may arise when two rules apply to a given factual situation and also where rules are expressly framed in such unspecific terms as "reasonable" or "material." Such cases can be resolved only by methods whose rationality cannot lie in the logical relations of conclusions to premises. Similarly, because precedents can logically be subsumed under an indefinite number of general rules, the identification of *the* rule for which a precedent is an authority cannot be settled by an appeal to logic.

These criticisms of traditional descriptions of the judicial process are in general well taken. It is true that both jurists and judges, particularly in jurisdictions in which the separation of powers is respected, have frequently suppressed or minimized the indeterminacy of legal rules or precedents when giving an account of the use of them in the process of decision. On the other hand, another complaint often made by the same writers, that there is an excess of logic or formalism in the judicial process, is less easy to understand and to substantiate. What the critics intend to stigmatize by these terms is the failure of courts, when applying legal rules or precedents, to take advantage of the relative indeterminacy of the rules or precedents to give effect to social aims, policies, and values. Courts, according to these critics, instead of exploiting the fact that the meaning of a statutory rule is indeterminate at certain points, have taken the meaning to be determinate simply because in some different legal context similar wording has been interpreted in a certain way or because a given interpretation is the "ordinary" meaning of the words used.

This failure to recognize the indeterminacy of legal rule (often wrongly ascribed to analytical jurisprudence and stigmatized as conceptualism) has sometimes been defended on the ground that it maximizes certainty and the predictability of decisions. It has also sometimes been welcomed as furthering an ideal of a legal system in which there are a minimum number of independent rules and categories of classification.

The vice of such methods of applying rules is that their adoption prejudges what is to be done in ranges of different cases whose composition cannot be exhaustively known beforehand: Rigid classification and divisions are set up which ignore differences and similarities of social and moral importance. This is the burden of the complaint that there is an excessive use of logic in the judicial process. But the expression "an excessive use of logic" is unhappy, for when social values and distinctions of importance are ignored in the interpretation of legal rules and the classification of particulars, the decision reached is not more logical than decisions which give due recognition to these factors: Logic does not determine the interpretation of words or the scope of classifications. What is true is that in a system in which such rigid modes of interpretation are common, there will be more occasions when a judge can treat himself as confronted with a rule whose meaning has been predetermined.

METHODS OF DISCOVERY AND STANDARDS OF APPRAISAL. In considering both descriptive and prescriptive theories of judicial reasoning, it is important to distinguish (1) assertions made concerning the usual processes or habits of thought by which judges actually reach their decisions, (2) recommendations concerning the processes to be followed, and (3) the standards by which judicial decisions are to be appraised. The first of these concerns matters of descriptive psychology, and to the extent that assertions in this field go beyond the descriptions of examined instances, they are empirical generalizations or laws of psychology; the second concerns the art or craft of legal judgment, and generalizations in this field are principles of judicial technology; the third relates to the assessment or justification of decisions.

These distinctions are important because it has sometimes been argued that since judges frequently arrive at decisions without going through any process of calculation or inference in which legal rules or precedents figure, the claim that deduction from legal rules plays any part in decision is mistaken. This argument is confused, for in general the issue is not one regarding the manner in which judges do, or should, come to their decisions; rather, it concerns the standards they respect in justifying decisions, however reached. The presence or absence of logic in the appraisal of decisions may be a reality whether the decisions are reached by calculation or by an intuitive leap.

CLEAR CASES AND INDETERMINATE RULES. When the various issues identified above are distinguished, two sets of questions emerge. The first of these concerns the decisions of courts in "clear" cases where no doubts are felt about the meaning and applicability of a single legal rule, and the second concerns decisions where the indeterminacy of the relevant legal rules and precedents is acknowledged.

Clear cases. Even where courts acknowledge that an antecedent legal rule uniquely determines a particular result, some theorists have claimed that this cannot be the case, that courts always "have a choice," and that assertions to the contrary can only be ex post facto rationalizations. Often this skepticism springs from the confusion of the questions of methods of discovery with standards of appraisal noted above. Sometimes, however, it is supported by references to the facts that even if courts fail to apply a clearly applicable rule using a determinate result, this is not a punishable offense, and that the decision given is still authoritative and, if made by a supreme tribunal, final. Hence, it is argued that although courts may show a certain degree of regularity in decision, they are never bound to do so: They always are free to decide otherwise than they do. These last arguments rest on a confusion of finality with infallibility in decisions and on a disputable interpretation of the notion of "being bound" to respect legal rules.

Yet skepticism of this character, however unacceptable, does serve to emphasize that it is a matter of some difficulty to give any exhaustive account of what makes a "clear case" clear or makes a general rule obviously and uniquely applicable to a particular case. Rules cannot claim their own instances, and fact situations do not await the judge neatly labeled with the rule applicable to them. Rules cannot provide for their own application, and even in the clearest case a human being must apply them. The clear cases are those in which there is general agreement that they fall within the scope of a rule, and it is tempting to ascribe such agreements simply to the fact that there are necessarily such agreements in the use of the shared conventions of language. But this would be an oversimplification because it does not allow for the special conventions of the legal use of words, which may diverge from their common use, or for the way in which the meanings of words may be clearly controlled by reference to the purpose of a statutory enactment which itself may be either explicitly stated or generally agreed. A full exploration of these questions is the subject matter of the study of the interpretation of statute.

Indeterminate rules. The decisions of cases that cannot be exhibited as deductions from determinate legal rules have often been described as arbitrary. Although much empirical study of the judicial process remains to be done, it is obvious that this description and the dichotomy of logical deduction and arbitrary decision, if taken as exhaustive, is misleading. Judges do not generally, when legal rules fail to determine a unique result, intrude their personal preferences or blindly choose among alternatives; and when words such as *choice* and *discretion*, or phrases such as "creative activity" and "interstitial legislation" are used to describe decisions, these do not mean that courts do decide arbitrarily without elaborating reasons for their decisions—and still less that any legal system authorizes decisions of this kind.

It is of crucial importance that cases for decision do not arise in a vacuum but in the course of the operation of a working body of rules, an operation in which a multiplicity of diverse considerations are continuously recognized as good reasons for a decision. These include a wide variety of individual and social interests, social and political aims, and standards of morality and justice; and they may be formulated in general terms as principles, policies, and standards. In some cases only one such consideration may be relevant, and it may determine decision as unambiguously as a determinate legal rule. But in many cases this is not so, and judges marshal in support of their decisions a plurality of such considerations which they regard as jointly sufficient to support their decision, although each separately would not be. Frequently these considerations conflict, and courts are forced to balance or weigh them and to determine priorities among them. The same considerations (and the same need for weighing them when they conflict) enter into the use of precedents when courts must choose between alternative rules which can be extracted from them, or when courts consider whether a present case sufficiently resembles a past case in relevant respects.

Perhaps most modern writers would agree up to this point with this account of judicial decision where legal rules are indeterminate, but beyond this point there is a divergence. Some theorists claim that notwithstanding the heterogeneous and often conflicting character of the factors which are relevant to decision, it is still meaningful to speak of a decision as *the* uniquely correct decision in any case and of the duty of the judge to discover it. They would claim that a judicial choice or preference does not become rational because it is deferred until after the judge has considered the factors that weigh for and against it.

Other theorists would repudiate the idea that in such cases there is always a decision that is uniquely correct, although they of course agree that many decisions can be clearly ruled out as incorrect. They would claim that all that courts do and can do at the end of the process of coolly and impartially considering the relevant considerations is to choose one alternative that they find the most strongly supported, and that it is perfectly proper for them to concede that another equally skilled and impartial judge might choose the other alternative. The theoretical issues are not different from those that arise at many points in the philosophical discussions of moral argument. It may well be that such terms as *choice, discretion,* and *judicial legislation* fail to do justice to the phenomenology of considered decision: It is the law felt involuntary or even inevitable character that often marks the termination of deliberation on conflicting considerations. Very often the decision to include a new case in the scope of a rule or to exclude it is guided by the sense that this is the "natural" continuation of a line of decisions or carries out the "spirit" of a rule. It is also true that if there were not also considerable agreement in judgment among lawyers who approach decisions in these ways, we should not attach significance and value to them or think of such decisions as reached through a rational process. Yet however it may be in moral argument, in the law it seems difficult to substantiate the claim that a judge confronted with a set of conflicting considerations must always assume that there is a single uniquely correct resolution of the conflict and attempt to demonstrate that he has discovered it.

RULES OF EVIDENCE. Courts receive and evaluate testimony of witnesses, infer statements of fact from other statements, and accept some statements as probable or more probable than others or as "beyond reasonable doubt." When it is said that in these activities special modes of legal reasoning are exhibited and that legal proof is different from ordinary proof, reference is usually intended to the exclusionary rules of the law of evidence (which frequently require courts, in determining questions of fact, to disregard matters which are logically relevant), or to various presumptions that assign greater or lesser weight to logically relevant considerations than ordinary standards of reasoning do.

The most famous examples of exclusionary rules are those against "hearsay," which (subject to certain exceptions) make inadmissible, as evidence of the facts stated, reports tendered by a witness, however credible, of statements made by another person. Another example is the rule that when a person is charged with a crime, evidence of his past convictions and disposition to commit similar crimes is not admissible as evidence to show that he committed the crime charged. An example of a rule that may give certain facts greater or less probative weight than ordinary standards do is the presumption that unless the contrary is proved beyond reasonable doubt, a child born to a woman during wedlock is the child of both parties to the marriage.

The application of such rules and their exceptions gives rise to results which may seem paradoxical, even though they are justifiable in terms of the many different social needs which the courts must satisfy in adjudicating cases. Thus, one consequence of the well-known exception to the hearsay rule that a report of a statement is admissible as evidence of a fact stated if it is made against the interest of the person who stated it, is that a court may find that a man committed adultery with a particular woman but be unable to draw the conclusion that she committed adultery with him. A logician might express the resolution of the paradox by saying that from the fact that p entails q it does not follow that "it is legally proved that p" entails "it is legally proved that q."

Apart from such paradoxes, the application of the rules of evidence involves the drawing of distinctions of considerable philosophical importance. Thus, although in general the law excludes reports of statements as evidence of the facts stated, it may admit such reports for other purposes, and in fact draws a distinction between statements of fact and what J. L. Austin called performatory utterances. Hence, if the issue is whether a given person made a promise or placed a bet, reports that he uttered words which in the context amounted to a promise or a bet are admissible. So, too, reports of a person's statement of his contemporary mental states or sensations are admissible, and some theorists justify this on the ground that such first-person statements are to be assimilated to behavior manifesting the mental state or sensation in question.

PROBLEMS OF THE CRITICISM OF LAW

ANALYSIS AND EVALUATION. A division between inquiries concerned with the analysis of law and legal concepts and those concerned with the criticism or evaluation of law prima facie seems not only possible but necessary, yet the conception of an evaluatively neutral or autonomous analytical study of the law has not only been contested but also has been taken by some modern critics to be the hallmark of a shallow and useless legal positivism allegedly unconcerned with the values or ends which men pursue through law.

Objections to pure analysis. Many different objections to a purely analytical jurisprudence have been made. By some it has been identified with, or thought to entail commitment to, the view that a legal system is a closed logical structure in which decisions in particular cases are "mechanically" deduced from clear antecedent rules whose identification or interpretation presents no problem of choice and involves no judgment of value. Other critics have contended that any serious demand for the definition of a legal concept must at least include a request for guidance as to the manner in which, when the relevant legal rules are unclear or indeterminate, particular cases involving the concept in question should best be determined. It is assumed by these critics that any question concerning the meaning of expressions such as "a right" or "a duty," as distinct from the question of what rights or duties should be legally recognized, are trivial questions to be settled by reference to a dictionary. Still others have urged that since the maintenance of a legal system and the typical operations of the law (legislation, adjudication, and the making of legal transactions) are purposive activities, any study that isolates law or legal phenomena for study without considering their adequacy or inadequacy for human purposes makes a vicious abstraction that is bound to lead to misunderstanding.

Replies to objections. None of the above seem to constitute serious objections. The difficulties of decision in particular cases arising from the relative indeterminacy of legal rules are of great importance, but they are distinct from analytical questions such as those illustrated earlier, which remain to be answered even when legal rules are clear. Thus the isolation and characterization of the normative and predictive standpoints from which law may be viewed and the precise manner of interplay between subjective and objective factors in legal transactions are not things that can be discovered from dictionaries. But attention to them is indispensable in the analysis of the notion of a legal obligation, a legal right, or a contract. There is of course much justice in the claim that in order to understand certain features of legal institutions or legal rules, the aims and purposes they are designed to fulfill must be understood. Thus, a tax cannot be distinguished from a fine except by reference to the purpose for which it is imposed; but to recognize this is not to abandon an analytical study of the law for an evaluative one. The identification of something as an instrument for certain purposes leaves open the question whether it is good or bad, although such identification may indicate the stan-

dards by reference to which this question is to be answered. In any case, there are many features of legal rules that may profitably be studied in abstraction from the purposes which such rules may be designed to achieve.

CRITERIA OF EVALUATION. Nonetheless, protests against the severance of analytical from critical or evaluative inquiries, even if misdirected in their ostensible aim, often serve to emphasize something important. These protests are usually accompanied by and sometimes confused with a general thesis concerning the standards and principles of criticism specifically appropriate to law. This is the thesis (which has appeared in many different forms in the history of the philosophy of law) that, whatever may be the case with value judgments in other fields or with moral judgments concerning the activities of individuals, the criteria which distinguish good law from bad do not merely reflect human preferences, tastes, or conventions, which may vary from society to society or from time to time; rather, they are determined by certain constant features of human nature and the natural environment with which men must contend.

The doctrine of natural law in its various traditional forms embodies this thesis. There are, however, obscurities and metaphysical assumptions involved in the use by natural-law theorists of the notions of nature and reason that make their formulations unacceptable to most modern secular thought; and they often confuse their important arguments concerning the principles by which law and social institutions should be judged with arguments designed to show that a reference to morality or justice must be introduced into the definition of law or legal validity. Nonetheless, it is possible to segregate these tangled issues, and some important modern philosophical arguments concern the possibility of restating in an acceptable form the claim that there are certain objective and rationally determined criteria for the evaluation and criticism of law. These arguments will be sketched here in relation to substantive law, procedural law, and the ideas of justice and utility.

SUBSTANTIVE LAW. The purposes that human beings pursue in society and for the realization of which they employ law as an instrument are infinitely various, and individuals may differ in the importance they attach to them and in their moral judgments about them. But the simplest form of the argument that there are certain constant criteria for the evaluation of a legal system consists in the elaboration of the truth that if law is to be of any value as an instrument for the realization of human purposes, it must contain certain rules concerning the basic conditions of social life. Thus it is not only true that the legal system of any modern state and any legal system which has succeeded in enduring have contained rules restricting the use of violence, protecting certain forms of property, and enforcing certain forms of contract; it is also clear that without the protections and advantages that such rules supply, people would be grossly hampered in the pursuit of any aims. Legal rules providing for these things are therefore basic in the sense that without them other legal rules would be pointless or at least would operate only fitfully or inefficiently. Criticism of a legal system on the grounds that it omitted such rules could be rebutted only by the demonstration that in the particular case they were unnecessary because the human beings to which the system applied or their natural surroundings were in some way quite extraordinary, that is, that they lacked certain of the salient characteristics that persons and things normally have. This is so because the need for such rules derives from such familiar natural facts as that people are both vulnerable to violence and tempted to use it against each other; that the food, clothes, and shelter necessary to existence do not exist naturally in limitless abundance but must be grown or manufactured by human effort and need legal protection from interference during growth and manufacture and safe custody pending consumption; and that to secure the mutual cooperation required for the profitable development of natural resources, people need legal rules enabling them to bind themselves to future courses of conduct.

Argument along these lines may be viewed as a modest empirical counterpart to the more ambitious teleological doctrine of natural law, according to which there are certain rules for the government of human conduct that can be seen by men endowed with reason as necessary to enable people to attain the specifically human optimum state or end (*finis, telos*) appointed for human beings by Nature or (in Christian doctrine) by God. The empirical version of this theory assumes only that, whatever other purposes laws may serve, they must, to be acceptable to any rational person, enable men to live and organize their lives for the more efficient pursuit of their aims. It is, of course, possible to challenge this assumption and to deny that the fact that there are certain rules necessary if fundamental human needs are to be satisfied has any relevance to the criticism of law. But this denial seems intelligible only as a specifically religious doctrine that regards law as the expression of a divine will. It may then be argued that people's lives should be regulated by the law not in order to further any secular human purposes

but because conformity to God's will is in itself meritorious or obligatory.

A more serious objection to the empirical argument conducted in terms of human needs for protection from violence to the person and property and for cooperation is the contention that although these are fundamental human needs, the coercive rules of a legal system need not provide for them. It may be said that the accepted morality of all societies provides a system of restraint which provides adequately for these needs, and that the vast majority of people abstain from murder, theft, and dishonesty not from fear of legal sanctions but for other, usually moral, reasons. In these circumstances it may be no defect in a legal system that it confines itself to other matters in relation to which the accepted morality is silent.

It seems clear, however, that social morality left to itself could not provide adequately for the fundamental needs of social life, save in the simplest forms of society. It may well be that most individuals, when they believe themselves to be protected from malefactors by the punishments, threats of punishment, and physical restraints of the law, will themselves voluntarily submit to the restraints necessary for peaceful and profitable coexistence. But it does not follow that without the law's protections, voluntary submission to these restraints would be either reasonable or likely. In any case, the rules and principles of social morality leave open to dispute too many questions concerning the precise scope and form of its restraints. Legal rules are needed to supply the detail required to distinguish murder and assault from excusable homicide and injury, to define the forms of property to be protected, and to specify the forms of contract to be enforced. Hence, the omission of such things from the legal system could not be excused on the ground that the existence of a social morality made them unnecessary.

PROCEDURAL LAW. Laws, however impeccable their content, may be of little service to human beings and may cause both injustice and misery unless they generally conform to certain requirements which may be broadly termed procedural (in contrast with the substantive requirements discussed above). These procedural requirements relate to such matters as the generality of rules of law, the clarity with which they are phrased, the publicity given to them, the time of their enactment, and the manner in which they are judicially applied to particular cases. The requirements that the law, except in special circumstances, should be general (should refer to classes of persons, things, and circumstances, not to individuals or to particular actions); should be free from contradictions, ambiguities, and obscurities; should be publicly promulgated and easily accessible; and should not be retrospective in operation are usually referred to as the principles of legality. The principles that require courts, in applying general rules to particular cases, to be without personal interest in the outcome or other bias and to hear arguments on matters of law and proofs of matters of fact from both sides of a dispute are often referred to as rules of natural justice. These two sets of principles together define the concept of the rule of law to which most modern states pay at least lip service.

These requirements and the specific value that conformity with them imparts to laws may be regarded from two different points of view. On the one hand, they maximize the probability that the conduct required by the law will be forthcoming, and on the other hand, they provide individuals whose freedom is limited by the law with certain information and assurances that assist them in planning their lives within the coercive framework of the law. This combination of values may be easily seen in the case of the requirements of generality, clarity, publicity, and prospective operation. For the alternative to control by general rules of law is orders addressed by officials to particular individuals to do or to abstain from particular actions; and although in all legal systems there are occasions for such particular official orders, no society could efficiently provide the number of officials required to make them a main form of social control.

Thus, general rules clearly framed and publicly promulgated are the most efficient form of social control. But from the point of view of the individual citizen, they are more than that: They are required if he is to have the advantage of knowing in advance the ways in which his liberty will be restricted in the various situations in which he may find himself, and he needs this knowledge if he is to plan his life. This is an argument for laws that are general in the sense of requiring courses of action and not particular actions. The argument for generality in the sense of applicability to classes of persons is different: It is that such rule confer upon the individual the advantage of knowing the restrictions to which the conduct of others besides himself will be subject. Such knowledge in the case of legal restrictions that protect or benefit the individual increases the confidence with which he can predict and plan his future.

The value of the principles of natural justice which concern the process of adjudication are closely linked to the principles of legality. The requirement that a court should be impartial and hear arguments and proofs from both sides of a dispute are guarantees of objectivity which increase the probability that the enacted law will be applied according to its tenor. It is necessary to ensure by such means that there will be this congruence between judicial decisions and the enacted law if the commitment to general rules as a method of government is taken seriously.

Care must be taken not to ascribe to these arguments more than they actually prove. Together they amount to the demonstration that all who have aims to pursue need the various protections and benefits which only laws conforming to the above requirements of substance and procedure can effectively confer. For any rational person, laws conferring these protections and benefits must be valuable, and the price to be paid for them in the form of limitations imposed by the law on one's own freedom will usually be worth paying. But these arguments do not show, and are not intended to show, that it will always be reasonable or morally obligatory for people to obey the law when the legal system provides them with these benefits, for in other ways the system may be iniquitous: It may deny even the essential protections of the law to a minority or slave class or in other ways cause misery or injustice.

JUSTICE AND UTILITY. The equal extension to all of the fundamental legal protections of person and property is now generally regarded as an elementary requirement of the morality of political institutions, and the denial of these protections to innocent persons, as a flagrant injustice. Even when these protections are denied, lip service is often paid to the principle of equal distribution by the pretense that the persons discriminated against are either criminal in intention, if not in deed, or are like children who are incapable of benefiting from the freedom which laws confer and are in need of some more paternalistic regime.

Inadequacy of utilitarianism. Different moral philosophies offer different vindications of the principle of equality. The matter is considered here in order to illustrate the philosophical problems that arose in the criticism of law concerning the relative place of the notions of utility and justice. The central principle of utilitarianism, insofar as it supplies a moral critique of law, may be stated as the doctrine that there is only one vice in legal arrangements, namely, that they fail to produce the greatest possible total of happiness in the population within their scope. The concept of a total of happiness or pleasure or satisfaction is of course open to well-known objections. But on any interpretation, utilitarian principles, if unrestricted, must endorse legal or social arrangements if the advantages they give to some persons outweigh the disadvantages imposed on others. For a consistent utilitarian there can be no necessary commitment to any principles requiring an equal distribution.

However, in some cases, if allowance is made for principles of diminishing marginal utility, it may be shown that an equal distribution is the most efficient, in the sense of producing the greatest total of happiness. But for the utilitarian this is a contingent matter to be established in each case, not a matter of moral principle or justice; and where the question concerns the distribution of the fundamental legal protections of person and property, there seems no compelling utilitarian argument in favor of an equal distribution. Thus, a slave-owning class might derive from the system of slavery benefits outweighing the misery of the slaves. Bentham urged that this was not the case, owing to the inefficiency of slave labor, and therefore he rejected slavery; but he rejected it as inefficient rather than as unjust. Plainly, this form of argument is a very insecure foundation for the principle that all people are morally entitled to the equal protection of the laws, and it seems clear that utilitarian principles alone cannot give any account of the moral importance attached to equality and in general to the notion of the just, as distinguished from an efficient, distribution as a means of happiness.

Moral argument for equality. The simplest moral argument in support of the equal distribution of the law's fundamental protections is one that combines the idea that no rational person could wish himself to be denied these fundamental legal protections with the principle of the universalizability of moral judgment: Moral judgments concerning social and legal arrangements must conform to the requirement that no man could regard as morally acceptable the withholding from others with needs and in circumstances similar to his own of those benefits which he would not wish to be withheld from himself. If this principle is admitted, it follows that it cannot be a sufficient moral ground for accepting legal arrangements that the advantages they give to some outweigh the disadvantages for others. The equal extension to all of the law's protections satisfies both the principle of utility, which requires that the law should advance human happiness, and the independent principle of justice, that the gain in happiness should be distributed fairly. According to this qualified form of utilitarianism, the best legal and social arrangements realize the most efficient of just distributions.

More ambitious arguments have been advanced to show that in spheres other than the distribution of the fundamental protections of the law, utilitarianism is acceptable only if qualified by independent principles of just distribution, and also to demonstrate that the distribution required by justice is in all spheres prima facie that of equality, unless inequalities can be shown to work ultimately for the equal benefit of all. Whatever the strength of these more general arguments may be, it is true that in relation to many legal institutions, utilitarianism unrestricted by other principles of justice yields results which would not be regarded as morally tolerable. This is particularly true of punishment. In all civilized legal systems it is recognized that no man should be punished except for his own conduct, and (with certain exceptions in the case of minor offenses) only then for such of his actions as were voluntary or within his power to control. Such limitations on the scope of punishment seem obvious requirements of justice to the individuals punished, but it is at least doubtful whether they can be adequately supported on purely utilitarian grounds.

THE OBLIGATION TO OBEY THE LAW. The philosophical investigation of the obligation to obey the law requires a distinction between the utilitarian and other moral aspects of this subject similar to that outlined in the case of justice. It seems clear that the mere existence of a legal system, irrespective of the character of its laws, is not sufficient in any intelligible theory of morality to establish that a person ought morally to do what its laws require him to do. Yet there are also powerful arguments against a purely utilitarian theory of the obligation to obey law which would regard this obligation as simply a special case of the obligation to promote happiness, with the corollary that disobedience to bad laws is justified if the consequences of disobedience (including any harm done to others through the weakening of the authority of the legal system) are better in utilitarian terms than the consequences of obedience. Among features of the moral situation for which this utilitarian theory fails to account there are two of peculiar importance. The first is that the obligation to obey law is one which is considered as owed by the citizen specifically to the members of his own society in virtue of their relationship as fellow members, and is not conceived merely as an instance of an obligation to men in general not to cause harm, injury, or suffering. Second, men are often held to be subject to an obligation to obey the law even though it is clear that little or no harm will be done to the authority of the legal system by their disobedience, as in cases (like that of the conscientious objector) where those who disobey the law willingly submit to punishment.

The theory of a social contract focused on these two aspects of the obligation of obedience to law, and it is possible to detach from what is mythical or otherwise objectionable in contract theory certain considerations which show that the obligation to obey the law may be regarded as the obligation of fairness to others, which is independent of and may conflict with utility. The principle involved, stated in its simplest form, is that when a number of persons restrict their liberty by certain rules in order to obtain benefits that could not otherwise be obtained, those who have gained by the submission of others to the rules are under an obligation to submit in their turn. Conflicts between this principle and the principle of utility are possible because often the benefits secured by such restrictions would arise even if considerable numbers failed to cooperate and submit to the rules in their turn. For the utilitarian, there could be no reason for anyone to submit to rules if his cooperation was not necessary to secure the benefits of the system. Indeed, if a person did cooperate, he would be guilty of failing to maximize the total happiness, for this would be greatest if he took the benefits of the system without submitting to its restraints. The consideration that the system would fail to produce the desired benefits or would collapse if all were to refuse their cooperation is irrelevant in a utilitarian calculation if, as is often the case, it is known that there will be no such general refusal.

See also Analytic Jurisprudence; Bentham, Jeremy; Equality, Moral and Social; Ethics and Morality; Guilt; Historical School of Jurisprudence; Justice; Legal Positivism; Natural Law; Persons; Philosophy of Law, History of; Property; Punishment; Religion and Morality; Responsibility, Moral and Legal; Rights; Utilitarianism.

Bibliography

DEFINITION OF LAW

The major classics of jurisprudence in which definitions of law are elaborated include Thomas Aquinas, *Summa Theologiae* I, 2, 90–97; Jeremy Bentham, *The Limits of Jurisprudence Defined* (New York, 1945) and *The Comment on the Commentaries* (Oxford: Clarendon Press, 1928); John Austin, *The Province of Jurisprudence Determined* (London: J. Murray, 1832); J. C. Gray, *The Nature and Sources of the Law* (New York, 1909); and Hans Kelsen, *General Theory of Law and State*, translated by Anders Wedberg (Cambridge, MA: Harvard University Press, 1945).

More recent contributions include Hermann Kantorowicz, *The Definition of Law* (Cambridge, U.K.: Cambridge University Press, 1958); H. L. A. Hart, *The Concept of Law* (Oxford: Clarendon Press, 1961); and Richard Wollheim, "The Nature of Law," in *Political Studies* 2 (1954): 128–142.

ANALYSIS OF LEGAL CONCEPTS

On legal obligations and duties, see Jeremy Bentham, "Essay on Logic," in *The Works of Jeremy Bentham,* edited by J. Bowring, 11 vols. (Edinburgh, 1838–1843), Vol. VIII, pp. 213–293 and *Fragment on Government* (London, 1776), Ch. 6; and O. W. Holmes Jr., "The Path of the Law," in *Collected Legal Papers* (New York: Harcourt Brace, 1920), pp. 167–202.

On legal transactions, see Axel Hägerström, *Inquiries into Law and Morals,* translated by C. D. Broad (Uppsala, 1953), Ch. 5; Morris R. Cohen, *Law and the Social Order* (New York, 1933), Ch. 2; John L. Austin, *How to Do Things with Words* (Oxford, 1962); and Wesley N. Hohfeld, *Fundamental Legal Concepts* (New Haven, CT: Yale University Press, 1964).

On intention, see Jeremy Bentham, *An Introduction to the Principles of Morals and Legislation* (London, 1789), Ch. 8; John Austin, *Lectures on Jurisprudence* (London, 1869), Chs. 18–19; G. L. Williams, *The Criminal Law: The General Part,* 2nd ed. (London: Stevens, 1961), Ch. 2; and G. E. M. Anscombe, *Intention* (Oxford, 1957).

PROBLEMS OF LEGAL REASONING

On logic and law, see Julius Stone, *The Province and Function of Law* (London: Stevens, 1947), Chs. 6–7; J. C. Jensen, *The Nature of Legal Argument* (Oxford: Blackwell, 1957); Norberto Bobbio, "Diritto e logica," in *Il problema della giustizia* (Milan, 1962), pp. 11–44; and Lars Bergstrom, "Imperatives and Ethics," in *Filosofiska Studier* 7 (1962): 94ff.

On rule and discretion in judicial decision, see John Dickinson, "Legal Rules: Their Function in the Process of Decision," in *University of Pennsylvania Law Review* 79 (1931): 833ff., and "The Problem of the Unprovided Case," in *Recueil d'études sur les sources de droit en honneur de F. Gény* (Paris, 1934), Vol. 11; Jerome Frank, *Law and the Modern Mind,* 6th printing (New York, 1949); Edward Levi, *Introduction to Legal Reasoning* (Chicago, 1949); John Wisdom, "Philosophy, Metaphysics, and Psycho-analysis," in his *Philosophy and Psycho-analysis* (Oxford, 1952); and Richard Wasserstrom, *The Judicial Decision* (Stanford, CA: Stanford University Press, 1961) and "The Obligation to Obey the Law," in *University of California Law Review* 10 (1963): 780–807. Also see *Jurimetrics: Law and Contemporary Problems* 28 (1963).

PROBLEMS OF THE CRITICISM OF LAW

On problems of the criticism of law, see Alf Ross, *On Law and Justice,* translated by Margaret Dutton (London: Stevens, 1958); John Rawls, "Justice as Fairness," in *Philosophical Review* 67 (1958): 164–194; H. L. A. Hart, *The Concept of Law* (Oxford: Clarendon Press, 1961), Chs. 8–9; Torstein Eckhoff, "Justice and Social Utility," in *Legal Essays: A Tribute to Frede Castberg* (Oslo, 1963), pp. 74–93; and Lon Fuller, *The Morality of Law* (New Haven, CT: Yale University Press, 1964).

H. L. A. Hart (1967)

PHILOSOPHY OF LAW, PROBLEMS OF [ADDENDUM]

One of the dominant issues in philosophy of law since Hart's main entry was published has been the dispute between Hart and Ronald Dworkin about the best way to characterize a legal system and the modes of legal reasoning (especially by judges) most appropriate to it.

RULES AND SOCIAL PRACTICES

THE RULE OF RECOGNITION. Hart identified two main kinds of rules in a complex and mature legal system. There are rules that tell people what to do or not do (tax laws, criminal laws, traffic laws), and there are rules that tell people how to do certain kinds of things (in order to accomplish such legal transactions as making valid wills or binding contracts and conveying property). Among the latter kind of rules he identified a small set that he regarded as fundamental to all but the most primitive legal systems: These rules tell how to identify a particular legal system and, within it, how to make laws and adjudicate claims arising under law. Hart's main entry does not address these fundamental rules.

The first kind of fundamental rule Hart famously styled the "rule of recognition." It identifies the primary sources of law (e.g., the Queen-in-Parliament) and it prioritizes these sources (e.g., statute law > common law > "customary law"). Because this and the other fundamental rules determine what is to count as valid law within that system, they have normative legal force there but are not themselves properly called *valid* laws.

SOCIAL PRACTICES AND LEGAL SYSTEMS. Hart's rule of recognition is more like a social practice (or, better, the presuppositions of such a practice) than it is like a black-letter rule of any sort. To follow or engage in a social practice is to conform reflectively to an existing, ongoing pattern or template as a matter of appropriate conduct. The practice functions as a standard and serves as a basis for criticizing deviations. Officials (almost all of them most of the time, in the standard case) simply follow the social practice: They presuppose it internally in what they actually do when they make and enforce given laws. They do so not out of fear of sanctions, but rather because so acting is the regular and expected thing to do. Ordinary citizens need not be aware of the authoritative sources of law (or the other fundamental rules) in their country; but they do need to know what the laws are, for it is these they

follow or conform to. In the standard case, a substantial number of them do so in the same way as the officials do—by taking an internal point of view. This concordance between officials and ordinary citizens constitutes law as a social practice. One of Hart's main objects in invoking the idea of a social practice (or rule) is to say that a system of laws, as an exemplar of such a practice, is distinguishable from a large-scale scheme of coercion.

VALID LAWS AND JUDICIAL DISCRETION. Any legal system, insofar as it is a social practice, is an effective legal system, one where laws are conformed to most of the time by most of the people. When laws and court decisions in an effective system are made (or almost always made) in strict conformity to the fundamental rules, such a system would be a full and proper legal system. Here all the laws and court decisions that are made in accordance with the fundamental rules would be valid ones.

Hart does not think that a given law or decision (simply as valid) can cover and determine the correct outcome for all the instances that come within its proper range. For reasons that he spells out in the main entry, there will always be some such cases where the "law runs out." In those cases judges and executive officials will have to use "discretion"; they will have to supplement the law with what he calls (in the main entry) "interstitial legislation."

PRINCIPLES AND INTEGRITY

ONE RIGHT ANSWER: HERCULEAN JURISPRUDENCE. Ronald Dworkin was Hart's main critic in the last three decades of the twentieth century. One of his main criticisms is that legal systems have inbuilt features such that judges, taking the law as it is, can be said to have a duty to make the best decision. In simplest terms, then, Dworkin closes Hart's alleged gaps in law (which allow for judicial discretion) by turning to the character of legal reasoning itself, within a determinate legal system.

Dworkin's theory, using a model judge (named Hercules) for purposes of illustration, is called "law as integrity." Dworkin's main argument may be put this way: If two different judges, both committed to law as integrity agreed literally on everything—agreed "preinterpretively" on what counts as law in a given system (an agreement one can expect from all lawyers, judges, and jurisprudents in the determinate legal system within which they work, say, the United States or the United Kingdom); agreed on the relevant facts of the case; agreed on the law (the relevant propositions of law) and on the history of politics/law and on an interpretation of the political institutions in their country; agreed about the relevance of the same governing principles in the case at hand; and agreed about the main substantive principles embedded in their own legal system (especially justice [e.g., rights] and fairness [e.g., democratic decision making]) and about the interpretation and the preferred ordering of each of these—they'd reach the same decision. Thus, there is one (and only one) determinate decision a given Herculean judge would reach in a given case within the existing resources of the law, in a determinate legal system.

The theory that there is always one and only one right answer (though it may not always be reached) runs into real problems, however, when one considers a panel of such judges who must reach a single decision through discussion and voting. Here different judges, deploying somewhat different interpretive choices than Judge Hercules, may come up with answers that are significantly different from Hercules's own answers. Such judges would reach their decisions in the right way, in accordance with the ideals and procedures of law as integrity; and each judge's decision, based on convictions grounded in the law's resources, would be a wholly sound one. There could in principle, then, be more than one right answer. Given the way the world is and given Dworkin's own statement in the matter at the end of *Law's Empire* (1986, pp. 412–413), there probably would in fact be more than one right answer.

This reading does not supplant the orthodox reading for a single judge; it continues to be the case here that there is, for that judge, one and only one determinate best answer in a given case. But it does force an amendment on the "one and only one right answer" thesis for a panel of judges, or for a whole judicial system. Here, though there continues to be no need for Herculean judges ever to go outside the law's resources to reach a judicial decision, and no need for them to use discretion (or "interstitial legislation") to fill in gaps in the law, more than one right answer is possible—indeed, is to be expected.

CONVERGENCES. Hart conceded, in the "Postscript" to his *Concept of Law* (1994), that he had not given sufficient attention to principles in the law or found an appropriate role for them in his theory. He also allowed that given legal systems could have a set of embedded substantive principles (a public morality, as Dworkin called it); such principles are, for Hart, typically enshrined in a written constitution and in judicial reasoning about that constitution.

On the other hand, Dworkin's acknowledgment of the important place of near unanimous "preinterpretive"

agreement on what counts as law in a given system marks an almost wholesale acceptance of Hart's idea of the nature and importance of a rule (or norm) of recognition in a mature and complex legal system. And there's much merit to Hart's observation that "Dworkin's later introduction of interpretive ideas into his legal theory [in *Law's Empire*] … brought the substance of [h]is position very close to my own" in recognizing that the courts have to deal interpretively with underdetermination in the written law. Hart continues, "Arguably [though] before the introduction of interpretive ideas into his theory there seemed to be a great difference between our respective accounts of adjudication.…" (Hart, "Postscript" to *Concept of Law* [1994], note to p. 272 on p. 307.)

UTILITARIANISM AND BASIC RIGHTS

Hart alluded in his main entry to difficulties utilitarianism had in accommodating within its normative frame the central issues of justice (that is, distribution of basic benefits and protections equally to all). But since the time at which Hart's main entry was written, significant attempts have been made within utilitarianism (under the name "indirect" utilitarianism) to address and perhaps resolve this problem.

Many people in the 1970s and 1980s—including John Rawls, Ronald Dworkin, and even thinkers broadly sympathetic to utilitarianism, such as David Lyons—concluded that utilitarianism was somehow incompatible in particular with basic rights (human or constitutional), or at least with the priority habitually given to such rights.

The problem they see is that no one can think that acting in accordance with any given right (especially if the social rules that formulate such things are kept fairly simple and easy to follow) will on every occasion yield up a result that is compatible with the general happiness principle. Sometimes deviating from that policy will have the greater welfare value. And, given the general happiness principle itself, the principle that the greater benefit should be preferred to the lesser and that normative requirements on action can always be set to achieve the greater benefit, that deviation should be taken. Sometimes a right ought to yield to these considerations: It should do so when so doing holds the prospect of greater well-being.

INDIRECT UTILITARIANISM. In an effort to deal with the problem the critics had identified, this new version of utilitarianism shifts the focus of attention from Jeremy Bentham, who did not countenance the idea of basic moral rights, to J. S. Mill, who did. Roughly, the theorists of indirect utilitarianism assert that direct appeals to general welfare are self-defeating, all things considered, and that putting standing constraints on the principle—such as a system of moral rules (typically relatively simple and easily followable rules) or a coherent set of civil or constitutional rights justifiable by the standard of general happiness—in fact produces the greater well-being.

Indirect utilitarians do not, however, assert that moral rules should never be overridden nor individual rights ever broached. Rather, on their view, where rules or rights conflict (as they inevitably will, many have argued), some sort of appeal to the general happiness is in order.

Here is where the notion of an indirect utilitarianism comes crucially into play. Its advocates argue that the principle of general happiness should not directly determine what is to be done even here. Rather, the principle operates only indirectly in all such cases. It bears down, not on individual actions per se but on the rules themselves. Here the general welfare principle is used merely to help determine which rule is weightier, a determination that occurs gradually (over time and with experience) and cumulatively, or used to help determine a policy (a second-order rule of conduct), all things considered, for conduct when these particular moral rules (or these particular rights) conflict.

Thus, on their account it is possible to have policies for action (to have both moral rules and rights) that are justifiable by the standard of general happiness and at the same time to shield these policies from direct confrontation with (and possible overthrow by) the happiness principle on individual occasions. Thus, indirect utilitarianism (if all its arguments and presumptions are allowed) seemingly establishes that utilitarianism is compatible with basic constitutional rights and their priority—at least in the case of those rights that are themselves justifiable in accordance with the general happiness principle.

CRITICISM. But considerations of corporate good and of aggregate welfare (including those that amount to nothing more than the increased well-being of some individuals at the expense of others) can and do in fact override constitutional rights on given occasions. Indirect utilitarians cannot really deny this. If they do, then the jumping-off point of indirect utilitarianism would disappear along with the problem it was designed to solve. There would simply be no point to a strategy of shielding moral rules and constitutional rights from being overridden by corporate or aggregate political policies on those occasions

when such policies were arguably supported as preferable by direct reference to the standard of general happiness.

Thus, indirect utilitarians are in effect forced to admit that social policies could override constitutional rights, within the utilitarian frame they have devised. After all, social policies in their view merely reflect, cumulatively, the results of applying general welfare considerations to occasions of acting in accordance with those policies. And they have admitted, necessarily, that sometimes corporate or aggregate political policies would in fact be supported as preferable over moral rules and constitutional rights by direct reference to the standard of general happiness.

If this is so, the general happiness principle could not support the assignment of constitutionally guaranteed benefits and protections to each and every individual person in advance, so to speak, and across the board. It could not do so if, in effect, such rights tied the utilitarian politician's hands against allowing corporate or aggregate interests to override or supersede constitutional rights when, cumulatively and all things considered, those aggregate interests could be seen to conduce to greater benefit. Indirect utilitarians cannot allow for politically fundamental constitutional rights that have a built-in, standing, and overriding priority over corporate or aggregate considerations. To this degree, then, philosophical utilitarianism is incompatible with the notion of basic rights (human or constitutional rights) as that idea is commonly understood.

RECENT CRITICAL PHILOSOPHY OF LAW: MODERN AND POSTMODERN

Recent decades have witnessed the birth of several noteworthy developments or movements within the philosophy of law. Broadly these divide into two camps. Those belonging to the first remain more or less faithful to a generally modernist and liberal orientation to legal philosophy. They include law and economics and the liberal humanist strand of feminist jurisprudence. Those belonging to the second camp take up a generally postmodernist and postliberal orientation to legal philosophy. They include critical legal studies in its various manifestations along with the more radical strands of feminist jurisprudence and critical race theory.

Characteristic of modernist liberal legal philosophy are the following assumptions:

(i) human reason is univocal and universal;

(ii) language represents reality and truth is correspondence to reality;

(iii) knowledge requires justification from foundations;

(iv) the methodological path to foundations is analysis (often drawing on methodological individualism or social atomism in the social sciences);

(v) all persons share some morally significant basic freedom and equality;

(vi) to be legitimate government must be constitutional and limited;

(vii) law serves legitimate government through its institutional subordination of power to reason; and

(viii) the true path to historical and moral progress is that marked by the rule of law.

Characteristic of postmodern and postliberal legal philosophy is the rejection of several if not all of these assumptions. Thus: human reason is multivocal and relativistic; language shapes or determines reality; truth is largely coherence; knowledge does not require justification from foundations; and so on. The most significant and general feature of postmodernist and postliberal legal philosophy, however, is its unwillingness to affirm the rule of law as either an empirical possibility or normative goal. On the postmodernist and postliberal view, it is not reason, but power, will, desire, the subconscious, the chance of history, or the forces of nature to which law is always in the end subordinate and through which any historical or moral progress must ultimately be won.

LAW AND ECONOMICS

As a development or movement within legal philosophy, law and economics took flight in the 1970s with Richard Posner's *The Economic Analysis of Law* (published originally in 1973). But its roots reach back to work in the early 1960s by Guido Calabresi, Ronald Coase, and others, as well as to legal realism's instrumentalist stance toward law and associated efforts to bring economic analysis to bear on legal issues in the early twentieth century. What unifies the law and economics movement is a commitment to putting the concepts, methods, and principles of microeconomics to work center stage in the study of law. Several law and economics theses have been advanced.

One thesis was straightforwardly descriptive. Some or all of the law was said to be best described exclusively or primarily in terms of economic efficiency. The law of tort, for example, was best understood as an institutional attempt to minimize the costs of accidents overall for society, including the cost of preventing accidents. A sec-

ond thesis was straightforwardly normative. Some or all of the law was said to be properly criticized or evaluated exclusively or primarily in terms of economic efficiency. Wherever the law failed to promote or realize economic efficiency, it was to be criticized and reformed. Subsequent theses claimed that considerations of economic efficiency were the key to making accurate predictions of future legal developments, or to explaining legal history, or to giving the best interpretation of various legal systems (e.g., the United States or the United Kingdom). The normative thesis remains today the most widely affirmed and discussed. But taken as a thesis about the primary or overriding aim of law it is not compelling.

ECONOMIC EFFICIENCY. Economic efficiency is a property of transactions or relations between persons and was developed as a proxy for aggregate utility, which was thought unmeasurable given the impossibility of interpersonal utility comparisons. If a transaction or relation makes all those it affects better off or at least no worse off by their own lights, then there is good reason to believe that it increases aggregate utility (though it is not possible to know by how much). Such a transaction or relation is Pareto superior to its status quo ante. Any state of affairs from which no Pareto superior transactions or relations is possible is Pareto optimal. The set of Pareto optimal states of affairs marks the limit of our ability rationally to act so as to improve aggregate utility.

Of course, some non-Pareto optimal states of affairs may actually represent gains in aggregate utility over any or all Pareto optimal states of affairs. But without being able to do interpersonal utility comparisons, there is no way of reliably picking them out. From a utilitarian perspective, then, using the law to facilitate or produce Pareto superior transactions and relations up to but not beyond a point of Pareto optimality is a normatively sound ambition. The law may do this in at least three ways: (i) distributing legal rights and entitlements to those who value them most; (ii) redistributing the costs and benefits of some transaction or relation so as to render it efficient on the Pareto criteria; or (iii) sustaining an open and transparent market with low transaction costs and few incentives for strategic holdout behavior so that persons can voluntarily exchange until they arrive at a Pareto optimal state of affairs (which, according to the Coase theorem, they will do).

The Pareto criteria of economic efficiency have limited application because most transactions or relations between persons generate transaction costs or adverse third-party effects. The Kaldor-Hicks criterion of efficiency accounts for this by picking out as efficient any transaction or relation in which those who gain enough that they could in principle (but need not actually) compensate from their gain those who lose, such that no person impacted by the transaction or relation would be made worse off by it relative to its status quo ante. The Kaldor-Hicks criterion, however, is problematic at the level of application because two different states of affairs may be reciprocally Kaldor-Hicks efficient (the Scitovsky paradox). As more refined criteria of efficiency continue to be introduced, the underlying idea remains the same: Economic efficiency is a proxy for aggregate utility.

DESCRIPTIVE THESIS. Whereas it is possible superficially to describe many areas of the law in terms of economic efficiency, the extent to which the law is well described in such terms is difficult to determine. It may be more efficient (reduce costs overall) for the law to deal with accidental harms through liability rather than property rules because the latter would require those who cause accidents to undertake the costly project of reaching agreements with their victims ex ante. But, because of the complexity and general unavailability of the information required, it is nearly impossible to defend any particular liability rule as privileged from the point of view of economic efficiency. The expected costs associated with any particular rule will be a function not just of the degrees and probabilities of harm from accidents covered by the rule, but also of such things as the costs of the care required to avoid liability and of administering and enforcing the rule. The descriptive thesis advanced by law and economics becomes less compelling as the picture of law to which it is applied is made more realistic and fine-grained.

NORMATIVE THESIS. Attention has shifted over recent years to the normative claim that regardless of how the law as it stands is best described, surely it ought primarily to aim at economic efficiency. This claim is problematic. First, prescriptions that make use of highly simplified economic models inattentive to the kinds of information alluded to above are of marginal use. But the costs (e.g., of information gathering) of building more useful models are likely prohibitive. Second, it is not clear why efficiency should be taken as normatively primary for the law. Whereas there may be good utilitarian reasons to insist that legal reforms always be efficient relative to their status quo ante, there are no good utilitarian reasons to insist that legal reforms either be Pareto optimal regardless of the path to them or be Kaldor-Hicks efficient, because neither guarantees a gain in aggregate utility over

the status quo ante. It is unlikely that there are any other good moral reasons (of fairness, or consent, or respect for autonomy) to privilege Pareto optimality or Kaldor-Hicks efficiency as the overriding aim of the law. Thus, the case for grounding legal criticism and reform exclusively in considerations of economic efficiency is weak. Still, economic efficiency may (and probably should) play a subordinate role in legal criticism and reform.

FEMINIST JURISPRUDENCE

Characteristic of feminist jurisprudence are two claims, one descriptive and explanatory, the other normative. The former is that the patriarchical oppression of women is fundamentally realized through law. The latter is that the ending of patriarchical oppression must rank at or near the top of the list of aims in terms of which the law is properly criticized and reformed. Apart from these claims, however, there is little general consensus within feminist jurisprudence. Positions vary with respect to whether women and men share the same fundamental interests, whether those interests are rooted in a biologically or psychologically given human nature, the extent to which those interests are malleable regardless of their genesis, and the proper relationship of the law to those interests.

Liberal humanist feminists generally regard the abolition of patriarchy as a substantially completed task, the completion of which is possible without radical change to the basic structure of modern liberal legal institutions and theory. They aspire to an egalitarian humanism realized under the rule of law. They endeavor to reveal and reform those remaining areas of the law—for example, rape law, employment law, and marriage law—through which patriarchical oppression continues to operate. Progressive feminists also generally regard the abolition of patriarchy as a substantially completed project, the completion of which is possible under the rule of law. But they argue for more radical substantive changes to modern liberal legal theory—for example, the recognition of special rights for women as distinct from men, or the redrawing of the lines marking a private domain presumptively immune to state intervention. These more radical changes to substantive law may be argued for on the grounds that women possess at least some fundamental interests distinct from men, or that under current conditions privacy merely secures a social space for the unchecked reproduction of patriarchical self-understandings.

So, for example, whereas liberal humanist feminists insist that the free speech and privacy rights common to men and women properly protect the private consumption of pornography, progressive feminists typically endorse legal restrictions on the private consumption of pornography, or at least that pornography that depicts women as mere sexual objects or as subordinate to men. The call for a "battered woman's syndrome" defense to homicide is also a progressive feminist initiative; it is a carefully limited but substantively radical revision to a particular legal doctrine (concerning intent) necessary if the fundamental interests of women are to be secured under the rule of law.

Whereas liberal humanists and progressive feminists divide over the means necessary and appropriate to a final victory over patriarchy, they both seek that victory within and through the rule of law and thus share a modernist orientation toward the law. Radical feminists are different. They argue that patriarchy depends on and is at least partially constituted through the rule of law. They reject the modernist aspiration to historical and moral progress through law and seek a more radical revision to the legal status quo ante. Radical feminists argue that the categories most basic to modern liberal legal theory and practice—such as due process, equal rights, fairness, state neutrality, consent, individual responsibility, privacy, justice, objectivity, impartiality, and rules—underwrite and obscure patriarchical oppression. They seek both to illuminate this fact and to suggest alternative, typically nonlegal or extralegal, frameworks for thinking about and realizing social order.

Feminist jurisprudence has been and remains theoretically diverse and rich. This is in part because it remains politically and methodologically open. Feminist legal theorists have often allied themselves with and drawn on the work of those pursuing other emancipatory political agendas. In its various strands, feminist jurisprudence draws on neo-Marxist and poststructuralist critical theory, queer theory, race theory, neopragmatism, Lacanian psychoanalytic theory, and rational choice theory.

CRITICAL LEGAL STUDIES

Critical Legal Studies (CLS) grew out of a conference in the 1970s that sought to bring together the New Left politics of the 1960s, American Legal Realism's instrumentalist stance toward law, and European social theory (structuralism and poststructuralism). At its inception, then, CLS was divided between modernist and postmodernist orientations toward the law, drawing from Nietzsche, Marx, Weber, Habermas, Foucault, and Derrida. In time, this division was settled in favor of a postmodernist orientation. What began as a radical critique of law under

conditions of modern capitalism became a more radical critique of the idea of law itself. At its most provocative, at least in the United States, CLS called into question the possibility of realizing justice under or through law.

Though CLS had some presence in England and Germany, it was and remains (to the extent that it remains at all) primarily an American development. Throughout its history, CLS organized itself generally around two theses. The first was that legal systems, both in their content and operations, were best understood as ideological systems of legitimation. The second was that legal systems were indeterminate and thus incapable of subordinating the exercise of coercive political power to reason. Together these theses underwrite the proposition that law is always and everywhere only the politics of power by another name.

CLS, like American Legal Realism, understood the content and structure of the law to derive in the end from nonlegal normative commitments. And, again like Legal Realism, it sought honesty about that fact. Just as legal realists had undertaken to show that much of American law was determined by a laissez-faire political ideology rather than any science of legal reasoning, so too did CLS scholars. What was not so determined was determined, on the CLS view, by patriarchical or racist or other morally suspect political commitments. Of course, legal realists sought to expose the ideological bases of law so as to place law in the service of morally more reputable nonlegal or extralegal political commitments (generally utilitarian and progressive). CLS scholars generally rejected this instrumentalist approach to law. They tended to argue that the law was always an effect, and could never be the genuine cause, of underlying political, social, and economic change. The point of demystifying the law and exposing it as ideological in nature was not to put it in the service of a more noble cause, but rather to encourage non- or extralegal means to social reform.

That the content and methods of mature legal systems almost always underdetermine the answer to at least some legal questions is neither a radical nor particularly controversial claim. By the 1960s, few legal philosophers thought mature legal systems were or could be fully autonomous and possessed of sufficient internal resources to generate, mechanically as it were, a single determinate answer to every legal question. The existence of so-called hard cases was taken for granted. That all cases were hard cases, however, was not. It is this thesis that CLS, in its most ambitious moments, advanced: that mature legal systems (or at least particular legal systems, e.g., the United States and the United Kingdom) are radically indeterminate and, accordingly, that the rule of law is impossible.

Three lines of argument were advanced for this thesis. The first and least ambitious rooted the indeterminacy of the law in the formal structures of law. Legal rules competed not only with one another, but with more flexible standards and principles. Precedents, often diverse themselves, could always be read narrowly or broadly. Principles of statutory construction pointed in multiple directions. And so on. While sufficient to debunk any vision of legal reasoning as scientific or mechanical, this argument is not sufficient to establish the radical indeterminacy of law. The sheer number of easy cases never litigated suggests that legal reasoning is not inherently radically indeterminate.

A second and more ambitious argument rooted the indeterminacy of the law in the inconsistency or incoherence of liberal political morality (presumably foundational at least in the United States and the United Kingdom and other contemporary liberal democracies). Liberal political morality valued both individual self-interest and the collective or common good, saw the individual as ultimately free and responsible and socially constituted, and committed itself to state neutrality while privileging secular modernist humanistic conceptions of the good. It was, in short, inconsistent and incoherent. But competing principles and commitments are not necessarily inconsistent or contradictory. Liberal political morality may indeed express and undertake to mediate rationally and reasonably the tension between several competing principles and commitments. It need not, for all that, be reducible to an irrational self-contradiction or to incoherence.

The third and most ambitious argument for the indeterminacy of the law appealed to the structure of language and thought itself. The argument here, drawn from poststructuralist linguistic and social theory, was that the possibility of language and thought, the possibility of meaning itself, presupposed for any particular utterance or expression the existence of a multiplicity of meanings. If legal language could mean even one thing, then, it must necessarily mean or potentially mean many things. For several years many CLS scholars made the case for this proposition by using "deconstructive" strategies of critical reading to "trash" legal propositions privileged within the conventional order of legal reasoning. But this argument ultimately proved to be its own undoing. It dissolved the purposeful human subject in an endless proliferation of meanings and reduced progressive poli-

tics to the obscure mysticism of such slogans as "deconstruction is justice."

The future of CLS as a movement in legal philosophy remains unclear. Its most provocative claims have been largely abandoned, whereas its more modest but also more plausible claims (about the relationship of law to politics and underdetermination within the law) have been largely assimilated into more mainstream jurisprudential thinking.

See also Bentham, Jeremy; Derrida, Jacques; Dworkin, Ronald; Feminist Legal Theory; Foucault, Michel; Habermas, Jürgen; Hart, Herbert Lionel Adolphus; Humanism; Justice; Legal Positivism; Legal Realism; Marx, Karl; Mill, John Stuart; Nietzsche, Friedrich; Philosophy of Law, History of; Rawls, John; Responsibility, Moral and Legal; Rights; Utilitarianism; Weber, Max.

Bibliography

HART AND DWORKIN ON SOCIAL PRACTICES AND PRINCIPLES

Coleman, Jules, ed. *Hart's Postscript: Essays on the "Postscript" of "The Concept of Law."* New York: Oxford University Press, 2001.

Dworkin, Ronald. *Law's Empire.* Cambridge, MA: Harvard University Press, 1986.

Dworkin, Ronald. *A Matter of Principle.* Cambridge, MA: Harvard University Press, 1985.

Dworkin, Ronald. *Taking Rights Seriously.* Cambridge, MA: Harvard University Press, 1978. Originally published 1977; important appendix added in 1978.

Hart, H. L. A. *The Concept of Law.* 2nd ed., with a postscript, edited by Penelope Bulloch and Joseph Raz. Oxford: Oxford University Press, 1994.

Rawls, John. *Political Liberalism.* 2nd ed. Lectures 6 and 8. New York: Columbia University Press, 1996.

UTILITARIANISM AND BASIC RIGHTS

Gray, John. *Mill on Liberty: A Defence.* London: Routledge, 1983.

Hart, H. L. A. *Essays in Jurisprudence and Philosophy.* Chs. 8 and 9. Oxford: Clarendon Press, 1983. Both of these essays were originally published in 1979.

Lyons, David. *Rights, Welfare, and Mill's Moral Theory.* New York: Oxford University Press, 1994. Collects together Lyons's "Utility and Rights," referred to below, with other of his relevant essays on Mill.

Lyons, David. "Utility and Rights." In *Ethics, Economics, and the Law,* NOMOS 24, edited by J. R. Pennock and John W. Chapman, 107–138. New York: New York University Press, 1982.

Lyons, David. "Utility as a Possible Ground of Rights." *Nous* 14 (1980): 17–28. This essay and "Utility and Rights" criticize the thesis that indirect utilitarianism is compatible with basic rights, but many of his earlier essays support that compatibility.

Martin, Rex. *A System of Rights*. Oxford: Clarendon Press, 1993. See especially chapter 13, section 1.

Rawls, John. *A Theory of Justice*. 2nd ed. Harvard University Press, 1999.

RECENT CRITICAL PHILOSOPHY OF LAW AND SUBSE-QUENT SECTIONS

Altman, Andrew. *Critical Legal Studies: A Liberal Critique*. Princeton, NJ: Princeton University Press, 1990.

Calabresi, Guido, and A. D. Melamed. "Property Rules, Liability Rules, and Inalienability: One View of the Cathedral." *Harvard Law Review* 85 (1972): 1089–1128.

Coleman, Jules, and Jeffrey Murphy. "Law and Economics." In *Philosophy of Law*. 2nd ed. Boulder, CO: Westview Press, 1990.

Frug, Mary Jo. *Postmodern Legal Feminism*. New York: Routledge, 1992.

Gilligan, Carol. *In a Different Voice: Psychological Theory and Women's Development*. Cambridge, MA: Harvard University Press, 1982.

Kairys, David, ed. *The Politics of Law: A Progressive Critique*. New York: Pantheon Books, 1982.

Kelman, Mark. *A Guide to Critical Legal Studies*. Cambridge, MA: Harvard University Press, 1987.

MacKinnon, Catherine. *Feminism Unmodified: Discourses on Life and Law*. Cambridge, MA: Harvard University Press, 1987.

Minow, Martha. *Making All the Difference*. Cambridge, MA: Harvard University Press, 1990.

Patterson, Dennis. *Law and Truth*. New York: Oxford University Press, 1996.

Polinsky, A. *An Introduction to Law and Economics*. 2nd ed. Boston, MA: Little Brown, 1989.

Posner, Richard. *The Economic Analysis of Law*. 5th ed. Boston, MA: Little Brown, 1998.

Smith, Patricia. *Feminist Jurisprudence*. New York: Oxford University Press, 1993.

Symposium: "Critical Legal Studies." *Stanford Law Review* 36 (1984): 1–674.

Symposium: "Deconstruction and the Possibility of Justice." *Cardozo Law Review* 11 (1990): 919–1734.

Symposium: "Efficiency in the Law." *Hofstra Law Review* 8 (1980): 485–770.

Unger, Roberto. *The Critical Legal Studies Movement*. Cambridge, MA: Harvard University Press, 1986.

Rex Martin (2005)
David Reidy (2005)

PHILOSOPHY OF MEDICINE

The subject matter unique to philosophy of medicine—as opposed to those issues that are best seen under the heading of philosophy of biology—is clinical medicine and its underlying methodology and assumptions. Crucial to philosophy of medicine is the family of terms *disease*, *malady*, *health*, *normal*, *abnormal*, *condition*, and *syndrome*, all of which have evaluative aspects to their definitions. For all its scientific base, medicine must be a value-laden practice guided by the values of its practitioners and its public. It is in this regard—but not only in this regard—that the claim "Medicine is an art and a science" should be understood.

DISEASE, HEALTH, AND NORMALITY

A stable departure from physiological normality that causes death, disability, pain, loss of pleasure, or inability to achieve pleasure is the sort of entity that is called disease (Clouser, Culver, and Gert 1981). The departure has to be stable enough so that it causes similar problems in similar people and so that it is recognizable by different medical practitioners as the same disease entity. When the departure is less clearly individuatable than a disease, the entity is referred to as a syndrome.

Normality and health are relative terms. They are relative to species, age, gender, (perhaps) social status, race, and ultimately to one's own physiology. A healthy (normal) eighty-five-year-old is different from a healthy (normal) twenty-year-old; and a healthy (normal) professional athlete is different from a healthy (normal) philosophy professor. Normal health is also relative to one's values. Unless a person feels comfortable doing what she wants to do, she can claim to be unhealthy by saying things like: "I just don't feel up to par." In this sense health is a theoretical state of a person.

The concept of biological variability derives its useful sense from the relativity of *normal*. Biological variability makes generalization problematic in a way that generalizing from one billiard ball to any such object is not. Biological variability—meaning that no two organisms are exactly alike—is trivially true. It is unhelpful, except as a reminder that generalization is problematic.

Diseases are real to the extent that they are stable departures from normality (sometimes called "baseline") as defined above. Obviously, diseases are not like traditional physical objects. They can overlap and be in two places at the same time. (Mental diseases present their sorts of problems, which parallel issues in philosophy of mind and philosophy of psychology.) Diseases are real in that they cause real pain, disability, or both; they are real in the sense that they can be reduced to physiological occurrences. Diseases are theoretical in the sense that they are not traditional physical objects, and they are identified only relative to a value structure that then becomes part of the medical theory. For example, given the current medical theory of European and North American scientific medicine, chronic fatigue syndrome is a disease. But against the backdrop of eighteenth-century medicine, it would have been seen primarily as a characteristic of some women and lazy men. Chiropractic medicine sees disease only in terms of misalignment of vertebrae. The reality of disease, a sense for reduction, and the theory-ladenness of disease exemplify traditional questions in philosophy of science.

What is classifiable as a disease is also a function of what physicians are willing to do, what they are interested in, and what will be reimbursed. Thus, infertility is treated as a disease in large part because it is a terrible burden to some, it is interesting to deal with medically, and people are willing to pay for treatment. Being short is also treated as a condition worth reversing (in children) for the same sorts of reasons. This makes disease relative to culture and economic conditions.

Treating a condition as if it were a disease makes it a disease in a stipulative sense but not in the physiological sense. Baldness and bad breath would be conditions that might be troublesome, most effectively treated medically, and yet still not classified as diseases. However, if they are caused by a disease, they may be considered signs of an underlying medical condition. Psychiatry periodically re-decides whether certain psychological conditions should be considered diseases.

Genetics adds an interesting twist to defining disease and thinking about health. Consider a disease such as sickle-cell anemia, where homozygous recessive is a serious disease but the heterozygous condition can be beneficial in malarial areas (heterozygotes have a better survival rate from malaria than do either homozygotic forms) but still can, in rare instances, cause serious medical problems. Thus, in a nonmalaria infested area, the heterozygous condition might be called a disease. Huntington's disease is caused by a dominant gene whose effects do not manifest themselves until (usually) middle age. Should one consider a teenager with the dominant gene diseased? One could say that the person is healthy now even though the gene is one that will cause a disease later in life. But this is not really correct, because there are subtle changes in body chemistry caused by the dominant gene even when there are no Huntington's symptoms. One normally would say something such as, "a mutation in the normal gene is what causes Huntington's disease." This locution is odd for two reasons: (1) the person (almost assuredly) never had a normal gene to mutate; and (2) using "normal" when speaking of the gene would seem to imply that "abnormal" and "diseased" might be

usable for genes as well. But, of course, the gene for Huntington's disease is not a normal gene with a disease.

THE LOGIC OF DIAGNOSIS

Diagnosis and scientific explanation present similar philosophical problems, especially with respect to explanation, causality, and laws. Diagnosis begins with history taking and moves on to the physical examination. The standard history questions assume that disease entities have a typical natural history to them.

Signs are objective characteristics, such as blood pressure and broken bones. Symptoms are the subjective characteristics reported by the patient—for example, pain and lightheadedness. The signs and symptoms of disease vary with the stage of the disease. Thus, an early stage of any disease may be confused for the later stage of another. Physicians look for the best overall explanation for the condition, given the patient's individuating factors such as age, gender, occupation, stress factors, and so forth. The best explanation is assumed to be the most probable explanation, where the disease is considered to be the cause of the condition being investigated.

A standard procedure in diagnosis is the rule-out test. A physician limits the diagnosis to a few conditions and then does a test, which, if negative, will rule out one of the possible causes. This procedure is repeated until only one likely answer is left. This is in keeping with a simplistic version of falsification.

Doctors also use a simple confirmation strategy in diagnosis. Usually, more than one confirmatory test result is required before the diagnosis is accepted. Other predictions will have to be borne out by test results as well as physical findings and consistent history. Laboratory tests are crucial to modern-day diagnoses, although they present problems. Results are subject to false positives (disease reported when absent) and false negatives (disease not reported when present). The best test has a high true positive ratio and a low false positive ratio. Bayes's theorem can be used to calculate the probability that a person with a positive test actually does have the disease in question.

Because test results are continuous, cutoff points must be chosen. The cutoff points are chosen based on how serious an error would be. If a disease is fatal and can be treated safely, then a high false positive rate would be acceptable. For less worrisome conditions, compromise between the two figures is possible. Again, values are part of what looks like a objective aspect of medicine. In this sense, medical diagnosis may be different from the usual picture of the scientific method. There are other differences as well.

Some of the crucial aspects of physical diagnosis—for example, interpreting heart sounds and kinds of rashes—are subjective and cannot be taught so much as they must be learned by practice. The apprenticeship of medical students and physicians (residents) is, in this sense, different from the time graduate students in science spend learning bench laboratory skills. Also, anecdotes play a role in diagnosis in a way that they would not in physics or most other sciences. Related to the reliance on anecdotes is that the best physicians just seem to sense that, no matter where the facts are pointing, something else is going on. Subjectivity, anecdotes, and intuition seem not, in general, to be good scientific methodology, and yet it seems to be precisely what separates the great clinicians from the ordinary ones. The key to understanding these great diagnosticians is probably pattern recognition.

Physicians often wait in order to let a disease show itself more clearly, sometimes confirming their diagnoses by follow-up: Did the condition follow its predicted course? Did the treatment have the expected effect and in the expected manner? If not, the diagnosis may well have been incorrect. Even if the follow-up is consistent with the diagnosis, the actual condition may have been different and may have remitted on its own or have been similar enough to the disease suspected so that it responded to the treatment. In these sorts of cases, physicians do not know that they were wrong; they will count these cases as successes and so use them to support a similar diagnosis the next time. There is no practical defense against this failing.

HOLISM AND REDUCTIONISM

Holistic medicine assumes that diseases are primarily a function of lifestyle and life events of the patient. A holistic approach to diagnosis will focus as much on psychosocial history as it will on traditional signs and symptoms. Stress as a factor in disease is important in holistic accounts. Reductionistic medicine focuses more on physiology as the key to diagnosis, treatment, and taxonomy of disease. The reductionistic approach is the legacy of scientific medicine begun in the mid-nineteenth century.

See also Bayes, Bayes' Theorem, Bayesian Approach to Philosophy of Science; Causation: Philosophy of Science; Explanation; Laws, Scientific; Laws of Nature; Philosophy of Biology; Philosophy of Mind; Reduction; Reductionism in the Philosophy of Mind.

Bibliography
Bursztajn, H., R. Feinbloom, R. Hamm, and A. Brodsky. *Medical Choices, Medical Chances.* pts. 1 and 2. New York: Routledge, Chapman and Hall, 1990.

Clouser, K. D., C. M. Culver, and B. Gert. "Malady: A New Treatment of Disease." *Hastings Center Report* 11 (June 1981): 29–37.

Collins, D. "Genetics of Huntington's Disease." University of Kansas Medical Center. Available from http://www.kumc.edu/hospital/huntingtons/genetics.html.

Kark, J. "Sickle Cell Trait." Information Center for Sickle Cell and Thalassemic Disorders. Available from http://sickle.bwh.harvard.edu/sickle_trait.html.

Kelley, W., ed. *Textbook of Internal Medicine.* Chps. 6–8. Philadelphia: Lippincott, 1992.

Margolis, J. "Thoughts on Definitions of Disease." *Journal of Medicine and Philosophy* 11 (3) (1986): 233–236.

Maull, N. "The Practical Science of Medicine." *Journal of Medicine and Philosophy* 6 (2) (1981): 165–182.

McNeil, B., et al. "Primer on Certain Elements of Medical Decision Making." *New England Journal of Medicine* 293 (5) (1975): 211–215.

Merskey, H. "Variable Meanings for the Definition of Disease." *Journal of Medicine and Philosophy* 11 (3) (1986): 215–232.

Munson, R. "Why Medicine Cannot Be a Science." *Journal of Medicine and Philosophy* 6 (2) (1981): 183–208.

Murphy, A. E. *The Logic of Medicine.* Baltimore, 1976.

Passmore, R., ed. *A Companion to Medical Studies.* Vol. 3. Oxford: Blackwell Scientific Publications, 1974.

Schaffner, K. "Philosophy of Medicine." In *Philosophy of Science,* edited by M. Salmon, et al. Englewood Cliffs, NJ: 1992.

Wulff, H. *Rational Diagnosis and Treatment.* Oxford: Blackwell Scientific Publications, 1976.

Arthur Zucker (2005)

PHILOSOPHY OF MIND

The mind seems to occupy a special place in the world. It is the seat of thought and feeling, of rationality and moral concern. Is it fundamentally different from the other things we find in the natural world? Is it possible for the mind to be investigated scientifically? Can one ever really know what is going on in the mind of someone else?

Such questions delineate the subject matter of the philosophy of mind. The central problem in this area is the *mind-body problem*: the project of finding an account of the mind that locates it in the broader physical world. While this problem does not exhaust the philosophy of mind, one's response to it imposes substantial constraints on what one may say about other questions in this area.

One of these questions concerns mental causation. It seems obvious that what happens in the mind can bring about physical events in one's body and vice versa. If, however, the mental is radically different from the physical, such causal commerce may seem problematic. A related question concerns the prospects for psychology. If there is difficulty in supposing that causal laws govern the mental, what sorts of results can we expect from the scientific investigation of the mind?

Another question concerns epistemology. The *problem of other minds* is the project of explaining how one can know about the minds of others. The problem arises as a result of an asymmetry between how one knows about one's own mental states and how one knows about others' mental states. I know what I am thinking or feeling by a peculiar means devoid of inference from more basic bits of knowledge. I do not have to make observations on the basis of which I find out what is going on in my mind. Indeed, I may be unable to err about my own mental states. By contrast, I cannot know what someone else is thinking or feeling without observing their behavior, and the inferences I make are plainly subject to error. One may wonder if such inferences are ever justified. Even if they are justified, one may wonder how it is possible that the very same kind of phenomena may be known in such radically different ways.

These questions presume, of course, that we know how to sort the mental from the nonmental in the first place. Two features seem especially characteristic of the mental. First, many mental states exhibit what is known as *intentionality*: They have content directed at the world; they are about things. The belief that the earth is flat, for example, has as its content the proposition that the earth is flat; the fear of flying, for another example, is about flying. Second, any mental state involving an experience displays the striking feature that it makes sense to speak of *what it is like* to be a particular kind of creature having that kind of experience. Mental states having this what-it-is-like character may be called *phenomenal* states, and if someone is in such a state, we may say that that person is *phenomenally conscious*.

Some remaining questions in the philosophy of mind aim at more specific kinds of mental phenomena. What is the difference between an emotion and a mood? How is an intention to act related to a desire to act? Such questions often branch into other areas of philosophy: the philosophy of action, of responsibility, and so on.

THE MIND-BODY PROBLEM

Leaving the notion of reduction at an intuitive level, we may distinguish the two dominant positions on the mind-body problem as follows. Materialism (or physicalism) is the thesis that that the mental reduces to the physical. More cautiously, every mental entity is ultimately nothing above and beyond the physical entities that exist. Once certain physical entities are in place, nothing extra is needed for the mental entities to exist as well. By contrast, dualism is the thesis that the mental and physical are ultimately distinct, so that neither reduces to the other. What makes the mind-body problem a problem is that we seem to have powerful evidence for both of these incompatible positions.

On the one hand, the physical workings of the brain apparently suffice to account for our behavior. If the mind is not in some way reducible to the brain, it is hard to see what room there could be for the mind to play any role in our behavior. Yet it surely does play such a role. Further, it is plain that events affecting the brain have systematic effects on the mind as well. So simplicity favors eliminating the mind as an extra entity.

On the other hand, the mind resists such a reduction. It is hard to see how the physical aspects of anything could add up to its having thoughts or feelings. Any putative creature with a mind may well be a mindless automaton. The point is made most vivid if we consider a physical organism built out of the very same physical ingredients as you, the reader. It seems possible that such an organism may yet be mindless, despite its physical and behavioral similarity to a creature that has a mind. If this is right, then clearly what makes you a creature with a mind does not automatically accompany your physical characteristics; it is something over and above the physical. Hence, materialism is false.

Materialism and dualism are not the only options. One other option is idealism (or phenomenalism), according to which it is the physical that ultimately reduces to the mental. Further, there is the view that neither the mental nor the physical reduces to the other. Rather, both reduce to some third, neutral entity. This position is sometimes known as neutral monism. Neither alternative has been widely endorsed. Idealism is apt to seem simply incredible, and neutral monism may seem frustratingly mysterious.

DUALISM

René Descartes developed the most famous form of dualism, a form known as Cartesian substance dualism. On this view, the mind is a substance (and hence capable of existing on its own without any distinct supporting entities, such as a body). It is distinct from any physical object in that it is essentially without spatial extension. A dualist need not adopt all of these tenets, however. A dualist need hold only that mental properties—such as being in pain or intending to leave the room—are in principle independent of any combination of physical properties.

As noted above, there is considerable pressure to opt for materialism in order to make sense of the causal role that the mental has in affecting our behavior. One route that the dualist might take in the face of this pressure is to endorse epiphenomenalism—the view that, contrary to appearances, mental events never cause physical events. There would then be no need to accommodate the causal role of the mind. This advantage is offset, however, by a grave difficulty in accounting for one's knowledge of other minds. When I know what someone else is thinking, my primary evidence is that person's behavior. In treating this as evidence, I presume that part of what brings about such behavior is the person's mental states. Epiphenomenalism undercuts this presumption and throws into doubt the value of such evidence.

There is no requirement that a dualist be an epiphenomenalist. Perhaps the most attractive form of dualism is one that maintains causal interaction between mind and body while rejecting the supposition that the mind is a substance. The view known as *emergentism* does exactly this. (For a classic defense of the view, see C. D. Broad's *The Mind and Its Place in Nature*.) Emergentism may be characterized by three theses. First, it rejects the view that the mind is a substance, maintaining only that there are two types of properties, mental properties and physical properties (property dualism). Second, it claims that once an organism reaches a certain level of complexity, the laws of nature dictate that it will then have various irreducible mental properties. Third, it holds that these mental properties subsequently make a difference to the organism's behavior. More precisely, in the presence of mental properties, the physical elements of the organism behave differently from what one would expect on the basis of just the general laws governing those physical elements when not assembled in this special fashion. The emergentist thus makes the bold empirical claim that we have in effect only an incomplete view of the laws of physics, that if one were to examine the physical events occurring in creatures with minds, one would find that the usual laws do not apply.

LOGICAL BEHAVIORISM

In the first half of the twentieth century, logical behaviorism held sway as the main alternative to dualism. On this view, any statement about the mental can be translated into a statement about behavioral dispositions. A statement such as "Amy is in pain" is synonymous with some such statement as "Amy is disposed to wince, cry out, etc." Since wincing and crying out are themselves physical events, it seems that something purely physical can be disposed to undergo such events. If being in pain is merely being thus disposed, then a purely physical thing can be in pain. (A seminal statement of this view may be found in Gilbert Ryle's *The Concept of Mind*.)

Logical behaviorism has several attractive aspects. First, it makes good sense of our knowledge of other minds. If pain is simply the disposition to wince, cry out, or the like, then I can know that someone is in pain simply by observing those behaviors. Second, it fits happily with the familiar picture of how we come to learn psychological terms, specifically, that one learns what others mean by the word "pain" by observing that pain is attributed to people on the basis of their overt behavior. Third, the view explains why we have apparent a priori knowledge of the links between certain mental states and certain behaviors. We do not have to gather empirical evidence to support the claim that wincing is typically a sign of pain.

Logical behaviorism nonetheless faces a very basic problem, namely, that no proposed translation is in fact plausible unless it makes use of further mental terms. Consider again the statement "Amy is in pain." It seems possible for this to be true even when she is not disposed to wince, cry out, or the like. Suppose, for instance, that she wishes not to let anyone discover her pain and is thus determined to suppress any overt indications of it. She will then not be inclined to behave in those ways.

Of course, we could try to understand the behavioral disposition in a more complex fashion. We might unpack the disposition claim as follows: "Amy is in such a state that *if she were to feel uninhibited*, she would wince, cry out, etc." The situation in which she never displays such behaviors because she is determined to suppress such signs is no counterexample to this translation. But if this is the translation on offer, then we have not succeeded in showing how a purely physical entity could be in pain, since the complex characteristic assigned to Amy is already mental in part in that it refers to feeling uninhibited—a mental characteristic in its own right. In general, any attempt to characterize a behavioral disposition seems bound to include such a reference.

THE IDENTITY THEORY

The identity theory rose to prominence in the middle of the twentieth century, succeeding logical behaviorism as the leading materialist theory. The view is simple: Every type of mental state is identical with some type of physical state, probably a neurophysiological state. (An extensive overview of the sorts of considerations that helped lead many philosophers to the identity theory can be found in Herbert Feigl's extensive essay "The 'Mental' and the 'Physical.'")

What is novel in the identity theory is not so much its simple positive claim as its disavowals: The identity claim is not accompanied by any claim about translation. This feature of the identity theory enables it to avoid many of the usual objections to materialism. This virtue can be illustrated by working with a well-known example. Consider the claim that being in pain is identical with some type of brain process, say, having one's C-fibers firing. Identity theorists suppose that the relation between "being in pain" and "having one's C-fibers firing" is analogous to the relation between "the morning star" and "the evening star": the terms have different senses, but the same referent. Other favored examples include the identity of lightning with a kind of electrical discharge, or the identity of heat with molecular motion. In each case, the identity can only be discovered empirically; it cannot be discovered by a priori analysis of the meanings of the terms.

While the a posteriori character of these identity claims is a key appeal of the identity theory, it is also the source of important objections. One such objection was made famous as "objection 3" in J. J. C. Smart's classic paper "Sensations and Brain Processes" (1959). If an identity statement of the form "$M = P$" is a posteriori, different concepts must be associated with "M" and "P." Those different concepts involve different properties that pin down the referent of "M" and "P." For example, with the identity "the morning star = the evening star," the first name is associated with certain properties, such as being visible in the morning, that are not associated with the second name. Now turn to the alleged identity of pain with C-fiber firing. By analogy, we should conclude that despite the truth of this identity, there are nonetheless two distinct sets of properties, those associated with "pain" and those associated with "C-fiber firing." The objection, finally, is that the property associated with "pain" is a mental property that has yet to be identified with anything physical. Any a posteriori identity between the mental and physical will leave an unreduced residue

of mental properties, and these mental properties undermine materialism.

Smart's response to this objection was to acknowledge that there must be different senses associated with the mental and physical terms of the identity while insisting that the sense of the mental term can be explained without appeal to any further mental properties. For instance, he claims that the sentence "I see a yellowish-orange afterimage" is equivalent in meaning to "There is something going on in me which is like what goes on in me when I see an actual orange in good light." The vocabulary in this second statement is topic-neutral in the sense that it is silent on the nature of what is going on; it may or may not be a physical process. When we identify the experience of a yellowish-orange afterimage with a type of brain process, that identity is justified by the empirical evidence that shows that the named type of brain process is in fact what is going on when one sees an actual orange in good light.

It is worth stressing here that, while the identity theorists advertised a lack of commitment to translations of psychological sentences, this sort of objection seems to force them to providing translations nonetheless. Their translations might prove to be just as dubious as the behaviorist's translations.

ANOMALOUS MONISM

One important challenge to the identity theory is posed by anomalous monism, the view championed by Donald Davidson and made famous in his essay "Mental Events." The view may be defined as a combination of one positive thesis and one negative thesis. Positively, it holds that each particular mental event is also a particular physical event, though categories of mental events cannot be equated with categories of physical events. Anomalous monism thus endorses a thesis of token identity, but not type identity. The negative thesis is that the mental is anomalous: there are no strict laws involving mental events as such. This anomalism allegedly blocks the discovery of laws relating the mental and the physical, laws apparently needed to justify a claim of identity between mental and physical properties.

The negative claim is aimed directly at the identity theory; it seeks to undercut potential sources of empirical support for that view. It is worth noting that even if anomalism is consistent with the identity theory, it is certainly significant for psychology, since it rules out the ambition of psychology to uncover strict laws governing the mental.

The positive thesis also challenges the identity theory, albeit indirectly, in that it suggests that one can be a materialist without being an identity theorist. If it suffices for materialism to say that each particular mental event is identical with some physical event, then a materialist may rest content with such instead of holding out for the more ambitious theory of type identity. Yet few philosophers are convinced that a thesis of token identity is sufficient for materialism. Intuitively, a materialist must hold, at a minimum, that how someone is mentally depends on how that person is physically. The thesis of token-event identity does not secure this result.

SUPERVENIENCE

The idea that how things are physically must determine how things are mentally may be captured by the notion of *supervenience*, also introduced into the philosophy of mind by Davidson. To say that mental properties supervene on physical properties is (roughly) to say that any two creatures that are exactly alike physically must also be exactly alike psychologically. There may be no neat match-up of mental and physical properties, but supervenience implies that how things are mentally is fixed by how things are physically.

The notion of supervenience is in this way useful for formalizing a kind of dependence of the mental on the physical, although there have been many subtly different ways of making the notion precise. There is an important limitation to any supervenience thesis, however, in that the thesis itself leaves unanswered questions as to why and how the mental is determined in this fashion. To answer these questions, it seems that a more committed theory of the nature of the mental is needed.

FUNCTIONALISM

A distinct challenge to the identity theory came in the form of functionalism. This is the view that mental properties are functional properties, that is, properties defined by the causal or functional roles they play. Consider the property of being a laundry detergent. Something is a laundry detergent if and only if it can combine with water in a washing machine to clean clothes. Various different chemicals can play this role equally well. When a particular chemical plays this role, it is said to *realize* the property of being a detergent. Since many different chemicals can play this role, the property of being a detergent is multiply realized and cannot be identified with any one of its realizers. (A seminal paper advocating functionalism is Hilary Putnam's "The Nature of Mental States.")

One motivation for functionalism is the conviction that it is in fact very unlikely that there is a single physical property to be found in all creatures sharing a given mental state. Functionalism accommodates this conviction by allowing mental properties to be multiply realized, and it does so without giving up on materialism, as an individual can have a functional property solely in virtue of his physical characteristics.

Functionalism has also been found attractive because of the apparent similarity between minds and computers. Consider what it is for a computer to run a program. The same program can be run by many different sorts of machines, so long as they have distinguishable states that play the right roles relating inputs, outputs, and each other. If the mind is akin to a computer, mental states may plausibly be classified as functional, relating sensory inputs, behavioral outputs, and different internal states. (For an important challenge to this analogy, see John Searle's "Minds, Brains, and Programs.")

A further appeal of functionalism is that it promises a degree of autonomy for psychology. If mental properties are multiply realized, then one can investigate what mental properties do without worrying about the specific physical characteristics of the underlying realizers. It is, of course, controversial how much autonomy this provides.

Even if we opt for functionalism, there remains much work to be done by way of locating the right sorts of functional properties to identify with various mental properties. The two distinctive features of the mind mentioned earlier—intentionality and phenomenal consciousness—provide targets for such work.

INTENTIONALITY

Theories of intentionality have generally taken either of two forms. They differ primarily in whether they determine the content of a mental state by appeal to the overall functioning of the mind in question or by appeal to individual mental states in isolation. On the former (interpretational) approach, a subject S has the belief that P just in case the belief that P appears in the overall assignment of intentional states providing the best interpretation of S. The details of the theory depend on what it takes to amount to a good interpretation. Typically, the idea is that the theory must predict the behavior of S and make S's thoughts and actions by and large *rational* for someone in that environment.

The other (causal/informational) approach, which focuses on specific connections between particular brain states and states in the world, is encouraged by the idea that we may be able to distinguish within states such as believing that P and hoping that P a common element—a *representation* that P—for which an independent physicalist theory can be given. The physical state N may represent that P by virtue of a causal link, in that someone in state N has the information that P. On a very simple version of this view, N represents that P if and only if the only thing that can cause someone to be in N is the fact that P. This simple version fails to make room for false representations, however; some way is needed to distinguish those causes of the representing state that fix its content and those that do not. (Seminal works in this area include Fred Dretske's *Knowledge and the Flow of Information* and Jerry Fodor's *Psychosemantics*. A useful survey may be found in the anthology *Mental Representation: A Reader*, edited by Stich and Warfield.)

CONTENT EXTERNALISM

Whatever theory of content one develops, an important constraint is imposed by content externalism. This is the view that the content of someone's mental states is determined not solely by that person's intrinsic features; the larger social and historical environment in which that person is embedded makes a difference. An easy route to seeing the point is to consider beliefs about particular individuals. Suppose that Amy and Basil are friends, that Amy believes that Basil is intelligent, and further, that Basil has a twin about whom Amy knows nothing. Amy's belief is plainly about Basil, not his twin. Yet if the situation were reversed, so that Amy was acquainted with Basil's twin instead of Basil, her belief would have had a different content, even though she would have been intrinsically the same in both cases. Hence, the contents of one's mental states may vary while one's intrinsic features remain unchanged. (Two fundamental papers about content externalism are Hilary Putnam's "The Meaning of 'Meaning'" and Tyler Burge's "Individualism and the Mental.")

This observation has raised two concerns. First, some worry that externalism is problematic for the view that intentional mental states can play a causal role in determining behavior. The worry, crudely put, is that since content is determined by wider environmental factors, content can play a causal role in behavior only if those wider environmental factors themselves play a causal role, which seems mysterious. A second concern is that externalism may be incompatible with the privileged access to our own minds that we seem to have. We need not investigate our environment to know what we think; yet if the contents of our thoughts depend on that envi-

ronment, it may seem mysterious how we manage such a feat. These two problems have motivated some philosophers to introduce a notion of narrow content—mental content determined solely by the intrinsic features of the agent. If there is such a thing as narrow content, any theory of intentionality needs to accommodate it as well as content individuated in a more ordinary fashion.

PHENOMENAL CONSCIOUSNESS

The second distinctive aspect of the mind with which materialists must contend is phenomenal consciousness. What sort of physical and/or functional property can ensure that its bearer is undergoing an experience?

Many positive approaches to phenomenal consciousness take their cue from the fact that phenomenal states seem bound up with intentionality. Consider, for instance, what it is like to look at a bright red tomato. That experience plausibly represents the world as being a certain way: as containing a bright red tomato. One may even argue that all phenomenal states include such content. The state of pain, for instance, may represent one's body as being damaged.

What makes a state phenomenal, however, is not simply its having a certain content. Something else must be added to distinguish the mere belief that there is a bright red tomato in front of one from the visual experience of a bright red tomato in front of one. A variety of proposals have been offered as to what might make the difference. On one option, the content of a phenomenal state plays a rather different functional role in the overall system than the content that attaches to a mere belief. On another, a phenomenal state is a representational state that itself is represented by some other, higher-order representational state.

Whatever the merits of these theories, few would hold that they can be seen to be true simply as a matter of conceptual analysis. It is simply too easy to imagine situations in which the proposed physical and functional conditions are met even while nothing is experienced at all. Indeed, it seems quite conceivable that a being could have all the various physical and functional properties that we ourselves have and yet be devoid of phenomenal consciousness. Such creatures are known as philosophical zombies—physical duplicates of ourselves for whom all is "dark inside." (For influential discussions, see David Chalmers, *The Conscious Mind*; Peter Ludlow et al., eds., *There's Something about Mary*; and Ned Block et al., eds., *The Nature of Consciousness*.)

The fact that we can easily conceive of such zombies does not, of course, settle the issue in favor of dualism. As is familiar from the work of the identity theorists, the identity in question may be a posteriori. Consider the case of heat and molecular motion again. There is, in fact, no possible situation in which heat is present without molecular motion; nonetheless, we can apparently conceive of such a situation. We may explain away that apparent conceivability, however, by pointing out that we could then be imagining a world in which something other than heat *appears* to be heat, because, we imagine, this other thing produces heat sensations. We have misdescribed the genuine possibility we imagined.

The materialist appears to be obligated to offer a similar sort of story explaining away our apparent ability to conceive of zombies. There is, however, an important difference between the psychophysical case and the case of phenomenal states. In the heat example, we could distinguish between the appearance of heat and the heat itself, but in the case of phenomenal states, it is unclear that a comparable distinction can be drawn. (This well-known argument is found in Saul Kripke's *Naming and Necessity*.)

The difficulty here is related to one discussed earlier—namely, that made famous as "objection 3" in Smart's classic defense of the identity theory. There the worry turned on the implications of saying that mental and physical terms are associated with quite distinct concepts. The materialist needs to offer some story about those concepts that allows us to explain the a posteriori character of the identity claim, and the apparent possibility of zombies, in a way consistent with the claim that *all* properties are ultimately nothing over and above physical properties. Whether any such story is available remains an extremely controversial question.

See also Behaviorism; Dualism in the Philosophy of Mind; Functionalism; Mind-Body Problem; Physicalism; Reductionism in the Philosophy of Mind.

Bibliography

Armstrong, David. *A Materialist Theory of the Mind*. Rev. ed. New York: Routledge, 1993.

Block, Ned, ed. *Readings in Philosophy of Psychology*. Cambridge, MA: Harvard University Press, 1980.

Block, Ned, Owen Flanagan, and Güven Güzeldere, eds. *The Nature of Consciousness: Philosophical Debates*. Cambridge, MA: MIT Press, 1997.

Broad, C. D. *The Mind and Its Place in Nature*. Paterson, NJ: Littlefield Adams, 1960.

Burge, Tyler. "Individualism and the Mental." *Midwest Studies in Philosophy* 4 (1979): 73–121.

Chalmers, David J. *The Conscious Mind: In Search of a Fundamental Theory*. Oxford, U.K.: Oxford University Press, 1996.

Chalmers, David J., ed. *Philosophy of Mind: Classical and Contemporary Readings*. Oxford, U.K.: Oxford University Press, 2002.

Davidson, Donald. "Mental Events." In *Essays on Actions and Events*. Oxford, U.K.: Oxford University Press, 1980.

Dretske, Fred. *Knowledge and the Flow of Information*. Cambridge, MA: MIT Press, 1981.

Feigl, Herbert. *The "Mental" and the "Physical": The Essay and a Postscript*. Minneapolis: University of Minnesota Press, 1967.

Fodor, Jerry. *Psychosemantics*. Cambridge, MA: MIT Press, 1987.

Fodor, Jerry. *Representations: Philosophical Essays on the Foundations of Cognitive Science*. Cambridge, MA: MIT Press, 1981.

Foster, John. *The Immaterial Self*. London: Routledge, 1991.

Kim, Jaegwon. *Supervenience and Mind*. Cambridge, U.K.: Cambridge University Press, 1993.

Kripke, Saul. *Naming and Necessity*. Cambridge, MA: Harvard University Press, 1980.

LePore, Ernest, and Brian McLaughlin, eds. *Actions and Events: Perspectives on the Philosophy of Donald Davidson*. Oxford, U.K.: Blackwell, 1985.

Levine, Joseph. *Purple Haze: The Puzzle of Consciousness*. Oxford, U.K.: Oxford University Press, 2001.

Lewis, David. "Psychophysical and Theoretical Identifications." *Australasian Journal of Philosophy* 50 (1972): 249–258.

Ludlow, Peter, Yujin Nagasawa, and Daniel Stoljar, eds. *There's Something about Mary: Essays on Frank Jackson's Knowledge Argument*. Cambridge, MA: MIT Press, 2004.

Putnam, Hilary. "The Meaning of 'Meaning.'" In his *Mind, Language, and Reality*. Vol. 2 of *Philosophical Papers*. Cambridge, U.K.: Cambridge University Press, 1975.

Putnam, Hilary. "The Nature of Mental States." In his *Mind, Language, and Reality*, Vol. 2 of *Philosophical Papers*. Cambridge, U.K.: Cambridge University Press, 1975.

Ryle, Gilbert. *The Concept of Mind*. Chicago: University of Chicago Press, 1984.

Searle, John. "Minds, Brains, and Programs." *Behavioral and Brain Sciences* 3 (1980): 417–424.

Smart, J. J. C. "Sensations and Brain Processes." *Philosophical Review* 68 (1959): 141–156.

Stich, Stephen P., and Ted A. Warfield, eds. *Mental Representation: A Reader*. Oxford, U.K.: Blackwell, 1994.

D. Gene Witmer (2005)

PHILOSOPHY OF PHYSICS

The philosophy of physics investigates the logical, conceptual, metaphysical, and epistemological foundations of the physical sciences, especially fundamental physics. It is concerned with general issues such as the subject matters and aims of physics, the nature of physical laws, the direction of time, and issues specific to particular theories such as the measurement problem in quantum mechanics and the status of the second law in thermodynamics. The philosophy of physics is enormously relevant to traditional metaphysics because it addresses the implications of physical theories for fundamental ontology, the natures of time and space, laws, causal relations, counterfactuals, and natural kinds. This encyclopedia includes entries on general, specific, and metaphysical issues in the philosophy of physics, so this entry will serve mainly as a guide to the main problems in philosophy of physics and to direct the reader to more specific articles.

The best short characterization of physics derives from Aristotle's view that physics is the science of motion and the causes of motion of material bodies; paradigmatically the motions of planets, projectiles, and pointers. The primary aim of fundamental physics has been to find a true theory (or theories) that specifies a fundamental ontology, spatiotemporal structure and laws, and that provides a complete (or as complete as possible) account of the motions of such material bodies. Many natural phenomena (e.g., the tides, the weather, rainbows, the growth of plants, the movements of animals, light, and even mental phenomena) either involve the motions of material bodies or are the causes of motions of material bodies. It follows that the scope of physics includes most everything. A true theory that accounted for the motions of all material bodies would be a theory of everything or at least of everything capable of making a difference to the positions and motions of material bodies.

The possibility of their being a complete physical theory was given a tremendous boost by the development of Newtonian or classical mechanics (see the "Classical Mechanics, Philosophy of" entry). The ontology of classical mechanics consists of dimensionless particles that possess inertial mass and certain other intrinsic properties and that move in a three-dimensional space in accordance with certain laws. Macroscopic material bodies are identified with more or less stable configurations of dimensionless particles and the motions of a particle are described in terms of the change of spatial position (or relative spatial position) over time.

The motion of a particle (and so the motions of the material bodies) is determined by the forces acting on it via the single dynamical law $F=m(p)a$ where F is the total force (the vector sum of all forces acting on particle p) on p, m(p) is the inertial mass of p and a is p's acceleration. A free particle (one on which the total force is 0) moves at a constant velocity. Newtonian forces are determined by the intrinsic natures of particles (their masses, charges,

and so on) and their relative positions. For example, the attractive gravitational force particles exert on one another is given by $F = Gm1m1/r^2$; where m1, m2 are the gravitational masses of the two particles and r is the distance between the two particles. Classical mechanics was enormously successful in accounting for the motions of material bodies in circumstances where the total force on a body could be (approximately) determined as in the motions of the planets, comets, projectiles, and so on.

Classical mechanics is usually understood as supporting determinism. This means, roughly, that the state of the universe at time t together with the dynamical laws determines the state of the universe at any other time. Pierre Simon de Laplace made this vivid by imagining a supreme intelligence that ascertains the state of the universe at one time and then, knowing the laws of mechanics, is able to predict the state of the universe at any other time. There are subtle issues concerning the relations between determinism and prediction and also issues concerning whether classical mechanics is genuinely deterministic. It is only given certain qualifications concerning the nature of the force laws and the assumption that the system is isolated (see the "Determinism and Indeterminism" entry). Many philosophers think that the issue of the truth of determinism has significant implications for issues concerning free will (see the "Determinism and Freedom" entry) and more generally the place of mind in nature.

During the latter half of the nineteenth century classical mechanics was extended to include light and other electromagnetic phenomena. This involved introducing electromagnetic fields and dynamical equations (Maxwell's equations) that described the dynamics of electromagnetic fields and interactions between the motions of charged particles and fields. Light was understood as a kind of wave disturbance in the aether—a posited substance that was supposed to fill all space and provide the ground for electromagnetic fields. Also, toward the end of the nineteenth century it became increasingly plausible that matter is composed of atoms of various kinds and that these can be identified with Newtonian particles. By the last decade of the nineteenth century the package of Newtonian mechanics, Maxwellian electromagnetic theory, and the atomic theory of matter looked like good candidates for the sought after complete theory of the motions of material bodies. Of course this turned out not to be so.

One of the main philosophical discussions inspired by classical mechanics concern the natures of space and time. Isaac Newton thought of space as a kind of arena in which particles move. Newtonian space is absolute in that its existence and nature is independent of the particles it contains. It is three-dimesional, infinite in each dimension, homogeneous, and Euclidian. The positions of and so distances between particles are defined in terms of their locations in space. It follows that for Newton there are distinct possible universes in which all the distances among particles are identical but the positions are translated. Famously, G.W. Leibniz argued that it is difficult to make sense of absolute space. He observed that God would have no reason to place the material contents of space in one region of absolute space rather than another and concluded that absolute space offends the principle of sufficient reason.

The dispute between Newton and Leibniz blossomed into a debate between those (absolutists) who think of space as an independent entity that provides spatial structure and those (relationists) who think of spatial relations between particles as primary. There are famous arguments on both sides. Relationists observe that by the lights of Newtonian physics, absolute position and motion are empirically inaccessible. Empiricist considerations suggest to them that we should not believe that absolute space exists. Absolutists respond that although we cannot determine absolute motion, absolute space is required to provide an adequate explanatory theory including the explanation of possible distance relations and of rotations. Relationists reply by arguing that the empirical content of Newtonian theory is that trajectories are physically possible only if they can be embedded into absolute space and satisfy the Newtonian laws, but that reference to absolute space is merely a convenient fiction. Only spatial relations are real. This debate has survived the demise of Newtonian mechanics and continues in discussions of the interpretations of relativity theories (see the entries "Space in Physical Theories" and "Relativity Theory").

Newton also thought of time as absolute. He suggests that time flows throughout the universe at a constant rate. It is assumed that a free particle traverses equal absolute distances in equal intervals of absolute time and so free motion measures absolute time. There is also an absolutist/relativist issue concerning the nature of time. Relativists observe that Newtonian theory provides no empirical access to absolute temporal locations. Again empiricist considerations suggest that physics can do without Newtonian time.

Some relativists claim that the empirical content of classical mechanics involve only facts about temporal sequences of interparticle distances. On a sophisticated relativist account, the laws of classical mechanics specify which sequences of interparticle distances are physically possible (see Julian Barbour's *The End of Time* and the "Time in Physics" entry for further detail). Exactly how far one can go in dispensing with apparent spatial and temporal structure in favor of spatial and temporal relations while maintaining the empirical core of classical mechanics—or relativity and quantum mechanics—remains a lively topic of discussion.

Another issue concerning time in classical mechanics involves the apparent direction or arrows of time. Many apparently lawful processes, in particular those associated with thermodynamics, are temporally directed. For examples, gasses diffuse, ice in warm water melts, and electromagnetic waves emanate from moving charged particles and the entropy of isolated systems never decreases. In addition, causation, counterfactuals, memory, decision, and so forth are temporally directed. However, the dynamical laws of classical mechanics are temporally symmetric in that for any sequence of particle positions that are in accord with those laws (i.e., is physically possible), the reversed sequence of positions is also physically possible. Where then does the arrow of time come from? Newton seems to have thought of time as possessing an intrinsic direction of flow. But it is hard to see how this flow—whatever "flow" amounts to—can account for the temporal asymmetries. It seems that the solution must lie in physical laws or conditions rather than the metaphysical nature of time.

There has been much work within physics on the problem of reconciling temporally asymmetric processes, in particular those of thermodynamics, with temporally symmetric fundamental laws. (see the "Philosophy of Statistical Mechanics" entry). Ludwig Boltzmann observed that most of the micro states compatible with, say, a block of ice floating in warm water are ones that evolve toward the future in accordance with their dynamical laws to ones in which the ice block melts. *Most* is determined relative to a natural measure on the set of micro states and Boltzmann understood this to mean that it is very likely that the ice block will melt. However, it turns out that, relative to the same probability measure, it is very likely that the ice cube evolved from one that was more melted in the past! This follows from the temporal symmetry of the laws. One response to this problem is that the explanation of temporal asymmetries lies in the macro state of the very early universe. It is posited that this state was one of enormously low entropy (and satisfies certain further conditions) and it is also posited that there is a probability distribution over micro states that realize this state. This is called "the past hypothesis" (Albert 2000).

It has been argued that it follows from the past hypothesis and the dynamical laws that macroscopic systems that become approximately energetically isolated (e.g., an ice cube in warm water) will satisfy (the appropriate statistical versions of) the laws of thermodynamics. Some philosophers have pursued his idea further and claimed that all of the temporal arrows are ultimately derivable from the past hypothesis and the dynamics. The foundations of statistical mechanics and the relations between fundamental laws of physics and special science laws (see the "Special Sciences" entry) remain controversial philosophical issues.

The idea that the package of classical mechanics, electromagnetic theory, the atomic theory of matter, and statistical mechanics constitute the complete theory of motion was undermined during the first decades of the twentieth century as it became clear that these theories are incompatible with one another and inadequate as a theory of the very small—atomic structure—and the very big—cosmology. One big problem is that in Maxwell's equations the speed of light appears as a constant of nature. It was thought that this speed is relative to the aether. This suggests that it ought to be possible to measure the absolute velocity of the Earth relative to the aether by sending light rays in various directions. However, experiments designed to measure the velocity of the Earth relative to the aether yielded null results. It appeared that measurements of the speed of light yield the same result no matter the velocity of the source or receiver. Obviously, some modification of classical mechanics/electromagnetic theory was required.

H. A. Lorentz proposed modification of the Newtonian laws so that clocks and measuring rods, which are in motion with respect to absolute space, systematically slow down and shorten. As a consequence, although there are facts about the velocities of bodies with respect to absolute space, it also turns out that those velocities cannot be detected. Albert Einstein's special theory of relativity (STR) makes a quite different and revolutionary proposal. It rejects absolute Newtonian space-time as the framework for the motions of matter in favor of Minkowski space-time.

In Minkowski space-time the fundamental notion is that of the space-time interval between events. Einstein posited that the interval between any two events connected by a light ray is 0. This has the consequence that there are no absolute (frame independent) facts about the elapsed time or spatial distance between two events. It

also follows that there are pairs of events (events that cannot be connected by a light ray) for which there are no absolute facts about their temporal order. Einstein's proposal entails the same phenomena as Lorentz's as a result of changing the underlying spatiotemporal structure.

The change from Newtonian space and time to Minkowski space-time suggested to Einstein the possibility of accounting for gravitation not as a force between bodies, but rather as a feature of space-time itself. He succeeded in doing this in the general theory of relativity (GTR). The main idea of the general theory is that the geometry of space-time itself has a geometrical structure that is not Euclidian (i.e., flat) but, rather, depends locally on the distribution of matter and energy. According to GTR, bodies freely move on geodesics (the shortest paths between points in space-time) and what counts as a geodesic is given by the geometry. Because gravitation is an effect of space-time in the GTR, not a force as in classical mechanics, it follows that it acts on all bodies in the same way. This is quite different from Newtonian mechanics in which gravitation is a force that acts the same on all bodies only because inertial mass and gravitational mass are equal. Where in Newtonian mechanics space is an inert arena, in the GTR space-time is a dynamical entity that changes over time through interactions with matter. Both the STR and the GTR are spectacularly successful in their empirical predictions (see "Relativity Theory" entry).

The STR and the GTR have been the objects of much discussion in the philosophy of physics. Among the main issue are: paradoxical scenarios; for example, the twin paradox and the possibility of closed causal loops and apparent time travel, the extent to which the metric of space-time is a real fact or is, to some extent, conventional (see the entry on "Conventionalism"), descendents of the absolutist/relationist dispute within relativistic frameworks, the formulation and viability of determinism within relativity theory (see the "Hole Argument" entry), the compatibility relativity, and quantum mechanics.

The other major failure of classical mechanics/electromagnetic theory concerned its inadequacy as accounts of atomic structure and interaction between atoms and light. According to these theories, atoms should be unstable. Further, it was found, contrary to these theories, that matter emits radiation only with certain specific frequencies, that light behaves in particle-like as well as wave-like ways, and that electrons behave in wave-like as well as particle-like ways. Over the first third of the twentieth century a novel theory—quantum mechanics—developed to account for these and many other phenomena. In quantum mechanics the state of a system at t is characterized by a wave function $\Psi(t)$.

$\Psi(t)$ specifies the values of certain "observables" (position, momentum, spin, and so on) and the probabilities of obtaining various measurement results. A novel feature of quantum mechanics is that $\Psi(t)$ specifies the values of only some observables; for example, if it specifies the value of x-spin, say spin up (in which case it is said to be an eigenstate of x-spin with value spin up), it specifies no value for other spin observables (e.g., y-spin). This is an instance of Werner Heisenberg's uncertainty principle. Ψ also specifies the probabilities of the results of measurements of other spin observables. If $\Psi1$ is an eigenstate of observable O with value v1 and $\Psi2$ is an eigenstate of O with value v2, then the superposition $c1\Psi1 + c2\Psi2$ is a well-defined state that specifies no value for O but says that the probability of a measurement of O yielding value v is c^2. $\Psi(t)$ evolves deterministically by Schrödinger's law except when measured. When measured, Ψ collapses probabilistically to an eigenstate of the measured observable.

Quantum mechanics is beset with puzzles. The dominant way of thinking about quantum mechanics—the Copenhagen interpretation—holds that an observable possesses a determinate value only when the state is an eigenstate of that observable. What does it mean for an electron to possess a position but no determinate momentum (or the other way round) and yet for there to be a probability of a measurement yielding a particular value? It turns out that, in typical (nonmeasurement) interactions, the macroscopic system will evolve into a state that is not an eigenstate of ordinary properties. This is the situation of Erwin Schrödinger's cat that ends up in a state that is not an eigenstate specifying whether it is alive or dead (see "Quantum Mechanics" entry). What can that mean?

Further, that measurement appears in the fundamental laws is immensely implausible and completely unsatisfactory without a precise characterization of measurement. There is also the novel feature that typical quantum states are nonlocal. As Einstein observed and John Bell demonstrated (see entries on "Einstein, Albert" "Bell, John, and Bell's Theorem," and "Non-locality"), there are quantum states involving pairs of particles for which a measurement on one of the pair instantaneously changes the probabilities of certain measurement results for the other particle. This appears to be a kind of influence at a distance that seems incompatible with special relativities apparent prohibition on superluminal causal influences. Whether or not the conflict is genuine is a subtle issue

For most of its history and up until the present, these problems encouraged an instrumentalistic construal of quantum mechanics (see entries on "Scientific Realism" and "Copenhagen Interpretation"). Instrumentalism amounts to giving up the ambition of a complete true theory of motion. However, in the last few decades a number of realist interpretations of quantum mechanics have been proposed. These include Bohmian mechanics, many world/minds theories, and spontaneous collapse theories. Each of these interpretations specify an explicit ontology (that interprets the wave function realistically and may include other items) and laws governing that ontology that yield results matching (or approximately matching) the predictions of orthodox quantum theory. In some, such as Bohmian mechanics, the dynamical laws are completely deterministic, whereas in others, such as the GRW collapse theory, are probabilistic. Because these interpretations are empirically equivalent (or approximately empirically equivalent), they provide an interesting real example of theory underdetermination (see the entry on "Underdetermination Thesis, Duhem-Quine thesis").

Among the notable features of realist interpretations of quantum mechanics are the difficulty squaring it with relativity theories. Currently, there is no satisfactory quantum version (realist or not) of general relativity. Producing such an account is one of the urgent problems of contemporary physics. Less often appreciated is the difficulty in reconciling quantum mechanics and Einstein's Minkowski formulation of special relativity. A realist understanding of the wave function seems to require (because of nonlocal states) more space-time structure than Minkowski space-time provides. Interpretations of quantum theory and connections with relativity will be of central concern in the philosophy of physics in the twenty-first century.

See also Bell, John, and Bell's Theorem; Classical Mechanics, Philosophy of; Conventionalism; Copenhagen Interpretation; Determinism and Freedom; Determinism and Indeterminism; Einstein, Albert; Hole Argument; Non-locality; Philosophy of Statistical Mechanics; Quantum Mechanics; Relativity Theory; Scientific Realism; Space in Physical Theories; Special Sciences; Time in Physics; Underdetermination Thesis, Duhem-Quine Thesis.

Bibliography

Albert, David Z. *Quantum Mechanics and Experience.* Cambridge, MA: Harvard University Press, 1992.

Albert, David Z. *Time and Chance.* Cambridge, MA: Harvard University Press, 2000.

Barbour, Julian. *The End of Time: The Next Revolution in Physics.* Oxford; New York: Oxford University Press, 2000.

Maudlin, Tim. *Quantum Non-locality and Relativity.* Oxford, U.K.; Cambridge, MA: Blackwell, 1994.

Barry Loewer (2005)

PHILOSOPHY OF RELIGION

Analytical "philosophy of religion," still in its infancy in the 1960s, has developed markedly since then. Other approaches have certainly continued to play a part in philosophy of religion written in English, even more so in other languages. Process philosophy, for example, inspired by the thought of Alfred North Whitehead and exemplified in the ongoing work of Charles Hartshorne and others, has retained influence in philosophy of religion and in theology, probably more than in other areas of philosophy. Phenomenology, postmodernism, and other approaches characteristic of the European continent inspire important contributions to the subject. Indeed, there is often not a sharp line between different approaches. Continental writers such as Søren Kierkegaard figure extensively in undoubtedly analytical writing about religion, and analytical philosophy of religion makes such extensive use of medieval material as to be more or less continuous with neoscholastic treatments of the subject.

Although there had been a few earlier analytical essays about various religious issues, the main development of analytical philosophy of religion may be said to have begun in the 1950s with discussion of the "logical positivist" challenge to the cognitive significance of religious language. Most analytical philosophers then held, or were strongly tempted to hold, as an empiricist principle, that every (logically contingent) assertion, in order to have any cognitive meaning, must be verifiable or, more broadly, testable, in principle, by experience. It was charged, by Alfred Jules Ayer, Antony Flew, and others, that the affirmations of religious belief typically do not satisfy this criterion of meaning (A. Flew, R. M. Hare, and B. Mitchell in Brody 1974).

How, then, were the apparent truth claims of religions to be understood? Some were prepared, with Ayer, to treat major religious assertions as mere expressions of emotion, without any cognitive significance. Others sought ways of understanding such assertions as empirically verifiable in principle. John Hick (in Brody 1974) argued, for instance, that "eschatological verifiability," in a life after death, provides at least a partial solution to the problem. Still others, while granting that empirical testability is decisive for the meaning of typical factual assertions, sought to establish a different, and not merely emotive, type of meaning that could be ascribed to religious assertions. The most influential attempts of this type were inspired by the later writings of Ludwig Wittgenstein, particularly by his account of "language games" and their relation to forms of life.

The Wittgensteinian approach, as developed, for example, by Norman Malcolm (in Brody 1992) and D. Z. Phillips (1970), has generated very interesting studies of the relation of religious language to religious life. It is widely criticized, by some as giving inadequate weight to the apparent straightforwardly realistic intent of typical religious assertions, and by some as improperly shielding religious claims from rational criticism by relativizing them to religious language games. It remains, nevertheless, an important strand in contemporary discussion. Of all that has been done in analytical philosophy of religion, it is probably the discussion of religious language in general, and Wittgensteinian themes in particular, that have most interested professional theologians, perhaps because these themes have seemed more relevant than more metaphysical discussions to the work of interpretation and reinterpretation of traditions in which theologians are so much engaged.

Within analytical philosophy during the 1950s the verifiability criterion of meaning was already undergoing severe criticism and has since been virtually abandoned in anything like its original form. Many analytical philosophers continue to consider themselves empiricists and seek alternative ways of excluding claims that they regard as objectionably metaphysical. Many others, however, see the permanent contribution of analytical philosophy, not in a form of empiricism, or in any set of doctrines, but in a method, style, or discipline that can be applied to virtually all the historic issues of metaphysics and ethics and can be used in developing and espousing almost any of the classic philosophical doctrines.

The majority of work done in analytical philosophy of religion since the 1960s has been inspired by the later conception of analytical philosophy and has not focused on issues about religious language. It is characterized by metaphysical realism, taking the religious claims under discussion to be straightforwardly true or false. (For defense of this stance, see, e.g., Swinburne 1977, chaps. 2–6.) Some have suggested calling it philosophical theology rather than philosophy of religion, because the principal subject of most of it is God rather than human religious phenomena, though atheists as well as theists have certainly been important participants in the discussion. On this basis, mainly since 1960, a very substantial body of literature, dealing with most of the traditional issues of philosophical theology and some new ones too, has been created.

Among the traditional topics the attributes of God received rather early analytical attention. (For general treatments see Swinburne 1977, chaps. 7–15; Kenny 1979; Wierenga 1989.) Analysis of the concept of God was easily seen as an appropriate subject for analytical philosophy, and issues about the attributes had been connected, since the Middle Ages, with problems about predication, an appealing point of entry into philosophical theology for those interested in the philosophy of language. According to some of the most influential medieval theologians, God is so different from creatures that positive attributes of creatures cannot in general be predicated of God univocally, that is, in the same sense in which they are predicated of creatures. How then can we predicate anything of God? Various Scholastic theologians developed various solutions, the best known being the theory of analogical predication of Thomas Aquinas. Analytical philosophers of religion have taken up the problem and some of the medieval views, along with more contemporary concerns—for instance, about the ascription of psychological predicates to a being who is supposed not to have a body. (Cf. Maimonides, Thomas Aquinas, and Alston in Brody 1992).

The two divine attributes that have received the most extensive analytical discussion are omniscience and eternity. The central issue about eternity is whether to understand it (as medieval and early modern theology generally did) as involving existence outside of time or rather as involving existence without beginning or end in time, as many contemporary thinkers have proposed. Critics of divine timelessness, such as Nelson Pike (1970) and Nicholas Wolterstorff (in Brody 1992), have questioned the compatibility of timelessness with God's consciousness or action or interaction with creatures. Eleanor Stump and Norman Kretzmann, however, have presented an influential defense of the traditional timeless conception (in Brody 1992), and the issue remains vigorously debated.

Omniscience and eternity are related topics, for one of the most discussed issues about God's knowledge concerns God's relation to time: Does God have complete knowledge of the future? In particular, does God know, infallibly and in every detail, how free creatures will use their freedom? Traditional theologies generally gave an emphatically affirmative answer to this question; but some modern philosophers and theologians have disagreed, arguing that the doctrine of total, infallible foreknowledge compromises the freedom of the creatures. The extensive analytical literature on this issue (e.g., in Fischer 1989) is continuous with older discussions, and opinion remains divided.

A related old debate, recently revived, concerns what has been called "middle knowledge": Does God know, completely and infallibly, what every actual and even merely possible free creature would freely do (or would have freely done) in every possible situation in which that creature could act freely? In the late sixteenth century, Luis de Molina, a Jesuit, proposed an ingenious theory of divine providence according to which God uses such subjunctive (and largely counterfactual) conditional knowledge to control the course of history without having to interfere metaphysically with the freedom of creatures. This theory of middle knowledge was widely embraced by Jesuits, but opposed by Dominicans, who argued that there cannot be such determinate conditional facts about everything that would be freely done by particular creatures in all possible circumstances. This historic controversy was introduced into current analytical discussion by Anthony Kenny (1979) and Robert Adams (1987), who have both defended the Dominican objection to middle knowledge; but the opposite position has been argued by a vigorous school of contemporary Molinists, including Alvin Plantinga (1974) and Alfred Freddoso (1988).

Regarding the relation of God to ethics, it was almost universally held in the 1960s that fundamental ethical principles must be independent of theology and that an acceptable theological account of the nature of ethical facts is impossible. Since then, however, it has come to be widely held by theists, and granted by many nontheists, that facts about God, if God exists, could play a central role in explaining the nature of ethics and that theistic philosophers should be expected to avail themselves of this possibility. The most discussed type of theological theory in this area is the divine-command theory of the nature of ethical obligation, or of right and wrong (Helm 1981). Several thinkers, such as Philip Quinn (1978), have tried to reformulate and explain the theory in such a way as to defend it against the traditional objections to it.

Adams (1987) has proposed a form of the theory that rests on semantical assumptions very similar to those of some of the most influential contemporary exponents of metaethical naturalism but employs different (theistic) metaphysical assumptions.

The grounds proposed for belief or disbelief in the existence of God have naturally claimed at least as much analytical attention as the attributes of God. This is a subject so intensively discussed for centuries that one might have expected little novelty in the treatment of it. But in fact investigations have been rather innovative, and the state of debate has changed significantly since 1960. One striking change is that the traditional arguments for the existence of God, then widely dismissed, even by theologians, as hopelessly discredited, have many defenders at the turn of the twenty-first century.

This is connected with a more general phenomenon, which is that analytical philosophers, especially those inclined to construct and defend constructive metaphysical theories, demand less of arguments than has commonly been demanded in the past. Virtually no one thinks any one "theistic proof" conclusive; but if arguments must be either conclusive or worthless, there would be little useful reasoning about any of the most important philosophical issues. Theistic apologists are accordingly less apt to seek a single "knockdown" proof than to try to show that several traditional (and perhaps also novel) arguments have something of value to contribute to a "cumulative case" for theism, an approach exemplified by Richard Swinburne (1979). Extensive work has been done interpreting, developing, and criticizing all the main types of theistic arguments. Those that have probably received the most attention and development are the "ontological" and the "teleological" (to give them their Kantian names).

The fallaciousness of any ontological argument and the contingency of all real existence had become such commonplaces, especially among empiricists, that it had a certain "shock value" when Norman Malcolm in 1960 published a defense of an ontological argument (reprinted in Brody 1992). Malcolm claimed to find in Anselm's *Proslogion*, besides the famous argument of its second chapter, a second ontological argument in which it is not existence but necessary existence that figures as a perfection. Malcolm also held that necessary existence cannot be excluded from theology on general philosophical grounds. Whether a statement expresses a necessary truth, he argued, depends on the language game in which it figures; and a religious language game can treat the existence of God as a necessary truth. These two features

of Malcolm's article foreshadow the main tendencies in the development of ontological arguments since then: (1) attention to more modal versions of the argument and (2) the attempt to rehabilitate the idea of necessary existence.

Ontological argument studies have been greatly influenced by the dramatic development of modal logic, which was gathering momentum in the 1960s and burst into the center of American philosophical consciousness in the 1970s. In 1962 Hartshorne published a modal proof of the existence of God relying only on the premises that God's existence must be necessary if it is actual and that God's existence is at least possible. Subsequent discussion has established that this proof, and related proofs from slightly slenderer assumptions, are valid in the system of modal logic (S5) most widely thought to be appropriate for the context. David Lewis (in Brody 1974) and Plantinga (1974) have given the argument a form that takes account of developments in modal predicate logic as well as modal propositional logic (or in *de re* as well as *de dicto* modality). The argument is still of limited value for proving the existence of God, because those who would otherwise doubt the conclusion are likely to doubt the possibility premise, given the rest of the argument. But the modal development of the argument is helpful in structuring discussion of questions about necessary existence.

In the 1950s it was the opinion of almost all analytical philosophers that the existence of a real being, such as God (as distinct from merely abstract objects, such as numbers), cannot be necessary in the strongest, "logical" sense. This opinion has come to be widely doubted, however, and the traditional view that God should be conceived as an absolutely necessary being has regained a following. (For contrasting views see Adams 1987, chaps. 13–14, and Swinburne 1977, chaps. 13–14.) Several factors have contributed to this change. The identification of necessity with analyticity, on which the rejection of necessary existence was commonly based, is under attack. W. V. O. Quine's influential doubts about the adequacy of the notion of analyticity led Quine himself to skepticism about necessity. But others, influenced in some cases by an interest in necessity *de re*, have been inspired to seek a more robustly metaphysical conception of necessity. Since a conception of the latter sort was generally held by the great philosophers of the Middle Ages and the seventeenth century, a growing and more sympathetic understanding of those periods of the history of philosophy has also tended to undermine the most dismissive attitudes toward the idea of necessary existence.

The most popular argument for the existence of God in the eighteenth century was the teleological or design argument, usually in a pre-Darwinian form drawing its evidence largely from biological adaptations. This type of argument was discredited both by the devastating critique it received in David Hume's *Dialogues concerning Natural Religion* and by the development of an alternative explanation of the biological phenomena in terms of natural selection. A major rehabilitation of the design argument has been undertaken by Swinburne (1979). Instead of the biological evidence, he takes as his principal evidence the most pervasive, highest-level regularities in the universe. Since they constitute the most fundamental laws of nature, to which all scientific explanations appeal, he argues, there cannot be any scientific explanation of them. There may therefore be no viable alternative to a theological explanation for them, if they are to be explained at all. Deploying the apparatus of Bayesian probability theory, and responding to Hume's objections, Swinburne tries to establish that a theological explanation is indeed more plausible than no explanation at all. Swinburne's argument depends at some points on controversial metaphysical theses and has inspired an extended atheistic response by J. L. Mackie (1982); but the teleological argument has at least been shown to have much more philosophical life in it than had been thought.

The leading argument for atheism, aside from the various critiques of theistic arguments, has long been the argument from evil. The evils that occur in the world are incompatible, it is argued, with the existence of an omnipotent, omniscient, perfectly good God. In the earlier years of analytical philosophy of religion this was usually a charge of demonstrable, logical incompatibility; and attempts to provide theists with a "solution" to the "problem of evil" concentrated accordingly on trying to show the possibility of a perfect deity having permitted the evils. Borrowing a Leibnizian idea, for instance, Pike argued that for all we know, this might be the best of all possible worlds (in Adams and Adams 1990). Plantinga (1974) developed a much-discussed version of the traditional "free will defense," arguing that even if there are possible worlds containing less evil, and as much moral good, as the actual world, an omnipotent God may have been unable to create them because it may be that creatures (whether humans or angels) would not have freely done what they would have to do freely in order for one of those worlds to be actual. The adequacy of such theistic responses to the "logical" form of the argument from evil has been keenly debated, but it has probably become the predominant view that the argument does not afford much hope of a tight, demonstrative proof of atheism.

There has therefore been increasing interest in probabilistic arguments from evil, as presented, for example, by William Rowe (in Adams and Adams 1990), whose thesis is that evils show theism to be implausible, or at least constitute evidence against theism, which might contribute to a cumulative case for atheism. Theistic responses to this type of argument must address issues of plausibility and not merely of possibility. Some have been methodological, attempting to show that the relevant probabilities cannot be determined, or that the explanatory structure of the situation keeps the evils from being even relevant evidence (e.g., Stephen Wykstra in Adams and Adams 1990). Others have tried to give plausible accounts of why evils might have been necessary for greater goods. One widely debated hypothesis, developed in different ways by Hick (in Adams and Adams 1990) and Swinburne (1979), for instance, is that evils, and possibilities of evil, play an essential part in making the world a context for the moral and spiritual development of free creatures.

All such explanations of why God would permit great evils have seemed to some morally or religiously objectionable. Among theists who take this view, Marilyn Adams has argued that we should accept that we simply do not know why God has permitted horrendous evils but that within a religion that affirms, as Christianity does, God's love for individuals who suffer them, it is important to have a coherent account of how God may be seen as redeeming them (Adams and Adams 1990). She points to traditional religious ideas of suffering shared with God or with Christ as suggesting how horrendous evils might be "defeated" by forming an organic whole with incommensurably great religious goods.

One of the more dramatic developments of the period under review is the development of a defense of the rationality of theism that professes not to be based on arguments or evidence. Plantinga maintains that belief in the existence of God can be "properly basic," a basic belief being one that is not inferentially based on any other belief (Plantinga and Wolterstorff 1983). It has been held by many that some beliefs (formed, perhaps, in sensation or memory) do not need inferential support from other beliefs for their justification. Plantinga argues that more beliefs than some have supposed are reasonably held without being based on the evidence of other beliefs and that there is no compelling reason to deny that some religious beliefs have this basic status. He suggests that religious beliefs not based on "evidence" constituted by other beliefs may nonetheless be based on other sorts of "grounds," which might be found, for example, in religious experience. Plantinga's view (which he has dubbed "Reformed epistemology") has been keenly debated. One of the most discussed issues is whether it allows an adequate basis for distinguishing between rational and irrational religious beliefs. (For a moderately critical view see R. Audi in Audi and Wainwright 1986).

A related but importantly different view has been developed by William Alston (1991). Religious experience has been a major subject of discussion in philosophy of religion (e.g., W. James, W. T. Stace, and C. B. Martin in Brody 1974; Wainwright, 1981), as it has been in modern theology. Not all of the discussion has been epistemological or focused on the justification of belief. Pike (1992), for instance, has written about the phenomenology of mysticism, arguing, against the older theory of Stace, that there are mystical experiences of theistic as well as non-theistic content. Alston's approach is thoroughly epistemological, however, and he focuses on the experience of more ordinary religious believers rather than of those adepts typically singled out as "mystics."

Relying on carefully discussed analogies with sense perception, Alston argues that in some circumstances experiences as of God addressing, or being present to, a person can reasonably be regarded as perceptions of God. His argument is placed in the context of a "doxastic practice" conception of the justification of beliefs. He argues that we are able to form and justify beliefs only in socially established practices in which we have learned to be responsive to such factors as experiential cues and communal traditions as well as to beliefs that we hold. In Alston's view we have no choice but to rely on socially established doxastic practices, and it is presumptively rational to do so, even though we typically have little or no independent evidence of the reliability of the practice. He argues that this presumption of rationality applies also to religious doxastic practices that are socially established, and in particular to practices in which participants have learned to form beliefs of having perceived God in various ways. Alston offers vigorous rebuttals of several major objections to basing religious beliefs on religious experience. In his opinion the most serious problem for his view, which he treats at some length, is that posed by the existence of diverse religious traditions whose well-established doxastic practices lead them to form apparently conflicting beliefs on the basis of their religious experience.

For philosophy of religion as for contemporary theology, the problem of conflicting truth claims of different religions is, if not a new issue, one that is coming into increasing prominence. Hick (1989) has done much to draw attention to it. He argues that it is not plausible to suppose that one traditional form of religious experience is veridical while others are not, and he tries to articulate a way in which many apparently conflicting forms could all be at bottom veridical, proposing to regard them as apprehending different "phenomenal" manifestations of a single "noumenal" transcendent "reality." Not that Hick thinks all religious beliefs equally acceptable; the main criterion he proposes for the value of religious traditions and belief systems is their fruitfulness in producing morally and spiritually recognizable saints, people notably advanced in a transformation from self-centeredness to Reality-centeredness. Among the issues in the vigorous debate about Hick's view are the adequacy of the conceptual apparatus he borrows from Immanuel Kant and whether it is compatible (as he means it to be) with a fundamentally realist and cognitivist conception of religious belief.

See also Atheism; Ayer, Alfred Jules; Bayes, Bayes' Theorem, Bayesian Approach to Philosophy of Science; Empiricism; Epistemology, Religious; Evil, The Problem of; God, Concepts of; Hare, Richard M.; Hume, David; James, William; Kant, Immanuel; Kierkegaard, Søren Aabye; Mackie, John Leslie; Malcolm, Norman; Modal Logic; Mysticism, Nature and Assessment of; Ontological Argument for the Existence of God; Phenomenology; Postmodernism; Quine, Willard Van Orman; Religious Experience; Religious Experience, Argument for the Existence of God; Religious Pluralism; Stace, Walter Terence; Teleological Argument for the Existence of God; Theism, Arguments For and Against; Thomas Aquinas, St.; Whitehead, Alfred North; Wittgenstein, Ludwig Josef Johann.

Bibliography

Adams, M. M., and R. M. Adams, eds. *The Problem of Evil.* New York: Oxford University Press, 1990.

Adams, R. M. *The Virtue of Faith and Other Essays in Philosophical Theology.* New York: Oxford University Press, 1987.

Alston, W. P. *Perceiving God.* Ithaca, NY: Cornell University Press, 1991.

Audi, R., and W. J. Wainwright, eds. *Rationality, Religious Belief, and Moral Commitment: New Essays in the Philosophy of Religion.* Ithaca, NY: Cornell University Press, 1986.

Brody, B. A., ed. *Readings in the Philosophy of Religion: An Analytic Approach.* Englewood Cliffs, NJ: Prentice-Hall, 1974; 2nd ed., 1992. Somewhat different selections, both comprehensive and both excellent, in the two editions.

Fischer, J. M., ed. *God, Foreknowledge, and Freedom*. Stanford, CA: Stanford University Press 1989.

Hartshorne, C. *The Logic of Perfection and Other Essays in Neoclassical Metaphysics*. La Salle, IL: Open Court, 1962.

Helm, P., ed. *Divine Commands and Morality*. Oxford: Oxford University Press, 1981.

Hick, J. *An Interpretation of Religion*. New Haven, CT: Yale University Press, 1989.

Kenny, A. *The God of the Philosophers*. Oxford: Clarendon Press, 1979.

Mackie, J. L. *The Miracle of Theism*. Oxford: Clarendon Press, 1982.

Molina, L. de. *On Divine Foreknowledge* (Part IV of the *Concordia*). Translated and with an introduction by A. J. Freddoso. Ithaca, NY: Cornell University Press, 1988.

Phillips, D. Z. *Faith and Philosophical Enquiry*. New York: Schocken, 1970.

Pike, N. *God and Timelessness*. New York: Schocken, 1970.

Pike, N. *Mystic Union*. Ithaca, NY: Cornell University Press, 1992.

Plantinga, A. *The Nature of Necessity*. Oxford: Clarendon Press, 1974.

Plantinga, A., and N. Wolterstorff, eds. *Faith and Rationality*. Notre Dame, IN: University of Notre Dame Press, 1983.

Quinn, P. L. *Divine Commands and Moral Requirements*. Oxford: Clarendon Press, 1978.

Swinburne, R. *The Coherence of Theism*. Oxford: Clarendon Press, 1977.

Swinburne, R. *The Existence of God*. Oxford: Clarendon Press, 1979; 2nd ed., 1991.

Wainwright, W. J. *Mysticism*. Madison: University of Wisconsin Press, 1981.

Wierenga, E. R. *The Nature of God*. Ithaca, NY: Cornell University Press, 1989.

Robert M. Adams (1996)

PHILOSOPHY OF RELIGION [ADDENDUM]

Philosophy of religion has recently focused on a range of issues regarding God: semantic (concerning the meaning of the term *God*), metaphysical (concerning the reality and attributes of God), epistemological (concerning justified belief and knowledge regarding God's reality), and ethical (concerning the bearing of God on personal and social morality and the meaning of life). The entry by Robert M. Adams illustrates some of these issues; longer representative discussions can be found in William E. Mann (2005) and William J. Wainwright (2005). Another area of recent philosophy of religion concerns whether, and if so how, claims regarding God fit with the natural sciences. With growing recognition that the natural sciences are not deterministic, many philosophers have found room for a God who freely acts in history and in human lives (see Draper [2005] and the exchange between Worrall and Ratzsch [2004]).

The term *God* joins *religion* as among the most elusive in English. Its uses are remarkably diverse, and this contributes significantly to the difficulty in settling many apparent disagreements regarding God. If I use the term *God* in one way, and you use it in a different way, then we may find ourselves appearing to disagree about God but actually talking at cross-purposes. For example, if I use the term in such a way that God is capable of suffering, rejection, and even incarnation, but you do not, we will diverge significantly in our questions and answers regarding God. The underlying semantic divergence regarding *God* will yield, sooner or later, divergence in claims deemed acceptable or true regarding God. As a result, philosophical illumination of one's concept of God continues to serve a valuable purpose.

One important semantic lesson is that the term *God* is typically used as a title rather than as a personal name (on which see Pike 1970). Such use can easily avoid begging the question whether God exists. The title *God* can have an intelligible use even if no one satisfies the title. The title *God*, however, does not enjoy just one understanding among its users, even its philosophical users. For instance, some philosophical writers use the title to connote a timeless transcendent agent, whereas others allow for a God in time.

Philosophers of religion have recently pursued the following longstanding question: What cognitive support, if any, is there for the claim that God exists? The question attracts a wide variety of interpretations of *cognitive support*. The most familiar understanding of cognitive support is in terms of evidence, that is, what indicates, even if fallibly and nondeductively, that a proposition is true. Evidence for the claim that God exists indicates, perhaps fallibly and only probabilistically, that it is true that God exists. Evidence can come in differing strengths and can enable a claim to be beyond reasonable doubt.

DIVINE HIDDENNESS

We can now approach the problem of *divine hiddenness* that is beginning to occupy many philosophers of religion: If God exists, why do not all competent people have evidence that makes it beyond reasonable doubt for them that God exists? Many competent people claim not to have adequate evidence (for reasonable belief) that God exists. Some philosophers, however, deny that an all-loving God would be hidden in a way that permits reasonable doubt about God's existence (see Schellenberg 2004).

FREEDOM RESPONSE

Proponents of the Freedom Response to divine hiddenness maintain that God hides to enable people freely to love, trust, and obey God (see Hick 1985, Murray 2002). Seeking to form truly loving relationships with people, God does not coerce people to respond in a particular way. As an all-loving being, God hides to avoid coercing people to respond, and some philosophers hold that this allows for inculpable nonbelief regarding God's existence. The Freedom Response, however, prompts this question: Could not God supply less obscure self-revelation without abolishing our freedom in responding to that revelation? God could, evidently, be significantly less hidden while preserving our freedom to deny that God exists. Some revelations of God's power would overwhelm us in a way that removes our freedom, but the removal of divine hiddenness seems not to require any such overwhelming revelation.

PROPER-MOTIVATION RESPONSE

A second response to divine hiddenness, the Proper-Motivation Response, implies that God hides to discourage a human response based on improper motives (see Pascal 1995, Swinburne 1992). According to this response, God's self-revelation without hiding would prompt us to selfish fear or arrogance. Aiming to discourage such fear and arrogance, God hides and, according to some philosophers, thereby allows for inculpable nonbelief regarding God's existence. However, the Proper-Motivation Response must face this issue: Could not God supply a less obscure self-revelation without eliciting improper motives in our response to that revelation? Must a world where God is less obscure be less susceptible to human pursuit of God that is humble and passionate? The mere fact of less obscurity in God's self-revelation seems not to undermine humble and passionate seeking after God. God could readily promote such seeking in a setting of less obscure divine revelation.

HIDDENNESS AND SIN

A third response to divine hiddenness is that human sinfulness accounts for typical failure to appreciate the evidence of God's reality through creation, history, and conscience (see the discussions in Moroney 2000, Plantinga 2000). Some proponents hold that every competent adult who does not believe that God exists culpably fails to believe and thus that there is no need to explain how

an all-loving God could allow for inculpable nonbelief that God exists, at least among competent adults. The main problem with this response is that it offers no straightforward way for itself to be justified. We seem to lack the needed avenue to evidence to infer that, with regard to every person who does not believe that God exists, that person is culpable, owing to sin, for nonbelief. Some people cannot plausibly be diagnosed so readily.

MULTIPURPOSE RESPONSE

A fourth response to divine hiddenness, the Multipurpose Response, acknowledges that God has various purposes in hiding and that we are not in a position to identify all of God's specific purposes in hiding (see Moser 2002). Divine hiding is sometimes a constructive effort on God's part to encourage (deeper) human focus, longing, and gratitude toward God. God thus aims to take us to our own deepest resources and their ultimate inadequacy, where we acknowledge our needing God at all times. In apprehending God's absence, we can achieve a deeper appreciation of God's presence. According to the Multipurpose Response, occasional divine hiding occurs in the context of God's main desire to have people lovingly know God and thereby to become loving as God is sacrificially loving. According to this response, God's primary aim is to include all people in God's kingdom family as beloved children under God's lovingly righteous guidance. So, God wants humans to love God and thus to treasure God, not just to believe, however reasonably, that God exists. Mere reasonable belief that God exists will not meet God's primary aim for humans. For our own benefit, according to this response, God is after something more profound and more transforming than simple reasonable belief that God exists.

COGNITIVE IDOLATRY

If we reject or neglect transformation toward God's character of sacrificial love, we may be blinded by our own counterfeit "intelligence" and "wisdom." We will then lack the kind of filial obedience and humility appropriate to relating, cognitively and otherwise, to God. We will then have assigned the authority of God to ourselves or to some other part of creation. We would then be guilty of idolatry, the mistake of exchanging God's rightful authority for a false authority. We commit cognitive idolatry when we demand a certain sort of knowledge or evidence of God inappropriate to a filial relationship with God (on which see Moser 2002). We thereby run afoul of God's rightful authority in the cognitive domain. The Multipurpose Response implies that we are in no position to demand that God be revealed in a particular way.

The problem of divine hiddenness has affinities with the traditional problem of evil. One might think of inculpable nonbelief as a certain sort of evil that would not exist if there were a loving God. In any case the problem of divine hiddenness occupies many philosophers of religion in ways that bear on epistemology, semantics, and metaphysics.

See also Hiddenness of God.

Bibliography

Draper, Paul. "God, Science, and Naturalism." In *The Oxford Handbook of Philosophy of Religion*, edited by William J. Wainwright, 272–303. New York: Oxford University Press, 2005.

Hick, John. *Evil and the God of Love.* 2nd ed. London: Macmillan, 1985.

Howard-Snyder, Daniel, and Paul K. Moser, eds. *Divine Hiddenness: New Essays.* New York: Cambridge University Press, 2002.

Mann, William E., ed. *The Blackwell Guide to the Philosophy of Religion.* Malden, MA: Blackwell, 2005.

Moroney, Stephen K. *The Noetic Effects of Sin: A Historical and Contemporary Exploration of How Sin Affects Our Thinking.* Lanham, MD: Lexington Books, 2000.

Moser, Paul K. "Cognitive Idolatry and Divine Hiding." In *Divine Hiddenness: New Essays*, edited by Daniel Howard-Snyder and Paul K. Moser, 120–148. New York: Cambridge University Press, 2002.

Murray, Michael J. "Deus Absconditus." In *Divine Hiddenness: New Essays*, edited by Daniel Howard-Snyder and Paul K. Moser, 62–82. New York: Cambridge University Press, 2002.

Pascal, Blaise. *Pensées and Other Writings.* Translated by Honor Levi. New York: Oxford University Press, 1995.

Peterson, Michael L., and Raymond J. VanArragon, eds. *Contemporary Debates in Philosophy of Religion.* Malden, MA: Blackwell, 2004.

Pike, Nelson. *God and Timelessness.* New York: Schocken Books, 1970.

Plantinga, Alvin. *Warranted Christian Belief.* New York: Oxford University Press, 2000.

Schellenberg, J. L. "Divine Hiddenness Justifies Atheism." In *Contemporary Debates in Philosophy of Religion*, edited by Michael L. Peterson and Raymond J. VanArragon, 30–41. Malden, MA: Blackwell, 2004.

Swinburne, Richard. *Revelation: From Metaphor to Analogy.* Oxford, U.K.: Clarendon Press, 1992.

Wainwright, William J., ed. *The Oxford Handbook of Philosophy of Religion.* New York: Oxford University Press, 2005.

Worrall, John, and Del Ratzsch. "Does Science Discredit Religion?" In *Contemporary Debates in Philosophy of Religion*, edited by Michael L. Peterson and Raymond J. VanArragon, 59–94. Malden, MA: Blackwell, 2004.

Paul K. Moser (2005)

PHILOSOPHY OF RELIGION, HISTORY OF

It is not easy to say when strictly philosophical thought about religion began, for religion has always involved thought or belief of some kind. Even in other fields much of our thought is incipiently philosophical, but this is much more so in an interest that tends to be all-embracing. Religion has always had a cognitive factor, observances of various kinds had a meaning and these would often be of a far-reaching kind, involving beliefs about an afterlife or the influence upon us of beings other than those who inhabit this world. At what stage such beliefs come to be questioned, and not just accepted as a matter of course or tradition, is difficult to determine. But there is evidence of early questioning of this kind, and of the consequent defense and speculation, in some cultures, for example in India. It is a moot point how much of this we would consider strictly philosophical. But it is certain that the period, from the eighth to the fourth century BCE, which saw such an upsurge of intellectual interest and culture simultaneously (and seemingly without much mingling of cultures) in different parts of the world, produced philosophical thought of a very explicit kind, including philosophical reflection about religion.

EASTERN TRADITIONS

HINDUISM. Perhaps the earliest example of philosophical reflection about religion is found in the *Upaniṣads*. These were committed to writing about the eighth century BCE but they reflect much that had been going on before. They are part of the corpus of Indian sacred writings known as the *Vedānta*. Even the earliest and simplest of these contain distinctive and shrewd anticipations of the views about life and the universe that came to be explicitly formulated in the *Upaniṣads*, and it would thus be misleading to say that religious thought began in India with the composition of the *Upaniṣads*. But it is in the body of writings known by that name that we have the first sustained and deliberate thought about religion in a form that has affinity with what we know as philosophy.

The *Upaniṣads* vary much in quality and purpose. There is also much variety within their more strictly philosophical content, but the dominant theme is that of the unity of the universe. This is sometimes thought of in a sense that eliminates all plurality, anticipating much that some mystics have held at later times. For others "the One" is involved in all things in a way which is transcendent and absolute but which leaves it vague what status is to be accorded to finite things. This comes closer to the way God's transcendence has been understood generally in Western thought. But on occasion the *Upaniṣads* venture to be more explicit; some of their themes come close to those of G. W. F. Hegel and of post-Hegelian idealists in the nineteenth century; there is a clear insistence on the interdependence of whole and part in an all-inclusive system of reality, and this led also to speculations about the nature of the system and the function of the parts within it which suggest much that we read in idealist writings in our own times. There are also parts of the *Upaniṣads* that come closer to the Western notion of God as creator of a world of beings distinct from Himself and from one another. This is not unlike Christian theism and, in this respect, some passages of the *Upaniṣads* anticipate much which has since been central in Christian thought.

"The One breathed breathless" is a typically cryptic summing up of much of the teaching of the *Upaniṣads*. What it expresses is the profound and persistent sense of some ultimate nature of reality which escapes our understanding. The world does not wholly explain itself, it is rooted in mystery, and this means more than that there are things which are beyond our particular understanding at a certain time. All things point beyond themselves to a mystery that is in principle beyond our grasp or to some unity of things in the universe which is in some way more complete and final than the interrelations of things as we trace them in our normal understanding of the world. This is the significance of the terms that occur so often in Indian thought—"not this, not that" and "I am that." In this context these reflect a sense of some ultimate transcendent reality which is very vigorously presented in the *Upaniṣads* and whose implications are sometimes very explicitly set forth. It is indeed a very significant fact that there should be so shrewd a philosophical grasp of this notion at such an early date, and this makes the *Upaniṣads* a work of considerable significance for our understanding of religion in general. They contain also much explicit philosophical argument that is highly relevant to philosophical controversies about religion today. This covers many aspects of religion besides those that directly concern the dominant theme of the unity of all reality.

The *Upaniṣads* contain also much reflection upon our practical attitudes. This tends to be of the "world-denying" type and severely ascetic; that is not surprising where the dominant theme is the ultimate oneness of all things. But we find also in the *Upaniṣads* much emphasis on social service, on compassion, virtue, and welfare.

Even if the views adopted on such matters seem to Western eyes too strictly determined by the sense of ultimate union with the whole, and even if it is true, as even some leading Hindus have stressed, that the otherworldly feature of Indian religion has led to apathy and indifference to present concern, there is also much to be learned from the insights we find in the *Upaniṣads,* as in later Indian thought, about the true nature of compassion and selflessness.

DAOISM AND CONFUCIANISM. Not much later than the time the *Upaniṣads* were committed to writing, there appeared in China philosophical teaching and writing about religion which had also at the center of it a sense of some ultimate unity of all reality. This is the essential significance of the doctrines of Dao (expounded in the *Dao-de Jing* traditionally ascribed to Laozi—born 604 BCE—and in later writings like those ascribed to Liezi and Zhuangzi); and this in turn reflects a generally more basic notion that lies behind most early Chinese thought about religion, the idea of a "heaven and earth relationship." What this implies is that there is some character of reality beyond what we find in the world around us but which cannot be explicitly defined or grasped. We can only know it in its requirements and in the sense of some kind of justice operative in the universe at large. The "beyondness" of the power which works for righteousness in this way is deliberately softened; it is almost as if it could only be known from within. But this is itself a very significant fact, and the elusiveness of the influence to which our lives are subject in this way in Chinese thought is no mean indication of the subtleness of their philosophical and religious insights. It has in fact led sometimes to the view that Chinese religion, and especially Confucianism, is entirely a moral or religious system. That impression could easily be derived from *The Analects* of Confucius (551–478 BCE), since they are concerned mainly with ethical and social matters, especially those which concern the appropriate "orders" in society. But Confucianism is in fact extensively determined and overlaid by notions like that of a heaven and earth relationship mentioned above. The distinctive thing, for philosophy, about early Chinese religion and thought about religion is the shrewd sense that the nature of what lies beyond present existence and gives it meaning is best discerned by following a Way or path. The goal is, as it were, best reflected for us in the way it is to be attained. If this is not the whole truth, it is a significant pointer to it.

BUDDHISM. At a slightly later date we have the founding of the Buddhist religion in India. This led to the composition of the Pali Canon, containing, it is alleged, the substance of the teaching of Buddha. The canon was closed in the reign of King Aśoka (273–231 BCE) but not committed to writing until the first century BCE. It is not implausible to conclude that it does reflect fairly closely the actual teaching of the historical Buddha. The Pali Canon is of exceptional interest to philosophers today. It contains acute philosophical thinking, and some incline even to think of Buddhism as being more a philosophical system than a religion. That is certainly a mistaken impression, but we have in Buddhism a very shrewd grasp of the nature of religion as philosophy illuminates it. The purport of this has often been grievously misunderstood, not least in the assumption that Buddhism is a religion without God. The mystery of transcendent being is at the center of Buddhism and has remained so through most of its history and in its many varieties. This may not take quite the same form as in the West or find closely parallel expressions elsewhere, but it is unmistakable to anyone who knows his way about the subject.

A peculiarly distinctive feature of the doctrines of the Pali Canon is the subtle understanding of the difficulty of characterizing a reality that is "beyond" in the sense in which the infinite must be. It is in this context that we are told that we must not say that God exists or that He does not exist. At one point we have a list of sixty-two typical metaphysical questions that must not be asked. This is closely in line with much that has been maintained today in various forms of antimetaphysical philosophy, and it is strange how little appreciation there has been, on the part of recent positivists and agnostics, of how much grist of a sort there is to their mill in the doctrines of the Pali Canon. But it might all the same not be grist they could altogether accept, least of all if they fully grasped its implications in its contexts. For here we have skepticism and positivism with a difference. It springs less from a radically empiricist outlook than from a profound sense of the elusiveness of transcendent reality, and this makes much of the teaching of the Pali Canon uniquely relevant to philosophical controversies about religion today. The account of such matters as Buddha's enlightenment reinforces this, for while this can plausibly in fact be given an atheistic interpretation, it does point suggestively to a subtle grasp of the transformation of present reality through the invasion of it by a reality of an entirely different order which beggars all description. In these and kindred ways the Pali Canon, like related further aspects of Buddhist and of Hindu thought, has close and instructive points of affinity with the cruxes of religious thought today; and this is being increasingly understood by some experts in this field.

PHILOSOPHERS. There has been a long line of impressive Asian thinkers who have attempted variations and refinements on the themes just outlined. Among the most important are Śankara (c. 788) and Rāmānuja (c. 1017). In recent times the more traditionalist type of Hindu thought is well represented in the works of Radhakrishnan, while we have in the very liberal writings of Śri Aurobindo an attempt at reform that is sharply opposed to the objectionably otherworldly aspect of Hinduism and that tries to come to grips with the notion of some divine disclosure which leaves the individual a free and responsible creature.

GREECE

In the Western tradition philosophy begins with the Greeks, and to give a full indication of the course of religious philosophy in the West would be to outline the main continuous progress of philosophy from the Greeks to the present day. For almost all the main philosophical notions and the main divisions of opinion in philosophy (realist, nominalist, idealist, and so forth) have entered into religious controversy in one way or another. The matters that can be noted in the remainder of this entry must thus be highly selective.

PARMENIDES AND HERACLITUS. In Greek thought, as in that of the Orient, there has been a central preoccupation with the problem of the one and the many. In the work of Parmenides this took a very distinctive and influential form. He proceeded by way of analysis of the nature of thought. This he found to involve predication, the affirmation of one thing about something else. To think is to say of an identifiable A that it is B; it is some relating of terms in a system that makes the relations possible. But there is an element of exclusion in such predication. If I say that this book is blue, that precludes its being black, although of course it says nothing about its being round or square, etc. All determination, as it is put, is negation. But does not this raise peculiar problems? For negation seems to be some odd sort of affirmation of what is not the case. It appears thus to deal with what is not. But what is not, Parmenides thought, is just altogether unreal—and no one can think or affirm this. But if negation becomes impossible in these ways, affirmation appears also to stand condemned, and there seems thus to be something radically unsatisfactory about thought itself and about the world as thinking apprehends it. Parmenides concluded that it was a mistake to suppose that the universe was a system of terms in relation, of the many which change and come into being and go, and that we must therefore think of all reality as one undifferentiated whole—conceived by him also as a sphere extending in the same way in all directions. There was given in this way a logical form to a profound religious sense of some ultimate all-embracing unity.

By contrast we find, in the work of other Greek philosophers, an emphatic insistence on the reality of the here and now and the world of variety and change. Protagoras took this to the length of insisting, in anticipation of much later empiricism and relativism, that nothing is real except as it appears. Neither the external world nor our moral ideas have any independent or objective reality; and this view of things received distinctive expression also in the thought of Heraclitus, who insisted that all things were in flux and that "we cannot step twice into the same river." But this was supplemented by Heraclitus by the notion of a pattern of change in which some principle or "logos" was expressed. For him, as for Parmenides, this carried with it a poetically mystical religious undertone. The idea of fire, as a central element, functioned as a symbol of that.

PLATO. In due course Plato was to take up the problems presented in the way described above. He carefully restated and developed the difficulties that troubled Parmenides and Heraclitus and started a program of reconstruction by dealing firmly with the problem of negation. He observed that this does not involve reference to a wholly unreal, to mere nothing. It could be amply provided for within the notion of terms in relation, for to say that something is not is just to say that it is other than something else, to indicate precise location within a system of interrelations. But if thought, as involving determination of this kind, is to function accurately, the system within which it operates must be a strict and tight one. Where is this to be found? Plato thought he found it preeminently in mathematics, and he thus came to regard mathematics as the true propaedeutic to philosophy and a paradigm of its method. The realities which could be properly thought and known had thus to be quasi-mathematical ones, and they consisted of general forms or principles which were real in their own right and bestowed on all other things whatever reality those could properly claim. This left Plato with the hard problem of accounting for the particulars and the changing course of things in the world, and it is not certain that he arrived at a view of this question which contented him. He sometimes spoke of particulars imitating the forms and sometimes of their participating in the reality of the forms, but the individual and unique existent had never more than a problematic place in Plato's philosophy.

Difficulties also arose in yet another way, for even in its more rarefied instances, as in mathematics, there appears to be something essentially inadequate about the process of relating terms in a system. Every relation, including the relation of whole to part, seems to require yet another, or another system, to make it possible. All explanations of one thing in terms of others leave us with further questions and matters unexplained—there is no natural limit to the process of thought—and for the Greeks in particular that which is without proper limit is unsatisfactory—evil, they said, is of the infinite. Plato was led in this way to the notion of some yet more perfect reality, some quite different mode of unified existence in which present imperfect relatedness disappeared, and he held that everything had its reality exhaustively determined by this ultimate nature of the universe. To this he gave the name "the Good," and he declared that, in the sense indicated, this Good was "beyond being and knowledge." He did not mean that it was not real, or a mere notion—far from it. But it could not be given the sort of determinate existence and intelligibility which we ascribe to the sort of entities our minds can understand and encompass.

This is the first explicit formulation in Western thought of the idea of transcendence as it came to dominate much subsequent thinking. It is evident that it owes much, not only to Parmenides' puzzles about predication and nonbeing, but also more directly to Parmenides' insistence on some ultimate all-encompassing unity of being. But it does not involve the elimination of all plurality. When his system seems to involve that, Plato turns back on himself in vigorous protest—as in the famous passage in the *Sophist* where he insists that there must be "place in that which is perfectly real" for "change, life, soul, understanding." The specific forms, metaphysical as well as mathematical, had their place in the one universe in which everything derived its significance from the central all-encompassing reality of the good, and these forms lent some sort of reality to the particulars and to individual lives in the normal sense. The relation of particular to universal and of this to the Good, the ultimate supreme reality, may not have been worked out in a satisfactory way. But at least we have the notion that all we find in the world derives eventually from some one transcendent source in which all imperfection is resolved.

The formulation of these ideas owed much to the influence upon Plato of the Eleusinian mysteries and Orphic cults with which he came into contact—and also to the religiously orientated teaching of Pythagoras. In turn, it affected his teaching on what may appear to be more specifically and recognizably religious conceptions, like his doctrine (in the *Timaeus* and the *Laws*) about the Demiurge who fashions the world according to the eternal patterns and his belief in preexistence and immortality. But it is not primarily in what he says about these more conventionally religious notions that Plato shows his main penetration or had his more abiding influence on religious thought. His notion of a system of forms held together in the transcendent unity of the Good was a more radically instructive and formative notion—although the teaching of the *Laws* and the *Timaeus* prescribed much of the form of later natural theology. It accorded best also with the element of mysticism which tempered the rationalism of his precursor to whom he was deeply indebted, namely Socrates. It is thus in the notion of the Form of the Good that Plato comes nearest to the idea of God in subsequent theism, but his approach to the subject left him no way in which his supreme and central principle of the Good could acquire the character of a person. That was precluded by the severely rationalist nature of Plato's main approach to his task and the consequent exclusion of any kind of revelation of an active concern, which could only be mediated through the actual particulars of life and history that figured in such an ambiguous and unimpressive way in Plato's philosophic outlook.

ARISTOTLE. Our next main landmark is the philosophy of Aristotle. He did not separate the universal as completely as Plato did from the particular, although it is a moot point, still much debated, how ultimate is the difference between Plato and Aristotle here. But the difference did lead in due course to notions of the union of form and matter and of mind as the informing principle of the body by which much subsequent thinking on questions of this kind was directed. For Plato the properly mental side of human life was sharply separated from the body, and along with this went a low estimate of the body—although the body was not thought to be evil, as in much subsequent teaching. The mind is apt to be thought of by Plato as imprisoned in the body and awaiting its release. On the slant given to the subject by Aristotle there is a much closer integration of mind and body and this has been the model for a great deal of later thinking about human personality and the belief in resurrection. The mind is thought to require at least some kind of body, and there are philosophers who regard mind and matter as coextensive in the universe in general. Others have taken the Platonic lead in propounding a very sharp dualism of mind and body.

In strictly religious matters the difference between Plato and Aristotle here seems to become narrow; for although we have no strict equivalent to the Form of the Good in Aristotle or the same insight into the transcendent character of the ultimate religious reality, we do have an "Unmoved Mover" whose relation to the course of events He affects is a somewhat remote and detached one. The God of Aristotle is little involved in the world; it would have been a sign of inferiority and imperfection for Him to be so. This reflected a typically Greek attitude. To be affected by something external to your self is an indication of weakness, and in Aristotle's ideal of the "Great-Minded Man" this is very marked—he will not be cruel to his inferiors just because they are beneath such notice.

The Stoics came later to pride themselves on their independence and self-sufficiency. Likewise the God of Aristotle is absorbed in contemplation of His own perfection; He takes no overt interest in other things, but He moves all other things by attraction. This is in sharp contrast with subsequent Christian teaching and represents the main way in which Christianity is "foolishness to the Greek." But the idea of an Unmoved Mover did nonetheless have a very extensive influence on later religious thought: It provided the model for the famous causal arguments for the existence of God. We have somehow to account for the world, and since we cannot account for it in terms of the way events determine one another within the world, we must have recourse to some altogether different mode of determination and explanation; and in due course this consideration became one of the main ways in which religious thinkers presented the idea that the world as we find it is dependent on some reality which is altogether "beyond" or transcendent. Here, as elsewhere, Aristotle determined very closely the style, if not always the substance, of later religious arguments.

This is evidenced specially in the way some of the further leading notions of Aristotle's philosophy, such as his distinction of potential and actual and his analysis of four types of cause and his notion of substance, became formative ideas in the religious thinking of later Christian times. It is in these ways, more than by very distinctively religious insight, that Aristotle made his main contribution to the philosophy of religion.

There is one further notion of great importance which had its place in Aristotle's system and became subsequently very influential. It is the idea of a law of nature. At times this was understood in a very relativistic way. To "follow nature" was taken to mean abiding by your own whims or impulses. It was sharply contrasted with convention, and the latter came to be much derided in some quarters in the period after Aristotle and Plato in Greece—indeed earlier to some extent among the Sophists. Here we see again, in an extreme form, the ideal of being self-sufficient. This was carried by some of the Cynics and Epicureans and the early Stoics to the extent of trying to "return to nature" and doing without society and its irksome restrictions altogether—a cry that was sounded vigorously again in the seventeenth century. But it came to be realized that this policy led to absurdity and chaos, in personal life and in society; and thus the idea of "Nature" underwent complete transformation—it came to be taught that there was a nature to the universe at large ("Nature" with a capital N, as it were) and that this disclosed itself to men's reason. This led, in the fusion of the idea of law of nature with the Roman idea of a "law of nations," to the conception of a number of basic moral principles which were bound up with our rational nature and which, for many, further owed their firmness and objectivity to their foundation in the ultimate nature of the universe. This notion had a long and varied history and played a very important part in Christian accounts of morality and its relation to religion. It has a close affinity with the teaching of early Chinese religions and the notion of some power from beyond the world working for righteousness within it and prescribing our basic moral principles. Reflection upon this affinity can be very fruitful in seeking the way forward with such problems in the way they present themselves today.

EARLY AND MEDIEVAL CHRISTIANITY

The thought of early Christian times was extensively affected by Greek philosophy. This is evident even in the New Testament itself, not only in the way its authors write about matters like soul and body, but also in the central theme of "the Word" or Logos which became flesh. The Greek notion of Logos provided the basic concept in terms of which the doctrine of the Incarnation was to be understood. Directly, the concept of Logos came into philosophical thought in Christian times from the Stoics, for whom it meant originally an immanent World-Soul. But it was later combined with the Platonic idea of *nous* and so was conceived as acting in accordance with archetypal patterns. The basic problem was how is it possible to have knowledge of a strictly transcendent being, and for this a solution was sought in terms of an intermediary, in this case a logos, which was also induced in due course to fill other roles and help in the solution of further problems. These procedures came into Christian thought in the first place through the work of a gifted Jewish

philosopher of the first century, namely Philo, and it had a prominent place in the subsequent Christology of formative thinkers like the Alexandrians, of whom Origen has most interest for philosophers. But what we have in the main during early Christian centuries is not so much philosophy of religion in the strict sense as theological writings that make extensive use of philosophical concepts. There were also some theologians of this period, as there have been of later times, who resented the intrusion of philosophy into the domain of faith. Of these the most outstanding was Tertullian.

The main exception to the normal course of thought in the early Christian period was Neoplatonism. Here we revert again to a profound sense of the Oneness of the Universe in a way that puts particulars and plurality in jeopardy, as they had been to some extent in the philosophy of Plato. But some account must be given of particulars, and there was developed in this way the difficult notion of emanation. God is the ultimate unity and He transcends all the categories of thought, but finite beings exist in the form of some falling away from the original perfection. This comes to terms in some fashion with the facts of finite existence and the reality of evil that occupied the minds of thinkers of this period a great deal. But it is very hard to make sense of the notion of emanation without calling in question the all-embracing nature of the one ultimate reality. The insistence on the latter notion did, however, influence the course of mystical thought and practice extensively. It also led, as in the case of Oriental mysticism, to attempts to draw away altogether from our present existence, with its limitations and evil, and to pass beyond the world of intellect as well as sense into total union with ineffable Being.

In sharp contrast to this teaching we have the position of thinkers who reflected anew on the significance of the Hebrew-Christian doctrine of creation. The Hebrews had come early to understand the elusive and transcendent character of God, and this had found very remarkable expression in parts of the Old Testament, the most famous passage here being the story of Moses at the burning bush. But this carried with it in Hebrew thought a subtle appreciation of the way a true discernment of God's transcendence required the recognition of our own distinctness as beings dependent on God. This sharpened, however, the question how such beings could in any way come to know God. The Hebrew answer was in terms of God's disclosure of Himself in history and experience, and this was deepened and extended in specifically Christian claims about the work and person of Christ. In this context the problem of revelation becomes a crucial one, and it has remained at the center of Christian philosophy at all times except when insistence on the distinctness of faith precluded all rational consideration of it.

AUGUSTINE. Preoccupation with the way human beings, being finite, can come to know an Infinite Being lies at the center of the more specifically philosophical parts of the writings of Augustine. In his attack on the problem Augustine gives prominence to our reflection on what we find our own souls to be like as a clue to our understanding of the relation of God to the world. He set the pattern for much subsequent reflection on our own nature and started a concern for the inward aspect of personality which persisted through formative later thinkers, such as René Descartes and George Berkeley, to such nineteenth-century theologians as F. R. Tennant and the phenomenologists and existentialists of the present day. This side of Augustine's achievement is, however, often obscured by another. For although he emphasized the distinctness and freedom of finite beings, he came in another way to put these ideas in considerable jeopardy. In seeking to account for the redemptive work of Christ he posited the notion of an initial abuse of man's freedom leading to subsequent enslavement to sin. This gave considerable impetus to a doctrine of the Fall which, although not prominent in this form in earlier Christian times, became a central theme of much later theology and Christian profession of faith. The personal experiences of Augustine and his African background are thought to have greatly influenced his view in these respects, and there have certainly been voices, like those of Pelagius in his own time and Abelard later, raised in sharp protest against the rigors of the Augustinian doctrine of humanity's sin. The doctrine of the Fall has also been invoked to simplify the problem of our knowledge of God by blunting the strictly epistemological character of the problem; this came about through emphasis on the way our own allegedly corrupted nature made us spiritually blind and stood in the way of a vision of God. In the same context the idea of a law of nature became the idea of what is practicable in the present sinful state of humankind and society by contrast with the ideal law of God. This distinction was given much prominence by St. Augustine and has been reaffirmed, in the sense in which he understood it, by his most notable followers to the present day.

ANSELM. The question of particulars and universals became prominent again in the controversy of realism and nominalism in the early Middle Ages. It had many implications for religious thought. For example, the view that individuals do not exist in themselves was thought to culminate in pantheism in the sense that "all visible things pass into intellectual, and intellectual into God." This period also saw further attempts to provide a rational defense of the faith, although without denying that faith had a firm foundation of its own. An outstanding feature of this activity in philosophical thinking is the formulation of the Ontological Argument by St. Anselm. This was intended to show that sound understanding of the idea of God yields us the necessity of His existence. The idea of God, it was urged, is the idea of a being than whom nothing greater can be conceived. But a being that does not exist is inferior to one who has the additional attribute of existence. Many changes have since been rung on this argument and it is being much canvassed at the present day.

THOMAS AQUINAS. The most impressive achievements of the Middle Ages in religious thought came about initially through the work of Muslim scholars (Mohammad al-Ghazali and Averroes in particular) who were much concerned about the question of reason and revelation in their own faith. Among these there had also been preserved important works of Greek philosophy, especially those of Aristotle, which were not properly known by Christian scholars. There came about in this way a revival of the study of Aristotle and a new concern about the way a transcendent being could be known by limited finite ones. This culminated in the very comprehensive work of St. Thomas Aquinas, which ranged over most religious questions, seeking a synthesis of religious claims and established philosophical principles. It set up firmly one of the main forms of natural theology. For Thomas this covered two things. First we have the attempt to establish the existence of God by argument. This took the form of the famous "Five Ways." The first three of these are variations on the Cosmological Argument, as the term came to be used in due course. They seek to pass from the limited or contingent nature of finite things to an ultimate First Cause or Ground. The least elaborate, and also the most plausible, is the third way, which proceeds directly from the contingency of the world to its absolute Source without presupposing any particular view of cause and effect as we understand it. This argument, in one form or another, has been central to a great deal of subsequent philosophy of religion. Many hold today that it gets us at least very near the truth about the initial relation of God to the world and the way we know this. The other two "Ways" depend on notions of a scale of being and value and on the adaptation of things to their purposes, which are at least alien to the way we normally think about the world today—though they have their defenders.

The second prong of natural theology was that which sought, through an extremely subtle and cautious doctrine of analogy, to determine the attributes of God more precisely. It was urged that we cannot know God as He is in Himself, we can only know that He must be; and because God is a transcendent Ground of all things, He cannot be mirrored in the world He has made in the way an effect normally tells us something about its cause. Thomas and his followers were therefore well aware of the need to move very circumspectly here, and what they maintained was that God must be thought to have certain attributes, like goodness or power, in whatever way is necessary for Him to be the Author of those in the form in which they appear in the created world. In presenting this doctrine some very careful distinctions were drawn between various types of analogies. The main difficulty which this approach involves is that of determining whether anything of substance is added in this way to what is originally claimed in regarding God as a transcendent Being. There is in any case needed in addition extensive recourse to revealed truth to supply the particular affirmations of a faith like the Christian one. These truths of faith could not, according to Thomas, conflict with the truths of reason, but they go beyond them.

WILLIAM OF OCKHAM. The most formidable opponent of natural theology was William of Ockham, who questioned the ability of natural reason to discover in any measure the inscrutable will of God or reduce the mystery of transcendent being. His methods of procedure, involving the reduction of our postulates to the minimum that the facts require, anticipates many features of modern thought where skepticism about affirmations and alleged entities which pass beyond the facts of sensible experience and science is sometimes combined with a dogmatic affirmation of faith in which reason plays no part.

MODERN PHILOSOPHY

Outstanding formative philosophers of the modern period, roughly the last five hundred years, were of two main sorts, rationalists and empiricists. The former, including Descartes, Benedict de Spinoza, and Gottfried Wilhelm Leibniz, had great confidence in the power of reason alone to establish ultimate metaphysical truths.

RATIONALISM. Descartes claimed to prove his own existence by the power of reason alone and drew a sharp distinction between mind and body. He then sought, by severely rational arguments, to prove the existence of God. Two of these arguments invoke the causal principle,

although they require also our having the idea of God; the third is a special form of the Ontological Argument; it contends that if we think of a being who does not exist we are withholding from our conception of it a "perfection," namely existence, which is essential to our conception of a perfect being. These arguments are not usually thought to succeed as they stand, but they can nonetheless be thought to be significant as indications of the insight into there having to be an ultimate reality in which essence and existence are one. They also illustrate the futility of seeking to establish the existence of such a being by arguments involving consideration of what limited finite things are like. Descartes's causal arguments are particularly illuminating in this way, as he imports into his premises, at every step in an elaborate argument, certain considerations derived from the notion of an infinite being which it is the aim of the argument to defend.

A further feature of Descartes's work is the insistence on the freedom of the individual—"liberty of indifference." This is bound up with the insistence on the distinctness of persons as nonmaterial entities. The same theme is taken up in Leibniz's monadology, in which every being is a distinct mental monad. But the genuineness of our freedom is jeopardized by Leibniz in his doctrine of preestablished harmony and the way each monad consistently unfolds in its history some destiny which its own nature prescribes for it from the start. In the ingenious monistic system of Spinoza freedom comes to be thought of in terms of accepting our place and destiny in the universe with adequate understanding and forbearance rather than in the form of genuine "liberty of indifference." Descartes's doctrine of the self as a distinct mental substance has been subjected to considerable criticism from time to time, not least at the present day. But there are many also who consider it an essential ingredient in a sound understanding of the relations of God to man and who stress, as did Descartes, the "interiority" and unextended character of the mind.

EMPIRICISM. Empiricism inclines to skepticism and is severely skeptical in its stricter forms. The great British empiricists did not all hold to their principle with the same consistency. We find John Locke departing from his avowed aim of showing that knowledge derives from sense impressions, not only in his theory of knowledge and his account of material and mental substances, but also in his expressly religious thought where he claimed, for example, that the existence of One Infinite Mind can be proved with the same certainty as we find in mathematics. There is much in fact in Locke's presentation of the causal argument in Chapter X, Book IV, of his *Essay concerning Human Understanding* that has close relevance to controversies about the subject today. Likewise Berkeley, while dispensing with the notion of independent material substances, found in his account of the world of nature as dependent on its being perceived a firm foundation for the belief in a Divine Being on whose Mind the whole world of nature depends. To Berkeley we owe also a subtle appreciation of the distinctiveness of the way minds are known and the essential inwardness of personality which is so central a feature of religious philosophy today.

David Hume, however, was little attracted to these compromises and, although he confessed to some admiration for the argument which seeks to prove God's existence from the evidence of design in the universe, he adhered generally to a ruthlessly empiricist position. This involved total skepticism about God, immortality, and all properly religious notions. Hume contended that religion had started in a thoroughly naturalistic way with the personification of natural objects and so forth and that only at a late and sophisticated stage of culture did people arrive at some unification of religious notions and the belief in one God. His presentation of this view is delightfully lucid and it set the pattern for much of the anthropological treatment of religion later in the nineteenth century. In Hume's *Dialogues* there are also canvassed some of the main arguments that are used to support or reject religious beliefs, ranging from the general belief in God to belief in miracle.

KANT'S CRITICISMS. The "critical" philosophy of Immanuel Kant sought to arrest the skepticism of Hume without retreating to the strict rationalism of Descartes and his followers. Kant's main contention was that the sort of experience of the world which we undoubtedly have presupposes a unified world of objects presented to an abiding subject. The modes of unification thereby involved, the necessary conditions of experience, provided a new basis for confident belief in causality and substance, though not in the same sense as that of Descartes; but it was also implied that knowledge is confined to the world of our experience and the principles involved in this, sometimes thought to be imposed by the mind itself. This did certainly yield us the belief in an unobservable subject of experience, but nothing could be known of this beyond its being required to account for the sort of knowledge we have of the external world. There was also a tendency to isolate this inner self so completely from the external world of known reality that the functioning of the "pure self," especially as will or active agent, became very hard to conceive and set for Kant some of his main difficulties, especially in his ethics.

The limitations involved in the alleged "critical" account of knowledge were, however, extensively corrected by Kant in his insistence that we have certain grounds for "faith," which supplements what we can strictly know. These grounds of faith are found in the operation of our practical reason or moral awareness which sets before us certain moral obligations, largely in the form of strictly universal rules, which have in turn far-reaching implications. It was urged, for example, that there is a moral requirement that justice be rewarded, but that, since the ethical motive would be impaired if we set our own happiness as the aim of moral actions, God must be postulated to guarantee the eventual relation between happiness and virtue in the universe. Freedom and immortality were similar postulates of practical reason. These contentions have been subjected to much criticism, and doubt has been cast on the success of even the limited undertaking of postulating certain principles of a unified world of experience. Religious thinkers have urged that "faith" in its Kantian form has little in common with properly religious faith and that the severely rationalist character of the appeal to postulates of practical reason neglects the distinctively religious element in religious belief. On the other hand the prominence given to moral considerations in religious thought has been widely welcomed, and many writers have sought to provide versions of the moral and teleological arguments which are not open to the difficulties of those provided by Kant.

IDEALIST RESPONSES TO KANT. A great deal of post-Kantian philosophy was concerned with the gap in the Kantian system between the world as we apprehend it and the ultimate or "noumenal" reality of the world as it really is. For Kant these tended to be two separate worlds, but many thought this unsatisfactory and sought in various ways to understand the ultimate reality or "thing-in-itself" as some completion of the world as we find it—a notion that is in many ways anticipated in some of Kant's own reflections. There were thus initiated various metaphysical enterprises concerned especially with finding within the world of our own experience some reliable clue to the nature of the universe as a whole. The most influential of these was that of Hegel, who found the ultimate principle of reality in reason. We cannot exhaustively understand the universe but the universe is in principle capable of being understood through and through as a system where everything has its place and nature determined by rational necessity. Others (like

Arthur Schopenhauer) gave to will the preeminent place as a metaphysical clue.

There were many variations on these themes in the nineteenth century, including the work of British idealists such as Thomas Hill Green, F. H. Bradley, and Bernard Bosanquet and of American thinkers such as Josiah Royce. Idealism became the dominant philosophical view, and within the perspective of it many views were advanced about the relation of God to the world, taking distinctive features of our own experience as the clues to what lies beyond it. This tended to leave nothing essentially or irreducibly mysterious about religion. But the leading post-Hegelian idealist, namely Bradley, argued that there were radically contradictory features of present experience which implied that the ultimate nature of the universe was suprarational. And with this emphasis we come back again to the idea of some transcendent reality on which everything depends in some way that in principle we cannot understand. It was argued also, in criticism of the more rationalist type of idealism, that it left little room for the distinctness and freedom of the individual, since all beings came to be regarded as elements or "phases" or "appearances" of an ultimate all-inclusive system—and in the same way the problem of evil became a very acute one for idealist defenders of religion.

NATURAL THEOLOGY. In correction of the rationalist temper of idealist philosophy many voices were raised from time to time during the nineteenth century, stressing the mystery and elusiveness of religion. The most impressive and influential of these were those of Friedrich Schleiermacher and Rudolf Otto, the former giving prominence to the "feeling of absolute dependence" in religion and the latter stressing our sense of the holy or the numinous, the *mysterium tremendum et fascinans*. Otto claimed, in sharp contrast to the earlier naturalistic theories of Hume and his nineteenth-century followers, that there was ample evidence of this sense of the holy in the rawest beginnings of religion and he sought to describe the way it became schematized and moralized to give riper and more distinctive forms of religion. Other writers sought to correct the somewhat a priori approach of idealist philosophers by resorting to what they described rather incorrectly as an empiricist defense of religion that consisted in drawing out the implications of various features of our experience. This was the form that much natural theology took in the late nineteenth century, exemplified especially in the work of F. R. Tennant. Even if this approach fails to do justice to the factor of transcendence in religion, it could nonetheless be thought to have provided many of the ingredients of a sound understanding of religious experience.

Toward the close of the nineteenth century and early in the twentieth century there appeared, however, a strong reaction against what was thought to be the facile and too liberal rationalization of religious philosophy at that time. This found expression most of all in the insistence, by Karl Barth and other eminent theologians such as Reinhold Niebuhr and Emil Brunner, on the "wholly other" character of God and the need, as they understood it, to fall back on a dogmatically orthodox theological position in which the central place was accorded to the idea of an exclusive revelation. This presented considerable difficulties, not least on the ethical side where elementary ethical principles seemed to be put in serious jeopardy. But it did give prominence again to the idea of God's transcendence, which is a focus for controversies about religion among philosophers of the present day.

PHILOSOPHY OF RELIGION. The philosophy of our time has become extensively empiricist again. This trend had been preparing for some time in America in aspects of the work of William James and Charles Sanders Peirce. But it gathered its momentum in the work of the Vienna circle and those, such as Ludwig Wittgenstein, who extended its influence in England, notably at Cambridge and Oxford. Recent empiricism represents a sharp reaction against the ambitious and occasionally turgid speculations of nineteenth-century metaphysical philosophers. It set a premium on clarity and claimed to be tough-minded and down to earth. Its policy was extensively that of Hume, and it reflected much of the skepticism of the period subsequent to World War I. To Hume's empiricism was added, however, an alleged linguistic technique which was intended, in its main early forms at least, to account for the persistence of seemingly bold nonempirical notions, like the idea of the soul or of God, by ascribing them to confusions engendered by misleading forms of speech. This set off a spate of philosophical criticism of religion aimed at showing that its basic conceptions were logically improper. This is sometimes known as the linguistic veto. A desperate attempt to save religion was undertaken by several other empiricist philosophers who seemed willing to sacrifice the strictly nonempirical elements in religion and reinterpret the main features of religious belief in terms of present experience—for example, by regarding religion as a matter of satisfying certain distinctive emotions or by identifying it, in essentials, with ethics.

There have been considerable recent variations on this theme of the attenuation of religious faith. The same method of apologetics has appealed also to many theological writers, some equating religion with morality and others finding the essence of religion in a certain depth and earnestness of our own activities. The most outstanding of these theologians have relied heavily on the work of existentialist philosophers who have brought into prominence the importance of certain searching present experiences and of deep inner aspects of them. Neither they nor their existentialist mentors are very systematic or lucid thinkers, and it is thus not very clear how far they mean to go in interpreting religion in terms of our human experience in the here and now.

RELIGIOUS EXISTENTIALISM. A typically elusive representative of this kind of philosophical theology was Paul Tillich. It is never quite clear whether he meant by his central conceptions of "the Ground of Being" and the "New Being" a transcendent reality (or some impact of this upon us) or some profound depth of our own experience and natures. Nor is it clear how far this skepticism about traditional beliefs, reinforced by much skepticism in the field of biblical scholarship, is meant to go; for the writers in question often give expression to seemingly skeptical views in the language of orthodoxy. The position is not made easier by considerable borrowings from phenomenological thinkers like Martin Heidegger who combine unusual perceptiveness with a veritable genius for elaborate and obscure modes of utterance.

LINGUISTIC APOLOGETIC. Equally uncertain and difficult is the work of certain more strictly philosophical thinkers who take their start from a new emphasis in linguistic philosophy derived largely from the later and much modified form of Wittgenstein's work. They stress the open texture and varieties of language and, on this basis, press the claims of religious language to a status not impaired by its not complying with the conditions of ordinary language or scientific language. This leaves the door open for a cautious but less skeptical approach to religion. But the question remains how much is accomplished unless we indicate how the distinctive language of religion is to be understood and what criteria may be applied to it. There is a tendency for some linguistic apologists of religion to be content with stressing the alleged oddity of religious language and thereby also to conflate major notions, like freedom and immortality, and to leave it very unclear in what sense the various affirmations made in religion are to be understood. These writers also tend to draw much support from existentialist insistence on the importance of formative and challenging present experiences. The details of their work, as in the case of I. T. Ramsey, is illuminating and imaginative, but it is not clear how much it can accomplish until their kind of sensitivity to religious language is accompanied by rigorous heed to the centrality and discipline of the more strictly epistemological considerations.

RESPONSE TO EMPIRICIST CRITICISMS. Epistemological considerations have again been uppermost in the work of a further body of recent philosophers who have taken up the challenge of empiricist and linguistic critics more boldly. They have welcomed the challenge in particular as a way of sharpening the question of the place of evidence in religious belief. They maintain that evidence is not strictly relevant to the question of the existence of God; we apprehend the necessity of God's existence in the contingent character of everything else. This, they maintain, is the element of truth misleadingly presented in the traditional arguments. Pioneers of this position in recent philosophy are Austin Farrer and E. L. Mascall, while another severe critic of linguistic empiricism, C. A. Campbell, has arrived, by way of some modifications of Bradley's thought, at a not dissimilar renewal of the emphasis on the suprarational character of the object of religious worship.

This takes the sting out of the challenge, given sharpness by John Wisdom and later by Antony Flew, to indicate what would count for or against the existence of God. The answer, it is said, is "nothing," for we are not here accounting for the way the world goes or some particular feature of it, but for there being anything at all. The question "Why is there something rather than nothing?" is regarded even by some skeptical philosophers as a significant one. This new appreciation of the uniqueness of the idea of God and of God's relation to the world has opened the way also for subtler understanding of religions other than Christianity, especially Buddhism, and with this has come a renewed philosophical interest in world religions. This is a more discerning interest than the one motivated by superficial notions of syncretism at the turn of the century.

But there has been accentuated in turn the problem of particular religious affirmations. Some have attacked this afresh through new presentations of the traditional doctrine of analogy; some, like A. C. Ewing, persist in a cautious restatement of idealism; others turn to fresh examination of the nature and sanction of religious imagery. There has also been much recourse to the analogy with our knowledge of one another, and in this context it has been thought, by the present writer among others, that a fresh examination of the nature of religious experience and of features of it that could afford justification of the claim to revelation in Scriptures and history, holds the best promise of a solution of the epistemological problems of religious faith. Some who follow this course are apt to lapse from a steady epistemological study, which their initial problem requires, into a psychological or phenomenological one; but when they do so, in the case of Gabriel Marcel for example, they may nonetheless provide highly relevant material for those who manage to keep the epistemological task steadily in mind. That may also be supplemented by the perceptive analysis of those whose concern is not mainly religious or who may be strictly atheistic like Jean-Paul Sartre. The work of Maurice Merleau-Ponty is thought by many to be especially suggestive and illuminating in this way.

Consideration of religious experience may thus prove the point of convergence of many of the approaches to religion which hold most promise today of deepening our understanding of its perennial problems. Advances in fields other than strictly religious studies, most of all perhaps the study of paranormal phenomena, will have much relevance to the present tasks of the philosophy of religion; and some writers, such as H. H. Price, C. D. Broad and C. J. Ducasse, have considered closely the implications of matters like paranormal phenomena for our general view of the world and for relevance to specific questions like immortality. Psychological studies, notably those that investigate the unconscious and the unconscious matrix of conscious imagery, have considerable relevance to the philosophers' problems. A further major preoccupation of those who study the philosophy of religion today is the relation of ethics to religion, not only in the form of fresh examination of the problems of freedom and grace or of variations on the traditional "moral argument," but also in reflections on the role of moral experience within the totality of religious experience. There have likewise been fresh examinations of the claims made for mystical experience, and one writer at least, namely W. T. Stace, is prepared to defend a very extreme form of monism as the ultimate truth about the universe to which mystical experience points. Other philosophers, including some such as J. N. Findlay who took their orientation at one time from Wittgensteinian philosophy, are beginning to embark on bold—too bold?—speculative ventures in the field of religious thought.

In these ways the philosophy of religion, of which fashionable philosophers fought very shy about twenty years ago, has become again one of the liveliest interests of philosophers. It is of considerable significance also that some of the major themes of contemporary fiction, including those that seem to have little overtly to do with religion, are found to bear closely on aspects of religion that have most importance for the philosophy of religion. In the blend of new philosophical investigations of religion, sharpened in the challenge and discipline of tough-minded philosophy, and a perceptive understanding of contemporary cultures (in their limitations as well as in their achievements) in other regards may be found a means of genuine advance in the life of religion itself which will enable it to have its place effectively in the sophistications of a developing culture and rapidly changing state of society.

See also Islamic Philosophy; Jewish Philosophy.

Bibliography

Allen, E. L. *Existentialism from Within*. London: Routledge and Paul, 1953.

Blackham, H. J. *Six Existentialist Thinkers*. London: Routledge and Paul, 1952.

Campbell, C. A. *Selfhood and Godhood*. London and New York, 1957.

Ewing, A. C. *Idealism*. London: Methuen, 1934.

Farrer, Austin. *Finite and Infinite*. 2nd ed. Naperville, IL, 1959.

Ferré, Frederick. *Language, Logic, and God*. New York: Harper, 1961.

Flew, A. G. N., and Alasdair MacIntyre, eds. *New Essays in Philosophical Theology*. London: SCM Press, 1955.

Hartshorne, Charles. *The Logic of Perfection*. La Salle, IL: Open Court, 1962.

Henson, H. H. *Christian Morality*. Oxford: Clarendon Press, 1936.

Hepburn, Ronald. *Christianity and Paradox*. London: Watts, 1958.

Hick, John. *Philosophy of Religion*. Englewood Cliffs, NJ: Prentice-Hall, 1963.

Hughes, E. R., and K. Hughes. *Religions in China*. London, 1950.

James, E. O. *The Worship of the Sky God*. London: Universtiy of London, Athlone Press, 1963.

Jayatilleke, K. N. *Early Buddhist Theory of Knowledge*. London, 1963.

Knowles, David. *Evolution of Medieval Thought*. London: Longmans, 1962.

Lewis, H. D. *Our Experience of God*. London: Allen and Unwin, 1959.

Lewis, H. D. "Survey of the History of Religion." *Philosophical Quarterly* (15) (April 1954) and (16) (July 1954).

Lewis, H. D. *Teach Yourself the Philosophy of Religion*. London, 1965.

MacGregor, Geddes, and J. W. Robb. *Readings in Religious Philosophy*. Boston: Houghton Mifflin, 1962.

Mascall, E. L. *Existence and Analogy*. London, 1949.

Mascall, E. L. *He Who Is*. London: Longmans, Green, 1943.

Mascall, E. L. *The Secularization of Christianity*. London: Darton, Longman and Todd, 1965.

Mascall, E. L. *Words and Images*. New York: Ronald Press, 1957.

Mitchell, Basil, ed. *Faith and Logic*. London: Allen and Unwin, 1957.

Moore, Edward C. *American Pragmatism*. New York: Columbia University Press, 1961.

Murti, T. R. V. *The Central Philosophy of Buddhism*. London: Allen and Unwin, 1955.

Paton, H. J. *The Modern Predicament*. London: Allen and Unwin, 1955.

Perry, R. B. *Present Philosophical Tendencies*. London: Longmans, Green, 1929.

Philosophy (122) (July 1957). On empiricism and religion.

Pringle-Pattison, Andrew Seth. *The Idea of God*. Oxford: Clarendon Press, 1917.

Ramsey, Ian. *Prospect for Metaphysics*. New York: Philosophical Library, 1961.

Ramsey, Ian. *Religious Language*. London: SCM Press, 1957.

Rogers, A. K. *A Student's History of Philosophy*. New York, 1940.

Rose, H. J. *Ancient Greek Religion*. London: Hutchinson's University Library, 1948.

Slater, R. H. L., and H. D. Lewis. *World Religions and World Community*. New York: Columbia University Press, 1963.

Smart, Ninian. *Historical Selections in the Philosophy of Religion*. New York: Harper and Row, 1962.

Smart, Ninian. *Reasons and Faiths*. London: Routledge and Paul, 1958.

Smith, John E. *Philosophy of Religion*. New York: Macmillan, 1965.

Taylor, A. E. "Theism," in *Encyclopedia of Religion and Ethics*, edited by James Hastings. New York, 1959.

Wolfson, H. A. *Religious Philosophy*. Cambridge, MA: Belknap Press of Harvard University, 1961.

H. D. Lewis (1967)

PHILOSOPHY OF RELIGION, HISTORY OF [ADDENDUM]

A remarkable revival of interest in philosophy of religion occurred during the final third of the twentieth century. The demise of logical positivism had freed philosophers of religion from their preoccupation with responding to its verificationist challenge to the meaningfulness of religious language. A narrow empiricism in epistemology ceased to play a foundational role in the philosophy of the Anglophone world. The philosophical community became more pluralistic in its views about the methods and assumptions that may fruitfully be brought to bear on the study of religion. At the same time, the philosophical community was growing in size, largely as a result of the rapid expansion of systems of higher education in countries such as the United States. As a result of these developments, philosophical reflection on religion came to be conducted by more philosophers with a greater variety of points of view than at any time in the past. Many philosophers approached religion from within well-established traditions of thought such as pragmatism, process philosophy, phenomenology, and Thomism. Remarks on religion in the later works of Ludwig Wittgenstein inspired discussions of religious forms of life. Some philosophers cast fresh light on classical topics in philosophical theology, whereas others focused on issues that contemporary culture has made salient. This entry provides a brief survey of some of the highlights of this flowering of philosophy of religion.

Natural theology, the enterprise of giving arguments for God's existence, was among the classical topics that attracted attention. Alvin Plantinga (2000) constructed a modal ontological argument that resembles earlier arguments discussed by Charles Hartshorne and Norman Malcolm, and William Rowe (1975) set forth a cosmological argument that resembles the version proposed by Samuel Clarke. Both of these arguments are clearly valid. However, as Plantinga and Rowe point out, each of them depends on a premise that one may rationally reject, and so neither is a successful proof of God's existence. Richard Swinburne (1979) produced a probabilistic cumulative case argument for God's existence. Making use of Bayesian reasoning, he tried to show that each one of several factors such as cosmic order, the existence of consciousness, and religious experience increases the probability of God's existence. According to Swinburne, the cumulative effect of all these factors is to render theism slightly more probable than not.

A controversial challenge to the view that belief in God is irrational or in some other way improper unless it is supported by arguments or other propositional evidence was mounted by Plantinga. Many theists do not, in fact, base their belief in God on such propositional evidence. Plantinga argued that such basic belief in God can be epistemically proper under certain conditions, typically conditions pertaining to how the belief is directly grounded in experience. In later work, he has gone on to contend that basic belief in God can have a good deal of warrant, which is the epistemic characteristic enough of which converts true belief into knowledge, despite its lack of support by arguments or other propositional evidence. Plantinga describes the position for which he has argued as Reformed epistemology because he finds it suggested in the writings of John Calvin. Influenced by Wittgenstein and Thomas Reid, William Alston (1991) argued for the practical rationality of engaging in a nonsensory perceptual practice whose outputs are beliefs about how God is manifested in the experience of the practitioner. Both Plantinga and Alston espouse views in religious epistemology according to which belief in God can have positive epistemic status even in the absence of a successful natural theology.

Of course evil constitutes a potential defeater for the positive epistemic status that theistic belief can acquire from experience. According to the logical problem of evil, the existence of an omnipotent, omniscient, and perfectly good God is logically inconsistent with the existence of evil. In his celebrated free will defense, Plantinga (2000) argued convincingly that the existence of God is consistent with the existence of evil The main focus of debate subsequently shifted to the evidential problem of evil, according to which evils of a certain sort count as evidence that renders the existence of God improbable. An influential version of this problem formulated by Rowe (1975) started from the notion of pointless suffering, which is defined as suffering an omnipotent and omniscient being could have prevented without losing some greater good or permitting some evil equally bad or worse. Rowe maintained that instances of suffering known to us are apparently pointless and hence count as compelling evidence against the existence of God. In an attempt to rebut Rowe, Stephen Wykstra argued against concluding that such instances of suffering are apparently pointless. On his view, even if such suffering has a point because without it God cannot secure some greater good, it is very likely that its point is completely beyond our ken.

As a result of the increasing religious pluralism of modern societies, religious diversity has become a salient threat to the positive epistemic status of conflicting systems of religious belief. Major world religions disagree about even such fundamental issues as whether the ultimate religious reality is a personal deity or an impersonal absolute. John Hick proposed that our response to this situation should be to adopt the hypothesis that all the world religions are somehow in touch with a single noumenal reality to which no substantive human concepts apply. On this hypothesis, the ultimates of different world religions are equally real but merely phenomenal realities, all of which are in part products of human cultures and traditions. Opponents of Hick's proposal, such as Alston and Plantinga, have argued for the rationality of remaining within the belief systems of particular religions despite the negative impact religious diversity has on the epistemic status of such beliefs, at least for those who are sufficiently aware of the conflict to which this diversity gives rise.

Important work has also been done on several other topics. One example is the metaphysics of theism. Philosophical reflection on God's nature has produced new accounts of such divine attributes as omniscience, omnipotence, eternity, and simplicity. Another example is religious ethics. John Finnis has developed a natural law theory influenced by the thought of Thomas Aquinas; Alasdair MacIntyre has argued in favor of moral inquiry within the tradition of Aquinas; Robert Adams and Philip Quinn have formulated and defended divine command theories of moral obligation. John Caputo and Merold Westphal have played a significant role in drawing to the attention of Anglophone philosophers the religious implications of the writings of major French and German thinkers. And promising first steps have been taken toward feminist and comparative philosophies of religion.

See also Islamic Philosophy; Jewish Philosophy.

Bibliography

Adams, Marilyn M., and Robert M. Adams, eds. *The Problem of Evil.* Oxford and New York: Oxford University Press, 1990. Reprints important contributions to the discussion of logical and evidential problems of evil.

Alston, William P. *Perceiving God: The Epistemology of Religious Experience.* Ithaca and London: Cornell University Press, 1991. Defends the rationality of engagement in nonsensory perceptual religious practices of belief formation.

Long, Eugene, T. *Twentieth Century Western Philosophy of Religion: 1900–2000.* Dordrecht: Kluwer, 2000. Offers a comprehensive historical account of Western philosophy of religion in the twentieth century.

Plantinga, Alvin. *Warranted Christian Belief.* Oxford and New York: Oxford University Press, 2000. Develops and argues for the author's mature position on topics in religious epistemology.

Quinn, Philip L., and Kevin Meeker, eds. *The Philosophical Challenge of Religious Diversity.* Oxford and New York: Oxford University Press, 2000. Reprints major contributions to the debate about the epistemological consequences of religious diversity.

Quinn, Philip L., and Charles Taliaferro, eds. *A Companion to Philosophy of Religion.* Oxford: Blackwell, 1997. Provides a comprehensive survey of philosophy of religion at the end of the twentieth century in seventy-eight original articles by leading contributors to the field.

Rowe, William L. *The Cosmological Argument.* Princeton, NJ: Princeton University Press, 1975. Contains a thorough analysis of Samuel Clarke's version of the cosmological argument for the existence of God.

Swinburne, Richard. *The Existence of God.* Oxford: Clarendon Press, 1979. Sets forth in detail the author's Bayesian cumulative case argument for the existence of God.

Philip L. Quinn (2005)

PHILOSOPHY OF RELIGION, PROBLEMS OF

The term *philosophy of religion* is a relative newcomer to the philosophical lexicon, but what is now so designated is as old as philosophy itself. One of the earliest spurs to philosophical reflection, in ancient Greece and elsewhere, was the emergence of doubts concerning the religious tradition; and religious beliefs and conceptions have always formed much of the staple of philosophical discussion.

If one surveys the various things philosophers have done in thinking about religion, it is difficult to find any unifying thread other than the fact that they all spring from reflection on religion. Philosophy of religion is occupied to a large extent with the consideration of reasons for and against various fundamental religious beliefs, particularly the various arguments for the existence of God. But we find many other matters treated in books that are regarded as being within the philosophy of religion. These include the nature and significance of religious experience, the nature of religion, the relation between religion and science, the nature of religious faith as a mode of belief and/or awareness, the nature of revelation and its relation to the results of human experience and reflection, the place of religion in human culture as a whole, the logical analysis of religious language, the nature and significance of religious symbolism, and possibilities for reconstructing religion along relatively nontraditional lines.

CENTRAL AIM

Some justification can be found for grouping all these topics under the heading "philosophy of religion" if we view them all as growing out of a single enterprise, the rational scrutiny of the claims of religion—the critical examination of these claims in the light of whatever considerations are relevant—with a view to making a reasonable response to them. A highly developed religion presents us with a number of important claims on our belief, our conduct, our attitudes and feelings. It gives answers to questions concerning the ultimate source of things, the governing forces in the cosmos, the ultimate purpose(s) of the universe, and the place of man in this scheme. It tells us what a supreme being is like, what demands he makes on men, and how one can get in touch with him. It offers a diagnosis of human ills, and it lays down a "way of salvation" that, if followed, will provide a way to remedy these ills and satisfy man's deepest needs. All this is very important. If the claims of a given religion

on these points are justified, discovering this is a matter of the greatest moment. At bottom the philosophy of religion is the enterprise of subjecting such claims to rational criticism.

It is worth noting that such claims are not made by religion in general but by particular religions exclusively and that although generally we can find claims of all these sorts in any given religion, the specific content will differ widely from one religion to another. This will have important consequences for the direction taken by the philosophizing that arises in response to each religion. This article is largely concerned with the Western tradition, and thus the philosophy of religion represented has grown out of concern with some aspect of the Judeo-Christian tradition, either through support or opposition. Philosophical reflection on a very different religious tradition will give rise to different preoccupations. Thus, Western philosophers, unlike their Indian counterparts, are much concerned with arguments for and against the existence of a supreme personal deity and with whether or not the occurrence of miracles is compatible with the reign of natural law. However, in a religious tradition like the Hindu or the Buddhist, which does not feature the notion of a supreme personal deity who has active personal dealings with his creatures, these problems do not arise. Philosophers in such a tradition, by contrast, will be concerned with trying to clarify the relation of a supreme ineffable One to the various things in the world that constitute its manifestations and with considering arguments for the ultimate unreality of the empirical world. There is, however, enough in common among different religions to ensure that all philosophy of religion will be directed to recognizably identical problems, though in very different forms.

Philosophers have raised critical questions about the justifiability and value of religious beliefs, rites, moral attitudes, and modes of experience. However, philosophers have largely focused their critical powers on the doctrinal (belief) side of religion. This selectivity might be attributed to an occupational bias for the intellectual, but there is a real justification for it. If our basic interest is in questions of justifiability, then it is natural that we should concentrate on the belief side of religion, for the justification of any other element ultimately rests on the justification of some belief or beliefs. If one asks a Roman Catholic why he goes to Mass, or what the value is of so doing, he would, if he knew what he was about, appeal to certain basic beliefs of his religion: that the universe, and all its constituents, owes its existence to and depends for its ultimate fate on a supreme personal being, God; that man inevitably fails to live up to the moral requirements God lays down for him; that God became a man in the person of Jesus of Nazareth and suffered death in order to save man from the fatal consequences of his sinfulness; that as a part of a program designed to enable men to benefit from this, God has ordained that they should participate in the rite of the Mass, in which, in some mysterious way, they actually incorporate the body and blood of Jesus and so partake of the salvation effected through him. The ritual, as conceived by the participants, is a reasonable thing to do if and only if these beliefs are justified.

However, the attention of philosophers is generally more narrowly concentrated than this. Not all the beliefs of a given religion, not even all the beliefs considered crucial by that religion, receive equal attention. In works on the philosophy of religion, one finds little discussion of relatively special doctrines that are peculiar to a given religion, such as the virgin birth of Jesus, the divine mission of the church, or the special status of the priesthood, however important these doctrines may be for the religion in question. Instead, attention is focused primarily on what might be called the metaphysical background of the doctrinal system, the worldview of the religion—the view of the ultimate source and nature of the universe; the nature of man; man's place in the universe; the end to which man is, or should be, tending; and so on. This preferential treatment is partly due to a desire to make philosophical discussions relevant to more than one religion; for example, roughly the same worldview underlies Judaism, Christianity, and Islam. It is also partly due to a conviction that philosophical reflection will yield definite results only with respect to the more general aspects of a religious outlook. Very few philosophers have supposed that one can establish the virgin birth by philosophical argument.

It might also be argued that if we abstract from commitment to any particular religion, the worldview aspect of religion is the most undeniably significant one. Without presupposing some particular religious beliefs, it would be difficult to show that the acceptance of elaborate theological dogmas like that of the Trinity, or participation in rites, or singling out certain objects as sacred is an essential part of a fully human life. However, it can be argued on the basis of facts concerning the nature of man and the conditions of human life that human beings have a deep-seated need to form some general picture of the total universe in which they live, in order to be able to relate their own fragmentary activities to the universe as a whole in a way meaningful to them; and that a life in which this is not carried through is a life impoverished in a most significant respect. This would seem to be an aspect of religion that is important on any religious position; and so it seems fitting that it should be at the center of the picture in a general philosophical treatment of religion.

OTHER INVESTIGATIONS AND THE CENTRAL AIM

In presenting, defending, and criticizing arguments for and against such fundamental beliefs as the existence of a supreme personal deity, the immortality of the human personality, and the direction of the universe toward the realization of a certain purpose, philosophers are directly engaged in critical evaluation. The other major topics listed at the beginning of this article do not have exactly this status, but they are all directly relevant to rational criticism of fundamental religious beliefs. In order to conduct a systematic scrutiny of such beliefs, one must start with an adequate conception of the nature and range of religion, so that he can be sure that he is dealing with genuine religious beliefs and with those which are most fundamental for religion, and so that he will not be unduly limited by the particular interests with which he starts.

Moreover, one needs an adequate understanding of the nature of religious belief in order to filter out irrelevant considerations and arguments. The charge of irrelevancy has been most trenchantly leveled against the traditional enterprise of presenting metaphysical arguments for the existence of God by Søren Kierkegaard, who maintained that anyone who tries to give an argument for the existence of God thereby shows that he has misunderstood the special character of religious belief. Whether or not such charges are justified, the mere fact that they can be made with any plausibility shows that it is incumbent on the philosopher of religion to look into the character of religious faith and to try to determine its similarities to and differences from other modes of belief; for example, those in everyday life and in science. With an increasing realization of the way in which thought and belief are shaped by language, this kind of investigation has increasingly taken the form of an inquiry into the type of utterances that express religious belief, an attempt to make explicit the logic of religious discourse—the special ways in which terms are used in religious utterances, the logical relations between religious statements themselves and between religious statements and statements in other areas of discourse, the extent to which religious statements are to be construed as expressive of feelings or attitudes or as directions to action, rather than as factual claims. Also, an appreciation of the extent to which language is used symbolically in religion can easily lead to a general concern with the nature and function of religious symbolism.

All the concerns listed thus far involve investigation of the relation of religion to other segments of human culture, such as science, art, and literature. The question of the relation of science and religion has a special importance for one who is critically examining religious beliefs in our society. For the last few hundred years the main challenges to religious doctrine in Western society have been made in the name of science. With respect to many segments of science, from Copernican astronomy through Darwinian biology to Freudian psychology, it has been claimed that certain scientific discoveries disprove, or at least seriously weaken, certain basic religious doctrines. Discussions of whether this ever does, or can, happen—and if so, what is to be done about it—have bulked large in works on philosophy of religion.

Philosophers of religion also investigate the nature of religious experiences because it is often claimed that such experiences provide direct warrant for the existence of God, or of other objects of religious worship. One is naturally led into a survey of the types of religious experience and into questions of their psychological bases. Finally, if a philosopher has decided that the basic beliefs of the traditional religion(s) of his society are unacceptable, he is naturally faced with the question of what to do about it. If he feels that religion is a crucially important aspect of human life, he will want to find some way of preserving religious functions in a new form. Hence, naturalistic philosophers, who reject the supernaturalistic beliefs of our religious tradition, sometimes attempt to sketch the outlines of a religion constructed on naturalistic lines. This will usually involve the substitution of some component(s) or aspect(s) of the natural world for the supernatural deity of the Judeo-Christian tradition. This may be Humanity (Auguste Comte), human ideals (John Dewey), those natural processes which make a contribution to the realization of the greatest good (H. N. Wieman), or some combination of these.

RELATIONS TO OTHER DISCIPLINES

The philosophy of religion is distinguished from theology and from sciences dealing with religion (such as psychology of religion and sociology of religion) in opposite ways. It is distinguished from theology by the fact that it takes nothing for granted, at least nothing religious; in the course of its examination it takes the liberty of calling

anything into question. Theology, in a narrow sense of that term, sets out to articulate the beliefs of a given religion and to put them into systematic order, without ever raising the ultimate question of their truth. The philosophy of religion is distinguished from sciences of religion by the fact that it is addressed to questions of value and justification and tries to arrive at some sort of judgment on religious claims. The psychology of religion—for instance, when pursuing strictly psychological questions—studies religious beliefs, attitudes, and experiences as so many facts, which it tries to describe and explain, without attempting to pass judgment on their objective truth, rationality, or importance.

The philosophy of religion, conceived of as an attempt to carry out a rational scrutiny of the claims made by a given religion, will always start from concern with some particular religion or type of religion and will basically aim at a judgment of that religion. It certainly is historically accurate to think of philosophy of religion as arising in this way and, furthermore, it may be taken as its common and most basic form. However, it is also possible for a philosopher to concern himself directly with the fundamental issues involved in the religious claims in question—the ultimate source of things, the destiny of man, and cosmic purpose, for example—without approaching them through the consideration of answers given to these questions by some organized religion. Benedict de Spinoza's *Ethics* is an outstanding example of this kind of investigation. Other examples are Samuel Alexander's *Space, Time and Deity* (2 vols., London, 1920) and Henri Bergson's *L'évolution créatrice* (*Creative Evolution,* New York, 1911). Whether we call philosophizing of this kind philosophy of religion is not important, but it is important to realize that these questions can be considered outside the context in which we are explicitly concerned with religion as such.

VARIOUS APPROACHES

One should not suppose that every philosopher of religion concerns himself with the whole range of problems. On the contrary, a given philosopher will usually restrict his attention because of his special interests, his conception of religion, and/or his general philosophical position. The second and third of these factors deserve further notice. Concerning the second, the types of problems that a given philosopher emphasizes will sometimes be influenced by the particular aspect of religion he regards as essential. Thus, the concentration on problems connected with religious belief in traditional philosophy of religion is partly due to the fact that most philosophers of religion have thought of religion primarily as a kind of belief (although this may, in fact, be less important than other factors). W. T. Stace in *Time and Eternity,* for example, considers mystical experience to be the essence of religion. Stace concentrated his main efforts on interpreting and justifying religious doctrine conceived as basically an expression of mystical experience. On the other hand, Kierkegaard thought of religion as basically a matter of an individual maintaining a certain general stance in life, and he devoted himself to an elaborate description of a variety of such stances, combined with indirect recommendations of one of these; he rarely mentioned any of the problems customarily discussed by philosophers of religion.

The operation of the third factor, the individual's philosophical position, is more apparent and, perhaps, more powerful. A few examples, selected more or less at random, will be helpful. Philosophers who are primarily speculative metaphysicians—Plato, Thomas Aquinas, Gottfried Wilhelm Leibniz, G. W. F. Hegel, and A. N. Whitehead—naturally take very seriously the enterprise of constructing metaphysical arguments for or against the existence of God, whereas predominantly antimetaphysical philosophers—David Hume, Immanuel Kant, and Dewey—will either criticize such arguments or, as is more common in recent times, ignore them altogether. Those who subscribe to the thesis that the only proper job of philosophy is the analysis (clarification) of concepts will observe the appropriate restrictions when and if they turn their attention to religion. There is a great deal of work of this kind to be done with the concepts of God, creation, revelation, faith, and miracle, to name a few. Traditionally this has been done in connection with attempts to reach substantive conclusions on the existence of God, immortality, and other major issues, but if one thinks that conclusions on such matters cannot be attained by philosophical reflection, as analytic philosophers do, he may still seek to make explicit the concepts involved in religious belief. Such philosophizing will regard itself as a humble servant of theology or of more ordinary religious belief and will pretend to no judicial functions, except where it locates internal confusions or inconsistencies.

The influence of philosophical orientation is clearly exemplified in naturalistic philosophers, who generally rule out all supernaturalism on the basis of their general philosophical position, without giving particular supernaturalistic beliefs any detailed examination. Naturalists devote their energies to revising religious belief and prac-

tice so that they will be acceptable within a naturalistic framework.

Finally, one may consider Hegel, who devoted his lectures on the philosophy of religion to demonstrating a dialectical progression in the history of religion. This reflected Hegel's basic philosophical conviction that reality consists of the process of the Absolute coming to full self-consciousness, that this process exhibits a dialectical pattern, and that it is manifested in the history of every cultural form.

In the task of classifying the positions that have been taken in the philosophy of religion, one confronts the difficulty that not all philosophers of religion, even in a single religious tradition, are dealing with the same problems. However, there is a common task underlying all the different approaches. All philosophy of religion is ultimately concerned with arriving at a rational judgment of the religion under discussion and, if the judgment is negative, to present some sort of alternative. The initial principle of division can then be taken as the affirmative or negative character of this judgment. (This cannot be absolutely clear-cut, partly because often some part of the religion is affirmed and some is rejected, partly because it is not absolutely clear what is to be included in the religion in question.) It can then be asked of those whose judgment is affirmative what the basis of their judgment is.

One major group, which includes the great majority of philosophers of religion, presents various arguments in support of such beliefs as the existence of God and the immortality of the soul, arguments that take their start from premises that are not themselves religious doctrines and that, it is assumed, any reasonable man would accept. In other words, they attempt to support religious belief by resting it on nonreligious premises. A smaller but still considerable group regards religious belief as not needing any such support from the outside; they regard it as somehow self-justifying or at least as justified by something from within religion. Some of them (Bergson and James) suppose that the belief in the existence of God, for example, is justified by religious experience. One can directly experience the presence of God, and therefore one does not need to prove his existence by showing that he must be postulated to explain certain facts. Others regard religious faith as different from other modes of belief in such a way that it does not need support of any kind, either from argument from effect to cause or from direct experience. Kierkegaard, Emil Brunner, and Paul Tillich, for example, all take this position, though there are great differences between them. (The case of Tillich illustrates the point that in some cases it is difficult to distinguish between those who accept the religious tradition and those who reject it. Tillich considered himself a Christian theologian, but his interpretation of Christian doctrine is so unorthodox that many feel he reconstrued it out of recognition and therefore should be classed with those who substitute a symbolic reinterpretation for traditional beliefs.)

In the other major group we can distinguish between those who simply reject traditional religion (Baron d'Holbach and Bertrand Russell) and those who in addition try to put something in its place. In the latter group we can distinguish between those who try to retain the trappings, perhaps even the doctrinal trappings, of traditional religion but give it a nonsupernaturalistic reinterpretation, usually as symbolic of something or other in the natural world (George Santayana), and those who attempt to depict a quite different sort of religion constructed along nonsupernaturalistic lines (Comte, Dewey, and Wieman).

Outside this classification are those analytical philosophers who restrict themselves to the analysis of concepts and types of utterances. We may regard them as not having a major position in the philosophy of religion, but rather as making contributions that may be useful in the construction of such a position.

See also Religion.

Bibliography

Edwin A. Burtt, *Types of Religious Philosophy*, rev. ed. (New York: Harper, 1951), and Robert Leet Patterson, *An Introduction to the Philosophy of Religion* (New York: Holt, 1958), are useful introductory textbooks. A wide variety of readings in the field can be found in *Philosophy of Religion*, edited by George L. Abernethy and Thomas A. Langford (New York: Macmillan, 1962), and in *Religious Belief and Philosophical Reflection*, edited by William P. Alston (New York, 1963).

The following works are important treatments of a wide variety of topics in this area: John Baillie, *The Interpretation of Religion* (New York: Scribners, 1928); H. J. Paton, *The Modern Predicament* (London: Allen and Unwin, 1955); A. E. Taylor, *The Faith of a Moralist* (New York: Macmillan, 1930); and F. R. Tennant, *Philosophical Theology* (Cambridge, U.K.: Cambridge University Press, 1928). These works are written from a standpoint more or less sympathetic to traditional theism. For fairly comprehensive discussions from a more critical standpoint, see J. M. E. McTaggart, *Some Dogmas of Religion* (London: Arnold, 1906), and Bertrand Russell, *Religion and Science* (New York: Holt, 1935).

Works dealing with the nature and significance of religious experience include William James, *The Varieties of Religious Experience* (New York: Longman, 1902), and Rudolf Otto, *The Idea of the Holy,* translated by J. W. Harvey (New York: Oxford University Press, 1958). The nature of religion is discussed in Josiah Royce, *The Sources of Religious Insight* (New York: Scribners, 1912), and in Julian Huxley, *Religion without Revelation* (New York: Harper, 1957). For the relation of religion and science, see Bertrand Russell, op. cit., and Michael Pupin, ed., *Science and Religion; a Symposium* (New York, 1931). J. H. Newman, *A Grammar of Assent* (London: Burns, Oates, 1870), and Paul Tillich, *Dynamics of Faith* (New York: Harper, 1957), cover the nature of religious faith as a mode of belief and/or awareness.

In Emil Brunner, *The Philosophy of Religion from the Standpoint of Protestant Theology,* translated by A. J. D. Farrer and B. L. Woolf (New York: Scribners, 1937), the nature of revelation and its relation to the results of human experience and reflection are considered. The place of religion in human culture as a whole is dealt with in G. W. F. Hegel, *Lectures on the Philosophy of Religion,* translated by E. B. Speirs and J. B. Sanderson, 3 vols. (London: K. Paul, Trench, Trubner, 1895), and in George Santayana, *Reason in Religion* (New York: Scribners, 1905). For the logical analysis of religious language, see A. G. N. Flew and Alasdair MacIntyre, eds., *New Essays in Philosophical Theology* (London: SCM Press, 1955), and C. B. Martin, *Religious Belief* (Ithaca, NY: Cornell University Press, 1959). Edwyn Bevan, *Symbolism and Belief* (Boston: Beacon Press, 1957), and W. T. Stace, *Time and Eternity* (Princeton, NJ: Princeton University Press, 1952), discuss the nature and significance of religious symbolism. Possibilities for reconstructing religion along relatively nontraditional lines appear in Immanuel Kant, *Religion within the Limits of Reason Alone,* translated by T. M. Greene and H. H. Hudson (La Salle, IL: Open Court, 1934); John Dewey, *A Common Faith* (New Haven, CT: Yale University Press, 1934); and Julian Huxley, op. cit.

William P. Alston (1967)

PHILOSOPHY OF SCIENCE, HISTORY OF

Philosophy of science emerged as a distinctive part of philosophy in the twentieth century. Its defining moment was the meeting (and clash) of two courses of events: the breakdown of the Kantian philosophical tradition and the crisis in the sciences and mathematics in the beginning of the century. But what we now call philosophy of science has a rich intellectual history that goes back to the ancient Greeks. It is intimately connected with the efforts made by many thinkers to come to terms with the distinctive kind of knowledge (*epistēmē, scientia*) that science offers. Though science proper was distinguished from natural philosophy only in the nineteenth century, the *philosophy* of natural philosophy had almost the very same agenda that current philosophy of science has.

ARISTOTLE

Aristotle (384–322 BCE) thought that there was a sharp distinction between our understanding of facts and our understanding of the reasons for those facts. Though both types of understanding proceed via deductive syllogism, only the latter is characteristic of science, because only the latter is tied to the knowledge of causes. In *Posterior Analytics*, Aristotle illustrates this difference by contrasting the following two instances of deductive syllogism:

Syllogism A
Planets do not twinkle.
What does not twinkle is near.
Therefore, planets are near.

Syllogism B
Planets are near.
What is near does not twinkle.
Therefore, planets do not twinkle.

Syllogism A, Aristotle said, demonstrates the fact that planets are near, but does *not* explain this fact, because the syllogism does not state its causes. However, syllogism B is explanatory because the syllogism gives the *reason why* planets do not twinkle: *because* they are near. Aristotle's point was that, besides being demonstrative, explanatory arguments should also be asymmetric: The asymmetric relation between causes and effects should be reflected in an asymmetric relation between the premises and the conclusion of the explanatory arguments: The premises should explain the conclusion, and not the other way around.

For Aristotle, scientific knowledge forms a tight deductive-axiomatic system whose axioms are *first principles*, which are "true and primary and immediate, and more known than and prior to and causes of the conclusion" (71b19–25). Being an empiricist, he thought that knowledge of causes has experience as its source. But experience on its own cannot lead, through induction, to universal and necessary first principles that state ultimate causes. Nor can first principles be demonstrated, on pain of either circularity or infinite regress. So something besides experience and demonstration is necessary for knowledge of first principles. This is the process of abstraction based on intuition, a process that reveals the essences of things, that is, the properties by virtue of which a thing is what it is. Though Aristotle called first principles "definitions," they are not verbal, but rather state the essences of things. In Aristotle's rich ontology, causes are essential properties of their effects and necessarily give rise to their effects. He thought that the logical necessity by which the conclusion follows from the premises of an explanatory argument mirrors the physical necessity by which causes produce their effects.

ARISTOTELIANISM

By the 1250s, Aristotle's works had been translated into Latin, either from the original Greek or through Arabic translations, and a whole tradition of writing commentaries on these works flourished. Aristotle's *Organon* was the main source on issues related to logic and knowledge. At about the same time, the first universities were founded in Paris and Oxford, and natural philosophy found in them its chief institutional home. Aristotelianism was the dominant philosophy throughout the Middle Ages, though it was enriched by insights deriving from religious beliefs and many philosophical commentaries. The new Aristotelianism put secular learning on almost equal footing with revealed truth, especially at the University of Paris.

Thomas Aquinas (c. 1225–1274) argued that science and faith cannot have the same object, since the object of science is something seen, whereas the object of faith is the unseen. He found in Aristotle's views the mean between two extremes, one being Plato's view, which demeaned experience and saw in it just an occasion in the process of understanding the realm of pure and immutable forms, the other being the Democretian atomist view, which reduced all knowledge to experience. Aristotelianism, Aquinas thought, was the golden mean. Experience is necessary for knowledge, since nothing can be in the mind if it is not first in the senses. But thought is active in that it extends beyond the bounds of sense and states the necessary, universal, and certain principles on which knowledge is based.

Aquinas inherited (and suitably modified) much of Aristotle's rich metaphysics. Aristotle, drawing a distinction between matter and form, argued that when a change takes place, the matter perdures (persists), while the form changes. He conceived of change as the successive presence of different (even opposing) forms in the substratum. Scholastic philosophers differentiated this substratum from the ordinary matter of experience and called it "prime matter" (*materia prima*). The form that gives prime matter its particular identity (making it a substance of a particular kind) they called "substantial form." Substantial forms were individuating principles that accounted for the specific properties of bodies (which all shared the same prime matter). Aquinas added that prime matter is pure potentiality, incapable of existing by itself. He adopted the view that change (as well as motion) was the passage from potentiality to actuality. Since a thing cannot be both actual and potential at the same time, he took it to be obvious that nothing can be the active source of its own motion, and hence that motion always requires a mover. Aquinas found solace in the Aristotelian doctrine of the first unmoved mover (the source of all motion), which immediately lent itself to being identified with God.

THE PROBLEM OF MOTION

The status of motion was heavily debated among the Scholastics. One central Aristotelian axiom was that everything that moves requires a mover. Another central axiom was that the mover is in contact with the thing moved. This might be borne out in ordinary experience, but some cases created problems. One of them was projectile motion, and another concerned natural motion, that is, motion toward the natural place of a thing. In both cases, it is not obvious that something does the moving, let alone by being in contact with the thing moved. There was no easy way out of these problems. Underlying them was the very issue of what motion is. Is motion merely the final form momentarily attained by the moving object at any instant? Or is it something in addition, a flux or transformation of forms (in medieval terminology, *forma fluens* or *fluxus formae*)?

The radical answer to this question was sharpened by William of Ockham (c. 1280–1349), who argued that motion is nothing over and above the moving body and its successive and continuous termini. He was a nominalist who thought that only particulars exist. He denied that universals exist and claimed that general terms, or predicates, refer to concepts that apply to many particulars. He argued that the key to the problem of motion was thus held by the abstract noun "motion." It is wrong, he claimed, to think that this and other abstract nouns refer to distinct and separately existing things. Only individual bodies, places, and forms are needed to explain what motion is. Another view came from Jean Buridan (c. 1295–1358). He argued that local motion involves *impetus*, a motive force transmitted from the mover to the moving body, which acts as an internal cause of its continued motion.

ARGUMENT ACCORDING TO IMAGINATION

On March 7, 1277, Etienne Tempier, Bishop of Paris, issued an act condemning 219 propositions drawn from the works of Aristotle and his commentators (including Aquinas). These propositions were supposed to be in conflict with Christian faith and in particular with the omnipotence of God. They included such claims as that the world is eternal, that God could not make several worlds, that God could not make an accident exist without a subject, that God could not move the entire cosmos in straight line. Ironically, this act opened up new conceptual possibilities that were hitherto regarded as closed. If Aristotle could err in matters theological, could he not err in matters philosophical too?

On the premise that only the law of noncontradiction constrains God's actions, it was argued that anything that can be conceived without contradiction is possible. This led to a new type of argumentation: arguing according to the imagination (*secundum imaginationem*). If something could be consistently imagined, then it was possible. New ideas were pursued on this basis, unconstrained by claims concerning the actual course of nature (*secundum cursus naturae*). Central elements of Aristotelian doctrine were given close logical scrutiny. For instance, in the Aristotelian scheme of things, where there is no void and the entire cosmos occupies no place, it made no sense to say that the entire cosmos could move. But what if, Buridan asked, God made the whole cosmos rotate as one solid body? Freed to inquire into the logical possibility of this rotation, Buridan argued that since we can imagine it, there must be something more to motion than the moving body, its forms, and the places it acquires. For if these were all there were to motion, then, contrary to our assumption, the entire cosmos could not move, simply because there would be no places successively acquired.

Ockham pushed argument according to imagination to its limits by arguing that there is no a priori necessity in nature's workings. God could have made things other than they are. Hence, all existing things are contingent. There are no necessary connections between distinct existences, and there is justification for inferring one distinct existence from another, Ockham forcefully argued. Accordingly, all knowledge of things comes from experience. Ockham claimed that there could never be certain causal knowledge based on experience, since God might intervene to produce the effect directly, thereby dispensing with the secondary (material) cause. Ockham thus gave a radical twist to empiricism, putting it in direct conflict with the dominant Aristotelian view.

FIRST PRINCIPLES

The status of scientific knowledge was heavily debated in the thirteen and fourteenth centuries. John Duns Scotus (c. 1265–1308) defended the view that first principles are knowable with certainty, as they are based only on the natural power of the understanding to see that they are self-evident, ultimately by virtue of the meanings of the terms involved in them. For him, the understanding is not caused by the senses, but only occasioned by them. Once it has received its material from the senses, the understanding exercises its own power in conceiving first principles. Interestingly enough, Scotus thought that there could be certain causal knowledge coming from experience. He asserted as self-evident a principle of induction. He held that this principle is known a priori by the intellect, since a free cause (that is, an act of a free agent) leads by its *form* to the effect that it is ordained to produce. It was then an easy step for him to extend this principle from free causes to natural causes: "Whatever happens frequently through something that is not free, has this something as its natural *per se* cause."

Ockham disagreed with Scotus's account of the first principles, but his central disagreement with his predecessors was about the *content* of first principles. Since he thought there was nothing in the world that corresponded to general concepts (such as universals), he claimed that first principles are, in the first instance, about mental contents. They are about concrete individuals only *indirectly* and insofar as the general terms and concepts can be predicated of concrete things. Ockham is famous for the principle known as Ockham's razor: Entities must not be multiplied without necessity. In fact, this principle of parsimony was well-known in his time. Robert Grosseteste (c. 1168–1253) had put it forward as the law of parsimony (*lex parsimoniae*).

Ockham's most radical follower, Nicolas of Autrecourt (c. 1300–after 1350), rejected the demand for certainty altogether and claimed that only probable knowledge is possible. He endorsed atomism, claiming that it is at least as probable as its rival, Aristotelianism. In reaction, the fourteenth-century Parisian masters—Buridan, Albert of Saxony (c. 1316–1390), and others—claimed that empirical knowledge can be practically certain and wholly adequate for natural science. For Buridan, if we fail to discover an instance of *A* that is not *B*, then it is warranted to claim that all *A*s are *B*. On the basis of this principle, he defended on empirical grounds the Aristotelian claim that there is no vacuum in nature, since, he said, we always experience material bodies.

THE PREROGATIVES OF EXPERIMENTAL SCIENCE

Despite their engagement with philosophical issues in natural science, thinkers such as Ockham and Scotus were little concerned with natural science itself. They saw little role for mathematics, the science of quantity, in physics. They neglected experiment altogether. This was a drawback of their thought in relation to some earlier medieval thinkers. Grosseteste was one of the first to emphasize the role of mathematics in natural science. Roger Bacon (1214–1292) went further by arguing that all sciences rest ultimately on mathematics, that facts should be subsumed under mathematical principles, and that empirical knowledge requires active experimentation. Bacon put forward three virtues of experimental science. First, it criticizes by experiment the conclusions of all the other sciences. Second, it can discover new truths (not of the same kind as already known truths) in the fields of science. Third, it investigates the secrets of nature and delivers knowledge of future and present events.

The emphasis on the mathematical representation of nature exerted important influence on the work of the masters of Merton College in Oxford, who, in the fourteenth century, by and large put aside the philosophical issues of the nature of motion and focused instead on its mathematical representation. Walter Burley (c. 1275–c. 1345), Thomas Bradwardine (c. 1295–1349), William of Heytesbury (before 1313–1372/1373), Richard Swineshead (d. c. 1355), known as the Mertonians, most of whom where nominalists, engaged in a project to investigate motion and its relation to velocity and resistance in an abstract mathematical way. Similar research, though more concerned with the physical nature of motion, was undertaken in Paris by Buridan, Albert of Saxony, and Nicole Oresme (c. 1320–1382), known as the Paris terminists. The mathematical ingenuity of the Mertonians and the Parisians led to many important mathematical results that spread throughout Western Europe and germinated in the thought of many modern thinkers, including Galileo Galilei (1564–1642). By the end of the fourteenth century, a protopositivist movement, concerned not with the ontology of motion, but with its measurement, started to spread.

THE COPERNICAN TURN

In *De revolutionibus orbium coelestium* (On the revolutions of the celestial spheres), Nicolaus Copernicus (1473–1543) developed his famous heliocentric model of the universe. The unsigned preface of the book, which was published posthumously in 1543, firmly placed it within the saving-of-appearances astronomical tradition favored by Plato and endorsed by many medieval thinkers. As it turned out, the preface was written not by Copernicus himself but by Andreas Osiander, a Lutheran theologian. Copernicus emphatically refused to subscribe to this tradition. He had a *realist* conception of his theory, according to which, as Pierre Duhem put it, "a fully satisfactory astronomy can only be constructed on the basis of hypotheses that are true, that conform to the nature of things" (1908, p. 62).

Before Copernicus, the dominant astronomical theory was that of Claudius Ptolemy (c. 85–c. 165). Pretty much like Aristotle and Plato, Ptolemy had assumed a geocentric model of the universe. To save the appearances of planetary motion, he devised a system of deferents (large circles centered on the earth) and epicycles. There were alternative mathematical models of the motion of the planets (e.g., one based on a moving eccentric circle), but Ptolemy thought that since all these models saved the appearances, they were good enough. The issue of their physical reality was not raised (though at least some medieval philosophers understood these models realistically). Geometry was then the key to studying the celestial motions, but there was no pretense that the world itself was geometrical (though Plato, in the *Timaeus*, did advocate a kind of geometrical atomism). The Copernican heliocentric model, though it made the earth move around the sun, continued to use epicycles. But Copernicus argued that his theory was true. He based this thought mostly on considerations of harmony and simplicity: His own theory placed astronomical facts into a simpler and more harmonious mathematical system.

THE BOOK OF NATURE

Galileo Galilei (1564–1642) famously argued that the book of nature is written in the language of mathematics. He distinguished between logic and mathematics. Logic teaches us how to derive conclusions from premises, but does not tell us whether the premises are true. Mathematics is in the business of demonstrating truth. Though Galileo emphasized the role of experiment in science, he also drew a distinction between appearances and reality, which set the stage for his own, and subsequent, explanatory theories of phenomena, which posited unobservable entities. He accepted and defended the Copernican system and further supported it with his own telescopic observations, which spoke against the dominant Aristotelian view that the heavens are immutable. But the possible truth of Copernicus's theory suggested that the world might not be as it is revealed to us by the senses. Indeed, Galileo understood that the senses can be deceptive, and hence that proper science must go beyond merely relying on the senses. The mathematical theories of motion that he advanced were based on idealizations

and abstractions. Experience provides the raw material for these idealizations (frictionless inclined planes, ideal pendula), but the key method of science was extracting, via abstraction and idealization, the basic structure of a phenomenon so that it could be translated into mathematical form. Then mathematical demonstration takes over and further consequences are deduced, which are tested empirically. So Galileo saw that understanding nature requires the use of creative imagination.

Galileo also distinguished between primary qualities and secondary qualities. Primary qualities—such as shape, size, and motion—are possessed by objects in themselves and are immutable, objective, and amenable to mathematical exploration. Secondary qualities, such as color and taste, are relative, subjective, and fleeting. They are caused on the senses by the primary qualities of objects. The world that science studies is the world of primary qualities. Subjective qualities can be left out of science without any loss. Galileo set for modern science the task of discovering the objective and real mathematical structure of the world. This structure, though mathematical, was also mechanical: All there is in the world is matter in motion.

THE INTERPRETATION OF NATURE

The emerging new science was leaving Aristotelianism behind. But it needed a new method. Better, it needed to have its method spelled out so that the break with Aristotelianism, as a philosophical theory of science, could be complete. Aristotelianism offered two criteria of adequacy for scientific method: epistemological adequacy and metaphysical adequacy. For epistemological adequacy, the scientific method had to meet some philosophical requirements as to what counts as knowledge. For metaphysical adequacy, the metaphysical presuppositions of scientific theories should coincide with the metaphysical presuppositions of philosophical theories. To different extents, the theories of scientific method developed in the seventeenth century were attempts to challenge these criteria, for they were considered more as fetters to science than enablers of its development.

In *Novum organum* (*The New Organon*; 1620/1960), Francis Bacon (1561–1626) placed method at center stage and argued that the world is knowable but only after a long process of trying to understand it—a process that begins with experience and is guided by a new method of induction by elimination. This new method differed from Aristotle's on two counts: on the nature of first principles and on the process of attaining them. According to Bacon, the Aristotelian method (which Bacon called "anticipation of nature") starts with the senses and particular objects but then flies to first principles and derives from them further consequences. He contrasted this method to his own, which aims at an interpretation of nature, and which gradually and carefully ascends from the senses and particular objects to the most general principles. He rejected induction by enumeration as childish (since it takes account only of positive instances).

Bacon's alternative proceeds in three stages. Stage 1 involves compiling a natural and experimental history to derive a complete inventory of all instances of natural phenomena and their effects. Here observation rules. Then at stage 2, one constructs tables of presences, absences, and degrees of variation. Take, for example, the case of heat, which Bacon discussed in some detail. The table of presences records all phenomena with which the nature under examination (heat) is correlated (e.g., heat is present in light, etc.). The table of absences is a more detailed examination of the list of correlations of the table of presences that seeks to find absences (e.g., heat is not present in the light of the moon). The table of degrees of variation consists of recordings of what happens to correlated phenomena if the nature under investigation (heat) is decreased or increased in its qualities. Stage 3 is induction. Whatever is present when the nature under investigation is present or increases, and whatever is absent when this nature is absent or decreases, is the *form* of this nature. The crucial element in this three-stage process is the elimination or exclusion of all accidental characteristics of the nature under investigation. On the basis of this method, Bacon claimed that heat is motion and nothing else.

Bacon's forms are reminiscent of Aristotelian substantial forms. Yet he also claimed that the form of a nature is the law(s) it obeys. Indeed, Bacon's view was transitional between the Aristotelian view and a more modern conception of laws of nature. Bacon, in his view of science, found almost no place for mathematics, however, though he did favor active experimentation and showed great respect for alchemists because they had laboratories. In an instance of a fingerpost, he claimed that an essential part of interpreting nature by the new method of induction consists in devising a crucial experiment that judges between two competing hypotheses for the causes of an effect. Accordingly, Bacon distinguished between two types of experiments: those that gather data for a natural and experimental history and those that test hypotheses.

THE METAPHYSICAL FOUNDATIONS OF SCIENCE

René Descartes (1596–1650) too sought to provide an adequate philosophical foundation of science. But unlike Bacon, he felt more strongly the force of the skeptical challenge to the very possibility of knowledge of the world. So he took it upon himself to show how there could be certain (indubitable) knowledge and, in particular, how science can be based on certain first principles. Knowledge, he thought, must have the certainty of mathematics. Though Bacon was fine with some notion of virtual certainty, Descartes was after metaphysical certainty, that is, knowledge beyond any doubt. But in the end, Descartes accepted that in science a lot of things (other than the basic laws of nature) can be known only with virtual certainty. He distinguished all substances into two sorts: thinking things (*res cogitans*) and extended things (*res extensa*). He took the essence of mind to be thought and of matter extension. The vehicles of knowledge he took to be intuition and demonstration. We can be certain only of things that we can form clear and distinct ideas of or truths that we can demonstrate. Descartes tried to base his whole foundation for knowledge on a single indubitable truth, namely, "Cogito, ergo sum" ("I think; therefore I exist"). But having demonstrated the existence of God, he took God as guaranteeing the existence of the external world and, ultimately, of our knowledge of it.

Descartes was not a pure rationalist who thought that *all* science could be done a priori. Nor was he an empiricist either, obviously. He did not think that all knowledge stemmed from experience. In *Principia philosophiae* (*Principles of Philosophy*; 1644/1985), he argued that the human mind, by the light of reason alone, can arrive at substantive truths concerning the fundamental laws of nature. These laws (for instance, that the total quantity of motion in the world is conserved) are discovered and justified a priori, as they supposedly stem directly from God's immutability. Accordingly, the basic structure of the world is discovered independently of experience, is metaphysically necessary, and is known with metaphysical certainty. But once this basic structure has been laid down, science can use hypotheses and experiments to fill in the details. This is partly because the basic principles of nature place constraints on whatever else there is and happens in the world, without determining it uniquely. The less fundamental laws of physics are grounded in the fundamental principles, but are not directly deducible from them. Hypotheses are needed to flesh out these principles. Hypotheses are also needed to determine particular causes and matters of fact in the world, such as the shape, size, and speeds of corpuscles. It is only through experience that the values of such magnitudes can be determined. Accordingly, Descartes thought that the less fundamental laws could be known only with virtual certainty. Descartes's view of nature was mechanical: Everything can be explained in terms of matter in motion.

NEWTON

The real break with the Aristotelian philosophical and scientific outlook occurred with the consolidation of empiricism in the seventeenth century. Empiricists repudiated the metaphysics of essences and the epistemology of rational intuition, innate ideas, and infallible knowledge. Modern philosophical empiricism was shaped by the work of three important figures: Pierre Gassendi (1592–1655), Robert Boyle (1627–1691), and Isaac Newton (1642–1727). Gassendi revived Epicurean atomism and stressed that all knowledge stems from experience. Boyle articulated the mechanical philosophy and engaged in active experimentation to show that the mechanical conception of nature is true.

Newton's scientific achievements, presented in his monumental *Philosophiae naturalis principia mathematica* (*Mathematical Principles of Natural Philosophy*) of 1687, created a new scientific paradigm. The previous paradigm, Cartesianism, was overcome. Newton's methodological reflections became the point of reference for all subsequent discussion concerning the nature and method of science. Newton demanded certain knowledge but rejected the Cartesian route to it. By placing restrictions on what can be known and on what method should be followed, he thought he secured certainty in knowledge. His famous dictum "Hypotheses non fingo" ("I do not feign hypotheses") was supposed to act as a constraint on what can be known. It rules out metaphysical, speculative, and nonmathematical hypotheses that aim to provide the ultimate ground of phenomena. Newton took Descartes to be the chief advocate of hypotheses of the sort he was keen to deny.

His official conception of the method of science was deduction from the phenomena. He contrasted his method with the broad hypothetico-deductive method endorsed by Descartes. Newton's approach was fundamentally mathematical and quantitative. He did not subscribe to the idea that knowledge begins with a painstaking natural and experimental history of the sort suggested by Francis Bacon. The basic laws of motion, in a sense, stem from experience. They are neither true a priori nor metaphysically necessary. Newton strongly disagreed with Gottfried Leibniz (1646–1716), who thought that laws of nature are contingent but knowable a priori through considerations of fitness and perfection. The empirically given phenomena that Newton started with are laws (e.g., Kepler's laws). Then, by means of mathematical reasoning and the basic axioms or laws of motion, he drew further conclusions, for example, that the inverse-square law of gravity applies to all the planets. This kind of deduction from the phenomena has been described as demonstrative induction. It is induction, since it ultimately rests on experience and cannot deliver absolutely certain knowledge. But it is demonstrative, since it proceeds in a mathematically rigorous fashion.

THE REVIVAL OF EMPIRICISM: LOCKE AND HUME

In his preface to *An Essay concerning Human Understanding* (1689), John Locke (1632–1704) praised "the incomparable Mr. Newton" and took his own aim to be "an Under-Labourer in clearing some Ground a little, and removing some of the Rubbish, that lies in the way of Knowledge." Locke was an empiricist and a nominalist. He thought that all ideas come from impressions and claimed that whatever exists is particular. He adopted as fundamental the distinction between primary and secondary qualities. He also drew a distinction between real essences and nominal essences. The real essence of a thing is its underlying internal constitution, based on its primary qualities. The nominal essence concerns the observable characteristics of a thing and amounts to the construction of a genus or a species. The nominal essence of gold, for instance, is a body yellow, malleable, soft, and fusible. Its real essence is its microstructure. Being a nominalist, he thought that real essences are individuals, whereas nominal essences are mere concepts or ideas that define a species or a kind. Though Locke argued that proper knowledge amounts to knowing the real essences of things, he was pessimistic about the prospects of knowing real essences. As he said, he suspected "that natural philosophy is not capable of being made a Science" (1689/1975, IV.12.10). To be sure, knowledge of nominal essences can be had, but Locke thought that this knowledge is trivial and uninteresting, since it is ultimately analytic. Even though Locke's famous book appeared after Newton's *Principia*, it is a pre-Newtonian work. It does not share Newton's optimism that the secrets of nature can be unlocked.

All empiricists of the seventeenth century accepted nominalism and denied the existence of universals. This led them to face squarely the problem of induction. Realists about universals, including Aristotle, who thought that universals can exist only *in* things, could accommodate induction. They claimed that after a survey of a relatively limited number of instances, thought ascended to the universals shared by these instances and thus arrived at truths that are certain and unrevisable. This route was closed for nominalists. They had to rely on experience through and through, and inductive generalizations based on experience could not yield certain knowledge. This problem came in sharp focus in the work of David Hume (1711–1776).

The subtitle of Hume's *A Treatise of Human Nature* (1739/1978) was *Being an Attempt to Introduce the Experimental Mode of Reasoning into Moral Subjects*. This was an allusion to Newton's achievement and method. Hume thought that the moral sciences had yet to undergo their own Newtonian revolution. He took it upon himself to show how Newton's rules for philosophizing were applicable to the moral sciences. All ideas should come from impressions. Experience must be the arbiter of everything. Hypotheses should be looked upon with contempt. His own principles of association by which the mind works (resemblance, contiguity, and causation) were the psychological analogue of Newton's laws.

Being an empiricist, Hume argued that all factual (and causal) knowledge stems from experience. He revolted against the traditional view that the necessity that links cause and effect is the same as the logical necessity of a demonstrative argument. He argued that there can be *no* a priori demonstration of any causal connection, since the cause can be conceived without its effect and visa versa. Taking a cue from Nicolas Malebranche (1638–1715), he argued that there is no perception of a supposed necessary connection between cause and effect. Hume also went one step further. He found worthless his predecessors' appeals to the power of God to cause things to happen. Hume completely secularized the notion of causation. He also found inadequate, because circular, his predecessors' attempts to explain the link between causes and effects in terms of powers, active forces, and the like.

But his far-reaching point was that the alleged necessity of the causal connection cannot be empirically proved either. As he famously argued, any attempt to show, on the basis of experience, that a regularity that has held in the past *will* or *must* continue to hold in the future is circular and begs the question. It presupposes a principle of uniformity of nature. But this principle is *not* a priori true. Nor can it be proved empirically without circularity. For any attempt to prove it empirically will have to assume what needs to be proved, namely, that since nature has been uniform in the past, it will or must continue to be uniform in the future. Hume's challenge to any attempt to establish the necessity of causal connections on empirical grounds has become known as his *skepticism* about induction. But Hume never doubted that people think and reason inductively. He just took this to be a fundamental psychological fact about human beings that cannot be accommodated within the confines of the traditional conception of Reason. Indeed, Hume went on to describe in detail some basic "rules by which to judge of causes and effects" (1739/1978, p. 173).

KANT'S AWAKENING

Hume's critique of necessity in nature awoke Immanuel Kant (1724–1804) from his "dogmatic slumber," as he famously stated. Kant thought that Hume questioned the very possibility of science, and Kant took it upon himself to show how science was possible. He claimed that although all knowledge starts with experience, it does not arise from it. It is actively shaped by the categories of the understanding and the forms of pure intuition (space and time). The mind, as it were, imposes conceptual structure on the world, without which no experience could be possible. His central thought was that some synthetic a priori principles must be in place for experience to be possible.

Unlike Newton, Kant thought that proper science is not possible without metaphysics. Yet his understanding of metaphysics contrasted sharply with that of his predecessors. Metaphysics, Kant thought, was a science, in particular, the science of synthetic a priori judgments. Mathematics is a key element in the construction of natural science proper; without mathematics no doctrine concerning determinate natural things is possible. On these grounds, Kant argued that the chemistry of his age was more of an art than a science. The irony, Kant thought, was that though many past great thinkers (Newton in particular) repudiated metaphysics and relied on mathematics to understand nature, they failed to see that such reliance on mathematics made them unable to dispense with metaphysics. For, in the end, they had to treat matter in abstraction from any particular experiences. They postulated universal laws without inquiring into their a priori sources.

As Kant argued in his *Critique of Pure Reason* (1781/1965), the a priori source of the universal laws of nature is the transcendental principles of pure understanding. These constitute the object of knowledge in general. Thought (that is, the understanding) imposes on objects in general certain characteristics in virtue of which objects become knowable. Phenomenal objects are constituted as objects of experience by the schematized categories of quantity, quality, substance, causation, and community. If an object is to be an object of experience, it must have certain necessary characteristics: It must be extended; its qualities must admit of degrees; it must be a substance in causal interaction with other substances. In his three Analogies of Experience, Kant tried to prove that three general principles hold for all objects of experience: that substance is permanent, that all changes conform to the law of cause and effect, and that all substances are in thoroughgoing interaction. These synthetic a priori principles make experience possible. In particular, there is the universal law of causation, namely, that "everything that happens, that is, begins to be, presupposes something upon which it follows by rule." This is nothing like an empirical generalization. Rather, it is imposed by the mind on objects.

Yet these transcendental principles make no reference to any objects of experience in particular. In his *Metaphysical Foundations of Natural Science* (1786/1970), Kant sought to show how these principles could be concretized in the form of laws of matter in motion. Kant thus enunciated the law of conservation of the quantity of matter, the law of inertia, and the law of equality of action and reaction, and he thought that these laws were the concrete mechanical analogues of his general transcendental principles. These laws were metaphysical laws in that they determined the possible behavior of matter in accordance with mathematical rules. They determine the pure and formal structure of motion, where motion is treated *in abstracto* purely mathematically. It is no accident, of course, that the last two of these laws (the law of inertia and the law of equality of action and reaction) are akin to Newton's laws and that the first law (the law of conservation of the quantity of matter) was presupposed by Newton too. Kant intended his metaphysical foundations of (the possibility of) matter in motion to show how Newtonian mechanics was possible. But Kant also thought that there are physical laws that are discovered empirically. Though he held as true a priori that matter and motion arise out of repulsive and attractive forces, he claimed that the laws of particular forces, even the law of universal attraction as the cause of gravity, can only be discovered empirically.

His predecessors, Kant thought, had failed to see the hierarchy of laws that make natural science possible: transcendental laws that determine the object of possible experience in general, metaphysical laws that determine matter in general, and physical laws that fill in the actual concrete details of motion. Unlike the third kind, laws of the first two kinds require a priori justification and are necessarily true. Though philosophically impeccable, Kant's architectonic suffered severe blows in the nineteenth and early twentieth centuries. The blows came, by and large, from science itself. Creating an explosive mixture that led to the collapse of Kant's synthetic a priori principles were the crisis of Newtonian mechanics, the emergence of Albert Einstein's special and general theories of relativity, the advent of quantum theory, the emergence of non-Euclidean geometries and their application to physics, Gottlob Frege's claim that arithmetic, far from being synthetic a priori, was a body of analytic truths, and David Hilbert's arithmetization of geometry, which proved that no intuition was necessary. It is no exaggeration to claim that much of philosophy of science in the first half of the twentieth century was an attempt to come to terms with the collapse of the Kantian synthetic a priori and to re-cast (or even cast to the wind) the concepts of the a priori and the analytic so as to do justice to developments in the sciences.

WHEWELL VERSUS MILL

The nineteenth century saw the culmination of Newtonian mechanics, mostly in the able hands of Pierre-Simon Laplace (1749–1827) and his followers. The Newtonian framework was extended to capture other phenomena, from optics, to heat, to electricity and magnetism. But Kant's philosophy was very much the doctrine that almost every serious thinker about science had to reckon with. William Whewell (1794–1866) took from Kant the view that ideas (or concepts) are necessary for experience in that only through them can facts be bound together. He noted, for instance, that induction gives rise to a "new mental element." The concept of elliptical orbit, he thought, was not already there in the astronomical data employed by Johannes Kepler, but was a new mental element added by Kepler. But, unlike Kant, he thought that history (and the history of science in particular) had a key role to play in understanding science and its philosophy. He analyzed this role in *The Philosophy of the Inductive Sciences, Founded upon Their History* (1840). Each science grows through three stages, Whewell thought. It begins with a "prelude," in which a mass of unconnected facts is collected. It then enters an "inductive epoch," in which the useful theories of creative scientists bring order to these facts—an act of "colligation." Finally, a "sequel" follows, where the successful theory is extended, refined, and applied. Whewell strongly emphasized the role of hypotheses in science. Hypotheses can be proven true, he thought, by a "consilience of inductions," by which he meant the theoretical unification that occurs when a theory explains data of a kind different from those it was initially introduced to explain, and when a theory unifies hitherto unrelated domains. Indeed, Whewell found in the consilience of inductions a criterion of truth.

His contemporary John Stuart Mill (1806–1873) took an empiricist turn. Mill was a thoroughgoing inductivist who took all knowledge to arise from experience through induction. He even held that the law of universal causation, namely, that for every event there is a set of circumstances upon which it follows as an invariable and unconditional consequent, is inductively established. Hence, Mill denied that there could be any certain and necessary knowledge. But Mill also tried to delineate the scientific method so that it leads to secure causal knowledge of the world. In *A System of Logic, Ratiocinative and Inductive* (1843/1911) he put forward the method of agreement and the method of difference. According to the first, the cause is the common factor in a number of otherwise different cases in which the effect occurs. According to the second, the cause is the factor that is different in two cases that are similar except that the effect occurs in one, but not the other. In effect, Mill's methods encapsulate what is going on in controlled experiments. Mill was adamant, however, that his methods work *only if* certain substantive metaphysical assumptions are in place: that events have causes, that events have a *limited* number of possible causes, and that the same causes have the same effects, and conversely.

Mill was involved in a debate with Whewell concerning the role of novel predictions. Unlike Whewell, Mill thought that no predictions could *prove* the truth of a theory. He suggested that a hypothesis could not be proved true on the basis that it accounts for known phenomena, since other hypotheses may fair equally well in this respect. He added that novel predictions cannot provide proof either, since they carry no extra weight over predictions of known facts. Mill's target was not just the crude version of the method of hypothesis. He wanted to attack the legitimacy of the rival substantive assumption featured in Whewell's more sophisticated view, namely, that elimination of rival hypotheses can and should be based on explanatory considerations. The difference between Mill and Whewell was over the role of substantive explanatory considerations in scientific method. The debate continues.

CONVENTIONALISM

The inductivist tradition that flourished in England in the nineteenth century was challenged by the rise of French conventionalism. The work of Henri Poincaré (1854–1912) on the foundations of geometry raised the question of whether physical space is Euclidean. In *La science et l'hypothèse* (*Science and Hypothesis*; 1902/1952), Poincaré took this question to be meaningless, because, he suggested, one can make physical space possess *any* geometry one likes, provided that one makes suitable adjustments to one's physical theories. Consequently, he called the axioms of Euclidean geometry "conventions" (definitions in disguise). He extended his geometric conventionalism further by arguing that the principles of mechanics are also conventions. Conventions, for Poincaré, are general principles that are held to be true but whose truth can neither be the product of a priori reasoning nor be established on a posteriori grounds. But calling general principles "conventions" did not imply, for Poincaré, that their adoption (or choice) was arbitrary. He stressed that some principles were more convenient than others. He thought that considerations of simplicity and unity, as well as certain experiential facts, could and should guide the relevant choice. Indeed, he envisaged a hierarchy of the sciences in which the axioms of Euclidean geometry and the principles of Newtonian mechanics are in place (as ultimately freely chosen conventions) so as to make possible empirical and testable physical science.

Though Poincaré took scientific theories to be mixtures of conventions and facts, he favored a structuralist account of scientific knowledge that was Kantian in origin. The basic axioms of geometry and mechanics are (ultimately freely chosen) conventions, and yet, he thought, scientific hypotheses proper, even high-level ones such as Maxwell's laws, are empirical. Faced with discontinuity in theory change (the fact that some basic scientific hypotheses and laws are abandoned in the transition from one theory to another), he argued that there is, nonetheless, substantial continuity at the level of the mathematical equations that represent empirical and theoretical relations. From this, he concluded that the theoretical content of scientific theories is structural, by which he meant that a theory, if successful, correctly represents the *structure* of the world. In the end, the structure of the world is revealed by structurally convergent scientific theories.

THE RISE OF ATOMISM

The beginning of the twentieth century was marked by a heated debate over atomism, an emergent scientific theory that posited unobservable entities, atoms, to account for a host of observable phenomena (from chemical bonding to Brownian motion). Though many scientists adopted atomism right away, there was strong resistance to it by other eminent scientists. Ernst Mach (1838–1916) resisted atomism on the basis of the empiricist claim that the concept of atoms was radically different from ordinary empirical concepts, and hence problematic. Resistance to atomism was best exemplified in the writings of Pierre Duhem (1861–1916). In *La théorie physique, son objet, sa structure* (*The Aim and Structure of Physical Theory*; 1906/1954), he put forward an antiexplanationist form of instrumentalism that sharply distinguished science and metaphysics, and claimed that explanation belongs to metaphysics and not to science.

But Duhem's theory of science rested on a restricted understanding of scientific method that can be captured by the equation "scientific method = experience + logic." On this view, whatever cannot be proved from experience with the help of logic is irredeemably suspect. To be sure, theories, as hypothetico-deductive systems, help scientists classify and organize the observable phenomena. But, for Duhem, the theoretical hypotheses of theories can never be confirmed or accepted as true. At best, they can be appraised as convenient or inconvenient, empirically adequate or empirically inadequate, classifications of the phenomena. Ironically, Duhem himself offered some of the best arguments against his own instrumentalist conception of theories. The most central one comes from the possibility of *novel* predictions. If a theory were just a "rack filled with tools," it would be hard to understand how it can be "a prophet for us" (Duhem 1906/1954, p. 27).

Duhem was a strong critic of inductivism. He argued that observation in science is not just the act of reporting phenomena. It is the interpretation of phenomena in the light of some theory and other background knowledge. This thesis, known as the view that observation is theory-laden, resurfaced in the 1960s, at that time drawing on a mass of empirical evidence coming from psychology to the effect that perceptual experience is theoretically interpreted. Duhem also stressed that there can be no crucial experiments in science, since no theory can be tested in isolation from other theories (and auxiliary assumptions), and consequently, that any theory can be saved from refutation by making suitable adjustments to collateral theories or auxiliary assumptions.

THE A PRIORI SET IN MOTION

Though battered by developments in physics and mathematics, the Kantian conception of a priori principles did find a place of sorts in the work of the neo-Kantian school of Marburg, Germany. In *Substance and Function* (1910/1923), Ernst Cassirer (1874–1945) argued that, though mathematical structures are necessary for experience, in that phenomena can be identified, organized, and structured *only* if they are embedded in such structures, these structures need not be fixed and immutable for all time. He thought that mathematical structures, though a priori (since they are required for objective experience), are revisable yet convergent: Newer structures accommodate old ones within themselves.

But it was Hans Reichenbach (1891–1953), in *The Theory of Relativity and A Priori Knowledge* (1921/1965), who unpacked the two aspects of Kant's conception of the a priori: that a priori truths are necessarily true, and that they structure objects of knowledge. Reichenbach rejected the first aspect of a priori knowledge, but insisted that the second aspect was inescapable. Knowledge of the physical world, he thought, requires principles of coordination, that is, principles that connect the basic concepts of the theory with reality. These principles he took to structure experience. Mathematics, he thought, was indispensable precisely because it provided a framework of general rules for coordinating scientific concepts and reality. Once this framework is in place, a theory can be presented as an axiomatic system, whose basic axioms (what Reichenbach called "axioms of connection") are empirical. Against Kant, Reichenbach argued that a priori principles of coordination, though they structure objects of knowledge, can be rationally revised in response to experience. He was naturally led to conclude that the only workable notion of the a priori is one that is *relativized*.

LOGICAL POSITIVISM

The influence of Moritz Schlick (1882–1936) on the philosophical course of events can hardly be exaggerated. Armed with the notion of convention, he and his followers, the logical positivists, tried to show that there can be no synthetic a priori at all. They extended conventionalism to logic and mathematics, arguing that the only distinction possible is between empirical (synthetic a posteriori) principles and conventional (analytic a priori) ones. In particular, though they thought that empirical science requires a logico-mathematical framework to be in place before theories can get any grip on reality, this conventional and analytic framework is purely *formal* and is *empty* of factual content. Accordingly, all a priori knowledge is analytic. Moreover, the logical positivists' conventionalist account of analyticity implies that grasping a priori (or analytic) truths requires no special faculty of intuition and that having epistemic access to a priori (or analytic) truths presents no deep philosophical problem. Accompanying the doctrine that analytic truths are definitions or stipulations was the so-called linguistic doctrine of necessity: that all and only analytic truths are necessary. In the spirit of Hume, this doctrine excised all necessity from nature, and had already played a key role in Ludwig Wittgenstein's *Tractatus Logico-Philosophicus*.

The logical positivists adopted an empiricist criterion of meaning known as the verification principle. Nonanalytic statements, that is, synthetic empirical statements, are meaningful (cognitively significant) if and only if their truth can be verified in experience. In slogan form, the meaning is the method of verification. The logical positivists used this criterion to show that statements of traditional metaphysics were meaningless, since their truth (or falsity) made no difference in experience.

Soon after the foregoing criterion of meaning was adopted, a fierce intellectual debate started among members of the Vienna Circle, a debate that spanned a good deal of the 1930s and came to be known as the "protocol-statements debate." Protocol statements were supposed to capture the content of scientists' observations in such a basic form that they can be immediately verified. One issue was whether protocol statements are (should be) expressed in physical-object language ("The needle points to 2 on the dial") or in phenomenal language ("A black line overlies a "2" shape on a white background"). Though the balance soon turned in favor of the former, Rudolf Carnap (1891–1970), following Schlick, did toy with the idea that protocol statements need no justification, for they constitute the simplest states in which knowledge can be had. But he was soon convinced by the arguments of Otto Neurath (1882–1945) that there are neither self-justified protocol statements nor statements not subject to revision, if only because the processes that yield them are fallible. Instead of abandoning the claim that science provides knowledge, on the grounds that this knowledge cannot be certain, Carnap opted for the view that scientific knowledge falls short of certainty. Armed with Alfred Tarski's account of truth, he claimed that the truth of a scientific statement is no less knowable than the statement itself.

In the course of the 1930s, the concept of verifiability moved from a strict sense of being provable on the basis of experience to the much more liberal sense of being confirmable. The chief problem was that the strong criterion of cognitive significance failed to deliver the goods. In addition to metaphysical statements, many ordinary scientific assertions, those that express universal laws of nature, turn out meaningless on this criterion,

precisely because they are not, strictly speaking, verifiable.

According to the logical positivists, Hilbert's approach to geometry and the Duhem and Poincaré hypothetico-deductive account of scientific theories, if combined, offer a powerful and systematic way to present scientific theories. The basic principles of the theory are taken to be the axioms. But the terms and predicates of the theory are stripped of their interpretation, or meaning. Hence, the axiomatic system itself is entirely formal.

The advantage of the axiomatic approach is that it lays bare the logical structure of the theory, which can then be investigated independently of the meaning, if any, one may assign to its terms and predicates. However, as a formal system, the theory lacks any empirical content. For the theory to acquire such content, its terms and predicates have to be suitably interpreted. It was a central thought of the logical positivists that a scientific theory need not be completely interpreted to be meaningful and applicable. They claimed that it is enough that only *some* terms and predicates, the so-called observational ones, be interpreted. The other terms and predicates of the theory, in particular, those that, taken at face value, purport to refer to unobservable entities, were deemed theoretical and were taken to be only partially interpreted by means of correspondence rules. It was soon realized, however, that the correspondence rules muddle the distinction between the analytic (meaning-related) part and the synthetic (fact-stating) part of a scientific theory—a distinction that was central in the thought of the logical positivists. For, on the one hand, the correspondence rules specify (even if only partly) the meaning of theoretical terms, and on the other hand, they contribute to the factual content of the theory.

A GHOSTLY DISTINCTION

A key idea developed in Carnap's *Logical Syntax of Language* (1934/1937) was that the development of a general theory of the logical syntax of the logico-mathematical language of science would provide a neutral framework in which scientific theories are cast and studied, scientific concepts (e.g., explanation, confirmation, laws, etc.) are explicated, and traditional metaphysical disputes are overcome. The project required a sharp analytic-synthetic distinction. Philosophical statements would be analytic (about the language of science), and scientific statements would be synthetic (about the world). A central (and stable) tenet of Carnap's was the principle of tolerance. Since the choice of a language is a conventional matter (to be evaluated only in terms of its practical fruitfulness), the aim of philosophy of science, Carnap held, is to make clear the different language *forms* adopted by rival parties in philosophical and scientific disputes (e.g., the dispute between logicists and intuitionists in mathematics, or between realists and idealists, Platonists and nominalists, scientific realists and instrumentalists in philosophy of science). Far from being genuinely factual, these disputes, Carnap thought, center on suitable choices of a language. The principle of tolerance is thus part of Carnap's attempt to eliminate metaphysical "pseudoproblems" from the sciences. It formulates a metatheoretical standpoint in which issues of ontology are replaced by issues concerning logical syntax.

Carnap's project in *The Logical Syntax of Language* came to grief. This was the result of many factors, but prominent among them were Tarski's work on truth (which suggested that truth is an irreducibly semantic notion) and Kurt Gödel's incompleteness theorem. Though Carnap was fully aware of Gödel's limitative results, his own attempt to provide a neutral, minimal metatheoretical framework (the framework of "General Syntax" [1934/1937, pt. IV]) in which the concept of analyticity was defined fell prey to Gödel's proof that some mathematical truths are not provable within such a system.

The notion of analytic a priori truths came under heavy attack from W. V. O. Quine (1908–2000). In "Two Dogmas of Empiricism" (1951), Quine argued that the notion of analyticity is deeply problematic, since it requires a notion of cognitive synonymy (sameness of meaning) and there is no independent criterion of cognitive synonymy. Quine's chief argument against the analytic/synthetic distinction rested on the view that "analytic" was taken to mean unrevisable. If analytic statements have no empirical content, experience cannot possibly have any bearing on their truth-values. So analytic statements cannot undergo truth-value revision. But, Quine argued, nothing (not even logical truths) is unrevisable. Hence, there cannot be any analytic truths. Here Quine took a leaf from Duhem's book (and also from Carnap's book). Confirmation and refutation are holistic; they accrue to systems (theories) as a whole and not to their constituent statements, taken individually. If a theory is confirmed, then everything it says is confirmed. Conversely, if a theory is refuted, then *any* part of it can be revised (abandoned) to restore accord with experience. The image of science that emerged had no place for truths with a special status: all truths are on a par. This leads to a blurring of the distinction between the factual and the conventional. What matters for Quine is

that a theory acquires its empirical content as a whole, by issuing in observational statements and by being confronted with experience.

The cogency of Quine's attack on the a priori rests on the cogency of equating the notion of a priori with the notion of unrevisable. We have already seen a strand in post-Kantian thinking that denied this equation, while holding onto the view that some principles structure experience. It might not be surprising, then, that Carnap was not particularly moved by Quine's criticism. For he *too* denied this equation. Quine, however, did have a point. For Carnap, (a) it is rational to accept analytic statements within a linguistic framework; (b) it is rational to reject them when the framework changes; and (c) all and only analytic statements share some characteristic that distinguishes them from synthetic statements. Even if Quine's criticisms are impotent against (a) and (b), they are quite powerful against (c). The point was simply that the dual role of correspondence rules (and the concomitant Hilbert-style implicit definition of theoretical terms) made drawing this distinction impossible, even *within* a theory. Carnap spent a great deal of effort to develop the characteristic specified in (c). In the end, he had to reinvent Ramsey sentences to find a plausible way to draw the line between the analytic and the synthetic (Psillos 1999, chap. 3).

The challenge to the very possibility of a priori knowledge was a key factor in the *naturalist turn* in the philosophy of science in the 1960s. The emergence of naturalism was a real turning point in the philosophy of science, because it amounted to an ultimate break with neo-Kantianism in all its forms. By the 1960s, philosophy of science had seen the advent of psychologism, naturalism, and history of science.

See also Bayes, Bayes' Theorem, Bayesian Approach to Philosophy of Science; Constructivism and Conventionalism; Laws of Nature; Laws, Scientific; Philosophy of Science, Problems of; Scientific Realism.

Bibliography

Aristotle. *Posterior Analytics*. 2nd ed. Oxford, U.K.: Clarendon Press, 1993.

Bacon, Francis. *The New Organon* (1620), edited by Fulton H. Anderson. New York: Macmillan, 1960.

Burtt, Edwin A. *The Metaphysical Foundations of Modern Physical Science*. 2nd ed. London: Routledge and Kegan Paul, 1932.

Carnap, Rudolf. *The Logical Syntax of Language* (1934). Translated by Amethe Smeaton. London: Kegan Paul, 1937.

Cassirer, Ernst. *Substance and Function* (1910). Translated by William Curtis Swabey and Marie Collins Swabey. Chicago: Open Court, 1923.

Cohen, I. Bernard. *The Birth of a New Physics*. London: Penguin, 1985.

Descartes, René. *Principles of Philosophy* (1644). In *The Philosophical Writings of Descartes*, Vol. 1. Translated by John Cottingham, Robert Stootfoff, and Dugald Murdoch. Cambridge, U.K.: Cambridge University Press, 1985.

Duhem, Pierre. *The Aim and Structure of Physical Theory* (1906). Translated by Philip Wiener. Princeton, NJ: Princeton University Press, 1954.

Duhem, Pierre. *To Save the Phenomena* (1908). Translated by Edmund Doland and Chaninah Mascher. Chicago: University of Chicago Press, 1969.

Duns Scotus, John. *Philosophical Writings: A Selection*. Translated by Allan Wolter. Indianapolis, IN: Hackett, 1987.

Gower, Barry. *Scientific Method: An Historical and Philosophical Introduction*. London: Routledge, 1998.

Grant, Edward. *Physical Science in the Middle Ages*. Cambridge, U.K.: Cambridge University Press, 1977.

Hume, David. *A Treatise of Human Nature* (1739), edited by L. A. Selby-Bigge. 2nd ed. edited by P. H. Nidditch. Oxford, U.K.: Clarendon Press, 1978.

Kant, Immanuel. *Critique of Pure Reason* (1787). Translated by Norman Kemp Smith. New York: St. Martin's Press, 1965.

Kant, Immanuel. *Metaphysical Foundations of Natural Science* (1786). Translated by James Ellington. Indianapolis, IN: Bobbs-Merrill, 1970.

Lindberg, David C., ed. *Science in the Middle Ages*. Chicago: University of Chicago Press, 1978.

Locke, John. *An Essay concerning Human Understanding* (1689). Oxford, U.K.: Clarendon Press, 1975.

Losee, John. *A Historical Introduction to the Philosophy of Science*. 4th ed. Oxford, U.K.: Oxford University Press, 2001.

Mill, John Stuart. *A System of Logic, Ratiocinative and Inductive* (1843). 8th ed. London: Longmans, Green, 1911.

Ockham, William. *Philosophical Writings: A Selection*. Translated by Philotheus Boehner. Indianapolis, IN: Hackett, 1990.

Poincaré, Henri. *Science and Hypothesis* (1902). New York: Dover, 1952.

Psillos, Stathis. *Scientific Realism: How Science Tracks Truth* (1999). London: Routledge.

Quine, W. V. O. "Two Dogmas of Empiricism." *Philosophical Review* 60 (1951): 20–43.

Reichenbach, Hans. *The Theory of Relativity and A Priori Knowledge* (1921). Translated by Maria Reichenbach. Berkeley: University of California Press, 1965.

Thayer, H. S., ed. *Newton's Philosophy of Nature: Selections from His Writings*. New York: Hafner, 1953.

Whewell, William. *The Philosophy of the Inductive Sciences, Founded upon Their History*. London: J. W. Parker, 1840.

Whewell, William. *Theory of Scientific Method*. Indianapolis, IN: Hackett, 1989.

Stathis Psillos (2005)

PHILOSOPHY OF SCIENCE, PROBLEMS OF

The scope of the philosophy of science is sufficiently broad to encompass, at one extreme, conceptual problems so intimately connected with science itself that their solution may as readily be regarded a contribution to science as to philosophy and, at the other extreme, problems of so general a philosophical bearing that their solution would as much be a contribution to metaphysics or epistemology as to philosophy of science proper. Similarly, the range of issues investigated by philosophers of science may be so narrow as to concern the explication of a single concept, considered of importance in a single branch of science, and so general as to be concerned with structural features invariant to all the branches of science, taken as a class. Accordingly, it is difficult to draw boundaries that neatly separate philosophy of science from philosophy, from science, or even from the history of science, broadly interpreted. But we can give some characterization of the main groups of problems if we think of science as concerned with providing descriptions of phenomena under which significant regularities emerge and with explaining these regularities. Problems thus arise in connection with terms, with laws, and with theories where a theory is understood as explaining a law and a law is understood as stating the regularities that appear in connection with descriptions of phenomena.

TERMS

Ordinary language provides us the wherewithal to offer indefinitely rich descriptions of individual objects, and, as a matter of logical fact, no description, however rich, will exhaustively describe a given object, however simple. Science chooses a deliberately circumscribed vocabulary for describing objects, and scientists may be said to be concerned only with those objects described with the vocabulary of their science and with these only insofar as they are so describable. Historically, the terms first applied by scientists were continuous with their cognates in ordinary speech, just as science itself was continuous with common experience. But special usages quickly developed, and an important class of philosophical problems concerns the relation between scientific and ordinary language, as well as that between those terms selected for purposes of scientific description and other terms that, though applicable to all the same objects as the former, have no obvious scientific use. Scientists from Galileo Galilei to Arthur Eddington have sometimes tended to impugn as unreal those properties of things not covered by scientific description or at least have thought that the question of which are the real properties is an important one. Certainly, it would destroy the very concept of science to suppose it possible to account for all the distinctions between things under all the descriptions of them that are feasible, but there is no recipe for selecting the scientifically relevant predicates.

In practice, terms have been chosen when there seem to be interesting and systematic patterns of change in the properties picked out by these terms—for instance, between the distance a body travels and the time it takes to do so, between the temperature and the pressure of a gas, between the density of a fluid and the deviation from a norm of a light ray passing into it, and so forth. It has often been immensely difficult to set aside manifest and cherished differences among objects and the subtle language for expressing these in favor of the spare vocabulary of science under which such seemingly crucial distinctions are obliterated, as, for example, between celestial and terrestrial objects or between "noble" and base metals.

Not only do scientific terms cut across the distinctions of common sense, but they also permit distinctions not ordinarily made and allow comparisons more precise than ordinarily demanded—for example, between differential amounts and precisely determinable degrees. For the class of terms discussed here are those that may be said to apply or not to apply to a given object by means of an act of observation rendered precise through some device of mensuration—for example, that the distance traveled is n units along a scale, that the temperature of a gas is n degrees along another scale, that the density of a fluid is m grams per cubic centimeter. The last measurement, which involves reference to different scales— namely, measures of mass and volume—is sometimes called a "derived" in contrast with a "fundamental" measurement, where only single scales are involved. But even when we speak of derived measurements, as with pressure (in terms of foot-pounds), velocity (in terms of feet per second), or stress (in terms of force per unit area), we remain within the domain of observation; the coincidence of a needle with a mark on a gauge, the angle of a balance, the appearance of a color, a bubble between lines, or a certain buzz, inform us that a given term is true or false with respect to whatever we are studying.

Philosophers may press for a further reduction of the observational language of a science to a favored idiom— for example, to a sense-datum language—but within science observational vocabulary enjoys a certain ultimacy. There are many questions as to whether observational language, thus construed, is sufficient for the entire conduct of science, whether the whole language of science can be expressed in purely observational terms so that recourse need never be made to covert entities, hidden processes, or occult structures unamenable to direct observation and measurement. This issue cannot be fruitfully discussed until we come to the topic of theories, but it has been recognized that while observation has an essential role to play as the occasion for framing and the basis for testing scientific hypotheses, the no less important feature of measurement sets a limit on the program of thoroughgoing observationalism. For the algorithms, in connection with which it first makes scientific sense to assign numerical values and to apply scales, require use of the real number system, the class of whose values has the power of the continuum.

Hence, as Carl G. Hempel remarked, "A full definition of metrical terms by means of observables is not possible." Nevertheless, it has been through the efforts of reductionists to assimilate the entirety of scientific language to observation terms that other sorts of terms, having logically distinct roles within science, have been discovered, and a main task in philosophy of science has been to identify and determine the relation between terms occurring at different levels, and variously related to observation, within the idiom of developed scientific theories.

LAWS

One cannot very readily treat the syntactical features of laws in isolation from their semantic properties or, for that matter, from pragmatic considerations. Syntax here concerns the formal conditions of "lawlikeness" for sentences, and semantics concerns the truth conditions for lawlike sentences, it being customary to define a law as a true lawlike sentence. But some philosophers will reject this definition since it might rule out any sentence as having the status of a law, inasmuch as laws are not, they feel, the sorts of sentences that it makes sense to regard as admitting truth-values in the normal way or even at all; for these a law would be a lawlike sentence which has a certain use.

It is commonly supposed that a universally quantified conditional sentence—$(x)(Fx \supset Gx)$—is the simplest form with which a lawlike sentence may be expressed. The chief syntactical problems arise, however in connection with the nonlogical terms F and G. For an important class of cases these will be observational, so that it is in principle possible to determine whether a given instance is both F and G, and the law is generally based upon some known favorable instances, Yet there are cases in which the terms satisfy observational criteria, in which there are a large class of favorable instances and no known counterinstances, and still the appearance of these terms in a lawlike sentence L disqualifies L as a law even if it is true. Such terms are unduly restricted in scope, whereas it is thought that the terms suitable for laws should be unrestricted in scope. "All the hairs on my head are black" employs the restrictive term "the hairs on my head" and thus is disqualified as a law.

A criterion sometimes advanced for identifying restrictive terms as antecedents in possible laws is that if the requisite universal conditional supports a true counterfactual, it is a law, but if the counterfactual is false, as (with reference to a certain white hair) "If that hair were on my head, it would be black" is false, then the corresponding sentence is not a law, and the term is restricted. However, this criterion begs the question insofar as it seems that counterfactuals must be analyzed in terms of general laws; at any rate, the analysis of counterfactuals, as well as the basis for distinguishing true from false counterfactuals, remains to be given by philosophers. In what sense "the hairs on my head" is restrictive, whereas *ravens* in "All ravens are black" is not, is difficult to specify, though the former does refer to a specific object (my head) and it is believed that the terms in a law must not make such references. This restriction, however, makes Johannes Kepler's laws laws in name only and forestalls the possibility of any laws for the universe as a whole. And though Kepler's laws may be retained since they are derivable from laws that employ unrestricted and generally referential terms, the laws of the universe hardly could be thus derived; moreover, it could be argued that "All the hairs on my head are black" might be derivable from some general laws of hirsuteness, making use only of purely qualitative predicates. Thus, precise and rigorous criteria for lawlikeness are difficult to specify.

If the terms of a lawlike sentence L must be unrestricted, L cannot be known as true through induction by finite enumeration; since there must in principle always be uninspected instances under F, the law $(x)(Fx \supset Gx)$ cannot be known true no matter how many known favorable instances there are. Of course, laws are not always (and perhaps not even often) inductive generalizations from large samples—Galileo's laws, for instance, were based upon few observations indeed—and it has been maintained by anti-inductivists (chiefly Karl Popper and his followers) that observations function as tests rather than inductive bases for laws; in this view laws need not be generalizations from observation but only be in prin-

ciple falsifiable on the basis of observation. Some lawlike sentences may be known false, at least to the extent that they admit of observational consequences, but often the antecedent of a lawlike sentence is sufficiently hedged with *ceteris paribus* riders, to which we may add indefinitely, that one need not surrender a law save as an act of will.

This suggests that the criteria for accepting a lawlike sentence as a law are more complex than either inductivists or their opponents have recognized, and an instrumentalist position may be taken, in accord with which laws are neither true nor false but serve as instruments in the facilitation of inference—"inference-tickets," as Gilbert Ryle put it. In this view, as Stephen Toulmin pointed out, the question is not "'Is it true?' but 'When does it hold?'" Here laws are regarded not as sentences about the world but as rules for conducting ourselves in it, and semantic considerations thus yield to pragmatic ones in that there is surely some agreement that a criterion for accepting L as a law is that it should, in conjunction with information, furnish successful predictions. Whether, in addition, a successful law is true and, if so, in what sense it is true other than that it successfully enables predictions cannot be discussed independently of larger philosophical considerations.

Many laws in science are statistical in form, but the suggestion that a law may be truly scientific and yet affirm a merely probable connection among phenomena has been offensive to scientists and philosophers with antecedent commitments to determinism as a metaphysical fact or a scientific ideal. For these nothing less than deterministic (nonstatistical) laws are ultimately tolerable, so that statistical laws, while countenanced as interim makeshifts, are, ideally, to be replaced in every instance with deterministic ones. As a program, however, the projected reconstruction of statistical laws and the theories that contain them has encountered an impressive obstacle in the quantum theory of matter, upon which the whole of atomic physics is based, for the laws here are demonstrably irreducible to deterministic form.

To be sure, there is a logical possibility that quantum theory could be replaced in toto. But there is no way—for instance through the discovery of hidden variables—in which its laws may be rendered deterministic, and since there is scant evidence for any alternative and the evidence for quantum theory is overwhelming, most members of the scientific community are reconciled to an obdurate indeterminism at the core of one of its most fundamental theories. If the quantum theory should be true, certain events are objectively probable, or indeterministic; that is, they are probable independently of the state of our knowledge or ignorance.

An epistemological sense of probability, connected with our concepts of induction and confirmation, is not incompatible with determinism; we may even speak of the probability of a deterministic law, meaning that relative to our evidence its degree of confirmation is equal to a number between 0 and 1. It is nonepistemological probability, according to which we could conceivably be certain that a given event were objectively probable, which is allegedly repugnant to determinism. It should be pointed out, however, that indeterministic laws may be deterministic in at least the sense that the values of certain probability variables are precisely determined by the values of other variables. At any rate, the extent of incompatibility between determinism and indeterministic laws and the precise explication of the two kinds of probability are topics of continuing philosophical investigation and controversy.

Laws are believed to play an important role in explanation as well as in prediction. It has been maintained that a necessary condition for explaining an event E consists in bringing E under the same general law with which it could have been predicted. Hempel regards the temporal position of the scientist vis-à-vis the event as the sole difference between explaining and predicting that event. This symmetry has been challenged (notably by Israel Scheffler), but we might still maintain Hempel's thesis by distinguishing among laws. Not every law used in prediction has explanatory force if we think of explanations as causal explanations, for causal laws do not exhaust the class of scientific laws, which also includes functional expressions of covariation among magnitudes, statistical laws, and so on, all of which are used in predicting. Even so, it has been questioned whether even causal explanation requires the use of causal laws, either in science or in history or the social sciences, where this controversy has been chiefly focused.

Be this as it may, the explanation of particular events has less importance in science proper than the explanation of regularities, and it is therefore the explanation of laws that characterizes scientific achievement in its most creative aspect. This brings us to theories, for it is commonly held that to explain a law L is to derive L from a theory T when T satisfies certain conditions.

THEORIES

Let us characterize a law all of whose nonlogical terms are observational as an empirical law. A theory may be regarded as a system of laws, some of which are empiri-

cal. Not every empirical law is part of a theory, nor are all the laws of a theory empirical, for some of a theory's laws employ theoretical terms, which are nonobservational. Theoretical terms, if they denote at all, refer to unobservable entities or processes, and it is with respect to changes at this covert level that one explains the observed regularities as covered by empirical laws. Thus one explains the regularities covered by the Boyle–Charles law (all the terms of which are observational) in terms of the (unobservable) behavior of the gas molecules of which the gas is theoretically composed. The status of theoretical terms (and the theoretical entities they would designate if they designated anything) has been the subject of intense philosophical investigation. It is not mere unobservability—Julius Caesar is at this point in time unobservable though his name is not a theoretical term—but unobservability in principle that characterizes these entities; it is unclear whether there would be any sense in speaking of observing, say, Psi-functions, electrons, fields, superegos, and the like. Moreover, the behavior of theoretical entities, supposing the theory to be true, is (as with certain fundamental particles) often so grossly disanalogous to the behavior of the entities they are invoked to explain that our ordinary framework of concepts fails to apply to them.

Yet theoretical terms seem deeply embedded in scientific language. Empiricist strategies of eliminating them by explicit definition in observational language or of tying them to observation by reduction sentences have failed, although there exist techniques by which they may be formally replaced with striking ease. William Craig demonstrated that any theory containing both theoretical and observational predicates may be replaced with another employing only observational ones but yielding, nevertheless, all the observational theorems (or empirical laws) of the original. Craig's result, however, has not been a victory for empiricism; the reasons for this are somewhat obscure, but it is due in part at least to the realization that theoretical terms play a role and have a meaning in terms of the total structure of the theory and therefore cannot be neatly extricated to leave anything to be called a "theory." Indeed, it often happens that rather than theoretical terms being defined in observational terms, observational terms are defined with reference to the theoretical vocabulary, so that one must, in effect, master the theory in order to make the relevant observations.

With the elaboration of a theory, however, the inferential route from observation to (predicted) observation becomes complex (there may be many intervening steps and intermediate computations) and far removed from the simple universal conditional used to represent a law. A theory, in Hempel's words, "may be likened to a complex spatial network [which] floats, as it were, above the plane of observation and is anchored to it by rules of interpretation." Theories, that is, impinge upon experience as wholes but not in all their parts, and the rules of interpretation, or correspondence, which permit them to be applied, are not part of the theory; indeed, the same formal theoretical network might, through different interpretations, have application to different domains of experience.

We may think of a theory as a formal system distinguishable, in principle, from its interpretation, regarding the former (in R. B. Braithwaite's terms) as a calculus and the latter as its model. In point of scientific history and practice, however, model and calculus emerge together. The distinction first began to be clear through the advent of non-Euclidean geometries and the consequent agitated question of which was physically descriptive, and geometry, perhaps because it has been almost paradigmatic of axiomatic systems, has served as a pattern, at least for analytical purposes, for the calculi of theories generally. Thus, philosophers think of theories as employing primitive and derived terms, primitive and derived sentences, satisfying explicit formation and transformation rules, and the like. But whether, apart from the purposes of philosophical representation, actual scientific theories exhibit axiomatized form and whether axiomatization is even a desideratum for scientific theory-formation are moot points.

At any rate, the framing of theories in the course of history has almost always involved some intuitive model on the scientist's part, the pattern of thought being (whether this is or is not the "logic of discovery" that N. R. Hanson suggested) this, that the regularities for which explanation is sought would hold as a matter of course if certain states of affairs (those postulated by the theory) held in fact. Whether the theoretical states do hold in fact is, of course, the immediate question, and it is through the obligation to provide an answer that the scientific imagination is disciplined. Without the formal means of deriving testable consequences from a theory, the theory would merely be ad hoc, and one wants more than the mere deduction of the laws that the theory was intended to explain. Indeed, it is by and large the ability of a theory to permit derivations far afield from its original domain that serves as a criterion for accepting a theory, for in addition to the obvious fruitfulness such a criterion emphasizes, such derivations permit an increasingly broad and diversified basis for testing the theory. The

great theories in the development of science—Isaac Newton's, Albert Einstein's, Paul Dirac's—have brought into a single comprehensive system great numbers of phenomena not previously known to have been connected.

It is impossible to say, of course, whether the whole of scientific knowledge might someday be embraced in a single unified theory, but piecemeal assimilation of one theory to another is constantly taking place, and the conceptual issues that arise through such reductions are of immense philosophical interest. The careful elucidation of the logic of scientific reduction—of thermodynamics to mechanics, of wave and matrix mechanics—draws attention to features that lie, far more obscurely, within the oldest philosophical problems and controversies: problems of emergence, of natural kinds, of free will and determinism, of body and mind, and so on. The treatment of these questions is often not so much philosophy of science proper as the philosophical interpretation of science, in which the philosophy of science serves as a technique of philosophical clarification, illuminating topics remote from the conceptual issues of science as such.

See also Braithwaite, Richard Bevan; Eddington, Arthur Stanley; Empiricism; Explanation; Force; Galileo Galilei; Hempel, Carl Gustav; Laws, Scientific; Matter; Popper, Karl Raimund; Quantum Mechanics; Ryle, Gilbert; Thought Experiments in Science.

Bibliography

The literature on the philosophy of science is immense and often technical. Many influential papers are anthologized in *Philosophy of Science*, edited by Arthur C. Danto and Sidney Morgenbesser (New York: Meridian, 1960), and in *Readings in Philosophy of Science*, edited by Herbert Feigl and May Brodbeck (New York: Appleton-Century-Crofts, 1953).

The following may be consulted as representative and excellent discussions. On preliminary definition of the field see R. B. Braithwaite, *Scientific Explanation* (Cambridge, U.K.: Cambridge University Press, 1953), pp. 1–9, and Israel Scheffler, *The Anatomy of Inquiry* (New York: Knopf, 1963), pp. 3–15. On the observational bases of science see Carl G. Hempel, *Fundamentals of Concept Formation in Empirical Science* (Chicago: University of Chicago Press, 1952), especially pp. 20–50, and Scheffler, op. cit., pp. 127–222. On measurement see Ernest Nagel "Measurement," in Danto and Morgenbesser, op. cit., pp. 121–140. On laws see C. F. Presley, "Laws and Theories in the Physical Sciences," in Danto and Morgenbesser, op. cit., pp. 205–215; Ernest Nagel, *The Structure of Science* (New York: Harcourt Brace, 1960), especially pp. 29–78; and Stephen Toulmin, *Philosophy of Science* (London: Hutchinson, 1953), pp. 57–104. On the nonlogical terms of laws see Carl G. Hempel and Paul Oppenheim, "The Logic of Explanation," in Feigl and Brodbeck, op. cit., pp. 319–352. On laws and falsifiability see Karl Popper, *The Logic of Scientific Discovery* (New York: Hutchinson, 1959), pp. 27–48. On explanation see Hempel and Oppenheim, op. cit. On the parity between explanation and prediction see Scheffler, op. cit., pp. 43–88. On theories see Braithwaite, op. cit., pp. 50–114; Nagel, *The Structure of Science*, op. cit., pp. 79–152; Presley, op. cit., pp. 215–225; Toulmin, op. cit., pp. 105–139. On Craig's theorem see Carl G. Hempel, "The Theoretician's Dilemma," in *Minnesota Studies in the Philosophy of Science*, edited by Herbert Feigl et al., Vol. II (Minneapolis: University of Minnesota Press, 1958), and Scheffler, op. cit., pp. 193–203. On the logic of discovery see N. R. Hanson, *Patterns of Discovery* (Cambridge, U.K.: Cambridge University Press, 1958), passim. On reduction of theories and related issues, see Nagel, *The Structure of Science*, pp. 336–397.

Arthur C. Danto (1967)

PHILOSOPHY OF SEX

In the last quarter of the twentieth century a distinct, new subarea of philosophy came to life, the philosophy of sex. Many philosophical books and professional journal articles on various aspects of sex appeared in print during this period; university-level courses devoted substantially or entirely to the philosophy of sex proliferated, as did textbooks for these courses (the first, the anthology *Philosophy and Sex*, was published in 1975, edited by Robert Baker and Frederick Elliston); and in 1977 a professional organization, The Society for the Philosophy of Sex and Love, was founded.

The new philosophical investigation of sexuality emerged partially in concert with second-wave feminism's critique of both the politics of sexual difference, including gender discrimination, and the politics of sexual desire and behavior, including widespread social and legal contempt for the sexual preferences and lifestyles of gays, lesbians, transsexuals, and the transgendered. But the philosophy of sex was (and has been) historically and thematically separate from any particular ethical, political, metaphysical, or religious perspective. Indeed, the discipline encompasses a host of viewpoints, schools, approaches, and methods, as shown by its eclectic teaching and research materials, for example, Igor Primoratz's collection *Human Sexuality* (1997) and Alan Soble's encyclopedia *Sex from Plato to Paglia* (2005).

By the early twenty-first century, scholars working in the philosophy of sex had exhumed much of its history, although many figures and movements remained to be explored. They had also written about numerous conceptual, ontological, ethical, and political matters. In addition to "sexual activity" and "sexual desire," perhaps the

two fundamental concepts (or phenomena) of the area, subjects investigated included marriage (same- and other-sex), fidelity and adultery, consent and coercion, seduction, exploitation, sexual objectification, sexual harassment, rape, date and acquaintance rape, pornography, prostitution (and other sex work), sexual perversion, incest, pedophilia, group sex, masturbation, sexual orientation, sadomasochism, and sex with and without love, commitment, or psychological intimacy (casual sex, promiscuity). Analytic, existentialist, phenomenological, poststructuralist, postmodernist, evolutionary, conservative, liberal, feminist, Marxist, and diverse religious philosophers have all had their say.

A HISTORY OF THE PHILOSOPHY OF SEX

The philosophical discussion of sex in the West began with the ancient Greek philosopher Plato (427–347 BCE). His dialogues *Symposium* and *Phaedrus*, which are about *eros* (identified in the former work as a powerful passion to possess the good and beautiful), are provocative, astute, and an indispensable foundation for anyone interested in pursuing the philosophy of sex. Although Plato's student Aristotle (384–322 BCE) had little to say about *eros*, he meditates at length in his *Nicomachean Ethics* (books 8, 9) about *philia* (friendship-love), arguing that genuine friends improve each other's virtue and want the good for each other for each other's sake. Those who engage in research in the philosophy of sex commonly also study the related phenomena of love and friendship. Furthermore, the philosophy of sex generates its most instructive results when approached interdisciplinarily, that is, when it pays attention not only (and most obviously) to the psychology of sex and love but also to the sociology and history of mating practices and marriage forms, the anthropology of sexual and fertility rites and rituals, and the anatomical, physiological, and genetic findings of biomedical science.

Between antiquity and the twenty-first century, many philosophers, theologians, and others in the humanities made significant contributions to the richness of the philosophy of sex. Among the figures who made a lasting impact is St. Augustine (354–430), the Bishop of Hippo (in North Africa). Augustine was a profound thinker about sex and the human condition, as can be seen in his *The City of God* (for example, book 14), in which he expresses apprehension (as Plato did) about the threat to self-mastery and individual contentment by the forcefulness of the sexual impulse. Also noteworthy are the people with whom Augustine had theological disputes over the nature of the prelapsarian sexuality of Adam and Eve and the effects on sexuality of the Fall: on the one side, the radically more sexually ascetic St. Jerome (the translator of a Latin Vulgate bible, in 380) and, on the other, the much more sexually relaxed Pelagians, including Julian (c. 386–454), Bishop of Eclanum—battles recounted well by Princeton University historian of religion Elaine Pagels (1988). Innumerable later medieval theologians were also important (see Brundage 1987), from Peter Abelard and his student, lover, and wife Heloise, whose tragic lives and impassioned letters are lessons in ardent sexual desire and an equally ardent Christianity, to St. Thomas Aquinas, tutored by Albertus Magnus (who also set about to merge Catholicism with Aristotle). In his stupendous *Summa theologiae* (1265–1273), Aquinas formulated a natural law theory that eventually (1879) became the authoritative foundation of Catholic teaching about sexuality.

After the medievalists, there came, from 1500 to 1900, a stream of colorful scholars: the skeptic Michel De Montaigne (1533–1592), author of the famous essay "On Friendship" and the lesser known "Of the Power of the Imagination," on sexuality; the French mathematician and rationalist philosopher René Descartes, whose last book (1649) was *The Passions of the Soul*; the Scottish empiricist philosopher David Hume, who proposed in his monumental *A Treatise of Human Nature* (1739–1740) that the amorous passion "betwixt the sexes" was composed of three discordant elements: kindness, lust, and a response to beauty (2.2.11); the Englishman Thomas Hobbes (life in the state of nature, he wrote in 1651, is "solitary, poor, nasty, brutish, and short" [*Leviathan*, sec. 1.13]), who contended in his earlier "Human Nature" (sec. 9.15) that sexual desire is actually composed of two distinct desires, a desire to be sexually pleased by the other person and (as anomalous as it sounds) a desire to please the other; his adversary, a defender of the state of nature, Jean-Jacques Rousseau (1712–1778), who promulgated terrifying warnings about the evils of self-abuse (the solitary vice) in his autobiography, *Confessions*, and in a treatise devoted to educational techniques, *Emile*; the philosopher and physician Bernard Mandeville, who, in *A Modest Defence of Publick Stews* (1724), praised prostitution in part because it prevented self-abuse, or so he was convinced; the bachelor Immanuel Kant (1724–1804), who alleged that sexual love not combined with "human love" is merely an appetite that, when satisfied, discards the other person like a lemon sucked dry (*Lectures on Ethics* 1997, Ak 27:384); the Marquis de Sade, whose inventory of acrobatic and monstrous sexual feats in *120 Days of Sodom* (c. 1785) proclaims that "anything goes,"

and who died in the Charenton insane asylum; G. W. F. Hegel, who, wielding dialectical logic in "On Love" (1797–1998), claimed that during sex (only during good sex?) "consciousness of a separate self disappears, and all distinction between the lovers is annulled" (p. 307); the Danish Christian-existentialist philosopher Søren Kierkegaard, whose brilliant "Diary of a Seducer" and portrayal of the aesthetic/sensual and ethical stages of life in *Either/Or* (1843) began the decade-long analysis of his broken engagement with his beloved Regine Olsen; a German fan of Kant, Arthur Schopenhauer (1788–1860), whose nineteenth-century metaphysics, philosophy of mind, and deification of the reproductive function of sexuality in *World as Will and Representation* uncannily anticipated both Charles Darwin and Sigmund Freud; Karl Marx and Friedrich Engels, whose *Communist Manifesto* (1848) equated being a prostitute and being a bourgeois wife, an idea far from dead among contemporary feminist scholars; John Stuart Mill, the author of the definitive feminist treatise *Subjection of Women*, who employed, in *On Liberty* (1859), his liberal utilitarianism to exonerate Mormon polygyny and pimps or brothels; and, closer to the fin-de-siècle, a German fan of Schopenhauer, Friedrich Nietzsche, who, with myriad scattered, sharp aphorisms about the sexes to his credit, still failed to negotiate benignly his crush on the vamp Lou Salomé and ended up dying in an insane asylum.

After Plato and Augustine, philosophical deliberation about sex became less urgent. With the exception of the thorough Thomas and the obsessed Sade, those mentioned above did most of their philosophy in epistemology, ontology, ethics, economics, and political theory, writing only sporadically on sexuality. The twentieth century, however, witnessed an outpouring of candid, sometimes shocking, inquiries into human sexuality. First was Sigmund Freud's *Three Essays on the Theory of Sexuality* (1905), which audaciously challenged myths about childhood sexual innocence and postulated that human sexual nature was polymorphously perverse. Freud's legacy includes the maverick psychoanalyst Jacques Lacan (1901–1981), who explored sex and language, and Lacan's Slovenian student Slavoy Žižek, who has explored nearly everything, from the role of power in human sexuality to cultural variations in the technology of toilets. Later came Bertrand Russell's *Marriage and Morals* (1929), which combined a prescient and formidable feminism with a well-reasoned critique of marital sexual fidelity. *Marriage and Morals*, called a "lecherous" book by some, cost Russell an appointment at the City University of New York. Then, during the thick of World War II (1943), Jean-Paul Sartre's *L'être et le néant* was published. Sartre unabashedly exposed the "bad faith" of the woman who allows an unwelcome male hand to remain on her knee without so much as a mild squawk. In sexual interactions, for Sartre, we always desire to capture the freedom of the other. That endeavor, however, is doomed to failure; consequently, he argued, sexual relations reduce to masochism or sadism.

Soon afterwards appeared *Le deuxième sexe* (*The Second Sex*) by Simone de Beauvoir, Sartre's long-standing companion, with its primordial yet fertile feminist accounts of love, sex, and gender: "One is not born, but rather becomes, a woman" (p. 267). Beauvoir's "Must We Burn Sade?" helped garner for the Divine Marquis a persisting scholarly interest. Coming before and after Sartre and Beauvoir were some social philosophers—Wilhelm Reich (1897–1957), Herbert Marcuse (1898–1979), Erich Fromm (1900–1980), and Norman O. Brown (1913–2002)—who tried to solder an alliance between Freud's psychology and Marx's humanist economics in the name of liberating sexuality from oppressive Victorian morality and twentieth-century political tyranny. (Marcuse's *Eros and Civilization* [1955] is a worthy successor to Freud's 1930 *Civilization and Its Discontents*.) Outside philosophy, Alfred Kinsey and his associates at Indiana University stirred up a hornet's nest by investigating in the late 1940s the extent of homosexual and other atypical sexual behaviors in America.

More recently, New York University philosopher Thomas Nagel domesticated Sartrean insights and fashioned from them, in "Sexual Perversion" (1969), an H. P. Gricean theory of psychologically natural human sexuality. It is routinely acknowledged that this essay inaugurated contemporary philosophy of sex. It was followed almost immediately by a swarm of sophisticated discussions and rebuttals that also boosted the field, including essays by Sara Ruddick, Robert C. Solomon, Janice Moulton, Jerome Shaffer, Robert Gray, and Alan Goldman. In his wide-ranging and erudite *Sexual Desire: A Moral Philosophy of the Erotic* (1986), politically conservative British philosopher Roger Scruton rehabilitated nearly everything traditional, from sexual fidelity in marriage to Rousseau's condemnation of the solitary vice and, in an already sexual-orientation sensitive climate, Scruton fearlessly raised doubts about homosexuality. In *Sex and Reason* (1992), law professor and Judge Richard Posner expounded a no-nonsense, pragmatic/utilitarian ethical and legal philosophy of sex, and articulated what we should expect sexually from *homo economicus* (e.g., male pederasty tends to increase in locales in which there is a relative scarcity of women).

Another law professor and political philosopher, Catharine MacKinnon, after her early innovative writings on sexual harassment, dramatically escalated (along with Andrea Dworkin) the feminist battle against sexism. In *Feminism Unmodified: Discourses on Life and Law* (1987) and *Toward a Feminist Theory of the State* (1989), she argued that women's consent to sex in patriarchy is chimerical, implying that all heterosexual intercourse is rape. A third philosopher with legal training, John Finnis, joined by other New Natural Lawyers and the Catholic theologian Germain Grisez, overhauled Thomistic philosophy of sex. Finnis defended, in the *Notre Dame Law Review* (1994), the crucial but, for many critics, dubious moral distinction between the permitted coital acts of a sterile heterosexual couple and the prohibited sexual acts of a lesbian or gay couple.

This distinction in Catholic ethics has affinities with another one, well worth contemplating, between (illicit) heterosexual coitus in which procreative potential is deliberately impeded by contraceptive devices and (licit) intercourse that is unlikely to be procreative because the couple has deliberately restricted engaging in the act to the infertile period in the wife's cycle (see Anscombe 1976, Wojtyła 1981, and Noonan 1986). The unconventional feminist Camille Paglia frankly told university women, in *Sex, Art, and American Culture* (1992), that if they go to fraternity parties and willingly drink excessively, it is partially their own foolish fault if their panties come down on a billiard table—thereby adding the cool voice of a humanist public intellectual to the often tempestuous debate in philosophical and legal circles about date and acquaintance rape.

Of special significance is the French Renaissance man Michel Foucault, who caused a thunderstorm among philosophers, historians, and social theorists of sex with the three volumes of his *Histoire de la sexualité* (1976–1984). Foucault sparked "genealogical" studies informed by the heuristic idea that not only are patterns of sexual desire and behavior socially engineered but also that the very concepts of our sexual discourse are "socially constructed." (He was in part reacting against the discourse of "natural" sexuality found in Reich and Marcuse.) Foucault influenced feminism, gender studies, queer theory, and the debate about the resemblance and continuity, or lack of them, between ancient same-sex relationships and their contemporary counterparts. (These questions are pursued in the collections edited by Edward Stein, by Nussbaum and Sihvola, and by David Halperin and his colleagues. This venture is sharply criticized by Paglia in "Junk Bonds and Corporate Raiders," in her *Sex, Art, and American Culture.*) One contested issue is whether homosexuality as a sexual orientation was first recognized in 1869 when the Magyar sexologist Károly Mária Benkert coined a word for it ("homosexuality"), a word unknown to the ancients, who could very well have invented it had they deemed that doing so was philosophically, socially, or medically meaningful. It was late nineteenth-century European sexology that detected value in picking out and labeling a class of persons as homosexual.

CONCEPTUAL ANALYSIS

Related to the question of the "birth" of the modern homosexual, there is the analytic task of defining "sexual orientation" and each of the various sexual orientations. It seems that neither sexual orientation in general nor any specific sexual orientation can be adequately understood in terms solely of behavior. Because there are many reasons and motives to engage in sex, and many intentions and desires are involved, outward behavior might not reveal anything interesting about a person's core sexual psychology (orientation). A closeted gay male who engages in coitus with his wife to impregnate her does not thereby make or declare himself heterosexual; the frustrated straight male in prison who reluctantly succumbs to mutual masturbation does not thereby become gay; the prostitute who participates in sexual acts with both the male and the female of a couple who has hired her for an evening is not thereby bisexual; an abstinent person who engages in no sexual activity, not even self-abuse, does not necessarily have an "asexual" orientation but may be heterosexual, homosexual, bisexual, or polysexual. What the examples suggest is that preferred sexual activity, or activity that one would engage in purely out of desire and for no other reason, is a better indicator of sexual nature than behavior, which might be induced by nonsexual motives. Counterfactual questions such as "What would you prefer to do, given your druthers and all real-life obstacles eliminated?" as well as straightforward questions about sexual fantasies, perhaps those entertained during the solitary vice, and about what a person finds arousing in anticipation (even if not during the anticipated act itself) are more revealing of sexual psychology than an accounting of acts performed. Orientation, then, is largely understood in terms of what sexual desire attaches to and the sources of sexual pleasure. But what are sexual desire and sexual pleasure?

Among the central concepts in the philosophy of sex are sexual desire, sexual activity, sexual pleasure, sexual perversion, sexual arousal, and sexual satisfaction. Philosophers have worked on these concepts, striving to provide clear analyses of them as well as illumination about the role and significance of sexual desire, and the others, in human life. Analytic philosophy of sex attempts to indicate, for example, how sexual desire is different from other kinds of desires; to explain how acts can be specifically sexual instead of some other kind of act; to discover what it is that makes a feeling or sensation one of sexual pleasure; and to determine what meaning, if any, can be given to the idea that some sexual acts (but not others) are unnatural or perverted. In the process of analyzing these central concepts, philosophers of sex have discerned or proposed that understanding any one of them might require understanding some other central concept. A chief case is sexual activity, which might be defined as activity that aims to satisfy sexual desire, or is motivated by sexual desire, or is intended to produce (or does produce) sexual pleasure. These candidate analyses seem to be on the right track, yet they all suffer from the same apparent defect.

The principal problem is that if sexual activity is defined as activity that is motivated by sexual desire or is intended to yield sexual pleasure (which works well for many paradigmatic instances), there are activities that are presumably sexual, are not uncommon, and yet are not captured by these or similarly fashioned definitions. Acts performed by a prostitute may produce pleasure for the paying client or are done by him to satisfy his sexual desires, but these definitions cannot explain why the acts of the prostitute (e.g., fellatio or coitus) are still sexual for her, assuming, which is plausible, that she participates for payment and not out of sexual desire for her client and that she derives no sexual pleasure from what she does or has done to her. The problem is not only that, given this type of analysis, the single act that the client and the prostitute perform together might be a sexual act for the client but not for the prostitute. The conundrum, more specifically, is that the feature (if any) in virtue of which her contribution to the act is sexual is not clear. It might be proposed that sexual activity be analyzed, instead, in terms of the involvement of salient sexual body parts—say, the genitals. If so, acts performed by a prostitute are sexual when and because her genitals are involved. But "involves the genitals" (or any other body part) seems neither necessary nor sufficient for an act to be sexual: some sexual acts are not genital (rubbing the breasts) and some acts that involve the genitals are not sexual (a gynecological exam). Perhaps "sexual body part" should be analyzed in terms of "sexual activity" (a body part is sexual exactly on those occasions when it is employed in a sexual act) rather than the other way around.

Analytic philosophy also tackles "derivative" sexual concepts, a large group of concepts (or phenomena) that include reference to sexuality. Derivative concepts that philosophers have attended to include adultery, jealousy, sexual harassment, casual sex, promiscuity, seduction, flirting, cybersex, and sexual fantasy.

Intriguing questions can be asked about adultery, in addition to standard moral questions, which are also explored by philosophers of sex. Does a nonmarried person who engages in sexual activity with a married person commit adultery? (In the law, the answer varies by jurisdiction.) Does a person commit adultery if she believes falsely that her spouse is deceased? Is adultery altogether a physical act or could desires and fantasies be not only adulterous in spirit but adultery itself? (See Matthew 5:28.) Some claim that in vitro fertilization, if carried out with donor (nonspousal) sperm, constitutes adultery. Can such a judgment be sustained? Casual sex and promiscuity, too, suggest questions beyond the ethical: For how many partners over what period of time is the judgment "promiscuous" accurate? Can one engage in casual sex with one's spouse? (Theologians argue that marital sex can be unchaste. Perhaps in this way it can be casual.) What distinguishes promiscuity from casual sex? Are there moral or perfectionist criticisms that can be made about casual sex and promiscuity other than condemning them for the absence of love, marriage, or commitment? There are difficulties in defining "sexual harassment"—what counts as a sexual advance, an improper sexual comment, or hostile work environment?—and explaining what is wrong with it, when (if) it is wrong—as sexual discrimination, immoral sexual conduct, or misuse of power, authority, or institutional position?

Seduction poses the analytic problem of carving out distinct logical space between rape, on the one side, and completely consensual sexual activity, on the other, and hence may pose novel ethical questions beyond those that apply to the other cases. But the moral issues concern not only the perpetrator of seduction. What about the person who welcomes and encourages being seduced, perhaps to be reassured of attractiveness or power? Sexual fantasy is a ubiquitous human phenomenon that suggests provocative questions: Does sexually fantasizing about a person "use" that person in any robust sense? Is it possible to criticize morally a person who fantasizes sexually about a third party during sexual activity with a partner, while not objecting to sexual fantasy *tout court*? What is the relationship between fantasy and sexual desire: Do we fantasize about something (or someone) because we desire it or do we desire it because we have fantasies about it? Jealousy, because of its intentional structure (its dependence upon beliefs), might arise in response to a fantasy. Is the fault with sexual jealousy (if it is faulty) exhausted by its being caused by a false belief or one arrived at negligently? Or can sexual jealousy be deplored because it frequently betrays a wrongful attitude of owning another person?

Cybersex highlights the intentionality of sexuality, because cybersexual arousal depends exquisitely on beliefs about unseen persons; it forces us to ask why another person's body is apparently so important—or not so important, after all—in sexual experiences, which also raises questions about masturbation; and cybersex makes us ponder whether some sexual activity—and therefore, for example, some adultery—may involve no physical touching in the ordinary sense (as does telephone sex). Similarly, flirting might be a sexual activity that falls somewhere between faithfulness and infidelity. To which is it closer? Does this depend on with whom one flirts, why, or the extent to which one is tempted or willing to turn flirting into physical contact? Flirting is interesting also because it is occasionally misread, conveying to some optimistic or deluded recipients an explicit invitation to engage in sex instead of registering merely as playful or teasing. As a result, flirting might sometimes precipitate date or acquaintance rape.

The derivative concept "rape" has long presented special problems. One controversial matter is whether rape should be defined in terms of the absence of consent or the presence of force. This has implications for how the occurrence of rape is established in a court of law. The choice is difficult: A force definition of rape might place too much emphasis on whether or to what extent a woman resists, which many see as irrelevant. A consent criterion implies that tough issues about mens rea become important: Did the accused believe that the woman had consented, even if she didn't; is the accused liable for something he might or should have believed but did not believe (that is, that consent was absent)? The difference between a force and a nonconsent criterion may be illustrated with acquaintance rape. A force criterion tends not to classify such acts as rape, whereas proponents of a nonconsent criterion argue that rape includes all nonforcible yet nonconsensual sex (see McGregor 2005). Further, like prostitution, rape seems to provide a counterexample to the analytic proposal that sexual activity be understood in terms of sexual desire or sexual pleasure.

Perhaps because both prostitution and rape are activities that involve coercion or are not engaged in (fully) voluntarily, they resist being characterized as sexual acts in terms of desire or pleasure. Indeed, it has been argued, on various grounds, that rape is not a sexual activity at all. (Maybe this point applies to prostitution as well.) If a woman, a virgin, is raped and does not thereby, automatically, lose her virginal sexual status, she has not taken part in a sexual activity, at least not one that was sexual for her. But the derivative concept "virginity" and similar notions—abstinence, chastity, celibacy—require careful analysis in their own right. Are they merely a matter of behavior or anatomical characteristics or does state of mind play a role, and how? Another issue concerns the extension of "rape," which accentuates problems in spelling out the meaning of coercion or consent and in deciding why and when coerced or nonconsensual sex is wrong. Suppose a man badgers his wife for sex until she acquiesces, and they engage in sexual activity even though she much prefers not to. Has she been coerced and therefore raped, and is this the reason the act is morally stained? Perhaps badgering does not amount to coercion, but it is still morally suspect. By contrast, some would say that even if the badgering coerces her into sex, it is not especially morally objectionable. Or suppose a woman hints to her husband, "No sex until you buy me that fur coat."

HUMANS AND OTHER ANIMALS

One debate in the philosophy of sex concerns the relevance of animal sexuality for understanding and judging human sexuality. Some philosophers, for example Thomas Aquinas in *Summa contra gentiles* (chap. 122, sec. 6), argue from observations of animal sexual behavior to the nature of human sexuality and draw ethically conservative conclusions. These philosophers emphasize (a subset of) that which is common between humans and animals. For example, many animals engage in sexual relations only to reproduce and that, too, is what is significant about human sexuality. Then there are philosophers—those who are sympathetic to sociobiology or evolutionary psychology are among them—who similarly stress what is common to animals and humans, yet draw ethically liberal conclusions. We are fundamentally animals and that fact should not be ignored or minimized; the robust sexuality that is due to our animal nature is suppressed at our peril.

What may distinguish the first group of philosophers from the second is the animal species invoked in drawing conclusions about humans. If one selects as the argu-

ment's observational basis monogamous birds (swans) and mammals (wolves), different conclusions will emerge than if one selects more sexually adventuresome species (dogs, the bonobo). The question—Which is the right animal model?—is murky, although similarity of DNA, testicle size, and other traits are potentially useful links. (Why even assume that the same animal model will be the right one for both human males and females?) Regardless, we must avoid the circularity of arguing that a species is the right model because these creatures are remarkably like humans—unless our methodology is a sophisticated "reflective equilibrium." Further, once we select some animal species from which to argue, we must take the "bad" with the "good": The aggression, dominance, promiscuity, and oddness (e.g., urolagnia in some llamas) of animal sexuality, along with its attractive features, have to be extrapolated to humans as well. Against both the conservative and the liberal who argue from animal sexuality to ethics, it can be protested that doing so commits the naturalistic fallacy. What cannot be excluded is that comprehensively studying animals can tell us something about human nature. It is a dangerous leap from there to ethics.

Some philosophers, by contrast, even though acknowledging that humans, as embodied, are undeniably in part animals, perceive sharp discontinuities or differences of kind, not degree, between animals and humans. There are physiological differences such as concealed ovulation and the absence of oestrus in human females that have extensive implications for sexual psychology and behavior. But more striking is the human cerebral cortex and hence cognitive differences between humans and animals. This view can also be taken in an ethically conservative or liberal direction. Conservatives—Scruton, for one, and many theologians—say that humans have mind or soul, something that lifts us above animals, so that even if we have animal urges, we can and should transcend them. Behaving in a humanly civilized fashion is to be accomplished by virtue of our spirit and for the sake of our spirit. But the discontinuity is also compatible with liberal sexual ethics. Nagel, in formulating his theory of psychologically natural human sexuality, emphasizes the differences between animal and human sexuality that result from the nearly unique faculties of the human mind, primarily intentionality and self-consciousness (which also figure prominently in Scruton's philosophy of sex). Yet Nagel comfortably embraces Millian liberal sexual ethics.

Further, for social constructionists animal and human sexuality are of course different, and nothing much is to be gained by comparing them. Human sexuality and sexual discourse vary as much as human culture varies, whereas animals have (by and large) no culture or language that might construct their sexuality or their (nonexistent) conceptions of it. The sociobiologists and their philosophical sympathizers retort: Yes, society constructs much of human sexuality, but human sexuality (to use E. O. Wilson's metaphors) is a twig bent at birth; it is on a leash, tied ultimately to a biological post, a substrate upon which society can work—and which it requires in order to work—its constructionist miracles. As suggested by the mixed results of the medical management of intersex conditions (neonates of ambiguous sex), the social cannot make everyone male, female, straight, or gay. How much of human sexual nature is due to animal biology, and how much to culture, is as difficult to resolve as analogous nature-nurture quandaries about the contribution of race or biological sex on various skills and personality traits. Often these disputes are replaced by (prematurely, perhaps, but not altogether baselessly) brute political machinations, à la Plato's Thrasymachus in the *Republic*.

One reason for looking at animal sexuality is that this knowledge may serve as a guide to what human sexuality would be like were it not for social interference, that is, in the absence of all cultural influence (although, unlike Freud, social constructionists do not speak of the cultural as an "interference" but as necessarily constitutive). It does not strain the imagination to conceive of cultureless animals as expressing pure state-of-nature sexuality. If humans arrange their sexuality consistently with what is seen among animals (by peeling back various social influences), we can have some faith that we are not too far away from humanly natural, healthy, satisfying sexuality. Such thinking builds on an absorbing and plausible thought, that animal sexuality cannot in any way be unnatural or "perverted." If nothing about morality can be learned from animal sexuality, at least we can get glimpse of normality. There is probably too much Rousseauvian utopianism in this thinking, and of course such a view remains vulnerable to the hitch of which animal model confers the best insight into "normal" humanity. Alternatively, well-founded speculation about the sexuality of prelapsarian Adam and Eve might, for some theologians, supply that information. The Garden of Eden is their Hobbesian state of nature.

SEXUAL PERVERSION

As far as popular culture and ordinary folk are concerned, the terms "[sexual] perversion," "[sexually] perverted,"

and "[sexual] pervert" are not problematic, even if they might not always be in good taste and cause distress to those singled out. "Sexual" is bracketed because "pervert" in ordinary talk implies that the domain of discourse is the sexual. (At least, that is the default position.) By contrast, some philosophers, psychologists, and other academics have argued that "sexual perversion" is outmoded, ontologically groundless, confused, offensive, unscientific, not applicable to anything in human sexual behavior, and hence happily dispensable. Despite the counsel of philosophers and other experts that "perversion" be extirpated from the language, ordinary people use it unflinchingly, as does the Religious Right. The American Psychiatric Association (APA) no longer officially uses "perversion" to refer to sexual disorders but has, since 1980, opted for the clinical "paraphilia," even if an ordinary person's list of perversions is nearly identical to the paraphilias listed in the *Diagnostic and Statistical Manual of Mental Disorders* (*DSM*). ("Paraphilia" is not a total improvement. It is an unlikely group that includes "Philadelphia," "philanthropy," "philosophy"—and "paraphilia.")

The fundamental problem about sexual perversion is distinguishing natural from unnatural sexuality. In carrying out this task, it is necessary to explain not only how certain sexual behaviors (desires, preferences) are perverted but also how they are sexual to begin with. For example, if being potentially procreative is the feature that defines sexual activity, then being nonprocreative cannot be a mark of the sexually perverted, because whatever is not procreative is not sexual. (The acts might still be "nonsexually [or fill in the blank] perverted.") Or if sexual activity is defined as activity that tries to satisfy sexual desire and sexual desire is defined, in turn, as desire for physical contact with another human being, the perversions cannot be sexual, because they typically do not involve desire for that contact: consider the wide variety of fetish objects that excite men. Some would call it special pleading or adhockery, whereas others would see it as a stroke of genius, to say that the fetishist does desire physical contact with a person, unconsciously, and achieves that in a psychologically safe way by substituting the fetish object.

Philosophers and psychologists have tried, with unclear success, to formulate theories about sexual perversion. An obvious contender, that only potentially reproductive sexual acts—acts that are reproductive in their anatomical and physiological forms—are natural, and all others perverted, has seemed plausible to many thinkers (Catholics and some evolutionists, mostly) but implausible to others. Certainly, being nonprocreative is a property that many (preanalytically) perverted sexual acts share: zoophilia, cross-dressing, exhibitionism, voyeurism, klismaphilia, necrophilia, urolagnia, sadomasochism.

But analyzing perversion as nonprocreative sexuality is not straightforward. Some nonprocreative sexual acts are not especially, or at all, perverted: masturbation (solitary or mutual) and oral sex to orgasm. And some purportedly perverted acts (cross-dressing, light sadomasochism) for some people often or regularly culminate in heterosexual intercourse, as if functioning as foreplay. Also note that both vertical (parent-child) and horizontal (sibling-sibling) incest can be procreative, yet many have thought them considerably unnatural (or maybe only repulsive). The sexual practices that are supposed to be subsumed under the label "perversion" or "paraphilia" are extraordinarily diverse, other than being nonprocreative, so finding common, essential features may be doomed—a reason to dispatch the concept. We could still investigate, without using "perversion," behaviors that are unusual, bizarre, harmful, or are done compulsively or exclusively, in preference to every other sexual activity (which category may well include a narrow interest in heterosexual coitus). That "unusual," "bizarre," and "harmful" are to a greater or lesser extent evaluative or culturally bound is why these features of sexual acts cannot be used to develop an objective, scientific, universally sound theory of sexual perversion. Social constructionists applaud this result.

Another question about sexual perversion has to do with its morality. The Roman Catholic position, that what is perverted is for that reason sinful, has not won over many secular adherents. "Premodern" philosophy of sex, which derives from the older Plato, Augustine, and Aquinas, understands sexual perversion teleologically as behavior that is incompatible with the (perhaps divinely ordained) species design. Premoderns frequently add that in virtue of this deviation, deliberately performed sexually perverted acts are immoral. But perhaps not every deviation is wrong. Mutual masturbation, cunnilingus, and fellatio, which in themselves are nonprocreative and hence unnatural, might be permissible when they function as preparation for heterosexual marital coitus. "Modern" philosophy of sex dates from the late nineteenth century and the rise of scientific sexology (e.g., Iwan Bloch, Magnus Hirschfeld, Richard Krafft-Ebing, Havelock Ellis, Freud). Some modern philosophers of sex retain the biological, teleological account of perversion,

whereas others (Freud, Nagel) replace that with a more sophisticated psychological account.

What the two branches of modern philosophy of sex share is a refusal to judge perverted sex immoral merely because it is perverted. Many modern philosophers of sex have reached, instead, for the evaluation "psychologically unhealthy." It is worthwhile to think of premodern judgments of sinfulness as superseded by modern judgments of sickness, as social authority residing over sexual perversion passed from the clergy and organized religion to the physician and biomedical science. The fate of homosexuality illustrates this progression, from being condemned as sin by all Western religions to being deprecated as sickness (although excused, in keeping with the medical model) by most Western psychology and psychiatry through the mid-twentieth century. But in 1973, the APA removed homosexuality from its list of mental disorders in *DSM*, thereby helping to usher in "postmodern" philosophy of sex, according to which no nonharmful, consensual sexual behaviors are perversions, sinful, or sick, but alternative sexual choices. The APA has not gone completely postmodern. It still classifies some innocuous sexual practices (fetishism, transvestism) as sexual mental disorders.

The American Psychiatric Association distinguishes between sexual dysfunctions and the paraphilias, which, even though they involve unusual or bizarre sexual desires or acts, do not necessarily involve inadequate functioning of the sexual organs. When homosexuality was still a mental sexual disorder, there was no doubt that gay men could sport firm erections and did not suffer from ejaculatory problems merely in virtue of their orientation. In addition to premature ejaculation, an inability to achieve or maintain an erection, insufficient lubrication, and pain during coitus, the APA includes as a dysfunction "Hypoactive sexual desire disorder," a deficit or absence of sexual desire that causes psychic distress or interpersonal (e.g., marital) problems (*DSM-IV*, sec. 302.71). Critics have pointed out that the clinical judgments that a person has too little sexual interest and is bothered too much by a perceived lack of desire are routinely influenced by all manner of social factors that seem irrelevant to a diagnosis of mental disorder. The *DSM* also lists a more extreme variant, "Sexual Aversion Disorder" (sec. 302.79), but (asymmetrically) contains no "hyperactive sexual desire disorder." The APA did, however, briefly flirt with Patrick Carnes's innovation, "sexual addiction" (a type of obsessive-compulsive promiscuity), as a sexual mental disorder, which was included only in the revised version of *DSM-III* (1987). Speaking of naturally pleasurable sexual activity as "addictive" is highly disputable, as is whether promiscuity (such as homosexuality) is sinful, sick, or a mere variation in human sexuality.

SEXUAL USE

Being unnatural is of course not the only way sexual activity might go astray morally. In the Kantian tradition, the central way that sexual activity is morally wrong is when one person uses another person sexually, treating the other as a means or object, thereby violating the second formulation of the categorical imperative. Coercing another person, as in rape or quid pro quo sexual harassment (boss to employee: "Have sex with me or you're fired"), or deceiving someone in order to obtain sexual relations (an identical twin sliding into the bed of his brother's wife) are frequently cited cases of treating another person as a means. On a Kantian view, and on some utilitarian views (such as Mill's), it is necessary for the moral permissibility of a sexual event that all parties furnish free and informed consent. Other instances of possible use are difficult to settle; even among confirmed Kantians, exactly what treating another person as a means or an object amounts to has long been disputed. One disagreement between conservative and liberal Kantians is over whether an adult's consent is sufficient (ceteris paribus) for the morality of sexual activity. Kant answered "no," arguing that sexual activity avoided mere use in, and only in, marriage, or that marriage made mutual sexual use permissible. (How to interpret Kant is an issue for Kant scholarship. See *Lectures on Ethics*, Ak 27:388.)

In this respect many conservative Kantians, such as Karol Wojtyła (Pope John Paul II, 1920–2005), have followed Kant, insisting that mutual consent alone neither eliminates nor blesses the mutual use in sexual relations that must occur if the persons are not married (although some conservatives would be satisfied were sexual relations confined to a genuinely committed even if nonmarital relationship). In any event, Kant and the conservative Kantians need to explain—a challenging task—how the additional ingredient, marriage or commitment, changes sexual activity from mere mutual use to something morally permissible, and why only commitment or marriage and nothing else (say, consent) has the ability to do this. For liberal Kantians, mutual consent is powerful enough by itself to make sexual acts permissible in the absence of marriage. The presence of consent, they argue, satisfies the demand of the second formulation of the categorical imperative for the reciprocal acknowledgment by each person of the rational autonomy (the humanity) of the other. In virtue of consent, much sex is permissible

that is condemned morally by Kantian and other conservatives: same-sex sexual acts, group sex, casual sex (say, between strangers), even adultery if all parties consent. Consent is sufficient only ceteris paribus for the liberal Kantian and the Millian utilitarian because third parties might be harmed or have their legitimate interests disregarded by the consensual sex of others (as often happens in adultery). For some conservative Kantians, mutual consent to use each other not only is not sufficient, but makes for an especially morally corrupt situation, for they take, as did Kant, the often slighted part of the second formulation seriously: one may not treat the humanity in one's own person merely as a means. This is what one does to oneself—willingly makes an object of oneself—when consenting to be sexually used by another person, even if that use is mutual. It is an interesting question how it might be decided whether mutual consent cancels or compounds the moral faults of mere use.

The opposite of sexual objectification is sexual personification, which occurs when, to mention the key instance, a person or a couple gives a name to an erotic body part. (Christening the genitals is an important theme in D. H. Lawrence's *Lady Chatterley's Lover*.) An example of nonsexual personification might be worshiping an idol, a golden lamb, treating a mere material symbol of the Almighty as if it were the Almighty. Personification can be understood as raising something's ontological status or treating it as if had a higher status. This is what happens when a couple gives proper names to their genitals, treating them as persons. In objectification, by contrast, one person reduces (or attempts to reduce) the ontological status of another. If a person manipulates another so that a goal of the first person is thereby attained, the first has used the second, has treated him or her as a mere material object, in that the second's personhood-defining feature, rational autonomy, has been minimized or ignored. One person is acting toward another as if the latter were no more ontologically elegant than an inanimate thing or a subhuman animal. In sexual objectification, even if there is no coercion or deception, a person is treated as a usable object fundamentally capable of (only) satisfying another's sexual desire. It is often claimed, by both Kantian conservatives and many feminist philosophers, that this is exactly what is morally wrong with prostitution and pornography: women are not respected fully as the persons they are but are seen and treated only or primarily as consumable and fungible providers of sexual pleasure, even when they consent to participate. Some theorists go further, claiming that these considerations apply as well to the institution of heterosexual marriage.

PORNOGRAPHY AND PROSTITUTION

Arguments about consent occur when philosophers, legal theorists, political activists, and women and men sex-industry workers discuss pornography and prostitution. If consent is present in a given instance of prostitution (which can be defined, but not unproblematically, as exchanging sexual activity for compensation), if neither the client nor the provider of sexual services is subject to coercion or is deceived, or if those hired to perform sexual acts in front of a camera (a type of prostitution) in the production of pornography (variously definable, notoriously with difficulty) have, similarly, freely and with reasonably full and relevant information agreed to do so, the issue still arises whether their consent is sufficient. In this debate, one side (the liberal, the libertarian, perhaps the Milton Friedman capitalist) points out that if consent is sufficient for other kinds of paid labor, from slinging slop in a fast food pub and collecting garbage to executing proctological examinations and fighting in a volunteer army, there can be no objection to a person's engaging in sex for payment. Anything is fodder for the market or, at least, nothing differentiates selling sexual services and performing other tasks that some people, but not all, find too repugnant or risky to undertake even for substantial financial compensation. The other side (some conservative theologians, Marxists, and feminists) insists, however, that sexuality is "different," that it does or should involve a quality of intimacy that is undermined by its being bought and sold, or that it is demeaning when sexuality is the means of making a living, or that sexuality is metaphysically or anthropologically too crucial an aspect of human personality or identity to be commodified. Doing so entails an immeasurable cheapening of humanity. Whether these claims about how sexuality differs from other aspects of human life are culturally bound (hence not so compelling?) or are deep, sustainable philosophical truths about the human person is unclear. Note that if they are overblown, exaggerating the significance of sexuality in an overall picture of the human person, it might be more difficult to explain why rape is an especially grievous harm (see Murphy 1994).

However, that women sex-industry workers participate consensually is debatable. There are various reasons, often advanced by feminists and Marxists, for doubting that the consent of the women who make pornography or sell sexual services is genuine (see, e.g., MacKinnon's *Only Words*). They might have been indoctrinated to devalue themselves and their sexuality or have been as children victims of sexual abuse, and in either case, they may be exceptionally vulnerable to being manipulated into pros-

titution and the production of pornography. Further, to the extent that women who participate in these activities come from the lower economic levels of society, the lure of making decent money despite lacking education or vocational training can be coercive, if their alternatives are even more dismal. The possibility of compulsion may be greater when the women, in addition to being relatively impoverished, are members of a disparaged ethnic minority or have dependent children. Their dire need creates a situation in which being offered money for sexual activity is coercive, even if engaging in those sexual events seems to them, at the moment, a small sacrifice of their sexual integrity.

It might also be argued that because women are willing to sell sexual services in either prostitution or pornography, this is by itself evidence that something is amiss in their rational autonomy; doing such things is not what someone "in her right mind" would choose to do. Several responses to this account of the plight of women sex-industry workers have been advanced. One rebuttal is that it overstates the victimization of women and underestimates their strength and resourcefulness. Another is that citing financial need as coercive may imply too much. Most people who sell their labor have financial needs, are in no position to refuse to work, and they, too, would have to be described as coerced. Finally, there are women who relish the opportunity to make good money in the sex industry and would not describe their situation as one in which they are pressured into doing something they prefer not to do.

CONCLUSION

Our personal understandings of the nature of sexuality and its significance in our lives, public discussion of ethical, religious, and social issues, and technical matters about sex that arise in medicine, social science, and the law—all these can profit from philosophical study. Students who take courses in the philosophy of sex are exposed to material they are unlikely to encounter elsewhere, material that gives them an opportunity to scrutinize their beliefs about sexuality and habitual behaviors. The law benefits from the philosophical analysis of concepts such as rape, harassment, and consent; theology is in a position to learn from the elaboration of theories of natural human sexuality and the examination of the conceptual connection between the goodness of the natural and the goodness of human actions; social scientific surveys of the frequency of sexual activity (by age, education, ethnicity, and other parameters) and the extent of non-heterosexual sexual orientations depend on analyses of

ENCYCLOPEDIA OF PHILOSOPHY
2nd edition

"sexual activity," "sexual desire," and "sexual preference" and effective ways of identifying and counting or measuring them; the pronouncements of psychiatry and medicine on sexual health, both physical and mental, can be (and have been) improved by the deliberations of philosophers who investigate the concepts of sexual perversion and mental illness. The philosophy of sex has proven that it is no idle enterprise.

See also Abelard, Peter; Albert the Great; Affirmative Action; Aristotle; Augustine, St.; Beauvoir, Simone de; Darwin, Charles Robert; Descartes, René; Engels, Friedrich; Feminist Social and Political Philosophy; Foucault, Michel; Freud, Sigmund; Grice, Herbert Paul; Hegel, Georg Wilhelm Friedrich; Heterosexism; Hobbes, Thomas; Hume, David; Kant, Immanuel; Kierkegaard, Søren Aabye; Lacan, Jacques; Mandeville, Bernard; Marx, Karl; Mill, John Stuart; Montaigne, Michel Eyquem de; Nagel, Thomas; Nietzsche, Friedrich; Nussbaum, Martha; Pelagius and Pelagianism; Plato; Reich, Wilhelm; Renaissance; Rousseau, Jean-Jacques; Russell, Bertrand Arthur William; Sartre, Jean-Paul; Schopenhauer, Arthur; Sexism; Thomas Aquinas, St.; Thomism; Utilitarianism; Wilson, Edward O.

Bibliography

Anscombe, G. E. M. "Contraception and Chastity." *The Human World*, no. 7 (1972): 9–30. Reprinted and revised in *Ethics and Population*, edited by Michael D. Bayles. Cambridge, MA: Schenkman, 1976.

Baker, Robert B., and Frederick A. Elliston, eds. *Philosophy and Sex*. 3rd ed., edited by Robert B. Baker, Kathleen J. Wininger, and Frederick A. Elliston. Amherst, NY: Prometheus, 1998.

Beauvoir, Simone de. "Must We Burn Sade?" Translated by Annette Michelson. In *The Marquis de Sade: The 120 Days of Sodom and Other Writings*, edited by Austryn Wainhouse and Richard Seaver. New York: Grove Press, 1966.

Beauvoir, Simone de. *The Second Sex*. Translated by Howard M. Parshley. New York: Knopf, 1953.

Ben-Ze'ev, Aaron. *Love Online: Emotions on the Internet*. Cambridge, U.K.: Cambridge University Press, 2004.

Blackburn, Simon. *Lust: The Seven Deadly Sins*. New York: Oxford University Press/New York Public Library, 2004.

Brundage, James A. *Law, Sex, and Christian Society in Medieval Europe*. Chicago: University of Chicago Press, 1987.

Burgess-Jackson, Keith, ed. *A Most Detestable Crime: New Philosophical Essays on Rape*. New York: Oxford University Press, 1999.

Cornell, Drucilla, ed. *Feminism and Pornography*. Oxford, U.K.: Oxford University Press, 2000.

Corvino, John, ed. *Same Sex: Debating the Ethics, Science, and Culture of Homosexuality*. Lanham, MD: Rowman and Littlefield, 1997.

Devine, Philip E., and Wolf-Devine, Celia, eds. *Sex and Gender: A Spectrum of Views*. Belmont, CA.: Wadsworth, 2003.

Dworkin, Andrea. *Intercourse*. New York: Free Press, 1987.

Dworkin, Andrea. *Pornography: Men Possessing Women*. New York: Penguin, 1989.

Epstein, Louis M. *Sex Laws and Customs in Judaism*. New York: Bloch, 1948. Reprint, New York: Ktav, 1967.

Finnis, John M. "Law, Morality, and 'Sexual Orientation.'" *Notre Dame Law Review* 69 (5) (1994): 1049–1076.

Foucault, Michel. *The History of Sexuality*. Translated by Robert Hurley. 3 vols. New York: Vintage, 1988–1990.

Freud, Sigmund. *Three Essays on the Theory of Sexuality*. In *The Standard Edition of the Complete Psychological Works of Sigmund Freud* Vol. 7, translated and edited by James Strachey. London: Hogarth Press, 1953–1974.

Gert, Bernard. "A Sex Caused Inconsistency in DSM-III-R: The Definition of Mental Disorder and the Definition of Paraphilias." *Journal of Medicine and Philosophy* 17 (2) (1992): 155–171.

Gilbert, Paul. *Human Relationships: A Philosophical Introduction*. Oxford, U.K.: Blackwell, 1991.

Giles, James. *The Nature of Sexual Desire*. Westport, CT: Praeger, 2004.

Gruen, Lori, and George F. Panichas, eds. *Sex, Morality, and the Law*. New York: Routledge, 1997.

Gudorf, Christine E. *Body, Sex, and Pleasure: Reconstructing Christian Sexual Ethics*. Cleveland: Pilgrim Press, 1994.

Halperin, David M., John J. Winkler, and Froma I. Zetlin, eds. *Before Sexuality: The Construction of Erotic Experience in the Ancient Greek World*. Princeton, NJ: Princeton University Press, 1990.

Halwani, Raja. *Virtuous Liaisons: Care, Love, Sex, and Virtue Ethics*. Chicago: Open Court, 2003.

Hegel, G. W. F. "Love." In *On Christianity: Early Theological Writings*, translated by Thomas M. Knox and Richard Kroner, 302–308. New York: Harper, 1961.

Hobbes, Thomas. "Human Nature, or the Fundamental Elements of Policy." In *The English Works of Thomas Hobbes of Malmesbury*. Vol. 4, edited by Sir William Molesworth. Aalen, Germany: Scientia Verlag, 1966.

Horowitz, Gad. *Repression: Basic and Surplus Repression in Psychoanalytic Theory; Freud, Reich, and Marcuse*. Toronto: University of Toronto Press, 1977.

Jackson, Stevi, and Sue Scott, eds. *Feminism and Sexuality: A Reader*. New York: Columbia University Press, 1996.

Kant, Immanuel. *Lectures on Ethics* [*Vorlesung*]. Translated by Peter Heath, edited by Peter Heath and J. B. Schneewind. Cambridge, U.K.: Cambridge University Press, 1997.

LeMoncheck, Linda, and Mane Hajdin. *Sexual Harassment: A Debate*. Lanham, MD: Rowman and Littlefield, 1997.

MacKinnon, Catharine A. *Feminism Unmodified: Discourses on Life and Law*. Cambridge, MA: Harvard University Press, 1987.

MacKinnon, Catharine A. *Toward a Feminist Theory of the State*. Cambridge, MA: Harvard University Press, 1989.

MacKinnon, Catharine A. *Only Words*. Cambridge, MA: Harvard University Press, 1993.

Mandeville, Bernard. *A Modest Defence of Publick Stews*. Edited by Richard I. Cook. Los Angeles: Augustan Reprint Society, 1973.

McGregor, Joan. *Is It Rape? On Acquaintance Rape and Taking Women's Consent Seriously*. Aldershot, U.K.: Ashgate, 2005.

Montaigne, Michel De. "Of the Power of the Imagination." In *The Complete Essays of Montaigne*. Translated by Donald M. Frame. Stanford, CA: Stanford University Press, 1958.

Murphy, Jeffrie G. "Some Ruminations on Women, Violence, and the Criminal Law." In *In Harm's Way: Essays in Honor of Joel Feinberg*, edited by Jules Coleman and Allen Buchanan. Cambridge, U.K.: Cambridge University Press, 1994.

Nagel, Thomas. "Sexual Perversion." *Journal of Philosophy* 66 (1) (1969): 5–17. Reprinted and revised in his *Mortal Questions*. Cambridge, U.K.: Cambridge University Press, 1979.

Noonan, John T. *Contraception: A History of Its Treatment by the Catholic Theologians and Canonists*, enlarged ed. Cambridge, MA: Harvard University Press, 1986.

Nussbaum, Martha C. *Sex and Social Justice*. New York: Oxford University Press, 1999.

Nussbaum, Martha C., and Juha Sihvola, eds. *The Sleep of Reason: Erotic Experience and Sexual Ethics in Ancient Greece and Rome*. Chicago: University of Chicago Press, 2002.

Pagels, Elaine. *Adam, Eve, and the Serpent*. New York: Vintage, 1988.

Paglia, Camille. *Sex, Art, and American Culture: Essays*. New York: Vintage, 1992.

Plato. *The Collected Dialogues of Plato*. Edited by Edith Hamilton and Huntington Cairns. Princeton: Princeton University Press, 1961.

Posner, Richard A. *Sex and Reason*. Cambridge, MA: Harvard University Press, 1992.

Priest, Graham, ed. *The Monist* ["Perversion"] 86 (1) (2003).

Primoratz, Igor. *Ethics and Sex*. London: Routledge, 1999.

Primoratz, Igor, ed. *Human Sexuality*. Aldershot, U.K.: Ashgate, 1997.

Rich, Adrienne. "Compulsory Heterosexuality and Lesbian Existence." *Signs* 5 (4) (1980): 631–660. Reprinted in *Blood, Bread, and Poetry: Selected Prose 1979–1985*. New York: Norton, 1986.

Robinson, Paul. *The Freudian Left: Wilhelm Reich, Geza Roheim, Herbert Marcuse*. New York: Harper and Row, 1969.

Rubin, Gayle S. "Thinking Sex: Notes for a Radical Theory of the Politics of Sexuality." In *Pleasure and Danger: Exploring Female Sexuality*, edited by Carole S. Vance. London: Routledge, 1984.

Russell, Bertrand. *Marriage and Morals*. London: George Allen and Unwin, 1929.

Sartre, Jean-Paul. (1943) *Being and Nothingness: An Essay on Phenomenological Ontology*. Translated by Hazel E. Barnes. New York: Philosophical Library, 1956.

Schopenhauer, Arthur. *The World as Will and Representation*. Translated by E. F. J. Payne. New York: Dover, 1966.

Schulhofer, Stephen. *Unwanted Sex: The Culture of Intimidation and the Failure of Law*. Cambridge, MA: Harvard University Press, 1998.

Scruton, Roger. *Sexual Desire: A Moral Philosophy of the Erotic*. New York: Free Press, 1986.

Shelp, Earl E., ed. *Sexuality and Medicine*. 2 vols. Dordrecht, Netherlands: Reidel, 1987.

Shrage, Laurie. *Moral Dilemmas of Feminism: Prostitution, Adultery, and Abortion*. New York: Routledge, 1994.

Snitow, Ann, Christine Stansell, and Sharon Thompson, eds. *Powers of Desire: The Politics of Sexuality*. New York: Monthly Review Press, 1983.

Soble, Alan. *Pornography, Sex, and Feminism*. Amherst, NY: Prometheus, 2002.

Soble, Alan. *Sexual Investigations*. New York: New York University Press, 1996.

Soble, Alan. *The Philosophy of Sex and Love: An Introduction*. St. Paul, MN: Paragon House, 1998.

Soble, Alan, ed. *The Philosophy of Sex: Contemporary Readings*. 4th ed. Lanham, MD, 2002.

Soble, Alan, ed. *Sex from Plato to Paglia: A Philosophical Encyclopedia*. Westport, CT: Greenwood Press, 2005.

Soble, Alan, ed. *Sex, Love, and Friendship: Studies of the Society for the Philosophy of Sex and Love, 1977–1992*. Amsterdam: Rodopi, 1997.

Solomon, Robert C., and Kathleen M. Higgins, eds. *The Philosophy of (Erotic) Love*. Lawrence: University Press of Kansas, 1991.

Stein, Edward, ed. *Forms of Desire: Sexual Orientation and the Social Constructionist Controversy*. New York: Routledge, 1992.

Stewart, Robert, ed. *Philosophical Perspectives on Sex and Love*. New York: Oxford University Press, 1995.

Strossen, Nadine. *Defending Pornography: Free Speech, Sex, and the Fight for Women's Rights*. New York: Scribner, 1995.

Taylor, Richard. *Having Love Affairs*. Buffalo, NY: Prometheus, 1982. Reissued, *Love Affairs: Marriage and Infidelity*. Amherst, NY: Prometheus, 1997.

Thomas Aquinas, St. *On the Truth of the Catholic Faith: Summa Contra Gentiles*. Book 3, pt. 2, *Providence*, translated by Vernon J. Bourke. Garden City, NY: Image Books, 1956.

Thomas Aquinas, St. (1265–1273) *Summa Theologiae*. Cambridge, U.K.: Blackfriars, 1964–1976.

Thurber, James, and White, E. B. *Is Sex Necessary? Or Why You Feel the Way You Do*. New York: Harper and Row, 1975.

Trevas, Robert, Arthur Zucker, and Donald Borchert, eds. *Philosophy of Sex and Love: A Reader*. Upper Saddle River, NJ: Prentice Hall, 1997.

Tuana, Nancy, and Laurie Shrage. "Sexuality." In *The Oxford Handbook of Practical Ethics*, edited by Hugh LaFollette. Oxford, U.K.: Oxford University Press, 2003.

Vannoy, Russell. *Sex Without Love: A Philosophical Exploration*. Buffalo, NY: Prometheus, 1980.

Verene, Donald, ed. *Sexual Love and Western Morality: A Philosophical Anthology*. 2nd ed.. Boston: Jones and Bartlett, 1995.

Watson, Francis. *Agape, Eros, Gender: Towards a Pauline Sexual Ethic*. Cambridge, U.K.: Cambridge University Press, 2000.

Wertheimer, Alan. *Consent to Sexual Relations*. Cambridge, U.K.: Cambridge University Press, 2003.

Wilson, Edward O. *On Human Nature*. New York: Bantam, 1979.

Wojtyła, Karol [Pope John Paul II]. *Love and Responsibility*. New York: Farrar, Straus and Giroux, 1981.

Alan Soble (2005)

PHILOSOPHY OF SOCIAL SCIENCES

The "philosophy of social sciences" comes in three varieties, as the metaideology, the metaphysics, and the methodology of the disciplines involved. The metaideology looks at how far different, traditional legitimations of social sciences succeed. The metaphysics looks at questions having to do with what social science posits—what things it says there are—and at how far those posits are consistent with more or less commonplace beliefs. And the methodology looks at questions regarding the nature of observations, laws, and theories in social science, the logic of induction and confirmation, the requirements of understanding and explanation, and so on.

METAIDEOLOGY

The social sciences were conceived and pursued, from the very beginning, under the influence of ideals (particularly of scientific objectivity and progress) deriving from the eighteenth-century enlightenment (Hawthorn 1976). The first social scientists were economists and sociologists, as we would call them today, and they were self-consciously concerned about producing something that would count, not as philosophy, not as literature, not as common sense, but as science: as a project faithful to the image forged by natural science.

The scientific intention—the intention to make science—has remained characteristic of work in the social sciences. It puts social scientists, paradoxically, under an obligation of an ideological kind: the obligation to show that the sort of analysis they pursue is of a properly scientific kind. The metaideology of social science interrogates and assesses the ideologies whereby the social sciences try to legitimate what they do, to show that what they do is genuinely scientific in character.

Broadly speaking, there are three main ideologies that have been invoked—individually or in various combinations—by social scientists in the scientific legitimation of their enterprise. Each of these marks a feature that putatively distinguishes social science from mere common sense, mere social lore. The first ideology hails social science as an explanatory enterprise of culturally universal validity; the second as an enterprise that is interpretatively neutral, not being warped by people's self-understanding; and the third as an enterprise that enjoys evaluative independence: value-freedom. The universality, neutrality, and independence claimed are each meant to establish social science as objective, and therefore scientifically respectable, in a way in which common sense is

not; each notion offers an explication of what scientific objectivity involves. Some approaches in the metaideology of social science, particularly those of a postmodern cast (Rosenau 1992), reject all three ideologies out of hand: They reject any notion of objectivity in the area (others consider them one by one, under the assumption that they may come apart.

Social lore is always lore about a particular social milieu and culture, and an aspiration to cultural universality, if it can be vindicated, would certainly give social science a distinctive status. Such an aspiration is supported in a variety of traditions: among anthropologists and sociologists of a Durkheimian cast, among many Marxist scholars, and among those economists who think that all human behavior, and the patterns to which it gives rise, can be explained by reference to *homo economicus.*

But the metaideologists of social science have claimed many reasons to question the possibility of any universalist, or at least any straightforwardly universalist, theory. Hermeneutic philosophy, which has long been dominant in Germany, and the analytical tradition sponsored by the work of the later Ludwig Wittgenstein both suggest that any explanation of human behavior has to start with the culturally specific concepts in which people understand their environment and cannot aspire, therefore, to a substantive universality (McCarthy 1978, Winch 1958). The debate on these questions ranges widely, encompassing issues of cultural and other forms of relativism (Hollis and Lukes 1982).

Social lore is not only particularistic, it is also designed to represent people as subjectively understandable or interpretable. We, the local consumers of such lore, know what it is like to be creatures of the kind represented and know how we would go about communicating with them. The second, and perhaps least persuasive, ideology of social science suggests that this disposition to represent people as subjectively understandable comes of a limited perspective that social science transcends. It suggests that social science can aspire to an objective explanation of people's behavior without worrying about whether the explanation fits with their self-understanding: without being anxious to ensure that it makes native sense of them and facilitates interpersonal communication. The ideology suggests that social science, in the received phrases, can aspire to a form of *Erklären,* or explanation, that need not service the needs of interpersonal *Verstehen,* or understanding.

Metaideologists of social science have claimed many reasons to question this aspiration to *Verstehen*-free explanation. Hermeneutic and Wittgensteinian thinkers both reject the idea that people can be properly understood without facilitating communication (Winch, 1958). And the many philosophers who follow the lead of Donald Davidson on interpretation argue that there is no interpreting human subjects without representing them as more or less rational and more or less interpersonally scrutable (Macdonald and Pettit 1981).

Social lore is often evaluatively committed as well as particularistic and oriented to subjective understanding. It takes a form premised on an evaluative characterization of the status quo. Thus, it may characterize the beliefs and explain the behavior of rulers on the assumption that the regime they sustain is unjust. The third and most common legitimating ideology of social science, one associated in particular with the German sociologist Max Weber, holds that in this respect—and perhaps in this respect only—social science can do scientifically better than social lore. It can acknowledge that the agents in the society have evaluative beliefs, and it can take account of these in its explanation of what they do, without itself endorsing any such beliefs; it can be objective, in the familiar sense of remaining uncommitted on evaluative questions.

Metaideologists of social science have also sought reasons to doubt this claim, but the debate has been confused by differences over what sorts of evaluative commitments would really be damaging to the pretensions of social science. The critique of social science on the grounds of not escaping a commitment to value has been nurtured by the appearance, in the later part of the century, of a variety of realist positions on the nature of value. If values are taken to be objective features of the world, then a social scientist's beliefs as to what those features are may well affect their interpretation of how certain subjects think and act; interpretation, after all, is bound to be influenced by the interpreter's view of the subject's environment (Hurley 1989, chap. 5; Macdonald and Pettit 1981, chap. 4; Taylor 1981).

The metaideology of social science may concern itself with other issues: for example, whether the models used in social science, in particular within economics, are really empirical, scientific models and not just pieces of mathematics or exercises in a conversational rhetoric (Hausman 1991, McCloskey 1985, Rosenberg 1992). These issues are not discussed here.

METAPHYSICS

The metaphysics of social science usually takes it as granted that there is no society without individual inten-

tional agents: without subjects who apparently act, other things being equal, on the basis of their beliefs and desires (Pettit 1993, pt. 1). The question that metaphysics raises bears on what more we should include in our metaphysical stock-taking of society; and on how the more we should include, if there is any, relates to individual intentional subjects.

There are two aspects of social life that are particularly relevant to this question. There is the social interaction between individuals in virtue of which various relationships get formed: relationships involving communication, affection, collaboration, exchange, recognition, esteem, or whatever. And there is the social aggregation of individual attitudes and actions in virtue of which various institutions get established: These institutions will include common instrumentalities such as languages, cultures, and markets; groups such as the club, union, or party, whose essence it is to have a mode of collective behavior; groups that may have only a nonbehavioral collective identity such as genders, races, and classes; and shared resources of the kind illustrated by museums, libraries, and states.

The metaphysics of social science concerns itself both with issues raised by interaction and with questions associated with aggregation, specifically with social interaction and aggregation. (On the definition of "social," see Ruben 1985.)

On the side of interaction the main issue in social philosophy is that which divides so-called atomists from nonatomists (Taylor 1985). The atomist holds that individual human beings do not depend—that is, noncausally or constitutively depend—on social relationships for the appearance of any distinctive, human capacities. The nonatomist holds that they do. The atomist defends an image of human beings under which they come to society with all the characteristic properties that they will ever display; social life does not transform them in any essential manner. The nonatomist denies this, believing that it is only in the experience of social relationships that human beings come properly into their own.

The debate between atomists and nonatomists has centered on the connection between thought and language. Atomists have taken their lead from Thomas Hobbes, who argues that, however useful language is for mnemonic, taxonomic, and communicative purposes, thinking is possible without speech, even without any inchoate form of speech. Nonatomists have tended to follow Jean-Jacques Rousseau and the Romantic tradition with which he is associated—a tradition also encompassing Johann Gottfried Herder and G. W. F. Hegel—in arguing, first, that language is social and, second, that thought requires language.

The atomist tradition has been dominant in English-speaking philosophy, while the nonatomist has had a considerable presence in France and Germany. One source of nonatomism in the English-speaking world has been the work of the later Wittgenstein, in which it is suggested that following a rule—and, therefore, thinking—is possible only in the context of social practices and relationships (Wittgenstein 1968). This very strong nonatomist thesis may also be weakened, so that the claim is that following a rule of a characteristic kind—say, a suitably scrutable kind—requires such a social context (Pettit 1993, chap. 4). Another source of nonatomism in recent English-speaking philosophy has been the argument that the content of a person's thoughts is fixed, not just by what goes on in his head, but by the linguistic community to which he belongs and to which he aspires to remain faithful (Burge 1979, Hurley 1989).

What now of the issues generated by the aggregative aspect of society? There are a number of interesting questions raised by the aggregative structure of society, some having to do with the reducibility of aggregative theory to theory of a more psychological cast, others having to do with the status of aggregative individuals and the standing of the causal relevance we ascribe to such entities (Gilbert 1992, James 1984, Ruben 1985, Tuomela 1996). Perhaps the most pressing question, however, is whether the entities that appear with the social aggregation of individual attitudes and actions give the lie to our ordinary sense of intentional agency: whether it means that, contrary to appearances, we are in some way the dupes of higher-level patterns or forces (Pettit 1993, chap. 3). The individualist, to use a name that also bears further connotations—see under "Methodology"—denies that aggregate entities have this effect; the nonindividualist insists that they do.

One extreme sort of individualism would say that intentional agency is not compromised by any aggregate, social entities, because in strict truth no such entities exist. A more plausible form of the doctrine would say that while there are indeed a variety of aggregate entities, there is nothing about those entities that suggests that our received, commonplace psychology is mistaken. No doubt, there are aggregate regularities associated with such entities: For example, a rise in unemployment tends to be followed by a rise in crime; the fact that something is in an organization's interest generally means that agents of the organization will pursue it; and so on. But the individualist will argue that those regularities do not signal the presence of forces unrecognized in commonplace psychology or the operation of any mechanism—say, any selection mechanism—that belies the assumptions of that psychology. That the regularities obtain can be explained within that psychology, given the context in which the relevant agents find themselves and given their understanding—perhaps involving relevant aggregate-level concepts—of that context.

METHODOLOGY

There are two sorts of methodological questions raised in the philosophy of social science: first, questions imported from the methodology of natural science having to do with such matters as observations and laws and theories, realism and nonrealism in theory interpretation, statistical inference, confirmation, and explanation; second, questions that arise only, or arise distinctively, within the social sciences. Perhaps the two major questions of the latter kind bear on whether it is good explanatory practice to follow the individualistic and economistic assumptions, respectively, that characterize much social science. Here the emphasis will be on the issues of individualism and economism.

The methodological individualist, as characterized in the literature, is associated with a number of more or less outlandish doctrines: for example, that individuals each play indispensable roles, so that things would always have been significantly different if the actual individuals had not been around or if they had not done the things they actually did; that individuals are unaffected by their circumstances, or their relationships with one another, in the things they come to think and want; or that all social facts can be expressed in terms of a nonsocial psychology and that all social laws can be derived from the laws of such a psychology.

Methodological individualism is better understood, however, as a doctrine that has more clearly had respectable defenders as well as opponents: specifically, as the doctrine that it is always good explanatory practice to try to explain social events in terms of finer-grain, individualistic factors rather than by reference to aggregative antecedents. Such an explanatory individualism has been defended by Jon Elster (1985). He argues that aggregative antecedents are causally relevant in virtue of the causal relevance of individual factors and that staying at the aggregative level means leaving the productive mechanism in a black box; it amounts to a willful neglect of relevant facts.

Suppose that we have found a good aggregative explanation of some social phenomenon: say we find that secularization is explained adequately by urbanization or a rise in crime by a rise in unemployment. We gain further information about the causal history of such a phenomenon as we are informed about the individual-level factors at work in producing secularization or crime. But it may still be that the aggregative story gives us equally important causal information. It may be, for example, that while we learn more about the detail of the actual causal process in going individualistic we learn more about what would be enough to ensure an increase in secularization or crime—that there should be urbanization or unemployment—in spotting the aggregative connections. After all, we might have known the individual-level explanations without having come to recognize the aggregative connections. Perhaps the right line is neither explanatory individualism nor explanatory nonindividualism but explanatory ecumenism (Jackson and Pettit 1992).

The second question bears on whether it is a good explanatory strategy in social science to make economistic assumptions about individual agents: to assume, as economists tend to do, that agents are rational in the way they form and reform their preferences and that their preferences are generally egoistic in character. There are lots of persuasive arguments for following an economistic strategy: arguments that point to the precision in model building and prediction that economistic assumptions allow (Becker 1976). But it seems manifest, on the other hand, that the economistic story is not the whole truth about human beings (Hollis 1977). For example, it is surely obvious that most of us do not make our decisions on the self-concerned, calculative basis that that story would seem to suggest.

But this consideration may not be decisive against economism. For what is possible is that while agents often do not calculate economistically, they tend sooner or later to give up on patterns of behavior that are not at least comparatively satisfactory in economistic terms (Pettit 1993, chap. 5). Perhaps the fact that a pattern of behavior satisfies such economistic constraints is necessary to explain the resilience, if not the actual production and reproduction, of the behavior.

See also Confirmation Theory; Davidson, Donald; Durkheim, Émile; Enlightenment; Explanation; Hegel, Georg Wilhelm Friedrich; Herder, Johann Gottfried; Hermeneutics; Hobbes, Thomas; Induction; Marxist Philosophy; Philosophy of Science, History of; Philosophy of Science, Problems of; Postmodernism; Realism; Rousseau, Jean-Jacques; Weber, Max; Wittgenstein, Ludwig Josef Johann.

Bibliography

Becker, G. *The Economic Approach to Human Behavior.* Chicago: University of Chicago Press, 1976.

Burge, T. "Individualism and the Mental." *Midwest Studies in Philosophy* 4 (1979): 73–121.

Elster, J. *Making Sense of Marx.* Cambridge, U.K.: Cambridge University Press, 1985.

Gilbert, M. *On Social Facts.* Princeton, NJ, 1992.

Hausman, D. *The Inexact and Separate Science of Economics.* Cambridge, U.K.: Cambridge University Press, 1991.

Hawthorn, G. *Enlightenment and Despair: A History of Sociology.* Cambridge, U.K.: Cambridge University Press, 1976.

Hollis, M. *Models of Man: Philosophical Thoughts on Social Action.* Cambridge, U.K.: Cambridge University Press, 1977.

Hollis, M., and S. Lukes, eds. *Rationality and Relativism.* Cambridge, MA: MIT Press, 1982.

Hurley, S. *Natural Reasons: Personality and Polity.* New York: Oxford University Press, 1989.

Jackson, F., and P. Pettit. "In Defence of Explanatory Ecumenism." *Economics and Philosophy* 8 (1992): 1–21.

James, S. *The Content of Social Explanation.* Cambridge, U.K.: Cambridge University Press, 1984.

Macdonald, G., and P. Pettit. *Semantics and Social Science.* London: Routledge and Kegan Paul, 1981.

McCarthy, T. *The Critical Theory of Jürgen Habermas.* Cambridge, MA: MIT Press, 1978.

McCloskey, D. *The Rhetoric of Economics.* Madison: University of Wisconsin Press, 1985.

Papineau, D. *For Science in the Social Sciences.* London: Macmillan, 1978.

Pettit, P. *The Common Mind: An Essay on Psychology, Society, and Politics.* New York: Oxford University Press, 1993.

Rosenau, P. M. *Post-Modernism and the Social Sciences: Insights, Inroads, and Intrusions.* Princeton, NJ: Princeton University Press, 1992.

Rosenberg, A. *Economics: Mathematical Politics or Science of Diminishing Returns?* Chicago: University of Chicago Press, 1992.

Ruben, D.-H. *The Metaphysics of the Social World.* London: Routledge and Kegan Paul, 1985.

Ryan, A. *The Philosophy of the Social Sciences.* London: Macmillan, 1970.

Taylor, C. *Philosophy and the Human Sciences.* Cambridge, U.K.: Cambridge University Press, 1985.

Taylor, C. "Understanding and Explanation in the *Geisteswissenschaften*." In *Wittgenstein: To Follow a Rule*, edited by S. H. Holtzman and C. M. Leich. London: Routledge and Kegan Paul, 1981.

Tuomela, R. *The Importance of Us.* Stanford, CA: Stanford University Press, 1995.

Winch, P. *The Idea of a Social Science and Its Relation to Philosophy.* London, 1958.

Wittgenstein, L. *Philosophical Investigations*, 2nd ed. Translated by G. E. M. Anscombe. Oxford: Blackwell, 1968.

Philip Pettit (1996)

PHILOSOPHY OF STATISTICAL MECHANICS

Probabilistic modes of description and explanation first entered into physics in the theory of statistical mechanics. Some aspects of the theory that are of interest to the general philosopher of science are the nature of probability and probabilistic explanations within the theory, the kind of intertheoretical relation displayed between this theory and the nonprobabilistic theory it supplants, and the role to be played in scientific explanations by the invocation of cosmological special initial conditions. In addition, this theory provides the framework for attempts to account for the intuitive sense that time is asymmetric by reference to asymmetric physical processes in time.

HISTORY OF THE THEORY

It was in the seventeenth century that thinkers first realized that many material systems were describable by a small number of physical quantities related to one another by simple laws—for example, the ideal gas law, relating the volume, temperature, and pressure of a gas.

It was soon understood that a fundamental notion was that of equilibrium. Left alone, systems might spontaneously change the value of their parameters, as when a gas expands to fill a box. But they would soon reach an unchanging final state, that of equilibrium. And it was realized that this process was asymmetrical in time, in that systems went from earlier non-equilibrium states to later equilibrium states, but not from earlier equilibrium states to later states of non-equilibrium.

Studies of steam engines initiated by S. Carnot showed that stored heat could be converted to mechanical work, but only by a process that converted stored heat at a higher temperature to residual heat at a lower temperature. This result was made mathematically elegant by R. Clausius, who introduced the notion of entropy as a measure of heat's ability to be converted into external work into physics. That heat was a form of stored energy and that the total amount of energy in heat and work was conserved became a fundamental principle of physics, as did the idea that energy could spontaneously only go from a more ordered to a more a less orderly state. These results were formalized in the First and Second Laws of Thermodynamics. But why were these laws true?

The latter half of the nineteenth century and the beginning of the twentieth saw the development of an intensive debate about the place of thermodynamics within the more general sciences that dealt with dynam-

ics and with the constitution of matter. P. Duhem, E. Mach, and others argued that the laws should be understood as autonomous principles. But others sought an account of heat as the hidden energy of motion of the microscopic constituents of matter. This was later understood for gases in terms of a simple model of molecules in free motion except for collisions among them. The early work on kinetic theory of W. Herepath and J. Waterston, followed by work of A. Kronig, made this a rich area for theoretical exploration. J. C. Maxwell and L. Boltzmann discovered laws governing the distribution of velocity of the molecules in the equilibrium state, and they developed a law governing how such distributions changes as a system in nonequilibrium approached equilibrium, at least for the simple system of a nondense gas.

The theory of approach to equilibrium soon met with profound objections. J. Loschmidt pointed out that the apparently demonstrated time-asymmetrical approach to equilibrium was hard to understand in light of the fact that the laws governing the underlying dynamics of the molecules allowed for the time reverse of each possible process to be possible as well. Later H. Poincaré showed that the kind of systems being dealt with would, except possibly for exceptional initial conditions in a class of probability zero, return over infinite time infinitely often to states arbitrarily close to their initial states. Once again this seemed incompatible with the monotonic increase of entropy described by thermodynamics and apparently deduced from the dynamics in kinetic theory.

Both Maxwell and Boltzmann introduced probabilistic elements into their theory. The equilibrium distribution might be thought of as the most probable distribution of the molecules in space and in velocity. Alternatively, in an approach later systematically developed by J. W. Gibbs, equilibrium values might be calculated by computing the average of macroscopic features over all possible distributions of the molecules. Both Maxwell and Boltzmann also argued that approach to equilibrium should also be thought of probabilistically. Maxwell discussed the possibility of a "demon" who could, by inspecting molecules one by one, change an equilibrium state of a system to a nonequilibrium state without doing external work on the system. Critics such as S. Burbury and E. Culverwell noted that the introduction of probabilistic notions was not sufficient by itself to overcome the puzzles of reversibility and recurrence.

In his last view of the theory, Boltzmann, following his assistant Dr. Scheutz, offered a time-symmetrical version of the theory. On this view, isolated systems spend most of their life near equilibrium over very long periods of time. There would be occasional fluctuations away from equilibrium. A system found in a nonequilibrium state would probably be closer to equilibrium both in the past and future. Our local region of the universe, a universe that as a whole was itself in equilibrium, was one such fluctuation. Scientists could only exist in such a nonequilibrium regions because only such a region could support sentient creatures. Why do we find our local world approaching equilibrium in the future and not in the past? Because the time direction of increase in entropy determined the future just as the local direction of gravitational force determined the down spatial direction.

In an important study of the foundations of the theory in 1910, P. and T. Ehrenfest (1959) surveyed the basis of the theory as understood in different ways by Maxwell, Boltzmann and Gibbs. They also offered an important interpretation of Boltzmann's equation describing approach to equilibrium in which the solution of the equation described not the inevitable or even probable behavior of an individual system but rather the sequence of states that would be found dominant at each time in a collection of systems all of whose members started in the same macroscopically nonequilibrium condition.

PROBABILITY AND STATISTICAL EXPLANATION

Probability is characterized formally by simple mathematical postulates, the additivity of probabilities over disjoint sets of events being the most important of these. Philosophers have long debated the interpretation of probability. Some interpretations are subjectivist, taking probabilities to be measures of partial belief. Others are logical, holding probabilities to represent partial entailments. Other interpretations are objectivist. Some varieties of this last are frequency, limits of frequency, or dispositional interpretations.

At least one proposal (by E. Jaynes) has held that the probabilities in statistical mechanics are subjective, or rather of a kind of logical sort resting upon a principle of indifference. Most interpreters of statistical mechanics hold to objectivist interpretations of probability, but even among them there is much debate. Are the probabilities somehow dependent on the underlying dynamical laws, as ergodic approaches suggest? Or are they reflective of a deeper lawlike structure of tychistic chance, as Albert suggests, referring to Ghirardi-Rimini-Weber (GRW) stochastic theories introduced in the interpretation of quantum mechanics? Or is it the case, rather, that the probabilities have an autonomous place within the theories requiring their independent postulation?

Philosophers analyzing statistical explanations have usually focused on uses of probabilistic explanation in everyday circumstances or in the application of statistics to such fields as biology. Here some suggestions have been that high probability is explanatory, that increased probability is what matters, or that explanations are only genuinely probabilistic when pure tychistic chance is relevant.

In statistical mechanics explanation in the nonequilibrium theory has many aspects that fit familiar patterns of statistical explanation as analyzed by philosophers. Within the theory the main areas of controversy are over the nature and rationale for the particular kind of probabilistic explanation that does justice to the empirical facts. In the equilibrium theory a kind of transcendental use of probability in the statistical explanations offered by ergodic theory is quite unlike the usual kind of causal-probabilistic explanations familiar in other contexts.

THE THEORY OF EQUILIBRIUM

Boltzmann and Maxwell developed a standard method for calculating the equilibrium values of the macroscopic parameters of a system. This became formalized by Gibbs as the method of the microcanonical ensemble. Here a probability distribution is placed over the microstates possible for the system, given its constraints. For each microstate the values of the macroscopic parameter are calculable. One takes as the observed equilibrium values the average value of these parameters calculated over all the possible microstates, using the stipulated probability distribution. But why does the method work? What rationalizes the choice of probability distribution and the identification of average values with equilibrium quantities?

Boltzmann argued that the method could be partly justified if one thought of equilibrium values as average values over an infinite time as the system changes its microstates under dynamic evolution. Another component of this way of thinking is a claim that, given the large numbers of molecules in a system, average values would coincide with overwhelmingly most probable values for a macroscopic parameter. Boltzmann and Maxwell argued that one could identify such time averages with so-called phase averages, calculated using the posited probability distribution over the microscopic conditions possible for the system, if one thought of any one system as going through all possible microstates compatible with the macroscopic constraints on the system as time went on.

This became formalized by the Ehrenfests in the form of the Ergodic Hypothesis.

Early versions of the Ergodic Hypothesis were provably false. Weaker versions, such as the claim that the microstate of the system would come arbitrarily close to every possible microstate over infinite time, were impossible to demonstrate and could not support the equality of time and phase averages even if true.

These early ideas gave rise to the mathematical discipline of ergodic theory. The results of J. von Neumann, and, in stronger form, those of G. Birkhoff, showed that for certain idealized dynamical systems, except for a set of initial conditions of zero probability in the standard probability distribution, the time average of quantities calculated from the microstate of the system over infinite time would, indeed, equal the phase average of that quantity calculated using the standard-probability distribution over all possible microstates of the system.

But did any realistic models of a system meet the conditions needed for these theorems to hold? Many decades of work, culminating in that of Sinai, showed that a familiar model of a dilute gas, hard spheres in a box, was a model of an ergodic system. On the other hand, important work in theoretical dynamics showed that more realistic models of the gas would necessarily fail to be strictly ergodic (the KAM theorem). So any hope of applying ergodicity to rationalize the standard theory would require subtle reasoning involving the fact that the system was composed of vast numbers of molecules and might be, therefore, "ergodiclike."

From ergodicity many consequences follow. Except for a set of initial points of probability zero, infinite time averages of a phase quantity will equal the phase average of that quantity. For any measurable region of the phase space, the proportion of time spent by the system in that region over infinite time will equal the probabilistic size of that region. Most important is the following: Boltzmann realized that the standard probability distribution was invariant over time under the dynamics of the system. But could there be other such time invariant distributions? If the system is ergodic, one can show that the standard distribution is the unique time-invariant distribution, which assigns zero probability to regions assigned zero probability by the standard distribution.

These results provide us with a kind of transcendental rationale for the standard equilibrium theory. Equilibrium is an unchanging state. So if we are to identify macroscopic features of it with quantities calculated by using a probability distribution over the microstates of the system, this probability distribution should be unchanging under the dynamics of the system. Ergodicity shows us, with a qualification, that only one such probability distribution, the standard one, will do the trick.

But as a full rationale for the theory, ergodicity must be looked at cautiously. Real systems are not genuinely ergodic. We need to simply swallow the claim that we may ignore sets of conditions of probability zero in the standard measure. And the kind of rationale we get seems to ignore totally the place of equilibrium as the end point of a dynamic evolution from nonequilibrium conditions.

THE THEORY OF NONEQUILIBRIUM

Maxwell and Boltzmann found equations describing the approach to equilibrium of a dilute gas. Later a number of other such kinetic equations were found, although attempts at generalizations to such situations as dense gases have proved intractable.

But how can such equations, whose solutions are time asymmetric, possibly be correct if the underlying dynamics of the molecules are symmetrical in time? Careful analysis showed that the Boltzmann equation depended upon a time-asymmetrical assumption, the Stosszahlansatz. This posited that molecules had their motions uncorrelated with one another before, but not after, collisions. Other forms of the kinetic equations made similar assumptions in their derivation. Two general approaches to deriving such equations are that of the master equation and the approach that works by imposing a coarse graining of cells over the phase space available to the system and postulating fixed transition probabilities from cell to cell. But the time-asymmetrical assumption must be imposed at all times and might even be inconsistent with the underlying deterministic dynamics of the molecules.

Many attempts have been made to understand the kinetic equations and to resolve the paradoxes. Some of these explore how an initial probability distribution over a collection of systems can, in a "coarse-grained" sense, distribute itself over the increased phase volume available to a system. This way of looking at things was first described by Gibbs. The coarse-grained spreading of the probability distribution is taken to represent the approach to equilibrium of the system. This interpretation fits with the understanding of the solution curve of the Boltzmann equation outlined by the Ehrenfests.

To show that such spreading of the initial probability distribution occurs, one relies upon the underlying dynamics and generalizations of the results of ergodic theory. Systems can be characterized as randomizing in a variety of senses of increasing strength such as being a mixing system, a K-system, or a Bernoulli system. Then one can rely upon the model of the system—hard spheres in a box, for example—and the dynamics to show the system randomizing in the specified sense. This approach often relies upon many idealizations, such as calculating what happens in the infinite time limit. And the results often depend upon the use of unrealistic models of systems. For these reasons the applicability of the results to real systems and their real finite time behavior requires care.

Crucially these results, following as they do from the time-symmetrical dynamics, cannot by themselves introduce time asymmetry into the account. To do that one must make a time-asymmetrical assumption about how the initial probability distribution over the microstates of the system is constrained. This problem was studied by N. Krylov and others. Krylov's solution was a kind of nonquantum uncertainty principle applicable to the preparation of systems. Others look for the solution in cosmological facts, as we shall later note. Still others seek to modify the underlying dynamics by postulating some time-asymmetrical fundamental physical principle in play, such as the time-asymmetrical GRW stochastic field proposed in some interpretations of quantum mechanics.

There are ways of trying to understand an approach to equilibrium quite at odds with the mixing approach just described. O. Lanford, for example, has produced a "rigorous derivation of the Boltzmann equation." Going to an idealized limit, the Boltzmann-Grad limit, Lanford imposes an initial probability distribution, and then shows that with probability one systems will evolve for a short time as described by the Boltzmann equation. Because the results can be proved only for very short times—less than the mean free time to the first collision—their applicability to the real world is again in question. As usual, interesting issues about time asymmetry arise, here in the form of the choice of the initial probability distribution.

IRREVERSIBILITY

Why is it that, although the underlying dynamic principles are symmetrical in time, the thermodynamic laws describe a world asymmetrical in time, a world in which entropy spontaneously increases in one time direction but not the other? Merely introducing probabilities into the account by itself will not provide the grounds for understanding the physical origins of irreversibility.

Throughout the history of thermodynamics and statistical mechanics, the suggestion has been repeatedly made that the source of thermodynamic time asymmetry lies in the existence of some time-asymmetrical law governing the underlying dynamics. The recent invocation of time asymmetric GRW stochastic influences is the latest such proposal.

Sometimes it has been suggested that the entropic increase experienced by an "isolated" system is to be accounted for in terms of the fact that systems can never really be fully causally isolated from their external environment. Even the most carefully insulated system, for example, has its molecules' motion influenced by gravitational forces exerted by matter outside the system. Whether the fact that isolation is an idealization is really relevant to thermodynamic time asymmetry has been much debated. Of great importance to this debate is the existence of systems that seem to show the usual macroscopic entropic increase familiar from thermodynamics, but which are systems sufficiently isolated from their surrounding environments such that a simple external trigger can have their microstates follow a reverse course, with the system recurring to its original nonequilibrium state—spin-echo experiments, for example. For these systems seem to show that a kind of entropic increase cannot be accounted for in terms of external interference with the system.

As noted above, it was Boltzmann's assistant, Dr. Scheutz, who first suggested a cosmological solution to the problem. Scheutz suggested that the universe as a whole is in a time-symmetrical equilibrium state, with our local portion of the cosmos in a rare fluctuation away from equilibrium. Such a region would be very likely, from a time symmetrical probabilistic perspective, to evince higher entropy in one time direction but lower entropy in the other direction of time, since it is unlikely to be at the turning point of maximal deviation from equilibrium. Boltzmann then supplemented this with his assertion that the very meaning of the future is that is the time direction in which entropy is increasing.

Current cosmological theories describe a very different sort of universe, one that, to the best of our knowledge, is in an overall nonequilibrium state and that has entropic increase in the same time direction in all its regions. In current Big Bang cosmology the universe is said to be spatially expanding from a singularity some tens of billions of years ago. Some theorists take the thermodynamic time asymmetry to have its roots in the cosmic expansion. The more general opinion is that this cannot be correct, since, according to the prevailing but not universal opinion, even if the universe began to contract, entropy would continue to increase.

In the dominant opinion, rather, the source of entropic increase is found in a special physical condition of the universe just after the Big Bang. In these accounts the matter of the universe is taken to be, at that early date, in thermal equilibrium. But matter is thought to be smoothly distributed in space. This is a very low entropy state because of the fact that gravity, unlike intermolecular forces in a gas, is a purely attractive force. The theory goes on to propose a clumping of matter into dense galactic clusters, galaxies, and stars, leaving most of space almost devoid of matter. This results in an enormous increase in spatial-gravitational entropy. Matter so clumped goes into a lower entropy state than its original equilibrium, since it now consists of hot stars in cold interstellar space. The general increase of entropy from the Big Bang onward is then accounted for by positing both the usual time-symmetrical probability assumptions and initial low entropy for the universe as a whole.

One question that then arises is why the initial state should be one of such low entropy. Here one is up against the usual perplexities that arise if we ask for an answer to a why question about "the initial state of everything." Why is such a low-probability state the one we find? Should one posit many universes, of which our low-probability case is a rare example? Here one is reminded of the speculation of Scheutz about our region of the universe just being an improbable sample from the whole. Can one explain why we find ourselves in such a universe by some version of the anthropic principle, first used by Boltzmann to explain why we find ourselves in a low-entropy region of his speculated high-entropy universe? Can one attribute probabilities to initial singular states or to universes at all? Here one thinks of the criticism offered by D. Hume of the teleological argument for the existence of God.

The second law of thermodynamics is not concerned, of course, with the entropy change of the entire cosmos, but rather with the parallel in time-entropic increases of small systems temporarily causally isolated from their external environments. The study of the connection between cosmic entropy increase and that of the "branch systems" was initiated by H. Reichenbach. Many of the arguments in the literature claiming to derive changes of entropy of branch systems that are parallel in time to the entropy increase of the cosmic whole are badly flawed, but a reasonable inference can likely be constructed using probabilistic posits that themselves do not smuggle time asymmetry into the derivation.

THERMODYNAMICS AND STATISTICAL MECHANICS

We often speak of an older theory being reduced to a newer theory, and it is often said that thermodynamics has been reduced to statistical mechanics. But, as we have learned in general, the relation of older theory to newer theory may be of some complexity and some subtlety.

Thermodynamics, traditionally, was not a theory framed in probabilistic terms. Its laws, especially the second law, could not be exactly true, as Maxwell noted, in the light of the new probabilistic account. Alternative ways of dealing with this problem are available. One way is to stick with traditional thermodynamics and offer an account of the relation between newer and older theory that is far from a simple derivation of the latter from the former. Another possibility is to use the new knowledge of the probabilistic aspects of thermal phenomena to construct a novel statistical thermodynamics that imports probabilistic elements directly into the older theory.

There must be a high degree of complexity in the relations between the concepts of the older theory—such as volume, pressure, temperature and entropy—and those of the newer theory—such as concepts dealing with molecular constitution, the dynamics governing the molecules, and probabilistically framed concepts dealing either with the distribution of states of constituents of the individual system or with the distribution of microstates of systems in a collection of systems characterized by some macroscopic parameters.

Consider, for example, thermodynamic entropy. Associated with it are many distinct entropy concepts in statistical mechanics. Boltzmann entropy, for example, is defined as the fluctuating property of an individual system, defined in terms of the actual spatial and momentum distribution of the molecules of the system at a time. Gibbs's entropies, on the other hand, are defined in terms of some probability distribution imposed over some imagined ensemble of systems characterized by some specified constraints. To make matters even more complicated, there is Gibbs's fine-grained entropy, defined by the probability distribution alone and useful for describing the equilibrium states of systems, and Gibbs's coarse-grained entropy, whose definition requires a specification of some coarse-grained partition of the phase space as well as the probability distribution, and whose place is in characterizing the approach to equilibrium of nonequilibrium systems. Other notion of entropy, such as those defined in terms of topology rather than measure theory, exist as well.

None of this complexity shows that one is wrong in thinking that in some appropriate sense, statistical mechanics explains the success of thermodynamics or that it might be plausible to speak of a reduction of thermodynamics to statistical mechanics. The complexity and subtlety of the relations between the two theories informs the philosopher of science of just how varied and complicated such reductive relations might be.

Philosophers outside the field of philosophy of physics might take some interest in the relationship that thermodynamics bears to the underlying physical description of the systems to which thermodynamic concepts are applied. A material object composed of atoms or molecules, for example, can exist in equilibrium with a system of electromagnetic radiation, leading physicists to speak of both such systems as having a common temperature. What this shows is that concepts such as entropy and temperature have a kind of functional role, with their meanings fixed by the place they play in a theory that is applicable to physical systems of many different kinds. This bears some analogy with the claim, so familiar in the philosophy of mind, that mental terms are functional and that mental states are multiply realizible in physical systems of varied natures.

THE DIRECTION OF TIME

The claim that our very notion of the asymmetry of time is rooted in entropic asymmetries of physical systems in time was first made by Boltzmann, as we have noted. The claim has often been repeated but remains controversial. Much needs to be done to provide a completely convincing case that our deepest intuitions about the difference between past and future are somehow grounded in entropic asymmetries.

A first question relates to what an entropic theory of the direction of time is claiming. It certainly cannot be that we find out which direction of time is the future by somehow checking up directly on the entropic behavior of systems around us, for that claim has little plausibility. So what does the claim come down to?

What intuitively distinguishes future from past? We think we have a direct insight into which of a pair of events is later than the other. We take it that we have asymmetric epistemological access into past and future, there being memories and records of the past and not of the future. We usually take it that causation goes from an earlier event as cause to a later event as effect. We are anxious about future events but not about past events, although we may regret the latter. We often think of the past as being over and done with and hence not subject to change, whereas the future is open to many possibilities. Some philosophers have argued that past events have determinate reality, whereas there is no such thing as a determinate being to the future.

The most plausible version of the entropic theory of the direction of time is best understood by looking at the analogy introduced by Boltzmann. What lies behind our intuitions that space is distinguished by an asymmetry because one direction is down and its opposite up? Surely it is the existence of gravitational force that fully accounts for the down-up distinction. It is gravity that explains why rocks fall down and, in our atmosphere, flames and helium balloons go up. Even the fact that we can tell, directly and without using our sensory awareness of the external world, which direction is down is explained in terms of the local direction of gravitational force. For it is the behavior of fluids in our semicircular canals that tells us which way is up, and the behavior of that fluid is entirely explained in terms of its gravitationally induced weight. In regions of the universe with no gravitational field, there is no distinction between the up and the down direction to be drawn.

The entropic theorist of the direction of time argues that the situation is exactly analogous to the case of down directionality and gravity. The claim is that we can account for all the intuitive differences by which we distinguish past from future by a scientific account at whose core are entropic asymmetries in the behavior of systems in time. If there were regions of the cosmos in which entropic changes were antiparallel to one another in time, the entropic theorist claims, the inhabitants of such regions would take opposite directions of time to be the future direction of time. And in regions of the cosmos in equilibrium, there would be no past-future distinction, although, of course, there would still be opposite directions in time.

There have been numerous proposals, starting with the seminal work of H. Reichenbach, to try to justify the claim that is it is, indeed, entropic change that lies at the heart of any explanation of why we have memories and records of the past and not of the future, of why we think of causation as going from past to future, of why we have differential concerns about past and future, and of why we think of the past as determinate but think of the future as an open realm of mere possibilities. Despite much important work on this problem, however, the very possibility of constructing such entropic accounts remains controversial.

See also Causal Approaches to the Direction of Time; Counterfactuals; Physics and the Direction of Time.

Bibliography

Albert, D. *Time and Chance*. Cambridge MA: Harvard University Press, 2000.

Brush, S. *The Kind of Motion That We Call Heat*. Amsterdam: North-Holland, 1976.

Brush, S., ed. *Kinetic Theory*. Oxford: Pergamon Press, 1965.

Ehrenfest, P. and T. *The Conceptual Foundations of the Statistical Approach in Mechanics*. Ithaca, NY: Cornell University Press, 1959.

Guttman, Y. *The Concept of Probability in Statistical Physics*. Cambridge, U.K.: Cambridge University Press, 1999.

Price, H. *Time's Arrow and the Archimedean Point*. Oxford: Oxford University Press, 1996.

Reichenbach, H. *The Direction of Time*. Berkeley: University of California Press, 1956.

Sklar, L. *Physics and Chance: Philosophical Issues in the Foundations of Statistical Mechanics*. Cambridge, U.K.: Cambridge University Press, 1993.

Lawrence Sklar (2005)

PHILOSOPHY OF TECHNOLOGY

The philosophy of technology brings logical, metaphysical, epistemological, ethical, and political philosophical questions to bear on the making and using of artifacts. The particular balance among these questions will differ within related regionalizations of philosophy, such as the philosophy of science or the philosophy of art. In the philosophy of technology, for instance, epistemology typically plays a lesser role than in the philosophy of science but a greater role than in the philosophy of art. Any philosophical assessment of technology is thus partially defined by its own inner balance in relation to philosophy as a whole.

HISTORICAL EMERGENCE

Although limited discussions of *techne* and associated or derivative phenomena can be found in ancient, medieval, and early modern philosophy, it was not until the late nineteenth and early twentieth centuries that technology, as something distinct from technics or technique, became a subject for theoretical examination. Among the earliest contributing texts, the mechanical engineer Franz Reuleaux's *Theoretische Kinematik* (1875) developed an extended conceptual analysis of different types of tools and machines. More generally, Ernst Kapp's *Grundlinien einer Philosophie der Technik* (1877), in the first book to use "philosophy of technology" in its title, outlined a theory of culture grounded in technics understood as the extension and differentiation of human anatomy and physiology. The hammer, for instance, functions as an extension of the fist, the camera as an extension of the eye, and the railroad as an extension of the circulatory system; and vice versa, the fist can be said to be like a hammer, the eye like a camera, and rail lines like blood vessels. Elaborations of this view of technology as organ projection are representative of a school of what Carl Mitcham (1994) calls engineering philosophy of technology, an approach that was further developed in the work of thinkers as diverse as the Russian Peter Englemeier, the German Friedrich Dessauer, the Frenchman Gilbert Simondon, and the Spaniard Juan David García Bacca (all of whom have been largely ignored in Anglo American philosophy).

The research engineer Dessauer, for instance, developed a neo-Kantian critique of the transcendental possibility of technological invention that sees technology as bringing noumenal power into the world. Dessauer was also instrumental in promoting philosophical discussion within the Verein Deutscher Ingenieure (VDI; Society of German Engineers). The psychologist Simondon explored relations among parts, artifacts, and technical systems and the evolutionary manifestation of what he called technicity. The engineer Englemeier and the philosopher García Bacca both saw technological change engendering world-historical transformations that were at once humanizing and transcending of the merely organically human. Additional contributions to this school can be found in theoretical discussions about cybernetics and artificial intelligence. Also illustrative of achievements in engineering-oriented philosophy of technology are the scientific philosopher Mario Bunge's (1985) systematic metaphysics, epistemology, and ethics of technology and the engineer Billy Vaughn Koen's (2003) brief for engineering as the one right method for problem solving.

In its emergence, however, philosophy of technology was more commonly associated with what might be called a counterphilosophy that interprets technology not as extending but as encroaching on or narrowing the dimensions of human experience. Following Immanuel Kant's attempt "to deny [scientific] *knowledge*, in order to make room for *faith*," this humanities philosophy of technology has sought to limit technological thought and practice to make room for human culture in all its rich diversity. A case in point is the public intellectual Lewis

Mumford's (1967) criticism of what he calls monotechnics, the technics of power, in contrast to poly- or biotechnics. The problem with monotechnics is that it promotes the pursuit of physical power and control at the expense of other aspects of human flourishing such as friendship and art. For Mumford the "myth of the machine" is to think that power is the source of all human benefit. In fact, it constitutes an unrealistic narrowing of human activity. Some version of this argument has been promoted especially by the continental European philosophical tradition in the works of José Ortega y Gasset (1939), Martin Heidegger (1954), and Jacques Ellul (1954). Indeed, even more broadly, the relation between technology and life—whether in the sense of *zoe* (organic existence) or *bios* (human flourishing)—has become one of the most crucial issues in both the metaphysics and ethics of technology.

Until the latter half of the twentieth century, the argument for delimitation had the unintended side effect of relegating technology to marginal status in professional philosophy. Only as technology became more than an engineering interest or a social problem has it begun to be a mainstream topic in philosophy. One of the challenges in the twenty-first century will be to pursue the professional development of philosophical reflection on technology in ways that bridge the oppositions inherent in its bimodal historical origins without compromising their basic if divergent concerns.

ETHICAL AND POLITICAL ISSUES

Because of their prominence in public affairs, the philosophy of technology properly highlights ethical and political issues. Indeed, contemporary work in practical or applied ethics—as in nuclear, environmental, biomedical, and computer ethics—emphasizes the moral challenges of technology, although in ways that sometimes reduce the field to an aggregate of different ethics for different technologies. Such subspeciation can deprive ethics of possible synergistic strengths. Access equity issues, for instance, occur in both biomedicine and computers, and the concepts and principles for dealing with one might well inform or enhance the other. Speaking generally, then, one can identify at least six competing and overlapping interpretations of technology as an ethical or political problem. Three of these arose initially before World War II, although they have continued to cast a shadow of concern, often in new and distinctive forms.

First, there is a problem of the just distribution of technological products and powers—that is, technology as a political issue. Since the Industrial Revolution the

social-justice question has found numerous expressions in authoritarian and democratic regimes, in developing and developed countries. Authoritarian regimes have often justified themselves as acting to promote access to technological benefits against entrenched special scientific, technical, or corporate interests or against those whose commitment to equality undermines the invention and production of goods and services. Democratic regimes have placed more emphasis on promoting equality by means of due process and regulatory agencies. One aspect of due process that has been given special philosophical attention concerns the legal protocols to promote free and informed consent, extending the concept from human experimentation to engineering at large (Martin and Schinzinger 2005).

With the engineered design of new products and processes social justice issues have often taken special form in association with some otherwise morally neutral concepts. The advent of electronic computer and Internet communications, for instance, has helped impart ethical significance to questions of privacy and the so-called "digital divide." Additionally, according to Ulrich Beck (1992), concerns for the fair distribution of goods and services were, during the late twentieth century, superseded by those dealing with the fair distribution of dangers and risks, thus giving social justice debates a special twist. One of the strongest criticisms of some of the resulting twists and turns has been Kristin S. Shrader-Frechette's (1991) careful dissecting of the antidemocratic assumptions of much risk-cost-benefit analysis.

Second is the problem of the alienation of workers from their labor in the industrial means of production, which has been presented especially by Marxists as an economic and by some non-Marxist social scientists as a psychological issue. Langdon Winner's (1977) analysis of the theory of autonomous technology or the idea that technology as resistant to human control is a more general statement of the issue. Critical theory work by Herbert Marcuse (1964) and Andrew Feenberg (1991, 1999) extended the classic Marxist discussion into situations reconfigured by consumerist culture and globalization. Opposing Marcuse's pessimism about transformation, Feenberg (especially 1995) has been more optimistic about alternative possibilities. Environmentalists, however, have further argued that technology in general alienates human beings from nature.

Don Ihde's (1990) phenomenology of the technolifeworld offers another take on this issue through an analysis of human—technology—world relations. Two fundamental types of such engagements are instrumental relations, in which the technology is integrated into the human sensorium as its extension (the blind man's cane), and hermeneutic relations, in which the technology becomes part of the world to be interpreted (a thermometer). Both engagements manifest an invariant structure that amplifies some aspect of the world (exact metric of temperature) while simultaneously reducing others (general sense of climate). The former tends to bring humans closer to the world, the latter to distance (or alienate) them from it.

Third is the problem of the destruction or transformation of culture by modern science and technology—either directly through new weapons and forms of military conflict or indirectly through the impact of new means of transportation, communication, and media. The destruction of World War I, the most violent in human history, was a manifestation of technology that only became worse during World War II with the development of nuclear weapons. The long cold war practice of nuclear deterrence and the early twenty-first-century challenges of terrorism present special problems for learning to manage the destructive potential in technology.

Between the two world wars concern for the more indirect technological transformation of culture took on special salience, as variously illustrated by the cultural lag theory of the American sociologist William Fielding Ogburn, the elegiac ruminations of the Catholic theologian Romano Guardini, or the active nihilistic enthusiasms of Ernst Jünger. In the latter half of the twentieth century the issue found small-scale manifestation in personal efforts to come to terms with new choices (e.g., in diet, drugs, and consumer lifestyle options) and large-scale manifestation in debates about the dynamics of sociotechnical change (e.g., the role of technology in economic development and technological determinism versus social constructionism). Questions can also arise about the transformed character of cultural life under the influence of information and image technologies, from television to the Internet and virtual reality machines.

Since World War II three more issues have emerged to ethical and political prominence. One is that of democratic participation. An anticipatory version of this issue emerged in interwar proposals for technocracy. For some theorists (such as Thorstein Veblen) rule by technical elites offered a better alternative than rule by economic or political elites. However, in the postwar revival of democratic theory, and with recognition that technology (like law) is a creation that also influences the creators, it was argued that the principle of "no taxation without representation" should be extended to "no innovation without representation" (Goldman 1992). Winner, for instance, describes "technologies as forms of life" and calls for the abandonment of "technological somnambulism" (1986, p. 10) in favor of public debate about the design of technological projects as diverse as highway bridges, tomato harvesters, and nuclear power plants. Efforts to determine how such democratic participation should be structured both within communities of technical expertise and in the negotiations between technical experts and the nontechnical public have been the subject of ongoing debates (see Sclove 1995).

Fifth is the industrial pollution of the natural environment, which has contributed to attempts to develop an appropriate environmental or ecological ethics. What is the difference between artifice and nature—and the moral status of wilderness or the nonhuman environment? As nature is humanly transformed, to what extent should contemporary technological action take into account the welfare of future generations, whether human or nonhuman? What is the relation between values that are divided between the anthropocentric and ecocentric, extrinsic or instrumental and intrinsic?

Another morally relevant concept, closely related to issues of both participation and environmentalism, is that of unintended consequences. To what extent are scientists and engineers responsible for the unexpected and perhaps even unforeseeable results of their technological actions? Two attempts to deal with the plethora of environmental issues, especially in relation to the challenge of unintended consequences, are those associated with sustainable development and the precautionary principle—with competing interpretations of both becoming major themes of moral and political deliberations.

Finally, there is the issue of responsibility: How are humans to respond ethically to the power placed in their hands by modern technology? Such a question has personal, professional, and policy dimensions. At the personal level, quantitatively and qualitatively enhanced choices, with expanding knowledge production relevant to such choices (scientific research and consumer reports), place existential pressures on individuals to increase conscious reflection. The principle of free and informed consent appears to require not only that medical professionals inform the subjects of human experimentation about the risks and benefits of their participation but also that medical patients of all sorts become reflective participants in their own treatment—and that consumers of any technological goods or services weigh multiple costs and benefits as if they were engineers designing their lives. Are such demands both reasonable and possible?

At the professional level, scientists and engineers, falling under similar existential pressures to expand the conscious exercise of responsibility, have formulated codes of conduct for technical practices related to both research and design. In engineering ethics, for instance, the primacy of protecting public safety, health, and welfare is now a well-established general principle. In what sense, however, are engineers qualified to make such judgments? Does technical expertise provide any basis for determining appropriate levels of public safety, health, or welfare?

Finally, at the level of public policy, responsibility takes two closely related forms. Policy for science and technology seeks out the best ways to fund or regulate developments in science and technology. Science and technology for policy searches for the best ways to bring scientific knowledge to bear on political decision making while making technological power most effectively available for political action. Responding to and exemplifying these dual drives scientific and technological research agencies such as the U.S. National Science Foundation, the Human Genome Project, and the National Nanotechnology Initiative have created specific programs to promote ethical reflection on the creation and use of new scientific knowledge and technological products, processes, and systems.

Again speaking broadly, it is possible to identify two fundamental attitudes toward this spectrum of ethical and political issues. One attempts to explain modern technology as rooted in human nature and culture (engineering philosophy of technology), the other interprets modern technical methods and effects as deformations of human action, however preferable in particular instances to those of nature (humanities philosophy of technology). The engineering approach in its expansive confidence calls in one way or another for more and better technology, the humanities approach in its restrictive questioning for some relinquishment or delimitation of technology. The tensions between such alternative attitudes repeatedly come to the fore in analysis of such key concepts as privacy, risk, participation, and the environment, and in assessments of new opportunities in virtual reality construction, biotechnological design, and nanotechnological research and development.

There is also a tendency for the engineering school to make alliances with the Anglo American analytic tradition in philosophy, and for the humanities school to find a convenient partner in the European phenomenological tradition. The former, viewing technology as a complex amalgam of artifacts, knowledge, activities, and volitions, each with diverse structural features scattered across historical epochs and societal contexts, prefers to deal on a case-by-case basis with one technology after another. The latter strives for bolder generalizations about technology as a whole, at least across each historical or societal context. From the phenomenological perspective, too great an emphasis on individual technological rocks can obscure the extent to which such geological specimens are constituents of mountains extended in both space and time.

METAPHYSICAL ISSUES

The attempt to speak of *technology* rather than *technologies* rests on an attempt to identify some inner or essential feature of diverse technologies. This hypothetical essential feature may be termed *technicity*. One can then immediately note that, before the modern period, technicity was at a minimum scattered throughout and heavily embedded within a diversity of human engagements, and indeed that philosophy took a stand against any separating of technicity from its embedding context. Plato's argument in the *Gorgias* is precisely an argument against disembedding *techne* from social or cultural contexts and traditions, not to mention ideas of the good. For Aristotle, *techne* is an intellectual virtue, and thus properly subordinate to the flourishing of human nature. What is distinctive about modern philosophy, by contrast, is the attempt, beginning with Galileo Galilei, Francis Bacon, and René Descartes to disembed technics from particular human activities, to study them in systematic ways, and thus to create technology.

John Stuart Mill in his *Logic* (1843) already assumes the success of this disembedding project when he explains the practical value of science. For Mill the rationality of any art is grounded in a corresponding science.

> The art proposes to itself an end to be attained, defines the end, and hands it over to the science. The science receives it, considers it as a phenomenon or effect to be studied, and, having investigated its causes and conditions, sends it back to art with a theorem of the combinations of circumstances by which it could be produced. Art then examines these combinations or circumstances, and according as any of them are or are not in human power, pronounces the end attainable or not.

> (*LOGIC*, BOOK 6, CH. 12, SECTION 2)

Remarkably, Mill's analysis does not recognize art (or traditional technics) as including any knowledge of means. Art is concerned solely with determining an end, to achieve which it deploys appropriate means as determined by science. It is the scientific study of means that constitutes what even during Mill's lifetime was coming to be called technology. Modern technicity may thus be defined as a systematic or scientific study of means that suspends examination of ends. Does such an approach have distinctive social and cultural implications, independent of any particular technologies and contexts?

Among the first philosophers to analyze such a disembedding of means from ends was Ortega. In the English translation of his *La rebelión de las masas* (1929), Ortega writes that "[t]hree principles have made possible [the] new world: liberal democracy, scientific experiment, and industrialism. The two latter may be summed up in one word: technicism" (1939, p. 56). Ortega himself actually uses the word *técnica*, but the term *technicism* is significant, and this in fact constitutes one of its first English occurrences with this sense. (Before the 1930s, *technicism* simply meant excessive reliance on technical terminology. The previous decade Max Scheler used the cognate *Technizismus* to name the industrial ethos.)

As part of a further "Meditación de la técnica" (1939), Ortega outlined a historical movement from the chance inventions that characterize archaic societies, through the trial-and-error techniques of the artisan, to the scientific technologies of the engineer. According to Ortega, the difference between these three forms of making lies in the way they create the means to realize a human project—that is, in the kind of technicity involved. In the first epoch, technical discoveries are accidental; in the second, techniques emerge from intuitive skill. In both instances they are preserved and elaborated within the confines of myth and craft traditions. In the third, however, the engineer undertakes scientific studies of technics and, as a result, "prior to the possession of any [particular] technics, already possesses technics [itself]" (*Obras*, 5:369). It is this third type of technicity that constitutes modern technicism (and here Ortega himself uses the term *tecnicismo*).

But technicism, understood here as the science of how to generate all possible technical means, disembedded from any lived making and using, creates a unique challenge. Before the modern period human beings were commonly limited by circumstances, within which they inherited a way of life and the technical means to achieve it. Now, however, they are given in advance many possible ways to live and a plethora of technical means but little in the way of a substantive vision of human flourishing. "To be an engineer and only an engineer is to be everything possibly and nothing actually," all form and no content (*Obras*, 5:366). There is in the midst of modern technicism what Ortega describes as a hidden ethical challenge to imagination and choice. Insofar as people can be anything they want, why should they take the trouble to be any one thing at all? Will not some extranatural motivation (not to say fanaticism) not be needed to help Buridan's cyborgs select among (rejecting some) the equally liberal options that surround them?

According to Heidegger modern technology is a challenge not just to ethics but to ontology. For Heidegger (1954) scientific technics constitutes a new kind of truth: truth not as correspondence, not as coherence, and not as functional knowledge, but as disclosure or revelation. Technology discloses Being in a historically unique way: as *Bestand* or resource. A castle constructed with traditional technics on a cliff overlooking the Rhine makes more fully present than before the stone that invests the landscape with its particular contours, while it sets off the curve of the river against the backdrop of its walls and towers. It invites people to settle near and experience the particularities of this place. By contrast, a poured concrete, hydroelectric power station compels the river to become an energy resource and converts the landscape into, not a place of human habitation, but a machine for the generation of electricity. It encourages people to draw on its energy for multitasking business in production and travel. The distinctly modern technicity that manifests itself in the disclosure of nature as resource Heidegger names *Gestell* (enframing).

Gestell at first sight appears to be a human work, something human beings in the course of history have chosen to practice for their own benefit. It gives them power over nature. However, as it digitalizes nature physically (dimensioned vectors), geographically (longitude and latitude), chemically (molecules, atoms, and subatomic particles), and biologically (genetic mapping), it also transforms language (computer signal processing) and art (pixel imaging) so that impact outstrips original intentions. Hidden in the midst of *Gestell* is Being as event, that which lets this dominating transformation come to pass. *Gestell* is at once destiny and, precisely because it appears so clearly to be the result of a human activity, an obscuring of the transhuman imparting of a destiny that is its ground.

In the same year that Heidegger's *Die Frage nach der Technik* appeared, Jacques Ellul published *La Technique*, later translated into English as *The Technological Society* (1954). For Ellul, too, what is happening is something transhuman, or at least transindividual, the emergence of a new social order in which people give themselves up to the systematic analysis of actions into constituent means that are then evaluated in terms of output/input metrics. The scientific analysis of techniques extends technoscientific methods into economics, politics, education, leisure, and elsewhere creating what he calls the technical milieu. After the milieux of nature and of society, technology is the third great epoch of human history. Ellul's characterology of this new reality—describing its rationality, artificiality, self-directedness, self-augmentation, indivisibility, universality, and autonomy—reveals the technical milieu as something more than simply human. Although more hospitable to human biological existence, it nevertheless also manifests certain inexorable laws of artifice (such as those of economics). Just as the natural milieu once provided a framework for human life, a differentiated but overriding order to which human beings adapted in a variety of ways, so now a much more homogeneous technical milieu presents itself, not simply as a realm of freedom that human beings have constructed, but as that which also constructs and constrains them even when they fail to recognize it.

FROM METAPHYSICS TO ETHICS

Efforts to make phenomenological metaphysics fruitful for ethics can be found in the work of two German American philosophers, Hans Jonas and Albert Borgmann. Jonas's (1966) work begins with a fundamental inquiry into the phenomenon of life, arguing that in the organic world there emerges a new kind of being. For Jonas the key features of human inner life (introspection and subjectivity) are present in embryo in the most primitive organisms, and in metabolism there emerges the primordial form of freedom. In metabolism a detachment enters the world insofar as being becomes distinguished from physical identity. However, in the materialism of modern science this unique reality is easily overlooked. Adopting a teleological approach to ontology, Jonas argues that only from the perspective of the more fully realized freedom manifest in humans can the reality of the organic as a whole be recognized for what it is. On this ontological basis Jonas (1984) undertakes an extended philosophical scrutiny of the technological projects of nuclear weapons and biomedical health care. In the presence of technical powers to end or alter human life Jonas reformulates the Kantian categorical imperative as: "Act so that the effects of your action are compatible with the permanence of genuine human life" (p. 11). Such a reformulation of the fundamental deontological principle constitutes an attempt at the re-embedding of technology in moral philosophy.

More broadly and in sustained dialogue with a range of discussions about the place of technology in human affairs, Borgmann's (1984) work draws a fundamental distinction between two kinds of artifice and action. On the one side are technological devices that obscure their inner functions to deliver without engagement commodities for easy and effortless consumption. This constitutes what Borgmann calls the device paradigm, an ideal type at which the products and processes of modern technology aim. On the other are focal things and practices whose workings are more transparent and that demand of their users some reordering of interests if they are to be used. The model for the first is the central heating system that only needs its thermostat set, for the second the wood-fired hearth.

In a series of studies arguing the nondeterminist importance of material culture to ethics and politics, Borgmann (1992, 1999) calls on citizens in the high-tech world to reconsider their ways of life to develop a deeper sense for the possibilities of human flourishing in the midst of liberal options for self-determined self-fulfillment. For Borgmann the ideal is not a forced return to the past but a voluntary recovery of the commanding presence of things in the technological present. As he concludes in a volume devoted to the critical assessment of his thought:

> Science makes reality ever more transparent, and technology makes it more and more controllable. But at the end of our inquiries and manipulations there is always something that reflects rather than yields to our searchlight and presents itself as given to us rather than constructed by us. It is intelligible not because we have seen through it or designed it but because it speaks to us [in the form of] an unforethinkable and uncontrollable reality. (Higgs, Lights, and Strong 2000, pp. 368–369)

It is such a reality to which human flourishing is ultimately in thrall even in the midst of its highest exercises of insight and mastery.

EPISTEMOLOGICAL ISSUES

Epistemology has often been treated as a stepchild in the philosophy of technology family of philosophical interests. Technological forms of knowledge are commonly thought to be derivative of scientific knowledge, so that any attempt to bring the theory of knowledge to bear in the examination of technology has regularly been part of a discussion of the relation between technology and science. At the same time this common privileging of science has been philosophically criticized, although the criticism has taken different forms in the European phenomenological and in the Anglo American analytic philosophical traditions.

From a phenomenological perspective the argument has been that technology is not so much applied science as science is theoretical technology. In his historico-philosophical studies of the scientific and technological revolutions of the seventeenth century and after, for instance, Jonas (1974) argues that from its origins modern science was animated by a technological interest that gives it an inherently applicable or technological character. Related studies of the dependency of science on technological instrumentation, from Galileo's telescopes to particle accelerators and PCR (polymerase chain reaction) machines (e.g., see Ihde 1991), suggest that science might even be described as applied technology. This approach to the epistemology of technology has parallels with the pragmatic tradition of conceiving scientific knowledge in fundamentally instrumentist terms (see Hickman 2001). The Venezuelan phenomenologist Ernesto Mayz Vallenilla (2004) likewise offers a more Husserlian-based but complementary effort to describe the unique epistemological features of what he calls meta-technical instruments.

From the analytic perspective there has been more of an effort to identify distinctive types of knowledge operative in technology. Summarizing the results from such an approach, Mitcham (1994) draws attention to at least four types of distinctly technological knowledge: sensorimotor skills, technical maxims (including rules of thumb and recipes), descriptive laws or technological rules (which take an "if A then B" form), and technological theories (either grounded in scientific theory or bringing scientific method to bear on human-technology interactions). German philosophers of technology such as Hans Lenk, Gunter Ropohl, and Bernhard Irrgang, all associated with the VDI promotion of philosophical reflection on technology, are pursuing efforts to develop epistemological analyses of the engineering sciences. And Joseph C. Pitt (2000) makes a determined effort to identify the distinctive forms of technological and engineering knowledge, drawing especially on the careful analyses of aeronautical engineering history by Walter G. Vincenti

(1990) to argue that engineering design possesses its own cognitive features.

Important issues for any theory of technological knowledge remain the characterization of whatever basic epistemic criteria might be analogous to those operative in science such as truth, simplicity, coherence, and explanation. There may be distinctive technological forms of such criteria. But two major candidates for uniquely technological criteria are effectiveness and efficiency. Certainly, many propositions of engineering knowledge are assessed in terms of effectiveness and efficiency more than truth or explanation. A further epistemological challenge is to explicate the distinctive character of models and modeling in the technological and engineering contexts. The relevance of such epistemological analyses nevertheless remains of problematic relevance to ethics and politics.

EMPIRICAL, ANTHROPOLOGICAL, AND POLICY TURNS

Concern for the adequacy of metaphysical definitions of technology—and perhaps exhaustion with endless ethical and political difficulties (with hopes that new approaches might prove more fruitful)—has given rise to what has been called an empirical turn in the philosophy of technology. As advocated by the Dutch philosophers Peter Kroes and Anthonie Meijers, this program argues that "philosophical reflection should be based on empirically adequate descriptions reflecting the richness and complexity of modern technology" (2000, p. xix) and promotes a greater analysis of what technologists and engineers actually do over any extended exegesis of texts, whether those of other philosophers of technology or even engineers and technicians. As such, a natural alliance has developed with social constructivist approaches to science, technology, and society studies in the pursuit of richer metaphysical or ontological understandings of artifacts, epistemological analyses of technical practice, and even ethical decision making among professional engineers. From the perspective of Jozef Keulartz et al. (2002), this also provides a solid opportunity for advancing a pragmatist ethics for technological culture.

Two topics of prominence in the empirical turn from the interpretation of texts to the interpretation of technical artifacts have been those of design and function. Design is often identified as the essence of engineering, and there have been numerous technical studies of design methodology. At the same time engineering design must be distinguished from aesthetic design as well as design by means of evolutionary processes in nature. Even within the realm of engineering design, studies such as those by Vincenti (1990), Louis Bucciarelli (1994), and Richard Buchanan and Victor Margolin (1995) have very different implications for assessing proposals for consumer, green, sustainable, or participatory design. With regard to technical functions, analyses have focused on the relation between functions in organisms, social institutions, and artifacts; on the relation between functional and physical descriptions of artifacts; and on the extent to which functions are determined by design or use.

A different sense for new beginnings has emerged in relation to prospects in the development of the new fields of bioengineering and biotechnology—especially when applied to humans. The leader in this case is the medical scientist and philosopher Leon Kass, the chair of the Bush administration's President's Council on Bioethics. In his turn Kass has tried to go outside the boundaries of standard bioethics in at least four ways: to promote thinking that enrolls more than professional bioethicists, that does more than piecemeal or specialized analyses, that references human nature as a norm, and that builds toward policy results. As in *Beyond Therapy: Biotechnology and the Pursuit of Happiness* (2003), Kass et al. at the council seek to raise broad issues about what it means to be human in the presence of possibilities for the reengineering not just of the external world but of the inner world of human birth, growth, and experience. He has been especially concerned about the possibilities for the deformation of humanity not from above by totalitarian governmental use of technology but from below by positive consumer endorsement of behaviors that would from a traditional perspective be assessed as temptations.

Beyond the policy-oriented work of Kass and colleagues, policy questions have become increasingly central not just as aspects of ethical responsibility but as issues in their own right. What precisely is technological policy, as opposed to technological politics? Does policy decision making take different forms in relation to science and to engineering? How are policies to be formulated and assessed?

The extent to which these turns in the philosophy of technology will define its future are questions that the professional community must examine. Any such examination will also need to include a self-criticism that considers the special responsibilities of a regionalization in philosophy that, more than the philosophy of science or of art, has as part of its heritage public responsibilities and a large measure of ethical concerns.

See also Applied Ethics; Aristotle; Artificial Intelligence; Bacon, Francis; Bioethics; Categorical Imperative; Computationalism; Computer Ethics; Descartes, René; Engineering Ethics; Environmental Ethics; Epistemology, History of; Ethics, History of; Galileo Galilei; Genetics and Reproductive Technologies; Heidegger, Martin; Human Genome Project; Kant, Immanuel; Machine Intelligence; Marxist Philosophy; Metaphysics, History of; Mill, John Stuart; Neo-Kantianism; Ortega y Gasset, José; Philosophy of Biology; Philosophy of Science, History of; Philosophy of Science, Problems of; Veblen, Thorstein Bunde.

Bibliography

Beck, Ulrich. *Risikogesellschaft: Auf dem Weg in eine andere Moderne.* Frankfurt am Main, Germany: Suhrkamp, 1986. Translated by Mark Ritter as *Risk Society: Toward a New Modernity.* London: Sage, 1992.

Borgmann, Albert. *Crossing the Postmodern Divide.* Chicago: University of Chicago Press, 1992.

Borgmann, Albert. *Holding on to Reality: The Nature of Information at the Turn of the Millennium.* Chicago: University of Chicago Press, 1999.

Borgmann, Albert. *Technology and the Character of Contemporary Life: A Philosophical Inquiry.* Chicago: University of Chicago Press, 1984.

Buccarelli, Louis. *Designing Engineers.* Cambridge, MA: MIT Press, 1994.

Buchanan, Richard, and Victor Margolin, eds. *Discovering Design: Explorations in Design Studies.* Chicago: University of Chicago Press, 1995.

Bunge, Mario. "Technology: From Engineering to Decision Theory." In *Treatise on Basic Philosophy, Vol. 7, Philosophy of Science and Technology*, Part 2, *Life Science, Social Science, and Technology.* Boston: D. Reidel, 1985.

Ellul, Jacques. *La technique ou l'enjeu du siècle.* Rev. ed. Paris: Economica, 1990. Translated by John Wilkinson as *The Technological Society* (New York: Vintage, 1965). See also two supplements: *Le système technicien* (Paris: Calmann-Lévy, 1977), translated by Joachim Neugroschel as *The Technological System* (New York: Continuum, 1980); and *Le bluff technologique* (Paris: Hachette, 1988), translated by Geoffrey W. Bromiley as *The Technological Bluff* (Grand Rapids, MI: W. B. Eerdmans, 1990).

Feenberg, Andrew. *Alternative Modernity: The Technical Turn in Philosophy and Social Theory.* Berkeley: University of California Press, 1995.

Feenberg, Andrew. *Critical Theory of Technology.* Rev. ed. New York: Oxford University Press, 1991.

Feenberg, Andrew. *Questioning Technology.* New York: Routledge, 1999.

Feenberg, Andrew. *Transforming Technology: A Critical Theory Revisited.* New York: Oxford University Press, 2002.

Goldman, Steven. "No Innovation without Representation: Technological Action in a Democratic Society." In *New Worlds, New Technologies, New Issues*, edited by Stephen H.

Cutcliffe et al., 148–160. Bethlehem, PA: Lehigh University Press, 1992.

Heidegger, Martin. "Die Frage nach der Technik." In *Vorträge und Aufsätze*. Pfullingen, Germany: Neske, 1954. Translated by William Lovittas "The Question concerning Technology," in *The Question concerning Technology and Other Essays* (San Francisco: Harper and Row, 1954).

Hickman, Larry. *Philosophical Tools for Technological Culture: Putting Pragmatism to Work*. Bloomington: Indiana University Press, 2001.

Higgs, Eric, Andrew Lights, and David Strong, eds. *Technology and the Good Life?* Chicago: University of Chicago Press, 2000.

Ihde, Don. *Instrumental Realism: The Interface between Philosophy of Science and Philosophy of Technology*. Bloomington: Indiana University Press, 1991.

Ihde, Don. *Technology and the Lifeworld: From Garden to Earth*. Bloomington: Indiana University Press, 1990.

Jonas, Hans. *The Phenomenon of Life: Toward a Philosophical Biology*. New York: Harper and Row, 1966.

Jonas, Hans. *Philosophical Essays: From Ancient Creed to Technological Man*. Englewood Cliffs, NJ: Prentice Hall, 1974.

Jonas, Hans. *Das Prinzip Verantwortung: Versuch einer Ethik für die technologische Zivilisation*. Frankfurt: Germany, 1979. Translated by Hans Jonas, with the collaboration of David Herr, as *The Imperative of Responsibility: In Search of an Ethics for the Technological Age* (Chicago: University of Chicago Press, 1984).

Keulartz, Jozef, Michiel Korthals, Maartje Schermer, and Tsjalling Swierstract, eds. *Pragmatist Ethics for a Technological Culture*. Dordrecht, Netherlands: Kluwer Academic, 2002.

Koen, Billy Vaughn. *Discussion of the Method: Conducting the Engineer's Approach to Problem Solving*. New York: Oxford University Press, 2003.

Kroes, Peter, and Anthonie Meijers, eds. *The Empirical Turn in the Philosophy of Technology, Vol. 20, Research in Philosophy and Technology*. Amsterdam, Netherlands: Elsevier, 2000.

Marcuse, Herbert. *One-Dimensional Man: Studies in the Ideology of Advanced Industrial Society*. Boston: Beacon Press, 1964.

Martin, Mike W., and Roland Schinzinger. *Ethics in Engineering*. New York: McGraw-Hill, 1983. 4th ed., 2005.

Mayz Vallenilla, Ernesto. *Fundamentos de la meta-técnica*. Caracas, Venezuela: Monte Avila, 1990. Translated by Carl Mitcham as *The Foundations of Meta-Technics*. Lanham, MD: University Press of America, 2004.

Mitcham, Carl, ed. *The Encyclopedia of Science, Technology, and Ethics*. 4 vols. Detroit, MI: Macmillan Reference, 2005.

Mitcham, Carl. *Thinking through Technology: The Path between Engineering and Philosophy*. Chicago: University of Chicago Press, 1994.

Mumford, Lewis. *The Myth of the Machine, Vol. 1, Technics and Human Development*. New York: Harcourt, Brace, 1967.

Ortega y Gasset, José. "Meditación de la técnica." In *Ensimismamiento y alteración*. Buenos Aires, Argentina: Espasa-Calp, 1939.

Ortega y Gasset, José. *Revolt of the Masses*. New York: W. W. Norton, 1932.

Pitt, Joseph C. *Thinking about Technology: Foundations of the Philosophy of Technology*. New York: Seven Bridges Press, 2000.

President's Council on Bioethics. *Beyond Therapy: Biotechnology and the Pursuit of Happiness*. New York: Regan, 2003.

Sclove, Richard. *Democracy and Technology*. New York: Guilford Press, 1995.

Shrader-Frechette, Kristin S. *Risk and Rationality: Philosophical Foundations for Populist Reforms*. Berkeley: University of California Press, 1991.

Vincenti, Walter G. *What Engineers Know and How They Know It: Analytical Studies from Aeronautical History*. Baltimore, MD: Johns Hopkins University Press, 1990.

Winner, Langdon. *Autonomous Technology: Technics-out-of-Control as a Theme in Political Thought*. Cambridge, MA: MIT Press, 1977.

Winner, Langdon. *The Whale and the Reactor: A Search for Limits in an Age of High Technology*. Chicago: University of Chicago Press, 1986.

Carl Mitcham (1996, 2005)

PHONOLOGY

"Phonology" is the branch of linguistics concerned with the articulatory and auditory domain of grammar—that is, with the theory of what John Langshaw Austin (1962) called phonetic acts. Its subject matter links with but is distinct from that of syntax, semantics, and pragmatics. It covers the forms in which the sounds of words are kept in memory and the manner in which the motions of speech organs are shaped by grammar.

Unlike syntax, semantics, and pragmatics (but like closely related morphology), phonology has been largely ignored by philosophers. On the whole, philosophers consider the fact that natural languages are primarily spoken rather than written as of little interest for what Michael Dummett (1986) calls a "philosophical explanation" of language. This attitude stems largely from the mistaken but widely held view that spoken signs are arbitrary sounds whose individuating traits are those of noises. On that view, utterances contemplated apart from their semantic and syntactic features are merely tokens of acoustical types, bereft of grammatical properties, fully described by the physics of noises, and available for human communication simply because humans can perceive and produce them; there is nothing intrinsically linguistic about them. Nor is this attitude an accident. Historically, philosophers have had little incentive to reflect on the sound of language. Most belong to traditions that admit no crucial differences (except perhaps those that pertain to pragmatics) between natural languages and notational systems developed by scientists, mathematicians, or philosophers for the elaboration of their theories. Such notational systems have a syntax and a semantics of sorts, but they have no phonology. Their constituent elements are typically spatial ideographs that share little with the phonological structures of natural languages. Studying language with such a bias offers few reasons, if any, to focus on what is spoken rather than written. It can, however, entrap one in a false conception of linguistic signs, so false, in fact, as seriously to weaken philosophic doctrines built on it.

Phonology rests on a series of presumptions—each supported by a vast body of observations—that together entail that the sounds of natural languages are not arbitrary human noises, on a par with grunts or snorts, whose individuating attributes lie entirely outside the domain of grammar.

The first such presumption is that when people acquire a word they memorize the underlying phonological representation of that word, a representation that defines—but often only partially—how the word is pronounced. These representations have the structure of linearly arrayed discrete timing positions that are assigned pointers to articulatory organs (lips, blade of tongue, dorsum of tongue, root of tongue, velum, vocal cords) implicated in the pronunciation of the word, and pointers to actions these organs execute during speech. The first timing position for the English *pin,* for instance, points to the lips, the vocal cords, the velum, full closure of the first, stiffening of the second, and nonlowering of the third.

A second presumption is that these pointers (called phonological features) on timing positions are drawn from a finite repertoire, common to all languages, and that they are combined within and across timing positions in rule-governed ways. Some rules are common to all languages and reflect innate linguistic endowments, others are language specific and reflect the influence of linguistic exposure. No language, for instance, avails itself of nasal snorts. French admits rounding of the lips in combinations of features that English excludes (thus the sound *ü* in French but not in English). Korean, unlike English (except for *h*), admits aspiration in underlying phonological representations. German, unlike English, admits initial sequences corresponding to sounded *k* followed by sounded *n.* All languages assemble features in similar (three-dimensional-like) structures.

A third presumption is that underlying phonological representations, in isolation or when compounded in complex words, are subject to rule-governed processes that add, subtract, or modify phonological features, which group them into syllables, feet, and prosodic words, which assign stresses and (in some languages) tones, and which ultimately yield final articulatory instructions, so-called surface phonological representations related to, but often very different from, the underlying representations in memory. Processes of this sort account for the fact that, for example, *leaf* occurs as *leavz* (with *v* instead of *f*) in the plural, or that *serene* is pronounced differently when alone than when a constituent of *serenity,* or that *p* gets aspirated in *pin* though not in *spin.* The details of these rules, the manner of their application, the universality of their formats, and the options fixed by different languages are all objects of intense research and controversies. But the evidence in behalf of their reality seems irrefutable.

Phonology is of philosophic interest, not only because it brings into question analogies between contrived notational systems and natural languages, but also because it raises conceptual issues of its own. Two can be mentioned here.

First, individual spoken utterances are analyzable in both acoustical and phonological terms. No generalizable exact correspondences between these two analyses are known. None may be forthcoming. For instance, nothing acoustical corresponds to word division. How can this dualism be reconciled? Is there a cogent sense in which the objects of speech production are the same (or belong to the same types) as those of speech perception? Offhand, the problem resembles that raised by other events amenable to multiple descriptions. But in this case solutions must be attuned to much that is already understood about both phonology and acoustics. It is not a simple task.

Second, phonological theory associates multiple representations with each utterance—including an underlying representation and a surface one—and it describes them all in the same notation. Surface representations can be conceptualized as instructions (or intentions) to move articulators in certain ways; their ontological status, though unclear, is at least comparable to that of other familiar cases. Not so the other phonological representations. They do not have familiar analogues. The semantic domain of phonological notation therefore cannot be ontologically homogeneous. Furthermore, part of that domain is deeply perplexing.

See also Austin, John Langshaw; Dummett, Michael Anthony Eardley; Philosophy of Language; Pragmatics; Semantics; Syntax.

Bibliography

Anderson, S. R. *Phonology in the Twentieth Century*. Chicago: University of Chicago Press, 1985.

Austin, J. L. *How to Do Things with Words*. Cambridge, MA: Harvard University Press, 1962.

Bromberger, S., and M. Halle. "The Ontology of Phonology." In *On What We Know We Don't Know*, edited by S. Bromberger. Chicago: University of Chicago Press, 1992.

Dummett, M. In *Truth and Interpretation: Perspectives on the Philosophy of Donald Davidson*, edited by E. LePore. Oxford and New York: Blackwell, 1986.

Kenstowicz, M. *Phonology in Generative Grammar*. Cambridge, MA: Blackwell, 1994. An introduction to the field and a complete bibliography.

Quine, W. V. O. *Word and Object*, chap. 3. Cambridge, MA: MIT Press, 1960.

Sylvain Bromberger (1996)
Morris Halle (1996)

PHRONÊSIS

See Appendix, Vol. 10

PHUSIS

See *Nomos and Phusus*

PHYSICALISM

Physicalism, of which materialism is a historical antecedent, is primarily an ontological doctrine concerning the nature of reality and, specifically, mental reality. It is the view that reality is ultimately constituted or determined by entities—objects, events, properties, and so on—that are physical. This thesis is often combined with a claim about the explanatory supremacy of physical theory (physics).

Any formulation of physicalism raises the question, What is meant by "physical"? It is difficult to formulate a conception of the physical that is neither too strong, making physicalism obviously false, nor too weak, making physicalism trivially true. For example, what is physical may be simply identified through the language of physics. However, a problem arises over the conception of physics appealed to. Current physics seems too narrow because future extensions of physics would not count as physical; but the idea of a completed physics is too indeterminate because there is no clear idea of what that physics might include. One could attempt to characterize the physical in more general terms such as having spatial location or

being spatiotemporal. However, this threatens to make physicalism trivially true because mental phenomena seem clearly to have spatial location in virtue of having subjects—persons—who have bodies. It may be preferable to appeal to the idea of a completed physics. Although at any particular time people may not know exactly what is physical and what is not (because they may not know whether they have completed physics), nevertheless what is physical is all and only what a completed physics countenances.

There are two main types of physicalist theses. First, there is eliminative materialism, or physicalism. According to this there are not, and never have been, any mental entities, events, properties, and so forth. Strictly speaking, this is not a view about the nature of mental reality. Second, there is a group of doctrines that fall under the general heading of identity theories, some of which are stronger than others. These can be divided into two main categories. The stronger doctrines may be called type-type identity theories, or type physicalist theories (Armstrong 1968, Lewis 1966, Place 1956, Smart 1959), and the weaker doctrines may be called token identity theories, or token physicalist theories (Davidson 1970, Macdonald 1989, Macdonald and Macdonald 1995).

Physicalist theories need to account for at least two different kinds of mental phenomena. First, there are the sensations, such as color experiences, pains, tingles, itches, and the like, which are typically, and perhaps essentially, identified in terms of how they feel to their subjects. Then there are the intentional states or events, such as beliefs, hopes, desires, and thoughts, which are typically, and perhaps essentially, identified in terms of their intentional contents, or their "aboutness." For example, a person's belief that water is transparent has the intentional content, *water is transparent*; a content that represents the world around that person in a certain way, irrespective of whether the world happens to be that way. One of the biggest difficulties for physicalism is accounting for both of these kinds of mental phenomena. In the late twentieth and early twenty-first centuries, philosophers have expressed skepticism as to whether a thoroughgoing physicalist position is possible, and have maintained that physicalism (either token, or type) is true of at most one of these two kinds of mental phenomena (Chalmers 1996, Kim 1998).

TYPE PHYSICALISM

Consider any mental phenomenon, such as being in pain now, or thinking right now that water is transparent. It is possible to talk about this phenomenon as an individual occurrence of a certain kind in the mental life of a person and discuss its properties. It is also possible to talk about the kind of phenomenon—pain, or the thought that water is transparent—of which this event is an individual instance. Physical phenomena too can be discussed in both of these ways. Type physicalism is the view that the mental types, properties, or kinds under which mental phenomena fall are identical with physical types, properties, or kinds. For example, pain—that type of phenomenon, occurrences of which are individual pains—is identical with some single type of physical phenomenon such as C-fiber stimulation.

Type physicalism has its origins in the doctrines espoused by the logical positivists and central-state materialists (Place 1956, Smart 1959). It is a strong form of physicalism because it is reductionist. Many who endorse it believe that nothing short of it counts as a proper physicalism. They argue that even if it is in practice impossible for sentences containing mental terminology to be translated into or replaced by sentences containing physical and topic-neutral terminology, any view that holds that all mental phenomena are physical phenomena, but mental properties or kinds are not physical properties or kinds, is not worthy of the name "physicalism."

THE FIRST OBJECTION TO TYPE PHYSICALISM. Type physicalism suffers from two serious objections. The first, from phenomenal properties, specifically concerns sensations such as color experiences, pain, afterimages, and the like. It is that phenomena of these kinds or types have "felt" properties, such as being reddish, stabbing, or vivid, whereas phenomena of physical types do not. Given this, and given Leibniz's principle of the indiscernibility of identicals, it follows that sensation types are not identical with physical types because the phenomena that fall under them do not share all of the same properties. A variant of this objection focuses on the distinctive point of view a subject has on its own experiences: A subject knows what it is like to have experiences in a way that others do not, and this subjective mode of access reveals the phenomenal aspect of the experience, whereas an "other"-oriented point of view does not (Nagel 1974).

One response is to argue that the problem is purely conceptual and does not threaten physicalism, which is an ontological view about what sorts of things there are in the world, not a view about concepts (Levine 2001, Loar 1997, Tye 1999). Consider the type-type identity expressed by "Brain State B is the red-feeling sensation." To the objection that such identities are false because first-person access to experiences reveals them to have

properties that physical states do not have, the response is that the apparent difference in properties arises from the distinctive nature of human experiential (or phenomenal) concepts alone. Certain concepts, such as the concept *red-feeling sensation* (or *reddish sensation*), are ones that can only be possessed by being put into direct contact with experiences that fall under them, without the mediation of other information or concepts that one might have of those states. Because the phenomenal concept *red-feeling sensation* enables subjects to be put in direct contact with their own red-feeling experiences in a way in which no concept of Brain State B could do, it puts them in a position to recognize directly and in an immediate way their own phenomenal red-feeling experiences. Possession of the concept *Brain State B* could not put any subject in a position to recognize directly and in an immediate way its own red-feeling experiences. So, even having met the experiential requirement on the possession of the concept *red-feeling experience*, a subject might be under the illusion of thinking that the red-feeling sensation has a property that Brain State B lacks. Whether or not this response succeeds depends on whether, in acquiring a new concept, such as the concept *red-feeling sensation*, one learns a new fact about the world that one did not know before, despite being in possession of the concept *Brain State B*.

THE SECOND OBJECTION TO TYPE PHYSICALISM. The second objection to type physicalism is that from multiple realizability. This claims that mental kinds or properties may be realized in physically diverse types of ways, hence there is no single physical property with which a given mental property may be identified. The point is that even if each mental property were in fact to be realized by a single physical one, it is possible for it to be realized by physically diverse ones. The reason is that the introspective and behavioral basis upon which attributions of mental properties are typically made is silent on the potential internal physical realizers of them. Given the claim that identical things are necessarily identical, the mere possibility that a given mental property should be realized by a physical property other than that which in fact realizes it is sufficient to refute the claim that that mental property is identical with any physical property that may realize it. This objection is not independent of a modal argument that trades on the thesis that identical things are necessarily identical (Kripke 1980). This begins with the conceivability of a mental state type's existence in the absence of any physical type of state, and argues that, because what is conceivable is possible, it is possible that mental state types could exist in the absence of any physical state type. The argument concludes that, because it is possible that mental types should exist in the absence of any type of physical phenomenon, mental state types are not identical with any type of physical phenomenon. A version of this argument is held to be particularly decisive against type physicalism with respect to sensation states.

One response is to argue that mental types are identical with disjunctions of physical types. For example, pain may not be identical with C-fiber stimulation, but it may be identical with the disjunctive property, C-fiber stimulation, or A-fiber stimulation, or … , and so on (properties picked out by predicates formed by disjoining predicates that pick out all the possible physical realizers of mental properties). However, it is unclear whether these are bona fide properties. They do not have a unity of their own, viewed from a physical perspective; and it is arguable that a reason is needed, apart from the fact that they all realize a given mental property, to think that they are properties in their own right (Macdonald 1989).

Against this, it might be claimed that because any given mental *predicate* may correlate with an indefinite number of physical *predicates*, this may pose problems for formulating laws connecting mental with physical properties; but it does not follow that there is not a single physical *property* that is the extension of a given mental predicate. Mental properties are identical with the physical properties picked out by disjunctive physical predicates, but their autonomy is secured by their participation in real regularities, and so they do have a unity of their own, despite being identical with disjunctive physical properties (Antony 2003).

In a similar but more radical vein, it might be claimed that although there are mental and physical predicates, there really are only physical properties, so there are no type-type identities of any kind that might be problematic for physicalism (Kim 1998). This reductionist response avoids the problem of multiple realizability altogether, but only by taking an eliminativist stand on mental properties. Alternatively, it might be claimed that the only type-type identities licensed by physicalism are species-specific (as in, for example, that expressed by "pain in humans is identical with C-fiber stimulation"). None of these claims is unproblematic: the first, because it threatens to make mental properties non-nomic, which seems to undermine the commitments of type physicalism; the second, because it is eliminativist; and the third, because it leaves questions such as "What makes pain in humans and pain in dogs both pain?" unanswered.

TOKEN PHYSICALISM

Many consider one or the other of the above objections to be decisive against type physicalism and have opted instead for a weaker view: token physicalism. According to this, each individual mental event or phenomenon is identical with some physical event. One influential version of this is the view known as anomalous monism (Davidson 1970). Token physicalism is compatible with the multiple realizability of mental properties by physical ones because it is not committed to the view that each individual occurrence of a given mental kind is identical with an occurrence of the same type of physical phenomenon. It also appears to avoid the objection from phenomenal properties in its original form because it can concede that mental kinds have associated with them felt aspects with which no physical kinds are associated. To the objection that mental events are not identical with physical events because it is no part of the nature of any physical event that it have a felt aspect, the following reply can be made. If token physicalism is true, no physical event is essentially of a mental type; but given that it is of a given mental type, it has what is essential to being of that type. Thus, if this pain is identical with this C-fiber stimulation, then it is not essentially a pain. However, given that it is, as it happens, a pain, it has (though not essentially) what is essential to being of that type, namely being felt.

Without an explanation of how mental types relate to physical ones, token physicalism threatens to succumb to the charge that it is dualist because it countenances the existence of nonphysical properties or types. A common strategy is to advance a supervenience doctrine concerning the relation between mental and physical properties, according to which physical properties, although distinct from mental ones, in some sense determine them (Hellman and Thompson 1975). There are many varieties of supervenience theses. One difficulty is in finding a thesis strong enough to do justice to the claim that physical properties determine mental ones without being so strong as to entail identities between mental and physical properties or types, and with these, reducibility. Another, related problem, is explaining how it could be that mental types or properties supervene on physical ones in a way that dispels the worry that mental properties have no causal powers of their own.

See also Causal Closure of the Physical Domain; Dualism in the Philosophy of Mind; Functionalism; Mind-Body Problem; Nonreductive Physicalism; Philosophy of Mind; Reduction; Reductionism in the Philosophy of Mind.

Bibliography

Antony, L. "Who's Afraid of Disjunctive Properties?" *Philosophical Issues* 13 (2003): 1–21. An argument for the identity of mental properties with disjunctive physical ones.

Armstrong, D. M. *A Materialist Theory of Mind*. London: Routledge & Kegan Paul, 1968. Defense of a type-type identity theory of the mental and physical.

Block, N., ed. *Readings in the Philosophy of Psychology*. Vol. 1. Cambridge, MA: Harvard University Press, 1980. Articles on type-type identity theories, token identity theories, reductionism, and functionalism.

Chalmers, D. *The Conscious Mind*. New York: Oxford University Press, 1996. A conceivability argument against type physicalism, specifically with regard to sensation states.

Davidson, D. "Mental Events." In *Experience and Theory*, edited by Lawrence Foster and J. W. Swanson. Amherst, MA: University of Massachusetts Press, 1970: 79–101. Highly influential argument for a token identity of the mental and physical.

Hellman, G., and F. W. Thompson. "Physicalism: Ontology, Determination, Reduction." *Journal of Philosophy* 72 (1975): 551–564. Defense of a supervenience doctrine.

Jackson, F., R. Pargetter, and E. Prior. "Functionalism and Type-Type Identity Theories." *Philosophical Studies* 42 (1982): 209–225. Discussion of the relation between functionalism and type-type identity theories.

Kim, J. "Supervenience as a Philosophical Concept." *Metaphilosophy* 12 (1990): 1–27. Discusses supervenience as a covariance relation and its relation to reduction.

Kim, J. *Mind in a Physical World*. Cambridge, MA: MIT Press, 1998. A reductionist physicalist position regarding intentional states only that suggests handling the multiple realizability objection either by denying that mental properties are genuine or by maintaining that mental properties are identical with disjunctive physical ones.

Kripke, S. *Naming and Necessity*. Oxford: Basil Blackwell, 1980. A modal argument against type-type and token identity theories.

Levine, J. *Purple Haze*. Oxford: Oxford University Press, 2001. A defense of the view that phenomenal property problems with type physicalism are purely conceptual.

Lewis, D. "An Argument for the Identity Theory." *Journal of Philosophy* 63 (1966): 17–25. An argument for a type-type identity theory.

Loar, B. "Phenomenal States." In *The Nature of Consciousness*, edited by N. Block, O. Flanagan, and G. Guzeldere, 597–616. Cambridge, MA: MIT Press, 1997. A defense of the view that phenomenal property problems with type physicalism are conceptual.

Macdonald, C. *Mind-Body Identity Theories*. London: Routledge, 1989. A survey of type-type and token identity theories, and a defense of a token identity theory.

Macdonald, C., and G. Macdonald. "How to Be Psychologically Relevant." In *Philosophy of Psychology: Debates on Psychological Explanation*, edited by C. Macdonald and G. Macdonald. Oxford Basil Blackwell, 1995. Advances an argument for a token identity theory that attempts to explain how mental properties could supervene on physical ones in a way that dispels the worry that mental properties have no causal powers of their own.

McGinn, C. "Can We Solve the Mind-Body Problem?" *Mind* 98 (1989): 349–366. An argument for the view that the mind-body problem cannot be solved because of the conceptual disparities between the mental and the physical.

Nagel, T. "What Is It Like to Be a Bat?" *Philosophical Review* 83 (1974): 435–450. Argues against identity theories of the mental and the physical on the basis of a disparity between the mental and physical in points of view.

Place, U. T. "Is Consciousness a Brain Process?" *British Journal of Psychology* 47 (1956): 44–50. A defense of central-state materialism for sensations.

Smart, J. J. C. "Sensations and Brain Processes." *Philosophical Review* 68 (1959): 141–156. A defense of central state materialism for sensations.

Tye, M. "Phenomenal Consciousness: The Explanatory Gap as a Cognitive Illusion." *Mind* 108 (1999): 705–725. A defense of the view that phenomenal property objections to type physicalism are due to a confusion about phenomenal concepts.

Cynthia Macdonald (1996, 2005)

PHYSICAL REALITY

See *Philosophy of Science, History of; Philosophy of Science, Problems of*

PHYSICOTHEOLOGY

"Physicotheology" is the aspect of natural theology that seeks to prove the existence and attributes of God from the evidence of purpose and design in the physical universe. The argument is very ancient, but it is from the Greeks that its medieval and modern forms principally spring. Socrates revolted against the materialist tendencies of earlier philosophers, and his pupil Plato sought to show that the order and harmony exhibited in the world sprang from the action of mind. Plato argued that since matter cannot move itself, motion is evidence of the presence of mind in nature. All the activity and change in the world have their origin in a supreme mind that moves itself and creates subordinate souls or gods, the heavenly bodies. The outer sphere of the universe is set in motion by the direct action of the changeless, transcendent God. Aristotle expounded more emphatically a teleological or purposive view of nature in which the members of the hierarchy of natural classes in the universe seek to realize their beings according to their stations. This perspective presupposes a rational design, a universal aspiration to fulfillment, and in one passage Aristotle describes God as the perfect being whom all things desire.

The theological aspects of Greek views of nature passed into later science and were readily translated into Christian thought. The animistic view of natural knowledge may be seen in the work of Galen (second century), for whom the processes of the human body are divinely planned. During the earlier medieval period the natural world appeared to the eye of faith to be a scene of symbols and ciphers veiling moral and spiritual doctrines. Later medieval philosophers were fond of discerning marks of providential direction in the operations of nature, and Thomas Aquinas rests one of his proofs of the existence of God upon the cooperation of all types of natural objects to make the order of the world and the pointing of that order to an intelligent author who devised it. There was abundant recourse to this argument during the later Middle Ages.

SEVENTEENTH CENTURY

The golden age of the Argument from Design was the two centuries following the rise of science in the seventeenth century, and it took place principally in England. The new philosophy of nature abandoned belief in the intrinsic teleology of physical objects. In place of the analogy with a creator of living organisms or an artist creating works of beauty it substituted the analogy of an inventor and manufacturer of elaborate machines. The new scientists combined faith in the sovereignty of God in nature and belief in the mechanistic bases of phenomena by conceiving the deity as the skillful contriver of instruments, a consummate engineer.

In England the doctrine was promoted by two trends of thought, the Baconian gospel of controlled observation and the revival of Greek atomism. The Baconian method inspired groups of inquirers in London and Oxford to collect a mass of detailed information in which they saw the confirmation of their religious faith; and it was the descriptions of the zoologists and botanists, such as Nehemiah Grew and Francis Willoughby, that strikingly illustrated the marvelous skill of the Creator. The second doctrine, the atomic, or corpuscular, theory of matter, incurred charges of materialism and atheism from moralists because of its association with Epicurean atomism, and in order to divide themselves from these imputations the virtuosi were intent on attaching theological conceptions to the elements of the material world. They were also acutely sensitive to the materialist dangers in the dualist philosophy of René Descartes. Neither their religion, which formed the frame of all their thought, nor their reason, which saw the marks of purpose and planning in nature, allowed them to accept the idea that the

world originated in the chance combination of material atoms. Ralph Cudworth, in his *True Intellectual System of the Universe* (1678), spoke for all the experimental philosophers when he argued at length that greater perfections and higher degrees of being cannot possibly arise out of senseless matter. The ancient metaphysics of cause, securely rooted in Christian theology, precluded any doctrine of natural evolution, and it is interesting to observe that when writers on biology mentioned the hypothesis that creatures have been produced by "millions of trials," as did John Ray, the hypothesis was dismissed with scorn. Species had been finally and completely created. There was no conceivable alternative to the Argument from Design.

ROBERT BOYLE. The Argument from Design was expounded with eloquence by Robert Boyle (1627–1691). In his multifarious researches he was concerned with the evidence of benevolent and ingenious contrivance in nature and found on all sides "curious and excellent tokens and effects of divine artifice." But first we may notice the way in which he associated the atomic view of matter with supernatural power. In embracing the corpuscular or mechanical philosophy, he writes, he is far from supposing with the Epicureans that atoms accidentally meeting in an infinite vacuum were able by themselves to produce a world and all its phenomena. The philosophy he pleads for teaches that in the beginning God gave motion to matter and so guided the motions of its parts as to "contrive them into the world he designed they should compose," establishing those rules of motion that we call the laws of nature (*The Excellence and Grounds of the Mechanical Philosophy,* 1674). In *The Origin of Forms and Qualities* (1666) he explains that the diversity of bodies must arise from motion and that motion in the beginning was from God, for it is not inherent in matter.

In the realm of animate nature Boyle points to numerous instances of ingenious design, such as the human eye, and he constantly speaks of organisms as engines or machines. For him an animal as a whole is an engine, and each part of it is a subordinate engine excellently fitted for some subordinate use. Here he reverts to a famous analogy that in a simpler context goes back to Cicero and even to Xenophon, the analogy of organisms and the world with clocks and watches. In Boyle's day, clocks were the most complex examples of machines available for comparison, and he takes a celebrated clock as a model of the machine of the world, the cathedral clock at Strasbourg, in which "the several pieces making up that curious Engine are so fram'd and adapted, and are put into such motion, as though the numerous wheels and other parts of it knew and were concerned to do its Duty" (*The Usefulness of Experimental Natural Philosophy*, 1663). The popularity of the analogy between a watchmaker and the author of nature in the following age issued largely from the writings of Boyle.

ROBERT HOOKE. During the early years of the Royal Society proofs of design multiplied. Robert Hooke's *Micrographia* (London, 1665) disclosed the astonishing beauty and ingenuity of the minute creatures revealed by the microscope, and in his Cutlerian lectures he spoke of the divine providence that in the eye "has so disposed, ordered, adapted, and empowered each part so to operate as to produce the wonderful effects which we see."

JOHN RAY. Before the end of the century there appeared treatises by the greatest zoologist of the age that were wholly devoted to the evidences in nature of the existence of God. John Ray's *The Wisdom of God Manifested in the Works of Creation* was first published in London in 1691, enlarged in three later editions before Ray's death in 1705, and reprinted more than twenty times by 1846. In the preface he declares that his discourse will serve to demonstrate the existence of the Deity and illustrate his principal attributes, his infinite power and wisdom. He proceeds to show the futility of attributing the world to the operation of chance events; it manifests all the marks of deliberate creation. Inanimate bodies are reviewed in order, the system of the stars and their planets, and the services performed for animals and man by water, air, fire, meteors, rain, and winds. Passing to regions of life, he ascends through the vegetable and animal kingdoms, discovering everywhere a complex arrangement of parts that contribute to the welfare of the plant or animal and to the uses of man.

Ray was too close an observer of nature to accept the crude doctrine that organisms are complex machines constructed by a divine watchmaker. His physicotheology borrowed from Cudworth the theory of plastic nature or vital force by which the growth, adaptation, and instinctive activities of living creatures are directed. This plastic virtue acts sympathetically, without reason, informing the movements of material bodies. Ray therefore diluted his physicotheology with an immaterial energy, a form of animism. But the plastic nature is nonetheless a subordinate instrument of divine providence, although it transcends the operations of local motion. Its relative independence of the immediate direction of God allowed Ray to meet a cardinal difficulty in the Argument from Design; he could accept the aberrations of nature without making the Deity responsible for them. Faced with this problem, Boyle has preserved his mechanistic view of creation by asserting that the irregularities we find in nature may serve ends that lie concealed in God's unsearchable wisdom.

Ray presided over the subsequent course of the Argument from Design, and theologians drew freely on his *Wisdom of God in Creation*. They studied also his *Three Physico-theological Discourses* (London, 1692), which supports the biblical narratives of the creation, the deluge, and the final dissolution of the world by arguments from natural philosophy.

ISAAC NEWTON. The appearance of Isaac Newton's *Principia* in 1687 had provided the argument with a great deal of new material. Natural theology became absorbed by the cosmology of the *Principia*, and preachers and poets acclaimed the almighty hand that "poised, impels and rules the steady whole." Newton's great treatises offered at many points notable arguments for the belief that the universe is the work of an intelligent being; indeed, Newton told Richard Bentley that in writing the *Principia* he had had an eye upon arguments for a belief in a deity, and in the *Opticks* he declared that the main business of natural philosophy was to deduce causes from effects until we arrive at the First Cause, which cannot be mechanical. In the *General Scholium* added to the second edition of the *Principia* and in the *Queries* of the Latin translation of the *Opticks* (1706), he set forth the religious conceptions that underlay his mathematical physics of the universe. Why is it, he asks, that all planets move the same way in concentric orbits? What prevents the stars from falling on one another? And, with a glance at the evidence of Boyle and Ray, how, he asks, did the bodies of animals come to be contrived with so much art? Whence, in short, arose all that order and beauty that we see in the world? Does it not appear that there is a Being incorporeal, living, intelligent, and omnipresent, who created the world?

For Newton, however, the admirable system of nature was not imposed by the deity upon an infinitely complex material mechanism; immaterial forces were introduced into the heart of the mechanism of nature. Newton asserted the atomic theory of matter in the manner of Boyle: It seemed probable that God in the beginning formed matter in solid, massy, hard, impenetrable, movable particles, but the forces that cause the particles to cohere and to form larger bodies are immaterial. It is not the business of experimental philosophy to discuss the nature of these forces, but it is clear that they provide the world with its structure and order. They could not have arisen from chaos by the mere laws of nature; the wonderful uniformity of the planetary system, for example, must be the effect of choice and must proceed from the counsel and dominion of an intelligent and powerful Being.

Other fundamental principles of Newton's system of physics are associated with theology. Absolute space is immovable, homogeneous, indivisible, and distinct from matter; like other thinkers of the time, Newton accorded space some of the attributes of God. He described infinite space as the boundless sensorium of the omnipresent God, whereby he perceives all things. Motion also presupposes a metaphysical agent, for if the motion of moving bodies is derived from the impact of bodies already in motion, some other principle was necessary for putting bodies in motion in the first instance and for conserving the motion of those in movement. The agent must be an all-powerful immaterial being, for pressure is constantly brought to move bodies throughout the universe. Furthermore, the variety of motion is always decreasing because at every impact between bodies, some motion is lost. It must be renewed by an immaterial power.

EIGHTEENTH CENTURY

The natural theology of Newton crowned the Argument from Design, and by the beginning of the eighteenth century the main stock of theory and of evidence on which the argument relied had been provided. Numerous writers repeated and enforced the case pronounced by John Locke that the works of nature everywhere sufficiently evidence a Deity. Prominent among those who vindicated the conclusions of the great men of the seventeenth century were the Boyle lecturers in the series instituted in Boyle's will with the purpose of confuting atheism. The lectures were inaugurated in 1692 by Richard Bentley, a renowned scholar who corresponded with Newton while preparing the lectures. In his letters to Bentley, Newton maintained that there are many features of the universe that cannot be explained in terms of mechanical principles, and he went on to assert that the cause that constructed the planetary system cannot be blind and fortuitous but must be one very skilled in mechanics and geometry. Bentley faithfully reported these opinions in the lectures.

CLARKE AND LEIBNIZ. The second Boyle lecturer was the celebrated Samuel Clarke, who delivered the course called "A Demonstration of the Being and Attributes of God" in 1704, an excellent survey of the accepted picture,

with some fresh touches. His famous correspondence with Gottfried Wilhelm Leibniz on natural theology was published in 1717; he probably received advice from Newton in composing his replies, and the letters further reveal Newton's position on such important topics as the divinity of space. But the vital interest of this correspondence is the conflict between Leibniz's conception of nature as mechanical, determined, self-sufficient, and self-perpetuating and the doctrine, defended by Clarke, of God's providential guidance of the world. Leibniz rejected the Newtonian contention that God corrects aberrations of the cosmic order, such as certain inequalities of planetary motions, as a watchmaker cleans and mends a watch—a view that implies that the creation of the system was imperfect and that God is lacking in foresight. Clarke, on his part, accused Leibniz of restricting the liberty of God to act as he will, independently of the laws of nature; indeed, but for his constant intervention, the world would lapse into chaos. The doctrine of supernatural intervention began to recede from the physics of astronomy and found its home before the end of the century in the realms of geology and biology.

JOSEPH BUTLER. The deists, in their war against revelation, caught at the notion that God, having created the world in the distant past, had left it to the action of the laws of nature. Deism provoked a stream of hostile pamphlets and treatises, but orthodox churchmen who opposed deism continued to harp on law, order, and design and the divine artificer. The greatest of these apologists was Bishop Butler. *The Analogy of Religion* (1736) shows that he had closely studied Newton, but his natural theology rises above that of other writers of the age in its candid recognition of the defects of nature, which he ascribes to our ignorance of God's purposes.

Another Boyle lecturer was William Derham, whose *Physico-theology* (London, 1713) and *Astro-theology* (London, 1715) rehearsed the testimony of Ray and of Newton at prodigious length, with some superficial reflections of his own. Many other utterances must be passed over. It is interesting to observe the large number of writers who discussed Clarke's (and Newton's) theology of space.

DAVID HUME. In the later years of the eighteenth century, natural theology encountered the penetrating criticism of David Hume, although few scientific theologians were shaken by it. In the *Dialogues concerning Natural Religion,* published posthumously in 1779, Hume exploded the logic of the Argument from Design, especially in the form in which it was presented by the disciples of Newton, such as the Scottish mathematician Colin Maclaurin. Hume confronted the analogy between the maker of a machine and the maker of the world with the point that while scientists like Nicolas Copernicus and Galileo Galilei made fruitful use of reasoning by analogy, the associations between cause and effect that provided the material of their arguments were derived from observation. The inference from machines and their makers to a world and its maker is not parallel. Order, arrangement, or the adjustment of final causes is not by itself any proof of design, but only insofar as it has been seen to be produced by design; since we have no experience of the invention and production of a world or of nature, we cannot maintain that an orderly universe must arise from thought or art. For all that we can know a priori, matter may contain the source of order within itself.

Hume attacked this argument by a reductio ad absurdum. If we are confined to speculative, a priori explanations of the origins of the world, they can lead to disturbing conclusions. Some natural philosophers have found nature to resemble an organism, a vegetable or an animal, and its origin ought to be ascribed to generation and vegetation rather than to reason or design. When the analogy with the manufacturers of machines is pressed, we might infer that several deities combine in contriving and framing the world. Hume now introduced fatal evidence against the belief in a benevolent Creator. The curious artifices of nature embitter the life of every living being. "The whole presents nothing but the idea of a blind nature, impregnated by a great vivifying principle, and pouring forth from her lap, without discernment or parental care, her maimed and abortive children." Faced with these difficulties the defender of traditional doctrine in the *Dialogues* is compelled to admit that belief in a beneficent Creator of the world cannot be rationally sustained. The sources of such a belief are "temper and education," and the defender of the Argument from Design falls back on utilitarian supports; belief in divine design promotes morality.

NINETEENTH CENTURY

Hume's *Dialogues concerning Natural Religion* failed to confound the deep-seated prepossessions of the natural theologians, nor were they discomposed by the refutation of the Argument from Design by Immanuel Kant in the *Critique of Pure Reason* (1781).

WILLIAM PALEY. At the turn of the century the argument was revived in William Paley's *Natural Theology* (1802). It marks the apotheosis of the analogy between a watch and a natural object, opening, in fact, with the discovery of a watch lying on a heath. The instrument must have been made by a being who comprehended its construction and designed its use. If we suppose that the watch contains a mechanism by which it can produce another watch (a supposition that exhibits the deficiency of the mechanical analogy), our admiration of the maker's skill will increase. Paley proceeds to describe numerous examples of natural contrivances, drawn from anatomy, physiology, botany, and entomology: the eyes of fish, animals, and men, the construction of the ear, the webbed feet of water birds, the elongated tongue of the woodpecker, and a catalog of other instances. These marvels of adaptation prove the existence of a superhuman designer, God. As for the suffering that nature displays, Paley attempts to minimize the spectacle; the pain of animals, he thinks, is exaggerated, and their happiness outweighs their pain. Even venomous bites and the preying of one species on another are shown to be necessary features of benevolent design.

BRIDGEWATER TREATISES. Leading men of science in this period duly acknowledged the action of divine providence in natural phenomena. In geology John Playfair and Sir Charles Lyell discovered in the adjustment of the strata of the earth to the accommodation of living creatures clear proofs of divine foresight, and James Prescott Joule saw in the interconvertibility of natural forces evidence of the sovereign will of God. The most sustained defense of the Argument from Design was advanced in the Bridgewater Treatises of the 1830s. Eight men of science, four of whom were clergymen, were chosen to discharge the intentions of the earl of Bridgewater to explore "the Power, Wisdom and Goodness of God, as manifested in the Creation." These writers added a wealth of new information from astronomy, physics, chemistry, and anatomy to the old theses of Ray and Derham, and they outstripped Paley in showing how all aspects of nature have been thoughtfully arranged for the comfort of the world's inhabitants and especially for man. John Kidd, Regius professor of medicine in the University of Oxford, in *On the Adaptation of External Nature to the Physical Condition of Man* (London, 1833); Peter Roget, secretary to the Royal Society, in *On Animal and Vegetable Physiology Considered in Relation to Natural Theology* (London, 1834); and William Buckland, professor of geology at Oxford, in *On Geology and Mineralogy* (London, 1836), showed how climates have been fitted to the character of the various races of humankind, horses invented for man's transport, minerals for his adornment, and water for his ablutions. In short, much of the reasoning of these writers recalls that of the lady who praised the goodness of the Creator in causing a great river to flow through the main cities of Europe.

Sir Charles Bell, the most distinguished physiologist of the time, in his *The Hand, Its Mechanism and Vital Endowments as Evincing Design* (London, 1833), argues that species were successively created to fit the conditions of geological epochs, changes in their anatomy being deliberately shaped to meet the circumstances of the creatures' life. Man is the center of a magnificent system, which has been prepared for his reception by a succession of revolutions affecting the whole globe, and the strictest relation is established between his intellectual capacities and the material world. The celebrated William Whewell, in his *Astronomy and General Physics considered with Reference to Natural Theology* (London, 1833), makes play with the ambiguous sense of the word *law,* a common procedure among scientific theologians of the period, confusing the idea of uniform sequence with the idea of legal and moral law; the confusion arose from Whewell's demonstration that the laws of nature, terrestrial and celestial, provide evidence of selection, design, and goodness. The tenacity and ingenuity with which the scientists vindicated the sovereignty of God over nature are illustrated in Charles Babbage's *Ninth Bridgewater Treatise* (London, 1837), where by means of his calculating machine he proves mathematically that miraculous interruptions of scientific laws can be predicted, and that the Being who called the laws into existence must have chosen them with the breaches of continuity in view.

The Bridgewater Treatises marked the final stage of the general confidence of men of science in the old natural theology, although religious thinkers long continued, and still continue, to appeal to it. However, when the treatises appeared the classical form of the Argument from Design was weakening. Whewell had difficulty in understanding the bearing of cosmology upon the support and comfort of sentient creatures, and geologists, led by James Hutton and Lyell, were abandoning the view that there had been sudden changes in the crust of Earth, occasioned by the mediation of God. The catastrophic picture of geological change was yielding to the uniformitarian view in which the laws operating at present could in the slow process of ages have caused all the changes of the past. The range of natural law in time and space was being extended, but the scientists failed to account for the processes by which fresh species had originated, and faith in the periodic agency of the Creator was encouraged.

CHARLES DARWIN. Charles Darwin opened a notebook on the transmutation of species in 1837, and in the unpublished "Essay on Species" of 1844 he proposed the machinery by which new species might result from the natural selection of fortuitous variations. The notion of special creations, he recorded in his private notebook, explains nothing, and the Essay concluded with a forceful reductio ad absurdum of the Argument from Design. *The Origin of Species* (1859) brought a wealth of material to substantiate the theory of natural selection in the evolution of species and in adaptations of the organs of living creatures to their circumstances, and it is interesting to see Darwin using the same examples that Paley did to show evidence of contrivances resulting not from purpose but from chance. By abolishing both transcendent and immanent teleology, Darwin undermined the ground on which physicotheology had stood since the seventeenth century. Yet in the last chapter of the *Origin* Darwin himself assumed a First Cause, though not a beneficent one, and he declared in 1873 that the impossibility of conceiving that this great and wondrous universe arose through chance seemed to him the chief argument for the existence of God. In the end, however, Darwin became a complete agnostic, as is shown most clearly in the unexpurgated edition of his *Autobiography* (first published in 1958).

J. S. MILL. In his *Three Essays on Religion,* published posthumously in 1874, J. S. Mill allowed some value to the Argument from Design, for the world contains marks of deliberate contrivance, and our experience of such devices is associated with an intelligent mind. Mill here seems to have exposed himself to Hume's objections against arguing from cases within the world to the world as a whole. But Mill recognized many features of the world that are incompatible with beneficent design, and he thought that God may be a limited Being circumscribed by matter and force. Mill maintained that if Darwin's doctrine of evolution were shown to be valid it would greatly weaken the evidence for the work of a divine intelligence in nature.

SUPPORT FROM SCIENTISTS. Other scientists contrived to fit the theory of natural selection into the frame of divine purpose. Samuel Houghton, a fellow of the Royal Society, described expressions of supernatural intentions in his book *Principles of Animal Mechanics* (London, 1873). Another book that exercised great influence was Professors P. G. Tait and Balfour Stewart's *The Unseen Universe* (1875), in which it was contended that science upheld the ideas of religion on the transcendental world and its connection with the physical world. A succession of eminent scientists proclaimed that nature is the sacred book of God. The most popular and, it must be added, most muddle-headed work that applied evolution to theistic principles was Henry Drummond's *Natural Law in the Spiritual World* (1883). The tendency of these scientific writers was to assert the view that Darwin's theory had deepened and widened the belief in the operation of purpose in nature, a view that was characterized as misplaced zeal by those who stood more closely to Darwin's findings.

A number of physicists of the period also employed classical versions of the design argument. The Celestial Engineer was reinstated by O. M. Mitchell in his widely read *The Orbs of Heaven* (4th ed., London, 1853) at the middle of the century, in which, after the manner of Newton, the deity is invoked to secure the stability of the solar system. It was a notion of the earlier apologists that the identical character of the fundamental materials of the physical world in all parts of the natural order indicated the action of an intelligent maker. The idea had been adopted by Sir John Herschel in his *Study of Natural Philosophy* (1830), and it was now revived by the greatest mathematical physicist of the age, James Clerk Maxwell. At the meeting of the British Association in 1873, he pointed out that every type of molecule in the universe is identical with every other type; a molecule of hydrogen, whether it occurs in Sirius or in Arcturus, executes its vibrations in precisely the same time. No theory of evolution accounts for this identity, for the molecule is not subject to change. Its similarity to other molecules proves that it is the product not of chance but of design. It is a manufactured article, and because they are the work of a Creator, the foundation stones of the material universe remain, whatever catastrophes may occur in the heavens. Even the argument from miracles reappeared in the *Natural Theology* (London, 1891) of a later mathematical physicist, Sir George Stokes: "If the laws of nature are in accordance with God's will, he who willed them may will their suspension." Stokes assumed that God's action in nature cannot be detected within the laws of physics but by interventions from beyond. *Natural Theology* embraces the arguments of physicotheology in the period.

A monumental exposition in a modern setting of the Argument from Design appeared in *Philosophical Theology* (London, 1928–1930) by F. R. Tennant. Recent discussions of the argument have abandoned the old mechanical analogies and have dwelled on the evidence for various types of vitalism in biology. On these views evolution is guided no longer from outside but by directive activities within organisms. In the human psychosocial phase of evolution these self-directed activities point toward moral ends; history becomes the education of humankind in the fulfillment of God's design. Teleological doctrines of this kind have drawn support from philosophers such as Samuel Alexander and A. N. Whitehead, who contend that the universe is informed by an immanent nisus to divinity. Present theological discussions, however, ignore natural theology, and for contemporary linguistic philosophers the Argument from Design possesses no validity whatsoever and is logically and morally indefensible, although it may serve to heighten religious emotions.

See also Alexander, Samuel; Atheism; Atomism; Boyle, Robert; Butler, Joseph; Cicero, Marcus Tullius; Clarke, Samuel; Copernicus, Nicolas; Cudworth, Ralph; Darwin, Charles Robert; Deism; Descartes, René; Epicureanism and the Epicurean School; Galileo Galilei; God, Concepts of; Hume, David; Kant, Immanuel; Leibniz, Gottfried Wilhelm; Locke, John; Materialism; Matter; Maxwell, James Clerk; Mill, John Stuart; Motion; Motion, A Historical Survey; Newton, Isaac; Paley, William; Plato; Socrates; Teleological Argument for the Existence of God; Tennant, Frederick Robert; Thomas Aquinas, St.; Whewell, William; Whitehead, Alfred North; Xenophon.

Bibliography

In addition to original works mentioned in the text, the reader may consult the following works as guides to the immense literature on the subject.

Adams, Robert. *Leibniz: Determinist, Theist, Idealist.* New York: Oxford University Press, 1994.

The Bridgewater Treatises on the Power, Wisdom and Goodness of God as Manifested in the Creation. 12 vols. London, 1833–1836.

Burtt, E. A. *The Metaphysical Foundations of Modern Physical Science.* London: K. Paul, Trench, Trubner, 1925.

Carré, M. H. "The Divine Watchmaker." *Rationalist Annual* (1965): 83–91.

Clark, Ronald. *The Survival of Charles Darwin: A Biography of a Man and an Idea.* New York: Random House, 1984.

Cohen, Bernard, and George Smith, eds. *The Cambridge Companion to Newton.* Cambridge, U.K.: Cambridge University Press, 2002.

Cohen, I. B., and H. M. Jones, eds. *Science before Darwin.* London: Deutsch, 1963.

De Beer, Gavin. *Charles Darwin.* London: Nelson, 1963. Bibliography.

Flew, Antony, and Alasdair MacIntyre, eds. *New Essays in Philosophical Theology.* New York, 1955.

Gillispie, Charles C. *Genesis and Geology.* Cambridge, MA: Harvard University Press, 1951.

Hodge, Jonathan, and Gregory Radick, eds. *The Cambridge Companion to Darwin.* Cambridge, U.K.: Cambridge University Press, 2003.

Hooykaas, R. *Natural Law and Divine Miracle.* Leiden: Brill, 1959.

Hurlbutt, R. M., III. *Hume, Newton and the Design Argument.* Lincoln: University of Nebraska Press, 1965.

Jolley, Nicholas, ed. *The Cambridge Companion to Leibniz.* Cambridge, U.K.: Cambridge University Press, 1994.

Koyré, Alexandre. *From the Closed World to the Infinite Universe.* Baltimore: Johns Hopkins Press, 1957.

LeMahieu, Dan. *The Mind of William Paley.* Lincoln: University of Nebraska Press, 1976.

Metzger, Henri. *Attraction universelle et religion naturelle chez quelques commentateurs anglais de Newton.* Paris, 1938.

Mossner, E. C. *Bishop Butler and the Age of Reason.* New York: Macmillan, 1936.

Norton, David, ed. *The Cambridge Companion to Hume.* Cambridge, U.K.: Cambridge University Press, 1993.

O'Connor, David. *Hume on Religion.* New York: Routledge, 2001.

Pendelhum, Terence, and Ted Honderich, eds. *Butler: The Arguments of the Philosophers.* London: Routledge, 1985.

Pilkington, Roger. *Robert Boyle; Father of Chemistry.* London: Murray, 1959.

Raven, C. E. *John Ray.* Cambridge, U.K., 1950.

Raven, C. E. *Natural Religion and Christian Theology.* Cambridge, U.K.: Cambridge University Press, 1953.

Redwood, John. *Reason, Ridicule, and Religion: The Age of Enlightenment in England, 1660–1750.* Cambridge, MA: Harvard University Press, 1976.

Ruse, Michael. *The Darwinian Paradigm: Essays on Its History, Philosophy and Religious Implications.* New York: Routledge, 1989.

Rutherford, Donald. *Leibniz and the Rational Order of Nature.* New York: Cambridge University Press, 1995.

Sargent, Rose. *The Diffident Naturalist: Robert Boyle and the Philosophy of Experiment.* Chicago: University of Chicago Press, 1995.

Strong, E. W. "Newton and God." *Journal of the History of Ideas* 13 (2) (April 1951): 147–167.

Westfall, R. S. *Science and Religion in Seventeenth Century England.* New Haven, CT: Yale University Press, 1958.

Westfall, Richard. *The Life of Isaac Newton.* New York: Cambridge University Press, 1993.

Young, Robert. *Darwin's Metaphor: Nature's Place in Victorian Culture.* Cambridge, U.K.: Cambridge University Press, 1985.

Meyrick H. Carré (1967)
Bibliography updated by Christian B. Miller (2005)

PHYSICS, PHILOSOPHY OF

See *Philosophy of Physics*

PHYSICS AND THE DIRECTION OF TIME

Our experience of the temporality of things seems to be an experience of a radically asymmetric feature of the world. Although we do know some things about what the future will be like, we have an access to past events that is not given to us of events in the future. We take ourselves as having memories of the past but not of the future and as having records of the past but not of the future. In our explanatory accounts of what happens in the world, we explain present and future by reference to what happened in the past, but we typically do not explain the past by referring to the future. We take it that there is causation in the world—that events determine one another to occur. But, intuitively, we think of causation and determination as directed from past to future. We have distinctive *attitudes* to past and future. Of the past we may have regrets, for example, but our concern for the future will be rather things such as anxiety or anticipation. So profound are these apparent differences between past and future that they are often promoted into the realm of deep metaphysics. Sometimes it is argued that the past is *fixed*, subject to some version or another of immutability, whereas the future remains merely a domain of open possibilities. In an even more extreme view it is argued that what is past has a *determinate reality* whereas the future remains a realm to which we cannot even attribute any kind of determinate being.

One might take these asymmetric features of time as irreducible, primitive properties of the world. And one might take our awareness of these features as somehow direct and not further explicable. Alternatively, one might argue for some basic, asymmetrical, metaphysical aspect of time as grounding all the asymmetries discussed above. For example, there are proposed *branching* models of the world in which a tree of possibilities is constantly pruned into a single actuality as time goes on and the present moves inexorably into the future. One problem with any such model is the need to respect the results of modern physics, especially special and general relativity, so as to reconcile the usual assumption in the metaphysical models of a unique global present with the denial of any such objective feature of the world in the relativistic accounts of spacetime. Another alternative would be to take a temporally asymmetric notion of causation as primitive and argue that all the other intuitive asymmetries follow from the fundamental asymmetry of causation.

NATURALISTIC THEORIES OF TIME ASYMMETRY

On the other hand, one could seek for some *naturalistic* account of the temporal asymmetries. Here, one looks at what our best available scientific theories tell us about the actual physical structure of the world in the hopes of finding some physical process characterized by fundamental physics that could serve to *ground* or *explain* the existence and nature of the fundamental temporal asymmetries. Much work has been done in this direction, but more needs to be done to make such a naturalistic account fully convincing. It is to this approach that this entry is directed.

Physics presents us with a *paradox*. Although most of its fundamental laws are often alleged to be time-reversal invariant and unable, it is therefore claimed, to ground any fundamental asymmetry in time of processes in the world, physics also describes a number of alleged time-asymmetric features of the world at a very general level. Measurement processes in quantum mechanics are often alleged to be asymmetric in time. We see radiation outbound in spherical waves from accelerated charged particles but not spontaneous collapsing spheres of radiation converging on a particle and accelerating it. Subtle experiments seem to show that some of the interactions of the elementary particles show asymmetries in time that may, indeed, require positing a fundamental law governing them that itself describes a lawlike asymmetry in time for the world. Most importantly, thermodynamics seems to reveal to us a world that is time asymmetric. A metal bar hot at one end and cold at the other when kept in isolation becomes uniformly warm all over. But an isolated uniformly warm bar does not spontaneously become hot at one end and cold at another.

A naturalistic account of the *direction of time* requires more than finding some physical process that is time asymmetric. It also requires even more than finding a fundamental process that has such time asymmetry. Suppose the weak interactions of the elementary particles obey a time-asymmetric law. How would such a fact be of any use in accounting for our intuitive sense that there are records and memories of the past and not of the future, or that causation proceeds from past to future, or that the past is determinate and fixed and the future a realm of mere possibilities? What is needed from a naturalistic theory of the direction of time is some appropriate connection between the physical facts introduced in the account as grounding the direction of time and those features that characterize our intuitive, deeply rooted sense of the asymmetry of time.

THERMODYNAMIC ASYMMETRIES

The thermodynamic asymmetries, being pervasive elements of our everyday experience, provide the most promising physical basis for a naturalistic account of the direction of time. Here, two fundamental questions must be explored: (1) Why does the world show these deep asymmetries in time of physical processes? (2) How could the existence of these asymmetric processes account for the intuitive asymmetries we attribute to the world in time? Neither question is trivially answered.

The contemporary explanation of the thermodynamic laws starts with the realization that macroscopic objects are composed of a vast number of microscopic constituents. Macroscopic thermodynamic properties, then, are thought of as grounded in such microscopic features of a system as the total energy of its microscopic constituents or the average energy of some one of these. The microscopic constituents are assumed to obey the standard dynamical laws, originally classical dynamics and now quantum mechanics. How the system behaves, then, will depend upon these laws and upon whatever initial conditions are possessed by the microscopic constituents, with the system also subject to such macroscopic constraints as exist (such as a gas being confined to a box).

Probabilistic methods were soon invoked to deal with the behavior of the vast number of microscopic constituents. These led to such theories as the kinetic theory of gases and the more abstract statistical mechanics. One consequence of this new viewpoint was a rethinking of the thermodynamic laws to allow for such possibilities as fluctuations away from the equilibrium state, even for an isolated system. A deep conceptual problem for this theory is the understanding of why the probabilistic posits that are made, and that work so well for prediction and explanation, hold in the world. Are they brute posits to be otherwise unexplained? To what degree can they be extracted from the dynamical laws governing the behavior of the microscopic constituents? Need the fundamental dynamical laws be modified to find an appropriate explanation for the fundamental probabilistic posits (and, perhaps, to solve other outstanding problems as well, such as the nature of the measurement process in quantum mechanics)? Another crucial question is the degree to which the probabilistic posits can be shown consistent with the underlying dynamics and the degree to which they can be weakened with the empirical results still forthcoming.

Furthermore, arguments that have existed from the early days of the theory indicate that introducing probability into the theory is not, by itself, enough to ground a theory of the direction of time. Probabilistic considerations would suggest that the world we live in should be a world where all systems are at equilibrium, not at all like the world we actually live in with its vast pool of nonequilibrium systems and its parallel movement from nonequilibrium to equilibrium of temporarily isolated systems. In addition, to obtain the desired nonequilibrium results in the theory, the theory's probabilistic posits must be applied in a temporally asymmetric way, being taken as correctly applicable to temporally initial, but not to temporally final, states of isolated systems.

COSMOLOGICAL CONSIDERATIONS

From early days of the theory, cosmology has been invoked as providing the needed supplementary posits. Ludwig Boltzmann's assistant Scheutz suggested the possibility that the cosmos was, in general, in equilibrium, with the part of it with which we were familiar in a local (if large from our perspective) fluctuation away from equilibrium. Our local cosmos, then, was in equilibrium in the past and will be again in the future. Boltzmann added the *anthropic* observation that we could not find ourselves in one of the pervasive equilibrium regions of the cosmos since such a region could not support the flows of energy necessary for life. To this Boltzmann added the additional proposal that the reason we found our region heading toward equilibrium in the future time direction and not in the past time direction is that our very meaning of the *future* direction of time was that the future time direction was determined by that temporal direction in which our local region of the cosmos had a succession of states closer to equilibrium (of higher entropy).

Current cosmology, insofar as it is a discipline open to observation and empirical test, is doubtful of this early cosmological speculation. The current model, rather, is of a universe (at least as far as we know) that is distinctly unsymmetrical in time. In particular, it is posited that there is a singularity in which the cosmos is all *at a single spatial point* in the past time direction some tens of billions of years ago, the so-called Big Bang cosmology.

Even accepting this model of the universe is not enough to get the thermodynamic asymmetries out of the cosmology. Instead, it is generally agreed, one must make a specific assumption about the Big Bang state of the cosmos, that it is a low-entropy, that is, a highly nonequilibrium, state. The usual posit is that the space of the world at the Big Bang is highly smooth, this being for gravitational force the low-entropy condition. The idea is that as matter clumps from uniformly distributed into stars (and galaxies, etc.), the matter, initially in thermal equilibrium, becomes highly nonuniform and in a grossly nonequilibrium state, with hot stars radiating out to cold space. The decrease in the matter's entropy is continually being paid for by the great increase in the entropy of the spatial distribution that has gone from uniform to clumped.

The idea, then, is that the universe as a whole must be posited to have an initial highly nonequilibrium starting point. It is this posit that must be added to the standard probabilistic assumptions to get us the result of a predicted nonequilibrium condition for the world as we find it, and a predicted, temporally asymmetric, approach to equilibrium in the future and not into the past, for system temporarily isolated from their environments. Here the grand cosmic initial condition is being invoked to generate the temporal asymmetry unobtainable from the allegedly time-symmetric dynamical laws alone. Getting the result about the temporarily isolated subsystems of the universe requires a little more, in the form of a demonstration that from the temporally asymmetric behavior of the universe as a whole one can derive, with either no additional temporally asymmetric assumptions at all or with some posited additional asymmetry of dynamics, parallel increase of entropy of so-called *branch systems* in the same time direction in which the entropy of the cosmos as a whole is increasing.

FROM ASYMMETRIES IN TIME TO THE DIRECTION OF TIME

But then there is the second question noted above as well. Why should we think that this pervasive asymmetry of physical systems in time has anything to do with our intuitive sense of the asymmetry of time itself? Once again, the mere fact that there is some asymmetry in time of systems of the world, even a lawlike temporal asymmetry, is not enough to establish the naturalist's claim. What else is required?

Boltzmann hinted at an answer in his famous paper "On Zermelo's Paper 'On the Mechanical Explanation of Irreversible Processes'" where he claimed that what we took to be the future direction of time was just the direction of time in which the entropy of our local portion of the universe was on the increase. In that paper he drew a trenchant analogy between the temporal case and an intuitive spatial asymmetry accounted for by gravity. Originally we might think of space as being asymmetric, with one direction being *down* and its opposite *up*. Eventually, though, we realize that what we call the *down* direction is just the direction of the local gravitational force. On antipodal points of the earth, the local *down-ward* directions are directed oppositely to one another. And in a region of space in which there was no gravitational force, there would be no downward direction. Just so in a region of the universe not in equilibrium, Boltzmann maintained, the direction of time in which entropy was increasing would be the future time direction, and in a region of the universe at equilibrium, there would be no future direction of time and no past direction (although there would still be two oppositely directed directions of time).

What makes Boltzmann's remarks about gravity and *down* so plausible? It is the fact that we have in gravity and its consequences a complete explanation of all the facts that we take as distinguishing the downward direction of space from all the other directions. Down is the direction in which, for example, rocks fall. We even have an explanation, invoking the fluid in our semicircular canals, of how it is that we can tell without external observation which direction is the downward one.

The analogous argument in the case of the direction of time would require a sustained argument to the effect that it is the existence of the asymmetric processes of systems in the world described by thermodynamics, and explained by statistical mechanics combined with cosmology, that provides a full explanatory account of all those features of the world that we take as marking out an asymmetric nature to time. What would need explaining is why we have memories and records of the past and not of the future, why we take causation as going from past to future and not the other way around, why we think of the past as fixed and determinate and of the future as a realm of possibility, and, also, of how it is that we think we can tell, without inference, of any pair of events which is the earlier and which the later.

Sometimes it is claimed that the entropic theory of time direction is supported by the fact that we cannot tell of a film of events whether it is being run in the right or the wrong direction except by reference to entropic facts portrayed by the film. Sometimes it is argued against the entropic account that we can tell of events in the world what their order is in time without noting any entropic features of them. Both arguments are misguided. What would be required of an entropic account would be some kind of explanation of all the intuitive asymmetries that constitute our sense of the direction of time, not a demonstration that our judgments of time order are always inferences from directly observed entropic facts.

A number of tentative suggestions have been made in this direction. Hans Reichenbach suggested that records

might be analyzed as causal interventions that induced a macro low-entropy change into what would otherwise be a macro high-entropy state. But many records do not fit his paradigm. There is no fully developed extant argument to the effect that the very existence of records, and presumably those mental records we call memories, can have their time asymmetry directly accounted for by the entropic asymmetry of processes in time.

One might argue that such intuitive asymmetries as the direction of causation and the difference in *fixedness* of past and future are derivative from the asymmetry of records, our taking as the fixed and the determining that which we can know to be the case from records. Or, alternatively, one might try to directly account for the asymmetry of causation out of entropic-like facts. An example of that can again be found in a tradition stemming from Reichenbach where it is noted that spatially separated correlated events can often have their correlation explained by some common past event casually connected to both correlated events but not by any such correlating event in the future of the correlated pair (the so-called *fork* asymmetry). Another approach stems from David Lewis. Here, causation is analyzed in terms of counterfactual conditionals. It is suggested that the fact that an even has a numerous extended range of effects in its future, but not in its past, grounds our intuition that there are forward looking but not *back tracking* counterfactual assertions that we accept, and that this underlies our intuitions about the time asymmetry of the causal relation.

Even though no fully worked-out account of these sorts exists, the naturalistic approach to the direction of time remains the only plausible alternative to *metaphysical* accounts. The latter remain hard to explicate, and it is hard to understand how they might provide new insights into the intuitive asymmetries of time. The former, in its usual thermodynamic version, is at least clear in its intentions and of an intrinsic plausibility. The further pursuit of this naturalistic program is well worthwhile.

See also Boltzmann, Ludwig; Lewis, David; Reichenbach, Hans; Time; Time, Being, and Becoming.

Bibliography

Albert, D. *Time and Chance*. Cambridge, MA: Harvard University Press, 2000.

Boltzmann, L. "On Zermelo's Paper 'On the Mechanical Explanation of Irreversible Processes.'" In *Kinetic Theory*. Vol. 2, edited by S. Brush, 239–245. Oxford: Pergamon Press, 1965–1972.

Davies, P. *Physics of Time Asymmetry*. Berkeley: University of California Press, 1974.

Earman, J. "An Attempt to Add a Little Direction to 'The Problem of the Direction Of Time.'" *Philosophy of Science* 41 (1974): 15–47.

Horwich, P. *Asymmetries in Time*. Cambridge, MA: MIT Press, 1987.

Lewis, D. "Counterfactual Dependence and Time's Arrow." In *Philosophical Papers*. Vol. 2. edited by D. Lewis, 32–66. Oxford: Oxford University Press, 1983–1986.

McCall, S. *A Model of the Universe*. Oxford: Oxford University Press, 1994.

Mehlberg, H. *Time, Causality and the Quantum Theory*. Dordrecht, Netherlands: Reidel, 1980.

Mellor, H. *Real Time, II*. London: Routledge, 1998.

Price, H. *Time's Arrow and Archimedes' Point: New Directions for the Physics of Time*. New York: Oxford University Press, 1996.

Reichenbach, H. *The Direction of Time*. Berkeley: University of California Press, 1956.

Sklar, L. *Physics and Chance*. Cambridge, U.K.: Cambridge University Press, 1993.

Sklar, L. "Up and Down, Left and Right, Past and Future." *Nous* 15 (1981): 111–129.

Strevens, M. *Bigger Than Chaos*. Cambridge MA: Harvard University Press, 2003.

Tooley, M. *Time, Tense, and Causation*. Oxford: Clarendon Press, 1997.

Lawrence Sklar (1996, 2005)

PHYSIS AND NOMOS

See *Nomos and Phusus*

PIAGET, JEAN

(1896–1980)

Jean Piaget, the psychologist and philosopher, was born in Neuchâtel, Switzerland. He studied zoology at the university there and in 1918 received his doctorate for a thesis on the subject of land mollusks in the Valais Alps. He then studied psychology for a year at Zürich and, from 1919 to 1921, abnormal psychology, logic, and the philosophy of science at the Sorbonne. From 1921 to 1925, he was director of studies at the Institut J.-J. Rousseau (now the Institut des Sciences de l'Éducation) in Geneva; he was its assistant director from 1929 to 1932 and became codirector in 1932. In 1925 he was appointed professor of philosophy at the University of Neuchâtel; in 1929, professor of the history of scientific thought at the University of Geneva; and in 1940, professor of experimental psychology and director of the psychological laboratory at Geneva. He served as professor of child psychology at the Sorbonne from 1952 to 1963. From 1955 to 1980 he was director of the Centre International de l'Épistémologie Génétique at Geneva. Piaget also took an active interest in international educational projects. He was director of the Bureau International de l'Éducation from 1929 to 1967 and was associated with UNESCO as its assistant director general.

THOUGHT

Although Piaget is usually considered a psychologist working in the field of child thought, his interests were always, broadly speaking, philosophical. As a young man he read widely in philosophy, and while in Paris he studied with André Lalande and Léon Brunschvicg. Even his earliest work, which appeared between 1925 and 1932, dealt with such topics as thought, causality, moral judgment, and the development of language. His logical and epistemological interests show themselves particularly in his later studies, starting about 1937. By means of simple, although highly ingenious experiments, Piaget set out to make a detailed investigation of the way in which logical, mathematical, and physical concepts develop in the individual. He thus studied experimentally many of the concepts and principles that philosophers had discussed in the past on a purely a priori level. Piaget would say that what he was really doing in this work was reexamining the whole question of the Kantian categories. This reexamination formed for him the basis of a new discipline that he called genetic epistemology.

In a series of studies Piaget examined in some detail the development not only of abstract concepts such as classes, relations, and numbers but also of physical concepts like space, time, speed, atomism, conservation, and chance, all of which he has regarded as constructed from our behavioral activities. In starting from the facts of observable child behavior rather than from adult introspections (or sensations), Piaget differed from such thinkers as Ernst Mach, Karl Pearson, and Bertrand Russell by the importance he attached to the part played by overt activities in building up the conceptual machinery of thought. Throughout his work Piaget placed considerable emphasis on the pragmatic aspect of logical and mathematical operations, as, for example, the way we actually handle symbols and formulas. From this point of view Piaget's account bears a marked resemblance to the views of Jules Henri Poincaré and the intuitionists; the construction of number, for example, had for Piaget a definite psychological aspect.

ABSTRACT CONCEPTS. Piaget believed that logical and mathematical notions first show themselves as overt activities on the part of the child and only at a later stage take on a conceptual character. They are to be conceived as internalized actions in which things are replaced by signs, and concrete actions by operations on these signs. Rational activity occurs in the child when his trial-and-error gropings attain a definite pattern of order that may be inverted in thought. At this rational stage, if the child makes a mistake in performing a task, he is able to return to his starting point. This characteristic of thought that enables us to reverse a train of ideas or actions Piaget calls "reversibility." It is the basis of our ability to perform mental experiments, as well as the psychological foundation of the deductive process.

Piaget contended that the more elementary forms of logical behavior in which the child compares, distinguishes, and orders the objects around him are largely concerned with the creation of concrete classificatory and relational systems. It is from these systems that we develop our later, more abstract, logical and mathematical modes of thinking. Piaget would rather not speak of the intuition of number before the child has developed logical concepts of invariance and has thereby grasped the operation of reversibility. The transition to number occurs in the child just when his activities of classifying and ordering objects take on the form of simple logical systems. What emerges from Piaget's experimental researches is that numerical concepts in their psychological development are ultimately based on simple logical notions. There is thus some resemblance between the way number comes to be constructed in a child's thought and the attempt on a purely normative plane by Russell and others to define number in logical terms.

PHYSICAL CONCEPTS. Among the other concepts studied by Piaget, those of time and space are of particular philosophical relevance. Immanuel Kant, for example, believed that these concepts were objects of an a priori intuition. Piaget, however, found that the abstract notion of time arises at a relatively late stage; at first time is connected with space. For example, the child first confuses the notion of age with that of height or other visible signs of age. As far as space is concerned, his ability to make spatial judgments is initially fairly rudimentary. He can differentiate between open and closed figures but has difficulty in distinguishing one shape from another. He is also incapable of imagining a perspective other than his own. Only at a later stage is he able to take account of several relations at once (before and behind, right and left)

and to coordinate them into a general system of perspectives.

PERCEPTION. For Piaget learning played an important part not only in the elaboration of intellectual structures but also in the field of perception. It is this that distinguishes his view from that of the Gestalt psychologists. For the latter, the perceptual constancies of shape and size belong directly to the perceived objects and are independent of age and ability. For Piaget, however, perception of figures is built up as a result of a series of random eye and other muscular movements, which are gradually corrected. The young child does not attribute a constant size or even identity to the objects around him. Piaget believed that the logical forms of activity that emerge in child behavior, namely classifying, relating, and so forth, arise as a result of his trial-and-error activities.

Piaget's views on perception have certain philosophical implications. In the past, he points out, philosophers have assumed a definite psychology of perception in their epistemologies. A good example of this is John Locke's sensationalism, in which it is assumed (1) that empirical facts are passively given in perception and (2) that they correspond to a certain range of linguistic expressions that designate them. For Piaget, however, even the notion of an object, one of the simplest forms of perceptual invariants, requires a definite learning process. Before the child is able to use linguistic expressions to refer unequivocally to definite objects, he must first have developed concrete classificatory and relational activities. Even the simple statement, "This is green," implies the acquisition of such skills and hence cannot be regarded as a reference to a simple perceptual datum. When we talk intelligently of green, this presupposes that we have learned to classify objects according to their color and to differentiate one color from another.

BEHAVIOR AND LOGIC. Piaget's work might be dismissed as philosophically irrelevant by philosophers of a Platonic turn of mind. It might be said that philosophical discussions of conceptual thinking are largely concerned with questions of validity and not with questions of origin. Piaget does not deny that logical notions as they appear in purely formal discussions differ from those occurring in ordinary thought. However, he asserts (1) that even our simpler kinds of intellectual performance have a logical character about them, which we can study formally, and (2) that when the logician constructs logical systems, performs deductions, tests for validity, and so on, his logical behavior can be studied in the same direct way as that of the child or unsophisticated adult. Piaget also believed that it may be illuminating to compare the simpler logical structures inherent in our behavior with the purely formal systems constructed by the logician, as we may find some continuity between them.

See also Brunschvicg, Léon; Intuitionism and Intuitionistic Logic; Kant, Immanuel; Mach, Ernst; Number; Pearson, Karl; Perception; Poincaré, Jules Henri; Psychology; Russell, Bertrand Arthur William.

Bibliography

WORKS BY PIAGET

Piaget was a prolific writer, and among the numerous volumes he wrote, the following have a specifically logical or philosophical character:

Le jugement et le raisonnement chez l'enfant. Paris, 1924. Translated by M. Warden as *Judgment and Reasoning in the Child.* New York: Harcourt Brace, 1928.

Le langage et la pensée chez l'enfant. Paris, 1924. Translated by M. Warden as *The Language and Thought of the Child.* New York: Harcourt Brace, 1926. 2nd ed. translated by M. Gabain. London, 1932.

La représentation du monde chez l'enfant. Paris: Alcan, 1926. Translated by J. Tomlinson and A. Tomlinson as *The Child's Conception of the World.* New York: Harcourt Brace, 1929.

La causalité physique chez l'enfant. Paris, 1927. Translated by M. Gabain as *The Child's Conception of Physical Causality.* New York: Harcourt Brace, 1930.

Le jugement moral chez l'enfant. Paris: Alcan, 1932. Translated by M. Gabain as *The Moral Judgment of the Child.* New York: Harcourt Brace, 1932.

La genèse du nombre chez l'enfant. Paris, 1941. Written with A. Szeminska and translated by C. Gattegno and F. M. Hodgson as *The Child's Conception of Number.* New York: Humanities Press, 1952.

Le développement des quantités chez l'enfant. Paris, 1941. Written with B. Inhelder.

Le développement de la notion du temps chez l'enfant. Paris: Presses Universitaires de France, 1946.

Les notions de mouvement et de vitesse chez l'enfant: Paris: Presses Universitaires de France, 1946.

La représentation de l'espace chez l'enfant. Paris: Presses Universitaires de France, 1948. Written with B. Inhelder and translated by F. J. Langdon and J. L. Lunzer as *The Child's Conception of Space.* New York: Humanities Press, 1956.

La géometrie spontanée chez l'enfant. Paris: Presses Universitaires de France, 1948. Written with B. Inhelder and A. Szeminska and translated by E. A. Lunzer as *The Child's Conception of Geometry.* New York: Basic, 1960.

La genèse de l'idée de hazard chez l'enfant. Paris: Presses Universitaires de France, 1951.

De la logique de l'enfant à la logique de l'adolescent. Paris: Presses Universitaires de France, 1955. Translated by Anne Parsons and Stanley Milgram as *The Growth of Logical Thinking.* New York: Basic, 1958.

La genèse des structures logiques elementaires. Paris, 1959. Written with B. Inhelder.

WORKS ON PIAGET

There have been few philosophical discussions of Piaget's work, but W. Mays, "The Epistemology of Professor Piaget," in *PAS* (London, 1953–1954) compares his epistemology with the views of contemporary philosophers. C. Parsons in "Inhelder and Piaget's 'The Growth of Logical Thinking: II.' A Logician's Viewpoint," in the *British Journal of Psychology* (1960), criticizes Piaget's logic from a theoretical standpoint.

John H. Flavell in *The Developmental Psychology of Jean Piaget* (Princeton, NJ: Van Nostrand, 1963) gives a good summary of Piaget's work from a psychological point of view. The book contains an excellent bibliography of primary and secondary sources. W. Mays, "How We Form Concepts," in *Science News* (1954) gives a simple introduction from a more philosophical viewpoint.

K. Lovell in *The Growth of Basic Mathematical Concepts in Children* (London, 1961) provides an introduction to Piaget's ideas from an educational standpoint. Z. P. Dienes in *Building up Mathematics* (London, 1960) shows how Piaget's work has influenced the introduction of new methods in the teaching of school mathematics.

OTHER RECOMMENDED WORKS

Battro, Antonio M. *Piaget: Dictionary of Terms.* New York: Pergamon Press, 1973.

Boden, Margaret A. *Jean Piaget.* New York: Viking Press, 1980.

Bringuier, Jean Claude, and Jean Piaget. *Conversations with Jean Piaget.* Chicago: University of Chicago Press, 1980.

Elkind, David. *Child Development and Education: A Piagetian Perspective.* New York: Oxford University Press, 1976.

Elkind, David, and John H. Flavell, eds. *Studies in Cognitive Development: Essays in Honor of Jean Piaget.* New York: Oxford University Press, 1969.

Furth, Hans G. *Piaget and Knowledge: Theoretical Foundations.* Englewood Cliffs, NJ: Prentice-Hall, 1969.

Ginsburg, Herbert, and Sylvia Opper. *Piaget's Theory of Intellectual Development.* 3rd ed. Englewood Cliffs, NJ: Prentice-Hall, 1988.

Kegan, Robert. *The Evolving Self: Problem and Process in Human Development.* Cambridge, MA: Harvard University Press, 1982.

Murray, Frank B., and Millie Corinne Almy. *The Impact of Piagetian Theory: On Education, Philosophy, Psychiatry, and Psychology.* Baltimore: University Park Press, 1979.

Piaget, Jean. *The Essential Piaget,* edited by Howard E. Gruber and J. Jacques Vonèche. Northvale, NJ: J. Aronson, 1977, 1995.

Piaget, Jean, and Bäbel Inhelder. *The Child's Conception of Space.* New York: W. W. Norton, 1967.

Piattelli-Palmarini, Massimo, ed. *Language and Learning: The Debate between Jean Piaget and Noam Chomsky.* Cambridge, MA: Harvard University Press, 1980.

Wolfe Mays (1967)
Bibliography updated by Michael J. Farmer (2005)

PICO DELLA MIRANDOLA, COUNT GIOVANNI
(1463–1494)

Count Giovanni Pico della Mirandola, the Renaissance philosopher, was born in Mirandola, near Modena. He was a younger son in a family of feudal lords who ruled the small territory of Mirandola and Concordia in northern Italy. He seems to have received at an early age his first humanistic training in Latin and, perhaps, in Greek. Being destined by his mother for a career in the church, he was named papal protonotary at the age of ten and began to study canon law at Bologna in 1477. Two years later he began the study of philosophy at the University of Ferrara, which he continued at the University of Padua from 1480 to 1482.

After a number of journeys that took him to Paris and repeatedly to Florence, Pico studied Hebrew and Arabic under the guidance of several Jewish teachers and in 1486 composed 900 theses, offering to defend them in Rome the following year in a public disputation to which he invited scholars from all parts of Europe. When some of these theses met with objections from various theologians, Pope Innocent VIII appointed a committee to have them examined. As a result of the investigation 7 theses were condemned as unorthodox, and 6 more were declared to be dubious. When Pico published a defense of these 13 theses, the pope condemned all 900, although Pico had signed an act of submission. Pico fled to France, where he was arrested in 1488 on the request of papal envoys.

Upon the intervention of several Italian princes Pico was released from prison by King Charles VIII. He returned to Italy and was allowed by the pope to settle in Florence, under parole, as it were, and under the personal protection of Lorenzo de' Medici. Except for a few short visits to Ferrara, Pico spent the remainder of his life in Florence and there wrote, or began to write, his most important works, remaining in close touch with the circle of the Medici, with the Platonic Academy of Marsilio Ficino, and with Girolamo Savonarola. In 1493 he was acquitted of all ecclesiastical censures and restrictions by Alexander VI. He died in 1494 on the very day (November 17) on which Charles VIII of France made his entry into Florence after the expulsion of Piero de' Medici.

Pico's numerous writings reflect the wide range of his interests. He composed Italian and Latin poems of which only some have survived. A number of his humanistic letters were published posthumously, as was his famous *Oration*, originally composed for the projected disputation. To the scholastic aspect of his work we may assign the 900 theses (1486) and especially the *Apologia* (1487), his defense of the condemned theses. Another early work is his lengthy commentary on the Platonic love poem of his friend Girolamo Benivieni (1486). His mature philosophical works include the *Heptaplus* (1489), a sevenfold interpretation of the first verses (1:1–27) of Genesis, and his *De Ente et Uno* (On Being and Unity), written in 1491 but published posthumously. His most extensive work is his *Disputationes Adversus Astrologiam Divinatricem* (Disputations against Astrology), in twelve books, published posthumously. To this we may add a few short religious and theological writings and several fragments of a commentary on the Psalms that have been preserved in a number of scattered manuscripts and are still for the most part unpublished.

A characteristic document of Pico's attitude on history and philosophy from his earlier years is his correspondence with Ermolao Barbaro (1485). Barbaro, a distinguished Venetian humanist and student of the Greek texts of Aristotle, had stated in a letter to Pico that the medieval philosophers were uncultured and barbarous and did not deserve to be read or studied. Pico replied in a long letter in which he praises and defends the medieval philosophers and insists with great eloquence that what counts in the writings of philosophers is not their words but their thoughts. Unlike Barbaro and many other humanists who despised the scholastic philosophers for their lack of elegance and classical learning, Pico is willing to recognize the solidity of their thought and to learn from them whatever truth they may have to offer. The line between humanism and Scholasticism, rhetoric and philosophy, is thus clearly drawn, and Pico, although deeply imbued with humanist learning, throws his weight on the side of Scholasticism or, at least, of a synthesis of both sides. Many years after Barbaro and Pico died, Philipp Melanchthon wrote a reply to Pico's letter in defense of Barbaro's position.

SYNCRETISM

Pico's defense of the scholastic philosophers was merely a special instance of a much broader historical and philosophical attitude that has been rightly emphasized as his syncretism. Pico was convinced that all known philosophical and theological schools and thinkers contained certain valid insights that were compatible and hence deserved to be restated and defended. This was the underlying idea of his projected disputation, for the 900 theses relied on the most diverse sources—Hermes Trismegistus, Zoroaster, Orpheus and Pythagoras, Plato and Aristotle and all their Greek followers and commentators, Avicenna and Averroes and other Arabic philosophers, Thomas Aquinas and John Duns Scotus and several other medieval Latin thinkers, and the Jewish kabbalists.

In using all these sources, Pico wished to emphasize his basic conviction that all of these thinkers had a genuine share in philosophical truth. His notion of a universal truth in which each of the schools and thinkers participates to some extent constitutes an attempt to deal with the apparent contrasts and contradictions in the history of philosophy. It may be compared with the positions of the ancient eclectics and of G. W. F. Hegel, yet it differs from both of them. For Pico truth consists in a large number of true statements, and the various philosophers participate in truth insofar as their writings contain, besides numerous errors, a number of specific statements that are true. That this was Pico's intent we may gather from the second part of his *Oration* and from a passage in the *Apologia* that repeats it almost verbatim. He insists that he is not bound by the doctrines of any master or school but has investigated all of them. Instead of confining himself to one school, he has chosen from all of them what suits his thought, for each has something distinctive to contribute.

Pico's syncretism presupposes that of Ficino, who had proposed a theory of natural religion; had traced the Platonic tradition back to Hermes, Zoroaster, and other early theologians; and had insisted on the basic harmony between Platonism and Christianity. Yet Pico made these notions part of a much wider and more comprehensive synthesis. He explicitly includes Aristotle and all his Greek, Arabic, and Latin followers, and he adds to these previously known sources the Jewish kabbalists, with whom he became acquainted through his Hebrew studies, thus being probably the first Christian scholar to use kabbalistic literature. This attitude toward Aristotelianism and kabbalism clearly distinguished Pico from Ficino and other predecessors; it was to find further development in Pico's own later thought and to exert a strong influence on the philosophy of the sixteenth century. Pico's broad syncretism has been rightly praised by several historians as a steppingstone to later theories of religious and philosophical tolerance.

Pico's use of kabbalism consisted not so much in accepting specific kabbalist theories as in gaining recognition for kabbalism in general. Some of the theories that he seems to have borrowed from kabbalist authors were not necessarily of kabbalistic origin, such as the scheme of the three worlds—elementary, celestial, and angelic—which he uses for the first three sections of his *Heptaplus*.

Pico accepted the claim made by the followers of kabbalism that their writings were based on a secret tradition that went back, at least in oral form, to biblical times. Kabbalism thus acquires a kind of authority parallel to that of the Bible and similar to that held by Hermes and Zoroaster in the eyes of Ficino and Pico. Moreover, Pico applied to kabbalism a principle that had been used for the Old Testament by all Christian writers since St. Paul: He tried to show that the kabbalistic tradition, no less than the Hebrew Scripture, was in basic agreement with Christian theology and hence could be taken as a prophecy and confirmation of Christian doctrine. With this argument he laid the foundation for a whole tradition of Christian kabbalism that found its defenders in Johannes Reuchlin, Giles of Viterbo, and many other thinkers in the sixteenth and later centuries.

In Pico's own work the kabbalistic influence is most noticeable, after the time of the 900 theses, in his *Heptaplus* and in his fragmentary commentary on the Psalms. In a manner that goes far beyond the usual medieval scheme of the four levels of meaning Pico assigns to the text of Scripture a multiple meaning that corresponds to the various parts of the universe. He also uses the kabbalistic method of scriptural interpretation, which assigns numerical values to the Hebrew letters and extracts secret meanings from the text by substituting for its words other words with comparable numerical values.

The other distinctive aspect of Pico's syncretism, his tendency to assume a basic agreement between Plato and Aristotle, also remained one of his major preoccupations during his later life. We know that he planned to write an extensive treatise on the agreement between Plato and Aristotle. The idea that Plato and Aristotle were in basic agreement, although differing in their words and apparent meaning, was not new with Pico. We find it in Cicero, who probably took it from his teacher Antiochus of Ascalon. It is also attributed as a program to Ammonius Saccas, the teacher of Plotinus, and endorsed by Boethius. We may also compare certain trends in recent scholarship that have attempted to bridge the gap between Plato's dialogues and Aristotle's extant later writings by interpolating the oral teaching of Plato and the lost early writings of Aristotle.

Pico's approach is known to us through his *De Ente et Uno*, a small treatise composed toward the end of his life and the only surviving fragment of his projected larger work on the harmony of Plato and Aristotle. The question he discusses is whether being and unity are coextensive, as Aristotle maintains in the tenth book of the *Metaphysics*, or whether unity has a broader diffusion and higher status than being, according to the view of Plotinus and other Neoplatonists. Following the scholastic doctrine of the transcendentals, Pico sets out to defend the position of Aristotle. He then tries to prove that Plato did not hold the opposite view, as claimed by the Neoplatonists. In support of his claim Pico cites a passage from Plato's *Sophist* and dismisses the testimony of the *Parmenides*, arguing that this dialogue is merely a dialectical exercise.

In the course of his discussion Pico sharply distinguishes between being itself and participated being, and it is thus possible for him to maintain that God is identical with being in the first sense but above being in the second. The harmony between Plato and Aristotle that Pico tries to establish turns out to be Aristotelian, at least in its wording, but in another sense it is neither Platonic nor Aristotelian, and the distinction between being itself and participated being is evidently indebted to the same Neoplatonists whom Pico tries to refute on the major issue of the treatise. As a result Pico's position was criticized, on the one side, by Ficino, who, in his commentary on the *Parmenides*, defended Plotinus and, on the other, by the Aristotelian Antonio Cittadini, who formulated a series of objections that were answered first by Pico himself and then by his nephew and editor Gianfrancesco Pico.

Another aspect of Pico's syncretism is his treatment of classical mythology. An allegorical interpretation of the myths of the Greek poets had been developed by the ancient Stoics and Neoplatonists, and for them it had been a device for reconciling pagan religion with philosophical truth. When the medieval grammarians continued to interpret the classical poets in this manner, they minimized the pagan religious element and emphasized the implied universal, or even Christian, truth that would justify the study of these authors. The method was taken over and further developed by the humanists and Ficino. Pico tends to be even more elaborate in his discussion and interpretation of ancient myths, especially in his commentary on Benivieni's love poem. Here he repeatedly mentions his plan to write a treatise on poetic theology, a work that probably remained unwritten. Pico apparently intended to construct a detailed system of the theology implicit in the myths of the ancient poets and thus to include them in his universal syncretism.

DIGNITY OF MAN

Much more famous than the ideas thus far discussed is Pico's doctrine of the dignity of man and his place in the universe. The *Oration*, in which this doctrine is developed, is probably the most widely known document of early Renaissance thought. In many editions the work is titled "Oration on the Dignity of Man," but this title properly belongs only to the first part of the oration; the original title was simply *Oration*. Man and his dignity are often praised by the early humanists, and some of them dedicated entire treatises to the subject. The topic was taken up by Ficino, who assigned to the human soul a privileged place in the center of the universal hierarchy and made it, both through its intermediary attributes and through its universal thought and aspirations, the bond of the universe and the link between the intelligible and the corporeal world. In his *Oration* Pico went beyond Ficino in several ways. He did not discuss the question merely in passing or in the context of a large work dedicated to other subjects but displayed it prominently in the opening section of a short and elegant speech. Moreover, he lays the accent not so much on man's universality as on his freedom; instead of assigning to him a fixed though privileged place in the universal hierarchy, he puts him entirely apart from this hierarchy and claims that he is capable of occupying, according to his choice, any degree of life from the lowest to the highest. He has God tell Adam:

> Neither a fixed abode nor a form that is thine alone, nor any function peculiar to thyself have We given thee, Adam, to the end that according to thy judgment thou mayest have and possess what abode, what form, and what functions thou thyself shalt desire. Constrained by no limits, in accordance with thine own free will, in whose hand We have placed thee, thou shalt ordain for thyself the limits of thy nature.... Thou shalt have the power to degenerate into the lower forms of life, which are brutish. Thou shalt have the power, out of thy soul's judgment, to be reborn into the higher forms, which are divine.

These words have a modern ring, and they are among the few passages in the philosophical literature of the Renaissance that have pleased, almost without reservation, modern and even existentialist ears. It is not absolutely certain that they were meant to be as modern as they sound, and it is hard to believe what has often been said—that when Pico wrote them, he had denied or forgotten the doctrine of grace. After all, the words are attributed to God and are addressed by him to Adam before the Fall. Yet they do contain an eloquent praise of human excellence and of man's potentialities, and they receive added vigor when we think of what the reformers, and even great humanists like Michel Eyquem de Montaigne, were to say about man's vanity and weakness.

Some scholars have tried to minimize Pico's praise of human dignity and regard it as a piece of mere oratory. This view is refuted by the testimony of the *Heptaplus*, a work written several years later and for an entirely different purpose. Here again, Pico places man outside the hierarchy of the three worlds—the angelic, celestial, and elementary—treats him as a fourth world by himself, and praises him and his faculties, although within a more obvious theological context.

Pico's insistence on man's dignity and liberty also accounts, at least in part, for his attack on astrology, to which he dedicates his largest extant work, probably composed during the last few years of his life. The *Disputationes Adversus Astrologiam Divinatricem* is full of detailed astronomical discussions and displays an amazing mastery of the astrological and antiastrological literature of previous centuries. It has often been hailed by historians as a landmark in the struggle of science against superstition. In fact, Pico does state that the stars act upon sublunar things only through their light and heat, not through any other occult qualities that may be attributed to them, and this statement sounds very sober, if not necessarily modern. Moreover, we learn that even a scientist such as Johannes Kepler at least modified his initial belief in astrology under the influence of Pico's treatise.

In Pico's time, however, the belief in astrology was more than a superstition, and the rejection of it was not necessarily scientific. As a general system astrology was closely linked with the scientific cosmology of the age and hence widely accepted not only by quacks but also by serious thinkers. There is no evidence that Pico was especially guided by scientific considerations in his polemics against astrology, and we must face the fact that he accepted natural magic while rejecting astrology. We happen to know that his work against astrology was composed as a part of a larger work he planned to write against the enemies of the church. The basic impulse of his attack was religious and not scientific, and he indicates more than once what his chief objection to astrology was—the stars are bodies, and our selves are spirits; it cannot be admitted that a corporeal and, hence, lower being should act upon a higher being and restrict its freedom.

Pico's conception of the relation between philosophy and religion is also significant. He became increasingly concerned with religious problems during his later years, a development in which his shock at the papal condemnation of his theses and the influence of Savonarola must have played a part. The fact appears in the religious and theological content of several of his later writings and in the religious motivation of his treatise against astrology. It also finds an unexpected expression in certain passages of the *De Ente et Uno*, a work that deals fundamentally with a very different problem. Here Pico tells us that God is darkness and that philosophical knowledge can lead us toward God only up to a certain point, beyond which religion must guide us. Unlike Ficino, Pico seems to regard religion as a fulfillment of philosophy; religion helps us to attain that ultimate end for which philosophy can merely prepare us.

Pico did not live long enough to develop his ideas into a coherent system. Fragmentary as his work was, it had wide repercussions for a long time. His universal syncretism came closer to subsequent efforts at formulating a universal religion than that of any of his predecessors, including Ficino. His study of Hebrew and Arabic, although not entirely without precedents, served as a widely known example and gave a powerful impulse to these studies in Christian Europe, leading to a study of the Hebrew Scripture and to many new translations of Jewish and Arabic texts. His study of the kabbalah started a broad and powerful current of Christian kabbalism, which flourished throughout the sixteenth century and included many distinguished scholars and thinkers. In his attempt to harmonize the traditions of Platonic and Aristotelian philosophy, of Hermetic and kabbalistic theology, and of the various strands of Arabic and scholastic thought with one another and with Christian doctrine, Pico pointed the way toward intellectual freedom and a universal truth that stands above the narrow limits of particular schools and traditions.

See also Antiochus of Ascalon; Aristotelianism; Aristotle; Averroes; Avicenna; Boethius, Anicius Manlius Severinus; Cicero, Marcus Tullius; Duns Scotus, John; Ficino, Marsilio; Hegel, Georg Wilhelm Friedrich; Humanism; Italian Philosophy; Kabbalah; Kepler, Johannes; Melanchthon, Philipp; Montaigne, Michel Eyquem de; Neoplatonism; Pico della Mirandola, Gianfrancesco; Plato; Platonism and the Platonic Tradition; Plotinus; Pythagoras and Pythagoreanism; Renaissance; Stoicism; Thomas Aquinas, St.

Bibliography

WORKS BY PICO

Three volumes of a critical edition of Pico's works by Eugenio Garin have appeared: *De Hominis Dignitate, Heptaplus, De Ente et Uno, e scritti vari* (Florence: Vallecchi, 1942) and *Disputationes Adversus Astrologiam Divinatricem*, 2 vols. (Florence: Vallecchi, 1946–1952). For the other works (especially the *Conclusiones, Apologia,* and *Letters*) one of the numerous editions of Pico's works must be used. The earliest and best was published in Bologna (1496); the most accessible is the Basel edition of 1572. For additional letters and texts see Léon Dorez, "Lettres inédites de Jean Pic de la Mirandole," *Giornale storico della letteratura italiana* 25 (1895): 352–361, and Eugenio Garin, *La cultura filosofica del Rinascimento italiano* (Florence: Sansoni, 1961). A few of Pico's letters and short religious works, along with the biography of Pico by his nephew, were translated by Sir Thomas More as *Pico, His Life by His Nephew,* edited by J. M. Rigg (London, 1890). The commentary on Benivieni was translated by Thomas Stanley in 1651 and later appeared as *A Platonick Discourse upon Love,* edited by Edmund G. Gardner (Boston: Merrymount Press, 1914).

There is a modern English version of the *De Ente et Uno,* translated by Victor M. Hamm as *Of Being and Unity* (Milwaukee, WI: Marquette University Press, 1943), and no less than three versions of the *Oration—The Very Elegant Speech on the Dignity of Man,* translated by Charles G. Wallis (Annapolis, MD: St. John's Book Store, 1940); *Oration on the Dignity of Man,* translated by Elizabeth L. Forbes in *The Renaissance Philosophy of Man,* edited by Ernst Cassirer, Paul Oskar Kristeller, and John H. Randall Jr. (Chicago: University of Chicago Press, 1948), and published separately with the Latin text (Lexington, KY, 1953); and *Oration on the Dignity of Man,* translated by A. Robert Caponigri (Chicago: Gateway, 1956). The correspondence with Ermolao Barbaro was translated by Quirinus Breen as "Giovanni Pico della Mirandola on the Conflict of Philosophy and Rhetoric," *Journal of the History of Ideas* 13 (1952): 384–426.

WORKS ON PICO

For Pico's thought the chief monograph is Eugenio Garin, *Giovanni Pico della Mirandola* (Florence: Le Monnier, 1937). Important is Ernst Cassirer's "Giovanni Pico della Mirandola," *Journal of the History of Ideas* 3 (1942): 123–144, 319–346. See also Giovanni Semprini, *La filosofia di Pico della Mirandola* (Milan, 1936); Eugenio Anagnine, *G. Pico della Mirandola* (Bari, Italy: Laterza, 1937); Pierre Marie Cordier, *Jean Pic de la Mirandole* (Paris: Nouvelles Éditions Debresse, 1957); E. Monnerjahn, *Giovanni Pico della Mirandola* (Wiesbaden, Germany: Steiner, 1960); and Eugenio Garin, *Giovanni Pico della Mirandola* (Mirandola, Italy, 1963).

For Pico's sources see Pearl Kibre, *The Library of Pico della Mirandola* (New York: Columbia University Press, 1936). For the condemnation of his theses see Léon Dorez and Louis Thuasne, *Pic de la Mirandole en France* (Paris: Leroux, 1897). For his scholastic background see Avery Dulles, *Princeps Concordiae: Pico della Mirandola and the Scholastic Tradition* (Cambridge, MA: Harvard University Press, 1941). For the *De Ente et Uno* and its background see Raymond Klibansky, "Plato's *Parmenides* in the Middle Ages and the Renaissance," *Mediaeval and Renaissance Studies* 1 (1941–1943): 281–330. For his kabbalism see Joseph L. Blau, *The Christian Interpretation of the Cabala in the Renaissance* (New York: Columbia University Press, 1944); F. Secret, *Le zôhar chez les kabbalistes chrétiens de la Renaissance* (Paris, 1958) and "Pico della Mirandola e gli inizi della Cabala cristiana," *Convivium,* n.s. 25 (1957): 31–47.

For Pico's influence on the iconography of Renaissance art see Edgar Wind, *Pagan Mysteries in the Renaissance* (New Haven, CT: Yale University Press, 1958).

Several long papers by Eugenio Garin, Robert Weiss, Paul Oskar Kristeller, and Frances A. Yates are included in *L'opera e il pensiero di Giovanni Pico della Mirandola nella storia dell'umanesimo. Convegno internazionale, Mirandola, 15–18 settembre 1963,* 2 vols. (Florence: Nella Sede dell'Istituto, 1965).

See also Brian P. Copenhaver, "The Secret of Pico's Oration: Cabala and Renaissance Philosophy," *Midwest Studies in Philosophy* (26 [2002]: 56–81).

Paul Oskar Kristeller (1967)
Bibliography updated by Tamra Frei (2005)

PICO DELLA MIRANDOLA, GIANFRANCESCO

(1469–1533)

Gianfrancesco Pico della Mirandola was the nephew of the great Florentine humanist Giovanni Pico della Mirandola. He, like his uncle, became interested in the reform movement of Girolamo Savonarola (1452–1498) that was centered in the Convent of San Marco. The younger Pico della Mirandola moved into the convent and joined the group of scholars who took part in the daily discussions of philosophy and religion. His uncle moved into the convent in 1492 and placed his library there. Among the manuscripts brought to the convent by Pico della Mirandola and other scholars were five manuscript copies of Sextus Empiricus. Savonarola became interested in making these texts in Greek available to modern readers and asked two of his monks to begin preparing an edition of the writings of Sextus. This project never came to fruition, but some of it seems to be incorporated in the younger Pico della Mirandola's own publications.

He edited his uncle's work on astrology that was left in 1494, after Pico della Mirandola had died. He himself authored another work criticizing astrology, as did Savonarola. Pico della Mirandola was writing in praise of Savonarola up to the moment when the latter was arrested, tried, and burned at the stake. Thereafter, his disciples had to flee for their lives. Pico della Mirandola went back to his ancestral home of Mirandola, Italy, and struggled for about ten years to secure control of his family's property.

He wrote on a variety of philosophical and theological subjects, supporting the views of his teacher, Savonarola. In 1520 he published the first presentation of Greek skepticism in modern times, *Examen vanitatis doc-*

trinae gentium et veritatis Christianae disciplinae: Distinctum in libros sex, quorum tres omnem philosophorum sectam universim: reliqui Aristoteleam et Aristoteleis armis particulatim impugnant: Ubicunque autem Christiana et asseritur, et celebratur disciplina (Examination of the vain doctrine of the gentiles and the true Christian teaching). The work was apparently written over at least fifteen to twenty years. Besides presenting arguments and analyses out of Sextus, it also contains a text by John Philoponus and Hasdai Crescas. It is curious that Pico della Mirandola includes the material from Crescas, which had not yet been published and only circulated in Hebrew manuscript. He may have gotten a text and its translation from Judah León Abrabanel (c. 1460–c. 1521), with whom he was in contact. Pico della Mirandola's skeptical work did not have wide circulation. It is cited by several people writing on philosophical topics, but it does not seem to have encouraged people to look further into skeptical thought. He was read by Gentian Hervetius (1499–1584), the translator of Sextus, and probably by Francisco Sanches, Pierre Gassendi, and Gottfried Wilhelm Leibniz. The more serious impact of Sextus on modern thought had to await the presentation of his doctrines in Michel Eyquem de Montaigne's writings.

See also Pico della Mirandola, Count Giovanni; Sextus Empiricus; Skepticism, History of.

Bibliography

WORKS BY PICO DELLA MIRANDOLA

Examen vanitatis doctrinae gentium, et veritatis Christianae disciplinae. Mirandulae, Italy: N.p., 1520.

WORKS ABOUT PICO DELLA MIRANDOLA

Cao, Gian Mario. "Gianfrancesco Pico, Reader of Sceptics." Paper presented at the Conference on Renaissance Scepticism, New York, April 2004.

Floridi, Luciano. *Sextus Empiricus: The Transmission and Recovery of Pyrrhonism.* New York: Oxford University Press, 2002.

Popkin, Richard H. *The History of Scepticism: From Savonarola to Bayle.* Rev. ed. New York: Oxford University Press, 2003.

Schmitt, Charles B. *Gianfrancesco Pico della Mirandola (1469–1533) and His Critique of Aristotle.* The Hague: Nijhoff, 1967.

Schmitt, Charles B. "The Rediscovery of Ancient Skepticism in Modern Times." In *The Skeptical Tradition,* edited by Myles Burnyeat. Berkeley: University of California Press, 1983.

Viti, Paulo, ed. *Pico, Poliziano e l'umanesimo di fine quottrocento: Beblioteca medicea laurenziana,* November 4–December 31, 1994. Florence, Italy: Leo S. Olschki editore, 1994.

Richard Popkin (2005)

PIETISM

Since the seventeenth century "Pietism" has been an important movement within German Protestantism, and it is still influential in some parts of Germany. It began as a reaction against the formal and conventional character that appeared in Protestantism in the aftermath of the Reformation. Pietism opposed on the one hand the intellectualism implicit in the orthodox tendency to equate faith with the giving of assent to correct doctrine, and on the other, the tendency to identify Christianity with conformity to the ecclesiastical establishments that had been set up in various parts of Germany. By stressing experience, feeling, and personal participation as essential to a true Christian faith, Pietists hoped to bring new life into the Lutheran Church. One can point to similar movements in other parts of Christendom, in the English-speaking world the movement most akin to Pietism was Methodism.

The founder of German Pietism was Philipp Jakob Spener (1635–1705). Influenced by the extreme Protestant sect of Jean de Labadie, he undertook the task of raising the devotional level of his congregation in Frankfurt am Main and eventually, he hoped, of German Protestantism as a whole. Devotional meetings in his home were the beginnings of the famous *collegia pietatis.* At its meetings his sermons were considered, the New Testament was expounded, and there was conversation on religious topics. Spener gave clear expression to the aims of his movement in *Pia Desideria* (Frankfurt am Main, 1675), in which he laid down six goals to be realized: (1) greater study of the Bible but with the aim of personal devotion rather than academic competence; (2) a serious commitment to Martin Luther's belief in the priesthood of all Christian believers, so that the laity might really participate in the life of the church instead of merely conforming outwardly; (3) a realization that Christianity is a practical faith rather than an intellectual belief and that this faith expresses itself in love; (4) corresponding to this, a new style in apologetics and controversy that must aim not so much at intellectual conviction as at winning the allegiance of the whole man; (5) following from the last two points, the reorganization of theological education in order to lay stress on standards of life and conduct rather than on academic achievement; (6) the renewal and revitalizing of preaching as an instrument for building up a genuine piety among the people.

Spener continued to advocate his views in many other writings, including *Das geistliche Priesterthum* (1677), *Des thätigen Christenthums Nothwendigkeit*

(1679), *Die allgemeine Gottesgelehrtheit aller gläubigen Christen und Rechtschaffenen Theologen* (1680), *Klagen über das verdorbene Christenthum* (1684), *Natur und Gnade* (1687), and *Evangelische Glaubenslehre* (1688), which were all published at Frankfurt. He became engaged in stormy controversies, both attracting supporters and arousing opposition. Through the support of the elector of Brandenburg, the University of Halle became a center for Pietist views. Spener himself seems to have been a reasonable man who avoided the extravagances of some of his followers and performed a genuine service for the Lutheran Church.

Also important in the history of Pietism is August Hermann Francke (1663–1727). He taught at the University of Halle and is noteworthy for his development of the practical emphasis of Pietism. He founded a school for the poor and an orphanage and also took an interest in the cause of foreign missions. Like Spener, he encountered opposition, especially among some of the theologians, because of his indiscriminate attacks on intellectualism and his depreciation of the academic disciplines in the interests of devotion and philanthropy. Francke, however, had his supporters and was favored by King Frederick William I of Prussia. Mention should also be made of Count Nikolaus Ludwig von Zinzendorf (1700–1760), a pupil of Francke, who spread the spirit of Pietism to Holland, England, and North America by founding communities there. He maintained close relations with John Wesley and the Methodists. Like the other Pietists, he stressed feeling and personal devotion in what seems to have been a mixture of mysticism and emotionalism.

The chief characteristics of Pietism can be seen from this sketch of its origins and early history. It made claims for the affective and sometimes also the conative aspects of religion, in devotion and in practical service, at the expense of the cognitive element. While this may have been a healthy corrective to a sterile dogmatic orthodoxy, it tended to lead to dangerous excesses. Its insistence on intense inward experience could easily lead to the emotionalism that is common in evangelical religion and to the contempt for intelligence and common sense that sometimes accompanies it. The moralistic tone encourages utopianism. Some of those who have been caught up in the enthusiasm of Pietism have underrated the complexities of the moral life and the limitations of what is possible for man; as a result they have shared with the Methodists a belief in perfectionism. Apart from these dangerous excesses, Pietism has contended for the breadth of the human spirit and guarded against too narrow a rationalism. That the tenets of Pietism can receive a sober formulation worthy of respectful consideration is shown above all by the work of F. D. E. Schleiermacher, whose analysis of religion in terms of the feeling of absolute dependence is a direct reflection of the Pietist tradition in Germany.

The influence of Pietism on philosophy is largely indirect. The Pietists themselves tended to be antiphilosophical, but their spirit and teaching became part of the German heritage and eventually influenced even philosophy. This influence showed itself above all in the rise of *Lebensphilosophie* of which the religious variety, as expressed in the work of Rudolf Christoph Eucken, comes nearest to being a philosophical version of Pietism. Yet even the nonreligious varieties of this philosophy probably owe something to the anti-intellectualism that Pietism has encouraged.

See also Eucken, Rudolf Christoph; Luther, Martin; Mysticism, Nature and Assessment of; Schleiermacher, Friedrich Daniel Ernst.

Bibliography

Crowner, David, and Gerald Christianson, eds. and trans. *The Spirituality of the German Awakening*. New York: Paulist Press, 2003.

Grünberg, Paul. *P. J. Spener*, 3 vols. Göttingen: Vandenhoeck and Ruprecht, 1893–1896.

Mahrholz, A. *Der deutsche Pietismus*. Berlin: Furche-verlag, 1921.

Nagler, Arthur W. *Pietism and Methodism*. Nashville, TN, 1918.

Petig, William E. *Literary Antipietism in Germany During the First Half of the Eighteenth Century*. New York: P. Lang, 1984.

Pinson, Koppel S. *Pietism as a Factor in the Rise of German Nationalism*. New York: Columbia University Press, 1934.

Ritschl, A. *Geschichte des Pietismus*, 3 vols. Bonn: Marcus, 1880–1886.

Sachsse, E. *Ursprung und Wesen des Pietismus*. Wiesbaden: Niedner, 1884.

Schmid, H. *Die Geschichte des Pietismus*. Nördlingen: Beck, 1863.

Stoeffler, Fred E. *German Pietism During the Eighteenth Century*. Leiden: Brill, 1973.

John Macquarrie (1967)
Bibliography updated by Tamra Frei (2005)

PISAREV, DMITRI IVANOVICH
(1840–1868)

Dmitri Ivanovich Pisarev, the Russian literary critic and social philosopher, was educated at St. Petersburg University (1856–1861). His studies were interrupted by a nervous breakdown requiring four months of institutionalization. At this time he twice attempted suicide. Pisarev was imprisoned from 1862 to 1866 for his outspoken criticism of the tsarist regime. He drowned while swimming in the Baltic Sea, under circumstances that suggest suicide, at the age of twenty-eight.

Pisarev called himself a "realist" and praised "fresh and healthy materialism," but his own philosophical position was a sense-datum empiricism. In his early writings on ethics and social philosophy, in the years 1859 to 1861, he advocated the "emancipation of the individual person" from social, intellectual, and moral constraints but particularly stressed the preservation of the wholeness of human personality in the face of the fragmenting pressures of functional specialization and the division of labor.

Among the constraints that the free individual must discard are those resulting from "the timidity of his thought, caste prejudices, the authority of tradition, the aspiration toward a common ideal" (*Polnoye Sobraniye Sochineniy*, Vol. I, Col. 339). Pisarev declared that common ideals have "just as little *raison d'être* as common eyeglasses or common boots made on the same last and to the same measure" (Col. 267). Eyes differ, feet differ, individuals differ; hence eyeglasses, boots, and ideals (for "every ideal has its author") should be individually fitted. Pisarev's moral relativism anticipated contemporary emotivist or noncognitivist doctrines in ethics—the claim that moral judgments are expressions of individual taste or preference. "When it is a matter of judging port or sherry," Pisarev wrote, "we remain calm and cool, we reason simply and soundly …, but when it is a question of lofty matters, we immediately … get up on our stilts…. We let our neighbor indulge his taste in hors d'oeuvres and desserts, but woe unto him if he expresses an independent opinion about morals" (Col. 266).

In his later writings Pisarev adopted a utilitarian ethics modified by the principle of "economy of intellectual energies." In the situation of cultural and intellectual deprivation of Russia at mid-century, he argued, the greatest-happiness principle precludes such luxuries as esoteric art that can be enjoyed "only by a few specialists" and abstruse science that is "in its very essence inaccessible to the masses" (Col. 366).

See also Empiricism; Ethics, History of; Noncognitivism; Russian Philosophy; Social and Political Philosophy; Utilitarianism.

Bibliography

WORKS BY PISAREV

Polnoye Sobraniye Sochinenii (Complete works). St. Petersburg, 1894. Six volumes.

Selected Philosophical, Social and Political Essays. Moscow: Foreign Languages Publishing House, 1958.

WORKS ON PISAREV

Coquart, Armand. *Dmitri Pisarev (1840–1868) et l'idéologie du nihilisme russe.* Paris: Institut d'études Slaves de l'Université de Paris, 1946.

Masaryk, Tomáš G. *Die geistigen Strömungen in Russland.* 2 vols. Jena, Germany, 1913. Translated by E. and C. Paul as *The Spirit of Russia: Studies in History, Literature, and Philosophy.* 2 vols., Vol. II, 53–81. New York: Macmillan, 1955.

George L. Kline (1967)

PLANCK, MAX
(1858–1947)

The German physicist Max Planck was the discoverer of the quantum of action, also called Planck's constant. Born in Kiel, he studied physics and mathematics at the University of Munich under Philipp von Jolly and at the University of Berlin under Hermann von Helmholtz and Gustav Kirchhoff. After receiving his Ph.D. at Munich (1879), he taught theoretical physics, first in Kiel, then (starting in 1889) in Berlin, as Kirchhoff's successor. "In those days," he wrote later, "I was the only theoretician, a physicist *sui generis,* as it were, and this circumstance did not make my *début* so easy." At this time Planck made important, and indeed quite fundamental, contributions to the understanding of the phenomena of heat, but he received hardly any attention from the scientific community: "Helmholtz probably did not read my paper at all. Kirchhoff expressly disapproved of its contents." The spotlight was then on the controversy between Ludwig Boltzmann and the Wilhelm Ostwald–Georg Helm–Ernst Mach camp, which supported a purely phenomenological theory of heat. It was via this controversy, and not because of the force of his arguments, that Planck's ideas were finally accepted. "This experience," he wrote, "gave me an opportunity to learn a remarkable fact: a new scientific truth does not triumph by convincing its opponents and making them see the light, but rather because its opponents eventually die."

Nevertheless, the discovery of the quantum of action in 1900, for which Planck received the Nobel Prize in physics (1918), was a direct result of these earlier studies. In 1912 Planck became permanent secretary of the (then)

Prussian Academy of Sciences, a post that he retained with only minor interruptions for the rest of his life. He used this position with excellent judgment for furthering the international collaboration of all scientists. From 1930 to 1935 he was president of the Kaiser-Wilhelm-Institut, which later became the Max-Planck-Institut.

Politically Planck was conservative, loyal to the Prussian ideas of the state and of honor, and loyal to Wilhelm II. During World War I he more than once expressed his devotion to the cause of the German people united in battle, and he received the order of "pour le mérite," one of the highest orders of Wilhelm's Germany. However, he opposed the Nazi regime. He defended Albert Einstein, first against his scientific opponents, then against his political enemies. Despite severe criticism by Johannes Stark, Phillip Lenard, and Ernst Müller, he continued to defend Einstein and other Jewish scientists (such as Walther Nernst) even after 1933. He later personally demanded of Adolf Hitler that those scientists who had been imprisoned be freed; as a consequence he was removed as president of the Physical Society, was refused the Goethe Prize of the city of Frankfurt (he was awarded it after the war, in 1946), and finally was forced to witness the execution of his only son, who had been connected with the German resistance. Antiquated as some of his political ideas may have been, he nevertheless put individual justice above all and defended it even at the risk of his own life. At the end of the war he was rescued by the Allied forces. He spent the last years of his life in Göttingen.

APPROACH TO SCIENCE

Planck's research was guided by his belief "of the existence in nature of something real, and independent of human measurement." He considered "the search for the absolute" to be the highest goal of science. "Our everyday starting point," he explained, "must necessarily be something relative. The material that goes into our instruments varies according to our geographical source; their construction depends on the skill of the designers and toolmakers; their manipulation is contingent on the special purposes pursued by the experimenter. Our task is to find in all these factors and data, the absolute, the universally valid, the invariant that is hidden in them."

This point of view was not allowed to remain a philosophical luxury, without influence upon the procedures of physics. One of the main objections that Planck raised against the positivistic creed was its sterility in the promotion of theory. "Positivism lacks the driving force for serving as a leader on the road of research. True, it is able to eliminate obstacles, but it cannot turn them into productive factors. For … its glance is directed backwards. But progress, advancement requires new associations of ideas and new queries, not based on the results of measurement alone."

SCIENTIFIC DISCOVERIES

Of new ideas Planck himself produced essentially two. He recognized and clearly formulated those properties of heat that separate it from purely mechanical processes, and he introduced and applied to concrete problems the idea of an atomistic structure not only of matter but of radiation also. In his doctoral dissertation he had already separated thermodynamic irreversibility from mechanical processes and had interpreted Rudolf Clausius's entropy as its measure. Later he showed (independently of Willard Gibbs) that "all the laws of physical and chemical equilibrium follow from a knowledge of entropy."

His conviction that the principle of the increase of entropy was a genuine and independent physical law and his belief in the universal (or, to use his term, *absolute*) validity of all physical laws led him to apply thermodynamic reasoning in domains that until then had been regarded as inaccessible to it. For example, he determined that the lowering of the freezing point of dilute solutions could be explained only by a dissociation of the substances dissolved, thus extending the science of thermodynamics to electrically charged particles. This tendency to strain laws to the limit rather than to restrict them to the domain of their strongest evidence caused a temporary clash with Boltzmann, who was quite unperturbed by the fact that in his approach the entropy of a system could both increase and decrease. But it also led to Planck's greatest triumph—his discovery of the quantum of action.

Planck was the only one to correlate the relevant features of radiation with the entropy, rather than the temperature, of the radiant body. "While a host of outstanding physicists worked on the problem of spectral energy distribution, both from the experimental and theoretical aspect, every one of them directed his efforts solely towards exhibiting the dependence of the intensity of radiation on the temperature. On the other hand I suspected that the fundamental connexion lies in the dependence of entropy upon energy. As the significance of the concept of entropy had not yet come to be fully appreciated, nobody paid attention to the method adopted by me, and I could work out my calculations completely at my leisure." These calculations furnished a formula that agreed with experiment and contained the existing theoretical results (Wien's formula and the

Raleigh-Jeans law) as limiting cases. In the attempt to find a rationale for this result, Planck used Boltzmann's statistical interpretation of entropy and was thus led to the discovery of the "atomic," or discontinuous, structure of action (energy).

REALISM, DETERMINISM, AND RELIGION

The discovery of the quantum of action was brought about not only by the specific physical arguments used but also by the philosophical belief in the existence of a real world behaving in accordance with immutable laws. The intellectual climate of the late nineteenth century was opposed to such a belief (Boltzmann was almost the only other figure to uphold it). This climate not only found expression in the philosophical superstructure but influenced physical practice itself. Laws were regarded as summaries of experimental results and were applied only where such results were available. However, it was the "metaphysics" of Planck, Boltzmann, and, later on, Einstein (whom Planck interpreted as a realist from the very beginning) that made possible many of the theories that are now frequently used to attack realism and other "metaphysical" principles.

Planck never accepted the positivistic interpretation of the quantum theory. He distinguished between what he called the "world picture" of physics and the "sensory world," identifying the former with the formalism of the ψ waves, the latter with experimental results. The fact that the ψ-function obeys the Schrödinger equation enabled him to say that while the sensory world might show indeterministic features, the world picture, even of the new physics, did not. His belief in the existence of objective laws also provided him with an important steppingstone to religious belief. Planck argued that the laws of nature are not invented in the minds of men; on the contrary, external factors force us to recognize them. Some of these laws, such as the principle of least action, "exhibit a rational world order" and thereby reveal "an omnipotent reason which rules over nature." He concluded that there is no contradiction between religion and natural science; rather, they supplement and condition each other.

See also Quantum Mechanics.

Bibliography

WORKS BY PLANCK

Theory of Heat Radiation. Translated by Morton Masius. Philadelphia: P. Blakiston's Son, 1914; 2nd ed., New York: Dover, 1959.

Eight Lectures on Theoretical Physics. Translated by A. P. Wills. New York: Columbia University Press, 1915. Lectures given at Columbia University in 1909.

The Origin and Development of the Quantum Theory. Translated by H. T. Clarke and L. Silberstein. Oxford: Clarendon Press, 1922. Nobel Prize address.

A Survey of Physics; A Collection of Lectures and Essays. Translated by R. Jones and D. H. Williams. London: Methuen, 1925. Reissued as *A Survey of Physical Theory.* New York: Dover, 1960.

Treatise on Thermodynamics. Translated by Alexander Ogg. London: Longmans, Green, 1927; 3rd rev. ed., New York, 1945.

Introduction to Theoretical Physics. Translated by Henry L. Brose, 5 vols. London, 1932–1933; New York, 1949. Includes *General Mechanics, The Mechanics of Deformable Bodies, Theory of Electricity and Magnetism, Theory of Light,* and *Theory of Heat.*

Scientific Autobiography and Other Papers. Translated by Frank Gaynor. New York: Philosophical Library, 1949.

The New Science. Translated by James Murphy and W. H. Johnston. New York: Meridian, 1959. Includes *Where Is Science Going?* (a defense of determinism with a preface by Albert Einstein), *The Universe in the Light of Modern Physics,* and *The Philosophy of Physics.*

WORKS ON PLANCK

Schlick, Moritz. "Positivism and Realism." In *Logical Positivism,* edited by A. J. Ayer. Glencoe, IL: Free Press, 1959. This essay was a direct reply to the criticisms of positivism that Planck expressed in *Positivismus und reale Aussenwelt.* Leipzig, 1931.

Vogel, H. *Zum philosophischen Wirken Max Plancks.* Berlin: Akadamie, 1961. Excellent biography with detailed bibliography.

Paul K. Feyerabend (1967)

PLANTINGA, ALVIN
(1932–)

Born in Ann Arbor, Michigan, Alvin Plantinga is one of the most important and influential philosophers of the twentieth and early twenty-first centuries. His publications range over a wide variety of fields, but his most enduring contributions have been in metaphysics, epistemology, and, especially, the philosophy of religion. He is best known for his work on the metaphysics of necessity and possibility, for his defense of the view that knowledge is to be analyzed partly in terms of proper function, for his development of the "free will defense" against the so-called "logical problem of evil," for his many and vigorous defenses of the rationality of religious belief, and for his much-discussed "evolutionary argument against naturalism."

Plantinga earned his BA in philosophy and psychology from Calvin College in 1953, and he cites his experience at Calvin as perhaps the single most significant intellectual influence in his life. There he studied with Henry Stob and Harry Jellema, the latter of whom played an especially formative role in his intellectual development. Plantinga received his MA in philosophy from the University of Michigan in 1955, and his PhD from Yale in 1958 under the supervision of Paul Weiss. He was elected to the American Academy of Arts and Sciences in 1975, co-founded the Society of Christian Philosophers in 1978, served as President of the Central Division of the American Philosophical Association in 1981 and 1982, and served as President of the Society of Christian Philosophers from 1983 to 1986. He has given the prestigious Gifford Lectures twice, and in a 1980 article he was heralded by *Time* magazine as "America's leading orthodox Protestant philosopher of God."

METAPHYSICS

Plantinga's most influential work in metaphysics has focused primarily on the metaphysics of modality. In *The Nature of Necessity* (1974), as well as in various papers, a central theme is the exposition and defense of a *realist* and *actualist* construal of possible worlds and modal properties. On his view, the standard possible worlds semantics for modal logic is to be taken with metaphysical seriousness: it is not a mere heuristic device; possible worlds are not merely useful fictions. Rather, possible worlds exist. They are abstract states of affairs of a certain kind—something like total or complete ways that a world history might have gone. Moreover, individual things have *modal properties*—properties such as *being possibly seven feet tall*, or *being necessarily even*—and, Plantinga thinks, realism about such properties requires one to believe that individual things exist in other worlds. On his view, a thing exists in another possible world only if, had that world been actual, the thing itself, not a mere stand-in or counterpart, would have existed. Thus, if Fred has the property *being possibly seven feet tall*, then there is a possible world such that, had that world been actual, Fred himself would have existed and would have been seven feet tall. Ultimately, this understanding of modal properties, together with his commitment to strong form of actualism, leads Plantinga to endorse the controversial view that objects have *individual essences*—properties that are both essential and essentially unique to them.

EPISTEMOLOGY

Plantinga's major works in epistemology are the volumes that comprise his *Warrant* trilogy (1993a, 1993b, 2000). Warrant, according to Plantinga, is that property or quantity that distinguishes knowledge from mere true belief. The main goals of the *Warrant* books are to identify the necessary and sufficient conditions for warrant, and to defend an affirmative answer to the question whether distinctively Christian belief can be warranted.

In the first volume of the trilogy, Plantinga surveys a broad range of post-Gettier analyses of knowledge, arguing that all of them founder on counterexamples involving cognitive malfunction. The basic problem is that, for each candidate analysis of "S knows that *p*," the conditions listed as necessary and sufficient for knowledge could be satisfied by a person whose cognitive faculties are malfunctioning in such a way that, intuitively, beliefs produced by faculties behaving in that way fail to count as knowledge. He also argues for the striking and controversial conclusion that *justification*, construed at least in part as a matter of epistemic duty-fulfillment, is not necessary for knowledge at all.

In the second volume, Plantinga articulates and defends a new analysis of knowledge, according to which (roughly) S knows that *p* if and only if S believes that *p*, *p* is true, and S's belief that *p* is the product of faculties that are properly functioning, successfully aimed at truth, and operating in an appropriate environment. The notions of *proper function* and *appropriate environment* are normative notions; but, Plantinga says, the normativity involved is of a sort commonly invoked in the natural sciences. Thus, Plantinga regards his analysis as, strictly speaking, an instance of "epistemology naturalized." But he also argues that his brand of epistemology naturalized flourishes best in the context of a supernaturalistic metaphysics. Toward establishing this conclusion, he begins by arguing that proper function is an irreducibly normative notion that does not admit of a purely naturalistic analysis. He then attacks naturalism directly, arguing that belief in naturalism and evolutionary theory together is epistemically self-defeating and therefore irrational. This latter argument is the so-called "evolutionary argument against naturalism."

The third volume of the *Warrant* trilogy applies the account of knowledge defended in the second volume in the service of an argument for the possibility of warranted Christian belief. The central and striking thesis of the book is that if Christian belief is true, then it is warranted. This conclusion is important because it implies, contrary to widespread opinion, that objections against the *rationality* of Christian belief are not independent of objections against the *truth* of Christian belief. In order to defend the conclusion that Christian belief is unwarranted, one must first defend the conclusion that it is false. In support of his central thesis, Plantinga begins by arguing that the only really philosophically interesting question about the rationality of Christian belief is the question that asks whether Christian belief is or can be warranted. He then notes that, in light of the analysis of knowledge proposed in the second volume, Christian belief can be warranted so long as it is produced by properly functioning faculties that are successfully aimed at truth and functioning in a suitable environment. Much of the rest of the volume, then, is devoted to establishing the conclusion that if Christian belief is true, then these conditions are satisfied.

PHILOSOPHY OF RELIGION

Plantinga's work in the philosophy of religion has focused on what is sometimes referred to as "negative apologetics": the task of showing that objections to religious belief are unsuccessful. Thus, to take just a few examples, Plantinga has argued that the proposition that God exists is logically consistent with the proposition that evil exists; that the existence of evil does not constitute a defeater for the rationality of Christian belief; that widespread religious pluralism and intractable disagreement on religious matters do not provide reason to doubt that one knows that one's own religious beliefs are true; and that what he takes to be the correct views about human freedom and moral responsibility are not in tension with the traditional belief that God has perfect knowledge of the future.

Plantinga's focus on negative apologetics stems in part from his view that the warrant for Christian belief need not, and, in the ordinary case, does not come from philosophical argument but rather from something like religious experience. This view is a central theme in his work on religious epistemology, especially in the third volume of his *Warrant* trilogy (discussed above), but also in two earlier works: *God and Other Minds* (1967), and "Reason and Belief in God." Nevertheless, he does make occasional forays into the territory of positive apologetics. For example, in *The Nature of Necessity* and *God, Freedom and Evil* (1977), Plantinga argues that a modal version of the ontological argument for God's existence is both valid and plausibly sound. Likewise, Plantinga has devoted considerable energy to rebutting naturalism and its common companion, materialism.

Besides introducing important arguments into the literature on the philosophy of religion, however, Plantinga has also played an important role in shaping the way in which many religious philosophers now approach topics in their own fields of specialization. In his highly influential paper, "Advice to Christian Philosophers,"

(1984) Plantinga urges philosophers who share his Christian worldview to allow the presuppositions of that worldview to inform their work not only on topics in the philosophy of religion but elsewhere as well. He advises them not to become swept up in projects that arise out of and embody presuppositions of rival worldviews (such as naturalism or creative anti-realism), but to pursue a philosophical agenda in which one explores how a person with a Christian perspective ought to think about the various topics central to her discipline. This advice, itself an apt expression of one of the distinctive features of Plantinga's own work, has had a significant impact on the sorts of philosophical projects that have been undertaken in the late twentieth and early twenty-first centuries.

See also Evil, the Problem of; Ontological Argument for the Existence of God.

Bibliography

PRIMARY WORKS

God and Other Minds. Ithaca, NY: Cornell University Press, 1967.

The Nature of Necessity. New York: Clarendon Press, 1974.

God, Freedom, and Evil. Grand Rapids, MI: Eerdmans, 1977.

"Reason and Belief in God." In *Faith and Rationality*, edited by Alvin Plantinga and Nicholas Wolterstorff, 16–93. Notre Dame: University of Notre Dame Press. 1983.

Warrant: The Current Debate. New York: Oxford University Press, 1993a.

Warrant and Proper Function. New York: Oxford University Press, 1993b.

"Advice to Christian Philosophers," *Faith and Philosophy* 1: 253–71. Reprinted in Sennett, 1998.

The Analytic Theist: An Alvin Plantinga Reader. Edited by James F. Sennett. Grand Rapids, MI: Eerdmans, 1998.

Warranted Christian Belief. New York: Oxford University Press, 2000.

Essays in the Metaphysics of Modality, edited by Matthew Davidson. New York: Oxford University Press, 2003.

SECONDARY WORKS

Tomberlin, James, and Peter van Inwagen, eds. *Alvin Plantinga*. Dordrecht, Netherlands: D. Reidel, 1985.

Michael C. Rea (2005)

PLATO
(428/427 BCE–337/336 BCE)

The philosopher Plato was born to an aristocratic Athenian family. His father Ariston was said to be descended from the legendary King Codrus; the family of his mother Perictione was prominent in more historical times.

Dropides, an ancestor of Perictione, was a relative and friend of Solon (as Plato himself reports in the *Timaeus*, 20e). After Plato's father's death, Perictione was remarried to Pyrilampes, a political associate of Pericles and Athenian ambassador to the Persian king. Perictione's brother Charmides and her cousin Critias had a more sinister career, as members (and in Critias's case, ringleader) of the Thirty Tyrants who ruled Athens in a bloody junta, after the defeat by Sparta in 404 BCE.

Plato's family is well represented in the dialogues, perhaps to compensate for his own absence. In the *Charmides*, situated thirty years before the rule of the Thirty, Plato introduces his uncle Charmides as a promising young nobleman, under the influence of his older cousin Critias. The reference here to Charmides' family allows Plato to sing the praises of his own household, as the union of two outstanding families "than which no more noble union can be found in Athens" (*Charmides* 157e). The two families in question are those of Perictione and Pyrilampes, Plato's mother and stepfather. It is Plato's cousin Critias the tyrant (and not, as some scholars have supposed, the tyrant's grandfather) who appears again as introductory speaker in the *Timaeus* and as narrator in the unfinished *Critias*. Plato's older brothers Glaucon and Adeimantus are the chief interlocutors in the *Republic*, his stepbrother Demos is mentioned as a reigning young beauty in the *Gorgias* (481d), and his half brother Antiphon appears in the *Parmenides* as the one who preserves the memory of the philosophical conversation between Socrates, Zeno, and Parmenides. Plato had no occasion to mention his sister Potone, the mother of his nephew Speusippus who succeeded him as head of the Academy.

We are largely dependent on the autobiographical sections of the *Seventh Letter* for information about Plato's life. (The authenticity of this *Letter* is disputed, but even scholars who doubt its authenticity generally assume that the author was well informed.) The author of the *Letter* reports that Plato's relatives in the anti-democratic coup of 404 BCE invited him to join them, and that he, as an upper-class young man of twenty-three with political ambitions, was initially sympathetic; he expected these men to lead the city "from a life of injustice to a just government." But Plato observed that in a short time "they made the previous (democratic) regime look like a Golden Age" (*Epist.* VII, 324d). Thus Plato was repulsed by the behavior of Critias and the oligarchs; on the contrary, he admired the courage of Socrates in refusing to obey the tyrants' command, when they ordered him to lead a death squad against a prominent democrat.

Plato's political ambitions revived in the restored democracy after 403, but after watching the politics of Athens for ten or fifteen years he concluded that the situation was hopeless, and that "the races of mankind would not cease from evils until the class of true philosophers come to political power or the rulers of the cities practice true philosophy" (*Epist.* VII 326b). At the age of about forty, Plato then departed for the Greek cities of southern Italy and Sicily.

Sometime after his return to Athens from Syracuse (c. 387 BCE), Plato began to gather together the group of students and researchers in science, mathematics and philosophy that became known as the school of the Academy. The early fourth century saw the creation in Athens of the first fixed schools of higher education, replacing the wandering Sophists of the fifth century. Antisthenes, the follower of Socrates, and the famous orator Isocrates had both recently established their schools. Unlike these institutions, Plato's community of scholars seems to have had no formally enrolled students and no tuition fees.

We know very little about the functioning of the Academy. The physical basis was a small estate with a garden owned by Plato, in the suburban neighborhood named after a park and gymnasium dedicated to the hero Academos. Formal instruction was probably offered in the gymnasium; the communal meals, or *syssitia*, presumably took place in Plato's villa. We happen to know of one public lecture given by Plato "On the Good." There is no evidence for a curriculum in mathematics and dialectic modeled on the studies of the guardians in *Republic* VII, as some scholars have supposed. There is in fact no evidence for any fixed curriculum. The only contemporary report (other than veiled attacks from Isocrates as head of the rival school) consists of quotations from Attic comedy, which make fun of the haughty manners and elegant dress of intellectuals from the Academy, and of their elaborate pedantry in the botanical classification of a pumpkin.

The intellectual caliber of the school is attested by the quality of its associates: on the one hand, Aristotle, who worked in the Academy for twenty years before Plato's death, and on the other hand Eudoxus, a great mathematician and astronomer, who seems to have maintained close contact with the school over many years, despite philosophical disagreement with Plato on central issues. Clearly, the members of the Academy were as much concerned with ethics and politics as with science and theoretical philosophy; the school is sometimes represented as a training program for statesmen. Plato's personal prestige is reflected in Aristotle's elegy to Friendship, where Plato is called "a man whom the bad do not even have the right to praise, who alone or who first among mortals clearly showed, in his own life as in his teachings, that to become good is also to become happy (*eudaimôn*)."

Plato's quiet life in the Academy was interrupted in 367 and 361 by two invited voyages to the court of Dionysius II in Syracuse. Plato was persuaded to accept the invitation by his close friend Dion, the uncle of the tyrant, whom Plato had converted to philosophy on his first visit to Syracuse some twenty years earlier. Since the young Dionysius displayed a passion for philosophy, Plato was unwilling to reject this opportunity to influence the politics of the most powerful Greek city of the time. He proved quite ineffective in the intrigues of the Syracusan court, and was barely able to escape safely from his final visit to Dionysius in 360 BCE at the age of sixty-eight. The *Seventh Epistle* presents a detailed account of the Syracusan adventure from Plato's point of view. It ended in disaster both for Plato and for Sicily. After driving the tyrant out of Syracuse, Dion himself was murdered in 353 BCE. Plato, at seventy-five, responded with an elegy on the death of Dion, ending with the verse "Dion, you who once drove my heart mad with *erôs*."

WRITINGS

Of the thirty-six dialogues preserved in the traditional canon (presumably as edited by Thrasyllus in the first century CE), some twenty-six or twenty-seven are generally recognized as the work of Plato. (The authenticity of the *Hippias Major* is contested; some scholars would also defend the *First Alcibiades* and perhaps a few others usually regarded as spurious.) The traditional corpus includes thirteen *Epistles*, most of them now recognized as spurious. Two or three of the *Epistles* have some claim to be authentic; the most important of these, for both philosophical and biographical reasons, is *Epistle* VII.

The only reliable guide to the chronology of the dialogues is the division into three stylistic groups, established by Campbell and Ritter in the late nineteenth century.

Group I: *Apology, Charmides, Crito, Cratylus, Euthydemus, Euthyphro, Gorgias,* [*Hippias Major*], *Hippias Minor, Ion, Laches, Lysis, Menexenus, Meno, Phaedo, Protagoras, Symposium*

Group II: *Republic, Phaedrus, Parmenides, Theaetetus*

Group III: *Sophist-Statesman, Philebus, Timaeus-Critias, Laws*

Group III was identified first (as the "late group") on the basis of several independent studies. These six dialogues are marked by very strong stylistic peculiarities typical of the *Laws*, which we know to have been written towards the end of Plato's life. Group II includes dialogues stylistically akin to the *Republic*, which show relatively few distinctive features of Plato's late style. Group I is the default class, the remaining sixteen or seventeen dialogues, from the *Apology* to the *Symposium* and *Phaedo*, in which Plato's brilliant conversational style bears none of the distinctive marks of the late period.

This chronological division into three groups is only partially in agreement with a conventional division of Plato's dialogues into early, middle, and late. The dialogues of Group III are all truly "late." (There was a brief attempt to date the *Timaeus* earlier for philosophical reasons, but that attempt has generally been recognized as a failure. The style of the *Timaeus* was from the beginning recognized as belonging to the latest period.) But the usual classification of "middle" dialogues ignores chronology altogether. It combines two dialogues of Group II (*Republic, Phaedrus*) with two from Group I (*Symposium, Phaedo*) solely on grounds of philosophical content. Despite their stylistic differences, all four works present the classical version of Plato's doctrine of Forms. A popular view of Plato's development locates these dialogues in a "middle period," divided on the one hand from the more "Socratic" dialogues of an earlier period, and, on the other hand, from the attack on the theory of Forms in the *Parmenides* and hence from the more critical philosophy of the *Theaetetus* and *Sophist*. This tripartite division is not supported by the Campbell-Ritter chronology of the three groups, since stylistically the *Parmenides* and *Theaetetus* are not later than the *Republic*. The notion of a "Socratic" period depends upon a particular interpretation of the role of Socrates in the earlier dialogues.

SOCRATES

The figure of Socrates appears in every Platonic dialogue except the *Laws*, and he is the chief speaker in all but five. This raises two difficult problems for interpreting Plato's work. How far does Socrates speak for Plato? And what is the relation between the Socrates of Plato's dialogues and the historical figure? We deal here with the historical question.

Since Socrates wrote nothing, we are entirely dependent on other writers for knowledge of his thought. The traditional attitude of historians has been to rely on the picture of Socrates presented in Plato's earlier dialogues, supplemented or confirmed by information from Xenophon and Aristotle. The result has been to take dialogues such as the *Laches*, *Euthyphro*, and *Protagoras* as providing a historical account of Socrates, as a moral philosopher who identifies virtue with knowledge, denies the reality of *akrasia* (weakness of will), and systematically pursues definitions of the moral virtues. In these "Socratic" dialogues Plato is thought to be closely following the thought and methodology of his master. On this view, Plato will only gradually develop his own philosophy, first with the doctrine of recollection in the *Meno* and then with the theory of Forms in the *Symposium* and *Phaedo*. This view can be supported by evidence from Aristotle, whose references to Socrates match the picture given in these "early" dialogues.

This account of Socrates has been treated with skepticism in much recent scholarship, because of a realization (pioneered by Gigon but developed by others) that the Socratic literature is a form of fiction rather than of historical biography. This fictional status is particularly clear in the remains of Socratic dialogues by other authors, such as Aeschines or Phaedo, but also in Xenophon's *Symposium* and in Platonic dialogues such as the *Menexenus*. Plato's portrait of Socrates is no doubt generally faithful to the moral character of the man as he saw him. But in regard to details of Socratic philosophy and argumentation, Plato would be at least as free as a modern novelist would be in dealing with historical figures. Furthermore, in the view of skeptical critics, Aristotle cannot serve as a reliable witness. He arrived in Athens as a youth more than thirty years after Socrates' death, and his picture of Socrates can be explained as his own inference from the Platonic dialogues. Judged as a historian of philosophy, Aristotle has serious faults. He generally sees his predecessors through the prism of his own scheme, and his account of the development of Plato's thought is particularly suspect. Aristotle's report of Cratylus's early influence on Plato is scarcely compatible with Plato's own portrait of Cratylus in the dialogue of that name; and Aristotle's claim that Plato's Theory of Forms was derived from the Pythagoreans is not supported by his own account of Pythagorean doctrine. Aristotle never mentions Plato's much more profound debt to Parmenides' concept of Being.

For all these reasons, a critical reader may well doubt that we have any reliable information about the philosophy of Socrates. It is perhaps in Plato's *Apology* that we can best catch a glimpse of the historical Socrates. The *Apology* is a special case among Plato's writings, since it is not a fictitious dialogue but a courtroom speech, the representation of a public event at which Plato claims to have been present. From this and other sources we can form a vivid picture of Socrates' powerful personality, his strong moral character, and his remarkable skill in elenchus, that is, in arguing his interlocutors into contradiction. But beyond the firm refusal to act unjustly and the conception of virtue (*aretê*) as care of one's self, or care of one's soul, our historical knowledge of Socrates' philosophical views seems to be limited to a handful of moral paradoxes: that no one does wrong voluntarily, that it is better to suffer than to do wrong, that virtue is knowledge, and that no evil can happen to a good man. In order to put philosophical flesh on this skeleton of doctrine, we must turn to the dialogues. But then we can no longer distinguish what derives from Plato's memory of the historical Socrates from what has its source in Plato's own artistic and philosophical imagination.

THE FIRST DIALOGUES: *APOLOGY*, *CRITO*, *ION*, *HIPPIAS MINOR*, *GORGIAS*

Although we do not know the chronological order of the dialogues in Group I, it is natural to begin with the two dialogues directly concerned with Socrates' trial and death, *Apology* and *Crito*, and with two other very short dialogues, *Ion* and *Hippias Minor*. We connect with this group a much more substantial work, *Gorgias*, which many scholars would put later. These five dialogues serve to illustrate the wide range of Plato's philosophical concerns, while at the same time revealing no trace of the metaphysics and epistemology that we recognize as distinctly Platonic.

Although it may have been written ten or twelve years after Socrates' death, the *Gorgias* presents a systematic exposition of Socratic moral doctrine and a strong defense of this view against anti-moralist attack. The *Gorgias* repeatedly recalls Socrates' trial and matches it with a judgment myth, in which the souls of those who are truly guilty of injustice will be punished. In the *Crito*, Socrates had formulated as his fundamental moral principle that one should never act unjustly, never return a wrong for a wrong. Socrates is prepared to die for this principle, and is unwilling to save his life by an unjust escape from prison. "It is not living that is of chief importance, but living well, and that is living honorably and justly" (*Crito* 48b). Crito agrees. Socrates recognizes that, between those who accept and those who reject these principles, "there is no common basis for discussion, no *koinê boulê*, but they must despise one another's views" (49d). In the *Gorgias* there is no such agreement, and the principle of justice is itself at stake. The Greek conception of justice (dikaiosunê) is broad enough to cover morality generally, understood as respect for the rights of others. (Thus Aristotle defines "justice" as virtue in regard to others.) Socrates in the *Gorgias* has much the same task as later in the *Republic*: to defend the principle of morality against opponents who endorse the ruthless pursuit of wealth and power. The question, "Why be moral?" is posed here in dramatic form, against the background of Socrates' own fate as a martyr for moral principle.

The Socratic elenchus as practiced in the *Gorgias* is able to show that the anti-moral positions of Polus and Callicles are basically incoherent, but Socrates is less successful in his positive defense of the principle of morality. He relies here on an analogy between virtue or moral integrity, as an internal order of the soul, and the role of order and harmony in other domains: in the health of the body, in the order of the cosmos, and in the successful products of the arts. But an argument from analogy has its limitations. What is lacking here is a positive psychological theory (like the tripartite theory of the *Republic*) as the basis for a constructive argument in support of the conception of virtue as the harmony and health of the soul.

The most important positive doctrine of the *Gorgias* is the claim that all actions are done "for the sake of the good," that is, for a goal or *telos* that the agent perceives as good (467c–468b). This remains the fundamental axiom in action theory for both Plato and Aristotle; it reappears in the *Republic* as the supreme Form of the Good, "which every soul pursues, and for the sake of which it performs all its actions" (*Rep.* 505d 11). In the argument for this principle in the *Gorgias*, Plato deliberately blurs the distinction between good-for-the-agent and intrinsically or absolutely good. Polus will acknowledge that what people really want is something good, namely good for them or in their interest, but he denies that this is necessarily the honorable or moral thing to do (*to kalon*). Plato's point will be that moral knowledge consists precisely in the recognition that what is good absolutely (i.e., virtue) is also good for you, so that it is in your interest to be virtuous. This is Plato's reading of the Socratic paradox that no one is voluntarily unjust.

The *Gorgias* thus expounds, both by paradox and by systematic argument, the principles of Socratic moral philosophy as exemplified in the *Apology* and *Crito*. By contrast, in the *Hippias Minor* we find Socrates arguing for a more perverse paradox, namely, for the blatantly false proposition that anyone who commits unjust and dishonorable actions *voluntarily* is a better person than the one who does such actions unintentionally. The inter-

locutor is unconvinced, and we can only wonder what point Socrates is supposed to be making. This is probably an indirect way of calling attention to the more authentic Socratic claim that in fact no one does such actions voluntarily. But why not? Why does the analogy fail with arithmetic, for example, where the good mathematician makes mistakes on purpose, whereas the bad mathematician does so unintentionally? If moral virtue is a form of knowledge, why is it not to be understood on the model of the arts and sciences? The implicit Platonic answer seems to point to the role of intentions (the verb *boulesthai*, "to want," is systematically repeated at 366b–367a), and thus to the universal desire (*boulêsis*) for the good recognized in the *Gorgias*. Whatever the implied answer to this paradox may be, the *Hippias Minor* demonstrates Plato's early preoccupation with the problem of moral knowledge.

Finally, in the *Ion* Plato develops a different Socratic theme concerning knowledge: the refutation of knowledge claims on the part of the poets (*Apology* 22b). Instead of attacking the poets directly, Plato begins with their representative, the *rhapsode* or performer. Socrates' argument in the *Ion* is a direct refutation only of the claim to knowledge or art (*technê*) on the part of the rhapsode, but the positive theory of poetic inspiration applies to the poet as well. According to this theory, the power of poetry comes from the Muse and is transmitted via the poet to the rhapsode, like the attractive power that is transmitted from the magnet stone via iron rings to other pieces of iron. Hence neither the poet nor the rhapsode needs to understand what is going on. Their divine inspiration is non-cognitive: being possessed by a god, they are out of their mind.

The *Ion* thus presents Plato's first move in the ancient quarrel between philosophy and poetry, a quarrel that will be dramatically represented in the confrontation between Socrates and the poets in the *Symposium* and will assume canonical form in the criticism of poetry in the *Republic*. The *Ion* is indirectly invoked in the last scene of the *Symposium*, since it provides us with the argument that the narrator has forgotten. In this final episode Socrates is proving to Agathon and Aristophanes, a tragic and a comic poet, that anyone who knows how to compose tragedy by art (*technê*) will know how to compose comedy as well (223d). The needed premise is given by a proposition of the *Ion*, namely, that anyone who possesses the relevant knowledge (*technê*) will be able to deal with poetry as a whole, since it is a single art (532c). With a slight revision, Socrates' argument against Ion will serve as well against Agathon and Aristophanes. In contrast with the *Republic*, where Plato criticizes poetry first on moral grounds (in Book 3), and then on principles of ontology (in Book 10), in the *Ion* and *Apology* Plato's criticism is more Socratic, rejecting the claims of poetry to be recognized as a kind of knowledge. It is thus aimed directly against the traditional conception of poets as *sophoi* or sages, sources of wisdom. For Plato the quarrel between philosophy and poetry is ultimately a culture war, a competition for the moral leadership of Greek society.

In the course of his attack on poetry in the *Ion*, Plato introduces the important epistemological principle of a one-to-one mapping between a *technê* and its object: "necessarily, the same art will know the same subject matter, and if the art is different, it will know a different subject" (538a). This correlation between a form of cognition and a definite content or subject matter appears frequently in other dialogues (for example *Gorgias* 464b, *Charmides* 171a). In the *Republic* this principle is invoked to show that knowledge and opinion must have different ontological objects (V, 478a); in the *Timaeus* a similar principle is implied as premise in an argument for positing Forms (51d). Problematic in its particular applications, this principle reflects Plato's fundamental realism in epistemology. Truth in cognition reflects reality in the object known: "What *is* completely is completely knowable; what is not in any respect is unknowable in every respect" (*Rep.* 477a 3).

DEFINITION AND APORIA: *LACHES*, *CHARMIDES*, *EUTHYPHRO*, *PROTAGORAS*

On a traditional view, these four dialogues provide something like a philosophical portrait of the historical Socrates: pursuing the topic of moral virtue, seeking definitions of the virtues (courage in *Laches*, temperance in *Charmides*, piety in *Euthyphro*), identifying virtue as a kind of knowledge, and denying the reality of *akrasia*. Most descriptions of the philosophy of Socrates are based upon the evidence of these dialogues, as supported by Aristotle's account. But if Aristotle's account of Socrates is derived from his own reading of these dialogues, his testimony is of no independent historical value. In at least one case Aristotle's report can be seen to be directly dependent on a Platonic dialogue, since for the Socratic denial of *akrasia* he quotes the *Protagoras* verbatim (*N.E.* VII.2, 1145b 24, citing *Prot.* 352c 1).

On the fictional view of the dialogues proposed above, what we have in the *Protagoras* and the dialogues of definition is not documentary evidence for the historical Socrates but rather Plato pursuing Socratic themes in his own way, and with his own philosophical goals in view. Thus the *Laches* and the *Euthyphro* offer a subtle lesson in the logic of definition, which will be completed in the *Meno*. And in the *Protagoras* we find something entirely new and problematic: a hedonistic anticipation of rational choice theory that is unparalleled in other dialogues.

Whatever Socrates' own concern with definition may have been (and there is no trace of this either in the *Apology* or the *Crito*, nor in the *Ion* and *Hippias Minor*), the treatment of definition in the *Laches-Charmides-Euthyphro-Meno* has a systematic quality and an epistemic orientation that is distinctly Platonic. Unlike the more straightforward search for a definition of rhetoric in the *Gorgias*, which does not raise epistemological issues but leads instead to a formula acceptable to all parties, the attempt to define virtues in these four dialogues of definition is formally aporetic and regularly unsuccessful. Although the search for a definition always fails, in two cases it points incidentally to an account of virtue as the knowledge of good and bad (*Laches* 198c–199e, *Charmides* 174b–e). In the *Protagoras* (as also in *Meno* and *Euthydemus*) virtue is again identified with some kind of knowledge.

The teachability of virtue is a topic debated at length in the *Protagoras* and *Meno*, and raised also in the *Laches* for the special case of courage. The claim of teachability seems to stand or fall with the conception of virtue as knowledge. The *Meno* makes explicit the principle implied at the end of the *Protagoras*: Virtue is teachable if and only if virtue is a kind of knowledge (*Meno* 87b). This assumption reflects the Greek sense that *technê* and teaching go together. But this principle raises the problem posed in the *Hippias Minor*: If virtue is a kind of knowledge, how is it different from other, more professional forms of *technê*? This question is briefly discussed at the beginning of the *Protagoras*: The young Hippocrates wants to study with Protagoras not for professional reasons, in order to become a sophist, but for liberal education, the training appropriate for a free man and citizen (312ab). This leaves open the question of what such training should consist in. We must wait for the *Republic* to get a definite answer to the question of the teachability of virtue. The *Protagoras* and *Meno* present arguments for both sides of the question (see below).

The dialogues of definition direct us to the theory of knowledge by two routes: first, by the suggestion that virtue, the target of definition, is itself a kind of knowledge. And second, by the claim that knowledge as such depends on knowledge of essences. Thus in the *Laches*, where the two generals Laches and Nicias are being consulted as experts on training in virtue, the request for a definition is proposed as a test of their expertise: "if we know *what virtue is*, we should be able to say *what it is*" (190c). For if we did not know at all what virtue is, how could we advise anyone how to acquire it? (190b). Similarly, if Charmides is temperate, he should have some notion of what temperance is (*Charmides* 159a). In the *Meno* this type of question is justified by the general principle of priority of definition: One cannot know anything whatsoever about X unless one knows what X is (*Meno* 71b). We will return to this principle below, in discussing the *Meno*.

It is in the *Euthyphro* that the notion of essence or whatness, what X is, is most fully articulated as the object to be captured in a definition. To define piety one must specify something quite general, for the pious is "the same as itself in every action... similar to itself and having some one character (*idea*)" (*Euthyphro* 5d). The definiens must be not only coextensive with the definiendum but explanatory of it; necessary and sufficient conditions are not enough for a Platonic definition. Socrates wants to find "the very feature (*auto to eidos*) by which all pious things are pious." Only then will he be able to "look to this character (*idea*) and use it as a model (*paradeigma*), so that when any action is of this sort I will say that it is pious, and when it is not of this kind I will say that it is not pious" (6e). The definition offered by Euthyphro ("piety is what is loved by the gods") turns out to fail this test; it is a proprium, an attribute uniquely true of piety, but not an explanatory essence. Socrates complains to Euthyphro: "When you were asked *what the pious is*, you were not willing to reveal to me its essence (*ousia*, literally its being or is-ness), but you gave me instead an attribute (*pathos*), saying that it belongs to the pious to be loved by all the gods" (11a).

The distinction between an essence and an accidental attribute, so fundamental for Aristotle's philosophy, is here sharply delineated for the first time, but without clear metaphysical implications. In the dialogues of definition, including the *Meno*, essences are presented as logical or epistemological concepts, as items corresponding to a definition, an item true of all the cases, and hence able to serve as a criterion for the use of a term, but without any definite ontological interpretation. Despite the terminology of *eidos* and *idea*, which in later dialogues will serve to designate the Forms of classical Platonic theory, the essences of the *Euthyphro* and *Meno* are not articulated as structures in the nature of things, neither as

immanent nor as transcendent forms. In this situation the reader is free to assume either that the author of these dialogues has not yet decided on an ontological interpretation for his definienda, or that he has chosen to reserve this task for other dialogues, such as the *Symposium* and the *Phaedo*.

TRANSITIONAL DIALOGUES? *LYSIS*, *EUTHYDEMUS*, AND *MENO*

These three dialogues present or allude to typical Platonic themes in epistemology and metaphysics, but without any definite formulation of what will be the standard theory of the *Phaedo* and *Republic*. Hence they are sometimes described as "transitional." It is again left to the reader to regard these statements either as deliberately incomplete or as reflecting Plato's own indecision.

Lysis and *Euthydemus* form with *Charmides* a literary group of dialogues with similar introductory episodes, presenting a charming school scene in which Socrates converses with handsome boys or adolescents. (The setting of the *Laches* is comparable, but in that dialogue Socrates converses only with the fathers and not with the boys.) The question of education is implicitly raised by the setting in each case, and discussed at length in the *Euthydemus* and *Meno*. Aside from the literary setting and the general theme of education, in other respects these three "transitional" dialogues are very different from one another.

The *Lysis* is concerned with the topic of friendship and love, a topic discussed below in connection with the *Symposium* and *Phaedrus*. There are a number of parallels between the *Lysis* and *Symposium*), the most striking of which is the concept of a final object of love for the sake of which everything else is loved. In seeking to explain in the *Lysis* why anything is dear or desirable (*philon*), Socrates suggests that one thing is dear for the sake of another, as a doctor is desirable for the sake of health, but that such a regress cannot go on indefinitely: "we must either give up or come to some starting-point (*archê*), which will no longer refer to some other dear, but we will come to "that which is primarily dear" (*prôton philon*), for the sake of which we say that all other things are dear ... This is what is truly dear; the other dear things are like its images" (*Lysis* 219c 5–d5). Since the form of the argument resembles Aristotle's thesis (in N.E. I.7) that happiness is the supreme good, for the sake of which everything else is good, some scholars have used this parallel to interpret the Lysis passage as a reference to happiness. But there is nothing in the text to justify this interpretation. On the contrary, the formula "for the sake of which" refers to the good in passages cited above from the *Gorgias* and *Republic* (section IV). Furthermore, the context in the *Lysis* identifies the "dear" (*philon*) as the good and the beautiful (216c 6–d2). Above all, the formula "that which is primarily dear" (*ekeino ho esti prôton philon*) is a close approximation to the standard terminology for the Forms in other dialogues, and specifically for the Form of Beauty in the *Symposium* (*auto ho esti kalon* 211d 1). This anticipation of the technical language for Forms, together with the generally quite abstract form of the arguments about friendship, sets the *Lysis* apart from more typical "early Socratic" dialogues such as the *Laches* or the *Euthyphro*.

The *Euthydemus* is equally non-standard for other reasons. Plato presents an entertaining satire on two elderly sophists, the brothers Euthydemus and Dionysodorus, who claim to teach virtue by a shortcut method, and who display their art by confounding the student with a rapid series of fallacious arguments. Their art of unscrupulous refutation, or eristic, is designed to provide the sharpest possible contrast with the genuine Socratic elenchus, represented here not by the usual refutation but by a constructive protreptic in which Socrates argues that wisdom is the only good, ignorance the only evil, and hence that in order to enjoy happiness and a good life (*eu prattein*) one must pursue wisdom and knowledge.

Both Socrates' protreptic and several of the Sophists' refutations contain enigmatic allusions to Platonic doctrines presented in other dialogues. In the most surprising of these allusive passages, the young Clinias compares mathematicians to hunters because they must turn over their findings to someone else. Just as hunters turn over their catch to cooks, who know how to make good use of it, mathematicians, if they are wise, will turn over their discoveries about reality (*ta onta*) to dialecticians (*hoi dialektikoi*) to make use of (*Euthydemus* 209c). This subordination of mathematics to dialect is scarcely intelligible without the epistemology of Books VI and VII of the *Republic*. But this is not the only case where the *Euthydemus* anticipates doctrines to be developed in later dialogues, including an allusion to recollection (296d 1) and a hint that the relativism of Protagoras may be self-refuting. (Compare *Euthydemus* 286c 2–4 with the *peritropê* argument of *Theaetetus* 170a–171c.) There is also a rough version of the principle of non-contradiction (293b 8–d 1), and a kind of caricature of the problem of the presence of "the beautiful itself" in the many beautiful things (300e–301a). The *Euthydemus* is thus one of the most comical and also one of the most puzzling of all the dialogues.

MENO AND RECOLLECTION

The *Meno* introduces the doctrine of recollection, which plays an important role in two later dialogues, the *Phaedo* and *Phaedrus*. Like the sixteenth-century theory of innate ideas which it inspired, Plato's doctrine of recollection is an antecedent both for the Kantian notion of a priori knowledge and for contemporary theories of innatism in psychology. The fundamental thesis of the Platonic doctrine is that there is something in the nature of the human mind that predisposes it to grasp the nature of reality: "the truth of beings (*ta onta*) is forever in our psyche" (*Meno* 86b 1). The supernatural form this doctrine takes in Plato is determined by its association with the Pythagorean doctrine of transmigration, which implies a previous existence for the human soul. The *Phaedrus* give a mythical account of prenatal experience, in which human souls travel with the gods outside the heavens, to a vision of ultimate reality described in terms of the Platonic theory of Forms. It is our recollection of this prenatal vision of transcendent Beauty that explains the phenomenon of falling in love.

In the *Phaedo* as well recollection takes as its object the eternal Forms, illustrated in this dialogue by the Equal itself, as distinct from sensible equals. This choice of the Form of Equality in the *Phaedo* connects recollection with mathematics, as in the *Meno*, where recollection is illustrated by the geometry lesson to an uneducated slave boy. (The boy is led by a series of questions to see, first, that he is unable to double a square by numerical additions to the side, and then to recognize the solution when Socrates draws the diagonal.) But it is not only mathematical concepts but conceptual thought generally that is involved in recollection. As the *Phaedrus* insists, a human soul must be able "to understand what is said according to a form (*eidos*), passing from many sense perceptions to a unity gathered together by rational thought. And this is recollection of what our soul once saw when it traveled together with a god and looked beyond what we now call reality and was able to rise up into the really Real" (*Phaedrus* 249bc). The myth of the *Phaedrus* thus represents Plato's most brilliant expression of the classical Greek view that reason (*nous*), the cognitive capacity to understand the world, constitutes the immortal, godlike element in the human psyche.

The *Meno* presents a simpler version of the doctrine, without any explicit reference to the theory of Forms. Recollection is introduced in response to Meno's paradox about learning something new, or seeking for something you do not know. Meno in turn is responding to the principle of "Priority of Definition," which claims that you cannot know anything about X unless you know "what X is." How then do we ever get started? Recollection answers that what we learn is not new; we only need to be reminded. In the fuller doctrine formulated in the *Phaedo* and *Phaedrus*, it is not Socratic questioning but sense perception that serves to trigger a conceptual understanding (of equality, beauty, and the like) that is provided by the mind from its innate resources.

The "transitional" status of the *Meno* is indicated not only by the fact that it presents the simplest version of recollection, but also by tentative statements of other themes that are more fully developed in the *Phaedo* and *Republic*: the distinction between knowledge and opinion, the method of hypothesis, and two levels of virtue, one dependent on right opinion and the other on knowledge (*Meno* 99a–100a).

PLATO'S THEORY OF ERÔS

Love is a central topic in three Platonic dialogues (*Lysis, Symposium, Phaedrus*); it also plays an important role in the moral psychology of the *Phaedo* and *Republic*. The fundamental idea is expressed symbolically in Plato's etymological reading of *philo-sophia* as love of wisdom or passion for knowledge (*Phaedo* 66e2, 68a). In the psychological theory of the *Republic*, all three parts of the soul are characterized as distinct forms of love: desire for learning (*to philomathes*), desire for honor, desire for pleasure and wealth. Thus for the rational part the object of desire is "to know the truth" (581b). Like the religious mystics, Plato makes use of the language of sexuality to express philosophical passion: the true lover of knowledge will not be relieved of his pangs of *erôs* "until he grasps the nature of each Form with the appropriate part of the soul, and clinging to and mingling with the truly real, he begets truth and understanding (*nous*)" (490b). Plato anticipates the Freudian notion of sublimation in his account of the channeling of desire (485d); the notion of unconscious Oedipal desires is recognized in his description of criminal dreams (571c–d). There is also a superficial analogy between Plato's tripartite psychology and the Freudian trio of ego, superego, and id, but the second principle is in fact quite different in each case. Plato's *thumos* or "spirit" is a principle of anger, pride, and self-assertion, in contrast to the guilt-producing and self-punishing aspects of the Freudian superego. What the two psychological theories have in common is the understanding of psychic conflict in terms of deep divisions within the soul.

Plato's theory of *erôs* has been criticized for devaluing the love for an individual person in favor of love for an abstract principle like the Forms. Thus in the ladder-of-love passage in the *Symposium*, the lover who follows Diotima's instructions will leave behind his initial passion for an individual beauty in order to rise to more spiritual beauties and finally to the Beautiful itself. Even in the *Phaedrus*, where the philosophical lovers assist one another in growing the wings of their souls and escape together from the cycle of rebirth, their real love is for the Form of Beauty. But it is misleading to evaluate the Platonic conception of *erôs* as if it were a contribution to the modern theory of love. Plato's concern with interpersonal love is better illustrated by his treatment of friendship (*philia*), as depicted in the case of the two boys Lysis and Menexenus in the *Lysis*. So it is the *Lysis* that provides Aristotle with the starting point for his own theory of friendship. The philosophical importance of *erôs* for Plato lies not in its role as a relation between persons but rather in its function as the energy driving us to pursue what we take to be good (or good-and-beautiful) and hence, when properly enlightened, to pursue the Good itself. Rightly directed, *erôs* is *philo-sophia*, the passion for wisdom. Only wisdom can recognize the true nature of the Good, "which every soul pursues and for the sake of which it performs all its actions" (*Rep.* VI, 505d11). It is in this sense, as knowledge of the good, that wisdom is equivalent to virtue, since it guarantees that the *erôs* of the wise will be directed to what is objectively good. The emotional drive in question is, however, intrinsically ambivalent; in the absence of wisdom, *erôs* can also become the criminal passion that impels the tyrant to psychological destruction in *Republic* Book IX.

VIRTUE AND KNOWLEDGE: PLATO'S MORAL PSYCHOLOGY

Many scholars have followed Aristotle in holding that Socrates identified virtue with wisdom and thus ignored the power of irrational emotion to influence action. The conception of virtue as a form of knowledge is represented in a number of dialogues. The neglect or denial of irrational emotion is most extreme in the *Protagoras*, where Socrates interprets *akrasia* as an error in measuring future pleasures and pains. What is generally understood as being overcome by passion is there explained as an intellectual mistake. No other Platonic text explicitly denies the reality of *akrasia*. But several passages in the *Gorgias* and *Meno* have been taken to imply this, by suggesting that everyone desires good things, and hence that virtue consists only in the knowledge of good and bad, that is, in the ability to choose the goal of action correctly.

Nowhere, however, does either Plato or Socrates maintain that *all* desires are desires for the good. On the contrary, the *Gorgias* implicitly distinguishes between *boulesthai* as desire for good things and *epithumia* as desire for pleasure (so explicitly at *Charmides* 167e; this distinction between rational desire or *boulêsis* and non-rational desire or *epithumia* becomes fixed in Aristotelian terminology). The doctrine that virtue is a kind of knowledge can be understood as a paradoxical exaggeration, designed to focus attention on the practical importance of a correct conception of the good, and hence on the value of the Socratic elenchus in leading interlocutors to recognize their own ignorance. But in the face of this exclusive focus on moral knowledge, the existence of *akrasia* (that is, of people acting against their better judgment) is a challenge. The last section of the *Protagoras* was written in response to this challenge. But some readers will doubt that either Plato or Socrates ever held the extreme view presented in this dialogue, namely, that the intellect is all-powerful in the control of human action, so that *akrasia* is simply an error of judgment and vice is always due to ignorance.

What is clear, in any case, is that if Plato ever held such an intellectualist view, he abandoned it in the *Republic*. The exposition of the tripartite psychology includes an unmistakable description of *akrasia* in the story of *Leontius* (who is disgusted at his own weakness in "being overcome by the desire" to gaze at corpses, *Republic* 440a 1). In this tripartite theory, two out of three psychic principles represent emotional drives that can conflict with, and sometimes overcome, the rational judgment of the *logistikon* (the calculating part) as to what is best to do. These two principles are the *thumos*, or "spirit" of anger and pride, and the *epithumêtikon* of animal appetite—hunger, thirst, and sexual desire. The division into three parts rests upon a careful distinction between sheer desire, for example thirst as desire to drink, and the rational desire for something good, as desire for a good drink. The aim of Plato's tripartite division is precisely to account for the phenomena of psychic conflict, in this case between the desire of a thirsty man to drink and his rational judgment that the water is not good to drink.

On the basis of this division into three parts of the soul, each with its characteristic desire, Plato provides a psychological definition of the virtues in terms of the harmonious working together of all three parts. It is the function of the rational part (*logistikon*) to rule over the others in deciding what is the best thing to do; and wisdom is the excellence of this part in judging well. Courage is the excellence of the spirited part, maintaining its loy-alty to the commands of reason and law in the face of danger and temptation. The other virtues consist in cooperation, that is, in willing obedience to the commands of the rational part. Hence virtue can be defined as psychic harmony, and vice defined as psychic disorder or *stasis*, civil war between the parts of the soul.

By this assimilation of virtue to psychological health, vice to psychological disorder, Plato formulates his first answer to the challenge to morality (formulated by Thrasymachus in Book I, reformulated by Glaucon and Adeimantus in Book II). But the *Republic* actually represents two different views of psychic disorder. In Book IV the vices are described in terms of disobedience or revolt on the part of the irrational emotions; in this context, there is no distinction to be drawn between vice and *akrasia*, conceived as unruly behavior by the lower parts. (This is also the picture of vice presented by the behavior of the disobedient horse in the *Phaedrus* myth.) In Books VII and IX, on the other hand, the irrational desires are presented not as disobedient subjects but as successful rebels, who have driven reason from the throne and taken its place as rulers in the acropolis of the soul (*Rep.* 553d, 560b–d). The *logistikon* now appears as their subject, carrying out their commands. Thus we have in Books VII–IX a conception of vice represented not as *akrasia*, not as a failure of reason to control the emotions, but rather as moral ignorance, that is, a mistaken conception of the good (as in Aristotle's distinction between vice and *akrasia*).

This Platonic distinction between two conceptions of vice, only one of which corresponds to *akrasia*, is developed in different ways in several later dialogues. Thus the *Sophist* (228a–229a) distinguishes moral ignorance from *ponêria*, vice as a kind of disease; the former is to be treated by instruction, the latter by punishment. The *Timaeus* 86b–e proposes a similar distinction between moral ignorance and madness due to excessive pleasures and pains; the latter is caused by a disordered condition of the body. The Socratic paradox will be maintained for both kinds of vice, since the loss of self-control from bodily causes can be seen as involuntary (*Tim.* 86e 3). The connection of the non-rational desires with the body rather than with the soul proper, hinted at in the *Phaedo* and in *Republic*, is most systematically developed in the *Timaeus* (42a–e), where the non-rational soul is created by the lesser gods in connection with their creation of the body.

POLITICAL CONSTRUCTION: FROM THE *REPUBLIC* TO THE *LAWS*

The tripartite psychology of the *Republic* has an exact parallel in the tripartite social structure of the envisaged polis. Corresponding to reason, spirit and appetite are the three classes of rulers, soldiers, and producers (the latter class consisting of farmers and craftsmen). Scholars have suggested that the psychic tripartition is an artifact of this parallelism, and that Plato's moral psychology would more properly take the form of a bipartition into reason and emotion, as in Aristotle's *Nicomachean Ethics* (I.13) and in modern theories of action based on belief and desire. (Plato actually flirts with such a bipartite psychology in Socrates' first speech in the *Phaedrus* 237d–e). However, Plato remains loyal to the tripartite psychology in non-political settings as well (in Socrates' second speech in the *Phaedrus*, and in the *Timaeus*). There is a theoretical advantage to recognizing more than one type of non-rational emotions, some of which are more amenable than others to rational control.

It is essential to the scheme of the *Republic* that the city is conceived as a great organism, just as the psyche is conceived as a micro-community. Unity and cohesion are fundamental principles of excellence for the city as much as for the individual. Plato's political aim, the greatest good for the city, is for the citizens to share one another's joys and sorrows with a unanimity like that of the parts of a human body, where the whole person suffers if a single part is in pain (V, 462a–e). But this organic unity can be achieved only on the basis of a functional division of labor between the three social classes. Thus the political definition of justice in terms of each group doing its proper job (in Book IV) is prefigured by the initial division of labor through which the city comes into being (in Book II). The first society arises from the mutual need of individuals for one another: one to grow food, one to build houses, one to make clothes. Hence the fundamental principle of specialization: one person, one work.

Instead of a social contract theory, in which civil society is conceived as an artifact designed to bring people out of the state of nature, Plato claims to find a natural basis for social life in reciprocal need and the advantages of cooperation (II, 369–370). He thus sees human beings as by nature friendly and cooperative, in deliberate contrast to the Hobbesian view of human nature presented by Glaucon in the ring of Gyges story earlier in the same book (II, 358e–362c). Since the division of labor is to the advantage of all in the political as well as in the economic sphere, the city of the *Republic* will have a natural cohesion that is absent from the historical cities of Greece, which are (as Socrates observes in a moment of Marxian insight) really two cities, the city of the rich and the city of the poor (IV, 422e–423a). This pathological split will be avoided in Plato's city, because there the ruling classes will have no private property, no money, and no nuclear family to generate selfish preferences. The needs of the rulers will be provided for by the farmers and craftsmen, who alone will have private belongings and wealth. Thus the ideal city will radically separate economic power from political power; the rulers, who alone possess the latter, will be systematically excluded from the former.

The political structure of the *Republic* is built up in successive stages, beginning with cooperation and division of labor, then the division into three classes, followed by three culminating waves of paradox in Book V. The first wave is the principle of equal education and access to political power for gifted women; the second wave is the community of wives and children, in other words, the abolition of the nuclear family. (This innovation brings with it some extraordinary marriage arrangements requiring a great deal of systematic deception on the part of the rulers. The principle of benevolent deception was established earlier, in presenting the myth of metals as a noble lie in Book III, 414b–415c.) The third wave, and the condition of possibility for the entire scheme, is rule by philosopher-kings. Only philosophers are competent to rule the city, because only philosophers have access to the Form of the Good and the Form of Justice, the knowledge of which is strictly necessary if the rulers are to make the city just and good. The system of education designed to produce these rulers will be discussed below.

Did Plato abandon these ideals in his later work? An answer to this question is provided in two documents, the *Statesman* and the *Laws*. The *Statesman* is a puzzling work. It purports to define the statesman, or *politikos*, and to show how he is different from the philosopher. It then defines *politikê*, the art of statesmanship as a kind of knowledge or understanding that is competent in giving orders, that is, in ruling. But the dialogue never specifies the content of this expertise. It says only that the possession of such knowledge by the ruler (or rulers) is the one indispensable condition of a genuine constitution; all other constitutions can be no better than imitations of this model. Constitutions are ranked by two criteria; the old classification according to rule by one, few or many is now crossed with the new criterion of lawful or lawless. As lawless one-man rule, tyranny is still the worst form of government, but democracy is now the least bad; the best imitation of the model is a constitutional monarchy (302b–303).

How is the ideal model of the *Statesman* essentially different from the constitution of the *Republic*? More precisely, how is this ruler with authoritative knowledge different from a philosopher-king? If we assume that the *Republic* is in the background, we can see Plato as returning here to familiar territory but from a very different point of view. The Forms are not mentioned as objects of the statesman's expertise (although the dialogue does refer to incorporeal and non-sensible realities); nothing whatever is said about the content of the statesman's knowledge or the nature of his training. We are told only that he will act with justice, and so as to make the city and the citizens better (293d8–9, 297b 2). So presumably the perfect statesman must know what is justice and what is good. Whether or not he knows them as transcendent Forms is left for the reader to surmise.

The one point of general theory that is carefully discussed in the *Statesman* is whether or not the true ruler's knowledge should in principle be supreme over and above the law, and the answer of this dialogue is a resounding "yes." The regime of legality is an imitation, a second-best, in the absence of the scientific ruler. But nothing in the human world can be superior to genuine knowledge.

At first sight, the position of the *Laws* is diametrically opposed, for here Plato provides the first philosophical argument in favor of the principle that a city should be ruled by laws rather than by men, and that human rulers should be servants of the law (*Laws* IV, 715c–d). Law, indeed, is said to be "the dispensation of reason (*nous*)" (714a). But on a closer look the two texts are not so far apart, since the omniscient ruler of the *Statesman* is not to be found among us, and according to that dialogue also the best human constitutions must be law-abiding. In the *Laws*, despite the shift in favor of the rule of law, Plato still yearns nostalgically for the unfettered authority of the truly wise ruler. He is now convinced that human nature is too weak to bear such unlimited power and still remain uncorrupted (IV, 713c with IX, 875b, the source of Acton's principle that absolute power corrupts absolutely). But if such a man could be found, he would not need to be controlled by laws. "For neither law nor any order is superior to knowledge; and it is not right for reason (*nous*) to be subordinate to anything" (IX, 875c). This is precisely the thesis of the *Statesman*.

But the author of the *Laws* has given up hope of the messianic politics sketched in the *Republic*. The detailed constitution of the twelve books of the *Laws* presents a complex political system tightly controlled by an extremely precise legal code, with many invasions of individual liberty, and a social structure very different both from that of the *Republic* and also from that of fourth-century Athens. The society of Plato's last city prefigures

that of Aristotle's *Politics*, Book VII. In both constructions one social class possesses all the property and is the only group to bear arms and to have political rights, while the mass of the population—the producer class of the *Republic*—is disenfranchised and reduced to slavery or limited to foreign residents. In the *Laws* the city has become a club of the leisured class, whose members can devote all of their time to the practice of political virtue, to the study of the law code. and to ritual celebrations in song and dance.

The city of the *Laws* is an entirely new project, based upon a different political philosophy in which the rule of law is supreme. The constitution includes several realistic political institutions, representing a compromise with Athenian democracy, which introduce a career of public service into the utopian life style of this privileged class of citizens. But despite all these innovations, one fundamental principle of the *Republic* has been preserved. Although there is no place for a supreme philosopher-king in this law-bound aristocracy, a kind of counterpart is nevertheless preserved in the institution of the Nocturnal Council, introduced at the end of the work. This Council is a group of high officials meeting daily to study the philosophical foundations of legislation, and to revise the laws if need be. To this extent the author of the Republic remains loyal to himself. The construction of a good constitution will still require the presence of philosophy in a position of the highest influence.

RHETORIC AND DIALECTIC: *GORGIAS* AND *PHAEDRUS*

Rhetoric, the art of public speaking, was developed by the Sophists into a powerful instrument of political leadership; and Plato's chief rival as an educator was the orator Isocrates. Corresponding to its important role in Greek society, rhetoric is a frequent topic of the dialogues, notably in the *Gorgias* and the *Phaedrus*, but implicitly also in the *Protagoras*. In the latter dialogue Socrates presents his own art of question-and-answer as an alternative to, and ultimately a victor over, the art of long speeches represented by Protagoras.

The contest between Socrates and Protagoras is thus a contest between two forms of *logos*, two methods for winning an argument. In the *Gorgias* this contrast of methods reflects the deeper contrast between values. The goal of Socrates' rhetorical opponents is wealth and power, and their speeches aim to persuade the majority. Socrates' goal is virtue and knowledge, and his methodology is designed to get only the agreement of his interlocutor (472b). Socrates' characteristic device is the elenchus: deriving a denial of the interlocutor's thesis from premises that the interlocutor will accept. This is the method that Plato describes retrospectively in the *Sophist*: if someone claims to have knowledge who is in fact ignorant, "since his opinions are confused, it is easy to examine him and to bring these opinions together in discussion and, setting them side by side, to show that they contradict one another" (230b). In the *Gorgias*, Socrates refers to this as the art of conversation (*dialegesthai*) in contrast to the art of speech-making (*rhetorikê*) (448d 10). But Socratic dialectic must also be distinguished from eristic, the pursuit of contradiction for its own sake (illustrated by the notorious behavior of the two sophists in the *Euthydemus*, above in section VI). Unlike this frivolous form of refutation, the Socratic elenchus is designed to free the interlocutor from the false conceit of knowledge, so that the way is opened for him to begin to learn.

In the *Republic* Plato will transform dialectic, as the art of question and answer, into a much more ambitious and constructive method. We look first at his treatment of rhetoric, which is quite different in the *Gorgias* and the *Phaedrus*. In the *Gorgias*, rhetoric is represented by Socrates' opponents, and in particular by Gorgias, the most famous orator of the late fifth century, and teacher of Plato's rival Isocrates. Gorgias stands for the political power of unscrupulous persuasion, and thus for power without moral responsibility or even, in the case of his followers Polus and Callicles, for power without moral restraint. In the *Gorgias*, Socrates argues that the rhetorical practice of public persuasion, without principles of justice and without knowledge, is not an art at all, not a *technê* but a mere empirical knack. To qualify as a *technê* rhetoric would need the theoretical clarity and contact with truth that are characteristic of knowledge. As seen in the *Gorgias*, rhetoric clearly lacks both.

In the *Phaedrus*, by contrast, Plato is concerned with rhetoric not as an instrument of political power but as the form of prose literature, and his sample is not a political speech but a series of epideictic displays on the topic of love. Socrates surprises his interlocutor by not limiting the rhetorical art to speeches in law courts and in public assemblies but generalizing it to cover "the bewitchment of the soul through discourse" (*psychagogia dia logôn*, 261a8). Rhetoric is here conceived as the art of speaking and writing well. Plato makes one of his notable contributions to literary criticism in the discussion of what he calls "literary necessity" (*logographikê anankê*) linking the parts of a composition to one another. Socrates observes that a discourse (*logos*) should have an organic form, like

a living creature, "so as to be neither headless nor footless, with middle parts and extremities that are fitting both to one another and to the whole" (262bc). It turns out that to produce discourse with this quality, the author must be able to gather similar things into unity, and also divide them by kinds. The art of these collections and divisions is called "dialectic" (266c), and it seems that a true art of writing or speaking must include or presuppose dialectic. If rhetoric is to be a *technê*, it will not follow the path of the professional orators (269d). True rhetoric would, for instance, require a philosophic understanding of the psyche and of its natural varieties (271d). Like the *Gorgias*, the *Phaedrus* ends by rejecting the claims of ordinary rhetoric to be regarded as a *technê*. But if Plato's judgment of rhetoric in this dialogue tends to be much more positive than in the *Gorgias*, that is because the art of *logoi* is here conceived constructively as the art of writing, including philosophical writing, and hence as an application of dialectic rather than an alternative to it.

While dialectic was introduced in the *Gorgias* and elsewhere as the Socratic art of conversation (*dialegesthai*) conducted in question-and-answer form, in the *Republic* it becomes the highest method of philosophy, the method by which the intellect ascends to the cognition of transcendent Forms. More specifically, it is the method of passing beyond the assumptions (hypotheses) that function as premises of reasoning in the deductive sciences of mathematics. Dialectic thus presupposes the method of hypothesis developed in the *Meno* and *Phaedo*, a method derived from mathematics, according to which a problem can be solved conditionally on the basis of an explicit assumption. By subjecting these assumptions to critical scrutiny, dialectic is somehow able to rise above them and thus reach the *anhypotheton*, the object of unconditional knowledge, in other words the Forms (VI, 511b). The actual practice of dialectic is not described, but its study follows ten years of training in mathematics. Its connection with the conversational method of question-and-answer is preserved in the requirement that the dialectician must be able to "give an account (*logos*) of the being (*ousia*) of each thing" (VII, 534), that is, to give a systematic answer to the question "What is it?" Giving such an account will necessarily involve a reference to permanent essences or Forms.

Dialectic is described quite differently in the later dialogues, but it remains the highest form of knowledge, the essential method of philosophy. It continues to proceed by question and answer, and to seek the definition of essences in answers to the question "What is X?" According to the *Philebus*, dialectic still takes as its object "true being which is forever unchanging," the reality "which neither comes to be nor passes away" (58a2, 61e2)," precisely the kind of Being represented by the Forms in Plato's classical theory. In the *Sophist* and *Statesman*, however, as in the *Phaedrus*, dialectic is described in more formal terms, as the method of gathering pluralities into unities and dividing them into kinds (*genê*), where the term *eidos*, which designates a transcendent entity in the classical theory of Forms, seems to be used in the more strictly logical sense of "species" or sub-kind. Instead of the relation to mathematics and the method of hypothesis, which is fundamental for the conception of dialectic in the *Republic*, it is the method of Division that is central for dialectic in the later dialogues, from the *Phaedrus* to the *Philebus*. This shift in the description of dialectic corresponds to a different, less metaphysical way of referring to the objects of knowledge (see further below).

ESTHETICS AND EDUCATION: PLATO AGAINST THE POETS

Can virtue be taught? That is the question raised dramatically in the school scenes of several early dialogues, and discussed at length in the *Protagoras* and *Meno*. The conclusion of the *Meno* is problematic. Socrates insists that we must first define virtue before we can answer this question. Since we have no definition, we must answer it conditionally. If (and only if) virtue is a kind of knowledge, it is clearly teachable. But such virtue is hard to find. What about virtue based on correct opinion (*doxa*)? It might give the same results as virtue based on knowledge, but would it be teachable? The *Meno* ends without any clear statement on the question of teachability.

If there is a Platonic answer to this question, it must be found in the educational scheme of the *Republic*. There is a different but parallel answer in the scheme of education in the *Laws*. For Plato (as later for Aristotle), an essential function of the city is to make its citizens good, that is, virtuous. Hence education is a central concern in both dialogues. The *Republic* describes two stages of education, one for the wider guardian class (in Books II and III) and one for the select group of future rulers (in Book VII). Corresponding to these stages we have two accounts of virtue, one based on right opinion (in Book IV) and one on philosophic knowledge (Books VI–VII). The limitations of the initial account of the virtues in Book IV are visible only retrospectively, after the distinction between knowledge and opinion is drawn in Book V. Only after this introduction of philosophy can we appreciate the ambiguous status of wisdom, and hence of virtue generally, as defined in Book IV.

In order to become virtuous, the entire guardian class must have the basic system of education described in terms of music and gymnastics. Only a smaller group will enjoy the training in philosophy, consisting of ten years of mathematical science followed by dialectic and culminating in the vision of the Form of the Good. The first stage of education will produce "citizen excellence" (*politikê aretê*); the higher education, accompanied by years of public service, will yield the unqualified virtue of the philosopher-kings. If we take this as Plato's answer to Meno's question "Is virtue teachable?" the answer is: yes, but not by the available means of education. Only a fundamental change in the conditions of social life would make it possible to produce in a regular way the kind of excellence that occurs sporadically today, by good luck or (as the *Meno* says) by divine dispensation.

Under the more favorable conditions of Plato's city, the character of the guardians will be shaped by a carefully controlled cultural environment, that will include a radical change in the literary and musical content of their education. Plato here defines his position in the culture war he describes as the ancient quarrel between philosophy and poetry (*Rep.* X, 607b; see above). All of the arts will play an essential role in the moral education of the young guardians, but it is poetry that is the center of Plato's attention, because of the fundamental influence of Homer and the tragedians on Greek moral thought. Since Plato regards their influence as essentially malignant, he would eliminate from his educational scheme major themes of Greek poetry (Books II–III). Following Xenophanes and others, he attacks as immoral the Homeric depiction of the gods. His basic theological principle is that the gods are good, and are therefore (by the law of transitive causation) cause only of the good, and they must be represented accordingly (III, 379a–380c). Plato thus avoids the thickets of theodicy; there is no problem of justifying the action of the gods, since they are never responsible for evil. The actions of glorified heroes must also be represented in such a way as to provide a moral paradigm for the young guardians.

Finally, when Plato returns in Book X to the restrictions on poetry, he attacks the imitative arts generally on epistemic grounds, as being at third remove from truth. He also blames the emotional impact of epic and tragedy for relaxing the moral discipline of the soul. Hence the poets are to be banned from Plato's city, and readmitted only if their influence can be morally justified (697b–e). This is a famous challenge to future aesthetic theory. Aristotle's *Poetics* and Sir Philip Sydney's *Defence of Poesie*

ENCYCLOPEDIA OF PHILOSOPHY
2nd edition

count among the more noteworthy responses to Plato's challenge.

At the same time, a properly controlled aesthetic environment is recognized as decisive for the development of virtue in the young. This includes the visual arts, but poetry and music are of particular importance, since rhythm and harmony, more than anything else, penetrate deep into the soul (III, 401d). Because of the close connection between the beautiful and the good, the young should be surrounded by beauty in all its forms, so that later, when moral principles are presented to them in rational teaching (*logos*), they will recognize these as familiar and congenial (402a). The positive use of the arts in education is developed further in the *Laws*, with special attention to dance, since there will be choruses for the citizens at all ages (Books I–II). Literature and lyre-playing will be essential in education, and the Athenian Stranger who speaks for Plato in the *Laws* holds up the Platonic dialogue, and specifically the text of the *Laws*, as a model for the literature to be used in schools (*Laws* VII, 802 ff; 811c-e). In both the *Republic* and the *Laws*, the content of literature and music is interpreted in moral terms: "rhythms and the performing arts as a whole (*pasê mousikê*) are the imitations of the characters of better and worse human beings" (*Laws* VII, 798e).

Plato's positive evaluation of poetry, implicit in his use of literature in these proposed schemes of education, receives a theoretical development in the account of poetic inspiration as divine madness in the *Phaedrus* (245a). In the *Ion* (as in the *Apology*) the notion of divine possession for the poet was employed ironically, in order to emphasize the poet's lack of cognitive competence. In the *Phaedrus*, on the other hand, the madness of artistic inspiration is presented as a positive force, in parallel with the divine madness of love which carries us back in recollection to a prenatal vision of the Forms. Plato never says that artistic experience, like erotic experience, can trigger recollection of the Forms. But it is easy to see how a later Platonist such as Plotinus (and his followers, such as Proclus), less fearful than Plato of the moral and intellectual dangers from poetry, could make use of the *Phaedrus* parallel between poetry and love to develop a powerful conception of art as a privileged mode of access to a higher level of metaphysical reality. This was a theory much in vogue among the Romantics of the nineteenth century, who took over Plato's theory of poetry as divine possession, deprived it of its ironic sting, and transformed it into a theory of creative genius.

THE CLASSICAL DOCTRINE OF FORMS

The centerpiece of Platonic philosophy is the metaphysical theory of Forms or Ideas, presented in three dialogues (*Symposium*, *Phaedo*, and *Republic*), utilized in two others (*Cratylus* and *Phaedrus*) and criticized in a sixth (*Parmenides*). Whether some version of this theory reappears in dialogues later than the *Parmenides* is a question to be discussed below. The term "idea" is a transliteration of *idea*, one of Plato's terms for the Forms. Since the English word suggests something mental or psychological, "idea" seems misleading as a designation for Platonic Forms, which are clearly intended to be mind-independent realities.

As we have seen above, the dialogues of definition present the object of definition as the being or essence (*ousia*) of the subject under discussion and distinguish it from an ordinary property or attribute (*pathos*). The essence is not only true of all and only instances of the subject, but it is also explanatory of *being the thing in question*. The answer to a question "What is *X*?" should say what *X* is, in the sense of explaining what makes something an *X*. (*Meno* 72c 8.; *Euthyphro* 6d 11). Thus being dear to the gods, although true of all and only pious actions, does not say *what pious is*, because it does not tell us why the gods favor some actions rather than others (*Euthyphro* 11a). These logical properties of essences prepare for, but do not imply, the metaphysical doctrine of the *Phaedo* and *Republic*.

Similarly, the terminology for *definienda* in the dialogues of definition prefigures the later terminology for the Forms, but in a pre-theoretical way: *eidos* and *idea* are ordinary terms for features, structures, or kinds of things. Aristotle says that Socrates was pursuing universal definitions, but that he did not separate the universals as Plato did (*Met.* 1078b 30). Hence some scholars have interpreted the essences of *Meno* and *Euthyphro* as immanent (Aristotelian) rather than transcendent (Platonic) forms. But the texts do not support such a distinction. For example, the idea of piety is described as a model (*paradeigma*) for deciding whether a given action is pious (*Euthyphro* 6e); but the *Euthyphro* does not tell us whether this model would be located in the mind or in the nature of things. The ontology of the *definienda* in these dialogues is left strictly indeterminate.

Plato supplies a metaphysical framework for the objects of definition in the *Symposium* and *Phaedo*, with a further development in the Republic. These dialogues introduce the conception of eternal, unchanging Being as location for the objects pursued in dialectic. Plato has taken over from Parmenides this notion of Being or

What-is (*to on*) as an unchanging reality accessible only to thought or rational understanding (*nous*), defined by contrast with the changing realm of Becoming that is accessible to the senses. Plato's conception differs from that of Parmenides in two respects: Platonic Being exists in the plural (*ta onta* or The-things-that-are), corresponding to the plurality of Forms, while for Parmenides, Being is a unique One; and Becoming is allotted a certain measure of reality, whereas its ontological status for Parmenides seems to be that of appearance only.

This metaphysical conception of the Forms, which is assumed throughout the argument of the *Phaedo*, is most succinctly formulated in the final description of the Beautiful in Diotima's lesson on love, as reported by Socrates in the *Symposium* (210e–211b). The Form of Beauty (literally "the Beautiful itself") is there distinguished from the many beautiful things by (1) being one (unique) rather than many; (2) being a Being rather than a Becoming, that is, being eternally and unchangeably beautiful, rather than becoming beautiful at one time and not beautiful at another; (3) being only and always beautiful, rather than beautiful in one respect or for one observer, but not beautiful in another respect or for another observer. Hence (4) the being of the Form, which is accessible only to thought or understanding, is distinct from its appearance in becoming, which is accessible to opinion (*doxa*) and sense-perception. (5) Anything else that is beautiful is such only because of its dependence on the Beautiful itself. This ontological dependence is described in terms of participating or sharing in the Form, or imitating the Form by being an image of the Form. (6) Reflecting this dependence is the notion of eponymy: everything called an *F* is named after the *F* itself. (7) The converse of the eponymy relation is the principle of one over many: For every plurality of things called *F*, there is the Form *F* itself.

The relation between Forms and their sensible eponyms is the most obscure feature in Plato's theory. In the *Phaedo*, Socrates insists on the derivation of sensible beauty from the Form, but expresses uncertainty as to how this derivation is to be understood: "Nothing else makes it [the sensible thing] beautiful except the presence or communion or whatever connection there may be with the Beautiful itself—I am not sure about this, but [I am sure] that it is by the Beautiful that all the many beautiful become beautiful" (100d). The terminology of participation occurs once in the *Symposium*, repeatedly in the *Phaedo*, and once again in the *Republic*. But this notion of participation as a Form-sensible relation is subjected to a withering critique in the *Parmenides* (131a–e).

In the *Republic* participation is generally replaced by the language of imitation and imaging or copying; and it is this terminology that reappears later in the *Timaeus*.

Difficulties with the classical theory will be discussed in the next section. We consider here the intended scope and motivation of Plato's theory. It is often presented as a solution to the problem of universals. This, however, is not only anachronistic but inaccurate, since the concept of universals (which are not properly *ousiai*, not substances in a strict sense) was introduced by Aristotle precisely as an alternative to Plato's conception of Forms. In the *Republic* the Being of the Forms is introduced on epistemic grounds as the object of knowledge, in contrast to the imperfect reality of the sensible manifold as object of *doxa*. (The deficient reality of the many beautiful things is reflected in the fact that they are beautiful in some respects, not beautiful in other respects. Hence they *are* in some respects, but they *are not* in other respects. The *is* of predication is thus taken to express a reality claim for the subject.) The underlying assumption, often reasserted in later dialogues, is that an object of knowledge must be eternally invariant; otherwise the cognition of it at one time would become false at another time (so explicitly at *Cratylus* 440a). But knowledge must be always true; hence an object of knowledge must be eternally unchangeable.

This is the argument underlying the presentation of Forms as invariant objects of knowledge in *Republic* V. To knowledge strictly understood corresponds Being strictly understood: "what is completely real (*to pantelôs on*) is completely knowable" (*Rep.* 477a 3). Anything less real can be the object only of imperfect cognition and partial truth. Plato hesitates to present this as an argument, however, since it might seem to imply the priority of epistemic considerations. That would be misleading. Epistemology and ontology go hand in hand for Plato, but it is the real that determines what is knowable and not conversely. It is the stability of Being that makes reliable cognition possible.

This Parmenidean insight constitutes the permanent basis for Plato's metaphysical speculation. It is worked out for the first time in the classical theory of Forms, but it persists as well in later dialogues such as the *Philebus* and *Timaeus*. It is in the *Sophist* that we have the most explicit statement that without stability and invariance there can be no knowledge or understanding (*nous*) whatsoever (249b–d). What is distinctive of the classical theory is not the invariance of Being but the one-many and eponymy relations between Forms and sensibles, as expressed at *Rep.* X, 596a: "We are accustomed to posit some one Form concerning each plurality to which we assign the same name." Thus there will be one Form of Beauty corresponding to all beautiful things, one Form of Good corresponding to all specific goods, and so on. But the passage just quoted from *Republic* X is destined to cause trouble, for many reasons. For example, it suggests that Forms will be as plentiful as common nouns and adjectives. Plato will have to speak more cautiously about cutting nature at the joints (*Phaedrus* 265e) and thus make clear that not every distinction between words will mark a distinction between Forms or Kinds of things (*Statesman* 262b–263b). The scope of the classical theory is originally undefined, but it does seem to be committed to Forms for artifacts as well as for natural kinds. Thus there is a Form for shuttle at *Cratylus* 389b and a Form for bed at *Rep.* 596b, 597a.

Less obvious than the Parmenidean-epistemic motivation for the doctrine of Forms, but equally important, is the distinctively Platonic conception of philosophy as a form of love or *erôs*, the conception expressed in Plato's etymological reading of *philo-sophia* as "the love of wisdom" (see above). This notion of the philosopher as lover with the Forms as the beloved object provides the original context for the introduction of the theory in the *Symposium*, where the Beautiful itself appears as the ultimate object of philosophic passion. In the *Phaedo* the philosopher is said to be ready for death because it is only when liberated from the body that he can hope to obtain the object of his desire, namely, full knowledge of the truth (67e–68b). The Form of Good is the ultimate Form, not only because it is the source of being and knowability for the other Forms, but also because it is "what every soul pursues and for the sake of which it performs all of its actions" (*Rep.* 505d 11). The doctrine of Forms is thus designed, from the beginning, to provide not only an epistemology and an ontology but also a philosophy of life, that is to say, a theoretical basis for ethics and politics. It is in virtue of his or her access to the Forms, and above all to the Form of the Good, that a philosopher-king is uniquely qualified to govern, since only such access enables them to know what is a good life for individuals and for the city.

These powerful practical implications of the theory of Forms reflect its origin in the Socratic conception of philosophy as a form of life and in the Socratic concern with defining the virtues as the mark of a good life. No interpretation of Plato's theory can be adequate unless it takes into account this profoundly practical bent of Plato's conception of philosophy. The unique character of Plato's metaphysics lies in this convergence between the Parmenidean demand for eternally unchanging reality

and the Socratic pursuit of what makes a human life worth living. Thus the original focus of the theory is not on the problem of meaning for general words or concepts but specifically on what we may identify as value terms: the noble and beautiful first of all (*to kalon*), the good (*agathon*) and the just (*dikaion*). The first generalization of the theory is to mathematical concepts (the equal, the greater, and the smaller) and then to health and strength and to every term defined in dialectic, that is, to every essence (*ousia*) "on which we put the stamp of what-it-itself-is" (*Phaedo* 65d 12, 75d 1: *auto to ho esti*, the most technical expression for the Forms). How far this generalization of the theory is meant to extend is a question to be raised and partially answered in later dialogues.

PARMENIDES AND THE CHALLENGE TO THE CLASSICAL THEORY

In the dialogue *Parmenides* Plato brings the two Eleatic philosophers, Parmenides and Zeno, to Athens for an imaginary confrontation with Socrates. This is the first of a series of dialogues in which Socrates is no longer the chief speaker, being replaced here by Parmenides. Since Parmenides was almost certainly dead by 450 BCE (the alleged time of the conversation, when Socrates was about twenty), Plato has ignored chronology in order to introduce Parmenides as a masterful critic of the doctrine of Forms. It is no accident that, in the dialogues generally, Parmenides is the only philosopher who is allowed to win an argument with Socrates. Furthermore, in view of the Eleatic inspiration of Plato's own conception of Being, Parmenides can be trusted as a sympathetic critic of the theory. He is the first to recognize that to give up the theory completely would mean to abandon philosophy (135b–c).

The dialogue divides into two parts. Part I present a series of objections to the Forms, objections that are never explicitly answered by Plato either in this dialogue or elsewhere. Part II contains eight rigorous deductions from the hypotheses *That the One Is* and *That the One Is Not*. The conclusions come in contradictory pairs. According to Deduction 1, the One has no properties; according to Deduction 2 the One has all properties, including contraries (e.g., it is both at rest and in motion, both greater than itself and smaller than itself). How the deductions of Part II are related to one another and to the objections in Part I are matters of extreme obscurity. Parmenides introduces these arguments simply as an example of how a philosopher should be trained before attempting to formulate a theory of Forms. These deductions are thus presented as a logical "exercise" (*gymnasia*) preliminary to philosophy proper. They nevertheless represent the only fully developed examples of formal dialectic in the dialogues.

Interpretation of the eight (or on some counts nine) baffling arguments of Part II has been a subject of controversy since antiquity. Skeptics saw these apparently contradictory deductions as purely destructive, whereas Plotinus identified the first three hypotheses with his three principal hypostases: the One, Nous and Soul (*Ennead* V.1.8). Modern views have emphasized the overlap with the mingling of Kinds in the *Sophist* and other topics discussed in the late dialogues, such as whole and part, rest and motion. Several interpreters have found in Part II Plato's answers to the difficulties raised in Part I. Some commentators assume that all the arguments of Part II are intended as valid; others regard some of the deductions as so obviously fallacious that the detection of fallacy must be intended as an essential part of the training.

Part I begins with a brief statement by Socrates of the classical theory of Forms, presented as a response to Zeno's paradoxes about plurality. Zeno is quoted as showing that, if things are many, they must have incompatible properties, for example they must be both similar and dissimilar. Socrates agrees that such contraries will be true of the sensible many but not of the corresponding Form: Similarity itself will never be dissimilar, and the One itself will never be plural. Socrates' brief statement here of the classical theory is peculiar in two respects: the relation between the many and the corresponding Form is consistently described as participation (*metechein*, *metalambanein*), and the Forms are said at one point to be "separate" (*chôris*) from their participants (129d 7). In responding, Parmenides will seize upon this last point: "And do you divide as separate certain Forms themselves, on the one hand, and as separate on the other hand the things which participate in them? And is there in your view some Similarity itself separate from the similarity that we have?" (130b 1–5). Socrates agrees, and thus accepts a fatal replication of the Forms as immanent properties.

Both features—the reliance on the concept of participation and the distinction between Magnitude itself and the magnitude in us—accurately reflect the formulation of the doctrine in the *Phaedo* (e.g. 102d 7). And both will be exploited by Parmenides in his criticism, where the notion of participation is shown to be incoherent, while the separation between Similarity itself and "the similarity that we have" (or the similarity "in us") leads to a two-world ontology in which our world is structured by immanent forms. In that case the transcendent Forms of Plato's theory become irrelevant and unknowable. This is the conclusion of the last difficulty, which Parmenides describes as the greatest (133b–134e).

As a consequence of Parmenides' criticism, two features of the classical theory as formulated here must be abandoned: namely, participation taken literally as the "sharing" of Forms by sensibles, and the existence of "forms that we have" or "forms in us" separate from the Forms themselves. Among Parmenides' other objections the best known is the so-called Third Man argument, according to which the one-over-many principle of *Republic* X (that for every group of *F*s we posit a Form, the *F*-itself) leads to an infinite regress. The nerve of this argument is the implicit premise that the *F*-itself is *F*; hence if we add the *F*-itself to the first group of *F*s, we get a larger group of *F*s calling for another *F*-itself; and so on indefinitely. Some scholars have claimed that this premise (the so-called self-predication principle, that *F*-itself is *F*) reflects a logical confusion on Plato's part between being a property and having a property. However, the *Sophist* makes clear that Plato remained committed to this principle, and recent interpretations have shown that no fallacy need be entailed. At the same time, the second implicit premiss required for the regress, the so-called Non-identity principle (that for any larger group of *F*s, a new and different *F*-itself is needed), has no deep Platonic motivation, and its role in generating the regress can be blocked in several different ways. More problematic than the Third Man argument is the parallel objection against the conception of Forms as models (*paradeigmata*), where the dependent relation of participation is understood in terms of similarity or being a likeness of the Form (132d–133a). This objection seems to attack the central concept of imaging or imitation, which replaces participation in the doctrine as reformulated in the *Republic* and *Timaeus*. How much of the classical theory of Forms can be thought to survive the critique of the *Parmenides* will depend in part on the interpretation of this model-copy relation as developed in the *Timaeus*.

THEAETETUS AND SOPHIST: SURVIVAL OF THE FORMS? THE LATER DIALECTIC

The *Theaetetus* and *Sophist* stand in the shadow of the *Parmenides*: both dialogues refer to the conversation between Socrates and Parmenides as if it were a historical event (*Theaet.* 183e 7; *Soph.* 217c 5). As a consequence, both dialogues distance themselves from the classical theory of Forms. Neither dialogue denies the existence of

Forms, and both refer to concepts or entities that recall Forms. But neither dialogue asserts the metaphysical dualism of the classical theory. The *Sophist* even subjects this theory to a new round of criticism. It is as if Plato in the *Parmenides* had wiped the slate clean, and was prepared to make a fresh start in the later dialogues in addressing the basic issues of epistemology and metaphysics.

The *Theaetetus* is almost the last dialogue in which Socrates appears as the chief speaker (only the *Philebus* is later), and the last one in which his elenchtic function is dramatically displayed. In fact the negative character of the elenchus is uniquely underscored here in the comparison of Socrates to a midwife. The official role of Socrates in this dialogue is not to produce theories on his own (as he did in the *Phaedo, Republic* and *Phaedrus*, and will again in the *Philebus*) but solely to extract definitions of knowledge from Theaetetus.

Theaetetus's attempts to define knowledge fall into two categories, dividing the dialogue into two unequal parts. The first and longer section corresponds to the initial definition of knowledge as sense perception (*aisthêsis*). This definition is ultimately rejected on the grounds that truth, and therefore knowledge, is not accessible to sense perception as such but only to the rational psychic activity that Theaetetus calls *doxazein*, "having an opinion" (187a). The remainder of the dialogue is then devoted to various accounts of knowledge and error based on this notion of *doxa*, that is, opinion, belief, or judgment. The results of this second section are equally negative, so that the *Theaetetus* has the external form of an aporetic dialogue like the *Laches* or *Meno*—an unsuccessful attempt to define knowledge. The philosophical content of the *Theaetetus* is, however, extremely productive in arguments and insights for epistemology and philosophy of mind. Why then is the outcome so negative?

If we relate this discussion to Plato's theory of knowledge as formulated in the *Republic*, we can see why the enterprise of the *Theaetetus* was doomed to fail. According to the view of *Republic* V–VI (reasserted in the *Timaeus*), sense perception and opinion (*doxa*) take as their object the realm of sensory Becoming, whereas knowledge proper takes as its object only invariant Being. Thus in the Divided Line of *Republic* VI, both sense perception and *doxa* belong to the lower sections of the line, devoted to the visible realm, but knowledge belongs at the top with the Forms as its object. In the *Republic* and *Timaeus* this view of knowledge as metaphysically grounded is presented as a basic assumption, without detailed supporting argument. In the *Theaetetus*, in contrast, all attempts to define knowledge avoid any recourse to Parmenidean ontology or to the classical doctrine of Forms. This systematic departure from Plato's classical epistemology can be seen as an application of the method proposed and exemplified by Parmenides in the dialogue named after him: See what follows not only from your own assumption but also from its denial (136a 1). Accordingly, in the *Theaetetus* we pursue an acount of knowledge from the opposing, non-Platonic point of view. Let us assume that knowledge can be defined either on the basis of sense perception, or on the basis of *doxa*, and see what follows from either assumption. The *Theaetetus* thus has the form of a double *reductio*. Since neither alternative gives a satisfactory result, we are justified in returning to our original point of view. There is still no explicit argument for the Parmenidean postulate (that knowledge in the full sense takes as its object Being in the full sense). But this assumption is supported indirectly, by the failure of the alternative attempt in the *Theaetetus* to give an account of knowledge that avoids this postulate.

Although the general form of the *Theaetetus* is thus negative, the positive content is extremely rich. The first section develops a subtle theory of subjective perceptual qualities within the framework of Protagorean relativism, on the basis of a neo-Heraclitean doctrine of flux. Commentators disagree on whether this theory of perception should be read as merely hypothetical or whether it in fact represents Plato's own view of the subject. A decision must depend upon whether or not the *Theaetetus* account of perception is compatible both with Plato's own version of cosmic flux in the Timaeus and also with his mechanistic account of sense qualities in that dialogue. Of great interest also is the argument known as the *peritropê*, or "overturning," according to which Protagorean relativism is shown to be self-refuting; since it could be true at most for those who believe it, but false for everyone else, therefore even those who believe it must admit its falsity for the others, that is, for most people (*Theaet.* 170a–171c).

The final rejection of sense perception as a candidate for knowledge relies upon a new distinction between sense-perception proper, that is, information derived through the sense organs of the body, and "common thoughts" (*koina*) like "same" and "different," "one" and "many," that apply to more than one sense modality. The argument concludes that the *being* of predication and existence, and hence of truth, is not available to sense perception as such. "But if one fails to grasp the truth of something, one cannot have knowledge of that thing" (186c 9). Hence sense perception cannot be knowledge.

The "common thoughts" or concepts (*koina*) introduced by this argument include "beautiful" and "ugly," "good" and "bad," as well as "same" and "different," "similar" and "dissimilar" (185a–186a). As non-sensible notions, these *koina* are clearly suggestive of Forms, but nothing whatsoever is said about their ontological status. There is a closer hint of the classical theory in the famous moral digression of the *Theaetetus* (where virtue is defined as *homoiôsis theôi*, "becoming like god" 176b 1): There resemblance at the human level is said to connect us with transcendent models (*paradeigmata*) of justice and injustice "established in reality" (*en tôi onti hestôta* 176e 3). These two paradigms represent two lives, one of which, as a model of injustice, is "godless and most wretched." The context of the digression clearly invokes both the judgment myths of *Phaedo* and *Republic* and the moral spirit of the *Gorgias*; but there is no unambiguous reference here to Forms as defined in the classical theory.

In the *Sophist*, Plato returns to questions of ontology with a vengeance. The central theme of the dialogue is the problem of Not-Being, and it is argued that the concept of Being is equally problematic, so that the two concepts must be clarified together. Accordingly, the dialogue surveys a series of metaphysical positions, including both Parmenidean monism and a materialist view that reduces Being to bodily existence. A clearly recognizable version of Plato's classical theory is discussed as the doctrine of "the friends of the Forms." As in the *Parmenides*, a sympathetic critique is guaranteed here by the presence of a metaphysically oriented philosopher as protagonist. As a pupil of Parmenides, this "visitor from Elea" can subject both Parmenides' account of Being and Plato's own theory to constructive criticism. In particular, the Stranger's critique of the Friends of Forms shows that the classical theory must expand its ontology to make room for motion and change as a kind of Being. How this is to be done is left for discussion elsewhere, presumably in the *Timaeus*. The *Timaeus* also pursues the most puzzling suggestion of the Stranger's critique, namely that there must be a place among the Forms for Intelligence (*nous*) and hence for life and soul (*Sophist* 248e–249d).

The doctrine of Forms reappears in the constructive argument of the *Sophist* as a theory of Kinds (*genê*) that are capable of combination or participation with one another; dialectic is accordingly redefined as the science of "dividing according to Kinds," knowing "which Kinds harmonize with which, and which do not admit one another" (253b–d). Although in this dialogue we set out to define the Sophist, we seem to have found the philosopher instead, since this dialectical art belongs only "to one who purely and rightly philosophizes" (253e). The description of the philosopher appeals here to the visual imagery of the classical theory: The philosopher is said to be so hard to see because of the brightness of the region "where he is attached always in reasoning to the form (*idea*) of Being; for the eyes of the soul of most people cannot bear for long the sight of what is divine" (254a). The metaphysical discussion is, however, left incomplete. The Eleatic Stranger speaks of participation only between Forms or Kinds; nothing is said of the relation between Forms and their sensible eponyms.

Instead of metaphysics the new theory of participation between Kinds offers something like transcendental logic. "It is through the weaving-together of Forms (*eidê*) with one another that rational discourse (*logos*) has been given to us" (259e). The most elementary weaving-together (*symplokê*) is between noun and verb to form the basic *logos* of a sentence or statement (262c 6). Plato thus introduces the subject-predicate analysis of sentence structure that served as the basis for Aristotle's own theory of predication. Exactly how this analysis is applied in the detailed account of Not-Being is a matter of dispute, but it is clear that the Form of Not-Being is explained by reference to two other Forms, Being and Otherness. (In effect, negation is analyzed in terms of non-identity.) The *Sophist* thus opens up an entirely new dimension in the theory of Forms: a network of logical and semantic relations between concepts or Kinds, such as whole-part or logical inclusion, combination or extensional overlap, and mutual exclusion.

This conception of dialectic as "dividing according to Kinds" is reflected in the method of Collection and Division that was described in the *Phaedrus* (265d–266c) and is systematically applied here in both dialogues, in successive definitions of the *Sophist* and the *Statesman*. As was noted above, in these definitions the terms *genos* (kind) and *eidos* (form) seem to be used in their logical sense simply as "genus" and "species," and the ontology of the Forms is apparently left indeterminate. At the same time, the Eleatic Stranger speaks more definitely of "incorporeal beings, the greatest and finest," which have no images adapted to sense perception but can be clearly indicated only by rational discourse (*logos*); it is for the sake of these beings that the dialectical definitions are pursued (*Statesman* 285e–286a). In such a passage, as in the reference to the divine *idea* of Being at *Sophist* 254a, there is a clear reminder of the classical theory. But nothing is said in either the *Sophist* or *Statesman* to indicate how the dualism of the *Phaedo* and *Republic* is to be altered or preserved.

PHILEBUS AND THE RETURN OF SOCRATES

In the *Philebus* the problems of ontological dualism and participation are directly confronted for the first time since the *Parmenides*. These issues are presented here within the broader context of relations between the One and the Many. As in the *Parmenides*, the problem of participation is distinguished from superficial or eristic ways of being at the same time one and many (as one subject with many properties, or one whole with many parts). The serious problem arises only when we distinguish unities that do not belong to "what comes to be and perishes" but are truly beings and truly unities, like the one Beautiful and the one Good. (Among the examples of ungenerated and imperishable unities listed at *Philebus* 15a are One Human Being and One Ox, thus providing a partial answer to the Population Problem of *Parmenides* 130c 1. Another partial answer is given in the discussion of Forms of Fire and other elements at *Timaeus* 51b–52a.) The question then is how such unities, "admitting neither generation nor corruption, can remain one and the same while coming to be in many and infinite cases of becoming, either one unity being scattered and becoming many, or (most impossible of all) being separate from itself as a whole" (15a–b, recalling the critique of participation at *Parmenides* 131a–c).

A full discussion of these metaphysical issues is avoided in the *Philebus*, however, because of pressure from the prior question whether pleasure or knowledge is the good and the cause of a good human life. The relation of eternal Forms or Monads to sensible becoming is reformulated here in the light of "an immortal and unaging attribute (*pathos*) of discourse (*logoi*)," an attribute rather cryptically identified as the claim that "the identity of one and many generated by discourse (*logoi*) circulates in every way among everything that is ever said" (15d). As the best way out of this confusion, the dialectical method of collecting unities and distinguishing pluralities is presented as a gift from the gods and the basis for all art or science (*technê*, 16c 2). The discussion thus shifts from the problems of ontological dualism to the dialectical project of discerning unity and plurality in the various kinds of pleasure and knowledge. Instead of metaphysics we are given the method of Division, based on the principle (tossed down from heaven by some Prometheus) that "things that are said to be in every case (or "things said to be forever," *ta aei legomena einai*) are derived from

one and many, and hence have Limit and Unlimited in their nature" (16c).

These principles of Limit and the Unlimited, introduced here by Plato for the first time, are apparently borrowed from the Pythagorean philosopher Philolaus, who claimed that "Nature in the world-order has been fitted together from unlimited [constituents] and from limiting ones, both the world-order as a whole and everything within it" (fragment 1). In the *Philebus* these two principles provide the basis for a fourfold cosmic scheme that includes several ideas figuring also in the cosmology of the *Timaeus*. "All the beings that are now present in the universe" are analyzed as a blended Mixture of Limit and Unlimited, under the causal influence of Intelligence (*nous*). In this scheme, as in the *Timaeus*, causality is interpreted as the purposeful act of a maker, or *dêmiourgos*. Also common to the *Timaeus* is the introduction of a world soul (*Philebus* 30a–d). But the *Philebus* principles of Limit and Unlimited do not correspond exactly to anything in the *Timaeus*; they figure here as immanent components of Becoming, entering as ingredients into a Mixture that represents both cosmic order and a good human life (23b–27c).

This fourfold scheme of Unlimited, Limit, Mixture, and rational Cause is said to be required in order to decide the contest between pleasure and knowledge for recognition as the good. It has already been settled that neither candidate deserves first place; pleasure and knowledge are each shown to be less choiceworthy alone than the Mixed Life that contains both (20d–22c). The issue for the rest of the dialogue is to assign second place in the competition for the good or, more precisely, to determine the relative position of knowledge and pleasure in accounting for the goodness of the good life. It will turn out that, in the ranking of ingredients in the final Mixture, forms of knowledge occupy third and fourth place, while a selected group of pleasures comes in only fifth. The first two constituents of the good life are principles first of measure (*metron, metrion*) and next of beauty and proportion (*kalon, symmetron*). The fourfold scheme permits Socrates to identify pleasure as a part or species of the Unlimited, while knowledge and intelligence (*nous*) belong to the genus of the Cause of successful mixtures.

The central section of the *Philebus* is a classification of different kinds of pleasure and knowledge. Socrates proceeds to give a subtle analysis of a number of kinds of pleasure, both mental and physical, in order to distinguish pleasures that are true and pure from various mixed and false pleasures. Only pure pleasures of sense and intellect will be admitted into the final construction of the good life. Although all forms of knowledge will be admitted, a ranking is nevertheless carried out between different forms of expertise, in a new version of the Knowledge Line of *Republic* V. The lowest division is between various manual crafts, including music; for such arts the level of cognition depends upon the extent and precision of the mathematical component. Mathematics in turn is divided into two, with philosophical mathematics representing a higher standard of precision. (Pure mathematics here recalls, but does not exactly correspond to, the higher form of measurement based upon "due measure" in the *Statesman*. The concept of due measure, to *metrion*, does, however, return to define the first constituent of the Good Life in the final ranking of the *Philebus*.)

Finally, the highest form of knowledge is identified as dialectic, which ranks above natural philosophy and cosmology on ontological grounds familiar from the classical theory. For only dialectic is concerned with what is "really real," with Being that is eternal and unchanging; whereas the science of the natural world is a study of what has comes to be and perishes (*Philebus* 59a, 61e; this is the same ontological contrast that will serve as foundation for the cosmology of the *Timaeus* 28a–b). Dialectic is here described in terms of classical dualism, including the epistemic contrast with *doxai* (at 59a 1). But the reader is inevitably reminded of the quite different account of dialectic given earlier in the *Philebus*, where there is reference not to Being and Becoming but rather to the recognition of unities and pluralities (16b–17a). The old and the new conceptions of dialectic are thus both presented but left uncombined. A similar ambivalence can be seen in the *Philebus* regarding the problems of metaphysical dualism, which are recognized but not resolved. And in another respect we are left with expectations unfulfilled. Much of the dialogue raises the question of the Good as such and the good-making properties of any mixture, but we reach at the end only "the threshold of the good," in a list of the essential ingredients of a good human life. Any hopes for an account of the Form of the Good are left unsatisfied. It is no wonder that the dialogue ends (67b 11) with the interlocutor reminding Socrates that something has been left out!

We may wonder why Plato brings Socrates back as protagonist in the *Philebus*, after replacing him with an Eleatic Visitor in the *Sophist-Statesman*, and again replacing him with Timaeus and an Athenian Stranger in the other late dialogues. No doubt the role of pleasure in the good life was familiar Socratic terrain. But the presence of Socrates might equally serve as a reminder of the dualism expounded by the same figure in the *Phaedo* and *Republic*, and also of the unresolved problems raised against Socrates' presentation of this doctrine in the *Parmenides*. Although the *Philebus* is not formally aporetic like the *Theaetetus*, it certainly concludes on a note of incompleteness. If there is a Platonic response to the metaphysical problem recalled here, one must look for it elsewhere, perhaps in the *Timaeus*.

TIMAEUS AND THE PLATONIC COSMOS

The *Timaeus* was for many centuries the most influential of all of Plato's works. After the rise of Christianity, it could be regarded as a philosophical exegesis of the creation story in the Book of Genesis. But the profound influence of the *Timaeus* derives from its mathematical conception of nature, which has also attracted modern admirers from Kepler and Galileo to Whitehead and Heisenberg. For students of Plato the *Timaeus* has the special interest of offering Plato's only radical reformulation of the classical theory of Forms. The introduction of a spatial Receptacle, on the one hand, and an intelligent Maker of cosmic order, on the other hand, permits Plato for the first time to give a systematic account of the natural world, while deploying new resources to counter the challenges to the classical theory that were formulated in the *Parmenides*.

In addition to the Receptacle and the Demiurge, Plato's new theory makes use of two other notions developed in the late dialogues: (1) The idea presented in the *Sophist* that the realm of Being must be enlarged to include motion and change is reflected in the theory of mixture in the *Philebus*, where the analysis of phenomenal unities gives rise to the new, paradoxical expressions *genesis eis ousian*, "becoming into being" (26d 8) and *gegenêmenê ousia*, "being that has come to be" (27b 8). Although the *Timaeus* reverts to the classical antithesis between Being and Becoming, the cosmological theory deals in fact almost exclusively with Becoming. (2) Without using the terms "Limit" and "Unlimited" from the *Philebus*, the *Timaeus* presents a comparable analysis of Becoming as the mixed result of an interaction between two principles, represented here allegorically as Reason and Necessity. The victory of the former over the latter is spelled out in the creation narrative as the shaping of the chaotic motions of the Receptacle by the purposeful action of the Demiurge, "structuring [the pre-cosmic elements] with figures (*eidê*) and numbers" (53b 4).

The *Timaeus* thus interprets the cosmic act of the divine Maker in terms of the normative notion of mathematical measure (*to metrion, to symmetron*) expounded in the *Statesman* and *Philebus*. Whereas in the epistemology of the *Republic* mathematics points only upward, to raise the mind towards the Forms, in the cosmology of the *Timaeus* (and, by anticipation, in the *Statesman* and *Philebus* as well) the function of mathematics is also directed downward, to impose order on the mixed products of Becoming, on the good human life as on the order of nature.

By the formal device of Timaeus's monologue, Plato has inserted into this dialogue a prose treatise *peri physeôs* in the Pre-Socratic tradition, applying a revised theory of Forms to produce his own account of the nature of things, that is to say, of the world of perceptible order and natural change. One goal of this account must be to avoid the "greatest aporia" of the *Parmenides* by giving an account of the visible cosmos, including human beings, that does not "separate" the phenomenal world from the Forms. Hence, instead of a sensible realm of immanent forms, Timaeus posits as an entity independent from the Forms only the Receptacle, the place where the Forms are imaged. As joint offspring of Forms and Receptacle, the sensible images are like the Mixtures of the *Philebus*, with no existence independent of their two principles. On the one hand, as modifications of the Receptacle their existence is adjectival rather than substantival. On the other hand, they are no more independent or separable from the Forms than the images in a mirror are independent from the objects mirrored. The *Timaeus* is insistent on this fact of double dependence. "Since in the case of an image even that on which it depends does not belong to it, but it is always carried about as an appearance (*phantasma*) of something else [namely, the Form], it is fitting that it come to be in something else [namely, the Receptacle], on pain of being nothing at all" (52c 2–5). This is Plato's strategy for avoiding the fatal separation between Forms and immanent features of the sensible world, conceived as the "forms that we have" or "forms in us." Properly conceived, images exist only as fleeting determinations of the Receptacle under the influence of one or more Forms.

Of course many questions are left open, including the problem of how Plato can avoid the reciprocity of Similarity which in the *Parmenides* (in a version of the Third Man argument at 132d–133a) threatens to undermine the explanatory role of images and likeness. Images are said to be impressed on the Receptacle " in an amazing way, hard to describe" (50c 6). The promise to return to this topic is not fulfilled, unless we take the theory of elementary triangles, introduced at 53b, to be the promised account of how images of the Forms are produced in the Receptacle. It is in any case the geometry of these invisibly small triangles that replaces the atomism of Democritus with a more strictly mathematical theory. And it is the same geometric account that provides the mechanism by which the mathematics of Limit and "due measure" imposes order and goodness on the realm of sensory flux. It would seem that the theory of elementary triangles in the *Timaeus* is the physical expression of the notion of normative mathematics developed in the *Statesman* and *Philebus*.

A famous problem, debated already in Plato's school, is whether the creation story is to be taken literally, as positing a chaotic condition of the Receptacle before the Demiurge goes to work, or whether the myth of creation is to be interpreted as an expository device to distinguish different explanatory factors. A non-literal reading of creation would avoid the apparent incompatibility between the *Timaeus* account of pre-cosmic motions before the creation of the world-soul and the account given in the *Phaedrus* and the *Laws*, where the soul as self-mover is the source of all motion and change. A non-literal reading would also dispense with some vexing problems about the ontological status of the Demiurge and his relation to the Forms. (He is described as *noêtos*, "intelligible" like the Forms at 37a 1.) If we do not have to take creation literally, the Maker simply represents the principle of reason as a causal agency among the Forms.

Some problems will nevertheless remain. Why is the eternal and unchanging model for creation presented as a *panteles zôon*, a "complete living thing," containing within itself as parts or species all the intelligible living beings (30c–31b)? On the one hand, this eternal model is described in terms that clearly identify it with the Forms of the classical theory. (Thus at 39e 8 the model is referred to as to *ho estin zôon*, "the what-living-thing-is." This technical expression for the Forms occurs in no other dialogue later than the *Parmenides*.) On the other hand, nothing in the classical theory prepares us for this conception of the Forms as alive. It is as if Plato in the *Timaeus* chose to respond to the criticism of the Eleatic Stranger in the *Sophist*, who complained that the Friends of Forms conceive the highest Being as neither living nor thinking, "but standing immobile like a pious statue, without intelligence" (249a 1). Since it is a fixed doctrine that intelligence (*nous*) requires a mind or *psychê*, and *psychê* entails life (*Sophist* 249a, *Philebus* 30c 9, *Timaeus* 30b), by bringing the Forms to life the *Timaeus* evades this criticism. But the reader is left without a clue as to how the life and thought of the Forms are to be understood. Does the divine Intelligence of the Forms possess a divine Psyche of its own, before the creation of the World-Soul? And how is this Intelligence among the Forms related to the divine Psyche established as first source of motion by the argument of *Laws* X? These are some of the many questions that the myth of the Demiurge allows Timaeus to avoid.

See also Aristotle; Platonism and the Platonic Tradition; Socrates.

Bibliography

WORKS BY PLATO

Editions and Translations

The standard edition of the Greek text is by John Burnet, *Platonis Opera*. 5 vols. Oxford: Clarendon Press, 1899–1907. Volume I has appeared in a second edition, edited by E.A. Duke, W. F. Hicken, D. B. Robinson, and J. C. G Strachen, 1995, and a new edition of the *Republic* has appeared as *Platonis Respublica*, edited by S.R. Slings, New York: Oxford University Press, 2003. There are also editions of the Greek text with French translations in the "Les Belles Lettres" series (13 vols. in 25 parts, Paris: Les Belles Lettres, 1920–1956), and with English translations in the Loeb series (12 vols., London and New York: Harvard University Press, 1921–1935). The best English translations are collected in J. M. Cooper, ed., *Plato: Complete Works* (Indianapolis, IN: Hackett, 1997).

Modern Editions and Translations of Individual Dialogues

Adam, James. *The Republic of Plato*. 2 vols. Cambridge, U.K.: Cambridge University Press, 1902.

Burnyeat, Myles. *The Theaetetus of Plato*. Translated by M. J. Levett. Indianapolis, IN: Hackett, 1990.

Cornford, F. M. *Plato and Parmenides*. Translation of the *Parmenides* with commentary. London: Routledge & Kegan Paul, 1939.

Cornford, F. M. *Plato's Cosmology*. Translation of the Timaeus with Commentary (1937). Indianapolis, IN: Hackett,1997.

Cornford, F. M. *Plato's Theory of Knowledge*. Translation of the *Theaetetus* and *Sophist* with commentary. London: Routledge & Kegan Paul, 1935.

Morrow, G. R. *Plato's Epistles*. Indianapolis, IN: Bobbs-Merill, 1962.

Plato. *Gorgias*. Translation and commentary by E. R. Dodds. Oxford: Clarendon Press, 1959.

Plato. *Meno*, edited with translation and commentary by R. W. Sharples. Warminster, U.K.: Aris & Phillips, 1985.

Plato. *Parmenides*. Translated by M. L. Gill and P. Ryan with an introduction by M. L. Gill.Indianapolis, IN: Hackett, 1993.

Plato. *Phaedo*. Translated with commentary by D. Gallop. Oxford: Clarendon Press, 1975.

Plato. *Phaedo*, edited by C. J. Rowe. Cambridge, U.K.: Cambridge University Press, 1993.

Plato. *Phaedrus*, edited with translation and commentary by C. J. Rowe. Warminster, U.K.: Aris & Phillips, 1986.

Plato. *Philebus*. Translated with Introduction by D. Frede. Indianapolis, IN: Hackett, 1993.

Plato. *Statesman*, edited with translation and commentary by C. J. Rowe. Warminster, U.K.: Aris & Phillips, 1995.

Plato. *Symposium*, edited by K. J. Dover. Cambridge, U.K.: Cambridge University Press, 1980.

Plato. *Symposium*, edited with translation and commentary by C. J. Rowe. Warminster, U.K.: Aris & Phillips, 1998.

Plato. *Timaeus*. Translated with introduction by D. J. Zeyl. Indianapolis, IN: Hackett, 2000.

WORKS ABOUT PLATO

General Accounts

Crombie, I. M. *An Examination of Plato's Doctrines*. 2 vols. London: Routledge & Kegan Paul, 1962–1963.

Friedländer, P. *Plato*. Translated by H. Meyerhoff. 3 vols. London: Routledge & Kegan Paul, 1958–1969.

Grote, G. *Plato and the Other Companions of Socrates*. 2nd ed., 3 vols. London: Murray, 1867.

Grube, G. M. A. *Plato's Thought* (1935). Indianapolis, IN: Hackett, 1980.

Guthrie, W. K. C. *A History of Greek Philosophy*. Vols. 3–5. Cambridge, U.K.: Cambrdige University Press, 1969–1978.

Kraut, R., ed. *Cambridge Companion to Plato*. Cambridge, U.K.: Cambridge University Press, 1992.

Robin, Léon. *Platon* Paris: F. Alcan, 1935.

Shorey, Paul. *What Plato Said*. Chicago: University of Chicago Press, 1933.

Taylor, A. E. *Plato: The Man and His Work*. London: Methuen, 1926.

Willamowitz-Moellendorff, Ulrich von. *Platon*. 2 vols. (1919). 3rd ed., vol. I. Berlin: Weidmann, 1948.

Zeller, Eduard. *Die Philosophie der Griechen*. 6th ed. Hildesheim, 1963.

Particular Aspects of Plato's Work

Allen, R. E., ed. *Studies in Plato's Metaphysics*. London: Routledge & Kegan Paul, 1965.

Bambrough, Renford, ed. *New Essays on Plato and Aristotle*. London: Routledge & Kegan Paul, 1965.

Bobonich, C. *Plato's Utopia Recast: His Later Ethics and Politics*. Oxford: Oxford University Press, 2002.

Burnyeat, M. "Plato on Why Mathematics is Good for the Soul." *Proceedings of the British Academy* 103 (2000): 1–81.

Cherniss, H. F. *Aristotle's Criticism of Plato and the Academy*. Baltimore, MD: Johns Hopkins Press, 1944.

Cherniss, H. F. *The Riddle of the Early Academy*. Berkeley: University of California Press, 1945.

Frede, M. "Prädikation und Existenzaussage." *Hypomnemata* 18. Göttingen: Vandenhoeck and Ruprecht, 1967.

Gosling, J. C. B., and C. C. W. Taylor. *The Greeks on Pleasure*. Oxford: Oxford University Press, 1982.

Irwin, T. *Plato's Moral Theory* (1977). Revised as *Plato's Ethics*. Oxford: Oxford University Press, 1995.

Kahn, C. H. *Plato and the Socratic Dialogue: The Philosophical Use of a Literary Form*. Cambridge, U.K.: Cambrdige University Press, 1996.

Klosko, G. *The Development of Plato's Political Theory*. New York: Methuen, 1986.

Meinwald, C. C. *Plato's Parmenides*. Oxford: Oxford University Press, 1991.

Morrow, G. R. *Plato's Cretan City: A Historical Interpretation of the Laws*. Princeton, NJ: Princeton University Press, 1960.

Patterson, R. *Image and Reality in Plato's Metaphysics*. Indianapolis, IN: Hackett, 1985.

Robinson, Richard. *Plato's Earlier Dialectic*. 2nd ed. Oxford: Clarendon Press, 1953.

Ross, W. D. *Plato's Theory of Ideas*. Oxford: Clarendon Press, 1953.

Santas, G. X. *Plato and Freud: Two Theories of Love*. Oxford: Blackwell, 1988.

Skemp, J. B. *The Theory of Motion in Plato's Later Dialogues*. Cambridge, U.K.: Cambridge University Press, 1942.

Solmsen, Friedrich. *Plato's Theology*. Ithaca, NY: Cornell University Press, 1942.

Stenzel, Julius. *Plato's Method of Dialectic*. Translated from the 2nd German edition by D. J. Allan. Oxford: Clarendon Press, 1940.

Vlastos, G. *Introduction to Plato's Protagoras*. New York: Liberal Arts Press, 1956.

Vlastos, G. *Platonic Studies*. 2nd ed. Princeton, NJ: Princeton University Press, 1981.

Vlastos, G. *Studies in Greek Philosophy*. Vol. 2. Princeton, NJ: Princeton University Press, 1995.

Wedberg, A. E. C. *Plato's Philosophy of Mathematics*. Stockholm: Almqvist & Wiksell, 1955.

On Socrates

Gigon, O. *Sokrates, sein Bild in Dichtung und Geschichte*. Bern: A. Francke, 1947.

Momigliano, A. *The Development of Greek Biography* Cambridge, MA: Harvard University Press, 1971.

Patzer, A., ed. *Der Historische Sokrates*. Darmstadt: Wissenschaftliche Buchgellschaft, 1987.

Vlastos, G. *Socrates, Ironist, and Moral Philosopher*. Cambridge, U.K.: Cambridge University Press, 1991.

On the Early Academy

Dillon, J. *The Heirs of Plato: A Study of the Old Academy*. Oxford: Clarendon Press, 2003.

Ostwald, M., and J. P. Lynch. "Plato's Academy." Cambridge Ancient History VI, 602–616. 2nd ed. Cambridge, U.K.: Cambridge University Press, 1994.

On the Chronology of the Dialogues

Brandwood, L. *The Chronology of Plato's Dialogues*. Cambridge, U.K.: Cambridge University Press, 1990.

Campbell, L. *The Sophistes and Politicus of Plato*. Oxford: Clarendon Press, 1867.

Kahn, C. H. "On Platonic Chronology." *New Perspectives on Plato, Modern and Ancient*, edited by J. Annas and C. Rowe, 93–127. Cambridge, MA: Harvard University Press, 2002.

Ritter, C. *Untersuchungen über Plato*. Stuttgart: n.p., 1888.

Bibliographies

Brisson, Luc, and Benoît Castelnérac. *Platon, 1995–2000: Bibliographie*. Paris: Vrin, 2004.

Brisson, Luc, and Frédéric Plin. *Platon, 1990–1995: Bibliographie*. Paris: Vrin, 1999.

Cherniss, H. F. "Plato Studies, 1950–1957." *Lustrum* 4 (1959): 5–308; 5 (1960): 323–648.

Rosenmeyer, T. G. "Platonic Scholarship, 1945–1955." *Classical Weekly* 50 (1957): 172–182, 185–196, 197–201, 209–211.

Saunders, Trevor, and Luc Brisson. *Bibliography on Plato's Laws*, revised and completed with an additional *Bibliography on the Epinomis* by Luc Brisson. Sankt Augustin, Germany: Academia Verlag, 2000.

Charles H. Kahn (2005)

PLATONISM, MATHEMATICAL

See *Realism and Naturalism, Mathematical*

PLATONISM AND THE PLATONIC TRADITION

The term "Platonism" is so widely used in modern scholarship that it is difficult to determine its meaning precisely as applicable either to a particular group of thinkers or to a specific collection of doctrines. Ancient sources frequently describe "Platonists" as those philosophers who further developed the known or presumed teaching of Plato himself and "Academics" as those who pursued the skeptical methodology believed to have been initiated by the Socrates of Plato's earlier dialogues. However, the substantive "Platonism" seems first to occur in scholarly literature only around the beginning of the eighteenth century when it was used to characterize doctrines that were not only derived from but also combined with Plato's own teaching by later exegetes.

In order to apply this relatively modern usage of the term "Platonism" legitimately to the history of Western philosophy in general, it is useful to distinguish between: (1) Platonism in the sense of a Platonic *tradition*, or a set of ideas that is viewed in a strongly historical sense in connection with Plato or his early exegetes and is sufficiently extensive and coherent to overwhelm any influences from other traditions; and (2) Platonism in the sense of a Platonic *influence*, or a set of ideas that is viewed in a weakly historical sense in connection with Plato or his early exegetes and is not sufficiently extensive or coherent to overwhelm any influences from other traditions. Within the former category, it is useful to distinguish further (a) the *direct* Platonic tradition, that is, various philosophical ideas which we know to form part of the Platonic legacy and which their proponents characterized similarly, and (b) the *indirect* Platonic tradition, that is, those philosophical ideas which we know to form part of the Platonic legacy but which their advocates characterized differently.

Throughout the ancient period of Western thought, there was a Platonic tradition when Platonic philosophers were either members of Plato's Academy or claimed to revive and continue the "Academy." For this discussion, the medieval period is considered in terms of distinct Byzantine, Arabic, Jewish, and Latin cultural components, and here the distinction between direct and indirect traditions of Platonism becomes important, especially with respect to the Arabic tradition in which a type of indirect Platonism was viewed as "Aristotelianism." During the modern period of Western thought there has been initially a Platonic tradition, when Platonic philosophers again claimed to revive and continue the "Academy," but subsequently only Platonic influence.

Although such a procedure risks oversimplification, it may be useful to introduce the detailed historical analysis with a statement of the "essence of Platonism," that is, the set of philosophical assumptions underlying Plato's own written works or oral teachings in the view of his immediate successors in the Academy. Scholars may perhaps be guided by the ancient summary of Platonism in Apuleius's *On Plato and His Doctrine* (2nd century CE), which can be shown to depend on the early Peripatetics and on the early Academy—both with respect to the individual doctrines attributed to Plato and the pedagogical framework presenting them. According to Apuleius, Plato developed his own philosophical viewpoint after being introduced to the teachings of Heraclitus, studying with Socrates, encountering the Pythagoreans, and absorbing the dialectics of Parmenides and Zeno—the philosophical notions influencing Plato here being obviously those of the world as a continuous flux (Heraclitus), of the pursuit of universal definitions and of the primacy of the moral sphere (Socrates), of number as the underlying reality and of the immortality of the soul (the Pythagoreans), and of the contrast between real being and mere appearance (Parmenides).

Also according to Apuleius, Plato brought philosophy to perfection by combining the physics, ethics, and logic that had been pursued independently by the Pythagoreans, Socrates, and the Eleatics respectively into a single curriculum organized into three parts. On the basis of these historical data, one might therefore summarize the "essence of Platonism" as follows: Platonism is specifically characterized by the establishment of a contrast between the realm of being that is the object of knowledge or reasoning and is not subject to change and the realm of becoming that is the object of opinion or sensation and is liable to change. The two realms are linked by the soul, which exists indestructibly before, during, and after the temporal period of its combination with the body and for which assimilation either to the realm of being or to the realm of becoming represents the primary ethical choice.

ANCIENT PLATONISM

Modern scholars customarily divide Platonism in the ancient world into four main periods by using a mixture of ancient and modern terminology.

The "Old Academy" (347–267 BCE) is what Cicero called the original succession of philosophers within the Academy itself. The first of these philosophers was Speusippus (the scholarch, or "head of the school," 347–339 BCE), whose written works do not survive but whose doctrines can be reconstructed somewhat from later reports. Apparently Speusippus was influenced by the Pythagoreans into advocating as the first principles of reality, the One and the Dyad, the former transcending being, goodness, and intellect and the latter coinciding with matter. Speusippus abandoned Plato's own doctrine that the Forms were Ideal Numbers, yet emphasized Plato's teaching regarding the mathematicals intermediate between intelligibles and sensibles. He also explained the various levels of being as resulting from the relation between the One and different levels of matter.

Whereas Speusippus's theories were not influential until the time of the Neoplatonists, what became the standard type of Old Academic doctrine seems to have originated with his successor Xenocrates (scholarch, 339–314 BCE). Although the latter's works do not survive, it is possible on the basis of later reports to conclude that he produced the official edition of Plato's works and that he began a process of systematizing Platonic thought. For example, he established the formal tripartite division of philosophy into physics, ethics, and logic and he continued to develop the Pythagorean side of Plato's oral teaching. As first principles of reality, Xenocrates opposed the monad conceived as good to the dyad conceived as evil—the former corresponding to a self-thinking intellect containing the Forms or Ideal Numbers—and derived the entire cosmos from their interaction. The higher and lower worlds were mediated by a soul that was defined as a "self-moving number": in other words, it was self-moving like the soul of the *Phaedrus* and mathematically structured like that of the *Timaeus*.

Xenocrates' successor was Polemo (scholarch, 314–267 BCE), who seems to have differed from his two predecessors in that he placed somewhat greater emphasis on ethics. According to later testimonies, Polemo advocated the view that the goal of human existence was "life according to nature," this principle however required neither the rejection of external goods nor the extirpation of passions. Besides the three scholarchs, the Old Academy included other significant thinkers, including Crantor of Soli, the first known author of formal commentaries on the dialogues of Plato.

The New Academy (267–80 BCE) is distinguished by Cicero from the Old Academy on the basis of its shift from a dogmatic to a skeptical mode of philosophizing. Although this radical change of direction seems to have occurred in reaction to the extreme dogmatism of the current Stoic school, it appealed to the aporetic method illustrated by Socrates in the early dialogues of Plato for its historical justification. Arcesilaus (scholarch, 267–241 BCE), who followed the Socratic practice of writing nothing, argued that the degree of cognitive certitude claimed by the Stoic notions of perspicuity and assent was unattainable and that the correct epistemological attitude to the physical world was one of "withholding assent" (epochē). In fact, Arcesilaus did not hold to the position that nothing could be known, but more radically to the viewpoint that one cannot be certain whether anything can be known or not.

Later thinkers in the New Academic tradition slightly modified Arcesilaus's teaching. Carneades (scholarch, c. 160–129 BCE) agreed that it would be possible to reject the Stoic notions of perspicuity and assent while being guided in practical matters by observing three levels of probability. The end of the New Academy seems to have been occasioned by a dispute, the precise details of which are somewhat obscure, between Philo of Larissa (c. 130–69 BCE) and Antiochus of Ascalon (160–80 BCE). According to one reading of the evidence, Philo attempted to reconcile the New Academy and the Old Academy, whereas Antiochus, who was particularly enraged by the interpretation gaining currency that Arcesilaus and Carneades had endorsed the skeptical position publicly while indulging in dogmatic activities in private, preferred to reestablish the Old Academy entirely.

Modern historians call the next phase of ancient Platonism (80 BCE–c. 250 CE) "Middle Platonism." This terminology has been established in order to characterize Platonism in the period between the revival of dogmatism in the Academy by Antiochus of Ascalon and the innovations of doctrine introduced by Plotinus. Although it is applied to a number of philosophers working at different times and in different places, it is perhaps possible to identify certain methods and doctrines as typical of this phase of the tradition. From the viewpoint of methods, the Middle Platonists concentrated on the dogmatic aspects of the tradition—although aporetic and dogmatic elements co-exist in the work of Plutarch of Chaeronea (c. 45–125 CE)—and within the dogmatic approach there is a strong tendency toward systematization. The practice becomes fully established of writing commentaries on Plato's work: Eudorus of Alexandria (fl. c. 25 BCE) is reported to have followed Crantor in commenting on the Timaeus—and also of producing handbooks of Platonic teachings—examples of this genre are extant in the form of the Didaskalikos of "Alcinous" (fl. c. 130 CE) and On Plato and his Doctrine by Apuleius of Madaura (b. c. 125 CE). The tendency toward systematization is accompanied by a tendency toward syncretism. From Aristotelianism, Plutarch can adopt the ethical doctrine of the mean and Alcinous the logical doctrine of the categories. The combination of Pythagoreanism and Platonism implicit in the assumption of monad and dyad as first principles continues with figures like Eudorus, this development being associated with the rise of Platonizing pseudo-Pythagorica around this time (for example, the treatises On the Soul of the Universe and On Nature by "Timaeus of Locri" and On the Nature of the Universe by Ocellus Lucanus).

From Stoicism, Antiochus of Ascalon can adopt the physical doctrine of active and passive principles and Atticus (fl. c. 170 CE) the ethical doctrine of extirpating passions. From the viewpoint of doctrines, the following physical ideas may be considered as particularly characteristic of Middle Platonism: (1) controversy over the corporeality or the incorporeality of the first principle—here the position of Antiochus should be contrasted very clearly with that of Eudorus and the rest of the tradition; and (2) postulation of a triadic group of first principles consisting of a first God that is One as in Pythagoreanism and Good as in the Republic and corresponds to a self-thinking Intellect containing the Forms; a second God having affinities with the Demiurge of the Timaeus and the Logos of Stoicism; and a World Soul sharing features with the principle of the same name in the Timaeus and the Indefinite Dyad of the Pythagoreans; and (3) tentative emergence of a first principle above Being itself in the work of Numenius of Apamea (fl. c. 150 CE). Among the ethical ideas characteristic of Middle Platonism might be mentioned the debate over the goal of human life. Here, the Antiochean notion of assimilation to nature should be contrasted with the Eudoran ideal of assimilation to God.

The phase in the history of Platonism initiated by the philosophy of Plotinus and in the twenty-first century called "Neoplatonism" may be divided into several "schools," in the sense of being associated with certain leading thinkers: namely, that of Plotinus and his students Porphyry and Amelius, that of Iamblichus and his followers, and the Athenian school from Plutarch of Athens, through Syrianus and Proclus, to Damascius. This last school claimed to be the successor of the ancient Academy and was closed by the Emperor Justinian in 529 CE.

Plotinus (204–269 CE) studied with Ammonius Saccas in Alexandria and later established his own school in Rome. He set out a metaphysical system, which, with various additions and modifications, became foundational for Platonic philosophy and for the reading of Plato until modern times. Thanks to the complete corpus of Plotinian writings called the *Enneads* and the biography attached by Porphyry to his edition of the latter, historians can understand the methods and doctrines of Plotinus more than they can those of any previous Platonist. The *Enneads* reveal precisely how Plato's works yielded systematic metaphysical tenets: The *Republic* provided the notion of the Good above Being; the *Parmenides* provided the postulation of the One, the One-Many, and the One-and-Many as the three first principles; the *Symposium* provided the identification of Beauty and Intellect; the *Sophist* provided the five Kinds constituting Intellect; the *Phaedrus* provided the relation between universal and individual Soul; the *Phaedo* provided the individual soul's attachment and detachment from the body and the notion of virtue as purification; the *Theaetetus* provided the notion of assimilation to the divine; and the *Timaeus* provided the distinction between being and becoming, the notion that the divine has no envy, the treatment of the intelligible living creature as a phase of Intellect, the treatment of the Demiurge as an intellective phase of Soul, the indivisible and divisible components of Soul, the cosmological reading of the lower gods, and the identification of the Receptacle and Matter.

Plotinus's philosophical approach was sometimes based on the interpretation of a specific passage, often quite brief, in Plato's dialogues, sometimes based on the discussion of a particular problem (e.g., that of the relation between Intellect and intelligible objects raised by Porphyry and recorded in *Enneads* V. 5), sometimes based on the critique of some false interpretation of Plato (e.g., that of the evil nature of the visible world maintained by the Gnostics and reported in *Enneads* II. 9) but usually based on a combination of the above. Porphyry's *Life of Plotinus* describes the role of sources other than Plato in these discussions, Aristotle's *Metaphysics* being particularly influential (a statement corroborated by Plotinus's use of the doctrines of potency and act and of the self-thinking intellect), both Platonic and Peripatetic commentators (e.g., Gaius and Alexander respectively) being sources of inspiration, and Stoic doctrines also being utilized (a statement corroborated by Plotinus's dematerialized reading of the *pneuma* as "procession and reversion").

The system emerging from this analysis might perhaps be summarized as follows. According to Plotinus, reality—understood dynamically as a descending hierarchy of "procession" (ontological founding and at certain points ethical fall) and as an ascending hierarchy of "reversion" (ontological completing and at certain points ethical perfecting)—consists of three principles or "hypostases": the One or Good (described less determinately as the Beyond, the Supreme, the First), which is cause or power; Intellect—a macrocosmic unity and microcosmic plurality that timelessly thinks itself is logically distinguishable into the five Platonic Kinds of Being, Sameness, Otherness, Motion, and Rest, and metaphysically contains the Platonic Forms; and Soul—a macrocosmic unity and microcosmic plurality that generates time and receives the Platonic Forms into itself as reason-principles. This hypostasis also contains a higher and a lower aspect: Soul proper and Nature. Below these three principles is the nonprinciple of Matter (in some but not all contexts called Evil), which receives the unfolding of Soul's lower aspect by projecting the Forms into three-dimensional space. The reversion is the more complex of the two dynamic aspects of reality given that it also comprises the epistemological transition from the discursive and propositional reasoning of Soul to the intuitive and nonpropositional thinking of Intellect to that which is approached in an entirely noncognitive manner.

Iamblichus (c. 245–325 CE) presided over an influential philosophical school at Apamea in Syria. He devoted himself to formal commentary on both Plato and Aristotle, a practice in which he followed his teacher Porphyry, and wrote an extensive study of Pythagorean mathematics. His approach to philosophy initiated certain tendencies especially characteristic of later Neoplatonism: namely, increasing emphasis on systematic and religious elements. In the former case, Iamblichus reinforced both the continuity and the discontinuity between the Plotinian hypostases by introducing numerous mediating terms; in the latter, he postulated a more radical fall of the human soul that could only be reversed by ritual observances. For Iamblichus, the systematic and religious aims came together since the discernment of more levels of reality provided a metaphysical foundation for traditional polytheism.

Proclus (412–485 CE) was the most influential representative of the Athenian school of Neoplatonism. In a number of extant works that include commentaries on Plato's *Alcibiades, Cratylus, Parmenides, Republic,* and *Timaeus,* a commentary on Euclid's *Elements,* and such independent treatises on Platonic philosophy as *The Platonic Theology* and the *Elements of Theology,* Proclus extended the emphasis on systematic and religious aspects of philosophy already detectable in Iamblichus. The systematization was particularly influential. This can be seen in his *Commentary on the Parmenides,* where he interpreted the famous dialectical discussion starting from the hypothetical proposition "If it is (there is a) one, the one will not be many" by applying the first five hypotheses to the One, the "ones" or gods together with the beings participating in them, nondivinized souls, Forms in Matter, and Matter; by associating three senses of "One" (above Being, with Being, and below Being) with the first three hypotheses; and by showing that all the attributes denied of the One in the first hypothesis are affirmed of the gods in the second.

Systematization can also be seen in the *Elements of Theology* where Proclus applied a method reminiscent of Euclidean geometry in order to "demonstrate" through a series of propositions, proofs, and corollaries and starting from certain initial propositions such as "All that is unified is other than the One itself" what philosophers must believe regarding the One itself (propositions 1–6), regarding the relation between the One and the other hypostases of the expanded post-Iamblichean order of being (propositions 7–112), and regarding the other hypostases themselves (propositions 113–211).

MEDIEVAL PLATONISM

The medieval Platonic tradition can be divided into the non-Latin and Latin traditions, the former in its turn being divisible into the Byzantine, Arabic, and Jewish traditions. But before turning to these, a few comments are necessary regarding certain transformations of ancient philosophy by patristic writers that formed a basis for later developments.

The most important intermediary between ancient and medieval Platonism in the West was Augustine of Hippo (354–430 CE). In the autobiographical *Confessions,* Augustine reported his encounter with "certain Platonic books translated from Greek into Latin" (Confessions VII. 9)—assumed to be writings of Plotinus and Porphyry by most scholars—and his consequent liberation from the dualistic and materialistic tenets of Manichaeism that had formerly impeded his progress toward Christian truth. What is being described here in narrative terms is the discovery of that synthesis of Platonism (specifically Neoplatonism) and Christianity that becomes a standard feature of Augustine's writing. This synthesis included two versions of a Platonic theory of first principles: (1) the identification of the Neoplatonic One and Being/Intellect with the Trinitarian Father and Word respectively (as in *Confessions* VII. 9); and (2) the identification of the One and Being/Intellect with God and the angels respectively (as in *On the Literal Interpretation of Genesis* II. 15ff.).

These two versions of Platonism are moving in opposite directions, since in the former case the universal aspect of the second principle is intensified while the hierarchical relation between the first and second principles is weakened; in the latter, the universal aspect of the second principle is weakened while the hierarchical relation between the first and second principles is intensified. The most important intermediary between ancient and medieval Platonism in the East was "Dionysius the Areopagite." This otherwise unknown fifth-century Christian achieved a posthumous authority by writing an important group of theological treatises, including *On the Celestial Hierarchy, On Divine Names* and *On Mystical Theology,* under the pseudonym of the first-century Dionysius famously converted by St. Paul.

On Divine Names in particular provides a skillful Christian adaptation of late pagan Neoplatonism in which the negative and affirmative predicates of hypotheses I and II of Plato's *Parmenides* are applied not to the One and the gods respectively—as in Proclus's commentary—but to a God or "Thearchy"—who is simultaneously transcendent of and immanent in created things. This important transformation in the direction of monotheism has as further philosophical consequences that the distinction between the transcendence and immanence of the deity by being partially mind-dependent introduces an element of idealism into the realist ontology characteristic of traditional Platonism. The Augustinian and Pseudo-Dionysian versions of the Neoplatonic theory of first principles should especially be compared with regard to their handling of the theory of Forms and the doctrine of Soul. With respect to the Forms, both writers understood Forms in the sense of physical paradigms as contained in the divine Intellect but Forms in the sense of moral absolutes as equivalent to divine attributes. With respect to the Soul, both authors removed the universal Soul from their system but, with suppression of the idea of transmigration between bodies, retained the function of individual souls.

The most important thinker within the Byzantine tradition of medieval Platonism is Michael Psellus (1018–1078). This author's claim to have revived the discipline of philosophy single-handedly is justified to the extent that, in an environment dominated by orthodox Christianity and methodological Aristotelianism, he reestablished the patristic notion of Platonism as a forerunner of Christianity and the later Neoplatonic notion of a relation between Aristotle and Plato in which the former's physics serves as an introduction to the latter's theology. Although Psellus is hardly responsible for metaphysical innovations in works like *On Plato's Psychogony* and *On the Ideas Which Plato Mentions*, the fact that he discussed philosophy by explicitly combining pagan Platonic sources such as Plato, Proclus, and Plotinus with Christian Platonic sources such as Gregory of Nyssa, Pseudo-Dionysius, and Maximus the Confessor represents an innovation in textual practice.

More specifically, this practice might be characterized as selective in that it isolates only certain aspects of traditional Platonism as compatible with Christianity—for example, by removing all theurgic elements (in *On the Activity of Demons*)—as allegorical in interpreting metaphysical principles in pagan texts as symbols of metaphysical principles in Christian scripture, and as combinatory in that it juxtaposes groups of notions drawn from traditional Platonism and Christianity without reducing the conflicting elements—for example, by combining Proclus's metaphysical interpretation of Jupiter's relation to the lower gods with the pseudo-Dionysius's of the Thearchy's relation to the angelic ranks (in *On Homer's Golden Chain*). This highly original textual manipulation of Platonism established an intellectual tradition that endured until the fall of Constantinople. Later representatives include John Italos (c. 1025–after 1082), Eustratios of Nicaea (fl. at the end of the eleventh and early twelfth centuries)—author of a commentary on Aristotle's *Nicomachean Ethics*, which includes material from Proclus and was translated into Latin by Grosseteste, and Nicholas of Methone (mid-twelfth century), author of a "refutation" of Proclus's *Elements of Theology*.

That Arabic writers were able to make a major contribution to the development of medieval Platonism not only in the Islamic but also subsequently in the Christian world resulted from a fortunate circumstance: the availability of some reasonable translations as sources. Under the Umayyad and 'Abbāsid caliphs, a vast enterprise of translating scientific and philosophical works from Greek into Arabic (sometimes through the intermediary of Syriac) was undertaken by such figures as Hunain b. Ishāq (808–873) and Qustā b. Lūqā (tenth century) with the result that all of Aristotle except the *Politics*, a certain amount of Plato, and many Greek philosophical commentaries, became available. It was in such a milieu that an important group of philosophical *apocrypha* arose.

This group consists of: (1) an Arabic "Plotinian" corpus (possibly the remains of a translation and commentary on *Enneads* IV–VI produced in the circle of al-Kindī [b. late eighth century and d. after 866]) comprising the *Theology of Aristotle*, the *Letter on Divine Science*, and the *Sayings of a Greek Sage*; (2) the adaptation of Proclus's *Elements of Theology*, later known to the Latins as the *Book of Causes* (the Arabic original of which was produced before 992); and (3) an Arabic translation of approximately thirty-five propositions from Proclus's *Elements of Theology* and *Elements of Physics*. These works are connected through their expression of metaphysical teachings that depart from their Plotinian or Proclean originals in identical ways: namely, in describing the first principle as Pure Being—meaning Being without Form—rather than as the One above Being; and as creating, without any preexistent term or materiate substratum—rather than as causing—all subsequent principles. Moreover, that the first principle or Creative Being does not relate indirectly—through the mediation of an order of gods or "ones"—but directly to the second principle or Created Being is the common doctrine of the *apocrypha*.

During the next few generations, various writers developed a uniquely Arabic approach to the reading of the philosophical tradition in which a Neoplatonic doctrinal component drawn from sources of the type mentioned was inserted into an overtly Aristotelian context. Within this tradition al-Fārābī (Latin: *Alfarabius* [d. 950]) outlined a program of harmonizing Aristotelian and Platonic doctrine in his *Reconciliation of the Two Sages*, *Philosophy of Plato*, *Philosophy of Aristotle*, *Attainment of Happiness*, and *Opinions of the Inhabitants of the Virtuous City*. According to his metaphysical system, the Supreme Being or One produces a series of intellects, each of which can think its cause (thereby giving rise to a further intellect) and itself (thereby giving rise to a celestial sphere), this theory being understandable as the transfer of the emanative causal mechanism from the Neoplatonic hypostases to the Aristotelian unmoved movers.

Also within this tradition Ibn Sīnā (Latin: *Avicenna* [980–1037]) organized knowledge into logic, physics, and metaphysics along Aristotelian lines in his encyclopedic *Book of Healing* and its abridgement the *Book of Salvation*. He further developed al-Fārābī's metaphysical system in proposing that, when the Supreme Being produces the subsequent terms, the first intellect in a threefold process first thinks the Being necessary in itself (thereby producing by emanation the second intellect), then itself as necessarily existing through its cause (thereby producing the soul of the first heaven), and finally itself as contingently existing through itself (thereby producing the body of the first heaven), this process being repeated until all the intellects, souls, and heavens have been generated. The inevitable reaction came when Ibn Rushd (Latin: *Averroes* [1126–1198]) attempted to liberate the authentic Aristotle from such Neoplatonizing tendencies. Of his two most famous interpretative innovations, the doctrines that the intellects are not connected by emanation and that there is a single agent and materiate intellect for all humanity, the first but not the second obviously runs counter to Neoplatonism. Ethical and political thought was not neglected by the Arabs and, since both Plato's *Laws* and *Republic* were available in Arabic, in this area they tended to be more Platonic than Aristotelian. Among examples of their work are al-Fārābī's compendium of the former dialogue and Ibn Rushd's commentary on the latter.

The most important thinker within the Jewish tradition of medieval Platonism is Solomon ben Judah ibn Gabirol (Latin: Avicebron [c. 1021–1058]). As the author of some excellent poetry in Hebrew, including the famous *Kingly Crown* and one philosophical treatise in Arabic, Ibn Gabirol stands within two cultural traditions. The philosophical work, which survives only in the Latin translation by Iohannes Hispanus and Domenicus Gundissalinus under the title of *Fountain of Life*, continues the speculative approach of the Arabic *apocrypha* but also develops the latter in an original style. Ibn Gabirol argued that the duality of form and matter underlies both the spiritual and the corporeal levels of reality, this combination of the formal and the material being used in subtle ways to explain the relation between unity and plurality. Although form and matter are also two closed doors between the human intellect and its Creator that are difficult to pass through, one can describe the Creator as Wisdom, Unity, and Will inasmuch as he is the cause of form and as Being inasmuch as he is the cause of matter.

Ibn Gabirol's duality of form and matter in created things represents the moments of determination and undetermined within an emanation, as indicated by his references elsewhere to the dynamic process whereby the inferior comes forth from and strives for union with the superior. Although a Hebrew translation of certain extracts was subsequently made by Ibn Falqera and there may have been some influence on the Jewish mystics of the Gerona circle, the philosophical afterlife of the *Fountain of Life* was mainly in the world of Latin scholasticism.

Because only the *Timaeus* was available in Latin (translated up to 53c with commentary by Calcidius [fourth century CE]) throughout the Middle Ages, the translations of the *Meno* and *Phaedo* (by Aristippus of Catania [d. 1166]) and of the *Parmenides* (included in Proclus's commentary up to 142a translated by William of Moerbeke [c. 1215–1286]) achieving only limited circulation towards the end of the period, one refers to a predominantly indirect transmission of doctrine in speaking of a "Platonic" tradition in the medieval Latin world. However, even this restricted definition of the latter is problematic given that the doctrines concerned are usually combined with Christianity and, during the thirteenth to fifteenth centuries especially, with Aristotelianism. One way of approaching the medieval Latin tradition of Platonism is perhaps to distinguish certain doctrinal clusters; that is, groups of philosophical teachings that exhibit sufficient coherence among themselves and predominate sufficiently in the context where they occur, and then to track the evolution of these clusters through medieval thought. The most important clusters are the following:

(1) A "Timaean" cluster. This group of doctrines, which is presented in passages of Augustine's *Against the Academics*, *On the City of God*, and *On Eighty-Three Different Questions* (qu. 46), based on Cicero's works (including his partial translation of the *Timaeus*) and also in Calcidius's *Commentary on the Timaeus* and Macrobius's *Commentary on the Dream of Scipio*, represents a systematic and cosmological Platonism. It emphasizes the metaphysical principles of Soul and Nature, interprets the transcendent Forms as thoughts in the divine mind, and in general has affinities with the Middle Platonic doctrine of Antiochus of Ascalon.

(2) A psychological and Augustinian cluster. Based on Augustine's *Soliloquies* and *On the Trinity*, this group identifies the relations between the macrocosmic and microcosmic aspects of the Neoplatonic hypostases of the One and Intellect respectively along Porphyrian lines in order to ground human cognition or rather supracognition of the First Principle.

(3) A mathematical cluster. Based on the ancient tradition dating back to Xenocrates, it is transmitted to the Middle Ages by Boethius's *On Arithmetic, On Music*, and *On the Consolation of Philosophy*. This group emphasizes the relations between the monadic and dyadic aspects of the hypostases and between monad, dyad, and number series.

(4) A "Proclean" cluster. This group of doctrines, which is presented in different ways by Latin translations of the Pseudo-Dionysian corpus (by John Scottus Eriugena [d. c. 877–879] and several later writers), of the Arabic *Book of Causes* (by Gerard of Cremona between 1160 and 1187), and of Proclus's *Elements of Physics* (by an unknown translator c. 1160), *Elements of Theology, Commentary on the Timaeus, Commentary on the Parmenides*, and *Minor Theological Tractates* (all by William of Moerbeke between 1268 and 1286), represents a systematic and theological Platonism. It emphasizes the metaphysical principles of the One and Intellect, interprets the transcendent Forms as divine attributes or names, and in general is aligned with the Neoplatonic doctrines of the Athenian School.

(5) A psychological and Avicennian cluster. Based on the Latin translation of the psychological portions of Ibn Sīnā's *Book of Healing* (probably by Ibn Daud [d. c. 1180] and Dominicus Gundissalinus [fl. 1126–1150]), this group equates the relation between the macrocosmic and microcosmic aspects of the Neoplatonic hypostasis of Intellect with the conjunction between the separate agent intellect and the human intellect used by Arabic Aristotelianism to combine the abstraction of universals with the emanation of Forms.

In the medieval Latin world, these clusters occur in the following combinations and sequence. In John Scottus Eriugena's *On Natures*, cluster 4 as it occurs in the pseudo-Dionysian corpus is developed into a comprehensive metaphysical doctrine in which everything that is and is not can be divided on the one hand into the four quasi-species of "creating and not created," "creating and created," "not creating and created," and "not creating and not created" and on the other into a procession and a reversion of the First Cause with respect to its effects and of the effects with respect to their First Cause.

In philosophers of the twelfth century there was a tendency to combine clusters 1 and 3. For example, Adelard of Bath (fl. c. 1110–1125), who also translated the writings of Euclid from Arabic, elaborated within the

context of cluster 1 a view of nature and of reason as theologically quasi-independent and also a theory of universals designed to harmonize the opinions of Plato and Aristotle; see his *On the Same and the Different and Natural Questions*. William of Conches (d. c. 1154), in his *Glosses on Plato's Timaeus, Glosses on Macrobius*, and *Philosophy of the World*, wrote extensively on an issue central to a naturalistic cosmology but problematic for Christian theology: namely the status and function of the Platonic world soul. Thierry of Chartres (fl. 1121–1148), who was described by contemporaries as the greatest Platonist of his era, elaborated within the contexts of cluster 1 and cluster 3 a metaphysics in which the interaction between God's unity and Matter produces the multiplicity of Forms equivalent to numbers, the Trinitarian nature of God also being expressible arithmetically as $1 \times 1 = 1$; see his *Commentary on Boethius's On the Trinity* and *On the Works of the Six Days*.

With the appearance of translations from Arabic into Latin and the rise of the medieval university after circa 1200, Platonism had to compete with Aristotelianism: a task that it accomplished most successfully within the sphere of what modern scholars term "Latin Avicennism." In the anonymous *Book of Avicenna on the First and Second Causes and the Emanation of Being*, cluster 2, cluster 4 as it occurs in the Pseudo-Dionysius and in the *Book of Causes*, and cluster 5 are combined to produce a metaphysical system in which the procession and reversion of effects with respect to the First Cause begins with the production of the first created intellect by Pure Being, and in which cognition takes place when the human soul ascends from the looking of reason to the vision of intellect and the tenth created intellect or agent intellect combines with the human intellect. This text represents a kind of standard late medieval Platonism to which all serious thinkers will have to react whether they are predominantly Aristotelian (e.g., Albert the Great [c. 1200–1280]) or predominantly Platonic (e.g., Dietrich of Freiberg [c. 1240–1318/1320], Meister Eckhart [c. 1260–1327]) in tendency.

MODERN PLATONISM

The modern Platonic tradition can be divided into a phase beginning with the impact of the early-fifteenth-century humanist movement and a phase beginning with Friedrich Daniel Ernst Schleiermacher's German translation of Plato (published 1804–1809). The former phase might also be termed the "early modern" or "Renaissance" phase of Platonism.

Humanism can be defined as an ideal of liberal education based on the study of grammar, rhetoric, poetry, history, and moral philosophy especially through the recovery of authoritative texts in Greek and Latin, the term "humanism" itself corresponding to the *studia humanitatis* advocated by the Roman rhetorician and philosopher Cicero. Although the beginnings of the humanistic movement can be detected in Northern France during the early twelfth century, the main development is usually traced from Francesco Petrarca (in English, "Petrarch," 1304–1374).

Taking their cue from the latter's pointed praising of Plato in preference to Aristotle, Italian humanists together with their Byzantine associates produced during the next century and a half a series of Plato translations based on newly imported manuscripts. These included Latin versions of the *Republic* by Manuel Chrysoloras and Uberto Decembrio, by Pier Candido Decembrio, and by Antonio Cassarino, versions of the *Phaedo, Gorgias*, several *Letters, Phaedrus* (partial), *Crito, Apology, Symposium* (partial) by Leonardo Bruni, of the *Axiochus* by Cencio de' Rustici, of the *Ion* by Lorenzo Lippi, of the *Crito, Axiochus*, and *Euthyphro* by Rinuccio Aretino, of several *Letters* and the *Euthyphro* by Francesco Filelfo, and of the *Charmides* (partial) by Angelo Poliziano. From this list of titles, one may conclude that the "humanists" interest in Plato was primarily focused on the literary, ethical, and political aspects of Plato's work.

The first Platonic philosopher affected by humanism was Nicholas of Cusa (originally Niklaus Krebs, 1401–1464), a fact indicated by his commissioning of a Latin translation of the *Parmenides* by the Byzantine émigré George of Trebizond, the manuscript of which exists, together with his own marginal notes (Volaterranus 6201, f. 61r–86v), in the twenty-first century. Although Nicholas was not familiar with the complete *Parmenides* when he wrote his most celebrated philosophical work *On Learned Ignorance* (1440)—and probably not even with the part reproduced in Moerbeke's Latin translation of Proclus's commentary—the teaching of the dialogue fitted naturally into the philosophical system already developed for that work on the basis of medieval sources.

In summary, that system involves the threefold distinction of an "absolute maximum" (God), a "contracted maximum" (the Universe), and a simultaneously absolute and contracted maximum (Christ). With respect to the absolute maximum (and also to the relation between the three maxima), one can discern a Pythagorean and Trinitarian metaphysical structure comprising unity, equality, and connection, which is applied to a Dionysian structure based on the contrast of negative theology (indicating divine transcendence) and affirmative theology (indicating divine immanence) in order to produce an original Cusan metaphysical structure consisting of what surpasses opposites, opposites as such, and the "coincidence of opposites." Although this system has many affinities with doctrines advocated during the Middle Ages, it is innovative in emphasizing the subjectivity of the negative-affirmative theological antithesis (by transferring the teaching of pseudo-Dionysius's *On Mystical Theology* to the cosmological sphere), in its frequent recourse to mathematical images: for example, the maximum, infinity, the circles and triangles of geometry, and the concord of music, and in emphasizing the coincidence inherent in opposition (again adapting the teaching of *On Mystical Theology* to a cosmological use), the combination of the first and last points epitomizing the "learned ignorance," which provided Nicholas with his title.

Marsilio Ficino (1433–1499) is a truly seminal figure who established a pattern of interpreting Platonic philosophy that remained fundamental for the next three centuries. By the late 1450s Ficino had acquired a sufficient reputation as a Platonic thinker and as a Greek scholar to be requested by the Florentine ruler Cosimo de' Medici in 1462 to translate Plato's complete works into Latin from a newly acquired manuscript, this translation appearing in a first edition in 1484 and a second edition in 1491. In addition to this commission, Ficino translated the Hermetic corpus (under the title *Pimander*), the *Enneads* of Plotinus (published in 1492), and various treatises by Porphyry, Iamblichus, Proclus, Synesius, and Michael Psellus for the first time, and also made a fresh translation of the pseudo-Dionysian corpus.

Historians rate him highly not only as an exegete of Plato and Platonism (on the basis of his translations and the commentaries published with the latter) but also as a constructive Platonic thinker (on the basis of his substantial independent treatise titled *The Platonic Theology or On the Immortality of the Soul*). Ficino is important as an exegete because he considered for the first time since antiquity the complete writings of Plato and was therefore able to draw material from dialogues unavailable during the Middle Ages and to engage more fully with the argumentative context of Plato's teaching. Moreover, he proposed a special interpretation of the history of philosophy under the influence of late ancient and Byzantine writers and of Diogenes Laertius's *Lives of the Philosophers* according to which the Christian revelation beginning from Moses is confirmed by a unified and harmonious system of pagan theology emerging as a six-fold transmission linking Hermes Trismegistus with Orpheus, Aglaophemus, Pythagoras, Philolaus, and Plato.

Dionysius the Areopagite plays a pivotal role in this theory, which basically unifies disparate ideas through allegorical reading. As a thinker of unique inspiration and apostolic authority, Dionysius disclosed the truths concealed in the ancient system to pagan Platonists like Plotinus, the latter in turn transmitting those truths back to Christian writers such as Augustine. Ficino is important as a constructive thinker because he developed the Neoplatonism not only of Proclus (which had become known toward the end of the medieval period) but also of Plotinus (which was almost totally unknown during the Middle Ages) in directions more consistent with the Christian sense of human dignity and individuality. For example, the hypostatic system is sometimes recast so that Soul, instead of being simply the lowest of the three principles of the One, Intellect, and Soul, becomes the third member of a series of five terms God, Angel, Soul, Quality, and Body. This arrangement not only gives Soul a mediating and therefore sustaining function but supplies a novel argument for Soul's immortality in that if Soul were dissoluble then the entire order could likewise suffer dissolution. The hypostatic system is also sometimes modified in that Soul, instead of ascending or descending by identifying with the adjacent term of the series conceived dynamically in the upward direction, ascends or descends by passing through static regions formed by the adjacent terms on both sides.

One work by Ficino was particularly influential both inside and outside philosophy: namely, *On Love* written in 1469 and published in 1484. In fact, it is largely owing to this free commentary on Plato's *Symposium* that Platonism was to become among all doctrines in the history of philosophy the most influential on literature, the visual arts, and music.

Another Platonic philosopher affected by humanism was Giovanni Pico della Mirandola (1463–1494). In his *Conclusiones*—a set of 900 philosophical theses that he would have defended in a public disputation had the Pope not intervened by declaring some of them heretical—Pico attempted to extend the notion of a universal system underlying philosophy by adding the Jewish Kabbalah to the Egypto-Hellenic tradition described by Ficino. On the basis of the number of theses drawn from different schools of philosophy in the more historical first part of the work, it would seem that Proclus (supplying fifty-five theses) and the Kabbalists (supplying forty-seven theses) are the most important influences, the

organization of the project itself into a set of propositions recalling Proclus's methodology (as in the *Elements of Theology*) and the ascription of numbers to the propositions reflecting the Kabbalistic approach (900 being the numerical value of the cruciform Hebrew letter *tsade*).

Other writings by Pico also respond to Ficinian ideas. The *Oration* (called *Oration on the Dignity of Man* after Pico's death) and the *Heptaplus* elaborate the notion of Soul as central in the order of reality, while *On Being and Unity* (part of a projected work *On the Concord of Plato and Aristotle*) discusses the question whether among first principles Unity is prior to Being or not. In the latter essay, Pico's conclusion that Unity is not prior to Being according to either Plato or Aristotle required him to argue that hypothesis I of the *Parmenides* forms part of a purely dialectical exercise and thereby to sustain the Porphyrian, Arabic, and Latin rather than the Plotinian version of the Neoplatonic theory of first principles. In both these cases his theories deviate from Ficino's normal view.

The question of the impact of Platonism on the generations after Ficino is an extremely complex one. Despite the reading of Plato's dialogues in Greek courses at the traditional universities, the attempt of Francesco Patrizi (1529–1597) to establish courses on Platonic philosophy at the Universities of Ferrara and Rome, and the rise of numerous Platonically inclined literary "academies" in Italy and France, Platonism never displaced Aristotelianism institutionally. In fact, with respect to the sixteenth century it is necessary to speak of Platonic influence rather than of a Platonic tradition. Platonism during this period is partially a continuation of earlier tendencies. This description would apply to various discussions of Soul, for example when the Lateran Council of 1512–1517 proclaimed the immortality of the human soul as official dogma perhaps under the influence of Ficino, and when Giordano Bruno (1548–1600) incorporated the Plotinian theory of the World Soul into his cosmological speculation. Closely connected with the theory of Soul and disseminated by the various "academies" were the Platonic doctrines of spiritual love (derived from Ficino's reading of the *Symposium*) and of divine madness (derived from Ficino's reading of the *Phaedrus* and *Ion*) whose influence can be detected in Bruno's *Eroici Furori* and Patrizi's *Della Poetica* respectively.

Sixteenth-century Platonism is also partially an adaptation to newer ideas. Here, Platonism was rightly seen as having more in common with the rising mathematical sciences and quantitative thought than did Aristotelianism. Of the two main concepts of traditional mathematical Platonism, the notion of the *a priori* validity of numbers and of the symbolic power of numbers, Johann Kepler (1571–1630) applied both the first and the second and Galileo Galilei (1564–1642) the first but not the second to the astronomical-physical sphere.

With respect to the seventeenth and eighteenth centuries it is even more necessary to speak of Platonic influence rather than of a Platonic tradition. Platonism during this period is partially a continuation of earlier tendencies. This description applies to the philosophy of inner spirituality advocated by the "Cambridge Platonists" Henry More (1614–1687) and Ralph Cudworth (1617–1688), the last European thinkers to explicitly place themselves within the Platonic tradition. Seventeenth- and eighteenth-century Platonism is also partially an adaptation to newer ideas. Here, the notion of the intellectual love of God in Benedictus de Spinoza (1632–1677), the notion of reality as a system of spiritual monads each of which reflects the entire universe from its own viewpoint in Gottfried Wilhelm Leibniz (1646–1716), and the notion of thought reaching the sphere of things-in-themselves in the precritical thought of Immanuel Kant (1724–1804) are particularly important.

Between the sixteenth and eighteenth centuries there is also a remarkable example of a Platonism that might be considered as standing on the borderline between Platonic tradition and Platonic influence. The treatise *Siris* by George Berkeley (1685–1753) is a recommendation of tar-water as a panacea taking the form of a chain of reflections linking the properties of this liquid first with the chemical and physical phenomena of air and fire respectively and secondly with the spiritual world ascending to God. The main philosophical aims of Berkeley's study, which obviously blends the chain of reflections with the chain of being itself, are to oppose the mechanistic, materialist, and pluralistic view of the universe—well established by his own day—with a spiritual, immaterialist, and unified one, and also to supplement the sensuous immaterialism of his own earlier works—notably the *Treatise concerning the Principles of Human Knowledge*—with a theological idealism. The substantial final section of the treatise achieves its aims by mustering an impressive array of explicitly cited Platonic sources, including Plato's dialogues *Alcibiades I*, *Phaedo*, *Republic*, *Theaetetus*, *Timaeus*, *Parmenides*, and *Letters*, Plotinus's *Enneads*, Proclus's *Platonic Theology*, Bessarion, Ficino (especially his commentary on the *Enneads*), Patrizi, and Cudworth.

On the basis of these authorities, it then argues that the three hypostases of Plotinian Neoplatonism are a reflection of the Christian Trinity. Here, the most important points to emerge are that Unity and Being are mutually convertible, that the placing of the hypostasis of the One before the hypostasis of Intellect or Being does not imply any atheism because there is nevertheless no time at which the One was without Intellect—an argument seemingly unprecedented within the Platonic tradition—and that the purely notional distinction between divine attributes allows the first point to be compatible with the second. The Platonic teachings quoted in *Siris* are clearly not to be taken too literally: Rather, the philosophical maxims of ancient times are proposed, as Berkeley put it, not as principles of logical demonstration but as hints to awaken and exercise the inquiring mind.

Schleiermacher's German translation of the writings of Plato (1804–1809), in which the necessity of distinguishing Plato's own doctrine from the teachings of later "Platonists" and the suggestion that the authentic teaching of the dialogues is superior to the pedantic systematizations of their later admirers was stressed, is rightly seen as the watershed in the history of Platonic interpretation. This new approach had already been gaining ground during the seventeenth and eighteenth centuries, as evidenced by various comments in Leibniz and reference books like J. J. Brucker's *Historia Critica Philosophiae* (1742–1744) and Denis Diderot's *Encyclopédie* (1751–1765). This approach underlines the change from the perception of a unified Platonic tradition to that of more fragmentary Platonic influences. But these changed circumstances present a new set of problems for any interpreter wishing to apply the term "Platonism" henceforth. In short, to what extent is it reasonable to speak of "Platonism" after 1800? A few comments on the "afterlife" of Platonism are perhaps in order.

One should begin by considering what might be termed *modern historical studies* on the question of "Platonism." Of relevance to the historical question are the distinctions intended by modern interpreters when employing the terms "Middle Platonism" (occasionally "Pre-Neoplatonism") and "Neoplatonism" with respect to the ancient tradition (see especially the works of Willy Theiler and Heinrich Dörrie). Although the application of such terminology assumes the principle of distinguishing between Plato's own doctrine and that of later exegetes, it does not exclude the possibility that a particular teaching originates with Plato himself, something that must be ascertained on a case by case basis. Also of relevance to the historical question is the notion that certain doctrines central to Plato's thought that were taught orally by the master but not included in his dialogues can be identified using the tools of modern criticism (see especially the works of Hans-Joachim Krämer and Konrad Gaiser). The study of such doctrines can yield clarification regarding both the meaning of certain teachings expressed obscurely in the dialogues and the origination of various doctrines associated with Middle or Neoplatonism.

These points represent historiography rather than philosophy in the wake of "Platonism." In order to identify a trajectory of modern philosophical Platonism, one might consider the following three cases in which influential doctrines have been or could be associated with Platonism:

(1) Georg Wilhelm Friedrich Hegel (1770–1831) in his *Lectures on the History of Philosophy* interpreted the Proclean triad of Being, Life, and Intellect within the intelligible world as corresponding to thought-determinations within the Hegelian Idea. One could tentatively propose this as a case of Platonism in that Hegel was explicitly reading a Platonic text and because his doctrine combines similarities with Platonism (the triadic structure occurs in Neoplatonism) with differences (the Platonic structure is abstractly universal whereas the Hegelian is concretely universal). But Hegel is obviously less a Platonist in either of the aforementioned senses than a creative reader of Platonism.

(2) Gottlob Frege (1848–1925) in his *Foundations of Arithmetic* postulated purely logical objects, which inhabit a logical realm of the objectively nonreal in contrast with the physical realm of the objectively real and the psychical realm of the subjectively real, and which especially include numbers. Scholars frequently describe his thinking as "logical Platonism" in that, although Frege was not explicitly reading a Platonic text, his doctrine combines similarities with Platonism (the establishment of an *a priori* element) with differences (the Platonic element is an essence whereas the Fregean is a proposition). But scholars label Frege a Platonist in an extremely loose sense, given that what is common to Platonism and Frege does not enter into any recognizably systematic structure of Platonism.

(3) Martin Heidegger (1889–1976) in his *The Essence of Truth: On Plato's Cave Allegory and Theaetetus* interpreted the Platonic Forms not as what is real as opposed to what is apparent but as the interplay of appearance and concealment. One could again tentatively propose this as a case of Platonism in that Heidegger was explicitly reading a Platonic text and because his doctrine combines similarities with Platonism (the dual structure occurs in Neoplatonism) with differences (the Platonic duality is metaphysical in character whereas the Heideggerian is phenomenological in character). But Heidegger is again less a Platonist in either of the senses distinguished previously than a creative reader of Platonism.

These ideas in Hegel, Frege, and Heidegger are undoubtedly among the more powerful philosophical thoughts since the 1800s. They reveal clearly that, although Platonism declined in significance as a tradition between 1600 and 1800, it has continued to provide a stimulus to philosophical activities of all kinds. There is no reason to think that this will not continue to be the case in the twenty-first century and beyond.

See also Agent Intellect; Alcinous; al-Fārābī; Ancient Scepticism; Antiochus of Ascalon; Arcesilaus; Augustine, St.; Averroes; Avicenna; Carneades; Cudworth, Ralph; Eckhart, Meister; Ficino, Marsilio; Frege, Gottlob; Hegel, Georg Wilhelm Friedrich; Heidegger, Martin; Ibn Gabirol, Solomon ben Judah; More, Henry; Neoplatonism; Nicholas of Cusa; Numenius of Apamea; Petrarch; Philo of Larissa; Pico Della Mirandola, Count Giovanni; Plato; Plotinus; Plutarch of Chaeronea; Porphyry; Proclus; Pseudo-Dionysius; Pythagoras and Pythagoreanism; Schleiermacher, Friedrich Daniel Ernst; Socrates.

Bibliography

Copenhaver, Brian P., and Charles B. Schmitt. *Renaissance Philosophy*. New York: Oxford University Press, 1992.

Dillon, John M. *The Middle Platonists: A Study of Platonism 80 BC to AD 220*. London: Duckworth, 1977.

Fakhry, Majid. *A History of Islamic Philosophy*. 2nd ed. New York: Columbia University Press, 1983.

Gersh, Stephen. *From Iamblichus to Eriugena: An Investigation of the Prehistory and Evolution of the Pseudo-Dionysian Tradition*. Leiden, Netherlands: E. J. Brill, 1978.

Gersh, Stephen. *Middle Platonism and Neoplatonism: The Latin Tradition*. Notre Dame, IN: University of Notre Dame Press, 1986.

Hankins, James. *Plato in the Italian Renaissance*. Leiden, Netherlands: E. J. Brill, 1990.

Klibansky, Raymond. *The Continuity of the Platonic Tradition during the Middle Ages*. Millwood, NY: Kraus International Publications, 1982.

Kristeller, Paul Oskar. *Eight Philosophers of the Italian Renaissance*. Stanford, CA: Stanford University Press, 1964.

Kristeller, Paul Oskar. *Renaissance Thought and Its Sources.* Edited by Michael Mooney. New York: Columbia University Press, 1979.

Merlan, Philip. *From Platonism to Neoplatonism.* 3rd ed. The Hague: Nijhoff, 1968.

Rosenthal, Franz. *The Classical Heritage in Islam.* Translated by Emile and Jenny Marmorstein. Berkeley: University of California Press, 1975.

Tigerstedt, Eugène N. *The Decline and Fall of the Neoplatonic Interpretation of Plato. An Outline and Some Observations.* Helsinki: Societas Scientiarum Fennica, 1974.

Tigerstedt, Eugène N. *Interpreting Plato.* Stockholm: Almqvist and Wiksell International, 1977.

Wallis, Richard T. *Neoplatonism.* London: Duckworth, 1972.

Zervos, Christian. *Un philosophe néoplatonicien du XIe siècle: Michel Psellos: Sa vie, son œuvre, ses luttes philosophiques, son influence.* Paris: Laroux, 1920. An English-language translation was published by Burt Franklin (New York) in 1973.

Stephen Gersh (2005)

PLEASURE

The concept of "pleasure" has always bulked large in thought about human motivation and human values and standards. It seems clear to most people that pleasure and enjoyment are preeminent among the things worth having and that when someone gets pleasure out of something, he develops a desire for it. Moreover, from the time of Plato much of the discussion of the topics of motivation and value has consisted in arguments for and against the doctrines of psychological hedonism (only pleasure is desired for its own sake) and ethical hedonism (only pleasure is desirable for its own sake). One can make an intelligent judgment on these doctrines only to the extent that he has a well-worked-out view as to the nature of pleasure. Otherwise he will be unable to settle such questions as whether a putative counterexample, for instance, a desire for the welfare of one's children, is or is not a genuine example of desiring something other than pleasure for its own sake.

DEMARCATION OF THE TOPIC

Pleasure and pain have usually been regarded as opposite parts of a single continuum. As pain diminishes, it tends toward a neutral point; by continuing in the same "direction" we move toward increasing intensities of pleasure. Thus Jeremy Bentham regarded amounts of pain as negative quantities to be algebraically summated with amounts of pleasure in computing the total hedonic consequences of an action or a piece of legislation. This was in accordance with the utilitarian principle that an action is justified to the extent that it tends to produce pleasure and the diminution of pain. Since *pain* is most commonly used as a term for a kind of bodily sensation, it is natural to think of pleasure as having the same status. And indeed there are uses of the term *pleasure* in which it seems to stand for a kind of bodily sensation. Thus we speak of "pleasures of the stomach" and thrills of pleasure. But as hedonists have often insisted, in any sense of the term in which psychological or ethical hedonism is at all plausible, the term *pleasure* must be used so as to embrace more than certain kinds of localized bodily sensations. When someone maintains that pleasure is the only thing which is desirable for its own sake, he certainly means to include states of the following sort:

(1) Enjoying (taking pleasure in) doing something, such as playing tennis.

(2) Getting satisfaction out of something, such as seeing an enemy humiliated.

(3) Having a pleasant evening; hearing pleasant sounds.

(4) Feeling good, having a sense of well-being.

(5) Feeling contented being.

It seems clear that phenomena of these sorts do not consist in localized bodily sensations of the same type as headaches, except for being of an opposite quality. When someone has enjoyed playing tennis, it makes no sense to ask where (in his body) he enjoyed it. Nor does it make sense to wonder whether the pleasure he got from the tennis came and went in brief flashes, or whether it was steady and continuous; but these would be sensible questions if getting pleasure from playing tennis were a localized bodily sensation like a headache. This is not to deny that various localized sensations might be involved in his enjoyment of the game, such as a swelling in his chest after making a good shot, or a sinking sensation in his stomach after muffing a shot. The point is that his enjoyment of the game cannot be identified with such sensations, for he could be enjoying the game throughout its duration, even though such sensations cropped up only from time to time.

In fact we are confronted with two distinguishable positive-negative dimensions. There is the pleasure-pain dimension, a dimension of bodily sensations ranging from intense pains to intense localizable pleasures of the sort experienced in sexual orgasm. To specify the other dimension we need a terminological convention. We shall use the term *getting pleasure* as a general designation for an experience like those specified in the above list. Thus, enjoying listening to music and feeling good on arising in the morning are special forms of "getting pleasure." Getting pleasure can, then, be thought of as the positive segment of a dimension, the negative segment of which will be termed *getting displeasure* and will include such things as feeling bad, feeling discontented, having a miserable time, being uncomfortable, being displeased by someone's action, being "pained" or distressed at the sight of something, and so on. We have variations of degree in this "pleasure-displeasure" dimension, as well as in the "pleasure-pain" dimension. One can enjoy oneself more or less and be displeased at something more or less. Moreover, it would seem that there is an intermediate neutral point at which one is neither pleased nor displeased at what is happening, neither enjoying oneself nor feeling miserable, and so on. It is the pleasure-displeasure dimension that philosophers are really trying to understand when they discuss "pleasure and pain." Hence we shall take the problem of the nature of pleasure to be the problem of understanding what it is to "get pleasure." For simplicity of exposition we shall largely confine the discussion to the positive segment of the pleasure-displeasure dimension; when dealing with the entire dimension we shall use the term *hedonic tone*.

It is important to realize that in posing the problem in this way philosophers (and psychologists) have assumed that there is something fundamental which is common to enjoying something, getting satisfaction out of something, being pleased at something, feeling good, and so on. It is conceivable that this assumption is mistaken, in which case virtually all the discussions of the problem have been misguided. In this article we shall follow tradition in supposing that there is an important common element to be found.

PLEASURE AS A NONLOCALIZED SENSATION

Admitting all the above, it still might be supposed that pleasure is a nonlocalized bodily sensation on the order of fatigue or "feeling energetic." (If pleasure is a sensation, it must be a bodily sensation rather than visual, auditory, tactile, olfactory, or gustatory; for it is evident that pleasure is not simply a function of the stimulation of external sense receptors.) If so, to get pleasure out of playing tennis would be to have the pleasure sensation while playing tennis. This view has been made the target of some acute critical attacks, most notably by the Oxford philosopher Gilbert Ryle. The main criticisms are as follows:

(1) Any sensation can be either pleasant or unpleasant, depending on further features of the context. A thrill can be either a thrill of pleasure or a thrill of horror. A masochist even gets pleasure out of painful sensations. Some sensations are generally pleasant (moderate warmth), others generally unpleasant (strong electric shock); but the fact that what one enjoys in a particular case depends on factors other than the kind of sensation involved, shows that we cannot identify taking pleasure in something with having a certain kind of sensation.

(2) It would seem that any sensation, if it becomes sufficiently acute, will tend to monopolize consciousness and interfere with concentration on anything else. On the view under consideration, the more pleasure we get out of, say, playing the piano, the more intense the sensation of pleasure would become, the more our attention would be taken up with the sensation of pleasure, and the harder it would become to concentrate on the playing. But the reverse is the case. The more pleasure we get out of doing something, the easier it is to concentrate on *it*.

(3) Any kind of sensation could conceivably occur without its usual conscious accompaniments and could, indeed, occupy the whole of consciousness. Even if sinking sensations in the stomach normally coincide with a perception or thought of something as dangerous, it is quite possible for one to have such sensations without being aware of anything else at the moment. Thus, on the sensation theory one could conceivably have the pleasure of playing tennis all by itself, without having it in conjunction with one's awareness that one is playing tennis. Pleasures do not seem to be detachable in the way this theory requires them to be. However, to this argument the sensation theorist could reply that we do have cases in which the pleasure sensation occurs all alone, such as feeling good or having a sense of well-being without consciously feeling good *about* anything in particular. Of course we cannot get the enjoyment of playing tennis without playing tennis, but that is just because of the way the complex phrase "enjoying playing tennis" is defined. We would not label the pleasure we get "the pleasure of playing tennis" unless the pleasure sensation occurred in conjunction with the awareness that one is playing tennis. But this verbal point does not disprove the contention that what makes enjoying playing tennis a case of getting pleasure is the presence of the

same sensation which occurs alone in feeling good (about nothing in particular).

(4) A more serious difficulty is posed by another respect in which the sensation theory represents enjoyment as loosely connected with what is enjoyed. According to the theory, to enjoy something is to have the pleasure sensation in conjunction with that something. But if "in conjunction with" means merely "in consciousness at the same time as," we are faced with the following difficulty. Let us suppose that while enjoying playing tennis at a given moment I am aware not only of playing tennis but also of oppressive humidity in the atmosphere and of a plane flying overhead. The pleasure sensation occurs in consciousness at the same time as all these cognitions. Therefore the sensation theory implies that I must be enjoying the oppressive humidity and the plane just as much as I am enjoying playing tennis. But this is contrary to the facts. A person knows immediately which of the various things he is aware of at the moment he is taking pleasure in; and the sensation theory can give no account of this discrimination. We must posit some more intimate connection between the pleasure and its object than simply being together in consciousness at the same time. But it seems that so long as we interpret getting pleasure as having a certain kind of sensation, no more intimate bond can be specified.

VARIANTS OF THE "CONSCIOUS-QUALITY" THEORY

The heavy emphasis on the bodily sensation theory in recent philosophical discussion has tended to obscure the fact that there are a number of other theories that belong to the same family, some of which have been much more important historically than the sensation theory. The general sort of view, of which the sensation theory is a variant, can be described as the view that pleasure is one of the ultimate immediate qualities (or data) of consciousness (experience). To say that it is a quality of consciousness is to say that it constitutes one of the ways in which one state of consciousness differs from another with respect to its own intrinsic nature rather than its relations to other things. (To say that a state of consciousness is a visual sensation of redness is to say something about its intrinsic nature, while to say that it belongs to Jones is not.) It is an immediate quality of consciousness because one is aware of it immediately, just by

virtue of its presence; nothing further is required to get at it. Analogously, in a visual sensation one is aware of the color just by virtue of having the sensation; the color is not something that could be there without being the object of awareness. It is an ultimate quality of consciousness, because it cannot be analyzed in any way with respect to its intrinsic nature. Again we may use the less problematic sensory qualities to illustrate the point. A felt pressure differs from a felt warmth, or a seen color from a heard sound, in a way that cannot be further analyzed. To know what the difference is, one must have experienced both. Henceforth, we shall use the terms *pleasantness* and *unpleasantness* for the supposed ultimate qualities, the awareness of which is, on this kind of theory, essential for getting pleasure or displeasure.

The thesis that

(A) Pleasure is a kind of bodily sensation (more exactly stated, a quality that defines a kind of bodily sensation)

is one variant of this view; for qualities that do define kinds of bodily sensation are ultimate immediate qualities of experience—tingling, nausea, dizziness, and so on. However, there are other variants that are deserving of more respect.

(B) Pleasure is a kind of feeling, or a quality that defines a kind of feeling, where feelings are taken to be elements of consciousness distinguishable from sensations, including bodily sensations.

(C) Pleasure is a quality that can occur only as one aspect or attribute of some larger conscious complex, as a certain pitch or timbre occurs only as an aspect of a sound that has other aspects. Theories of this sort differ according to the sort of conscious element pleasure is thought to qualify: sensations, complexes of sensations, feelings, and so on. However, once we abandon the project of identifying pleasure with a certain kind of mental element, there is no reason not to take the most liberal alternative and consider the quality of pleasantness attachable to any sort of conscious state. This would have the advantage of not forcing us to explain away the fact that thoughts, realizations, memories, and mental images all seem to be accompanied by pleasure in the same way as sensations. For purposes of further discussion we shall take as our formulation of (C): *Pleasure is a quality that can attach to any state of consciousness.*

Let us consider whether the arguments against (A) cited above have any force against (B) and (C). Both the

ENCYCLOPEDIA OF PHILOSOPHY
2nd edition   • 619

first argument (that any sensation can be pleasant or unpleasant) and the second (that any sensation is capable of monopolizing consciousness) depend on specific features of bodily sensations; one could hardly expect them to have any bearing on theories that do not identify getting pleasure with having a certain kind of bodily sensation. With respect to thesis (C), it is not clear that every quality of conscious states is inherently neutral between being pleasant and unpleasant, nor is it clear that every quality of conscious states will monopolize attention in proportion to its degree. With respect to thesis (B), there are, of course, feelings that are, or essentially involve, bodily sensations (feeling nauseated, feeling tired), and the arguments do apply to these. But thesis (B) identifies pleasure with feelings that are distinct from bodily sensations. Apart from this qualification there are feelings, ordinarily so called, which, no matter how "strongly" one has them, do not tend to monopolize attention (feeling calm), and there are feelings that are not, by their nature, neutral between pleasantness and unpleasantness (feeling contented, feeling distressed). Such examples show that the consideration adduced in the first two arguments cannot be used to rule out the possibility that pleasure is some kind of feeling.

The third argument (that any sensation should be capable of occurring without its usual conscious accompaniments), on the other hand, does rule out the possibility of pleasure being a feeling, if a feeling is conceived as a mental element that could occur alone. However, we must remember that thesis (B) is distinguishable from thesis (A) only to the extent that it is restricted to feelings that are not identifiable, in whole or in part, with bodily sensations. And insofar as such feelings exist, it is doubtful that they are capable of occupying the whole of consciousness.

To make this point more concrete, let us look at the way position (B) developed. Its historical roots are to be found in the tripartite division of the mind into faculties of cognition, will, and feeling, a scheme developed in Germany in the eighteenth century by such men as Moses Mendelssohn and Immanuel Kant. Roughly speaking, the faculty of feeling is the faculty of being consciously affected, positively or negatively, by things of which one becomes aware through the faculty of cognition. Already the suggestion appears that a feeling is something that arises only in reaction to one or more cognitions and hence does not have the essential autonomy of a sensation. The introspective psychologists of the nineteenth and early twentieth centuries who tried to work out a doctrine of feeling as a distinctive kind of element of consciousness, most notably Wilhelm Wundt and E. B. Titchener, wound up with a notion of feelings as, in effect, simply hypostatized bearers of the supposed ultimate qualities of pleasantness and unpleasantness. Wundt, indeed, tried to incorporate other qualities into feelings, namely, the dimensions of strain-relaxation, and excitement-quiescence; but other workers in the field tended to regard these as features of associated bodily sensations.

More generally, it seems likely that insofar as two feelings, ordinarily so called, differ in their immediate "feel," other than with respect to pleasantness and unpleasantness, this difference can be attributed to the bodily sensations involved. Thus, if we contrast feeling homesick and feeling relieved, or feeling distressed and feeling contented, the difference in "feel," apart from different degrees of pleasantness and unpleasantness, will come down to differences in the kinds of bodily sensations involved. Hence, we are left with pleasantness and unpleasantness as the only qualitative dimension of feelings, construed as elements distinguishable from bodily sensations. Since it was generally held that such feelings could occur only in reaction to "cognitive" mental elements, including sensations, the third argument has no force against the thesis that getting pleasure out of something consists in having a pleasant feeling in conjunction with that something. But immunity from those criticisms is purchased at the price of any significant distinction between theses (B) and (C). Instead of saying that pleasantness and unpleasantness are qualities of special mental elements termed *feelings*, which can occur only in conjunction with other mental elements, we might just as well say that pleasantness and unpleasantness are qualities that can attach to any mental element. For since on the feeling theory nothing can be said about the intrinsic nature of feelings, other than that they "bear" the qualities of pleasantness and unpleasantness, it would be in principle impossible to determine by introspection whether, when I am relieved at discovering that my child is out of danger, the pleasantness I experience attaches to my awareness of the situation or to a feeling that occurs in response to my awareness. There would be a point in adopting the more complex categorization of the experience in terms of special feeling-elements if the postulation of such elements were needed for the construction of a theory as to the causes and/or effects of getting pleasure and displeasure. But the notion of feeling-elements has not so far demonstrated any theoretical fertility. Thus, when probed, thesis (B) reduces to thesis (C).

Thesis (C)—that pleasure is a quality that can attach to any state of consciousness—escapes the third and fourth arguments, as well as the first two. The third argument obviously has no application since, according to this thesis, pleasure can exist only as a quality of some more concrete entity. It escapes the fourth argument (that according to the sensation theory, pleasure would attach to any awareness present in consciousness at the same time) because it is possible that the quality of pleasantness would attach to one apprehension and not another, even if both are in the same consciousness at the same time. Thus, in the example given, pleasantness could attach to my awareness of playing tennis but not to my awareness of the humid atmosphere, even though I am aware of both simultaneously.

Thus thesis (C) emerges as the only serious contender from the ranks of quality-of-consciousness theories, and historically most such theories can be regarded as approximations to it. John Locke treated pleasure and pain as "simple ideas obtained both from sensation and reflection," and for David Hume pleasure and pain were "impressions of sensation." Neither Locke nor Hume distinguished in any systematic way between kinds of sensations, qualities of sensations, feelings, and qualities of feelings. If we look at the way they actually used the notions of an "idea of pleasure" or "impression of pleasure," we can see that in effect they took pleasure to be a qualitative feature that can attach to any state of consciousness. The "sensationist" psychologists, such as David Hartley and James Mill (whose psychology, in the hands of Jeremy Bentham and John Stuart Mill, became the basis of the utilitarian ethics and social philosophy), took pleasure and pain to be ultimate, unanalyzable properties of sensations, copies of sensations (ideas), and combinations of sensations and ideas; pleasure and pain were thought to be transferred, via association, to any mental content. None of these thinkers distinguished between the pleasure-pain and the pleasant-unpleasant dimensions, but once we clear up that confusion their view, as applied to the latter, can be seen to be a form of thesis (C).

CONSIDERATION OF CONSCIOUS-QUALITY THEORY

The main support for the conscious-quality theory comes from the fact, already noted, that a person knows immediately when he is getting pleasure from something. He knows it in a way no one else could conceivably know it—just by virtue of being the one who is getting the pleasure. He has an epistemologically "privileged access" to the fact. Since it is natural to take the awareness of sensory qualities, especially visual ones, as a paradigm of immediate knowledge of one's psychological states, it is natural to construe what one knows when he knows that he is enjoying something as some ultimate quality of consciousness.

Nevertheless, on further probing, the thesis that pleasure is a quality that can attach to any state of consciousness is not very plausible phenomenologically. When we reflect on a wide variety of cases of getting pleasure, as indicated by the list at the beginning of this article, we are unable to isolate a felt quality that they all share, in the way in which we can easily isolate a quality of redness which a number of different visual sensations share, or a quality of painfulness that a number of different bodily sensations share. On the contrary, enjoying playing tennis feels very different from getting satisfaction out of seeing an enemy in distress, and both feel very different from the sense of well-being one has when, in good health, one arises carefree from a good night's sleep. Nor does it seem possible to find *in* these experiences some respect in which they are qualitatively the same, as two sounds, otherwise very different, can be the same in pitch. Even if we stick to one term in the "pleasure family," such as *getting satisfaction,* it seems equally implausible to suppose that there is some felt quality common to getting satisfaction out of seeing an enemy in distress and getting satisfaction out of the realization of a job well done. The enjoyment or satisfaction seems to take whatever felt quality it has from what one is enjoying or getting satisfaction from. Thus John Stuart Mill was on sound ground in insisting, against Bentham, that there are qualitative differences between "pleasures."

These doubts are reinforced by the fact that here we are without external support for the postulation of basic conscious qualities. In the case of sensory qualities, at least those of the external senses, we can tie down the quality to a certain kind of stimulation; people ordinarily get red visual sensations when and only when their optic nerves are stimulated by stimuli of a certain physical description. Moreover, certain kinds of variations in the physical properties of the stimulus can be correlated with judgments of degrees of properties of the sensation, such as hue, saturation, and shade. These correlations support our confidence in purely introspective discriminations between visual qualities. Nothing of the sort is possible with pleasantness. This quality, if such there be, does not vary with variations in physical stimuli in any discernible fashion. Nor can anything much better be found on the response side. It is true that there are gross typical differences in bearing and manner between a person enjoying himself and a person having a miserable time, between a person satisfied with the way things are going and a person who feels terribly frustrated. On the positive side of these contrasts we are more likely to get relaxation, expansiveness, and smooth coordination; on the negative side tenseness, constriction, and disruption of ongoing activities. But these manifestations differ so much from case to case because of other factors—general personality characteristics and state of health, for example—that they cannot be taken as reliable indications of how much pleasure or displeasure a given person is getting at the moment.

MOTIVATIONAL THEORIES

No doubt there is something that all the experiences we have classified under "getting pleasure" have in common. If it is not an immediately felt quality, what is it? In searching for an alternative we might well take note of a different tradition in which the notion of pleasure was analyzed motivationally, in terms of the realization of the good, of the object of striving. In many systematic schemes of the "passions of the soul," the basic notion is appetite, inclination, striving, or tendency of the person toward some object he apprehends as good or desirable. Pleasure, delight, or joy is then defined as the state in which this object is actually present, in which the appetite has reached fruition. Versions of this view are to be found in Thomas Aquinas, Thomas Hobbes, Benedict de Spinoza, and many other philosophers, as well as in some more-recent psychologists, notably William McDougall. The basic presuppositions of this approach to the subject are quite different from those of Locke and Hume. For Locke and Hume, and British empiricists generally, the way to understand any psychological concept is either to find it among the immediate data of introspection or to show how it is to be analyzed into such data. This approach ultimately stems from the Cartesian insistence that one knows one's own states of consciousness better than anything else, in particular, better than physical objects and events, since it is possible to doubt the existence of all the latter but not of all the former. Hence it is natural for one in this tradition freely to posit immediate qualities of consciousness whenever there is any plausibility to doing so. Thinkers in the other tradition have a more objectively oriented epistemology, according to which conscious experience has no priority over, for instance, overt behavior as an object of investigation and an object of knowledge. This leaves them free to explore the possibility of analyzing the notion of pleasure in

terms of notions like appetite, or tendency, which could not be regarded as immediate objects of introspection.

Their view of the nature of pleasure might be formulated as follows:

(D) To get pleasure is to be in a state of consciousness which includes the awareness that one has obtained something one wants.

There are serious difficulties with this version of a motivational theory of pleasure. No doubt there are many pleasures that do presuppose a want in the absence of which no such pleasure would be forthcoming. I would not take pleasure in the discomfiture or prosperity of a certain person unless I wanted him to be discomfited or to prosper, as the case may be. But it seems that there are many pleasures which do not presuppose any such preexisting want. Simple sensory pleasures, such as the pleasure of eating a good steak, are the most obvious cases. Having found steak pleasant, we may then develop a desire for a steak; but here the want presupposes the prior experience of pleasure, not vice versa. The view under consideration does not deny that wants can be reinforced or strengthened by the experience of pleasure in their satisfaction. But it does deny that one can get pleasure from anything except by way of that thing satisfying some previously existing want. And this seems contrary to experience. Surely infants take pleasure in many things, such as throwing a ball, when they encounter them for the first time. Prior to this encounter they could not have had a desire for it, for they did not yet know what throwing a ball is. It is noteworthy that proponents of this position maintain it in the face of these difficulties only by generously positing instincts and other nonconscious "tendencies" and "strivings."

However, there are other versions of a motivational theory that do not presuppose a preexisting desire for each pleasure. The most promising is a view put forward by Henry Sidgwick, among others:

(E) To get pleasure is to have an experience that, as of the moment, one would rather have than not have, on the basis of its felt quality, apart from any further considerations regarding consequences.

This account makes pleasure a function not of a preexisting desire but of a preference one has at the moment of the experience. To say that one has the preference at the moment is not to say that one expresses the preference even to oneself; it is not to say anything about what is before one's consciousness at the moment. It is, rather, to say something dispositional—for example, that one would choose to have an experience just like this rather than not if one were faced with such a choice at this moment and if no considerations other than the quality of the experience were relevant. This, unlike thesis (D), allows for the possibility of taking pleasure in something one did not previously have a tendency to seek. On the other hand, it is also clearly distinct from the conscious quality theory. According to thesis (E), when one says that he is enjoying something, he is saying something about the quality of his experience; he is saying that the quality of his experience is such that on that basis alone he would prefer to have it rather than not to have it. But he is not saying what the quality of his experience is; he is saying, rather, how it is related to his preferences, likes, or desires. More particularly, he is not saying that there is some particular quality, "pleasantness," present in the experience. On this view, the felt qualities on the basis of which the experience is valued can be as diverse as the range of human likes. They can involve calm, excitement, warmth, cold, thrills, and sinking feelings.

It might seem that the strongest reason for the conscious-quality view, the fact that pleasure is something to which the subject has privileged access, would pose a difficulty for thesis (E), but this is not necessarily so. It is natural to think that the only things an individual can know about immediately, in a way no one else can, are the qualities of his experience; and indeed sensory qualities have this status. But there are many things to which an individual has privileged access that cannot be regarded as immediately felt qualities, such as intentions, attitudes, and beliefs. If I intend to quit my job tomorrow, I know that I have this intention without having to do any investigation to find out; I know just by virtue of having the intention; I know this as immediately as I know that I am now aware of a reddish patch. And it is in principle impossible for anyone else to know in this way that I have that intention. Yet an intention is neither a felt quality nor a complex of felt qualities. Hence the epistemological status of pleasure is not a conclusive reason for construing it as a quality of experience. The epistemological status of pleasure does place a constraint on the range of possible theories; we cannot identify pleasure with something to which the subject does not have privileged access, such as a certain pattern of neuron firings in the brain. However, among the nonsensory quality items to which a person has privileged access are his likes, preferences, and wants. It seems reasonable to suppose that a person's knowledge that he would choose to have an experience just like his present one on the basis of its felt quality can be just as immediate as his knowledge that he is aware of a red patch.

Motivational theories have the following superiority over conscious-quality theories. It does not seem to be merely a contingent fact that pleasure is desirable, or that the fact that an activity is enjoyable is a reason for doing it. "I get a lot of satisfaction out of teaching, but I see absolutely no reason to do it" sounds like a self-contradiction. This is not to say that the fact that one will get pleasure out of something is a conclusive reason for doing it; there may well be other considerations that outweigh this. I would enjoy playing tennis now, but if an urgent job has to be completed, that is a good reason for not playing tennis. What we are suggesting to be necessarily true is (P) the fact that one gets pleasure out of x is a reason for doing or seeking x. This reason must be put into the balance along with other relevant reasons in making a decision in any particular case. The conscious-quality theory can throw no light on this necessity. If pleasure is an unanalyzable quality of experience, there is nothing about the meanings of the terms involved in (P) that would make it necessarily true. Why should it be necessarily true that a certain unanalyzable quality of experience is something to be sought? It would seem that any such quality is something that would or would not be taken as desirable by a given person, or people in general, depending on further factors. A motivational theory, on the other hand, analyzes the concept of pleasure in such a way as to make principles like (P) necessary. If to enjoy an experience is just to be disposed to choose an experience exactly like it if nothing other than the felt quality is relevant, then it follows trivially that the fact that something involves enjoyment is a reason for choosing it.

Superficially it might appear that opting for a motivational theory would involve a commitment to psychological hedonism, but this would be a mistake. The motivational theory commits us to holding that pleasure is (always) intrinsically desirable, but it carries no implication that pleasure is the only thing intrinsically desirable. One could adopt thesis (E) as his theory of the nature of pleasure and still regard other things as intrinsically desirable, such as fulfillment of one's potentialities and intellectual consistency, independent of any pleasure they might bring. It is an analysis of desire in terms of pleasure that would stack the cards in favor of psychological hedonism. If we hold that to desire something is to think of it as pleasant, it does follow that we do not desire anything except pleasure or what is believed to lead to pleasure.

THE MEASUREMENT OF PLEASURE

The problem of measuring hedonic tone has occupied both psychologists and philosophers. Psychologists have addressed themselves to such problems as the physiological basis of pleasure, the dependence of pleasantness on various aspects of sensory stimulation (such as contrast), and the effect of pleasure and displeasure on the speed and efficiency of learning. To deal with these problems they have to study the effect of variation of sensory stimulus conditions, for instance, on degree of hedonic tone, or the effect of variations in hedonic tone on something else, such as ease of recall of learned material. To do this, one must be able to specify the degree or amount of hedonic tone present at a given moment. Philosophical concern with the measurement of pleasure has grown out of utilitarianism and other hedonistic ethical theories. According to utilitarianism, an action is justified if and only if it will probably lead to a greater balance of pleasure over displeasure for everyone affected than any possible alternative action. Applying this principle to a particular case would involve estimating the total quantity of pleasure and displeasure that would be produced by each of the possible choices. To do this we would first have to list the ways in which one choice or another would make the situation, patterns of activities, and so on of a given person different from what they would be if that choice had not been made. Second, we would have to obtain information concerning how much pleasure or displeasure that person has derived from the situations and activities in question. Third, we would have to project how much pleasure and displeasure the person would derive from each of these in the future, taking into account any changes in circumstances, age, and so on that could be expected to make a difference. Fourth, we would have to sum up the hedonic consequences for that person. Fifth, having done this for each person likely to be affected, we would have to sum these results, arriving at a figure representing the probable total hedonic consequences of that choice.

Some of the problems relevant to these procedures fall outside the scope of this article. These include the problem of determining just what the objective consequences of a choice are likely to be, the problem of determining what features of a situation are responsible for the pleasure or displeasure felt, and the problem of projecting probable future pleasure from past pleasures. These are all essentially general problems of inductive reasoning. The problems having to do specifically with the measurement of pleasure are (1) How can one determine the degree of pleasure or displeasure experienced by a given person at a given moment? (2) How can one compare the amount of pleasure felt by one person at a given time with the amount of pleasure felt by another person at a given time?

In everyday discourse we compare pleasures and displeasures. We say things like "I didn't enjoy that party as much as the last one," "I get more pleasure out of gardening now than I used to," and "That interview was not as unpleasant as I had expected it to be." Even granting the reliability of such comparative judgments, the utilitarian needs something more. He needs to be able to specify the hedonic value of particular experiences in numbers that he can meaningfully subject to arithmetical operations, so that if a person gets four positive units (pleasure) from one minute of playing tennis and one negative unit (displeasure) from the next minute of playing tennis, the total hedonic value of the two minutes is greater than that of two minutes spent lying in the sun, from which he derived one positive unit per minute.

An obvious move is to try to refine everyday comparative judgments in such a way as to yield these kinds of results. (In fact, all the methods that have actually been used have been of this sort.) We might ask the subject to consider a large number of his past experiences and to make a comparative judgment on each pair. Possibly after ironing out a few inconsistencies, we would arrange a series such that each experience is more pleasant, or less unpleasant, than any experience lower in the series. We could then have the subject locate a point of hedonic indifference, after which we could assign positive and negative integers to the ranks diverging in either direction from the point of indifference. This would constitute a hedonic scale for that individual. Any other experience would be assigned a number by matching it with an experience on the scale from which it is hedonically indistinguishable. (If it fell between two experiences on the scale, the scale would have to be revised.)

Even assuming that subjects make responses that would enable us to set up an unambiguous scale, one might still doubt that it provides an adequate measuring procedure. First, it relies heavily on the subject's memory of how much pleasure or displeasure he got out of something in the past, and such memories are notoriously fallible. Second, even if we have constructed a scale such that, given two adjoining experiences, the subject is unable to think of an experience which would lie between them, it is still an open question whether the intervals between the items are equal. We have as successive items (*a*) taking a shower after a game of tennis, (*b*) being complimented on a performance, and (*c*) seeing one of one's children receive a prize. What reason is there to think that (c) is just exactly as much more pleasant than (b) as (b) is than (a)? And yet we have to make that assumption if we are going to use the numerical assignments to compare one "sum" of pleasures with another.

A different procedure would be to have the subject rate an experience, when it happens, by an absolute scale, for instance, a nine-point scale ranging from +4 to –4. This would avoid the problem about memory, but it brings fresh difficulties in its stead. Why suppose that the subject is in fact using the same standards every time we get him to make a rating? For that matter, why suppose that ratings which people are forced to make on an artificially constructed scale correspond to any real differences in experience at all? Moreover, there is still the question of whether the intervals on our "absolute scale," as used by the subject, reflect equal differences in actual degree of hedonic tone. If one of these procedures yielded measurements that entered into well-confirmed hypotheses relating hedonic tone to, for example, various properties of learning, this would bolster our confidence in the procedure. At least it would show that we were measuring something important. But such results have not been obtained to any considerable extent.

Even if all the above problems were surmounted, it would still be very difficult to compare the amount of pleasure or displeasure experienced by two different people. Suppose that I am trying to determine whether the total balance of pleasure over displeasure (or the reverse) is greater for my wife or for myself with respect to a given party. Even if the foregoing problems could be surmounted and we could find a valid way of assigning a hedonic number for each of us, relative to a scale for each, how are we to calibrate the two scales? How are we to determine whether a rating of +3 on my scale represents the same amount of pleasure as a rating of +3 on her scale?

So long as we restrict ourselves to refinements of the method of introspective judgment, the problem of intersubjective comparison seems insoluble. On the other hand, if there were some intersubjectively measurable variable, or complex of variables, which we had reason to think is intimately related to hedonic tone and which correlated well enough with rough introspective judgments to be taken as a measure of hedonic tone, all problems would be solved. Such a development is still in the future. Attempts to correlate introspective hedonic judgments with gross physiological variables on the order of pulse rate or patterns of respiration have not been fruitful. There has been no end of speculation concerning the

neurological basis of hedonic tone. Pleasantness has been thought to depend on the degree to which assimilation counteracts dissimilation in the activity of any group of central neurones (A. Lehmann), the degree of the capacity of a neural element to react to stimulation (H. R. Marshall), the average rate of change of conductance in the synapses (L. T. Troland), and so on. Thus far, none of these theories has yielded effective physiological measures.

See also Bentham, Jeremy; Cartesianism; Empiricism; Good, The; Hartley, David; Hedonism; Hobbes, Thomas; Hume, David; Kant, Immanuel; Locke, John; McDougall, William; Mendelssohn, Moses; Mill, James; Mill, John Stuart; Pain; Plato; Ryle, Gilbert; Sensa; Sidgwick, Henry; Spinoza, Benedict (Baruch) de; Thomas Aquinas, St.; Utilitarianism; Wundt, Wilhelm.

Bibliography

Plato discusses the nature of pleasure in his dialogues *Philebus* and *Timaeus*. Aristotle's main discussion is in Book X of the *Nicomachean Ethics*. A very illuminating history of the topic is H. M. Gardiner, R. C. Metcalf, and J. G. Beebe-Center, *Feeling and Emotion, A History of Theories* (New York, 1937).

Important discussions by contemporary analytical philosophers include Gilbert Ryle, *The Concept of Mind* (London: Hutchinson, 1949), Ch. 4, and *Dilemmas* (Cambridge, U.K.: Cambridge University Press, 1954), Ch. 4; a symposium, "Pleasure," between Ryle and W. B. Gallie in *PAS*, Supp. 28 (1954): 135–164; Terence Penelhum, "The Logic of Pleasure," in *Philosophy and Phenomenological Research* 17 (1957): 488–503; Anthony Kenny, *Action, Emotion, and Will* (London: Routledge and Kegan Paul, 1963), Ch. 6; P. H. Nowell-Smith, *Ethics* (London: Penguin, 1954), Chs. 8–10; and R. B. Brandt, *Ethical Theory* (Englewood Cliffs, NJ: Prentice-Hall, 1959), Ch. 12.

Karl Duncker's article "Pleasure, Emotion and Striving," in *Philosophy and Phenomenological Research* 1 (1940): 391–430, is a brilliant phenomenological analysis of the varieties of pleasure and their relation to desire. The psychological research on hedonic tone is well summarized in J. G. Beebe-Center, *The Psychology of Pleasantness and Unpleasantness* (New York, 1932). More recent developments are surveyed in Beebe-Center's article "Feeling and Emotion," in *Theoretical Foundations of Psychology*, edited by Harry Helson (New York: Van Nostrand, 1951).

The measurement of pleasure is discussed in Jeremy Bentham, *Introduction to the Principles of Morals and Legislation* (2nd ed., Oxford, 1907), Ch. 4; Henry Sidgwick, *The Methods of Ethics* (London: Macmillan, 1874), Book II, Chs. 2 and 3 (also good on the nature of pleasure); R. B. Perry, *General Theory of Value* (New York: Longmans Green, 1926), Ch. 21; and Robert McNaughton, "A Metrical Conception of Happiness," in *Philosophy and Phenomenological Research* 14 (1954): 172–183.

William P. Alston (1967)

PLEKHANOV, GEORGII VALENTINOVICH
(1856–1918)

Georgii Valentinovich Plekhanov, the Russian Marxist, revolutionary, philosopher, sociologist, and historian of social thought, was the son of a poor nobleman. After graduating from a military academy in Voronezh, he studied at the Mining Institute in St. Petersburg. As a student he joined the revolutionary movement and became one of the leaders of the revolutionary organization of the Narodniki (Populists), called Zemlia i volia (Soil and freedom). After Zemlia i volia split into the terroristic Narodnaia volia (People's freedom) and the Bakuninist-anarchist Chernyi peredel (Redistribution of soil) groups, Plekhanov became the leading theoretician of the Chernyi peredel group.

In the beginning of 1880, Plekhanov emigrated to France and then settled in Switzerland. Between 1880 and 1882 he turned from Populism to Marxism, and in 1883 he founded in Geneva the first Russian Marxist group, Osvobozhdenie truda (The emancipation of labor). In the summer of 1889 he took part in the founding congress of the Second International. In the late 1890s Plekhanov was one of the first to criticize both the international revisionism of Eduard Bernstein and its Russian variant, "economism."

In 1900, Plekhanov's group joined forces with a new group headed by V. I. Lenin. The two groups organized the second congress of the Russian Social-Democratic Labor Party in London in 1902. The congress accepted a party program written mainly by Plekhanov. Disagreements over the nature of the party led to the split of the party into Bolsheviks and Mensheviks. Plekhanov supported Lenin at the congress, but he became neutral soon afterward and even leaned to the Menshevik side.

During the first Russian revolution (1905), Plekhanov severely criticized the tactics of the Bolsheviks, but after the defeat of the revolution he again came closer to Lenin. The onset of World War I led to the final parting of Plekhanov and Lenin. Plekhanov urged socialists to support the Allied governments, but Lenin declared war on the imperialist war.

After the February revolution of 1917 Plekhanov returned to Russia. Believing that Russia was not yet sufficiently mature for socialism, he regarded the October revolution as a fateful mistake. Nevertheless, he refused to engage in active struggle against Soviet authority.

As the founder of the first Russian Marxist group, Plekhanov is rightly called the father of Russian Marxism and of Russian social democracy. He was also an outstanding leader of the Second International. But the workers' movement is indebted to Plekhanov for his theoretical work, especially in philosophy, even more than for his practical organizational activity.

GENERAL PHILOSOPHICAL VIEWS

Plekhanov regarded himself as an orthodox follower of Karl Marx and Friedrich Engels and severely criticized those who tried to "revise" the basic teachings of Marx or to "supplement" them with the ideas of Immanuel Kant, Ernst Mach, or some other philosopher. But he insisted that the views of Marx and Engels should be developed further.

In his early writings Plekhanov exhibited the tendencies to reduce philosophy to the philosophy of history and to regard philosophy as a preliminary to science. He later stressed the independent tasks and problems of philosophy and defined philosophy in a broader way, as a study of the basic principles of being and knowledge and of their mutual relationships. Whereas Marx and Engels often insisted on the methodological character of their philosophy, Plekhanov stressed its systematic character. Marxist philosophy, according to Plekhanov, is a system, which Plekhanov named dialectical materialism.

Following Engels, Plekhanov maintained that the basic question of every philosophy was "the question about the relationship of subject to object, of consciousness to being," and he regarded materialism and idealism as two basic answers to the question. Dualism was a possible, but weaker, answer. A consistent thinker must choose between an idealistic and a materialistic monism, but vulgar materialism is not the only alternative to idealism. The real solution is dialectical materialism.

As the concept of matter was not clearly defined by Engels, Plekhanov made several attempts to do so. His formulations were more or less modifications of the traditional materialist view that matter is what exists independently of man's consciousness, affects his sense organs, and produces sensations. Plekhanov tried to show that opposing philosophies that maintain the world exists only in the consciousness of one man (solipsism), only in the consciousness of humankind (solohumanism), or only in that of some superindividual objective spirit (objective idealism) all lead to contradictions. The belief in the existence of the external world is, according to Plekhanov, an unavoidable leap in philosophy. Lenin reproached Plekhanov for such Humean terminology,

ENCYCLOPEDIA OF PHILOSOPHY
2nd edition

and Soviet philosophers later exploited this criticism to accuse Plekhanov of Humeanism.

In criticizing idealistic views that *mind, spirit, consciousness,* or *psyche* (he used these terms more or less interchangeably) is the only reality, Plekhanov at the same time rejected the view of those materialists who regard mind as a part of matter or (as Engels did) as a form of the movement of matter. Nevertheless, he held that mind is one of the properties of substance, or matter. In some earlier writings Plekhanov affirmed that mind is merely a mode of matter, a property characteristic of matter organized in a certain way. Later he modified his view, maintaining that mind is an attribute of matter, a property that, at least to a minimal, nonobservable degree, belongs to all matter. This theory led to his being accused of hylozoism. Plekhanov first thought that mind could be regarded as a consequence of another, more fundamental property of matter, movement. Later he changed this view and asserted that consciousness is an "inner state" of matter in motion, a subjective side of the same process whose objective side is motion.

Accepting the traditional correspondence theory of truth, Plekhanov tried to explain in a more specific way the character of correspondence or agreement holding between thought and reality. Against naive realism he stressed that "correspondence" does not mean "similarity." He maintained that sensations are "hieroglyphs" because although they can adequately represent things and their properties, they are not "similar" to them. To avoid misinterpretation of his views, Plekhanov later renounced this terminology; nevertheless, he was severely criticized for it by some Soviet philosophers, who held that it was a concession to Kantianism.

Plekhanov often stressed that Marxist philosophy is *dialectical* materialism and that dialectics is the soul of Marxist philosophy. But in explaining his conception of dialectics, he added little to what had already been said by Marx and Engels. He was more original in his view of the relationship between formal logic and dialectics. Starting from Engels, who likened the relationship between the two to that between lower and higher mathematics, Plekhanov maintained that thinking according to the laws of formal logic is a special case of dialectical thinking. By the help of a number of distinctions, like those between motions and things, between changing and relatively stable things, and between simple and compound things, he tried to determine more precisely the limits of fields in which the two logics could be applied. These explanations, although they gave no final clarification of the problem, nevertheless were the most explicit treatment of the problem in classical Marxist literature and served as the starting point for many later discussions.

PHILOSOPHY OF HISTORY

Plekhanov's views on the philosophy of history have sometimes been misinterpreted. The fault is partly his own. Trying to present Marx and Engels's view on the relations between the economic foundation and the superstructure in a simple schematic way, he produced a formula involving:

> 1. The state of the forces of production; 2. Economic relations conditioned by these forces; 3. The socio-political regime erected upon a given economic foundation; 4. The psychology of man in society, determined in part directly by economic conditions and in part by the whole socio-political regime erected upon the economic foundation; 5. Various ideologies reflecting this psychology. (*Fundamental Problems of Marxism,* edited by D. Ryazanov, p. 72)

This formula may be regarded as an adequate schematization of economic materialism, the theory according to which the economic factor (the forces of production) is ultimately predominant in history. However, in other places Plekhanov maintained that neither man as man nor society as society can be characterized by a constant relationship between economic and other factors because such relationships are always changing. He even explicitly criticized the view that the economic factor must always be decisive and called it a "libel against mankind." Plekhanov admitted that so far men have been the "slaves of their own social economy," but he insisted that "the triumph of human reason over the blind forces of economic necessity is possible" (*Izbrannye filosofskie proizvedeniia* [Selected philosophical works], Vol. II, p. 233).

In his best writings Plekhanov criticized not only the theory of the predominant role of the economic factor but also the theory of factors as such. In polemics against those who attributed the theory to Marx, he maintained that genuine materialists are averse to dragging in the economic factor everywhere and that "even to ask which factor predominates in social life seems to them pointless" (*The Materialist Conception of History,* p. 13). The question is unjustified because, "strictly speaking, there exists only one factor of historical development, namely—social man" (*Izbrannye Filosofskie Proizvedeniya,* Vol. V, p. 363); different branches of the social sciences—ethics, politics, jurisprudence, political economy—investigate one and the same thing, the activity of social man.

AESTHETICS

Plekhanov was one of the few Marxist thinkers interested in aesthetics and the sociology of art. Criticizing the view that art expresses only feelings, he insisted that it expresses both feeling and thoughts, not abstractly, however, but in lively pictures. He added that the pictorial expression of feelings and thoughts about the world is not an end in itself but is done in order to communicate one's own thoughts and feelings to others. Art is a social phenomenon.

The first task of an art critic, according to Plekhanov, is to translate the idea of a work of art from the language of art into the language of sociology in order to find what could be called the sociological equivalent of a literary phenomenon. After the first act of materialistic criticism, the second act—the appreciation of the aesthetic values of the work in question—must follow.

Investigating the social roots of the theory of art for art's sake and of the utilitarian view of art, Plekhanov came to the conclusion that the inclination toward art for its own sake emerges from a hopeless separation of the artist from the surrounding social milieu, whereas the utilitarian view of art emerges when a mutual understanding between the larger part of society and the artist exists. The utilitarian view of art can thus be combined with both conservative and revolutionary attitudes.

The value of a work of art is primarily dependent on the value of the ideas it conveys, but correct ideas are not enough for a valuable work. A work of art is great only when its form corresponds to its ideas.

IMPORTANCE AND INFLUENCE

Although Plekhanov is not one of those greatest of philosophers who have opened up new vistas to humankind, he was not a mere popularizer of Marxist philosophy. Starting from Engels's interpretation of Marxist philosophy, he improved it and developed it in many directions. He greatly influenced Lenin's conception of Marxist philosophy, and through both his own works and Lenin's he decisively influenced Soviet philosophy between the two world wars. The leaders of the Soviet "philosophical front" in the 1920s, A. M. Deborin and Deborin's most outstanding opponent, L. I. Aksel'rod, were Plekhanov's immediate disciples.

In 1930 a new period in Soviet philosophy began, a period that included severe criticism of Plekhanov. All kinds of accusations were made against Plekhanov, but the Stalinist criticism abated in the 1940s and 1950s, and Plekhanov's philosophical views survived. Nevertheless, the publication of previously unpublished writings of Marx in the 1930s and 1940s and new discussions of Marx's philosophy in the 1950s and the 1960s seem to have produced an interpretation of Marxist philosophy that is more profound than that offered by Engels and developed by Plekhanov and Lenin.

See also Aesthetics, History of; Art, Expression in; Art, Value in; Correspondence Theory of Truth; Deborin, Abram Moiseevich; Dialectical Materialism; Engels, Friedrich; Kant, Immanuel; Lenin, Vladimir Il'ich; Mach, Ernst; Marx, Karl; Marxist Philosophy; Panpsychism; Russian Philosophy.

Bibliography

WORKS BY PLEKHANOV

Collections

Sochineniya (Works). 24 vols, edited by D. Ryazanov. Moscow and Leningrad, 1922–1927.

Literaturnoe nasledie G. V. Plekhanova (The literary heritage of Plekhanov). 8 vols. Moscow, 1934–1940.

Selected Philosophical Works. 5 vols. Moscow: Progress, 1974–76.

Other Works

Anarchism and Socialism. Westport, CT: Hyperion Press, 1981.

The Development of the Monist View of History. Moscow: Progress Publishers, 1974.

Essays in the History of Materialism. Translated by Ralph Fox. New York: H. Fertig, 1967.

The Materialist Conception of History. New York: International Publishers, 1964.

K Voprosu o Razvitii Monisticheskogo Vzglyada na Istoriyu. St. Petersburg, 1895. Translated by Andrew Rothstein as *In Defense of Materialism: The Development of the Monist View of History.* London, 1947; 2nd ed., published as *The Development of the Monist View of History*, Moscow: Foreign Languages Publishing House, 1956.

"K Voprosu o Roli Lichnosti v Istorii." *Nauchnoe Obozrenie,* Nos. 3–4 (1898). Translated as *The Role of the Individual in History.* New York, 1940.

Fundamental Problems of Marxism. Moscow: Progress Publishers, 1977.

Art and Society & Other Papers in Historical Materialism. New York: Oriole Editions, 1974.

Materialismus militans: Reply to Mr. Bogdanov, edited by Richard Dixon, Moscow: Progress, 1973.

WORKS ON PLEKHANOV

Baron, Samuel H. *Plekhanov in Russian History and Soviet Historiography.* Pittsburgh: University of Pittsburgh Press, 1995.

Baron, Samuel H. *Plekhanov: The Father of Russian Marxism.* Stanford, CA: Stanford University Press, 1963.

Fomina, V. A. *Filosofskie vzgliady Plekhanova* (Philosophical views of Plekhanov). Moscow, 1955.

Hook, Sidney. *The Hero in History.* New York: John Day, 1943.

Howard, M. C., and J. E. King. "The Political Economy of Plekhanov and the Development of Backward Capitalism." *History of Political Thought* 10 (1989): 329–344.

Kolakowski, Leszek. "Plekhanov and the Codification of Marxism." In *Main Currents of Marxism*. Vol. 2. Oxford: Oxford University Press, 1978.

Petrović, Gajo. *Filozofski pogledi G. V. Plehanova* (Philosophical views of G. V. Plekhanov). Zagreb, Yugoslavia, 1957.

Steila, Daniela. *Genesis and Development of Plekhanov's Theory of Knowledge: A Marxist between Anthropological Materialism and Physiology*. Dordrecht: Kluwer Academic, 1991.

Vaganyan, V. *G. V. Plekhanov: Opyt kharakteristiki sotsial'no-politicheskikh Vozzrenii* (G. V. Plekhanov: An essay on the characteristics of his sociopolitical views). Moscow, 1924.

Vaganyan, V. *Opyt bibliografii G. V. Plekhanova* (Bibliographical essay on G. V. Plekhanov). Moscow and Leningrad, 1923.

Volfson, S. *G. V. Plekhanov*. Minsk, U.S.S.R., 1924.

Walicki, A. *A History of Russian Thought from the Enlightenment to Marxism*. Oxford: Clarendon Press, 1980.

Yovchuk, M. T. *G. V. Plekhanov i ego trudy po istorii filosofii* (G. V. Plekhanov and his works in the history of philosophy). Moscow, 1960.

Zinoviev, Grigori. *G. V. Plekhanov*. Petrograd, 1918.

Gajo Petrović (1967)
Bibliography updated by Vladimir Marchenkov (2005)

PLESSNER, HELMUT
(1892–1985)

Helmut Plessner, was, with Max Scheler, the founder of modern philosophical anthropology. Born in Wiesbaden, Germany, he studied medicine, and then zoology and philosophy, at the universities of Freiburg, Heidelberg, and Berlin. He received a doctorate in philosophy from Erlangen in 1916 and his *Habilitation* in philosophy with Scheler and Hans Driesch at Cologne in 1920. His academic career in Germany was terminated by the National Socialist regime, and in 1934 he went to Groningen, the Netherlands, first as a guest of the Physiological Institute (where he was associated with F. J. J. Buytendijk), then as Rockefeller fellow, and from 1929 to 1942 as professor of sociology. Again dismissed by the Nazis, he was reinstated at Groningen by the Dutch in 1945 and occupied the chair of philosophy from 1946 to 1951. In 1951 he accepted the chair of sociology at the University of Göttingen in Germany. He became professor emeritus in 1962 and lectured as a visiting professor at the New School for Social Research in New York in 1962–1963. He received an honorary doctorate from Groningen in 1964.

Plessner's work—he published twelve books and approximately ninety monographs, essays, and papers—ranges over an extraordinarily wide area, including animal physiology, aesthetics, phenomenology, the history of ideas, the history of philosophy, sociological theory, sociology of knowledge, sociology of education, and political sociology. Most of these studies are linked to the problems of philosophical anthropology, the discipline to which he devoted his most important publications. His background in zoology and physiology, his phenomenological training under Edmund Husserl, and his sociological orientation led him to redefine the problems and findings of the modern sciences of man.

Plessner agrees with the view that man artificially creates his nature, or more precisely, that what man makes of himself is contingent on history. However, man is bound by the structural principle of his position in the world; in contrast to the centricity of animals, who are, simply, what they are as organisms, in their *Umwelt*, man is "eccentric." Plessner rejects the dualism of spirit and matter present in Scheler's anthropology. He sees man as being a body (with such organically determined traits as upright posture, impoverishment of instincts, and drive surplus) and consequently exposed to his environment, and also as having a body and acting by means of it, as being open, within certain limits, to the world. Man is both "inside" and "outside" himself. Social and historical order is based on the precarious balance of these two dialectical moments. This order enables man to maintain a distance from things, from situations, and from himself, making it possible for him to use language and to plan actions. Man's eccentricity leads him to enter history, "to make himself" in history. However, when man faces ambivalent or insuperable situations, the balance on which order is founded is disrupted; planned action, speech, and all historically determined "orderly" ways of coming to terms with the world are blocked. His indirect, socially mediated relationship with the world momentarily breaks apart. In such marginal situations man responds in a prehistorical, presocial, and yet peculiarly human manner: by laughter or by tears.

See also Driesch, Hans Adolf Eduard; Husserl, Edmund; Philosophical Anthropology; Scheler, Max.

Bibliography

Plessner's most important works are *Die Einheit der Sinne* (Bonn: Cohen, 1923), *Die Stufen des Organischen und der Mensch* (Berlin and Leipzig: de Gruyter, 1928; 2nd ed., Stuttgart, 1964), *Das Schicksal deutschen Geistes im Ausgang seiner bürgerlichen Epoche* (Zürich and Leipzig: Niehans, 1935; 2nd ed. published as *Die verspätete Nation*, Stuttgart: Kohlhammer, 1959), *Lachen und Weinen* (Munich, 1941), and *Zwischen Philosophie und Gesellschaft* (Berlin and Munich, 1953).

For literature on Plessner see Jürgen Habermas, "Anthropologie," in *Fischer Lexikon*, Vol. II, *Philosophie*, edited by Alwin Diemer and Ivo Frenzel (Frankfurt, 1958).

OTHER RECOMMENDED WORKS

Essbach, Wolfgant, et al. *Plessners "Grenzen der Gemeinschaft": eine Debatte*. Frankfurt am Main: Suhrkamp, 2002.

Marx, Werner, and Helmut Plessner. *Das Spiel, Wirklichkeit und Methode*. Freiburg i. Br., Schulz, 1967.

Schultz, Walter, and Helmut Fahrenbach, eds. *Wirklichkeit und Reflexion: Walter Schulz zum 60. Geburtstag*. Pfullingen: Neske, 1973.

Thomas Luckmann (1967)
Bibliography updated by Michael Farmer(2005)

PLETHO, GIORGIUS GEMISTUS

(c. 1355–1452)

Giorgius Gemistus Pletho, the leading Byzantine scholar and philosopher of the fifteenth century, was born in Constantinople, the son of a cleric. Pletho is noted primarily for advocating a restoration of ancient Greek polytheism and, above all, for inspiring the interest of the Italian humanists of the *quattrocento* in the study of Plato. His studies followed the usual pattern of Byzantine education, emphasizing the classical Greek heritage. Influenced by certain of his teachers, Pletho became interested primarily in the philosophy of Plato, whose writings had again been brought into vogue in Byzantium during the eleventh-century renaissance under the influence of the Neoplatonic philosopher-statesman Michael Psellus. In 1380, Pletho went to the Turkish court at Brusa, or Adrianople, where he is reputed to have studied under the Jewish scholar Elisaeus. There Pletho presumably received training in the Muslim commentators on Aristotle, in Zoroastrianism, and in Chaldean astronomy and astrology and was encouraged by Elisaeus to further his study of Greek philosophy. Indeed, Gennadius Scholarius, who later condemned Pletho for his belief in polytheism, credits Elisaeus with leading Pletho to apostasy. About 1390, Elisaeus was burned at the stake by the Turks, probably for heterodoxy, and Pletho returned to Constantinople, from which he moved in 1393 to Mistra in the Peloponnese, near the ancient site of Sparta. It was at this administrative and cultural center of Mistra, which ranked second only to Constantinople and Thessalonica, that he spent the most important years of his life.

In 1438 Pletho appeared as adviser to the Greek delegation at the Council of Ferrara-Florence, convoked in order to effect a union between the Eastern and Western churches. An antiunionist and in some respects even anti-Christian, he took little interest in the council's proceedings. He preferred to consort with the Italian humanists, themselves fascinated by his knowledge of the works of Plato, which had for centuries been virtually unknown to the West. He left the council before the final ceremony of union to return to Mistra, where he remained until his death.

Pletho's works reveal a deep insight into Platonic philosophy and, remarkably, a devotion to Greece rather than to the crumbling Byzantine Empire. Many of his treatises aim at the revivification and restoration of Greece's ancient glory. In his famous tract "On the Differences between Plato and Aristotle," he asserts the superiority of Platonism to Aristotelianism, and his *Laws,* inspired by Plato's *Laws* and *Republic,* advocates a return to the polytheism of ancient Greece. Two memoirs based on a Platonic reconstruction of the state present a systematic plan of social and economic reform for Greece. Pletho felt that the collapse of the Byzantine Empire was due primarily to Christianity, the adoption of which had caused the alteration of the institutions of ancient Greece. In order to restore Greece to its former greatness it was necessary to foster a return to the ancient religion and to adopt a philosophy based on Platonic principles, which could serve as a guide in the process of governing. Pletho's numerous works include treatises on Zoroastrianism, Chaldean astronomy, music, history, rhetoric, the "philosophic virtues," geography, and various theological subjects. Among his theological writings is a treatise on the procession of the Holy Spirit composed in response to the Latin view presented at the Council of Ferrara-Florence.

Despite some modern opinion to the contrary, Pletho's apostasy from Christianity seems certain. Scholarius, his Aristotelian opponent, condemns him for advocating paganism in his *Laws,* and George of Trebizond quotes Pletho as asserting that a new religion, neither Christian nor Islamic but similar to that of the ancient Greeks, would sweep the world. Why then did Pletho attend the Council of Ferrara-Florence and evidently acquiesce in the act of union? Pletho was taken to the council by the Byzantine emperor John VIII, probably as a learned layman philosopher who could buttress the arguments of the theologians. Pletho's opposition to union was more on nationalistic grounds than dogmatic. As a patriot he feared that the consummation of union would precipitate a fresh Turkish attack on Constantinople. Moreover, he seemed to fear the Latinization of the Greeks, as for example in the possible suppression of

Greek in favor of Latin in the ritual of the church. Finally, as a propagandist for the formation of a "Greek" nation and a restored Hellenism (in contrast to a "Byzantine" or, more correctly, "Roman" state), he was opposed to the international papal control implicit in the union of the two churches. His acceptance of the union can then be explained only as an act of political expediency with the aim of aiding Greece, not as the result of conviction that any particular doctrinal position was correct.

Almost every Greek humanist scholar of the fifteenth century was in some way influenced by Pletho, the most notable being his pupil, Cardinal Bessarion. A great many Italian humanists were also influenced by his writings and presence at the council. Through Pletho, ancient doctrines of the Chaldeans and Pythagoreans were transmitted to the West. More important, he set in motion at Florence the passionate interest in Platonism that was soon to permeate much of western Europe. Marsilio Ficino credits Pletho with inspiring Cosimo de' Medici to found the famous Platonic Academy. By introducing into Italy (especially through Paolo dal Pozzo Toscanelli) the geographical concepts of Strabo, Pletho may have prepared the ground for the correction of Ptolemy's geographical errors. Pletho consequently helped to alter the Renaissance conception of the configuration of Earth, thus indirectly influencing Christopher Columbus, for whom Strabo was an important authority. The high esteem in which Pletho was held by the Italian humanists is attested by the transfer of his remains from Mistra to Rimini, where they were interred in the Church of St. Francis.

See also Aristotelianism; Aristotle; Byzantine Philosophy; Ficino, Marsilio; Greek Academy; Humanism; Neoplatonism; Plato; Platonism and the Platonic Tradition; Pythagoras and Pythagoreanism; Zoroastrianism.

Bibliography

TEXTS

Traité des vertus. Edited by Brigitte Tambrun-Krasker. Athens: Academy of Athens, 1987.

Contra Scholarii pro Aristotele objections. Edited by E. V. Maltese. Leipzig: Teubner, 1988.

Oracles Chaldaïques. Recension de Georges Gémiste Pléthon. Edited by Brigitte Tambrun-Krasker. Athens: Academy of Athens, 1995.

STUDIES

Athanassiadi, Polymnia. "Byzantine Commentators on the Chaldaean Oracles: Psellos and Plethon." In *Byzantine Philosophy and Its Ancient Sources,* edited by Katerina Ierodiakonou, 237–252. Oxford: Oxford University Press, 2002.

Karamanolis, George. "Plethon and Scholarios on Aristotle." In *Byzantine Philosophy and Its Ancient Sources,* edited by Katerina Ierodiakonou, 253–282. Oxford: Oxford University Press, 2002.

Lagarde, B. "Le *De Differentiis* de Pléthon d' après l'autographe de la Marcienne." *Byzantion* 43 (1973): 312–343.

Tardieu, M. "Pléthon lecteur des Oracles." *Mêtis* 2 (1987): 141–164.

Woodhouse, C. M. *Gemistos Plethon: The Last of the Hellenes.* Oxford: Clarendon Press, 1986.

Deno J. Geanakoplos (1967)
Bibliography updated by Katerina Ierodiakonou (2005)

PLOTINUS
(c. 205–270)

Plotinus, usually considered the founder of Neoplatonism, was probably born in Lykopolis, Upper Egypt, and he may have been a Hellenized Egyptian rather than a Greek. He turned to the study of philosophy when he was twenty-eight. Disappointed by several teachers in Alexandria, he was directed by a friend to Ammonius Saccas, who made a profound impression on him. Of Ammonius's teachings we know extremely little, but a promising line of investigation has been opened up in a comparison of Plotinus's doctrines with those of Origen the Christian, also a student of Ammonius. Of other students of Ammonius, Origen the Pagan and Longinus deserve special mention.

Plotinus was Ammonius's pupil for eleven years. He left Ammonius to join the expeditionary army of Emperor Gordianus III that was to march against Persia, hoping to acquire firsthand knowledge of Persian and Indian wisdom, in which he had become interested through Ammonius. When Gordianus was slain in Persia in 244, probably at the instigation of his successor, Philip the Arabian, Plotinus had to flee from the army camp—which could mean that he was politically involved in some way. Plotinus reached Antioch in his flight and from there proceeded to Rome, where he arrived in the same year. In Rome he conducted a school of philosophy and after ten years started writing. At about this time he gained influence over, or the confidence of, the new emperor, Gallienus, and it is possible that his philosophy was meant to aid the emperor in some way in his attempted rejuvenation of paganism. In any case, Plotinus asked the emperor to grant him land in order to found some kind of community, the members of which would live according to the laws (or *Laws*) of Plato.

Despite the emperor's favorable attitude, a cabal of courtiers brought the plan to nothing, indicating that they may have seen in it some political implications. However, because the contents of Plotinus's writings and some facts of his life seem to point to a complete absence of political interests, the problem of Plotinus's involvement in affairs of state is controversial. Nevertheless it is strangely coincidental that his literary activity began in the first year of Gallienus's rule. Moreover, when Plotinus died (probably from leprosy, about two years after the assassination of Gallienus), he was not in Rome but on the estate of one of his friends (of Arabic origin), and only one of his pupils, a physician, was present. These circumstances make it difficult to rule out the possibility that Plotinus had left Rome and that his pupils had all dispersed at the death of Gallienus (between March and August of 268) because he and they were afraid they would be affected by the anti-Gallienus reaction; this would again contradict a completely apolitical interpretation of Plotinus.

Plotinus's works, which were all written in the sixteen years after 253, have come down to us only in the edition by his pupil Porphyry. Porphyry arranged the works according to content into six sections called enneads because each contains nine treatises; he arbitrarily created some treatises by dissecting or combining the originals. Independent of this arrangement, he indicated when each treatise was written by assigning it to one of three periods in the life of Plotinus: before Porphyry became Plotinus's student, 253–263; while Porphyry was his student, 263–268; after Porphyry left him, 268–270. Whether Porphyry numbered the treatises within each period in strictly chronological order is open to some doubt. The presentation of Plotinus given here follows the three periods of Porphyry with only a few forward or backward references. The standard citation to Plotinus's work designates the number of the ennead first, by Roman numeral; the treatise second, by Arabic numeral; and the place of the treatise in Porphyry's chronological enumeration third, in brackets. The chapter number and, where relevant, the line number are also given in addition to the standard citation.

Contrary to the frequent attempts to present Plotinus's philosophy as a consistent whole, this presentation will stress all tensions by which the philosophy is permeated and leave it an open question whether Plotinus succeeded in reconciling them.

INFLUENCES

To understand the philosophy of Plotinus, a knowledge of some of the doctrines of Plato, Aristotle, the Neo-Pythagoreans, and the Stoics is very important.

In his dialogues Plato divided all reality into the realm of ideas (intelligibles) and the realm of sensibles, treating intelligibles alone as that which truly is (*ousia*), which implied that they are eternal and changeless (but see below). One of these ideas, the idea of the Good, he elevated above others, calling it beyond being (*epekeina ousias*). Comparable to the sun, it is the source of being and cognizability of all existents. In a lecture (or a lecture course) he seems to have identified the Good with the One.

Plato discussed the concept of the One in his dialogue *Parmenides*, ostensibly without any conclusion. In one passage he asserts hypothetically that if the One existed, it would be ineffable and unknowable. Whether this assertion was supposed to reveal the self-contradictory and, therefore, unacceptable character of the One, or on the contrary to express Plato's positive assertion as to the character of the One, is controversial. In another dialogue, *The Sophist*, Plato seems to contradict his standard doctrine concerning the unchangeable character of the ideas by ascribing life, change, and knowledge to the realm of ideas.

As to the realm of the sensible, Plato in his *Timaeus* explains the origin of the cosmos in the form of a myth—as the work of a divine artisan (demiurge) who uses an ideal cosmos as model and fashions it out of something Plato calls "receptacle" and describes as void of any qualities, after ideas have in some way "entered" this void and by so doing created rudiments of the four elements. In addition to the physical universe the demiurge also fashions a cosmic soul and the immortal part of individual souls. The cosmic soul and the individual souls consist of a mixture of the same ingredients, on which mixture the demiurge imposes a numerical and a geometrical structure.

The immaterial and substantial character of the individual souls (or at least part of them) guarantees their preexistence and postexistence (immortality). They are all subject to the law of reincarnation.

In the *Second Letter* (the authenticity of which was never doubted in antiquity, though today it finds virtually no defender), Plato, in a brief, and entirely obscure passage, seems to compress his whole philosophy into a formula reading: There are three realms, the first related to "the king," the second to the second, the third to the third. Plotinus was convinced that Plato is here describing the three realms of the One, Intelligence, and the Soul (whereas many Christian writers were convinced that Plato must have darkly anticipated the doctrine of the Trinity).

From Aristotle, Plotinus drew an important presentation of Plato's philosophy, ostensibly different from the one professed by Plato in his dialogues. According to Aristotle, Plato had assumed a realm of mathematicals mediating between ideas and sensibles (other sources identified this realm with that of the soul). Aristotle also attributed to Plato the view that two opposite principles, the One and the Indeterminate Dyad, are the supreme principles constitutive of everything, particularly of ideas and mathematicals—a doctrine Aristotle related to a similar, equally dualistic doctrine of the Pythagoreans. Aristotle represented Plato as having identified the Indeterminate Dyad with the receptacle and as having seen in it the principle of evil.

Plotinus also adopted Aristotle's doctrine of Intelligence (nous) as superior to the rest of the soul. Aristotle implied that it alone is immortal, the rest being merely the "form" of the body, hence incapable of separate existence. Aristotle designated the supreme deity as Intelligence contemplating (that is, intelligizing) itself; the cognitive activity of the Intelligence differed from sensation in that its objects (immaterial intelligibles) are identical with the acts by which Intelligence grasps them.

Plotinus was also aware of Academic and Neo-Pythagorean attempts to take over and modify the two-opposite-principles doctrine by elevating the One above the Indeterminate Dyad (sometimes above another One, coordinated with the Dyad), which thus changed Plato's dualism into monism culminating in a transcendent One. Plotinus also knew of the syntheses of Plato's and Aristotle's philosophy attempted by some Platonists, especially of the second century CE, most prominently Albinus and Apuleius. Another influence was the strictly materialistic and immanentistic Stoic doctrine of the omnipresence of the divine in the cosmos. Finally, two Neo-Pythagorean teachers are particularly relevant as sources for Plotinus: Moderatus, who seems to have taken his cue from Plato's *Parmenides*, distinguishing a first One above being from a second and a third; and Numenius, who distinguished the supreme god from the divine artisan, creator of the cosmos.

PLOTINUS'S PHILOSOPHY FIRST PERIOD, 253–263

Plotinus subdivided Plato's realm of intelligibles into three: the One, Intelligence, and the Soul (presupposed in IV 8 [6], Ch. 6; V 4 [7], Ch. 1; VI 9 [9], Chs. 1f.; V 1 [10], Ch. 10; V 2 [11]).

THE ONE. Following what are at best hints in Plato, Plotinus developed a full-fledged theory of the One as the highest principle, or cause. Precisely because it is the principle of everything that is—and is therefore omnipresent—it is itself above being (absolutely transcendental: VI 9 [9], Ch. 4, ll. 24f., Ch. 7, ll. 28f.; V 4 [7], Ch. 1, ll. 4–8; V 2 [11], Ch. 1). Since it is above being, it is fully indetermined (qualityless), although it may be called the Good as the object of universal desire. Because it is one, it is entirely undifferentiated (without multiplicity: V 4 [7]; VI 9 [9], Ch. 3, ll. 39–45). As every act of cognition, even of self-cognition, presupposes the duality of object and subject, Plotinus repeatedly and strongly states that the One is void of any cognition and is ignorant even of itself (VI 9 [9], Ch. 6, l. 42; III 9 [13], Chs. 7, 9). He tries to mitigate this statement in some places, hesitatingly attributing to the One some kind of self-awareness (V 4 [7], Ch. 2, l. 16) or quasi awareness of its "power" to engender being (V 1 [10], Ch. 7, l. 13). In other places he distinguishes the ordinary kind of ignorance from the ignorance of the One and says that there is nothing of which the One is cognizant but that there is also nothing of which it is ignorant (VI 9 [9], Ch. 6, ll. 46–50).

INTELLIGENCE. The realm of the One is "followed" by that of Intelligence (intellect, spirit, mind—all somewhat inadequate translations of the Greek word *nous*). Here, for the first time, multiplicity appears. Roughly, this realm (hypostasis) corresponds to Plato's realm of ideas and, therefore, to that of true being. But whereas Plato's ideas are self-sufficient entities outside the Intelligence that contemplates them, Plotinus develops a doctrine of the later Platonists (perhaps originating with Antiochus of Ascalon) that interpreted ideas as thoughts of God and insists that intelligibles do not exist outside the Intelligence (V 9 [5], Chs. 7f.; III 9 [13], Ch. 1). The structure of the second hypostasis also differs from that of Plato's ideal realm in that Plotinus assumes the existence of ideas of individuals; the resulting difficulty that the infinity of individuals would demand an infinity of ideas Plotinus meets by assuming that the sensible world is, as the Stoa had it, subject to cyclical destruction and regeneration and that in each of these worlds the same indistinguishable individuals, for which one idea would suffice, would exist (V 7 [18], Ch. 1).

Another difference between Plato's and Plotinus's realm of ideas is that Plotinus assumed the existence of souls in this realm (IV 8 [6], Ch. 3). This doctrine creates a special problem. The ideal Socrates, unlike the soul of Socrates, must be composed of soul and body. It should follow that the soul of the empirical Socrates should be only a copy of that of the ideal Socrates, a consequence that, however, Plotinus rejects in places (V 9 [5], Ch. 13; VI 4 [22] Ch. 14) and approaches in others (III 9 [13], Ch. 3; V 2 [11], Ch. 1, l.19). Finally, Plotinus's realm of Intelligence contains even archetypal matter.

Despite all this multiplicity Intelligence remains one. In it everything is contained in everything without losing its identity, just as in mathematics every theorem contains all the others and, thus, the totality of mathematics (V 9 [5], Chs. 6, 9; IV 3 [27], Ch. 2).

Plotinus found it necessary to relate his doctrine of the One and Intelligence to the doctrine of the two opposite principles that figures in Aristotle's obscure presentation of Plato's philosophy in the *Metaphysics* (A6, 987a29ff.). In that difficult passage (the text of which may be faulty), Plato is said to have identified ideas with numbers. Plotinus also found it necessary to relate his philosophy to the doctrine identifying the soul with number, the best-known example of which was Xenocrates' definition of the soul as self-changing number. Thus, Plotinus calls the realm of Intelligence the realm of number and calls the soul number (V 1 [10], Ch. 5). But as he conceives number to be derived from the interaction of One with plurality and yet elevates the One above the realm of Intelligence (being), he seems to assign to his One a double role, a doctrine very close to the Neo-Pythagorean assumption of a double One, one superior and transcendental and another inferior, present in the realm of Intelligence, or number (V 1 [10], Ch. 5).

SOUL. Below the hypostasis of Intelligence Plotinus locates that of the Soul. Some souls remain unembodied; others "descend" into bodies. These bodies are either celestial or terrestrial. Celestial bodies offer no resistance to the soul's dwelling in them and thus these souls do not suffer from their incarnation (IV 8 [6], Ch. 2); terrestrial bodies, however, do offer resistance, and governing them may involve the soul to such an extent that it becomes alienated from Intelligence, its true home, and thus "sinks." In addition to these souls of individual bodies, Plotinus also assumes the existence of a cosmic soul (IV 8 [6], Ch. 7; III 9 [13], Ch. 3; II 2 [14], Ch. 2; I 2 [19], Ch.

1); thus, the world at large is one living organism. Probably the realm of the Soul does not consist of these individual souls alone; rather, they are all only individualizations of something we could call Soul in general (compare IV 3 [27], Ch. 4). In any case, all souls form only one Soul, and this unity implies that all souls intercommunicate by extrasensory means (IV 9 [8]).

Plotinus sometimes proves, sometimes merely assumes, not only the incorporeality, substantiality, and immortality of all the individual souls of humans, animals, and even plants (IV 7 [2], Chs. 2–8[iii], 14), but also proves or assumes reincarnation, in the course of which the same soul may pass from the body of a human into that of a beast or a plant (III 4 [15], Ch. 2). Plato's best-known proof of immortality is based on the absolute simplicity and, therefore, indissolubility of the human soul. But Plato also taught that the soul is tripartite, and perhaps in an effort to reconcile these two doctrines, Plotinus assumes that the simple and, therefore, immortal soul on its "way" to the body receives additional, lower parts as accretions. This seems to be similar to a doctrine usually associated with Gnosticism—a downward journey of the soul, during which it passes the several planetary spheres, each of which adds something to it.

EMANATION. The explanation of the relation of the three hypostases to one another leads to one of the most characteristic doctrines of Plotinus, but it is a strangely ambiguous one. This relation is described as "emanation," or "effulguration," of Intelligence from the One and of Soul from Intelligence—an emanation that, however, leaves the emanating entity undiminished (VI 9 [9], Ch. 9; V 1 [10], Chs. 3, 5–7; compare III 8 [30], Ch. 8, l. 11). The emanating entity thus remains outside of its product and yet is also present in it (VI 4 [7], Ch. 3; VI 9 [9], Ch. 7), a position sometimes described as dynamic pantheism to distinguish it from immanentist pantheism. This emanation Plotinus describes as entirely involuntary: What is full must overflow, what is mature must beget (V 4 [7], Ch. 1, ll. 26–41; V 1 [10], Ch. 6, l. 37; V 2 [11], Ch. 1, l. 8; compare IV 3 [27], Ch. 13).

Seen in this way, there is no fault, no guilt involved in emanation, nor is any justification of why the One had to become multiple necessary. On the contrary, the process deserves praise; without it the One would have remained mere potentiality, and its hidden riches would not have appeared (IV 8 [6], Ch. 5f.). But sometimes, particularly when discussing the Soul's descent, Plotinus speaks of emanation in an entirely different manner. Even the emanation of Intelligence from the One, let alone that of Soul from Intelligence, he describes in such terms as *apostasy* and *falling away*. It is recklessness and the desire to belong to nobody but oneself that cause Intelligence to break away from the One (VI 9 [9], Ch. 5, l. 29). The Soul is motivated to break away from Intelligence by the desire to govern, which causes the Soul to become too immersed in bodies; by a craving for that which is worse; by a will to isolation (V 2 [11], Ch. 1; IV 8 [6], Ch. 4, I. 10; V 1 [10], Ch. 1). Matter emanates from Soul as the result of the Soul's wish to belong to itself (III 9 [13], Ch. 3). The "lowest" kind of Soul (the vegetative) is called the most foolhardy (V 2 [11], Ch. 2, l. 6). Thus, instead of an outflow, we should speak, rather, of a fall—with all its implications of will, guilt, necessity of punishment, and so on. These two interpretations—we shall call the former optimistic and the latter pessimistic—are difficult to reconcile.

INTELLIGENCE AND SOUL. Let us now consider the constitution of the second and third hypostases in additional detail. On the whole, Plotinus teaches that the One is in no way engaged in producing Intelligence. But sometimes he speaks as if Intelligence were the result of some kind of self-reflection of the One: The One turns to itself; this turning is vision; and this vision is Intelligence (V 1 [10], 7, l. 6—but the text is uncertain). Once more, we see that it is not easy for Plotinus to deprive the One of all self-awareness (consciousness). In any case, Intelligence is already multiple and, thus, less perfect than the One. However, the outflow from the One would not be sufficient to produce Intelligence. Rather, this flow must come to a stop—congeal, as it were. Incipient Intelligence must turn back to its source to contemplate it, and only by this act does Intelligence become fully constituted (V 2 [11], Ch. 1, l. 10). The emanation continues, and Soul emerges, again constituted by its turning toward the source, which is Intelligence (V 1 [10], Ch. 6, l. 47; V 2 [11], Ch. 1, l. 18; III 9 [13], Ch. 5). In Soul, multiplicity prevails over unity, and perfection has therefore decreased.

From Soul emanates matter, the totally indetermined (III 9 [13], Ch. 3; III 4 [15], Ch. 1). Because Plotinus tends to split the Soul into a higher, lower, and lowest kind, it is only the lowest that is the source of matter. Matter, when illuminated by the Soul, becomes the physical world, the model of which is in the realm of Intelligence (Soul thus corresponds to Plato's divine artisan, the demiurge). Thus, Plotinus's system would seem to be entirely monistic. But sometimes Plotinus speaks as if matter existed by and in itself, "waiting" to be ensouled (IV 8 [6], Ch. 6, ll. 18–20; V 2 [11], Ch. 1).

Emanation must be described in temporal terms. But, of course, it is in fact an entirely timeless event (VI [10], Ch. 6, l. 19). Once the sensible world, particularly the human body, has been constituted, the Soul in the acts of incarnation becomes submerged in the realm of the temporal. The clash between a pessimistic and an optimistic evaluation of the emanative process can now be repeated in Plotinus's evaluation of incarnation.

INCARNATION. The Platonist cannot easily ignore either the myth of the *Phaedrus*, implying that souls "fall" by some kind of failing, or the otherworldly mood of the *Phaedo*, implying that the soul should try to flee the body and be polluted as little as possible by it. But just as it is difficult for a Platonist to forget that according to the *Timaeus*, the first incarnation of the soul is the work of the divine artisan himself and, thus, a blameless event, so it is equally difficult for him to forget the myth of the *Republic*, according to which embodiment seems to be the result of some universal necessity. As a result, Plotinus had to resolve a contradiction. Sometimes he did so by trying to prove that there is no true contradiction (IV 8 [6], Ch. 5). But recognizing that such an assertion is in the last resort unsatisfactory, even when it is assumed that only part of the Soul descends (IV 7 [2], Ch. 13, l. 12; IV 8 [6], Ch. 7, l. 7), he adopted a theory that he explicitly claims as his innovation (he otherwise presents himself as an orthodox Platonist).

According to this theory, a true fall has never taken place. Actually, even when in a body, the soul still lives its original "celestial" life and remains unseparated from Intelligence. Only we are not aware of this "hidden" life of the soul; in other words, we are partly unconscious of what happens in our minds (IV 8 [6], Ch. 8). What is true of the Soul in relation to Intelligence is even truer of the relation between our embodied selves and Intelligence. Not even when present in us does Intelligence discontinue its activity (V 1 [10], Ch. 12).

Plotinus also makes an optimistic and a pessimistic evaluation of the deterioration that has taken place in the soul as a result of its incarnation. On the whole, he tries to prove that no real deterioration has taken place, but he often feels that he must find reasons why the soul should try to escape the body and return home. One of these reasons is that the body prevents the soul from exercising the activity peculiar to it (IV 8 [6], Ch. 2, l. 43), which means, of course, that some deterioration does take place.

DUALISM. There are some dualistic traits in the philosophy of Plotinus, particularly the recognition of the Indeterminate Dyad (as opposed to the One), to which he also refers simply as the Indeterminate (II 4 [12], Ch. 11, l. 37). Aristotle presented Plato's philosophy as a dualistic system, identifying the Indeterminate Dyad with Plato's receptacle and also with matter, in his own sense of the word; in other words according to him, Plato's ideas, being the product of the interaction of the two opposite principles, contain matter. Aristotle furthermore asserted that the Indeterminate Dyad is also the principle of evil. Plotinus is willing to recognize the Indeterminate as a second principle and to see in matter the principle of evil, but he refuses to recognize the existence of evil in the realm of Intelligence (ideas). He is thus forced to recognize the existence of two kinds of matter, one in the realm of the sensible and the result of the last emanative step, the other in the realm of Intelligence ("intelligible matter"), which does not have some of the properties usually associated with matter—specifically, it is not evil. He justifies this by the assumption that everything, including matter in the physical world, must have its archetype in the realm of Intelligence (II 4 [12], Chs. 2f., 11, 14). Whether the assumption of intelligible matter can be reconciled with monism appears dubious; its "origin" is never made clear by Plotinus.

As to matter in the realm of the sensible, it is sheer indeterminacy, incorporeal, and, thus, different from the Stoic conception of matter (II 4 [12], Chs. 1, 4, 9, 10). It remains as unaffected by the ideas (or "ratios," logoi, by which Stoic term Plotinus often designates ideas as present in the soul qua formative powers) as the mirror is unaffected by what it reflects. Precisely because this matter is indeterminate, it is evil (II 4 [12], Ch. 16, l. 19), which means that evil is not something positive, but sheer privation.

There is a strange parallelism between matter and the One, because both are entirely indeterminate. Therefore, they both elude ordinary concepts, and Plotinus faces the question of what it means to know them. As far as matter is concerned, Plotinus likens it sometimes to darkness, and the mental act by which we grasp it to "unthinking thinking," or the soul's reduction to indefiniteness (II 4 [12], Chs. 6, 11)—concepts reminding us of Plato's pseudo thinking (nothos logismos), declared by him to be the appropriate way to think the receptacle.

KNOWLEDGE OF THE ONE. But much more important for Plotinus is the problem how the One, in spite of its being ineffable, can be known. In the pseudo(?)-Platonic Epinomis (992B), the author insists that in order to know the One (whatever "knowledge" means here), the soul must itself become one; the Platonic Letters also seem to teach some kind of suprarational insight. Perhaps starting from passages such as these and also from passages in Aristotle and Theophrastus in which some kind of infallible knowledge of certain objects is described as a kind of touching (thinganein), Plotinus asserts that to "know" the One means to become one with it, which the soul can accomplish only by becoming as simple or as "alone" as the One. In the moment of such a union the soul has become God or, rather, is God; the soul has reascended to its original source (VI 9 [9], Ch. 9f.). Among the terms Plotinus uses to describe this condition are ecstasy, simplicity, self-surrender, touching, and flight of the alone to the alone (VI 9 [9], Chs. 3, 11). This ecstasy—repeatedly experienced by Plotinus himself—is undoubtedly the climactic moment of man's life. It is not expressible in words (compare Plato, Epistle VII, 341D); only he who has experienced it knows what it means to be ravished away and full of God.

For this reascent man prepares himself by the acquisition of all the perfections (virtues, aretai). However, each of these perfections acquires different meanings according to the level on which man's spiritual life takes place—thus, there is a social fairness, above it another kind of fairness, and so on. Man also prepares himself by the exercise of dialectics (I 2 [19]; I 3 [20]). The preliminary stages of achievement Plotinus calls "becoming Godlike" (I 6 [1], Ch. 8), a condition often described by Platonists preceding Plotinus as the ultimate goal of Plato's philosophy.

FREE WILL AND DEMONOLOGY. Among the other topics treated in this period, Plotinus's defense of the freedom of the will—only "reasonable" souls are free; others are subject to fate, εἱμαρμένη (III 1 [3])—and his demonology deserve special mention. In regard to demonology Plotinus tries to steer a middle course between two theories, one identifying demons with the supreme parts of our soul, and the other assuming the existence of demons as extrapsychical beings (III 4 [15]).

SECOND PERIOD, 263–268

POLEMICS. More than two-fifths of Plotinus's total literary output was produced during the brief period between 263 and 268, when Porphyry was studying with Plotinus. Perhaps Porphyry's presence worked as a powerful stimulus. A considerable part of the output of this period is devoted to polemics with other schools, notably on the doctrine of categories and against Gnosticism.

Categories. Plotinus rejects both the Aristotelian and the Stoic versions of this doctrine, adhering to the principle that there can be no categories common to the realms of the sensible and the intelligible. In application to the realm of the sensible he corrects and modifies Aristotle's categories; to the realm of Intelligence he tries to apply Plato's five genera—being, identity, diversity, rest, and change (VI 1–3 [42–44]).

Ideal numbers. Aristotle presented Plato as professing the existence of ideal numbers (twoness, threeness, and so on, as distinguished from ordinary numbers—two, three, and so on). And he devoted much effort to the criticism of the theory of ideal numbers. Plotinus defends the theory of ideal numbers—which differ from nonideal numbers in that they do not consist of addible unities and are therefore not addible themselves (V 5 [32], Ch. 4)—and, objecting to any nominalist or abstractionist theory of numbers, attributes to them subsistence. Specifically, after having divided the realm of Intelligence into three layers—Being, Intelligence (in a restricted sense of the word), and the original Living Being—he assigns ideal numbers to the uppermost layer and explains that only because of their existence can Being divide itself into beings (VI 6 [34]), Chs. 8, 16). In this context he also introduces a peculiar concept of infinity: The truly infinite is a thing that has no limits imposed on it from without but only from within (VI 6 [34], Chs. 17f., but compare V 5 [32], Ch. 4).

Polemic against Gnosticism. Of all the polemics of Plotinus, the most significant is the one against Gnosticism. One could say that when facing Gnostic pessimism point-blank, Plotinus overcompensates for the pessimistic and Gnostic strand present in himself and responds with an almost unlimited optimism. The fundamental mood underlying Gnosticism is alienation from a hostile world, and Gnosticism undertakes to explain this mood and to open the road to escape from the world. The explanation is in the form of a history of the origin of the visible cosmos; according to Gnosticism, this cosmos is the result of the activity of an evil god sometimes identified with the Creator-God of the Old Testament or with Plato's divine artisan. This evil god is only the last in a succession of beings. The manner in which this succession takes place consists in a number of voluntary acts by which divinities of an ever lower order originate. The relation between these deities is often personal, based on such traits as curiosity, oblivion, daring, ambition. Man, as he exists in this evil world, contains in himself a spark of what was his original, divine substance, now imprisoned in his body owing to the scheming of the evil god.

At a certain moment a messenger-savior in some way breaks the power of the evil god and makes it possible for those who hear the whole story (acquire gnosis) to regain their original standing and free themselves from the tyranny of the evil god.

Plotinus treats Gnosticism as a strictly philosophic system. He simply compares its doctrines with his own and with those of Plato; its salvationary aspects are of little interest to him (compare III 2 [47], Ch. 9). In the succession of divine beings he sees only a superfluous multiplication of the three hypostases of his own system (compare V 5 [32], Chs. 1f.). To the cosmic drama that results in the creation of the visible cosmos he opposes his view of a totally undramatic, unconscious emanation, a product of necessity without arbitrariness and, contradicting even Plato's *Timaeus* (40B–45A), without planning (V 8 [31], Ch. 7) and, therefore, entirely blameless. The cosmos, product of the activities of the Soul (or Intelligence or both), he considers to be beautiful. Whereas Gnosticism sees the visible universe filled with spirits inimical to man, most outstanding among them being the rulers of the celestial bodies (planets), Plotinus sees in these spirits powers related to man in brotherly fashion. What is true in Gnosticism can, according to him, be found in Plato. The Gnostic objection that Plato did not penetrate the mysteries of the intelligible world Plotinus considers ridiculously presumptuous (II 9 [33]; compare V 8 [31], Ch. 8).

PROBLEMS. In the second period Plotinus was also concerned with the problems inherent in his own system, especially with the relation between the intelligible world and the sensible world and with the structure of the intelligible world.

The One. First, Plotinus tries to elucidate the nature of the One still further. He does this particularly in the context of a discussion concerning the nature of human freedom, in which he also asks whether the One should be considered as a necessary being or as a free one (*ens necessarium* or *ens liberum*)—in theistic terms, whether God must exist or has freely chosen to exist. In what is perhaps his most profound theological discussion, Plotinus tries to establish the concept of the One as Lord of itself and thus not having to serve even itself, so that in the One freedom and necessity coincide (VI 8 [39], Chs. 7–21). And without any vacillation he excludes any kind of consciousness from the One (V 6 [24], Chs. 2, 4f.).

Intelligence and Soul. As far as Intelligence is concerned, Plotinus reiterates his doctrine that it contains ideas within itself (V 5 [32], Chs. 1f.), and he again tries to explain how, in spite of being one, it still contains multiplicity (VI 4 [22], Ch. 4; VI 5 [23], Ch. 6). With regard to souls Plotinus tries to explain how they can remain distinct from one another although they all are only one soul (VI 4 [22], Ch. 6; IV 3 [27], Chs. 1–8; compare IV 9 [8], Ch. 5).

Both Intelligence and Soul are supposed to be present in the sensible world and, therefore, present in what is extended, although they themselves are not extended. Starting from the famous discussion in Plato's *Parmenides* (131B), in which the attempt is made to explain how one idea can be present in many particulars, Plotinus tries to show that just because Intelligence and Soul are not extended, they can be omnipresent and ubiquitous in what is extended (VI 4 [22], especially VI 5 [23], Ch. 11). And also in this context he tries to establish the concept of differentiated unity (VI 4 [22], Ch. 4), that is, the noncontradictory character of "one" and "many."

Intelligence, Soul, change. Probably the most formidable difficulty facing Plotinus is the result of his theory treating Intelligence and Soul as metaphysical principles on the one hand and as present in man on the other (that is, as both transcendent and immanent) and, therefore, in some way engaged in mental life, particularly in sensing and remembering. As metaphysical principles—that is, members of the realm of the intelligible—Intelligence and Soul should be unchangeable, whereas in man they seem to be involved in change. From this difficulty Plotinus tries to extricate himself in many ways, of which two will be presented.

On the one hand he keeps even the human soul away as much as possible from the processes of sensing, remembering, desiring, experiencing pleasure and pain, and so on (III 6 [26], Ch. 1–5). Sometimes he insists that the soul simply notices all these processes without being affected by what it perceives (IV 6 [41]; IV 4 [28], Ch. 19). Sometimes he insists that it is not the soul itself but only some trace of it which is engaged in these activities (IV 4 [28], Chs. 18f.; compare VI 4 [22], Ch. 15, l. 15), and this ties in with the theory that the soul did not really—or not in its entirety—descend (VI 4 [22], Ch. 16). Sometimes he introduces the concept of a double soul, a higher and a lower, with only the lower being changeable. This doubling of the soul Plotinus carries to such extremes that he assumes two imaginative faculties and two faculties of memory, each belonging to its respective soul and each remembering in a different manner and different events. This is particularly the case after man's death; the higher soul no longer remembers anything it experienced while in the body, whereas the lower soul still remembers (IV 3

[27], Chs. 25–32; IV 4 [28], Ch. 1, l. 5). Sometimes he suggests that all the mental activities involving change happen not to the soul but to the composite of soul and body (IV 4 [28], Ch. 17), leaving undecided how anything can affect a whole without affecting the part that belongs to it.

On the other hand, when it comes to Intelligence and Soul as metaphysical principles (and even to the world soul and astral souls), Plotinus disallows them memory entirely (IV 4 [28], Chs. 6–17). As to sensing, he distinguishes two kinds, one serving such practical purposes as self-preservation, the other purely theoretical; it is only the theoretical kind that he ascribes to metaphysical entities, the implication obviously being that this kind of sensation does not cause any change in the perceiver (IV 4 [28], Ch. 24). Why they should still be called Intelligence and Soul remains somewhat unclear. Perhaps the most striking example of the real effects of the Soul's falling away from Intelligence (despite everything said by Plotinus to minimize these effects) is that the cosmic soul, as it falls away, engenders time because of an inability to contemplate the totality of Intelligence simultaneously (III 7 [45], Ch. 11).

Ethics. The difficulties created for the explanation of the cognitive aspects of man's mental life without the assumption of a real change (passibility) of the soul return with even greater significance in the field of ethics. If there is no actual fall of the soul and if no deterioration of its nature has taken place as the result of incarnation (III 6 [26], Ch. 5), why is purifying the soul necessary? Yet the concept of purification plays a central role in the ethics of Plotinus (compare I 6 [1]; I 2 [19]); he even describes the perfections—wisdom, self-control, justice, courage—as purifications. Plotinus tries to help himself by a metaphor: The soul is merely covered with mud, which, however, has never penetrated it. According to another explanation, what the soul has acquired because of its fall is nothingness, and all it has to do, therefore, is to get rid of nothing (VI 5 [23], Ch. 12, ll. 16–23).

Cosmic sympathy. The insistence that memory and sensation, in their ordinary senses, are absent from the realm of Intelligence and even from that of the celestial sphere Plotinus explains with his theory that the universe is one animated organism. The sympathy existing among parts of one organism make memory and sensation superfluous, since the mutual affection need not be perceived. This leads to characteristic explanations of the efficacy of magic, prayers, and astrology. All these activities (and prophecies) are made possible by the fact that each part of the universe affects the others and is affected by them, not by mechanical causation nor by influencing the will of deities—particularly stars—but exclusively by mutual sympathy (IV 3 [27], Ch. 11; IV 4 [28], Chs. 40f.). In this doctrine of sympathy many scholars see the influence of the Stoa, particularly Posidonius, on Plotinus.

Matter. As to matter, Plotinus in the writings of this period—with less ambiguity than in other periods—characterizes it as the result of the last step of the emanative process, thus fully preserving the monistic character of his system (II 5 [25], Ch. 5; compare I 8 [51], Ch. 7). Some other problems discussed by Plotinus are distinctly occasional pieces and somewhat peripheral with regard to the system. Thus, we find a theory of vision, explained by sympathy (IV 5 [29]; II 8 [35]); a discussion of the Stoic concept of the complete interpenetration of bodies (II 7 [37]); a cosmology without the assumption of ether (II 1 [40]).

THIRD PERIOD, 268–270

As is to be expected, some earlier themes recur in the third period. In fact, one of the essays of the third period (V 3 [49]) contains what is perhaps the most comprehensive presentation of the basic tenets of Plotinus's philosophy. Plotinus proves that there must be a One preceding all multiplicity and that this One must be ineffable (V 3 [49], Chs. 12f., 17). To explain its presence in us and the fact that we know about it although we do not know it, he says that those full of and possessed by the divine also feel that something greater than themselves is present in them, although they cannot say what it is (V 3 [49], Ch. 14). Once more facing the problem of how the One, which is absolutely simple, can be the source of multiplicity, Plotinus is on the verge of admitting that the One is at least potentially (though it is a potentiality sui generis) many (V 3 [49], Chs. 15f.; compare VI 5 [23], Ch. 9). The same essay contains what is probably the most detailed and the most impressive description of the upward journey of the soul to reach the goal of ecstatic union, described by the formula "through light light" (V 3 [49], Ch. 17, ll. 28–37; compare V 5 [32], Chs. 4–9). As advice on how to achieve this union, Plotinus says "strip yourself of everything" (V 3 [49], 17, l. 38). Furthermore, Plotinus still feels he must prove that ideas are not external to Intelligence (V 3 [49], Chs. 5–13).

On the whole, the writings of Plotinus's last period are dominated by two themes. The first concerns theodicy, the origin and justification of evil, and the second asks what man's true self is.

THEODICY. To explain the origin of evil, Plotinus tries to reconcile the view that matter, though void of any

quality and actually only deficiency, is still evil in some sense of the word and is the source of all evil (I 8 [51], Chs. 8, 10). In so doing, he sometimes comes dangerously close to the Gnostic theory that matter imprisons the soul (I 8 [51], Ch. 14, ll. 48–50) and to a completely dualistic system (I 8 [51], Ch. 6, l. 33). Nevertheless, his optimism is particularly strong in this period; he has high praise for the beauty of the visible cosmos (III 2 [47], Ch. 12, l. 4), and rejects the idea of an evil creator of the cosmos (III 2 [47], Ch. 1). His theodicy is a blend of Platonic arguments, drawn especially from Book X of the *Laws*, and Stoic arguments. Perfection of the whole demands imperfection of the parts (III 2 [47], Chs. 11, 17; III 3 [48]) and the existence of evil (I 8 [51], Chs. 8–15). At the same time he minimizes the importance of evil by insisting that it exists only for the wicked one (III 2 [47], Ch. 6). Furthermore, he points out that the cosmic order rewards and punishes everybody according to his merits and assigns each one an appropriate place, thus making for a completely harmonious whole (III 2 [47], Ch. 4). Ultimately, his theodicy is based on convictions characteristic of most theodicies—that to designate a particular as evil is to lose sight of the whole, that everything participates in the good as far as it can, and that evil is only absence of the good (III 2 [47], Chs. 3, 5; I 8 [51], Chs. 1–5).

Providence. Closely connected with the problem of theodicy is the problem of providence. Plotinus insists on the all-pervasive character of providence, thus rejecting Aristotle's dichotomy of the universe into a sublunar sphere dominated by necessity and a supralunar world to which providence is restricted. He replaces Aristotle's distinction by the dichotomy of good and wicked men; only the wicked are subject to necessity (III 2 [47], Ch. 9; compare III 1 [3], Chs. 8–10). But this providence is entirely impersonal (compare VI 7 [38], Ch. 1) and actually coincides with the order of the universe.

TRUE SELF AND HAPPINESS. The second major theme of Plotinus's last period is that of ascertaining what man's true self is—that is, of ultimately obeying the divine command "Know thyself." Attendant subproblems are the explanations of wherein man's true happiness consists and of the concept of self-knowledge. It is extremely difficult for Plotinus to give a consistent account of what constitutes man's true self. He cannot simply identify it with Intelligence or Soul (as he did in IV 7 [1], Ch. 1, l. 24 or in I 4 [46], Chs. 8–16, where it is identified with the "higher" soul), precisely because both, in their character of metaphysical entities, remain transcendent; however, he rejects the idea that man is truly the composite of soul and body (I 4 [46], Ch. 14, l. 1) because this would grant the body too much importance. One of the solutions favored by Plotinus is that Intelligence is man's true self, but only if and when he succeeds in identifying himself with it. On the other hand, no such identification is actually necessary, because Intelligence is always in and with us even though we are not aware of it. (*Mutatis mutandis* this can also be applied to the relation of man and whatever is to be conceived the highest divinity: compare VI 5 [23], Ch. 12). Once more the concept of the unconscious plays a decisive role in the system of Plotinus (I 4 [46], Chs. 9f.; V 3 [49], Chs. 3f.). All this ties in with the idea that self-knowledge occurs only when the subject, the act, and the object of knowledge coincide—which takes place only on the level of Intelligence—whereas neither man as a whole nor Soul can possess full self-knowledge (V 3 [49], Chs. 3, 6). The One is, of course, above any kind of self-knowledge (V 3 [49], Chs. 10–13).

The thesis that only Intelligence is man's true self (if and when he makes full use of it) serves also as a basis for a discussion of the problem of man's happiness. If by "man" we mean the composite of body and soul, man cannot experience happiness, nor can he if he is body alone. However, if by "man" we mean the true self, it is obvious that happiness consists in the exercise of Intelligence—that is, in contemplation. But as the activity of Intelligence is uninterrupted (here in the argument Plotinus switches from Intelligence as immanent to transcendent Intelligence; see I 1 [53], Ch. 13, l. 7) man is actually always happy, although he may remain unconscious of it (I 4 [46], Chs. 4, 9, 13–16). Why this should apply only to the sage remains unclear.

The formidable problem of how the soul, the essence of which is unchangeability, can ever become evil also vexed Plotinus to the end (compare I 8 [51], Ch. 4, 12, 15). In the work of his last period he explains that as the soul at its descent acquires additional parts, evil resides only in them. Thus, the ethical task of man is not so much to separate the soul from the body as it is to separate it from these adventitious parts (I 1 [53], Ch. 12, l. 18). In this context the problem of who is the subject of punishments in afterlife also emerges; Plotinus answers that it is that "composite" soul (I 1 [53], Ch. 12). Why we should call soul an entity that is or can become evil, "suffer" punishment, and so on, after Soul has been presented as belonging to the realm of the unchangeable, remains unanswered; so do virtually all questions resulting from the dual character of Intelligence and Soul as metaphysical (transcendental) entities on the one hand and human (immanent) entities on the other.

There is almost something providential in the fact that the very last of Plotinus's essays, written at a time when death was approaching him, reasserts that all things participate in the One (the Good) and discusses the question of how to reconcile the two theses that life is good and yet death no evil, though it deprives us of something good (I 7 [54], Ch. 3). The battle between the pessimistic and the optimistic strands in Plotinus continued to the very end of his activity. Optimism ultimately won: Life is good—though not for the wicked one; death is good, because it will permit the soul to live an unhampered life.

See also Alcinous; Antiochus of Ascalon; Aristotle; Categories; Cosmos; Emanationism; Evil, The Problem of; Gnosticism; Good, The; Neoplatonism; Nous; Numenius of Apamea; Origen; Plato; Platonism and the Platonic Tradition; Porphyry; Posidonius; Pythagoras and Pythagoreanism; Socrates; Stoicism.

Bibliography

WORKS BY PLOTINUS

The standard edition of the Greek text of the *Enneads* and of Porphyry's *Life of Plotinus* is by Paul Henry and Hans-Rudolf Schwyzer, *Plotini Opera*, in 3 vols. (Oxford: Clarendon Press, 1964–1982) (*editio minor* with concise apparatus). For full critical apparatus and an English translation of the important Arabic tradition see their *editio maior*, in 3 vols. (Paris: Desclée de Brouwer, 1951–1973).

Modern translations (some including ancient text and/or valuable notes) are available in English by A. H. Armstrong, in 7 vols. (Cambridge, MA, and London: Harvard University Press and Heinemann, 1966–1988); in French by É Bréhier, in 6 vols. (Paris: Belles Lettres, 1924–1938); in German by R. Harder, R. Beutler, and W. Theiler, in 5 vols. (Hamburg: F. Meiner, 1956–1962); in Spanish by J. Igal, in 3 vols. (Madrid: Gredos, 1982–1998); and in Italian by M. Casaglia, C. Guidelli, A. Linguiti, and F. Moriani, in 2 vols. (Torino: Unione Tipografico-Editrice, 1997). A new French translation of individual treatises with extensive commentary, under the direction of Pierre Hadot (Paris: Cerf, 1988–), comprises, so far, 8 vols.

WORKS ON PLOTINUS

A complete lexicon for Plotinus' writings is J. H. Sleeman and Gilbert Pollet, *Lexicon Plotinianum* (Leiden: Brill, 1980). For a comprehensive bibliography, see Richard Dufour, *Plotinus: A Bibliography 1950–2000* (Leiden: Brill [*Phronesis*, vol. 46, No. 3], 2001). This is updated in: http://rdufour.free.fr/BibPlotin/Anglais/Biblio.html.

GENERAL WORKS

Gerson, Lloyd P. *Plotinus*. London: Routledge, 1994.

Hadot, Pierre. *Plotinus, or the Simplicity of Vision*. Translated by M. Chase, with an introduction by A. I. Davidson. Chicago, IL: University of Chicago Press, 1993.

O'Meara, Dominic J. *Plotinus: An Introduction to the* Enneads. Oxford: Clarendon Press, 1993.

Rist, John M. *Plotinus: The Road to Reality*. Cambridge, NY: Cambridge University Press, 1967.

Schwyzer, Hans-Rudolf. "Plotinos." In *Realencyklopädie der classischen Altertumswissenschaft*, edited by A. Pauly and G. Wissowa. Vol. 21 (1951): 471–592, with supplement in *SupplementBand*, 15 (1978): 310–328.

COMMENTARIES ON INDIVIDUAL TREATISES

Atkinson, Michael. *Ennead V, 1, On the Three Principal Hypostases: A Commentary with Translation*. Oxford: Oxford University Press, 1983.

Fleet, Barrie. *Ennead III, 6, On the Impassivity of the Bodyless*. Oxford: Clarendon Press, 1995.

Meijer, P. A. *Plotinus On the Good or the One (Enneads VI, 9): An Analytical Commentary*. Amsterdam: Gieben, 1992.

Tornau, Christian. *Plotin: Enneaden VI, 4-5 (22–23): Ein Kommentar*. Stuttgart: Teubner, 1998.

STUDIES OF DETAIL

Adamson, Peter. *The Arabic Plotinus: A Philosophical Study of the Theology of Aristotle*. London: Duckworth, 2002.

Armstrong, A. H. *Plotinian and Christian Studies*. London: Variorum Reprints, 1979.

Blumenthal, Henry J. *Plotinus' Psychology: His Doctrines of the Embodied Soul*. The Hague: Nijhoff, 1971.

Bussanich, John R. *The One and its Relation to Intellect in Plotinus: A Commentary on Selected Texts*. Leiden: Brill, 1988.

Corrigan, Kevin. "Body's Approach to Soul. An Examination of a Recurrent Theme in the *Enneads*." *Dionysius* 9 (1985): 37–52.

Corrigan, Kevin. *Reading Plotinus: A Practical Introduction to Neoplatonism*. West Lafayette IN: Purdue University Press, 2005.

Dillon, John M. "Plotinus and the Transcendental Imagination." In his *Religious Imagination*. Edinburgh: Edinburgh University Press, 1986.

Dillon, John M. "Plotinus, the first Cartesian?" *Hermathena* 149 (1990): 19–31.

Emilsson, Eyjólfur Kjalar. *Plotinus on Sense-Perception: A Philosophical Study*. Cambridge, U.K.: Cambridge University Press, 1988.

Emilsson, Eyjólfur Kjalar. "Plotinus on the Objects of Thought." *Archiv für Geschichte der Philosophie* 77 (1995): 21–41.

Ferwerda, R. *La signification des images et des métaphores dans la pensée de Plotin*. Groningen: J. B. Wolters, 1965.

Gerson, Lloyd P., ed. *The Cambridge Companion to Plotinus*. Cambridge, NY: Cambridge University Press, 1996.

Hadot, Pierre. "Les niveaux de la conscience dans les états mystiques selon Plotin." *Journal de Psychologie Normale et Pathologique* 77 (1980): 243–266.

Igal, Jesus. "The Gnostics and 'The Ancient Philosophy' in Porphyry and Plotinus." In *Neoplatonism and Early Christian Thought: Essays in Honour of A. H. Armstrong*, edited by H. J. Blumenthal and R. A. Markus. London: Variorum Publications, 1981.

Jackson, B. Darrell. "Plotinus and the *Parmenides*." *Journal of the History of Philosophy* 5 (1967): 315–327.

Kalligas, Paul. "Forms of Individuals in Plotinus: a Re-examination." *Phronesis* 42 (1997): 206–227.

McCumber, J. "*Anamnesis* as Memory of Intelligibles in Plotinus." *Archiv für Geschichte der Philosophie* 60 (1978): 160–167.

O'Brien, Denis. *Plotinus on the Origin of Matter: An Exercise in the Interpretation of the* Enneads. Napoli: Bibliopolis, 1991.

O'Daly, G. J. P. *Plotinus' Philosophy of the Self*. Dublin: Irish University Press, 1973.

Rist, John M. "Monism: Plotinus and Some Predecessors." *Harvard Studies in Classical Philology* 69 (1965): 329–344.

Schibli, Hermann S. "Apprehending our Happiness. *Antilepsis* and the Middle Soul in Plotinus, *Ennead I, 4, 10*." *Phronesis* 34 (1989): 205–219.

Schniewind, Alexandrine. *L'éthique du sage chez Plotin: Le paradigme du* spoudaios. Paris: J. Vrin, 2003.

Schroeder, Frederic M. *Form and Transformation: A Study in the Philosophy of Plotinus*. Montréal, London: McGill-Queen's University Press, 1992.

Sorabji, Richard. "Myths about Non-propositional Thought." In *Language and Logos: Studies in Ancient Greek Philosophy Presented to G. E. L. Owen*, edited by M. Schofield and M. C. Nussbaum. Cambridge, U.K.: Cambridge University Press, 1982.

Strange, Steven Keith. "Plotinus, Porphyry and the Neoplatonic Interpretation of the *Categories*." In *Aufstieg und Niedergang der römischen Welt: Geschichte und Kultur Roms im Spiegel der neueren Forschung*, edited by Wolfgang Haase. Vol. II, 36.2. Berlin: De Gruyter, 1987.

Strange, Steven Keith. "Plotinus on the Nature of Eternity and Time." In *Aristotle in Late Antiquity*, edited by L. P. Schrenk. Washington DC: The Catholic University of America Press, 1994.

Philip Merlan (1967)
Bibliography updated by Paul Kalligas (2005)

PLOTINUS [ADDENDUM]

What is it, Plotinus asks (Plotinus 1956), that lures the eye toward a beautiful sight and that draws the ear to a beautiful sound? It is the thrill that the soul feels in sensing its affinity with the noble being that manifests itself in those beautiful sights and sounds. Material things become beautiful by sharing in Form and thus in Unity. This applies to the productions of artists as much as to the beauties of nature. Thus the true objects of artistic imitation are Form and Unity; and so the artist is always entitled to "add where nature is lacking" (Plotinus 1956). Beauty is also found in noble conduct, in excellent laws, and in human virtue. The virtuous soul acquires Beauty and becomes godlike by purifying itself from evil. Thus Beauty in general has a metaphysical significance through its relation to Form, the One, and to the divine. In Plotinus's eyes, Beauty's significance is not only metaphysical but quasi-religious, not only because of its relationship to the divine, but also because Beauty is what draws the soul onwards in its ascent to the suprasensible world whence it came (Plotinus 1956).

See also Beauty.

Bibliography

Beardsley, Monroe C. *Aesthetics from Classical Greece to the Present: A Short History*. New York: Macmillan, 1966.

Plotinus. *The Enneads*. Translated by Stephen McKenna, revised by B. S. Page, with a foreword by E R Dodds and an introduction by P Henry. 2nd ed. London: Faber and Faber, 1956.

Paul Thom (2005)

PLOUCQUET, GOTTFRIED
(1716–1790)

Gottfried Ploucquet, the German philosopher and logician, studied philosophy and theology at Tübingen, experiencing both Wolffian and Pietist influences. After serving as a pastor, he was professor of logic and metaphysics at Tübingen from 1750 to 1782. He was elected to the Berlin Academy in 1748. Ploucquet was one of the few logicians between Gottfried Wilhelm Leibniz and George Boole to study a symbolic calculus. In metaphysics, despite his Wolffian training, he developed a quite personal position inspired by René Descartes and Nicolas Malebranche and aimed at revising Leibnizianism on a theological basis.

Ploucquet regarded the problems of theology, cosmology, and psychology as inextricably intertwined, with theology as the predominant discipline. There were some variations in Ploucquet's doctrines, but typically he held that a monad is a spiritual substance, and that even being is spiritual. Spiritual substances and material things can interact because God represents both and connects them. Human perceptions are an effect of God's "real vision." Spiritual and material things are both real because God represents them; material things are real in a further sense, as *phaenomena substantiata*, insofar as God represents them as real. This divine representation is the cause of the real existence of things; but we perceive only an appearance of this real existence. Ploucquet showed, by an examination of the logical difficulties of the concept of infinity, that space and time cannot exist outside of human representation.

Ploucquet's philosophy was basically a pronounced metaphysical subjectivism and phenomenalism. But in order to escape the consequent idealism of this position,

Ploucquet reintroduced a variety of realism based on God. Ploucquet's was one of the most significant attempts before Immanuel Kant to develop a phenomenalism that asserted the real existence of things but denied (contrary to Leibnizian and Wolffian phenomenalism) that we can know such things on the basis of their appearances.

See also Descartes, René; Leibniz, Gottfried Wilhelm; Logic, History of: Precursors of Modern Logic; Malebranche, Nicolas; Phenomenalism; Wolff, Christian.

Bibliography

PRINCIPAL WORKS BY PLOUCQUET
Primaria monadalogiae capita. Berlin, 1747.
Principia de substantiis et phaenomenis. Frankfurt and Leipzig, 1752.
Fundamenta philosophiae speculativae. Tübingen, 1759.
Institutiones philosophiae theoreticae. Stuttgart, 1772.
Sammlung der schriften, welche den logischen Calkul des Herrn Prof. Ploucquets betreffen, mit neuen Zusätzen. Edited by F. A. Böck. Tübingen, 1773.
Elementa philosophiae contemplativae. Stuttgart, 1778.
Commentationes philosophicae selectiores. Utrecht, 1781.

WORKS ON PLOUCQUET
Aner, Karl. *Gottfried Ploucquets Leben und Lehre*. Bonn, 1909.
Bornstein, Paul. *Gottfried Ploucquets Erkenntnistheorie und Metaphysik*. Potsdam: Buchdr. von A.W. Hayn's Erben, 1898.

Giorgio Tonelli (1967)

PLURALISM

Pragmatism and Continental hermeneutics combined to produce a decided turn toward forms of "pluralism" in twentieth-century philosophy (Geyer 1993, B. Singer 1990). This has led to the rejection of any one favored epistemological method (e.g., the scientific method, scriptural exegesis, introspection) and any one favored basis for the reconstruction of reality (e.g., mind, matter). Neopragmatists propose to replace the notion of truth with notions such as "fitting," "useful," and "warranted." Given that what is "fitting" is relative to the problem being faced and the means at one's disposal, we are left with the possibility of a plurality of ways of conceiving the world and of achieving our aims within it.

Moral pluralism opposes the monistic view that there is any one method of determining what is morally right (e.g., the utilitarian calculus or Kantian universalizability), and it also opposes the relativistic view that all things have value only with respect to a particular cultural context. Pluralists insist that a good life typically involves the desire, not for one, but for many kinds of "goods," often of incommensurable value; moreover, the realization of certain "goods" may conflict with and even preclude the realization of others. As such, pluralists believe that moral conflicts are inevitable and that there are not one but many alternative ways of resolving such conflicts (Kekes 1993). The trend toward pluralism has also been influenced by our growing awareness of different cultures with nonequivalent conceptions of reality and "the good life."

The modern nation-state has evolved beyond the belief that it manifests the cultural orientation of a single "race," usually its majority. The reality is that every nation is composed of numerous groups with different cultural orientations. And the state is considered the primary guarantor that minority views will be presented, respected, and given a voice in determining policy (Guttman 1993). The rejection of the view that a Eurocentric male-dominated culture is the norm to be achieved universally has led to the demand that the cultures of non-Europeans, women, and minorities be recognized and granted equal voice (Taylor 1992). In this way pluralism is considered by many to be an essential part of the liberal democratic state, and this has manifested itself in terms of educational policy as the rejection of monoculturalism and the demand for a multicultural orientation.

One form of multiculturalism has focused on the need of suppressed groups to have their cultures recognized. Such a demand for recognition may motivate certain proposals—for example, to replace a Eurocentric focus with an Afrocentric focus or a male-centered orientation with a feminist-centered orientation. Some argue that because of the past harms inflicted upon such groups, ostensibly because they were different, they are justified in embracing those differences in order to cleanse them of the negative valuations imposed by the hegemonic culture. It is right for such groups to adopt a separatist posture if this is the best means of achieving a redefinition of themselves that is positive and self-affirming (Young 1990). Where members of the hegemonic culture have inflicted unjust harms on members of an oppressed group, some argue that the oppressed group has the right to cultural restitution. The domination of culture A by culture B may not be the result of culture A's not offering viable options; rather, it may be the result of unjust injuries and harms visited on culture A by culture B. In such cases groups sharing culture A have a right to "moral deference," affirmative action, and the preserva-

tion of their culture (Mosley 1990, Nickel 1994, Thomas 1992–1993).

Many have been concerned that multiculturalism might degenerate into a bedlam of different groups, each espousing its own brand of cultural authenticity. Critics argue that this would amount to merely replacing one culture's hegemony with another culture's hegemony. Multiculturalism in this sense would fail to reflect the pluralist maxim that no orientation is "fitting" for every situation and that for a given end there may be several equally "fitting" means (West 1993, Yates 1992).

An alternative form of multiculturalism, closer to pluralism, emphasizes the importance of diversity and cross-cultural communication. On this view the more cultural orientations there are for consideration, the better the likelihood of finding or constructing a "fitting" adaptation to some current problem (Rorty 1992). For this reason every culture should be allowed the opportunity of articulating itself to the public at large and of thereby influencing the manner in which individuals construct their character.

Pluralism does not end with the insistence on an equal voice for every culture but extends itself to the view that different biological species often have interests that may conflict with the interests of human beings. Some have argued that, just as racism and sexism accord special preference to white males and victimize women and non-Europeans, so speciesism accords special preference to the interests of human beings and unjustly victimizes nonhuman species (P. Singer 1990). The insistence on a plurality of interests and capacities has been extended to include the interests of other animal species, as well as trees, rivers, and ecological systems (Wenz 1990).

See also Affirmative Action; Animal Rights and Welfare; Pragmatism; Racism; Sexism; Social and Political Philosophy; Speciesism.

Bibliography

Baghramian, Maria, and Attracta Ingram, eds. *Pluralism: The Philosophy and Politics of Diversity.* London: Routledge, 2000.

Barry, Brian M. *Culture and Equality: An Egalitarian Critique of Multiculturalism.* Cambridge, MA: Harvard University Press, 2001.

Geyer, M. "Multiculturalism and the Politics of General Education." *Critical Inquiry* 19 (1993): 499–533.

Guttman, A. "The Challenge of Multiculturalism in Political Ethics." *Philosophy and Public Affairs* 22 (3) (Summer 1993): 171–206.

Kekes, J. *The Morality of Pluralism.* Princeton, NJ: Princeton University Press, 1993.

Mosley, A. "Preferential Treatment and Social Justice." In *Terrorism, Justice, and Social Values,* edited by C. Peden and Y. Hudson. Lewiston, NY: Mellen Press, 1990.

Nickel, J. W. "Ethnocide and Indigenous Peoples." *Journal of Social Philosophy* 25 (1994): 84–98.

Okin, Susan Moller. *Is Multiculturalism Bad for Women?* Edited by Joshua Cohen, Matthew Howard, and Martha Nussbaum. Princeton, NJ: Princeton University Press, 1999.

Rorty, A. "The Advantages of Moral Diversity." *Social Philosophy and Policy* 9 (2) (Summer 1992): 38–62.

Singer, B. "Pragmatism and Pluralism." *Monist* 75 (4) (October 1992): 477–491.

Singer, P. *Animal Liberation.* New York: New York Review of Books, 1990.

Taylor, C. *Multiculturalism and the Politics of Recognition.* Princeton, NJ: Princeton University Press, 1992.

Thomas, L. "Moral Deference." *Philosophical Forum* 24 (1–3) (Spring 1992–1993): 233–250.

Walzer, Michael. *On Toleration.* New Haven, CT: Yale University Press, 1997.

Wenz, P. "Minimal, Moderate, and Extreme Moral Pluralism." *Environmental Ethics* 15 (1993): 61–74.

West, C. *Beyond Eurocentrism and Multiculturalism.* Monroe, ME: Common Courage Press, 1993.

Yates, S. A. "Multiculturalism and Epistemology." *Public Affairs Quarterly* 6 (1992): 435–456.

Young, M. Y. *Justice and the Politics of Difference.* Princeton, NJ: Princeton University Press, 1990.

Albert Mosley (1996)
Bibliography updated by Philip Reed (2005)

PLURALS AND PLURALITY

Plurality falls under the concept of grammatical number. So, one prefaces the discussion of plurality with a brief overview of grammatical number. Since this entry is written in English, one can consider grammatical number in English.

English nouns are either plural or singular, which is usually signaled by the presence or absence of the inflectional ending *s*. Thus, *book* (singular) contrasts with *books* (plural). However, some nouns have peculiar forms for singular and plural. For example, the plural of *louse* (singular) is *lice* (plural). Some nouns, like *deer*, do not take the suffix *s*, yet behave as both singular and plural. This is shown by the form of its preceding determiner and, should the noun be in the subject position, by the form of the main verb. Thus, in the sentence *That deer is crossing the road*, *deer* behaves like a singular noun, while in the sentence *Those deer are crossing the road*, it behaves like a plural noun. Still other nouns, such as *police*, behave only as grammatically plural.

While every English noun must appear in either a singular or plural form, not every English noun may appear in both forms. On the contrary, English pronouns have both a singular (e.g., *he, she,* or *it*) and a plural form (*they*), which, for the most part, share no stem. In addition, as illustrated earlier, many English common nouns, known as count nouns, occur as both singular and plural nouns. By contrast, English proper nouns appear in the singular or plural form, but not both. The singular proper noun *Aristotle* does not occur in the plural (in the same relevant sense), nor does the plural proper noun *the Andes* occur in the singular. Moreover, English common nouns, such as *dust* and *advice*, called mass nouns, occur typically only in the singular. This division between nouns that can occur both in the singular and in the plural and those that do not occur is crosscut by words that cannot be preceded by the full range of English determiners and those that can be. Thus, English nouns can be partitioned into four classes. On the one hand, proper nouns and pronouns cannot be preceded by determiners, while common nouns can be; and on the other, count nouns and pronouns occur in both singular and plural forms, while mass nouns and proper nouns do not.

	Occurs with a determiner	Admits the contrast of singular and plural
Proper name	−	−
Pronoun	−	+
Mass noun	+	−
Count noun	+	+

The contrast between singular and plural forms is signaled by the inflection of the noun, but the distinction applies to the noun phrase containing the noun. This is manifested by the fact that conjoined proper nouns behave as though they are plural. For example, while the sentence *Russell and Whitehead was coauthors* is unacceptable in English, the sentence *Russell and Whitehead were coauthors* is not.

Bearing in mind these facts about English grammatical number, one may ask what contribution grammatical number makes to a noun phrase. The commonsensical view, the one of traditional grammar, maintains that a plural noun phrase, such as *these books*, denotes more than one thing, whereas a singular noun phrase, such as *this book*, denotes precisely one thing. Matters, however, are not so simple. Some singular noun phrases, such as *Pegasus*, and some plural noun phrases, such as *the Furies*, denote nothing at all. Some singular nouns denote more than one thing. The proper noun *Benelux* denotes Belgium, The Netherlands, and Luxemburg; the collective count noun phrase *the team* denotes the people making up the team; and *this furniture* may denote a roomful of furniture comprising, say, two tables and a sofa, each of which is, of course, a piece of furniture. At the same time, plural count nouns such as *these pants* (compare *this pair of pants*) may denote only a single thing. Finally, what single thing, if any, does the singular noun phrase *the average Roman legionnaire* denote?

Common nouns contrast with pronouns and proper names in that they tolerate being preceded either by almost any determiner or by no determiner. When a common count noun is not preceded by any determiner, it must appear in the plural form. Such noun phrases are known as bare plurals. As Greg Carlson (1977) notes, such noun phrases are liable to different construals. The noun *dogs* in the sentence *dogs are barking* can be paraphrased as *Some dogs are barking*; however, when it occurs in the sentence *dogs bark* it is not paraphrased as *some dogs bark*. Rather, it seems to express a quasi-universal statement, something like *almost all dogs bark*, often known as the generic construal. Carlson notices that a similar contrast applies to mass nouns in the bare usage. *Water is liquid* as opposed to *water is dripping* (see Carlson and Pelletier 1995).

Further questions arise with quantified noun phrases. The singular noun phrase *some boy* might be thought to contrast with the plural noun phrase *some boys* because the former pertains to a single boy, while the latter pertains to more than one boy. This contrast does not appear to obtain for the singular noun phrase *each boy* and the plural noun phrase *all boys*, nor for the singular noun phrase *no woman* and the plural noun phrase *no women*.

An important source of data for the investigation of plural noun phrases is their susceptibility to so-called collective and distributive construals. One useful way to determine what these construals consist in is to use an equivalence between plural noun phrases and conjoined noun phrases, where the conjoined noun phrases contain proper nouns. If *the men* denotes Bertrand Russell and Alfred Whitehead, then (1.0) is paraphrasable by (1.1):

(1.0) The men wrote a book.

(1.1) Whitehead and Russell wrote a book.

It has long been recognized that sentences such as (1.0) and (1.1) have different construals, distinguishable with the help of adverbs:

(2.0) The men wrote a book.

(2.1) The men wrote a book *together*.

(2.2) The men *each* wrote a book.

These are paraphrasable by the following sentences, respectively:

(3.0) Whitehead and Russell wrote a book.

(3.1) Whitehead and Russell wrote a book *together*.

(3.2) Whitehead and Russell *each* wrote a book.

The sentences in (1) are true on the collective construal, since *Principia Mathematica* was written as a collaborative effort of Whitehead and Russell. This construal can be forced by the use of the adverb *together*, as in (2.1) and (3.1). The sentences in (1) are also true on the distributive construal, since Russell wrote at least one book on his own, for example, *An Inquiry into Meaning and Truth*, and Whitehead also wrote a book on his own, for example, *A Treatise on Universal Algebra*. This construal can be enforced by the use of the adverb *each*, as in (2.2) and (3.2).

As shown by the next example, the susceptibility of plural noun phrases to collective and distributive construals is not confined to collaboration:

(4.0) These two suitcases weigh fifty kilograms.

(4.1) These two suitcases *each* weigh fifty kilograms.

(4.2) These two suitcases weigh fifty kilograms *together*.

Moreover, collective and distributive construals seem to be the extremes of a range of construals. If *the men* denotes Richard Rodgers, Oscar Hammerstein, and Lorenz Hart, it is true to say that

(5) The men wrote musicals.

even though none of them wrote a musical on his own and the three never wrote a musical together. What is true is that Rodgers and Hammerstein wrote musicals and Rodgers and Hart wrote musicals (see Gillon 1987).

Next, it should be noted that susceptibility of collective and distributive construals is not confined to plural noun phrases in the subject position. Every argument position containing a plural noun phrase—be it the subject, object, indirect object, or object of a preposition—is liable to these construals, regardless of whether the noun phrase is an argument of a verb or of a noun (see Gillon 1996).

(6.1) Isabelle gave the girls a cookie.

(6.2) Rick drove through the Redwood trees. (Compare *Rick drove through the Redwood tree.*)

(6.3) The two suitcases' weight is fifty kilograms.

(6.4) The writing of *Principia Mathematica* by Russell and Whitehead.

Finally, even singular count nouns give rise to collective and distributive construals. Suppose that someone has two suitcases and says:

(7) This luggage weighs fifty kilograms.

The sentence could be taken to mean that altogether the luggage weighs fifty kilograms or that each piece of luggage weighs fifty kilograms.

Two crucial questions arise for the semantics of plural noun phrases: First, what do plural noun phrases denote? Second, how does one account for the various construals to which they are liable?

One can begin with the first question. According to the earliest researchers to address the question, such as Michael Bennett (1974) and Roland Hausser (1974), plural noun phrases denote sets. This view was roundly criticized by Godehard Link (1983) and Peter Simons (1983), who argued, independently of each other, that plural noun phrases do not denote sets, but what Simons called pluralities. Whereas a set of concrete individuals is an abstract mathematical entity, without spatial or temporal location, a plurality of concrete individuals is a concrete entity, with the spatial and temporal location of its membership. However, for both a set and a plurality, identity is determined by membership.

A plurality, then, is nothing more than the sum of its members. At the same time, a plurality is different from a collective, which may be more than the sum of its members. Thus, while a plurality is identified by its membership, so that if it acquires or loses a member, it becomes a different plurality, a collective is not identified simply by its members, for it can remain the same, even if its membership changes. Thus, an orchestra can remain the same, even though its members change. Inversely, the exact same individuals might constitute two collectives. Indeed, Simons (1982) reports that once the same musicians made up the Chapel Orchestra, the Court Opera Orchestra, and the Vienna Philharmonic. Nonetheless, a plurality can also be seen as the limiting case of a collective: that is, a plurality is a collective without conditions governing its constitution (Simons 1987, chapter 4.4).

The set of pluralities on a finite domain has the structure of a join semilattice. For example, consider three people: Dan, Paul, and Rick. They can form seven pluralities: three improper—Dan, Paul, and Rick; and four improper—Dan + Paul, Dan + Rick, Paul + Rick, and Dan + Paul + Rick. The algebraic operation symbolized here by $+$, is a join operation. It is idempotent ($x + x = x$), since there is no difference between Dan and Dan + Dan; it is commutative, since there is no difference between Dan + Paul and Paul + Dan; and it is associative, since Dan + (Paul + Rick) is the same plurality as (Dan + Paul) + Rick. The seven pluralities are all concrete individuals.

The join semilattice just described is isomorphic to the join semilattice obtained by assigning each plurality, proper and improper, a set: An improper plurality is assigned a singleton set. Thus, Dan is assigned {*Dan*}, a plurality comprised of two people is assigned a doubleton set. Thus, Dan + Rick is assigned {*Dan, Rick*}. And the plurality comprising three people is assigned a set of three people. The operation on these sets corresponding to + is that of union. Since every join semilattice of pluralities is isomorphic to a join semilattice of sets, a number of semanticists, including Fred Landman (1989a, 1989b), Roger Schwarzschild (1996), and Yoad Winter (2001), are content to treat pluralities as sets.

Link (1983) develops a semantics for a formal notation, designed to simulate singularity and plurality. Like Simons (1983, 1987), Link views the denotations of plural count noun phrases as distinct from the denotations of singular mass noun phrases, the former having their denotation based on individuals, the latter on so-called masses (see the mass noun entry). This distinction in denotation seems implausible, in view of the near synonymy of mass nouns such as *footwear*, *luggage*, *traffic*, and *advice*, with count nouns such as *shoes*, *suitcases*, *vehicles*, and *suggestions*. In light of such facts, Gillon (1992) provides a semantics of common nouns whereby a plural noun phrase such as *shoes* and a singular noun phrase such as *footwear* may have the same denotation; after all, all shoes are footwear, even if some footwear are not shoes. Another semanticist to provide a uniform domain for the interpretation of mass nouns and count nouns is Almerino Ojeda (1993), who takes all nouns to denote, in the first instance, kinds.

One can now turn to the second question: How are the various construals of plural noun phrases to be explained? A few authors such as Gillon (1987, 1992, 1996) and Schwarzschild (1996) think that the collective and distributive construals are extremes of a variety of construals, which, in their view, is pragmatically determined. However, the preponderance of authors recognize only two construals—the collective and distributive construals of traditional grammar—and take them to be the result of an ambiguity arising from the presence or absence of an unpronounced adverb. For some, like Link (1983), the adverb is essentially a phonetically null version of the English adverb *each*. For others, like Landman (1989a, 1989b), it is a phonetically null collectivizing operator applying to noun phrases. In fact, each of these views require no less than three kinds of phonetically null operators. Since virtually every plural noun phrase, no matter where it occurs in a sentence, is liable to collective and distributive construals, no fewer than three such phonetically null words are required (see Gillon 1996). Finally, several authors (Schein 1993, Lasersohn 1995, Landman 2000) have tried to develop a theory of events and their parts and participants to account for collective and distributive construals.

See also Generics; Nouns, Mass and Count.

Bibliography

Bäuerle, Rainer, Christoph Schwarze, and Arnim von Stechow, eds. *Meaning, Use, and Interpretation of Language.* Berlin, Germany: Gruyter, 1983.

Bennett, Michael R. "Some Extensions of a Montague Fragment of English." PhD diss., University of California, Los Angeles, 1974.

Carlson, Greg. "A Unified Analysis of the English Bare Plural." *Linguistics and Philosophy* 1 (1977): 413–457.

Carlson, Greg, and Jeff Pelletier, eds. *The Generic Book.* Chicago: University of Chicago Press, 1995.

Gillon, Brendan S. "Collectivity and Distributivity Internal to English Noun Phrases." *Language Sciences* 18 (1–2) (1996): 443–468.

Gillon, Brendan S. "A Common Semantics for English Count and Mass Nouns." *Linguistics and Philosophy* 15 (6) (1992): 597–639.

Gillon, Brendan S. "The Readings of Plural Noun Phrases in English." *Linguistics and Philosophy* 10 (1987): 199–220.

Hausser, Roland. *Quantification in an Extended Montague Grammar.* PhD diss., University of Texas, Austin, 1974.

Landman, Fred. *Events and Plurality: The Jerusalem Lectures.* Dordrecht, Netherlands: Kluwer Academic, 2000.

Landman, Fred. "Groups I." *Linguistics and Philosophy* 12 (5) (1989a): 559–606.

Landman, Fred. "Groups II." *Linguistics and Philosophy* 12 (6) (1989b): 723–744.

Lasersohn, Peter. *Plurality, Conjunction, and Events.* Dordrecht, Netherlands: Kluwer Academic, 1995.

Link, Godehard. "The Logical Analysis of Plurals and Mass Terms." In *Meaning, Use, and Interpretation of Language,* edited by Rainer Bäuerle, Christoph Schwarze, and Arnim von Stechow, 302–323. Berlin, Germany: Gruyter, 1983.

Ojeda, Almerindo. *Linguistic Individuals.* Stanford, CA: Center for the Study of Language and Information, 1993.

Schein, Barry. *Plurals and Events.* Cambridge, MA: MIT Press, 1993.

Schwarzschild, Roger. *Pluralities.* Dordrecht, Netherlands: Kluwer Academic, 1996.

Simons, Peter M. "Class, Mass, and Mereology." *History and Philosophy of Logic* 4 (1983): 157–180.

Simons, Peter. *Parts: A Study in Ontology.* New York: Oxford University Press, 1987.

Simons, Peter M. "Plural Reference and Set Theory." In *Parts and Moments: Studies in Logic and Formal Ontology,* edited by Barry Smith, 199–260. Munich, Germany: Philosophia (Analytica), 1982.

Smith, Barry, ed. *Parts and Moments: Studies in Logic and Formal Ontology.* Munich, Germany: Philosophia (Analytica), 1982.

Winter, Yoad. *Flexibility Principles in Boolean Semantics: The Interpretation of Coordination, Plurality, and Scope in Natural Language.* Cambridge, MA: MIT Press, 2001.

Brendan S. Gillon (2005)

PLUTARCH OF CHAERONEA
(c. 46–after 119, before 127 CE)

Plutarch, a Greek biographer and Platonic philosopher, was born in Chaeronea, Boeotia. His teacher was Ammonius, an Egyptian Platonist who resided in Athens and was head of a school that he called the Academy. After his studies (c. 90?) Plutarch established a philosophical school in Chaeronea. Plutarch held important public offices and was a priest at Delphi for twenty years or more. His extant writings include forty-eight biographies and various other works (*Moralia*): dialogues; diatribes; theoretical treatises; essays; collections of anecdotes; moralistic lectures; and polemical, antiquarian, and exegetical works. Several dialogues have Delphi as their setting and are concerned with the oracle and other religious problems. *Socrates' Daemonic Sign* has a historical setting. It portrays Plutarch's circle of friends and students. *Table-Talks* is a long collection of conversations on a wide range of questions.

INFLUENCES

Plato's dialogues, especially the *Timaeus*, but also Platonic school philosophy, as it could be found in manuals and introductory works, provide the basis of Plutarch's philosophy. In Plutarch's day, Platonism was dominated by Pythagorean tendencies, most importantly the tendency to construct a hierarchy of metaphysical principals based on an ontological derivation from the principals "one" and "dyad." Plutarch himself, however, was just as much influenced by the skepticism of the Hellenistic Academy, though in the mitigated form it took under Philo of Larissa. This influence shows in the limited epistemic status he granted to empirical science, his cautious attitude regarding the epistemic claims of popular religion, and his reflections on the unreliability of the senses. This epistemology can be traced back to Plato's *Timaeus*, and Plutarch explicitly did so. He developed a kind of fallibilism that allowed him provisionally to accept various physical doctrines, for example, about the nature of the moon, or the function of specific organs of the body. The Hellenistic Academy provided Plutarch with numerous arguments against Stoics (*Common Notions, Stoic Contradictions*) and Epicureans (*Reply to Colotes* and *That Epicurus Actually Makes a Pleasant Life Impossible*).

COSMOLOGY AND METAPHYSICS

Plutarch devoted a separate treatise to Plato's description of the composition of the world soul in the *Timaeus* and discussed this issue in several other places. Contrary to the large majority of his fellow Platonists, Plutarch understood Plato's story of the creation of the cosmos by a divine craftsman literally, in that he believed that the cosmos had existed only for a finite time. It came into being when the craftsman, or demiurge, imposed order on a preexisting chaos. Previous to his intervention, there was matter and a precosmic soul, as the principle of motion, both in a disordered state. The Platonic forms too existed, as their existence is eternal, but the world did not yet participate in them. When the demiurge imparted something of himself—namely intelligibility, or mathematically expressible rationality—to this preexisting soul, it became the world soul. The world soul then started to organize matter and create a structured, beautiful world (or cosmos).

Time, in the Platonic sense of succession characterized by cyclic regularities, was born together with the world. Plutarch leaves unspecified the relation between the craftsman and the forms. The forms and the craftsman belong to the same realm, and when the craftsman imparts something of himself to the preexisting soul, the latter, and through it the world, partake of the forms. The world is not perfect, as the original irrational soul, now integrated into the world soul, at times makes its influence felt. Soul itself, that is, soul in abstraction from the order it has received, is thus Plutarch's principle of evil. Plutarch espouses a mitigated metaphysical dualism: The rational and the irrational, order and disorder, good and evil are engaged in an unending struggle, but the good always dominates. The good he attributed to the gods, whereas higher forces responsible for evil can be mere demons, not gods. Plutarch linked his dualist views to an antagonism, at the level of metaphysical principles,

between the One and the indeterminate Dyad. This doctrine was attributed to Plato from as early as Aristotle and was cherished by Pythagorean Platonists. Plutarch equates the demiurge with the highest deity. In his dialogue *The Delphic E*, Plutarch has his master Ammonius define the supreme god as true being, eternity, and absolute unity, and call this god the One. In his treatise on Egyptian religion, *Isis and Osiris*, Plutarch interprets Egyptian myths allegorically and explains how they conform with Plato's cosmology and metaphysics, as he understands them.

MORAL PSYCHOLOGY AND ETHICS

The human soul, being an image of the world soul, is analogously constituted. It too consists of rational and irrational parts, the latter being more prominent than it is in the world soul, however. The irrational is part of the human soul itself, is the cause of disorder and the passions, but is also the dynamic force of our mental life. Rationality is intellect and the truly divine coming from outside.

In the eschatological myth at the end of *The Face in the Moon*, Plutarch develops a theory of a double death: In "ordinary death," the human soul frees itself from the body and ascends to the moon; after purification a second death ensues wherein the intellect sheds the irrational part. In *Moral Virtue*, Plutarch transposes his cosmological views onto the human soul and on this basis erects a theory of virtue as the mean and the moderation of the passions (*metriopatheia*). Plutarch's virtue ethics stands in a Peripatetic tradition, yet has its theoretical foundations in Platonic traditions as well. Our souls have a rational and an irrational part or force—the passions. The passions have to be made obedient to reason. Reason imposes limit and structure, or even in a sense *is* the limit, establishing the right mean between extremes, moral virtue between opposite vices. When the passions obey reason, the human soul achieves psychic harmony, which is a necessary and perhaps even sufficient condition for happiness in this life (though not necessarily for success in one's undertakings) and leads to felicity in the next. This is also the fundamental lesson of Plutarch's texts on practical ethics. Plutarch was a keen observer of human behavior, virtues, and vices. His *Lives* essentially consists of character studies, and some two dozen of his *Moralia* are on moral themes. Titles include *Advice to Bride and Groom, How to Tell a Flatterer from a Friend, Inoffensive Self-Praise, Exile, Compliancy, Superstition, Control of Anger, Tranquillity of Mind, Brotherly Love, Talkativeness*. Moral considerations dominate his approach to literature in *How to Study Poetry*. He even wrote on the behavior of animals: *The Cleverness of Animals* and *Beasts Are Rational*.

PLATONISM, STOICISM, AND EPICUREANISM

Plutarch incorporated ideas, examples, and terminology from other schools into his texts, but he subordinated them to his overall Platonism. This is especially obvious in his dialogues: He presents and examines various views; this typically leads to a Platonic position in which he combines what is sound in the views of other schools and adds an additional, transcendental, perspective. Plutarch construed his Platonism as occupying a middle position between Stoicism and Epicureanism. Whereas the Epicureans denied providence and the Stoics made the gods responsible for everything, the Platonic god is causally responsible for good things only. Plutarch combated the Stoic monolithic view of the mind and the Stoic ideal of being passionless: The passions constitute an intrinsic, indelible part of our psychic make-up; hence we have to learn to manage and control them.

See also Ancient Skepticism; Aristotle; Epicureanism and the Epicurean School; Neoplatonism; Plato; Pythagoras and Pythagoreanism; Stoicism; Virtue Ethics.

Bibliography

All the extant works of Plutarch have been edited and translated in *The Loeb Classical Library*. Among the more important spurious works included in the Plutarchan corpus are *Philosophical Opinions* (a doxography), *Music* (drawn from Peripatetic sources), *Fate* (a product of syncretistic Platonism of the second century CE), and, on the level of popular philosophy, *The Education of Children* and *Consolation to Apollonius*.

GENERAL INTRODUCTIONS TO PLUTARCH

Russell, D. A. *Plutarch*. London: Duckworth, 1973.

Sirinelli, Jean. *Plutarque de Chéronée: Un philosophe dans le siècle*. Paris: Fayard, 2000.

Ziegler, Konrat. *Plutarchos von Chaironea*. In Pauly's Realenzyklopädie, 41. Halbband, 1951: 636.18-962.14 (also published as a monograph: Stuttgart, 1949)

IMPORTANT STUDIES ON PLUTARCH'S PHILOSOPHY

Babut, Daniel. *Plutarque et le stoïcisme*. Paris: Presses Universitaires de France, 1969.

Brenk, Frederick E. "An Imperial Heritage: The Religious Spirit of Plutarch of Chaironeia." *Aufstieg und Niedergang der Römischen Welt* 2.36.1 (1987): 248–349.

Dillon, John. *The Middle Platonists: A Study of Platonism, 80 B.C. to A.D. 220*. Rev. ed. London: Duckworth, 1996.

ON THE *LIVES*

Duff, Tim. *Plutarch's Lives: Exploring Virtue and Vice*. Oxford, U.K.: Clarendon Press, 1999.

Jan Opsomer (2005)

PNEUMA

Ancient Greek thought early posited a connection between breath and life. The notion that wind or breath—*pneuma*—accounted for the functions of living things persisted in philosophical and medical accounts of organisms, sometimes alongside the notion of an immaterial soul or *psychē*. The idea that a distinct kind of *pneuma* played a role in the functioning of organisms seems to have developed in early medical theory. Some texts refer to *pneuma* as a kind of nutriment. The idea that there is a specifically "psychic" *pneuma* is found in the doctor Diocles of Carystus (fourth century BCE), who had connections to Aristotle's school.

In Aristotle's biology an innate *pneuma* is mentioned in connection with a number of functions of the organism and is even compared to the *ether*, the fifth element from which the heavenly bodies are composed. In the case of sexual generation *pneuma* is used to explain the ability of the male seed to convey its movements to the female matter without contributing matter to the resulting embryo; in animal movement it helps explain the movement of the limbs. There is room for doubt about how systematically Aristotle used the concept, however, or its relationship to the elements. His second successor, Strato of Lampsacus, seems to have considered *pneuma* to be the material substance of the soul, perhaps in recognition of the discoveries of Hellenistic medicine; a treatise on *pneuma* survives in the Aristotelian corpus.

Praxagoras (fourth century BCE), who distinguished veins from arteries, theorized that the latter contain only *pneuma*; this was eventually rejected by Galen. The Hellenistic doctors Herophilus (c. 335–c. 280 BCE) and Erasistratus (flourished c. 250 BCE) recognized a system of *neura* or nerves originating from the brain, responsible for motor and perceptual functions. Because some nerves were seen to be hollow, they were thought to contain a special kind of *pneuma* suited to their functions. In Galen's physiology the "vital *pneuma*" is distributed through the arteries; the brain refines this into "psychic *pneuma*," which, through the nerves, is the instrument by which the soul performs its functions.

Unlike these medical theories associating *pneuma* with the vascular systems, Epicurus describes the material soul as like, or partly composed of, *pneuma*. In Stoic philosophy it played a broader role. The Stoics hypothesized that *pneuma*—for them, a kind of hot air—is distributed throughout all other matter in the cosmos. Supposing that all action happens by bodies in contact, yet needing to account for apparent cases of action at a distance, the Stoics held that the pervasiveness of this single material accounted for the "sympathy" between distant bodies, as well as the cohesiveness of the cosmos as a whole and the qualities of individual things. Associated with the divine intelligence pervading the cosmos, the part of the cosmic *pneuma* pervading living things is the soul.

The Greek term *pneuma* was later used in religious contexts and associated with spirit and the divine. The physiological use of *pneuma* to account for functions of living things is echoed in the early modern notion of "animal spirits."

See also Aristotle; Epicurus; Stoicism; Strato and Stratonism.

Bibliography

Freudenthal, Gad. *Aristotle's Theory of Material Substance: Heat and Pneuma, Form and Soul.* Oxford, U.K.: Clarendon Press, 1995.

Solmsen, Friedrich. "Greek Philosophy and the Discovery of the Nerves." In *Kleine Schriften.* Vol. 1, 536–582. Hildesheim, Germany: Georg Olms Verlagsbuchhandlung, 1968.

Staden, Heinrich von. "Body, Soul, and Nerves: Epicurus, Herophilus, Erasistratus, the Stoics, and Galen." In *Psyche and Soma: Physicians and Metaphysicians on the Mind-Body Problem from Antiquity to Enlightenment,* edited by John P. Wright and Paul Potter, 79–116. Oxford, U.K.: Clarendon Press, 2000.

Sylvia Berryman (2005)

POINCARÉ, JULES HENRI
(1854–1912)

Jules Henri Poincaré, the French mathematician and philosopher, was born into a distinguished family at Nancy. His cousin Raymond was both prime minister and president of the Third French Republic. At an early age Poincaré showed an interest in natural history and the classics, and at the age of fifteen he developed an interest in mathematics. However, he trained first as a mining engineer, studying mathematics on his own during this training. In 1879 he was appointed to teach courses in mathematical analysis in the Faculty of Science at Caen. In 1881 he moved to the University of Paris, where he was soon given charge of the courses in mathematics and experimental physics. He lectured on mechanics, mathematical physics, and astronomy. Poincaré wrote an enormous number of papers on mathematics and physics and several important books on the philosophy of science and mathematics, as well as popular essays on science. His most important mathematical contributions were in differential equations, number theory, and algebra. In 1887 he was elected a member of the Académie des Sciences, and in 1899 he was made a knight of the Légion d'Honneur for his work on the three-body problem. In 1906 he became president of the Académie des Sciences, and in 1908 he was elected to the Académie Française.

Poincaré's work in the philosophy of science was in the tradition of Ernst Mach and Heinrich Hertz, and he admitted a debt to Immanuel Kant. His work was clearly influenced by his mathematical approach, and his interest was largely in the formal and systematic character of theories in the physical sciences. He showed less concern with epistemological problems connected with their support and establishment although he did write on the psychology of discovery. Albert Einstein had a profound respect for his work in both mathematics and the philosophy of science. He is often claimed as an ancestor of logical positivism, although the justification is not always easy to see.

AIMS AND GENERAL CHARACTER OF SCIENCE

Underlying scientific procedures, Poincaré held, is a belief in a general order in the universe that is independent of us and our knowledge. This is what mainly distinguishes the sciences from mathematics, which presupposes, if anything, merely the ability of the human mind to perform certain operations. The aim of the scientist is to discover as much as possible of the order of the universe, a point which must be borne in mind when Poincaré's view is called "conventionalism."

The method of discovery is basically inductive, proceeding by generalizing from observed facts; its lack of finality is due to its basis in a belief in a general order, since we can never be sure that the discovered order is absolutely general. Modifications in scientific conclusions spring from the constant pursuit of this generality. The discovery of facts depends upon observation and experiment, but these, in turn, depend upon selection because scientists cannot observe and absorb everything at once. There must be some principle of selection, but this principle must not be one of morality or practical utility. The search for an acceptable principle of selection led Poincaré to the idea of simplicity and a somewhat unusual defense of this idea. The best scientists are motivated by disinterested curiosity about how the world is, and their interest in general truths leads them to select those facts that "have the greatest chance of recurring." These are simple facts—that is, facts with few constituents. On grounds of probability there is more chance of the recurrence of a few constituents together than of the recurrence of many constituents together. However, familiar facts are more likely to appear simple to us than are unfamiliar facts. This seems to involve an unresolved conflict between two conceptions of simplicity.

What did Poincaré mean by "facts"? This is a question to which he gave less attention than it deserves. He held that science is to some extent objective. He toyed with sensationalism, but as a means of obtaining the necessary objectivity, he asserted that many sensations have external causes. Thus, he cannot strictly be regarded as a sensationalist. Objects are groups of sensation but not merely this; the sensations are "cemented by a constant bond," and science investigates this bond, or relation. Our sensations reflect whatever it is in the external world between which relations hold; science teaches us not the true nature of things but only the true relations between things. Scientific conclusions may thus be true of the world since they can give us a picture of its structure, though not of its content. We should expect theories of light, for example, to tell us not what light is but only what relations hold between the various occurrences of whatever light is.

The two main aims of scientific investigations are to relate what previously appeared unrelated and to enable us, by using these relations, to predict new phenomena.

CONVENTIONS

Poincaré constantly compared the physical sciences with pure mathematics and said that their methods of discovery are similar even though their methods of supporting conclusions are different. His view of science emerges most clearly from his comparison of it with geometry, in *Science and Hypothesis*. The space of geometry is not the space of sense experience; we can arrange conditions so that two things that look equal to a third thing do not look equal to each other. The mathematical continuum is invented to remove this disagreement with the law of contradiction; then, in mathematics things equal to the same thing are equal to one another *whatever* our senses tell us. This is one of those axioms of analysis, not geometry, which Poincaré called "analytical a priori intuitions."

Some geometrical axioms look superficially like this—for example, the Euclidean axiom that through one point only one line parallel to a given line can be drawn. The development of non-Euclidean geometries has shown that such axioms do not, as was formerly supposed, state fundamental properties of observable space. Coherent systems of geometry can be constructed based on the denial of Euclid's axioms, and these new geometries, when suitably interpreted, are translatable into Euclidean geometry. Moreover, they have physical applications. The applicability of the various systems is a function of context, or scale. The representation is purely structural.

Poincaré concluded that geometrical axioms are not synthetic a priori truths, for they are not of necessity true, and not experimental truths, for geometry is exact. They are conventions, or disguised definitions. It does not follow, as some critics have supposed, that they are arbitrary, for our choice is controlled by observation, experiment, and the need to avoid contradictions; nevertheless, such axioms cannot be either true or false. They are adopted because in certain contexts they are useful for saying how the world is. For most purposes Euclidean geometry is the most convenient. The application of geometry to the world involves an idealization. "Thus we do not *represent* to ourselves external bodies in geometrical space, but we *reason* about these bodies as if they were situated in geometrical space." No experimental support for Euclidean or any other geometry is possible, since experiments tell us only about the relations between bodies and nothing about the relations of bodies to space or of one part of space to another.

The physical sciences contain a conventional element as well as experimental, mathematical, and hypothetical elements, a fact which has been missed by most scientists. For example, the principle of inertia, according to which a body under the action of no force can move only at a constant speed in a straight line, is neither a priori nor experimental. It was originally conceived as experimental but has become a definition and so cannot now be falsified by experiment. Scientific conclusions are always conventional to some extent since alternatives to any hypothesis are always possible and, other things being equal, we choose those that are most economical. Because we have no means of knowing that the qualitative features of our hypothesis correspond to the reality, it does not make sense to regard the chosen hypothesis as the one true hypothesis.

In the physical sciences there are two kinds of statement—laws, which are summaries of experimental results and are approximately verified for relatively isolated systems, and principles, which are conventional postulates, completely general, rigorously true, and beyond the reach of experimental testing because for reasons of convenience we have made them so. Science is not entirely conventional because it does not consist wholly of principles. We begin with a primitive law, or experimental conclusion, but this is broken up into an absolute principle (definition) and a revisable law. Poincaré's example is the empirical statement "The stars obey Newton's law," which is broken up into the definition "Gravitation obeys Newton's law" and the provisional law "Gravitation is the only force acting upon the stars." Gravitation is an invented, ideal concept, but the provisional law is empirical and nonconventional because it predicts verifiable facts. The law of the conservation of energy is an outstanding example of a convention; it defines the concept of energy.

Prediction involves generalization, and generalization involves idealization. We connect a number of points on a graph by a smooth curve which does not pass through every one of them, and so we presuppose that the law we seek is best represented by a smooth curve even if this does not exactly fit the experimental results.

Points chosen midway between the existing points have a much better chance of showing which curve we should draw by eliminating one of them. A hypothesis is most strongly supported when it passes the tests that it was most likely to fail.

UNITY AND SIMPLICITY

We can obtain new knowledge only through experiment, and the role of mathematics in the physical sciences is to direct our generalizations from experiment. But experiment and generalization depend on presuppositions, most of which we make unconsciously. Among our presuppositions the most important are beliefs in the unity and simplicity of nature. Unity involves the possibility that various parts of the universe act upon one another as do the various parts of the human body, in the limited sense that to understand and describe one phenomenon, we may have to investigate other, superficially unrelated phenomena. The presupposition of simplicity is weaker: We can generalize any fact in an infinite number of ways, and we actually generalize in the simplest way until we have evidence against this way.

Two opposing trends can be discerned in the history of science. There is a movement toward simplicity and unity when we discover new relations between apparently unconnected objects and a movement toward complexity and diversity when, with the help of improved techniques, we discover new phenomena. The progress of sci-

ence depends upon the first tendency, for "the true and only aim is unity." The second tendency is important, but it must ultimately give way to the first. Poincaré argued, referring to the growing unification of the studies of light, magnetism, and electricity, that there are signs of a continued victory for the tendency toward unity. But there are also signs that this does not always go along with simplicity since unity can sometimes be achieved only by revealing the increased complexity in things when shown to be related. However, unity is essential and simplicity merely desirable.

Poincaré's account, like many others, suffers from a lack of clarity concerning precisely what is meant by "simplicity."

HYPOTHESES

Poincaré distinguished three kinds of hypotheses. The first kind he called "natural and necessary," and they are the very general hypotheses that we use in making judgments of relevance—for instance, when in physics we judge that the effect of very distant bodies is negligible. These form the common basis of theories in mathematical physics and should be the last to be abandoned.

The second kind he called "indifferent," and these are useful artifices for calculation or pictorial aids to understanding. Hypotheses are of this kind when they are alternatives that cannot be distinguished by experiment. Thus, he said, the two hypotheses that matter is continuous and that matter has an atomic structure are indifferent because experiment cannot establish the real existence of atoms. Such hypotheses may be useful, but they may also be seriously misleading if they are not seen for what they are.

The third kind of hypotheses he called "real generalizations." They are direct generalizations from observations and are indefinitely open to further testing. Whether or not they are finally accepted, they are always valuable, if only for their suggestiveness.

THEORIES AND THE ROLE OF MATHEMATICS

The aim of experiments in physical science is to break up complex phenomena into simple ones with respect to time and space, to connect each moment in the development of phenomena with immediately contiguous moments and each point in space with immediately contiguous points. We also aim to break up complex bodies and events into elementary bodies and events. Because observable phenomena may be analyzed in this way and

ENCYCLOPEDIA OF PHILOSOPHY
2nd edition

be regarded as the result of large numbers of elementary phenomena similar to one another, they are conveniently described by differential equations. This accounts for the ease with which scientific generalization takes a mathematical form. Mathematical physics depends upon the approximate homogeneity of the matter studied, since this enables us to extrapolate.

A physical theory may be superseded by another that uses qualitatively different concepts but the same differential equations; the equations are merely given different interpretations in the two theories. The superseded theory will be just as valuable for prediction because it contains the same relations as the new one, and as long as these stand up to testing, we can say that these are the real relations between things in the world. Both theories are true in the only way in which it makes sense to talk of the truth of a theory. Any advantage that the new theory has over the old will be merely psychological and will lie in its suggestions rather than in its implications. It is relatively unimportant that one theory of light refers to the movement of an ether and another refers to electric currents; what is important is the extent to which their equations agree, and it is on this that their truth must be judged.

Theories do not set out to explain, although they may provide possible explanations. They are devices enabling us to connect and predict phenomena but not to describe reality in all its details. The assertion that, for example, atomic theories explain the behavior of matter implies that we are able to establish the actual existence of atoms as delineated by the theories. But this is a metaphysical and not a scientific assertion because such existence can never be established by scientific means.

MATHEMATICS AND LOGIC

In mathematics Poincaré was, on the whole, an intuitionist, holding that the integers are indefinable and that underlying all mathematics is the principle of mathematical induction whose validity is intuitively recognized—that is, synthetic a priori.

In his last years Poincaré made a lively attack on the logic of Giuseppe Peano, Bertrand Russell, and others, especially on the logistic attempt to reduce mathematics to logic (*Mathematics and Science: Last Essays,* Chs. 4–5). He thought it important to study not only the consequences of adopting given conventions but also the reasons for adopting these conventions rather than others. He argued that it is impossible to derive all mathematical truths from the accepted logical principles without further appeals to intuition. He pointed, for example, to the difficulty of defining numbers without begging the question, and he saw even in the foundations of Russell's logic a reliance, inescapable on any satisfactory account, on synthetic a priori principles. He objected to the idea of an actual infinity, which he claimed was essential to Russell's system, and held that the logical paradoxes could be avoided by excluding nonpredicative definitions—that is, definitions of particular members of a class which refer to all the members of that class (*Science and Method,* Book II, Chs. 4–5). He expressed a general dissatisfaction with the extensional interpretation of logical constants.

See also Mathematics, Foundations of.

Bibliography

WORKS BY POINCARÉ

Oeuvres de Jules Henri Poincaré. 11 vols. Paris: Gauthier-Villars, 1928–1956. Contains all Poincaré's important scientific papers together with part of his own account of his work, a biography by G. Darboux (Vol. II), and centenary lectures on his life and work (Vol. XI).

La science et l'hypothèse. Paris: Flammarion, 1902. Translated by W. J. Greenstreet as *Science and Hypothesis.* London, 1905. Poincaré's most important book on the philosophy of science and mathematics.

La valeur de science. Paris: Flammarion, 1905. Translated by G. B. Halsted as *The Value of Science.* New York: Science Press, 1907.

Science et méthode. Paris: Flammarion, 1908. Translated by Francis Maitland, with a preface by Bertrand Russell, as *Science and Method.* London: Nelson, 1914.

Dernières Pensées. Paris: Flammarion, 1912. Translated by John W. Bolduc as *Mathematics and Science: Last Essays.* New York: Dover, 1963.

"Analyse des travaux scientifiques de Henri Poincaré, faite par lui-même." *Acta Mathematica* 38 (1921): 1–385. Partly reprinted in *Oeuvres.* This is a Poincaré issue of the journal and contains an extensive bibliography and appreciations by J. Hadamard, H. A. Lorenz, P. Painlevé, M. Planck, L. Fuchs, and others.

WORKS ON POINCARÉ

Carnap, Rudolf. *Logical Syntax of Language.* London: Kegan Paul, 1937.

Einstein, Albert. "Geometry and Experience." In *Sidelights on Relativity,* translated by G. B. Jeffery and W. Perrett. London, 1922.

Frank, Philipp. "Einstein, Mach and Positivism." In *Albert Einstein, Philosopher-Scientist,* edited by P. A. Schilpp. Evanston, IL: Library of Living Philosophers, 1949. Other articles also mention Poincaré.

Frank, Philipp. *Modern Science and Its Philosophy.* Cambridge, MA, 1949. Logical positivism's debt to Poincaré.

Grünbaum, Adolf. "Carnap's Views on the Foundations of Geometry." In *Philosophy of Rudolf Carnap,* edited by P. A. Schilpp. La Salle, IL: Open Court, 1964.

Hadamard, J. S. *The Early Scientific Work of Henri Poincaré.* Rice Institute Pamphlet (Houston, TX) 9 (3) (1922).

Hadamard, J. S. *The Later Scientific Work of Henri Poincaré.* Rice Institute Pamphlet (Houston, TX) 20 (1) (1933).

Le Roy, É;douard. "Science et philosophie. "*Revue de métaphysique et de morale* 7 (1899): 375, 503, 706; 8 (1900): 37.

Popper, K. R. *The Logic of Scientific Discovery.* London: Hutchinson, 1959. For a somewhat misleading criticism of Poincaré's conventionalism.

Revue de métaphysique et de morale 21 (1913): 585–718. Obituary number of journal.

Rey, A. *La théorie de la physique chez les physiciens contemporains.* Paris, 1907.

Schlick, Moritz. *Raum und Zeit in der gegenwärtigen Physik* Berlin, 1917. Translated by H. L. Brose as *Space and Time in Contemporary Physics.* Oxford, 1920.

Volterra, V. "H. Poincaré." *Book of the Opening of the Rice Institute* 3 (Houston, TX, 1912): 899–928.

Peter Alexander (1967)

POLITICAL PHILOSOPHY, HISTORY OF

The history of political philosophy is the succession of notions about the actual and proper organization of people into collectivities and the discussion of those notions. It is philosophical in character, because it is concerned with obedience and justice as well as with description; the persistent preoccupation of political philosophers has been the definition of justice and of the attitude and arrangements that should create and perpetuate justice.

A distinctive characteristic of political philosophizing is that it has usually been undertaken in response to some particular political event, or possibility, or threat, or challenge. This has led to a raggedness, even an incoherence, in works devoted to it and to an emphasis on intuitive argument which compares unfavorably with the content of other philosophical literature. Political philosophy has sometimes been supposed to confine itself to a particular entity called "the state," but in fact political philosophers have always concerned themselves with the collectivity as a whole, even when they have drawn a distinction between "state" and "society."

Problems of definition and description might appear to be prior to problems of analysis and prescription in political philosophy. In fact, however, ethical doctrine has always had a powerful effect on the view that a political thinker takes of the collectivity; he has tended to see it in terms of what he thinks it ought to be. Nevertheless, it has become usual to separate the empirical element from the normative. Empirical study has been further divided into sociology and political science. These definitions and divisions are no more satisfactory than others devised for similar purposes, and although we talk with some confidence of "sociologists," "political scientists" have only very recently emerged as an independent class of thinkers.

It is often useful to look upon political philosophy as in some sense systematic, proceeding from a view of reality and knowledge (ontology and epistemology) to a view of the individual (psychology) and a view of the social bond (sociology), and so to a general ethic, a political ethic, and finally to a set of recommendations about the form of the state and about political conduct. The expression "political philosophy" will be used in this sense here, and it will be considered solely in terms of the Mediterranean-European tradition.

CRITIQUE OF THE SUBJECT

There are several ways in which the history of political philosophy has been found important. Every thinker who engages in speculating about state and society and in formulating principles concerning them is anxious to know of the performance of his predecessors, to learn from them and to share their minds. Every thinking citizen is in this position too, to some extent, at least in the democracies: The questions raised in political life are frequently philosophical questions. Both thinkers and citizens, moreover, have good reason to believe that the intellectual and cultural life which they share with their contemporaries, together with the institutions which make political and social life possible for them, in some sense embody notions inherited from past political philosophy and philosophies. Certainly neither political attitudes nor political behavior nor political machinery can be understood without knowledge of this kind.

These various requirements have led to differing standards for the study. Insofar as it is the record of thought about state and society, its level of accuracy has to be as high as possible. For academic historical purposes, every word of the text of Aristotle, or Marsilius of Padua, or Jefferson must be correctly registered, his intentions known, the circumstances of the writing and publication of his work discovered and recorded. But neither the conscientious citizen nor the inquiring political theorist need be much affected by the particular version of a given work which he reads, even if it is an indifferent version, clumsily translated and abbreviated perhaps, or a brief and tendentious summary in a general history. The complete book need not be known, nor the attitude of its author. It may even help if little fables are allowed to grow up around such works. The misunderstanding of one political philosopher by another, or the misreading of authoritative books by citizens and constitution makers, has often been fruitful.

Moreover, historians of thought and of society have not been content with the role of annalists or of mere recorders of what was once written. They have sought to discover why the works were composed at all, to trace interconnections and influences covering whole generations, whole centuries of intellectual development. More recently they have been concerned to study literature in the light of ideology and to see in the writings of political philosophers especially the "reflection" or "expression" of the social structure at the time of writing, with its discontinuities, inconsistencies, and ambivalencies. Classics have come to be regarded not only as determined in this way but also as instruments in the social process, intellectual weapons in the hands of interested men and groups of men.

Although these differing motives can be distinguished in the historiography of political philosophy, individual commentators are seldom moved by one alone and often fail to see them as distinct. To this confusion must be added the unfortunate consequence of confining attention to a particular selection of authorities, a selection perhaps made originally for good philosophical reasons but which persists for reasons of convenience, curriculum, or plain conservatism. This, which is itself an example of a confusion between the interests and outlook of the historian and of the philosopher, has led to the creation of a canon of "classics" which alone go to make up "the history of political philosophy." Taken together, these circumstances are responsible for a number of persistent weaknesses in the study of this subject, some of which are listed below:

(1) The scripturalist tendency to criticize works as if their authors should have written out the final truth with complete coherence and as if, therefore, their failure to do so, their incoherencies and inconsequences must conceal some inner truth to be unraveled.

(2) The philosophizing tendency to relate the select thinkers to each other and to no others, as if contrasts between them and them alone are significant and as if they can be thought of as addressing each other. The reader's task becomes that of welding the various works into some philosophic whole.

(3) The tendency to mistake the theoretical interest of a work for its significance in other directions. This tendency is the general form of the failure to distinguish the separable interests and objectives of historians (as annalists and explainers), of philosophers, and of citizens.

(4) The tendency toward what might be called "naive sociologism": The particular circumstances of a thinker are seen as expressed in his thinking in a literal and unconvincing way, and the dominant social conditions of the present are read almost unchanged into apparently analogous conditions of the past.

Each of these tendencies can be disabling enough in itself; when they are present in combination, the results can be strange indeed. The search for Hobbist elements in John Locke, for example (tendency 2), can become an attempt to prove that he was really a Hobbist altogether and that his work on government must be examined for cryptic signs of those elements. More familiar are the exaggerations that come from stressing the relations of influence between the canonical works (tendency 2) and seeing all other intellectual elements as "anticipations" and "derivations" of these to such an extent that the relationships between bodies of thought and past societies are entirely distorted (tendency 3). Worst of all, perhaps, is a commentator who allows his thought to be so dominated by his experiences as a citizen in his own day that he betrays himself into an extreme form of the fourth tendency. When this happens, not only do Plato's or Rousseau's politics appear "totalitarian," but they are also made distantly responsible for the totalitarian proclivities of the twentieth century.

Weaknesses of this kind, however, do not necessarily deprive the commentaries concerned of their interest. In the historiography of political philosophy, as in many other inquiries, the intrusion of obvious but stimulating fallacies helps to maintain the enterprise.

GREEK POLITICAL PHILOSOPHY

The Greek city-state, or polis, gave us the word *political* and is usually supposed to have been the social organization which provided the necessary conditions for men to take for the first time a rational-critical view of the relation of the individual to the collectivity. The claim might be made that only in completely autonomous, small-scale, urban societies, like those of the Mediterranean area from the tenth century before Christ on, could an attitude of this kind develop. Because of the small size of these political entities, deliberations could take place, and decisions be made, in face-to-face discussion among all citizens, who could also see their collectivity as parallel with numerous other collectivities of the same character. It is certainly the case that the mold in which political philosophy has been set ever since is patently recognizable as Greek, and the assumption of face-to-face discussion and decision persists to this day, with not entirely fortunate results.

SOCRATES AND PLATO. The issues of freedom versus tyranny, of the various forms of the state (monarchy, aristocracy, or democracy), and of the nature and operation of law are not certainly known to have been debated until very close to the time of Socrates, who was born about 470 BCE, well into the famous fifth century. The Sophists, or teachers of the art of rhetoric and persuasion for use in the law courts and in Greek public life generally, are usually credited with initiating political discussion properly defined. Although he was unsparing in his criticism of these professionals in the techniques of influence, of *sophistry* in fact, it is hard not to classify Socrates himself as a Sophist.

A determined effort has been made, by Karl Popper and others, to separate the political doctrine of Socrates, the champion of the critical discussion of dogmas and of institutions, from that of Plato, "the enemy of the open society," and their thinking has been related to the political events of late fifth-century Athens in a way which betrays many of the weaknesses described above. It seems best, however, to take Socrates and Plato as the dual spokesmen in the first known critical inquiry into the nature of the collectivity, with the peculiarity that one of them, Plato, did all the recording. The point at issue was the perennial point of how justice can be secured between men, organized as they have to be for the purposes of making a livelihood, propagating their kind, and cultivating the humane arts and accomplishments.

The answer given in Plato's *Republic*, probably composed about 365 BCE and the most powerful of his dialogues, is straightforward enough in principle, perhaps even a little banal, but it is argued on the very loftiest plane. Justice is secured only when every member of the polis is doing what he is best suited to do, and those who are best suited to do the ruling are the philosophers themselves—lovers of wisdom, those who really know. "Unless," says Socrates at the end of Book V, "either philosophers become kings in our states or those whom we now call kings and rulers take to the pursuit of philosophy seriously and adequately, and there is a conjunction of these two things, political power and philosophic intelligence, … there can be no cessation of troubles for our states, dear Glaucon, nor I fancy for the human race either."

The steps of the argument before and after this passage are by no means a matter of formal political-theoretical demonstration, and the *Republic* is at one and the same time many different treatises, a characteristic which it shares with most of its successors as classics of political philosophy. What has probably sunk deepest into the European political imagination is its utopian element, the description of an ideal condition of the collectivity when it is ruled by a select society of guardians.

The famous Platonic guardians were to be brought into the world in accordance with premeditated principles of eugenics and were not to know who their parents were. They were to live in conditions of complete communism and poverty, without privacy and outside the family; both men and women were to spend their whole lives in the service of the polis and to undergo thirty years of education—gymnastics and military training to prepare the body, music and philosophical instruction to prepare the mind. Although it is implied that the guardians would be a small minority of the whole population, and that their undisturbed rulership would ensure justice, their actual relationship with the other two elements in the polis, the soldiery and the consumers (by which term Plato presumably meant the mass of handicraftsmen and peasants, producing and consuming), is never specified. These divisions of the polis are presented as analogues of the divisions of the soul; indeed, the polis is the soul writ large. Insofar as there is a positive political doctrine in this most famous of all works of political philosophy, it seems to be hypothetical—if the polis-soul could be constructed in this way, then all problems would be solved.

Several other Platonic dialogues are concerned with political issues, and the last of them, the *Laws*, can be looked upon as the complete recasting of the Socratic-Platonic political philosophy in the light of a lifetime's reflection and experience, some of it Plato's own practical experience in advising a pupil of the Platonic Academy in the administration of the polis at Syracuse, in Sicily. But although Plato's *Politicus* (otherwise called the *Statesman*) presents an account of political life and political ideals rather different from that of the *Republic*, and although his *Laws* clashes at certain points with the *Politicus*, the ideal state of the *Republic* is that element of the political thought of Socrates and Plato which has interested posterity and influenced its thinking, almost to the exclusion of their other views.

ARISTOTLE. Aristotle, Plato's pupil, was the first of many later philosophers and thinkers who addressed themselves to the Platonic utopia, and he rejected a great deal of it. Aristotle was even more of a synoptic thinker than Plato and was much more interested in the amassing and classification of knowledge. The gathering of information about politics and political organization was, therefore, only one of the many tasks on which Aristotle spent his extraordinarily industrious life (384–322 BCE), along with his Herculean studies of logic, psychology, biology, literature, economics, physics and other subjects. But there is evidence to show that, like Plato and other Greek thinkers, Aristotle considered politics the most important subject of all.

The Aristotelian treatises on political philosophy, the *Eudemian Ethics* and *Nicomachean Ethics* and the *Politics* itself, appear to have been based on a monumental assemblage of material of a political-scientific character, including a record of no fewer than 158 constitutions of Greek poleis. These writings had even more impressive experience behind them, because Aristotle, a Macedonian by birth, had actually been tutor to Alexander the Great, who in Aristotle's lifetime subjugated Greece and Athens. Nevertheless, Aristotle's political theory was properly philosophical, that is, it proceeded from a general view of the world and of knowledge.

He was no more disposed than any other citizen of the polis to see the individual as a reality apart from the collectivity, but he did provide a critique of the reasons why human life implied compulsory association. Man, he claimed, is a species of animal that possesses intelligence and is found in intelligently collaborative groups; therefore "man is a political animal." The natural unit of the human family forms part of the natural unit of the village, which in turn forms part of the natural unit of the polis; but the polis is not merely the family enlarged, it is an association for leading the good life, which is otherwise incapable of realization—and this means a difference in classificatory, in logical, order. States (poleis—Aristotle significantly dismisses all larger organizations as capable of ordered living only by religious means) must be judged by the extent to which they enable citizens to become virtuous and to live the good life, a life of moderation, the mean. This line of argument led Aristotle to sketch his own ideal state, but it also led him, in the *Politics*, to raise a series of crucial issues which have endured almost unchanged as decisive questions for political science as well as for political philosophy.

Probably the most conspicuous are the claims of fundamental inequality between humans: Slaves and barbarians are by nature inferior to Greeks and to citizens, although Aristotle conceded that inequality in some respects does not mean inequality in all respects. Within every collectivity, however, quite apart from the division between citizens and those incapable of citizenship, there are three classes: an upper class of aristocrats; a middle class of substantial men, mainly merchants, craftsmen, and farmers; and a lower class of laborers and peasants. The interests of these classes conflict: in sharp contrast with Plato and his anxiety for a harmony, a unity, in the polis-soul, Aristotle recognized politics as a conflict-defining, conflict-resolving activity. The actual distribution of political power among these classes—Aristotle himself insisted on the political virtue of the middle class—together with the web of manmade laws, goes to make up the particular constitution (*politeia*, the same word as the Greek title of Plato's *Republic*) of that polis. In spite of his fundamental inegalitarianism and his Greek inability to conceive of consent or representation as relevant to politics, Aristotle has often been hailed as the initiator of constitutionalism, as "the first Whig."

JUDAIC AND CHRISTIAN POLITICAL PHILOSOPHY

It is conventional to reckon the death of the polis at the death of Aristotle in 322 BCE and to believe that nothing new of importance to political philosophy appeared until the Roman Stoics evolved the universalistic dogmas of natural law. It is undoubtedly true that no systematic philosophical discussion of political principles can be traced in Judaic thought or in early Christian thought. But it is important to recognize that the symbols and the symbol system of subsequent political thinking derives from Judaic as well as from Greek sources and that its psychological assumptions are deeply tinged with Christian revelationism.

The three social institutions of the ancient Hebrews, whose significance for the history of political thinking has only recently come to be recognized, are patriarchalism, the sense of the people, and kingship. The text of the Old Testament that proclaimed the duty of obedience as the basis not only of political discipline but of all social order, including economic order, was the commandment "Honor thy father and thy mother." Throughout the Christian centuries, therefore, all questions of obedience were seen in a patriarchal context, and the political power of the Hebraic patriarch (Judah, who condemned his daughter to death for playing the harlot, or Abraham, with his fighting army of servants) was the model for the power exercised by kings and ministers. Quite as significant was the Judaic sense of the chosen people, the people led by the hand of God through the wilderness because they had an enduring purpose and being. Whenever Christian political theorists thought of the people as having a voice in the appointment of a king or a regime, or of the king as having a duty to his people, their model was the peculiar people of Israel. European kingship was also conceived in biblical terms, and the tribal hero-king whose actions committed the people before God and whose power came from God can be seen behind the western European dynastic regimes.

Even more authoritative, of course, were the words of Jesus himself on political matters, and the few texts which could be made to bear at all upon them have been perpetually cited throughout the Christian era. Christ's submission to the Roman authority, his use of an inscription on a Roman penny ("Render unto Caesar the things that are Caesar's"), and his repeated insistence that his kingdom was not of this world made it difficult to find authority in the New Testament for any doctrine of resistance. Saint Paul's sayings pointed in the same quietist direction ("The powers that be are ordained of God"). But more interesting to the twenty-first century are those fragments of evidence from the apostolic era that make it possible to believe that Christ's immediate followers lived a communistic existence.

ROMAN STOICISM AND NATURAL LAW

The belief that there is a universal and eternal moral ordering which is common to all men and which therefore carries weight on certain issues in every collectivity is a widespread ethical and religious notion, and it need have very little specific content. Its origins have been sought in Plato's immutable Ideas and, further back, in Greek poetry. The source most often favored, however, is the religious-philosophical sect of the Stoics, who took their name from the *stoa,* or porch, before which Zeno, their reputed founder, preached and taught in Athens soon after the time of Aristotle, about 390 BCE. Stoicism was brought to Rome during the classical generations of Roman republicanism, and it continued to be a system widely accepted, although changing in content, from the time of the Scipios (about 100 BCE) until about 200 CE, when even the great Roman political families began to feel the attraction of Christianity.

The orator-statesman Cicero, although eclectic in his intellectual outlook and not usually thought of as a philosopher, wrote probably the most widely read of all works in political philosophy until recent times, *On the Laws* (*De Legibus,* c. 46 BCE) and *On the Duties of the Citizen* (*De Officiis,* a year or two later). The *Laws* was composed in deliberate imitation of Plato and was intended to complement Cicero's *De Re Publica* (his *Republic* of a year or two before), a work that was lost until 1820. *De Re Publica* contains, however, the classic text for the universalistic theory of natural law as it entered into political philosophy:

> True law is right reason in agreement with Nature; it is of universal application, unchanging and everlasting ... there will not be different laws at Rome and at Athens, or different laws now and in the future, but one eternal and unchangeable law will be valid for all nations and all times, and there will be one master and one ruler, that is, God, over us all, for He is the author of this law, its promulgator and its enforcing judge. (Book III, Ch. 22, Sec. 33)

The cosmopolitan character of this doctrine—a society of all humanity ruled by one God—is in sharp contrast with the earlier Greek outlook, which assumed that only the small-scale polis could embody political good. The individual is recognizably the unit of this universal society and is the subject of the rights conferred on all citizens, all Roman citizens, by the Roman law. The identification of law with reason must be noticed in this process; reason carries its own claims to the individual's obedience. The final sanction of law and authority is placed here outside the collectivity altogether, in the Deity. Nevertheless, nothing in Stoicism could be taken as an argument against the deification of the later emperors, and one of them, Marcus Aurelius, was himself a Stoic thinker. So also was Epictetus, who began life as a slave. A rough doctrine of original freedom and equality, even the use of the contractarian model for the collectivity, has been read into Stoic texts—"All seats," so the Stoic proverb went, "are free in the theatre, but a man has a right to the one he sits down in"—but it was religious rather than specifically social equality. Much of the intellectual groundwork, in fact, of subsequent political philosophy can be sighted in the intellectual-religious tradition of Stoicism, and it is only the philosophizing tendency of historians which has prevented its attracting more attention than it has done.

ST. AUGUSTINE

The City of God (*De Civitate Dei*), written between 410 and 423 by St. Augustine, bishop of Hippo in north Africa (354–430), traditionally occupies an important place in the canon of great works on political philosophy. This extraordinary treatise raises in an acute form the problem of the historical reputation and effect of a body of thought in contrast with its actual content and the intention of its writer. *The City of God* was undoubtedly read in medieval times and afterward as the authoritative statement of the superiority of ecclesiastical power over the secular, because it was believed to identify the visible Christian church with the mystical city of God, thought of as the bride of Christ or, even more mystically, as the body itself of the Christian Saviour. But it is very doubtful whether this was St. Augustine's intention or is even implied by his text. What is more, the conscientious political scientist finds it very difficult to decide whether *The City of God* contains any positive political doctrine at all, theoretical or otherwise.

Very recent political philosophy might, therefore, justifiably claim this work as an antipolitical classic, stating in very different terms the position sketched out by Karl Marx and V. I. Lenin as "the withering away of the state." There is the same tendency to identify all arrangements in the collectivity with evil, with the unjustifiable exercise of naked power, and the same confidence that in the fullness of time this monstrous regimentation will disappear. Moreover, Augustine was a historicist: He sought to show how God's plan to fill up the places left in Heaven when Satan and his angels revolted was being fulfilled. The creation of man and the world was intended to reveal candidates for the heavenly choir, and some few men on earth at any one time, the pilgrims (*peregrinati*), were destined at the last trumpet to be among them. They and they only were the living members of the City of God, but no one would know who constituted this select few until the judgment. It seems to have been a matter of almost complete indifference to St. Augustine how those who were to be saved behaved toward society, secular or spiritual, or what was the nature of political arrangements.

The occasion of Augustine's beginning *The City of God* was the sack of Rome by Alaric the Goth in 410, and the fall of the Roman Empire, which this event presaged, could not possibly affect the Christian who held such views about history, state, and society. The complement of the City of God was the city of the devil (*civitas diaboli*), and although it seems unjustifiable to identify the one city with the church, it seems that Augustine did quite often refer to the Roman Empire as the other. Since the heathen Romans could not possibly do justice to God and since kingdoms without justice are but great robberies (*Remota itaque justitia quid sunt regna nisi magna latrocinia?*—Ch. 4, Bk. 4), what could the Roman Empire be but thievery on a colossal scale? If by the Roman Empire Augustine implied all possible forms of the collectivity—and there are passages to confirm this assumption—then he must indeed be supposed to have had a completely negative political philosophy. Justice could

never be found in any of them. In this final work of ancient political theory, then, the overriding concern is with justice, just as it had been with Socrates at the very beginning, but in it justice is viewed from an anarchist, antipolitical outlook.

MEDIEVAL POLITICAL PHILOSOPHY: POPE AND EMPEROR

Apart from the development of natural law in Christian form, the Middle Ages did not give rise to much speculation about the nature of the collectivity that has affected subsequent attitudes, nor to any great body of specifically political philosophy. Before the time of St. Thomas Aquinas in the thirteenth century, what little critical analysis there was seems to have been dominated by the Church Fathers and especially by Augustine. Although these early medieval thinkers knew of the great Greek philosophers, the actual treatises of Plato, Aristotle, and others had been lost in the West. There seems to have been a certain amount of political awareness among the subjects of the Germanic kingdoms which had come to spread over Europe, and during the nineteenth century a great deal was made of the primitive Germanic sense of community (*Gemeinschaft*), people (*Volk*, folk), and corporation (*Gesellschaft*). But unless jurisprudence is counted a part of political philosophy, neither these arrangements nor the universal social institutions associated with feudalism seem to have been the subjects of much corresponding theorization. It is remarkable how little headway the analysis of political theories in ideological terms has made with the Middle Ages.

ST. THOMAS. John of Salisbury's *Policraticus* (1159) was still Ciceronian and Augustinian in content, in spite of the fact that by his time the text of Aristotle had already reached the Latin West from the Arabs. It was left to St. Thomas to arrange the enormous access of Aristotelian information and principle in a form acceptable to a Christian Europe, which he did in his great *Summa Theologiae*. The frank acceptance of natural man—man as revealed by Aristotelian science; man not incurably maimed by sin and therefore indifferent to social-political arrangement; man whose nature is perfected, not taken away by the grace of God (*gratia non tollit naturam, sed perfecit*)—distinguished the sociology of Thomas from that of his predecessors. But although of enduring importance for politics, indeed still the final authority for the Thomist thinkers of our own day, the *Summa* and its Christian doctrine of natural law contains no developed political philosophy. For this we must turn to the *De Regimine Principum* (*Of the Rulership of Princes*) and other works, including Thomas's commentaries on Aristotle's *Politics* and *Ethics.*

In these works St. Thomas presented his theory of the relationship between pope and emperor, which had already preoccupied Christian Europe for centuries and would continue to do so until the end of the medieval period. He developed the traditional distinction of *regnum* and *sacerdotum* (secular and spiritual jurisdiction) in Aristotelian terms, in terms of ends, the ends of humanity. "We are confronted," as A. P. d'Entrèves says, "with the doctrine of the distinction and interrelation of two great spheres of human life within one single society—the Christian society, *respublica christiana.*" But although Thomas is moderate in his claims for the pope against the emperor, although he never talks of the direct sovereignty of the pope, he is firmly convinced that all kings in Christendom should be subject to the Vicar of Christ as to Christ himself. Yet willing as he was to temper Aristotelian inegalitarianism with Christian grace, anxious as he was to give every Christian his share in the affairs of the collectivity, Thomas was absolutely intolerant of the Jew and the infidel: They remain outcasts in the Christian community.

Authority in St. Thomas's system must be legitimate, otherwise it may be resisted. An evil ruler exceeding his powers and burdening his subjects must be resisted—resisted not by the individual citizen in virtue of his individual rights (Thomas had no room for such rights) but presumably by the church. This is the sense in which Thomas's thinking has been hailed, like that of Aristotle, as the forerunner of constitutionalism.

DANTE AND MARSILIUS. The other two medieval thinkers usually accorded a place in the history of political philosophy are Dante Alighieri, the supreme poet of the city of Florence, whose political essay *Monarchia* was composed between 1310 and 1313, and Marsilius of Padua, whose *Defensor Pacis* (Defender of peace) was completed in 1324. Both were imperialists, on the opposite side of the pope-emperor controversy from St. Thomas, but both were Aristotelians. Dante's work was an idealization of the position of the medieval European emperor, who was in fact a ruler of Germany to whom the traditional trappings of the Western Roman emperor still attached as the secular ruler of all humanity, whose powers were derived directly from God and not indirectly through the pope. Marsilius approached somewhat closer to realism and had a recognizably empirical sociology: He insisted on the Aristotelian class analysis of political society and regarded the clergy as one among the classes, and therefore not in the privileged position which papal theory claimed.

The twenty-first-century observer is far more at home in the Greek polis or in a Roman province than at the papal *curia* or the court of a feudal king. So much was the medieval collectivity a religious whole, embracing not only all the territory occupied by Christians but also the whole of intellectual and cultural life, that it may be doubted whether there existed anything which corresponds to the term *state* as political philosophers ordinarily use it. Apart from the metaphysics of the papal-imperial argument, most "political thought" of the European Middle Ages is recognizable as advice to a ruler, wise reflections on commonplace situations that are entirely traditional in context and object and show no trace of the analytic attitude. Nevertheless, the medieval collectivity and the reflections of medieval theologians upon it can be appreciated under more headings than that of record.

Apart from the paradigm for the metaphysical approach to the final problem of ethics and politics provided by Thomas, the medieval situation provides the extreme example of territorial political relationships, in which the psychological mechanism usually called religious can be seen most clearly at work in providing the consensus on which such collective action as went forward had to rely. Any properly empirical account of how a collectivity in fact works, at any time, has to recognize that this mechanism is still very much in operation and that the mistake of supposing it to be replaced by rational-technical cooperation has still to be properly appreciated.

MACHIAVELLI AND REALPOLITIK

Although the polis began to lose its independence of policy as early as the lifetime of Aristotle, the towns of the Roman Empire continued to maintain a collective life that differed very little from the life of the classical polis. The decline of the cities was the outstanding feature of the fall of the empire, but they never entirely disappeared, at least in Italy. By the time of Dante and Marsilius such cities as Florence, Venice, and Milan were again in the formal position which Athens had occupied: They were independent urban communities having diplomatic relationships with each other and with the territorial monarchies. The cities possessed their own hinterlands, too, and colonies. It is not surprising, therefore, that the rational-critical attitude reappeared and that a consuming interest in ancient culture, in Plato and Aristotle, in Rome and

Greece, led to an appreciation of classical political philosophy on something like its own terms.

Nevertheless, Niccolò Machiavelli's *The Prince* (written 1513, first printed 1532), in some ways the most effective and interesting of all works of political philosophy, was in form merely one more piece of advice to a ruler. It was not presented as a philosophical work, and it contained neither abstract argument about politics nor any systematic discussion of the nature of state and society. Its analysis is confined to situations between a prince and his people and between princes (or cities) themselves. Its method is historical, the citing of significant instances. The outcome of discussion is advice, with occasional reflective aphorisms. Some of these aphorisms have become famous, and all of them show an astonishing realism and insight: "Above all a prince should abstain from the property of others; because men sooner forget the death of their father than the loss of their patrimony." "Whoever is responsible for another becoming powerful ruins himself." "Fortune is a woman and if she is to be submissive it is necessary to beat and coerce her." The headings of the twenty-six brief chapters of *The Prince* are even more significant than the sayings; Chapter 17 is titled "Cruelty and Compassion, Whether It Is Better to Be Loved Than to Be Feared."

Machiavelli's well-known answer is that it is far better to be feared than to be loved, if you cannot be both. His cool discussion of the effects of cruelty and unscrupulousness, his detached attitude toward Christianity and the traditional virtues, and his professed admiration for men of his time who are known to have been villainous and contemptible, especially the political gangster Cesare Borgia, have given Machiavelli the reputation of being the theorist of power politics, deliberate immoralism, and irresponsible, tyrannical government. But the contents of his major work on politics, the *Discourses on Livy*, have been cited to show that he was a believer in republican, not monarchical, government, and they have been used with the famous last chapter of *The Prince* itself to demonstrate that he was in fact a virtuous, patriotic Italian, worthy of the reputation he enjoyed among the English Whigs, for example, for political probity and insight. It has even been suggested, not for the first time in our generation, that *The Prince* was a satirical work. But there can be no doubt that from the time of its appearance this book was regarded as a textbook for tyrants and an exposition of the principles of power politics.

THE REFORMATION AND SECULAR NATURAL LAW

If Machiavelli's writing is looked upon as philosophical in intent, its most remarkable feature is its failure even to mention the doctrine of Christian natural law, which since the time of Thomas had dominated discussion of the nature of the collectivity and of the duties of citizens. The arrival of Protestantism raised the question of political obligation in an acute form for the first time in the history of political philosophy. It challenged a believing Lutheran or Calvinist to decide whether he should go on obeying a Catholic prince, and a Catholic subject to make the same decision about a Protestant prince. This had the effect of emphasizing, crystallizing, and codifying natural-law doctrine, since it was only under a legal or quasi-legal system of natural law that most citizens felt that they could claim a right to disobey and ultimately to resist political authority which commanded actions against their faith. Once this codification was made, systematic reflection on the philosophical problems raised by political allegiance began in earnest, and in the process natural law began to lose its exclusively religious sanction and become secularized.

It took a long time for the breakdown of universal religious consensus to have effects of this kind, even though many other influences going far back into the Middle Ages tended toward the secularization of political life. Martin Luther himself offered no systematic political teaching, certainly no doctrine of the right to resist princes for conscience sake'. In fact, in his treatise *Of Good Works* (1520) Luther wrote out traditional patriarchal rules for submission in a particularly emphatic form. John Calvin preached nonresistance too, but the religious wars in France in the later sixteenth century gave rise to a multitude of theories of the social contract that provided justification for disobedience and even for revolution on the basis of natural law. In England the Calvinists went even further, or so it seemed to the great doctor of the English Reformed church, Richard Hooker, when he sat down to write *The Laws of Ecclesiastical Polity* (written in the 1590s, first four books published in 1594 but not in print complete until 1662). Hooker believed that the claims to inspiration made by the extreme Puritans amounted to a denial of the efficacy of reason itself and to a complete rejection of natural-law principles. His response was a majestic reformulation of Thomas's natural-law philosophy that took account of the changes brought about by the Reformation, particularly of the doctrine of the final sovereignty of each individual state and its ruler, which had come to replace the ultimate authority of emperor or pope in Christendom. The absolute sovereignty of the secular ruler, from whose decree there was no appeal, a doctrine which might be called that of ethical self-sufficiency of every political system, was given its classical expression in the *Six Books of the Republic*, published by the eminent French lawyer Jean Bodin in 1576.

Along with these developments went another that can be seen very clearly, as early as Machiavelli. This was the recognition that the body politic—the people and their political instruments, such as their parliament or their local institutions—might itself be an object of governmental action, worked on and molded by an enlightened ruler, just as the body politic might in its turn take action against government, rebel against it, replace and change its constitution. Meanwhile, secular natural law was providing a framework within which such processes could go forward and within which—as a code of international law—the various sovereign states could negotiate with one another. By the time that Hugo Grotius came to write that source book of all subsequent international law, *De Jure Belli ac Pacis* (The law of war and of peace; 1625), these relationships had come to include Islamic and Buddhist societies and societies entirely alien to the Christian point of view, even societies with no apparent belief in a deity. Natural law therefore had to become independent of Christian revelation, and Grotius stated that his principles would endure even if God did not exist. The stage was set for the first great classic of modern European, as opposed to classical ancient, political philosophy, the *Leviathan* of Thomas Hobbes (1651).

HOBBES

Although Hobbes is rightly regarded as above all a philosopher, with his own view of knowledge and of the nature of the physical world, his point of departure was political, as much as Plato's or Aristotle's was. Hobbes's declared object was "to set before men's eyes the mutual relation between protection and obedience, of which the condition of human nature, and the laws divine require an inviolable observation." This relation required the absolute submission of each individual to the dictates of an arbitrary sovereign, of "That great LEVIATHAN, or rather (to speak more reverently) of that *Mortal God*, to which we owe under the Immortal God, our peace and defence" (*Leviathan*, Ch. 17). Political science—though Hobbes did not use the phrase itself, he insisted that the proper name for the knowledge he was examining was in fact "science," on the geometrical model then beginning

to take hold on men's minds—implied absolutism, despotism.

But Hobbesian political doctrine was no doctrine of the divine right of kings, nor even of one-man rule, for in this system democracies, aristocracies, and monarchies should all equally be absolute sovereigns, whose every dictate is law. Monarchy was to be preferred, as might be expected, and democracy, "the government of a few orators," was least desirable. The power of government is a part of the divine providence, but its sanctions are much more tangible. They rest on the unqualified alienation of all the rights of every individual into the hands of the sovereign at the time of the making of the social contract—of compact, as Hobbes called it—and thereafter every attribute of every citizen, even his property, depended on the sovereign's will. So anxious was Hobbes to remove any possible grounds that might be used to justify resistance to authority that he advanced two positions entirely unacceptable to most of his contemporaries. One was the reformulation of natural law in a form that gave no rights to the citizen and the other was to confer on the sovereign the function of pronouncing on the interpretation of Scripture itself.

Perhaps the most famous element in the Hobbesian system was the account of the state of nature, and the best-remembered passage reads:

> during the time men live without a common power to keep them all in awe, they are in that condition which is called war; and such a war, as is of every man against every man.... In such condition, there is no place for industry, because the fruit thereof is uncertain: and consequently no culture of the earth, no navigation, nor use of the commodities that may be imported by sea; no commodious building; no instrument of moving, and removing such things as require much force; no knowledge of the face of the earth; no account of time; no arts; no letters; no society; and which is worst of all, continual fear, and danger of violent death; and the life of man, solitary, poor, nasty, brutish and short. (*Leviathan*, Ch. 13)

If this fighting anarchy is in fact the natural state of man, then it does seem to follow that the only possibility of cooperation in the collectivity is by absolute submission, and every human value must depend on the existence and efficacy of "the great Leviathan." The law, or rather the laws, of nature did exist at that repulsive stage of human development but only as rules of prudence, for "Reason suggesteth convenient articles of peace, which otherwise are called the laws of nature." Whatever the status of these principles, they could not possibly be used to justify resistance to the sovereign, although Hobbes did provide for the transfer of allegiance to another sovereign when the one established can no longer provide protection. He also allowed to the individual the right to refuse to confess to a crime or to take his own life. The appeal to revelation and to conscience, which Hobbes believed was responsible for the political instability of his own time, and especially for the Puritan rebellion in England, was completely precluded by his interpretation of the claims of his sovereign.

In spite of Hobbes's confident belief that his elucidation of the true principles of political science would resolve conflict, his work aroused immediate opposition and has given rise to unending controversy. There is first the question of whether his state of nature, succeeded by a covenant, or social contract, was intended to be taken literally as a historical and anthropological claim, or whether it was simply hypothetical. A recent ideological interpretation has claimed that the state of nature was hypothetical but that the aggressive, competitive emphasis arose from Hobbes's observing the possessive individualism informing the increasingly capitalist society in which he lived. The second question concerns the continuity between his state of nature and his state of society. How could men with the characteristics Hobbes gives them ever form themselves into a collectivity? A third question is whether he ever intended men to be morally obliged to obey the sovereign, or, if this was his intention, whether he succeeded in tying them down ethically. A further question is how far he was indeed abandoning the whole natural-law position and advancing an entirely utilitarian political ethic; men obey always and only because they see it is to their advantage.

WHIG CONSTITUTIONALISM AND LOCKE

Hobbes was not the first writer to invoke what came to be called the "pleasure-pain principle" in political discussion, and his radical contemporaries, the Levellers of the English Civil War, also made claims which seemed to rest on strictly utilitarian grounds, although in an unphilosophical and unsystematic form. The appearance of writings of this character, which have claims to be the first emanating from the common man, raises an important issue about the career of political philosophy from the seventeenth century on. The Levellers were democrats, and the political rights they claimed were meant to be exercised by a far greater proportion of the population

than ever had been previously contemplated, even by the English Parliamentarians locked in their struggle with the house of Stuart. It has been recently and justifiably questioned whether all individuals were intended to be covered by Leveller declarations, or even all male householders, but from that time on, there is a recognizable class content in the doctrines of the political philosophers. Until the late eighteenth century most thinkers continued to share the universal assumption that "citizen" must be confined to the fully literate, propertied, elite minority, but they showed an increasing awareness that this was a tiny minority and that the right of this minority to stand for the whole might need justification.

Paradoxically enough, this crucial question was raised in an awkward form by one of Hobbes's exact contemporaries, Sir Robert Filmer, a traditionalist rather than a progressive. Sovereignty is a patriarchal matter, Filmer claimed, a matter of natural subordination, and unless this is recognized, the inequality of distribution of property and the subjection of poor men, men without the vote, servants, and women could never be justified. Much of Filmer's thinking, and that of the commonsensical Englishmen who came to accept his authority, is present in the writing of Hobbes. Nevertheless, for historical reasons it was against Filmer rather than against Hobbes that in the years 1679 and 1680 Locke wrote out the classic statement of Whig constitutionalism and government by consent, *Two Treatises of Government* (revised and published in 1689).

This modification of the accepted account of the relation of Locke to Hobbes is due to very recent scholarship, and the same evidence goes to show that the work of Benedict de Spinoza, the only immediate follower Hobbes had among philosophers, was more of an intellectual preoccupation for Locke than Hobbes ever was. Spinoza (*Tractatus Theologicopoliticus*, 1670; *Tractatus Politicus*, 1677), if easily the least influential, was in some ways the most engaging of all the political thinkers of the early modern age in Europe. Unfortunately, we cannot dwell here on his modification of the Hobbesian system; his overt insistence that the contract was hypothetical; his specific insistence that all obligations had to be utilitarian, based on self-interest; or his attempt to ensure that the enlightened sovereign must seek the welfare of his people.

Locke's *Second Treatise*, with its subtitle *Of Civil Government*, seems to have been the first composed of the two, and it begins with the following assertion against Filmer's claim that all men are born unfree, unequal, and in patriarchal subjection:

To understand political power right, and derive it from its original, we must consider what state all men are naturally in, and that is, a state of perfect freedom to order their actions and dispose of their possessions, and persons, as they think fit, within the bounds of the law of nature, without asking leave, or depending on the will of any other man. A state also of equality, wherein all the power and jurisdiction is reciprocal, no one having more than another. (Sec. 4)

The law of nature, then, was real, and it governed all men in the peaceable condition which preceded the foundation of the collectivity, when order was maintained by what Locke called "the executive power of the law of nature" in the hands of every man. This law of nature gave men tangible rights, even before the contract. It ensured them the right to their religious opinions (not argued for, or even mentioned, in the work on government but in a succession of *Letters on Toleration,* the first published in 1689); it guaranteed them the right to property, whose acquisition was brought about by men "mixing their labour" with the goods of nature; it made it legitimate for every person to take some political responsibility and in due course to act as sovereign himself or as part of the sovereign power, for the vital political right was that of insisting that government rested on the consent of the governed, the consent of the majority expressed constitutionally through representation. The stage of contract came about because the predominantly peaceful state of nature was liable to war and because property was insecure under it. When it arrived, political power was "a right of making laws for the regulating and preserving of property, and of employing the force of the community, in the execution of such laws, and in defence of the commonwealth from foreign injury, and this only for the common good" (*Second Treatise,* Sec. 3).

Contract, to Locke, was an agreement to pool the natural political virtue of individuals and to establish a sovereign power thereby which was in a perpetual trust relationship with the people. If the trust was broken, the people had a right to cashier their governors and put others in their place or, if necessary, to alter the constitution, and all this without the return of the state of nature. In this sense, and in allowing a final appeal to God if the compact itself was dissolved, Locke can be said to have held to a doctrine of the sovereignty of the people and to a perpetual reserved right of revolution. He believed in a form of the separation of powers and in the rule of majorities, but he shows little sympathy with representative democracy.

Recent studies have shown that Locke's political philosophy, as contrasted with his general philosophy, was much less influential in the eighteenth century than had been supposed. Nevertheless, the Lockean outlook, along with that of his friend and contemporary Sir Isaac Newton, must be counted as the point of departure of the intellectual movement known as the Enlightenment.

THE ENLIGHTENMENT AND MONTESQUIEU

Locke could not deal adequately with Newtonian mathematics, but in spite of the intellectual barrier between them, the two men shared one passionate curiosity: to know all that could be known about societies, customs, and religions outside Europe. Confidence in the efficacy of mathematico-physical methods to solve all problems, including those of social and political organization, and cultural relativism leading to doubt about religious revelation and the necessary value of any familiar institution underlie much Enlightenment thought. Meanwhile, the steady spread of literacy and the consequent growth of the size of the politically conscious, curious, and ambitious community, especially in France and England, was changing the conditions of political and social speculation.

The result was a proliferation of works of political philosophy which from now on defeats the summary historian. Sir Isaiah Berlin has said that "the conflict of the rival explanations (or models) of social and individual life had by the late eighteenth century become a scandal." Except as a critical movement, compelling all established dogma to give an account of itself, the Enlightenment cannot be called a uniform current of thought at all. Of the multiple works of Voltaire, Baron de Montesquieu, David Hume, Claude-Adrien Helvétius, Adam Ferguson, Jean-Jacques Rousseau, Gabriel Bonnot de Mably, D'Argenson, Richard Price, Thomas Paine, Thomas Jefferson, Edmund Burke, and their successors, we can comment here on only one or two that find a place in the traditional canon.

MONTESQUIEU. Charles Louis de Secondat, Baron de Montesquieu, may serve as the example of the early sociological attitude, presented with great literary skill and at considerable length in his *Esprit des lois* (in preparation from 1734, published 1748). To Montesquieu, who sought to examine and record social uniformities, natural laws describe necessary human behavior, and because they are necessary, they also oblige men ethically, or, rather, they are the basis of legal systems which men are

ENCYCLOPEDIA OF PHILOSOPHY
2nd edition

morally obliged to obey. At this point it is usual to say that Montesquieu's attitude touches that of Hume in his *Treatise of Human Nature* (1739), containing his famous aphorism about all systems of morality imperceptibly changing from propositions containing "is" and "is not" to propositions containing "ought" and "ought not." But the French author's interest was not in obligation as such; rather, it was in the structure of the collectivities which men find themselves obeying and in the ways in which these structures or their "spirits" (*esprits*) express environment.

ROUSSEAU AND THE GENERAL WILL. Montesquieu is scarcely representative of the most characteristic feature of the political philosophy of his age, at least when viewed from the somber century we now inhabit, because he was neither an optimist nor a believer in the perfectibility of man. Rousseau was skeptical of progress too, for in some moods he seems to have believed that human nature had once been perfect but had been corrupted by society. This was the position which he defended in his first *Discourse* (1751). In his second *Discourse*, the *Discourse on Inequality* (1755), not society but property was the evil attacked.

Neither of these works contained Rousseau's specific contribution to political philosophy. In the *Social Contract* (*Du contrat social*, 1762) Rousseau elaborated a doctrine that was both original and potentially revolutionary; the relation of the individual to the collectivity was seen as a matter of will, not of agreement, and the solution of the problem of obligation was the discovery of a general will directed to universal moral ends, which the individual had only to obey in order to secure justice. Rousseau presented the general-will model in individualistic, contractarian terms:

> Man was born free, and everywhere he is in chains. What is it that can make this legitimate? … The moment men leave the state of nature and set up society, that act of association brings into being a moral, collective body in the place of the particular persons of each contracting party, composed of as many members as there are voices in the assembly, which from this same act receives its unity, its common personality (*moi commun*), its life and its will. This passage from the state of nature to the state of society produces a very remarkable change in man, in substituting justice for instinct in his conduct, and giving to his actions the morality which before they lacked. (*Du contrat social*, Book I, Chs. 1 and 6)

In spite of the care that Rousseau took to effect a moral reconciliation of the will of the individual and that of society, the collectivist possibilities of his approach to political obligation are evident. Since he insisted that a collectivity which has no general will is unworthy of the obedience of its citizens, its revolutionary potentialities are also obvious. The most conspicuous element supporting the interpretation that the *Social Contract* is a statement of tyrannical revolutionary nationalism is its final chapter, "The Civil Religion," which can be interpreted as justifying the condemnation to death of anyone who flouts Rousseau's own dogmatic statement about the relation of the individual to the state.

THE FEDERALIST, BURKE, AND PAINE. The supposed direct relationship of Rousseau's thinking with the revolutionary movements of the late eighteenth century, particularly with the American and French revolutions—even with the Reign of Terror and the despotism of Napoleon Bonaparte—is a conspicuous example of that interplay between intellectual speculation and political movement in which both citizens and historians seem to want to believe. It is of course doubtful whether any element from the multifarious theorization about politics which went on during the Enlightenment could ever be shown to be causally related to what happened in France after 1789, and it is certain that the rebelling American colonists took little trouble to justify their actions in philosophical terms. Nevertheless, the foundation of the American political attitude is of importance to political philosophy, and *The Federalist* (written jointly by James Madison, Alexander Hamilton, and John Jay in the form of a collection of papers published in the New York press in 1787 and 1788) is an outstanding instance of a book's being taken as a compendium of the theoretical content of a nation's political outlook. Max Beloff has said that the sociology of this work was static; in their day there had been founded in America a society, a prefabricated, premeditated structure that would endure unchanged forever. It had the characteristic common to all ethically justified institutions: "Justice is the end of government. It is the end of civil society. It ever has been and ever will be pursued, until it be obtained, or until liberty be lost in the pursuit." But justice is not the imposition of equality—it is the protection of the weak against the stronger. Government will otherwise be content to hold the ring, and liberty will be ensured by the separation of the powers and by the balance between the state and federal governments.

Edmund Burke was a champion of the Americans against the arbitrary powers of the British crown, and he must have approved of much of the argument of the *Federalist,* especially that concerning the benefits of unequal distribution of property. The exercise of political power was the greatest challenge to the wisdom and responsibility of an individual and to his capacity to decide weighty issues on behalf of others. Where were such men to be found but among those experienced in the proper administration of great possessions and of the people who went with them?

Each of Burke's voluminous writings on politics, which occupied his whole life, contains a remark or two of importance to the philosophy of politics. But the work that has caught the eye of posterity is the one he wrote in horrified protest against the actions of the French revolutionaries, *Reflections on the Revolution in France* (published in 1790). The famous passage remembered from this book goes as follows:

> Society is indeed a contract. Subordinate contracts for objects of mere occasional interest may be dissolved at pleasure—but the state ought not to be considered as nothing better than a partnership in a trade of pepper and coffee, calico or tobacco, or some other such low concern, to be taken up for a little temporary interest, and to be dissolved by the fancy of the parties. It is to be looked upon with other reverence; because it is not a partnership in things subservient only to the gross animal existence of a temporary and perishable nature. It is a partnership in all science; a partnership in all art; a partnership in every virtue, and in all perfection. As the ends of such a partnership cannot be obtained in many generations, it becomes a partnership not only between those who are living, but between those who are living, those who are dead, and those who are to be born. Each contract of each particular state is but a clause in the great primeval contract of eternal society, linking the lower with the higher natures, connecting the visible and invisible world, according to a fixed compact sanctioned by the inviolable oath which holds all physical and moral natures each in their appointed place. (pp. 163–164)

The extravagance of the language and the lamentable vagueness of the statements are typical of Burke, and typical also of the uncritical acceptance of the contractarian model long after it had become unnecessary. Indeed, Burke's account of obligation, insofar as he presented one

at all, was far closer to Rousseau's general-will argument than he would have admitted.

But the phrases that have interested posterity are those that limit the freedom of each generation to act against the expectations of the past and the interests of the future, and those in which he condemns as immoral the action of any society which allows fundamental revolution. It was an offense against all humanity to act as the French revolutionaries were doing. The very language of abstract natural right was excoriated by Burke, and he challenged all subsequent political thinkers with the problem of the status of political principles in relation to political action and practice.

Burke's effusive, skeptical conservatism was too much for Thomas Paine, his acute Anglo American contemporary, whose *The Rights of Man* (Part I, 1791, a direct answer to Burke) is often acclaimed a minor classic of political philosophy. There has been no writer more optimistic about the effects of violent political action, or more indifferent to the existence of established government. "The instant formal government is abolished, society begins to act. A general association takes place and common interest produces common security." But in the second part of *The Rights of Man* (1792) Paine identified himself with the nascent working class, and added to the responsibilities of government policies that were hitherto scarcely contemplated and are hailed in our day as the first discernible sign of welfare legislation, even down to family allowances and maternity benefits. The talk of property, representation, and the will and wants of all, which had increased steadily since the time of Hobbes, had issued at last into something like universalistic claims for participation in political activity, into that "numerical democracy" which has characterized the industrialized world ever since.

THE UTILITARIAN TRADITION

BENTHAM. "It is the greatest happiness of the greatest number that is the measure of right and wrong." This famous tag appears in the second paragraph of Jeremy Bentham's *Fragment on Government* (1776) and may be looked upon as the original formulation of the utilitarian principle for specifically political purposes, although Bentham had the law in mind. (Utilitarian ethics of course goes back as far as Hobbes, and Bentham's use of it may be directly referred to Hume.) Bentham went on to offer a definition of the collectivity which was followed more or less faithfully by all his successors in the utilitarian tradition: "When a number of persons (whom we may style subjects) are supposed to be in the habit of paying obedience to a person, or an assemblage of persons, of a known and certain description (whom we may call governors) such persons altogether (subjects and governors) are said to be in a state of political society."

The unsatisfactory character of crude utilitarian ethics is plain in Bentham's best-known book, the *Introduction to the Principles of Morals and Legislation* (1789). "It seems to me," John Plamenatz has said of this work, "that Bentham, without quite knowing what he is doing, is trying to reconcile two couples of irreconcilable doctrines; egoistic hedonism with utilitarianism on the one hand, and a psychological with an objective theory of morals on the other." But in clarifying legal principles and in giving directions to lawyers and politicians, Bentham was much more effective, perhaps the most effective writer of principle for the purpose of advice. So anxious was he to make it crystal clear what men should do tomorrow that he went so far as to proclaim that the motives from which men act are morally irrelevant; only the consequences matter. Carrying out this advice made Bentham into an advocate of the doctrine that government is a necessary evil, since all that government can do is to coerce, and coercion must be kept to that minimum (Bentham's coinage) which will prevent even greater pain. In this way, with Paine as well as with Bentham, utilitarianism was used to justify equality between citizens and representative democracy.

J. S. MILL.

The logical difficulties of utilitarian ethics and the possible dangers of numerical democracy—leaving every man to make up his mind about his own and the general happiness and giving him an equal right to a part in decisions about them—are also evident in the classic statement of liberalism, John Stuart Mill's *On Liberty* (written 1854, published 1859). It was followed in 1861 by *Utilitarianism* and *Representative Government*.

Mill's *On Liberty* shares some of the social unreality that is so evident in Bentham's definition of the collectivity, but to a very much smaller degree. "Wherever," says Mill, "there is an ascendant class, a large portion of the morality of the country emanates from its class interests, and its feelings of class superiority." In his later life Mill might well have described himself as socialist. But the doctrinal legacy of his text is very different:

> The object of this Essay is to assert one very simple principle, … that the sole end for which mankind are warranted, individually or collectively, in interfering with the liberty of action of any of their number, is self-protection, … to prevent harm to others.… The only part of the

conduct of any one, for which he is amenable to society, is that which concerns others.… The only freedom which deserves the name, is that of pursuing our own good in our own way, so long as we do not attempt to deprive others of theirs. (*On Liberty,* Ch. 1)

This principle of other-regarding actions being distinguished from self-regarding actions, and being alone amenable to control from outside, is one of extreme difficulty in practice but of great convenience in argument. With it goes a deep suspicion of the "tyranny of the majority," not simply as expressed in governmental action but even more in the form of intolerant conformism of opinion. Mill is at his most persuasive when he argues that "all silencing of discussion is an assumption of infallibility" and when he insists that it is to the universal advantage that the truth should be known. His book may be regarded as the most forceful of all pleas for freedom of thought and expression. He ends it by insisting on three very general reasons against "government interference." States should not do things better done by individuals, things which it is better for the individuals to do themselves, and things which might unnecessarily add to governmental power.

SIDGWICK.

Mill was by no means the last of the utilitarian thinkers, although the positive grounds for freedom and justice put forward by the idealists were already beginning to replace the negative arguments summarized above. Henry Sidgwick's *Elements of Politics* (1891) may be taken as the final statement of political utilitarianism, although in its later editions it is marked by repeated concessions to socialism, always referred to in quotes. Sidgwick's definition of the collectivity is still Bentham's, although he admits that the principles of politics are not absolutely true but are based on psychological propositions approximately true of civilized man. He adopts from the great utilitarian jurist, John Austin, the claim that in every state the legislature must be legally unlimited, but he also qualifies this. He comes down emphatically on the side of individualism, "which takes freedom—the absence of physical and moral coercion—as the ultimate and sole end of governmental interference."

GERMAN IDEALISM

KANT.

The general-will model associated with Rousseau underwent some development at the hands of the great German philosopher Immanuel Kant in various works written in the 1780s and 1790s. His idea of a "general and public will" is not a particularly lucid concept, but it does express for political purposes the supreme ethical principles of the Kantian philosophy that each man should treat each other man as if he were an end, never as a means, and that each act should be such that it might become a universal law. V. F. Carritt has also praised him highly for the recognition that obligation is a condition of political societies, not a product of them. More influential for subsequent political philosophy, however, was Kant's theory of history. In the course of this complex argument he proposes that the attainment of political society which shall enforce justice requires that man have a master to force him to be free and that this master be the will of the community.

HEGEL. Most philosophers have tried to bring to bear on the problems of political philosophy an overall view of the world and of knowledge. No philosopher has been so devoted to system and the whole as Georg Wilhelm Friedrich Hegel. Political philosophy has its appointed and necessary place within the dialectic exposition of reality. Reality is spiritual, the Absolute, and collectivities have their part to play in the teleological "unfolding" of the Absolute. Collectivities—the family, "civil society," and the state—are manifestations of objective spirit, and the state is the culmination of objective spirit. Collectivities arise when the manifestation of objective spirit in the individual reveals itself as inadequate. The individual can be truly himself only in some society. Formal ethics is bare and empty, and it must be made concrete. Concrete ethics can only be social. Thus the family is a dialectical necessity.

But the family is not a permanent institution; although the members of the family are united in the family and hence are one, the children grow up and leave the family. This "negation" of the family is negated in a new collectivity, civil society. Civil society embraces the economic order and the economic organizations and institutions through which it is expressed, as well as the legal system and the enforcement facilities necessary to it. But the legal system implies something over and above civil society, namely, the state, without which a legal system is impossible. Family and civil society are both embraced within the state; they are at the same time fulfilled by it and manifestations of it. The same is true of the individual. In the state the individual rises above his mere particularity to become a person and truly free.

What the concept of a state fully embraces can be known only through the historical development of actual states. Among the many possible forms of the actual state,

the most rational is a monarchy. A corporative state, in which individuals participate in governmental affairs by virtue of their standing in the corporative bodies of civil society rather than as individuals, is more rational than representative democracy, in which individuals are represented merely as individuals. Nevertheless, the constitution which is best for any particular state is that one which has developed slowly in that state over the course of centuries. A constitution imposed artificially is bound to fail.

It might seem that Hegel's conceptual scheme would require that the state be embraced in some other form of collectivity, but this is not the case. The state is the highest form of objective spirit, and, at this point of the dialectic, objective spirit is negated by absolute spirit—the realm of art, religion, and philosophy. Thus Hegel rejected the Kantian notion of a federation of states and regarded war as not only natural but the motive force of history.

GREEN AND BOSANQUET

The meaning and implications of Hegel's political philosophy provoked immediate and lasting controversy. The central points of discussion have been the relation of the individual to the collectivity, whether state, society, race, or nation; the meaning of the notion of state; and the application of dialectic to the discovery of a necessary pattern in political history. The first point was the dominant problem of the social thought of the British idealist philosophers of the later nineteenth and early twentieth centuries. In political philosophy the two chief figures, with rather opposed views, were T. H. Green and Bernard Bosanquet. Green undertook the task of updating British liberalism to meet the changing circumstances of a rapidly industrialized society. To do so, he sought to divorce liberalism from the ethical egoism of utilitarianism and the laissez-faire economic doctrines of David Ricardo and to replace them with an idealist theory of society based broadly on Kant and Hegel.

For Green, as for earlier liberals, the effect upon freedom was the criterion by which a piece of legislation was to be judged. Did it tend to enlarge or to restrict freedom? Green held that Benthamite liberals had arbitrarily identified freedom with absence of legal restraint, implying that any piece of legislation must necessarily restrict freedom. Green pointed out that it had become evident that a person could be legally free and still not have the power to act for his own benefit. Where one party to a contract has all the powers of coercion on his side and the other party cannot help but agree to the terms proposed by the first party, then the state has the right and the obligation to interfere to restore the original freedom. There are other restraints on freedom than those imposed by the state.

Nevertheless, freedom was not, for Green, a natural right, for he held that there are no natural rights in the eighteenth-century sense. No one possesses abstract rights independent of his membership in a society in which the members recognize some common good as their own ideal good. Thus Green, more a Kantian than a Hegelian, held that the basis of all political obligation is the moral obligation to treat the other members of one's own society as ends in themselves, as having wills whose realization should not be interfered with. The state, on Green's view, has the duty to foster the conditions that permit each member so to act, and to lead him to regard and treat the other members as ends. The members in turn obey the state because they recognize it as the embodiment of their common right.

Green's liberalism stressed the positive function of the state in supporting the moral well-being of all its citizens, and it was not far from the Fabian conception of a national minimum of physical well-being below which the state should not allow any of its citizens to fall—for otherwise they could not participate fully as moral and political beings in society. The liberal side of Green's thought has greatly influenced British political philosophy, which has tended to remain idealist or partially idealist long after idealism passed out of fashion in other areas of British philosophy. But it has been certain antiliberal tendencies which have come to be generally thought of as most typical of idealist political thought, especially since the publication of L. T. Hobhouse's *The Metaphysical Theory of the State* (London and New York, 1918). This work was a direct attack on Hegel and on Bosanquet's *Philosophical Theory of the State* (London, 1899).

Bosanquet developed the notion of the relation between individual and society beyond Green's claim that individuals are individuals only insofar as they are social. He claimed that society itself is more real and more of an individual than any of its members can ever be. And within each member of society it is the social self, rather than any purely individual desires or aims, that is most real. The social self is somehow identical with society, and thus social coercion is coercion by the higher, social self of the lower, individual self. In short, social coercion is self-mastery and true freedom.

Hobhouse charged that this revival of Rousseau's (and Locke's) notion that a man can be forced to be free

is in itself dangerous and illiberal. He further charged that this notion, combined with Bosanquet's failure to distinguish properly between society and the state, or indeed to give any clear or unambiguous definition of the state, leads to the doctrine that the state can do no wrong, and hence to the justification of almost any action on the part of the government in power. There is no doubt that idealist claims have in fact so been used; however, Bosanquet held not that individual governments can do no wrong but that they can do wrongs of a kind totally different from those which individuals can commit—a government can confiscate property, but it cannot commit theft. And individual states can be judged by how well or poorly they fulfill the functions of a state.

MARX AND MARXISM

The Marxian development of Hegelianism is of an entirely different order from the academic philosophies of Green and Bosanquet. The difference is epitomized in Marx's famous eleventh thesis on Ludwig Feuerbach: "The philosophers have only *interpreted* the world, in various ways; the point is to *change* it."

Karl Marx, the great theoretician of socialism, applied the Hegelian dialectic of history to the Hegelian analysis of collectivities. Hegel's family, civil society, and state are not three eternal ideas partially or imperfectly manifested at all periods of history. Rather, they are abstractions from the particular socioeconomic arrangements of the period in which Hegel and Marx lived. Hegel was right in stressing the central role of the economic function in civil society and in holding that, as now constituted, civil society requires a police power and hence a state. But he failed to see that civil society is not necessarily the same as capitalist, bourgeois society (civil society and bourgeois society are designated by the same phrase in German), and he did not see that those who determine the economic arrangements of society are not abstract individuals but are those who exercise control over the economic resources and forces available at the time. Since all others are excluded from having a voice in these economic arrangements, the result is class divisions and the need for the dominant class to defend its economic and political position against the other classes. Thus, as Hegel said, the state is necessary, but it is necessary as an instrument of the oppression of one class by another and not as something inherent in the very notion of social life. If class divisions were done away with, then there would be no one to oppress and the state would disappear. Civil society would be all that there was.

Marx, of course, believed that although in all previous periods (except for an initial period of primitive communism) the state had been necessary, the economic forces of capitalism had so developed that it was not only possible but also necessary for the state to disappear. The complexity of previous class divisions was becoming polarized into two antagonistic classes: the bourgeoisie, who controlled the instruments of production, and the proletariat, who had no choice but to work for the bourgeoisie at subsistence wages. Once the proletariat rises up and takes over the means of production from the bourgeoisie, there will be no more classes to oppress. In the classless society the state, the government of persons, will be "replaced by the administration of things and by the conduct of processes of production" (Friedrich Engels, *Anti-Dühring*, Moscow, 1962, p. 364).

Three intellectual tasks emerge from this view of the historical situation: a study of the laws according to which one era passes into another; a study of the present bourgeois era to discover in it those forces and movements tending toward its breakup and the emergence of the inevitable next era of the classless society; and some sort of preparation and anticipation, however blind, of the period of transition and its aftermath. Thus, economic history and political sociology become pressing practical subjects, and the central problem of politics becomes that of revolution.

The problem of justifying revolution had often been raised before. For Marxists, justification is no longer in question; revolution is inevitable, and only its date is unknown. Marxists must know how to bring about a revolution, whether it must be violent, and whether the revolution can be hastened if the productive forces are not yet ripe. Marx was sure that the bourgeoisie would not yield power without a struggle and that the revolution must be violent. He also held that it could not be hastened: "No social order ever disappears before all the productive forces for which there is room in it have been developed" (*A Contribution to the Critique of Political Economy*, translated by N. I. Stone, Chicago, 1904, preface).

Those later developments of Marxist thought that have been serious and not merely propagandistic justification of a position have generally been attempts at adjusting or revising the theory of revolution to changing historical situations—the growth of mass socialist parties with the apparent possibility of their coming into power by peaceful means; abortive revolutionary governments like those of the Paris Commune of 1870 and the soviets of workers and peasants of the Russian revolution of 1905

(both as interpreted somewhat mythically by Marxist writers); the rapid succession in 1917 of a bourgeois revolution in Russia by a proletarian one before all the possibilities of the bourgeois era could come to flower; the conspiratorial character ascribed to that proletarian revolution; the imposition of socialist regimes in Eastern Europe by Soviet intervention; and the greater or lesser success of Marxist-inspired revolutions in countries, notably China, where modern bourgeois capitalism had only the most tenuous foothold. These revolutions in countries with precapitalist economies were totally inexplicable on classical Marxist grounds, and interpretations of them generally rely on some variant of Lenin's doctrine that in the latter part of the nineteenth century capitalism developed into a higher, final phase of international imperialism, with a corresponding internationalized proletariat and an interaction between the proletariat of the imperialist states and of the populations of the colonies.

ANARCHISM

Socialism, both Marxist and non-Marxist, has since the time of Marx generally favored some sort of centralized control at least of economic life, despite the Leninist prominence given to Friedrich Engels's phrase "the withering away of the state." Although in general it has been held impossible to predict the exact character of a communist society, it has not been claimed that there would be no central authority. In opposition to this collectivist view were most of those early socialists whom Marx classified as utopian, as well as the anarchists and the later guild socialists, such as G. D. H. Cole.

The anarchists differed enormously in their attitudes toward social and economic arrangements, especially in their attitudes toward the institution of private property, but they were united in their opposition to the state, and hence to any centralized authority and to any participation in governmental functions. Engels expressed the Marxist's difference with the anarchist ideal succinctly:

In this society there will, above all, be no *authority,* for authority = state = absolute evil. (How these people propose to run a factory, operate a railway, or steer a ship without a will that decides in the last resort, without single management, they of course do not tell us.) The authority of the majority over the minority also ceases. Every individual and every community is autonomous, but as to how a society of even only two people is possible unless each gives up some of his autonomy Michael Bakunin again maintains silence. (Letter to Theodor Cuno, January 24, 1872)

The anarchists see the primary fault of the present economic order not in the economic arrangements, as do socialists, but in the existence of the state. The state is to be overthrown (although many anarchists, despite the popular identification of anarchism with terrorism, would stop short of violence), and then society will take care of itself. The actual order that will emerge is variously pictured as anything from an extreme individualism to voluntarily cooperating groups of various sizes. Marxists deny this primacy to the state, which, they hold, will collapse when the economic order of which it is the instrument collapses.

Ideas resembling the doctrines of the anarchist thinkers can be found in writings of various periods from Greek times onward, but the first fully articulated anarchist theory is to be found in William Godwin's *Enquiry concerning Political Justice* (1793). Like later anarchists, Godwin was as much an ethical writer as a political theorist. All social organization, and especially all governments, are necessarily corrupting. Society creates prejudices—preconceived ideas. We see people in terms of their social function and status rather than as individuals, and we judge in terms of false ideals—honor in a monarchy and public-spiritedness, a concern for the good of the state rather than of the individual, in a republic. Neither is a substitute for the ideal of benevolence. Godwin's solution is a small, classless community without rules in which individuals cooperate without compulsion, out of friendship, understanding, and benevolence.

Pierre-Joseph Proudhon, a self-educated Besançon printer, was the first theorist to describe himself as an anarchist. Despite his famous definition, "Property is theft," Proudhon was not against property as such but only against its unequal distribution. His ideals were equality and independence. As political science discovers the natural laws according to which society functions, then the arbitrary laws of governments become unnecessary. Proudhon favored individual ownership of the means of production by peasants and artisans. As political science revealed their mutual interests to them, they would freely join together in an ever-widening system of interlocking economic contracts that would make government unnecessary. Only in the case of some large-scale industries and public utilities would workers' syndicates be necessary.

With Bakunin anarchism became associated with the nineteenth-century revolutionary tradition. The son of a Russian nobleman, Bakunin was involved in a number of revolutionary movements from the 1840s on, took part in abortive revolutions in France, Prague, Dresden, and Bologna, and was imprisoned in Saxony, Austria, and Russia. Bakunin was influenced by Proudhon but also by Hegel, Comte, Arnold Ruge, Charles Darwin, and Marx. Like Proudhon, he held that what is produced should be distributed according to the amount of labor the recipient has provided, but he differed in advocating public ownership of the means of production. He differed from Marx in advocating the early destruction of the state rather than its seizure by the workers.

Another Russian writer, Prince Peter Kropotkin, was also influenced by Proudhon. His chief differences from Proudhon and Bakunin were that he favored the small local community as the unit of social organization and argued that goods should be distributed on the basis of need rather than on the basis of what the recipient had produced. Thus he envisaged warehouses where goods would be distributed freely rather than earlier schemes of distribution based on some measure of the recipient's production. Kropotkin also tended to stress the notion that man is naturally social, which was a factor in earlier anarchist theories, even going so far as to find that cooperation, and not merely competition, is a factor in animal evolution.

Far too complex in his views to be classed merely as an anarchist is the French philosopher Georges Sorel. Sorel is important less for his programmatic views than for his analysis of social systems into consumers' and producers' societies, each with its own system of morality, and of the roles of violence and of political myths in revolutionary movements. In a consumers' society the good is things to be obtained—welfare, prosperity, distributive justice, or the classless society. The consumers' society is based on envy. A producers' society sees the good in the cooperative creative endeavor of self-reliant individuals. But this creative endeavor tends in the end to decay into a consumers' society. Violence is a sign of moral health in a revolutionary movement. It ranges from a violence of principles to, occasionally, physical violence. It is intended as much to discourage the "reasonable" sympathizer who feels the time is not ripe for revolution and the man of good will seeking reconciliation as it is to intimidate the enemy. A myth is the revolutionary morality stated in terms of a hoped-for future. Thus, the notion of the general strike may be self-contradictory, but this is beside the point. It is not scientific prophesy but the expression of the aspirations of the revolutionary masses.

FASCISM AND NATIONAL SOCIALISM

Marxism and anarchism are representative of a modern tendency to see political arrangements in terms of a program and often of one dominant idea. There have been others, notably racism and the various forms of nationalism, but only two can be mentioned here. Like Marxism, fascism and national socialism were official philosophies, justifications of particular revolutions and of the regimes that ensued from them. Unlike Marxism, they were not coherent doctrines, and their proponents never made more than a pretense of reconciling theory and practice. New situations called out new theoretical pronouncements in diametrical opposition to earlier ones—but the earlier pronouncements were deliberately allowed to remain as part of the doctrine, with no attempt at harmonizing them with the new claims. Complicating any systematic interpretation is their deliberate irrationalism. Benito Mussolini tended to glorify action—any action; Adolf Hitler relied on his own intuition.

Of these two ideologies, fascism had the twin advantages for clarity and consistency, if not for ideological use, of being largely confined to a conception of the right arrangement of politico-economic life and of having an official formulation compiled by a philosopher, Giovanni Gentile (although Gentile's formulation was worked over by Mussolini himself). Both fascism and national socialism pretended to be nationalist and socialist. In Italy this meant the corporative state and the denial of class antagonisms. Political power was supposed to pass upward through organizations embracing all those who worked in an industry, workers and owners alike, but these organizations would naturally merge their own interests in the national interest. In practice, although not as efficiently as in Germany, this meant totalitarian political control. The fascist glorification of the leader and the attempted revival of the glories of the Roman Empire seem peripheral to fascism when compared with the role played by similar claims in national socialist doctrine.

The tenets of national socialism, unlike those of fascism, were purposely left vague and were allowed to shift as circumstances warranted. The actual doctrines could only be what Hitler said they were, yet he deliberately tolerated or encouraged conflicting outlines of national socialism by Alfred Rosenberg and others. Even statements by Hitler himself were authoritative for the doctrine only at the time they were made. What can be said is that national socialism, like anarchism, was an antipolitical doctrine, but at the same time it was paradoxically a doctrine that aimed at total control. It was antipolitical in that this control was centered outside the state even

though it might work through the state. The authority of the governmental workers and even of national socialist party leaders was diffused, indistinct, and broken on the lower levels so that it could be centered at the top. Hitler's own authority was held to derive not so much from his political position as chancellor of the Reich as from his being the *Führer*, or leader, of the people. He somehow embodied, and knew nonrationally, their strivings and desires; his will was theirs.

Of the various doctrines of national socialism, the central one was undoubtedly that of the racial war between Aryans and Jews. In this war the Jews were seen as the aggressors. They were guilty of constant and unceasing conspiratorial attacks on the superior Aryan race, which in self-defense was forced to undertake their extermination. All other violence instigated by Hitler, both against other nations and against the Germans themselves, was an incidental means to the strengthening of the Aryan race in its main battle. Nevertheless, even the race doctrine could have been dropped unceremoniously, or aimed at some other target, if circumstances had seemed to warrant, just as, for expediency, Hitler dropped first the anticapitalist claims of national socialism and then its anti-Bolshevist ones.

TWENTIETH-CENTURY POLITICAL THOUGHT

With the growing professionalization of political thought into political science and its various branches, and the development of related sociological disciplines, there has been a decline in the Anglo-Saxon countries of political philosophy in the tradition with which Hobbes, Locke, Burke, Mill, and Green are identified. Books of traditional political philosophy have continued to be written, but not generally by those who are writing the most vital works in the more central areas of philosophy, and the new works have not generally been regarded as major contributions to philosophy by those working in the newer analytic modes of philosophy. Perhaps only the subtle and persuasive Burkean traditionalism of Michael Oakeshott has attracted the continuing interest, if not the agreement, of contemporary analytic philosophers.

The dearth of major systematic treatises of the nineteenth-century kind written by contemporary philosophers does not mean that they have completely neglected political philosophy. Despite the recent claim that political philosophy is dead, contemporary philosophers have applied new techniques developed in other fields to the study of the political realm. The apparent death of one tradition of political philosophizing has per-

ENCYCLOPEDIA OF PHILOSOPHY
2nd edition

haps been confused with the death of political philosophy. Two main contemporary trends, which overlap to some extent, can be distinguished.

METHODOLOGY. The first trend consists in the application of the insights gained by the logical positivists and other philosophers of science into the logical status of laws, theories, and concepts in the physical sciences to the problems of political philosophy and to the methodology of political science. The most eminent representative of this trend was Karl Popper. Popper's conception of politics depended on his conception of scientific research, and its exposition is closely intertwined with his critique of earlier political philosophies. It is thus difficult to do justice to his view on how politics should be practiced without explaining his scientific methodology and his reasons for holding that the notions of historical development held by Hegel, Marx, Comte, and Mill are mistaken, and that therefore their notions of what the aims and methodology of the social and political sciences should be are fallacious. But in general he took a cautious attitude toward social change. He used the analogy of scientific investigations to advocate what he terms "piecemeal engineering"; small-scale social changes are to be preferred, because our predictions are always fallible, and mistakes on a small scale are more easily rectifiable than large-scale ones. A total change of society, or the prophecy of the results of a total change, is logically impossible; but the broader the change, the more factors which we must predict and which may go wrong or be overlooked. Connected with this viewpoint is his limited utilitarianism: It is better to attempt to alleviate pain by rectifying an existing evil than to try to increase pleasure by initiating some apparently beneficial change.

The writings of Popper and others on the logic and methodology of the social and political sciences has pioneered in a field that was little more than discovered in the nineteenth century by Mill, Comte, and Spencer—a field in which there is much important work to be done. For example, philosophers have begun to study the logic of political decision making, a subject that has heretofore been left largely to the political scientists themselves.

ANALYTIC POLITICAL PHILOSOPHY. The other main trend in contemporary political philosophy consists in the manipulation of the methods of philosophical analysis developed in the English-speaking countries in the middle decades of the twentieth century. However, neither the variety of philosophical tasks undertaken nor the results achieved present a unified picture, since the approach analytic philosophers take to political philosophy is no more unified than their approach to other groups of philosophical problems.

The first full-scale analytic treatment of the problems of political philosophy, T. D. Weldon's *The Vocabulary of Politics* (Harmondsworth, U.K., 1953), is popularly supposed to have proclaimed the death knell of political philosophizing. Weldon claimed that the various philosophical theories put forth as foundations for liberal democracy, communism, and authoritarianism cannot do what they are held to do. Either they are logically empty and thus have no consequences, or they are mistaken and harmful empirical generalizations open to refutation. Thus Weldon made short work of the social contract theory. Assume, he said, that the Mayflower Compact was shown to be a forgery and that the laws of Massachusetts are held to be based on it. If the citizens of Massachusetts then claimed that because the compact was a forgery, they had lost faith in their democratic institutions, we would feel that this reason was a cover for some other reason.

But despite his denial of the usefulness or the possibility of providing foundations for a political viewpoint, Weldon's alternative description of the political process is a good example of philosophizing about politics, and he himself claimed that "a great deal needs to be done about the language in which discussions of political institutions are conducted" (p. 172).

Other contemporary philosophers have not taken as negative an attitude toward traditional philosophizing about politics as Weldon's. Rather than rejecting out of hand notions like the social contract or general will, they have sought to give new interpretations of such notions, regarding them, for example, as models of the political process. When so interpreted, new sorts of questions arise, questions appropriate to the relation between a model and reality rather than to the analysis of an empirical description. Many other new analyses of traditional political problems and of earlier answers to them are being given, particularly of such problems as sovereignty and natural law, on the borderline between philosophy of law and political philosophy. But the variety of work being done precludes any overall description.

See also General Will; Natural Law; Social Contract.

Bibliography

GENERAL HISTORIES

The standard work is still G. H. Sabine, *A History of Political Theory* (New York, 1938, and revisions). More recent inclusive works, such as John Plamenatz, *Man and Society,* 2 vols. (London: Longman, 1963), tend to be much more restricted in range.

CRITIQUE OF THE SUBJECT

No reasoned survey has yet appeared, but in such works as Karl Popper, *The Open Society and Its Enemies* (Vol. I, *The Spell of Plato*, Vol. II, *The High Tide of Prophecy, Hegel, Marx and the Aftermath*; London: Routledge, 1945; Princeton, NJ: Princeton University Press, 1950), and C. B. Macpherson, *The Political Theory of Possessive Individualism* (Oxford: Clarendon Press, 1962), examples of contemporary critical attitudes will be found. They are themselves instances of an approach criticized in the first part of the article; for works sharing the view taken there, see the continuing collections titled *Philosophy, Politics and Society,* edited by Peter Laslett, W. G. Runciman, et al. (Oxford: Blackwell, 1957–).

ANCIENT POLITICAL PHILOSOPHY

Ernest Barker's books are the most useful for the ancient period: *Greek Political Theory, Plato and His Predecessors,* 3rd ed. (London: Metheun, 1947), *The Politics of Aristotle* (Oxford: Clarendon Press, 1946), and *From Alexander to Constantine* (Oxford: Clarendon Press, 1956). The editions of the ancient classics are innumerable, but the student is recommended to use the Loeb editions if he possibly can, with the original and its English translation on facing pages. All the relevant works (Plato, Aristotle, Cicero, Augustine, etc.) are now in print, although the edition of *The City of God* has yet to be completed.

MEDIEVAL POLITICAL PHILOSOPHY

The great works on medieval political philosophy are those of R. W. Carlyle and A. J. Carlyle (*A History of Mediaeval Political Theory in the West,* 6 vols., London: Blackwood, 1903–1936) and of Ernst Troeltsch (*The Social Teaching of the Christian Churches,* translated by Olive Wyon, 2 vols., New York: Macmillan, 1931). The books of Walter Ullmann, beginning with *The Medieval Idea of Law* (London: Methuen, 1946), contain a stimulating if highly individual interpretation. The important texts are available in Thomas Aquinas, *Selected Political Writings,* edited by A. P. d'Entrèves (Oxford: Blackwell, 1948); Marsilius of Padua, *Defensor Pacis,* translated with an introduction by Alan Gewirth as Vol. II of his *Marsilius of Padua, Defender of Peace* (New York: Columbia University Press, 1956); and Dante, *De Monarchia,* translated and annotated by P. H. Wicksteed (1896).

MACHIAVELLI AND THE SIXTEENTH CENTURY

The Prince was edited in Italian by L. H. Burd (Oxford: Clarendon Press, 1891), but there is a more recent critical edition in English of the *Discourses* (by L. J. Walker, London: Routledge and K. Paul, 1950) which is valuable for Machiavelli generally. A useful if uninspired book is J. W. Allen, *A History of Political Thought in the 16th Century* (reprinted, London, 1957). Jean Bodin's *Republic* has been edited in English by K. D. Macrae (Cambridge, MA: Harvard University Press, 1962). Hooker is still best read in John Keble's Victorian edition of his *Works,* 3 vols. (London, 1836).

THE SEVENTEENTH AND EIGHTEENTH CENTURIES

The general authority on the seventeenth and eighteenth centuries is Otto von Gierke, *Natural Law and the Theory of Society,* translated by Ernest Barker (Cambridge, U.K.: Cambridge University Press, 1934). Hobbes's *Leviathan* has been edited by Michael Oakeshott (Oxford, 1947); Spinoza's *Political Works* by A. G. Wernham (Oxford: Blackwell, 1958); Locke's *Two Treatises* by Peter Laslett (Cambridge, U.K.: Cambridge University Press, 1960); and Robert Shackleton has written a standard work on Montesquieu: *Montesquieu, a Critical Biography* (Oxford: Oxford University Press, 1961); Montesquieu's *De l'esprit des lois* is available in English, edited by F. Neumann (New York, 1949). Rousseau studies are still dominated by C. E. Vaughan, *The Political Writings* (1915; reprinted, Oxford: Blackwell, 1962); there is also a translation of the *Social Contract* by F. M. Watkins (London, 1953). There are many reprints, but so far no critical editions, of the books of Burke, Paine, Bentham, Mill, and Green quoted in the text.

THE ENLIGHTENMENT AND UTILITARIANISM

Ernst Cassirer wrote a definitive work, *The Philosophy of the Enlightenment,* translated by F. C. A. Koelln and J. P. Pettegrove (1932, English ed., Princeton, NJ: Princeton University Press, 1951), and J. L. Talmon one with a more tendentious if stimulating thesis, *The Origins of Totalitarian Democracy* (London: Secker and Warburg, 1952). John Plamenatz prefixed a brilliant essay, "The English Utilitarians," to his reprint of Mill's *Utilitarianism* (Oxford: Blackwell, 1949). Élie Halévy, *The Growth of Philosophic Radicalism,* translated by Mary Morris (London: Faber and Gwyer, 1928), is still important.

HEGEL AND GERMAN IDEALISM

Hegel's main work on political philosophy is *Naturrecht und Staatswissenschaft im Grundrisse* (Berlin, 1821), 2nd ed. edited by E. Gans as *Grundlinien der Philosophie des Rechts* (Berlin, 1833), translated by T. M. Knox as *The Philosophy of Right* (Oxford: Clarendon Press, 1942). His *Phänomenologie des Geistes* (Würzburg and Bamberg, 1807), translated by J. B. Baillie as *Phenomenology of Mind* (London: S. Sonnenschein, 1910), and *Vorlesungen über die Philosophie der Geschichte,* edited by E. Gans (Berlin, 1837) and translated by J. Sibree as *Lectures on the Philosophy of History* (London: Bohn, 1857), should also be consulted. See also *Hegel's Political Writings,* translated by T. M. Knox with an introductory essay by Z. A. Pelczynski (Oxford: Clarendon Press, 1964). On Hegel's political thought, see M. B. Foster, *The Political Philosophies of Plato and Hegel* (Oxford: Clarendon Press, 1935); Franz Rosenzweig, *Hegel und die Staat,* 2 vols. (Oldenburg, 1920); Eric Weil, *Hegel et l'état* (Paris: J. Vrin, 1950), and the works by Popper and Plamenatz cited above.

Hermann Lübbe, ed., *Die Hegelsche Rechte* (Stuttgart and Bad Canstatt, 1962), and Karl Löwith, ed., *Die Hegelsche Linke* (Stuttgart and Bad Canstatt, 1962), contain selections from right-wing and left-wing German successors of Hegel, respectively. The second is more directly relevant to political philosophy. From the voluminous writing on this period, see Sidney Hook, *From Hegel to Marx* (New York: Humanities Press, 1950); Georg Lukács, *Die Zerstörung der Vernunft* (Berlin: Aufbau, 1954); and Herbert Marcuse, *Reason and Revolution: Hegel and the Rise of Social Theory,* 2nd ed. (New York: Humanities Press, 1954). Johann Gottlieb Fichte was an idealist contemporary of Hegel whose writings are of considerable political interest. See especially his *Der geschlossene Handelsstaat* (The closed commercial state; Tübingen, 1800).

BRITISH IDEALISM

Green's *Lectures on the Principles of Political Obligation* were first published in *The Works of Thomas Hill Green,* edited by R. L. Nettleship, 3 vols. (London, 1885–1888). See Melvin Richter, *The Politics of Conscience: T. H. Green and His Times* (London: Weidenfeld and Nicolson, 1964). On Bosanquet, besides Hobhouse, see F. Houang, *Le néo-Hegelianisme en Angleterre: La philosophie de Bernard Bosanquet* (Paris, 1954). For a general account of British Neo-Hegelian political and social thought, see A. J. M. Milne, *The Social Philosophy of English Idealism* (London: Allen and Unwin, 1962). *The Philosophy of Loyalty* (New York: Macmillan, 1908) by the American idealist Josiah Royce shows a related development. On Royce, see J. E. Smith, *Royce's Social Infinite* (New York: Liberal Arts Press, 1950). Other works by Hobhouse are *Liberalism* (London: Williams and Nirgate, 1911) and *The Elements of Social Justice* (London: Allen and Unwin, 1922). See J. A. Hobson and Morris Ginsberg, *L. T. Hobhouse, His Life and Work* (London: Allen and Unwin, 1931). Of the many British political writings broadly following in the tradition of Green, the following may be mentioned: Ernest Barker, *Reflections on Government* (London: Oxford University Press, 1942); A. D. Lindsay, *The Modern Democratic State* (London: Oxford University Press, 1943); and J. D. Mabbott, *The State and The Citizen* (London: Hutchinson's University Library, 1948). A curious wartime idealist work with an intent similar to that of Hobhouse's *Metaphysical Theory of the State* is R. G. Collingwood's *The New Leviathan* (Oxford: Clarendon Press, 1942).

MARXISM

Almost any writing of Marx or Engels is relevant to their political philosophy. See especially Marx's *Das Kapital,* 3 vols. (Hamburg, 1867–1894), translated by Samuel Moore, Edward Aveling, and Ernest Untermann as *Capital,* 3 vols. (Chicago, 1915); Marx and Engels's *Die deutsche Ideologie,* edited by V. Adoratsky (Vienna, 1932), translated as *The German Ideology,* edited by S. Ryazanskaya (Moscow: Progress, 1964); Marx and Engels's *Manifest der kommunistischen Partei* (London, 1848), translated as *The Communist Manifesto,* edited with an introduction by Harold Laski (London: Allen and Unwin, 1948); and Engels's *Der Ursprung der Familie, des Privateigentums und des Staat* (Zürich, 1884), translated by Ernest Untermann as *The Origin of the Family, Private Property, and the State* (Chicago: Kerr, 1902). Two convenient anthologies are Lewis S. Feuer, ed., *Basic Writings on Politics and Philosophy* (Garden City, NY: Doubleday, 1949), and T. B. Bottomore and Maximilien Rubel, eds., *Selected Writings in Sociology and Social Philosophy* (London: Watts, 1956). Of the writings of Lenin, see especially *Chto Delat?* (*What Is to Be Done?*; Stuttgart: Dietz, 1902), *Shag Vperyod, Dva Shaga Nazad* (*One Step Forward, Two Steps Back*; Geneva: Partii, 1904), *Imperializm, kak Vysshara Stadiya Kapitalizma* (*Imperialism, the Highest Stage of Capitalism*; Petrograd: Zhizn' i znznie, 1917), and *Gosudarstvo i Revolutsiya* (*State and Revolution*; Petrograd: Zhizn' i znznie, 1918). There are various English editions of all of these. Of the many other Marxist writers on political philosophy, one of the most interesting is Antonio Gramsci. See his *Opere,* 6 vols. (Turin, 1947–1954), and *The Modern Prince and Other Writings,* translated by Louis Marks (London: Lawrence and Wishart, 1957). For other Marxist writings and for writings on Marxism, consult the bibliographies to the entries Dialectical Materialism, Historical Materialism, and Marxist Philosophy.

ANARCHISM

Among the chief anarchist works are William Godwin, *An Enquiry concerning Political Justice and Its Influence on General Virtue and Happiness* (London: GGJ and J. Robinson, 1793); the writings of Michael Bakunin, translations of which appear in *The Political Philosophy of Bakunin: Scientific Anarchism* (Glencoe, IL: Free Press, 1953); Prince Peter Kropotkin's *The State, Its Part in History* (London: Freedom office, 1898), *Mutual Aid, a Factor of Evolution* (London, 1902), and *Modern Science and Anarchism* (Philadelphia, 1903); Pierre-Joseph Proudhon's *Qu'est-ce que la Propriété?* (Paris, 1840), translated by Benjamin R. Tucker as *What Is Property; An Inquiry into the Principle of Right and of Government* (New York: Humboldt, 1890); Henry David Thoreau, "Civil Disobedience," in *The Writings of Henry David Thoreau,* Vol. X (Boston and New York, 1863); Benjamin R. Tucker, *Instead of a Book: A Fragmentary Exposition of Philosophical Anarchism* (New York, 1897); and Georges Sorel, *Réflexions sur la violence* (Paris: Librairie de "Pages Libres," 1908), translated by T. E. Hulme and J. Roth as *Reflections on Violence* (New York: Huebsch, 1914). On anarchism, see George Woodcock, *Anarchism: A History of Libertarian Ideas and Movements* (Cleveland, OH: World Publishing, 1962); James Joll, *The Anarchists* (London: Eyre and Spottiswoode, 1964); and Alexander Gray, *The Socialist Tradition* (London: Longmans, 1946).

NATIONAL SOCIALISM AND FASCISM

For further pronouncements by national socialists, see Josef Goebbels, *Goebbels Tagebücher,* edited by Louis Lochner (Zürich, 1948); Adolf Hitler, *Mein Kampf,* 2 vols. (Munich, 1925–1927), and *Hitler's Secret Conversations 1941–1944* (New York: Farrar, Straus and Young, 1953). German Philosophy and National Socialism contains an extensive bibliography of relevant works, which may be supplemented by bibliographies in many of the works cited there. On fascism, consult Benito Mussolini, *Scritti i discorsi,* 12 vols. (Milan, 1934–1939) and *The Doctrine of Fascism,* translated in *Social and Economic Doctrines of Contemporary Europe,* edited by Michael Oakeshott, 2nd ed. (New York, 1942); and Giovanni Gentile, *Che cosa è il fascismo* (Florence: Vallecchi, 1925) and *Origini e dottrine del fascismo* (Rome: Libreria del Littorio, 1929).

CONTEMPORARY POLITICAL THOUGHT

The best picture of contemporary analytic political philosophy can be gathered from the series of collections titled *Philosophy, Politics and Society,* edited by Peter Laslett, W. G. Runciman et al. (Oxford, 1957–). Popper's main works on political philosophy are *The Open Society and Its Enemies* and *The Poverty of Historicism* (London: Routledge, 1957). Weldon also published *States and Morals* (London: J. Murray, 1946). On Oakeshott, consult his inaugural address in the first volume of *Philosophy, Politics and Society* and his

Rationalism in Politics (New York: Basic, 1962). Other examples are H. L. A. Hart, "The Ascription of Responsibility and Rights," *PAS* 49 (1948–1949): 179–194, reprinted in *Essays on Logic and Language,* edited by A. G. N. Flew (Oxford: Blackwell, 1951); Margaret Macdonald, "The Language of Political Theory," in *PAS* 41 (1940–1941), reprinted in Flew, op. cit.; J. W. N. Watkins, "Epistemology and Politics," in *PAS* 58 (1957–1958): 79–102; and S. I. Benn and R. S. Peters, *Social Principles and the Democratic State* (London: Allen and Unwin, 1959).

Peter Laslett (1967)
(Introduction through Kant)
Philip W. Cummings (1967)
(Hegel through recent political thought)

POLITICAL PHILOSOPHY, HISTORY OF [ADDENDUM]

Political philosophy, theory, and thought all focus on the arguments that have been advanced—by prominent thinkers from around the world and throughout human history—for various conceptions of a just human community. Different schools of such political thinking have developed over time and here some of these schools will be sketched and the major contributors will be listed. The bibliography lists sources for further study of these ideas.

LIBERTARIANISM AND CAPITALISM

Libertarianism is the political system wherein the highest political good is the protection of the individual citizen's right to life, liberty, and property. Capitalism is the economic system of libertarianism because in libertarian societies the institution of the right to private property, that is, to own anything of value (not, of course, other human beings, who are themselves owners), is fully respected and protected.

Libertarian law rests on the idea that the individual is the most important member of society, with all groups to be formed by the consent of individual members, including the military, corporations, universities, clubs, and the government itself. What is primarily prohibited in a libertarian society is involuntary servitude. What is primarily promoted via the political administration is the liberty of all persons to advance their own objectives provided they do not in this process violate anyone's equal rights. The major contributors to libertarian political thought have been Murray N. Rothbard, Ayn Rand (although she eschewed that term, preferring *radical capitalism* instead), Robert Nozick, Loren Lomasky, Jan Narveson, Douglas B. Rasmussen, Douglas J. Den Uyl, and Tibor R. Machan.

There is dispute about the label *capitalism* as the proper way to call the economic order under libertarianism, mostly because its definition is often a precondition of having either a favorable or unfavorable view of the system. Some have insisted on the use of laissez-faire, in memory of the French entrepreneurs who responded to the king's question as to what the government can do to help the economy by exclaiming: "Laissez-faire, lassize passe," or "Leave us to do, leave us to act." Some use F.A. Hayek's term *the spontaneous order* to stress such a system's support of uncoerced behavior. There is also the more popular term *free enterprise*.

Yet capitalism is most widely used, by both critics and supporters of an economic order in which individuals have the right to own property and to use of it on their own terms. By itself capitalism is an economic arrangement of an organized human community or polity. Often, however, entire societies are called capitalist, mainly to stress their thriving commerce and industry. More rigorously understood, however, capitalism presupposes a libertarian legal order governed by the rule of law in which the principle of private property rights plays a central role. Such a system of laws was historically grounded on various classical liberal ideals in political thinking. These ideals can be defended by means of positivism, utilitarianism, natural rights theory and/or individualism, as well as notions about the merits of laissez-faire (no government interference in commerce), the invisible hand (as a principle of spontaneous social organization), prudence and industriousness (as significant virtues), the price system as distinct from central planning (for registering supply and demand), and so on.

Put a bit differently, *capitalism* or *economic libertarianism* are the terms used to describe that feature of a human community whereby citizens are understood to have the basic right to make their own (more or less wise or prudent) decisions concerning what they will do with their labor and property, or whether they will engage in trade with one another involving nearly anything they may value. Thus capitalism includes freedom of trade and contract, the free movement of labor, and the protection of property rights against both criminal and official intrusiveness.

The concept of freedom plays a central role in the understanding of both libertarianism and capitalism. There are two prominent ways of understanding the nature of freedom as it pertains to human relationships. The one that fits with capitalism is negative freedom: the condition of everyone in society not being ruled by others with respect to the use and disposal of themselves and what belongs to them. Citizens are free, in this sense, when no other adult person has authority over them that they have not granted of their own volition. In short, in capitalism one enjoys negative freedom, which amounts to be free from others' intrusiveness. The other meaning of freedom is that citizens have their goals and purposes supported by others or the government so as to prosper. Under this conception of freedom one is free to progress, advance, develop, or flourish only when one is enabled to do so by the efforts of capable others.

In international political discussions the concept of capitalism is used very loosely, so that such very diverse types of societies as Italy, New Zealand, the United States of America, Sweden, and France are all considered capitalist. Clearly, no country today is completely capitalist. None enjoys a condition of economic laissez-faire in which governments stay out of one's commercial transactions except when conflicting claims over various valued items are advanced and the dispute needs to be resolved in line with due process of law. But many Western type societies protect a good deal of free trade, even if they also regulate most of it as well. Still, just as those countries are called democratic if there is substantial suffrage—even though many citizens may be prevented from voting—or if there exists substantial free trade and private ownership of the major means of production (labor, capital, intellectual creations, and so on), the country is usually designated as capitalist.

The most common reason among political economists for supporting capitalism is this system's support of wealth creation. This is not to say that such theorists do not also credit capitalism with other worthwhile traits, such as encouragement of progress, political liberty, innovation, and so on. Those who defend the system for its utilitarian virtues—its propensity to encourage the production of wealth—are distinct from others who champion the system—or the broader framework within which it exists—because they consider it morally just.

The first group of supporters argue that a free market or capitalist economic system is of great public benefit, even though this depends on private or even social vice, such as greed, ambition, and exploitation. As Bernard Mandeville, the author of *The Fable of the Bees*, put it, this system produces "private vice, public benefit." Many moral theorists see nothing virtuous in efforts to improve one's own life. They believe, however, that enhancing the overall wealth of a human community is a worthwhile goal. Those who follow along lines of Man-

deville in the twentieth century, including Ludwig von Mises, Milton Friedman, F. A. Hayek, Gary Becker, and James Buchanan, stress the practical merits of this economic system rather than its moral justification.

Those who stress the moral or normative merits of capitalism, mostly libertarians, say the system rewards prudence, hard work, ingenuity, industry, entrepreneurship, and personal or individual responsibility in all spheres of human life, and this is all to the good. This alone makes the system morally preferable to alternatives. Yet, another reason given why libertarianism or capitalism is not only useful but morally preferable is that it makes possible the exercise of genuine moral choice and agency, something that would be obliterated in noncapitalist, collectivist systems or economic organization. Most of the libertarians (see previous paragraph) advance this type of normative argument for capitalism.

Capitalist theorists note that most critics of capitalism demean wealth. Indeed, they virtually attack the pursuit of human individual well-being itself and, especially, luxury, anytime there are needy people left anywhere on earth, as well as, more recently, if any portion of nature is overrun by human beings (as if they were not natural creatures). But, the champions of capitalism argue, this stems from utopian thinking and has the consequence of begrudging anyone a measure of welfare because some people will always be poor some of the time and nature will continue to be transformed by people.

Yet the capitalist advocate need not be seen as reckless toward the environment. Indeed, arguably the strict and consistent institution of the principle of private property rights—through, for example, privatization and prohibition of dumping waste into other private as well as public realms—may solve the environmental problems we face better than any central planning champions of the environment tend to propose. Libertarians and capitalists think that the environment suffers worst when the "tragedy of the commons" is permitted, whereby commonly owned values are overused because everyone is deemed to have a right to such use, while no one in particular is left with the responsibility to care for it.

Capitalism rests in large part on the belief that human beings are essentially individuals and a society's laws must value individuals above all else. Most historians of ideas admit that whether the importance of human individuality should have been recognized in earlier times, it certainly was not much heeded until the modern age. Even in our time it is more often that groups—ethnic, religious, racial, sexual, national, and cultural—are taken to have greater significance than individuals. The latter are constantly asked to make sacrifices for the former. In capitalism, however, the individual (e.g., as the sovereign citizen or the consumer) is king. Undoubtedly a capitalist system does not give prime place to economic equality among people, something that group thinking seems to favor because, in groups, all are deemed to be entitled to a fair share.

WELFARE STATISM

The welfare state or, from the economic viewpoint, the mixed economy, may be understood as a combination of the principles of capitalism and socialism. Sometimes the emphasis in this system is placed not so much on economic dilemmas as on certain moral considerations. Basically the welfare state consists of a legal system that aims at securing for everyone the negative right to liberty and the positive right to well-being. The main defenders of this system in the later twentieth century are John Rawls, Amartya Sen, Martha Nussbaum, and Jurgen Habermas.

The welfare state, which is to say most Western countries, balances the two values that together seem to its advocates to be the bedrock of a civilized society. No one ought to have his or her sovereignty seriously compromised, nor should anyone be permitted to fall below a certain standard of living. This is difficult to maintain because at different times one or another of these objectives will probably take priority and, in mostly democratic systems, political leaders will vacillate between giving more support to one or the other. The right to strike, for example, which is the negative liberty to quit one's job in an effort to gain respect for one's terms of employment, may conflict with the positive right to be provided with various services (e.g., health care, mail delivery, or education).

It is indeed a prominent feature of the welfare state that both negative and positive rights receive their legal protection. Negative rights involve respect for a person's life, liberty, and property—that is, everyone is by law supposed to abstain from interfering with these. Positive rights, in turn, involve respect for a person's basic needs—that is, everyone who is unable to secure the requirements of survival, and even flourishing, is supposed to have those provided by way of the appropriate public policy (e.g., taxation, mandated services, public education, and national health care).

The moral underpinnings of the welfare state can be utilitarianism, altruism, or certain intuitively held moral precepts. Utilitarianism requires that the general welfare be pursued by all and whatever public policies to facilitate this were needed would be justified. Although many utilitarians believe that the general welfare is best achieved when government operates in a largely laissez-faire fashion, there is no objection to government intervention in social affairs if without those many in the society may fail to achieve a decent and prosperous form of life. Altruists, in turn, often hold that to make certain that people fulfill their primary obligation to help others, it is necessary to introduce public measures that will secure such help, given that many might wish to breach their duty to do the right thing. Finally, there is the claim that, by our common intuitions, it is evident that both a measure of personal liberty and social welfare must be guaranteed to all, lest the quality of life in society fall below what it should be.

Whereas the welfare state is objected to by people from several other perspectives, it is thought by its supporters to be the most stable modern political order. Although it is characterized by much dispute and controversy, in the long run, its supporters maintain, the system seems to be overall satisfactory and just.

COMMUNITARIANISM

Communitarianism could be viewed as a sort of halfway house between the collectivist system of socialism and the individualist one of capitalism. The idea is less capable of being sharply defined than these others. Roughly it comes to the view that human beings are necessarily or essentially parts of distinct human groups, communities, with their diverse values, histories, priorities, practices, laws, and cultures. The organizing principles of these different groups will themselves vary. There is no overriding true social and political order, not even any universal ethics. Rather it is the particular character of the communities that establish for its parts or members what is the proper way to live, what laws should be enacted, and what aesthetic and religious values need to be embraced.

Some communities can be Spartan, others Stoic, yet others bohemian and so forth. Each can have its peculiar way of life without implying any objective condemnation of some alternative form. Yet participation in the community's form of life is not a matter of individual consent. Such an idea derives from a mistake: There is a transcendent or general human nature that requires every community to adhere to certain minimal standards of justice. No such transcendent human nature exists, as far as many communitarians see things, so those that, say, grant individuals certain rights are not superior to those that do not—they are simply different. Among those who are prominent communitarians, Charles Taylor, Amitai

Etzioni, Thomas Spragens, Michael Sandel, and Richard Rorty stand out.

Actually there is not much more that can be said about communitarianism because there are simply too many types of community, each with its own framework and priorities. The main point is that the rules, laws, ideals, and so forth are all the result of the often slowly evolving consensus or collective practices of the community's membership. Just as socialism sees humanity as the whole to which individuals belong, communitarianism sees different ethnic, national, racial, gender, cultural, professional, or similar distinguishable groups as the whole to which the individual member belongs. One may imagine, for example, that languages have developed, in part, to meet the requirements, imagination, and circumstances of different linguistic communities, with no language superior or completely translatable to any other.

Communitarians often unite in their criticism of bourgeois society or liberal capitalism because of their emphasis on individuality, privacy, personal freedom, consent, and competition. Communitarians believe that the view of human nature underlying such liberal capitalist views is seriously flawed. They are convinced, also, that the central idea of liberal capitalism is what has come to be known as *homo economicus* or *economic man*. That idea figures heavily in economic analysis and views individuals as autonomous entities who enter the world fully formed, ready to make choices in the market, and self-sufficient. While there are other conceptions of the human individual that might support liberal capitalism, it is this that has occupied the attention of communitarians and it is in contrast to this view that they have advanced their position.

ISLAMIC POLITICAL THEORY

Muslims are divided into two communities, the Sunni majority and Shii minority, and they adhere to different ideas as to political rule. They are known as the Sunni caliphate and the Shii Imamate.

When Muhammad died, most Muslims, since they thought that Muhammad did not name a successor, relied upon the decision of a group of his cohorts. The caliphate, chosen by way of consultation (called *shura*) and agreement (called *ijma*), an oath of loyalty (called *baya*) that is sworn by those who elect him, and the compact (called *ahd*) with the people to govern by Islamic law (Sharia) developed into what is widely regarded as legitimate government for Sunni Islam.

But the Shii rejected the Sunni caliphs and regarded them as subverting Islamic law. They adhered to the idea that Muhammad had selected Ali, who was reported to be his cousin and son-in-law, to be the ruler (*Imam*) of Muslims. They held that the oldest (male) descendant (*Ahl al-Bait*) must be the divinely anointed, religious, and political chief. Abbasid rule (750–1250) formed Islamic political theory as theocratic, with theologians as the legal authorities who had royal privilege and professed to uphold the divine goal for the Muslim community under Abbasid edicts. In the last analysis, as matters now stand, there is no unified Muslim political theory that enjoys widespread acceptance.

In geopolitical affairs a very influential version of Muslim politics comes from the clerics and adherents of the Wahhabi branch of radical Islam, based mainly in Saudi Arabia and considered to be the most virulently anti-Western in light of the belief that any accommodation of Western values is an intolerable compromise with the words of the Prophet. The main point of contention is that the West legally tolerates freedom of religion and even nonbelief, which undermines the virtuous life demanded of the faithful, leading to their corruption.

JEWISH POLITICAL THEORY

Jews, as such, do not adhere to a firm political creed, unlike many Muslims, but tend to embrace varieties of democratic, even liberal, institutions, while also encouraging some socialist economic practices and certain mild forms of theocracies, depending on the version of Judaism they embrace. Jewish political ideas derive mainly from the belief that Jews are a separate, unique—chosen—people, not merely adherents to a different religion or a system of moral principles that emerge from such a religion (of course this idea is shared by nearly all traditional and organized religious groups). Jewish political ideas pertain to how the Jews as a unified people have held on to a political community throughout the centuries, without becoming amalgamated into communities wherein they lived as exiles and how they shaped these by giving clear expressions of their own culture and forms of political conduct.

Jews often choose to demonstrate a Jewishness via political means and this for many of them consists of loyalty to modern Israel as well as various Jewish missions, including various communal groups (for example, the kibbutz) constituted almost exclusively by Jews. As is common in politics everywhere, Jews will often stress the need for power as they advance the causes of their various groupings, although this also includes extensive education and proselytizing.

CONCLUSION

None of the systems we have sketched here are fully exemplified anywhere, although some—for example, Islamic theocracy—are approximated in some parts of the world (e.g., Iran). There are, however, no purely capitalist, socialist, or communist societies and the welfare states are also quite different, with various ways of balancing the values of personal autonomy and social security. Instead, most societies—countries—exhibit mixed systems and often where democratic decision-making takes place, the main topic of debate is which of these values should be stressed more, as well as how much state support should be given to various special interests.

See also Civil Disobedience; Cosmopolitanism; Postcolonialism; Republicanism

Bibliography

Mitchell, Joshua. *Not by Reason Alone: Religion, History, and Identity in Early Modern Political Thought*. Chicago: University of Chicago Press, 1996.

Novak, David. *Covenantal Rights: A Study in Jewish Political Theory*. Princeton, NJ: Princeton University Press, 2000.

Skoble, Aeon J., and Tibor R. Machan, eds. *Political Philosophy: Essential Selections*. Upper Saddle River, NJ: Prentice Hall, 1999.

Strauss, Leo, and Joseph Cropsey, eds. *History of Political Philosophy*. 3rd ed. Chicago: University of Chicago Press, 1987.

Watt, William. *Islamic Political Thought*. Edinburgh: Edinburgh University Press, 1998.

Tibor Michan (2005)

POLLA

See *Hen/Polla*

POMPONAZZI, PIETRO
(1462–1525)

Pietro Pomponazzi, the Italian Renaissance Aristotelian, was born in Mantua. He studied philosophy at the University of Padua, where, after obtaining his degree, he became extraordinary professor of philosophy in 1488 and ordinary professor in 1495. When war caused the university to close in 1509, he left Padua. After a short period at Ferrara he became a professor of philosophy at the University of Bologna, where he taught from 1512 until his death. He married three times and had two children.

Of Pomponazzi's writings only a few were published during his lifetime. Best known is the treatise *De Immortalitate Animae* (On the immortality of the soul, 1516), which immediately provoked a large controversy. It was publicly attacked by several philosophers and theologians and was followed by the author's two treatises in defense—the *Apologia* (1518) and the *Defensorium* (1519)—which were longer than the original work. Probably as a result of this experience Pomponazzi did not publish anything else except for a few short philosophical questions that he added to the 1525 reprint (*Tractatus Acutissimi*) of his three writings on immortality. Equally important are his treatises *De Incantationibus* (On incantations) and *De Fato* (On fate), both written about 1520, which were published posthumously in Basel by a Protestant exile in 1556 and 1567, respectively. A sizable body of other writings has been preserved in manuscript, and the study and publication of this material have barely begun. The most important among these unpublished writings are questions on Aristotelian and other problems, which Pomponazzi probably worded himself and that therefore directly reflect his thought. A much larger group consists of his class lectures on various works of Aristotle. Since they were taken down by students and show a certain amount of oscillation from year to year and from copy to copy, they must be used with caution in any attempt to reconstruct Pomponazzi's thought and philosophical development.

Pomponazzi was a product and in many ways a typical representative of the tradition of scholastic Aristotelianism that flourished at Bologna, Padua, and other Italian universities from the thirteenth to the seventeenth century. This school, often referred to as Paduan Averroism, had no institutional or doctrinal connections with theology, as did its northern counterparts, but rather with medicine, and this accounts for its secular orientation. In the study of Aristotle, whose writings served as the prescribed texts for the teaching of the philosophical disciplines, the emphasis was, as in Paris and elsewhere, on logic and natural philosophy rather than on ethics and metaphysics.

Pomponazzi's main sources were the writings of Aristotle and of his commentators, and his style, far removed from classical or humanistic elegance, is a rather harsh example of scholastic terminology and argument, although he was at times capable of concise formulation and caustic wit. His reasoning shows great subtlety and acumen, but he is repetitious and sometimes inconsistent. He obviously enjoyed spinning out an argument and following reason wherever it led, and out of intellectual honesty he was prepared to admit his puzzlement before certain dilemmas and to modify his views whenever he felt compelled to do so by some strong argument. Thus, we may well understand the outburst in *De Fato* (III, 7) in which he compares the philosopher with Prometheus. In his efforts to understand the secrets of God the philosopher is eaten up by his continual worries and thoughts; stops eating, drinking, and sleeping; is held up to ridicule by all; is taken as a fool and a faithless person; is persecuted by the Inquisition; and is laughed at by the multitude.

In spite of his general scholastic orientation Pomponazzi was by no means unaffected by other currents. He knew and respected Plato and was clearly influenced by Marsilio Ficino (and Giovanni Pico della Mirandola) in his remarks about the place of man in the universe and perhaps in his preoccupation with the immortality of the soul. Like the humanists he cultivated the monographic treatise in addition to the question and the commentary, occasionally injected personal remarks about himself, and cited such sources as Cicero and Plutarch. His doctrine that virtue is its own reward has Stoic rather than Aristotelian antecedents, and his insistence that the end of man consists in practical virtue rather than in contemplation is at variance with Aristotle and may owe something to Cicero and to such humanists as Leonardi Bruni and Leon Alberti.

One may even link with humanism Pomponazzi's interest in Alexander of Aphrodisias. Alexander was not entirely unknown during the Middle Ages, but his writings acquired a much wider diffusion through new translations around the turn of the sixteenth century. The label of Alexandrism often attached to Pomponazzi is dubious and misleading. We know from a question composed by Pomponazzi in 1504 that his view on the problem of immortality, as adopted in his treatise of 1516, was derived from that of Alexander. We also learn that the writing of his treatise *De Fato* was occasioned by his reading a new Latin translation of Alexander's treatise on the subject (Pomponazzi knew no Greek). However, *De Fato* is actually a defense of the Stoic position against Alexander.

Pomponazzi's *De Incantationibus* is an attempt to offer natural explanations for a number of occurrences popularly ascribed to the agency of demons and spirits. The effects ascribed to the stars by the astrologers form for Pomponazzi a part of the system of natural causes.

This work is the only one by Pomponazzi that was once on the Index of Prohibited Books (it no longer is) because of its implied criticism of miracles. It contains an interesting passage on prayer that shows a certain affinity to some ideas expressed in the treatise on immortality. The value of prayer, he said, consists not in the external effects it may have but in the pious attitude it produces in the person who prays.

The *De Fato*, which is divided into five books, is by far the longest of Pomponazzi's works. He discusses in great detail and with a great number of intricate arguments the problems of fate, free will, and predestination. His conclusions are by no means simple or clear-cut, but it appears from his final remarks that he regarded the Stoic doctrine of fate, on purely natural grounds, as relatively free from contradictions. Yet, because human wisdom is subject to error, Pomponazzi was willing to submit to the teaching of the church and to accept the doctrine that God's providence and predestination are compatible with man's free will. However, he was not satisfied with the way in which this compatibility is customarily explained and tried to propose an explanation that he considered more satisfactory.

De Fato has been unduly neglected by students of Pomponazzi, perhaps because of its length and difficulty. It is now available in a critical edition and may be studied within the twofold historical context in which it belongs: first, the philosophical controversy between determinism and indeterminism as it appeared in antiquity in the works of the Stoics and Alexander and again in more modern discussions and, second, the specifically theological problem of reconciling providence and predestination with free will. The second question has occupied Christian theologians of all centuries; it had been discussed before Pomponazzi by Lorenzo Valla in his treatise on free will, and it was to be debated by Martin Luther, Desiderius Erasmus, and many other theologians during and after the Reformation.

DE IMMORTALITATE ANIMAE

Pomponazzi's treatise *De Immortalitate Animae* is much better known, and it had far wider repercussions during the sixteenth century and even later. Pomponazzi explains the origin of the treatise as follows: He had stated in a class lecture that Thomas Aquinas's view on immortality, though perhaps true, did not agree with Aristotle's, and he was subsequently asked by a Dominican friar who was his student to express his own opinion on the question, staying strictly within the limits of natural reason. In complying with this request, Pomponazzi begins with the statement that man is of a manifold and ambiguous nature and occupies an intermediary position between mortal and immortal things (Ch. 1). The question is in what sense such opposite attributes as mortal and immortal may be attributed to the human soul (Ch. 2). Pomponazzi first lists six possible answers, and after having discarded two of them because they had never been defended by anybody, he promises to discuss the remaining four (Chs. 2–3).

The first of the four answers is the view attributed to Averroes and others, according to which there is only one immortal soul common to all human beings and also an individual soul for each person, which, however, is mortal. Pomponazzi rejects this opinion at great length (Ch. 4). The Averroist position maintains that the intellect is capable of acting without a body and can therefore be considered as separable and immortal. Yet in our experience, Pomponazzi argues, the intellect has no action that is entirely independent of the body, and therefore we have no evidence that the intellect is separable. If we wish to understand the relationship of the intellect and the body, we must distinguish between being in the body as having the body for its organ or subject or substratum and depending on the body as having the body, its perceptions, and imaginations for its object. Pomponazzi insists that the intellect does not have the body as its subject as do the souls of animals and the lower faculties of the human soul. Yet the human intellect cannot know anything without the perceptions or imaginations offered to it by the body, and this fact alone proves that the intellect is not separable from the body.

Second, Pomponazzi discusses an opinion he attributes to Plato, according to which each person has two souls, one immortal and the other mortal (Ch. 5). This position is rejected on the ground that the subject of perception and that of intellectual knowledge must be the same and that it is therefore impossible to distinguish two separate natures within the human soul (Ch. 6).

Third, he examines the view, attributed to Thomas Aquinas, which holds that the human soul has but a single nature and that it is absolutely (*simpliciter*) immortal and only in some respects (*secundum quid*) mortal (Ch. 7). Elaborating on some of the arguments he had already advanced against Averroes, Pomponazzi insists that he finds no evidence to prove the absolute immortality of the soul. He has no doubt, he adds, that the doctrine of the absolute immortality of the soul is true, since it is in accordance with Scripture, but he wonders whether it is in agreement with Aristotle and whether it can be estab-

lished within the limits of natural reason without recourse to the evidence of faith and revelation (Ch. 8).

Fourth, Pomponazzi discusses a position according to which the human soul, having only one nature, is absolutely mortal and only in certain respects immortal (Ch. 9). He then proceeds to defend this position, which he had identified elsewhere as that of Alexander of Aphrodisias. Insisting once more on the middle position of humankind, he argues that the human intellect, unlike that of the pure intelligences, always needs the body for its object and has no way of acting without the help of the images of sense or imagination. It must therefore be considered absolutely mortal and only relatively, or improperly speaking, immortal. However, unlike the souls of the animals, the human intellect does not have the body as its subject because it does not use a bodily organ in knowing. If it resided in an organ, the intellect could not reflect on itself or understand universals. The fact that the human intellect is capable of some knowledge of itself and of universals shows that it participates somewhat in immortality and, hence, that it is in some respect immortal. This interpretation of immortality is claimed to be more probable than the others and to be more in accordance with the teachings of Aristotle (Chs. 9–10).

Having reached this conclusion, Pomponazzi continues in good scholastic fashion to formulate several sets of objections to his view (Chs. 11 and 13) and to answer these objections in great detail (Chs. 12 and 14). In addition to repeating and elaborating some of the same arguments presented in the preceding chapters, he introduces, especially in Chapter 14, several new arguments and conclusions that are of great intrinsic interest.

Along with other objections to his view Pomponazzi cites (Ch. 13) the argument that, according to Aristotle's *Ethics*, the ultimate end of man is contemplation and that the satisfactory fulfillment of this end requires immortality. In his reply he states that man has a threefold intellect—speculative, practical, and technical. Only a few persons have a share in the speculative intellect, whereas the technical intellect is shared by some animals. We may thus conclude that the practical intellect, in which all human beings and only all human beings share, is the faculty peculiar to human beings. Every normal person can attain the practical intellect in a perfect way, and a person is called absolutely good or bad with reference to this practical intellect but merely in some respect good or bad with reference to the other two intellects. For a man is called a good man or a bad man with reference to his virtues and vices, yet a good metaphysician with reference to his speculative intellect and a good architect with reference to his technical intellect. However, a good metaphysician or a good architect is not always a good man. Hence, a man does not mind so much if he is not called a good metaphysician or a good architect, but he minds very much if he is called unjust or intemperate, for it seems to be in our power to be good or wicked, but to be a philosopher or an architect does not depend on us and is not necessary for a man. The ultimate end must thus be defined in terms of the practical intellect, and every man is called upon to be as virtuous as possible.

By contrast, it is neither necessary nor even desirable that all men should be philosophers or architects but only that some of them should be. Moreover, since the perfection of the practical intellect is accessible to almost everybody, a farmer or a craftsman, a poor man or a rich man, may be called happy and is actually called happy and is satisfied with his lot whenever he is virtuous. In other words, Pomponazzi departs in this important respect from Aristotle and identifies the end of human life with moral virtue rather than with contemplation, because this end is attainable by all human beings.

There had been another objection—that God would not be a good governor of all things unless all good deeds found their reward and all bad deeds their punishment in a future life. To this Pomponazzi replies that the essential reward of virtue is virtue itself, and the essential punishment of vice is vice itself. Hence, it makes no difference whether the external or accidental reward or punishment of an action is sometimes omitted, since its essential reward and punishment are always present. Moreover, if one man acts virtuously without the expectation of a reward and another with such an expectation, the act of the latter is not considered to be as virtuous as that of the former. Thus, he who receives no external reward is more fully rewarded in an essential way than he who receives one. In the same way the wicked person who receives no external punishment is punished more than he who does, for the punishment inherent in guilt itself is much worse than any punishment in the form of some harm inflicted upon the guilty person.

Pomponazzi further develops this idea in reply to another objection. It is true that religious teachers have supported the doctrine of immortality, but they have done so in order to induce ordinary people to lead virtuous lives. Yet persons of a higher moral disposition are attracted toward the virtues by the mere excellence of these virtues and are repelled from the vices by the mere ugliness of these vices; hence, they do not need the expectation of rewards or punishments as an incentive. Rejecting the view that without a belief in immortality no

moral standards could be maintained, Pomponazzi repeats that a virtuous action without the expectation of a reward is superior to one that aims at a reward and concludes that those who assert that the soul is mortal seem to preserve the notion of virtue much better than those who assert that it is immortal. In thus stating that moral standards, as defined by the philosopher, do not depend on religious sanctions, he does not deny the validity of religious beliefs but asserts the autonomy of reason and philosophy, drawing upon certain passages in Plato and above all on Stoic doctrine and anticipating to some extent the views of Benedict de Spinoza and Immanuel Kant.

Having presented all arguments against the immortality of the soul, Pomponazzi states in the last chapter that the question is a neutral one, as is that of the eternity of the world. That is, he does not believe there are any natural reasons strong enough to demonstrate the immortality of the soul or to refute its mortality, although he knows that many theologians, notably Thomas Aquinas, have argued otherwise. Since the question is thus doubtful on purely human grounds, it must be resolved by God himself, who clearly proved the immortality of the soul in the Holy Scriptures. This means that the arguments to the contrary must be false and merely apparent. The immortality of the soul is an article of faith, for it is based on faith and revelation. It must thus be asserted on this ground alone and not on the basis of inconclusive or unconvincing rational arguments.

This conclusion and a similar one found in the *De Fato* have given rise to a variety of interpretations on the part of Pomponazzi's contemporaries and of modern historians. The statement made by some that Pomponazzi simply denied the immortality of the soul is patently false. He merely said that the immortality of the soul cannot be demonstrated on purely natural grounds or in accordance with Aristotle but must be accepted as an article of faith. This position is widely and somewhat crudely referred to as the theory of the double truth. The term is inadequate, for neither Pomponazzi nor anybody else ever said that something is true in theology and its opposite true in philosophy. What Pomponazzi did say, and what many respectable thinkers before and after him said, is that one theory—for example, that of the immortality of the soul—is true according to faith but that it cannot be demonstrated on the basis of mere reason and that its opposite would seem to be supported by equally strong or even stronger probable arguments.

This view has been called absurd by many modern historians and, ironically, by some who actually take a similar position themselves, though perhaps on other issues and with different words. Yet the persistent charge made against Pomponazzi and against many other medieval and Renaissance thinkers who took a similar position has been that the so-called theory of the double truth is merely a hypocritical device to disguise their secret disbelief and to avoid trouble with the church authorities. Thus, in saying that immortality cannot be demonstrated and that mortality may be defended by strong rational arguments whereas immortality is to be held as an article of faith, Pomponazzi, according to these historians, merely concealed his opinion that the soul was really mortal and substituted for it a formula that would protect him against ecclesiastic censure or punishment.

This is a serious and delicate problem. We cannot deny that a thinker of the past may have entertained opinions that we do not find expressed in his writings or that he may have put into writing views which he did not hold in his innermost heart. On the other hand, unless we have some text or document in support of this assertion, we are not entitled to claim that a thinker held some specific views that he failed to express in his writings or that are even in contrast with his expressed views. As a theologian of the eighteenth century said on this matter, we must leave it to God to look into Pomponazzi's heart and to see what his real opinion was. The human historian has no basis other than the written document, and the burden of proof, in history as in law, rests with those who want to prove something that is contrary to the overt evidence. Neither innuendo nor the assertions made by unfriendly critics or extremist followers can be accepted as valid evidence in lieu of some original statement or testimony concerning the author's view.

According to this standard, we have no real grounds for maintaining that Pomponazzi was hypocritical. The position he takes in the treatise on the immortality of the soul is fundamentally retained in two lengthy works composed afterward in defense of the first and, with a few dubious exceptions, also in his questions and class lectures. He was attacked by some theologians but defended by others, and his treatise was not condemned by the church authorities. The general position that immortality could not be rationally demonstrated, if not all the specific opinions that Pomponazzi associated with it, was held also by John Duns Scotus and even by the leading Thomist of Pomponazzi's time, Cardinal Cajetan. After the first excitement had passed, Pomponazzi continued to teach at a university located in the papal states, had among his students many clergymen who apparently found nothing offensive in what he said, and died peacefully as a widely respected scholar. The pupil who took his remains to his hometown and erected a monument for him was Ercole Gonzaga, later a cardinal and president of the Council of Trent. If there is any presumptive evidence, it hardly favors the opinion that Pomponazzi was a secret disbeliever or atheist.

INFLUENCE

Pomponazzi's influence, although not easily traceable, was considerable. The school of Italian Aristotelianism to which he belonged flourished for a hundred years or more after his death, and within this tradition his name remained famous and his views on such questions as the immortality of the soul and the unity of the intellect continued to be cited and discussed, if not adopted. The posthumous publication of several of his writings later in the century also gives testimony to his continued fame. His lectures and questions were copied in a large number of manuscripts, an indication of his popularity among his students; moreover, a considerable number of manuscripts containing the *De Incantationibus* and the *De Fato* prove that these works circulated widely, although, or perhaps because, they were not published during the author's lifetime. A few anecdotes associated with his name that we find in biographies, short stories, and dialogues of the period suggest that he made some personal impression even on the larger public outside university circles. He obviously was read by students and writers who did not belong to the Aristotelian tradition, and we may cite as an example Giulio Cesare Vanini, who seems to have used him as one of his favorite sources.

During the seventeenth century the Aristotelian school that had dominated the teaching of philosophy for such a long time finally lost its hold, especially in the field of natural philosophy, which was gradually replaced by the new mathematical physics of Galileo Galilei and his successors. Aristotelianism persisted much longer in the fields of logic, biology, and metaphysics. Yet because physics was the center and stronghold of medieval and Renaissance Aristotelianism, especially in Italy, most of Pomponazzi's specific teachings lost their immediate validity when the Aristotelian system within which he had developed his ideas came to be abandoned. Nevertheless, we may say that his view of the relation between natural reason and faith was capable of being reformulated in terms of the new physics and that in certain instances this did happen.

Even more important is another development. The seventeenth century, and still more the eighteenth, witnessed the rise and diffusion of free thought and overt atheism, especially in France. Some of the freethinkers who set out to discard faith and established religion came to consider the Aristotelian rationalists such as Pomponazzi as their forerunners and allies. Pomponazzi's treatise on the immortality of the soul was praised by the free thinkers and condemned by Catholic apologists, although moderate thinkers like Pierre Bayle tried to preserve a proper perspective. Pomponazzi's treatise was even reprinted in a clandestine edition with a false early date.

The use to which the French Enlightenment put Pomponazzi and the other Italian Aristotelians has had a strong influence on modern historians of the school, beginning with Ernest Renan. Again, a distinction is needed. It is one thing to say that Pomponazzi and the Aristotelians held the same views as later freethinkers, and it is another to state that they represent an earlier stage in a development that was to produce the views held by the freethinkers. In the first sense Pomponazzi was a forerunner of the freethinkers; in the second sense the evidence says he was not. Hence, we should not praise or blame him, depending on our own preferences and values, for being a freethinker, since we lack the factual basis for judgment. Yet in a different sense we may praise him. He belongs to the long line of thinkers who have attempted to draw a clear line of distinction between reason and faith, philosophy and theology, and to establish the autonomy of reason and philosophy within their own domains.

See also Alexander of Aphrodisias; Aristotelianism; Aristotle; Averroes; Averroism; Bayle, Pierre; Cajetan, Cardinal; Cicero, Marcus Tullius; Duns Scotus, John; Erasmus, Desiderius; Ficino, Marsilio; Galileo Galilei; Humanism; Kant, Immanuel; Luther, Martin; Pico della Mirandola, Count Giovanni; Plato; Plutarch of Chaeronea; Reformation; Renan, Joseph Ernest; Spinoza, Benedict (Baruch) de; Stoicism; Thomas Aquinas, St.; Valla, Lorenzo.

Bibliography

WORKS BY POMPONAZZI

Pomponazzi's *De Immortalitate Animae* is available in several modern editions—edited by G. Gentile (Messina, 1925), by G. Morra (Bologna, 1954), and by W. H. Hay II in a facsimile of the original edition of 1516 (Haverford, PA, 1938). It is also included, along with the *Apologia*, the *Defensorium*, and several shorter treatises, in the collection titled *Tractatus Acutissimi* (Venice, 1525).

The *De Naturalium Effectuum Causis Sive de Incantationibus* was printed separately in Basel (1556) and with the *De Fato* in the *Opera* (Basel, 1567); the volume contains only these two works. There is also a French translation—*Les causes des merveilles de la nature*, translated by Henri Busson (Paris, 1930).

There is a modern critical edition of the *De Fato* edited by Richard Lemay (Lugano, 1957). Of the *De Immortalitate* there is an English translation by W. H. Hay II, first published with the facsimile edition of the text and then in a revised and annotated version in *The Renaissance Philosophy of Man*, edited by Ernst Cassirer, Paul Oskar Kristeller, and John H. Randall Jr. (Chicago: University of Chicago Press, 1948).

For the unpublished works of Pomponazzi see L. Ferri, "Intorno alle dottrine psicologiche di Pietro Pomponazzi …," in *Atti della Reale Accademia dei Lincei, Memorie della classe di scienze morali, storiche e filologiche*, Series 2, Vol. 3 (1875–1876), Part III, 333–548; C. Oliva, "Note sull'insegnamento di Pietro Pomponazzi," in *Giornale critico della filosofia italiana* 7 (1926): 83–103, 179–190, 254–275; Bruno Nardi, "Le opere inedite del Pomponazzi," in *Giornale critico della filosofia italiana*, 29–35 (1950–1956); and Paul Oskar Kristeller, "A New Manuscript Source for Pomponazzi's Theory of the Soul …," in *Revue internationale de philosophie* 2 (1951): 144–157, and "Two Unpublished Questions on the Soul of Pietro Pomponazzi," in *Medievalia et Humanistica* 9 (1955): 76–101, and 10 (1956): 151.

WORKS ON POMPONAZZI

For the general background see Ernest Renan, *Averroès et l'averroïsme* (Paris: Durand, 1852); Bruno Nardi, *Saggi sull'Aristotelismo Padovano dal secolo XIV al XVI* (Florence, 1958), and John H. Randall Jr., *The School of Padua and the Emergence of Modern Science* (Padua, 1961).

For Pomponazzi's doctrine see Francesco Fiorentino, *Pietro Pomponazzi* (Florence: Successori Le Monnier, 1868); Andrew H. Douglas, *The Philosophy and Psychology of Pietro Pomponazzi* (Cambridge, U.K.: Cambridge University Press, 1910); E. Weil, "Die Philosophie des Pietro Pomponazzi," in *Archiv für Geschichte der Philosophie* 41 (1932): 127–176; Ernst Cassirer, *Das Erkenntnisproblem in der Philosophie und Wissenschaft der neueren Zeit*, Vol. I (Berlin: Cassirer, 1922), 105–117; and Bruno Nardi, *Studi su Pietro Pomponazzi* (Florence, 1965). For the immortality controversy see Giovanni Di Napoli, *L'immortalità dell'anima nel Rinascimento* (Turin: Società editrice internazionale, 1963).

See also Martin Pine, "Pomponazzi and Double Truth," *Journal of the History of Ideas* (29 [1968]: 163–176; John L. Treloar, John L., "Pomponazzi: Moral Virtue in a Deterministic Universe," *Midwest Studies in Philosophy* (26 [2002]: 44–55; John L. Treloar, "Pomponazzi's Critique of Aquinas' Arguments for the Immortality of the Soul," *Thomist* (54 [3] [1990]: 453–470; Margaret M. Van De Pitte, Margaret M., "Pietro Pomponazzi and the Debate Over Immortality," in *Philosophy and Culture, Vol. 3*, edited by Venant Cauchy (Montreal: Montmorency, 1988).

Paul Oskar Kristeller (1967)
Bibliography updated by Tamra Frei (2005)

POPE, ALEXANDER
(1688–1744)

Alexander Pope, England's leading poet of the Age of Reason, was born in London, the son of a prosperous Roman Catholic linen draper. His Catholicism barred him from public school and university; and he was educated by private tutors and by extensive reading and study on his own, largely at Binfield in Windsor Forest, where his father had retired. About the age of twelve, a severe illness stunted Pope's growth and deformed his spine, and for the rest of his life he was infirm. His devotion to poetry came early, and his genius was immediately recognized by William Wycherley and William Walsh. Early publications of note include the *Pastorals* (1709), *An Essay on Criticism* (1711), *The Rape of the Lock* (1712, enlarged 1714), and *Windsor Forest* (1714). During frequent visits to London, he became the friend of many prominent literary figures: Jonathan Swift, Joseph Addison, Richard Steele, John Arbuthnot, John Gay, and Lord Bolingbroke. Although not an ardent party man, Pope inclined more to the Tory than to the Whig. In 1718, after the death of his father, he removed to Twickenham, on the Thames near London. Pope's translations of the *Iliad* (1715–1720) and the *Odyssey* (1725–1726) were well received and financially successful. The edition of William Shakespeare appeared in 1725.

Author of the *Essay on Man* (1733–1734), *Moral Essays* (1731–1735), and *Imitations of Horace* (1733–1737), and of the *Dunciad* (1728–1743) and various other satires, Pope was a philosopher-moralist-poet. He was generally so regarded throughout the eighteenth century, both at home and abroad. There is little of the original in Pope's thought, nor did he pretend to any, the very notion of originality being distasteful to the rationalistic mind. In the *Essay on Criticism*, he stated that his aim was to present "What oft was thought, but ne'er so well expressed." His writing in general admirably fulfills this precept, and his memorable formulations of traditional and familiar ideas bear the stamp of literary genius.

Despite frequent allegations to the contrary, Pope was not a deist. Indeed, in the *Dunciad* he specifically attacks Anthony Collins, Bernard Mandeville, Thomas Morgan, Matthew Tindal, John Toland, and Thomas Woolston, the leading deists of the day. He eschewed the role of Christian (Catholic) poet, however, preferring to represent what he considered the best in Western thought, both pagan and Christian. His universality is best seen in the *Essay on Man*, where in Epistle I a rationalistic metaphysics is presented, centering on the "Great Chain of Being," a concept as old as Plato's *Timaeus* that was a part of the heritage of Western man and was influential until well into the eighteenth century. The rationalistic myth of a "chain of being" extending from the Godhead at the one extreme to the lowliest atom at the other, with man as the middle link between the pure reason of angelic spirits and the pure instinct of lower animals, is presented by Pope as a means of chastising presumptuous man for attempting to be too rational, for attempting to deny the earthbound aspect of his nature. Such generic "pride" on the part of man would necessarily push him into a higher link and thus destroy the entire chain. The moral is clear: "The bliss of Man (could Pride that blessing find)/Is not to act or think beyond mankind." Man must submit to his ordained place in the universe because "Whatever is, is Right."

Pope has been frequently ridiculed for ending Epistle I on this seeming note of "easy optimism," as it has been erroneously labeled. A moment's recollection, however, of the fact that Pope devoted much of his career to satirizing contemporary mores and morality will make it evident that his "optimism" was not ordinary or glandular optimism but strictly metaphysical optimism, which is not necessarily of any comfort to humankind. Granted the "chain of being" as ordained by Deity, that plan and that chain must be right, even though, according to the "principle of plenitude," evil is just as necessary as good. Thus, apart from the totality of cosmic rightness, many circumstances of life may not be good for man himself. Small comfort, therefore, to man to be assured that what seems evil to him personally is actually good from the cosmological point of view: God, but not man, can afford to be optimistic. In fact, the theme of the entire *Essay* is the problem of reconciling the contrary, apparently irreconcilable elements of man's nature with the infinite wisdom of a God of order and harmony. Thus it is that in the opening lines of Epistle II, Pope makes an effort to dismiss the prior metaphysical optimism with the homely precept: "Know then thyself, presume not God to scan;/The proper study of Mankind is Man." The remainder of the *Essay* is concerned with the world of real existence, insofar as this is possible given the background of rationalistic formalism. Epistle II treats of man as an individual; Epistle III treats of man and society; and Epistle IV treats of man and happiness. Here there is little "easy optimism."

Pope teaches that self-love is superior to reason and that the passions are requisite for action. The "dominant passion" (which varies from man to man) rules life in different ways, and virtue and vice are joined in man's mixed

ENCYCLOPEDIA OF PHILOSOPHY
2nd edition

nature. In the second epistle reason is "The God within the mind" that distinguishes between virtue and vice, to which in the third epistle are added instinct and social love. The fourth epistle, after much deliberation, declares that only in virtue is happiness to be found. Pope then ends the *Essay* with the affirmation that he has

> Shew'd erring Pride, *Whatever is, is Right*;
> That *Reason, Passion*, answer one great aim;
> That true *Self-Love* and *Social* are the same;
> That *Virtue* only makes our Bliss below;
> And all our Knowledge is, *Ourselves to Know*.

The major sources of Pope's philosophy have been much disputed, with Gottfried Wilhelm Leibniz, the earl of Shaftesbury, Bolingbroke, and William King the most frequently mentioned modern authors. There is no direct evidence that Pope knew Leibniz, and he specifically denied any influence by him. Pope had certainly read parts of Shaftesbury's *Characteristics* and undoubtedly acquired something from the reading. The case for Bolingbroke's *Fragments or Minutes of Essays* was widely accepted until recent investigations adduced evidence that the *Fragments* were composed later than Pope's *Essay;* what Pope may have received from Bolingbroke in the course of conversation, however, remains unknown. Archbishop King's *De Origine Mali* (1702), probably in Edmund Law's translation of 1731, contains much of the metaphysical thinking of the first epistle of the *Essay on Man;* and there is little doubt that Pope found much useful information and many references in Law's elaborate notes. Gleanings from the ancient Platonists, Neoplatonists, and Stoics are to be assumed, as are, of course, some from the Christian tradition.

The *Essay on Man* first appeared anonymously, and Pope did not claim it until 1735. On the Continent it was translated (poorly) into French prose in 1736 and the following year into French verse (even more poorly). It ran through several editions with considerable praise until attacked in 1737 by J. P. de Crousaz in his *Examen de l'essai de M. Pope sur l'homme*. The Swiss theologian, ignorant of English, deliberately used the poem as a means of assailing the Spinozistic and the Leibnizian philosophies, of which Pope was innocent. The attack was taken up by several English pamphleteers until William Warburton (later bishop of Gloucester and editor of Pope's *Works*), that colossus of controversy, came to the defense with a series of articles in the *History of the Works of the Learned*, published as a book in 1739 and revised in 1742. Warburton vindicated Pope against allegations of unorthodoxy, including that of deism.

Another Continental attack came in 1742 from Louis Racine in a poem titled *La religion*. In 1755 Gotthold Lessing and Moses Mendelssohn, in *Pope ein Metaphysiker!*, ridiculed both the Prussian Royal Academy for using a poet as the subject of a prize essay in philosophy and Pope for attempting to be a metaphysician in poetry. To Immanuel Kant, on the contrary, Pope was a favorite poet from whom he quoted frequently and whose thought he took seriously. Arthur O. Lovejoy has ventured the statement that "it would be hardly excessive to say that much of Kant's cosmology is a prose amplification and extension of the 'philosophy' of the First Epistle of the *Essay on Man*." Scorned or admired, at any rate, Pope's venture into verse philosophy was exceedingly popular, as is indicated by its translation into at least fifteen European languages and by scores of editions in English during the eighteenth century. And his century was the last that would have approved of such a venture.

Pope's original plan as poetical philosopher and moralist was ambitious, although somewhat vague. His magnum opus, to be titled "Ethic Epistles," was to consist of four books: the *Essay on Man*, as we now have it in four epistles; four more epistles dealing with "the extent and limits of human Reason," arts and sciences both "useful" and "unuseful," "the different Capacities of Men," and the "Use of Learning," science and wit; the "Science of Politics," to treat "of Civil and Religious Society in their full extent"; and "Private Ethics or Practical Morality." The plan—but not the philosophy—is curiously reminiscent of that of David Hume as stated in the "Advertisement" to the *Treatise of Human Nature* (1739). (Incidentally, Hume probably took from Pope such terms as "the science of man," "the science of human nature," "the soul's calm sunshine," and "the Feast of Reason.") In 1741 Hume was to devote an entire essay, "That Politics may be reduced to a Science," to the refutation of Pope's lines (*Essay on Man*, III, 303–304): "For Forms of Government let fools contest;/Whate'er is best administer'd is best."

The *Essay on Man* was the only part of the magnum opus completed as planned. However, the *Epistles to Several Persons*, commonly known as the *Moral Essays*, constitute part of the original design and would have been portions of the fourth book, "Private Ethics or Practical Morality." These four epistles or essays are "To Cobham" ("Of the Knowledge and Character of Men"); "To a Lady" ("Of the Characters of Women"); "To Bathurst" ("Of the Use of Riches"); and "To Burlington" (also "Of the Use of Riches"). Pope was always the philosopher-moralist-poet whose description of his own career (*Epistle to Dr. Arbuthnot*, ll. 340–341) is essentially accurate: "not in

Fancy's Maze he wander'd long,/But stoop'd to Truth, and moraliz'd his song."

See also Addison, Joseph; Bolingbroke, Henry St. John; Collins, Anthony; Deism; Gay, John; Hume, David; Kant, Immanuel; Leibniz, Gottfried Wilhelm; Lessing, Gotthold Ephraim; Lovejoy, Arthur Oncken; Mandeville, Bernard; Mendelssohn, Moses; Morgan, Thomas; Neoplatonism; Plato; Platonism and the Platonic Tradition; Shaftesbury, Third Earl of (Anthony Ashley Cooper); Stoicism; Swift, Jonathan; Tindal, Matthew; Toland, John; Woolston, Thomas.

Bibliography

Primary sources include *The Twickenham Edition of the Poems of Alexander Pope*, John Butt, general editor, 6 vols. in 7 (London, 1939–1961); and *Pope: The Correspondence*, edited by George Sherburn, 5 vols. (Oxford, 1956).

Secondary sources include Arthur Friedman, "Pope and Deism," in *Pope and His Contemporaries: Essays Presented to George Sherburn*, edited by J. L. Clifford and Louis A. Landa (Oxford: Clarendon Press, 1949); Arthur O. Lovejoy, *The Great Chain of Being* (Cambridge, MA: Harvard University Press, 1936); Geoffrey Tillotson, *The Moral Poetry of Pope* (Newcastle upon Tyne, U.K.: Literary and Philosophical Society of Newcastle upon Tyne, 1946), *On the Poetry of Pope*, 2nd ed. (Oxford, 1950), and *Pope and Human Nature* (Oxford: Clarendon Press, 1958); Jonathan Barnes, "Partial Wholes," *Social Philosophy and Policy* (8 [1] [1990]: 1–23; David J. Leigh, "Alexander Pope and Eighteenth Century Conflicts about Ultimacy," *Ultimate Reality and Meaning* (20 [1] [1997] 23–40.

Ernest Campbell Mossner (1967)
Bibliography updated by Tamra Frei (2005)

POPPER, KARL RAIMUND
(1902–1994)

Karl Raimund Popper, the Austrian philosopher of natural and social science, was born in Vienna and was a student of mathematics, physics, and philosophy at the university there. Although he was not a member of the Vienna circle of logical positivists and was in sharp disagreement with many of its doctrines, he shared most of the group's philosophical interests and was in close touch with several of its members, having a considerable influence on Rudolf Carnap. His first book, *Logik der Forschung*, was published in 1935 in the circle's series Schriften zur wissenschaftlichen Weltauffassung. In 1937 Popper went as senior lecturer to Canterbury University College in Christchurch, New Zealand, and remained there until his move in 1945 to a readership at the London School of Economics in the University of London. From 1949 to 1969 he was professor of logic and scientific method at the London School of Economics, and then became professor emeritus. He was knighted in 1964.

REJECTION OF VERIFIABILITY THEORY

The foundation of Popper's wide-ranging but closely integrated philosophical reflections is the bold and original form he first gave in 1933 to the problem of demarcating science from pseudo science in general and from metaphysics in particular. The logical positivists had taken this problem to be one of distinguishing meaningful from meaningless discourse and had proposed to solve it by making empirical verifiability the necessary condition of a sentence's meaningfulness or scientific status—in their eyes one and the same thing. Popper dissented both from their formulation of the problem and from their solution. His view had always been that the important task is to distinguish empirical science from other bodies of assertions that might be confused with it: metaphysics, such traditional pseudo sciences as astrology and phrenology, and the more imposing pseudo sciences of the present age, such as the Marxist theory of history and Freudian psychoanalysis. To identify this distinction with that between sense and nonsense is, he held, to make an arbitrary verbal stipulation. It is also an unreasonable stipulation because the line between science and pseudo science is neither precise nor impermeable. Pseudo science, or "myth," as he sometimes called it, can both inspire and develop into science proper: Indeed, the general progress of human knowledge can be considered as a conversion of myth into science by its subjection to critical examination.

FALSIFIABILITY CRITERION

A crucial difficulty for the verifiability theory of meaning was David Hume's thesis that inductive generalization was logically invalid. Being unrestrictedly general, scientific theories cannot be verified by any possible accumulation of observational evidence. Moritz Schlick sought to interpret scientific theories as rules for the derivation of predictive statements from observational ones and not as statements themselves at all, but this attempt came to grief on the fact that theories can be empirically falsified by negative instances. This logical asymmetry in the relation of general statements to observations underlies Popper's view that falsifiability by observation is the criterion of the empirical and scientific character of a theory. He maintained, first, that scientific theories are not, in fact, arrived at by any sort of inductive process. The formation of a hypothesis is a creative exercise of the imagination; it is not a passive reaction to observed regularities. There is no such thing as pure observation, for observation is always selective and takes place under the guidance of some anticipatory theory. Second, even if induction were the way in which hypotheses were arrived at, it would still be wholly incapable of justifying them. As Hume showed, no collection of particular observations will verify a general statement; nor, Popper added, is such a statement partially justified or rendered probable by particular confirming instances, since many theories that are known to be false have an indefinitely large number of confirming instances.

For Popper the growth of knowledge begins with the imaginative proposal of hypotheses, a matter of individual and unpredictable insight that cannot be reduced to rule. Such a hypothesis is science rather than myth if it excludes some observable possibilities. To test a hypothesis, we apply ordinary deductive logic in order to derive singular observation statements whose falsehood would refute it. A serious and scientific test consists in a persevering search for negative, falsifying instances. Some hypotheses are more falsifiable than others; they exclude more and thus have a greater chance of being refuted. "All heavenly bodies move in ellipses" is more falsifiable than "All planets move in ellipses," since everything that refutes the second statement refutes the first but much that refutes the first does not refute the second. The more falsifiable a hypothesis, therefore, the less probable it is, and by excluding more, it says more about the world, has more empirical content. Popper goes on to show that the obscure but important concept of simplicity comes to the same thing as falsifiability and empirical content. The proper method of science is to formulate the most falsifiable hypotheses and, consequently, those that are simplest, have the greatest empirical content, and are logically the least probable. The next step is to search energetically for negative instances, to see if any of the potential falsifiers are actually true.

CORROBORATION

If a hypothesis survives continuing and serious attempts to falsify it, then it has "proved its mettle" and can be provisionally accepted. But it can never be established conclusively. The survival of attempted refutations corroborates a theory; the corroboration being greater to the degree that the theory is falsifiable. Popper's critics have fastened on this theory of corroboration as the point at which the inductive procedure he ostensibly rejects

makes an implicit reappearance. Is there any real difference, they ask, between the view that a theory depends for justification on the occurrence of confirming instances and the view that it depends on the failure of falsifying ones to occur?

Furthermore, his critics claim, there is apparently an inductive inference embedded in Popper's doctrine—the inference from the fact that a theory has thus far escaped refutation to the conclusion that it will continue to do so. Popper could reasonably reply that the formal likeness between confirming and falsifying instances conceals an important difference in approach—that between those who glory in confirmations and those who ardently pursue falsifications. However, a certain disquiet about the inductivist flavor of the positive support that his theory allows a hypothesis to derive from the failure of attempted refutations is expressed in Popper's leanings toward a rather skeptical view of the status of unrefuted hypotheses: "Science is not a system of certain, or well-established, statements.... Our science is not knowledge (epistēmē): it can never claim to have attained truth, or even a substitute for it, such as probability.... *We do not know: we can only guess.*" (*The Logic of Scientific Discovery,* Ch. 10, Sec. 85, p. 278).

EMPIRICAL BASIS

To complete his account of the growth of scientific knowledge, Popper had to explain the empirical basis of the falsificatory operation, that is, he had to make clear the formal character of the observation statements that are logically deduced from theories. It follows from the falsifiability criterion that unrestricted existential statements of the form "There is (somewhere at some time) an *X*" are unempirical because however many spatiotemporal positions have been examined for the presence of an *X*, an infinity of further positions remains to be examined. This is not true, however, of circumscribed existential statements reporting the existence of something at a specified place and time. Popper takes the basic observation statements to be of this form, to refer to publicly observable material objects, and to be capable of being straightforwardly affirmed or denied as true or false. Such basic statements are motivated by perceptual experiences, but they do not, as they are held to in the usual empiricist tradition, describe them. They can themselves be empirically tested in the light of the further basic statements that follow from them, together with accepted scientific theories. The infinite regress that this conception involves is not a vicious one: It can be halted by a conventional assignment of truth to basic statements at any point. But this convention is not dogmatic, since it is only provisional; if the basic statements in question are challenged, they can always be exposed to empirical tests.

EPISTEMOLOGY

In his later writings Popper drew many further inferences from his initial body of ideas. One is that knowledge has no foundations or infallible sources, either in reason or the senses. He sees the rationalist and empiricist epistemologies of the modern age as united in a determination to replace one sort of authority—a sacred text or an institution—with another—a human mental capacity. Both kinds of intellectual authoritarianism hold the mistaken opinion that truth is manifest and consequently that error is a sin and its propagation the outcome of some kind of conspiracy to deceive. There is no more comprehensive critique of the quest for certainty in the work of any other modern philosopher.

A second conclusion Popper drew is that the traditional empiricist account of concept formation—essentially Hume's idea that concepts are acquired by perceiving the similarity of sets of particular impressions—is mistaken because it embodies the same inductivist error as Francis Bacon's and J. S. Mill's accounts of scientific knowledge. Resemblance is not passively stumbled upon; rather, we classify things together in the light of antecedent preconceptions and expectations. Popper rejects innate ideas strictly so called but believes that we approach the world of experience with innate propensities—in particular, with a general expectation of regularity that is biologically explicable even if not logically justifiable. The influence of Immanuel Kant is especially evident in this side of Popper's thought. In a sense the proposition that nature contains regularities is for him synthetic a priori: It is neither a logical truth nor an empirical truth (since it is unfalsifiable), but it has a kind of psychological necessity as a general feature of the active human intellect.

THEORETICAL ENTITIES

Popper's dissent from the usual empiricist and positivist view that private, experiential propositions constitute the empirical foundation of knowledge and his insistence on the provisional and incompletable nature of scientific theorizing together determine his attitude to the subject matter or ontological significance of scientific theory. He rejects the essentialism of the rationalist philosophy of science, which conceives the goal of inquiry to be a complete and final knowledge of the essences of things, on the grounds that no scientific theory can be completely justi-

fied and that the acceptance of a new theory creates as many problems as it solves. He is equally opposed to the instrumentalist or conventionalist doctrine of those who, like Ernst Mach, Henri Poincaré, and Pierre Duhem, take the theoretical entities of science to be logical constructions, mere symbolic conveniences to assist us in the prediction of experience. The entities of scientific theory (such as molecules and genes) are not distinguishable in nature from the medium-sized public observables (such as chairs and trees) referred to in basic statements: Both are possible objects of genuine knowledge.

PROBABILITY

A difficulty arises for Popper's falsifiability criterion from the presence in normal scientific discourse of statements about probability in the sense of frequency. No finite sequence of A's of which none are B decisively refutes the proposition that most A's are B. In his first book Popper put forward a modified version of Richard von Mises's view that the probability of the occurrence of a property in an unrestrictedly open class is the limit of the frequencies of its occurrence in finite segments of the open sequence, a version that made probability statements accessible to decisive empirical refutation. Since then he had argued that probability statements, although they may rest on statistical evidence, should not themselves be interpreted statistically but rather as ascribing objective propensities to natural objects.

DETERMINISM AND VALUE

Popper's conviction that the mind is essentially active in the acquisition of knowledge and that its progress in discovery cannot be subsumed under a law and made the subject of prediction led him far beyond the philosophy of natural science, with which his central doctrines were concerned. Scientific knowledge is a free creation; it follows that the mind is not a causal mechanism. He contended that no causal model of the most elementary acts of the mind in empirical recognition and description can be constructed, since such a model would leave out the intention to name that is essential to any real act of description. Although the pursuit of knowledge is guided by an innate propensity to expect deterministic regularity in the world, the existence of knowledge as developed by a series of unanticipatable novelties is the strongest reason for rejecting general, metaphysical determinism.

Popper's theory of mind and knowledge also has ethical implications. Judgments of value are not empirical statements but decisions or proposals. Our valuations are not determined by our natural preferences but are the outcome of autonomous acts of mind—a further link with Kant. Popper's own basic moral proposal was, however, not very Kantian. Popper was a negative utilitarian for whom the primary moral imperative is "diminish suffering."

HISTORY AND SOCIETY

In *The Open Society and Its Enemies* (1945) and in *The Poverty of Historicism* (1957), Popper applies his theory of knowledge to humankind and society in the form of an attack on historicism, the doctrine that there are general laws of historical development that render the course of history inevitable and predictable. In *The Open Society* historicism is examined in three influential versions, those of Plato, G. W. F. Hegel, and Karl Marx. In *The Poverty of Historicism*, historicism is formally refuted and attributed to two oppositely mistaken views about the nature of social science. The formal objection is that since the growth of knowledge exercises a powerful influence on the course of history and itself depends on the anomalous initiatives of original scientific genius, neither the growth of knowledge nor its general historical effects can be predicted. Some historicists have been motivated by the mistaken idea that a science of society would have a general evolutionary law as its goal. This is a naturalistic error. The evolutionary process is not a lawlike regularity at all; rather, it is a loosely characterized trend whose phases exemplify the laws of genetics, for example. The historicists who have made this error are right in believing that scientific method applies to society, but they have a false idea of what scientific method is. However, among historicists there are antinaturalists who hold that ordinary scientific method does not apply to society, for which laws of a special historicist form must be found. Popper asserts that scientific method applies both to nature and to society, and in the same way—to particular isolable aspects of the whole. Social science can discover laws that make clear the unintended consequences of human action, but there can be no laws of the whole system. It follows that social reform must proceed by piecemeal social engineering, not by total revolutionary reconstructions of the social order. Popper presents the central problem of politics in a characteristically falsificationist way: The question "Who should rule?," he says, should be replaced by the question "How can institutions be devised that will minimize the risks of bad rulers?"

PHILOSOPHY AND KNOWLEDGE

Popper did not believe, as do most analytic philosophers, that philosophy is sharply distinguishable from science,

either in its methods—which, like science's, must be those of trial and error, conjecture and attempted refutation—or in its subject matter—which is not only language but also the world to which language refers. Furthermore, there is no uniquely correct philosophical method. Both the examination of actual language and the construction of ideal languages can contribute to the philosophical understanding of particular problems, but they are not universal keys to truth. Popper believed that if philosophy is to be of any general importance, it must stand in a close relation to the work of other disciplines. When it is isolated, as a special autonomous craft, from the general pursuit of knowledge, it degenerates into scholasticism and triviality.

See also Basic Statements; Carnap, Rudolf; Confirmation Theory; Conventionalism; Determinism in History; Duhem, Pierre Maurice Marie; Hegel, Georg Wilhelm Friedrich; Historicism; Hume, David; Induction; Kant, Immanuel; Laws, Scientific; Logic, History of: Modern Logic; Logical Positivism; Mach, Ernst; Marx, Karl; Philosophy of Science, History of; Plato; Poincaré, Jules Henri; Political Philosophy, History of; Probability and Chance; Progress, The Idea of; Schlick, Moritz; Scientific Method; Verifiability Principle.

Bibliography

WORKS BY POPPER

Books

Logik der Forschung. Berlin: Springer, 1935. Translated by Popper, with the assistance of Julius Freed and Lan Freed, as *The Logic of Scientific Discovery.* New York: Basic, 1959.

The Open Society and Its Enemies. 2 vols. London: Routledge, 1945; 4th, rev. ed., with addenda, London, 1961.

The Poverty of Historicism. London: Routledge, 1957; 2nd ed., with some corrections, 1961.

Conjectures and Refutations; The Growth of Scientific Knowledge. London: Routledge, 1963. Collected essays.

Essays

"Logic without Assumptions." *PAS*, n.s., 47 (1946–1947): 251–292.

"New Foundations for Logic." *Mind*, n.s., 56 (1947): 193–235; corrections and additions, n.s., 57 (1948): 69–70.

"Indeterminism in Quantum Physics and in Classical Physics," I and II. *British Journal for the Philosophy of Science* l (1950–1951): 117–133; 173–195.

"On the Theory of Deduction." Proceedings of the *Koninklijke Nederlandse Akademie van Wetenschappen* 51 (1 and 2) (1948).

"Probability, Magic or Knowledge out of Ignorance?" *Dialectica* 2 (1957): 354–374.

"The Propensity Interpretation of Probability." *British Journal for the Philosophy of Science* 10 (1959): 25–42.

WORKS ON POPPER

Bunge, Mario, ed. *The Critical Approach to Science and Philosophy.* Glencoe, IL: Free Press, 1964. Contains 29 articles largely concerned with the whole range of Popper's views. Includes a bibliography of Popper's publications, complete up to the beginning of 1964.

Kaufmann, Walter. *From Shakespeare to Existentialism.* New York, 1959. Chapter 7, "The Hegel Myth and Its Method," is a sympathetic but powerful criticism of Popper's account of Hegel in *The Open Society.*

Levinson, Ronald B. *In Defense of Plato.* Cambridge, MA, 1953. This substantial critique of Plato's modern opponents gives Popper pride of place.

Neurath, Otto. "Pseudorationalismus der Falsifikation." *Erkenntnis* 5 (1935): 290–294.

Reichenbach, Hans. "Über Induktion und Wahrscheinlichkeit. Bemerkungen zu Karl Poppers *Logik der Forschung.*" *Erkenntnis* 5 (1935).

Schilpp, P. A., ed. *The Philosophy of Karl Popper.* 2 vols. La Salle, IL: Open Court, 1974.

Warnock, G. J. Review of *The Logic of Scientific Discovery. Mind,* n.s., 69 (1960): 99–101.

Anthony Quinton (1967)

POPPER-LYNKEUS, JOSEF
(1838–1921)

Josef Popper-Lynkeus was an Austrian inventor, social reformer, and philosopher. Now almost completely forgotten, Popper enjoyed great fame in the early years of the twentieth century and on several topics his writings are far from dated.

LIFE AND WORKS

Popper grew up in the ghetto of the small Bohemian town of Kolin. At the age of sixteen he began his studies in mathematics and physics at the German Polytechnikum in Prague. Four years later he moved to Vienna, where he attended lectures first at the Imperial Polytechnikum and later at the University of Vienna. In spite of his acknowledged brilliance, Popper was not able to secure a teaching position, partly because he was Jewish and partly because of his radical opinions on religious and social questions. For some time he had a minor clerical job with the National Railways in southern Hungary. Returning to Vienna, he earned his living as a private tutor and as the owner of a scientific-technical literary agency. He attended scientific conferences and lectures, taking notes in longhand. These he wrote up, making ten to twelve carbon copies which he sold to the city's newspapers. In his autobiography, Popper recalls that during those years his income barely equaled that of the lowest-paid unskilled laborer. Popper's extreme poverty came to an end at the age of thirty with his invention of the so-called *Kesseleinlagen*—a device that significantly improved the working capacity of engine boilers. Although this, as well as several other of Popper's inventions, became generally used, he did not acquire wealth and it was not until he was almost sixty that he could retire from active participation in the production and selling of his various appliances in order to devote himself to literary pursuits.

During the last twenty years of his life, when Popper's books on social and philosophical questions had a very wide circulation, he became the center of what amounted almost to a cult. Popper's books give the impression of a man of transparent honesty and uncompromising hostility to every kind of humbug, especially of the kind that infested German public life in the late nineteenth and early twentieth centuries, but they do not, according to those who knew him, convey an adequate idea of his character and personal impact. His friends and admirers included Ernst Mach, Wilhelm Ostwald, Albert Einstein, Sigmund Freud, Arthur Schnitzler, Hermann Bahr, Stefan Zweig, Philipp Frank, and Richard von Mises. Mach referred to him as a "genius of freethinking"; Einstein, who visited Popper when a young man, spoke of him as a "saintly and prophetic person"; and all who met Popper were impressed by his deep serenity, warmth, and unusual and genuine kindness.

Popper was not a scientist of the first rank, but several of his publications dealing with problems in physics are favorably mentioned in standard histories of the subject. He was the first person to suggest the possibility of transmitting electric power, he was a pioneer in aerodynamics, and he was one of the first to see the full implications of the work of Robert Mayer. Popper's treatise "Über die Quelle und den Betrag der durch Luftballons geleisteten Arbeit" (On the sources and the amount of the work done by balloons; *Sitzungsberichte der Kaiserlichen Akademie der Wissenschaften,* 1875) led to correspondence with Robert Mayer, who requested Popper to review the second edition of his *Die Mechanik der Wärme* (*Mechanics of Heat,* 1874). Popper's article, published under the title "Über J. R. Mayer's Mechanik der Wärme" in the periodical *Das Ausland* (1876), did not confine itself to a discussion of Mayer's conservation principle but also contained a statement of a phenomenalistic philosophy of physics. In its "sharpness and fresh originality," according to Philipp Frank, "it equals the best that is found in Mach's works." In this essay there are also some remarkably perceptive criticisms of the common view that the law of entropy implies the "heat-death" of the universe. In his later work, *Physikalische Grundsätze der elektrischen Kraftübertragung* (Physical principles of the transmission of electricity; Vienna, 1884), Popper emphasized the analogies between different forms of energy and suggested that every type of energy be regarded as a product of two factors, one of which can be regarded as a kind of quantity and the other as a "difference of level." This idea was subsequently employed in the "energetics" of Georg Ferdinand Helm and Ostwald, both of whom made due acknowledgment to Popper.

Popper's first work dealing with religious and social questions was published in Leipzig on May 30, 1878, the hundredth anniversary of Voltaire's death. It was titled *Das Recht zu Leben und die Pflicht zu Sterben, sozialphilosophische Betrachtungen, anknüpfend an die Bedeutung Voltaires für die neuere Zeit* (The right to live and the duty to die, social-philosophical reflections in connection with Voltaire's significance for our times). This work contains most of the ideas that Popper was to develop in later writings—a defense of the value of the individual in opposition to the national policies of all existing states, proposals for various social welfare measures totally at variance with the prevailing laissez-faire philosophy, recommendations for drastic reforms of the criminal law and judicial procedures, and reflections about the baleful influence of religion and metaphysics, accompanied by suggested methods for their elimination from the human scene. Both here and in a later more detailed study, *Voltaire, eine Charakteranalyse* (Voltaire—a character analysis; Vienna, 1905), Popper went out of his way to rebut the charges of German nationalists and romantics about Voltaire's disruptive (*zersetzende*) influence on morals and society, praising Voltaire for his great honesty, humanity, and courage, which, in Popper's opinion, were not matched by any of his German detractors.

In 1899 Popper published, under the pseudonym of Lynkeus (Lynkeus was the helmsman of the Argonauts, famous for his keen sight), a two-volume book titled *Phantasien eines Realisten* (Fantasies of a realist), which consisted of eighty sketches in the form of short stories or dialogues, most of them centering on some controversial philosophical or social topic. One story, "Gährende Kraft eines Geheimnisses" (The fermenting power of a secret), is set in fifteenth-century Florence and deals with the incestuous relations between a mother and her adolescent son, both of whom were burned at the stake. The *Phantasien* was banned in Vienna, and clerical members of the Austrian parliament demanded a criminal prosecution of the author. Since the book was published in Dresden and the German authorities took no action, it remained in circulation and went into no fewer than twenty-one editions. Philosophically of more interest than "Gährende Kraft eines Geheimnisses" are various sketches illustrating the influence of religion on human life, including an imaginary conversation between David Hume, Denis Diderot, Baron d'Holbach, and other outstanding figures of the French Enlightenment. One of the stories, "Träumen wie Wachen" (Dreaming like waking), independently arrived at several of the key doctrines of Freud's theory about dreams. Like Freud, Popper insisted that there is a continuity between waking thought and dream content and that dreams cannot be dismissed as "nonsense." Freud did not read Popper's story until after the first edition of *The Interpretation of Dreams* had been published, but later he repeatedly complimented Popper on his insights.

Of Popper's other books, three deserve special mention. *Über Religion* (Vienna, 1924), which was written in 1905 but could not be published before the overthrow of the monarchy with its clerical censorship, contains the fullest statement of Popper's criticism of religion and metaphysics. *Das Individuum und die Bewertung menschlicher Existenzen* (The individual and the evaluation of human lives; Dresden, 1910) is the most complete statement of Popper's individualistic ethics and his objections to the many theorists from G. W. F. Hegel to Friedrich Nietzsche whose writings bristle with contempt for the common man.

Popper himself regarded *Die allgemeine Nährpflicht* (Vienna, 1912) as his most important work. It develops in detail the system which, in Popper's words, should replace "our dreadful economic conditions" by such as are "good and moral." Society, according to Popper, has the duty to secure every individual against want, irrespective of his talents and qualifications. He classifies goods and services into "necessities" and "luxuries," the former including food, clothing, shelter, medical attention, and basic education. To ensure for every human being a "guaranteed subsistence-minimum," Popper proposes a term of labor service in the *Nährarmee* (Nourishment army). Utilizing an elaborate analysis of agricultural and industrial conditions in Germany at the beginning of the century, he calculates that twelve years of service by men and seven by women, working a thirty-five-hour week, would be sufficient for this purpose. There is to be a double economy: The provision of necessities is to be regulated by the state, while private enterprise is to handle the production and distribution of luxuries. After a person has completed his term of service, he is free to work in any occupation he chooses, or not to work at all. In the latter event, he is still fully entitled to receive all "necessities." As technology advances, the period of service in the Nourishment Army will become progressively shorter.

Popper deliberately used the term *Nährpflicht* (literally "the duty to furnish nourishment") to express the key concept of his program, since it rhymes with *Wehrpflicht*, the German for compulsory military service, which Popper resolutely opposed. Popper's idea of a "compulsory civil service" is similar to one proposed by William James in his essay "The Moral Equivalent of War," but Popper anticipated James by several decades. If Popper's ideas about the duty of society to secure the individual against economic uncertainty do not sound exciting to the contemporary reader now that the concept of the welfare state is accepted by the majority of the populations of western Europe and the United States, and even the notion of a guaranteed income is advocated by leading economists, it should be remembered that at the time of their first publication, these ideas were extremely radical and were in fact received with violent hostility. In 1878 the great majority of political theorists, economists, and statesmen still adhered to the view that people are poor because of their laziness and ineptitude and that any state intervention in economic matters is a highly dangerous tampering with natural laws.

In spite of his courage and independent spirit, Popper failed to emancipate himself in some important areas of thought from the prejudices of his times. For example, he accepted without any question the view that masturbation "shatters" (*zerrütet*) the nervous system. He also had no doubt about the soundness of the prevailing hereditarian theories, according to which mental disturbances are largely the result of an innately weakened nervous system, and Popper frequently indulged in generalizations about the basically weak or strong nervous system of this or that national group. Although he knew of Freud's high esteem of his own work, Popper had no appreciation whatsoever of any of the ideas of psychoanalysis. Fritz Wittels, a psychoanalyst who was one of Popper's most devoted and trusted followers, called his attention to Freud's books and there was some polite correspondence between Popper and Freud. However, according to Wittels, Popper scarcely did more than look at Freud's books. In one case, when the subject was society (Freud's *Group-Psychology and the Analysis of the Ego*), Popper went to the trouble of reading the book. "I enjoyed what he quoted from the Frenchman [Le Bon]," he later told Wittels, but as for Freud's own theories, Pop-

per added, "I must tell you that I did not understand one word."

THE SANCTITY OF HUMAN LIFE

None of Popper's theories is philosophically more interesting than the ethical individualism on which he bases his program of social reform. On the opening page of *Das Individuum und die Bewertung menschlicher Existenzen* (from now on referred to as *Das Individuum*) Popper announces what he calls his "motto," and the rest of the book consists of its elaboration and defense as well as of detailed criticism of the anti-individualist positions of various influential writers, including Hegel, Nietzsche, Thomas Carlyle, Herbert Spencer, Heinrich von Treitschke, and Popper's own friend Wilhelm Ostwald. Popper formulates the motto as follows:

Basic Principle of a Moral Social Order

When any individual, of however little account, but one who does not deliberately imperil another's existence, disappears from the world without or even against his will, this is a far more important happening than any political or religious or national occurrence, or the sum total of the scientific and artistic and technical advances made throughout the ages by all the peoples of the world.

Should anybody be inclined to regard this statement as an exaggeration, let him imagine the individual concerned to be himself or his best beloved. Then he will understand and accept it.

To make clear what he means, Popper lists a number of propositions that he terms "the value-arithmetic" of human lives. The valuation of a person's life by the person himself, he writes, is something indefinite, varying, according to the mental state of the individual, from nothing to infinity. His life means nothing to him in moments of extreme unhappiness or when he is willing to sacrifice it for a cause in which he believes; but in other circumstances he regards it as possessing infinite value. "From an ethical point of view," Popper writes, "the existence of a stupid peasant-boy is just as infinitely valuable as the existence of a Shakespeare or a Newton" (*Das Individuum*, p. 193). "There is not the remotest equivalence," he remarks, "between the existence of a human being who wants to go on living and who is not trying to destroy another one, and any other value; the former exceeds the latter infinitely" (p. 189). Let us suppose that the angel of death were to allow William Shakespeare and Isaac Newton, in the most creative periods of their lives, to go on living only on condition that we surrender to him "two stupid day-laborers or even two incorrigible thieves." As moral beings we must not so much as consider an exchange of this kind. It would be far better if Shakespeare and Newton were to die. One may call attention, as much as one wishes, to the pleasure produced in countless future ages by Shakespeare's plays; one may point to the immense progress of science which would be the consequence of the prolongation of Newton's life—by comparison with the sacrifice of a human being, these are mere "luxury-values."

However, all of these considerations, Popper repeatedly insists, apply solely to "non-aggressive individuals." A person whose life is threatened by another may, in self-defense, kill the aggressor without having to feel the slightest remorse or misgivings. In such a case, the person's own life rightly counts as something infinite, while the life of the aggressor, be he one or many, counts as nothing. It is in fact a person's *duty,* and not merely his right, to defend himself in such a case with all means at his disposal. In addition to helping himself, he also "exerts a beneficial influence on millions of others if he demonstrates to them by his example what importance and value a non-aggressive human being attaches to his life" (p. 218). In one place Popper goes so far as to assert that it would be better if all the aggressors in the world, even if they numbered millions, were to be destroyed than if a single human being succumbed to them without resistance.

On occasions Popper concedes that his own principles cannot be proved and that the principles of his assorted opponents cannot be disproved, but for the most part he maintains that they can be shown to be "true" by means of an "evident deduction" from premises granted by most civilized men (p. 64). He employs two types of arguments, the first of which consists in calling attention to the way in which civilized persons actually judge and behave in a great many situations, when their vision is not clouded by special bias or prejudice. Suppose, for example, a fire were to break out in the Louvre; in such a situation. Popper maintains, it would not occur to any of the firemen or any of the voluntary helpers to save the paintings in preference to the human beings present. If somebody were to save a painting and let a human being die, his behavior would be generally condemned and he might in fact be subjected to punishment. It is true, Popper admits, that sometimes when people *hear* that in a fire in some distant location a number of human beings perished but that certain valuable manuscripts or collections were saved, they respond with greater satisfaction

than if it had been the other way around; but this only proves that distance from the place of a disaster produces indifference and makes people forget the enormous value of somebody else's life. "It becomes altogether different," Popper observes, "if one stands in front of the burning house." To take another illustration, in all civilized nations a person may not be subjected to vivisection or become the involuntary subject of a medical experiment, regardless of the benefits that might accrue to medical science and, indirectly, to future generations.

Popper also considers at great length another type of case that, in his opinion, shows particularly clearly that civilized people do in fact adhere to his principles. In fortresses or on ships, where the shortage of food may become so acute as to necessitate the sacrifice of some individuals, civilized men would always decide the issue by the casting of lots; in such a situation it would not occur to anybody to refer to the special literary or scientific talents of some member of the group. Shakespeare and Newton would here count no more than anybody else, and nobody would dare to propose that a less talented person be killed so that the great dramatist or the great physicist be kept alive instead. This is very evident in a case of this kind because "once the terror of death is so close, everybody perceives that the naked existence of a human being is something so elevated and infinite that compared with it everything else—be it genius, scholarship, or physical beauty—becomes quite inferior in value and a mere luxury" (ibid., p. 208).

The analysis of these and many other cases makes it clear, Popper contends, that his principles, which seem so strange and unrealistic when first stated in general terms, are quite commonly invoked. It is true that they are widely ignored when it comes to certain questions, such as compulsory military service, the death penalty, and the duty of society to guarantee the basic subsistence of every human being. However, in these cases it can be shown that people are simply inconsistent and have not perceived the implications of their own principles.

Popper's second type of argument, which is already indicated in his "motto," is much more interesting and original. It may not unfairly be labeled an ad hominem technique. Arguments of this type consist of two steps: (*a*) If a person, *X*, recommends a policy that involves the killing of one or more nonaggressive human beings, we extract from him the admission that the policy would not be justified if he, *X*, were the individual to be killed; (*b*) we then extract from him the admission that other human beings have the same right to live and not to be sacrificed to some biological, cultural, or aesthetic goal.

Popper observes that, except in special "periods of hate," most human beings are ready to make the latter of these admissions, at the very least for other members of their own nation or class. It does not, of course, mean, Popper explains, that a human being should mourn the death of any given person the way he mourns the death of somebody close to him; but human beings should realize that the mourning of somebody else in a similar situation is as justified as one's own and that to this other person his life or the life of somebody dear to him is more important than anything else in the world.

Popper employed his ad hominem strategy with relish in dealing with assorted philosophers and aesthetes who flaunted their readiness to approve the killing or enslavement of millions of ordinary human beings if this were necessary to achieve a biologically superior race or to produce great works of art. Thus, Popper devoted a good deal of attention to Spencer's conclusions that in giving artificial aid to the weakest members of a society, its physical and moral qualities are undermined and that, furthermore, all acts by the state to protect the weak and the sick are a "sin against the natural laws of life." After pointing out the dubious analogies on which such conclusions are based and the arbitrary preference for the value of future lives to those now in existence, Popper turns to his "frequently employed method." Suppose, he writes, Spencer or those taking such a "biological viewpoint" were themselves to become sick or unable to look after themselves. Would they approve of a society that turned to them and said: "Perish miserably! To help you is to make future generations less perfect." Will Spencer and his followers then be prepared to be treated as damaged goods, as refuse in a human breeding institution? Will they then still hold to the theories which they so calmly advocated while they were in good health and *others* were sick and in need of assistance?

Apparently nobody, not even the "monstrous" Nietzsche, irritated Popper more than the anti-Semitic historian and aesthete Heinrich von Treitschke, who in his essay "Der Sozialismus und seine Gönner" (Socialism and its patrons) had claimed that "the one statue of Phidias more than makes up for all the misery of the millions of slaves in Antiquity." One may well believe, Popper comments, that Treitschke can look at the statue of Phidias with great delight when *others* were compelled to labor as slaves. "A person holding such a view," Popper proceeds, "ought to have his own principles applied to himself to determine whether he will adhere to them after he has come to feel in his own person what they mean" (ibid., p. 166). It would have been a good idea to condemn Tre-

itschke to five years of service as a slave and then offer him an apartment in the Berlin Museum, where he could spend all his days admiring antique statues. That would be the time to ask Treitschke how he feels about Phidias and the slaves. Perhaps this is the only method, Popper concludes, to make people like Treitschke have some respect for human life.

It would lead too far afield to attempt a detailed assessment of Popper's principles here, particularly of his rather curious "value-arithmetic" of human lives. A few words, however, are perhaps in order about his *ad hominem* technique, both because arguments of this kind are in fact very common (although few employ them with Popper's deliberateness and persistence) and because there may be a tendency to dismiss them too readily. Anybody with a training in logic is apt to regard all such arguments as flagrant instances of the fallacy of *ignoratio elenchi*. If a person makes a moral judgment but violates it in his own behavior, this is surely no argument against the soundness of the moral judgment. We all tend to smile at the familiar stage figure of the preacher of temperance who takes out his whiskey flask as soon as the congregation has departed, but his failure to practice what he preaches does not by itself invalidate his preaching—it does not even prove that he is insincere. A doctor, unable to break his own smoking habit, is not necessarily giving bad advice and also may be perfectly sincere when he advises his patients to stop smoking. Turning to one of Popper's examples, if Spencer, after becoming ill and helpless, were to abandon his views concerning the social or biological undesirability of aiding the weak, this would not disprove his views; nor, conversely, would it be evidence for Spencer's position if, upon falling ill, he refused all aid and cheerfully disintegrated in the belief that he was thereby promoting biological progress.

Yet surely this is not the end of the matter. In reading Popper, one cannot help feeling that he is doing a great deal more than expressing his indignation at the defenses of callousness and inhumanity by writers like Spencer, Nietzsche, and Treitschke. Granting that Popper's ad hominem arguments do not disprove the positions he attacks and that they do not prove his own ethical individualism, it might nevertheless be held that his strategy helps to bring out at least two points of some interest. In the first place, Popper may be said to call attention to a double use of "understand" and related expressions which seems of special importance in ethical controversy.

Bernard Shaw once remarked that nobody should be allowed to be a judge unless he had spent at least six months in prison. The average judge, he explained, does not really know what he is doing when he sends a man to prison. In a sense this is no doubt false, but in another and deeper sense it may well be true. A judge can of course understand the statement "You are hereby sentenced to imprisonment for a period of five years" without having been a prisoner and even without having visited a prison—he obviously knows the difference in meaning between "two years" and "five years," and he also knows when to apply and when not to apply the word *prison*. At the same time, however, he might not know what he is doing in the sense that he has no clear conception of what it is like to languish for years in prison—what conditions really prevail in most prisons and what such a term of imprisonment frequently does to a man's character.

It may very plausibly be held that when intellectuals like Nietzsche, Spencer, and Treitschke advocate or condone the destruction or enslavement of millions of men, they do *not*, in this latter sense of the word, understand what they are recommending and that they could properly understand their own recommendations only if they became slaves or if they themselves experienced the prospect of being forcibly done away with. If we are satisfied that a person who recommends a certain policy does not himself understand, in this deeper sense, what he is recommending, this does not indeed show his policy to be mistaken, but it does undermine his standing in the discussion. For it means that he is ignorant of relevant, perhaps crucially relevant, facts, and hence, on almost any normative theory, his recommendation would not be adequately supported.

Second, Popper's strategy may help to determine the true *status* of the recommendations under discussion. Most people would want to make a distinction between a genuine moral or evaluative judgment and the mere expression of a desire or feeling; and it is the mark of the former but not of the latter—so, at least, a defender of Popper would argue—that it is universalizable: In passing a moral judgment on somebody, one is, in virtue of its being a moral judgment, committed to passing the same judgment about *anybody else* in similar circumstances, including oneself and those one cares for. Now, the writers whom Popper was opposing presumably wished their pronouncements to be treated as genuine evaluative judgments, as the advocacy of certain ideals and not merely as expressions of their desires. However, unless they were willing to maintain that they, too, ought to be enslaved or killed or left without assistance in order to further the goals in question, their original assertions will not qualify as genuine evaluations.

It will be instructive to see how Popper's challenge, thus interpreted, helps to determine the status of Treitschke's recommendation. Treitschke, we will assume, has just declared that certain "inferior" human beings ought to be enslaved for the purpose of producing a sublime work of art. Let us also assume that, in the sense under discussion, Treitschke admits that he, as well as his children (whom he loves), is "inferior." Now, if Treitschke, in this hypothetical situation in which he imagines himself and his children to be inferior, is ready to maintain that he and his children, no less than other inferior human beings, ought to be enslaved, his original declaration has the status of a genuine evaluative judgment. If, however, Treitschke wishes to exempt himself and his children, not merely in the sense that he would resist any attempt to be sold into slavery but in the sense of declaring that he and his children, although inferior beings, ought not to be enslaved, it would follow that his initial statement was not a genuine evaluation—that "ought" was not used there in its moral or evaluative sense. (More accurately: It would follow either that Treitschke was not offering a genuine evaluation or that he was inconsistent in denying a proposition entailed by one asserted previously.) Popper would probably add to this that in actual fact the great majority of those who talk like Treitschke, and very likely Treitschke himself, would insist that they and those they love ought not to be enslaved or otherwise mistreated. While it may be disappointing to realize that the callous positions against which Popper wrote have not been refuted, it is not a mean achievement to have shown that certain pronouncements masquerading as value judgments are in fact nothing more than the expressions of certain desires.

ELIMINATION OF RELIGION AND METAPHYSICS

Popper's positivism, like that of Mach, may be regarded as a midway stage between the philosophy of Auguste Comte and the logical positivism of the Vienna circle. Although he knew a great deal about mathematics, Popper did not advance beyond J. S. Mill's position that mathematical statements are extremely well supported empirical propositions. Metaphysics he dismissed as futile, but he wavered between dismissing metaphysical questions as meaningless and treating them as meaningful but unanswerable.

He never wavered, however, in regarding metaphysics, and more especially the theological varieties associated with Western religions, as exceedingly harmful. No change in economic arrangements, however rational and beneficial it may be, can bring about a happy world unless all forms of supernaturalism are banished. There can be no peace in the world, Popper insists, as long as there is the slightest vitality in organized religious superstition, which is something "necessarily aggressive." Some of Popper's more conservative followers have done their best to play down his antireligious sentiments. It is therefore necessary to insist that he himself regarded the *Ausrottung* (extermination) of religion and metaphysics—and of all "enthusiasm for transcendent ideals"—as an essential part of his philosophical and social program, one that was necessarily implied by his humanitarian individualism. Margit Ornstein, his literary executor, relates how Popper, very shortly before his death, when be was revising the manuscript of *Über Religion*, remarked to her with a smile, "This is my Parthian arrow," adding, "When the Parthians left the battle scene they turned around once more to aim a final arrow at the enemy" (*Über Religion*, p. 3).

Purely ceremonial or "civil" religions, such as those practiced by the ancient Greeks and Romans or most of the people of China and Japan, are relatively harmless: Unlike the religions that we know in the West, they lack any kind of metaphysical foundation, anything that can be called a theological system, and above all, they do not possess a powerful priestly caste. Religion begins to have an evil influence only when it is given a systematic formulation and when it becomes "an affair of the heart." Popper's condemnation is sweeping and is meant to apply to the kind of belief fostered by rationalistic theologians no less than to the pietistic enthusiasm found in many religious groups all over the world. "At first it [religious zeal] is just nonsense, then it becomes obstinacy and spite, and in the end it is wildness and insanity beyond all limits" (*Über Religion*, p. 2). The harmfulness of religion is exactly proportional to the degree of religious fervor. Popper approvingly quotes Pierre Bayle's saying that "the person who is convinced that he is promoting the Kingdom of God by the extermination of heretics will step on all moral laws," and he offers numerous examples from the history of the "genuine positive," as opposed to the merely ceremonial and civil religions, to support his indictment that the former increase bad feeling in the world, that they encourage malicious tendencies which are then covered up and justified in high-sounding language, that they place love of man below the love of religious conceptions, that they multiply situations of strife and conflict by promoting the intervention of priests in even the most intimate details of everyday living, that they weaken and indeed destroy respect for truth and justice, and, finally, that they use, wherever they can, the

power of the state for their purposes, especially in matters of education.

Popper disliked Christianity most of all, and in a section of *Dos Individuum* (A digression on the valuation of human lives in the Christian religion) he undertakes to correct the long-standing and, he claims, erroneous notion that Christianity encourages respect for the individual. Christianity does indeed speak of the value of the individual *soul,* but both in doctrine and in practice this notion has coexisted with contempt for the individual's body and life here on Earth. Popper does not deny that now and then religious belief has given people hope and consolation and that some of the expressions of religious devotion have been touchingly beautiful. However, such considerations must not be allowed to affect our overall judgment—"the burning of one heretic more than cancels ten thousand beautiful and deep feelings" (*Dos Individuum*, p. 72).

Popper had no doubt that the ideal of a "superstition-free culture," which, for him, meant a world without religion, was entirely attainable. He repeatedly takes issue with the widespread view that religious belief or religious needs are innate. This, he argues, is clearly disproved by the existence of entire nations without religion and of numerous persons in our own culture who are entirely devoid of religious belief and whose lives are no less happy or responsibly conducted than those of most believers. Moreover, the existing statistics on the prevalence of religious faith are suspect in the sense that, as far as religious issues are concerned, most people are not allowed to develop freely but live under the constant pressure of proreligious propaganda and the threat of social disapproval and economic loss if they avow their disbelief. "The masses of Europe," he writes, live in effect "in a religious penitentiary" (*Dos Individuum*, p. 59). Once the social and political power of the churches is shattered and education, uninfected by proreligious bias, becomes universal, religious belief is bound to vanish. "A person who has learned about the history and origin of religions, including Christianity, who has absorbed the main results of the sciences and the relations of these to the claims of religion, will not for a moment be afraid of or express gratitude to imaginary entities or persons" (p. 223).

Prior to the elimination of religious influences from the public schools, freethinkers must band together into a powerful "International League for the Liberation from Superstition." Such a league would publish and obtain the vast circulation of what Popper calls "counter-books"—works written in simple and clear prose, which would refute point by point the fallacies, the lies, and the distortions in the religious and proreligious textbooks used in the schools. This league would also open "counter-schools" and train "wandering counter-preachers," whose function it would be to bring enlightenment to the peasant population. The counter-preachers would conduct meetings in the villages immediately after the Sunday services. In the beginning the peasants, incited by the priests, would try to chase away the "godless intruders," but with some courage and persistence it would be possible to receive a hearing, to catch the interest of the peasants, and in the end to make them see the soundness and good sense of the unbeliever's position. In his first formulation of this program in 1878, Popper estimated that such a "gigantic cleansing operation" would take several hundred years, but writing thirty years later, apparently encouraged by the constant decline in religious belief, he thought that a "few generations" would be quite sufficient.

In some places Popper admits that the teaching of science and of the history of religions and the exhibition of the conflict between scientific conclusions and religious assertions is not enough to banish supernaturalism. We also have to take into account the "metaphysical need" which is commonly found in Europeans, though it is for the most part lacking in the peoples of east Asia. This metaphysical need can be eliminated by "improved epistemological instruction." The metaphysical need is "nothing other than the longing to find a resting place in the exploration of the universe, to reach a stage at which there will be no urge to ask new questions" (p. 62). It is however, a senseless drive and must be recognized as such if we are to have a healthy mental constitution. Our knowledge of the world consists in the establishment of functional relations between experienced data (Mach's "elements"). Knowing the world means discovering correlations and subsuming these under ever wider correlations. "We cannot do anything further," writes Popper, "than to determine ever richer relations between elements already known or to insert new ones as connecting links between them." The world may be likened to a carpet spread out in front of us, between whose webs we go on weaving ever-new webs without limit. It is a vain effort "to try to see behind the carpet," as the metaphysicians and mystics do, in the hope of finding there all kinds of wonderful happenings. In discovering causal relations, "we do not descend step by step into the Ground of the World ... rather we crawl like an insect on that colorful carpet which we call the world and which, as a consequence of our explorations, becomes ever more dense" (p. 63). This carpet has no "other side" transcending the one we explore.

See also Bayle, Pierre; Carlyle, Thomas; Comte, Auguste; Diderot, Denis; Dreams; Einstein, Albert; Ethics, History of; Freud, Sigmund; Hegel, Georg Wilhelm Friedrich; Holbach, Paul-Henri Thiry, Baron d'; Holism and Individualism in History and Social Science; Hume, David; James, William; Logical Positivism; Mach, Ernst; Mill, John Stuart; Newton, Isaac; Nietzsche, Friedrich; Ostwald, Wilhelm; Positivism; Voltaire, François-Marie Arouet de.

Bibliography

In addition to the works by Popper mentioned in the body of the article, the following deserve to be mentioned. *Fürst Bismarck und der Antisemitismus* (Vienna, 1886) is an examination of the violent anti-Semitic fulminations of Eugen Karl Dühring and Richard Wagner, as well as of the milder anti-Semitic arguments of Eduard von Hartmann. Popper's *Selbstbiographie* (Leipzig, 1917) reprints the complete text of "Über J. R. Mayer's Mechanik der Wärme," as well as the correspondence between Mayer and Popper. *Die Philosophie des Strafrechts* (Vienna: R. Löwit, 1924) presents the details of Popper's objections to existing penal systems and his own alternative, based on his ethical individualism. Parts of a major epistemological treatise that Popper had planned to write were posthumously published under the title "Über die Grundbegriffe der Philosophie und die Gewissheit unserer Erkenntnisse" in *Erkenntnis* 3 (1932–1933): 301–324.

Very little by Popper is available in English. "Dreaming and Waking," translated by A. A. Brill, can be found in *Psychoanalytic Review* 34 (1947): 188–197. The story about incest is translated by S. Rosenzweig as Appendix I of his article "The Idiocultural Dimension of Psychotherapy—Pre- and Post-History of the Relations between Sigmund Freud and Popper-Lynkeus," in *Psychoanalysis and the Social Sciences* 5 (1958): 9–50. Extracts from various of Popper's writings are translated in H. 1. Wachtel, *Security for All and Free Enterprise; A Summary of the Social Philosophy of Josef Popper-Lynkeus* (New York: Philosophical Library, 1955), which has an introduction by Einstein.

A. Gelber, *Josef Popper-Lynkeus, sein Leben und sein Wirken* (Vienna, 1922), and F. Wittels, *Die Vernichtung der Not* (Vienna, 1922), are full-length studies of Popper's life and work. The latter is available in English, translated by Eden and Cedar Paul as *An End to Poverty* (London: Allen and Unwin, 1925). There is a shorter but very informative study by Richard von Mises in Vol. VII of the series Neue Österreichische Biographic (Vienna, 1931), pp. 206–217. Popper's scientific work is discussed in P. Frank, "Josef Popper-Lynkeus zu seinem achtzigsten Geburtstag," in *Physikalische Zeitschrift* 19 (1918): 57–59; and in T. von Karman, "Lynkeus als Ingenieur und Naturwissenschaftler," in *Die Naturwissenschaften* 6 (1918): 457–463. Popper's contributions to "energetics" are discussed in G. Helm, *Die Energetik nach ihrer geschichtlichen Entwickelung* (Leipzig: Veit, 1898), Part VII, Ch. 2. A most interesting excerpt from the correspondence between Mach and Popper, containing a remarkable anticipation of the quantum theory, is reprinted in H. Löwy, "Historisches zur Quantentheorie," in *Die Naturwissenschaften* 21 (1933): 302–303.

Freud's estimate of Popper is found in his article "My Contact with Josef Popper-Lynkeus," which is reprinted in Vol. V of Freud's *Collected Papers* (New York, 1959) and also in his *Character and Culture* (New York, 1963). Popper's remark about Freud quoted in this article will be found in F. Wittels, "Freud's Correlation with Popper-Lynkeus," in *Psychoanalytic Review* 34 (1947): 492–497.

In recent years there has been a good deal of discussion of ad hominem arguments of the kind employed by Popper against writers like Spencer, Nietzsche, and Treitschke. This discussion is in large measure due to the work of the influential British philosopher R. M. Hare, who in his *Freedom and Reason* (Oxford: Clarendon Press, 1963) employed a strategy strikingly similar to that used by Popper. Among discussions of how much (or how little) can be established by means of such arguments, the following are especially noteworthy: A. C. Ewing, "Hare and the Universalization Principle," in *Philosophy* 39 (1964): 71–74; D. H. Munro, "R. M. Hare's *Freedom and Reason*." in *Australasian Journal of Philosophy* 42 (1964): 119–134; G. Madell, "Hare's Prescriptivism," in *Analysis* 26 (1965): 37–41; and G. Ezorsky, "Ad Hominem Morality," in *Journal of Philosophy* 63 (1966): 120–125.

There is a complete bibliography of writings by Popper on philosophical, political, and scientific topics in H. I. Wachtel, *Security for All and Free Enterprise* (see above).

Paul Edwards (1967)

POPULAR ARGUMENTS FOR THE EXISTENCE OF GOD

Argument about the existence of God is rare, for religious beliefs are effectively supported in our society by means that are not principally rational. It is common to answer the question "Why are you a believer?" with "Because I was taught to be," uttered in the tone of voice, or in the context, of one presenting reasons, not mere causes, of belief. It is even more common to speak of faith in God as if this were a specially compelling reason for belief and, moreover, one beyond logical criticism. Faith, however, is merely determination to believe and no kind of reason. Literature giving such justifications is not considered in this entry. Despite this omission of the greater part of the popular writing and what one might call the traditional verbal folklore of religion, a vast quantity of material remains that can be considered argumentative. After omitting further the grossest absurdities among these arguments, it has still been necessary to choose in a rather arbitrary way what should be dealt with, and no claim to completeness is made.

GENERAL REMARKS

Most of the arguments in popular literature may be seen as variants of the more strictly philosophical arguments, such as the Cosmological and Teleological arguments, or those from morals and common consent. The variants are popular largely because they are posed as probable rather than as valid arguments; that is, they are not offered as arguments whose premises entail their conclusions. Almost all of them fall into a common class of arguments of the form "The universe contains some puzzling feature, F (design, an objective morality). God's existence explains F, and no other known hypothesis does. Therefore, God exists." That they have this form is a matter of no small importance; it affects the whole question of what kind of objection is likely to succeed against a given popular argument.

It is beside the point to demonstrate the formal invalidity of such arguments, although their invalidity is very easy to show in almost every case. However, it is entirely relevant to require of such an argument that it should make clear just how God's existence explains F. (Similarly, the real force of the well-known infinite regress counter to the Cosmological, or First Cause, Argument, is that it demonstrates the failure of this argument to provide the promised explanation. The argument merely postpones the explanation. That God's nature is mysterious does not, of course, fill any explanatory bill.) On this score, popular arguments are universally unsatisfactory, appealing tacitly (for the most part) to the claim on the one hand that all things are possible to God and on the other that, God being a transcendental mystery, it is presumptuous to expect any account of his efficacy to be actually intelligible. As the substance of an explanation, this is thin. Further, it is an entirely relevant question to ask whether any explanation is required of some singled-out feature, and whether alternative explanations are simply not known or whether there appears to be a reason to suppose there are none.

ARGUMENT FROM COMMON CONSENT

The argument from common consent is an old and constantly recurring popular argument (see J. A. O'Brien, *God: Can We Find Him?*). The argument has a large measure of plausibility, despite the fact that it is formally invalid; for it is very often overwhelming evidence for some view that the majority holds it. For example, if a huge majority of spectators at a football game believes that a certain team won the game, that is exceedingly good evidence that this team indeed won it; and any minority dissent can be written off in some way, such as irrational partisanship for the beaten team. However, the proportion of majority to minority views is not the only, or by any means the most important, factor in such situations. It is also crucial whether the majority has any competence to judge the issue. On the outcome of football games the majority of spectators is well placed to judge, but on the significance of some scientific experiment the majority is not at all well placed. Obviously, the general run of humankind has always been and still is poorly placed to pronounce on such a question as the existence of a Deity. This requires a competence in logical reasoning on highly abstract matters and an ability to assess complex evidence that the majority does not possess. Their vote carries no weight on this issue.

ARGUMENT FROM MORALS

An argument widely used, especially by evangelists who aim at the most general audience, is the argument from the intelligibility of morals. (On a more sophisticated level it has been argued by A. E. Taylor in *The Faith of a Moralist*.) Many who urge it seem to have dimly in mind an essentially rather sophisticated argument, encapsulated in naive remarks like "But if God doesn't exist, why do you not murder or plunder?" and "If God doesn't exist, then a morality could amount only to doing what you please." The rather sophisticated argument thus hinted at is as follows: To call an action moral (immoral) is, first, to provide a motive for doing (avoiding) it. Second, the claim that an action is moral can be a subject of rational dispute, which requires that the claim be not simply a disguised subjective remark about the speaker's tastes. The existence of God explains these two features of normal discourse. Therefore, God exists.

As was pointed out earlier, the first question must be "Does the existence of God explain these features of moral discourse?" If the question whether an action is moral is equivalent to the question whether the action is consistent with God's commands, then moral questions are not purely subjective. On the other hand, it is doubtful whether the theory accounts for the sort of discussion that actually goes on when moral issues are argued. God's commands must, according to the hypothesis, be arbitrary. It cannot be that he consults something beyond his own will, since that external thing or principle would then be the source of morality and God its mere interpreter and announcer, not its creator. However, moral reasoning surely requires empirical knowledge of other persons and the world generally—and a very great deal of intelligence if the reasoning is to be satisfactory. It is far from clear that the hypothesis allows for the relevant play of intelligence and knowledge in arriving at moral conclusions.

Again, it is rarely stated just which motive for behaving morally is provided under the hypothesis of God's existence. It cannot be suggested that we have a moral duty to obey God's commands because the whole point of the proposed explanation is that his commands are the source of all moral duties. It could be claimed that terror of punishment and desire for reward are perfectly adequate motives for obeying the commands. However, despite the undoubted efficacy of these motives, they are seldom urged because they do not adequately account for what we feel our motives really are in moral behavior. The most satisfactory suggestion as to the motive provided under the hypothesis seems to be that one obeys the commands out of love of God.

In sum, it is uncertain how the hypothesis clearly explains the required features of moral discourse. Further, it seems quite possible to account for them at least as well without being committed to the theistic view. For if love of God is an adequate motive for moral behavior, why should not love of one's fellows also be adequate? And if it is, then it further seems an objective empirical question that courses of action promote those almost universally desired ends of continuance of life, adequate food and shelter, and freedom from violence, as well as less fundamental and more subtle ends that promote smooth social intercourse.

TELEOLOGICAL ARGUMENTS

Versions of the classical Teleological Argument are by far the most popular of all popular arguments. The variety of changes rung upon this old theme in respect of its premises is astonishingly wide, as may be gathered from the following brief examples: The smallness of the human gene has been cited by A. C. Morrison, for no very clear reason, as an instance of God's designing hand, and so has the immensity of the orbital velocity of an electron. More markedly odd are such suggestions as "This old world has three times as much water as land but with all of its twisting and turning not a drop sloshes off into space" (*Ebony* symposium, November 1962, p. 96) and that the annual progress of Earth round the sun, although it is much more rapid, is also much smoother than the most sophisticated jet airliner yet designed. Although it is difficult to see what relevance these considerations may be thought to have, they perhaps involve a confusion between a good argument to the conditional conclusion that if these things are designed, then the technology of their production is well beyond our present reach, and a bad argument to the conclusion that these things have, in fact, been designed.

An ingenious variant, heard in conversation but apparently never published, neatly turns the tables on a standard polemic against belief in a God that stems from Freudian psychology—that such belief is caused by a psychological mechanism arising from various sexual stresses in an infant's relationship with its father. This mechanism, it is claimed, far from showing that belief in God is pathological and irrational, really demonstrates his loving care for his creatures in providing a psychological mechanism that promotes belief, thus preventing the damnation of his creatures as heretics and infidels. This does not at all answer the point that insofar as belief depends upon the psychological stresses, it is irrational and pathological. (Irrational and pathological beliefs may, of course, be true.)

ARGUMENTS FROM THE SCIENCES

Only more recent arguments taken from the biological and the physical sciences will be discussed. First, however, there is a general argument from the very existence of science, or as it is more likely to be put, from the intelligibility of nature (see D. Elton Trueblood, *Philosophy of Religion,* pp. 94–98). It is felt that the universe must be rational if science, using logic and mathematics, is able to comprehend it. But logic and mathematics are concerned with deriving some propositions or formulas from others. It is not the conclusions or the premises of arguments that may properly be called rational, but only the procedure of deriving conclusion from premises. This procedure reflects no rational process in nature. It would be more accurate (although still not very accurate) to call this a linguistic procedure. We can move from "If there is lightning, then there is thunder" and "There is lightning" to the conclusion "There is thunder" by the rational procedure known as *modus ponens,* but it is not even intelligible to suppose that *modus ponens* is a natural physical process by means of which lightning produces thunder. Scientists may discover the important equation that relates the speed of a falling body to the square of the time of its fall. They may differentiate this equation, $v = t^2$, to show that the body's acceleration is constant. Differentiation is a mathematical procedure of derivation, but it is not intelligible to say that the body or the gravitational field in which it falls undergoes any such process of differentiation, or that it undergoes some nonmathematical counterpart of it.

ARGUMENTS FROM BIOLOGY. It has been argued—by Pierre André Lecomte du Noüy and Pierre Teilhard de Chardin, for example—that the pattern of evolution as displayed by modern biology shows clear marks of a designing hand. The direction of evolution, it is claimed, is toward progressively more intelligent life forms, thus showing the desire of the Creator (Omega, as Teilhard de Chardin called him) to bring about beings like himself. The claim is highly dubious. It induces "a certain shuffling of the feet" (to quote P. B. Medawar's review) in Teilhard, when he discusses the fact that insects and plants do not seem to evolve in this way at all. Lecomte du Noüy solved the difficulty by defining the problematic cases not as evolutions but as adaptations. The direction of adaptation is toward usefulness; that of evolution, toward liberty. Thus he made the claim perfectly, if trivially, safe. Even so, there is a difficulty, for if it is all a plan, why does God not bring about immediately and at a stroke the desired state of affairs now being so laboriously approached with such a plethora of wasteful products? Lecomte du Noüy's apparent answer is merely that since God is an eternal Being, what seems to us simple mortals as a drear immensity of wasted time is to him but the twinkling of an eye. The irrelevance of this to the original objection is obvious enough. The waste is still waste, and the existence of so many pointless dinosaurs (whose lives played no part in future evolution) can scarcely have escaped the attention of him who takes note of the fall of a sparrow.

One prevalent argument, put forward by Morrison, among others, is based on the allegedly remarkable hospitality of our planet to complex forms of life. Temperatures are neither too high nor too low, and there is an abundance of water and oxygen and an atmospheric blanket against lethal doses of cosmic radiation. But the argument inverts the situation. We now have good reasons (of a Darwinian kind) to believe that the surviving life forms are those that adapt to the environment rather than those for whom the environment has been adapted by a beneficent Overseer. So far as is known, only one of the nine major planets of our particular star is hospitable to complex life forms. It might be surprising if every planet of every star fulfilled the quite detailed set of conditions that favor life as we know it and that prevail over most (not all) of our planet. But that there is one such planet is not so surprising that we need recourse to metaphysical entities to explain it.

Similar arguments from alleged improbabilities also spring from biology. Lecomte du Noüy and others have claimed that life is inconsistent with the Second Law of

Thermodynamics. This law states that entropy increases, which means, roughly, that in any isolated system energy breaks down from various differentiated forms that are usable in doing work to an undifferentiated state of uniform heat. In statistical thermodynamics, increase of entropy is defined roughly as increase of the randomness of systems, that is, their movement toward more probable forms. But, it is said, living organisms decrease in entropy as they grow; they build up differentiated forms of energy and hence are improbable structures.

However, the phenomena of life are quite consistent with the law, for living organisms are not thermodynamically isolated systems. In whatever way life may be improbable, it is certainly not improbable in any sense that makes it inconsistent with statistical thermodynamics.

A second, more plausible, claim of this kind is that even a simple protein molecule is a highly improbable structure, so improbable that it is simply incredible that it should ever have come into existence by pure chance. A calculation cited by V. H. Mottram puts the odds against a chance "manufacture" of a simple protein molecule as 10^{160} to 1, a small chance by any standards. Mottram also claimed that 10^{243} years would be needed for such an event to occur on this planet (a much longer period than that accepted for the cool Earth) and that it would require sextillion sextillion sextillion times more material than is believed to be in the entire universe. Another calculation shows that the probability of such a molecule's arising by chance manipulation of amino acids (already quite complex structures) is still as low as $1:10^{48}$ and hence very improbable indeed.

The ways of statistical arguments are notoriously complex. We must always ask "Relative to what assumptions are these probability figures reached?" This was not made clear by Mottram. Presumably we are to assume at least that the atoms are rearranged in various positions by a process of mechanical shuffling of some sort in which all the rearrangements so envisaged are equally probable.

The possibility of such a rearrangement is very dubious. Even elementary chemistry informs us that certain combinations are not possible—for example, five hydrogen atoms may not be linked to one carbon atom. There is no evidence that such groups were excluded from the class of equiprobable arrangements considered in constructing this figure. If one considers the various linkages of more complex groups in which, say, a group of fifty atoms hooks on to another group of fifty, the number of chemically possible combinations is, presumably, very small. But this cannot have been taken into consideration

in constructing the figures, because we do not have sufficient knowledge of the chemical possibilities at this level. The theists appear to have committed at this point the fallacy of assuming equal probabilities in cases where we have no positive knowledge of what the probabilities are.

Consider a liter of hydrogen containing, say, 10^{22} atoms. If we attempt to assign a number to all the conceivable arrangements of those atoms, the number is enormous. Yet we invariably find them divided into hydrogen molecules, 0.5×10^{22} pairs of atoms extremely close together. The improbability of this always coming about as a random arrangement of atoms is immense, and certainly far greater than any of the figures quoted by Mottram, yet this is presumably not evidence of design. Without more information about and justification of the assumption of equiprobability on which Mottram's calculation is based, plainly no reliance can be placed upon it.

ARGUMENTS FROM PHYSICS. Perhaps even more than biology, modern physics has given rise to a group of widely circulated arguments purporting to show that, despite the fact that God nowhere appears in the calculations of physicists, modern physics demands, suggests, or allows for the existence of God.

Although most apologists agree that the views of a scientist have no special authority outside the field of his expertise, this does not prevent their citing a vast mass of material produced by those physicists who spend their less strenuous hours philosophizing on their findings. The view almost universally favored among such writers, and perhaps most forcefully expressed by Sir Arthur Eddington and Sir James Jeans, is that modern physics establishes the subjectivity of all knowledge and that reality is mental, not material. It is often further concluded that physics has shown the world to be a nonrational place about which clear logical argument is out of place.

Relativity theories are alleged to have shown the subjectivity of all knowledge and to have confirmed Protagoras's doctrine that man is the measure of all things. But the special theory of relativity is concerned with relations between inertial systems (a notion definable wholly within objective dynamics). It is not at all concerned with any observers who may be reading clocks or using measuring rods within these systems. The general theory only extends the results of the special theory to cover relations between systems of a wider class. Neither theory is subjectivist or mentalistic.

A similar example of needless obscurantism concerns the primary place given the concept of energy by the relativistic notion that mass (matter) may be converted into energy, and vice versa. Few of us are sure just what energy is; and, when a scientist such as E. J. Bing informs us that everything is energy, that it may exist in the form of electromagnetic vibration, and that it is a vehicle of universal thought (a gratuitous addition), we are apt to think that, while we do not know what this really means, perhaps everything is, in some obscure way, thought and hence in the mind of God.

Trueblood (op. cit., pp. 102–105) has invoked the science of thermodynamics to yield a theistic conclusion. The Second Law of Thermodynamics shows that the universe is steadily increasing its thermodynamic randomness—it is dissipating its stores of differentiated energy usable in doing work. It also shows that, as we trace the history of the universe in time according to the law, we come to a state of minimum energy, a sort of beginning in time of the universe. But this is far from lending support to the theistic hypothesis. It simply means that the law leads us to a point beyond which it will not take us. It gives no warrant for the conclusion that the minimum entropy state has a supernatural cause.

The greatest number of arguments are derived from the difficult and puzzling field of quantum mechanics. It is possible to give some indication of the relevant state of affairs in physics in terms of two features: (1) The Schrödinger wave equation, which is fundamental to quantum physics, contains the ψ function. This gives as its square the probability that an electron, for example, is in a certain spatiotemporal region. This feature leads to the result that the exact later states of electrons are unpredictable even from the fullest statement of their earlier states. (2) Beams of radiation or of electrons show some features characteristic of beams of particles but others characteristic of beams of waves, although their being particles is inconsistent with their being waves.

Feature (2) leads directly to such distortions as "If an electron can be two wholly inconsistent things, it is a little narrow to expect so much less of God." The electron, of course, is not, nor can it be, two inconsistent things—and (2) does not entail this. But the claim, together with the breakdown of the Laplacean view that given the complete mechanical state of the universe at any one time, any future or past state could be rigorously deduced in every detail, is generally hailed by religious apologists. Very few apologists claim that quantum physics actually provides evidence for God's existence. It is simply that in quantum theory mechanical determinism breaks down and there is no mechanical picture of quantum processes that is an adequate interpretation of the mathematical formalism of the theory. To religious apologists it appears that these facts allow for occult nonphysical causes and forbid rational understanding. They appear to feel that in the overthrow of reason itself lies their best defense.

More specific in their trend toward the admission of occult or physically transcendent causes are the following characteristic arguments. Arguing from the bad habit some physicists have of speaking about unpredictable electron jumps as the electron "choosing" one rather than another energy state, E. J. Bing wrote, "Let's call a spade a spade. To say that an electron 'chooses' to do anything *is to attribute free will to the electron.*" The theory gives no warrant for taking this obvious metaphor literally. It is quite unclear what real meaning there could be for such terms as *choice* and *free will* if their use is extended from describing living things to describing those that are nonliving. Such extension can result only in confusion.

Some physicists (Jeans, for example) have an equally deplorable habit of speaking of the Schrödinger wave equation as "waves of knowledge" in discussing the behavior of subatomic particles. This is presumably because the Schrödinger equation, which describes the behavior, is a wave equation and contains a function whose square is a probability. Apparently they regard probability as purely a matter of knowledge and thus suppose that some occult mental principle is at work in the quantum world. These suggestions won no assent from such authoritative quantum physicists as Niels Bohr and Werner Heisenberg, who most strongly insisted on the indeterminacy of quantum physics. Their notion is not that quantum phenomena have occult causes (acts of free will on the part of electrons) or unknown causes, but that they have no causes at all. Although there have been many distinguished scientists, including Albert Einstein, who believe it is possible that in the future we shall have a fully deterministic theory of the subatomic world, they have all taken for granted that the theory would postulate only physical causes.

See also Common Consent Arguments for the Existence of God; Cosmological Argument for the Existence of God; Degrees of Perfection, Argument for the Existence of God; Moral Arguments for the Existence of God; Ontological Argument for the Existence of God; Religious Experience, Argument for the Existence of God; Teleological Argument for the Existence of God.

Bibliography

FAVORABLE VIEWS

Bing, E. J. "Modern Science Discovers God." *American Mercury* (June 1941).

Corbishley, Thomas. *Religion Is Reasonable.* London: Burns & Oates, 1960.

Ebony, symposium. "Why I Believe in God" (December 1961 ff.).

Eddington, A. S. *Nature of the Physical World.* London: Cambridge University Press, 1928.

Gittelsohn, R. B. "Have We Outgrown God?" *Saturday Review* (September 16, 1961).

Griffith, A. L. *Barriers to Christian Belief.* London: Hodder and Stoughton, 1962.

Jeans, Sir James. *The Mysterious Universe.* London: Cambridge University Press, 1930.

Lecomte du Noüy, Pierre. *Human Destiny.* London: Longmans Green, 1947.

Lewis, C. S. *Miracles.* London: Bles, 1948.

Morrison, A. C. "Seven Reasons Why a Scientist Believes in God." *Reader's Digest* (October 1960).

Mottram, V. H. "Scientific Basis for Belief in God." *Listener* (April 22, 1948).

O'Brien, J. A. *God: Can We Find Him?* New York: Paulist Press, 1942.

Robinson, J. A. T. *Honest to God.* London: SCM Press, 1963.

Rosten, Leo, ed. *Guide to the Religions of America.* New York: Simon and Schuster, 1955.

Taylor, A. E. *The Faith of a Moralist.* London: Macmillan, 1930.

Taylor, F. Sherwood. *Man and Matter.* London: Chapman and Hall, 1951.

Teilhard de Chardin, Pierre. *The Phenomenon of Man.* Translated by Bernard Wall. New York: Harper, 1959.

Trueblood, D. Elton. *Philosophy of Religion.* New York: Harper, 1957.

Weaver, Warren. "A Scientist Ponders Faith." *Saturday Review of Literature* (January 3, 1959).

Whittaker, Sir Edmund. "Religion and the Nature of the Universe." *Listener* (June 1, 1950).

SKEPTICAL VIEWS

Cohen, Chapman. *God and Me.* London, 1946.

Cohen, Chapman. *God and the Universe.* London: Pioneer Press, 1946.

Feyerabend, Paul. "Niels Bohr's Interpretation of the Quantum Theory." In *Current Issues in the Philosophy of Science,* edited by Herbert Feigl and Grover Maxwell. New York: Holt, Rinehart and Winston, 1961. The relevant features of quantum physics are well discussed in this difficult but not highly mathematical paper.

Jack, H. "A Recent Attempt to Prove God's Existence." *Philosophy and Phenomenological Research* 25 (1965): 575–579. Critically discusses one of the arguments by A. C. Morrison and a very similar argument by Lecomte du Noüy in *Human Destiny.*

Medawar, P. B. "Critical Notice of 'Phenomenology of Man.'" *Mind* 70 (1961): 99–106.

Russell, Bertrand. *Religion and Science.* London: Butterworth-Nelson, 1936.

Russell, Bertrand. *The Scientific Outlook.* London: Allen and Unwin, 1931.

Russell, Bertrand. *Why I Am Not a Christian.* New York: Simon and Schuster, 1957.

Stebbing, L. Susan. *Philosophy and the Physicists.* London: Methuen, 1937.

OTHER RECOMMENDED TITLES

Behe, Michael. *Darwin's Black Box: The Biochemical Challenge to Evolution.* New York: Free Press, 1998.

Behe, Michael et al., eds. *Science and Evidence for Design in the Universe.* San Franciso: Ignatius Press, 2000.

Buckman, Robert. *Can We Be Good without God? Biology, Behavior, and the Need to Believe.* Amherst, MA: Prometheus, 2002.

Capra, Fritjof. *The Tao of Physics,* 4th ed. Boston: Shambhala, 2000.

Davies, Paul. *God and the New Physics.* New York: Simon and Schuster, 1984.

Davis, Jimmy, and Harry Poe. *Designer Universe: Intelligent Design and the Existence of God.* Broadman and Holman, 2002.

Dawkins, Richard. *The Blind Watchmaker.* New York: Norton, 1996.

Dembski, William. *Intelligent Design: The Bridge between Science and Theology.* Downers Grove, IL: InterVarsity Press, 2002.

Dembski, William, ed. *Mere Creation: Science, Faith and Intelligent Design.* Downers Grove, IL: InterVarsity Press, 1998.

Dennett, Daniel. *Darwin's Dangerous Idea: Evolution and the Meanings of Life.* New York: Simon and Schuster, 1995.

Hare, John. *Why Bother Being Good? The Place of God in the Moral Life.* Downers Grove, IL: InterVarsity Press, 2002.

Johnson, Philip. *Darwin on Trial.* Downers Grove, IL: InterVarsity Press, 1993.

Ross, Hugh. *The Fingerprint of God.* New Kensington, PA: Whitaker House, 2000.

Schroeder, Gerald. *The Hidden Face of God: Science Reveals the Ultimate Truth.* New York: Free Press, 2002.

G. C. Nerlich (1967)
Bibliography updated by Christian B. Miller (2005)

PORPHYRY
(c. 232–c. 304)

Porphyry, one of the principal founders of Neoplatonism, was born of Syrian parents at Tyre. He studied philosophy at Athens. In 263 he went to Rome, joined the group that regarded Plotinus as its master, and, apparently some years after Plotinus's death, took over his school. He died some time in the first six years of the fourth century.

Porphyry can be called a founder of Neoplatonism because, while the philosophy he upheld was in the main that of Plotinus, he made it possible for this philosophy to become, as it did, an institution throughout the Roman Empire. He arranged Plotinus's lectures for publication in their present form; he defended and developed their content in independent works of his own; third, he enabled some of the much more systematic, not to say more teachable, philosophy of Aristotle to be included even by Platonic professors in a university curriculum.

In the so-called *Sententiae ad Intelligibilia Ducentes* (Aids to the Study of the Intelligibles; a short, difficult summary, incomplete as we have it, of Neoplatonism) he presents methodical proofs of two Plotinian theses which were unacceptable to the more conservative Platonists and to Porphyry himself when he first came to Rome: the independence and priority of the One to Being or Intellect, and the identity of Intellect or Thought with its objects. Plotinus, however, had been ambiguous over the extent to which the lower hypostases, Intellect (embracing the Platonic forms) and Soul (embracing nature and the Aristotelian forms), each existed in its own right. It is the monistic strand that seems to dominate in Porphyry: Everything that is not the One is an appearance of the One and is the result of the inadequacy of our thought about the One. The serious consequence of this doctrine is for the ordinary notion of personality. The individual, embodied soul and intellect, themselves appearances (he also calls them parts) of some universal soul and intellect, will be unreal; Porphyry calls the individual soul "the soul in a relation"—for it is related to a body—which implies its nonsubstantiality according to Aristotle's doctrine of categories. This consequence was vigorously challenged by Iamblichus. Union with the One can be achieved, according to Porphyry, by the unaided effort of intellect, but we do not have enough evidence to know how he met the philosophical problems of this thesis even if he had a consistent doctrine about it.

Porphyry's ethics followed Plotinus in stressing the universal equation between pursuit of the good, becoming what one "essentially" is, the self-awareness that accompanies thought, and "reversion" to the "cause" of one's being. Evil, together with matter, was the result of a "deviation from reality." In schematizing *Ennead* I 2 [19], Porphyry gave Plotinus's scale of virtues a nomenclature which became conventional for later Neoplatonists. *A*, the virtues of the soul, are (1) civic, (2) purificatory; *B*, the virtues of the intellect, are (3) contemplative, (4) paradigmatic. Less abstractly and on less philosophical grounds he was attracted like many Neoplatonists by the asceticism and taboos of Pythagoreanism.

Nothing has survived of a book that Porphyry wrote comparing Platonism and Aristotelianism. It undoubtedly maintained that there was no substantial conflict between the two, which was commonplace for Platonists of the empire. His commentaries on Plato have perished too; so have those on Aristotle, except for the introduc-

tion to the *Categories* known as the *Isagoge* and an elementary commentary on the same work. But his views were often quoted; and it is clear that what is distinctive about his treatment of Aristotle is twofold—a facility in expounding him without trying to Platonize him or to score against him, and a remarkable gift of clear exposition that does not depend (as it does in some later commentators) on ignoring the difficult issues. Most of the formulas that aimed at accommodating the metaphysical presuppositions of Aristotle's logic to Platonism had probably been worked out already. But since it was only the metaphysics that was objectionable, the way was open to the full acceptance of a purely formal logic. This meant not the Aristotelian logic of terms from which the nonexistent, the negative, and the particular were excluded, but something roughly equivalent to the Boolean algebra of classes.

This logic without metaphysics is roughly, too, what we find in Porphyry; and it is what has sometimes been inaptly called Porphyry's nominalism. With some debt to the Stoics, it enabled logic to develop as an autonomous science. For his *Isagoge* was translated into Arabic and Syriac as well as Latin, and his more advanced work was incorporated in Boethius's logic. The *Isagoge* is traditionally said to have made species a fifth predicable in place of definition. If it had it would have misrepresented Aristotle by implying that the subject was not a universal term, like those of the other predicables, but a particular. The implication might not have disturbed Porphyry, but in fact the *Isagoge*, or *Quinque Voces*, is not about predicables but what it says it is about, the five words that are essential to the understanding of the *Categories*. It does, however, introduce "inseparable accidents" which are an uneasy intermediate between essential attributes and pure or separable accidents.

Porphyry was a man of wide learning and wide interests. He studied many of the religious beliefs and practices with which he came into contact, and though generally sympathetic to them as various if inferior ways to salvation, he was renowned for centuries as the author of a detailed work against the Christians. But this and ventures of a more or less occultist nature—allegorical interpretations of poetry, descriptions of the soul's "vehicles," and the like—have mostly survived only in statements from controversial sources; and while respectable as philosophy in their day they are of small philosophical interest in the modern sense.

See also Logic, History of; Neoplatonism; Plotinus.

Bibliography

Porphyry's "Life of Plotinus" is included in editions of Plotinus' works.

Sententiae ad Intelligibilia Ducentes (Aids to the study of the intelligibles), edited by Erich Lamberz. Leipzig, 1975.

Opuscula Selecta, edited by A. Nauck. Leipzig, 1886, rpr. 1963.

On Abstinence from Killing Animals. Translation and commentary by Gillian Clark. London, 2000.

Isagoge, with Boethius' translation. In *Commentaria in Aristotelem Graeca*. Vol. IV, Part I, edited by A. Busse. Berlin, 1887.

Porphyry Introduction (Isagoge). Translation and commentary by Jonathan Barnes. Oxford, 2003.

Porphyrii Fragmenta, edited by Andrew Smith. Leipzig, 1993.

On Porphyry's life and works see:

Beutler, R. "Porphyrios." No. 21 in Pauly and Wissowa, *Realencyklopädie der classischen Altertumswissenschaft*. Vol. XXII, Sec. 1. Stuttgart, 1953.

Bidez, J. *Vie de Porphyre, Le philosophe néo-platonicien*. Ghent, 1913, rpr. 1964.

Dörrie, H., et al. *Porphyre*. Vandoeuvres-Genève, 1966.

Smith, Andrew. *Porphyry's Place in the Neoplatonic Tradition*. The Hague, 1974.

Smith, Andrew. "Porphyrian Studies since 1913." *Aufstieg und Niedergang der Römischen Welt* II 32 (1987): 717–773.

Zambon, Marco. *Porphyre et le Moyen-Platonisme*. Paris, 2002.

A. C. Lloyd (1967)
Bibliography updated by Andrew Smith (2005)

PORTER, NOAH
(1811–1892)

Noah Porter was an American Congregationalist clergyman, philosopher, and psychologist, and president of Yale College from 1871 to 1886. As a student in the Yale Divinity School, Porter had become a disciple of Nathaniel W. Taylor's modified version of New England Calvinism. For ten years he preached Taylorism at churches in New Milford, Connecticut (1836–1843), and Springfield, Massachusetts (1843–1846). He was then appointed Clark professor of moral philosophy and metaphysics at Yale, holding this chair throughout his tenure of the presidency of the college. On retiring from the office of president, he resumed a small teaching load until his death.

Porter's thought until 1853 was dominated by the conventional Scottish commonsense realism that pervaded American colleges. Then two years spent in Europe, largely in study at the University of Berlin, increased his familiarity with more recent and more daring philosophical systems. He became particularly interested, through the German philosopher Friedrich Adolf Trendelenburg, in the central epistemological problems of modern philosophy. Porter was convinced that these problems had to be solved before any advance in ontology could be expected. Moreover, he believed that the epistemological questions themselves required a foundation in scientific psychology.

This conviction and a much keener appreciation of the value of the history of thought than was usual among American philosophers of his time, led Porter to the preparation and publication of his important treatise *The Human Intellect*, the best work on psychology in English before William James. Porter presented and critically examined the leading ideas of both English and European (chiefly German) schools of psychology, as well as summarizing earlier work in the field. Because he regarded psychology as a necessary prelude to epistemology which, in turn, he considered prior to metaphysics, he insisted that psychology had to be an inductive science and roundly criticized G. W. F. Hegel for attempting to ground psychology in his metaphysical system. Although inductive, however, psychology cannot be a material or experimental science. Its subjects are the data of consciousness, which must be discovered introspectively; physiological experiments and investigations must be kept in mind by the psychologist, but these studies are ancillary to the direct study of the data of consciousness.

The influence of this major work and of Porter's many lesser writings was one of the chief forces in liberating academic philosophy in America from domination by naive realism and in introducing the study of German philosophy and psychology.

Among the nonphilosophical activities of Porter, special note should be taken of his editorship, with Chauncey A. Goodrich, of a revised edition of Noah Webster's *An American Dictionary of the English Language* (Springfield, MA, 1864). This work was revised under Porter's sole supervision as *Webster's International Dictionary of the English Language* (1890).

See also Common Sense; Consciousness; Hegel, Georg Wilhelm Friedrich; James, William; Psychology; Realism.

Bibliography

WORKS BY PORTER

The Human Intellect. New York: Scribners, 1868.

The American Colleges and the American Public. New Haven, CT: Chatfield, 1870.

Science and Sentiment. New York: Scribners, 1882.

The Elements of Moral Science. New York: Scribners, 1885.

Kant's Ethics. A Critical Exposition. Chicago: S.C. Griggs, 1886.

WORKS ON PORTER

Blau, Joseph L. *Men and Movements in American Philosophy.* New York: Prentice-Hall, 1952.

James, Walter T. *The Philosophy of Noah Porter.* 1951. An unpublished doctoral dissertation, available in typescript in the Columbia University library.

Merriam, George S., ed. *Noah Porter: A Memorial by Friends.* New York: Scribners, 1893. Biographical and expository discussion.

Schneider, H. W. *A History of American Philosophy.* New York: Columbia University Press, 1946. Contains additional comment.

J. L. Blau (1967)

PORT-ROYALISTS

See *Arnauld, Antoine; Logic, History of; Nicole, Pierre*

POSIDONIUS
(135–51? BCE)

Posidonius of Apameia, the Stoic philosopher, was famous in his own time and continued to influence writers into the first and second centuries CE. Soon after, his writings seem to have been lost, and even his name is rarely mentioned. Known to modern historiography mainly from the mention of his views in Cicero, Strabo, Seneca, and Galen, he was considered from the Renaissance to the beginning of the nineteenth century as a minor figure in the development of Stoicism. Then his thought began to be discovered in an ever-increasing number of writers, who were believed to follow him although they do not quote him, and he was established as the mediator between the Orient and the Occident, the reconciler of philosophy with religion and mysticism, the foremost representative of dualism. In the early twentieth century the reconstruction of Posidonius's work through *Quellenforschung* ("source criticism") was replaced by a reconstruction based on the inner form of his thought, and Posidonius was represented as a visual thinker, the defender of monism, the proponent of the doctrines of cosmic sympathy and vitalism, and the last Hellenistic philosopher. Both interpretations pay little attention to the fragments preserved under the name of Posidonius and therefore remain largely conjectural. What will be said here is based exclusively on the attested material.

This material leaves no doubt about the fundamentally dualistic character of Posidonius's system. His ethics, which is the best-known part of his thought, teaches, contrary to the general Stoic dogma, that passions are not simply false judgments but an irreducible force in human nature. This distinction is also echoed in Posidonian physics in the again unorthodox definition of matter as endowed with its own form and quality, which is merely reshaped and remodeled by divine reason. His logic establishes reason as a criterion of truth independent of sense perception. On the other hand, the duality of matter and reason is bridged by the realm of mathematical forms; among the Stoics only Posidonius was a mathematical realist. The macrocosm and the microcosm are in the end viewed as gradated, as hierarchies as it were, in which reason governs the subordinate irrational forces. God pervades the world; the passions follow the leadership of rational insight; man is here to contemplate and to act.

The Platonic and Aristotelian elements in this Stoicism were noted even by ancient critics. In Posidonius's opinion the founders of the Stoa, Zeno and Cleanthes themselves, had been Platonizing and Aristotelianizing. The strict monism of the school was due to Chrysippus, whose work Posidonius thought had to be undone. Yet although Posidonius harked back to the older teaching and in this sense remained in the Greek tradition—he was innocent of the later Orientalizing—he undoubtedly made an original contribution to philosophy. His ethics is a greatly refined analysis of the emotions that refutes the rationalistic position by pointing to its inner inconsistency and its inconsistency with observed facts. He stressed the importance of the will. Although only a few details of his physics can be rediscovered, it is clear that he was intent on explaining things; he was famous for his etiologies, and he carefully distinguished the various causes, assigning first place to teleology. Cosmic sympathy is but one of the factors he invoked in his exegesis of nature. His logical investigations furthered the understanding of syllogistic thinking, which seemed to him validated not by linguistic connections but by implied axioms. In short, his system marks a step forward in the history of Greek rationalism, and this is in accord with Posidonius's belief in the gradual development of knowledge and in the idea of progress, which he, like so many earlier Greek rationalists, upheld.

Posidonius's contributions were, however, not restricted to the field of philosophy proper. He wrote a history of his own time and in it, if not separately, dealt copiously with the rise of civilization, which he claimed began with practical inventions made by philosophers. In the historical process itself he detected the dominance of freedom over circumstance. Several of his books were devoted to natural sciences, such as astronomy and meteorology; he also investigated problems of mathematics and of military tactics. Perhaps the greatest significance of these works lies in the fact that they do not isolate scholarly and scientific research but put it in a philosophical framework. Events are seen as part of the history of the cosmos. Scientific explanations are hypotheses, the correctness and adequacy of which must be judged through philosophical reflection. It was as a philosopher that Posidonius felt impelled to reject the heliocentric theory in favor of the geocentric theory. Although he erred in this respect, he did enforce the idea of the hypothetical character of all scientific knowledge and did restore the unity of the sciences which Hellenistic thought had destroyed.

The stoa of the empire, initially influenced by Posidonius, tended more and more to follow Chrysippus. Thus, the philosopher Posidonius soon lost importance. His scientific writings kept the Greek heritage alive much longer and carried it, through Seneca's *Naturales Quaestiones*, into the Middle Ages. If one judges his achievement and his influence, one cannot compare him with Plato, Aristotle, or Democritus or with Zeno, Epicurus, or Plotinus. It is fair to say, however, that his personality, which he allowed to intrude into his work, makes him one of the most attractive figures among ancient philosophers. He was a man of dignity and not without a sense of irony and humor. He lived the dogma he preached, studying and teaching as well as participating in the political affairs of Rhodes, his adopted city. The variety of his gifts is amazing—his dialectical skill, traced by Galen to his mathematical erudition; the keenness of his powers of observation of men and things, which is especially marked in his reports on the travels that took him throughout almost the whole of the then-known world; and the strength of his analytical ability, along with his love of literature and art. It was perhaps the universalism of his nature that made it possible for him not only to attempt a new explanation of the universe in all its aspects, doing justice to both man's cognitive and his practical concerns, but also to root human existence—for the last time in antiquity, it seems—in the world of reality without depriving this world of the reign of human reason, which he considered of the same nature as the divine spirit ruling the cosmos.

See also Aristotelianism; Aristotle; Chrysippus; Cicero, Marcus Tullius; Epicurus; Galen; Hellenistic Thought; Plato; Platonism and the Platonic Tradition; Plotinus; Rationalism; Renaissance; Seneca, Lucius Annaeus; Stoicism; Vitalism; Zeno of Citium.

Bibliography

The approach of *Quellenforschung* has been criticized, and criticized fairly, by J. F. Dobson, "The Posidonius Myth," in *Classical Quarterly* 12 (1918): 179ff. For Posidonius as a monist see K. Reinhardt, *Poseidonios* (Munich: C.H. Beck, 1921); see also his *Kosmos und Sympathie* (Munich: C.H. Beck, 1926) and A. Pauly and G. Wissowa, *Realencyclopädie der classischen Altertumswissenschaft*, Vol. XXII (Stuttgart, 1953), Part I, Cols. 558–826. I. Heinemann, *Poseidonios' metaphysiche Schriften*, 2 vols. (Breslau, 1921–1928), considers Posidonius especially in relation to his predecessor Panaerius.

For a reconstruction of Posidonius's philosophy according to the attested fragments see Ludwig Edelstein, "The Philosophical System of Posidonius," in *American Journal of Philology* 57 (1936): 286ff. For the historical fragments see F. Jacoby, *Die Fragmente der griechischen Historiker*, Vol. II, No. 87 (Berlin: Weidmann, 1926). The collection of fragments by I. Bake, *Rhodii Reliquiae Doctrinae* (Leiden, 1810), is antiquated.

Ludwig Edelstein (1967)

POSIDONIUS [ADDENDUM]

Modern study of Posidonius has been transformed since the mid-1960s by the collection of ancient evidence compiled by Ludwig Edelstein and Ian G. Kidd (1972), and minutely analyzed by Kidd (1988, 1999), which contains only texts that name Posidonius explicitly. The picture presented is undoubtedly too narrow, and an accurate assessment of Posidonius's achievement and influence must await further study of other texts in which his influence may be reliably detected. But even the newly circumscribed picture has made it increasingly clear that Posidonius largely adhered to basic Stoic doctrines and principles and that his main innovations lie in his breathtakingly comprehensive effort to integrate both natural and human sciences into Stoic cosmology, epistemology, and ethics. His range was encyclopedic, and while the bulk of his massive output was in physics (embracing also metaphysics, theology, and the special sciences), there is little he neglected.

In metaphysics Posidonius sought to reconcile Stoic materialism with its quasi-dualist principles of matter and God (which are thoroughly blended together throughout the universe), and to explicate the incorporeal status of time, void, and bodily limits (points, lines, and surfaces). In logic relatively little is securely attested: work on the logic of relations and on axiomatic method in mathematics. He also analyzed the structure of scientific explanation (etiology): Subordinating mathematical sciences to philosophy, he emphasized material and teleological factors in ways that suggest Aristotelian influence (Rhodes, where he worked most of his life, had a tradition of Aristotelian studies, and Andronicus of Rhodes [first century BCE], a younger contemporary, had a prominent role in reviving study of Aristotle's treatises).

Posidonius's scientific work had substantial impact on many later Stoics (notably Lucius Annaeus Seneca, Cleomedes [fl. c. 100 CE], and Geminus [10 BCE–60 CE]) and on ancient science and philosophy more widely (including Strabo [c. 64 BCE–after 23 CE] and Galen). Spanning astronomy, meteorology, geophysics, and geography, his work shows a concerted effort to extend the scope and empirical basis of Stoic theories. Problems he tackled include the size and distance of the sun and moon, the size and climatic zones of the earth, eclipses, comets, rainbows, clouds, thunder, winds, earthquakes, volcanoes, hydrodynamics, and mineralogy. Especially impressive is his theory of oceanic tides, which he correlated with the daily, weekly, and annual periodic motions of the moon; detailed observation here revealed systematic links between celestial and terrestrial phenomena that exemplify the principle of cosmic interaction (sympathy) underlying Stoic determinism and its providential design.

In ethics Posidonius upheld the central doctrines of Stoic Eudaemonism: virtue is a form of knowledge, only it (and anything possessing it) is genuinely good, and it is entirely sufficient for happiness (eudaimonia). He also brought new rigor to Stoic psychology by subjecting previous accounts of emotion and emotional behavior to precise critical analysis. Tendentious evidence in Galen has convinced many scholars that Posidonius rejected the monistic psychology of Chrysippus in favor of a Platonizing dualism, but recent studies (Cooper, Tieleman) argue that he sought rather to defend Stoic intellectualism by analyzing the structure of human motivation more closely. Similar concerns are evident in his massive *History* (fifty-two books covering 146 to 80s BCE—from a Roman defeat of federated Greece to an invasion of Athens), where ethics and ethnography combine with climatology and geography to explain both customs and historical events.

See also Aristotle; Chrysippus; Eudaimonia; Galen; Plato; Seneca, Lucius Annaeus; Stoicism.

Bibliography

TEXTS AND TRANSLATIONS

Edelstein, Ludwig, and Ian G. Kidd, eds. *Posidonius. Vol. 1, The Fragments.* New York: Cambridge University Press, 1972. The standard collection of ancient testimony.

Kidd, Ian G. *Posidonius. Vol. 2, The Commentary.* New York: Cambridge University Press, 1988. Meticulous analysis, with full reference to earlier scholarship.

Kidd, Ian G. *Posidonius. Vol. 3, The Translation.* New York: Cambridge University Press, 1999.

Theiler, Willy. *Die Fragmente/Poseidonios.* 2 vols. Berlin: de Gruyter, 1982. An insufficiently cautious collection of texts but often helpful for its commentary.

STUDIES

Algra, Keimpe. "Posidonius' Conception of the Extra-cosmic Void: The Evidence and the Arguments." *Mnemosyne* 46 (4) (1993): 473–505. Establishes his Stoic orthodoxy on some basic questions of cosmology.

Cooper, John M. "Posidonius on Emotions." In *The Emotions in Hellenistic Philosophy*, edited by Juha Sihvola and Troels Engberg-Pedersen. Dordrecht, Netherlands: Kluwer Academic, 1998. Argues that Posidonius's account has affinities with Plato but remains fundamentally Stoic.

Tieleman, Teun. *Chrysippus' On Affections: Reconstruction and Interpretation.* Leiden, Netherlands: Brill, 2003. Argues, contrary to prevailing views, that Posidonius sought to refine rather than undermine Stoic moral psychology.

Stephen A. White (2005)

POSITIVISM

The term *positivism* was used first by Henri, Comte de Saint-Simon to designate scientific method and its extension to philosophy. Adopted by Auguste Comte, it came to designate a great philosophical movement which, in the second half of the nineteenth century and the first decades of the twentieth, was powerful in all the countries of the Western world.

The characteristic theses of positivism are that science is the only valid knowledge and facts the only possible objects of knowledge; that philosophy does not possess a method different from science; and that the task of philosophy is to find the general principles common to all the sciences and to use these principles as guides to human conduct and as the basis of social organization. Positivism, consequently, denies the existence or intelligibility of forces or substances that go beyond facts and the laws ascertained by science. It opposes any kind of metaphysics and, in general, any procedure of investigation that is not reducible to scientific method.

The principal philosophical sources of positivism are the works of Francis Bacon, the English empiricists, and the philosophers of the Enlightenment; but the cultural climate that made it possible was that of the eighteenth-century Industrial Revolution and the grand wave of optimism to which the first successes of industrial technology gave rise. Positivism made this climate into a philosophical program—that is, a universal project for human life. It exalted science without concerning itself (as does contemporary positivism) with the conditions and the limits of the validity of science, and it claimed that not only ethics and politics but also religion would become scientific disciplines. In one direction, this led to an attempt to establish a "positive" religion in place of traditional theological religions.

Through its acceptance of the concept of the infinity of nature and of history and, therefore, of necessary and universal progress, positivism had affinities with the other important nineteenth-century philosophical movement, absolute idealism, and belongs with it in the general range of romanticism.

There are two fundamental kinds of positivism: social positivism, with a professedly practicopolitical character, and evolutionary positivism, with a professedly theoretical character. Both share the general idea of progress, but whereas social positivism deduces progress from a consideration of society and history, evolutionary positivism deduces it from the fields of physics and biology. Comte and John Stuart Mill are the principal representatives of social positivism, and Herbert Spencer of evolutionary positivism. A materialistic or spiritualistic metaphysics is often associated with evolutionary positivism. A third, critical type of positivism, also known as empiriocriticism, should be distinguished from both social and evolutionary positivism. Contemporary forms of positivism—logical positivism and neopositivism—are directly connected with critical positivism.

SOCIAL POSITIVISM

Social positivism arose in France through the work of Saint-Simon and other socialistic writers (Charles Fourier, Pierre Joseph Proudhon) and in England through that of the utilitarians (Jeremy Bentham and James Mill), who, in turn, considered their work closely associated with that of the great economists Thomas Malthus and David Ricardo. Social positivism sought to promote, through the use of the methods and results of science, a more just social organization. According to Saint-Simon, men now lived in a critical epoch because scientific progress, by destroying theological and metaphysical doctrines, had eliminated the foundation of the social organization of the Middle Ages. A new organic epoch, in which positive philosophy would be the basis of a new system of religion, politics, ethics, and public education, was required. Through this system society would regain its unity and its organization by basing itself on a new spiritual power—that of the scientists—and a new temporal power—that of the industrialists. In his last writing, *The New Christianity* (1825), Saint-Simon considered the new organic epoch to be a return to primitive Christianity.

COMTE. Saint-Simon's ideas inspired the work of Auguste Comte. The point of departure of Comte's philosophy is his law of the three stages. According to this law, both the general history of humanity and the development of the individual man, as well as that of every branch of human knowledge, passes through three stages: the *theological*, or fictitious, stage in which man represents natural phenomena as products of the direct action of supernatural agents; the *metaphysical* stage, in which the supernatural agents are replaced by abstract forces believed to be capable of generating the observable phenomena; and, finally, the *positive* stage, in which man, refusing to seek the ultimate causes of phenomena, turns exclusively toward discovering the laws of phenomena by observation and reasoning. The positive stage is that of science, whose fundamental task is to predict phenomena in order to use them.

"Science whence comes prediction; prediction whence comes action" is the formula in which Comte epitomized his theory of science. The formula, as Comte himself recognized, expresses exactly Francis Bacon's point of view. The law of the three stages permits the classification of the sciences according to the order in which they entered into the positive phases—an order determined by the degree of simplicity and generality of the phenomena which are the objects of each science as it reaches the positive phase. Thus, according to Comte the following hierarchy constitutes "a necessary and invariable subordination": astronomy, physics, chemistry, biology, and sociology. Mathematics remains outside this order because it is at the basis of all the sciences; psychology, because it is not a science, also remains outside. Psychology should be based on introspective observation. But introspective observation is impossible, because the observed and observing organ would have to be identical. The apex of the hierarchy of sciences is sociology, or social physics, which Comte divided into social statics, or theory of order, and social dynamics, or theory of progress.

Progress is a necessary law of human history: The realization of progress is entrusted not to individuals, who are only the instruments of progress, but to the true subject of history—humanity, conceived as the Great Being in which past, present, and future beings partake. "We always work for our descendants, but under the impulse of our ancestors, from whom derive the elements and procedures of all our operations" (*Politique positive*, Vol. IV, pp. 34–35). Humanity is the continuous and uninterrupted tradition of the human race, and it is the divinity that must replace the God of traditional religions. The wisdom and providence of humanity preside infallibly over the realization of progress. At the end of progress there is sociocracy, a new absolutist social regime based on science and the religion of humanity and directed by a corporation of positivist philosophers. Sociocracy, by limiting liberties, will make impossible any deviation from the fundamental beliefs of the positivistic cult.

In his last work, *Philosophy of Mathematics* (1856), Comte proposed a new kind of religious trinity, the Great Being (humanity), the Great Fetish (Earth), and the Great Way (space). The religious aspect of Comte's philosophy drew a great number of followers and generated the greatest wave of enthusiasm. Pierre Lafitte and Émile Littré in France, Richard Congreve and G. H. Lewes in England were the most philosophical of Comte's first disciples. The influence of Comte's religious thought, however, rapidly exhausted itself, except among small groups of devotees, while his philosophical ideas (the law of the three stages; the conception of science as description and prediction; the theory of progress; and sociology as a positive science) have exercised a lasting influence on science and philosophy.

BENTHAM AND THE MILLS. Comte's English contemporaries, the utilitarians Jeremy Bentham and James Mill, presented with equal force, although more modestly, the fundamental requirement of positivism: that every kind of valid knowledge be included within science. They sought to establish a science of mind based on facts, as is the science of nature, and tried to make ethics itself, as Bentham used to say, an "exact science." They considered the mind to be an associative mechanism, ruled by precise laws whose constitutive elements are sensations, which were regarded as the ultimate facts of mind. Traditional ethics was substantially a theory of the end of human conduct: It established by a priori means what that end was and deduced from it the rules of conduct. Bentham and Mill intended to substitute for traditional ethics a theory of the motives of conduct—that is, of the specific causes of conduct. If it were ascertained what are the motives and the rules that human beings obey, Bentham and Mill believed, it would be possible to direct human conduct in the same way that nature can be controlled by knowing its causal laws.

These principles remained fundamental in later developments of positivism, first in the work of John Stuart Mill, who was influenced by both Saint-Simon and Comte. Mill, like Saint-Simon and Comte, spoke of reorganizing society on new foundations. He rejected, however, the doctrinaire political and religious absolutism of Comte and defended instead the freedom and development of the individual, to whom he considered the social organization subordinate. Mill's classic *Principles of Political Economy* (1848) concluded by determining the limits of governmental intervention in economic affairs—limits required so that there would be in human existence "a sacred fortress safe from the intrusion of any authority."

Mill's *System of Logic* (1843), which is perhaps the most important work of nineteenth-century positivism, contains a fundamental correction of Comte's view of science. Comte had stressed the rational aspect of science and considered its experimental basis, the verification of facts, as merely preparatory to the formulation of laws. He had excluded the notion that once they were formulated, laws could again be subjected to the test of facts and eventually placed in question by "a too detailed investigation," and he had prescribed for scientific investigation a series of limitations to keep it from being transformed into "a vain and at times a seriously disturbing curiosity." Mill's logic, instead, appealed to a radical empiricism and avoided any dogmatizing of scientific results. The very principles of logic, according to Mill, are generalizations of empirical data, and induction is the only method that science has at its disposal. The basis of induction itself, the principle of the uniformity of the laws of nature, is, in turn, an inductive truth, the fruit of many partial generalizations. Prediction is possible in science only on the basis of past experience, which alone furnishes the evidence both for the major premise and for the conclusion of the traditional syllogism. "'All men are mortal' is not the proof that Lord Palmerston is mortal; but our past experience of mortality authorizes us to infer *both* the general truth and particular fact with the same degree of certainty for one and the other" (*System of Logic*, Bk. II, Ch. 3).

Like the other utilitarians, John Stuart Mill held that the human mind has the same structure as natural phenomena and is knowable in the same ways. "If we knew the person thoroughly, and knew all the inducements which are acting upon him, we could foretell his conduct with as much certainty as we can predict any physical event" (*System of Logic,* Bk. VI, Ch. 2, 2). To make such predictions possible, he held that a new science, ethology, was needed to study the laws of the formation of character. Mill placed this science alongside Comtian sociology, to which he attributed the task of discovering the laws of progress that make it possible to predict social events infallibly (ibid., Ch. 10, 3).

Mill held that even religion should be based on experience. Experience, by suggesting that there is a limited and imperfect ideological order in nature, permits belief in a divinity of limited power, a kind of demiurge. Such belief encourages a religion of humanity based upon an altruistic ethics and the "supernatural hopes" of humankind.

SOCIAL POSITIVISM IN ITALY AND GERMANY.

In Italy social positivism had two defenders, Carlo Cattaneo and Giuseppe Ferrari. Both were influenced by the work of Saint-Simon, and both saw him as a continuer of the work of Giambattista Vico, whom they credited with having founded "a science of man in the very heart of humanity."

The German social positivists Ernst Laas, Friedrich Jodl, and Eugen Dühring appealed to Ludwig Feuerbach rather than to Saint-Simon and Comte. But faith in science, in progress based on science, and in a perfect social form to which this progress must lead was the inspiration of all social positivists.

EVOLUTIONARY POSITIVISM

Evolutionary positivism shared the faith in progress of social positivism but justified it in a different way. Evolutionary positivism is based not on society or history but on nature, the sphere of physics and biology. Its immediate forerunners were the work of the geologist Charles Lyell and the doctrine of biological evolution. Lyell, in *The Principles of Geology* (1833), demonstrated that the actual state of Earth is the result not of a series of cataclysms (as Georges Cuvier had argued) but rather of the slow, gradual, and imperceptible action of the same causes that are acting before our eyes. The doctrine of evolution triumphed in 1859 with the publication of Charles Darwin's *Origin of Species,* which first presented adequate proofs of biological evolution and formulated the doctrine in a rigorous way. Lyell's and Darwin's doctrines made possible the formulation of the idea of a natural and necessary progress of the whole universe, beginning with a cosmic nebula and, through the unin-

terrupted development of the inorganic and organic world, continuing into the "superorganic" development of the human and historical world. It is superfluous to note that the scientific theories that furnish the occasion for the rise of the idea of evolutionary positivism do not constitute the elements of a sufficient proof of it, since it is so highly generalized a hypothesis that it seems to be of a metaphysical nature. Darwin himself remained "agnostic" (to use the term created by another biological evolutionist, T. H. Huxley) with respect to all problems that concern the universe in its totality.

SPENCER.

The importance of Herbert Spencer, however, and the lasting influence of his work, depends on his defense of universal progress as a continuous and unilinear evolution from a primitive nebula to the more refined products of human civilization. Spencer used the term *evolution* in preference to progress in an early programmatic article of 1857, and even then he saw universal progress as modeled on biological evolution. His definition of evolution as "the passage from the homogeneous to the heterogeneous" or from the simple to the complex was suggested by the development of vegetable and animal organisms, whose parts are chemically and biologically indistinct at first but which then differentiate to form diverse tissues and organs. Spencer held that this process can be discovered in all fields of reality and that each of these fields has a specific science whose task is to recognize and clarify its characteristics. Philosophy is (as Comte conceived of it) the most generalized knowledge of the process of evolution. The role of philosophy begins with the widest generalizations of the individual sciences; from these generalizations it seeks to realize a "completely unified" knowledge. However, neither philosophy nor science, according to Spencer, can take the place of religion.

The truth of religion is that "the existence of the world with all that it contains and all that it encompasses is a *mystery* that always needs to be interpreted" (*First Principles,* London, 1862, Par. 14). All religions, however, fail in giving this interpretation; therefore, the sole task of authentic religion is to serve as a reminder of the mystery of the ultimate cause. The task of science, on the other hand, is to extend indefinitely the knowledge of phenomena. Like William Hamilton and Henry Mansel, Spencer held that human knowledge is enclosed within the limits of the relative and the conditioned, that is, within the limits of phenomena. Beyond these limits there is the unlimited and unknown force on which all phenomena depend. The unknowability of this force is revealed in the insolubility of certain problems at the limits of philosophy and science, such problems as those concerning the essence of space, of time, of matter, and of energy, the duration of consciousness (whether finite or infinite), and the subject of thought (whether it is the soul or not).

If Comte's religion of humanity had little success among philosophers and scientists, Spencer's agnosticism found many adherents among them, and for a few decades it was a required attitude for intellectuals generally. Other positivists, however, such as Roberto Ardigò, rejected agnosticism and denied that one could speak of an "unknowable" in an absolute sense. Ardigò;, moreover, wanted to redefine the process of evolution by considering it as "a passage from the indistinct to the distinct," referring to psychological experience rather than to biology.

Spencer wrote on many fields of knowledge—biology, sociology, ethics, politics, and education. When he turned his attention to sociology, he attempted to rescue it from the practical and political task that Comte had assigned to it and to consider it as a theoretical discipline whose task is to describe the development of human society to its present state. This change was accepted by such positivist sociologists as John Lubbock, Edward Tylor, Émile Durkheim, and William Graham Sumner, who were strongly influenced by Spencer.

Evolutionary positivism is, in its more rigorous form, as far from materialism as it is from spiritualism. Spencer affirmed (*First Principles,* Par. 194) that the process of evolution can be interpreted both in terms of matter and movement and in terms of spirituality and consciousness: The Absolute that it manifests can be defined neither as matter nor as mind. Positivism embraces both trends that interpret the concept of evolution materialistically and trends which interpret it spiritualistically. The laws of the conservation of matter discovered by Antoine Lavoisier (1789) and the laws of the conservation of energy implicit in Robert Mayer's discovery of the equivalence of heat and work (1842) were taken as proofs of the hypothesis that a single substance, of which matter and energy are inseparable attributes, is the eternal subject of cosmic evolution and necessarily determines all its characteristics.

HAECKEL AND MONISM. The German philosopher Ernst Haeckel termed the view that matter and energy are inseparable attributes of one basic substance "monism" and utilized it to combat the dualism that he held was proper to all religious conceptions based on the duality of spirit and matter, of God and the world. Haeckel also found a decisive confirmation of biological evolution and of its necessity in what he termed the "fundamental

biogenetic law" of a parallelism between ontogeny, the development of an individual, and phylogeny, the development of the species to which that individual belongs. Monism was accepted by many chemists, biologists, and psychologists and became popular through the diffusion of Haeckel's writings and of such other works as Ludwig Büchner's *Force and Matter* (1855).

Monism also inspired literary and historical criticism. A passage from the introduction to Hippolyte Taine's *History of English Literature* (1863) has remained famous as an expression of this tendency: "Vice and virtue are products just as vitriol and sugar are, and every complex datum is born from the encounter of other simpler data on which it depends."

LOMBROSO. The positive school of penal law, founded by Cesare Lombroso, drew its inspiration from materialistic and especially from deterministic positivism. This school taught that criminal behavior depends on inevitable tendencies which are determined by the organic constitution of the delinquent. The structures of this constitution would be analyzed by a corresponding science—criminal anthropology.

WUNDT. Evolutionary positivism was also interpreted spiritualistically, notably by Wilhelm Wundt, who sought to substitute "psychophysical parallelism" for materialistic monism. Wundt's doctrine was that mental events do not depend on organic events but constitute a causal series by themselves and correspond point for point to the series of organic events. He made this doctrine the basis of his psychological investigations (Wundt founded the first laboratory of experimental psychology), and for many decades it remained the working hypothesis of experimental psychology. Wundt cultivated, moreover, a "psychology of peoples" that is descriptive sociology, in Spencer's sense. Like Spencer, Wundt intended it to be the study of the evolutionary process that produces institutions, customs, languages, and all the expressions of human society.

INFLUENCE OF EVOLUTIONARY POSITIVISM. Evolutionary positivism has left as a legacy to contemporary philosophy the idea of a universal, unilinear, continuous, necessary, and necessarily progressive evolution—an idea that forms the background and the explicit or implicit presupposition even of many philosophies which do not recognize their debt to positivism and which, in fact, argue against it. The idea of evolution is fundamental to the philosophies of C. S. Peirce, William James, and John Dewey, as well as to those of George Santayana, Samuel

Alexander, and A. N. Whitehead. Some of these philosophers have sought to remove the necessitarian character from the idea of evolution and to include within it an element of chance or freedom (Peirce, James, Dewey) or of novelty and creativity (Henri Bergson, C. Lloyd Morgan). Bergson, who interpreted evolution in terms of consciousness and insisted upon its creative character, explicitly acknowledged his debt to Spencer (*La pensée et le mouvant*, 3rd ed., Paris, 1934, p. 8). It is not without reason that his disciple Édouard Le Roy termed Bergson's doctrine a "new positivism," which means a new spiritualistic interpretation of cosmic evolution.

The vitality and the broad diffusion of the legacy of positivism is no sign of its validity. No scientific discipline is as yet able to adduce any sufficient proof in favor of a unilinear, continuous, and progressive cosmic evolution. In fact, in the very field where the phenomena of evolution have been most closely considered—biology—evolution seems to lack precisely those characteristics that positivism attributes to it.

CRITICAL POSITIVISM

EMPIRIOCRITICISM. In the last decade of the nineteenth century, positivism took on a more critical form through the work of Ernst Mach and Richard Avenarius. In Germany and Austria this critical positivism was known as empiriocriticism. Mach and Avenarius both held that facts (which for them, as for the other positivists, constituted the only reality) were relatively stable sets or groups of sensations connected to and dependent on each other. Sensations are the simple elements that figure in the constitution both of physical bodies and of perceptions or consciousness or the self. These elements are neutral, neither physical nor psychical, and every substantial difference between the physical and the psychical disappears. From this point of view, a "thing" is a set of sensations and the thought of the thing is the same set considered as "perceived" or "represented." For Avenarius, however, the process of interiorization, which he called introjection, and by which the thing is considered as a modification of the subject or as a part of consciousness, is a falsification of "pure" (that is, authentic or genuine) experience. For Avenarius and Mach, science, and knowledge in general, is only an instrument that the human organism uses to confront the infinite mass of sensations and to act in the light of those sensations in such a way as to conserve itself. The function of science is, therefore, economic, not contemplative or theoretical. It conforms to the principle of least action, and its end is the progressive adaptation of the organism to the environment.

Theories concerning concepts, scientific laws, and causality very different from those of classical positivism are the chief results of empiriocriticism. According to Mach a concept is the result of a selective abstraction that groups a large number of facts and considers those elements of these facts that are biologically important—that is, those adapted to excite the appropriate reaction in the organism. Since the variety of the biologically important reactions is much smaller than the variety of facts, the first task is to classify and simplify the facts by means of concepts, each of which constitutes the project of an appropriate reaction. And since the interests with which people confront facts are different, there are different concepts which refer to the same order of facts. The laborer, the doctor, the judge, the engineer, and the scientist all have their own concepts, and they define them in those restricted ways which are appropriate for stimulating the reaction or set of reactions in which each is interested.

The concept of law, which classical positivism conceived of as a constant relationship among facts (a relationship which in turn was considered as a fact) underwent a radical transformation in critical positivism. The Englishman Karl Pearson, in *The Grammar of Science* (1892), gave a kind of *summa* of the fundamental principles of the science of the time. Although Pearson's work utilized Machian concepts, it supplied Mach himself with many inspirations. Pearson affirmed that scientific law is a description, not a prescription: It "never explains the routine of our perception, the sense-impressions we project into an 'outside world.'" Instead of description, Mach preferred to speak of a restriction that the law prescribes on our expectation of phenomena. In any case, he added, "Whether we consider it a restriction of action, an invariable guide to what happens in nature, or an indication for our representations and our thought which bring events to completion in advance, a law is always a limitation of possibilities" (*Erkenntnis und Irrtum*, Leipzig, 1905, Ch. 23).

Mach and Pearson sought to free the notion of causality from the notion of force, which they regarded as an anthropomorphic interpolation. Mach held that the mathematical notion of function should be substituted for that of cause. When science succeeds in gathering various elements into one equation, each element becomes a function of the others. The dependence among the elements becomes reciprocal and simultaneous, and the relation between cause and effect becomes reversible (*Die Mechanik in ihrer Entwicklung*, 4th ed., Leipzig, 1901, p. 513). From this point of view, time, with its irreversible order, is real at the level of sensations and as a sensation.

The time of science is, on the other hand, an economic notion which serves for the ordering and prediction of facts.

Along the same lines, a disciple of Mach, Joseph Petzoldt, proposed to substitute for the principle of causality the "law of univocal determination," which would also be applicable to cases of reciprocal action. According to this law, one can find for every phenomenon means that permit determination of the phenomenon in a way which excludes the concurrent possibility of different determinations. According to Petzoldt this law permits the choosing, from among the infinite conditions that either determine a phenomenon or are interposed between it and its cause, of those conditions which effectively contribute to the determination of the phenomenon itself.

Pearson drew from his descriptive concept of law the consequence that scientific laws have only logical, not physical, necessity: "The theory of planetary motion is in itself as logically necessary as the theory of the circle; but in both cases the logic and necessity arise from the definition and axioms with which we mentally start, and do not exist in the sequence of sense-impressions which we hope that they will, at any rate, approximately describe. The necessity lies in the world of conceptions, and is only unconsciously and illogically transferred to the world of perceptions" (*The Grammar of Science,* 2nd ed., London, 1900, p. 134).

The empiriocritical branch of positivism is the immediate historical antecedent of the Vienna circle and of neopositivism in general. The sense impressions spoken of by Pearson and the sensations spoken of by Mach, Avenarius, and Petzoldt as neutral elements that constitute all the facts of the world, both physical and psychical, correspond exactly to the objects (*Gegenstände*) spoken of by Ludwig Wittgenstein in his *Tractatus Logico-philosophicus* as the constituents of atomic facts and to the elementary experiences (*Elementarerlebnisse*) spoken of by Rudolf Carnap in *Der logische Aufbau der Welt.* The restriction of necessity to the domain of logic, and the consequent reduction of natural laws to empirical propositions, is also a characteristic of the neopositivism of Wittgenstein, Carnap, and Hans Reichenbach. The critique of the principle of causality frequently recurs in neoempiricism reinforced by consideration of quantum mechanics (Philipp Frank, Reichenbach). The emphasis on prediction, important at all levels of science, is also a result of both empiriocriticism and logical positivism, as is the principle of the empirical verifiability of scientific propositions and the need to test and correct them constantly.

What empiriocriticism lacks is the stress on logic and language that is central to contemporary neopositivism. This stress developed out of work done in mathematical logic, especially by Bertrand Russell. Empiriocriticism lacks the concern with logic and the preoccupation with the nature of mathematics and of logical principles that is characteristic of contemporary neopositivism. The view that the proper business of philosophy is the clarification of concepts or the analysis of meanings derives largely from Russell, as does the preoccupation with problems about the status of logical and mathematical principles. The so-called linguistic theory about the nature of logical and mathematical principles, although subsequently endorsed by Russell, was developed by Wittgenstein. The use of the verifiability principle to demarcate meaningful from meaningless sentences and questions derives ultimately from David Hume's theory of impressions and ideas, but it is not to be found in any systematic form prior to the publications of the Vienna circle.

See also Logical Positivism.

Bibliography

There are no complete studies on positivism. For the individual philosophers, see J. Watson, *Comte, Mill and Spencer: An Outline of Philosophy* (New York: Macmillan, 1895); Leslie Stephen, *The English Utilitarians*, 3 vols. (London: Duckworth, 1900); D. G. Charlton, *Positivist Thought in France during the Second Empire, 1852–1870* (Oxford: Clarendon Press, 1959); and W. M. Simon, *European Positivism in the Nineteenth Century* (Ithaca, NY: Cornell University Press, 1963), which is limited to Comte's positivism and reactions to it.

The best comprehensive exposition of positivism as a philosophy and general world view is Richard von Mises, *Kleines Lehrbuch des Positivismus: Einführung in die empiristische Wissenschaftsauffassung* (Den Haag: van Stockum, 1939), translated under the author's supervision as *Positivism: A Study in Human Understanding* (Cambridge, MA: Harvard University Press, 1951). A briefer and more historical account, by another member of the logical positivist movement, is Hans Reichenbach, *The Rise of Scientific Philosophy* (Berkeley, CA: University of California Press, 1951). A less partisan overview (by a non-positivist) of positivist thought as a whole, emphasizing its unity while acknowledging its diverse ramifications and placing each episode in historical context, is Leszek Kolakowski, *The Alienation of Reason: A History of Positivist Thought,* translated by Norbert Guterman (New York, NY: Doubleday, 1968).

On the Enlightenment forerunners to nineteenth-century positivism, Charles Coulston Gillispie, *Science and Polity in France: The Revolutionary and Napoleonic Years* (Princeton, NJ: Princeton University Press, 2004) provides the political and social background, while the ideas are the focus in Keith Michael Baker's *Condorcet: From Natural Philosophy to*

Social Mathematics (Chicago: University of Chicago Press, 1975).

There are a number of valuable studies of the major nineteenth-century figures. On Comte, Robert C. Scharff, *Comte after Positivism* (Cambridge, U.K.: Cambridge University Press, 1995) and Juliette Grange, *La philosophie d'Auguste Comte: Science, politique, religion* (Paris: Presses Universeritaires de France, 1996) both focus primarily on philosophical ideas. On Mill, John Skorupski, *John Stuart Mill* (London: Routledge, 1989) also puts philosophical content in the foreground. On the evolutionary positivists, however, most studies have focused on social, political, and cultural aspects. David Weinstein, *Equal Freedom and Utility: Herbert Spencer's Liberal Utilitarianism* (Cambridge, U.K.: Cambridge University Press, 1998), for instance, focuses entirely on political ideas, and the Monist movement is situated in its social context by Gangolf Hübinger. "Die monistische Bewegung: Sozialingenieure und Kulturprediger," in *Kultur und Kulturwissenschaften um 1900 II: Idealismus und Positivismus*, G. Hübinger, R. von Bruch, and F.W. Graf, eds. (Stuttgart: Steiner, 1997, 246–259). Two of the three major figures of critical positivism have been the subjects of informative life-and-works studies: John T. Blackmore, *Ernst Mach: His Work, Life, and Influence* (Berkeley: University of California Press, 1972), and Theodore M. Porter, *Karl Pearson: The Scientific Life in a Statistical Age* (Princeton, NJ: Princeton University Press, 2004). The importance of Mach in particular for later positivist thought is brought out by Richard von Mises in "Ernst Mach and the Scientific Conception of the World," in *Unified Science: The Vienna Circle Monograph Series Originally Edited by Otto Neurath, Now in an English Edition*, edited by Brian McGuinness, translated by Hans Kaal (Dordrecht: Reidel, 1987: 166–190), and by Philipp Frank in "The Importance for our Times of Ernst Mach's Philosophy of Science," in his *Modern Science and its Philosophy* (Cambridge, MA: Harvard University Press, 1949: 61–78).

A great deal of scholarly effort has been devoted since the 1980s to the excavation and philosophical reconstruction of logical positivism, particularly the Vienna Circle. One important strand in this literature has regarded the neo-Kantian roots of logical positivism as more important than the positivist influence going back to Comte, Mill, and the western Enlightenment; exemplary for this trend is Michael Friedman, *Reconsidering Logical Positivism* (Cambridge, U.K.: Cambridge University Press, 1999). The continuity between the Enlightenment and logical positivism, in contrast, has been stressed by Thomas Uebel, e.g. "Enlightenment and the Vienna Circle's Scientific World-Conception," in *Philosophers on Education; Historical Perspectives*, edited by A. O. Rorty (London: Routledge, 1998, pp. 418–438), and *Vernunftkritik und Wissenschaft: Otto Neurath und der erste Wiener Kreis* (Vienna: Springer, 2000). The occlusion of the political, social, and educational dimensions in logical positivism after its main figures emigrated to North America is discussed by George Reisch, *How the Cold War Transformed Philosophy of Science: To the Icy Slopes of Logic* (Cambridge, U.K.: Cambridge University Press, 2005). A useful handbook with comprehensive bibliographies of the major figures and many peripheral ones is Friedrich Stadler, *The Vienna Circle: Studies in the Origins, Development, and Influence of Logical Empiricism*, translated by Camilla Nielsen et al (Vienna: Springer, 2001).

Nicola Abbagnano (1967)
Translated by Nino Langiulli
Bibliography updated by A. W. Carus (2005)

POSITIVISM, LEGAL

See *Legal Positivism*

POSITIVISM, LOGICAL

See *Logical Positivism*

POSNER, RICHARD
(1939–)

Richard Allen Posner, legal academic and federal court judge, was born in 1939 in New York. He was educated at Yale and Harvard Law School and has taught at the University of Chicago for many years. He was appointed to the federal appellate bench in 1981 and served as the chief judge of his court from 1993 to 2000. He is a leading advocate of the economic analysis of law and, by his own description, a legal pragmatist.

ECONOMICS OF LAW

Posner has argued that the various doctrines of the common law can best be explained as wealth maximizing. To say that a transaction or institution is wealth maximizing is to say that it creates more wealth than alternative possible transactions or institutions. Wealth, in this usage, is the value that goods have in the hands of their owners, and the value that a thing will have in the hands of a particular person is, qualifications aside, the amount that that person is willing to pay for it. Thus, the goal of wealth maximization is reached when goods are placed in the hands of those who would be willing to pay the most for them. An example of a wealth-maximizing rule, according to Posner, is the negligence rule in tort law: Under the rule of negligence, properly understood, injurers are liable for the losses they cause only when they could have taken precautions that would have prevented the accidents for less than the expected cost (that is, the cost discounted by the likelihood) of the accidents themselves. If prospective injurers take precautions when and only when it would be cost effective to do so—which the rule of negligence gives them an incentive to do—then the cost of accidents overall will tend to be minimized and the wealth of society will tend to be maximized.

Similarly, but more controversially, Posner has offered an economic explanation of the criminal law. Its major function, according to Posner, is to prevent people from bypassing the market system of voluntary exchange. When goods are exchanged voluntarily, as in a sale, wealth is increased since parties necessarily value what they have received in an exchange more highly than what they traded for it. When the market is bypassed, as in theft, there is no guarantee that the stolen good is valued more highly by the thief than by its owner. Similarly, Posner has argued (thereby creating a great deal of controversy) that one of the things wrong with rape is that it bypasses the marriage and sex market so that wealth tends to be decreased. For Posner this is one of the virtues of wealth maximization over utilitarianism: Wealth maximization can explain why rape is always a crime whereas he believes that utilitarianism would have to condone rape if the enjoyment of the rapist were greater than the pain and unhappiness caused to the victim.

Even if the common law does promote the maximization of wealth, the question remains whether it *should*. Posner believes that wealth maximization is an ethically attractive guide not only for the common law but for social institutions generally. A system that maximized wealth overall would maximize everyone's chance for a higher income and thus would elicit *nearly* universal consent *ex ante*—though Posner's consenting parties would not have to do so in ignorance of their personal attributes. All persons would know of their own productive capacity—the extent to which they can benefit others—so they would know approximately how they would do under wealth-maximizing laws. It is only the unproductive who would not consent: They would be less well off under a wealth-maximizing system.

LEGAL PRAGMATISM

Posner believes that philosophical pragmatism is largely irrelevant to the law. By contrast, he believes that what he calls *everyday pragmatism* has a great deal to say. The everyday pragmatist—for example, the pragmatic judge—is an instrumentalist in law as in other things. Pragmatic judges are not bound by some conception of the law as an immutable body of rules but rather use their office to try to achieve reasonable resolutions to legal disputes. They reject moral, legal, and political theory (including constitutional theory) as guides to decision making. They are not bound by precedent, but neither are they bound to ignore it. Wise judges realize the virtues of

following precedent—the value of certainty in law, the importance of the reliance interest, the wisdom that inheres in some of the common law—but they are free to ignore it when they can do more good by ignoring it. When pragmatic judges must look beyond the law to settle legal disputes, as they often must, they will find no help in academic moral theory. They must rely on common sense and economics and other sciences, as well as on values that are widely shared.

Although Posner's pragmatic judges are free to follow precedent or not, as they see fit, Posner counsels restraint in constitutional adjudication, placing himself among those judges and theorists that belong to what he calls the *outrage* school: The problem is that most judges are lacking the factual knowledge and expertise in social science that would justify them in striking down legislation. Hence, judges should only declare legislation unconstitutional when it stirs a strongly negative reaction in them. When in the future judges do in fact have a better grasp of social science and the factual underpinnings of the various areas of law, the need for law itself as we understand it will begin to disappear—the *supersession* thesis. Antitrust law and administrative law are two areas of American law that illustrate the thesis: "It is fair to say that at the beginning of its second century antitrust law has become a branch of applied economics" (Posner 1999, p. 229).

Posner calls himself a moral relativist. He believes that there is no rational road to agreement with those of fundamentally different moral beliefs and—what is now largely uncontroversial—that there is no way to reach certainty in moral matters. It follows, he believes, that we cannot call the actions of someone in another culture immoral unless we add *by our lights*, though he does not explain what the difference is between saying that something is immoral and saying that it is immoral by our lights.

See also Ethics and Economics; Philosophy of Law.

Bibliography

WORKS BY POSNER

"Utilitarianism, Economics, and Legal Theory." *Journal of Legal Studies* 8 (1979): 103.

"The Ethical and Political Basis of the Efficiency Norm in Common Law Adjudication." *Hofstra Law Review* 8 (1980): 487.

Problems of Jurisprudence. Cambridge, MA: Harvard University Press, 1990.

Overcoming Law. Cambridge, MA: Harvard University Press, 1995.

Problematics of Moral and Legal Theory. Cambridge, MA: Harvard University Press, 1999.

Frontiers of Legal Theory. Cambridge, MA: Harvard University Press, 2001.

Michael Louis Corrado (2005)

POSSIBILITY

The subject of possibility is a central topic in philosophy. It was frequently discussed in the history of philosophy, and it is actively debated by contemporary philosophers.

HISTORICAL DEVELOPMENTS

ARISTOTLE. The first comprehensive treatment of possibility occurs in the work of Aristotle. Aristotle's writing on this subject is difficult and confusing, but he seems to have held that the idea of possibility is derivative from that of necessity and negation, "It is possible that P" meaning "It is not necessary that not-P" (see *On Interpretation* 13.22b). Necessity of this basic kind is absolute necessity, and like absolute possibility it is applicable to sentences or propositions (*logoi*). According to his *Posterior Analytics* (4.21), a necessary proposition truly predicates something of a thing's essence; an example would be "A man is a rational being." A possible proposition, one that may be asserted to be such by a proposition containing the words "It is possible that … ," attributes an accident to a thing, an accident being a character that, because it is not excluded by a thing's essence, may or may not belong to it, as being seated may or may not belong to a man or woman. Because Aristotle held that what belongs to a thing's essence is given by a "real" definition, necessary propositions for him are either real definitions or logical consequences of such definitions.

Formal possibility. Although Aristotle's explicit remarks on absolute necessity relate to his theory of essences, he also uses a formal notion of necessity and, thus, of possibility, as when he argues that "Necessarily, every S is L" follows from "Necessarily, every M is L" and "Necessarily, every S is M." That the necessity and, correlatively, the possibility involved here is not the same as the real necessity and possibility just discussed is evident from the fact that the necessity of the conclusion "Every S is L" (and the impossibility of "Some S is not L") is justified wholly by the logical connection signified by "Every … is …" and by the sub-occurrences of "necessarily" in the modal syllogism. Important as this type of necessity and possibility obviously is to his theory of modal syllogisms, Aristotle does not seem to have reached the point

of formulating its meaning explicitly. (See the discussion of Aristotle's modal syllogisms in *The Development of Logic* [1963] by William Kneale and Martha Kneale.) There can be little doubt, however, that this formal notion of necessity is rooted in the necessity of the first principles of all reasoning, such as the principle of contradiction. These principles cannot be demonstrated, Aristotle said, because all demonstration presupposes them (see *Posterior Analytics* 1.3.72b). They are known immediately and intuitively, and they cannot be consistently questioned.

Relative possibility. In the *Prior Analytics* (1.19.23a) Aristotle distinguishes absolute from relative necessity, and he implicitly makes a similar distinction for possibility in various passages of the *Organon* (for instance, in *De Sophisticis Elenchis* 4.166a22–166a30). Just as a proposition that does not state an absolute necessity may be considered necessary relative to certain other propositions (as a contingent statement constituting the conclusion of a valid deductive argument may be considered necessary relative to the truth of the premises), so a proposition like "Jones is walking" may be considered impossible relative to the proposition "Jones is sitting," and "Jones is sitting" may be considered possible relative to "Jones is not running." Although this distinction is intuitively clear, Aristotle does not explicitly say whether relative necessity and relative possibility are to be understood by reference to the sort of real absolute necessity and possibility discussed earlier or whether, as is likely, they are to be understood in relation to the formal notions that he sometimes uses but does not explicitly define.

Potentiality. Another sort of possibility discussed by Aristotle is potentiality, for certain possibilities can be said to exist as potentialities of concrete things. The possibility of a person's reading this or that may be understood in relation to a potentiality (we would say an ability) that the person has. For Aristotle a person who can read is a potential reader. Although the notion of potentiality is basic to Aristotle's metaphysics, he thought it could be understood only by analogy: "As a man who is building is to one who knows how to build, as waking is to sleeping, that which sees to that which has sight but has eyes shut, that which is shaped out of matter to its matter, the finished product to the raw material, so in general is actuality to potentiality" (*Metaphysics* 1048b).

MEGRIANS AND STOICS. A definition of possibility widely accepted in the Hellenistic period was that of Diodorus Cronus of Megara, who said, "The possible is that which either is or will be true" (Kneale and Kneale

1963, p. 117f). This identification of possibility with, in effect, present and future actuality was challenged by the Stoics (for example, by Chrysippus), who defined real possibility as "that which is not prevented by any thing from happening even if it does not happen" (Kneale and Kneale 1963, p. 123). Because the Stoics tended to be strict determinists, holding that whatever happens is necessitated by something else, they typically argued that our assessment of nonactuals as possibles could be based only on ignorance, for any conceivable occurrence that does not take place at some time or other is presumably prevented from taking place by the course of nature. Thus, their conception of real possibility developed into a conception of what is now known as epistemic possibility, or possibility as consistency with our knowledge.

Because the Stoics were especially interested in formal logic, they had another conception of possibility, however. According to this conception, necessary propositions (that is, necessary sentences) are those that are always true, such as the propositions of logic and mathematics. Possible propositions are those that are sometimes true. Since today's utterance of "A sea battle will occur tomorrow" is sometimes true according to the Stoics, then even though the course of nature may determine its truth with respect to tomorrow, the fact it states still belongs to the category of the possible (in the sense of sometimes true). It is perhaps worth adding that some commentators—for instance, Jaakko Hintikka (1959)—find this conception of possibility in Aristotle as well.

NEOPLATONISTS. The next distinctive conception of possibility, which turned out to be of great importance in medieval and modern philosophy, was worked out by the Neoplatonists—although it can be said to have its roots in Plato. According to this tradition, possibilities are not facts or states of affairs (that is, items properly expressed by sentences or propositions) but beings or essences that belong to Nous or Intelligence, the "first emanation of the One." Aristotle had spoken of potential beings inherent in various matters—for instance, a statue of Hermes existing potentially in a chunk of marble—but the idea of a possible being, which cannot be understood in relation to what substances or matter will become under certain conditions or when operated on in a certain way, is evidently new.

Admittedly, the idea may in a sense be traced back to Plato, for a possible being thus conceived is essentially something thinkable or intelligible, and Plato identified the intelligible with the world of Ideas or Forms. But Plato's Ideas were always general rather than specific, of humanity rather than of Socrates, and this means that the only possibilities, in this sense, that Plato could accommodate were kinds or species. Such Neoplatonists as Plotinus admitted Ideas of individual souls, and these, being nongeneral, may be regarded as the prototypes of the possible beings that occur in the theories of later philosophers such as Leibniz.

An extremely important aspect of the Neoplatonist treatment of possibles is that all possible beings were held to be actualized; possibility and actuality were regarded, that is, as precisely coextensive. The basic reason for this was that the infinite perfection or "goodness" of the One, which "overflows" into the emanation constituting the world of diverse actuality, requires that every possible being be brought into existence or actualized. This principle of plenitude among actualities was thought to be necessary according to the nature of things, because it is an essential feature of the One's perfection "to produce otherness" and "necessarily to do this in the maximum degree" (Lovejoy 1936, p. 66).

The Neoplatonic conception of possibles as Ideas in a divine mind that, owing to the perfection of that mind, are necessarily actualized was a recurrent and problematic theme in medieval philosophy. As A. O. Lovejoy pointed out in *The Great Chain of Being* (1936), medieval writers tended to conceive the love or goodness of the Christian God (in whose mind the Ideas were now said to exist) as an "immeasurable and inexhaustible energy," a love of which "the only beneficiaries … were not actual sentient creatures or already existing moral agents, but Platonic ideas, conceived figuratively as aspirants for the grace of actual existence" (p. 68).

ABELARD. Abelard, writing in the early twelfth century, was led to maintain that what can be is the same as what can be produced by God and that "it is intrinsically impossible for God to do (or make) or to leave undone (or unmade) anything other than the things that he actually does at some time do or omit to do; or to do anything in any other manner at any other time than that in which it actually is done" (Lovejoy 1936, p. 71).

AQUINAS. Because Abelard's view of possibility and actuality seemed not only to deny God's divine freedom but also, in implying that the created world was so good that it could not be better, to "make the creation equal to the Creator," it was regarded as heretical (Lovejoy 1936, p. 73). Accordingly, other Schoolmen, who like Aquinas agreed that "all things preexist in God by their types (*rationes*)," had to maintain that the creation involved a selection among the ideas. In this view not all possibles are actual, and what is actual is not necessary: There are, that is, possible beings that God could have created but did not create, and he did not have to create the things that he did create. To square this claim with God's goodness, Aquinas found it necessary to invoke the Aristotelian distinction between absolute and relative necessity and possibility. Although it is absolutely possible for God, good as he is, to have created things other than what he did create, it may nevertheless be admitted that, relative to his choice, which was "becoming to" rather than necessary to his goodness, the existence of what is actual is necessary and could not be otherwise. That is, relative to this premise, it is impossible for anything to exist that does not sooner or later actually exist.

Even granting the distinction between absolute and relative possibility, it might be objected that Aquinas is still imposing a limit on God's freedom. If what actually exists is determined by God's selection from a class of possibilities, it would appear that God could not, in an absolute sense, have created anything not belonging to this class. In reply to this Aquinas maintained that what is absolutely impossible is self-contradictory and that what is self-contradictory is contrary to God's nature, repugnant to being, and therefore not an object at all. ("So it is better to say that what involves a contradiction cannot be done rather than God cannot do it," *Summa Theologica* 1.25.3–4.) In making this reply, Aquinas may seem to be introducing a formal notion of absolute possibility of the sort defended in more recent times. Yet, as with Aristotle, the category of possibility in question is grounded not in linguistic or purely logical considerations but wholly in intelligible essences ("intelligible forms"). In other words, the definitions relevant to ascertaining the consistency or intelligibility of a term or idea are "real" rather than nominal or analytical, which means that the possibility in question is the absolute kind espoused by Aristotle, not the formal or conceptual sort allowed by most modern philosophers.

HOBBES. In the modern period we find in Hobbes a view that not only contrasts vividly with the typical medieval one but which, confused as it is, is occasionally defended by philosophers of the twenty-first century. Hobbes's view contrasts with the medieval one because he held that conceivable beings are not necessarily possible beings. If a being is conceivable, the only conclusion Hobbes would draw is that words standing for it are not gibberish. To be possible, the necessary conditions for a thing's existence must be satisfied. Hobbes therefore contended that every possible being, event, or state of affairs is actual at some

time or another: "If it shall never be produced, then those things will never concur which are requisite for the production of it" (*Elements of Philosophy* 10.4). Because for Hobbes whatever exists does so by virtue of necessary causes, we can call something possible (or contingent), as opposed to necessary, in his opinion only when we do not know the cause that will produce it. This view plainly goes back to that of the Stoics, for it implies that the only legitimate possibilities that are not also necessities are epistemic possibilities—that is, things or states of affairs whose existence is consistent with our knowledge at a given time.

DESCARTES. Descartes's approach to possibility is important mainly because it is essentially psychologistic: what is possible is what is clearly and distinctly conceivable. Descartes admitted that if the idea of a thing involves a contradiction, the thing is impossible, but he held that its impossibility is owing to the fact that contradictory ideas cannot be clearly and distinctly conceived. This latter criterion is basic for Descartes because some impossibilities do not, in his view, involve contradictions. As he saw it, there are *a priori* truths that are necessary and guaranteed to be true by the goodness of God but whose denials, which state impossibilities, are consistent. To know firsthand whether a given idea—for instance, the idea of a circular polygon—does represent a possibility, one must therefore be able to form a clear and distinct idea of it. If one is able to form such an idea, one has God's assurance that it represents a real possibility, the sort of thing that God could actualize if he chose to do so.

SPINOZA. According to Spinoza, "A thing is said to be impossible either because the essence of the thing itself or its definition involves a contradiction, or because no external cause exists determinate to the production of such a thing" (Spinoza, *Ethics*, 1, prop. 33, note I). Because Spinoza in effect adopted the Neoplatonic principle of plenitude, he held that if the idea of a thing does not involve a contradiction, it must be actual, for all self-consistent beings are determined to exist, and necessarily exist, by the very nature of reality, which he calls "God":

[Accordingly, a] thing cannot be called contingent unless with reference to a deficiency of our knowledge. For if [and here Spinoza introduces the notion of epistemic possibility] we do not know that the essence of a thing involves a contradiction, or if we actually know it involves no contradiction, and nevertheless can affirm nothing with certainty about its existence because the order of causes is concealed from us, that thing can never *appear to us* as necessary or impossible, and therefore we call it either contingent or possible (Spinoza, *Ethics*, 1, prop. 33, note I).

LEIBNIZ. To general readers, Leibniz is best known for his metaphysical optimism, the doctrine that this is the best of all possible worlds. He conceived of a possible world as a maximal collection of absolutely possible beings each of which is "compossible" with the other beings contained in that world; the totality is maximal in the sense that it contains everything compossible with its contents. Two things are compossible, Leibniz said, when it is absolutely possible for them to exist together; and something is absolutely possible, for him, when God's conception of it is free from contradiction. Because Leibniz held that God's concept of a thing includes all facts about it, including such apparently accidental facts as that it once crossed a certain river in Peru or that it once was bitten by a dog called "Rover," he concluded that if a thing is absolutely possible, it is so only relative to its place in a possible world, one including certain possible rivers, perhaps, and certain possible dogs. A possible being is strictly a being, therefore, whose existence is compossible with the members of a possible world. This conception comprehends the less restrictive idea, common in recent metaphysics, that a possible thing or state of affairs is one that "exists at," or belongs to, some possible world.

Like Aristotle, Leibniz drew a distinction between absolute and relative possibility. (Leibniz used the term "hypothetical" here instead of "relative," but his distinction was the same as Aristotle's.) Because God created the best of all possible worlds, any existing thing that is not, like God, an absolutely necessary being depends on God's creative choice. A thing that is absolutely possible but dependent this way on God's creative choice is hypothetically necessary: its nonexistence is hypothetically impossible, ruled out by the choice God actually made. Everything that has occurred, will occur, or is now occurring is necessary in this hypothetical sense, according to Leibniz. But hypothetical necessity is not the same as absolute necessity, he insisted; Diodorus Cronus (see above) erred in not recognizing this important fact. All human behavior is hypothetically necessary, but it is not thereby inevitable in an absolute sense. This is why one can rightly maintain that free choice remains possible for human beings. A free action, for Leibniz, is one that results from a "rationally spontaneous" choice; its originating principles lie within the agent. Free actions spring from motives and other causes, but these "incline without necessitating," he said; absolutely necessity is not imposed upon them (see Mates 1986, p. 119)

HUME. The British empiricists, typically rejecting the claims of conceptualism as defended by most epistemic rationalists, seemed to embrace more fully the idea that possibility is a matter of logical consistency. In remarking that, "The contrary of every matter of fact is still possible, because it can never imply a contradiction," Hume appears firmly committed to a view of logical possibility. But in adding to the quoted sentence, "And is conceived by the mind with the same facility and distinctness," Hume discloses his tacit commitment to a psychologistic conception of possibility (what is possible is what is conceivable), which was held by Descartes and is often assumed even today. (See Hume's *Enquiry concerning Human Understanding*, 4.1.)

KANT. In Kant there is not only a clear identification of *a priori* possibility but an explicit distinction between logical and physical (or nomological) possibility. For philosophers like Spinoza, who identified the logical with the real order, there was plainly no sense in this distinction, and there was little place for it in the philosophies of the Greek and medieval thinkers. It is, however, essential to the contemporary outlook. Kant expresses the distinction a bit clumsily thus:

> A concept is always possible [he means "represents a possibility"] if it is not self-contradictory. This is the logical criterion of possibility, and through it objects are distinguished from the *nihil negativum*. But it may nonetheless be an empty concept, unless the objective reality of the synthesis through which the concept is generated has been specifically proved; and such proof … rests on principles of possible experience, and not on the principle of analysis (the law of contradiction). This is a warning against arguing directly from the logical possibility of concepts to the real possibility of things. (*Critique of Pure Reason*, A597/B625, note)

> [Thus, the possibility of such things as] a special fundamental power of our mind to *intuit* the future (not merely, say, to deduce it), or, finally, a faculty of our mind to stand in a community of thoughts with other men (no matter how distant they may be)—these are concepts the possibility of which is entirely groundless, because it cannot be grounded in experience and its known laws, and without this it is an arbitrary combination of thoughts that, although it contains no contradiction, still can make no claim to objective reality, thus to the possibility of the

sort of object that one would here think. (*Critique of Pure Reason* A223/B270)

To ascertain that such things are empirically (as opposed to merely logically) possible, we must ascertain whether the nature of things so described agree with the formal conditions of actual experience.

CONTEMPORARY DEVELOPMENTS

Not all the conceptions of possibility discussed in the previous section on the history of philosophy are equally acceptable to contemporary philosophers, and new conceptions are topics of current debate. Generally speaking, possibility is now discussed in relation to two principal subjects: basic metaphysics, which takes some kind of absolute possibility as fundamental, and the compatibility of freedom and determinism, which introduces possibilities of other kinds. The conceptions of possibility now considered tenable by most philosophers (there is disagreement on this) can be identified by reference to these two subjects.

BASIC METAPHYSICS. Until the 1970s, most analytic philosophers described absolute *a priori* possibilities as "logical possibilities" and identified them, as Leibniz did, by reference to logical consistency: An absolute possibility is something that can be exhaustively described without contradiction. In logic a contradiction has the form of "p and not-p" however; and this syntactical structure is not explicit in many statements that fail to express genuine possibilities: it is not present, for instance, in "Some bachelors are married" or "Mary is both taller and shorter than Sally." To expose the contradictions implicit in these statements one must make use of definitions and conceptual truths such as "For any x and y, if x is taller than y then x is not shorter than y." Conceptual truths and statements true by definition were called "analytic" truths, and the full range of absolute possibilities was generally conceded to be identifiable only by reference to them. An absolute possibility was then said to be expressed by a statement that is consistent with all relevant analytic truths. According to this conception, a statement that is not so consistent would fail to express a genuine possibility.

This way of identifying absolute possibilities was undermined by Saul Kripke in lectures given in 1970 and subsequently published under the title *Naming and Necessity* (1980). Kripke's criticism featured two striking examples. The first involved what most philosophers would call an analytic truth pertinent to the standard meter located in Paris. The truth is that the rod is one meter long. Although this truth is a consequence of an arbitrarily chosen standard specifying what is to count as a meter in length, and thus would be acknowledged to be analytic by most philosophers, it is not necessary because the rod in question does not of necessity possess its current length: it could have a different one. This latter possibility is genuine, but it is identified by reflection on how the rod might change, what might happen if, say, it were heated—not by the consistency of "The rod is not a standard meter long" with the truth that the length it now has equals one meter. The analytic consistency conception of absolute possibility does not give the right result in this kind of case.

Kripke's second example concerned the identity of Hesperus and Phosphorus, the morning star and the evening star. The statement that Hesperus = Phosphorus is not an analytic truth; it was discovered to be true by empirical investigation. The two "stars" turned out to be a single planet, Venus, seen in the sky at different times and presumed to be different. The fact that the statement is not an analytic truth does not prove that it is not necessary, however. It is in fact necessary because it concerns a single planet, and that planet, like everything else, is necessarily self-identical. Because the identity of Hesperus and Phosphorous had to be discovered empirically, the necessity of their identity had to be inferred from the fact of their identity. If "a" and "b" are used "rigidly," as Kripke said, to pick out the same objects in actual as well as counterfactual situations, then the following principle provides a basis for the inference: If $a = b$ then it is necessary that $a = b$. Because the necessity of "a" being "b" is equivalent to the impossibility of *a* not being *b*, a certain possibility is ruled out by our empirical investigation: We learn that it is not possible for *a* to differ from *b*. This impossibility is not known *a priori* by the discovery that some statement (or proposition) is self-contradictory or analytically inconsistent.

In developing his metaphysical views, Kripke drew a distinction between *de dicto* and *de re* necessity and possibility. A *de dicto* possibility is in effect the possible truth of some proposition; it is expressed in words by a sentence beginning "It is possible that …" A *de re* possibility, by contrast, is attached to a particular thing, such as a person or chair. We are concerned with such possibilities, Kripke said, when we wonder whether a certain person might have done this or that in some counterfactual situation. Kripke spoke of "contingent properties" in describing such possibilities. A property is contingent for a thing when the thing may or may not possess it in some situation or other. Such a property contrasts with a necessary or "essential" one, this being a property that a thing possesses in every situation, actual and counterfactual, in which it may exist. *De re* possibilities correspond to Aristotle's potentialities; *de re* necessities correspond to his "actualities," or the components, as he conceived them, of a thing's "form" or essence.

Kripke emphasized that the notions of necessity and possibility he discussed belong to metaphysics, not epistemology, and he sometimes spoke of them as metaphysical necessity and metaphysical possibility (see Kripke 1980, p.19). In commenting on the formal semantics he invented for the logic of statements affirming such necessities and possibilities, Kripke used Leibniz's notion of a possible world. A statement, S, is necessary with respect to the actual world, Kripke said, just when S is true with respect to all possible worlds—more exactly, all worlds that are possible relative to the actual world. S is possible with respect to the actual world (it is, for members of this world, possible that S) just when S is true with respect to some possible world—with some world that is possible relative to the actual world. Kripke spoke of worlds possible "relative to" the actual world because different assumptions may be made about this relativity, and these different assumptions are associated with modal principles that are characteristic of different systems of modal logic (see Kripke 1971).

Although Kripke informally used the notion of a possible world in describing the truth-condition for statements affirming metaphysical possibilities and necessities, he did not believe that such statements were understandable only in relation to possible worlds or that the framework of possible worlds provides a reductive analysis of modal discourse. In fact, to avoid philosophical confusions and anxieties regarding possible worlds, he recommended that "possible state (or history) of the world" or "counterfactual situation" might provide a preferable terminology (see Kripke 1980, pp. 18f). As far as modal knowledge is concerned, he seems to believe that intuitiveness (or perhaps intuitive obviousness) is basic. As he put it in *Naming and Necessity* (1980), "Some philosophers think that something's having intuitive content is very inconclusive evidence in favor of it. I think it is very heavy evidence in favor of anything, myself. I really don't know, in a way, what more conclusive evidence one can have about anything, ultimately speaking" (p. 42). In speaking of intuitive content this way Kripke appears to favor an epistemically rationalist (or Cartesian) view of modal knowledge, but he did not discuss the matter in greater detail, and it remains uncertain what the details of his view actually are.

An influential writer about possibility who appears to regard possible worlds and the possible individuals that compose them as basic realities is David Lewis (1986). Lewis believes that all possible worlds actually exist but that only one world, at least from our perspective, is actual: our world. Like Leibniz, Lewis holds that the possible individuals of other possible worlds do not include the individuals of our world; in fact, he thinks the individuals of different worlds cannot be shared. When we consider a counterfactual possibility involving a person belonging to our world—George W. Bush, say—the possibility is grounded in (or actually involves) a counterpart to that person, a being relevantly similar to him, belonging to another possible world. Lewis accepts this counterpart theory because he thinks a given thing cannot have incompatible features. If a thing belonged to two different worlds, the worlds would overlap in it, and this could happen only if the thing's nonrelational features were exactly the same in both worlds: A thing cannot possibly differ from itself. Lewis ably defends his position against a multitude of objections in *On the Plurality of Worlds* (1986), and he also provides a non-Cartesian account of how he thinks we can have genuine knowledge of worlds that, although existing, are possible rather than actual.

FREEDOM AND DETERMINISM. The conceptions of possibility relevant to this topic are brought to mind by the question, "If the world is a deterministic system, is it possible for human beings to do anything that they do not actually do?" Not every responsible philosopher agrees that this question requires an affirmative answer if human beings can reasonably be considered capable of acting of their own free will, but the question is commonly asked and different kinds of possibility are mentioned in answering it (see Austin 1961).

Possibility as ability. This kind of possibility corresponds to Aristotle's potentiality. We often have this sort of possibility in mind when we wonder what a person is capable of doing, and what he or she could do in specific circumstances. Can Tom do fifty push-ups? Can he do that many after a big meal? What is relevantly possible here? The basic idea pertinent in answering these questions is that of an ability or capacity. To have an ability or capacity a person must be capable of doing something; and to be thus capable is to be such that if conditions are of the right kind, appropriate behavior will occur. In discussions involving human freedom the abilities under consideration are voluntary: they are abilities that a person can manifest "at will." If Sally has the ability to swim, then she will normally succeed in swimming if she is immersed in water and attempts to swim. The qualification "normal" is important here because a failure to swim would not be evidence of an inability to swim if one's legs were encased in concrete. Success is required only in "favorable" conditions.

Sometimes we are concerned with what a person can do in special conditions, which may be far from what are considered favorable. Can Tom swim in a rough sea? Can Betty solve an algebra problem when her roommate's stereo is pounding in her ears, when she is seething with irritable frustration? The relevant test here is success under the specified conditions. In a particular case the test to be satisfied is specified by a conditional statement in the subjunctive mood: If conditions C were to obtain and the subject attempted to exercise the relevant capacity, the subject would succeed in the attempt.

The most important recent work on the logic of subjunctive conditionals is contained in Davis Lewis's book *Counterfactuals* (1973). Lewis gives the truth-conditions for these statements by reference to possible worlds. A statement of the form "If it were the case that p, it would be the case that q" is true, according to Lewis, just when q is true at the possible worlds that satisfy p and are otherwise most similar to the actual world. (There may or may not be a single most similar p-world.) Thus, to decide whether Tom could do fifty push-ups after a certain meal, one in effect has to decide, Lewis says, whether a possible world in which he (or his "counterpart") does fifty push-ups after such a meal would be minimally different from the actual world, or whether it would require him to have undergone a course of training, say, that he did not experience in the actual world. Because the negation, according to Lewis, of the conditional "If A were to happen, B would happen" is "If A were to happen, B might not happen," one can use his theory to identify another kind of possibility, which might be called a "contingent" possibility. Suppose it is false both that if A were to happen, B would happen and that A does happen. Under these circumstances it could be said that B's not happening is a contingent possibility.

Relative or hypothetical possibility. A conception of possibility ultimately vital to the subject of human freedom is that of what is possible given the laws of nature and the occurrence of remotely prior causal factors. Aristotle and Leibniz both acknowledged this conception, but the idea that it represents a genuine kind of possibility is often questioned by contemporary philosophers. Benson Mates (1986), in his commentary on Leibniz, says that the distinction between absolute and hypothetical necessity (and therefore between absolute and hypothetical possi-

bility) seems to originate in a confusion of "Necessarily, if P then Q" and "If P, then necessarily Q." There is no doubt that this confusion is often made, but it was certainly not made by Leibniz, who explicitly distinguished statements of these kinds and accused Diodorus Cronos, who denied that any possibility could fail to be a necessity, of confusing hypothetical necessity with absolute necessity (see Mates 1986, pp. 117ff).

Peter van Inwagen (1983, 2000), wishing to avoid the confusion Mates mentioned, introduced a new modal operator in formulating an argument against the compatibility of freedom and determinism. The formula "Np" containing his special operator "N" is to be understood as meaning "p [is true] and no one has or ever had any choice as to whether p." If "O" is a modal operator representing a kind of necessity, there is no doubt that an argument having "Op" and "O(if p then q)" as premises and "Oq" as a conclusion is valid. Accordingly, van Inwagen formulates a corresponding argument featuring his operator "N" and argues that it is valid. The remotely prior causes C occurred and no one now has or ever had any choice about their occurrence; hence "N(C)." Similarly, the laws of nature hold true and no one has or ever had any choice about this fact. The laws also imply that if C then B, where B is a representative item of behavior in a deterministic world. Because this implication is necessary and something no one has or ever had any choice about, van Inwagen concludes that N(B)—that B occurs and no one has or ever had any choice about it: an alternative to B is out of the question.

Van Inwagen's argument has been seriously criticized since his book was published in 1983, and he has gone on to sketch a new argument to express his sense of the "sheer inescapablity" of determined behavior (see van Inwagen 2000). But it is obvious that the sheer inescapability of B is tantamount to the fact that it is relatively (or hypothetically) necessary in Leibniz's sense, and van Inwagen's conclusion "N(B)" amounts to nothing more than an assertion that B is a logical consequence of natural laws and the occurrence of initial conditions (or previous causes) that cannot be altered when B occurs. Van Inwagen's worry about human freedom depends, in effect, on the relative impossibility of behavior that does not occur. So this sense of possibility is vital to the freedom-determinism issue, at least as philosophers such as van Inwagen understand it.

See also Analytic and Synthetic Statements; Modal Logic.

Bibliography

POSSIBILITY IN THE HISTORY OF PHILOSOPHY

Aquinas, Thomas. *Basic Writings of Saint Thomas Aquinas*, edited by Anton C. Pegis. 2 vols. New York: Random House, 1945.

Aristotle. *The Complete Works of Aristotle: The Revised Oxford Translation*, edited by Jonathan Barnes. 2 vols. Princeton, NJ: Princeton University Press, 1984.

Copleston, Frederick. *A History of Philosophy*. 8 vols. London. 1959–1965.

Descartes, René. *The Philosophical Writings of Descartes*. Translated and edited by John Cottingham, Robert Stoothoff, and Dugald Murdoch. 2 vols. Cambridge, U.K.: Cambridge University Press, 1984.

Hintikka, Jaakko. "Necessity, Universality, and Time in Aristotle." *Adjatus* 20 (1959): 65–90.

Hobbes, Thomas. *Hobbes: Selections*, edited by Frederick J. E. Woodbridge. New York: Scribners, 1930.

Hume, David. *Enquiry concerning Human Understanding*. 3rd ed., edited by L. A. Selby-Bigge. Revised by P. H. Nidditch. Oxford: Clarendon Press, 1975.

Kant, Immanuel. *Critique of Pure Reason*. Translated and edited by Paul Guyer and Allen Wood. Cambridge, U.K.: Cambridge University Press, 1998.

Kneale, William, and Martha Kneale. *The Development of Logic*. Oxford: Clarendon Press, 1963.

Leibniz, Gottfried von. *Leibniz: Selections*, edited by Philip P. Wiener. New York: Scribners, 1951.

Lovejoy, A. O. *The Great Chain of Being: A Study of the History of an Idea*. Cambridge, MA: Harvard University Press, 1936.

Mates, Benson. *The Philosophy of Leibniz: Metaphysics and Language*. New York: Oxford University Press, 1986.

Spinoza, Baruch. *Philosophy of Benedict de Spinoza*. Translated by R. H. M. Elwes. New York, 1955.

POSSIBILITY IN CONTEMPORARY PHILOSOPHY

Austin, J. L. "Ifs and Cans." In his *Philosophical Papers*. Oxford: Clarendon Press, 1961.

Kripke, Saul. *Naming and Necessity*. Cambridge, MA: Harvard University Press, 1980.

Kripke, Saul. "Semantical Considerations on Modal Logic." In *Reference and Modality*, edited by Leonard Linsky. London: Oxford University Press, 1971.

Lewis, David. *Counterfactuals*. Oxford: Blackwell, 1973.

Lewis, David. *On the Plurality of Worlds*. Oxford: Blackwell, 1986.

van Inwagen, Peter. *An Essay on Free Will*. Oxford: Clarendon Press, 1983.

van Inwagen, Peter. "Free Will Remains a Mystery." In *Philosophical Perspectives*. Vol. 14: *Action and Freedom, 2000*, edited by James E. Tomberlin. Boston: Blackwell, 2000.

Bruce A. Aune (1967, 2005)

POSSIBLE WORLDS

See *Modality, Philosophy and Metaphysics of*

POSTCOLONIALISM

Not unlike the Renaissance, the Enlightenment, and postmodernism, postcolonialism refers not only to a temporal marker that signals a shift in mentalities and metaphilosophical questioning but also to a decolonizing movement enabled by new material conditions and to a theoretical and philosophical methodology. As a temporal marker postcolonialism is caught in a series of paradoxes. On the one hand, postcolonialism signals the alleged *end* of colonialism and the beginning of a new historical period. On the other hand, at the center of postcolonialism is the exploration of what postcolonial theorists have called the *postcolonial present*, namely, the enduring legacy of colonialism in contemporary times. Still, one of the most basic goals of postcolonialism is to foreground the movements of decolonization that began as early as the end of World War II, peaked during the 1950s and 1960s, and have lasted into the twenty-first century. For this reason many postcolonial theorists argue that postcolonialism is less an "ism" that describes an already past movement, but is more a series of philosophical issues that emerge from the ongoing process of decolonization in the midst of the global hegemony of Europe and the United States.

Undoubtedly, postcolonialism also refers to all the movements of decolonization that emerged during the 1950s, movements that predominantly took the form of so-called Third World nationalism. These movements of national liberation and anti-European imperialism and decolonization spread throughout the so-called Third World, a noun that conceals the specific Cold War context of many of these anticolonial struggles. *Third World* makes reference to all those recently created nations that were part neither of the developed, capitalist, industrialized, democratic *First World* nor the developing, industrializing, and socialist *Second World*. Critical theorist Robert J. C. Young (1950–) has for this reason argued that instead of referring to Third World postcolonialism, we should make reference to *Tricontinentalism*, by which he means, the deliberate and explicit joining of former colonial societies in Latin America, Africa, and Asia in anticolonial struggles. What postcolonialism as the collective name for a series of movements seeks to foreground is precisely the engagement with what is called by some postcolonial theorists the postcolonial condition, or postcoloniality. Latin American sociologist and critical theorist Anibal Quijano has called this condition the *postcoloniality of power*, a felicitous expression that expresses what Homi K. Bhabha (1949–) has called the *ongoing colonial present*.

As a theoretical and philosophical methodology, postcolonial theory is no less heterogeneous and at times internally contradictory than the Renaissance and the Enlightenment were. Postcolonial theory finds many of its philosophical sources in the discourse of, to use Paul Ricoeur's apropos phrasing, *the hermeneutics of suspicion*: Marxism, psychoanalysis, deconstruction, semiotics, structuralism, and postmodernism. More concretely, most of postcolonial thinking takes place through demystifying readings of canonical figures in Western philosophy. Such demystification is exemplified in the works of Louis Althusser (1918–1990), Jacques Derrida, Michel Foucault, Sigmund Freud, Jacques Lacan, Karl Marx, Friedrich Nietzsche, Jean-Paul Sartre. As a methodology, postcolonialism submits both the production and effects of all cultural artifacts, whether they be novels, philosophical texts, or sociological treatises, to a type of X-ray that shows the ways in which these texts and their effects are caught in the dialectical tension between colonialism, imposed and internalized, and anticolonialism, both internal to the West, and from without, from the colony, the liberated postcolonial nations, and emergent social movements.

This type of double reading that traces the effects of colonialism on colonial consciousness and culture, and that unearths and names the voice and gaze of the colonial other, has been amply developed by what has been called *postcolonial criticism*. With this term some critics seek to differentiate between the kinds of work that literary criticism performs from that which theory or philosophy produces. Yet, the attempt to differentiate between postcolonial criticism and theory reproduces one of the most contested *disciplinary* divisions that postcolonialism, as a methodology of analysis, continuously aims to challenge. As the works of Bhabha and Gayatri Chakravorty Spivak (1942–) illustrate and explore, literary criticism cannot be separated from and made to dispense with philosophical analysis, and the latter cannot dispense with literature nor be made to speak in a language purified of rhetoric, simile, metaphor, and the thick historicity of its diction. Furthermore, postcolonial theorists can neither negate nor neglect the ways in which disciplinary divides have been utilized to silence and deauthorize other forms of questioning—in what postcolonial theorists call the production of knowledge—precisely because of postcolonial theory's own hybrid and interdisciplinary sources.

Postcolonialism can be said to be a phenomenology of the social world that analyses in tandem the mutually conditioning effects of the objective on the subjective and vice versa. Social existence conditions the ways in which subjects are able to live and experience their subjectivities, and such subjectivities in turn, whether subjugated or insurrected, transform the social world. Postcolonialism is therefore also simultaneously a type of critical epistemology and historical ontology that studies the sources and effects of modes of representation and the ways in which social being is historically conditioned. As Spivak has put it, appropriating and displacing the phenomenological hermeneutics of Martin Heidegger, colonialism has *worlded*—that is to say, woven a thick web of material relationships that made possible meanings and the subjects that are mediated by them—the worlds of both the colonizer and the colonized. What makes postcolonialism different from other forms of phenomenology, ontology, and epistemology is that it has deliberately sought to disclose the world worlded by colonialism from the standpoint of the subaltern. By the term *subaltern* postcolonial critics mean those agents who have been expropriated, exploited, marginalized, racialized, bestialized, and rendered part of the fauna of continents empty of people and subjects. Every social agent and epistemic subject occupies a location, whether this location be literally geographical or figuratively political, epistemological, racial, or gendered. Edward W. Said (1935–2003) has called the analysis of this localization of all agents the *geographical inquiry into historical existence*.

Postcolonial theorists argue that to analyze the world from the perspective of the colonizer—the sovereign European political subject ensconced on the pedestal of racial privileged—would distort at best and conceal at worst the ways in which the colonized, the subaltern of colonial cultures, have been disempowered, rendered invisible and silent, reduced to a mere tabula rasa for the evangelizing, civilizing, and commercializing mission of Europe. The postcolonial critique of Western domination is simultaneously a critique of the imposition of a global economic system of structural inequality, or what is also called the globalization of capitalism through colonialism and imperialism. For this reason postcolonial theory shares many important insights and methods with standpoint feminist epistemological critique. All social location, as both of these positions argue, is mediated by representations: cultural, gendered, racial, religious. Postcolonial critique, as a form of Marxism, thus also aims to unmask the fetishizing and alienating effects of the systems of cultural representation imposed by European colonialism.

Postcolonialism, therefore, maintains that since no cultural or personal identity exists outside representation, and all representation is mediated by the history of its production, imposition, or rejection, all identities are thus contaminated by instability, hybridity, or creolization. A postcolonial corollary to the hybridity of all identity is that there is no subjectivity and agency that is not affected by power. All subjectivity and agency, argue postcolonial theorists, are forms of power. The postcolonial analysis, however, maintains that some forms of power are genocidal, subjugating, and narcissistic while others are enabling, benign, and indispensable. Power, in this analysis, is neither a stable substance nor a force that emanates from a center but a configuration of relationships that condition modes of social interaction. For postcolonial theorists, however, the uses and abuses of power are discerned from the standpoint of its effects on the subaltern in history and society.

At the center of postcolonial theory, notwithstanding its variegated sources and heterogeneous forms of articulation, is a series of epistemological innovations. Whether one studies the work of Bhabha, Frantz Fanon (1925–1961), Said, or Spivak, to mention just some of the canonical figures in postcolonial theory, we encounter an in-depth and unmitigated analysis of what has been called variously the space of enunciation, the discursive fields, or the structure of attitude and reference. Postmodern theorists mean by these terms that all epistemic locations, statements, and responses of affect are either allowed or disallowed by certain rules, syntax, or injunctions. To claim epistemic authority, make statements, and submit to feelings is to be interpellated by the syntax of a discursive matrix that already also anticipates their assent, response, or evocation.

Some postcolonial theorists have focused their attention on the structures of attitude and reference that condition how subjects and agents are made to know, speak, and feel *from* a location of privilege and plenipotentiary sovereignty *about* other subjects and agents who are located somewhere else in history and space. Said's classic work *Orientalism: Western Representations of the Orient* (1979) documented and analyzed the ways in which orientalism, the collective name for a group of disciplines that studied the Orient, operated as a power-knowledge apparatus that interpellated European agents to adopt imperial affective, epistemological, and enunciative spaces and comportments. Other postcolonial critics have focused on the knowing, speaking, and feeling *to* of all colonial discourse and the ways in which their reifying, objectivifying, and alienating effects are both unsustainable and contested by the other of their addressee. In Fanon's work, for instance, we discover one of the most

elaborate phenomenologies of oppression and liberation as well as a psychoanalytical analysis of the devastating effects of the powers of torture on both colonizer/torturer, and colonized/tortured. Yet other postcolonial theorists have focused on the *how* and by *what* means the mater-slave relationship between colonizer and *subaltern* have been mediated in such a way that neither the master nor the slave are entirely inured to each other's power of conquest or resistance. Spivak's work is without a doubt the most sophisticated, extensive, and sustained engagement with this dialectic of complicit and resisted knowledge production and insurrected agency.

Not unlike how Immanuel Kant illustrated his transcendental method by way of antinomies, postcolonial critics have developed a type of critical philosophy that proceeds also by way of the disclosure of a series of antinomies at the heart of contemporary Western thinking: universalism versus European exceptionalism; rationalism versus racial supremacy; humanism versus racial genocide; technophilia versus Romantic idolatry of the primitive; historicism versus teleological theodicy. As a critical methodology that inherits the discourse of what has been called a second Enlightenment, namely, the discourse of suspicion (Marx, Freud, Nietzsche), postcolonialism can be said to constitute a third Enlightenment, one that awakens the postcolonial world to the enduring legacies of five centuries of colonialism, imperialism, and now, globalization.

Postcolonialism is neither anti-Western, obdurately rejecting all European thinking, nor Third-Worldist, naively celebrating all that is produced and thought by the subaltern. Postcolonialism is a type of thinking that aims to situate us beyond the epistemological, ontological, and phenomenological Manichaeisms that have informed colonialism and postcolonial nationalism. Postcolonialism urges us to think beyond the either/or, for/against and in the proper space of the hybrid of the neither/nor, and/but, not with/but not without. For postcolonial thinkers, the philosophical inheritance of the West, of Europe, is at stake, not solely because it bears the traces of its complicity with colonialism, but because it is also the archive of resistance to that colonialism.

See also Deconstruction; Derrida, Jacques; Enlightenment; Epistemology; Foucault, Michel; Freud, Sigmund; Heidegger, Martin; Humanism; Kant, Immanuel; Lacan, Jacques; Mani and Manichaeism; Marxist Philosophy; Nietzsche, Friedrich; Ontology; Phenomenology; Postmodernism; Renaissance; Ricoeur, Paul; Romanticism; Psychoanalysis; Sartre,

Jean-Paul; Structuralism and Post-structuralism; Teleology.

Bibliography

Appiah, Anthony Kwame. *In My Father's House: Africa in the Philosophy of Culture*. New York: Oxford University Press. 1992.

Bhabha, Homi K. *The Location of Culture*. London: Routledge, 1994.

Brydon, Diana, ed. *Postcolonialism: Critical Concepts in Literary and Cultural Studies*. 5 vols. London: Routledge, 2000.

Cabral, Amilcar. *Return to the Source: Selected Speeches*. New York: Monthly Review Press, 1973.

Del Sarto, Ana, Alicia Ríos, and Abril Trigo, eds. *The Latin American Cultural Studies Reader*. Durham, NC: Duke University Press, 2004.

Fanon, Frantz. *Black Skins, White Masks*. Translated by Charles Lam Markmann. New York: Grove Press, 1967.

Fanon, Frantz. *A Dying Colonialism*. Translated by Haakon Chevalier. New York: Grove Press, 1967.

Fanon, Frantz. *The Wretched of the Earth*. Translated by Richard Philcox. New York: Grove Press, 2004.

Moore-Gilbert, Bart. *Postcolonial Theory: Contexts, Practices, Politics*. London: Verso, 1997.

Said, Edward W. *Culture and Imperialism*. New York: Alfred A. Knopf. 1993.

Said, Edward W. *Orientalism: Western Representations of the Orient*. New York: Vintage, 1979.

Said, Edward W. *Reflections on Exile and Other Essays*. Cambridge, MA: Harvard University Press, 2000.

Spivak, Gayatri Chakravorty. *A Critique of Postcolonial Reason: Toward a History of the Vanishing Present*. Cambridge, MA: Harvard University Press, 1999.

Spivak, Gayatri Chakravorty. *In Other Worlds: Essays in Cultural Politics*. New York: Routledge, 1988.

Spivak, Gayatri Chakravorty. *Outside in the Teaching Machine*. New York: Routledge, 1993.

Young, Robert J. C. *Postcolonialism: An Historical Introduction*. Malden, MA: Blackwell, 2001.

Eduardo Mendieta (2005)

POSTMODERNISM

The term "postmodernism" first emerged in the 1950s to describe new architectural and literary movements that opposed commonly accepted canons regarding the unity and coherence of narratives and artistic styles. Sociologists, meanwhile, have used "postmodernism" to indicate discordant trends such as the parallel growth in cosmopolitan globalization and parochial traditionalism. The term has also been appropriated by mainly French and German philosophers to designate a criticism of reason, regarded as a universal and certain foundation for knowledge and morality, and of modern culture, understood as a progressive unfolding of knowledge and morality. An examination of the works of these philosophers shows that many of the postmodern themes regarding the fragmentation (or deconstruction) of the rational subject and its object can be explained from the standpoint of conceptual tensions implicit within post-Kantian philosophy, which remains the main target of postmodern criticism.

A true son of the Enlightenment, Immanuel Kant defended reason as a universal faculty whose untrammeled exercise irresistibly leads to questioning all dogma and all authority, and from there leads to the complete emancipation of all individuals from the fetters of tradition. Faith in reason as it is deployed in science and morality fuels faith in the interminable progress of humanity. However, as postmodernists like Michel Foucault point out, the very reason that develops modern culture disintegrates under its own self-critical gaze, thereby issuing in oscillating and often discordant trends between absolutism and nihilism, totalitarianism and anarchism, humanism and multiculturalism, and universalism and parochialism. The end of rational idealism in turn spells the end of the subject as an autonomous, self-identifying, and self-determining locus of agency.

Ironically, it was Kant himself who initiated the critique of reason that later inspired postmodern philosophy. Kant observed that reason recognizes no limits in questioning the ultimate metaphysical grounds underlying reality, but that any answer it gives in response to its own questions entails contradiction. Rational inquiry must therefore be limited to phenomena within everyday experience. Kant's critique of pure, experience-transcending reason already anticipated postmodern skepticism regarding the completeness of our knowledge of things in their totality, while rejecting such skepticism with regard to our knowledge of things in their experiential finitude. Kant's rejection of this latter form of skepticism, whose main exponent is David Hume, requires that reason be seen as a synthetic power that infuses experience of objects with causal necessity as it imposes rational identity on the experiencing subject. However, to reconcile the causal necessity of the world with the uncaused freedom of the moral subject, Kant had to divide reason into two *opposed* deployments—theoretical and practical—only one of which was a source of knowledge (he later added a third, aesthetic deployment to mediate between the moral and the theoretical). Subsequent postmodernists continued to divide reason into an indefinite number of context-specific applications, thereby undermining any certain belief in a common reason, a common world, and a common humanity.

Also postmodern is Kant's view that reason questions even its own authority as a certain foundation of knowledge. As G. F. W. Hegel astutely noted, this self-referential (or reflexive) use of reason is paradoxical. By limiting the valid deployment of cognitive reason to natural science, critical philosophy undermines its own claim to validity as a *nonscientific* form of reflective knowledge. Conversely, by grounding natural science in a nonnatural form of transcendental subjectivity, it unwittingly shows natural science and its object to be partial and superficial forms of cognition and reality, respectively.

According to postmodernists, Hegel's system marks the last great attempt to resolve the crisis of reason bequeathed by Kantian philosophy. It does so by affirming what Kant had denied: reason's infinite demand to know the infinite totality. As noted above, this demand issues in contradiction. However, Hegel thought that this was true only if philosophical reflection did not completely grasp all possible metaphysical categories in a manner that showed how each implied all the others. Hegel's circular reasoning would show that the apparent contradictions implicit in metaphysical reasoning ultimately establish a closed system of resolved complementarities. In contrast, any attempt to found one kind of belief deductively on another in a noncircular way, as Kant had proposed, must issue in unresolved contradiction.

Postmodernists question whether reason can establish a complete and coherent system of thought. From Hegel's thought they retain his dialectical view that the fundamental reasons that define, categorize, and ground our beliefs about things effectively refer to properties that are thought to be external or opposed to these things. Thus, while logic (analytic reason) seeks to establish categorical distinctions between self and other, nature and society, reason and unreason, philosophical reasoning about logic undermines these distinctions. Postmodernists therefore conclude that nothing is certain and definite, not even our certainty that we as rational subjects exist.

The undermining of categorical distinctions has an important bearing on the meaningfulness of language. Postmodernists point to the futility of trying to ground the meaning of concepts in empirically verifiable objects or in what is immediately given in experience. As Ludwig Wittgenstein noted in his *Tractatus Logico-philosophicus*, the logical and philosophical metalanguage that is supposed to ground the meaningfulness of the object language in immediate experience is not itself an object language referring to immediate experience. Citing simi-

lar self-referential paradoxes made famous by Bertrand Russell, Kurt Gödel, and Werner Heisenberg, Jean François Lyotard has argued that epistemic and logical indeterminacy, incompleteness, and uncertainty necessarily infect any scientific or philosophical metanarrative that claims to be all-encompassing. At the beginning of the twenty-first century, the common acceptance by philosophers of language that meaning is relative to context and usage and yet is underdetermined by them has led philosophers as diverse as Donald Davidson and Jacques Derrida to suggest that meaning is at the very least an indefinite project of textual interpretation, if not, as Lyotard and Foucault argue, an anarchic war of contesting and inventing.

For postmodernists, acknowledging the uncertainty, ambiguity, and loss of identity that comes with the demise of rationalism, humanism, and idealism need not commit us to nihilism. On the contrary, as Friedrich Nietzsche observed, by insisting on impossible norms of certainty, clarity, and identity, we end up devaluing those common unfathomable and uncanny modes of moral and religious experience that open us up to novelty, fantasy, and vulnerability. Worse, by insisting on these impossible norms, we become arrogant and drunk on our own "will to power." It was in the name of pure reason, after all, that "enlightened" Europeans sought to eliminate or assimilate to themselves the "unenlightened" peoples of Africa, Asia, and the Americas. Genuine postmodern responsibility, by contrast, endeavors to promote an active, nondomineering receptivity to the other, no matter how different it may appear.

See also Art, Interpretation of; Art, Value in; Foucault, Michel; Language; Lyotard, Jean François; Rationality.

Bibliography

Best, Steven, and Douglas Kellner. *The Postmodern Turn*. New York: Guilford Press, 1997.

Derrida, Jacques. *Margins of Philosophy*. Translated by Alan Bass. Chicago: University of Chicago Press, 1982.

Derrida, Jacques. *Writing and Difference*. Translated by Alan Bass. Chicago: University of Chicago Press, 1978.

Foucault, Michel. *The Order of Things*. New York: Pantheon, 1970.

Habermas, Jürgen. *The Philosophical Discourse of Modernity*. Translated by Frederick G. Lawrence. Cambridge, MA: MIT Press, 1987.

Horkheimer, Max, and Theodor W. Adorno. *The Dialectic of Enlightenment*. Translated by John Cumming. New York: Herder and Herder, 1972.

Kristeva, Julia. *Revolution in Poetic Language*. Translated by Margaret Waller. New York: Columbia University Press, 1984.

Lyotard, Jean François. *The Postmodern Condition*. Translated by Geoff Bennington and Brian Massumi. Minneapolis: University of Minnesota Press, 1984.

Lyotard, Jean François. *The Postmodern Explained: Correspondence, 1982–1985*. Translated by Julian Pefanis and Morgan Thomas. Minneapolis: University of Minnesota Press, 1993.

Lyotard, Jean François. *Toward the Postmodern*. Translated by Robert Harvey and Mark S. Roberts. Atlantic Highlands, NJ: Humanities Press, 1993.

Natoli, Joseph, and Linda Hutcheon, eds. *A Postmodern Reader*. Albany: State University of New York Press, 1993.

Silverman, Hugh J., ed. *Postmodernism: Philosophy and the Arts*. New York: Routledge, 1990.

Vattimo, Gianni. *The End of Modernity*. Translated by Jon R. Snyder. Baltimore, MD: Johns Hopkins University Press, 1988.

David Ingram (2005)

POTENTIALITY

See *Possibility*

POWER

The meanings of *power, influence, control,* and *domination* are uncertain, shifting, and overlapping. Although two of these words may be interchangeable in one context, in another context one of the words may refer to a genus and another to a species, or one may refer to a cause and another to an effect. To substitute *power* for *influence* would not matter much in the sentence "The United States has very great influence in South American politics," but to interchange them would radically change the meaning of the sentence "Colonel House's power derived not from any constitutional authority but from his influence over President Wilson."

Shifts like this account for much of the intractability of problems associated with power. For instance, power is often said to be a relation (Lasswell 1950, Friedrich 1950, Partridge 1963), yet we talk about the distribution of power, about the power of speech, about seeking power as a means to future enjoyment (Hobbes 1946), or about power as "the production of intended effects" (Russell 1938). If power is a relation, between what kind of terms or things does it hold? Does power over men require a minimum of acquiescence, consent, or cooperation (Hume; Friedrich 1956–1957), or can it be analogous to a physical force acting on an otherwise inert object? Is to exercise power always to succeed in what one intends (Russell 1938, Lasswell 1950), or can a man exercise

power in ignorance of what he is doing (Dahl 1961, Partridge 1963, Oppenheim 1961), like a ruling elite that neither knows nor cares about the effects of its actions on other classes?

Instead of seeking a single analysis of *power,* it is more helpful to think of diverse uses of *power* and of associated words like *influence* as instances of different members of a family of concepts that do not all share any one particular characteristic but have various relations and resemblances by which they are recognizably kin. One might construct a power paradigm combining as many of these family features as possible. Thus, "*A*, by his power over *B*, successfully achieved an intended result *r;* he did so by making *B* do *b,* which *B* would not have done but for *A*'s wishing him to do so; moreover, although *B* was reluctant, *A* had a way of overcoming this."

There are five main features of this paradigm: (1) an intention manifest in the exercise of power; (2) the successful achievement of this intention; (3) a relationship between at least two people; (4) the intentional initiation by one of actions by the other; and (5) a conflict of interest or wishes engendering a resistance that the initiator overcomes. Not every feature would be present, of course, in every instance in which we properly speak of power; but we can examine how different instances are related to the paradigm and to one another, and thus throw some light on a few of the questions listed above.

POWER AND CONFLICT

Some instances of power do not involve overcoming resistance to an initiative. A charismatic leader's power over his followers consists in being able merely by suggestion to move them to do willingly what he wants, even though their interests might have led them to act differently. The family of power concepts might be arranged along a conflict scale (Partridge 1963): At the end at which conflict is least would lie instances of influence, while at the other end would lie instances of domination, and in between, instances of authority. In the extreme case, exercising influence would not involve overcoming resistance, for to manipulate a man's actions by shaping what he considers to be his interests is not to impose action upon him *in the face of* his interests. Yet this would still be an instance of power satisfying the first four features of the paradigm.

The limiting case at the end of the scale at which conflict is least would be rational persuasion, for to offer a man good reasons for doing something is not to exercise power over him, although it may influence his decision. One possible difference between influence and power, then, seems to be that power generally implies a difference of standing between the two parties: The one stimulates, the other reacts. Rational persuasion, on the contrary, to the extent that it criticizes and invites criticism, presupposes at least the possibility of a dialogue between equals. To the extent that persuasion is really rational, the influence is not so much that of the persuader as of his arguments; the same arguments from anyone else would do as well. (By contrast, a threat of violence is more effective coming from a strong man than from a weak man.) Of course, if A rationally persuades B to help him, A may get power—not over B, however, but over C or D, or even simply the power to do something he could not otherwise do.

POWER, INJURY, AND INTEREST

In the case of the man who punishes another for disobedience, conditions (1), (3), and (5) of the paradigm would be satisfied, but not (2) and (4), for the initiative has been refused. Instead, it suffices for an instance of power if the power-holder successfully and intentionally makes the subject suffer for refusing the initiative. And by yet a further extension of meaning, one can exercise power over someone by deliberately making him suffer, whether or not he has refused an initiative. Just as in the limiting case of rational persuasion one could speak of influence but hardly of power, so at the other end of the scale one can talk of power but not of influence, for influence is manifest in what a man is, does, or believes, not in what is simply made to happen to him by another man.

A stoic would probably resist the extension of the concept of power to cover the mere infliction of suffering. By not caring about physical pain or external conditions, he might say, one can remove oneself from the power of another man. So too Martin Luther believed that a true Christian is free because no outer things can touch him at any significant point. It would seem that what characterizes a power situation of this kind is not just the ability to make someone suffer, which after all a dentist possesses, but rather to do him harm—that is, to attack his interests. Thus, by revising the notion of a man's interests, and therefore the notion of harm, the stoic or the Christian can deny the reality of one man's power over another, since nothing that another man can do to me can affect my real interests; I am always free, if once I see what those interests are. This argument is a little odd, because the concept of power generally implies a restriction on choice; but according to the stoic or Christian view, one can always choose to make the restriction insignificant, and therefore one can choose whether to be in the power

of another. In that case, there could not be a real restriction, and all power would be illusory. But then, what would power be like if it were real?

The stoic argument demonstrates, however, that whether one man has power over another depends not merely on what he can do to the other but also on the importance to be attached to his action and on whether the subject can reasonably be expected to disregard it. One would not say that X was in Y's power if one thought that what Y could do to X was trivial—something that X could or should readily ignore.

Again, although threats of real harm are an exercise of power, bribes or promises of reward are not, unless some special feature of character or situation makes them irresistible—that is, unless no one so placed could reasonably be expected to resist them (although some in fact might). This is not to say, of course, that a man cannot exercise power by bribery. However, it need not be power *over* his hirelings but power over others *through* them; or it may be power only in the still more general sense of an ability to bring about an intended result. Thus, we speak of power in situations in which a man could either successfully determine another's actions or do him harm. An ability to do him some good is not in itself power over him, although the threat of withholding a good that he has come to count on may well be.

PROBLEMS OF POWER AS A RELATION

Power may not be a relation between people but between a person and a thing. There is a nonsocial kind of power that is simply an ability to produce an intended result, like a tenor's power to smash a tumbler with a high C. And even in a social context, the financier's power to destroy a government comes very close to this, for in this instance too power is manifest merely in the active achievement of an intended result. Although the financier no doubt works by initiating actions on the part of others, the relation between him and his object (the government) is that which exists between agent and patient. This case can be distinguished both from that in which power is exercised by punishing a subject for noncompliance and from that in which power is used to inflict deliberate injury. For in the present case the object of the exercise may be only to remove an obstacle. The manifestation of power does not consist in the government's being made to suffer, for it would be just as much a manifestation of power if the financier had chosen instead to prop it up or if the government welcomed its downfall as a blessed release from responsibility. Power is manifest simply in that what happens is the result of the financier's intentional action, just as the tenor's power is manifest in his being able to break a glass whenever he likes.

Power is of course relational in a logical sense in that it requires more than one term for a complete statement; and if more than one of the terms is a person, and the relation presupposes institutions, rules, and so forth, power will certainly be a social relation. But writers who stress that power is a relation usually mean that it is an initiative-response relationship of the kind that C. J. Friedrich had in mind when he wrote, "The power seeker must find human beings who value the things [he controls] sufficiently to obey his orders in return" (*Constitutional Government and Democracy*, p. 12).

Now, Friedrich's point is substantially true in those instances in which power implies a successful initiative and even perhaps in those instances in which power tends to injure its subject. To set about hurting someone, one must know how to get the right kind of response: There is no point in depriving nonsmokers of tobacco. It is not so clear, however, that the financier's power is of this type, for he does not secure a response from the government; he merely makes something happen to it. Although his agents respond to his initiatives, one must distinguish the power he has over them from the power he has over the government. These powers would be of the same kind only if he were able not just to destroy the government, but to use it as he wished. But it is presumably because he cannot do this that he uses his power to destroy it.

This analysis further elucidates the relation between power and consent. We have seen that at one extreme a man may exercise power over another by influencing his desires, or a man may do whatever he is told by another because he believes that he ought to do so, which is an instance of authority. Both cases imply some measure of consent or acquiescence, if not to the particular initiative, then to the right of the initiator to issue it. But in cases in which power depends on threats or on physical coercion, the subject's acquiescence amounts to no more than that he continues to value whatever is being used as a lever against him—an acquiescence that only the stoic, perhaps, would seriously regard as a matter of choice. However, political power cannot be entirely coercive. The few can rule the many because the many believe either that the few are entitled to do so or that they could harm them if they disobeyed. But they would not think that coercion were possible if they did not also believe that most of the people were prepared to obey without coercion. A political power situation, therefore, must almost always contain some elements of acquiescence as well as coercion—*almost* always because it is at least theoretically possible that a reign of terror might enslave a whole people simply by sowing such mistrust that its opponents could never know their own potential strength.

POWER AND INTENTION

Still further from the paradigm is the case in which one says quite generally that a person is powerful, or that he seeks power, without specifying the range of possible intended action or the persons subject to the power. Usually it would not be difficult to supply terms to complete either one or both of these blanks. Political theorists commonly insist that comparisons of power, without reference to its "domain" and "scope," are meaningless (Lasswell and Kaplan 1950, Oppenheim 1961). However, some have tried to generalize the concept by disregarding intentionality. R. A. Dahl defines power as "the difference in probability of an event, given certain actions by *A*, and the probability of the event given no such action by *A*" ("The Concept of Power," p. 214). At this level of abstraction, *power* is freed not only from intentionality but also from achievement and conflict; what remains is a relation between a stimulus and a reaction. Elsewhere (*Modern Political Analysis*, p. 40), Dahl defines *influence* as a relation among actors in which one induces others to act in some way in which they would not otherwise act. Dahl would want to purge, if he could, the hint of intentionality in the word *induce*. Like a field of force in mechanics, power is a potential for creating disturbance, like the potential of a stone cast in a pond for creating ripples. But this has some odd results. Instead of suffering a *loss* of power, the crashing financier who brings down thousands with him in his fall would be exercising a power that is perhaps greater than ever before. Admittedly, it is a mark of power if a man's actions cause disturbances, even if he is careless or even ignorant of them. Nevertheless, if powerful men cause incidental and unintended disturbances, they do so in the course of *getting what they want*. (C. Wright Mills's conception of a "power elite" seems to be of this kind.) One would not call someone powerful who, like a careless smoker constantly causing fires, was forever causing disturbances but never achieving anything he intended; nor is it clear that any useful methodological purpose in political science would be served by a definition of power that permitted the production of unintended effects alone to serve as a criterion.

To possess power or to be powerful is, then, to have a generalized potentiality for getting one's own way or for bringing about changes (at least some of which are intended) in other people's actions or conditions. *Influence*, it is true, is used in a more general sense. If a parent has the unintended influence of stiffening his child's determination to be as different from him as possible, this would not be described as an instance of power: It is more like "the influence of climate on national character." The use of the term *influence* suggests that there is a causal relationship between the behavior of the parent and that of the child (cf. P. H. Partridge, "Some Notes on the Concept of Power," p. 114). "A writer's influence on succeeding generations" stands somewhere between this case and that of influence by rational persuasion. For a writer may have influence only to the extent that other writers recognize his merits and choose to imitate him. Although such influence may not be intended, still it is not a cause, at least in the sense that climate is a possible cause of national character. In any case, none of these is an instance of an influence in the sense that House *had* influence with Wilson. "To *use* one's influence" usually implies actively and intentionally working through or on other people, and one who can do this recurrently "*has* influence." Of course, people who have power (that is, who can do many things they want and induce many other people to accept their initiative) are likely on that account to influence (that is, to have effects on) other aspects of society in ways that neither they nor their social inferiors necessarily understand. Other classes, envying and admiring them, may imitate their tastes and practices, and in this sense they may be influenced by them. But this influence is not a manifestation of power; it is only one of its effects.

See also Authority; Feminist Legal Theory; Freedom; Luther, Martin; Rights; Sovereignty; Stoicism; Violence.

Bibliography

CLASSIC THEORIES OF POLITICAL POWER

Aiken, H. D., ed. *Hume's Moral and Political Philosophy*. New York: Hafner, 1948.

Hobbes, Thomas. *Leviathan*, edited by M. Oakeshott. Oxford: Blackwell, 1946.

Hume, David. "Of the First Principles of Government." In *Essays Literary, Moral and Political* (1741). London, 1963.

Hume, David. *Treatise of Human Nature* (1740), edited by L. A. Selby-Bigge. Oxford, 1951. Book III.

Plamenatz, John. *Man and Society*. 2 vols. London: Longmans, 1963. A critical discussion of classic theories.

Spinoza, Benedict de. *The Political Works*. Translated and edited by A. G. Wernham. Oxford: Clarendon Press, 1958.

Spinoza, Benedict de. *Tractatus Politicus* (1677).

Spinoza, Benedict de. *Tractatus Theologico-Politicus*. Hamburg, 1670.

GENERAL PHILOSOPHICAL DISCUSSIONS

Acton, H. B. "Logique et casuistique du pouvoir." In *Annales de philosophie politique: Tomes I et II: Le Pouvoir*, Vol. II, 69–86. Paris, 1956–1957.

Emmet, Dorothy. "The Concept of Power." *PAS* 54 (1953–1954): 1–26.

Friedrich, C. J. "Le probleme de pouvoir dans la theorie constitutionnaliste." In *Annales de Philosophie Politique: Tomes I et II: Le Pouvoir*, Vol. I, 33–51. Paris, 1956–1957.

Jouvenel, Bertrand de. *Le pouvoir*. Geneva, 1945. Translated by J. F. Huntington as *On Power; Its Nature and the History of Its Growth*. Boston, 1962.

Jouvenel, Bertrand de. *Pure Theory of Politics*. Cambridge, U.K.: Cambridge University Press, 1963.

Partridge, P. H. "Politics and Power." *Philosophy* 38 (1963): 117–136.

Partridge, P. H. "Some Notes on the Concept of Power." *Political Studies* 2 (1963): 107–125.

Polin, R. "Sens et fondement du pouvoir chez John Locke." In *Annales de Philosophie Politique: Tomes I et II: Le Pouvoir*, Vol. I, 53–90. Paris, 1956–1957.

Russell, Bertrand. *Power*. London: Allen and Unwin, 1938.

SOCIOLOGY AND METHODOLOGY OF POLITICAL SCIENCE

Bierstedt, Robert. "An Analysis of Social Power." *American Sociological Review* 15 (1950): 730–738.

Dahl, R. A. "The Concept of Power." In *Introductory Readings in Political Behavior*, edited by Sidney S. Ulmer. Chicago: Rand McNally, 1961.

Friedrich, Carl J. *Constitutional Government and Democracy*. Boston: Ginn, 1950.

Friedrich, Carl J. *Man and His Government*. New York: McGraw-Hill, 1963.

Lasswell, Harold D., and Abraham Kaplan. *Power and Society: A Framework for Political Inquiry*. New Haven, CT: Yale University Press, 1950.

Merriam, Charles E. "Political Power." In *A Study of Power*, by H. D. Lasswell, C. E. Merriam, and T. V. Smith. Glencoe, IL: Free Press, 1950.

Oppenheim, Felix E. *Dimensions of Freedom*. New York: St. Martin's Press, 1961.

Walter, E. V. "Power and Violence." *American Political Science Review* 58 (1964): 350–360.

Weber, Max. *From Max Weber; Essays in Sociology*. Translated and edited by H. H. Gerth and C. Wright Mills. London: Routledge and Kegan Paul, 1948.

ADDITIONAL SOURCES

Arendt, Hannah. *On Violence*. New York: Harcourt Brace, 1970.

Connolly, William E. *The Terms of Political Discourse*, 2nd ed. Princeton, NJ: Princeton University Press, 1983.

Dahl, R. A. *Modern Political Analysis*, 5th ed. Englewood Cliffs, NJ: Prentice Hall, 1984.

Foucault, Michel. *Power*, edited by James D. Faubion; translated by Robert Hurley. New York: New Press, 2000.

Lukes, Steven. *Power: A Radical View*. London: Macmillan, 1974.

Morriss, Peter. *Power: A Philosophical Analysis*. Manchester, U.K.: Manchester University Press, 1987.

Parsons, Talcott. *Politics and Social Structure.* New York: Free Press, 1969.

Scott, John. *Power.* Cambridge, U.K.: Blackwell, 2001.

Wrong, Dennis H. *Power: Its Forms, Bases, and Uses.* New York: Harper and Row, 1979.

Stanley I. Benn (1967)
Bibliography updated by Philip Reed (2005)

PRACTICAL REASON

Reason can and should guide one in deciding what to believe, at least in large part. But can reason also guide one's actions and the goals that one aims to achieve through them? This question is at the heart of philosophical interest in practical reason. One's thoughts and discourse about practical matters are full of references to reason, and each day brings with it a fresh round of deliberation over such things as the costs and benefits of alternative lines of conduct. Disagreement over how best to understand these phenomena has focused on two distinct questions: First, is reason itself ever a genuine source of considerations for or against conduct, or is our everyday thought and discourse simply a *façon de parler*? Second, to what extent, if at all, can such considerations make a difference to what one does? Under the first question, which is address in the first three sections of this entry, the central issues concern whether and the extent to which the deliberative process that culminates in a decision or intention can be dubbed *reasoning*. The second question, with which the article ends, concerns the nature of motivation and action and, in particular, what role (if any) reason plays in the explanation of one's behavior.

INSTRUMENTAL PRACTICAL REASON

Most agree that if any conduct is contrary to reason, then not acting to achieve one's goals with some level of efficiency and effectiveness is. Once one decides to lose weight, for instance, overeating seems unreasonable. But what precisely is reason's role here? Many, such as those who follow the eighteenth-century Scottish philosopher David Hume, argue that its role is limited to delivering and evaluating beliefs about connections between behaving in certain ways and achieving goals. If one's goal is to lose weight, reason's work is done once it delivers the news that eating less will bring that about. This implies that reason concerns itself only with delivering causal information about how to realize one's goals and hence does work in the realm of action that is no different from the work it does in the realm of belief.

To see precisely how little reason does on such a view, consider the following: Suppose my goal is to have the doorbell to ring and I am told to push the button. However, I perversely insist that it is a trick door and that standing motionless will make it ring. If I stand motionless, I will as a consequence frustrate my goal. Reason seems against my conduct. For the minimalist, however, that means only that the belief on which my conduct was based was false. Suppose, alternatively, that I have no idea how to make a doorbell ring. I stand in puzzled silence, and again reason fails to support my behavior. This time, the problem is not that I have incorrect beliefs about how to achieve my goal; it is that I have no beliefs about this at all. Nevertheless, it is again really just in lacking a belief that I've fallen foul of reason. Conforming to practical reason, on this minimalist view, means simply ensuring that I have the right stock of beliefs about how to achieve my ends. Reason does not pass judgment on what I do per se. It is thus not practical in this more interesting sense. Indeed, when I do what I falsely believe will bring results, my action displays a kind of fit with my belief, even if my belief is itself defective.

Suppose, however, that my actions did not display this kind of fit with my beliefs, even while my beliefs were flawless. Imagine, for instance, I failed to push the button when my goal was that the doorbell ring and I correctly believed that pushing the button would achieve this. Was my conduct *then* contrary to reason insofar as it did not fit with my goal and my true means–ends belief? A minimalist such as Hume would deny that it was. An action itself cannot be contrary to reason because an action cannot be evaluated for its truth or falsity. *A fortiori* reason cannot justify an action either, for justification of something is just support for its truth. Thus, no action seems contrary to reason in the way that a false or unjustified belief is.

Reason will be practical in an interesting sense, it seems, only if one of two things is true: Either there exists some special realm of facts about the *to-be-doneness* of certain actions themselves, information about which reason can deliver, or else reason is more than an information-delivering faculty. Philosophers have tended to avoid views requiring special facts although in the case of ethical reasoning, some have thought the idea worth developing. This case will be returned to below. For many, a more attractive strategy is to argue that reason issues distinctive rules of conduct. The most likely candidate for such a rule would be a rule of instrumental reason, for instance: Do what is necessary to achieve your goals. For an action to be contrary to reason would then be for it to fail to conform to such a rule. The key issue, then, is whether practical reason is indeed *normative* in this sense, that is, whether there are any genuine rules of reason.

Arguments that a given rule is a norm of reason can be grouped into two kinds: those appealing to the concept of reasonableness, and those appealing to substantive considerations beyond that concept. The eighteenth-century Prussian philosopher Immanuel Kant, for instance, employed the first style of argument regarding conformity to a *hypothetical imperative*. The concept of *reasonable behavior*, he argued, contains the idea of conformity to the rule *take the means necessary to achieve your goals*. The twentieth-century political philosopher John Rawls is an example of a philosopher who also employed the second style of argument. Rawls argued that reasonableness includes a willingness to propose and abide by fair terms of cooperation if assured that others will likewise do so, on the grounds that, although it is not a conceptual truth, the contention enjoys much intuitive support.

REASONING ABOUT GOALS

Goals can share many of the above features of actions. Suppose, again, my goal is that the doorbell ring. Typically, I don't just want that. Perhaps I believe that the ring will bring my friend to the door. My goal is really an instrumental goal, a goal that is desirable because its achievement is instrumental to achieving a further distinct goal. Suppose, however, that I am standing in front of the wrong house. Even though I am right to believe that pushing the button will achieve the ring, reason is against my pushing the button because it is against achieving the ring. To this instrumental extent at least, our goals can be contrary to reason.

Minimalists will be led say about goals *mutatis mutandis* what they say about action: The defect, as in the case of action, is in the belief that the ring will bring my friend to the door. It is only because of this false belief that my goal falls foul of reason. Goals are just like actions in the sense that they cannot be evaluated as true or false, and *a fortiori* cannot be justified or unjustified either. So, if reason were practical in any interesting sense, there would either have to be a distinctive realm of facts about the *to-be-pursuedness* of certain goals or else reason would have to issue distinctive norms concerning goals such as *pursue intermediate goals necessary to reach your primary goals*.

This sort of reasoning need not exhaust practical reasoning about ends. For instance, suppose I have not one, but two goals: that the doorbell ring and that those behind the door not be disturbed. Do I conform to reason if I push, or rather fail to push, the button? Given the bell cannot ring and leave the inhabitants undisturbed, the answer must wait until I resolve this conflict. Having goals that are not *jointly realizable* seems contrary to reason. However, goals are jointly realizable only if some can be dropped in favor of others in cases of conflict. We could do this willy-nilly, of course. But ranking seems more reasonable. We should decide whether having the doorbell ring is more or less important than disturbing those behind the door. Given reason counsels joint realizability, it thus also counsels ranking. Moreover, rankings conform to requirements of consistency. For instance, they are transitive: If ringing is ranked above not disturbing the inhabitants, and not disturbing them above not wearing out the button very slightly, then ringing should be ranked above not wearing out the button. This would explain why we would think it unreasonable for me to worry about wearing out the button given that I'm not worried about the more important fact that it will disturb them.

Presumably, one does not pursue all of one's goals for the sake of other goals, however. Some things one cares about for their own sakes; they are *final* goals. Can reason evaluate such final goals? One way that it might is this (Schmidtz 1995): Suppose I am a philistine, but then decide to become the sort of person for whom art is a final end. Suppose further that I decide this because I believe that becoming that sort of person will enhance my standing in the eyes of others. I aim, in other words, to come to pursue something for its own sake, but my reasoning is clearly instrumental. If I find out that learning to love art for arts sake will not lead others to think better of me, then reason will counsel me not to learn that.

REASON IN ETHICAL DELIBERATION

When one deliberates about what to do, one often considers whether what one proposes is morally permissible, right, virtuous, and so on. One seems to care about such things for their own sakes, so this seems to constitute a final end. But does reason ever really guide one to moral conclusions?

Those who think that it does can be divided into two camps: those who think that moral reasoning can be explained in terms of reasoning from individual goals, and those who think it involves a special kind of reasoning. The former think that moral reasoning is, in fact, not fundamentally different from the above forms of practical reasoning but in some way facilitates the achievement of one's goals—typically, by being based on principles of social conduct that reasonable individuals would accept and act on. Such, for instance, is found in game-theoretic explanations of morality. On a standard version, game theorists argue that people seeking to achieve their goals will want ground rules for their interactions with each other. They will thus freely engage in a series of bargains with others in which each person tries to secure practices most favorable to their goals. Bargaining would continue until no viable alternative agreement can be struck under which someone would be better off. Moral practices represent these agreements, and because they do, they are justified in light of their being the upshot of these reasonable goal-oriented bargains. Along these lines, David Gauthier (1986) argues that reasonable agents will be disposed to cooperate with others who likewise cooperate, even when doing so will not be the best way to achieve their own goals (as is often the case in moral matters).

A more controversial idea is that moral reasoning is fundamentally different from nonmoral reasoning. There are two main lines of thought here: The first is that there is a distinct realm of moral facts, as real as any scientific fact but accessible only through the exercise of a special faculty of reason. On this view, practical reason operates quasi-perceptually to deliver putative moral facts such as that lying is wrong. Some (McDowell 1979) have held that this is analogous to sense perception, such as is exercised by informed palates when they perceive differences between wines. Others (Ross 1939) think of it as more akin to intellectual perception, such as is exercised in the perception of mathematical truths. Many, however, find this postulation of a *sui generis* faculty of reason too mysterious to accept.

The second line of thought does not appeal to the exercise of a special faculty and access to special facts but to a special rule distinct from those connected to advancing individual goals. The most famous attempt to defend this line of thinking comes from Kant. Moral reasoning is based, he argued, on a rule he referred to as the *Categorical Imperative*. This rule requires one not to act in ways that one could not want everyone else also to act. Every rational agent is committed to this rule, Kant argued, simply by engaging in practical reasoning. Committing oneself to this rule is a presupposition of taking up the point of view of practical deliberation. Therefore, he concluded, it is a rule of practical reason. Few have found Kant's arguments convincing. Nevertheless, some contemporary philosophers have tried to develop and defend some version of Kant's ideas. Rawls's idea of reasonableness is one attempt. Another is Thomas Scanlon (1998) who argues that reasonableness requires being responsive to the appropriateness of principles of conduct to serve as foundations for mutual recognition and accommodation.

REASON AND MOTIVATION

Suppose deliberating to conclusions about what to do is genuinely a form of reasoning. These conclusions may still make no difference to what one does. Reason, that is, may not be practical in another sense—in the sense that it cannot motivate one to comply with its conclusions. When one acts contrary to conclusions of practical deliberation, is one unreasonable in the sense of being insufficiently motivated by this deliberation?

Internalists about practical reason hold that one can be: The conclusions of practical reasoning must motivate reasonable agents. This is especially the case, they argue, in moral reasoning: It is not possible to believe it to be wrong to lie, for instance, yet remain unmotivated to tell the truth. One reason internalism is attractive is that it explains the magnetism conclusions of practical reasoning exhibit. To be sure, the conclusions of practical reasoning do not always motivate everyone. If one is depressed or weak-willed, for instance, practical conclusions may have no motivational effect on one. So, internalists must stipulate which psychological condition a reasonable agent is in such that that agent must be motivated. This has not proven to be an easy task.

Internalism, however, appears inconsistent with an attractive conception of motivation, often referred to as the Humean view. On this view, motivation requires, in addition to belief, a desire. Michael Smith (1995) has offered an influential defense of this view. Briefly, the leading idea is that the best functional account of belief and desire gives them different directions of fit with the world. A belief is an attitude toward a given proposition *p*, such that the perception of not-*p* disposes the believer to change attitude to not-*p*. Desire has the reverse direction of fit: an attitude toward *p* such that the perception of not-*p* disposes the desirer to change the world to *p*. If these accounts are basically right, then three things seem clear: Motivation requires a desire, beliefs and desires are only contingently related, and no state could have both directions of fit. Smith himself argues that, nonetheless, one's beliefs about what one has reason to do must motivate agents in the right psychological condition. His position is controversial, however, and the prospects for internalism remain unclear.

See also Decision Theory; Game Theory; Hume, David; Kant, Immanuel; Normativity; Rationalism in Ethics (Practical Reason Approaches); Rawls, John; Reason.

Bibliography

Blackburn, Simon. *Ruling Passions*. Oxford: Clarendon, 1998.

Bratman, Michael. *Intention, Plans, and Practical Reason.* Cambridge, MA: Harvard University Press, 1987.

Broome, John. "Normative Practical Reasoning." 175–193. *Aristotelian Society: Supplementary Volume.* 2001.

Dancy, Jonathan. *Moral Reasons.* Oxford: Basil Blackwell, 1993.

Darwall, Stephen. *Impartial Reason.* Ithaca, NY: Cornell University Press, 1983.

Gauthier, David. *Morals by Agreement.* Oxford: Oxford University Press, 1986.

Gibbard, Alan. *Wise Choices, Apt Feelings.* Cambridge, MA: Harvard University Press, 1992.

Hill, Thomas E., Jr. *Dignity and Practical Reason.* Ithaca, NY: Cornell University Press, 1992.

Hume, David. *A Treatise of Human Nature,* edited by D. F. Norton and M. Norton. New Ed. Oxford: Oxford University Press, 2000.

Kant, Immanuel. *Groundwork of the Metaphysics of Morals,* edited by A. Zweig and T. E. Hill, Jr. Translated by A. Zweig. Oxford: Oxford University Press, 2002.

Korsgaard, Christine. "The Normativity of Instrumental Reason." In *Ethics and Practical Reason,* edited by Garrett Cullity and Berys Gaut. Oxford: Oxford University Press, 1997.

Korsgaard, Christine. "Skepticism about Practical Reason." *Journal of Philosophy* (1986): 5–25.

McDowell, John. "Are Moral Requirements Hypothetical Imperatives?" *Aristotelian Society Supplementary Volume* (1978): 13–29.

McDowell, John. "Virtue and Reason." *Monist* 62 (1979): 331–50.

Nagel, Thomas. *The Possibility of Altruism.* Princeton, NJ: Princeton University Press, 1978.

Parfit, Derek. *Reasons and Persons.* Oxford: Clarendon Press, 1984.

Rawls, John. "Kantian Constructivism in Moral Theory." *Journal of Philosophy* 77 (1980): 515–572.

Rawls, John. *A Theory of Justice.* Cambridge, MA: Harvard University Press, 1972.

Raz, Joseph. *Practical Reason and Norms.* Oxford: Oxford University Press, 1975.

Ross, W. D. *Foundations of Ethics.* Oxford: Clarendon Press, 1939.

Scanlon, Thomas. *What We Owe to Each Other.* Cambridge, MA: Harvard University Press, 1998.

Schmidtz, D. *Rational Choice and Moral Agency.* Princeton, NJ: Princeton University Press, 1995.

Smith, Michael. *The Moral Problem.* New York: Routledge, 1995.

Stocker, Michael. "Desiring the Bad: An Essay in Moral Psychology." *Journal of Philosophy* 76 (1979): 738–53.

Velleman, David. "The Possibility of Practical Reason." *Ethics* 106, No. 4 (1996): 694–726.

Wallace, R. Jay. "How to Argue About Practical Reason." *Mind* 99 (395) (1990): 355–385.

Wallace, R. Jay. "Normativity, Commitment, and Instrumental Reason." *Philosopher's Imprint.* 1 (3) (2001): 1–26, http://www.philosophersimprint.org/001003.

Wiggins, David. "Deliberation and Practical Reason." In *Essays on Aristotle's Ethics,* edited by A. O. Rorty. Berkeley: University of California Press, 1980.

Williams, Bernard. "Internal and External Reasons." In *Moral Luck: Philosophical Papers, 1973–1980.* Cambridge, U.K.: Cambridge University Press, 1981.

Robert N. Johnson (2005)

PRACTICAL REASON APPROACHES

See *Rationalism in Ethics (Practical Reason Approaches)*

PRAGMATICISM

See *Peirce, Charles Sanders; Pragmatism*

PRAGMATICS

"Pragmatics" was defined by Charles W. Morris (1938) as the branch of semiotics that studies the relation of signs to interpreters, in contrast with semantics, which studies the relation of signs to designata. In practice, it has often been treated as a repository for any aspect of utterance meaning beyond the scope of existing semantic machinery, as in the slogan "Pragmatics = meaning minus truth conditions" (Gazdar 1979). There has been some doubt about whether it is a homogeneous domain (Searle, Kiefer, and Bierwisch 1980).

A more positive view emerges from the work of Herbert Paul Grice, whose *William James Lectures* (1967) are fundamental. Grice showed that many aspects of utterance meaning traditionally regarded as conventional, or semantic, could be more explanatorily treated as conversational, or pragmatic. For Gricean pragmatists, the crucial feature of pragmatic interpretation is its inferential nature: the hearer is seen as constructing and evaluating a hypothesis about the communicator's intentions, based, on the one hand, on the meaning of the sentence uttered, and on the other, on contextual information and general communicative principles that speakers are normally expected to observe. (For definition and surveys see Levinson 1983.)

THE SEMANTICS-PRAGMATICS DISTINCTION

In early work, the semantics-pragmatics distinction was often seen as coextensive with the distinction between truth-conditional and non-truth-conditional meaning

(Gazdar 1979). On this approach, pragmatics would deal with a range of disparate phenomena, including (a) Gricean conversational inference, (b) the inferential recognition of illocutionary-force, and (c) the conventional meanings of illocutionary-force indicators and other non-truth-conditional expressions such as *but, please, unfortunately* (Recanati 1987). From the cognitive point of view, these phenomena have little in common.

Within the cognitive science literature in particular, the semantics-pragmatics distinction is now more generally seen as coextensive with the distinction between decoding and inference (or conventional and conversational meaning). On this approach, all conventional meaning, both truth-conditional and non-truth-conditional, is left to linguistic semantics, and the aim of pragmatic theory is to explain how the gap between sentence meaning and utterance interpretation is inferentially bridged. A pragmatic theory of this type is developed in D. Sperber and D. Wilson (1986).

IMPLICATURE

Grice's distinction between saying and implicating crosscuts the semantics-pragmatics distinction as defined above. For Grice, "what is said" corresponds to the truth-conditional content of an utterance, and "what is implicated" is everything communicated that is not part of what is said. Grice saw the truth-conditional content of an utterance as determined partly by the conventional (semantic) meaning of the sentence uttered, and partly by contextual (pragmatic) factors governing disambiguation and reference assignment. He saw conventional (semantic) implicatures as determined by the meaning of discourse connectives such as *but, moreover* and *so,* and analyzed them as signaling the performance of higher-order speech acts such as contrasting, adding and explaining (Grice 1989). An alternative analysis is developed in D. Blakemore (1987).

Among nonconventional (pragmatic) implicatures, the best known are the conversational ones: These are beliefs that have to be attributed to the speaker in order to preserve the assumption that she was obeying the "cooperative principle" (with associated maxims of truthfulness, informativeness, relevance, and clarity), in saying what she said. In Grice's framework, generalized conversational implicatures are "normally" carried by use of a certain expression, and are easily confused with conventional lexical meaning (Grice 1989). In Grice's view, many earlier philosophical analyses were guilty of such confusion.

Grice's account of conversational implicatures has been questioned on several grounds:

(1) The status and content of the cooperative principle and maxims have been debated, and attempts to reduce the maxims or provide alternative sources for implicatures have been undertaken (Davis 1991, Horn 1984, Levinson 1987, Sperber and Wilson 1986).

(2) Grice claimed that deliberate, blatant maxim-violation could result in implicatures, in the case of metaphor and irony in particular. This claim has been challenged, and alternative accounts of metaphor and irony developed, in which no maxim-violation takes place (Blakemore 1992, Hugly and Sayward 1979, Sperber and Wilson 1986).

(3) Pragmatic principles have been found to make a substantial contribution to explicit communication, not only in disambiguation and reference assignment, but in enriching the linguistically encoded meaning in various ways. This raises the question of where the borderline between explicit and implicit communication should be drawn (Sperber and Wilson 1986, 1995). It has even been argued that many of Grice's best-known cases of generalized conversational implicature might be better analyzed as pragmatically determined aspects of what is said (Carston 1988, Recanati 1989).

(4) The idea that the context for utterance interpretation is determined in advance of the utterance has been questioned, and the identification of an appropriate set of contextual assumptions is now seen as an integral part of the utterance-interpretation process (Blakemore 1992, Sperber and Wilson 1986).

PROSPECTS

Within the cognitive science literature, several approaches to pragmatics are currently being pursued. There are computational attempts to implement the Gricean program via rules for the recognition of coherence relations among discourse segments (Asher and Lascarides 1995, Hobbs 1985). Relations between the Gricean program and speech-act theory are being reassessed (Tsohatzidis 1994). The cognitive foundations of pragmatics and the relations of pragmatics to neighboring disciplines are still being explored (Sperber and Wilson 1995, Sperber 1994). Despite this diversity of approaches, pragmatics now seems to be established as a relatively homogenous domain.

See also Cognitive Science; Grice, Herbert Paul; Metaphor; Philosophy of Language; Reference; Semantics.

Bibliography

Asher, N., and A. Lascarides. "Lexical Disambiguation in a Discourse Context." *Journal of Semantics* 12 (1995): 69–108.

Blakemore, D. *Semantic Constraints on Relevance.* Oxford: Blackwell, 1987.

Blakemore, D. *Understanding Utterances.* Oxford: Blackwell, 1992.

Carston, R. "Explicature, Implicature and Truth-Theoretic Semantics." In *Mental Representations: The Interface between Language and Reality,* edited by R. Kempson. Cambridge, U.K.: Cambridge University Press, 1988.

Davis, S., ed. *Pragmatics: A Reader.* New York: Oxford University Press, 1991.

Gazdar, G. *Pragmatics: Implicature, Presupposition and Logical Form.* New York: Academic Press, 1979.

Grice, H. P. "Logic and Conversation." *William James Lectures.* Cambridge, MA, 1967.

Grice, H. P. *Studies in the Way of Words.* Cambridge, MA: Harvard University Press, 1989.

Hobbs, J. "On the Coherence and Structure of Discourse." Center for the Study of Language and Information (October 1985).

Horn, L. "A New Taxonomy for Pragmatic Inference: Q-Based and R-Based Implicature." In *Meaning, Form and Use in Context,* edited by D. Schiffrin. Washington, DC, 1984.

Hugly, P., and C. Sayward. "A Problem about Conversational Implicature." *Linguistics and Philosophy* 3 (1979): 19–25.

Levinson, S. "Minimization and Conversational Inference." In *The Pragmatic Perspective,* edited by J. Verschueren and M. Bertuccelli-Papis. Amsterdam: Benjamins, 1987.

Levinson, S. *Pragmatics.* Cambridge, U.K.: Cambridge University Press, 1983.

Morris, C. "Foundations of the Theory of Signs." In *International Encyclopedia of Unified Science,* edited by O. Neurath, R. Carnap, and C. Morriss. Chicago: University of Chicago Press, 1938.

Recanati, F. *Meaning and Force.* Cambridge, U.K.: Cambridge University Press, 1987.

Recanati, F. "The Pragmatics of What Is Said." *Mind and Language* 4 (1989): 295–329.

Searle, J., F. Kiefer, and M. Bierwisch, eds. *Speech-Act Theory and Pragmatics.* Dordrecht: Reidel, 1980.

Sperber, D. "Understanding Verbal Understanding." In *What Is Intelligence?,* edited by J. Khalfa. Cambridge, U.K.: Cambridge University Press, 1994.

Sperber, D., and D. Wilson. *Relevance: Communication and Cognition.* Oxford, 1986.

Sperber, D., and D. Wilson. "Postface" to the second edition of *Relevance.* Oxford, 1995.

Tsohatzidis, S., ed. *Foundations of Speech-Act Theory: Philosophical and Linguistic Perspectives.* London: Routledge, 1994.

Deirdre Wilson (1996)

PRAGMATICS [ADDENDUM]

A major focus of post-Gricean pragmatics is the role that pragmatic inference plays in determining the explicit content of utterances (as opposed to their conversational implicatures). As well as disambiguation and reference fixing, there are pragmatic processes of propositional completion, as in the examples in (1), and, more controversially, processes of "free" enrichment, as in (2):

(1) a. It's too late.   *[for what?]*
     b. Cotton is better.   *[than what?]*
(2) a. I've had breakfast.   *[today]*
     b. John's car hit Tom's and   *[causal relation]*
         Tom stopped illegally.

The pragmatic completions in (1) are mandated by aspects of the linguistic semantics of the sentences, specifically by the lexical items *too* and *better*. However, this does not seem to be the case for the examples in (2), which express complete, truth-evaluable propositions without the bracketed addition. These pragmatic inferences seem to be entirely pragmatically motivated (i.e., "free" from linguistic indication); they are undertaken in order to satisfy standing communicative presumptions concerning the informativeness and relevance of utterances. For instance, (2a) is strictly speaking true provided the speaker has had breakfast sometime in her life, but in most contexts a speaker intends a more specific proposition and relevant implications hinge on the enriched content (e.g., "that she is not hungry at this moment"). Another kind of free pragmatic process is "lexical modulation": the encoded meaning of a word may be narrowed down in context (e.g., *drink* used to mean "alcoholic drink"), broadened (e.g., *square* used to mean "squarish") or metaphorically extended (e.g., *nightmare* used to mean "unpleasant experience").

The view that "free" pragmatic inferences can affect explicit content in these ways is labeled "truth-conditional pragmatics" and is held by pragmatists across different theoretical persuasions. Various accounts of the phenomenon and its relation to conversational implicature are being developed. Stephen Levinson (2000) argues for a system of "default" pragmatic inferences triggered by particular linguistic forms (e.g., *and, some, drink*), which are distinct from the kind of inferences responsible for more context-specific implicatures. François Recanati (2003) makes a different distinction between two kinds of pragmatic processes: "primary" processes, such as free enrichment, which contribute to truth-conditional content, are a matter of local associative processing, whereas "secondary" ones, which account for implicatures, are cases of global propositional inference, constrained by Gricean maxims. Relevance theorists, led by Dan Sperber and Deirdre Wilson, argue that all pragmatic inference can be accounted for by a single principle geared to the recovery of an "optimally relevant" interpretation and that pragmatic enrichment of explicit content often occurs in order to ensure an inferentially sound basis for an antecedently derived conversational implicature.

An alternative, more semantically oriented position, represented by Jason Stanley (2000), denies the existence of processes of "free" pragmatic enrichment and claims that all aspects of an utterance's truth-conditional content are indicated in its linguistic form. So the examples in (2) are to be explained in the same way as the examples in (1): There is a covert indexical element in their linguistic form and it is this that triggers the pragmatic process of finding the relevant contextual value.

Which of these views is correct (if either) remains to be seen.

See also Grice, Herbert Paul; Metaphor; Non-Truth-Conditional Meaning; Reference; Semantics; Semantics, History of.

Bibliography

Bach, Kent. "Speaking Loosely: Sentence Nonliterality." In *Midwest Studies in Philosophy*. Vol. 25, *Figurative Language*, edited by Peter French and Howard Wettstein. Oxford, U.K.: Blackwell, 2001.

Carston, Robyn. *Thoughts and Utterances: The Pragmatics of Explicit Communication*. Oxford, U.K.: Blackwell, 2002.

Levinson, Stephen. *Presumptive Meanings: The Theory of Generalized Conversational Implicature*. Cambridge, MA: MIT Press, 2000.

Recanati, François. *Literal Meaning*. Cambridge, U.K.: Cambridge University Press, 2003.

Stanley, Jason. "Context and Logical Form." *Linguistics and Philosophy* 23 (2000): 391–434.

Wilson, Deirdre, and Dan Sperber. "Relevance Theory." In *Handbook of Pragmatics*, edited by Laurence Horn and Gregory Ward. Oxford, U.K.: Blackwell, 2004.

Robyn Carston (2005)

PRAGMATISM

"Pragmatism" was the most influential philosophy in America in the first quarter of the twentieth century. Viewed against the widely diversified intellectual currents that have characterized American life, pragmatism stands out as an energetically evolved philosophical movement. As a movement it is best understood as, in part, a critical rejection of much of traditional academic philosophy and, in part, a concern to establish certain positive aims. It is in these respects, rather than because of any one idea or exclusive doctrine, that pragmatism has been the most distinctive and the major contribution of America to the world of philosophy. Among the Continental thinkers it has influenced and with whose philosophy it has been in harmony are Georg Simmel, Wilhelm Ostwald, Edmund Husserl, Hans Vaihinger, Richard Müller-Freienfels, Hans Hahn, Giovanni Papini (leader of the Pragmatist Club in Florence), Giovanni Vailati, Henri Bergson, and Édouard Le Roy.

BACKGROUND

The origins of pragmatism are clear in outline, if not in detail. The familiar capsule description is as follows: Pragmatism is a method of philosophizing—often said to be a theory of meaning—first developed by Charles Sanders Peirce in the 1870s; revived and reformulated in 1898 by William James, primarily as a theory of truth; further developed, expanded, and disseminated by John Dewey and Ferdinand Canning Scott Schiller.

This glossing of the facts is useful as a summary or for directing us where to look if we want to find out more about pragmatism. But it can be misleading. A reexamination or rewriting of the history is not to be embarked upon here; but the following cautionary points deserve mention. The specific formative conditions of the early evolution of pragmatism are not entirely clear for several reasons. The historical occasion of the birth of pragmatism is complicated because it was to some extent the product of cooperative deliberation and mutual influences within the "Metaphysical Club," founded by Peirce, James, and others in the 1870s in Cambridge. This may be one of the very few cases in which a philosophy club produced something notable philosophically (compare John Locke's account of the "club" in the 1670s that stimulated the writing of his great *Essay*). But the paper (now lost) that Peirce drew up as a memento lest the club dissolve without leaving behind anything substantial, the paper in which pragmatism was first expressed, was not the free creation of one mind, even though the major credit surely goes to Peirce. Years later, undertaking to write on pragmatism, Peirce queried James: "Who originated the term *pragmatism*, I or you? Where did it first appear in print? What do you understand by it?" And James replied with the reminder: "You invented 'pragmatism' for which I gave you full credit in a lecture entitled 'Philosophical Conceptions and Practical Results.'"

In addition to some uncertainty as to the facts in the evolution of pragmatism, there are—as we shall see—several problems of interpretation. Peirce and James often gave very different accounts of what they understood by "pragmatism." Usually this is explained by holding James responsible for distorting or even misunderstanding Peirce's ideas. That there were differences between Peirce and James on this score is clear. Peirce, despairing of what James (and his followers) were making of the idea, rebaptized his own view as "pragmaticism," a word ugly enough, he commented, to keep it safe from kidnapers. Historians usually side with Peirce, tending to discredit James's overzealous pronouncements upon pragmatism and applications of it to issues of the moral value and truth of religious belief. But with equal justice it can be maintained that James was developing a substantially different approach to a different type of philosophical problem, related in some ways to Peirce's thought, but mostly superficially; only his habitual overgenerosity led him to call what he was doing "pragmatism" and to cite Peirce as the "inventor."

There is, however, a more serious and persistent problem of interpretation entrenched in the history of pragmatism. This is the problem of determining with some precision what "pragmatism" means or stands for as a philosophical doctrine. As already suggested, pragmatism, by virtue of being an evolving philosophical movement, is to be viewed as a group of associated theoretical ideas and attitudes developed over a period of time and exhibiting—under the differing influences of Peirce, James, and Dewey—rather significant shifts in direction and in formulation. We have the advantage of historical perspective and can make use of it to survey and select distinctive themes and phases in the formation of pragmatism, but a single definitive statement of a single thesis is not to be hoped for.

In the heyday of pragmatism its rapidly changing character proved to be a source of embarrassment and confusion to pragmatists and critics alike. Arthur O. Lovejoy, in a welcome effort at clarification, in 1908 distinguished thirteen possible forms of pragmatism. And Schiller, in an almost intoxicating pluralistic spirit, commented that there were as many pragmatisms as there were pragmatists (at the time a considerable company). Additional confusion over pragmatism was caused by the tendency of its spokesmen to find the philosophical past well populated with pragmatists. Thus Socrates, Protagoras, Aristotle, Francis Bacon, Benedict de Spinoza, Locke,

George Berkeley, David Hume, Immanuel Kant, J. S. Mill, and an assorted variety of scientists were included in the fold.

These perplexities, once hotly debated in the journals, are now only of historical interest. They need not concern us in surveying and assessing what are undoubtedly the leading ideas of pragmatism. It suffices to note the irony in the fact that while pragmatism was supposed to have made its appearance in the paper by Peirce titled "How to Make Our Ideas Clear" (1878), pragmatists continued to have so much trouble in doing so.

CHARLES SANDERS PEIRCE

What has come to be known as Peirce's pragmatism grew out of his study of the phenomenology of human thought and the uses of language. For Peirce, the investigation of thought and language—and, therefore, the way into specific studies of all kinds of claims, assertions, beliefs, and ideas—depended upon the understanding of "signs." One of Peirce's lasting ideals, resolutely pursued but never completely achieved, was to work out a general theory of signs—that is, a classification and analysis of the types of signs and sign relations and significations that, in the broadest sense, make communication possible. A sign is anything that stands for something else. While this ancient way of putting it admits of a trivial construction (signs are signs), for Peirce, the main thing was that signs are socially standardized ways in which something (a thought, word, gesture, object) refers us (a community) to something else (the interpretant—the significant effect or translation of the sign, being itself another sign). Thus, signs presuppose minds in communication with other minds, which in turn presupposes a community (of interpreters) and a system of communication.

PRAGMATIC METHOD. Put roughly, Peirce's pragmatism is a rule of procedure for promoting linguistic and conceptual clarity—successful communication—when men are faced with intellectual problems. Because the emphasis is upon method, Peirce often remarked that pragmatism is not a philosophy, a metaphysic, or a theory of truth; it is not a solution or answer to anything but a technique to help us find solutions to problems of a philosophical or scientific nature.

One of Peirce's best-known statements of the technique was in "How to Make Our Ideas Clear" (1878): "Consider what effects, that might conceivably have practical bearings, we conceive the object of our conception to have. Then our conception of these effects is the whole of our conception of the objects." In a somewhat clearer account he said that "in order to ascertain the meaning of an intellectual conception one should consider what practical consequences might conceivably result by necessity from the truth of that conception; and the sum of these consequences will constitute the entire meaning of the conception" (*Collected Papers*, Vol. V, paragraph 9).

While Peirce often spoke of pragmatism as a method of clarifying the meaning variously of words, ideas, concepts (sometimes of objects), we can take his intended purpose to be as follows:

(1) Pragmatism is a method of clarifying and determining the meaning of signs. We must note the comprehensive status Peirce gives to signs in this connection, for example: "All thought whatsoever is a sign, and is mostly of the nature of language." The pragmatic method, however, does not apply to all the various kinds of signs and modes and purposes of communication. Peirce considered pragmatism "a method of ascertaining the meaning of hard words and abstract concepts" or, again, "a method of ascertaining the meanings, not of all ideas, but … 'intellectual concepts,' that is to say, of those upon the structure of which, arguments concerning objective fact may hinge."

(2) The aim of the method is to facilitate communication, and in particular cases, the degree to which this is accomplished determines the relevance and justification of the method. This aim takes two main forms illustrated in Peirce's writings. The first is of a critical nature: Where disputes or philosophical problems seem to have no discoverable or agreed-upon solution, pragmatism advises that words are being used in different ways or without definite meaning at all. For example, says Peirce, pragmatism will "show that almost every proposition of ontological metaphysics is either meaningless … or else … absurd." And it is in this critical capacity that Peirce remarked: "Pragmatism solves no real problem. It only shows that supposed problems are not real problems."

But the second role the method performs is much less negative: Where signs (that is, ideas, concepts, language) are unclear, the method supplies a procedure for reconstructing or explicating meanings. Here the method is directed to translating (or systematically replacing) unclear concepts with clearer ones. It is in this spirit that Peirce offered his explications of the concepts of "hardness," "weight," "force," "reality." His procedure consisted

in translating and explicating a sign (a term, such as *hard*, or sentences of signs, such as "*x* is hard") by providing a conditional statement of a given situation (or class of situations) in which a definite operation will produce a definite result. Thus, to say of some object *O* that it is "hard" is to mean that "if in certain situations the operation of scratch-testing is performed on *O*, then the general result is: *O* will not be scratched by most substances." The sign (or concept) "hard" in statements asserting that some object is hard is replaceable and clarified pragmatically with a conditional statement of the sort just given. Peirce refers to this method of conditional explication of signs as a "prescription" or "precept." The conditionals are recipes informing us what we must do if we wish to find out the kind of conditions determining the meaningful use of a sign.

MEANING. For Peirce, two points are of considerable importance in the pragmatic procedure for determining meaning, (*a*) Where one cannot provide any conditional translation for a sign, its (pragmatic) meaning is empty. This is what Peirce intended by such characteristic statements as that our conception of an object is our conception of its "practical effects" or "sensible effects." He did not mean (as James sometimes did) that the meaning of a concept is the practical effect it has in particular cases when you use it. All Peirce argued was that a concept must have some conceivable consequences, or "practical bearings," and that these must be specifiable in the manner just discussed if the concept is to play a significant role in communication, (*b*) Peirce's pragmatism thus is offered as a schema for getting at the meaning, or empirical significance, of language. As a schema it is not a theory of meaning in the sense of some general definition of meaning; it is a theoretical device for getting at the empirically significant content of concepts by determining the roles they play in classes of empirically verifiable statements. This procedure, or schema, clearly foreshadowed the later programs of operationalism and the verifiability theory of meaning.

Despite some serious difficulties that jeopardize portions of Peirce's method, the general aspects of his approach appear to be sound canons of scientific practice. Peirce's recondite statements of pragmatism have created considerable confusion. But Peirce seemed less concerned with the problem of providing an accurate and complete statement of the "maxim" of pragmatism than with its use and justification. This he attempted to show in much of his later philosophical inquiries of a scientific and metaphysical sort.

Peirce's schema, or prescriptive method, for "determining the meaning of intellectual concepts" has several sources in addition to his familiarity with scientific technique. Suggestions of it are to be found in Berkeley and in Kant. Peirce's view that meanings take a general form expressed in schema or formulas that prescribe kinds of operations and results and conceivable consequences and rules of action was directly linked to Kant. Peirce says he was led to the method of pragmatism by reflecting on Kant's *Critique of Pure Reason* and on the Kantian use of *pragmatisch* for empirical, or experimentally conditioned, laws, "based on and applying to experience."

INQUIRY AND TRUTH. It should be noted, finally, that Peirce's pragmatism is part of a more general account of "inquiry," aspects of which he elaborated with some care and most of which was taken up into Dewey's extensive construction of a theory of inquiry. Peirce described the function of thought as a form of behavior initiated by the irritation of doubt and proceeding to some resolution in a state of belief. Belief is a condition of organic stability and intellectual satisfaction, but these latter do not determine the truth of beliefs. Peirce outlined a scientific and pragmatic method of clarifying and justifying belief. It was this aspect of Peirce's analysis of inquiry and belief that suggested a pragmatic theory of truth. On this matter he was unclear and wavering. Sometimes truth and pragmatic meaning overlapped or coalesced in his discussions of them. But Peirce also argued that truth theory and pragmatism are entirely separate considerations. Generally, the idea of truth, for Peirce, is drawn from Kant and is to be understood as a regulative idea, one that functions solely to order, integrate, and promote inquiry. Taken as a "correspondence" or "coherence" theory—or criticized from the point of view of such theories— Peirce's account of truth looks strange, cumbersome, and naive.

WILLIAM JAMES

It was James who launched pragmatism as a new philosophy in a lecture "Philosophical Conceptions" in 1898; it was under his leadership that pragmatism came to be famous; and it was primarily his exposition that was received and read by the world at large.

Although Peirce and James were lifelong friends and exerted much intellectual influence upon each other, they differed in ways that had important effects upon their respective versions of pragmatism. Peirce was a realist (calling himself a scholastic realist); James was far more of a nominalist. Where Peirce sought meaning in general

concepts and formulas of action, James sought meaning in experienced facts and plans of action. James looked to the concrete, immediate, practical level of experience as the testing ground of our intellectual efforts; for Peirce, the immediate sensory experience is all but destitute of "intellectual purport." Furthermore, while Peirce's pragmatism took a logical and scientific character, James, despite being an eminent man of science, was first and foremost a moralist in his pragmatism.

VALUE. Moral interests and moral language appear in almost every important passage of James's writing on pragmatism. In *Pragmatism* James made his moral conception of philosophy unmistakably evident in saying that "the whole function of philosophy ought to be to find out what definite difference it will make to you and me, at definite instants of our life, if this world-formula or that world-formula be the true one." The phrase "what definite difference … at definite instants of our life" is by and large James's way of critically judging the meaning and truth of ideas. For James, meaning and truth are included in a more fundamental category of value; to determine the meaning or truth of ideas one must evaluate their "practical consequences," "usefulness," "workability." In several famous pronouncements, James spoke of truth as what is good or expedient in our beliefs. In a phrase that permanently shocked some of his readers, James described the meaning and truth of ideas as their "cash value."

Generally, for James, the function of thought is that of assisting us to achieve and sustain "satisfactory relations with our surroundings." The value of ideas, beliefs, and conceptual dealings is to be determined accordingly, on each of numerous occasions, by their effectiveness and efficiency as the means of carrying us propitiously "from any one part of our experience to any other part, linking things satisfactorily, working securely, simplifying, saving labor."

James was thus primarily concerned with issues of belief and conceptual renditions of experience in their role of enabling men to deal with environments and to enrich the fare of daily experience. It is the level of life experience that interested James. Hence, his own statements of pragmatism resemble those of Peirce but emphasize the importance of immediate experience and practical consequences and clues to action. For James, our thoughts of an object pragmatically considered lead us to "what conceivable effects of a practical kind the object may involve—what sensations we are to expect from it, and what reactions we must prepare. Our conception of these effects, whether immediate or remote, is then for us the whole of our conception of the object." If we compare this statement from *Pragmatism* with those cited earlier from Peirce, it is not difficult to see that in James's pragmatism the emphasis is upon the way individuals interpret environing conditions for purposes of successful action. The passage also reflects how James's view differed from Peirce's Kantian conception; James explained "pragmatism" as coming from the Greek πράγμα, meaning "practice," "action." Indeed, so fundamental are action, exploration, and life experience in James's philosophy that some of his critics have taken great pains to demonstrate the value of inaction and the general uselessness of philosophy. In this endeavor, it may be said, they have been on the whole successful.

BELIEF. It was James's conception of truth that became a *cause célèbre* for pragmatism and its critics, until eventually James, tiring of the matter, turned his attention to other philosophical pursuits, leaving to Dewey the defense and development of pragmatism. Aside from truth, the other major critical issue in pragmatism was James's argument for the justification of moral and religious belief. James's interest in the meaning and function of belief was that of a skilled and perceptive psychologist and moralist. His general view was this: When, for a given person P, a belief B answers or satisfies a compelling need (of P to see or interpret the world in a certain way), the "vital good" supplied by B in the life of P (the difference it makes as a beneficial causal condition in the psychological and physiological behavior of P) justifies B. It must be noted that James argued for this justification procedure only when (*a*) the choice of B or not-B is, for a given individual at a given time, "live," "forced," and "momentous"; (*b*) the evidence for or against B is equal, or admits of no rational adjudication of one over the other; (*c*) the effect or consequences of B are a "vital benefit." These three qualifications work against ascribing to James some popular defense or universal apologia for religious belief. He thought he was correct in pointing to a psychological and moral right to belief analogous to the justification of postulates or posits (in Kantian and Fichtean transcendental philosophizing) or of certain theoretical hypotheses in science.

Peirce and Dewey, among others, were highly critical of this defense of the will to believe. James the psychologist and literary artist brilliantly described the working consequences of types of religious belief for characteristic types of persons. But James the philosopher tended to confuse a descriptive analysis of how belief functions and why men believe with questions of the evaluation or ver-

ification of specific cases of belief. (Thus, for example, the fact that B answers a need of P is not of itself evidence that the content of belief B is warranted or that P has correctly understood his "need.")

However, it was this side of James that was enthusiastically received as the moral core of his pragmatism by Schiller in England and Giovanni Papini in Italy. Here also James's views have affinities with those of Bergson, Vaihinger, and Simmel. James seemed to be a democratic, energetic, and lovable Johann Gottlieb Fichte, an artist and scientist exhorting men to trust their beliefs and, above all, to leave the classroom and cloister and start living and acting in the world.

JOHN DEWEY

In the article "The Development of American Pragmatism," Dewey described Peirce's views as stemming from an "experimental, not a priori, explanation of Kant" and James's pragmatism as inspired by British empiricism. But he also noted this difference: "Peirce wrote as a logician and James as a humanist." There was, in fact, a crossfertilization of these strains; but the characterization is apt and traceable enough in the history of pragmatism and in Dewey, too, to be of expository aid. Dewey began to appreciate James while still under the influence of Hegelian and Kantian idealism; later he recognized the importance of Peirce, whose insights and ideas were in many respects anticipations of those Dewey had started to work out on his own. The Hegelian synthesis of the logical and humanistic sides of pragmatism was achieved by the disenchanted Hegelian Dewey.

INSTRUMENTALISM. Through Dewey's patient, critical, and indefatigable efforts, pragmatism was carefully and thoroughly reformulated into what Dewey called Instrumentalism, "a theory of the general forms of conception and reasoning." Instrumentalism was a single philosophical theory within which the two evolving aspects of pragmatism found coherent expression. Instrumentalism was both theory of logic and a guiding principle of ethical analysis and criticism. For Dewey, this theory bridged the most persistent and noxious of "dualisms" in modern thought—the separation of science and values, knowledge and morals.

Instrumentalism was Dewey's theory of the conditions under which reasoning occurs and of the forms, or controlling operations, that are characteristic of thought in establishing future consequences. In the paper cited above, Dewey wrote:

Instrumentalism is an attempt to constitute a precise logical theory of concepts, of judgments and inferences in their various forms, by considering primarily how thought functions in the experimental determinations of future consequences ... it attempts to establish universally recognized distinctions and rules of logic by deriving them from the reconstructive or mediative function ascribed to reason. It aims to constitute a theory of the general forms of conception and reasoning.

A suggestive and vital feature of this theory for Dewey was that while the subject matters of scientific inquiry and moral and social experience differ, the method and forms of thought functioning "in the experimental determinations of future consequences" do not differ in kind. The method of thought and the forms of reflective behavior exhibit a common functional pattern whenever problematic situations become resolved through inquiry yielding "warranted assertion."

INQUIRY AND TRUTH. "Warranted assertion" is the term for Dewey's version of truth. Inquiry is initiated in conditions of doubt; it terminates in the establishment of conditions in which doubt is no longer needed or felt. It is this settling of conditions of doubt, a settlement produced and warranted by inquiry, which distinguishes the warranted assertion. Whereas Dewey once defined "truth" as the "working" or "satisfactory" or "verified" idea or hypothesis, he was led, later—partly as a result of several critical controversies over truth with Bertrand Russell during the 1930s and 1940s—to restate his view of truth as warranted assertion.

In his *Logic* Dewey gave his general definition of inquiry as "the controlled or directed transformation of an indeterminate situation into one that is so determinate in its constituent distinctions and relations as to convert the elements of the original situation into a unified whole." The theory of inquiry was developed over many years and in many writings; into it went the products of Dewey's reflections on the nature of thought, his contributions to psychology and education, the influence of the biological and functional aspects of James's *Principles of Psychology*, and the influence of Peirce on the nature of scientific inquiry. In his analysis of the biological and cultural conditions of inquiry and in his account of intelligence as a function of these interacting conditions in a particular situation with respect to a problem and its outcome, Dewey was also guided by some of the basic ideas in the philosophical social psychology of G. H. Mead,

once Dewey's colleague at Michigan and Chicago and one of his closest friends. The definitive statement of the theory is in Dewey's *Logic: The Theory of Inquiry* (1938).

For Dewey, the theory of inquiry is a generalized description of the organic, cultural, and formal conditions of intelligent action. Such action is provoked by problems of diverse kinds—political, ethical, scientific, and aesthetic. But irrespective of the specific content of human problems or the nature of problem situations, inquiry is a reflective evaluation of existing conditions—of shortcomings and possibilities—with respect to operations intended to actualize certain potentialities of the situation so as to resolve what was doubtful. The purpose of inquiry is to create goods, satisfactions, solutions, and integration in what was initially a wanting, discordant, troubled, and problematic situation. In this respect all intelligence is evaluative, and no separation of moral, scientific, practical, or theoretical experience is to be made. So commanding an achievement was Dewey's last-mentioned work that "pragmatism" is often identified with the position he expounded there as a naturalistic logic for evaluating and reconstructing human experience.

MORE RECENT TENDENCIES

A somewhat different articulation of pragmatism, deriving less from James and Dewey than from Peirce, was set forth by C. I. Lewis in the 1920s as "conceptualistic pragmatism." Lewis emphasized the role of mind in supplying the a priori principles and categories by which we proceed to organize and interpret sense experience. But he also stressed the plurality of categories and conceptual schemes by which experience can be interpreted and the evolutionary character of our systems. Because a priori principles impose no necessary order on the world or upon sense experience (determining only our ways of organizing experience), Lewis argued for a "pragmatic a priori." Decisions to accept or reject conceptual principles, indeed the very function of those principles, rest upon socially shared needs and purposes and upon our interest in increased understanding and control over experience. According to Lewis (in *Mind and the World Order*), "The interpretation of experience must always be in terms of categories ... and concepts which the mind itself determines. There may be alternative conceptual systems giving rise to alternative descriptions of experience, which are equally objective and equally valid.... When this is so, choice will be determined, consciously or unconsciously, on pragmatic grounds."

Lewis's pragmatism resulted in a theory of conceptual and empirical meaning and in an analysis of empirical judgments as probable and evaluative modes of acting upon passing and future experience.

In more recent literature, under the influence of Dewey and Lewis as well as Rudolf Carnap, Charles Morris, Ernest Nagel, Willard Van Orman Quine, and others, "pragmatism" connotes one broad philosophical attitude toward our conceptualization of experience: Theorizing over experience is, as a whole and in detail, fundamentally motivated and justified by conditions of efficacy and utility in serving our various aims and needs. The ways in which experience is apprehended, systematized, and anticipated may be many. Here pragmatism counsels tolerance and pluralism. But, aside from aesthetic and intrinsic interests, all theorizing is subject to the critical objective of maximum usefulness in serving our needs: Our critical decisions, in general, will be pragmatic, granted that in particular cases decisions over what is most useful or needed in our rational endeavors are relative to some given point of view and purposes.

An expression of this attitude that is of current interest was advanced by Peirce, James, and Dewey, as well as by F. P. Ramsey, the brilliant English philosopher influenced by Peirce and James. This is an interpretation of the laws and theories of science as "leading principles," or instrumental procedures, for inferring stated conditions from others. Construed as leading principles, theories function as guides for logical inference, indicating how certain formulations are to be derived from other formulations of events, rather than as descriptively true statements of reality serving as premises from which conclusions are deduced. Pragmatically, theories are inference policies, neither true nor false (except pragmatically) but nonetheless critically assessable as to their utility and clarity and the fruitfulness of the consequences that result from adopting them.

While there continues to be an interest in the philosophies of Peirce, James, Dewey, and Schiller, pragmatism as a movement, in the form outlined in these pages, cannot be said to be alive today. But pragmatism has succeeded in its critical reaction to the nineteenth-century philosophical background from which it emerged; it has helped shape the modern conception of philosophy as a way of investigating problems and clarifying communication rather than as a fixed system of ultimate answers and great truths. And in this alteration of the philosophical scene, some of the positive suggestions of pragmatism have been disseminated into current intellectual life as practices freely adopted and taken for granted to an extent that no longer calls for special notice.

The measure of success pragmatism has achieved in encouraging more successful philosophizing in our time is, by its own standards, its chief justification. To have disappeared as a special thesis by becoming infused in the normal and habitual practices of intelligent inquiry and conduct is surely the pragmatic value of pragmatism.

See also Pragmatics; Pragmatist Epistemology.

Bibliography

GENERAL WORKS ON PRAGMATISM

Ayer, A. J. *The Origins of Pragmatism: Studies in the Philosophy of Charles Sanders Peirce and William James.* San Francisco: Freeman, Cooper, 1968.

Dewey, John. "The Development of American Pragmatism." In his *Philosophy and Civilization.* New York: Minton Balch, 1931. Ch. 2.

Murphy, J. P. *Pragmatism: From Peirce to Davidson.* Boulder, CO: Westview Press, 1990.

Quine, W. V. O. "Two Dogmas of Empiricism" In his *From a Logical Point of View.* Cambridge, MA: Harvard University Press, 1951.

Rorty, Richard. *Objectivity, Relativism, and Truth.* Cambridge, U.K.: Cambridge University Press, 1991.

Rorty, Richard. "A Pragmatist View of Contemporary Analytic Philosophy." *Utopia y Praxis Latinoamericana* 7 (2002): 29–40.

Scheffler, I. *Four Pragmatists: A Critical Introduction to Peirce, James, Mead, and Dewey.* London: Routledge and Kegan Paul, 1974.

Schneider, H. W. *History of American Philosophy.* New York: Columbia University Press, 1946. Chs. 39–41.

Thayer, H. S. *Meaning and Action: A Critical History of Pragmatism.* Indianapolis: Bobbs-Merrill, 1968.

Thayer, H. S. "Pragmatism." In *A Critical History of Western Philosophy*, edited by D. J. O'Connor, 437–462. New York: Free Press of Glencoe, 1964.

Wiener, Philip P. *Evolution and the Founders of Pragmatism.* Cambridge, MA: Harvard University Press, 1949.

WORKS BY PEIRCE

Collected Papers. 8 vols, edited by C. Hartshorne, P. Weiss, and A. W. Burks. Cambridge, MA: Harvard University Press, 1931–1958. Vols. V and VIII especially.

Charles S. Peirce: Selected Writings, edited by P. P. Weiner. New York: Dover, 1966.

WORKS ON PEIRCE

Buchler, Justus. *Charles Peirce's Empiricism.* New York: Harcourt Brace, 1939.

Gallie, W. B. *Peirce and Pragmatism.* Harmondsworth, U.K.: Penguin, 1952.

Murphey, Murray G. *The Development of Peirce's Philosophy.* Cambridge, MA: Harvard University Press, 1961.

Rosenberg, Jay F. "How not to Misunderstand Peirce—A Pragmatist's Account of Truth." In *What Is Truth?*, edited by Richard Schantz. Berlin: de Gruyter, 2002.

WORKS BY JAMES

"Philosophical Conceptions and Practical Results." University of California *Chronicle* (1898). Reprinted in his *Collected Essays and Reviews*, 406–437. New York: Longman, 1920.

Pragmatism and the Meaning of Truth. Cambridge, MA: Harvard University Press, 1979.

The Will to Believe and Other Essays in Popular Philosophy. Cambridge, MA: Harvard University Press, 1979.

WORKS ON JAMES

Myers, G. E. *William James: His Life and Thought.* New Haven, CT: Yale University Press, 1986.

Perry, R. B. *The Thought and Character of William James.* 2 vols. Boston: Little Brown, 1935.

WORKS BY DEWEY

Democracy and Education. New York: Macmillan, 1916.

Essays in Experimental Logic. Chicago: University of Chicago Press, 1916.

Reconstruction in Philosophy. New York: Holt, 1920. Reprinted in paperback edition with a new introduction. New York, 1950.

Human Nature and Conduct. New York: Holt, 1922.

Logic: The Theory of Inquiry. New York: Holt, 1938.

The Early Works, the Middle Works, the Later Works. Carbondale: Southern Illinois University Press, 1990.

WORKS ON DEWEY

Geiger, G. R. *John Dewey in Perspective.* New York: Oxford University Press, 1958.

Hook, Sidney. *John Dewey.* New York: Day, 1939.

Thayer, H. S. *The Logic of Pragmatism.* New York: Humanities Press, 1952.

White, Morton. *The Origin of Dewey's Instrumentalism.* New York: Columbia University Press, 1943.

OTHER PRAGMATISTS

Abel, Reuben. *The Pragmatic Humanism of F. C. S. Schiller.* New York: King's Crown Press, Columbia University, 1955.

Lewis, C. I. *An Analysis of Knowledge and Valuation.* La Salle, IL: Open Court, 1946.

Lewis, C. I. *Mind and the World Order.* New York: Scribners, 1929.

Lewis, C. I. "A Pragmatist Conception of the A Priori." *Journal of Philosophy* 20 (1923): 169–177.

Mead, George H. *Mind, Self, and Society.* Edited by C. W. Morris. Chicago: University of Chicago Press, 1934.

Mead, George H. *The Philosophy of the Act.* Chicago: University of Chicago Press, 1938.

Mead, George H. *Selected Writings.* Edited by Andrew J. Reck. Indianapolis: Bobbs-Merrill, 1964.

Schiller, F. C. S. "Axioms as Postulates." In *Personal Idealism,* edited by Henry Sturt, 47–133. London: Macmillan, 1902.

Schiller, F. C. S. *Logic for Use.* London: G. Bell, 1929.

Schiller, F. C. S. *Studies in Humanism.* New York: Macmillan, 1907.

H. S. Thayer (1967)
Bibliography updated by Benjamin Fiedor (2005)

PRAGMATISM [ADDENDUM]

Not unexpectedly, given that "pragmatism" is not a doctrine but a method (as Charles Sanders Peirce put it), the tradition of classical pragmatism is formidably diverse. Even the method—the pragmatic maxim—is differently interpreted by different pragmatists; and this diversity is compounded by the different doctrines and interests of the various pragmatists. But there is a pattern discernible within the diversity: a shift from Peirce's reformist, scientific philosophy, anchored by his realism about natural kinds and laws and about the objects of perception, through William James's more nominalist pragmatism, his insistence that "the trail of the human serpent is over everything" (1907, p. 37), through John Dewey's proposal that the concept of warranted assertibility replace the concept of truth, to the radicalism of Ferdinand Canning Scott Schiller's avowedly Protagorean relativization of truth to human interests.

Contemporary pragmatisms are no less diverse, but the spectrum has shifted to the left. The more conservative neopragmatists are as akin to James as to Peirce, and the most radical go beyond Schiller's relativism to an antiphilosophical, sometimes antiscientific, even anti-intellectual, stance—a stance so much at odds with the aspirations of the founders of pragmatism as to put one in mind of Peirce's complaints about writers who persisted in "twisting [the pragmatists'] purpose and purport all awry" (*Collected Papers*, 5.464).

Nicholas Rescher describes his philosophy as pragmatic idealism: idealism, because it holds that "reality … as humans deal with it is *our* reality—our thought-world as we conceive and model it" (1994, p. 377); pragmatic, because it holds that, though our picture of reality is a mental construction, it is not a free construction but is objectively constrained by success or failure in practice, in prediction and attainment of purpose.

In some ways—not least in philosophizing unapologetically in the grand systematic manner—Rescher is much like Peirce; indeed, his conception of the interlocking cognitive, evaluative, and practical aspects of rationality takes him further than Peirce into some of the territory of value theory. In other ways Rescher's pragmatism is more reminiscent of James: inter alia, for its stress on practical consequences and on a pluralism of perspectival truth-claims. So, too, is his idealism. Qua pragmatist Peirce denies the intelligibility of the in-principle-incognizable: Qua "objective idealist" he maintains that "matter is just effete mind" (*Collected Papers*, 6.25).

Rescher's idealism sounds more like the Jamesian serpent—or Deweyan interactionism.

In repudiating metaphysical realism and endorsing internal realism, Hilary Putnam evinced some sympathy with Peircean conceptions of truth and reality. But his conceptual relativism—"Our language cannot be divided into two parts, a part that describes the world 'as it is anyway' and a part that describes our conceptual contribution" (1992, p. 123)—sounded more like James. However, his argument against the irrealism of Nelson Goodman (himself classifiable as a left-wing Jamesian of the boldest nominalist stripe) stressed the distinction between wholly conventional names such as "Sirius" and only partially conventional general terms such as *star*. Putnam thus recalled Peirce's realism of natural kinds, and perhaps divided our language after all. It is not surprising, then, to find that most recently, in his Dewey lectures, he tends to a more realist stance.

Sympathetic in the 1950s and 1960s to the positivists' aspiration to a scientific single theory that explains everything" (Putnam 1992, p. 2), Putnam is since then inclined to a pluralistic, problem-centered approach to philosophy. Here, as in his defense of democracy as a precondition for the application of intelligence to the solution of social problems, he acknowledges Dewey.

A year before the publication of W. V. O. Quine's "Two Dogmas," Morton G. White had invoked Dewey in describing the analytic-synthetic distinction as "an untenable dualism." Rejecting that distinction, adopting a holism of verification, insisting on the underdetermination of theory by data, Quine describes himself as going beyond C. I. Lewis's pragmatic a priori to a "more thorough pragmatism" that emphasizes pragmatic considerations in theory-choice generally. "Pragmatic" here suggests the relatively unconstrained rather than, as in Rescher, a kind of constraint. Quine refers approvingly to Schiller's view of truth as manmade as one of pragmatism's main contributions to empiricism. But he hopes to avoid Schiller's relativism by means of a naturalism that views philosophy as internal to science. This differs significantly from Peirce's and Dewey's aspiration to make philosophy scientific by applying the method of science to philosophical questions.

As another of pragmatism's main contributions Quine mentions Peirce's and Dewey's connecting belief and meaning to behavior. But Quine's behaviorism is more stringent, in part because of the influence of B. F. Skinner, and in part because Quine's extensionalism leaves him uneasy, as Peirce was not, with any irreducibly dispositional talk.

As Putnam's allusions to the existentialist character of James's ethics indicate, some hope a neopragmatism might heal the analytic-Continental rift. One example is Karl-Otto Apel's grafting of pragmatic elements from Peirce and Jürgen Habermas onto Alfred Tarski's semantic conception of truth. Another is Joseph Margolis's attempt, emphasizing both the biological roots and the "deep historicity" of human injury, and proposing a reconciliation of a modest realism with a weak relativism, to marry themes from Peirce with themes from Martin Heidegger.

Richard Rorty describes himself as accommodating themes from Dewey with themes from Heidegger. Maintaining that "revolutionary movements within an intellectual discipline require a revisionist history of that discipline" (1983, p. xvii), Rorty dismisses Peirce as having merely given pragmatism its name. And he urges in the name of pragmatism that the project of a philosophical theory of knowledge should be abandoned; that science is exemplary only as a model of human solidarity; that philosophy is more akin to literature than to science: that it should be in the service of democratic politics; that truth is "not the kind of thing one should expect to have a philosophically interesting theory about" (1983, p. xiv) and that to call a statement true is just to give it "a rhetorical pat on the back" (1983, p. xvii); that pragmatism is antirepresentationalism.

There is some affinity between Rorty and Schiller. But Peirce, who was a pioneer of the theory of signs, of representation, and who desired "to rescue the good ship Philosophy for the service of Science from the hands of the lawless rovers of the sea of literature" (*Collected Papers*, 5.449), would disagree with Rorty's pragmatism in every particular. So too, except perhaps for his description of the best ethical writing as akin to "novels and dramas of the deeper sort" (1891, p. 316), would James. And so, most to the point, would Dewey, who hoped to renew the philosophical theory of knowledge by making it more scientific, and whose political philosophy is infused by the hope that the application of scientific methods would enable intelligent social reform, and by the conviction that a free society is a prerequisite of a flourishing science.

See also Behaviorism; Democracy; Dewey, John; Empiricism; Goodman, Nelson; Habermas, Jürgen; Heidegger, Martin; Idealism; James, William; Lewis, Clarence Irving; Naturalism; Peirce, Charles Sanders; Putnam, Hilary; Quine, Willard Van Orman; Rationality; Realism; Schiller, Ferdinand Canning Scott; Tarski, Alfred.

Bibliography

Apel, K.-O. "C. S. Peirce and the Post-Tarskian Problem of an Adequate Explication of the Meaning of Truth: Towards a Transcendental-Pragmatic Theory of Truth." In *The Relevance of Charles Peirce*, edited by E. Freeman. La Salle, IL: Open Court, 1983.

Bernstein, R. "The Resurgence of Pragmatism." *Social Research* 59 (1992): 813–840.

Brandom, Robert. "Pragmatics and Pragmatisms." In *Pragmatism and Realism*, edited by Hilary Putnam. New York: Routledge, 2002.

Dewey, John. *The Early Works, the Middle Works, the Later Works.* Carbondale: Southern Illinois University Press, 1990.

Dewey, John, and J. Tufts. *Ethics.* New York: Holt, 1932.

Goodman, N. *Ways of Worldmaking.* Hassocks, U.K.: Harvester Press, 1978.

Haack, Susan. "The Relevance of Psychology to Epistemology." *Metaphilosophy* 6 (1975): 161–176.

James, William. *Essays in Radical Empiricism.* Cambridge, MA: Harvard University Press, 1976.

James, William. "The Moral Philosopher and the Moral Life." *International Journal of Ethics* 1 (1891). Reprinted in *William James: Selected Writings*, edited by G. Bird. 1994.

James, William. *Pragmatism*, edited by F. Burkhardt and F. Bowers. Cambridge, MA: Harvard University Press, 1975.

Joas, H. *G. H. Mead: A Contemporary Re-examination of His Thought.* Translated by R. Meyer. Cambridge, MA: MIT Press, 1985.

Lewis, C. I. "A Pragmatist Conception of the A Priori." *Journal of Philosophy* 20 (1923): 169–177.

Margolis, J. *Pragmatism without Foundations.* Oxford: Blackwell, 1986.

Mead, G. H. *Selected Writings: George Herbert Mead,* edited by A. J. Reck. Chicago: University of Chicago Press, 1964.

Murphy, J. P. *Pragmatism: From Peirce to Davidson.* Boulder, CO: Westview Press, 1990.

Okrent, M. *Heidegger's Pragmatism.* Ithaca, NY: Cornell University Press, 1988.

Peirce, C. S. *Collected Papers,* edited by C. Hartshorne, P. Weiss, and A. Burks. Cambridge, MA: Harvard University Press, 1931–1958.

Putnam, Hilary. *Renewing Philosophy.* Cambridge, MA: Harvard University Press, 1992.

Putnam, Hilary. "Sense. Nonsense and the Senses: An Inquiry into the Powers of the Human Mind." *Journal of Philosophy* 91 (9) (1994): 447–517.

Putnam, Hilary. *Words and Life.* Cambridge, MA: Harvard University Press, 1994. Sec. 3, "The Inheritance of Pragmatism."

Putnam, Hilary, James Conant, and Urszula Zeglen, eds. *Pragmatism and Realism.* New York: Routledge, 2002.

Quine, W. V. O. "The Pragmatists' Place in Empiricism." In *Pragmatism: Its Sources and Prospects*, edited by R. J. Mulvaney and P. M. Zeltner. Columbia: University of South Carolina Press, 1981.

Quine, W. V. O. "Two Dogmas in Retrospect." *Canadian Journal of Philosophy* 21 (1991): 265–274.

Quine, W. V. O. "Two Dogmas of Empiricism." *Philosophical Review* 60 (1951): 20–43. Reprinted in his *From a Logical Point of View.* Cambridge, MA: Harvard University Press, 1951.

Rescher, Nicholas. *Pluralism: Against the Demand for Consensus.* New York: Oxford University Press, 1993.

Rescher, Nicholas. *A System of Pragmatic Idealism.* 3 vols. Princeton, NJ: Princeton University Press, 1992–1994.

Rescher, Nicholas et al. *Philosophy and Phenomenological Research* 54 (1994): 377–457.

Rorty, Richard. *The Consequences of Pragmatism.* Hassocks, U.K., 1983.

Rorty, Richard. *Objectivity, Relativism, and Truth.* Cambridge, U.K.: Cambridge University Press, 1991.

Sellars, Wilfrid. "Empiricism and the Philosophy of Mind." In his *Science, Perception, and Reality.* London: Routledge and Kegan Paul, 1956.

Stich, Stephen. *The Fragmentation of Reason: Preface to a Pragmatic Theory of Cognitive Evaluation.* Cambridge, MA: MIT Press, 1990.

Thayer, H. S. *Meaning and Action: A Critical History of Pragmatism.* Indianapolis: Bobbs-Merrill, 1968.

White, M. G. "The Analytic and the Synthetic: An Untenable Dualism." In *John Dewey, Philosopher of Science and Freedom*, edited by Sidney Hook. New York: Dial Press, 1950.

Susan Haack (1996)
Bibliography updated by Benjamin Fiedor (2005)

PRAGMATIST EPISTEMOLOGY

William James's observation that "when … we give up the doctrine of objective certitude, we do not thereby give up the quest or hope of truth itself" (1956, p. 17) succinctly expresses one important epistemological theme of traditional pragmatism: accommodation of a thoroughgoing fallibilism with a modest optimism about the possibility of successful truth seeking. Also characteristic of that tradition is its naturalism, its acknowledgment of the biological, and the social as well as the logical elements in the theory of knowledge, and its respect for science as, in Charles Peirce's words, "the epitome of man's intellectual development" (*Collected Papers*, 7.49). Since 1968 these ideas have been variously worked out by some who are fully aware of their roots in pragmatism and have also entered the thinking of many who are not. More surprising, some self-styled neopragmatists defend epistemological positions (or antiepistemological positions) quite unlike these classically pragmatist themes.

Both fallibilism and naturalism are prominent themes in W. V. O. Quine's epistemology, themes of which he acknowledges the pragmatist ancestry; his fallibilism, furthermore, like Peirce's, extends to mathematics and logic, and his naturalism, like Peirce's, has an evolutionary character. And he shares the pragmatists' regard for science. However, he seems drawn beyond a view of epistemology as resting in part on empirical assumptions about human cognitive capacities to conceiving of it as internal to the sciences of cognition; and thence, under pressure of the implausibility of supposing that psychology or biology could answer the questions about evidence, justification, and so forth, with which epistemology has traditionally been concerned, he seems drawn to a revolutionary scientism that would abandon the traditional questions in favor of questions the sciences can be expected to answer. Unlike his fallibilism and his modest, reformist naturalism, neither his scientism nor his revolutionary displacement of epistemology falls within the tradition of pragmatism.

Nicholas Rescher's approach, from its insistence that we humans "cannot function, let alone thrive, without knowledge of what goes on around us" (1994, p. 380) to its stress on the provisional, tentative character of all our estimates of truth, is unambivalently within the pragmatist tradition. But Rescher takes issue with Peirce's definition of truth, and therefore conceives of progress in terms of improvement over earlier stages rather than closeness to a supposed final stage.

Focusing on criteria of evidence and justification rather than on guidelines for the conduct of inquiry, Susan Haack adapts from the pragmatist tradition: Her fallibilism, expressed in the thesis that justification comes in degrees; her weak, reformist naturalism, expressed in the thesis that our criteria of evidence have built into them empirical presuppositions about human cognitive capacities; her account of perception; and her strategy for the metajustification of criteria of justification.

In stark contrast to Rescher or Haack, Richard Rorty urges in the name of pragmatism that the philosophical theory of knowledge is misconceived; and, in contrast to Quine, that epistemology should be, not replaced by the psychology of cognition, but simply abandoned. Rorty likens his repudiation of epistemology to John Dewey's critique of the "spectator theory." What Dewey intended, however, was to reform epistemology, to replace the quest for certain knowledge of eternal, unchanging objects with a realistic account of fallible, experimental, empirical inquiry. Rorty's revolutionary attitude derives from his conception of justification as a matter exclusively of our practices of defending and criticizing beliefs, not grounded in any connection of evidence and truth. This "conversationalist" conception of justification is motivated by his rejection of any conception of truth as meaning more than "what you can defend against all comers."

Often accused of relativism, Rorty denies the charge. He escapes it, however, only by shifting from contextualism ("A is justified in believing that p iff (if and only if) he can defend p by the standards of *his* community") to tribalism (" … iff he can defend p by the standards of *our* community" [1979, p. 308]). But tribalism is arbitrary if our practices of criticizing and defending beliefs are, as Rorty holds, not grounded in any connection of evidence and truth.

In not-so-stark contrast to Rorty, Stephen Stich (1990) urges in the name of pragmatism that it is mere epistemic chauvinism to care whether one's beliefs are true, and that justified beliefs are those that conduce to whatever the subject values. True, Stich cheerfully embraces relativism (and rejects tribalism since he thinks our epistemic practices too preoccupied with truth); and he looks to the sciences of cognition to help us "improve" our cognitive processing so as better to achieve what we really value. But, as more overtly in Rorty, the effect is profoundly antiepistemological and "pragmatist" in quite another sense than the traditional one.

See also Dewey, John; Epistemology; James, William; Naturalism; Peirce, Charles Sanders; Quine, Willard Van Orman.

Bibliography

Haack, S. *Evidence and Inquiry*. Oxford: Blackwell, 1993.

James, W. *The Will to Believe* (1897). New York, 1956.

Peirce, C. S. *Collected Papers*, edited by C. Hawthorne, P. Weiss, and A. Burks. Cambridge, MA: Harvard University Press, 1931–1958.

Quine, W. V. O. "Epistemology Naturalized." In *Ontological Relativity and Other Essays*. New York: Columbia University Press, 1967.

Quine, W. V. O. "Natural Kinds." In *Ontological Relativity and Other Essays*. New York: Columbia University Press, 1967.

Quine, W. V. O. "The Pragmatists' Place in Empiricism." In *Pragmatism: Its Sources and Prospects*, edited by R. J. Mulvaney and P. M. Zeltner, 21–40. Columbia: University of South Carolina Press, 1981.

Quine, W. V. O. *Pursuit of Truth*. Oxford: Oxford University Press, 1990.

Rescher, N. "Précis of *A System of Pragmatic Idealism*," *Philosophy and Phenomenological Research* 54 (1994): 377–390.

Rescher, N. *A System of Pragmatic Idealism*. Vol. 1: *Human Knowledge in Idealistic Perspective*. Princeton, NJ: Princeton University Press, 1992.

Rorty, Richard. *Consequences of Pragmatism*. Minneapolis: University of Minnesota Press, 1982.

Rorty, Richard. *Philosophy and the Mirror of Nature*. Princeton, NJ: Princeton University Press, 1979.

Stich, S. P. *The Fragmentation of Reason*. Cambridge, MA: MIT Press, 1990.

Susan Haack (1996)
Bibliography updated by Benjamin Fiedor (2005)

PRECOGNITION

Etymologically, *precognition* is simply the Latin equivalent of *foreknowledge*. But it has come to have a more specialized meaning as a semitechnical term for one of the phenomena or putative phenomena of parapsychology (psychical research). This entry touches on the wider issues of foreknowledge only insofar as they appear in a rather special form in the narrower context of parapsychology. Again, since the philosophical problems centering on some of the other concepts of parapsychology are examined at length elsewhere, telepathy, clairvoyance, and psychokinesis are mentioned here only when necessary to the main goal of becoming clearer about the logical geography of parapsychological precognition. Nor will there be any discussion of what the facts actually are. We shall be concerned only with theoretical questions of implication and explanation.

Precognition is one of a group of terms that also includes *telepathy, clairvoyance*, and—more peripherally—*psychokinesis* (PK). Telepathy is thought of, initially at any rate, as consisting in the acquisition of information by one person from another without the use of any of the senses normally indispensable to communication. Clairvoyance, at the same initial stage, is conceived of as being generically identical with telepathy; the specific difference is that in the case of clairvoyance the information is supposed to be obtained not from another person but from an object. Telepathy would be termed "precognitive" if the information so acquired was not going to become available to the other person until later. Clairvoyance would be termed precognitive if the information so acquired was not, until later, even going to become available in things, as opposed to minds.

It is thus possible to consider precognitive telepathy and precognitive clairvoyance as being two species of the genus precognition. Straight telepathy, straight clairvoyance, and both sorts of precognition are all supposed to be both nonsensory and noninferential. It is partly for this reason that all these alleged phenomena are frequently classed together as varieties of extrasensory perception (ESP). It is important to recognize that both these negative characteristics are in all four cases defining. To show that the information was acquired by the use, whether conscious or unconscious, of sensory cues, clues, or signs is a sufficient reason for disqualifying as genuine telepathy, or what have you, any ostensible case of telepathy or other such phenomenon. Similarly, to show that this acquisition was the result of a feat of inference, however heroic and remarkable in itself, again constitutes a completely sufficient reason for insisting that we are not confronted with a genuine case of precognition. At most we must describe it as a pseudo precognition, "precognition" only in quotation marks.

Suppose someone has an intuition or a dream or a waking vision that is found to correspond to some actual later happening. Suppose that it seems out of the question either (1) to account for the correspondence as the result of successful inference, conscious or unconscious, from materials available to the subject at the time, or (2) to trace it back to some causal ancestor common to both the "anticipation" and the "fulfillment," or (3) to say that the "fulfillment" was somehow a result of the "anticipation," or (4) even to refuse to account for the correspondence in any way on the grounds that it was just a coincidence. (The counterargument in this last case would be that some intuitions, dreams, visions, and so forth, are bound to prove veridical and that presumably this was just one of those striking cases that is—as the catch phrase has it—"by the law of averages" bound to occur occasionally.) If such an intuition, or what have you, were to occur we would—provided that all four conditions seemed to be met—have at least a prima facie case of precognition. Three theoretical questions must then be considered.

OPERATIONAL DISTINCTIONS

The first question is whether there are real operational distinctions to be made between all the supposed varieties of ESP or whether any of them can be regarded as alternative descriptions of the same logically possible phenomena. For instance, some ingenuity is required to work out an experimental design that would enable us to distinguish decisively between straight clairvoyance and precognitive telepathy.

To make this clear, consider a stylized ESP experiment. The experimenter equips himself with a pack of cards, perhaps the special Zener type, which consists of five suits of five identical cards. He devises a procedure for randomizing the order in which the cards are to be offered as targets. He recruits a subject whose function is to guess the values of the cards chosen as targets. The experimenter takes drastic and thorough precautions to ensure that it is quite impossible for the subject to tell by any combinations of inference and sensory perception what is or is going to be the value of any target card. (This is, of course, very much more easily said than done. But here our concern is with theory only.) The subject in due course makes his guesses, and these guesses are recorded. If enough guesses are made—provided always that the experiment has been properly designed and properly executed—we should expect "by the law of averages" that when the guesses are scored against their targets about one-fifth of the total will turn out to have been right and the remaining four-fifths wrong. But if significantly more hits have been scored than this mean-chance expectation, then it seems that *some* ESP factor must have been involved.

Suppose now that the experimenter has taken care to ensure that no one at all, himself included, should know, at the time when the subject makes his guesses, what is the value of each target card. It might seem that his experimental results can be interpreted as evidence only for clairvoyance and not for telepathy. But once we have allowed the possibility of precognition, then these same results can be described equally well in terms of precognitive telepathy. The subject is perhaps precognitively "picking" the brains of whoever later does the scoring.

The problem is further complicated if one is also prepared to allow the possibility of PK. Literally, "psychokinesis" means movement by the mind. The idea is that perhaps some people sometimes may be able, whether consciously or unconsciously, to move or otherwise affect things without pushing or pulling them and, indeed, without in any way touching either the things in question or any other things involved in the process. Perhaps, it is suggested, these people or, indeed, all of us really can in some conditions bring about changes in things by simply "willing," as a gambler might wish that by simply "willing" and without any detectable cheating he could get dice to fall in the ways he desires.

Once this suggestion is allowed there seems to be room for an alternative description of many experiments that might otherwise have appeared to be unambiguous evidence of the reality of precognition. Such a description will be in terms of psychokinesis, guided perhaps by a measure of straight telepathy or straight clairvoyance. The subject may not, after all, really be precognizing the target. Perhaps he or somebody else is consciously or unconsciously influencing psychokinetically the target-determining mechanism in order to increase the degree of correspondence between the guess series and the target

series. With appropriate alterations the same suggestion can be applied to spontaneous, as opposed to experimental, cases of ostensible precognition. The "fulfillment" or "fulfillments" become partly or wholly the results of the "anticipations," and, by specification, any such cases are disqualified from being classed as genuinely precognitive. Confronted by this kaleidoscopically changing confusion of alternative descriptions, we need not wonder that PK was once described as the parapsychological equivalent of a universal solvent.

IMPLICATIONS

The second sort of theoretical question concerns the implications of precognition. Suppose it were to be established that there really is such a phenomenon, which actually does satisfy all the conditions stipulated; what would follow?

THE FUTURE AS PRESENT. One consequence that has often been thought to follow from the existence of precognition is that, sensationally, the future must somehow be already here—or at any rate there. This is usually derived from a conception of precognition as a mode of perception, of ESP. Thus, J. W. Dunne, in *An Experiment with Time* (3rd ed., London, 1939, p. 7), claims that in precognition "we habitually observe events before they occur." By valid inference from this misdescription he concludes that the future must therefore really be present. Upon this absurdity he proceeds to erect his logical extravaganza "the serial theory of time." Or again, in a useful survey of the field, D. J. West remarks: "precognition—foreseeing arbitrary events in the future that could not by any stretch of the imagination be inferred from the present—that is something which is almost impossible for our minds to grasp. How can anyone see things which do not yet exist?" (*Psychical Research Today*, London, 1954, p. 104).

Now it is necessarily true that if anything is to be seen or otherwise perceived—and not just "seen" or "perceived" (in discrediting quotation marks)—that thing must be presently available. (We ignore for present purposes the peripheral problems presented by very distant stars.) West is therefore more right than perhaps he realizes in suggesting that it is inconceivable that anyone should be able to see things that do not yet exist. Nevertheless, the correct conclusion to draw is not, as some have been inclined to think, that precognition is logically impossible. The correct conclusion is, rather, that if the phenomenon specified was to occur, it could not be conceived of as any sort of perception. The argument reduces to absurdity not the notion of precognition as such but the assumption that such precognition can be assimilated to perception. (There are indeed further reasons, applying equally to all varieties of ESP, which tend to destroy this analogy and therefore make unfortunate the use of the expression "extrasensory perception." But the present reason, applying only to precognition, is in this case by itself entirely decisive.)

PRECOGNITION AS FOREKNOWING. Suppose one begins by thinking of precognition not as foreseeing but as foreknowing. Suppose then that one happens to be one of those who conceives of cognition on the model of perception. This is, of course, a misconception, but one with a most ancient and distinguished pedigree. One relevant reason for insisting that this model is inapplicable is that whereas it is logically possible for me to know now that certain things happened in the past and that other things will happen in the future, it is not logically possible for me now to perceive anything but what is now available to be perceived. Thus, anyone who thinks of precognition as a form of knowing and of knowing as a sort of perceiving will arrive by a rather longer route at exactly the same conclusions—that the future is present—as the person who begins by thinking of precognition as a type of perception. In either case the treatment indicated is essentially the same.

C. D. Broad comments:

> The fact is that most people who have tried to theorize about non-inferential precognition have made needless difficulties for themselves by making two mistakes. In the first place, they have tried to assimilate it to sense-perception, when they ought to have assimilated it to memory. And, secondly, they have tacitly assumed an extremely naive prehensive analysis … [which] is simply nonsensical when applied to ostensible remembering or ostensible foreseeing. ("The Philosophical Implications of Foreknowledge")

By "prehensive analysis" Broad means believing, mistakenly, that for an occurrence to be remembered it must somehow be present.

FATALISM. The model of memory is, as Broad urged, much less inapt than that of perception. But it, too, has its dangers. It has beguiled some into thinking that precognition must necessarily involve fatalism. The suggestion is that precognition would be an exact analogue and complement of memory, but where memory operates backward, precognition would be remembering forward. (See,

for instance, Lewis Carroll, *Through the Looking Glass*, Ch. 5.) Now, if someone remembers that he himself killed Cock Robin, and provided that he really does remember and that he is not merely claiming, mistakenly or even dishonestly, to remember that he committed this crime, then it follows necessarily that he did kill Cock Robin. But if he has done it, then he has done it, and it must now be too late for anyone to intervene to save the victim. It is, notoriously, a tautology that what is done is done and cannot be undone. The past is unalterable. The temptation is to argue that the same must, in exactly the same sense, apply to the future. If I can truly precognize that I will kill Cock Robin—provided that it really is a precognition and that I am not merely claiming mistakenly, or even dishonestly, to be precognizing—then it follows necessarily that I will kill Cock Robin.

The false step is to go on to urge that by parity of reasoning, since he will do it, then he will do it, and therefore it must now be too late for anyone to save Cock Robin. For the conclusion does not follow. From the proposition that he will kill Cock Robin we are entitled to infer that he will kill Cock Robin and hence that no one will in fact save the bird. But what we are not entitled to infer is that it must now be too late to take any steps to save Cock Robin, that no one could possibly do anything to help. It is one thing to know that some catastrophe will in fact occur; it is quite another to know that there is now nothing that anyone could do to prevent it, even if he so wished. To know that he will in fact do it, it is sufficient to know that he in fact will: tautology. It is not necessary also to know, what may very well not be the case, either that he would not have been able to do otherwise had he been going to want to or that no one else would have been able to stop him had they been going to be so inclined.

This point is, of course, involved in the much wider question of whether foreknowledge in the general sense must carry any such fatalist implications. The wider question is beyond the scope of this article, but the argument offered here is as applicable to the wider context as to this narrower one. The problem remains why it should be thought, as obviously it often is, that to establish the reality of noninferential precognition, even as an extremely weak and rare faculty, ought to raise fatalist anxieties in a much more acute form than does, for instance, the present possibility of inferring the outcome of some not too distantly future election—on the basis of a knowledge of the present preferences, psychological traits, beliefs, and expressed voting intentions of the electors concerned.

The threat to autonomy. One possible suggestion is that it may be thought that whereas predictions on the basis of knowledge of human beings do not constitute any threat to the autonomy and dignity of the persons concerned, a precognitive forecast about someone's future actions, made without reference to his peculiar characteristics, plans, and desires, would tend to show that his decisions to act in those ways will not be as causally necessary as he might like to believe. To show that human wishes, plans, and decisions do not affect what happens would indeed be to demonstrate a fatalist conclusion; for this is precisely what "fatalism" means. But to show that someone can know, without reference to that other person's wishes and plans, what another person is going to do is, surely, not sufficient to show that those wishes and plans will not determine his course of action.

It might be argued that knowledge presupposes grounds and that, insofar as the grounds contain no reference to the wishes and plans of the agent, this shows that he cannot properly be held responsible for what he is going to do. This argument would have more force if knowledge of what is going to occur always had to be grounded on knowledge of the presence of particular causes sufficient to bring about the occurrence. But quite apart from any question of whether it is true that all knowledge must be grounded on something else, the argument must be ineffective as long as we have to allow that some knowledge is quite sufficiently grounded simply on a recognition of reliable signs. Suppose precognition does actually occur, and suppose that it is properly to be classed as a form of knowledge; then it can be only either a variety that is not grounded at all or one which is based upon just such a recognition of signs—the recognition, namely, that some particular class of guesses, intuitions, visions, or whatnot are in fact reliable pointers to the future. For any inference, whether conscious or unconscious, from any knowledge, however acquired, of the causes of what is going to happen to the true conclusion that just that is indeed going to happen must by definition disqualify that conclusion as a genuine noninferential precognition.

Perceptual model and fatalism. A second suggestion is that the special anxiety felt in this case of precognition is just one more consequence of thinking in terms of a perceptual model. If in having a precognitive experience you were, as it were, seeing the future, then indeed it would be absurd to insist, once that experience has taken place, that there are any steps that anyone could take that could prevent the fulfillment of the precognition. It would be absurd so to insist because on this assumption of a literal foreseeing, the event precognized would by now have been seen happening. But once an event has

happened there cannot be anything that anyone could possibly do to prevent it from happening.

Precognitive infallibility. A third suggestion is adapted to a rather different conception of the problem. It is common enough to find people who (at any rate, in their most self-consciously philosophical moments) would be reluctant to concede that there is any such thing as real knowledge of future events, or at least of future human actions. To such a person precognition might appear to present a special problem precisely because of the analogy to memory. This might, of course, be because he naively assimilated memory to perception. But he might in a rather more complicated way be arguing that since from the occurrence of a genuine memory one is entitled to deduce that the past was as that memory represents it to have been, therefore the occurrence of an authentic precognition would, insofar as precognition is to be conceived on the model of memory, provide a similarly inexpugnable guarantee that the future must necessarily be as it is precognized to be going to be. The idea would be, presumably, that whereas inferences can be invalid and their conclusions false, memory is necessarily infallible. Thus, if precognition is a reality, and if it is a faculty exactly analogous to memory, then it, too, must be similarly infallible. In that case there can be nothing which anyone could do to prevent the fulfillment of any such precognitive anticipations.

Insofar as this claim really represents a different contention from any so far considered, and it is not altogether clear that it does, the crucial error seems to lie in a confusion between remembering and mistakenly or dishonestly claiming to remember. True memory is, if you like, infallible, but only in the weak sense that "I remember doing it" entails "I did it," not in the strong sense that "I claim to remember doing it" entails "I did it." This is because it is always possible that in making such a memory claim I may either be mistaken or be acting dishonestly. Thus, to be exactly analogous to memory, precognition would have to be infallible in this and only this sense. But this sort of infallibility pertains equally to knowledge: for "He knows that the dogmas of his Roman Catholic faith are true" entails "The dogmas of his Roman Catholic faith are true"; whereas "He claims with absolute conviction that he knows that the dogmas of his faith are true" is by itself not even evidence for "The dogmas of his faith are true." And we have already devoted enough space to urging that from the possibility of knowledge as such of future human actions no fatalist conclusions follow necessarily.

"Forward memory" and fatalism. Another, and perhaps the most important, consideration encouraging the

idea that parapsychological precognition must constitute a fatalist threat more serious than any arising from ordinary possibilities of foreknowledge is that what we remember is always and necessarily something in which somehow we ourselves were previously involved: We remember, that is, only what we have learned or what happened to us or what we did. Therefore, insofar as precognition is to be thought of as "remembering forward," its contents must be similarly restricted to what we shall later come to know by other means, to what will happen to us, or to what we will do. But now, as long as I remain the sort of creature that I am, it will clearly not be possible for me to precognize something very unpleasant as going to happen to me without my casting about for ways in which the unpleasantness may be avoided.

Hence, if there is to be precognition, at least one of three further conditions must be satisfied: Either (1) the contents of my precognitions must be restricted to terms that even in an unchanged universe would not provoke me to effective avoiding action, or (2) I as the precognizer must be so changed that I no longer attempt any avoiding action, or (3) the universe around me must be so changed that my attempts are all in fact now ineffective. Obviously both the second and the third of these options would constitute major steps towards a fatalistic universe. Yet neither of these represents a necessary corollary of precognition as such. On the other hand, to take the first option is to accept a limitation that drastically reduces the analogy between precognition and memory. The conclusion is that any fatalist consequences belong to precognition as a faculty fully analogous to memory, not simply to precognition as such.

CAUSE AND EFFECT. It has sometimes been suggested that to establish the reality of precognition would be to show that in some cases effects can precede their causes. Surprising and disturbing though the effects reported certainly are, this at least is something that neither these nor any other phenomena could ever establish. The reason is, quite simply, that "a cause must either precede or be simultaneous with its effect" is a necessary truth. It is no more possible to discover an effect preceding its cause than to light upon a bachelor husband—and the impossibility is of the same sort in both cases.

Someone who had appreciated this point might well be inclined to dismiss it as merely verbal and trifling. He might claim that nevertheless we have here some radically new and theoretically highly recalcitrant facts and that to take account of them we must revise some of our old ideas.

Not every verbal point is trifling, however, and not all matters of definition are mere matters of definition. What looks like a piece of obstructive lexicography can be justified at a deeper level. The implicit definitions to which appeal was originally made are grounded on a more fundamental necessity. We cannot simply brush off the objection by prescribing a small revision in usage whereby causes may in future be spoken of as succeeding their effects, and then proceed exactly as before. The crux is that causes are—and in principle can always be used by us as—levers for bringing about their effects. But a cause that succeeded its effect could not be, or be used as, a lever for producing it. Once the "effect" has happened it must be too late for any "cause" to bring it about—and too late also for it to be prevented by preventing the occurrence of this "cause." To make this suggested change in the usage of the terms *cause* and *effect* would be not to modify but to disrupt the concept of cause. The refusal to accept the claim that in precognition we would be confronted with causes operating backward in time may therefore spring from something less discreditable than complacency. It might even be one manifestation of a conviction that to accommodate such a phenomenon we should need something much more radical and much more ratiocinative than a paradoxical but really not particularly significant set of adjustments in the usage of one or two common terms.

POSSIBLE EXPLANATIONS

The third kind of theoretical question about precognition is "What sort of explanation or account could we hope to find, supposing it were to be definitely established that precognition does indeed occur?" Presumably this would have to cover whatever other parapsychological phenomena were also found to be genuine. To provide such a theory would be enormously difficult, if not impossible. In any case, in the present confusing and apparently contradictory state of the evidence in this field, a state that should no doubt be attributed (at least in part) to the lack of any theory adequate to serve as even the most tentative of working hypotheses, it is impossible to say with confidence and precision just what are the phenomena of which we need to take account. Nevertheless there are three suggestions that it may perhaps be useful to consider.

CAUSAL EXPLANATION. The first suggestion concerns the possibility of interpreting precognitive correlations in causal terms. To give a causal account of the subsistence of a statistically significant correlation between two series of events A and B involves showing either (1) that A results from B, or (2) that B results from A, or (3) that both A and B result from some third cause or set of causes, or (4) that both A and B are causally independent results of separate chains of causation. Suppose A is a series of precognitive guesses or anticipations and B a series of fulfillments or verifications. Series A cannot result from series B, for that would involve the logical impossibility of future occurrences bringing about events in the past. Series B cannot result from series A, for if it does, then the case is ipso facto disqualified by definition. And A and B cannot both result from some third cause or set of causes, for if they do, then again the case is by definition disqualified from rating as genuinely precognitive. The only remaining possibility is to say that A and B are both the causally independent results of separate chains of causation.

But to say this is precisely not to display a causal connection between A and B; it is, rather, to imply that the statistically significant correlation between the two series is a coincidence. This conclusion may be disturbing, but at least it has the merit of not involving any actual self-contradiction. For to establish a statistically significant correlation between two series of events is not thereby and necessarily to establish that these series are in any way connected causally. In the face of any correlation, however perfect and however extended, it is always significant, although often foolishly misguided, to insist that there is nevertheless no causal connection. Statements of constant conjunction do not entail statements of causal connection. Anyone who insists on a stronger sense of statistical significance, which would entail the subsistence of a causal connection, and who then proceeds to stipulate that a precognitive correlation would have to be statistically significant in this stronger sense, will succeed only in making his concept of precognition self-contradictory from the start.

COINCIDENCE. It seems that any explanation or, if that now becomes too strong a word, any account of precognition as such will have to center on the notion of coincidence or of something very like it. The laws, if there are any laws to be discovered, will describe the conditions under which we may expect to find precognitive correlations. One is reminded of C. G. Jung's talk about "synchronicity phenomena." For "synchronicity phenomenon" is in fact only a pretentious neologism for "coincidence," with perhaps a built-in suggestion that such phenomena are both more common and also somehow more significant than might be thought. It is a similarity that might easily be overlooked because of Jung's terminological peculiarities, because he associates the idea with many of his own more bizarre inventions, and because he exploits it for his own, it seems, often willfully antiscientific and antirational ends. A law of the kind suggested might paradoxically but pointedly be characterized as a law about the regularities in the conditions for the occurrence of a certain sort of coincidence.

STATISTICAL EXPLANATION. Theorists seem to have taken far too little notice of the surely remarkable fact that it seems to be impossible either for the subjects or for anyone else to achieve any significant success in identifying, without reference to the targets, the particular guesses that are going to prove to be hits. Another similar and similarly neglected fact is that even after the guesses have been scored against the targets we have no criterion for distinguishing any particular hit as precognitive. In each case the reason for talking of precognition is not that any particular guess can, at some stage, be identified as precognitive but that, after the guesses have been checked against the targets, the proportion of hits in a series of guesses is found to be significantly above mean-chance expectation.

With appropriate alterations the same thing seems to be true of all ostensible parapsychological phenomena. It is usually argued that whereas this perhaps has to be allowed in the case of quantitative experiments in card guessing, dice throwing, and so forth, it does not apply at all to what appear to be spontaneous cases of telepathy and clairvoyance, precognitive or straight. But this is surely wrong. For suppose we find that someone who had no means of inferring that the *Titanic* might meet disaster nevertheless had a dream that is later found to have corresponded in amazing detail with what actually happened on the night when that great ship went down. Still, our only warranty for describing his dream as precognitive lies precisely in that extraordinary degree of correspondence: Any single item of correspondence might be dismissed as something that was bound to happen "by the law of averages," and so no single item can be picked out as unequivocally precognitive.

Of course this situation may conceivably at any time be transformed by the progress of the research. But at the time of writing it remains true that all the putative varieties of ESP, precognition in particular, are and must be defined in essentially statistical terms. This is no reason to ignore or to dismiss the evidence. But it may very well prove to be a significant theoretical pointer.

See also Parapsychology.

Bibliography

For general discussion consult C. J. Ducasse, "Broad on the Relevance of Psychical Research to Philosophy," pp. 375–410, A. G. N. Flew, "Broad on Supernormal Precognition," pp. 411–436, and C. D. Broad, "A Reply to My Critics," pp. 709–830, in *The Philosophy of C. D. Broad*, edited by P. A. Schilpp (New York: Tudor, 1959); and W. G. Roll, "The Problem of Precognition," in *Journal of the Society for Psychical Research* 41 (1961): 2ff. Roll's article is valuable especially for its bibliography.

There have been many ingenious discussions of ways of making operational distinctions between the various forms of ESP phenomena in the parapsychological journals since about 1930. For an excellent example, see C. W. K. Mundle, "The Experimental Evidence for PK and Precognition," in *Proceedings of the Society for Psychical Research* 49 (1949–1952): 61–78.

For a criticism of Dunne's "Serial Theory of Time," see A. G. N. Flew, *A New Approach to Psychical Research* (London: Watts, 1953), Appendix II: "An Experiment with 'Time.'"

C. D. Broad's "The Philosophical Implications of Foreknowledge" was published in *PAS*, Supp. 16 (1937): 177–209. Broad referred the empirically curious to H. F. Saltmarsh's "Report on Cases of Apparent Precognition," in *Proceedings of the Society for Psychical Research* 42 (1934): 49–103. With Saltmarsh's paper one may compare D. J. West's considerably more skeptical "The Investigation of Spontaneous Cases," in *Proceedings of the Society for Psychical Research* 48 (1948): 264–300. The weight of both evidence and research has now shifted away from ostensible spontaneous cases of ESP toward quantitative experiments in card guessing. The classic series is that reported by S. G. Soal and K. M. Goldney in "Experiments on Precognitive Telepathy," in *Proceedings of the Society for Psychical Research* 47 (1942–1945): 21–150. This work was hailed by Broad in 1944 in "The Experimental Establishment of Telepathic Communication." Soal and Frederick Bateman have since produced a general survey, *Modern Experiments in Telepathy* (New Haven, CT: Yale University Press, 1954).

On the infallibility of precognitive experiences and on cause and effect, see M. A. E. Dummett, "Can an Effect Precede Its Cause?" in *PAS*, Supp. 28 (1954): 27–44, and the reply with the same title by A. G. N. Flew in that volume, on pp. 45–62. See also Flew's *Hume's Philosophy of Belief* (London: Routledge and Paul, 1961), Ch. 6.

For a fuller criticism of Jung's theory of synchronicity phenomena, see A. G. N. Flew's "Coincidence and Synchronicity," in *Journal of the Society for Psychical Research* 37 (1953–1954): 198–201.

OTHER RECOMMENDED TITLES

Braude, Stephen E., ed. *The Limits of Influence: Psychokinesis and the Philosophy of Science*. New York: Routledge, 1991.

Braude, Stephen E. "Psi and Our Picture of the World." *Inquiry* 30 (1987): 277–294.

Brier, Robert. "Mundle, Broad, Ducasse, and the Precognition Problem." *Philosophy Forum* 14 (1974): 161–169.

Brier, Robert. *Precognition and the Philosophy of Science: An Essay on Backwards Causation*. New York: Humanities Press, 1974.

Craig, William Lane. "Divine Foreknowledge and Newcomb's Paradox." *Philosophia* 17 (1987): 331–350.

Dummett, Michael. "Causal Loops." In *The Nature of Time*, edited by Raymond Flood and Michael Lockwood. Oxford: Blackwell, 1986.

Lucas, J. R. "Foreknowledge and the Vulnerability of God." In *The Philosophy of Christianity*, edited by Godfrey Vesey. Cambridge, U.K.: Cambridge University Press, 1989.

Meehl, Paul. "Precognitive Telepathy II." *Nous* 12 (1978): 371–395.

Werth, Lee F. "Normalizing the Paranormal." *American Philosophical Quarterly* 15 (1978): 47–56.

Zagzebski, Linda. *The Dilemma of Freedom and Foreknowledge*. Oxford: Oxford University Press, 1991.

Zagzebski, Linda. "Recent Work on Divine Foreknowledge and Free Will." In *The Oxford Handbook of Free Will*, edited by Robert Kane. Oxford: Oxford University Press, 2002.

Antony Flew (1967)
Bibliography updated by Benjamin Fiedor (2005)

PREDESTINATION

See *Determinism, A Historical Survey*

PREDICATE

See *Subject and Predicate*

PREFERENTIAL TREATMENT

See *Affirmative Action*

PRESCRIPTIVISM

See *Metaethics; Noncognitivism*

PRE-SOCRATIC PHILOSOPHY

"Pre-Socratic" is the term commonly used (and the one that will be used here) to cover those Greek thinkers from approximately 600 to 400 BCE who attempted to find universal principles that would explain the whole of nature, from the origin and ultimate constituents of the universe to the place of man within it. Yet 400 was the last year of Socrates' life, and among the Sophists, who are also excluded, Protagoras and Gorgias were older than he and others were his contemporaries. "Pre-Socratic" therefore indicates not so much a chronological limit as an outlook and a range of interests. This outlook Protagoras and Socrates deliberately attacked, condemning natural philosophy as worthless compared with the search for a good life, the discussion of social and political questions, and individual morality. Socrates also dismissed its explanations as inadequate because expressed predominantly in terms of origins and internal mechanisms. In his view explanation should be functional, looking to the end rather than the beginning. Thus, for the last sixty or so years of the fifth century, both points of view existed, and a lively controversy went on between them. It was not that the natural philosophers excluded human nature from their investigations but that they saw man and society in a larger framework, as a particular late stage in cosmic development, whereas the others deliberately turned their backs on the external world. The universal and speculative character of pre-Socratic thought was also combated by some of the fifth-century medical writers, and it was in the fields of physiology and hygiene that observational science reached its highest point in this period.

NATURE OF THE EVIDENCE

Before attempting to describe the pre-Socratic doctrines, it is necessary to emphasize the peculiar nature of our sources of knowledge. None of the pre-Socratics' works has survived independently. We have a few references in Plato, some more systematic discussion in Aristotle, and information from later compilers and commentators of which the greater part goes back to a history by Aristotle's pupil Theophrastus. Actual quotations occur and are in some cases extensive, as with the prose fragments of Heraclitus and the 450 surviving lines of Empedocles. Yet, from Aristotle onward, the men who passed on this information were not historians in the modern sense but wrote from a particular philosophical viewpoint (most often Peripatetic), searching the past for anticipations of their own ideas and selecting and arranging their material accordingly. The task of reconstruction and interpretation is thus very different from and more precarious than that of interpreting a philosopher whose original writings are still available for study.

THE MILESIAN SCHOOL

Pre-Socratic philosophy differs from all other philosophy in that it had no predecessors. Philosophy has been a continuous debate, and even highly original thinkers can be seen developing from or reacting against the thought of a predecessor. Aristotle is unimaginable without Plato; Isaac Newton, without René Descartes, Johannes Kepler,

Galileo Galilei, and many others. But with the Greeks of the sixth century the debate begins. Before them no European had set out to satisfy his curiosity about the world in the faith that its apparent chaos concealed a permanent and intelligible order, and that this natural order could be accounted for by universal causes operating within nature itself and discoverable by human reason. They had predecessors of a sort, of course. It was not accidental that the first pre-Socratics were citizens of Miletus, a prosperous trading center of Ionian Greeks on the Asiatic coast, where Greek and Oriental cultures met and mingled. The Milesian heritage included the myths and religious beliefs of their own peoples and their Eastern neighbors and also the store of Egyptian and Babylonian knowledge—astronomical, mathematical, technological. The influence of this heritage was considerable. Yet the Milesians consciously rejected the mythical and religious tradition of their ancestors, in particular its belief in the agency of anthropomorphic gods, and their debt to the knowledge of the East was not a philosophic one. That knowledge was limited because its aim was practical. Astronomy served religion; mathematics settled questions of land measurement and taxation. For these purposes the careful recording of data and the making of certain limited generalizations sufficed, and the realm of ultimate causes was left to dogmatism. For the Greeks knowledge became an end in itself, and in the uninhibited atmosphere of Miletus they gave free play to the typically Greek talent for generalization, abstraction, and the erection of bold and all-embracing explanatory hypotheses.

Consciously, the revolt of the Milesian philosophers against both the content and the method of mythology was complete. No longer were natural processes to be at the mercy of gods with human passions and unpredictable intentions. In their place was to come a reign of universal and discoverable law. Yet a whole conceptual framework is not so easily changed. Poetic and religious cosmogonies had preceded the schemes of the Milesians, and the basic assumptions of these can be detected beneath the hypotheses of their philosophic successors. Nevertheless, the achievement of abandoning divine agencies for physical causes working from within the world itself can hardly be overestimated.

It was common to the mythologies of Greece and neighboring civilizations (and, indeed, to others) that the world arose from a primitive state of unity and that the cosmogonic process was one of separation or division. This was the first act of the Hebrew Creator. In the Babylonian *Enuma Elish* the original state of the universe was an undefined mass of watery cloud. The Greek theogony of Hesiod speaks of Heaven and Earth, conceived as anthropomorphic figures, lying locked in an embrace until their son forced them apart as Marduk formed heaven and earth by splitting apart the body of the monster Tiamat. Euripides relates an old tale according to which earth and heaven were once "one form" and after their separation brought to birth the whole variety of living things. In Egypt (like Babylonia, a river culture) everything arose out of the primeval waters.

THALES. It is not surprising, therefore, that the first people to seek a universal explanation of the world along rational lines assumed that it was in substance a unity from which its variety had been produced by some process of segregation. The key, they thought, lay in identifying the single substance that must satisfy the condition of being able to produce variety out of itself. Thales (active in 585 BCE), who chose water or moisture, may still have had the myths at the back of his mind. For him the earth floated on water as it did for the Egyptians. Little else certain is known of him, and we can only guess at his reasons. Water can be seen as solid, liquid, and vaporous. Aristotle thought it more probable that Thales was influenced by the essential connection of moisture with life, as seen in such substances as semen, blood, and sap. With the removal of external personal agents, the world must initiate its own changes, and at this early stage of speculation the only possibility seemed to be that life of some kind is everywhere and that the universe is a growing, organic structure. This may be the explanation of the saying attributed to Thales: "Everything is full of gods."

ANAXIMANDER. With Anaximander, Thales' younger contemporary, there emerges the notion of the four primary opposites that later, when the concepts of substance and attribute had been distinguished, gave rise to the four elements adopted by Aristotle and destined for a long and influential history. Anaximander spoke of only the hot and the dry, which were inevitably in conflict with the cold and the wet. This led him to a momentous idea. The original substance of the universe could not be anything definitely qualified like water, for how could the cold and wet produce their opposites, the hot and dry? Water quenches fire; it cannot engender it. Prior to all perceptible body there must be an indefinite something with none of the incompatible qualities implied by perceptibility. Although still regarding all that exists as corporeal, Anaximander is the first to find ultimate reality in the nonperceptible.

This primary substance he called the apeiron, a word of many meanings all related to the absence of limits—everlasting, infinite, indefinite. Because it was imperishable, the origin of all things, and the author of their changes, he called it (says Aristotle) divine. From it all things have been "separated out," though in what sense they were previously "in" it while the apeiron itself remained a unity is a question that probably did not present itself to him. Somewhere in the apeiron, Theophrastus asserts, a "germ" or "seed" of hot and cold was separated off, and from the interaction of these two flowed the whole cosmic process. A sphere of flame enclosed a moist mass, more solid at the center where the earth formed, vaporous between. The sphere burst into rings around which the dark vapor closed, leaving holes through which we see what appear as sun, moon, and stars. Wet and dry continue to separate, forming land and sea, and finally life itself is produced by the same action of heat (sun) on the cold and moist portions of the earth. The first animals were born in water and crawled onto dry land. Human infants were originally born and nurtured within the bodies of fishlike creatures, for under primitive conditions unprotected babies could not have survived.

Earth, a flat cylinder, hangs freely in space because of its equal distance from all parts of the spherical universe. The sun is the same size as Earth. Eclipses are caused by the closing of the holes in the vapor tubes of the sun and moon. In this first of all attempts at a rational cosmogony and zoogony, the sudden freedom from mythical modes of thought is almost incredible.

ANAXIMENES. Further reflection led Anaximenes, the youngest member of the Milesian school, to a different conclusion about the primary substance: It was air. In its elusiveness and invisibility as atmospheric air, it could almost match the apeiron, and, whereas apeiron, once differentiated into a universe, could no longer be so called, air could become hotter and colder, rarer and denser, and still remain the same substance. Moreover, this theory allowed Anaximenes to break with the notion of separation, which was, at bottom, mythical, and account for the universe by the extension of a known natural process. This was condensation and rarefaction, the former of which he associated with cold and the latter with heat. Air as it rarefies becomes fire; condensed, it turns first to wind, then to cloud, water, earth, and stones. In other words, it is all a question of how much of it there is in a given space, and for the first time the idea enters science that qualitative differences are reducible to differences of quantity. This is Anaximenes' main achievement, although there is no evidence that he applied the principle with any mathematical exactness.

With air as his basic, self-changing substance, Anaximenes could find room for the ancient belief that life was identical with breath. Macrocosm and microcosm were animated by the same principle: "Just as our soul, which is air, integrates us, so breath and air surround the whole cosmos."

The few details that we have of his cosmology suggest that compared with Anaximander's, it was reactionary and timid. His contribution lies elsewhere.

THE PYTHAGOREANS

Pythagoras (c. 570–490 BCE) was also an eastern Greek but migrated from his native Samos to Croton in southern Italy. As a result the western or Italian Greek philosophers, even when not actual members of his school, became known for a characteristic outlook very different from that of the materialistic and purely rational Milesians and stamped with the impress of his remarkable genius. He founded a brotherhood dedicated to *philosophia* (the word was believed to be his invention) as a way of life, with a strong religious, and also a political, element. Philosophically, his importance lies in the shift of interest from matter to form. Inspired, it is said, by the discovery that the musical intervals known to the Greeks as consonant (and marked by four fixed strings on the seven-stringed lyre) were explicable in terms of ratios of the numbers 1 through 4, Pythagoras saw the universe as one glorious *harmonia*, or mathematico-musical structure. Number was the key to nature. This idea had incalculable consequences for science even if it led at the time to some rather fanciful equations of natural objects and moral qualities with particular numbers. In spite of that, by the time of Socrates the school had made real progress in mathematics. Since the cosmic harmony included everything, all life was akin. The soul was immortal and underwent a series of incarnations, both human and animal. Philosophy was the effort to understand the structure of the cosmic harmony, with the ultimate aim of integrating the philosophic soul more closely into that harmony on the principle that knowledge assimilates the knower to its object. This aim also demanded the observance of certain religious precepts of which the most important was abstention from animal food.

HERACLITUS

Heraclitus (active c. 500 BCE) objected to the Pythagorean emphasis on harmony, maintaining that, on the contrary, strife and opposition were the life of the world.

Life was maintained by a tension of opposites fighting a continuous battle in which neither side could win final victory. Thus, movement and the flux of change were unceasing for individuals, but the structure of the cosmos remained constant. This law of individual flux within a permanent universal framework was guaranteed by the Logos, an intelligent governing principle materially embodied as fire, the most subtle element and identified with soul or life.

Philosophy had thus far meant the search for an essentially simpler reality underlying the bewildering confusion of appearances. The answers fell into two broad categories, matter and form: Reality was a single material substance (the Milesians) or an integral principle of structure that could be expressed in terms of numbers (the Pythagoreans). Heraclitus, with a statement like "You cannot step twice into the same river," reaches the logical conclusion of the materialistic answer. The water will be different water the second time, and, if we call the river the same, it is because we see its reality in its form. The logical conclusion of form-philosophy is the opposite of flux—namely, a belief in an absolute, unchanging reality of which the world of change and movement is only a quasi-existing phantom, phenomenal, not real. (This conclusion was reached in the idealism of Plato, which was largely of Pythagorean inspiration.)

ELEATIC SCHOOL: UNITY OF REALITY

At this time the direction of philosophy was changed by the precocious and uncompromising logic of Parmenides of Elea, who was perhaps twenty-five years younger than Heraclitus. For the first time abstract, deductive reasoning is deliberately preferred to the evidence of the senses: "Ply not eye and ear and tongue, but judge by thought." He concluded that if there is any reality at all (in the language of his time, if "it is"), it must be (1) one only (for if more than one, its units could be separated only by "what is not"); (2) eternal and unchanging (for to speak of change or perishing is to say that reality at some time "is not" what it was, but to say of "what is" "it is not" is contradictory and impossible); (3) immovable (this follows from his statement that "all is full of what is"; since it cannot admit discontinuity or lack of homogeneity and since "what is not is not," the spatial requirements of locomotion cannot be provided).

In this way he "proved" that, on the premise of his predecessors that reality is one, differentiation of the real can never occur. It remains one—a timeless, changeless, motionless, homogeneous mass, which he compared to a sphere. The multiple, changing world of appearances is an illusion of our senses. Only as a concession to human weakness, and in recognition of our practical need to come to terms with the show of a natural world, did he append a cosmology of the conventional type, beginning with two principles, heat-light and cold-darkness. Cosmogony from a single origin was no longer possible, yet he explicitly warns his hearers that reality is in truth a unity and that the cosmos is only a deceitful appearance to mortals.

It is disputed whether the One Reality of Parmenides is material. The question can hardly be answered, since we are still in a period before the distinction between material and nonmaterial could be drawn. The important thing is that it was nonsensible and could be reached only by thought. Parmenides was the first philosopher to distinguish explicitly between the sensible and the intelligible and to condemn the former as unreal. Plato himself, though fully aware of the distinction between material and spiritual, usually preferred to call them sensible and intelligible, and it is very doubtful whether the philosophy of Platonic idealism would ever have been possible without Parmenides.

ZENO AND MELISSUS. Parmenides had two followers, who, with him, are known as the Eleatic school. Zeno of Elea (born c. 490 BCE) concentrated on a defense of the proposition that reality is one and immovable by the dialectical method of showing up absurdities in the contrary view. His famous paradoxes are aimed at demonstrating the impossibility of plurality and movement. Melissus of Samos (active in 440 BCE) modified Parmenides' ideas to the extent of saying that reality is infinite. He explicitly denied the possibility of empty space (which Parmenides had only hinted at) and said that if there were many things, each would have to have the characteristics of the Parmenidean One. It is therefore probable that the atomists had him especially in mind when they boldly explained the world in terms of space plus tiny entities, each of which had many of the Eleatic qualities—indivisibility, homogeneity, unalterability.

The naïveté of Parmenides' logic and the purely linguistic nature of some of his difficulties seem obvious now, but at the time his questions appeared unanswerable. There were only two ways out: either to abandon monism and admit the ultimate plurality of the real or to admit the unreality of the natural world. The latter solution was Plato's, with his contrast between "what always is and never becomes" and "what is continually becoming (like the flux of Heraclitus) but never truly is." The remainder of pre-Socratic thought is occupied with

attempts to save the phenomena by adopting some form of pluralism.

THE PLURALISTS: EMPEDOCLES

The first of the pluralistic systems was that of Empedocles (c. 490–430 BCE), a Sicilian poet-philosopher steeped in the Western tradition, with its combination of rationalism and mystical religion so different from the purely scientific outlook of the Ionians. His proposal was the first clear enunciation of the four-element theory. Fire, air, water, and earth are the ultimate roots of all things, themselves ungenerated and indestructible. Everything in nature comes into being and perishes by the mixture and separation of these substances. The first premise is no longer "It is" but "They are." Thus, trees and animals, clouds and rocks, are not mere illusion. However, since they are only temporary combinations of the four "realities" in varying proportions, we can admit that they themselves are not "real." Nor need the forbidden concepts of "becoming" and "perishing" be invoked; mixture and separation will account for all. Locomotion is, of course, necessary, and, although he accepts the Eleatic denial of empty space, Empedocles seems to have thought that this could occur by some reciprocal and simultaneous exchange of place, the whole remaining full.

The four elements are not self-moving (another concept that Parmenides had rendered difficult), and the blend of mystic and rationalist in Empedocles appears especially in his motive causes. These were two, Love and Strife, the former bringing disparate elements together and the latter drawing them apart. They are in endless opposition and prevail in turn, bringing about a double evolutionary cycle. Under Love all four elements are indistinguishably fused in a sphere; under Strife the same sphere contains them in separate layers. During the contest, when neither Love nor Strife is in complete control and when the elements are partly joined and partly separated, a world like our own is formed. Nothing existent is as yet incorporeal, though Love and Strife are of finer and more tenuous substance than the elements. Their names are no metaphors, nor is their action purely mechanical. Under Love the elements are dear to and desired by one another; Strife makes them grim and hostile. Nothing is purely inanimate, and everything has its share of consciousness.

Besides his poem on nature, Empedocles also wrote a religious one, in which the moral character of Love and Strife is emphasized—Love is good, Strife evil. In the present world Strife is gaining, and men have fallen from a previous blessed state by giving themselves to Strife and sin, above all the sin of killing and eating animals. All life is akin, as it was to the Pythagoreans, and our souls are fallen spirits that must undergo a series of incarnations before they can win back their former state by abjuring Strife and cultivating Love. What the substance of the spirits was is not clearly stated, but most probably in their pure state they were portions of Love that are now contaminated with Strife.

ANAXAGORAS

Anaxagoras of Clazomenae (c. 500–428 BCE) brings us back to Ionia both geographically and in spirit. His motive is rational curiosity entirely uncomplicated by religious preoccupations. Even Parmenides, a Westerner like Empedocles, had written in verse and represented his deductive arguments as a revelation from a goddess. In his return to prose, as in his purely scientific aims, Anaxagoras is the heir of the Milesians. At Athens, where he lived until exiled for atheism, he was a member of the brilliant and freethinking circle of Pericles. His prosecution seems to have had a political flavor, but the charge is nevertheless significant: He declared the sun to be not a living divinity but a lump of incandescent rock larger than the Peloponnese.

To save the phenomena without admitting the coming into being or destruction of what exists, he adopted an extreme form of pluralism plus a first cause of motion, which he called Mind. It is described as knowing all things and having the greatest power, and, in order to control the material world, it is entirely outside the mixture of which the material world is formed. It is not easy to be sure whether Anaxagoras is at last trying to express the notion of incorporeal being without an adequate vocabulary or whether he still thinks of Mind as an extremely subtle and tenuous form of matter. At any rate, its separateness from the constituents of the cosmos is emphasized at every turn. In spite of the references to its knowledge and power, it action seems to be confined to the earliest stages of cosmogony, except in the case of living creatures. They are an exception to the rule that Mind is in nothing else, and them it still controls.

In the beginning "all things were together," a stationary mass in which nothing could be distinguished. Mind is the agent that has produced from this an ordered cosmos. It did so by starting a rotatory movement or vortex, which by its own increasing speed brought about the gradual separation of different forms of matter. Anaxagoras's highly subtle and ingenious theory of matter seems to have been especially prompted by the need to explain nourishment and organic growth: How can flesh and hair come out of the not-flesh and not-hair of the food we eat? After Parmenides the coming into being of new substances is disallowed. Anaxagoras answered that there is a portion of everything in everything—that is, every distinguishable substance, in however small a quantity, contains minute particles of every other but is characterized by that which predominates. He boldly asserted the existence of the infinitesimal (which Zeno had denied) in the words: "Of the small there is no smallest."

THE ATOMISTS

Perhaps around 430 BCE Leucippus promulgated the much simpler theory of atomism, which was further developed by his famous pupil Democritus of Abdera (born c. 460 BCE). Like the other theories, this one arose in direct response to the Eleatic challenge. Its most striking innovation for its time was the assertion of the existence of genuine empty space. Thus far, everyone had believed that "what is" must be some form of body, and, when Parmenides brought into consciousness the implicit consequence that space, not being "what is," must be "what is not" (that is, nonexistent), his conclusion seemed logically inescapable. Hence, even the atomists had to use the paradoxical expression that it is no more correct to say of "what is" than of "what is not" that it *is*.

At this particular point in the philosophic debate, this was the only way of expressing the conviction that, though not any kind of stuff, space must be assumed if the plain facts are to be explained. Democritus, said Aristotle, is to be commended for refusing to be dazzled by the abstract logic of Parmenides and for relying on the kind of argument more proper to a natural scientist. Reality consists of innumerable microscopic and indivisible (*a-tomos* = uncuttable) bodies in motion in infinite space. They are solid and homogeneous but infinitely variable in size and shape. At different places in the infinite, they have collided and become entangled. Projections hook together, convex fits into concave, and so on. Their continued motion sets up a vortex in which the larger and heavier fall into the center and the smaller and lighter are extruded to the circumference; in this way a cosmos is formed. There are many worlds, and not all are similar to our own. The first atomists appear to have provided no separate cause of motion, perhaps because they deemed it sufficient to free the atoms by setting them loose in infinite space. After all, the chief Eleatic arguments against motion had been the continuity of being and the nonexistence of a void.

Only atoms and the void exist. Sensible qualities other than size and shape are subjective, caused by interaction between the atoms of external objects and those in our own bodies. This was worked out in considerable detail. For instance, hard objects have their atoms more closely packed than do soft. Sweet flavors are caused by smooth atoms, bitter and astringent by sharp or hooked. Colors vary according to the positions of surface atoms, which cause them to reflect in different ways the light that falls upon them. Objects are continually throwing off films of atoms, and sight is the reception of these films by the eye. The soul, or life principle, is composed of smooth, round atoms that are even more mobile than the rest and impart to the body the power of motion and cognition, for "soul and mind are the same"—that is, composed of the same kind of atoms. Soul is dispersed throughout the body, alternating with body atoms, but the mind appears to have been a collection of these finest particles that is located probably in the breast. Although the direct objects of sight and hearing, taste and smell, are unreal, they lead the mind to the truth about reality, and Democritus quoted with approval a saying of Anaxagoras: "Phenomena are a glimpse of the unseen."

Ancient atomism (including its revival by Epicurus a century or more after Democritus) has acquired a partly adventitious reputation through its resemblances to nineteenth-century physical theories, but its hard, solid, unbreakable particles have little in common with the ultimate entities of modern science. Its most striking features are the distinction between primary and secondary qualities (upheld by Descartes, Galileo, and John Locke), the explanation of directly observable objects by hypothetical constituents below the level of perception, and the outspoken championship of discrete quanta as opposed to a continuum. Its inadequacy in allowing no mode of action other than direct contact, collision, and interlocking was evident in some physical problems—for example, in its attempted explanation of magnetism and, most of all, in the effort to include within its purview the phenomena of life and thought. The atomic structure of matter has indeed been a fruitful hypothesis, but the intention of its authors is best understood in the context of their time and as an attempt to escape the Eleatic dilemma, rather than as an anticipation of postmedieval science.

DIOGENES OF APOLLONIA

The teleological explanation, which one would naturally associate with Anaxagoras's adoption of Mind as first cause, appears more strongly in the second half of the fifth century in a less gifted thinker, Diogenes of Apollonia. He put Mind back into the mixture by returning to Anaximenes's idea that the primary substance is air or

breath and by identifying this air in its purest (dry and warm) state with intelligence. The regularity of cosmic events he regarded as evidence of intelligent control, going so far as to say that anyone who reflects will agree that all is arranged in the best possible way. Breath is also the life of humans and animals, so that all owe their soul and mind to the same material principle—"a small portion of the god"—which they share in varying degrees of purity. He probably thought he avoided the Eleatic arguments against a materialistic monism by the admission of void, which, by the time he wrote (after Melissus and Leucippus), would in any case be recognized as necessary for the process of condensation and rarefaction by which air produced the variety of nature.

When we consider the grotesqueness of some of the mythological background from which the pre-Socratic thinkers started, we must be amazed by the intellectual insight and firm grasp of universal principles that at their best they were capable of displaying. But a dispassionate assessment of their contribution to the history of philosophy would probably show that, to use a metaphor, although they manufactured many of the pieces and set them on the board, Plato and Aristotle were the first players who learned the rules and started the game. The pieces are those opposed concepts by means of which philosophical discussion is maintained: being and becoming, sensible and intelligible, analytic and synthetic, appearance and reality, time and eternity, materialism and idealism, mechanism and teleology, and so forth. Once these stand out clearly, a philosopher may champion one or the other, but the pre-Socratics could not yet do this. One cannot speak realistically of a controversy among them between, say, materialists and idealists. The achievement of their intellectual effort and controversy was that by the end of this period a clear notion of what was meant by matter and mind, sensible and intelligible, phenomenal and real, and the rest was at last emerging, so that succeeding generations had the set in their hands and could begin the game in earnest. For the first of all philosophers, this was no mean achievement.

Their interests were, of course, in modern terms, as much scientific as philosophical, and in this sphere also they could claim some remarkable results. For instance, before the end of the period the true cause of both lunar and solar eclipses had been discovered (probably by Anaxagoras), and certain Pythagoreans had abandoned the geocentric cosmology, asserting that Earth, the sun, and the planets all circled round a central fire. But it is probably fair to say that their scientific discoveries appeared only as by-products of the main controversies and of the few universal principles from which they confidently deduced even the details of the physical world. The true and lasting discoveries were not picked up and developed as they would have been by post-Renaissance scientists because, owing to the different preoccupations of philosophy at their time, they had no firm basis in established fact and did not in any way stand out from other and, to us, more fanciful assumptions.

See also Alcmaeon of Croton; Anaxagoras of Clazomenae; Anaximander; Anaximenes; Apeiron/Peras; Appearance and Reality; Archē; Chaos Theory; Cosmology; Cosmos; Diogenes of Apollonia; Empedocles; Hen/Polla; Heraclitus of Ephesus; Infinity in Theology and Metaphysics; Leucippus and Democritus; Logos; Materialism; Melissus of Samos; Monism and Pluralism; Orphism; Parmenides of Elea; Philolaus of Croton; Pre-Socratic Philosophy; Pythagoras and Pythagoreanism; Thales of Miletus; Xenophanes of Colophon; Zeno of Elea.

Bibliography

Fränkel, Hermann. *Early Greek Poetry and Philosophy: A History of Greek Epic, Lyric, and Prose to the Middle of the Fifth Century*. Translated by Moses Hadas and James Willis. New York: Harcourt Brace Jovanovich, 1973.

Guthrie, W. K. C. *A History of Greek Philosophy*. Vol. 1: *The Earlier Presocratics and the Pythagoreans*. Cambridge, U.K.: Cambridge University Press, 1962. Vol. 2: *The Presocratic Tradition from Parmenides to Democritus*. Cambridge, U.K.: Cambridge University Press, 1965.

COLLECTIONS OF ESSAYS

Allen, R. E., and David J. Furley, eds. *Studies in Presocratic Philosophy*. Vol. 2: *The Eleatics and the Pluralists*. London: Routledge & Kegan Paul, 1975.

Curd, Patricia, and Daniel W. Graham, eds. *The Oxford Handbook of Presocratic Philosophy*. Oxford: Oxford University Press, 2006.

Furley, D. J., and R. E. Allen, eds. *Studies in Presocratic Philosophy*. Vol. 1: *The Beginnings of Philosophy*. London: Routledge & Kegan Paul, 1970.

Long, A. A., ed. *The Cambridge Companion to Early Greek Philosophy*. Cambridge, U.K.: Cambridge University Press, 1999.

Mourelatos, A. P. D., ed. *The Pre-Socratics: A Collection of Critical Essays*. Garden City, NY: Doubleday, 1974; second printing, with revised introduction and bibliography, Princeton, NJ: Princeton University Press, 1993.

Taylor, C. C. W., ed. *From the Beginning to Plato*. Routledge History of Philosophy, 1. London: Routledge, 1997.

PARTICULAR THINKERS OR SCHOOLS

Burkert, Walter. *Lore and Science in Ancient Pythagoreanism*. Translated by E. L. Minar, Jr. Cambridge, MA: Harvard University Press, 1972.

Huffman, Carl A. *Philolaus of Croton: Pythagorean and Presocratic, Commentary on the Fragments and Testimonia with Interpretive Essays*. Cambridge, U.K.: Cambridge University Press, 1993.

Kahn, Charles H. *Anaximander and the Origins of Greek Cosmology*. New York: Columbia University Press, 1960. Repr. Philadelphia: Centrum, 1982. Repr. Indianapolis: Hackett, 1994.

Kahn, Charles H. *The Art and Thought of Heraclitus: An Edition of the Fragments with Translation and Commentary*. Cambridge, U.K.: Cambridge University Press, 1979.

Mourelatos, A. P. D. *The Route of Parmenides*. New Haven. CT: Yale University Press, 1970.

Sider, David. *The Fragments of Anaxagoras*. Beiträge zur klassischen Philologie, 118. Meisenheim am Glan: Hain, 1981.

"Phoenix Pre-Socratics," a series published by the University of Toronto Press, comprises volumes that provide ancient text, English translation, and explanatory comments: (1) David Gallop, *Parmenides of Elea*, 1984, rev. ed. 1991; (2) Robinson, T. M., *Heraclitus*, 1987; (3) Inwood, Brad, *The Poem of Empedocles*, 1992, rev. ed. 2001; (4) Lesher, J. H., *Xenophanes of Colophon*, 1992; (5) Taylor, C. C. W., *The Atomists: Leucippus and Democritus*, 1999.

W. K. C. Guthrie (1967)
Bibliography updated by Alexander Mourelatos (2005)

PRESUPPOSING

The notions of "presupposing" and of contextual implication, which we shall compare and contrast in what follows, have come to play increasingly prominent roles in the philosophical literature of the English-speaking world since the 1940s. This development is not accidental but arises from the stress the twentieth century put upon analysis as a fundamental mode of philosophical inquiry. The notions of presupposing and of contextual implication play both negative and positive roles within this general orientation. Negatively, they are devices that contemporary thinkers employ in order to minimize the tendency of philosophers and other reflective persons to view the world in terms of oversimplified conceptual models. Positively, they function as instruments in the dissection and ultimate understanding of certain human activities, especially those that involve the efforts of human beings to communicate with one another, as in promising, stating, saying, implying, a task that, some philosophers feel, is hindered or obstructed by the natural disposition of reflective individuals to subsume such activities under excessively simple descriptions. The appeal to the notions of presupposing and of contextual implication has thus served to widen—and at the same time to make more accurate—our conceptions of the circumstances in which human communication takes place. This entry will describe the history (all of it relatively recent, of course) of the major developments that have taken place with regard to these subjects, and will in this way attempt to bring out their essential features.

SIMILARITIES AND DIFFERENCES

It is no simple matter to show why presupposing and contextual implication are two separate concepts, since the differences between them are subtle. Most writers have, in fact, not discriminated between them, in part because both notions are slippery but also because they have similar functions. Their similarities may be elucidated as follows. If we distinguish between what a person explicitly states, or asserts, when he utters certain words in certain circumstances and what he (or perhaps his statement) implies, then the concepts of presupposing and of contextual implication belong to the latter category rather than to the former. This crude distinction must be refined further, however, for the sense of "implies" that is being marked out here is not that of logical implication in any of the various senses of that term—for example, the sense involved in saying that "X is a husband" implies "X is married." Indeed, both presupposing and contextual implication are to be contrasted with logical implication.

The kinds of implications that fall into this category may be indicated by simple examples. In saying "alas!" in certain circumstances, I am normally taken as implying that I am unhappy. But I am not taken to be asserting that I am unhappy, as I would be if I were to utter the words "I am unhappy." Or, to vary the example, when a person says, "All my children are now in college," he is normally taken to be implying that he has children (although not to be asserting that he has), and his auditors are justified in making this assumption. Or again, when one says in such sorts of contexts, "Smith has just gone out," he implies, or his words imply, that he believes or knows that Smith has gone out, and those to whom he is speaking are justified in assuming that he does. That the sense of "implication" expressed by these examples is not that of logical implication may be illustrated by the observation that there is no formal contradiction in asserting "All my children are in college, but I have no children" or in asserting "Smith has gone out, but I don't believe he has." Indeed, in standard systems of mathematical logic, the first statement is true whenever the speaker has no children, and the second is true whenever Smith has gone out but the speaker does not believe he has.

Sentences like "All my children are in college, but I have no children" and "Smith has gone out, but I don't believe he has" thus satisfy the rules of logical syntax and, indeed, the rules for correct English. Yet they fall upon the ear as decidedly odd. If employed at all in everyday speech, they would occur only in unusual circumstances—"I don't believe he has" might be whispered as an aside to a confederate, for example. But except for situations like this, they would be perplexing things to say. What, then, is the source of their oddity, given that they do not involve any formal mistake?

It is now generally agreed that the oddity we feel upon hearing such sentences stems from a disparity between the conditions we assume will have been satisfied whenever someone is trying to communicate with another and the utterances we expect will be employed in those circumstances. In effect, this is to say that certain assumptions, or presuppositions, that communicating human beings make in the everyday give-and-take of verbal intercourse, assumptions that thus form the ground of such intercourse, fail to hold or are violated in such circumstances.

Talk about presuppositions and talk about what is contextually implied by a speaker's words thus have in common a reference to the background conditions normally expected to obtain when an utterance is made. If stating and asserting are conceived of as elements constituting part of the foreground of the situation in which communication takes place (that is, as activities that bring an item of information into the immediate focus of attention), then presupposing and contextual implication may be thought of as elements constituting part of the background of the situation (that is, as factors that remain implicit unless they are otherwise articulated but that nonetheless are essential factors in communication). Part of the task that faces the student of informal logic is to specify what these conditions are, how they contribute to the background that makes communication possible, and what sorts of relations exist between them and the utterances that occupy the foreground during the transmission of information.

Let us then call the concepts referring to such conditions background concepts. Because such concepts play covert roles in daily discourse and because their functions are remarkably similar, it is not surprising that many writers have failed to discriminate between them. But not all writers have blurred the distinction. Isabel C. Hungerland is one notable exception. In her important paper "Contextual Implication" (*Inquiry*, Vol. 4, 1960, pp. 211–258), she writes, "The relation (presupposing) defined by Strawson is *not* that of contextual implication.... The relation between the two may be indicated as follows: When *S* presupposes *S'*, a speaker in making the statement *S*, contextually implies that he believes that *S'*" (p. 239). Following Mrs. Hungerland's suggestion and overlooking the many subtleties a full treatment of the subject would demand, we may say that the key distinctions that mark off the one notion from the other are those of scope: Neither the conditions subsumed under the two notions nor the range of entities to which the notions apply are in all cases the same.

Presupposing is a concept referring to those conditions that must be satisfied before an utterance can count as a statement, or if "statement" is so defined that statements need be neither true nor false (see P. F. Strawson, "Identifying Reference and Truth-Values," in *Theoria* 30 [2] [1964]), then presupposing applies to those conditions that must be satisfied before statements can be either true or false. Contextual implication, on the other hand, is a concept that applies to those conditions that must be satisfied before an utterance can count as "normal" in the circumstances in which it is made—that is, it applies to those beliefs a speaker has when he makes the utterance he does in certain circumstances and which rule out that he is lying or deliberately deceiving someone. The range of entities thus referred to by the concept of presupposing is either the class of statements as such or the class of those statements that are either true or false, whereas the range of entities referred to by the notion of contextual implication is the class of beliefs held by the speaker (and, derivatively, by his auditors).

Examples may be invoked at this point to illuminate the above remarks. Suppose during the course of a conversation I say, "The store on the corner sells such goods," not realizing that there is no longer a store on the corner. My remark in this circumstance is neither true nor false; as R. G. Collingwood puts it, the question of its truth or falsity "does not arise." For it is a presupposition of my using that utterance to make a statement (that is, an utterance that can be either true or false) that there be such a store. We may say in such a case that it is a condition of the truth or falsity of the remark that the store exist. But I may well believe that there is such a store, and in making the remark, I imply that I have this belief at the time of my utterance. One of the conditions for the normality of the remark (that is, that I was not lying) is that I had this belief at the time of saying what I did. We may say therefore that the conditions determining the normality of the background from which my remark issued and the conditions determining the background from

which a statement would have issued are different conditions. It is this sort of difference in the background conditions that determines the difference between the concepts of presupposing and of contextual implication.

HISTORY OF CONTEXTUAL IMPLICATION

The genesis of the notions of contextual implication and of presupposing differs considerably. As a philosophical subject, contextual implication, under another name, has a longer traceable history in the modern period than does presupposing. The history of contextual implication is mainly connected with developments in moral philosophy, especially with efforts to give a correct analysis of the use of moral language. In G. E. Moore's *Ethics* (London, 1912), for example, we find the following comments:

> There is an important distinction, which is not always observed, between what a man *means* by a given assertion and what he *expresses* by it. Whenever we make any assertion whatever (unless we do not mean what we say) we are always *expressing* one or other of two things— namely, either that we *think* the thing in question to be so, or that we *know* it to be so." (p. 125)

In the subsequent history of moral philosophy the distinction referred to by Moore became the key distinction invoked by those authors who espoused the emotive theory of ethics. According to advocates of this doctrine, the sorts of utterances used in moral contexts ("That's good," "Stealing is wrong") are not being used to make assertions and hence are neither true nor false, as both naturalists and nonnaturalists had assumed. The primary use of such utterances is to express the attitude or the feelings of the speaker toward whatever he is talking about and to arouse comparable attitudes in the auditor. The later history of contextual implication is deeply concerned with the import of this distinction, and the main works in which it is discussed, sometimes critically, are *Language, Truth and Logic* by A. J. Ayer (London, 1936); *The Philosophy of G. E. Moore*, edited by P. A. Schilpp (Evanston, IL, 1942), pp. 540–554; *Ethics and Language* by C. L. Stevenson (New Haven, CT, 1944); *Ethics* by P. H. Nowell-Smith (Harmondsworth, U.K., 1954); *The Emotive Theory of Ethics* by Avrum Stroll (Berkeley, CA, 1954); *The Logic of Moral Discourse* by Paul Edwards (Glencoe, IL, 1955); and "Contextual Implication" by Isabel Hungerland (see above). Various formulas are proposed by some of these writers.

Nowell-Smith says, for example, "A statement *p* contextually implies *q* if anyone who knew the normal conventions of the language would be entitled to infer q from p *in the context in which they occur*" (*Ethics*, p. 80). According to Hungerland all such early attempts to characterize the relation that obtains between what a speaker expressly asserts and what he implies suffer either from vagueness or from mistakenly thinking that the relation is a special case of inductive inference. Her own contention is that it is neither vague nor a case of inductive inference, but is, rather, the presumption that in a situation of communication, acts of stating are normal. She thus likens contextual implication to the juridical principle that a man is presumed to be innocent until proved guilty, a principle that is not arrived at inductively, by surveying the evidence, but which serves to place the onus of proof in a legal contest upon the prosecution. As she puts it, "Contextual inference (if we wish to use the word) is a matter, rather, of a communal assumption in the absence of evidence to the contrary, that, in a situation of communication, acts of stating are normal" (p. 233). Her view is that contextual implication depends upon three factors: (1) The presence of a stating context (since the question of a man's believing what he says does not arise in a nonstating context); (2) the presumptions of normality (that is, that within a stating context the implication holds only if the presumptions are principles of communication); and (3) rules for the correct use of an expression (that is, whether belief is implied when a man says p will be in part determined by rules for the correct use of p).

HISTORY OF PRESUPPOSING

Unlike contextual implication, the notion of presupposing has its genesis in logical theory, especially in those developments involving alternative accounts of Bertrand Russell's theory of descriptions and of the so-called square of opposition. The writer most closely identified with both of these matters is P. F. Strawson of Oxford University. He has dealt with the theory of descriptions in his papers "On Referring" (*Mind*, 1950), "Presupposing" (*Philosophical Review*, 1954) and "Identifying Reference and Truth-Values" (see above) and in his book *Individuals* (London, 1959; Ch. 8 especially). In *Introduction to Logical Theory* (London, 1952) Strawson considers both the theory of descriptions and the square of opposition.

In the works that deal only with the theory of descriptions, Strawson rejects Russell's analysis of sentences containing definite descriptive phrases (that is, phrases of the form "the so and so" used in the singular in English). According to Russell, the analysis of a sentence like "The queen of England is beautiful" contains in part an assertion to the effect that the queen of England exists.

Strawson argues, cogently, that this statement is not an explicit part of what is asserted by "The queen of England is beautiful" but is presupposed by a speaker who would use such a sentence in normal circumstances to make a statement. In *Introduction to Logical Theory*, Strawson goes on to define the statement "S presupposes S'" as follows: "The truth of S' is a necessary condition of the truth or falsity of the statement that S" (p. 175).

This characterization has been objected to by various writers, including David Rynin, who points out that when "necessary condition" and "truth or falsity of the statement that" are interpreted in the ordinary, truth-functional way, the definition has the paradoxical consequence that all presupposed statements are true. Rynin's demonstration is that $(S \supset S')$ and $(-S \supset S')$, but $(S \lor -S)$; therefore S'. Avrum Stroll has also suggested that Strawson's account suffers from the difficulty that if "The king of France no longer exists" is used to make a true statement, then by Strawson's criterion one who employs it thereby presupposes the existence of the king of France. It is now generally agreed that neither Russell's nor Strawson's analysis does full justice to all uses of sentences in everyday English containing "the" phrases in the singular. But regarded as proposals for the development of explanatory models for subparts of everyday discourse, each has considerable merit. In this interpretation Strawson's doctrine belongs to the logical tradition of analyzing descriptive phrases initiated by Gottlob Frege in "Über Sinn und Bedeutung" (1892) and supported by David Hilbert and Paul Bernays in their *Grundlagen der Arithmetik* (Berlin, 1934; Vol. I, p. 384) and by Rudolf Carnap in *Meaning and Necessity* (Chicago, 1947; pp. 33–42).

Strawson has also argued that if universal statements ("All my children are in college") are interpreted as presupposing the existence of the items mentioned by the subject term, paradoxes stemming from modern symbolic interpretations of the square of opposition can be eliminated without affecting the logical relations that one intuitively feels ought to hold between the elements of the square. This matter is persuasively discussed by S. Peterson in "All John's Children" (in *Philosophical Quarterly*, 1960).

PRESUPPOSING IN METAPHYSICS

The notion of presupposition plays an important role in various metaphysical constructions, including Collingwood's *An Essay on Metaphysics* (Oxford, 1940) and Michael Polanyi's *Personal Knowledge* (Chicago, 1958). Collingwood distinguishes (Chs. 3–4) between absolute and relative presuppositions, arguing that the former are neither true nor false and that metaphysics is the science that ascertains what these absolute presuppositions are. His view is that absolute presuppositions form the basis of the civilizations developed at various times in history and the ground of the science developed in such civilizations. When a civilization changes, its presuppositions change and are succeeded by others. According to this view, metaphysics is therefore a branch of the historical sciences.

See also Ayer, Alfred Jules; Carnap, Rudolf; Collingwood, Robin George; Entailment, Presupposition, and Implicature; Frege, Gottlob; Hilbert, David; Moore, George Edward; Questions; Russell, Bertrand Arthur William; Strawson, Peter Frederick.

Bibliography

Anscombe, G. E. M. *An Introduction to Wittgenstein's Tractatus.* London: Hutchinson, 1959. Ch. II.

Asher, Nicholas, and Alex Lascarides. "The Semantics and Pragmatics of Presupposition." *Journal of Semantics* 15 (1998): 239–300.

Baker, A. J. "Presupposition and Types of Clause." *Mind* 65 (1956): 368–378.

Bar-Hillel, Yehoshua. "Analysis of 'Correct' Language." *Mind* 55 (1946): 328–340.

Black, Max. *Models and Metaphors.* Ithaca, NY: Cornell University Press, 1962. Ch. 4.

Black, Max. *Problems of Analysis.* Ithaca, NY: Cornell University Press, 1954. Chs. 2–3.

Cavell, Stanley. "Must We Mean What We Say?" *Inquiry* 1 (1958).

Collingwood, R. G. *An Autobiography.* London: Oxford University Press, 1939. See especially pp. 66–76.

Donagan, Alan. *The Later Philosophy of R. G. Collingwood.* Oxford: Clarendon Press, 1962.

Frege, Gottlob. "Über Sinn und Bedeutung." *Zeitschrift für Philosophie und philosophische Kritik* 100 (1892): 25–50. Translated by Max Black as "On Sense and Reference." In *Translations from the Philosophical Writings of Gottlob Frege*, edited by P. T. Geach and Max Black. New York: Philosophical Library, 1952.

Geach, P. T. "Russell on Meaning and Denoting." *Analysis* 19 (1959): 69–72.

Grant, C. K. "Pragmatic Implication." *Philosophy* 33 (1958): 303–324.

Grice, Paul. "Presupposition and Conversational Implicature." In *Radical Pragmatics*, edited by Peter Cole. New York: Academic Press, 1981.

Griffiths, A. P. "Presuppositions." *Analysis* 15 (1955).

Hall, Roland. "Assuming: One Set of Positing Words." *Philosophical Review* 67 (1958): 52–75.

Hall, Roland. "Presuming." *Philosophical Quarterly* 11 (1961): 10–21.

Hampshire, Stuart. "On Referring and Intending." *Philosophical Review* 65 (1956): 1–13.

Hancock, Roger. "Presuppositions." *Philosophical Quarterly* 10 (1960): 73–78.

Hart, H. L. A. "A Logician's Fairy Tale." *Philosophical Review* 60 (1951): 198–212.

Kemeny, John G. *A Philosopher Looks at Science.* Princeton, NJ: Van Nostrand, 1959. Ch. 3.

Langford, C. H. "The Notion of Analysis in Moore's Philosophy." In *The Philosophy of G. E. Moore*, edited by P. A. Schilpp. Evanston, IL: Northwestern University Press, 1942.

Lewis, David. "Scorekeeping in a Language Game." *Journal of Philosophical Logic* 8 (1979): 339–359.

Llewelyn, John E. "Collingwood's Doctrine of Absolute Presuppositions." *Philosophical Quarterly* 11 (1961): 49–60.

Llewelyn, John E. "Presuppositions, Assumptions, and Presumptions." *Theoria* 28 (1962): 158–172.

Lycan, William. "The Myth of the 'Projection Problem for Presupposition.'" *Philosophical Topics* 15 (1987): 169–175.

MacIver, A. M. "Some Questions about 'Know' and 'Think.'" *Analysis* 5 (1937–1938).

Nelson, Everett J. "Contradiction and the Presupposition of Existence." *Mind* 55 (1946): 319–327.

Nowell-Smith, P. H. "Contextual Implication and Ethical Theory." *PAS*, Supp. 36 (1962).

O'Connor, D. J. "Pragmatic Paradoxes." *Mind* 57 (1948): 358–359.

Quine, W. V. "Meaning and Inference." In *From a Logical Point of View.* Cambridge, MA: Harvard University Press, 1953. See especially pp. 164–166.

Rynin, David. "Donagan on Collingwood on Metaphysics." *Review of Metaphysics* 18 (1964).

Sellars, Wilfrid. "Presupposing." *Philosophical Review* 63 (1954): 197–215.

Shwayder, D. S. "Self-Defeating Pronouncements." *Analysis* 16 (1956).

Shwayder, D. S. "Uses of Language and Uses of Words." *Theoria* 26 (1960).

Soames, Scott. "Presupposition." In *Handbook of Philosophical Logic*, edited by D. Gabbay. Dordrecht: Kluwer, 1989.

Stalnaker, R. C. "Pragmatic Presupposition." In *Pragmatics: A Reader*, edited by S. Davies. New York: Oxford University Press, 1991.

Strawson, P. F. *Introduction to Logical Theory.* London: Methuen, 1952.

Strawson, P. F. "On Referring." *Mind* 59 (1950): 320–344. Reprinted in *Logico-Linguistic Papers.* London: Methuen, 1971.

Strawson, P. F. "A Reply to Mr. Sellars." *Philosophical Review* 63 (1954): 216–231.

Stroll, Avrum. "The Paradox of the First Person Singular Pronoun." *Inquiry* 6 (1963): 217–233.

Urmson, J. O. "Parenthetical Verbs." In *Essays in Conceptual Analysis*, edited by A. Flew. London: Macmillan, 1956.

Wolterstorff, Nicholas P. "Referring and Existing." *Philosophical Quarterly* 11 (1961): 335–349.

Avrum Stroll (1967)
Bibliographic assistance by J. Ornstein (1967)
Bibliography updated by Benjamin Fiedor (2005)

PRESUPPOSITION

Consider the following famous example from Bertrand Russell.

(1) The present king of France is bald.

According to Russell, (1) is false because it asserts the existence of the present king of France. However, following P. F. Strawson (1952), a number of philosophers and linguists have maintained that, if there is no present king of France, an utterance of (1) fails to have a determinate truth-value—in Strawson's words, the question of whether (1) is true or false "does not arise." On this view, (1) therefore does not assert or even entail the existence of the present king of France but rather "presupposes" his existence.

THE RANGE OF PHENOMENA

Sentences like (1) are argued to presuppose the existence of a particular individual, but there are many other "presupposition" effects. It has been argued, for example, that factive verbs such as *know* and *regret* presuppose the truth of their complement clauses and that "certain aspectuals"—a class of verbs such as *quit* and *continue*—also presuppose certain actions having taken place (this class covers the example "Have you stopped beating your dog?"). It also appears that a number of modifiers introduce presupposition effects, for example *again, too, even,* and so forth. L. Karttunen (1973) argued that in propositional-attitude environments such as "Fred wants to sell his unicorn" it is presupposed that Fred believes he has a unicorn. A number of additional constructions that invoke presupposition effects have been explored, including those triggered by phonological stress. So, for example, if I say "I didn't go to the baseball game," it arguably presupposes that I went to some other kind of game.

PRESUPPOSITION VERSUS ENTAILMENT

The philosophical controversy surrounding presupposition comes in at the very beginning—determining whether these are genuine cases of presupposition or are merely cases of entailment. To illustrate, consider (2)–(4):

(2) Fred stopped washing the dishes.

(3) Fred didn't stop washing the dishes.

(4) Fred had been washing the dishes.

According to the presupposition thesis, both (2) and (3) presuppose (4). Hence, if (4) is false, then (2) and (3) must lack determinate truth-values. Alternatively, according to the entailment analysis, (2) entails (4). Should (4) be false, then according to the entailment analysis (2) will be false and (3) will be true. This dispute has all the makings of a stalemate, since it turns on speakers' intuitions about whether sentences lack genuine truth-values under the relevant conditions or are merely false. Indeed, Strawson (1964) came to doubt whether the matter could in fact be settled by "brisk little formal argument[s]" and offered that each view could be reasonable, depending on one's interests. Others have put more stock in brisk little formal arguments, notably D. Wilson (1975), who offered an extensive critique of the presuppositional analysis.

THE PROJECTION PROBLEM

One of the most interesting questions to surface is the so-called projection problem for presupposition, first observed by D. T. Langendoen and H. Savin (1971). This problem involves the question of what happens when a construction with a presupposition is embedded in more complex constructions (e.g., in propositional-attitude constructions or in the scope of negation). To illustrate, when (2) is negated, yielding (3), it continues to presuppose (4)—the presupposition is said to be projected. Other constructions, such as "doubts that," do not always project presuppositions, and still others (such as the "wants" case from Karttunen, discussed above) project something weaker than the original presupposition. The question is therefore whether projection presupposition is arbitrary or whether it obeys certain specific rules. Much subsequent work has attempted to articulate those "projection rules" (see Gazdar, 1979, Heim 1991, Karttunen 1973, and Soames 1979, 1982, for important examples).

SEMANTIC VERSUS PRAGMATIC PRESUPPOSITION

If one accepts that there are genuine instances of presupposition, there remains the question of whether presupposition is a reflex of semantics or pragmatics—that is, whether the presupposition follows from the meaning of the sentence or is merely part of the conversational background. R. Stalnaker (1974) gave several arguments in favor of the pragmatic alternative, including the interesting observation that, in a case like (5),

(5) If Eagleton hadn't been dropped from the Democratic ticket, Nixon would have won the election

there seems to be a presupposition that Nixon lost, although the effect is weak, and, in the right context or given appropriate information, that presupposition can be overruled. This graded effect suggests that pragmatic phenomena are in play. Stalnaker also observed that the pragmatic alternative is useful in separating the question of entailment relations from the question of presupposition and in working out solutions to the projection problem. (But see Wilson 1975 for criticism of pragmatic accounts of presupposition.)

APPLICATIONS

The doctrine of presupposition remains somewhat controversial, but at the same time it has found interesting applications. For example, B. van Fraassen (1968, 1970) argued that presupposition might be employed in the treatment of the "liar paradox" and proposed that liar sentences are neither true nor false owing to a presupposition failure. Presupposition has also played an important role in work on the semantics of propositional attitudes, much of it extending from the work of Karttunen (1973). I. Heim (1992), for example, has updated the initial Karttunen analysis with features of Stalnaker's presuppositional analysis. Still other research (including unpublished work by Saul Kripke) has investigated the interplay of presupposition and the analysis of discourse anaphora.

See also Anaphora; Kripke, Saul; Liar Paradox, The; Philosophy of Language; Russell, Bertrand Arthur William; Strawson, Peter Frederick.

Bibliography

Gazdar, G. *Pragmatics.* New York: Academic Press, 1979.

Grice, P. "Presupposition and Conversational Implicature." In *Radical Pragmatics,* edited by P. Cole. New York: Academic Press, 1981.

Heim, I. "On the Projection Problem for Presuppositions." In *Pragmatics,* edited by S. Davis. New York: Oxford University Press, 1991.

Heim, I. "Presupposition Projection and the Semantics of Attitude Verbs." *Journal of Semantics* 9 (1992): 183–221.

Karttunen, L. "Presuppositions of Compound Sentences." *Linguistic Inquiry* 4 (1973): 169–193.

Langendoen, D. T., and H. Savin. "The Projection Problem for Presupposition." In *Studies in Linguistic Semantics,* edited by C. Filmore and D. T. Langendoen. New York: Holt, Rinehart and Winston, 1971.

Soames, S. "How Presuppositions Are Inherited: A Solution to the Projection Problem." *Linguistic Inquiry* 13 (1982): 483–545.

Soames, S. "A Projection Problem for Speaker Presuppositions." *Linguistic Inquiry* 10 (1979): 623–666.

Stalnaker, R. "Pragmatic Presuppositions." In *Semantics and Philosophy,* edited by M. Munitz and D. Unger. New York, 1974.

Strawson, P. "Identifying Reference and Truth-Values." *Theoria* 3 (1964): 96–118.

Strawson, P. *Introduction to Logical Theory.* New York: Wiley, 1952.

van Fraassen, B. "Presupposition, Implication, and Self-Reference." *Journal of Philosophy* 65 (1968): 136–152.

van Fraassen, B. "Truth and Paradoxical Consequences." In *The Paradox of the Liar,* edited by R. L. Martin. New Haven, CT: Yale University Press, 1970.

Wilson, D. *Presuppositions and Non-Truth-Conditional Semantics.* London: Academic Press, 1975.

Peter Ludlow (1996)